Mobil Travel Guide

Southwest

2005

Arizona

Colorado

Nevada

New Mexico

ExxonMobil
Travel Publications

Acknowledgements

We gratefully acknowledge the help of our representatives for their efficient and perceptive inspections of the lodging and dining establishments listed; the establishments' proprietors for their cooperation in showing their facilities and providing information about them; and the many users of previous editions who have taken the time to share their experiences. Mobil Travel Guide is also grateful to all the talented writers who contributed entries to this book.

Printing Acknowledgement: North American Corporation of Illinois

www.mobiltravelguide.com

Front cover photo: Taos Pueblo, New Mexico

ISBN: 0-7627-3592-9

ISSN: 1550-0284

Manufactured in the United States of America.

10 9 8 7 6 5 4 3 2 1

Contents

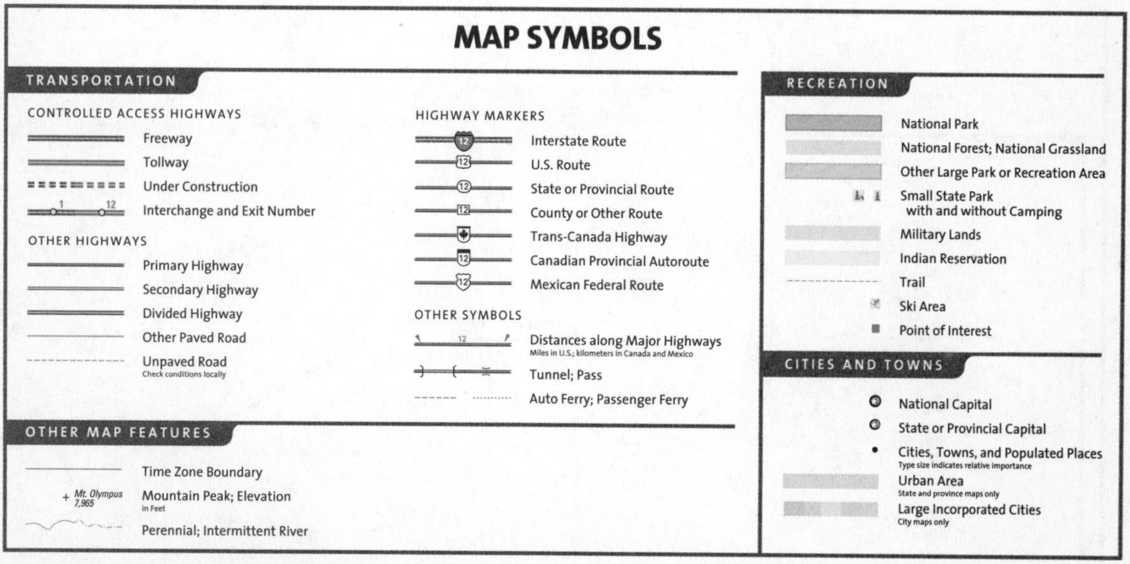

MAP SYMBOLS
TRANSPORTATION
CONTROLLED ACCESS HIGHWAYS
Freeway
Tollway
Under Construction
Interchange and Exit Number
OTHER HIGHWAYS
Primary Highway
Secondary Highway
Divided Highway
Other Paved Road
Unpaved Road
Check conditions locally
HIGHWAY MARKERS
Interstate Route
U.S. Route
State or Provincial Route
County or Other Route
Trans-Canada Highway
Canadian Provincial Autoroute
Mexican Federal Route
OTHER SYMBOLS
Distances along Major Highways
Miles in U.S.; kilometers in Canada and Mexico
Tunnel; Pass
Auto Ferry; Passenger Ferry
RECREATION
National Park
National Forest; National Grassland
Other Large Park or Recreation Area
Small State Park with and without Camping
Military Lands
Indian Reservation
Trail
Ski Area
Point of Interest
CITIES AND TOWNS
National Capital
State or Provincial Capital
Cities, Towns, and Populated Places
Type size indicates relative importance
Urban Area
State and province maps only
Large Incorporated Cities
City maps only
OTHER MAP FEATURES
Time Zone Boundary
Mt. Olympus 7,965
Mountain Peak; Elevation
in Feet
Perennial; Intermittent River

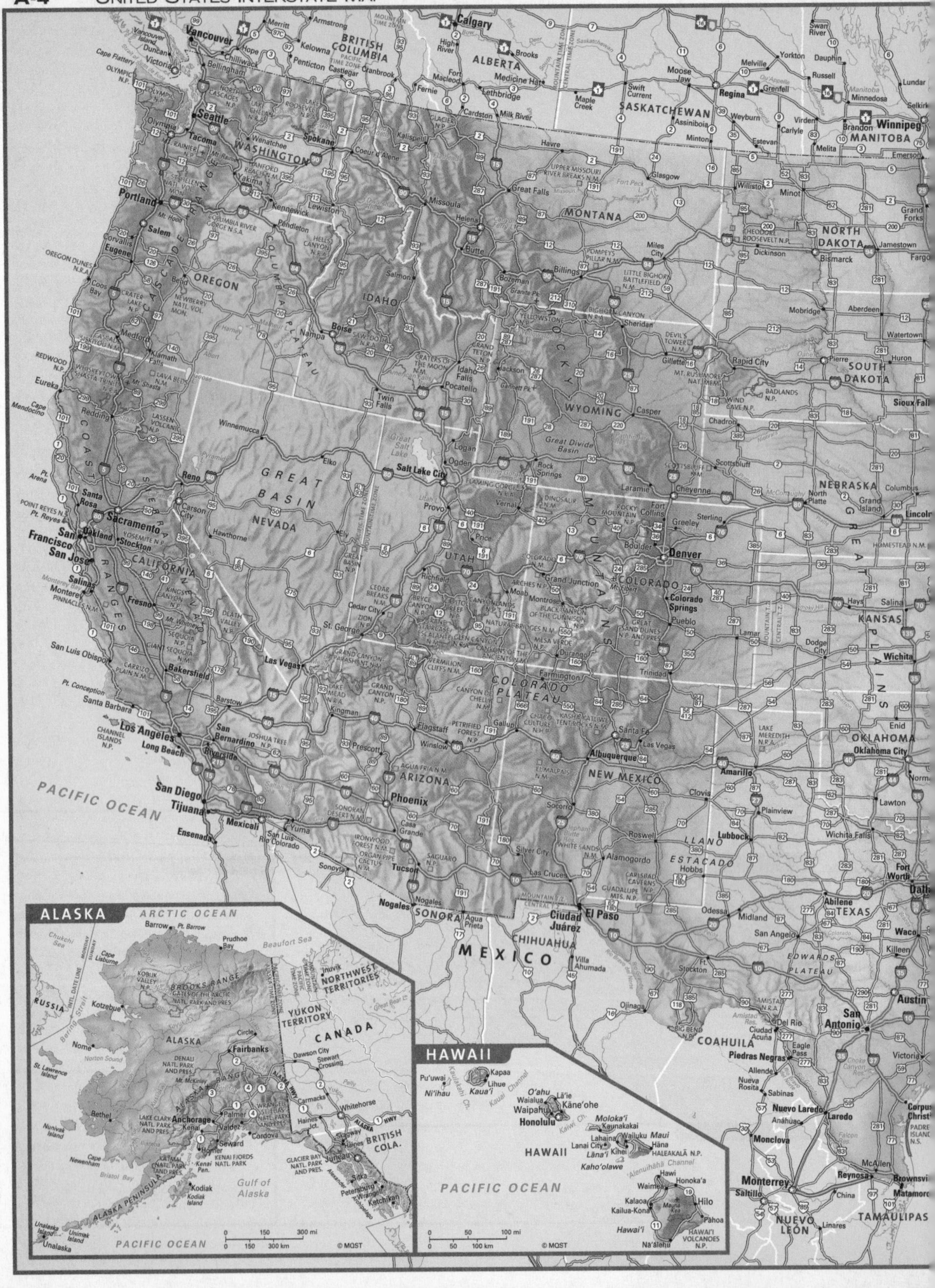
BRITISH COLUMBIA
ALBERTA
SASKATCHEWAN
MANITOBA
WASHINGTON
OREGON
IDAHO
MONTANA
WYOMING
NORTH DAKOTA
SOUTH DAKOTA
NEBRASKA
KANSAS
OKLAHOMA
TEXAS
NEW MEXICO
ARIZONA
UTAH
COLORADO
NEVADA
CALIFORNIA
MEXICO
SONORA
CHIHUAHUA
COAHUILA
NUEVO LEÓN
TAMAULIPAS
PACIFIC OCEAN
GREAT BASIN
COLUMBIA PLATEAU
COLORADO PLATEAU
ROCKY MOUNTAINS
GREAT PLAINS
LLANO ESTACADO
EDWARDS PLATEAU
CASCADE RANGE
SIERRA NEVADA
COAST RANGES
Vancouver
Calgary
Regina
Winnipeg
Seattle
Spokane
Portland
Salem
Eugene
Boise
Missoula
Helena
Billings
Sacramento
San Francisco
San Jose
Fresno
Bakersfield
Los Angeles
San Diego
Tijuana
Las Vegas
Reno
Salt Lake City
Phoenix
Tucson
Albuquerque
Santa Fe
Denver
Colorado Springs
Cheyenne
El Paso
Ciudad Juárez
Amarillo
Lubbock
Oklahoma City
Wichita
San Antonio
Austin
Monterrey
ALASKA
ARCTIC OCEAN
Beaufort Sea
BROOKS RANGE
ALASKA RANGE
NORTHWEST TERRITORIES
YUKON TERRITORY
CANADA
BRITISH COLA.
RUSSIA
Fairbanks
Anchorage
Juneau
Gulf of Alaska
PACIFIC OCEAN
© MQST
HAWAII
Kaua'i
O'ahu
Honolulu
Moloka'i
Maui
Lāna'i
Kaho'olawe
Hawai'i
Hilo
PACIFIC OCEAN
© MQST

CANADA
ONTARIO
QUÉBEC
NEW BRUNSWICK
MAINE
N.H.
VT.
MASS.
NEW YORK
CT.
R.I.
PENNSYLVANIA
NEW JERSEY
MD.
DE.
OHIO
MICHIGAN
WISCONSIN
MINNESOTA
IOWA
ILLINOIS
INDIANA
WEST VIRGINIA
VIRGINIA
KENTUCKY
MISSOURI
TENNESSEE
NORTH CAROLINA
SOUTH CAROLINA
GEORGIA
ALABAMA
MISSISSIPPI
ARKANSAS
LOUISIANA
FLORIDA
BAHAMAS
Lake Superior
Lake Michigan
Lake Huron
Lake Ontario
Lake Erie
APPALACHIAN MOUNTAINS
OZARK PLATEAU
ATLANTIC OCEAN
GULF OF MEXICO
Thunder Bay
Sault Ste. Marie
Sudbury
Ottawa
Montréal
Québec
Toronto
Hamilton
London
Windsor
Minneapolis
St. Paul
Duluth
Milwaukee
Madison
Green Bay
Chicago
Detroit
Cleveland
Toledo
Columbus
Cincinnati
Pittsburgh
Buffalo
Rochester
Syracuse
Albany
Boston
Providence
Hartford
New Haven
New York
Newark
Philadelphia
Baltimore
Washington, DC
Richmond
Norfolk
Virginia Beach
Indianapolis
Louisville
Lexington
St. Louis
Kansas City
Des Moines
Springfield
Memphis
Nashville
Knoxville
Chattanooga
Atlanta
Birmingham
Montgomery
Charlotte
Raleigh
Durham
Greensboro
Winston-Salem
Columbia
Charleston
Savannah
Jacksonville
Tallahassee
Orlando
Tampa
St. Petersburg
Miami
Fort Lauderdale
Key West
Mobile
New Orleans
Baton Rouge
Jackson
Little Rock
Shreveport
Houston
Galveston
Beaumont
Nassau
©MAPQUEST
0 150 300 mi
0 150 300 km

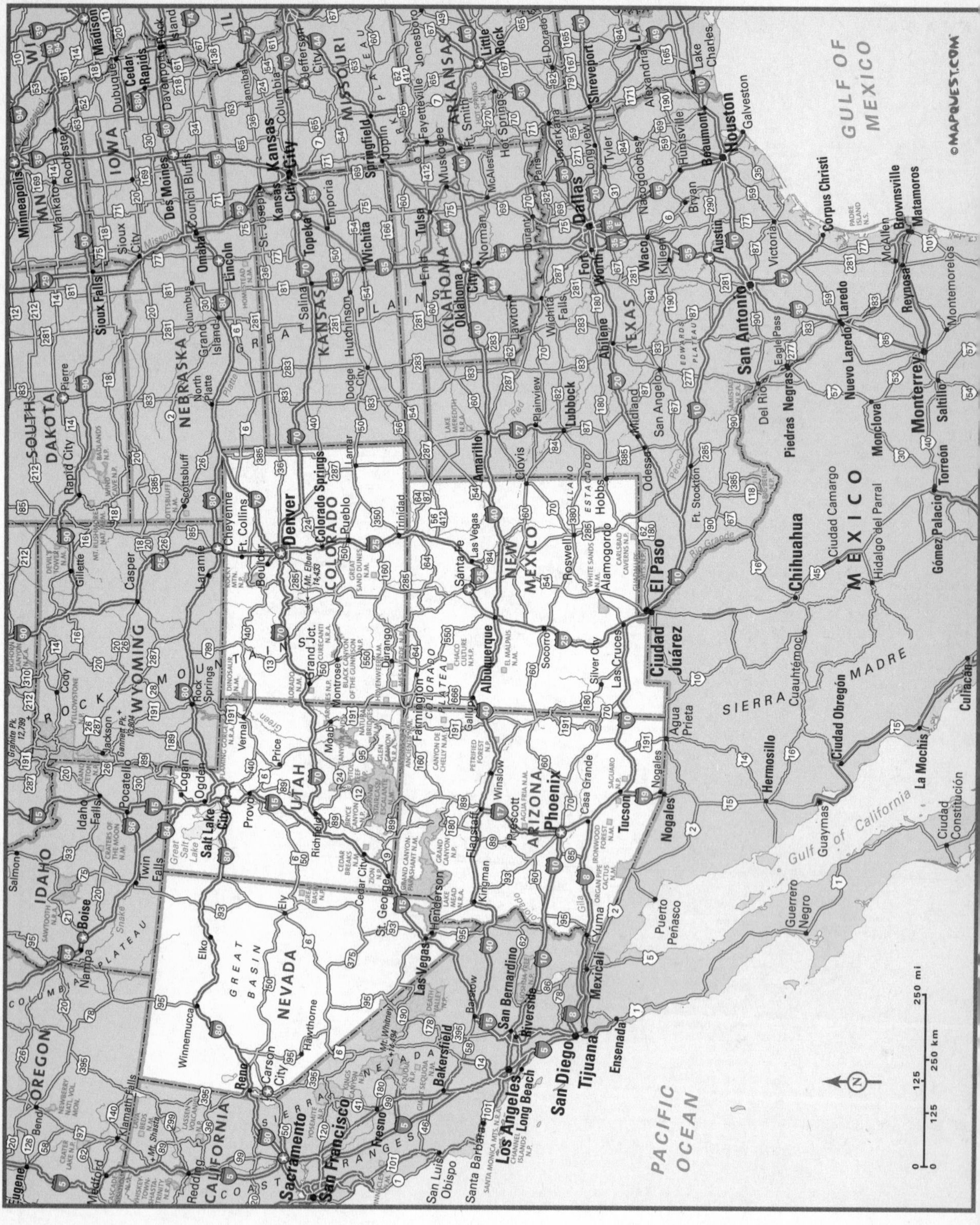
OREGON
IDAHO
WYOMING
SOUTH DAKOTA
NEBRASKA
IOWA
MISSOURI
KANSAS
COLORADO
UTAH
NEVADA
CALIFORNIA
ARIZONA
NEW MEXICO
OKLAHOMA
TEXAS
ARKANSAS
MEXICO
GULF OF MEXICO
PACIFIC OCEAN
GREAT BASIN
GREAT PLAINS
ROCKY MOUNTAINS
COLORADO PLATEAU
SIERRA MADRE
Gulf of California
Sacramento
San Francisco
Los Angeles
Long Beach
San Diego
Tijuana
Las Vegas
Phoenix
Tucson
Salt Lake City
Denver
Albuquerque
Santa Fe
El Paso
Ciudad Juárez
Dallas
Fort Worth
Houston
San Antonio
Austin
Oklahoma City
Kansas City
Omaha
Lincoln
Des Moines
Minneapolis
Little Rock
Shreveport
Chihuahua
Monterrey
Hermosillo
Boise
Reno
Cheyenne
0 125 250 mi
0 125 250 km
©MAPQUEST.COM

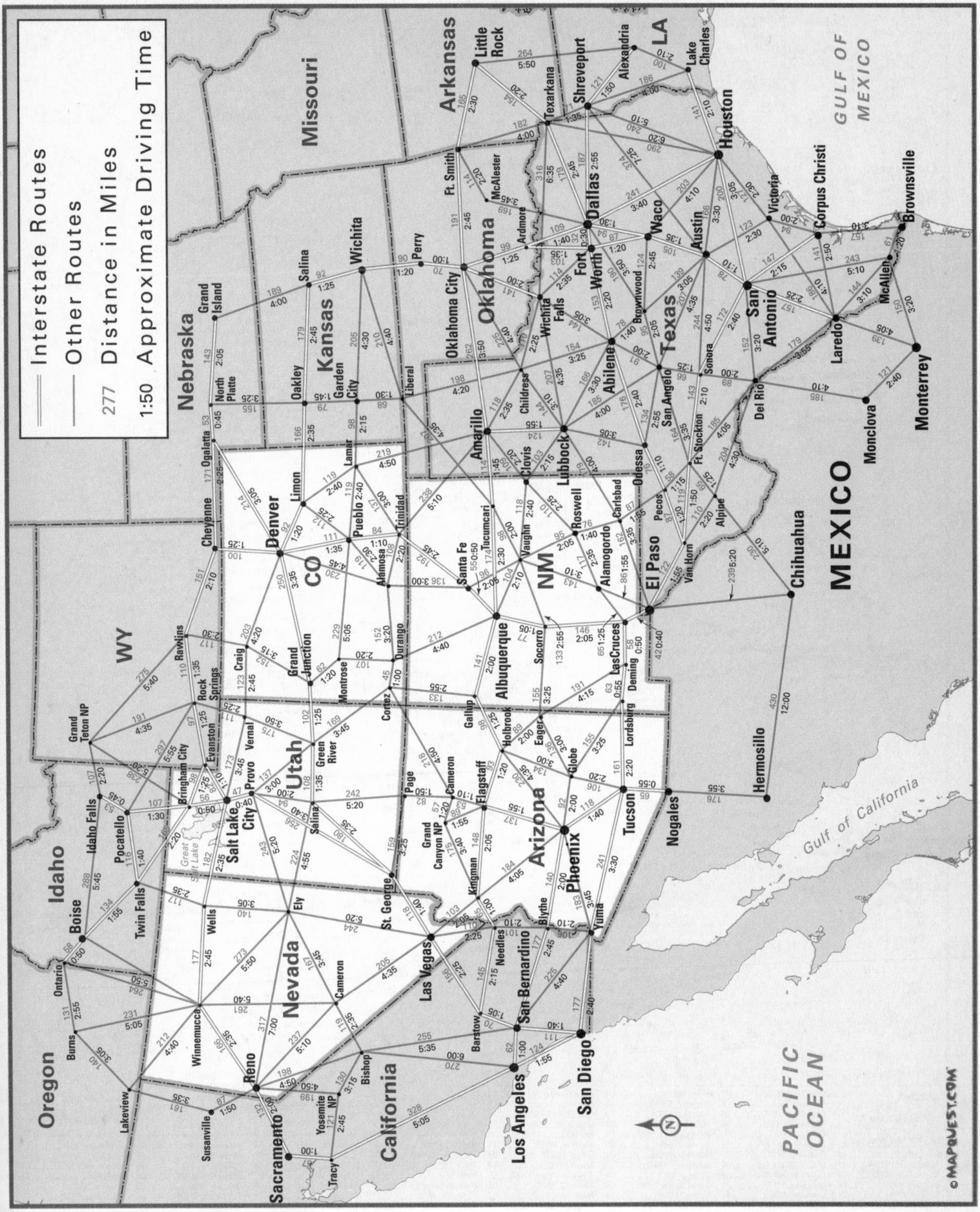

Interstate Routes
Other Routes
277 Distance in Miles
1:50 Approximate Driving Time
Oregon
Idaho
WY
Nebraska
Kansas
Missouri
Arkansas
LA
Oklahoma
Texas
Nevada
Utah
CO
Arizona
NM
California
MEXICO
GULF OF MEXICO
PACIFIC OCEAN
Gulf of California
Great Salt Lake
Boise
Ontario
Burns
Lakeview
Susanville
Sacramento
Tracy
Yosemite NP
Reno
Winnemucca
Wells
Twin Falls
Pocatello
Idaho Falls
Grand Teton NP
Rock Springs
Rawlins
Cheyenne
Ogalatta
North Platte
Grand Island
Evanston
Brigham City
Salt Lake City
Provo
Vernal
Craig
Grand Junction
Denver
Limon
Pueblo
Lamar
Trinidad
Alamosa
Durango
Montrose
Cortez
Green River
Salina
Ely
Cameron
Bishop
Las Vegas
St. George
Page
Grand Canyon NP
Flagstaff
Kingman
Needles
Barstow
San Bernardino
Los Angeles
San Diego
Blythe
Yuma
Phoenix
Tucson
Nogales
Globe
Eager
Holbrook
Gallup
Albuquerque
Santa Fe
Tucumcari
Vaughn
Socorro
Las Cruces
Deming
Lordsburg
El Paso
Alamogordo
Roswell
Carlsbad
Clovis
Amarillo
Lubbock
Odessa
Pecos
Van Horn
Alpine
Ft. Stockton
Sonora
San Angelo
Abilene
Childress
Wichita Falls
Oakley
Garden City
Liberal
Salina
Wichita
Perry
Oklahoma City
Ardmore
McAlester
Ft. Smith
Little Rock
Texarkana
Shreveport
Alexandria
Lake Charles
Houston
Dallas
Fort Worth
Brownwood
Waco
Austin
San Antonio
Victoria
Corpus Christi
Laredo
McAllen
Brownsville
Del Rio
Monterrey
Monclova
Chihuahua
Hermosillo
©MAPQUEST.COM

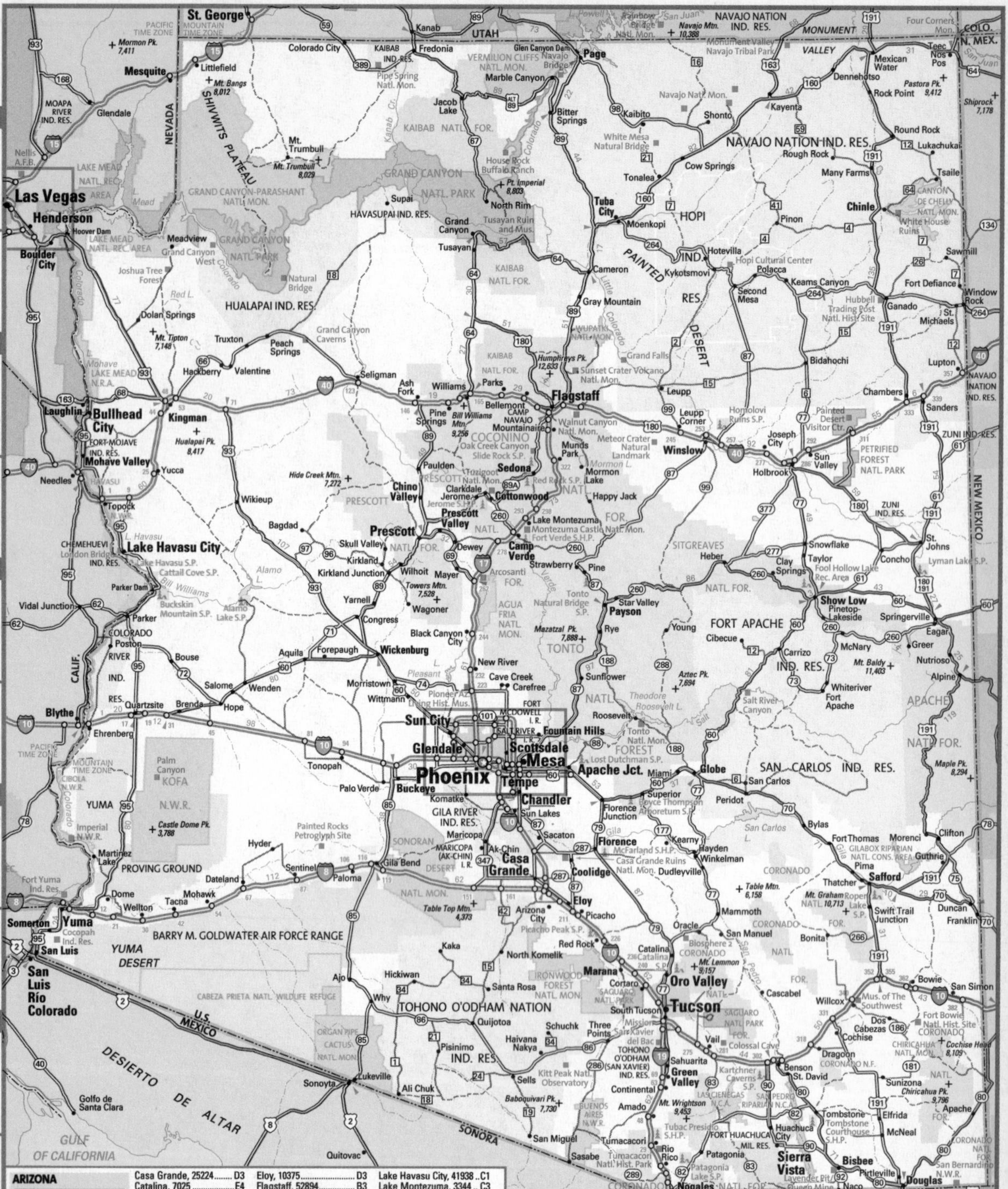

ARIZONA

POP: 5,130,632, rank 20

AREA: 114,000 sq mi, rank 6

Ajo, 3705 .... E2
Apache Jct., 31814 .... D3
Arizona City, 4385 .... D3
Bagdad, 1578 .... C2
Benson, 4711 .... E4
Bisbee, 6090 .... F5
Black Canyon City, 2697 C3
Buckeye, 6537 .... D3
Bullhead City, 33769 .... B1
Camp Verde, 9451 .... C3
Carefree, 2927 .... D3
Casa Grande, 25224 .... D3
Catalina, 7025 .... E4
Cave Creek, 3728 .... D3
Chandler, 176581 .... D3
Chinle, 5366 .... A5
Chino Valley, 7835 .... C3
Clarkdale, 3422 .... C3
Clifton, 2596 .... D5
Colorado City, 3334 .... A2
Congress, 1717 .... C2
Coolidge, 7786 .... D3
Cortaro, 1700 .... E4
Cottonwood, 9179 .... C3
Dewey, 6295 .... C3
Dolan Sprs., 1867 .... B1
Douglas, 14312 .... F5
Eagar, 4033 .... C5
Eloy, 10375 .... D3
Flagstaff, 52894 .... B3
Florence, 17054 .... D3
Ft. Defiance, 4061 .... B5
Fountain Hills, 20235 .... D3
Ganado, 1505 .... B5
Gila Bend, 1980 .... D2
Glendale, 218812 .... D3
Globe, 7486 .... D4
Green Valley, 17283 .... E4
Heber, 2722 .... C4
Holbrook, 4917 .... C4
Huachuca City, 1751 .... E4
Kaibito, 1607 .... A4
Kayenta, 4922 .... A4
Kearny, 2249 .... D4
Kingman, 20069 .... B1
Lake Havasu City, 41938 .. C1
Lake Montezuma, 3344 .. C3
Lukachukai, 1565 .... A5
Mammoth, 1762 .... E4
Many Farms, 1548 .... A5
Marana, 13556 .... E4
Mesa, 396375 .... D3
Miami, 1936 .... D4
Mohave Valley, 13694 .... B1
Morenci, 1879 .... D5
New River, 10740 .... C3
Nogales, 20878 .... F4
Oracle, 3563 .... E4
Oro Valley, 29700 .... E4
Page, 6809 .... A3
Parker, 3140 .... C1
Paulden, 3420 .... C3
Payson, 13620 .... C4
Phoenix, 1321045 .... D3
Pima, 1989 .... D5
Pine, 1931 .... C3
Pinetop-Lakeside, 3582 .. C5
Pirtleville, 1550 .... F5
Prescott, 33938 .... C3
Prescott Valley, 23535 .... C3
Quartzsite, 3354 .... D1
Rio Rico, 3164 .... F4
Sacaton, 1584 .... D3
Safford, 9232 .... D5
Sahuarita, 3242 .... E4
St. David, 1744 .... E4
St. Johns, 3269 .... C5
Salome, 1690 .... D2
San Carlos, 3716 .... D4
San Luis, 15322 .... E1
San Manuel, 4375 .... E4
Scottsdale, 202705 .... D3
Sedona, 10192 .... C3
Sells, 2799 .... E3
Show Low, 7695 .... C5
Sierra Vista, 37775 .... F4
Snowflake, 4460 .... C5
Somerton, 7266 .... E1
S. Tucson, 5490 .... E4
Springerville, 1972 .... C5
Sun City, 38309 .... D3
Sun Lakes, 11936 .... D3
Superior, 3254 .... D4
Swift Trail Jct., 2195 .... D5
Taylor, 3176 .... C5
Tempe, 158625 .... D3
Thatcher, 4022 .... D5
Three Pts., 5273 .... E4
Tombstone, 1504 .... E5
Tuba City, 8225 .... A4
Tucson, 486699 .... E4
Vail, 2484 .... E4
Wellton, 1829 .... E1
Whiteriver, 5220 .... D5
Wickenburg, 5082 .... C2
Willcox, 3733 .... E5
Williams, 2842 .... B3
Window Rock, 3059 .... B5
Winslow, 9520 .... B4
Yuma, 77515 .... E1

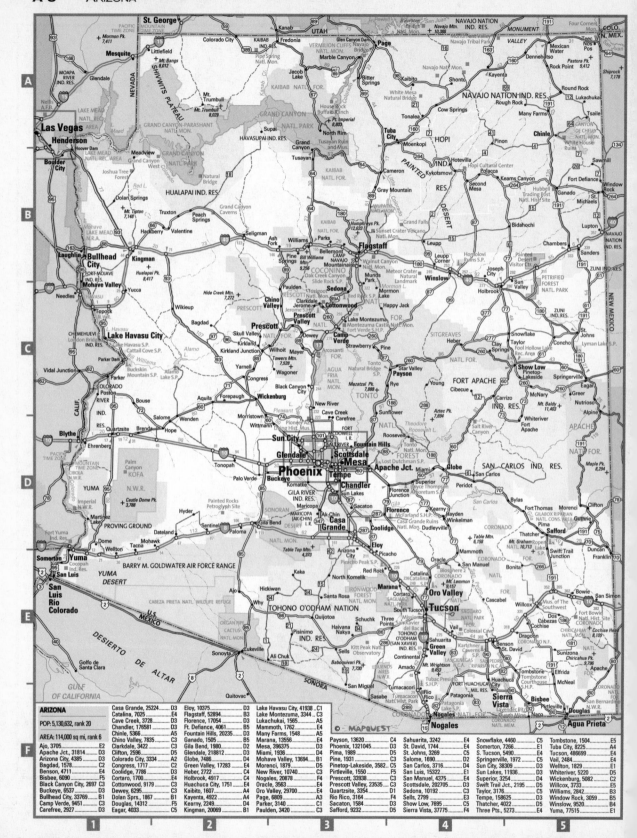

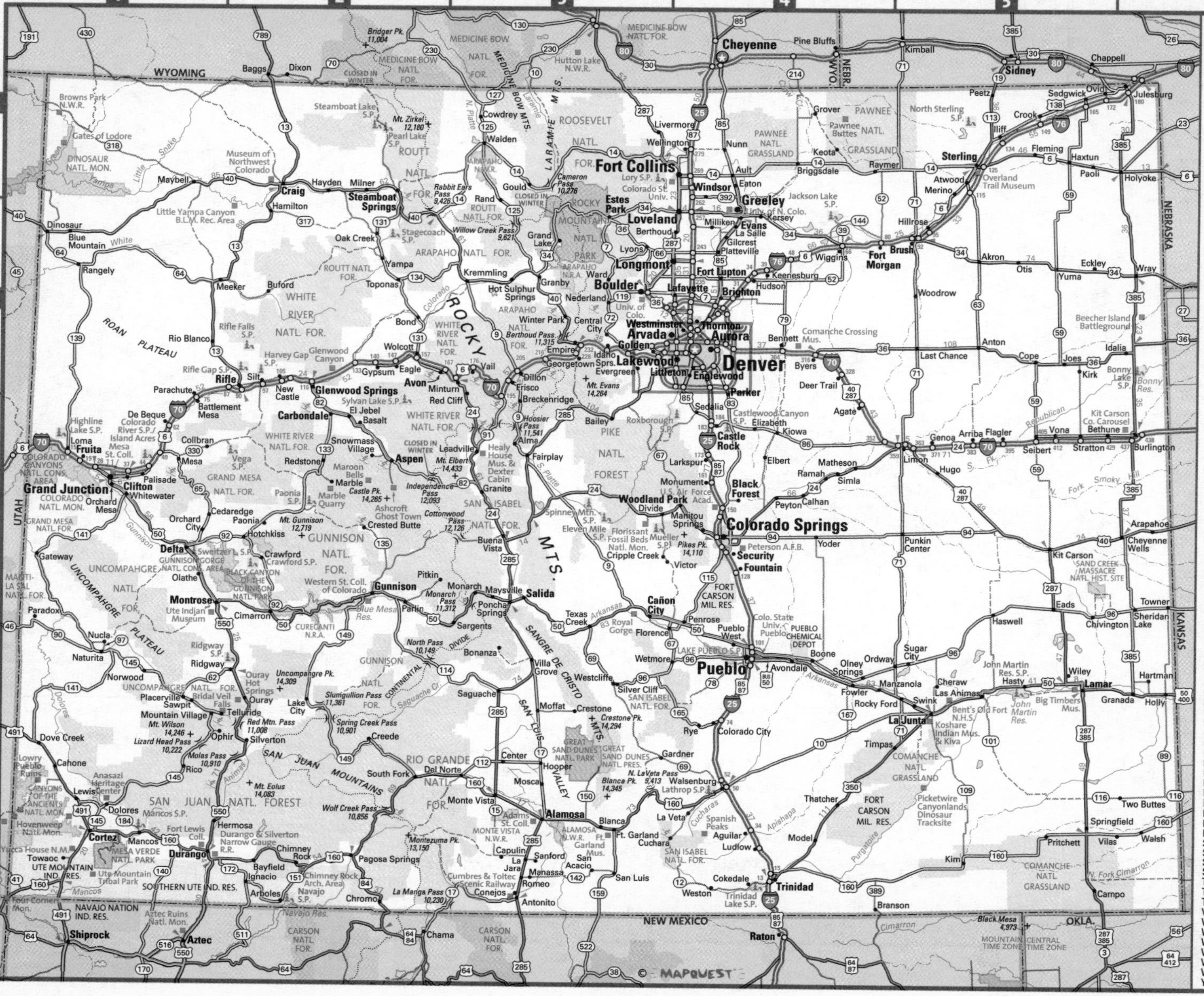

COLORADO

POP: 4,301,261, rank 24

AREA: 104,091 sq mi, rank 8

Alamosa, 7960	E3
Arvada, 102153	B4
Aspen, 5914	C2
Aurora, 276393	B4
Avon, 5561	B2
Basalt, 2681	C2
Battlement Mesa, 3497	C1
Bennett, 2021	B4
Berthoud, 4839	B4
Black Forest, 13247	C4
Boulder, 94673	B3
Breckenridge, 2408	B3
Brighton, 20905	B4
Brush, 5117	B5
Buena Vista, 2195	C3
Burlington, 3678	C6
Canon City, 15431	D3
Carbondale, 5196	C2
Castle Rock, 20224	C4
Center, 2392	D3
Clifton, 17345	C1
Colorado City, 2018	D4
Colorado Sprs., 360890	C4
Cortez, 7977	E1
Craig, 9189	A2
Delta, 6400	C1
Denver, 554636	B4
Durango, 13922	E1
Eagle, 3032	B2
Eaton, 2690	A4
El Jebel, 4488	C2
Englewood, 31727	B4
Estes Park, 5413	B3
Evans, 9514	B4
Evergreen, 9216	B3
Florence, 3653	D4
Ft. Collins, 118652	A4
Ft. Lupton, 6787	B4
Ft. Morgan, 11034	B4
Fountain, 15197	C4
Frisco, 2443	B3
Fruita, 6478	C1
Glenwood Sprs., 7736	B2
Golden, 17159	B3
Grand Jct., 41986	C1
Greeley, 76930	A4
Gunnison, 5409	C2
Gypsum, 3654	B2
Holyoke, 2261	A6
Lafayette, 23197	B4
La Junta, 7568	D5
Lakewood, 144126	B4
Lamar, 8869	D5
Las Animas, 2758	D5
Leadville, 2821	C3
Limon, 2071	C5
Littleton, 40340	B4
Longmont, 71093	B4
Loveland, 50608	B4
Manitou Sprs., 4980	C4
Meeker, 2242	B1
Milliken, 2888	B4
Monte Vista, 4529	E3
Montrose, 12344	D1
Orchard City, 2880	C1
Orchard Mesa, 6456	C1
Palisade, 2579	C1
Parker, 23558	B4
Penrose, 4070	D4
Platteville, 2370	B4
Pueblo, 102121	D4
Pueblo West, 16899	D4
Rangely, 2096	B1
Rifle, 6784	B2
Rocky Ford, 4286	D5
Salida, 5504	C3
Security, 29845	C4
Steamboat Sprs., 9815	A2
Sterling, 11360	A5
Telluride, 2221	D2
Thornton, 82384	B4
Trinidad, 9078	E4
Vail, 4531	B3
Walsenburg, 4182	D4
Wellington, 2672	A4
Westminster, 100940	B4
Windsor, 9896	A4
Woodland Park, 6515	C4
Wray, 2187	B6
Yuma, 3285	B5

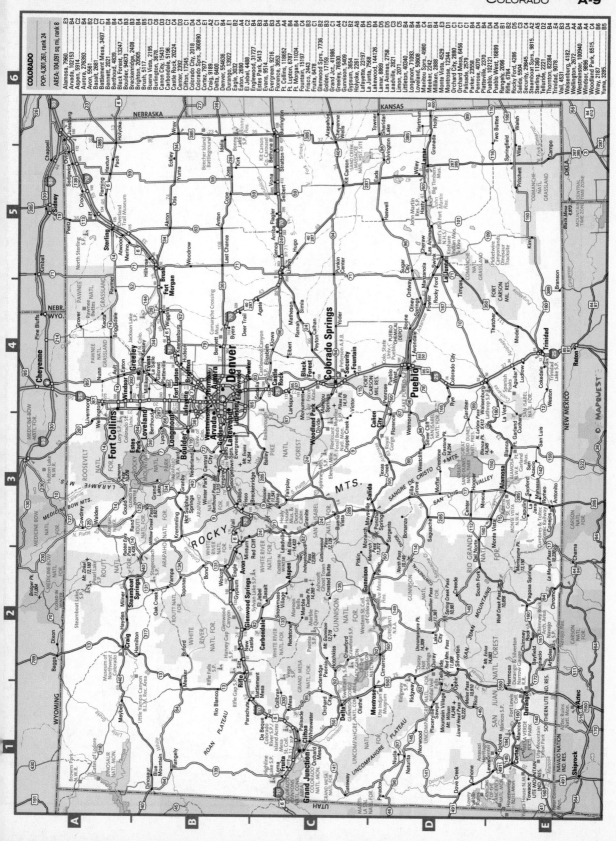

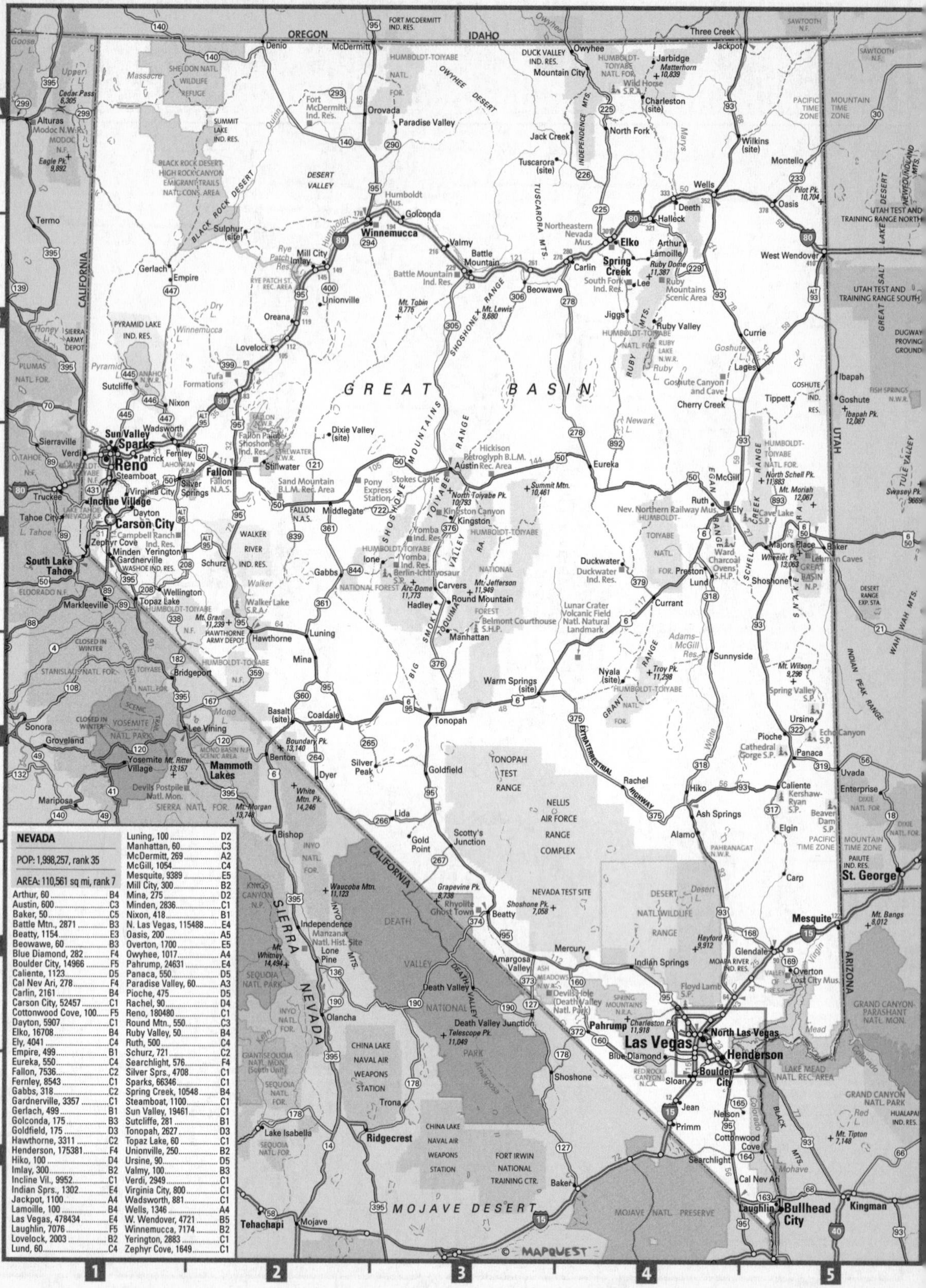

NEVADA

POP: 1,998,257, rank 35

AREA: 110,561 sq mi, rank 7

Arthur, 60	B4	Luning, 100	D2
Austin, 600	C3	Manhattan, 60	C3
Baker, 50	C5	McDermitt, 269	A2
Battle Mtn., 2871	B3	McGill, 1054	C4
Beatty, 1154	E3	Mesquite, 9389	E5
Beowawe, 60	B3	Mill City, 300	B2
Blue Diamond, 282	F4	Mina, 275	D2
Boulder City, 14966	F5	Minden, 2836	C1
Caliente, 1123	D5	Nixon, 418	B1
Cal Nev Ari, 278	F4	N. Las Vegas, 115488	E4
Carlin, 2161	B4	Oasis, 200	A5
Carson City, 52457	C1	Overton, 1700	E5
Cottonwood Cove, 100	F5	Owyhee, 1017	A4
Dayton, 5907	C1	Pahrump, 24631	E4
Elko, 16708	B4	Panaca, 550	D5
Ely, 4041	C4	Paradise Valley, 60	A3
Empire, 499	B1	Pioche, 475	D5
Eureka, 550	C4	Rachel, 90	D4
Fallon, 7536	C2	Reno, 180480	C1
Fernley, 8543	C1	Round Mtn., 550	C3
Gabbs, 318	C2	Ruby Valley, 50	B4
Gardnerville, 3357	C1	Ruth, 500	C4
Gerlach, 499	B1	Schurz, 721	C2
Golconda, 175	B3	Searchlight, 576	F4
Goldfield, 175	D3	Silver Sprs., 4708	C1
Hawthorne, 3311	C2	Sparks, 66346	C1
Henderson, 175381	F4	Spring Creek, 10548	B4
Hiko, 100	D4	Steamboat, 1100	C1
Imlay, 300	B2	Sun Valley, 19461	C1
Incline Vil., 9952	C1	Sutcliffe, 281	B1
Indian Sprs., 1302	E4	Tonopah, 2627	D3
Jackpot, 1100	A4	Topaz Lake, 60	C1
Lamoille, 100	B4	Unionville, 250	B2
Las Vegas, 478434	E4	Ursine, 90	D5
Laughlin, 7076	F5	Valmy, 100	B3
Lovelock, 2003	B2	Verdi, 2949	C1
Lund, 60	C4	Virginia City, 800	C1
		Wadsworth, 881	C1
		Wells, 1346	A4
		W. Wendover, 4721	B5
		Winnemucca, 7174	B2
		Yerington, 2883	C1
		Zephyr Cove, 1649	C1

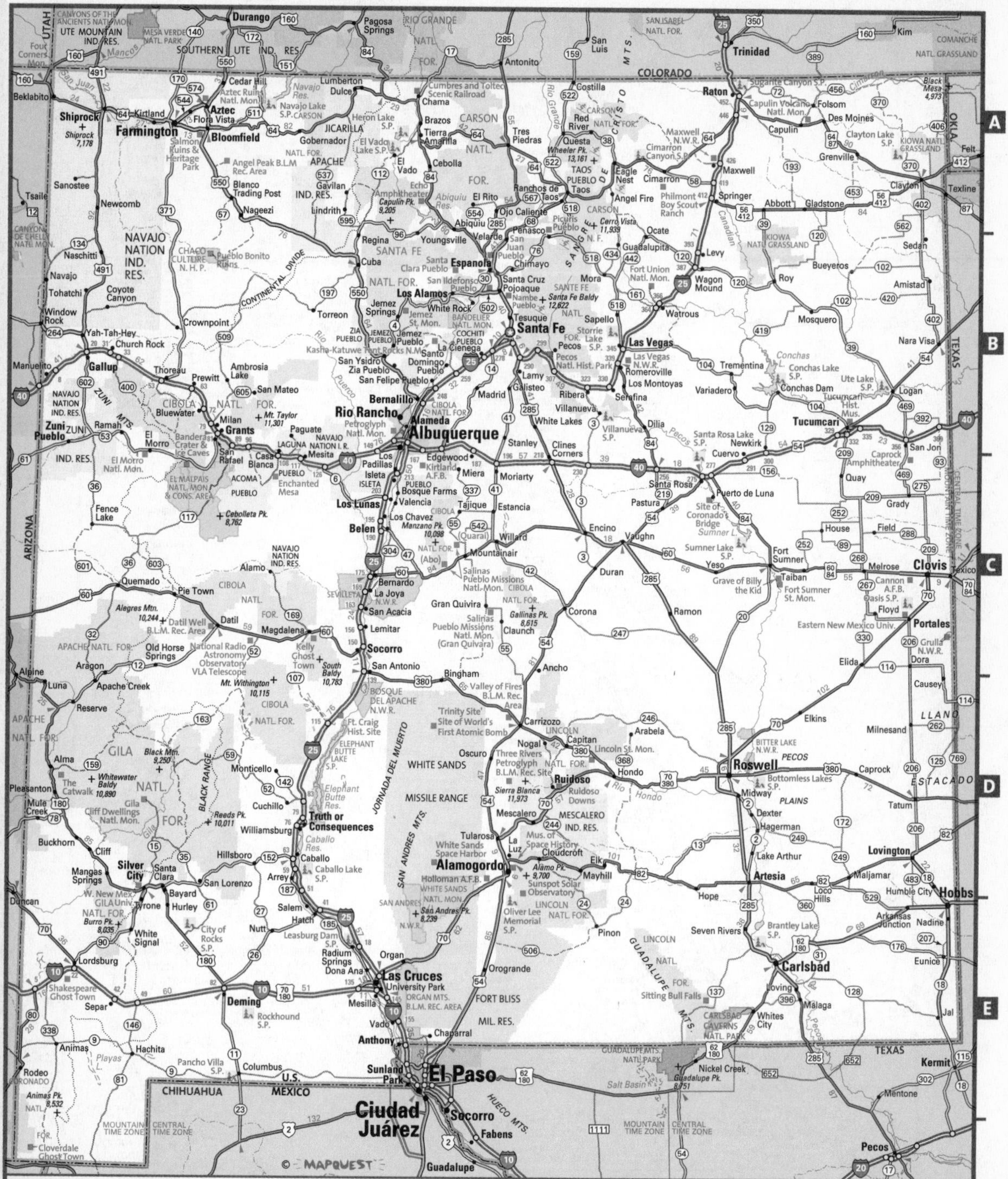

NEW MEXICO

POP: 1,819,046, rank 36

AREA: 121,593 sq mi, rank 5

Alameda, 4200 .... B3
Alamo, 1183 .... C2
Alamogordo, 35582 .... D3
Albuquerque, 448607 .... B3
Angel Fire, 1048 .... A4
Anthony, 7904 .... E3
Artesia, 10692 .... D4
Aztec, 6378 .... A2
Bayard, 2534 .... E1
Belen, 6901 .... C2
Bernalillo, 6611 .... B3
Bloomfield, 6417 .... A2
Bosque Farms, 3931 .... C3
Capitan, 1443 .... D3
Carlsbad, 25625 .... E4
Carrizozo, 1036 .... D3
Casa Blanca, 669 .... C2
Chama, 1199 .... A3
Chaparral, 6117 .... E3
Chimayo, 2924 .... B3
Church Rock, 1077 .... B1
Cimarron, 917 .... A4
Clayton, 2524 .... A5
Cloudcroft, 749 .... D3
Clovis, 32667 .... C5
Columbus, 1765 .... E2
Crownpoint, 2630 .... B1
Deming, 14116 .... E2
Dexter, 1235 .... D4
Doña Ana, 1379 .... E2
Dulce, 2623 .... A2
Edgewood, 1893 .... C3
Espanola, 9688 .... B3
Estancia, 1584 .... C3
Eunice, 2562 .... E5
Farmington, 37844 .... A1
Flora Vista, 1383 .... A1
Ft. Sumner, 1249 .... C4
Gallup, 20209 .... B1
Grants, 8806 .... B2
Hagerman, 1168 .... D4
Hatch, 1673 .... E2
Hobbs, 28657 .... E5
Hurley, 1464 .... E1
Jal, 1996 .... E5
Jemez Pueblo, 1953 .... B2
Kirtland, 6190 .... A1
La Cienega, 3007 .... B3
La Luz, 1615 .... D3
Las Cruces, 74267 .... E2
Las Vegas, 14565 .... B4
Logan, 1094 .... B5
Lordsburg, 3379 .... E1
Los Alamos, 11909 .... B3
Los Chavez, 5033 .... C2
Los Lunas, 10034 .... C2
Los Padillas, 1800 .... C2
Loving, 1326 .... E5
Lovington, 9471 .... D5
Magdalena, 913 .... C2
Melrose, 736 .... C5
Mescalero, 1233 .... D3
Mesilla, 2180 .... E2
Mesita, 776 .... C2
Midway, 700 .... D4
Milan, 1891 .... B2
Moriarty, 1765 .... C3
Mountainair, 1116 .... C3
Navajo, 2097 .... B1
Pecos, 1441 .... B3
Pojoaque, 1261 .... B3
Portales, 11131 .... C5
Questa, 1864 .... A3
Radium Sprs., 1518 .... E2
Ranchos de Taos, 2390 .... A3
Raton, 7282 .... A4
Rio Rancho, 51765 .... B3
Roswell, 45293 .... D4
Ruidoso, 7698 .... D3
Salem, 795 .... E2
San Felipe Pueblo, 2080 .... B3
Santa Clara, 1944 .... D1
Santa Fe, 62203 .... B3
Santa Rosa, 2744 .... C4
Santo Domingo Pueblo, 2550 .... B3
Shiprock, 8156 .... A1
Silver City, 10545 .... D1
Socorro, 8877 .... C2
Springer, 1285 .... A4
Sunland Park, 13309 .... E3
Taos, 4700 .... A3
Tatum, 683 .... D5
Tesuque, 909 .... B3
Texico, 1065 .... C5
Thoreau, 1863 .... B1
Tohatchi, 1037 .... B1
Truth or Consequences, 7289 .... D2
Tucumcari, 5989 .... B5
Tularosa, 2864 .... D3
University Park, 2732 .... E2
Vado, 3003 .... E2
Valencia, 4500 .... C2
White Rock, 6045 .... B3
Zuni Pueblo, 6367 .... B1

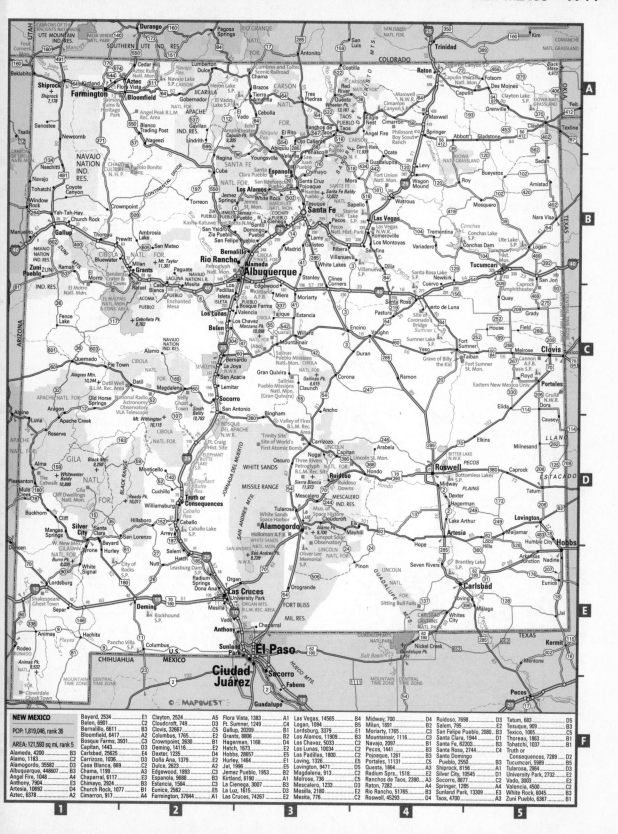

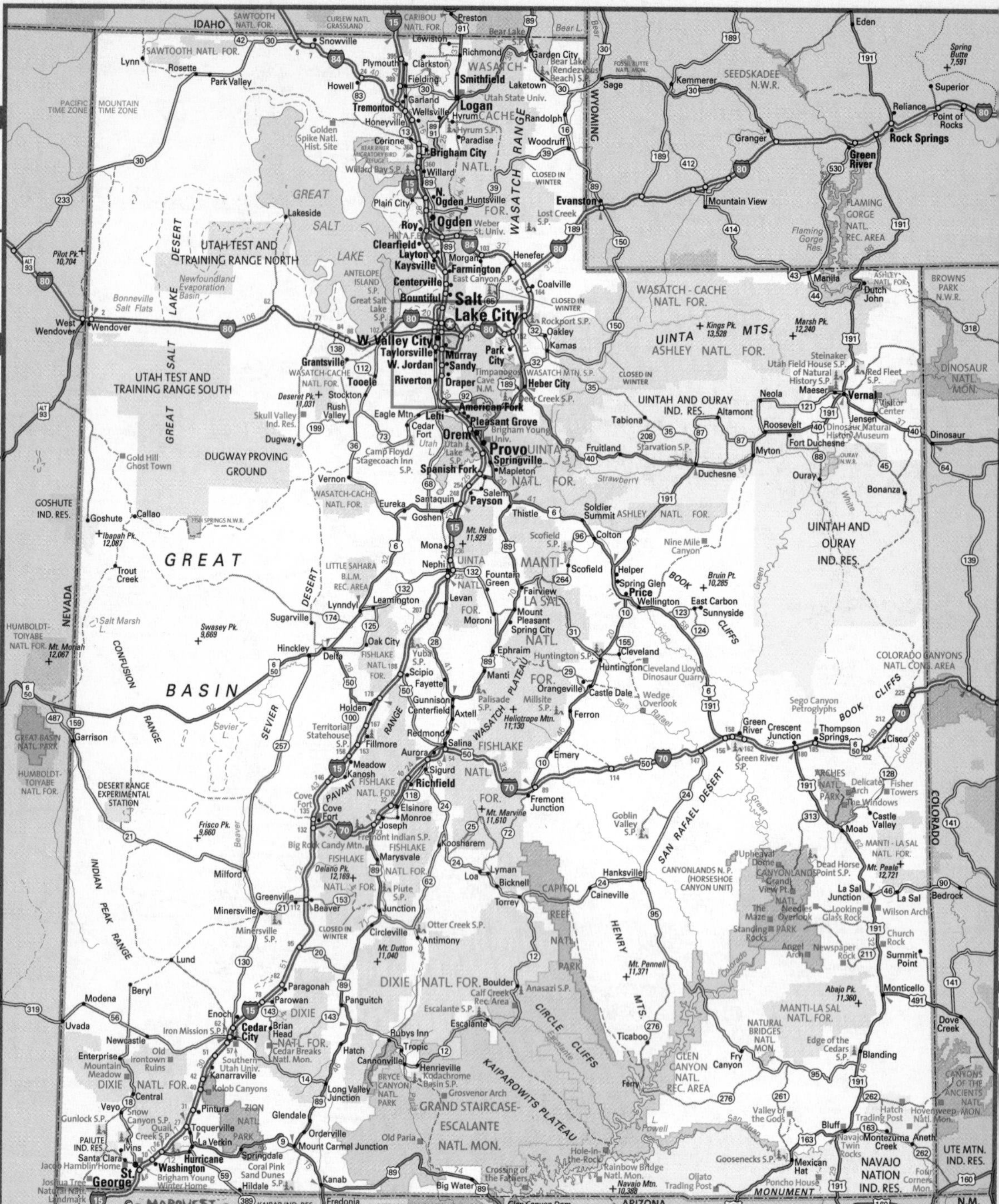

UTAH	
POP: 2,233,169, rank 34	
AREA: 84,899 sq mi, rank 11	
American Fork, 21941	B3
Aurora, 947	D3
Beaver, 2454	D2
Blanding, 3162	E5
Bountiful, 41301	B3
Brigham City, 17411	A3
Castle Dale, 1657	D3
Cedar City, 20527	E2
Centerfield, 1048	D3
Centerville, 14585	B3
Clearfield, 25974	B3
Coalville, 1382	B3
Delta, 3209	C2
Draper, 25220	B3
Duchesne, 1408	C4
Eagle Mtn., 2157	B3
E. Carbon, 1393	C4
Enoch, 3467	E2
Enterprise, 1285	E1
Ephraim, 4505	C3
Fairview, 1160	C3
Farmington, 12081	B3
Ferron, 1623	D3
Fillmore, 2253	D2
Fountain Green, 945	C3
Garland, 1943	A3
Grantsville, 6015	B2
Green River, 973	D4
Gunnison, 2394	D3
Heber City, 7291	B3
Helper, 2025	C4
Hildale, 1895	F2
Honeyville, 1214	A3
Huntington, 2131	C4
Hurricane, 8250	F1
Hyrum, 6316	A3
Ivins, 4450	F1
Kamas, 1274	B3
Kanab, 3564	F2
Kaysville, 20351	B3
La Verkin, 3392	F1
Layton, 58474	B3
Lehi, 19028	B3
Lewiston, 1877	A3
Logan, 42670	A3
Maeser, 2855	B5
Manti, 3040	C3
Mapleton, 5809	C3
Milford, 1451	D2
Moab, 4779	D5
Monroe, 1845	D2
Monticello, 1958	E5
Morgan, 2635	B3
Moroni, 1280	C3
Mt. Pleasant, 2707	C3
Murray, 34024	B3
Nephi, 4733	C3
N. Ogden, 15026	A3
Oakley, 948	B3
Ogden, 77226	A3
Orangeville, 1398	D3
Orem, 84324	B3
Panguitch, 1623	E2
Park City, 7371	B3
Parowan, 2565	E2
Payson, 12716	C3
Plain City, 3489	A3
Pleasant Grove, 23468	B3
Price, 8402	C4
Provo, 105166	B3
Richfield, 6847	D3
Richmond, 2051	A3
Riverton, 25011	B3
Roosevelt, 4299	B4
Roy, 32885	B3
St. George, 49663	F1
Salem, 4372	C3
Salina, 2393	D3
Salt Lake City, 181743	B3
Sandy, 88418	B3
Santa Clara, 4630	F1
Santaquin, 4834	C3
Smithfield, 7261	A3
Spanish Fork, 20246	C3
Spring City, 956	C3
Spring Glen, 1000	C4
Springville, 20424	C3
Taylorsville, 57439	B3
Tooele, 22502	B2
Tremonton, 5592	A3
Vernal, 7714	B5
Washington, 8186	F1
Wellington, 1666	C4
Wellsville, 2728	A3
Wendover, 1537	B1
W. Jordan, 68336	B3
W. Valley City, 108896	B3
Willard, 1630	A3

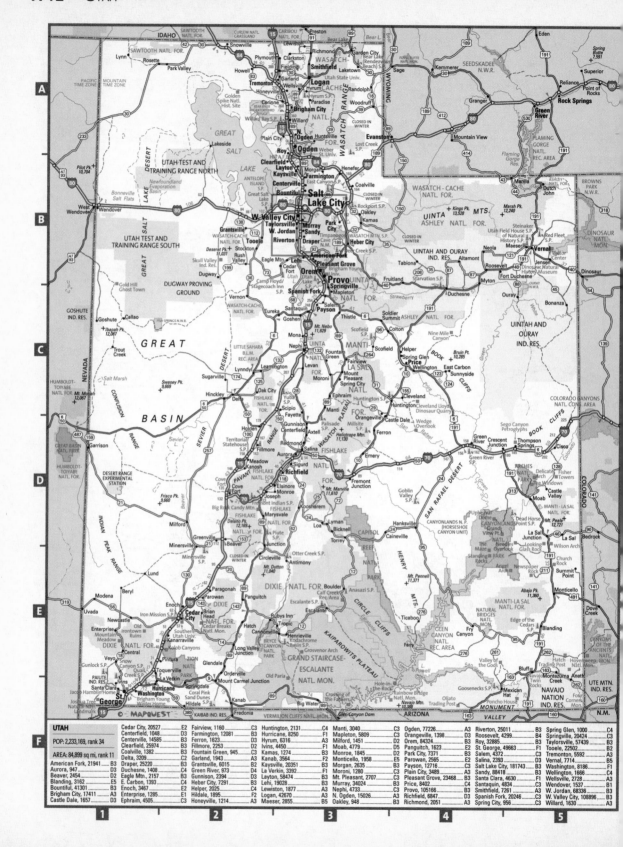

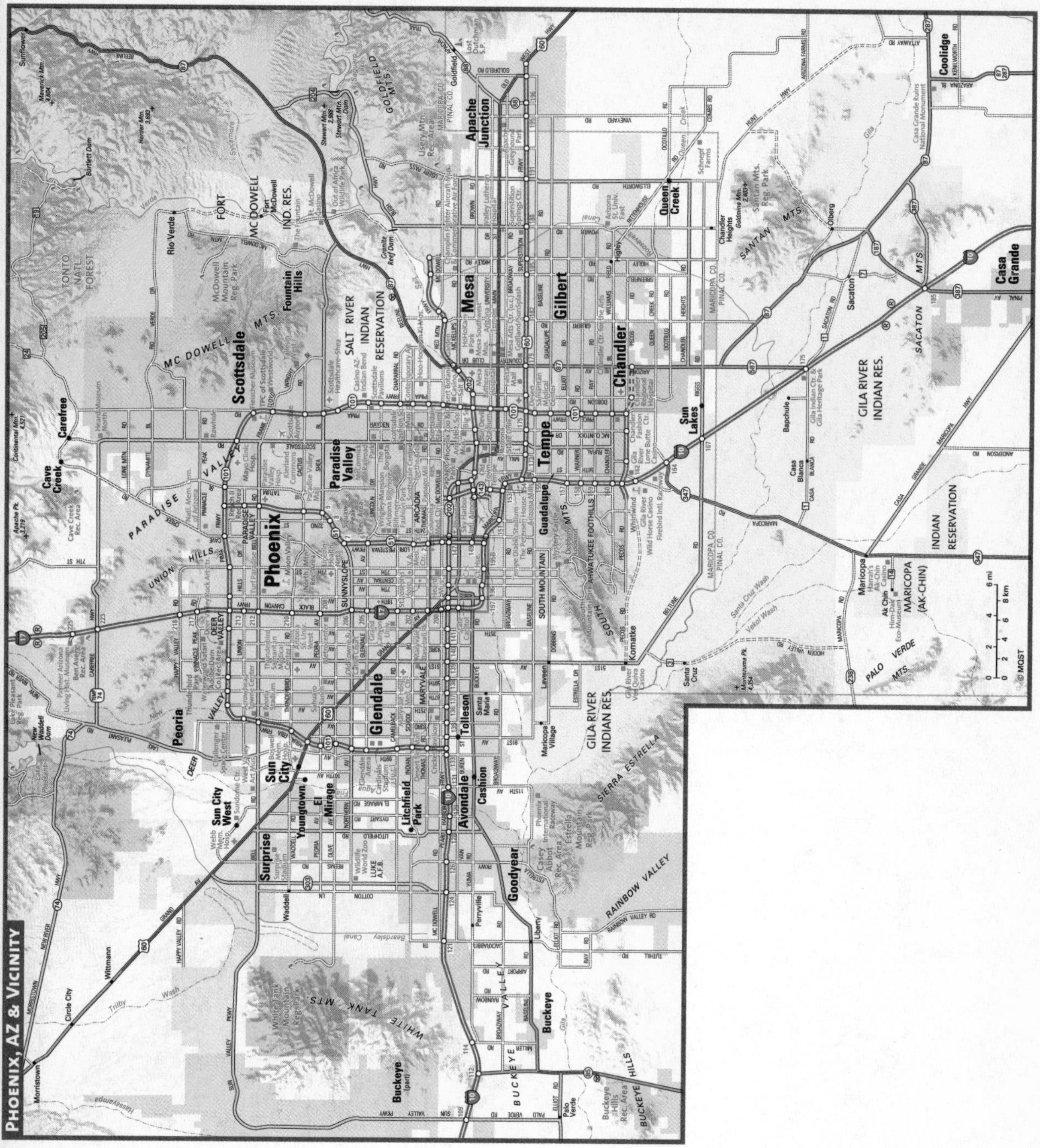
PHOENIX, AZ & VICINITY
Phoenix
Scottsdale
Mesa
Tempe
Chandler
Gilbert
Glendale
Peoria
Apache Junction
Fountain Hills
Paradise Valley
Queen Creek
Sun Lakes
Guadalupe
Avondale
Goodyear
Tolleson
Cashion
Litchfield Park
Sun City
Sun City West
Youngtown
El Mirage
Surprise
Buckeye
Carefree
Cave Creek
Casa Grande
Coolidge
Maricopa
Sacaton
Komatke
Laveen
Wittmann
Circle City
Morristown
Waddell
Liberty
Palo Verde
Santa Cruz
Rio Verde
SALT RIVER INDIAN RESERVATION
GILA RIVER INDIAN RES.
FORT MC DOWELL IND. RES.
MARICOPA (AK-CHIN) INDIAN RESERVATION
TONTO NATL. FOREST
MC DOWELL MTS.
WHITE TANK MTS
SIERRA ESTRELLA
SOUTH MOUNTAIN
SANTAN MTS.
SACATON MTS.
GOLDFIELD MTS.
PALO VERDE MTS.
BUCKEYE HILLS
RAINBOW VALLEY
PARADISE VALLEY
UNION HILLS
© MQST

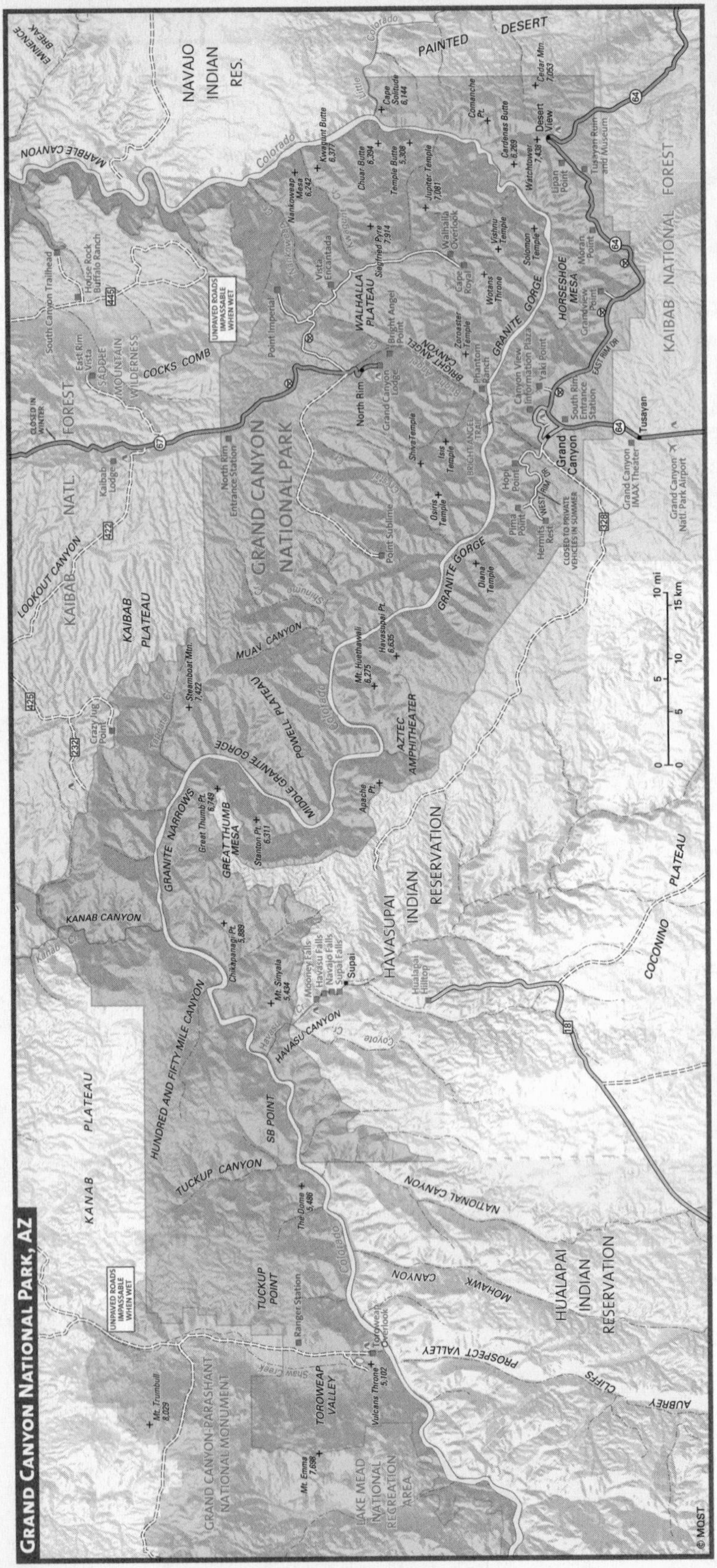
GRAND CANYON NATIONAL PARK, AZ
GRAND CANYON NATIONAL PARK
KAIBAB PLATEAU
HAVASUPAI INDIAN RESERVATION
HUALAPAI INDIAN RESERVATION
NAVAJO INDIAN RES.
KAIBAB NATIONAL FOREST
COCONINO PLATEAU
PAINTED DESERT
GRAND CANYON-PARASHANT NATIONAL MONUMENT
LAKE MEAD NATIONAL RECREATION AREA
© MOST

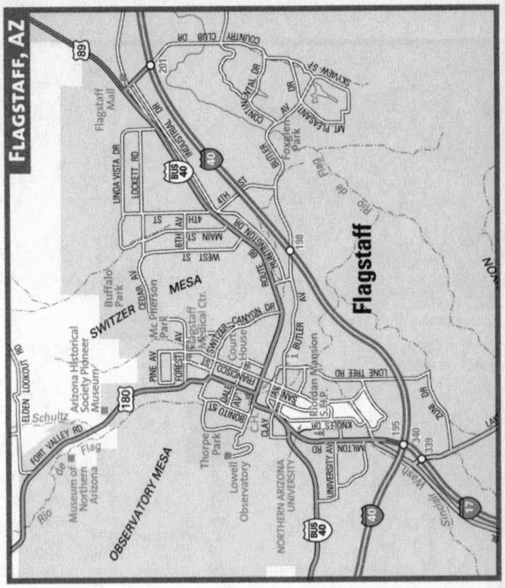
FLAGSTAFF, AZ
Flagstaff
OBSERVATORY MESA
SWITZER MESA

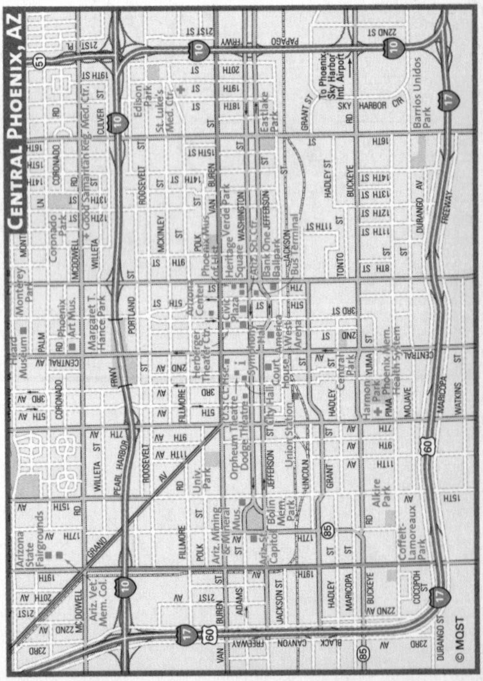
CENTRAL PHOENIX, AZ
© MOST

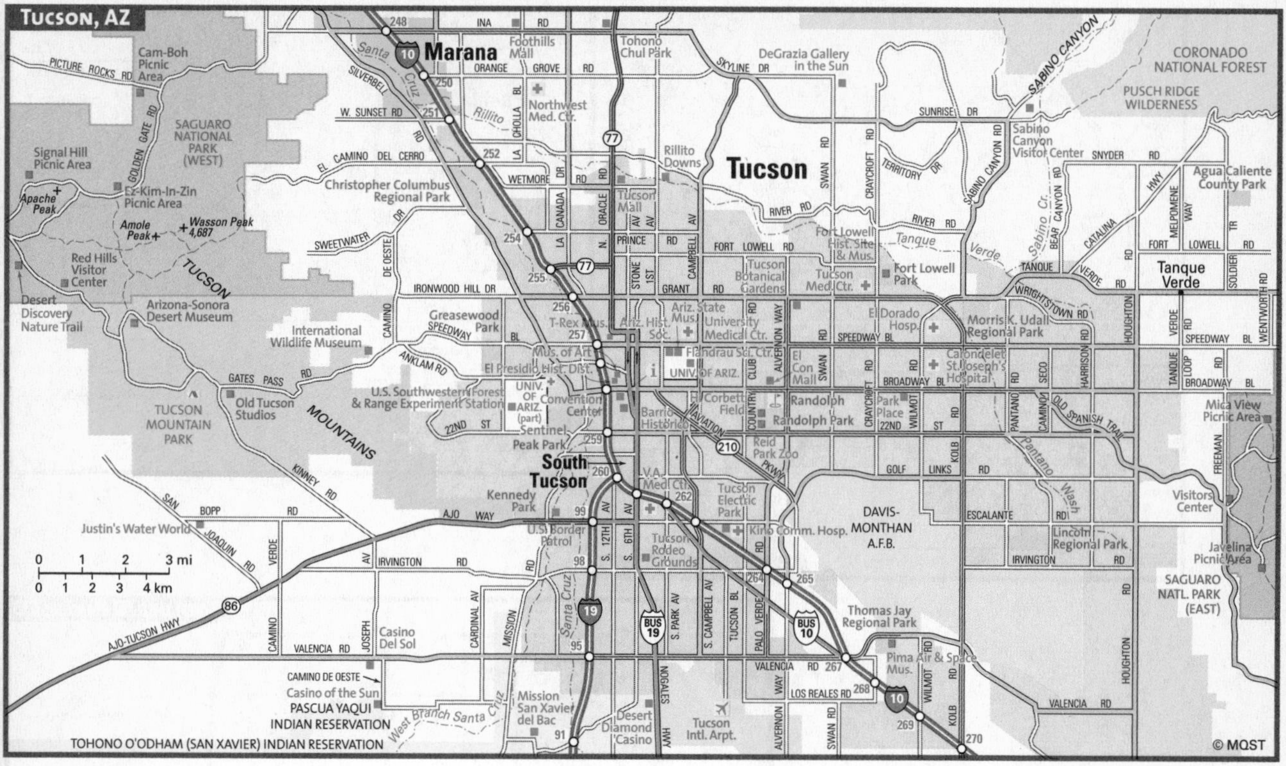
TUCSON, AZ
Marana
Tucson
South Tucson
Tanque Verde
Cam-Boh Picnic Area
Signal Hill Picnic Area
SAGUARO NATIONAL PARK (WEST)
Ez-Kim-In-Zin Picnic Area
Apache Peak
Amole Peak
Wasson Peak 4,687
Red Hills Visitor Center
Desert Discovery Nature Trail
Arizona-Sonora Desert Museum
International Wildlife Museum
Greasewood Park
Christopher Columbus Regional Park
Foothills Mall
Northwest Med. Ctr.
Tohono Chul Park
Rillito Downs
Tucson Mall
DeGrazia Gallery in the Sun
CORONADO NATIONAL FOREST
PUSCH RIDGE WILDERNESS
Sabino Canyon Visitor Center
Agua Caliente County Park
Fort Lowell Hist. Site & Mus.
Fort Lowell Park
Tucson Botanical Gardens
Tucson Med. Ctr.
El Dorado Hosp.
Morris K. Udall Regional Park
T-Rex Mus.
Ariz. Hist. Soc.
Ariz. State Mus.
University Medical Ctr.
Flandrau Sci. Ctr.
Mus. of Art
El Presidio Hist. Dist.
UNIV. OF ARIZ.
UNIV. OF ARIZ. (part)
Convention Center
U.S. Southwestern Forest & Range Experiment Station
Sentinel Peak Park
Barrio Historico
Corbett Field
El Con Mall
Randolph
Randolph Park
Park Place
Carondelet St. Joseph's Hospital
Reid Park Zoo
Mica View Picnic Area
Old Tucson Studios
TUCSON MOUNTAIN PARK
TUCSON MOUNTAINS
Kennedy Park
V.A. Med. Ctr.
Tucson Electric Park
DAVIS-MONTHAN A.F.B.
Visitors Center
Lincoln Regional Park
Javelina Picnic Area
SAGUARO NATL. PARK (EAST)
Justin's Water World
U.S. Border Patrol
Kino Comm. Hosp.
Tucson Rodeo Grounds
Thomas Jay Regional Park
Casino Del Sol
Pima Air & Space Mus.
CAMINO DE OESTE
Casino of the Sun
PASCUA YAQUI INDIAN RESERVATION
Mission San Xavier del Bac
Desert Diamond Casino
Tucson Intl. Arpt.
TOHONO O'ODHAM (SAN XAVIER) INDIAN RESERVATION
Santa Cruz
Rillito
Tanque Verde
Sabino Cr.
Pantano Wash
West Branch Santa Cruz
INA RD
ORANGE GROVE RD
PICTURE ROCKS RD
W. SUNSET RD
EL CAMINO DEL CERRO
WETMORE RD
SKYLINE DR
SUNRISE DR
SNYDER RD
RIVER RD
FORT LOWELL RD
PRINCE RD
GRANT RD
TANQUE VERDE RD
WRIGHTSTOWN RD
SPEEDWAY BL
BROADWAY BL
22ND ST
GOLF LINKS RD
ESCALANTE RD
IRVINGTON RD
VALENCIA RD
LOS REALES RD
AJO WAY
BOPP RD
GATES PASS RD
ANKLAM RD
IRONWOOD HILL DR
SWEETWATER DR
KINNEY RD
SAN JOAQUIN RD
AJO-TUCSON HWY
SILVERBELL RD
GOLDEN GATE RD
OLD SPANISH TRAIL
AVIATION PKWY
SABINO CANYON RD
TERRITORY DR
BEAR CANYON RD
CATALINA HWY
HOUGHTON RD
FREEMAN RD
SOLDIER TR
WENTWORTH RD
MELPOMENE WAY
CRAYCROFT RD
SWAN RD
WILMOT RD
KOLB RD
PANTANO RD
CAMINO SECO
HARRISON RD
ALVERNON WAY
COUNTRY CLUB RD
CAMPBELL AV
STONE AV
1ST AV
ORACLE RD
CANADA DR
LA CHOLLA BL
DE OESTE
CAMINO DE OESTE
VERDE
JOSEPH
CARDINAL AV
MISSION RD
S. 12TH AV
S. 6TH AV
S. PARK AV
S. CAMPBELL AV
TUCSON BL
PALO VERDE RD
NOGALES HWY
VERDE LOOP
TANQUE
248
250
251
252
254
255
256
257
259
260
262
264
265
267
268
269
270
91
95
98
99
0 1 2 3 mi
0 1 2 3 4 km
© MQST

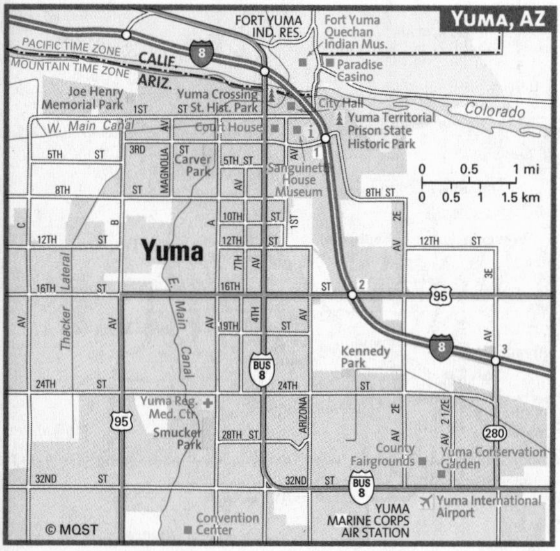
YUMA, AZ
Yuma
FORT YUMA IND. RES.
Fort Yuma Quechan Indian Mus.
Paradise Casino
PACIFIC TIME ZONE
MOUNTAIN TIME ZONE
CALIF.
ARIZ.
Joe Henry Memorial Park
Yuma Crossing St. Hist. Park
City Hall
Yuma Territorial Prison State Historic Park
Court House
Carver Park
Sanguinetti House Museum
Colorado
W. Main Canal
E. Main Canal
Lateral
Thacker
Kennedy Park
Yuma Reg. Med. Ctr.
Smucker Park
County Fairgrounds
Yuma Conservation Garden
Yuma International Airport
YUMA MARINE CORPS AIR STATION
Convention Center
1ST
3RD
5TH ST
8TH ST
10TH
12TH ST
16TH ST
19TH ST
24TH ST
28TH ST
32ND ST
MAGNOLIA AV
ARIZONA
0 0.5 1 mi
0 0.5 1 1.5 km
© MQST

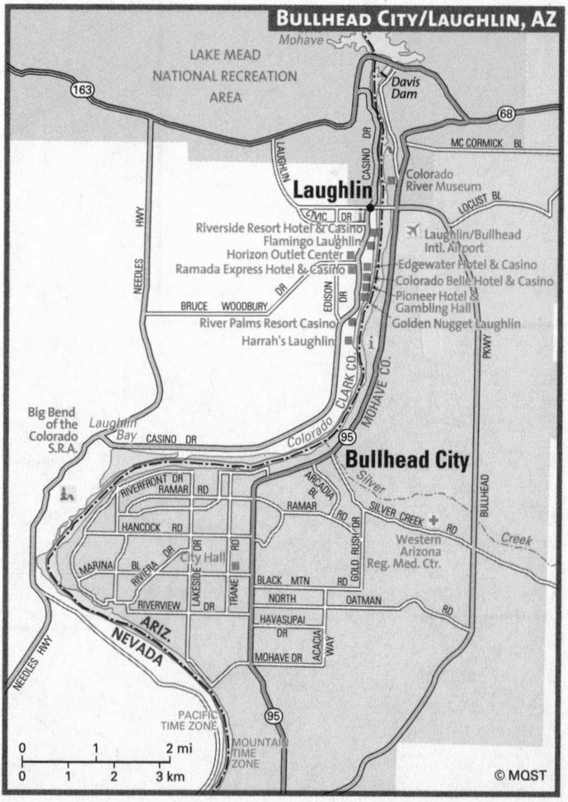
BULLHEAD CITY/LAUGHLIN, AZ
LAKE MEAD NATIONAL RECREATION AREA
Mohave
Davis Dam
Laughlin
Bullhead City
Colorado River Museum
MC CORMICK BL
LOCUST BL
CASINO DR
CIVIC DR
LAUGHLIN
NEEDLES HWY
Riverside Resort Hotel & Casino
Flamingo Laughlin
Horizon Outlet Center
Ramada Express Hotel & Casino
Laughlin/Bullhead Intl. Airport
Edgewater Hotel & Casino
Colorado Belle Hotel & Casino
Pioneer Hotel & Gambling Hall
Golden Nugget Laughlin
River Palms Resort Casino
Harrah's Laughlin
BRUCE WOODBURY DR
EDISON DR
CLARK CO.
MOHAVE CO.
Big Bend of the Colorado S.R.A.
Laughlin Bay
Colorado
RIVERFRONT DR
RAMAR RD
HANCOCK RD
MARINA BL
RIVERA DR
City Hall
RIVERVIEW DR
LAKESIDE DR
TRANE RD
ARCADIA BL
GOLD RUSH DR
SILVER CREEK RD
Silver Creek
Western Arizona Reg. Med. Ctr.
BLACK MTN
NORTH
OATMAN RD
HAVASUPAI DR
MOHAVE DR
ACACIA WAY
BULLHEAD PKWY
ARIZ.
NEVADA
PACIFIC TIME ZONE
MOUNTAIN TIME ZONE
0 1 2 mi
0 1 2 3 km
© MQST

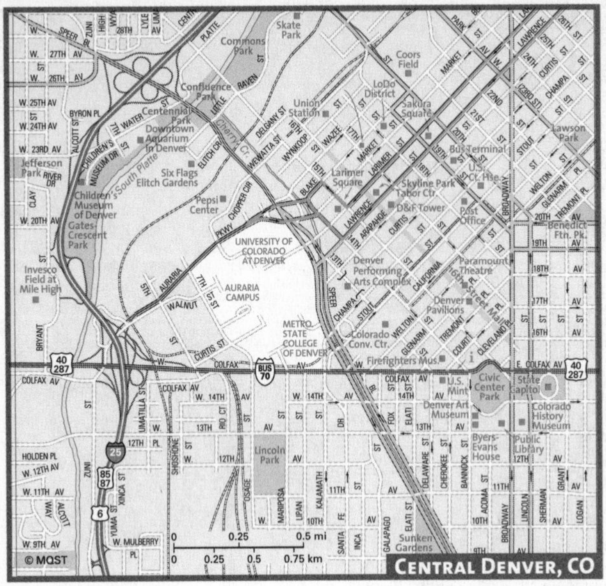
CENTRAL DENVER, CO
Commons Park
Skate Park
Coors Field
LoDo District
Confluence Park
Union Station
Sakura Square
Centennial Park
Downtown Aquarium in Denver
Lawson Park
Six Flags Elitch Gardens
Bus Terminal
Jefferson Park
Larimer Square
U.S. Ct. Hse.
Skyline Park
Tabor Ctr.
Children's Museum of Denver
D&F Tower
Pepsi Center
Post Office
Gates-Crescent Park
Benedict Ftn. Pk.
UNIVERSITY OF COLORADO AT DENVER
Paramount Theatre
Invesco Field at Mile High
Denver Performing Arts Complex
AURARIA CAMPUS
Denver Pavilions
METRO. STATE COLLEGE OF DENVER
Colorado Conv. Ctr.
Firefighters Mus.
U.S. Mint
Civic Center Park
State Capitol
Denver Art Museum
Colorado History Museum
Lincoln Park
Byers-Evans House
Public Library
Sunken Gardens
0 0.25 0.5 mi
0 0.25 0.5 0.75 km
© MQST

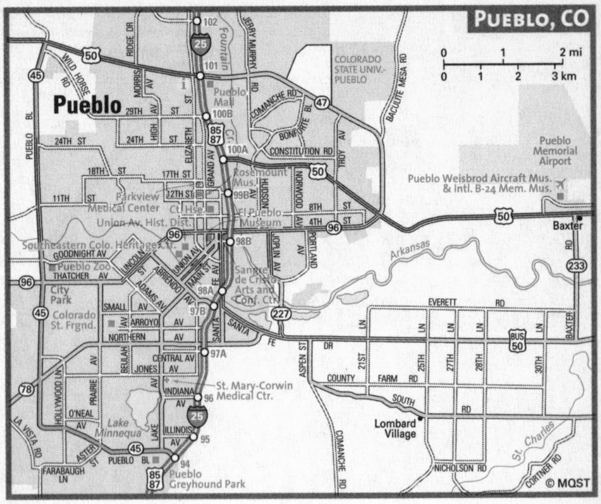
PUEBLO, CO
Pueblo
COLORADO STATE UNIV.-PUEBLO
Pueblo Memorial Airport
Pueblo Weisbrod Aircraft Mus. & Intl. B-24 Mem. Mus.
Pueblo Mall
Rosemount Mus.
Parkview Medical Center
Ct. Hse.
El Pueblo Museum
Union Av. Hist. Dist.
Southeastern Colo. Heritage Ctr.
Pueblo Zoo
City Park
Sangre de Cristo Arts and Conf. Ctr.
Colorado St. Frgnd.
Baxter
Arkansas
St. Mary-Corwin Medical Ctr.
Lake Minnequa
Lombard Village
Pueblo Greyhound Park
St. Charles
0 1 2 mi
0 1 2 3 km
© MQST

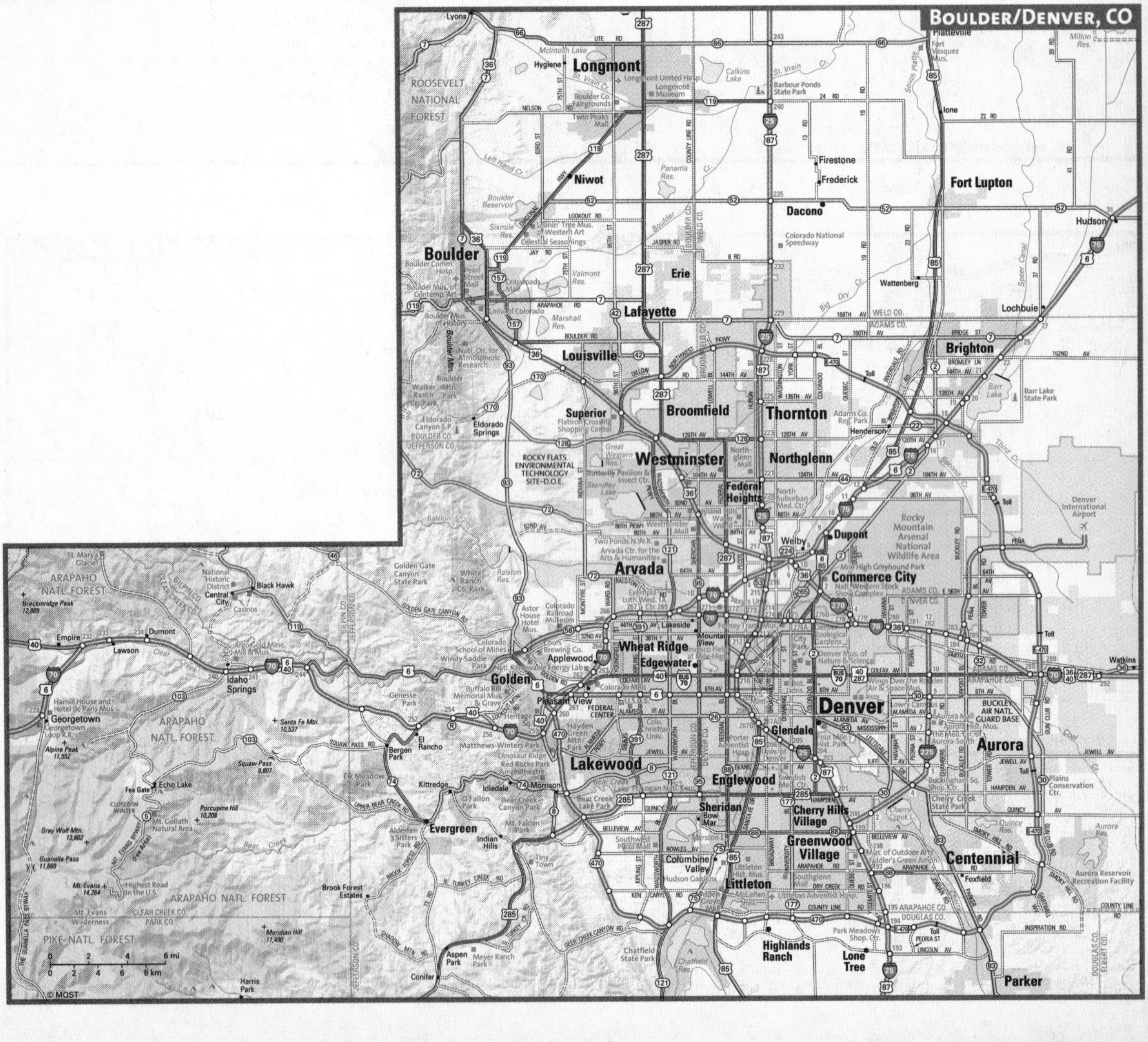
BOULDER/DENVER, CO
Lyons
Platteville
Longmont
ROOSEVELT NATIONAL FOREST
Hygiene
Firestone
Frederick
Niwot
Fort Lupton
Dacono
Hudson
Boulder
Erie
Wattenberg
Lafayette
Lochbuie
Louisville
Brighton
Superior
Broomfield
Thornton
Eldorado Springs
Westminster
Northglenn
ROCKY FLATS ENVIRONMENTAL TECHNOLOGY SITE-D.O.E.
Federal Heights
Denver International Airport
Rocky Mountain Arsenal National Wildlife Area
Dupont
Welby
Arvada
Commerce City
Black Hawk
Central City
ARAPAHO NATL. FOREST
Golden Gate Canyon State Park
Empire
Dumont
Lawson
Idaho Springs
Wheat Ridge
Edgewater
Golden
Watkins
Georgetown
Denver
Glendale
Aurora
Lakewood
Englewood
Sheridan
Cherry Hills Village
Greenwood Village
Centennial
Evergreen
Morrison
Kittredge
Idledale
Bergen Park
El Rancho
Indian Hills
Tiny Town
Columbine Valley
Littleton
Foxfield
Highlands Ranch
Lone Tree
Parker
Aspen Park
Conifer
Harris Park
Brook Forest Estates
Chatfield State Park
PIKE NATL. FOREST
Mt. Evans
Echo Lake
0 2 4 6 mi
0 2 4 6 8 km
© MQST

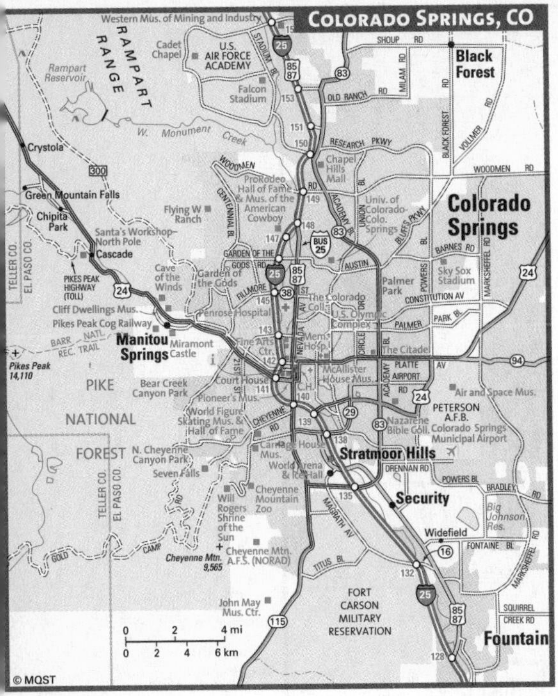
COLORADO SPRINGS, CO
Western Mus. of Mining and Industry
RAMPART RANGE
Cadet Chapel
U.S. AIR FORCE ACADEMY
Falcon Stadium
Rampart Reservoir
Black Forest
W. Monument Creek
Crystola
Green Mountain Falls
Chipita Park
Cascade
Santa's Workshop–North Pole
Flying W Ranch
ProRodeo Hall of Fame & Mus. of the American Cowboy
Chapel Hills Mall
Univ. of Colorado-Colo. Springs
Colorado Springs
Cave of the Winds
Garden of the Gods
PIKES PEAK HIGHWAY (TOLL)
Cliff Dwellings Mus.
Pikes Peak Cog Railway
Manitou Springs
Miramont Castle
Penrose Hospital
The Colorado College
U.S. Olympic Complex
Palmer Park
Sky Sox Stadium
The Citadel
Pikes Peak 14,110
PIKE NATIONAL FOREST
Bear Creek Canyon Park
Court House
McAllister House Mus.
Pioneer's Mus.
World Figure Skating Mus. & Hall of Fame
Air and Space Mus.
PETERSON A.F.B.
Nazarene Bible Coll.
Colorado Springs Municipal Airport
N. Cheyenne Canyon Park
Carriage House Mus.
World Arena & Ice Hall
Stratmoor Hills
Seven Falls
Cheyenne Mountain Zoo
Will Rogers Shrine of the Sun
Security
Widefield
Big Johnson Res.
Cheyenne Mtn. 9,565
Cheyenne Mtn. A.F.S. (NORAD)
FORT CARSON MILITARY RESERVATION
John May Mus. Ctr.
Fountain
TELLER CO.
EL PASO CO.
0 2 4 mi
0 2 4 6 km
© MQST

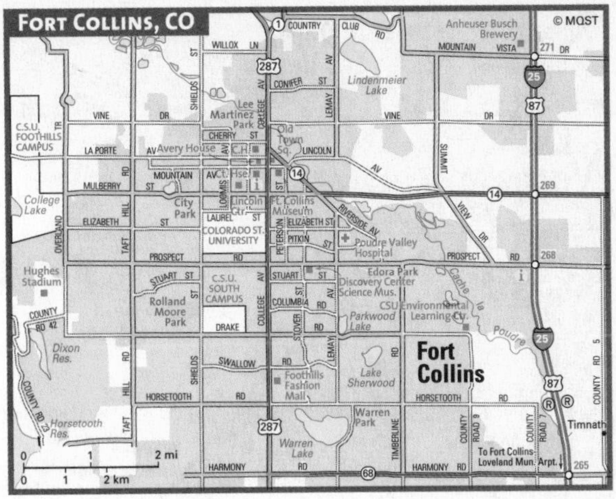
FORT COLLINS, CO
© MQST
Anheuser Busch Brewery
Lindenmeier Lake
C.S.U. FOOTHILLS CAMPUS
Lee Martinez Park
Avery House
Old Town Sq.
College Lake
City Park
Lincoln Ctr.
Ft. Collins Museum
COLORADO ST. UNIVERSITY
Poudre Valley Hospital
Hughes Stadium
C.S.U. SOUTH CAMPUS
Rolland Moore Park
Edora Park
Discovery Center Science Mus.
CSU Environmental Learning Ctr.
Parkwood Lake
Dixon Res.
Fort Collins
Lake Sherwood
Foothills Fashion Mall
Horsetooth Res.
Warren Park
Warren Lake
Timnath
To Fort Collins-Loveland Mun. Arpt.
0 1 2 mi
0 1 2 km

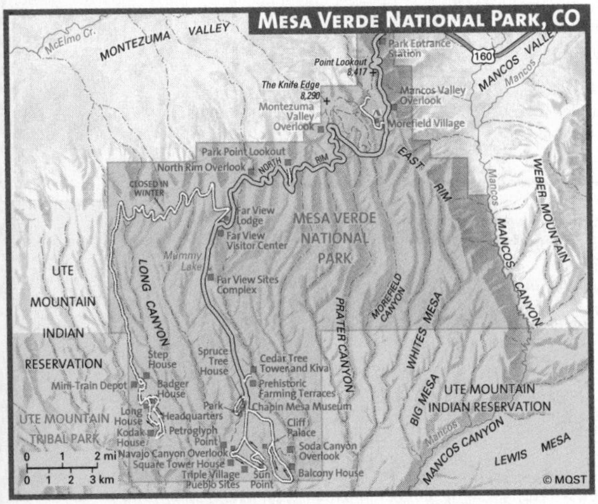
MESA VERDE NATIONAL PARK, CO
MONTEZUMA VALLEY
McElmo Cr.
Park Entrance Station
Point Lookout 8,417
The Knife Edge 8,290
Montezuma Valley Overlook
Mancos Valley Overlook
Morefield Village
MANCOS VALLEY
Park Point Lookout
North Rim Overlook
CLOSED IN WINTER
EAST RIM
WEBER MOUNTAIN
Far View Lodge
Far View Visitor Center
MESA VERDE NATIONAL PARK
Mummy Lake
Far View Sites Complex
UTE MOUNTAIN INDIAN RESERVATION
LONG CANYON
PRATER CANYON
MOREFIELD CANYON
WHITES MESA
MANCOS CANYON
Step House
Spruce Tree House
Cedar Tree Tower and Kiva
Prehistoric Farming Terraces
Chapin Mesa Museum
Mini-Train Depot
Badger House
Long House
Park Headquarters
UTE MOUNTAIN TRIBAL PARK
Kodak House
Petroglyph Point
Cliff Palace
BIG MESA
Navajo Canyon Overlook
Square Tower House
Soda Canyon Overlook
Triple Village Pueblo Sites
Sun Point
Balcony House
LEWIS MESA
0 1 2 mi
0 1 2 3 km
© MQST

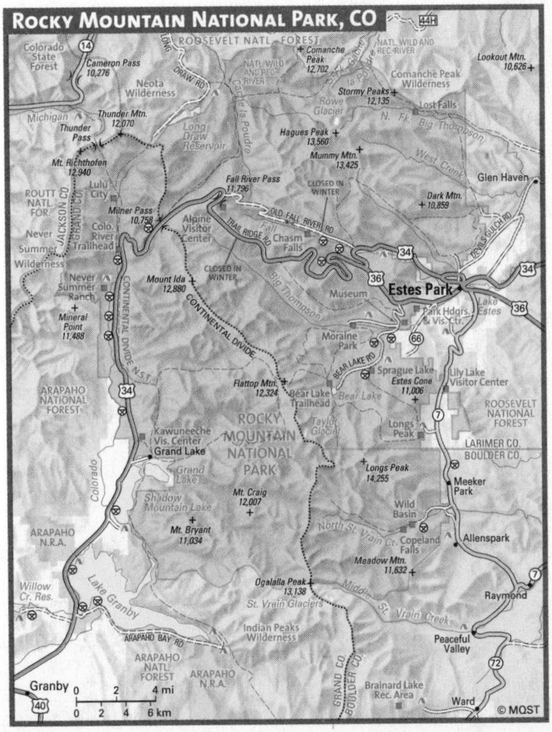
ROCKY MOUNTAIN NATIONAL PARK, CO
ROOSEVELT NATL FOREST
Colorado State Forest
Cameron Pass 10,276
Comanche Peak 12,702
Lookout Mtn. 10,626
Neota Wilderness
Comanche Peak Wilderness
Stormy Peaks 12,135
Michigan
Thunder Mtn. 12,070
Thunder Pass
Long Draw Reservoir
Lost Falls
Rowe Glacier
Hagues Peak 13,560
Mummy Mtn. 13,425
Mt. Richthofen 12,940
Glen Haven
Fall River Pass 11,796
CLOSED IN WINTER
Dark Mtn. 10,859
Lulu City
ROUTT NATL FOR.
Milner Pass 10,758
Alpine Visitor Center
Colo. River Trailhead
Chasm Falls
Never Summer Wilderness
Mount Ida 12,880
Estes Park
Museum
Never Summer Ranch
Mineral Point 11,488
Park Hdqrs. & Vis. Ctr.
Lake Estes
Moraine Park
Sprague Lake
Estes Cone 11,006
Lily Lake Visitor Center
Flattop Mtn. 12,324
Bear Lake Trailhead
ARAPAHO NATIONAL FOREST
ROOSEVELT NATIONAL FOREST
Kawuneeche Vis. Center
ROCKY MOUNTAIN NATIONAL PARK
Longs Peak
Grand Lake
Longs Peak 14,255
LARIMER CO.
BOULDER CO.
Mt. Craig 12,007
Shadow Mountain Lake
Meeker Park
Wild Basin
Mt. Bryant 11,034
Copeland Falls
Allenspark
ARAPAHO N.R.A.
Meadow Mtn. 11,632
Willow Cr. Res.
Ogalalla Peak 13,138
St. Vrain Glaciers
Raymond
Lake Granby
Indian Peaks Wilderness
Peaceful Valley
ARAPAHO NATL FOREST
ARAPAHO N.R.A.
Granby
Brainard Lake Rec. Area
Ward
0 2 4 mi
0 2 4 6 km
© MQST

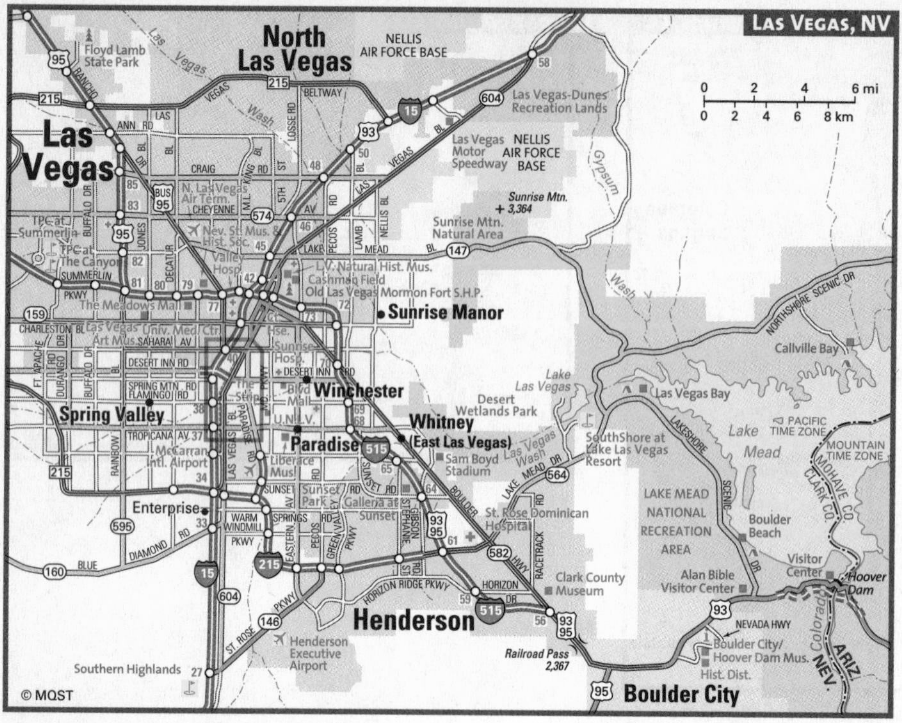
LAS VEGAS, NV
North Las Vegas
NELLIS AIR FORCE BASE
Floyd Lamb State Park
Las Vegas
Las Vegas-Dunes Recreation Lands
Las Vegas Motor Speedway
NELLIS AIR FORCE BASE
Sunrise Mtn. 3,364
Sunrise Mtn. Natural Area
Gypsum
N. Las Vegas Air Term.
Nev. St. Mus. & Hist. Soc.
Valley Hosp.
L.V. Natural Hist. Mus.
Cashman Field
Old Las Vegas Mormon Fort S.H.P.
Sunrise Manor
TPC at Summerlin
TPC at The Canyons
The Meadows Mall
Las Vegas Art Mus.
Univ. Med. Ctr.
Sunrise Hosp.
Blvd. Mall
Winchester
The Strip
U.N.L.V.
Spring Valley
Paradise
Whitney (East Las Vegas)
Desert Wetlands Park
Lake Las Vegas
Las Vegas Bay
Callville Bay
NORTHSHORE SCENIC DR
McCarran Intl. Airport
Liberace Mus.
Sam Boyd Stadium
SouthShore at Lake Las Vegas Resort
Lake Mead
PACIFIC TIME ZONE
MOUNTAIN TIME ZONE
MOHAVE CO.
CLARK CO.
LAKE MEAD NATIONAL RECREATION AREA
Boulder Beach
Enterprise
Sunset Park
Galleria at Sunset
St. Rose Dominican Hospital
Clark County Museum
Alan Bible Visitor Center
Visitor Center
Hoover Dam
Henderson
Henderson Executive Airport
Railroad Pass 2,367
Boulder City/Hoover Dam Mus.
Hist. Dist.
Southern Highlands
Boulder City
ARIZ.
NEV.
Colorado
© MQST
0 2 4 6 mi
0 2 4 6 8 km

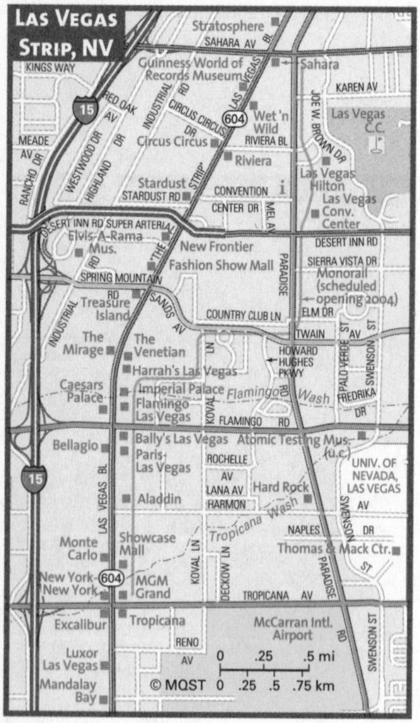
LAS VEGAS STRIP, NV
Stratosphere
Sahara
Guinness World of Records Museum
Wet 'n Wild
Circus Circus
Riviera
Las Vegas C.C.
Stardust
Las Vegas Hilton
Las Vegas Conv. Center
Elvis-A-Rama Mus.
New Frontier
Fashion Show Mall
Monorail (scheduled opening 2004)
Treasure Island
The Mirage
The Venetian
Harrah's Las Vegas
Caesars Palace
Imperial Palace
Flamingo Las Vegas
Flamingo Wash
Bellagio
Bally's Las Vegas
Atomic Testing Mus. (u.c.)
Paris-Las Vegas
Hard Rock
UNIV. OF NEVADA, LAS VEGAS
Aladdin
Tropicana Wash
Monte Carlo
Showcase Mall
Thomas & Mack Ctr.
New York-New York
MGM Grand
Excalibur
Tropicana
McCarran Intl. Airport
Luxor Las Vegas
Mandalay Bay
© MQST
0 .25 .5 mi
0 .25 .5 .75 km

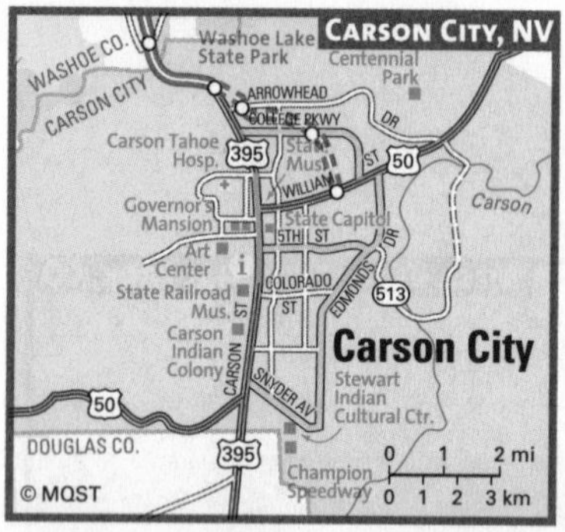
CARSON CITY, NV
WASHOE CO.
Washoe Lake State Park
Centennial Park
Carson Tahoe Hosp.
State Mus.
Governor's Mansion
State Capitol
Art Center
State Railroad Mus.
Carson Indian Colony
Carson City
Carson
Stewart Indian Cultural Ctr.
DOUGLAS CO.
Champion Speedway
© MQST
0 1 2 mi
0 1 2 3 km

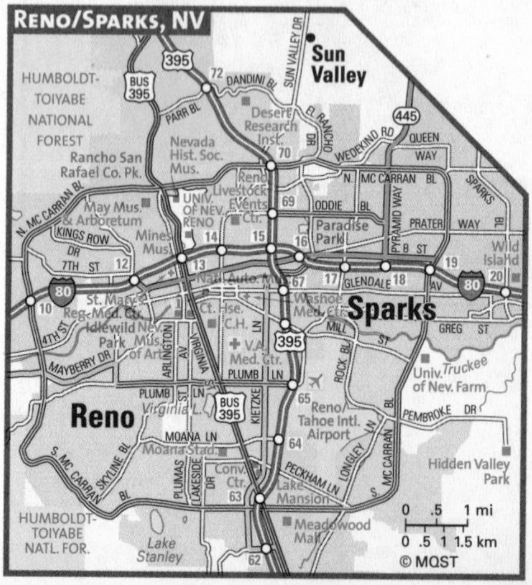
RENO/SPARKS, NV
Sun Valley
HUMBOLDT-TOIYABE NATIONAL FOREST
Desert Research Inst.
Rancho San Rafael Co. Pk.
Nevada Hist. Soc. Mus.
UNIV. OF NEV. RENO
Reno Livestock Events Ctr.
May Mus. & Arboretum
Mines Mus.
Paradise Park
Wild Island
Natl. Auto. Mus.
St. Mary's Reg. Med. Ctr.
Idlewild Park
Nev. Mus. of Art
Ct. Hse.
C.H.
Washoe Med. Ctr.
Sparks
V.A. Med. Ctr.
Univ. of Nev. Farm
Truckee
Reno
Virginia L.
Reno/Tahoe Intl. Airport
Moana Stad.
Conv. Ctr.
Lake Mansion
Hidden Valley Park
HUMBOLDT-TOIYABE NATL. FOR.
Lake Stanley
Meadowood Mall
0 .5 1 mi
0 .5 1 1.5 km
© MQST

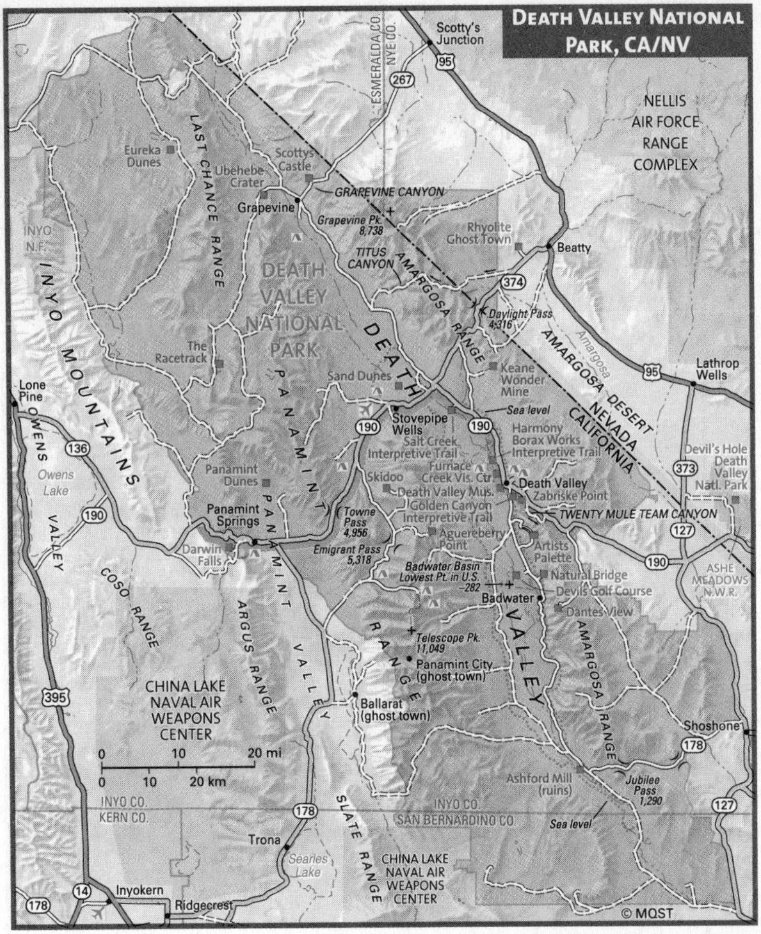
Death Valley National Park, CA/NV
Scotty's Junction
Nellis Air Force Range Complex
Eureka Dunes
Last Chance Range
Ubehebe Crater
Scottys Castle
Grapevine Canyon
Grapevine
Grapevine Pk. 8,738
Rhyolite Ghost Town
Beatty
Inyo N.F.
Titus Canyon
Amargosa Range
Death Valley National Park
Daylight Pass 4,316
Amargosa Desert
Inyo Mountains
The Racetrack
Panamint
Sand Dunes
Death
Keane Wonder Mine
Lathrop Wells
Lone Pine
Owens
Stovepipe Wells
Sea level
Nevada
California
Salt Creek Interpretive Trail
Harmony Borax Works Interpretive Trail
Devil's Hole Death Valley Natl. Park
Owens Lake
Panamint Dunes
Skidoo
Furnace Creek Vis. Ctr.
Death Valley Mus.
Death Valley
Zabriskie Point
Golden Canyon Interpretive Trail
Twenty Mule Team Canyon
Panamint Springs
Towne Pass 4,956
Aguereberry Point
Valley
Darwin Falls
Emigrant Pass 5,318
Artists Palette
Natural Bridge
Ashe Meadows N.W.R.
Badwater Basin Lowest Pt. in U.S. -282
Badwater
Devils Golf Course
Coso Range
Argus Range
Dantes View
Telescope Pk. 11,049
Panamint City (ghost town)
China Lake Naval Air Weapons Center
Ballarat (ghost town)
Shoshone
Jubilee Pass 1,290
Ashford Mill (ruins)
0 10 20 mi
0 10 20 km
Inyo Co.
Kern Co.
San Bernardino Co.
Slate Range
Trona
Searles Lake
Inyokern
Ridgecrest
Esmeralda Co.
Nye Co.
© MQST

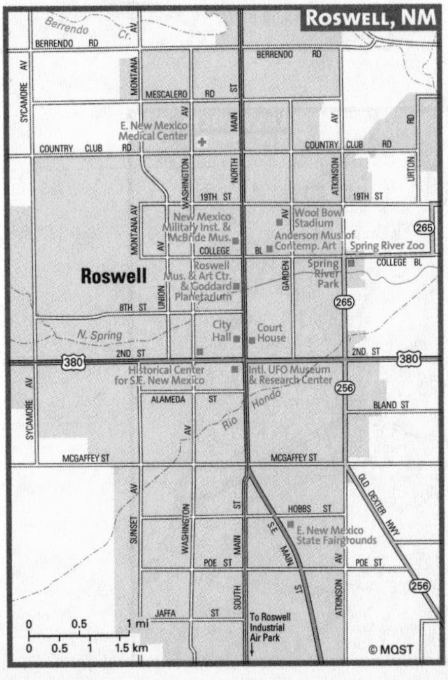
Roswell, NM
Berrendo Cr.
Berrendo Rd
Mescalero Rd
E. New Mexico Medical Center
Country Club Rd
Sycamore Av
Montana Av
Washington Av
North Main St
Atkinson Av
Urton Rd
19th St
New Mexico Military Inst. & McBride Mus.
Wool Bowl Stadium
Anderson Mus. of Contemp. Art
Spring River Zoo
College Bl
Roswell
Roswell Mus. & Art Ctr. & Goddard Planetarium
Spring River Park
Garden
Union
8th St
N. Spring
City Hall
Court House
2nd St
Historical Center for S.E. New Mexico
Intl. UFO Museum & Research Center
Alameda St
Rio Hondo
Bland St
McGaffey St
Old Dexter Hwy
Hobbs St
E. New Mexico State Fairgrounds
Sunset Av
S.E. Main St
Poe St
South
Jaffa St
To Roswell Industrial Air Park
0 0.5 1 mi
0 0.5 1 1.5 km
© MQST

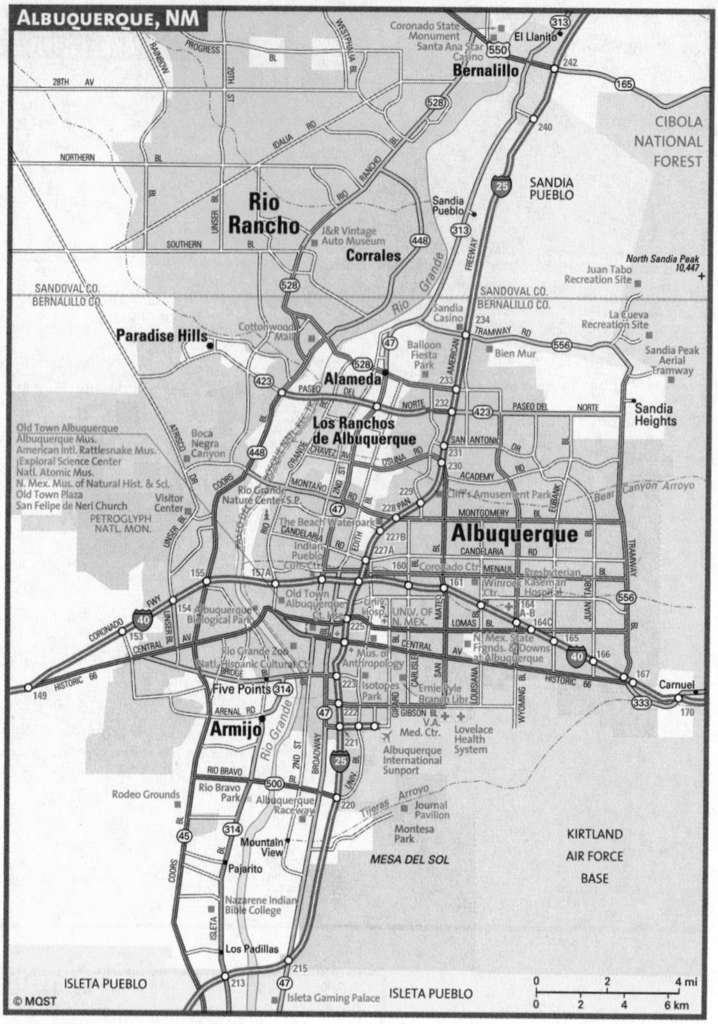
ALBUQUERQUE, NM
Coronado State Monument
Santa Ana Star Casino
El Llanito
Bernalillo
CIBOLA NATIONAL FOREST
SANDIA PUEBLO
Sandia Pueblo
Rio Rancho
J&R Vintage Auto Museum
Corrales
North Sandia Peak 10,447
Juan Tabo Recreation Site
SANDOVAL CO.
BERNALILLO CO.
Sandia Casino
La Cueva Recreation Site
Paradise Hills
Cottonwood Mall
Balloon Fiesta Park
Bien Mur
Sandia Peak Aerial Tramway
Alameda
Sandia Heights
Los Ranchos de Albuquerque
Old Town Albuquerque
Albuquerque Mus.
American Intl. Rattlesnake Mus.
Explora! Science Center
Natl. Atomic Mus.
N. Mex. Mus. of Natural Hist. & Sci.
Old Town Plaza
San Felipe de Neri Church
Boca Negra Canyon
Visitor Center
PETROGLYPH NATL. MON.
Rio Grande Nature Center S.P.
Cliff's Amusement Park
Bear Canyon Arroyo
The Beach Waterpark
Indian Pueblo Cultural Ctr.
Albuquerque
Coronado Ctr.
Presbyterian Kaseman Hospital
Winrock Ctr.
Old Town Albuquerque
Albuquerque Biological Park
Univ. Hosp.
UNIV. OF N. MEX.
N. Mex. State Frgnds. & Downs at Albuquerque
Rio Grande Zoo
Natl. Hispanic Cultural Ctr.
Mus. of Anthropology
Five Points
Isotopes Park
Ernie Pyle Branch Libr.
Carnuel
Armijo
V.A. Med. Ctr.
Lovelace Health System
Albuquerque International Sunport
Rodeo Grounds
Rio Bravo Park
Albuquerque Raceway
Tijeras Arroyo
Journal Pavilion
Montesa Park
Mountain View
KIRTLAND AIR FORCE BASE
MESA DEL SOL
Pajarito
Nazarene Indian Bible College
Los Padillas
ISLETA PUEBLO
Isleta Gaming Palace
ISLETA PUEBLO
Rio Grande
© MQST
0 2 4 mi
0 2 4 6 km

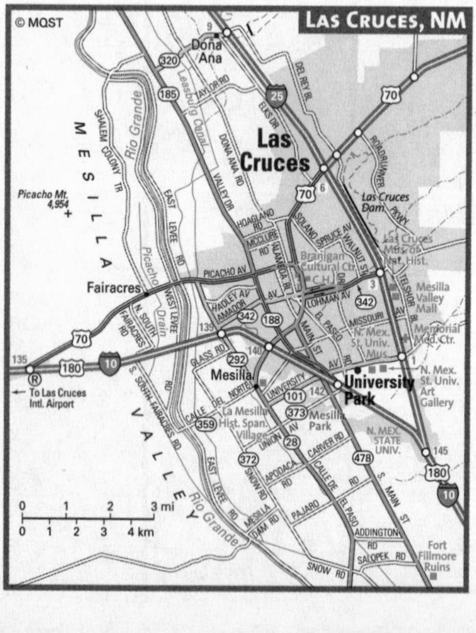
© MQST
LAS CRUCES, NM
Dona Ana
Las Cruces
MESILLA VALLEY
Picacho Mt. 4,954
Las Cruces Dam
Las Cruces Mus. of Nat. Hist.
Branigan Cultural Ctr.
Fairacres
Mesilla Valley Mall
Memorial Med. Ctr.
N. Mex. St. Univ. Golf
Mesilla
University Park
N. Mex. St. Univ. Art Gallery
La Mesilla Hist. Span. Village
Mesilla Park
N. MEX. STATE UNIV.
To Las Cruces Intl. Airport
Rio Grande
Fort Fillmore Ruins
0 1 2 3 mi
0 1 2 3 4 km

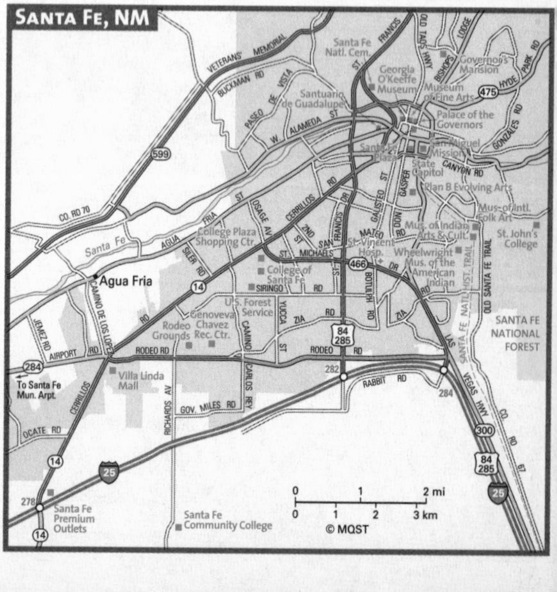
SANTA FE, NM
Santa Fe Natl. Cem.
Georgia O'Keeffe Museum
Museum of Fine Arts
Governor's Mansion
Santuario de Guadalupe
Palace of the Governors
Santa Fe Plaza
San Miguel Mission
State Capitol
Plan B Evolving Arts
Mus. of Intl. Folk Art
Mus. of Indian Arts & Cult.
St. John's College
College Plaza Shopping Ctr.
St. Vincent Hosp.
Wheelwright Mus. of the American Indian
Agua Fria
College of Santa Fe
U.S. Forest Service
Genoveva Chavez Rec. Ctr.
Rodeo Grounds
SANTA FE NATIONAL FOREST
To Santa Fe Mun. Arpt.
Villa Linda Mall
Santa Fe
Santa Fe Premium Outlets
Santa Fe Community College
0 1 2 mi
0 1 2 3 km
© MQST

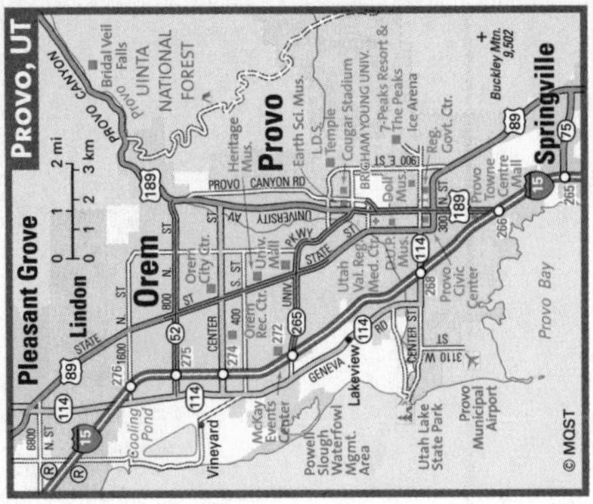
PROVO, UT
Provo
Orem
Pleasant Grove
Lindon
Springville
Vineyard
Provo Bay
© MOST

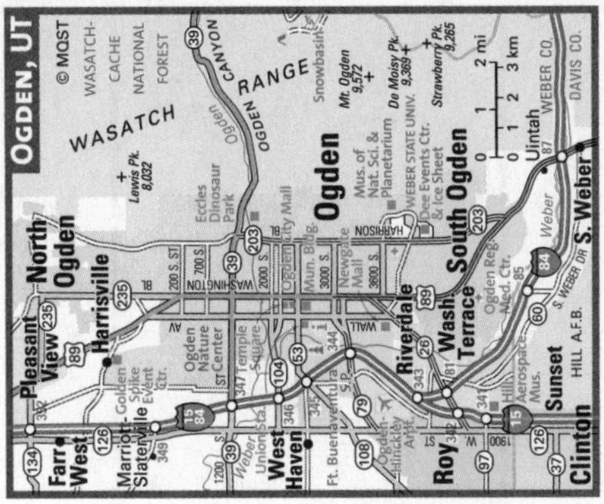
OGDEN, UT
Ogden
North Ogden
Harrisville
South Ogden
Riverdale
Roy
Clinton
Sunset
S. Weber
WASATCH
© MOST

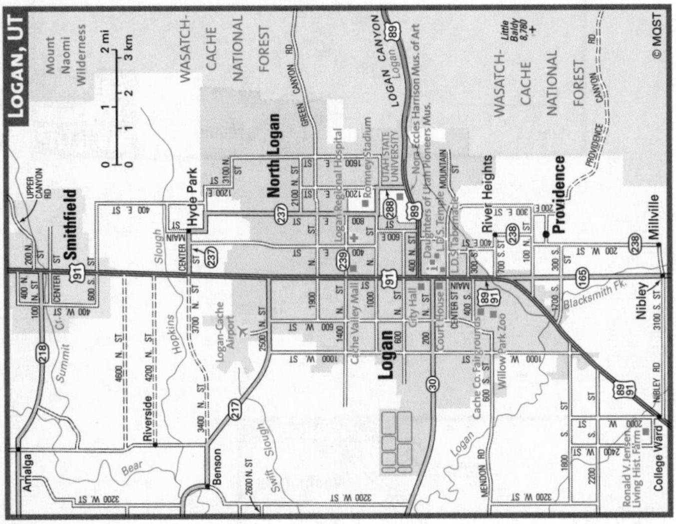
LOGAN, UT
Logan
North Logan
Smithfield
Hyde Park
Providence
River Heights
Millville
Nibley
College Ward
Benson
Amalga
© MOST

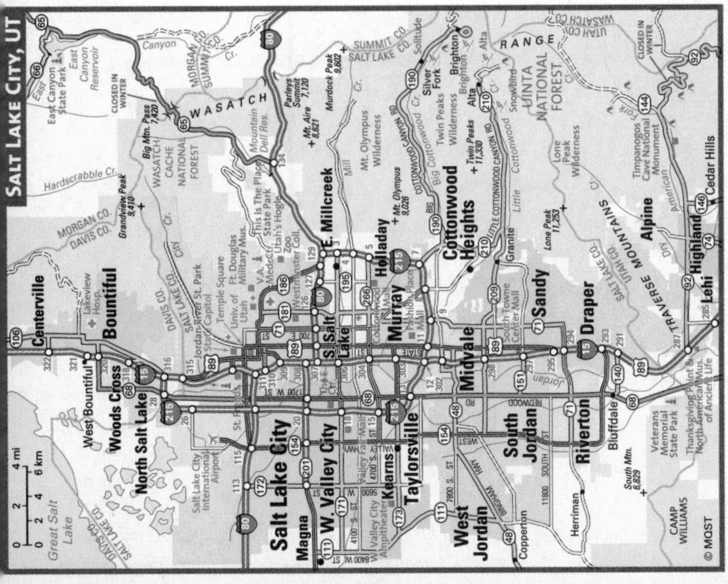
SALT LAKE CITY, UT
Salt Lake City
W. Valley City
Magna
Kearns
Taylorsville
West Jordan
South Jordan
Riverton
Draper
Sandy
Midvale
Murray
Holladay
Cottonwood Heights
E. Millcreek
Bountiful
Centerville
Woods Cross
North Salt Lake
West Bountiful
Lehi
Highland
Alpine
Cedar Hills
© MOST

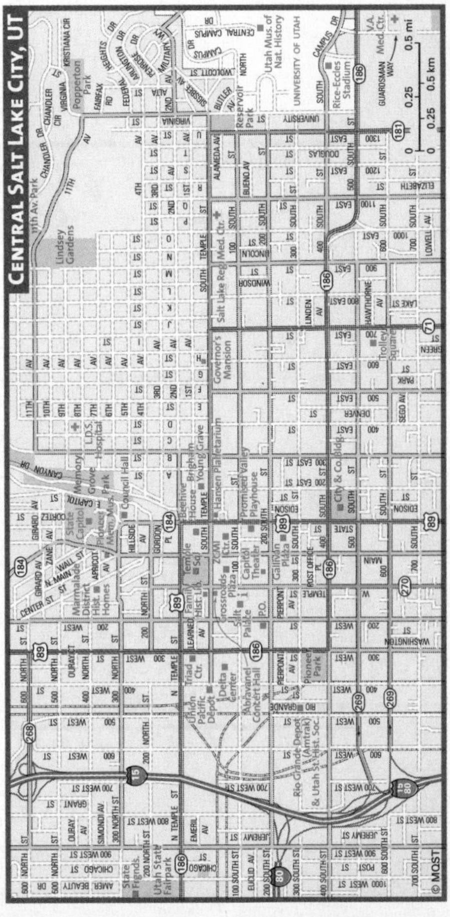
CENTRAL SALT LAKE CITY, UT
© MOST

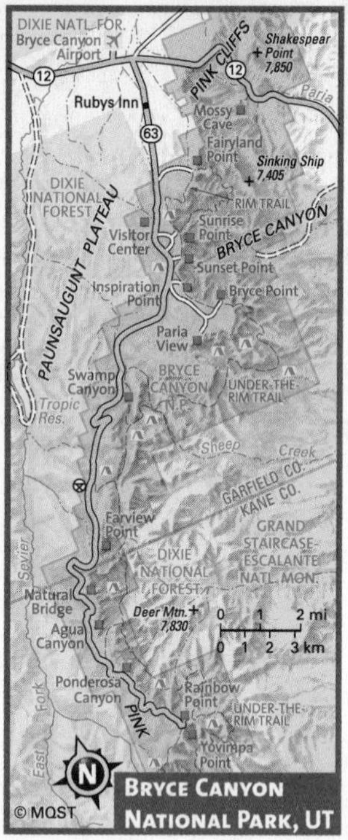
BRYCE CANYON NATIONAL PARK, UT
DIXIE NATL. FOR.
Bryce Canyon Airport
Shakespear Point 7,850
PINK CLIFFS
Paria
Rubys Inn
Mossy Cave
Fairyland Point
Sinking Ship 7,405
DIXIE NATIONAL FOREST
RIM TRAIL
Sunrise Point
Visitor Center
BRYCE CANYON
PAUNSAUGUNT PLATEAU
Sunset Point
Inspiration Point
Bryce Point
Paria View
Swamp Canyon
BRYCE CANYON N.P.
UNDER-THE-RIM TRAIL
Tropic Res.
Sheep Creek
GARFIELD CO.
KANE CO.
Farview Point
Sevier
GRAND STAIRCASE-ESCALANTE NATL. MON.
DIXIE NATIONAL FOREST
Natural Bridge
Deer Mtn. 7,830
Agua Canyon
0 1 2 mi
0 1 2 3 km
Ponderosa Canyon
Rainbow Point
UNDER-THE-RIM TRAIL
PINK
East Fork
Yovimpa Point
© MQST

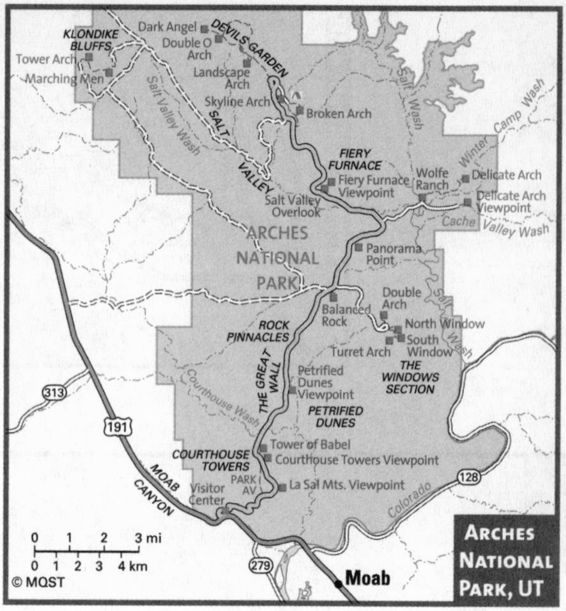
ARCHES NATIONAL PARK, UT
KLONDIKE BLUFFS
Dark Angel
DEVILS GARDEN
Double O Arch
Tower Arch
Marching Men
Landscape Arch
Skyline Arch
Broken Arch
Salt Valley Wash
SALT VALLEY
Salt Wash
Winter Camp Wash
FIERY FURNACE
Fiery Furnace Viewpoint
Wolfe Ranch
Delicate Arch
Delicate Arch Viewpoint
Salt Valley Overlook
Cache Valley Wash
ARCHES NATIONAL PARK
Panorama Point
Double Arch
Balanced Rock
North Window
South Window
ROCK PINNACLES
Turret Arch
THE WINDOWS SECTION
THE GREAT WALL
Petrified Dunes Viewpoint
PETRIFIED DUNES
Courthouse Wash
Tower of Babel
Courthouse Towers Viewpoint
COURTHOUSE TOWERS
PARK AV
La Sal Mts. Viewpoint
Visitor Center
MOAB CANYON
Colorado
0 1 2 3 mi
0 1 2 3 4 km
Moab
© MQST

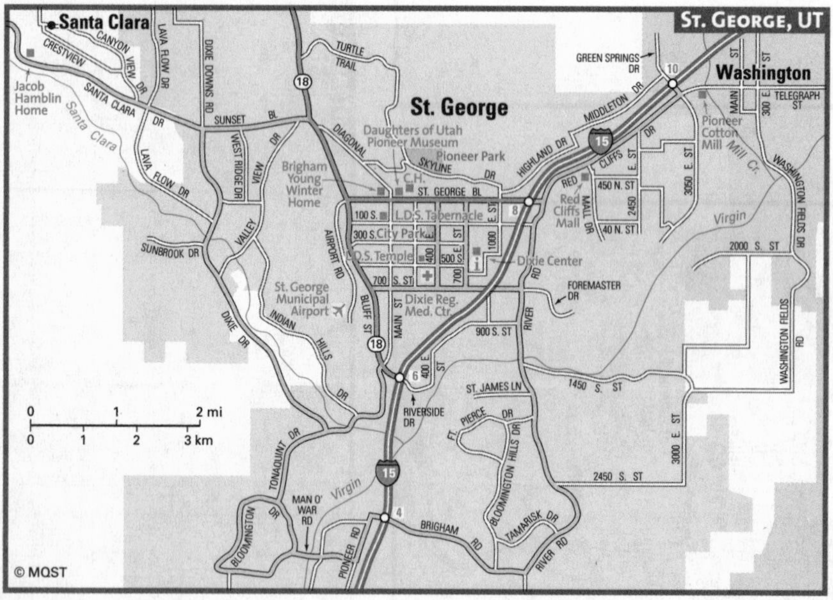
ST. GEORGE, UT
Santa Clara
CANYON VIEW DR
LAVA FLOW DR
DIXIE DOWNS RD
TURTLE TRAIL
GREEN SPRINGS DR
Washington
CRESTVIEW
Jacob Hamblin Home
SANTA CLARA DR
Santa Clara
SUNSET BL
St. George
MIDDLETON DR
TELEGRAPH ST
DIAGONAL
Daughters of Utah Pioneer Museum
Pioneer Park
Pioneer Cotton Mill
WEST RIDGE DR
VIEW DR
Brigham Young Winter Home
SKYLINE DR
HIGHLAND DR
C.H.
ST. GEORGE BL
CLIFFS DR
RED CLIFFS
Red Cliffs Mall
450 N. ST
Mill Cr.
WASHINGTON FIELDS DR
L.D.S. Tabernacle
City Park
L.D.S. Temple
Dixie Center
40 N. ST
Virgin
2000 S. ST
SUNBROOK DR
VALLEY
AIRPORT RD
FOREMASTER DR
St. George Municipal Airport
Dixie Reg. Med. Ctr.
INDIAN HILLS
BLUFF ST
MAIN ST
900 S. ST
RIVER RD
DIXIE DR
WASHINGTON FIELDS RD
ST. JAMES LN
1450 S. ST
RIVERSIDE DR
FT. PIERCE DR
0 1 2 mi
0 1 2 3 km
TONAQUINT DR
BLOOMINGTON HILLS DR
2450 S. ST
3000 E. ST
Virgin
MAN O' WAR RD
BLOOMINGTON DR
BRIGHAM RD
TAMARISK DR
PIONEER RD
RIVER RD
© MQST

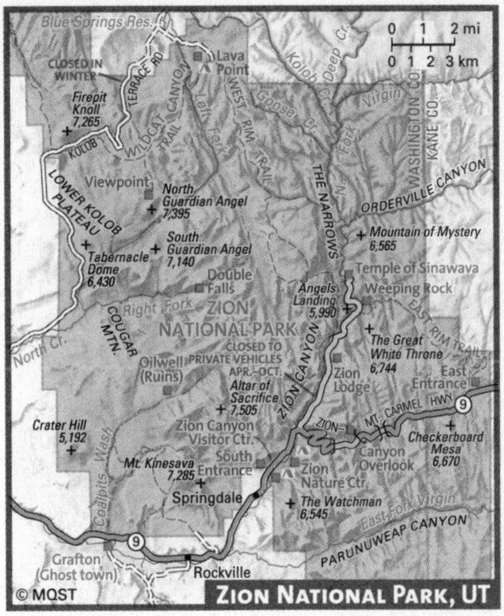

ZION NATIONAL PARK, UT

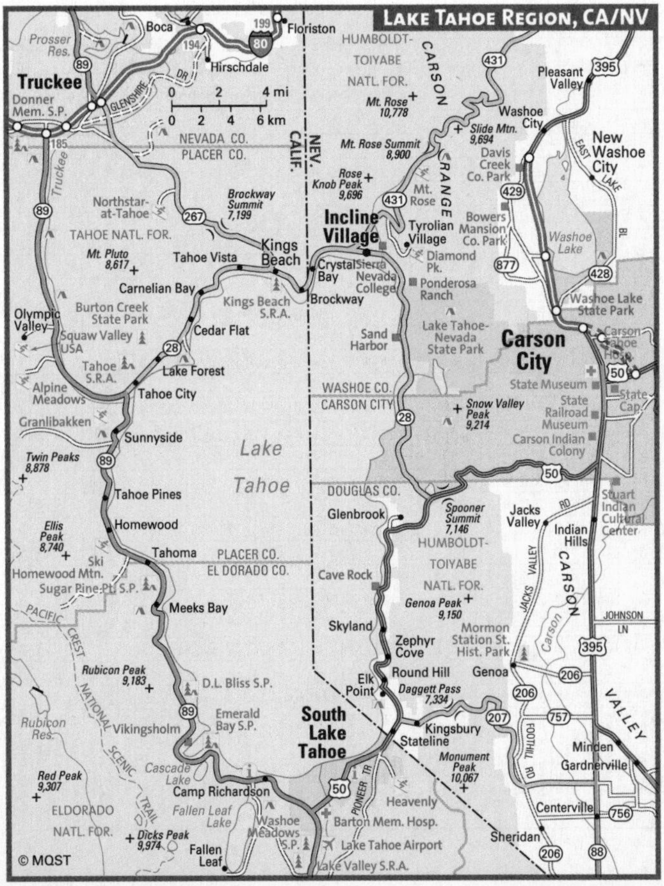

LAKE TAHOE REGION, CA/NV

Distances in chart are in miles. To convert miles to kilometers, multiply the distance in miles by 1.609

Example: New York, NY to Boston, MA = 215 miles or 346 kilometers (215 x 1.609)

	ALBUQUERQUE, NM	ATLANTA, GA	BALTIMORE, MD	BILLINGS, MT	BIRMINGHAM, AL	BISMARCK, ND	BOISE, ID	BOSTON, MA	BUFFALO, NY	BURLINGTON, VT	CHARLESTON, SC	CHARLESTON, WV	CHARLOTTE, NC	CHEYENNE, WY	CHICAGO, IL	CINCINNATI, OH	CLEVELAND, OH	DALLAS, TX	DENVER, CO	DES MOINES, IA	DETROIT, MI	EL PASO, TX	HOUSTON, TX	INDIANAPOLIS, IN	JACKSON, MS	KANSAS CITY, MO	LAS VEGAS, NV	LITTLE ROCK, AR	LOS ANGELES, CA	LOUISVILLE, KY	MEMPHIS, TN	MIAMI, FL	MILWAUKEE, WI	MINNEAPOLIS, MN	MONTRÉAL, QC	NASHVILLE, TN	NEW ORLEANS, LA	NEW YORK, NY	OKLAHOMA CITY, OK	OMAHA, NE	ORLANDO, FL	PHILADELPHIA, PA	PHOENIX, AZ	PITTSBURGH, PA	PORTLAND, ME	PORTLAND, OR	RAPID CITY, SD	RENO, NV	RICHMOND, VA	ST. LOUIS, MO	SALT LAKE CITY, UT	SAN ANTONIO, TX	SAN DIEGO, CA	SAN FRANCISCO, CA	SEATTLE, WA	TAMPA, FL	TORONTO, ON	VANCOUVER, BC	WASHINGTON, DC	WICHITA, KS
ALBUQUERQUE, NM		1490	1902	991	1274	1333	966	2240	1808	2178	1793	1568	1649	538	1352	1409	1619	754	438	1091	1608	263	994	1298	1157	894	578	900	806	1320	1033	2155	1426	1339	2172	1248	1276	2015	546	973	1934	1954	466	1670	2338	1395	841	1020	1876	1051	624	818	825	1111	1463	1949	1841	1597	1896	707
ATLANTA, GA	1490		679	1889	150	1559	2218	1100	910	1158	317	503	238	1482	717	476	726	792	1403	967	735	1437	800	531	386	801	2067	528	2237	419	389	661	813	1129	1241	242	473	869	944	989	440	782	1868	676	1197	2647	1511	2440	527	549	1916	1000	2166	2618	2705	455	958	2838	636	989
BALTIMORE, MD	1902	679		1959	795	1551	2401	422	370	481	583	352	441	1665	708	521	377	1399	1690	1031	532	2045	1470	600	1032	1087	2445	1072	2705	602	933	1109	805	1121	564	716	1142	192	1354	1168	904	104	2366	246	520	2830	1626	2623	152	841	2100	1671	2724	2840	2775	960	565	2908	38	1276
BILLINGS, MT	991	1889	1959		1839	413	626	2254	1796	2181	2157	1755	2012	455	1246	1552	1597	1433	554	1007	1534	1255	1673	1432	1836	1088	965	1530	1239	1547	1625	2554	1175	839	2093	1648	1955	2049	1227	904	2333	2019	1199	1719	2352	889	379	960	2053	1341	548	1500	1302	1176	816	2348	1762	949	1953	1067
BIRMINGHAM, AL	1274	150	795	1839		1509	2170	1215	909	1241	466	578	389	1434	667	475	725	647	1356	919	734	1292	678	481	241	753	1852	381	2092	369	241	812	763	1079	1289	194	351	985	729	941	591	897	1723	763	1313	2599	1463	2392	678	501	1868	878	2021	2472	2657	606	958	2791	758	838
BISMARCK, ND	1333	1559	1551	413	1509		1039	1846	1388	1773	1749	1347	1604	594	838	1144	1189	1342	693	675	1126	1597	1582	1024	1548	801	1378	1183	1702	1139	1337	2224	767	431	1685	1315	1734	1641	1136	616	2003	1611	1662	1311	1944	1301	320	1372	1645	1053	960	1599	1765	1749	1229	2018	1354	1362	1545	934
BOISE, ID	966	2218	2401	626	2170	1039		2697	2239	2624	2520	2182	2375	737	1708	1969	2040	1711	833	1369	1977	1206	1952	1852	2115	1376	760	1808	1033	1933	1954	2883	1748	1465	2535	1976	2234	2491	1506	1234	2662	2462	993	2161	2795	432	930	430	2496	1628	342	1761	1096	646	500	2677	2204	633	2395	1346
BOSTON, MA	2240	1100	422	2254	1215	1846	2697		462	214	1003	741	861	1961	1003	862	654	1819	2004	1326	741	2465	1890	940	1453	1427	2757	1493	3046	964	1353	1529	1100	1417	313	1136	1563	215	1694	1463	1324	321	2706	592	107	3126	1921	2919	572	1181	2395	2092	3065	3135	3070	1380	570	3204	458	1616
BUFFALO, NY	1808	910	370	1796	909	1388	2239	462		375	899	431	695	1502	545	442	197	1393	1546	868	277	2039	1513	508	1134	995	2299	1066	2572	545	927	1425	642	958	397	716	1254	400	1262	1005	1221	414	2274	217	560	2667	1463	2460	485	749	1936	1665	2632	2677	2612	1276	106	2745	384	1184
BURLINGTON, VT	2178	1158	481	2181	1241	1773	2624	214	375		1061	782	919	1887	930	817	567	1763	1931	1253	652	2409	1916	878	1479	1366	2684	1437	2957	915	1297	1587	1027	1343	92	1086	1588	299	1632	1390	1383	371	2644	587	233	3052	1848	2845	630	1119	2322	2036	3020	3062	2997	1438	419	3130	517	1554
CHARLESTON, SC	1793	317	583	2157	466	1749	2520	1003	899	1061		468	204	1783	907	622	724	1109	1705	1204	879	1754	1110	721	703	1102	2371	900	2554	610	760	583	1003	1319	1145	543	783	773	1248	1290	379	685	2184	642	1101	2948	1824	2741	428	850	2218	1310	2483	2934	2973	434	1006	3106	539	1291
CHARLESTON, WV	1568	503	352	1755	578	1347	2182	741	431	782	468		265	1445	506	209	255	1072	1367	802	410	1718	1192	320	816	764	2122	745	2374	251	606	994	601	918	822	395	926	515	1022	952	790	454	2035	217	839	2610	1422	2403	322	512	1880	1344	2393	2620	2571	845	537	2705	346	953
CHARLOTTE, NC	1649	238	441	2012	389	1604	2375	861	695	919	204	265		1637	761	476	520	1031	1559	1057	675	1677	1041	575	625	956	2225	754	2453	464	614	730	857	1173	1003	397	713	631	1102	1144	525	543	2107	438	959	2802	1678	2595	289	704	2072	1241	2405	2759	2827	581	802	2960	397	1145
CHEYENNE, WY	538	1482	1665	455	1434	594	737	1961	1502	1887	1783	1445	1637		972	1233	1304	979	100	633	1241	801	1220	1115	1382	640	843	1076	1116	1197	1217	2147	1012	881	1799	1240	1502	1755	773	497	1926	1725	1004	1425	2059	1166	305	959	1760	892	436	1046	1179	1176	1234	1941	1468	1368	1659	613
CHICAGO, IL	1352	717	708	1246	667	838	1708	1003	545	930	907	506	761	972		302	346	936	1015	337	283	1543	1108	184	750	532	1768	662	2042	299	539	1382	89	409	841	474	935	797	807	474	1161	768	1819	467	1101	2137	913	1930	802	294	1406	1270	2105	2146	2062	1176	510	2196	701	728
CINCINNATI, OH	1409	476	521	1552	475	1144	1969	862	442	817	622	209	476	1233	302		253	958	1200	599	261	1605	1079	116	700	597	1955	632	2215	106	493	1141	398	714	815	281	820	636	863	736	920	576	1876	292	960	2398	1219	2191	530	350	1667	1231	2234	2407	2368	935	484	2501	517	785
CLEVELAND, OH	1619	726	377	1597	725	1189	2040	654	197	567	724	255	520	1304	346	253		1208	1347	669	171	1854	1328	319	950	806	2100	882	2374	356	742	1250	443	760	588	531	1070	466	1073	806	1045	437	2085	136	751	2469	1264	2262	471	560	1738	1481	2437	2478	2413	1101	303	2547	370	995
DALLAS, TX	754	792	1399	1433	647	1342	1711	1819	1393	1763	1109	1072	1031	979	936	958	1208		887	752	1218	647	241	913	406	554	1331	327	1446	852	466	1367	1010	999	1772	681	525	1589	209	669	1146	1501	1077	1246	1917	2140	1077	1933	1309	635	1410	271	1375	1827	2208	1161	1441	2342	1362	367
DENVER, CO	438	1403	1690	554	1356	693	833	2004	1546	1931	1705	1367	1559	100	1015	1200	1347	887		676	1284	701	1127	1088	1290	603	756	984	1029	1118	1116	2069	1055	924	1843	1162	1409	1799	681	541	1847	1744	904	1460	2102	1261	404	1054	1688	855	531	946	1092	1271	1329	1862	1512	1463	1686	521
DES MOINES, IA	1091	967	1031	1007	919	675	1369	1326	868	1253	1204	802	1057	633	337	599	669	752	676		606	1283	992	481	931	194	1429	567	1703	595	720	1632	378	246	1165	725	1117	1121	546	136	1411	1091	1558	791	1424	1798	629	1591	1126	436	1067	1009	1766	1807	1822	1426	834	1956	1025	390
DETROIT, MI	1608	735	532	1534	734	1126	1977	741	277	652	879	410	675	1241	283	261	171	1218	1284	606		1799	1338	318	960	795	2037	891	2310	366	752	1401	380	697	564	541	1079	622	1062	743	1180	592	2074	292	838	2405	1201	2198	627	549	1675	1490	2373	2415	2350	1194	233	2483	526	984
EL PASO, TX	263	1437	2045	1255	1292	1597	1206	2465	2039	2409	1754	1718	1677	801	1543	1605	1854	647	701	1283	1799		758	1489	1051	1085	717	974	801	1499	1112	1959	1617	1530	2363	1328	1118	2235	737	1236	1738	2147	432	1893	2563	1767	1105	1315	1955	1242	864	556	730	1181	1944	1753	2032	2087	2008	898
HOUSTON, TX	994	800	1470	1673	678	1582	1952	1890	1513	1916	1110	1192	1041	1220	1108	1079	1328	241	1127	992	1338	758		1033	445	795	1474	447	1558	972	586	1201	1193	1240	1892	801	360	1660	449	910	980	1572	1188	1366	1988	2381	1318	2072	1330	863	1650	200	1487	1938	2449	995	1561	2583	1433	608
INDIANAPOLIS, IN	1298	531	600	1432	481	1024	1852	940	508	878	721	320	575	1115	184	116	319	913	1088	481	318	1489	1033		675	485	1843	587	2104	112	464	1196	279	596	872	287	826	715	752	618	975	655	1764	370	1038	2280	1101	2073	641	239	1549	1186	2122	2290	2249	990	541	2383	596	674
JACKSON, MS	1157	386	1032	1836	241	1548	2115	1453	1134	1479	703	816	625	1382	750	700	950	406	1290	931	960	1051	445	675		747	1735	269	1851	594	211	915	835	1151	1514	423	185	1223	612	935	694	1135	1482	988	1550	2544	1458	2337	914	505	1813	644	1780	2232	2612	709	1183	2746	996	771
KANSAS CITY, MO	894	801	1087	1088	753	801	1376	1427	995	1366	1102	764	956	640	532	597	806	554	603	194	795	1085	795	485	747		1358	382	1632	516	536	1466	573	441	1359	559	932	1202	348	188	1245	1141	1360	857	1525	1805	710	1598	1085	252	1074	812	1695	1814	1872	1259	1028	2007	1083	192
LAS VEGAS, NV	578	2067	2445	965	1852	1378	760	2757	2299	2684	2371	2122	2225	843	1768	1955	2100	1331	756	1429	2037	717	1474	1843	1735	1358		1478	274	1874	1611	2733	1808	1677	2596	1826	1854	2552	1124	1294	2512	2500	285	2215	2855	1188	1035	442	2444	1610	417	1272	337	575	1256	2526	2265	1390	2441	1276
LITTLE ROCK, AR	900	528	1072	1530	381	1183	1808	1493	1066	1437	900	745	754	1076	662	632	882	327	984	567	891	974	447	587	269	382	1478		1706	526	140	1190	747	814	1446	355	455	1262	355	570	969	1175	1367	920	1590	2237	1093	2030	983	416	1507	600	1703	2012	2305	984	1115	2439	1036	464
LOS ANGELES, CA	806	2237	2705	1239	2092	1702	1033	3046	2572	2957	2554	2374	2453	1116	2042	2215	2374	1446	1029	1703	2310	801	1558	2104	1851	1632	274	1706		2126	1839	2759	2082	1951	2869	2054	1917	2820	1352	1567	2538	2760	369	2476	3144	971	1309	519	2682	1856	691	1356	124	385	1148	2553	2538	1291	2702	1513
LOUISVILLE, KY	1320	419	602	1547	369	1139	1933	964	545	915	610	251	464	1197	299	106	356	852	1118	595	366	1499	972	112	594	516	1874	526	2126		386	1084	394	711	920	175	714	739	774	704	863	678	1786	394	1062	2362	1215	2155	572	264	1631	1125	2144	2372	2364	878	589	2497	596	705
MEMPHIS, TN	1033	389	933	1625	241	1337	1954	1353	927	1297	760	606	614	1217	539	493	742	466	1116	720	752	1112	586	464	211	536	1611	140	1839	386		1051	624	940	1306	215	396	1123	487	724	830	1035	1500	780	1451	2382	1247	2175	843	294	1652	739	1841	2144	2440	845	975	2574	896	597
MIAMI, FL	2155	661	1109	2554	812	2224	2883	1529	1425	1587	583	994	730	2147	1382	1141	1250	1367	2069	1632	1401	1959	1201	1196	915	1466	2733	1190	2759	1084	1051		1478	1794	1671	907	874	1299	1609	1654	232	1211	2390	1167	1627	3312	2176	3105	954	1214	2581	1401	2688	3140	3370	274	1532	3504	1065	1655
MILWAUKEE, WI	1426	813	805	1175	763	767	1748	1100	642	1027	1003	601	857	1012	89	398	443	1010	1055	378	380	1617	1193	279	835	573	1808	747	2082	394	624	1478		337	939	569	1020	894	880	514	1257	865	1892	564	1198	2063	842	1970	899	367	1446	1343	2145	2186	1991	1272	607	2124	799	769
MINNEAPOLIS, MN	1339	1129	1121	839	1079	431	1465	1417	958	1343	1319	918	1173	881	409	714	760	999	924	246	697	1530	1240	596	1151	441	1677	814	1951	711	940	1794	337		1255	886	1337	1211	793	383	1573	1181	1805	881	1515	1727	606	1839	1216	621	1315	1257	2014	2055	1654	1588	924	1788	1115	637
MONTRÉAL, QC	2172	1241	564	2093	1289	1685	2535	313	397	92	1145	822	1003	1799	841	815	588	1772	1843	1165	564	2363	1892	872	1514	1359	2596	1446	2869	920	1306	1671	939	1255		1094	1632	383	1625	1300	1466	454	2637	607	282	2963	1758	2756	714	1112	2232	2043	2931	2972	2907	1522	330	3041	600	1547
NASHVILLE, TN	1248	242	716	1648	194	1315	1976	1136	716	1086	543	395	397	1240	474	281	531	681	1162	725	541	1328	801	287	423	559	1826	355	2054	175	215	907	569	886	1094		539	906	703	747	686	818	1715	569	1234	2405	1269	2198	626	307	1675	954	2056	2360	2463	701	764	2597	679	748
NEW ORLEANS, LA	1276	473	1142	1955	351	1734	2234	1563	1254	1588	783	926	713	1502	935	820	1070	525	1409	1117	1079	1118	360	826	185	932	1854	455	1917	714	396	874	1020	1337	1632	539		1332	731	1121	653	1245	1548	1108	1660	2663	1643	2431	1002	690	1932	560	1846	2298	2731	668	1302	2865	1106	890
NEW YORK, NY	2015	869	192	2049	985	1641	2491	215	400	299	773	515	631	1755	797	636	466	1589	1799	1121	622	2235	1660	715	1223	1202	2552	1262	2820	739	1123	1299	894	1211	383	906	1332		1469	1258	1094	91	2481	367	313	2920	1716	2713	342	956	2189	1861	2839	2929	2864	1150	507	2998	228	1391
OKLAHOMA CITY, OK	546	944	1354	1227	729	1136	1506	1694	1262	1632	1248	1022	1102	773	807	863	1073	209	681	546	1062	737	449	752	612	348	1124	355	1352	774	487	1609	880	793	1625	703	731	1469		463	1388	1408	1012	1124	1792	1934	871	1727	1331	505	1204	466	1370	1657	2002	1403	1295	2136	1350	161
OMAHA, NE	973	989	1168	904	941	616	1234	1463	1005	1390	1290	952	1144	497	474	736	806	669	541	136	743	1236	910	618	935	188	1294	570	1567	704	724	1654	514	383	1300	747	1121	1258	463		1433	1228	1440	928	1561	1662	525	1455	1263	440	932	927	1630	1672	1719	1448	971	1853	1162	307
ORLANDO, FL	1934	440	904	2333	591	2003	2662	1324	1221	1383	379	790	525	1926	1161	920	1045	1146	1847	1411	1180	1738	980	975	694	1245	2512	969	2538	863	830	232	1257	1573	1466	686	653	1094	1388	1433		1006	2169	963	1422	3091	1955	2884	750	993	2360	1180	2467	2918	3149	82	1327	3283	860	1434
PHILADELPHIA, PA	1954	782	104	2019	897	1611	2462	321	414	371	685	454	543	1725	768	576	437	1501	1744	1091	592	2147	1572	655	1135	1141	2500	1175	2760	678	1035	1211	865	1181	454	818	1245	91	1408	1228	1006		2420	306	419	2890	1686	2683	254	895	2160	1774	2779	2900	2835	1062	522	2968	140	1330
PHOENIX, AZ	466	1868	2366	1199	1723	1662	993	2706	2274	2644	2184	2035	2107	1004	1819	1876	2085	1077	904	1558	2074	432	1188	1764	1482	1360	285	1367	369	1786	1500	2390	1892	1805	2637	1715	1548	2481	1012	1440	2169	2420		2136	2804	1335	1308	883	2343	1517	651	987	358	750	1513	2184	2307	1655	2362	1173
PITTSBURGH, PA	1670	676	246	1719	763	1311	2161	592	217	587	642	217	438	1425	467	292	136	1246	1460	791	292	1893	1366	370	988	857	2215	920	2476	394	780	1167	564	881	607	569	1108	367	1124	928	963	306	2136		690	2590	1386	2383	341	611	1859	1519	2494	2599	2534	1019	321	2668	240	1046
PORTLAND, ME	2338	1197	520	2352	1313	1944	2795	107	560	233	1101	839	959	2059	1101	960	751	1917	2102	1424	838	2563	1988	1038	1550	1525	2855	1590	3144	1062	1451	1627	1198	1515	282	1234	1660	313	1792	1561	1422	419	2804	690		3223	2019	3016	670	1279	2493	2189	3162	3233	3168	1478	668	3301	556	1714
PORTLAND, OR	1395	2647	2830	889	2599	1301	432	3126	2667	3052	2948	2610	2802	1166	2137	2398	2469	2140	1261	1798	2405	1767	2381	2280	2544	1805	1188	2237	971	2362	2382	3312	2063	1727	2963	2405	2663	2920	1934	1662	3091	2890	1335	2590	3223		1268	578	2925	2057	771	2322	1093	638	170	3106	2633	313	2824	1775
RAPID CITY, SD	841	1511	1626	379	1463	320	930	1921	1463	1848	1824	1422	1678	305	913	1219	1264	1077	404	629	1201	1105	1318	1101	1458	710	1035	1093	1309	1215	1247	2176	842	606	1758	1269	1643	1716	871	525	1955	1686	1308	1386	2019	1268		1151	1720	963	628	1335	1372	1368	1195	1970	1429	1328	1620	712
RENO, NV	1020	2440	2623	960	2392	1372	430	2919	2460	2845	2741	2403	2595	959	1930	2191	2262	1933	1054	1591	2198	1315	2072	2073	2337	1598	442	2030	519	2155	2175	3105	1970	1839	2756	2198	2431	2713	1727	1455	2884	2683	883	2383	3016	578	1151		2718	1850	524	1870	642	217	755	2899	2426	898	2617	1568
RICHMOND, VA	1876	527	152	2053	678	1645	2496	572	485	630	428	322	289	1760	802	530	471	1309	1688	1126	627	1955	1330	641	914	1085	2444	983	2682	572	843	954	899	1216	714	626	1002	342	1331	1263	750	254	2343	341	670	2925	1720	2718		834	2194	1530	2684	2934	2869	805	660	3003	108	1274
ST. LOUIS, MO	1051	549	841	1341	501	1053	1628	1181	749	1119	850	512	704	892	294	350	560	635	855	436	549	1242	863	239	505	252	1610	416	1856	264	294	1214	367	621	1112	307	690	956	505	440	993	895	1517	611	1279	2057	963	1850	834		1326	968	1875	2066	2125	1008	782	2259	837	441
SALT LAKE CITY, UT	624	1916	2100	548	1868	960	342	2395	1936	2322	2218	1880	2072	436	1406	1667	1738	1410	531	1067	1675	864	1650	1549	1813	1074	417	1507	691	1631	1652	2581	1446	1315	2232	1675	1932	2189	1204	932	2360	2160	651	1859	2493	771	628	524	2194	1326		1419	754	740	839	2375	1902	973	2094	1044
SAN ANTONIO, TX	818	1000	1671	1500	878	1599	1761	2092	1665	2036	1310	1344	1241	1046	1270	1231	1481	271	946	1009	1490	556	200	1186	644	812	1272	600	1356	1125	739	1401	1343	1257	2043	954	560	1861	466	927	1180	1774	987	1519	2189	2322	1335	1870	1530	968	1419		1285	1737	2275	1195	1714	2410	1635	624
SAN DIEGO, CA	825	2166	2724	1302	2021	1765	1096	3065	2632	3020	2483	2393	2405	1179	2105	2234	2437	1375	1092	1766	2373	730	1487	2122	1780	1695	337	1703	124	2144	1841	2688	2145	2014	2931	2056	1846	2839	1370	1630	2467	2779	358	2494	3162	1093	1372	642	2684	1875	754	1285		508	1271	2481	2601	1414	2720	1531
SAN FRANCISCO, CA	1111	2618	2840	1176	2472	1749	646	3135	2677	3062	2934	2620	2759	1176	2146	2407	2478	1827	1271	1807	2415	1181	1938	2290	2232	1814	575	2012	385	2372	2144	3140	2186	2055	2972	2360	2298	2929	1657	1672	2918	2900	750	2599	3233	638	1368	217	2934	2066	740	1737	508		816	2933	2643	958	2834	1784
SEATTLE, WA	1463	2705	2775	816	2657	1229	500	3070	2612	2997	2973	2571	2827	1234	2062	2368	2413	2208	1329	1822	2350	1944	2449	2249	2612	1872	1256	2305	1148	2364	2440	3370	1991	1654	2907	2463	2731	2864	2002	1719	3149	2835	1513	2534	3168	170	1195	755	2869	2125	839	2275	1271	816		3164	2577	140	2769	1843
TAMPA, FL	1949	455	960	2348	606	2018	2677	1380	1276	1438	434	845	581	1941	1176	935	1101	1161	1862	1426	1194	1753	995	990	709	1259	2526	984	2553	878	845	274	1272	1588	1522	701	668	1150	1403	1448	82	1062	2184	1019	1478	3106	1970	2899	805	1008	2375	1195	2481	2933	3164		1383	3297	916	1448
TORONTO, ON	1841	958	565	1762	958	1354	2204	570	106	419	1006	537	802	1468	510	484	303	1441	1512	834	233	2032	1561	541	1183	1028	2265	1115	2538	589	975	1532	607	924	330	764	1302	507	1295	971	1327	522	2307	321	668	2633	1429	2426	660	782	1902	1714	2601	2643	2577	1383		2711	563	1217
VANCOUVER, BC	1597	2838	2908	949	2791	1362	633	3204	2745	3130	3106	2705	2960	1368	2196	2501	2547	2342	1463	1956	2483	2087	2583	2383	2746	2007	1390	2439	1291	2497	2574	3504	2124	1788	3041	2597	2865	2998	2136	1853	3283	2968	1655	2668	3301	313	1328	898	3003	2259	973	2410	1414	958	140	3297	2711		2902	1977
WASHINGTON, DC	1896	636	38	1953	758	1545	2395	458	384	517	539	346	397	1659	701	517	370	1362	1686	1025	526	2008	1433	596	996	1083	2441	1036	2702	596	896	1065	799	1115	600	679	1106	228	1350	1162	860	140	2362	240	556	2824	1620	2617	108	837	2094	1635	2720	2834	2769	916	563	2902		1272
WICHITA, KS	707	989	1276	1067	838	934	1346	1616	1184	1554	1291	953	1145	613	728	785	995	367	521	390	984	898	608	674	771	192	1276	464	1513	705	597	1655	769	637	1547	748	890	1391	161	307	1434	1330	1173	1046	1714	1775	712	1568	1274	441	1044	624	1531	1784	1843	1448	1217	1977	1272	

Welcome

Dear Traveler,

Since its inception in 1958, Mobil Travel Guide has served as a trusted advisor to auto travelers in search of value in lodging, dining, and destinations. Now in its 47th year, the Mobil Travel Guide is the hallmark of our ExxonMobil family of travel publications, and we're proud to offer an array of products and services from our Mobil, Exxon, and Esso brands in North America to facilitate life on the road.

Whether you're looking for business or pleasure venues, our nationwide network of independent, professional evaluators offers their expertise on thousands of travel options, allowing you to plan a quick family getaway, a full-service business meeting, or an unforgettable Mobil Five-Star celebration.

Your feedback is important to us as we strive to improve our product offerings and better meet today's travel needs. Whether you travel once a week or once a year, please take the time to contact us at www.mobiltravelguide.com. We hope to hear from you soon.

Best wishes for safe and enjoyable travels.

Lee R. Raymond
Chairman and CEO
Exxon Mobil Corporation

A Word to Our Readers

Travelers are on the roads in great numbers these days. They're exploring the country on day trips, weekend getaways, business trips, and extended family vacations, visiting major cities and small towns along the way. Because time is precious and the travel industry is ever-changing, having accurate, reliable travel information at your fingertips is critical. Mobil Travel Guide has been providing invaluable insight to travelers for more than 45 years, and we are committed to continuing this service well into the future.

The Mobil Corporation (known as Exxon Mobil Corporation since a 1999 merger) began producing the Mobil Travel Guide books in 1958, following the introduction of the US interstate highway system in 1956. The first edition covered only five Southwestern states. Since then, our books have become the premier travel guides in North America, covering all 50 states and Canada.

Since its founding, Mobil Travel Guide has served as an advocate for travelers seeking knowledge about hotels, restaurants, and places to visit. Based on an objective process, we make recommendations to our customers that we believe will enhance the quality and value of their travel experiences. Our trusted Mobil One- to Five-Star rating system is the oldest and most respected lodging and restaurant inspection and rating program in North America. Most hoteliers, restaurateurs, and industry observers favorably regard the rigor of our inspection program and understand the prestige and benefits that come with receiving a Mobil Star rating.

The Mobil Travel Guide process of rating each establishment includes:

- Unannounced facility inspections
- Incognito service evaluations for Mobil Four-Star and Mobil Five-Star properties
- A review of unsolicited comments from the general public
- Senior management oversight

For each property, more than 450 attributes, including cleanliness, physical facilities, and employee attitude and courtesy, are measured and evaluated to produce a mathematically derived score, which is then blended with the other elements to form an overall score. These quantifiable scores allow comparative analysis among properties and form the basis that we use to assign our Mobil One- to Five-Star ratings.

This process focuses largely on guest expectations, guest experience, and consistency of service, not just physical facilities and amenities. It is fundamentally a relative rating system that rewards those properties that continually strive for and achieve excellence each year. Indeed, the very best properties are consistently raising the bar for those that wish to compete with them. These properties proactively respond to consumers' needs even in today's uncertain times.

Only facilities that meet Mobil Travel Guide's standards earn the privilege of being listed in the guide. Deteriorating, poorly managed establishments are deleted. A Mobil Travel Guide listing constitutes a positive quality recommendation; every listing is an accolade, a recognition of achievement. Our Mobil One- to Five-Star rating system highlights its level of service. Extensive in-house research is constantly underway to determine new additions to our lists.

- The Mobil Five-Star Award indicates that a property is one of the very best in the country and consistently provides gracious and courteous service, superlative quality in its facility, and a unique ambience. The lodgings and restaurants at the Mobil Five-Star level consistently and proactively respond to consumers' needs and continue their commitment to excellence, doing so with grace and perseverance.
- Also highly regarded is the Mobil Four-Star Award, which honors properties for outstanding achievement in overall facility and for providing very strong service levels in all areas. These

award winners provide a distinctive experience for the ever-demanding and sophisticated consumer.

- The Mobil Three-Star Award recognizes an excellent property that provides full services and amenities. This category ranges from exceptional hotels with limited services to elegant restaurants with a less-formal atmosphere.
- A Mobil Two-Star property is a clean and comfortable establishment that has expanded amenities or a distinctive environment. A Mobil Two-Star property is an excellent place to stay or dine.
- A Mobil One-Star property is limited in its amenities and services but focuses on providing a value experience while meeting travelers' expectations. The property can be expected to be clean, comfortable, and convenient.

Allow us to emphasize that we do not charge establishments for inclusion in our guides. We have no relationship with any of the businesses and attractions we list and act only as a consumer advocate. In essence, we do the investigative legwork so that you won't have to.

Keep in mind, too, that the hospitality business is ever-changing. Restaurants and lodgings—particularly small chains and stand-alone establishments—change management or even go out of business with surprising quickness. Although we make every effort to double-check information during our annual updates, we nevertheless recommend that you call ahead to make sure the place you've selected is still open and offers all the amenities you're looking for. We've provided phone numbers; when available, we also list fax numbers and Web site addresses.

We hope that your travels are enjoyable and relaxing and that our books help you get the most out of every trip you take. If any aspect of your accommodation, dining, or sightseeing experience motivates you to comment, please drop us a line. We depend a great deal on our readers' remarks, so you can be assured that we will read your comments and assimilate them into our research. General comments about our books are also welcome. You can write to us at Mobil Travel Guide, 1460 Renaissance Drive, Suite 401, Park Ridge, IL 60068, or send an e-mail to info@mobiltravelguide.com.

Take your Mobil Travel Guide books along on every trip you take. We're confident that you'll be pleased with their convenience, ease of use, and breadth of dependable coverage.

Happy travels!

How to Use This Book

The Mobil Travel Guide Regional Travel Planners are designed for ease of use. Each state has its own chapter, beginning with a general introduction that provides a geographical and historical orientation to the state and gives basic statewide tourist information, from climate to calendar highlights to seatbelt laws. The remainder of each chapter is devoted to travel destinations within the state—mainly cities and towns, but also national parks and tourist areas—which, like the states, are arranged in alphabetical order.

The following sections explain the wealth of information you'll find about those travel destinations: information about the area, things to see and do there, and where to stay and eat.

Maps and Map Coordinates

At the front of this book in the full-color section, we have provided state maps as well as maps of selected larger cities to help you find your way around once you leave the highway. You'll find a key to the map symbols on the Contents page at the beginning of the map section.

Next to most cities and towns throughout the book, you'll find a set of map coordinates, such as C-2. These coordinates reference the maps at the front of this book and help you find the location you're looking for quickly and easily.

Destination Information

Because many travel destinations are close to other cities and towns where travelers might find additional attractions, accommodations, and restaurants, we've included cross-references to those cities and towns when it makes sense to do so. We also list addresses, phone numbers, and Web sites for travel information resources—usually the local chamber of commerce or office of tourism—as well as pertinent statistics and, in many cases, a brief introduction to the area.

Information about airports, ground transportation, and suburbs is included for large cities.

Driving Tours and Walking Tours

The driving tours that we include for many states are usually day trips that make for interesting side excursions, although they can be longer. They offer you a way to get off the beaten path and visit an area that travelers often overlook. These trips frequently cover areas of natural beauty or historical significance.

Each walking tour focuses on a particularly interesting area of a city or town. Again, these tours can provide a break from everyday tourist attractions. The tours often include places to stop for meals or snacks.

What to See and Do

Mobil Travel Guide offers information about nearly 20,000 museums, art galleries, amusement parks, historic sites, national and state parks, ski areas, and many other types of attractions. A white star on a black background ★ signals that the attraction is a must-see—one of the best in the area. Because municipal parks, public tennis courts, swimming pools, and small educational institutions are common to most towns, they generally are not mentioned.

Following an attraction's description, you'll find the months, days, and, in some cases, hours of operation; the address/directions, telephone number, and Web site (if there is one); and the admission price category. The following are the ranges we use for admission fees, based on one adult:

- **FREE**
- **$** = Up to $5
- **$$** = $5.01-$10
- **$$$** = $10.01-$15
- **$$$$** = Over $15

Special Events

Special events are either annual events that last only a short time, such as festivals and fairs, or longer, seasonal events such as horse racing, theater, and summer concerts. Our Special Events listings also include infrequently occurring occasions that mark certain dates or events, such as a centennial or other commemorative celebration.

Side Trips

We recognize that your travels don't always end where state lines fall, so we've included some side trips that fall outside the states covered in this book but that travelers frequently visit when they're in the region. Nearby national parks, major cities, and other prime tourist draws fall into this category. You'll find side trips for a particular state at the end of that state's section.

Listings

Lodgings, spas, and restaurants are usually listed under the city or town in which they're located. Make sure to check the related cities and towns that appear right beneath a city's heading for additional options, especially if you're traveling to a major metropolitan area that includes many suburbs. If a property is located in a town that doesn't have its own heading, the listing appears under the town nearest it, with the address and town given immediately after the establishment's name. In large cities, lodgings located within 5 miles of major commercial airports may be listed under a separate "Airport Area" heading that follows the city section.

LODGINGS

Travelers have different wants and needs when it comes to accommodations. To help you pinpoint properties that meet your particular needs, Mobil Travel Guide classifies each lodging by type according to the following characteristics.

Mobil Rated Lodgings

- **Limited-Service Hotel.** A limited-service hotel is traditionally a Mobil One-Star or Mobil Two-Star property. At a Mobil One-Star hotel, guests can expect to find a clean, comfortable property that commonly serves a complimentary continental breakfast. A Mobil Two-Star hotel is also clean and comfortable but has expanded amenities, such as a full-service restaurant, business center, and fitness center. These services may have limited staffing and/or restricted hours of use.
- **Full-Service Hotel.** A full-service hotel traditionally enjoys a Mobil Three-Star, Mobil Four-Star, or Mobil Five-Star rating. Guests can expect these hotels to offer at least one full-service restaurant in addition to amenities such as valet parking, luggage assistance, 24-hour room service, concierge service, laundry and/or dry-cleaning services, and turndown service.
- **Full-Service Resort.** A resort is traditionally a full-service hotel that is geared toward recreation and represents a vacation and holiday destination. A resort's guest rooms are typically furnished to accommodate longer stays. The property may offer a full-service spa, golf, tennis, and fitness facilities or other leisure activities. Resorts are expected to offer a full-service restaurant and expanded amenities, such as luggage assistance, room service, meal plans, concierge service, and turndown service.
- **Full-Service Inn.** An inn is traditionally a Mobil Three-Star, Mobil Four-Star, or Mobil Five-Star property. Inns are similar to bed-and-breakfasts (see below) but offer a wider range of services, most significantly a full-service restaurant that serves at least breakfast and dinner.

Specialty Lodgings

Mobil Travel Guide recognizes the unique and individualized nature of many different types of lodging establishments, including bed-and-breakfasts, limited-service inns, and guest ranches. For that reason, we have chosen to place our stamp of approval on the properties that fall into these two categories in lieu of applying our traditional Mobil Star ratings.

- **B&B/Limited-Service Inn.** A bed-and-breakfast (B&B) or limited-service inn is traditionally an owner-occupied home or residence found in a residential area or vacation destination. It may be a structure of historic significance. Rooms are often individually decorated, but telephones, televisions, and private bathrooms may not be available in every room. A B&B typically serves only breakfast to its overnight guests, which is included in the room rate. Cocktails and refreshments may be served in the late afternoon or evening.

- **Guest Ranch.** A guest ranch is traditionally a rustic, Western-themed property that specializes in stays of three or more days. Horseback riding is often a feature, with stables and trails found on the property. Facilities can range from clean, comfortable establishments to more luxurious facilities.

Mobil Star Rating Definitions for Lodgings

- ★★★★★ : A Mobil Five-Star lodging provides consistently superlative service in an exceptionally distinctive luxury environment, with expanded services. Attention to detail is evident throughout the hotel, resort, or inn, from bed linens to staff uniforms.
- ★★★★ : A Mobil Four-Star lodging provides a luxury experience with expanded amenities in a distinctive environment. Services may include, but are not limited to, automatic turndown service, 24-hour room service, and valet parking.
- ★★★ : A Mobil Three-Star lodging is well appointed, with a full-service restaurant and expanded amenities, such as a fitness center, golf course, tennis courts, 24-hour room service, and optional turndown service.
- ★★ : A Mobil Two-Star lodging is considered a clean, comfortable, and reliable establishment that has expanded amenities, such as a full-service restaurant on the premises.
- ★ : A Mobil One-Star lodging is a limited-service hotel, motel, or inn that is considered a clean, comfortable, and reliable establishment.

Information Found in the Lodging Listings

Each lodging listing gives the name, address/location (when no street address is available), neighborhood and/or directions from downtown (in major cities), phone number(s), fax number, total number of guest rooms, and seasons open (if not year-round). Also included are details on business, luxury, recreational, and dining facilities at the property or nearby. A key to the symbols at the end of each listing can be found on the page following the "A Word to Our Readers" section.

For every property, we also provide pricing information. Because lodging rates change frequently, we list a pricing category rather than specific prices. The pricing categories break down as follows:

- **$** = Up to $150
- **$$** = $151-$250
- **$$$** = $251-$350
- **$$$$** = $351 and up

All prices quoted are in effect at the time of publication; however, prices cannot be guaranteed. In some locations, short-term price variations may exist because of special events, holidays, or seasonality. Certain resorts have complicated rate structures that vary with the time of year; always confirm rates when making your plans.

Because most lodgings offer the following features and services, information about them does not appear in the listings:

- Year-round operation
- Bathroom with tub and/or shower in each room
- Cable television in each room
- In-room telephones
- Cots and cribs available
- Daily maid service
- Elevators
- Major credit cards accepted

Although we recommend every lodging we list in this book, a few stand out—they offer noteworthy amenities or stand above the others in their category in terms of quality, value, or historical significance. To draw your attention to these special spots, we've included the magnifying glass icon to the left of the listing, as you see here.

SPAS

Mobil Travel Guide is pleased to announce its newest category: hotel and resort spas. Until now, hotel and resort spas have not been formally rated or inspected by any organization. Every spa selected for inclusion in this book underwent a rigorous inspection process similar to the one Mobil Travel Guide has been applying to lodgings and restaurants for more than four decades. After spending a year and a half researching more than 300 spas and performing exhaustive incognito inspections of more than 200 properties, we narrowed our list to the 48 best spas in the United States and Canada.

Mobil Travel Guide's spa ratings are based on objective evaluations of more than 450 attributes. Approximately half of these criteria assess basic expectations, such as staff courtesy, the technical proficiency and skill of the employees, and whether the facility is maintained properly and hygienically. Several standards address issues that impact a guest's physical comfort and convenience, as well as the staff's ability to impart a sense of personalized service and anticipate clients' needs. Additional criteria measure the spa's ability to create a completely calming ambience.

The Mobil Star ratings focus on much more than the facilities available at a spa and the treatments it offers. Each Mobil Star rating is a cumulative score achieved from multiple inspections that reflects the spa management's attention to detail and commitment to consumers' needs.

Mobil Star Rating Definitions for Spas

- ★★★★★ : A Mobil Five-Star spa provides consistently superlative service in an exceptionally distinctive luxury environment with extensive amenities. The staff at a Mobil Five-Star spa provides extraordinary service above and beyond the traditional spa experience, allowing guests to achieve the highest level of relaxation and pampering. A Mobil Five-Star spa offers an extensive array of treatments, often incorporating international themes and products. Attention to detail is evident throughout the spa, from arrival to departure.
- ★★★★ : A Mobil Four-Star spa provides a luxurious experience with expanded amenities in an elegant and serene environment. Throughout the spa facility, guests experience personalized service. Amenities might include, but are not limited to, single-sex relaxation rooms where guests wait for their treatments, plunge pools and whirlpools in both men's and women's locker rooms, and an array of treatments, including at a minimum a selection of massages, body therapies, facials, and a variety of salon services.
- ★★★ : A Mobil Three-Star spa is physically well appointed and has a full complement of staff to ensure that guests' needs are met. It has some expanded amenities, such as, but not limited to, a well-equipped fitness center, separate men's and women's locker rooms, a sauna or steam room, and a designated relaxation area. It also offers a menu of services that at a minimum includes massages, facial treatments, and at least one other type of body treatment, such as scrubs or wraps.

RESTAURANTS

All Mobil Star rated dining establishments listed in this book have a full kitchen and offer seating at tables; most offer table service.

Mobil Star Rating Definitions for Restaurants

- ★★★★★ : A Mobil Five-Star restaurant offers one of few flawless dining experiences in the country. These establishments consistently provide their guests with exceptional food, superlative service, elegant décor, and exquisite presentations of each detail surrounding a meal.
- ★★★★ : A Mobil Four-Star restaurant provides professional service, distinctive presentations, and wonderful food.
- ★★★ : A Mobil Three-Star restaurant has good food, warm and skillful service, and enjoyable décor.
- ★★ : A Mobil Two-Star restaurant serves fresh food in a clean setting with efficient service. Value is considered in this category, as is family friendliness.
- ★ : A Mobil One-Star restaurant provides a distinctive experience through culinary specialty, local flair, or individual atmosphere.

Information Found in the Restaurant Listings

Each restaurant listing gives the cuisine type, street address (or directions if no address is available), phone and fax numbers, Web site (if available), meals served, days of operation (if not open daily year-round), and pricing category. Information about appropriate attire is provided, although it's always a good idea to call ahead and ask if you're unsure; the meaning of "casual" or "business casual" varies widely in different parts of the country. We also indicate whether the restaurant has a bar, whether a children's menu is offered, and whether outdoor seating is available. If reservations are recommended, we note that fact in the listing. When valet parking is available, it is noted in the description. In many cases, self-parking is available at the restaurant or nearby.

Because menu prices can fluctuate, we list a pricing category rather than specific prices. The pricing categories are defined as follows, per diner, and assume that you order an appetizer or dessert, an entrée, and one drink:

- **$** = $15 and under
- **$$** = $16-$35
- **$$$** = $36-$85
- **$$$$** = $86 and up

Again, all prices quoted are in effect at the time of publication, but prices cannot be guaranteed.

Although we recommend every restaurant we list in this book, a few stand out—they offer noteworthy local specialties or stand above the others in their category in terms of quality, value, or experience. To draw your attention to these special spots, we've included the magnifying glass icon to the left of the listing, as you see here.

SPECIAL INFORMATION FOR TRAVELERS WITH DISABILITIES

The Mobil Travel Guide symbol indicates that an establishment is not at least partially accessible to people with mobility problems. When the symbol follows a listing, the establishment is not equipped with facilities to accommodate people using wheelchairs or crutches or otherwise needing easy access to doorways and rest rooms. Travelers with severe mobility problems or with hearing or visual impairments may or may not find the facilities they need. Always phone ahead to make sure that an establishment can meet your needs.

AMERICA'S BYWAYS™

Mobil Travel Guide is pleased to announce a new partnership with the National Scenic Byways Program. Under this program, the US Secretary of Transportation recognizes certain roads as National Scenic Byways or All-American Roads based on their archaeological, cultural, historic, natural, recreational, and scenic qualities. To be designated a National Scenic Byway, a road must possess at least one of these six intrinsic qualities. To receive an All-American Road designation, a road must possess multiple intrinsic qualities that are nationally significant and contain one-of-a-kind features that do not exist elsewhere. The road or highway also must be considered a destination unto itself.

America's Byways are a great way to explore the country. From the mighty Mississippi to the towering Rockies to the Historic National Road, these routes take you past America's most treasured scenery and enable you to get in touch with America's past, present, and future. Bringing together all the nationally designated Byways in the Southwest, this bonus section of the book is a handy reference whether you're planning to hop in the car tomorrow or you're simply looking for inspiration for future trips. Look for it at the end of the front section, before page 1.

Understanding the Symbols

What to See and Do

★	=	One of the top attractions in the area
$	=	Up to $5
$$	=	$5.01 to $10
$$$	=	$10.01 to $15
$$$$	=	Over $15

Lodgings

$	=	Up to $150
$$	=	$151 to $250
$$$	=	$251 to $350
$$$$	=	Over $350

Restaurants

$	=	Up to $15
$$	=	$16 to $35
$$$	=	$36 to $85
$$$$	=	Over $85

Lodging Star Definitions

★★★★★ A Mobil Five-Star lodging establishment provides consistently superlative service in an exceptionally distinctive luxury environment with expanded services. Attention to detail is evident throughout the hotel/resort/inn from the bed linens to the staff uniforms.

★★★★ A Mobil Four-Star lodging establishment is a hotel/resort/inn that provides a luxury experience with expanded amenities in a distinctive environment. Services may include, but are not limited to, automatic turndown service, 24-hour room service, and valet parking.

★★★ A Mobil Three-Star lodging establishment is a hotel/resort/inn that is well appointed, with a full-service restaurant and expanded amenities, such as, but not limited to, a fitness center, golf course, tennis courts, 24-hour room service, and optional turndown service.

★★ A Mobil Two-Star lodging establishment is a hotel/resort/inn that is considered a clean, comfortable, and reliable establishment, but also has expanded amenities, such as a full-service restaurant on the premises.

★ A Mobil One-Star lodging establishment is a limited-service hotel or inn that is considered a clean, comfortable, and reliable establishment.

Restaurant Star Definitions

★★★★★ A Mobil Five-Star restaurant is one of few flawless dining experiences in the country. These restaurants consistently provide their guests with exceptional food, superlative service, elegant décor, and exquisite presentations of each detail surrounding the meal.

★★★★ A Mobil Four-Star restaurant provides professional service, distinctive presentations, and wonderful food.

★★★ A Mobil Three-Star restaurant has good food, warm and skillful service, and enjoyable décor.

★★ A Mobil Two-Star restaurant serves fresh food in a clean setting with efficient service. Value is considered in this category, as is family friendliness.

★ A Mobil One-Star restaurant provides a distinctive experience through culinary specialty, local flair, or individual atmosphere.

Symbols at End of Listings

- Facilities for people with disabilities not available
- Pets allowed
- Ski in/ski out access
- Golf on premises
- Tennis court(s) on premises
- Indoor or outdoor pool
- Fitness room
- Major commercial airport within 5 miles
- Business center

Making the Most of Your Trip

A few hardy souls might look back with fondness on a trip during which the car broke down, leaving them stranded for three days, or a vacation that cost twice what it was supposed to. For most travelers, though, the best trips are those that are safe, smooth, and within budget. To help you make your trip the best it can be, we've assembled a few tips and resources.

Saving Money

ON LODGING

Many hotels and motels offer discounts—for senior citizens, business travelers, families, you name it. It never hurts to ask—politely, that is. Sometimes, especially in the late afternoon, desk clerks are instructed to fill beds, and you might be offered a lower rate or a nicer room to entice you to stay. Simply ask the reservation agent for the best rate available. Also, make sure to try both the toll-free number and the local number. You may be able to get a lower rate from one than from the other.

Timing your trip right can cut your lodging costs as well. Look for bargains on stays over multiple nights, in the off-season, and on weekdays or weekends, depending on the location. Many hotels in major metropolitan areas, for example, have special weekend packages that offer leisure travelers considerable savings on rooms; they may include breakfast, cocktails, and/or dinner discounts.

Another way to save money is to choose accommodations that give you more than just a standard room. Rooms with kitchen facilities enable you to cook some meals yourself, reducing your restaurant costs. A suite might save money for two couples traveling together. Even hotel luxury levels can provide good value, as many include breakfast or cocktails in the price of a room.

State and city taxes, as well as special room taxes, can increase your room rate by as much as 25 percent per day. We are unable to include information about taxes in our listings, but we strongly urge you to ask about taxes when making reservations so that you understand the total cost of your lodgings before you book them.

Watch out for telephone-usage charges that hotels frequently impose on long-distance, credit-card, and other calls. Before phoning from your room, read the information given to you at check-in, and then be sure to review your bill carefully when checking out. You won't be expected to pay for charges that the hotel didn't spell out. Consider using your cell phone if you have one; or, if public telephones are available in the hotel lobby, your cost savings may outweigh the inconvenience of using them.

Here are some additional ways to save on lodgings:

- Stay in B&B accommodations. They're generally less expensive than standard hotel rooms, and the complimentary breakfast cuts down on food costs.
- If you're traveling with children, find lodgings at which kids stay free.
- When visiting a major city, stay just outside the city limits; these rooms are usually less expensive than those in downtown locations.
- Consider visiting national parks during the low season, when prices of lodgings near the parks drop by 25 percent or more.
- When calling a hotel, ask whether it is running any special promotions or if any discounts are available; many times reservationists are told not to volunteer these deals unless they're specifically asked about them.
- Check for hotel packages; some offer nightly rates that include a rental car or discounts on major attractions.
- Search the Internet for travel bargains. Web sites that allow for online booking of hotel rooms and travel planning, such as *www.mobiltravelguide .com,* often deliver lower rates than are available through telephone reservations.

ON DINING

There are several ways to get a less expensive meal at an expensive restaurant. Early-bird dinners are popular in many parts of the country and offer considerable savings. If you're interested in visiting a Mobil Four- or Five-Star establishment, consider going at lunchtime. Although the prices are probably still relatively high at midday, they may be half of those at dinner, and you'll experience the same ambience, service, and cuisine.

ON ENTERTAINMENT

Although many national parks, monuments, seashores, historic sites, and recreation areas may be used free of charge, others charge an entrance fee and/or a usage fee for special services and facilities. If you plan to make several visits to national recreation areas, consider one of the following money-saving programs offered by the National Park Service:

- **National Parks Pass.** This annual pass is good for entrance to any national park that charges an entrance fee. If the park charges a per-vehicle fee, the pass holder and any accompanying passengers in a private noncommercial vehicle may enter. If the park charges a per-person fee, the pass applies to the holder's spouse, children, and parents as well as the holder. It is valid for entrance fees only; it does not cover parking, camping, or other fees. You can purchase a National Parks Pass in person at any national park where an entrance fee is charged; by mail from the National Park Foundation, PO Box 34108, Washington, DC 20043-4108; by calling toll-free 888/467-2757; or at www.nationalparks.org. The cost is $50.
- **Golden Eagle Sticker.** When affixed to a National Parks Pass, this hologram sticker, available to people who are between 17 and 61 years of age, extends coverage to sites managed by the US Fish and Wildlife Service, the US Forest Service, and the Bureau of Land Management. It is good until the National Parks Pass to which it is affixed expires and does not cover usage fees. You can purchase one at the National Park Service, the Fish and Wildlife Service, or the Bureau of Land Management fee stations. The cost is $15.
- **Golden Age Passport.** Available to citizens and permanent US residents 62 and older, this passport is a lifetime entrance permit to fee-charging national recreation areas. The fee exemption extends to those accompanying the permit holder in a private noncommercial vehicle or, in the case of walk-in facilities, to the holder's spouse and children. The passport also entitles the holder to a 50 percent discount on federal usage fees charged in park areas, but not on concessions. Golden Age Passports must be obtained in person and are available at most National Park Service units that charge an entrance fee. The applicant must show proof of age, such as a driver's license or birth certificate (Medicare cards are not acceptable proof). The cost is $10.
- **Golden Access Passport.** Issued to citizens and permanent US residents who are physically disabled or visually impaired, this passport is a free lifetime entrance permit to fee-charging national recreation areas. The fee exemption extends to those accompanying the permit holder in a private noncommercial vehicle or, in the case of walk-in facilities, to the holder's spouse and children. The passport also entitles the holder to a 50 percent discount on usage fees charged in park areas, but not on concessions. Golden Access Passports must be obtained in person and are available at most National Park Service units that charge an entrance fee. Proof of eligibility to receive federal benefits (under programs such as Disability Retirement, Compensation for Military Service-Connected Disability, and the Coal Mine Safety and Health Act) is required, or an affidavit must be signed attesting to eligibility.

A money-saving move in several large cities is to purchase a **CityPass.** If you plan to visit several museums and other major attractions, CityPass is a terrific option because it gets you into several sites for one substantially reduced price. Currently, CityPass is available in Boston, Chicago, Hollywood, New York, Philadelphia, San Francisco, Seattle, southern California (which includes Disneyland, SeaWorld, and the San Diego Zoo), and Toronto. For more information or to buy one, call toll-free 888/330-5008 or visit www.citypass.net. You can also buy a CityPass from any participating CityPass attraction.

Here are some additional ways to save on entertainment and shopping:

- Check with your hotel's concierge for various coupons and special offers; they often have two-for-one tickets for area attractions and coupons for discounts at area stores and restaurants.

- Purchase same-day concert or theater tickets for half-price through the local cheap-tickets outlet, such as TKTS in New York or Hot Tix in Chicago.
- Visit museums on their free or "by donation" days, when you can pay what you wish rather than a specific admission fee.

ON TRANSPORTATION

Transportation is a big part of any vacation budget. Here are some ways to reduce your costs:

- If you're renting a car, shop early over the Internet; you can book a car during the low season for less, even if you'll be using it in the high season.
- Rental car discounts are often available if you rent for one week or longer and reserve in advance.
- Get the best gas mileage out of your vehicle by making sure that it's properly tuned up and keeping your tires properly inflated.
- Travel at moderate speeds on the open road; higher speeds require more gasoline.
- Fill the tank before you return your rental car; rental companies charge to refill the tank and do so at prices of up to 50 percent more than at local gas stations.
- Make a checklist of travel essentials and purchase them before you leave; don't get stuck buying expensive sunscreen at your hotel or overpriced film at the airport.

FOR SENIOR CITIZENS

Always call ahead to ask if a discount is being offered, and be sure to carry proof of age. Additional information for mature travelers is available from the American Association of Retired Persons (AARP), 601 E St NW, Washington, DC 20049; phone 202/434-2277; www.aarp.org.

Tipping

Tips are expressions of appreciation for good service. However, you are never obligated to tip if you receive poor service.

IN HOTELS

- Door attendants usually get $1 for hailing a cab.
- Bell staff expect $2 per bag.
- Concierges are tipped according to the service they perform. Tipping is not mandatory when you've asked for suggestions on sightseeing or restaurants or for help in making dining reservations. However, a tip of $5 is appropriate when a concierge books you a table at a restaurant known to be difficult to get into. For obtaining theater or sporting event tickets, $5 to $10 is expected.
- Maids should be tipped $1 to $2 per day. Hand your tip directly to the maid, or leave it with a note saying that the money has been left expressly for the maid.

IN RESTAURANTS

Before tipping, carefully review your check for any gratuity or service charge that is already included in your bill. If you're in doubt, ask your server.

- Coffee shop and counter service waitstaff usually receive 15 percent of the bill, before sales tax.
- In full-service restaurants, tip 18 percent of the bill, before sales tax.
- In fine restaurants, where gratuities are shared among a larger staff, 18 to 20 percent is appropriate.
- In most cases, the maitre d' is tipped only if the service has been extraordinary, and only on the way out. At upscale properties in major metropolitan areas, $20 is the minimum.
- If there is a wine steward, tip $20 for exemplary service and beyond, or more if the wine was decanted or the bottle was very expensive.
- Tip $1 to $2 per coat at the coat check.

AT AIRPORTS

Curbside luggage handlers expect $1 per bag. Car-rental shuttle drivers who help with your luggage appreciate a $1 or $2 tip.

Staying Safe

The best way to deal with emergencies is to avoid them in the first place. However, unforeseen situations do happen, so you should be prepared for them.

IN YOUR CAR

Before you head out on a road trip, make sure that your car has been serviced and is in good working order. Change the oil, check the battery and belts, make sure that your windshield washer fluid is full and your tires are properly inflated (which can also improve your gas mileage). Other inspections recommended by the vehicle's manufacturer should also be made.

Next, be sure you have the tools and equipment needed to deal with a routine breakdown:

- Jack
- Spare tire
- Lug wrench
- Repair kit
- Emergency tools
- Jumper cables
- Spare fan belt
- Fuses
- Flares and/or reflectors
- Flashlight
- First-aid kit
- In winter, a windshield scraper and snow shovel

Many emergency supplies are sold in special packages that include the essentials you need to stay safe in the event of a breakdown.

Also bring all appropriate and up-to-date documentation—licenses, registration, and insurance cards—and know what your insurance covers. Bring an extra set of keys, too, just in case.

En route, always buckle up! In most states, wearing a seatbelt is required by law.

If your car does break down, do the following:

- Get out of traffic as soon as possible—pull well off the road.
- Raise the hood and turn on your emergency flashers or tie a white cloth to the roadside door handle or antenna.
- Stay in your car.
- Use flares or reflectors to keep your vehicle from being hit.

IN YOUR HOTEL

Chances are slim that you will encounter a hotel or motel fire, but you can protect yourself by doing the following:

- Once you've checked in, make sure that the smoke detector in your room is working properly.
- Find the property's fire safety instructions, usually posted on the inside of the room door.
- Locate the fire extinguishers and at least two fire exits.
- Never use an elevator in a fire.

For personal security, use the peephole in your room door and make sure that anyone claiming to be a hotel employee can show proper identification. Call the front desk if you feel threatened at any time.

PROTECTING AGAINST THEFT

To guard against theft wherever you go:

- Don't bring anything of more value than you need.
- If you do bring valuables, leave them at your hotel rather than in your car.
- If you bring something very expensive, lock it in a safe. Many hotels put one in each room; others will store your valuables in the hotel's safe.
- Don't carry more money than you need. Use traveler's checks and credit cards or visit cash machines to withdraw more cash when you run out.

For Travelers with Disabilities

To get the kind of service you need and have a right to expect, don't hesitate when making a reservation to question the management about the availability of accessible rooms, parking, entrances, restaurants, lounges, or any other facilities that are important to you, and confirm what is meant by "accessible."

The Mobil Travel Guide [D] symbol indicates establishments that are not at least partially accessible to people with special mobility needs (people using wheelchairs or crutches or otherwise needing easy access to buildings and rooms). Further information about these criteria can be found in the earlier section "How to Use This Book."

A thorough listing of published material for travelers with disabilities is available from the Disability Bookshop, Twin Peaks Press, Box 129, Vancouver, WA 98666; phone 360/694-2462; disabilitybookshop.virtualave.net. Another reliable organization is the Society for Accessible Travel & Hospitality (SATH), 347 Fifth Ave, Suite 610, New York, NY 10016; phone 212/447-7284; www.sath.org.

Border-Crossing Regulations

In addition to a driver's license or military ID, proof of citizenship—a passport or certified birth certificate—is required for travel into Mexico for US citizens ages 18 and over. Children under age 18 traveling with their birth certificates are not required to have photo IDs, but it is highly recommended. A child under age 18 traveling to Mexico without both legal guardians must have a notarized letter of consent from the nontraveling parent(s) granting permission for the child to travel. The notarized letter of consent is not waived even when the minor has his or her own passport.

Canadian citizens crossing into Mexico must have a valid Canadian passport or government-issued birth certificate along with a government-issued photo ID, such as current driver's license or military ID. Mexican citizens residing in the US must have a Mexican passport, or Matricula Consular; a Certificate of Nationality issued by the Mexican Consulate with photo ID; a birth certificate with recent photo ID; or Mexican voter registration papers with photo ID. A US Resident Alien Registration Card is no longer an acceptable travel document for entry into Mexico.

Resident aliens of the US must carry a valid national passport; a Mexican visa may be required. A US Alien Registration Card is no longer an acceptable travel document for entry into Mexico.

If you plan to travel beyond the border cities or stay in Mexico for longer than 72 hours, you must purchase a Mexican tourist card, available from Mexican consulates, Mexican border crossing points, Mexican tourism offices, airports within the border zone, and most airlines serving Mexico. If you're driving your car beyond the border area, you are required to purchase an automobile permit, which costs about $20. Get a copy of the current border regulations from the nearest Mexican consulate or tourism office before crossing, and make sure that you understand them. A helpful booklet, Know Before You Go, can be obtained free of charge from the nearest office of the US Customs Service or online at www.customs.treas.gov.

Your automobile insurance is not valid in Mexico; for a short visit, get a one-day policy before crossing. You may find it more convenient to unload all baggage before crossing than to go through a thorough customs inspection upon your return. At customs, you must declare your purchases. Each traveler may bring up to $800 worth of goods purchased in Mexico back into the United States duty free. In addition, federal regulations permit each US citizen 21 years of age or older to bring back 1 quart of alcoholic beverage duty free in a 30-day period. Travelers are not permitted to bring in plants, fruits, or vegetables. State regulations vary, so check locally before entering Mexico. New regulations may be issued at any time.

US currency is accepted in all border cities.

For more information about traveling to Mexico, including safety information, look for the US State Department's Consular Information Sheet at travel.state.gov/mexico.html, or request it by fax by calling 202/647-3000.

Important Toll-Free Numbers and Online Information

Hotels

Adams Mark 800/444-2326
www.adamsmark.com
AmericInn 800/634-3444
www.americinn.com
AmeriHost Inn 800/434-5800
www.amerihostinn.com
Amerisuites 800/833-1516
www.amerisuites.com
Baymont Inns 877/BAYMONT
www.baymontinns.com
Best Inns & Suites 800/237-8466
www.bestinn.com
Best Value Inn 888/315-BEST
www.bestvalueinn.com
Best Western 800/780-7234
www.bestwestern.com
Budget Host Inn 800/BUDHOST
www.budgethost.com
Candlewood Suites 888/CANDLEWOOD
www.candlewoodsuites.com
Clarion Hotels 800/252-7466
www.choicehotels.com
Comfort Inns and Suites 800/252-7466
www.choicehotels.com
Country Hearth Inns 800/848-5767
www.countryhearth.com
Country Inns & Suites 800/456-4000
www.countryinns.com
Courtyard by Marriott 800/321-2211
www.courtyard.com
Cross Country Inns (KY and OH) 800/621-1429
www.crosscountryinns.com
Crowne Plaza Hotels and Resorts 800/227-6963
www.crowneplaza.com
Days Inn 800/544-8313
www.daysinn.com
Delta Hotels 800/268-1133
www.deltahotels.com
Destination Hotels & Resorts 800/434-7347
www.destinationhotels.com
Doubletree Hotels 800/222-8733
www.doubletree.com
Drury Inn 800/378-7946
www.druryinn.com
Econolodge 800/553-2666
www.econolodge.com
Embassy Suites 800/362-2779
www.embassysuites.com
ExelInns of America 800/FOREXEL
www.exelinns.com
Extended StayAmerica 800/EXTSTAY
www.extstay.com
Fairfield Inn by Marriott 800/228-2800
www.fairfieldinn.com
Fairmont Hotels 800/441-1414
www.fairmont.com
Four Points by Sheraton 888/625-5144
www.starwood.com/fourpoints
Four Seasons 800/545-4000
www.fourseasons.com
Hampton Inn 800/426-7866
www.hamptoninn.com
Hard Rock Hotels, Resorts, and Casinos 800/HRDROCK
www.hardrock.com
Harrah's Entertainment 800/HARRAHS
www.harrahs.com
Hawthorn Suites 800/527-1133
www.hawthorn.com
Hilton Hotels and Resorts (US) 800/774-1500
www.hilton.com
Holiday Inn Express 800/465-4329
www.hiexpress.com
Holiday Inn Hotels and Resorts 800/465-4329
www.holiday-inn.com
Homestead Studio Suites 888/782-9473
www.homesteadhotels.com
Homewood Suites 800/225-5466
www.homewoodsuites.com
Howard Johnson 800/406-1411
www.hojo.com
Hyatt 800/633-7313
www.hyatt.com
Ian Schrager .... Contact individual hotel
www.ianschragerhotels.com
Inns of America 800/826-0778
www.innsofamerica.com
InterContinental 888/567-8725
www.intercontinental.com
Joie de Vivre 800/738-7477
www.jdvhospitality.com
Kimpton Hotels 888/546-7866
www.kimptongroup.com
Knights Inn 800/843-5644
www.knightsinn.com

La Quinta 800/531-5900
www.laquinta.com
Le Meridien 800/543-4300
www.lemeridien.com
Leading Hotels of the World 800/223-6800
www.lhw.com
Loews Hotels 800/235-6397
www.loewshotels.com
MainStay Suites 800/660-6246
www.choicehotels.com
Mandarin Oriental 800/526-6566
www.mandarin-oriental.com
Marriott Hotels, Resorts, and Suites 800/228-9290
www.marriott.com
Microtel Inns & Suites 800/771-7171
www.microtelinn.com
Millennium & Copthorne Hotels 866/866-8086
www.mill-cop.com
Motel 6 .... 800/4MOTEL6
www.motel6.com
Omni Hotels 800/843-6664
www.omnihotels.com
Pan Pacific Hotels and Resorts 800/327-8585
www.panpac.com
Park Inn & Park Plaza 888/201-1801
www.parkhtls.com
The Peninsula Group .... Contact individual hotel
www.peninsula.com
Preferred Hotels & Resorts Worldwide 800/323-7500
www.preferredhotels.com
Quality Inn 800/228-5151
www.qualityinn.com
Radisson Hotels 800/333-3333
www.radisson.com
Raffles International Hotels and Resorts 800/637-9477
www.raffles.com
Ramada Plazas, Limiteds, and Inns 800/2RAMADA
www.ramada.com
Red Lion Inns 800/733-5466
www.redlion.com
Red Roof Inns 800/733-7663
www.redroof.com
Regal Hotels 800/222-8888
www.regal-hotels.com
Regent International 800/545-4000
www.regenthotels.com
Relais & Chateaux 800/735-2478
www.relaischateaux.com
Renaissance Hotels 888/236-2427
www.renaissancehotels.com
Residence Inn 800/331-3131
www.residenceinn.com
Ritz-Carlton 800/241-3333
www.ritzcarlton.com

Rockresorts 888/FORROCKS
www.rockresorts.com
Rodeway Inn 800/228-2000
www.rodeway.com
Rosewood Hotels & Resorts 888/767-3966
www.rosewood-hotels.com
Select Inn 800/641-1000
www.selectinn.com
Sheraton 888/625-5144
www.sheraton.com
Shilo Inns 800/222-2244
www.shiloinns.com
Shoney's Inn 800/552-4667
www.shoneysinn.com
Signature/Jameson Inns 800/822-5252
www.jamesoninns.com
Sleep Inn 800/453-3746
www.sleepinn.com
Small Luxury Hotels of the World 800/525-4800
www.slh.com
Sofitel 800/763-4835
www.sofitel.com
SpringHill Suites 888/236-2427
www.springhillsuites.com
SRS Worldhotels 800/223-5652
www.srs-worldhotels.com
St. Regis Luxury Collection 888/625-5144
www.stregis.com
Staybridge Suites 800/238-8000
www.staybridge.com
Summerfield Suites by Wyndham 800/833-4353
www.summerfieldsuites.com
Summit International 800/457-4000
www.summithotels.com
Super 8 Motels 800/800-8000
www.super8.com
The Sutton Place Hotels 866/378-8866
www.suttonplace.com
Swissôtel 800/637-9477
www.swissotel.com
TownePlace Suites 888/236-2427
www.towneplace.com
Travelodge 800/578-7878
www.travelodge.com
Vagabond Inns 800/522-1555
www.vagabondinns.com
W Hotels 888/625-5144
www.whotels.com
Wellesley Inn and Suites 800/444-8888
www.wellesleyinnandsuites.com
WestCoast Hotels 800/325-4000
www.westcoasthotels.com
Westin Hotels & Resorts 800/937-8461
www.westin.com

Wingate Inns 800/228-1000
www.wingateinns.com
Woodfin Suite Hotels 800/966-3346
www.woodfinsuitehotels.com
Wyndham Hotels & Resorts 800/996-3426
www.wyndham.com

Airlines

Air Canada 888/247-2262
www.aircanada.ca
AirTran 800/247-8726
www.airtran.com
Alaska Airlines 800/252-7522
www.alaskaair.com
American Airlines 800/433-7300
www.aa.com
America West 800/235-9292
www.americawest.com
ATA 800/435-9282
www.ata.com
Continental Airlines 800/523-3273
www.flycontinental.com
Delta Air Lines 800/221-1212
www.delta.com
Frontier Airlines 800/432-1FLY
www.frontierairlines.com
Jet Blue Airways 800/JET-BLUE
www.jetblue.com
Midwest Express 800/452-2022
www.midwestexpress.com
Northwest Airlines 800/225-2525
www.nwa.com
Southwest Airlines 800/435-9792
www.iflyswa.com
Spirit Airlines 800/772-7117
www.spiritair.com
United Airlines 800/241-6522
www.ual.com
US Airways 800/428-4322
www.usairways.com
Vanguard Airlines 800/VANGUARD
www.flyvanguard.com

Car Rentals

Advantage 800/777-5500
www.arac.com
Alamo 800/327-9633
www.goalamo.com
Avis 800/831-2847
www.avis.com
Budget 800/527-0700
www.budgetrentacar.com
Dollar 800/800-4000
www.dollarcar.com
Enterprise 800/325-8007
www.pickenterprise.com
Hertz 800/654-3131
www.hertz.com
National 800/227-7368
www.nationalcar.com
Payless 800/729-5377
www.800-payless.com
Rent-A-Wreck.com 800/535-1391
www.rent-a-wreck.com
Thrifty 800/847-4389
www.thrifty.com

Meet the Stars

Mobil Travel Guide 2005 ***Five-Star*** *Award Winners*

CALIFORNIA
Lodgings
The Beverly Hills Hotel, *Beverly Hills*
Chateau du Sureau, *Oakhurst*
Four Seasons Hotel San Francisco, *San Francisco*
Hotel Bel-Air, *Los Angeles*
The Peninsula Beverly Hills, *Beverly Hills*
Raffles L'Ermitage Beverly Hills, *Beverly Hills*
The Ritz-Carlton, San Francisco, *San Francisco*

Restaurants
The Dining Room, *San Francisco*
The French Laundry, *Yountville*
Gary Danko, *San Francisco*

COLORADO
Lodgings
The Broadmoor, *Colorado Springs*
The Little Nell, *Aspen*

CONNECTICUT
Lodging
The Mayflower Inn, *Washington*

FLORIDA
Lodgings
Four Seasons Resort Palm Beach, *Palm Beach*
The Ritz-Carlton, Naples, *Naples*
The Ritz-Carlton, Palm Beach, *Manalapan*

GEORGIA
Lodgings
Four Seasons Hotel Atlanta, *Atlanta*
The Lodge at Sea Island Golf Club, *St. Simons Island*

Restaurants
The Dining Room, *Atlanta*
Seeger's, *Atlanta*

HAWAII
Lodging
Four Seasons Resort Maui at Wailea, *Wailea, Maui*

ILLINOIS
Lodgings
Four Seasons Hotel Chicago, *Chicago*
The Peninsula Chicago, *Chicago*
The Ritz-Carlton, A Four Seasons Hotel, *Chicago*

Restaurants
Charlie Trotter's, *Chicago*
Trio, *Evanston*

MASSACHUSETTS
Lodgings
Blantyre, *Lenox*
Four Seasons Hotel Boston, *Boston*

NEW YORK
Lodgings
Four Seasons Hotel New York, *New York*
The Point, *Saranac Lake*
The Ritz-Carlton New York, Central Park, *New York*
The St. Regis, *New York*

Restaurants
Alain Ducasse, *New York*
Jean Georges, *New York*
Masa, *New York*

NORTH CAROLINA
Lodging
The Fearrington House Country Inn, *Pittsboro*

OHIO
Restaurant
Maisonette, *Cincinnati*

PENNSYLVANIA
Restaurant
Le Bec-Fin, *Philadelphia*

SOUTH CAROLINA
Lodging
Woodlands Resort & Inn, *Summerville*

Restaurant
Dining Room at the Woodlands, *Summerville*

TEXAS
Lodging
The Mansion on Turtle Creek, *Dallas*

VERMONT
Lodging
Twin Farms, *Barnard*

VIRGINIA
Lodgings
The Inn at Little Washington, *Washington*
The Jefferson Hotel, *Richmond*

Restaurant
The Inn at Little Washington, *Washington*

Mobil Travel Guide has been rating establishments with its Mobil One- to Five-Star system since 1958. Each establishment awarded the Mobil Five-Star rating is one of the best in the country. Detailed information on each award winner can be found in the corresponding regional edition listed on the back cover of this book.

Four- and Five-Star Establishments in Southwest

Arizona

★★★★ Lodgings

The Boulders Resort and Golden Door Spa, *Carefree*
Four Seasons Resort Scottsdale at Troon North, *Scottsdale*
The Phoenician, *Scottsdale*
The Ritz-Carlton, Phoenix, *Phoenix*

★★★★ Restaurants

Acacia, *Scottsdale*
Golden Swan, *Scottsdale*
Mary Elaine's, *Scottsdale*
The Ventana Room, *Tucson*

Colorado

★★★★★ Lodgings

The Broadmoor, *Colorado Springs*
The Little Nell, *Aspen*

★★★★ Lodgings

The Brown Palace Hotel, *Denver*
The Ritz-Carlton, Bachelor Gulch, *Avon*
The St. Regis Aspen, *Aspen*

★★★★ Restaurants

Flagstaff House Restaurant, *Boulder*
Mirabelle at Beaver Creek, *Beaver Creek*
Montagna, *Aspen*
Penrose Room, *Colorado Springs*
Restaurant Kevin Taylor, *Denver*

Nevada

★★★★ Lodgings

Bellagio, *Las Vegas*
Four Seasons Hotel Las Vegas, *Las Vegas*
The Ritz-Carlton, Lake Las Vegas, *Henderson*

★★★★ Restaurants

Aqua, *Las Vegas*
Aureole, *Las Vegas*
Bradley Ogden, *Las Vegas*
Picasso, *Las Vegas*
Renoir, *Las Vegas*

New Mexico

★★★★ Lodging

Inn of the Anasazi, *Santa Fe*

★★★★ Restaurant

Geronimo, *Santa Fe*

Utah

★★★★ Lodgings

The Grand America Hotel, *Salt Lake City*
Stein Eriksen Lodge, *Park City*

★★★★ Restaurant

Riverhorse on Main, *Park City*

America's Byways™ are a distinctive collection of American roads, their stories, and treasured places. They are roads to the heart and soul of America. In this section, you'll find the nationally designated Byways in Arizona, Colorado, Nevada, New Mexico, and Utah.

Kaibab Plateau–North Rim Parkway

ARIZONA

QUICK FACTS

Length: 42 miles.

Time to Allow: 1 hour or more.

Best Time to Drive: Fall; high season is May through October.

Special Considerations: To avoid long lines at the entrance gate, enter the park before 10 am or after 2 pm. Make arrangements for accommodations and special activities in advance. All roads are winding and steep. You may come upon cows, deer, logging trucks, road construction, or visitors stopping to take photographs, so please drive carefully. Arizona's climate is dry and hot, so be sure to carry plenty of water. Wear proper footwear to minimize the risk of serious injury. There is also the danger of fires, lightning, and flash floods. Ridgetops seem to receive the most lightning strikes.

Restrictions: Most roads are not maintained during the winter. The Grand Canyon National Park North Rim section is closed from November 15 to May 1; Highway 67 is closed from mid-December to mid-May. However, Highway 89A is plowed and maintained year-round. Pets are allowed in Grand Canyon National Park, but they must be restrained at all times and are not allowed below the rim, in park lodgings, or on park buses. The only exception is for certified service dogs.

Bicycle/Pedestrian Facilities: Bicycles are not available for rent in the Grand Canyon. Bicyclists are permitted on all paved and unpaved park roads open to automobile traffic and must obey all traffic regulations. Shoulders are narrow, and vehicle traffic is heavy. Bicycles are prohibited on park trails.

This route crosses over the gorgeous Kaibab Plateau and travels through two forests: the Kaibab National Forest and Grand Canyon National Park. Along the route, you'll find plenty of places to hike and camp. Groves of golden aspen, flowery meadows, ponds, outcrops of limestone, and steep slopes on all sides break up the dominance of the regal coniferous forest. Also, the Colorado and Kanab rivers flow right around the Byway, so opportunities for water sports abound.

The Byway Story

The Kaibab Plateau–North Rim Parkway tells archaeological, cultural, historical, natural, recreational, and scenic stories that make it a unique and treasured Byway.

ARCHAEOLOGICAL

People have occupied the Kaibab Plateau for at least 8,000 years. The earliest people inhabiting this region were hunter-gatherers who utilized the plateau extensively for its big game opportunities and for plant and mineral resources. These people, referred to as the Archaic people, were highly nomadic. Between 500 BC and 300 BC, the life and methods of the people using the Grand Canyon area began to change. The first evidence of plant domestication is linked to this period. Archaeologists refer to the people of this era as the Basketmaker people. Although they still depended heavily on hunting and gathering, they were slowly incorporating horticulture into their lifestyle. The Basketmaker period lasted until around AD 800.

Toward the end of the Basketmaker period, pottery was made and people became less mobile. Over time, it is believed that the Basketmaker culture transitioned into what is now known as the Pueblo culture. The Pueblo people relied more heavily on farming than the Basketmaker people; they also built more permanent village sites that included upright masonry structures and cliff dwellings known as pueblos. They also developed beautiful painted pottery styles. The Pueblo people abandoned the area by the late 1200s. Archaeologists are unsure as to why they left; they suspect that prolonged drought and increased population levels forced the Pueblos to leave.

The Paiute people moved into the area shortly after the Pueblo people left. These people continue to live in the area today. The Paiute people were a hunting and gathering culture that utilized the Kaibab Plateau for its wild plant and animal resources. While some of the Paiute farmed in historic times, they were not originally a farming people. As with the earlier archaic cultures, the Paiute were highly nomadic. Unlike the Pueblo people, who built masonry pueblo structures, the Paiute lived in temporary brush structures called wikiups. This form of housing allowed them to move their camps on a regular basis to where resources were seasonably available. The Paiutes gave the region the name we still use today; Kaibab is the Paiute term meaning "mountain lying down." Today, the Paiute live on the Kaibab Paiute Indian Reservation located near Fredonia, Arizona. They continue to use the Kaibab Plateau for traditional cultural practices.

CULTURAL

The rich cultural diversity of Arizona is proudly displayed on the Kaibab Plateau–North Rim Parkway. Here, you find a diverse cross-section of Native Americans and pioneer stock. Visit the local towns of Kanab, Glendale, and Fredonia to see the rich heritage that is still maintained today. From good ol' country fairs to the vibrant Western Legends Round Up, everyone is sure to have a good time. Don't forget Glendale's Apple Festival in October, where you can experience archery contests, booths, crafts, and an apple Dutch-oven cooking contest that is sure to please even the most discerning tastes.

HISTORICAL

The Kaibab is rich with the history of preservation and conservation. In 1893, the Grand Canyon Forest Reserve was created, and in the first decade of the 20th century, national forests were designated. Then, in 1906, President Theodore Roosevelt created the Grand Canyon National Game Preserve to protect the Kaibab mule deer, and in 1908, the Grand Canyon Forest Reserve became the Kaibab National Forest. The historic Jacob Lake Ranger Station was built in 1910 to help administer lands that included what is now Grand Canyon National Park. The ranger station is located along the road that originally led to the North Rim of the Grand Canyon. Eventually, the road to Grand Canyon National Park was moved to its present location, but the Jacob Lake Ranger Station continued to be utilized to administer Kaibab National Forest lands. It is one of the oldest remaining ranger stations in the country and is now an interpretive site presenting the life of a forest ranger. It can be accessed from Highway 67.

After a devastating wildfire in 1910 burned through much of the Idaho panhandle and parts of western Montana, the United States ushered in an era of fire suppression. Prior to that time, little was done to suppress fires. However, after 1910, fire lookouts and trail systems began to be developed in earnest throughout the national forest system. The earliest fire lookouts on the Kaibab consisted of platforms built at the tops of tall trees that were accessed by ladders. Eventually, lookout buildings and towers were built, including the Jacob Lake Tower in 1934. The tower is located on the east side of Highway 67 and can be viewed from the Kaibab Plateau–North Rim Parkway.Today, the Jacob Lake Ranger Station and Fire Lookout Tower are on the National Register of Historic Places, and the Jacob Lake Fire Lookout Tower is on the National Register of Fire Lookouts.

NATURAL

The Kaibab Plateau could be called an island of forest; sage and grass cover the lower elevations that surround it. The plateau is bordered on the south by the Grand Canyon and on the east and west by the Colorado River, sometimes reaching elevations of 9,000 feet. Some of the trees found at its higher elevations include Ponderosa pine, Englemann spruce, aspen, blue spruce, oak, piñon, pine, and juniper. At lower elevations, you'll find bitter brush, Gambel oak, sagebrush, and cliffrose.

Within the forest are irregular areas entirely free of tree growth. These parks are found in canyon bottoms, dry southern exposures, and ridge tops near the forest's exterior limits. Naturally occurring water is scarce in the North Kaibab Ranger District; Big Springs and North Canyon are the only two places in the district where the surface water flows year-round.

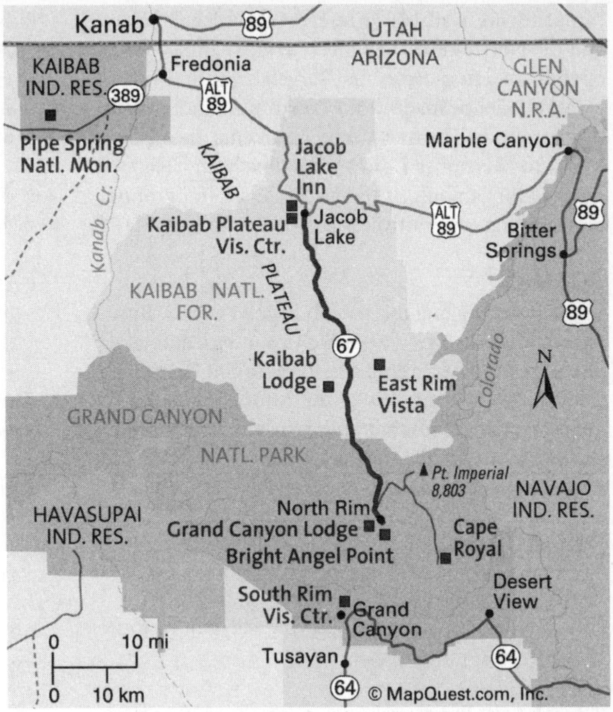

Melting snow seeps through the gravelly soil to emerge as springs several hundred feet below the plateau rim.

The Vermilion Cliffs are spectacular because of their brilliant colors. It is also thrilling to watch the Grand Canyon walls change color as the sun sets; watching the morning sun hit the canyon is just as unforgettable.

The Grand Canyon stands alone as the world's most awesome natural wonder, and the surrounding Kaibab National Forest offers plenty of native forest wildlife. Keep an eye open for large, soaring birds; the endangered California condor was recently introduced to this area.

RECREATIONAL

Nonmotorized and motorized trails are maintained for hikers, walkers, bikers, equestrians, cross-country skiers, four-wheel drivers, and snowmobilers. Fifty miles of the cross-state nonmotorized Arizona Trail traverse the district, providing opportunities for day hiking or multi-night trips. Many miles of closed roads provide outstanding mountain biking opportunities for all rider levels. (Remember that wilderness areas do not allow mountain bikes.) Spring and fall are the best seasons for enjoying both the wilderness and the Grand Canyon National Park trails due to extreme summer temperatures and winter inaccessibility. If you plan to stay overnight below the rim of the Grand Canyon, purchase a permit from the Grand Canyon National Park Backcountry Office.

For hunters, the Kaibab Plateau is famous for producing record-class mule deer, with established seasons for bow, black powder, and rifle hunting. Game birds, such as the chukar partridge and Merriam's turkey, also have established seasons. The Arizona Game and Fish Department sets the hunt dates and numbers, and hunters are selected by drawings.

The winter season on the Kaibab Plateau is a unique experience. Lodging is available on the plateau at Jacob Lake and Kaibab Lodge. Nordic skiing and snowmobiling are the most popular activities on the plateau in the winter. The area east of Highway 67 is open only to nonmotorized activities. The North Rim is also open only to nonmotorized activities, with no facilities or services during the winter season. All areas west of Highway 67 are open to motorized and nonmotorized activities. Winter conditions are surprisingly severe on the Kaibab Plateau. Be prepared for 4 to 8 feet of snow, along with cold and windy weather.

On national forest lands, camping is not limited to campgrounds; instead, camping is permissible off of any dirt road or out of the sight of a paved highway at no charge. Backcountry camping is prohibited within 1/4 mile of water to allow wildlife undisturbed access. Backcountry campers also must stay at least 1/2 mile from a developed campground or other facility. Campers are also asked to stay out of meadows, due to the fragile environment.

Jacob Lake area campgrounds open May 15 and close about October 20. Forest Service and National Park Service campgrounds have water and toilets, but no RV hook-ups. Private campgrounds at Jacob Lake or off the plateau do have full RV hook-ups, however. Tents and RVs are welcome at all campgrounds. DeMott Campground is not suitable for large RVs; all other campgrounds can handle any size. Group campsites are available by reservation at Jacob Lake and the North Rim. The Forest Service campgrounds operate on a first-come, first-served basis, and reservations can be made at the North Rim and private campgrounds. The free Jacob Lake picnic area is open May 1 to November 1 during daytime hours. No fee is charged for camping at Indian Hollow Campground, but camping is primitive, and no water is available.

SCENIC

In many areas along the Kaibab Plateau–North Rim Parkway, you can get out, stretch your legs, and take one of the trails to scenic overlooks in the Grand Canyon. The golden glow of the red rocks and the lonely sound of the wind in the early morning are enough to inspire the most inexperienced of poets. Be sure to bring a journal and a camera.

Highlights

While visiting the Kaibab Plateau–North Rim Parkway, you can take the following self-guided tour of the Byway.

- **Jacob Lake Junction:** Highway marker 579 or the junction of Highway 67 and Highway 89A. The **Kaibab Plateau Visitor Center** offers information and interpretive displays about the natural and cultural resources of the plateau. The visitor center also offers books, videos, postcards, and other interpretive sales items through the Public Lands Interpretive Association. **Jacob Lake Inn** is a historic lodge offering accommodations, a restaurant/café, and a gift shop. At **Jacob Lake Campground,** you'll find family sites and group sites available.

- **Jacob Lake Fire Lookout Tower:** Highway marker 580.3 or 1 mile south of the Jacob Lake Junction/ Highway 67 and 89A. Visit this historic tower and find out how fires are detected. Views of the **Grand Staircase** are visible from the tower. The tower is usually staffed between 9 am-6 pm and may be closed for two days during the week; check in at the visitor center for current opening.

- **Demotte Park Overlook:** Highway marker 604 or 22 miles south of the Jacob Lake Junction on the Byway. Vehicle pull-off overlooking Demotte Park. Demotte Park is one of the largest meadows on the Kaibab Plateau, and it's filled with deer, coyotes, and numerous species of birds. Wildflower enthusiasts will also enjoy the diversity and abundance in this meadow. One mile south of this stop is the historic **Kaibab Lodge.** Rustic cabins and restaurant, gift shop, gas station, and convenience store are available.

- **Grand Canyon National Park–North Rim:** 44 miles south on Highway 67. The end of this scenic parkway leads to a spectacular view of the North Rim of the Grand Canyon. Several hiking trails are located at or near the rim. The **North Rim Visitor Center** is open seven days a week 8 am-8 pm. Visitor information, interpretation, and interpretive sale items are available. The **North Rim's Historic Lodge** offers hotel accommodations, restaurant, mule rides, and a gift shop.

Dinosaur Diamond Prehistoric Highway

COLORADO

Part of a multistate Byway; see also UT.

Echoes of the past resonate along the Colorado stretch of the Dinosaur Diamond, with artifacts, such as dinosaur bones and rock art, from an earlier time. The most prominent example of rock art along the Byway may be found at Canyon Pintado, which features visible marks of the Fremont Indians. At the Colorado National Monument, visitors get a chance to view the striking landscape of western Colorado; the openness around Grand Junction fades into the majestic cliffs and canyons that are characteristic in the area. Around Fruita are examples of excavation sites, such as at Dinosaur Hill; Fruita is also home of the Museum of Western Colorado, where dinosaurs come alive. The Byway is a travel back in time, with recreational opportunities; such as biking, hiking, and camping awaiting you along the route.

Quick Facts

Length: 112 miles.

Time to Allow: 2.5 hours to several days.

Best Time to Drive: Year-round; high season is summer.

Byway Travel Information: Dinosaurland Travel Board: phone toll-free 800/477-5558; Byway local Web site: www.dinosaurdiamond.org.

Special Considerations: The mountain passes at Douglas Pass on Highway 139 can be treacherous during winter storms. This road is rarely, if ever, officially closed, but sometimes a few hours' delay would be prudent. All points along the Byway are subject to snowfall, with snow cover lasting longer in the northern and higher elevation areas than in the lower elevation and southern portions. Dinosaur trackways are difficult, if not impossible, to see under snow cover.

Bicycle/Pedestrian Facilities: The Dinosaur Diamond Byway includes portions of the interstate (I-70) and various US Highways. Because of this, bicycle and foot travel along the actual route may be prohibited and/or dangerous. However, numerous trails off the Byway delight visitors who come to the area. The Kokopelli Trail is designed and built for mountain bike travel between Moab and Fruita. Hiking for recreation, solitude, or sightseeing in the area of the Dinosaur Diamond is very popular, and you'll find many trails to follow.

The Byway Story

The Dinosaur Diamond Prehistoric Highway tells archaeological, cultural, historical, natural, recreational, and scenic stories that make it a unique and treasured Byway.

ARCHAEOLOGICAL

The Dinosaur Diamond Prehistoric Highway showcases the archaeological qualities of a time about 1,000 years ago, when Native American cultures lived and hunted in the area. These cultures maintained their way of life in the desert and today, remnants of this culture are located along the Byway. The best evidence of these ancient people is the abundance of petroglyphs and pictographs in the area. (Petroglyphs are pictures that are pecked into rock surfaces using harder rocks, often made into tools; pictographs are pictures painted onto the rocks.)

Ancient petroglyph panels show up on cliff sides and rock surfaces along the Byway, because the sheer rock cliffs and walls served as an ideal place to create this rock art. There are panels in both Utah and Colorado, and they are spread out along the Byway. The most prominent petroglyphs are in the Colorado National Monument near Grand Junction. In addition to these, Canyon Pintado, between

Douglas Pass and Rangely, has significant examples of rock art, along with roadside interpretive displays.

CULTURAL

Because of the rural nature of living in the desert, many cultural events have sprung up to give people a reason to congregate and enjoy the splendid outdoors. Festivals and events honoring the heritage and natural features of the area give the Byway a cultural flair.

Stroll by Colorado's largest and most diverse outdoor sculpture exhibit, on display along Grand Junction's downtown shopping park. The exhibit, entitled "Art Around the Corner," highlights a unique variety of work by local artists. The nearly 20-year-old ongoing event introduces visitors to many distinct artistic approaches. Informative brochures are available at the Downtown Development Authority Visitor's Center at 350 Main Street, Suite 204; phone 970/245-2926.

HISTORICAL

The high mountain desert of western Colorado has drawn people to the area of the present-day Dinosaur Diamond Prehistoric Highway. Evidences of Native American cultures, such as the Fremont and Ute, can be seen in the rock art along the Byway. The Escalante-Dominguez Expedition, followed by scientific and paleontologic expeditions, undertook early exploration of the area, while Mormon settlers, miners, and immigrants from Europe all settled in the area and created a unique and colorful history.

The first recorded venture of Europeans into the area was the Escalante-Dominguez Expedition in 1776. This expedition came from Santa Fe, New Mexico, attempting to blaze a trail to California in order to access the missions located there; however, their journey was unsuccessful due to the barriers formed by the western Utah deserts. The expedition was led by Father Silvestre Velez de Escalante and Father Francisco Dominguez, accompanied by Captain Bernardo dè Miera y Pacheco, a retired military engineer. They explored Canyon Pintado from Douglas Pass toward what is now Rangely, Colorado, crossed the Green river near Jensen, Utah, and traveled as far west as Spanish Fork, Utah, before turning back south to return to Santa Fe, New Mexico.

While Escalante and Dominguez came to the area in search of another route west, others have been drawn to western Colorado for more than 150 years because of scientific exploration. Beginning with John C. Fremont in the early 1840s, reports about the majesty of the mountains, the roaring rivers, the expanse and austerity of the deserts, the abundance of game, and the clues to vast mineral resources have enticed adventurers to the intermountain west of the United States. John Wesley Powell, Clarence King, and Ferdinand V. Hayden led extensive geological surveys that helped quantify these resources. In addition, their reports tempted paleontologists with a vast array of undescribed fossils, particularly dinosaurs and prehistoric mammals.

Settlement in the area inevitably brought about great changes on the landscape, such as mining. In the Uintah Basin, gilsonite was the first hydrocarbon to be mined, bringing a small narrow-gage railroad (the Uintah Railroad) into the southeastern edge of the basin near Dragon. Although several attempts were made to build more railroads into the basin, none was successful. As a result, the Uintah Basin remains one of the largest areas of the US to be undeveloped by railroads. After World War II, petroleum development and phosphate mining became integral to the rural economy. The railroad from Grand Junction, Colorado, to Price, Utah, brought development of the coal resources in both Carbon and Emery counties. As a result of this mining industry, an influx of some 18 different ethnic groups from across southern and eastern Europe and Asia came to work in the mines. This economic development was a great boost to the area.

NATURAL

The area encompassed by this diamond-shaped Byway is the best place in the world to see dinosaurs in a variety of ways: dinosaurs on display in museums, dinosaur bones still in the ground at the sites where they were discovered, dinosaur bones currently being excavated by paleontologists, and dinosaur trackways preserved in rocks.

Dinosaurs ruled the Earth long ago, and today, the bones and tracks of these extinct animals can be seen at various sites along the Byway. Many of these sites are located in their natural settings, which makes this Byway one of a kind. Actual dinosaur quarries, which are areas where dinosaur bones are excavated, are along the Byway. The Mygatt-Moore Quarry near Fruita preserves the history of dinosaurs in their natural state.

RECREATIONAL

River rafting is one popular sport to participate in along the Byway. Both calm water and white water river trips are available through companies out of Grand Junction. The whitewater sections can be frightening even to experienced river runners during the high water levels of spring melt, yet some stretches of both the Green and Colorado rivers have flatwater that may be enjoyable in canoes. Grand scenery awaits the visitor around every bend in the river. In fact, the Green River in Desolation Canyon has cliffs higher than the Grand Canyon in Arizona.

Hiking opportunities are everywhere along the Byway. The terrain is varied, giving visitors a feel for the many aspects of the Byway. In the mountains, numerous spectacular peaks and lakes are accessible to the hiker; the Uinta Mountain Range is the largest east-west mountain range in the 48 contiguous United States. The desert is another popular place to go hiking, and it is an entirely different experience from alpine hiking. All of the national parks and monuments along the Byway are outstanding places for hiking and camping. Outfitters are available all along the Byway for visitors who want guides, horses, or even llamas to help with the load. Hunting and fishing are also popular recreational activities in the area. Fruita also has excellent mountain biking trails to challenge the expert rider and lure the beginner.

Winter sports are also popular for visitors. Snowshoeing, cross-country skiing, snowmobiling, and ice fishing can be enjoyed in the high country, while hiking without the summer heat is a popular activity in the southern desert areas.

SCENIC

The Dinosaur Diamond Prehistoric Highway has many scenic views that capture the expansive area of land surrounding the Byway. Wide vistas are normal in this desert country, with the horizon stretching on for miles. During hot summer days, it seems like the blue sky is an endless expanse, and sunsets—going on forever—are magnified because of the open sky.

Vistas can include features that are over 100 miles away. Canyons with walls of red, green, beige, purple, gray, and white greet you. These scenes are intermingled with forested mountain passes and snowcapped mountains. As you travel winding roads out of canyons, sweeping views of the valleys below open up before you. Along the northern facet of the Dinosaur Diamond, the Uinta Mountains cut the skyline. Ancient faults and tectonics controlled the development of this maverick mountain range, creating the largest east-west trending mountain range in the lower 48 states. It is unlike the rest of the Rock Mountains that are aligned north to south.

The Green River joins the Yampa River in Dinosaur National Monument at Steamboat Rock. The canyon it forms is spectacular whether viewed from the canyon rim or from the river edge. Farther downstream, the river cuts through Split Mountain and then the Gray Tertiary badlands of the Uinta and Green River formations of Desolation Canyon, the main drainage for the Book Cliffs. The Colorado River provides further scenic aspects to the Byway, meandering through canyons of red rock. The green vegetation near the river is a nice contrast to the sheer red rock cliffs of the canyons, while snowcapped mountain ranges in the distance offer a break in the desert landscape.

Frontier Pathways Scenic and Historic Byway

COLORADO

Quick Facts

Length: 103 miles.

Time to Allow: 4 hours.

Best Time to Drive: Winter and summer; high season is summer.

Byway Travel Information: Greenhorn Valley Chamber of Commerce: phone 719/676-3000; Byway local Web site: www.coloradobyways.org.

Special Considerations: Wildfires are an ever-present danger in the dry summer months; follow all posted signs regarding campfires and do not throw cigarettes out the car window. Abandoned mines are extremely dangerous–look and take pictures but do not explore. This Byway traverses high mountain passes; be prepared for all types of weather. High altitudes bring increased sun exposure and reduced oxygen, so wear sunscreen and sunglasses and don't overexert yourself.

Restrictions: There are rare winter closures due to snowfall.

Bicycle/Pedestrian Facilities: This area is a mountain biker's paradise, with many roads and trails to choose from. Tour biking is also a popular activity, and the highway's paved shoulders, typically 4 feet in width, accommodate these bikers. Virtually every type of pedestrian-based recreational activity is accommodated. Whether you take a walking tour of Pueblo's Union Avenue Historic District, hike a meadow or mountain, take a backpacking trip, or opt for the historic walking tour of Westcliffe and Silver Cliff, you'll experience many wonderful natural attractions. The nationally renowned Rainbow Trail attracts many visitors each year as well.

During the winter of 1806, Lt. Zebulon Pike nearly froze to death in the Wet Mountain Valley within sight of the peak bearing his name. Nevertheless, this valley and its mountain became a beacon to 19th-century settlers, who came to take advantage of the good soil and climate. Today, the valley boasts one of the state's finest collections of historic ranches and farmsteads (some dating to the 1840s), trading posts, and stage stops. Also, this pastoral paradise contrasts with the more severe-looking Hardscrabble Canyon, the white-capped Sangre de Cristos, and the sharp mesas and hogbacks that flank the Arkansas River.

The Byway Story

The Frontier Pathways Scenic and Historic Byway tells cultural, historical, natural, recreational, and scenic stories that make it a unique and treasured Byway.

CULTURAL

This Byway chronicles the joys and sorrows that its early residents experienced while breaking in the land. It is a living showcase of the evolution of architecture, transportation, and agriculture that you can experience by visiting the Frontier Pathway's old homesteads, cabins, barns, stage-stops, and settlements. This landscape hasn't changed much in the last 100 years, so you can still see how different groups of people used their ingenuity to harness the land. Evidence of their resourcefulness is found in the area's nationally important high-country homesteading.

HISTORICAL

The Frontier Pathways Scenic and Historic Byway is seeping with nationally significant history. For example, some of the first high-country homesteads, ranches, and farms were developed here. In 1779, the Spanish Governor De Anza, with the help of the Utes, defeated Comanche Chief Cuerno Verde (Greenhorn) right in this very valley. Also, German and English colonists settled here in the mid-1800s, and their heritage still pervades this area.

NATURAL

The Wet Mountains and Greenhorn Valleys are not well known, even to long-time Coloradoans, making this Byway an excellent getaway. Home for a remarkable number of diverse species of plants and animals, this area attracts naturalists, nature lovers, and botanists. (Note that the Wet Mountains are neither an extension of Colorado's Front Range—the mountains immediately west of Denver—nor are they part of the Continental Divide.)

As the only trout native to Colorado, the greenback cutthroat trout was believed to be extinct until it was rediscovered in a stream near the Frontier Pathways and successfully reintroduced statewide.

RECREATIONAL

Year-round opportunities at this recreational mecca include climbing 14,295-foot-high Crestone Peak, shopping and dining in Pueblo's Historic Union Avenue District, and playing in the Wet Mountain Wilderness. You can also trout fish on the banks of Lake Isabel, backpack on the nationally renowned Rainbow Trail, and hike in the Sangre de Cristos or Greenhorn Wilderness.

While the summer sun is out, you may enjoy fishing for trout in streams, mountain biking, and horseback riding. You can also get in some sailing, power boating, or water-skiing at the Lake Pueblo State Recreation Area. Consider taking time to discover Pueblo Mountain Park, which is on the National Register of Historic Places. During the winter, be sure to cross-country ski, downhill ski, or ice fish on the Pueblo Reservoir.

SCENIC

Photographers will need to long-focus their cameras in order to capture a sliver of the 100-mile-long Sangre de Cristo Range. As the backbone of the Rocky Mountains, the Sangre de Cristos' many grand peaks jut into the clear blue sky; seven peaks reach over 14,000 feet, while 39 peaks rise over 13,000 feet.

You can also discover other intriguing photographic subjects among the shops and streets of Pueblo's Union Avenue Historic District or during your descent into dramatic Hardscrabble Canyon.

Highlights

To take in the highlights of the Frontier Pathways Scenic and Historic Byway, consider this must-see tour.

- **Pueblo Museum:** This museum, located in the town of Pueblo, gives you an opportunity to learn about the interaction of several different cultures: American Indian, Mexican, and American. Fascinating artifacts, colorful murals, and interesting stories bring the history of the Pueblo area to life.

- **Wetmore and Early Settlements (on Highway 96 at mile marker 26.4):** More than 150 years ago, buckskin-clad French traders, scrappy American farmers, and fur traders lived in nearby settlements. In the 1830s, three French trappers built a fort on Adobe Creek to facilitate trade with the Ute Indians. It was called Buzzard's Roost, or Maurice's Fort, after Maurice LeDuc. Later settlements in the area included Hardscrabble in 1844 and Wetmore in the late 1870s.

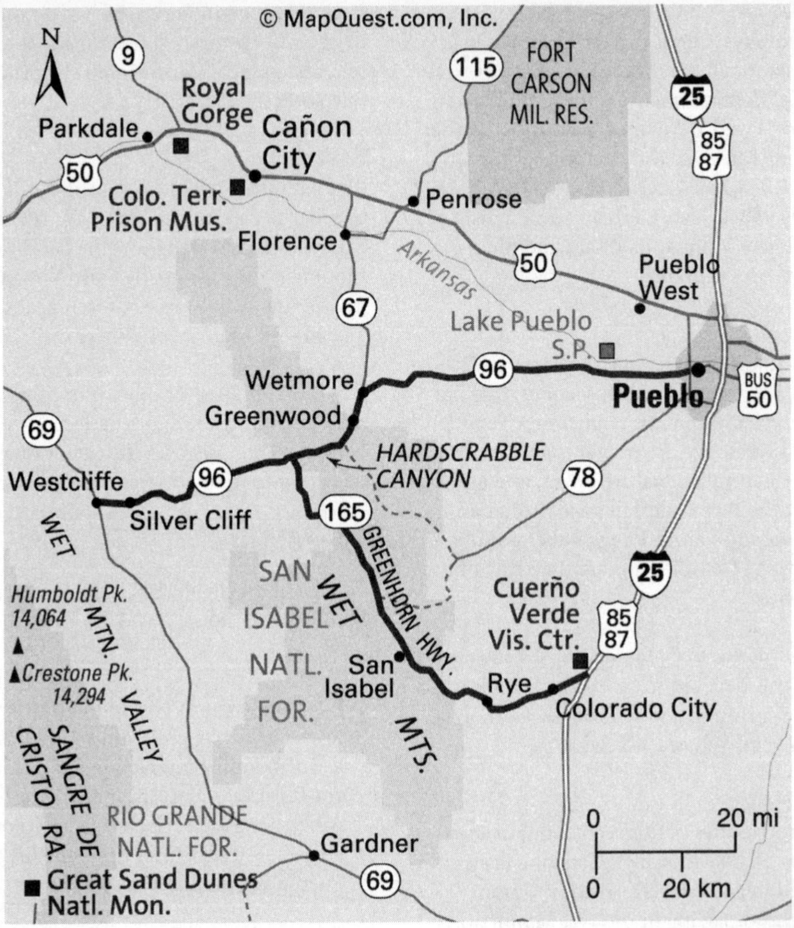

- **Sangre de Cristo Mountains (west of Silvercliff):** Miners, ranchers, and modern-day motorists have all marveled at this breathtaking view of the Sangre de Cristos. This 50-mile stretch of mountains includes 22 peaks that are over 13,000 feet in elevation.

- **Westcliff Schoolhouse:** This schoolhouse, located in the town of Westcliffe, was built in 1891 and dedicated on Christmas Eve of the same year. No one knows why the school name, still visible above the front doors as "Westcliff," was spelled without the *e*.

Gold Belt Tour Scenic and Historic Byway

COLORADO

On the Gold Belt Tour, the roads themselves are part of the personality of the Byway. The Byway follows historic railroad and stagecoach routes, leading you to North America's greatest gold camp, three world-class fossil sites, and numerous historical sites. The Shelf and Phantom Canyon roads offer adventurous driving experiences along unpaved routes through winding canyons. Paved roads wind through the gently rolling mountain parklands of the High Park route, where Colorado's highest mountain ranges rise in the distance. Teller 1 (a county road) travels through the pastoral Florissant Valley, with Pikes Peak in the background.

The five Byway communities invite you to share in their rich history. In Cripple Creek, the historical hub of the mining district and a National Historic Landmark, visitors enjoy the variety and beauty of the early 1900s architectural styles in the downtown district. The area's mining heritage continues in Victor, the City of Mines. Surrounded by hundreds of historic mines, Victor is the headquarters for a modern gold mine. Victor's downtown district, a National Historic District, includes beautifully restored buildings. To the south, you can enjoy the Royal Gorge as well as restaurants, museums, and historic sites in Cañon City and Florence. Florissant, the Byway's northern gateway, offers the Florissant Heritage Museum to interpret the area's numerous historic sites and Ute cultural sites.

Quick Facts

Length: 135 miles.

Time to Allow: 8 hours.

Best Time to Drive: Year-round.

Byway Travel Information: Gold Belt Tour Information/Cañon City Chamber of Commerce: phone 719/275-2331; Byway local Web site: www.goldbeltbyway.com

Special Considerations: The Phantom Canyon and Upper Shelf roads have rough, gravel surfaces, so it is better to avoid them in wet weather. A 4-mile segment of the Shelf Road becomes soft and slippery during wet periods and is not recommended for two-wheel-drive vehicles. A four-wheel-drive vehicle is recommended on the Upper Shelf Road.

Restrictions: Vehicles over 25 feet long are not permitted to travel the Phantom Canyon Road. RVs are not suitable for Shelf Road or Phantom Canyon Road.

Also located along the Byway are the Garden Park Fossil Area, the Florissant Fossil Beds National Monument, and the Indian Springs Trace Fossil Site. These sites form an internationally important area for paleontological discovery and research. The Florissant Fossil Beds Visitor Center, Dinosaur Depot Museum, wayside exhibits, and trails offer visitors the opportunity to experience these natural wonders.

The Byway Story

The Gold Belt Tour Scenic and Historic Byway tells archaeological, cultural, historical, natural, recreational, and scenic stories that make it a unique and treasured Byway.

ARCHAEOLOGICAL

Archaeological sites can be found throughout the Byway and provide a comprehensive look at the past and the creatures that lived in this area millions of years ago. With three fossil beds along the Byway, gold was clearly not the only treasure to be found within the mountains and hills of this section of Colorado. When settlers were done digging for gold, many excavations of the fossil beds in the area began, and the discovery and search for fossils on the Byway continues today. What has been found is one of the most diverse and complete collections of fossils on the continent.

For millions of years, creatures have been preserved in the rock and stone along the Gold Belt Tour; in fact, 460-million-year-old tracks of arthropods have been found at Indian Springs Trace. This discovery led scientists and even visitors to conjecture about the way the world was so many ages ago, and scientists use these fossils to explore new ideas in evolution. The Florissant Fossil Beds include imprints and fossils of creatures and their environment from 35 million years ago. Garden Park Fossil Beds hold bones of many of the favorite dinosaurs, including brachiosaurus and stegosaurus. Exploration of the fossil beds along the Gold Belt Tour gives you a glimpse of the Earth's age and fascinating history. Although visitor fossil hunting is prohibited at these places, in areas outside these parks, you may find a fossil of a prehistoric plant or insect.

CULTURAL

The Gold Belt Tour once sported a classic culture of the Wild West. Gold miners, saloons, and the untamed land of the Rocky Mountains are all part of the cultural past of this Byway. Although you probably won't experience a gun fight in the streets of a Byway town, the towns along the Gold Belt Tour are fiercely proud of their heritage and bring pieces of the past to the surface for visitors throughout the year.

The mining culture was not the first culture to inhabit the mountains of the Gold Belt Tour. Many native cultures, including the Ute, lived here and developed their own unique way of life. The area was a prime hunting spot and a good place to spend the winter because of its relatively mild climate. The history of these cultures has faded to only a few stories and archaeological artifacts.

In the 1800s, a new culture came to the Gold Belt Tour. Settlers from the east brought with them a new organization of towns, roads, and mines, coupled with all the lawlessness of gunfights and hangings. Respect for the land by the area's predecessors was replaced by a way of life that used up the resources around the people. When the gold boom subsided, however, the communities of the area decreased to smaller sizes, allowing the surrounding regions to continue in their natural beauty.

Now, the culture of the Byway is one that appreciates the natural wonders of the Byway while still remembering the days of miners and cowboys. Many of the towns that exist today along the Byway hold festivals and events throughout the year that both visitors and residents attend.

HISTORICAL

The three roads that constitute the Gold Belt Tour are the historic routes that connected the Cripple Creek Mining District to the communities to the north and south. The historic communities of Cripple Creek, Victor, Cañon City, Florence, and Florissant along with the Byway played important roles in what was the most productive gold mining district in North America.

Cripple Creek was the center of the Gold Boom. Bob Womack discovered gold in 1890, setting off a gold rush that brought people from all over the country and put Cripple Creek on the map. By the year 1900, three railroads, two electric tram lines, modern water and sewer systems, and many other conveniences separated Cripple Creek from the average western mining camp. Cripple Creek became the financial and commercial center of what is known as the Cripple Creek Mining District. Today, many of the historic buildings that played such a prominent role in the days of gold have been restored, and the entire downtown area of Cripple Creek is a National Historic Landmark.

Victor, which lies just southeast of Cripple Creek, was historically the home of the miners and their families. The downtown area of the city boasts several buildings that are on the National Register of Historic Places, and Victor's downtown itself is a National Historic District.

Florissant is north of the Cripple Creek mining district. It stands at the crossroads of two important Ute Indian trails. It was a stopover for Indians, trappers, traders, and mountain men long before silver and gold were discovered in the mountains to the west. In 1886, the railroad came through Florissant and was the closest rail connection to the mining district in the early years of the gold boom.

South of the Cripple Creek Mining District lies the Arkansas River Valley and two more communities that have historical significance. Cañon City and Florence both sought the overflow of wealth coming out of Cripple Creek during the golden years. Both cities were established in the second half of the 1800s and have a rich historical past. Cañon City's downtown area is a National Historic District; visitors can enjoy a tour of some early railroad depots that have been restored.

Along with the communities found on the Gold Belt Tour, the routes themselves have historical significance. The Phantom Canyon Road follows the abandoned railroad grade of the Florence and Cripple Creek Railroad, the first railroad to reach the gold mines. Today, travelers on the Phantom Canyon Road go through tunnels, drive over bridges, and see past remnants of train stations used by the railroad back in the 1890s. Shelf Road was constructed in 1892 and was the first direct route from Cripple Creek to the Arkansas River Valley. Today, travelers experience the shelf—a narrow, winding section of road perched high above Fourmile Creek—much the same way that people experienced it in the 1890s.

After you reach the outskirts of Cripple Creek, you pass several historic mines and mills. High Park Road travels through a high-elevation park that is home to modern cattle ranchers. This land and the ranches along High Park Road represent 150 years of ranching history. Historic ranch buildings, such as the Fourmile Community building, lie along the Byway route. Other roads like Skyline Drive near Cañon City provide beautiful views and interesting historical background as well.

NATURAL

Located in the Rocky Mountains, the Gold Belt Tour is a worthwhile visit for anyone who enjoys outdoor splendor. The landscape along the Byway resulted from multiple alternating periods of mountain-building and flooding by an inland sea; you can see sandstone formations and limestone cliffs that were formed as a result of this geological history. The remains of ancient plants and animals deposited during the flooding produced the rich coal and oil fields in the Arkansas Valley near Florence. It also produced the fossil beds at Garden Park and Indian Springs.

In addition to its unique collection of fossil beds, the Gold Belt Tour is a land with a volcanic history. In the areas of Cripple Creek and Victor, volcanic activity that occurred 6 million years ago formed the terrain. One volcanic cone was nearly 15 miles wide and rose 6,000 feet above surrounding hills. This volcanic activity is the reason the Byway is called the Gold Belt Tour today; it influenced the formation of the gold that was discovered in the early 1800s.

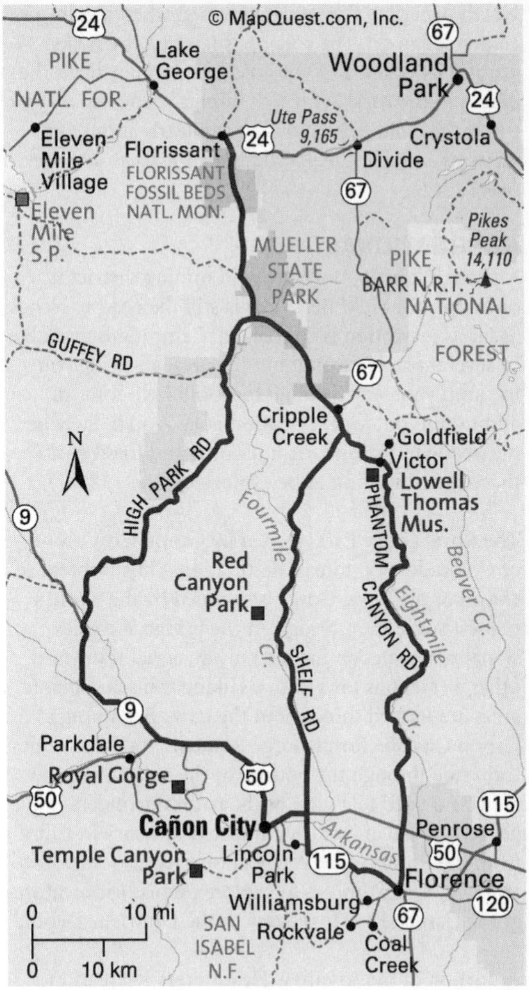

Visitors here can see a wide variety of fossils, from those of insects to petrified trees. The fossils provide insights into the environment of 34 million years ago. Garden Park Fossil Area, located along Shelf Road, has provided the world with many unique and complete dinosaur skeletons. The first major discoveries of large, plant-eating dinosaurs were made here in the 1870s, while the best example of a complete stegosaurus skeleton was found in 1992. You can take a guided tour and view the fossil quarries where these miraculous discoveries were made. Adjacent to Phantom Canyon Road lies the Indian Springs Trace Fossil Area, which contains portions of an ancient sea floor and was designated a National Natural Landmark in 1979.

The Cripple Creek Caldera, a 24-square-mile basin, is the site of the most productive gold mining area in

North America. The caldera formed when a volcanic center collapsed. The collapse shattered the rocks around its edges, and volcanic activity later filled the cracks in the rocks with rich mineral deposits. As you travel the Gold Belt Tour, you can learn about and view the Cripple Creek Caldera at the Cripple Creek overlook.

RECREATIONAL

Although it is no more the gold mining district it once was, the Gold Belt Tour is still the road to riches as far as recreation is concerned. Camping is available in several places throughout the area, allowing you to camp your way through the Gold Belt Tour. In addition to outdoor recreation areas, you'll likely be pleased with the historic museums and fossil parks that are just waiting to be explored.

The Royal Gorge Park, owned by Cañon City, is one of Colorado's top tourist destinations. The impressive chasm of the Royal Gorge is spanned by the world's highest suspension bridge. At the bridge, a concessionaire operates an incline railway, aerial tram, and other attractions for visitors. Hiking trails and picnic areas are located throughout the park. Beginning at Cañon City, the Royal Gorge Route leaves on a scenic train ride through the bottom of the gorge. Not only are you treated to a view of the natural wonders in the gorge, but you also catch glimpses of history in ruins from the Royal Gorge War. Cañon City also provides you with opportunities to explore prehistoric creatures at the Garden Park fossil area or the Dinosaur Depot.

A portion of the Arkansas Headwaters Recreation Area is located along the Byway. Colorado's Arkansas River between Leadville and Cañon City is among the nation's most popular whitewater boating destinations, hosting over 300,000 boaters annually. The river also offers some of Colorado's best fly fishing.

Shelf Road Recreation Area attracts rock climbers from around the world. The limestone cliffs offer short but extremely difficult climbs in some places. In other places, they are over 100 feet high and are enticing even to expert climbers. An extensive trail network along the cliffs provides hiking opportunities for climbers and non-climbers alike. On Lower Shelf Road, climbers can picnic at Red Canyon Park. Camping, hiking, and photographing are also excellent pastimes at Red Canyon Park. Many travelers also enjoy picnicking along Phantom Canyon Road after a drive through the forested areas. Here, you may glimpse wildlife or vegetation that are an indication of the area's pristine natural condition.

SCENIC

The Gold Belt Tour offers you a wide variety of scenic experiences. From majestic Pikes Peak to the depths of the Royal Gorge, the Gold Belt Tour is a scenery lover's delight. The dramatic changes in terrain and the majestic Rocky Mountains are the elements that give this Byway its unique flavor. The territory echoes with the Old West and the days when gold miners filled the countryside. Historic buildings, scenic roads, and natural splendor give the Gold Belt Tour even more scenic qualities.

Red Canyon Park, along Shelf Road, is filled with spires, windows, and other amazing rock formations eroded from red sandstone monoliths. The park roads provide easy access to a variety of scenic viewpoints. Skyline Drive, located on the western edge of Cañon City, climbs a 600 foot-high tilted sandstone ridge called a hogback. It offers a panoramic view of Cañon City and the lower Arkansas River Valley. The Royal Gorge, located along the High Park segment of the Byway, is one of Colorado's most famous tourist destinations: you can cross the bridge in a car or on foot or take the incline railway to the bottom of the gorge.

Historic buildings and museums are part of the picturesque towns you drive through along the Gold Belt Tour. Old West main streets and store fronts create a feeling from another time, although they offer modern amenities and attractions. You may drive past an old homestead framed against a Colorado grassland and imagine yourself in the days when gold glittered in the hills and the railroad brought new and interesting people everyday.

Plains and grasslands characterize the southern portion of the Byway near Cañon City. Phantom Canyon and Shelf roads climb out of the valley to the high country, following creeks or clinging to canyon walls hundreds of feet above the canyon floor. As you make your way up the canyons, the plains give way to the forest. As the road nears Cripple Creek and Victor, the scenery opens up to a view of high mountain ranges and majestic Pikes Peak. The area is covered with subalpine forests of Engelmann spruce, subalpine fir, and quaking aspen. Travelers driving through this area are very likely to catch a glimpse of some of the best wildlife the Gold Belt Tour has to offer. In addition, High Park Road and Teller 1 travel through rolling mountain parkland, offering awe-inspiring views of two of Colorado's highest mountain ranges—the Sawatch and Sangre de Cristo ranges.

Highlights

As you travel the Gold Belt Tour, consider following this itinerary.

- **Royal Gorge Bridge:** The first place you'll want to stop is the Royal Gorge Bridge. Travel south out of Cañon City on High Park Road for about 8 miles, turn right, and you'll come to the bridge (and Royal Gorge State Park) in about half a mile. The Royal Gorge Bridge is the world's tallest suspension bridge, spanning the Royal Gorge some 1,053 feet above the waters of the Arkansas River. You can walk or drive the bridge, have a picnic in the surrounding park, or take the world's steepest incline railway to the bottom of the Royal Gorge.

- **Dinosaur Depot and Garden Park Fossil Area:** As you drive back through Cañon City, take time to stop at Dinosaur Depot on Royal Gorge Boulevard. The Depot is a museum that shows some the fossils found at the Garden Park Fossil Area. You can take a guided tour of the museum that includes an informative video showing the removal of famous dinosaur fossils. This is also the place to set up a tour of Garden Park Fossil area, located just north of Cañon City. Garden Park Fossil Area has been the location of some of the most important discoveries about dinosaurs in North America. Tours should be made in advance; self-guided trails and exhibits are also available at the Garden Park Fossil Area.

- **View of Pikes Peak:** As you travel Shelf Road north to Cripple Creek, you will be treated to a beautiful vista of the west slope of Pikes Peak, named for explorer Zebulon Pike. Pikes Peak towers 14,110 feet and is one of the most breathtaking sights in Colorado.

- **Cripple Creek:** Take the Shelf Road north out of Cañon City, and you'll drive through a scenic canyon and across what's called the shelf, a narrow section of road perched high above Fourmile Creek. When you're 26 miles out of Cañon City, you'll reach historic Cripple Creek, the center of the Cripple Creek Mining District. Cripple Creek is a National Historic Landmark, and many of the buildings that were built during the early 1900s have been restored to their original likeness. Cripple Creek is a great place to stop, have lunch, and see a true piece of American history.

- **Florissant Fossil Beds National Monument:** From Cripple Creek, travel west on Bennett Ave to Teller 1. Seventeen miles from the junction on Teller 1, stop at Florissant Fossil Beds National Monument, which offers walking and guided tours. The fossils found here are renowned for their variety of species: over 80,000 fossilized specimens of tree stumps, insects, seeds, and leaves have been catalogued. The historic **Hornbek Homestead** is also located here. Picnic areas, a visitor's center, and hiking trails are available.

Grand Mesa Scenic and Historic Byway

COLORADO

The Utes called the Grand Mesa "Thunder Mountain." This name is fitting because, when standing at the Lands End Overlook, the Grand Valley unfolds more than a mile below, and you can imagine yourself as Zeus, ready to hurl thunderbolts from the top. Indeed, this playground in the sky seems too heavenly for mere mortals. The 63-mile route is transcendent as it climbs through the dusty canyon of Plateau Creek to the cool evergreen forests of the mesa top more than 11,000 feet above sea level.

Quick Facts

Length: 63 miles.

Time to Allow: 2 hours.

Best Time to Drive: Late spring through September; high season is summer.

Byway Travel Information: Grand Mesa Scenic Byway Welcome Center: phone 970/856-3100; Grand Mesa Byway Association: phone toll-free 800/436-3041; Byway local Web site: www.coloradobyways.org.

Special Considerations: There are no services between Cedaredge and Mesa. Wildfires are an ever-present danger in the dry summer months; follow all posted signs regarding campfires and do not throw cigarettes out the car window. Abandoned mines are extremely dangerous–look and take pictures but do not explore. This Byway traverses high mountain passes; be prepared for all types of weather. High altitudes bring increased sun exposure and reduced oxygen, so wear sunscreen and sunglasses and don't overexert yourself.

Restrictions: The main road is open year-round. However, Spur Road to Lands End is closed October through May.

Many scenic overlooks along the Byway allow you to glimpse the extraordinary landscape below. The Lands End Road follows the rim of the mesa for much of the way. From here, you may be able to see the peaks of the LaSal Mountains 60 miles to the west in Utah and may even see the San Juan Mountains in Colorado 90 miles to the south. You won't forget the grand views of the unfolding beauty below.

Every season has its highlights along the Grand Mesa Scenic and Historic Byway. Fall brings a splash of red and yellow to the valleys and mountains, while the mild climate encourages a variety of wildlife to wander in the area of the Byway. Summertime is the season for enjoying the many activities along the Byway. Hiking one of the many trails, fishing in the mesa's 300 lakes, hunting big game, or enjoying a roadside picnic with family or friends makes the Grand Mesa Scenic and Historic Byway one to remember.

The Byway Story

The Grand Mesa Scenic and Historic Byway tells historical, natural, recreational, and scenic stories that make it a unique and treasured Byway.

HISTORICAL

The first Europeans known to have come to the Grand Mesa were members of the famous Dominguez-Escalante expedition. In 1776, Ute guides led them over the Mesa because the expedition couldn't find a good land route to California on their own; more Europeans came as fur traders in the mid-1800s.

Early treaties "gave" this land to the Utes, but as white settlers moved to Colorado, the US government made a series of treaties with the Utes that reduced the territory by degrees. In the early 1880s, the Utes were moved to reservations in Utah and southwestern Colorado, and cattle and sheep ranchers soon dominated the area.

Since 1881, the valley floor has been home to farmers, who rely on water from the Grand Mesa for their crops and orchards. Beginning in the late 1800s, numerous water storage and irrigation projects were initiated to bring the water from the mesa. These water conservation systems continue to operate today with enhancements for hydroelectric production and municipal watersheds.

Fishing has been promoted since 1893, when the Mesa Resort Company was established. The company, still in existence today, built several lodges and over 300 summer homes. Skiing on the mesa dates back to 1939, with the construction of the Mesa Creek Ski Area. Relocated in 1964, it is now The Powderhorn of the Grand Mesa Ski Area.

Touring the scenic Grand Mesa began with horse and buggy trips that lasted several days. Access was improved in 1895 with the completion of the first road through Plateau Canyon. A stage line and freight wagons regularly traveled the route. The road was improved with convict labor in 1911 and later became part of the Pikes Peak Ocean-to-Ocean Highway.

A second access route to the top of the mesa was constructed in 1933 by ex-servicemen on a Civilian Conservation Corps (CCC) crew. The twisting, rocky road was then known as the Veteran Road in their honor. It is now called Lands End Road. With the advent of better roads and automobiles, the popularity of Grand Mesa touring has continued to expand.

NATURAL

Geologically, the Grand Mesa is a lava-capped plateau. Lava flows occurred in ancient river valleys about 10 million years ago. However, unlike many lava flows, no volcanic cone or crater was associated with the Grand Mesa flows. Instead, these flows rose through fissures in the Earth's surface on the eastern part of the mesa. Geologists have identified 25 individual flows, ranging in thickness from less than 10 feet to more than 70 feet. The total thickness of the lava cap of the Grand Mesa ranges from 200 to 600 feet.

Erosion over the last 10 million years has removed the hills that were composed of softer rocks that surrounded the harder lava-filled valleys, leaving the lava-capped terrain as a high plateau. During the Wisconsin Ice Age that occurred 100,000 to 50,000 years ago, glaciers formed on Grand Mesa. Some of these glaciers flowed down the north side of the mesa, over the area where The Powderhorn of the Grand Mesa Ski Area is now located and into the valley of Plateau Creek. The town of Mesa is built upon glacial gravels, and many of the lava boulders in Plateau Canyon were deposited by a glacial river that was much larger than the present-day Plateau Creek.

The drive along the Grand Mesa Scenic and Historic Byway takes you up through numerous ecological transitions that you would normally have to travel a much longer route to see. The ecology includes 5,000-foot elevation piñon-juniper desert canyons, aspen foothills, lily ponds, and alpine forest at 11,000 feet. The animal life found in each zone changes with the seasons. During the summer, elk and deer roam the cool alpine forests, while winter snow depths of 5 feet or more drive them to the lower elevations. There is a significant change in temperature as the elevation changes, as well. Although it can be hot and dry on the valley floor, the mesa's top may have enough snow for a snowball fight.

RECREATIONAL

The Grand Mesa offers excellent outdoor recreational opportunities. Over 300 stream-fed lakes are scattered across the mesa, teaming with rainbow, cutthroat, and brook trout. Numerous roads and trails offer sightseeing and hiking adventures. In the winter, the Grand Mesa provides premier cross-country skiing, downhill skiing at The Powderhorn of the Grand Mesa Ski Area, and snowmobiling. Big game hunting, horseback riding, mountain biking, and boating are also popular activities.

SCENIC

The Grand Mesa Scenic and Historic Byway offers a unique experience to travelers seeking an alternative to the typical fast-paced travel routes. Colorado

Highway 65 provides for safe, comfortable year-round passage along this nationally designated Byway, which incorporates the world's largest flat-top mountain. Lands End Road provides a unique and safe travel experience seasonally, offering magnificent vistas from a 10,000-foot elevation. The Byway passes through shimmering aspen and aromatic pine forests, by meadows of wildflowers, and among endless sparkling lakes. You have the opportunity to observe major changes and diversity in the landscape, from desert-like approaches to dense forests atop the Grand Mesa. Scenic overlooks, rest areas, trails, and picnic areas are clearly marked along the Byway, offering easy access to a variety of opportunities to take in the scenery. Interpretive and other information is available at two visitor centers on the Byway and at the Byway Welcome Center in Cedaredge.

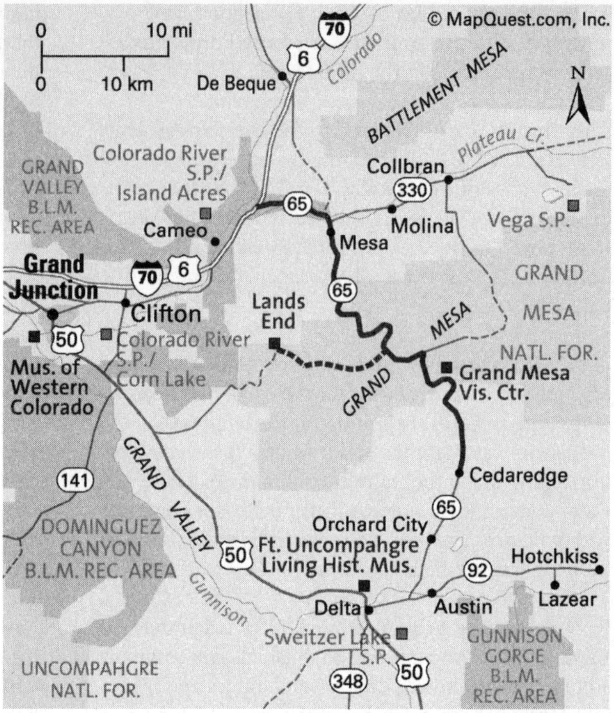

Highlights

You can begin this Grand Mesa must-see tour in either of two locations: starting from the Lands End Observatory and proceeding south or starting from the town of Cedaredge and proceeding north. If you are beginning this tour from Cedaredge, start at the bottom of the list and work your way up.

- **Lands End Observatory:** This spur of the Byway ends at the spectacular views around the Lands End Observatory. This structure, which is listed on the Register of Historic Sites, was built in the late 1930s as a public-works project. It is perched on the edge of Grand Mesa and offers views of the valley 6,000 feet below and the LaSal mountains in Utah to the west.

- **Land-O-Lakes Overlook:** When you return back to Highway 65, proceed south to the sign for the Land-O-Lakes Overlook. Due to the area's unique geology, the Grand Mesa is dotted with over 300 streams and reservoirs. A 100-yard trail to this overlook provides a great view that displays many of these lakes and the West Elk Mountains in the east.

- **Grand Mesa Visitor Center:** This beautiful log structure is located at the intersection of Highway 65 and Forest Development Road 121. It is open from 9 am to 5 pm, seven days a week from June to September, with the same hours on weekends for most of the rest of the year. This facility provides visitor information, sales of interpretive materials, and an interpretive hiking trail.

- **Cedaredge Welcome Center and Pioneer town:** These facilities are located together in the town of Cedaredge. Exhibits are open to the public daily from 9 am to 5 pm, Memorial Day to Labor Day. The facilities provide visitor information, exhibits, and a tour of a reconstructed town that depicts the life of early pioneers in the area.

San Juan Skyway

COLORADO

An All-American Road

Quick Facts

Length: 233 miles.

Time to Allow: 1 to 2 days.

Best Time to Drive: June through October. The Byway can be enjoyed year-round, and each season has its own attractions. Fall is one of the most spectacular seasons along the Byway because of the many fall colors. High season is in July and August.

Byway Travel Information: San Juan National Forest Visitors Center: phone 970/247-4874; Byway local Web site: www.coloradobyways.org.

Special Considerations: The country along the San Juan Skyway is exciting to explore, but safety should always be a major concern. Old, unstable mills, mines, and timber structures may be decaying and hazardous. Be prepared for changing weather both while driving and while hiking. If you are not accustomed to high altitudes, get plenty of rest and resist overdoing activities during your first two days at high altitude.

Restrictions: This Byway is maintained year-round. Mountain passes are sometimes closed for an hour or two (sometimes even a day or two) in the case of heavy snowstorms or slides during the winter. The two-lane road between Ouray and Silverton has incredibly beautiful views; it is also narrow and steep, has many hairpin switchbacks and a tunnel, includes tremendous drop-offs with no railings or shoulders, and offers few places to pass. Some curves are signed at 10 mph.

Bicycle/Pedestrian Facilities: The San Juan Skyway is a popular and extremely challenging bicycle route. Shoulders are always adequate, but in some places they are tight. Be particularly alert on the Ouray to Silverton segment, where the road is narrow, high, steep, and curvy, and views ahead are limited.

Travel to the top of the world and back in time on the San Juan Skyway. This loop trip through the San Juan Mountains of southwest Colorado follows more than 200 miles of state-maintained highways on a journey from towering mountains and alpine forests to the rolling vistas and ancient ruins of Native American country.

On this Byway, you drive through the heart of 5 million acres of the San Juan and Uncompahgre national forests. The skyway takes you over high mountain passes and through quaint historic towns. Crashing waterfalls can be seen in the spring as the snow melts in the higher mountains; wildflowers are in full bloom during the pleasant summer months; the golden colors of aspens delight visitors in the fall; and winter brings a quieting blanket of snow to the Byway.

You also find plenty of action along the route: four-wheeling, hiking, backpacking, bicycling, hunting, fishing, kayaking, dirt biking, and motorcycle touring.

You find rest and relaxation, too, by browsing town shops, soaking in historic hot springs, staying in a Victorian lodge, or sleeping under the stars in a forest campground. During the winter, skiing is one of the premier activities you can enjoy at quality resort areas like Telluride and Purgatory. The beauty of the surrounding mountains and the historic towns will remind you of the varied and complex history of the area. Ancestral Pueblos lived and worked the land long ago, and the cliff dwellings at Mesa Verde National Park exemplify the complexity of this culture. Spanish exploring parties made their way through the area, and the discovery of gold in the Rocky Mountains forever changed the nature of the surrounding country. Mining towns sprung up in the mountains, and the railroad helped maintain this growth.

The Byway Story

The San Juan Skyway tells archeological, historical, natural, recreational, and scenic stories that make it a unique and treasured Byway.

ARCHAEOLOGICAL

Among this Byway's many archaeological sites, Mesa Verde (located in Mesa Verde National Park) is arguably the most outstanding site. Mesa Verde (Spanish for "green table") offers an unparalleled opportunity to see and experience a unique cultural and physical landscape. The culture represented at Mesa Verde reflects more than 700 years of history. From approximately AD 600 through AD 1300, people lived and flourished in communities throughout the area. They eventually built elaborate stone villages, now called cliff dwellings, in the sheltered alcoves of the canyon walls. In the late 1200s and within only one or two generations, they left their homes and moved away.

The archaeological sites found in Mesa Verde National Park are some of the most notable and best preserved in the United States. Mesa Verde National Park offers visitors a spectacular look into the lives of the ancestral Pueblo. Scientists study the ancient dwellings of Mesa Verde in part by making comparisons between the ancestral Pueblo and their descendants who live in the Southwest today—24 Native American tribes in the Southwest have an ancestral affiliation with the sites at Mesa Verde.

HISTORICAL

The discovery of precious metals led to the exploration and settlement of areas along the San Juan Skyway during the late 19th century. Narrow-gauge railroads played an important role during the mining era and in the history of Southwest Colorado as a whole.

With their rails set 3 feet apart as opposed to the standard gauge of nearly 5 feet, the narrow-gauge lines made it possible for trains to operate in mountainous country with tight turns and steep grades. Evidence of these defunct, narrow-gauge lines is manifested by the water tanks, bridges, trestles, and sections of railroad bed found along the Byway. One narrow-gauge railroad, the Durango & Silverton, continues to operate as a tourist line. It was constructed in 1881-1882 by the Denver & Rio Grande Railroad to haul ore and provisions, and in 1968 the line was designated a National Historic Civil Engineering Landmark. As it travels along the Animas River amidst majestic mountains, the Durango & Silverton Railroad offers you spectacular scenic vistas and the experience of riding an authentic coal-fired, steam-powered railroad. It is one of southwest Colorado's major attractions and carries more than 200,000 passengers a year.

NATURAL

The already spectacular San Juan Skyway takes on especially vibrant beauty in the fall. The lush green of deciduous vegetation on the mountainsides is transformed into shades of gold, red, bronze, and purple, with evergreens adding their contrasting blues and greens.

The aspen trees are the first to turn shades of gold and rosy red. With their shimmering leaves, the aspen groves glow when the sun shines through them. The cottonwood trees, located along rivers and creeks, are next to turn gold, and a variety of shrubs complement the scene with their fall hues of red, purple, bronze, and orange.

Autumn is a favorite time for locals and tourists alike to enjoy the warm days, cool and crisp nights, and breathtakingly beautiful scenery of the San Juan Skyway.

RECREATIONAL

Summer activities include hiking, mountain biking, kayaking, four-wheeling, hunting, and fishing. Winter activities include snowshoeing, ice climbing, snowmobiling, and downhill and cross-country skiing.

Durango Mountain Resort at Purgatory offers downhill skiing and a Nordic center with a groomed track. In summer, the lift takes visitors up the mountain for sightseeing and wildflower viewing. The lift is also a way to get to the top of the mountain biking trail system and to the top of the toboggan-like Alpine Slide.

SCENIC

The brawny and pine-furrowed Rockies lounge around this Byway, and their uneven ridges yield to tree-packed forests, flashing streams, and slate-blue lakes. The scene extends into stretches of breezy grasslands divided occasionally by hand-hewn weathered fences. This Byway is known as the Million Dollar Highway not only for its connection to gold and silver mining, but also for its first-class scenery.

Highlights

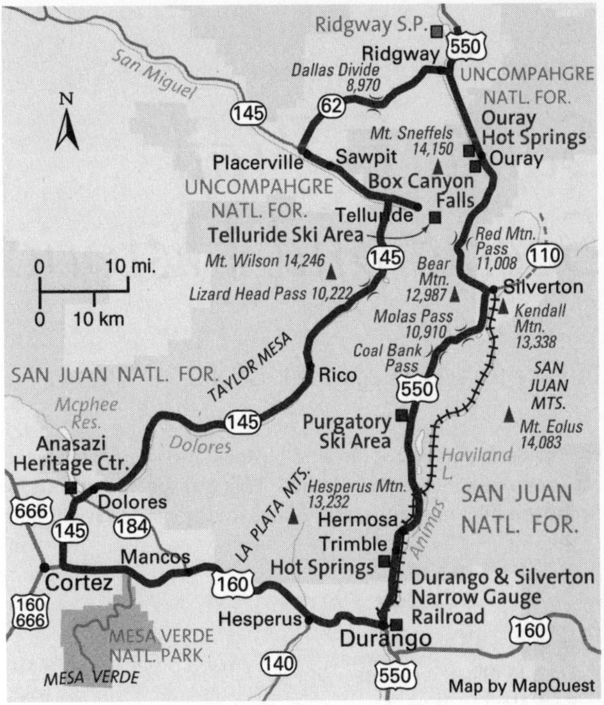

The following tour begins in Mesa Verde National Park and ends in the town of Ouray. If you are beginning the tour from Ouray, simply begin at the bottom of the list and work your way up.

- **Mesa Verde:** At this national park, explore cliff dwellings made by the Anasazi Indians. These dwellings were mysteriously abandoned by the Anasazi approximately 200 years before Columbus discovered America.

- **Durango:** This authentic Old West town, founded in 1880, still retains its Victorian charm. Restored historic landmarks line downtown streets, while nearby ski resorts beckon to adventurous winter travelers.

- **Silverton:** This remote mining community can be reached either by taking the historic Durango & Silverton narrow-gauge railroad or by driving over the 10,910-foot Molas Divide pass. Many of the beautiful Victorian buildings in Silverton are registered as National Historical Sites.

- **Ghost towns:** The ghost towns of Howardsville, Eureka, and Animas Forks are all located within 14 miles of Silverton. At Animas Forks, you can walk through the remnants of a 19th-century mining town or wander through beautiful meadows of wildflowers.

- **Million Dollar Highway:** The section of highway from Silverton to Ouray has been named the Million Dollar Highway because of the immense amounts of silver and gold that were carted through these passes. This road is quite possibly the most beautiful section of byway anywhere in the country and is not to be missed.

Santa Fe Trail Scenic and Historic Byway

COLORADO

Part of a multistate Byway; see also NM.

The Santa Fe Trail Scenic and Historic Byway is a rich legacy of the many people who made their way across southeastern Colorado. This transportation route served as a corridor to the West and resulted in the meshing of many cultures and traditions. Today along the Byway, festivals and museums honor the many men and women who left a distinctive mark on the area, including early Native Americans, military personnel, ranchers, miners, and railroad passengers.

QUICK FACTS

Length: 188 miles.

Time to Allow: 4 hours.

Best Time to Drive: Early spring through late fall.

Byway Travel Information: Colorado Welcome Center in Lamar: phone 719/336-3483; Byway local Web site: www.coloradobyways.org.

Bicycle/Pedestrian Facilities: This Byway is well equipped for passenger vehicles and bicyclists, offering flat or slightly rolling terrain. Highways 160 and 350 from Trinidad to La Junta have two undivided lanes. From La Junta east to the Kansas border on State Highway 50, the highway varies between two and four lanes. These road segments can easily accommodate passenger vehicle traffic because they have light traffic volume, 12-foot-wide lanes, and good sight lines. However, the road shoulders are fairly narrow at 2 feet wide. Even though specifically designated bicycle routes are not available, long-distance bicyclists can be found riding the route on a typical day. The communities along the Byway are small, with populations under 10,000 people, so local traffic has minimal impact on visiting pedestrians, bicyclists, and vehicle traffic. Bicyclists are permitted on I-25 because there are no alternative routes. Pedestrian usage is concentrated in commercial areas where sidewalks are available.

On a clear spring day, a sharp observer can still discern the wagon-wheel ruts of the Santa Fe Trail wending their way across the prairie. The cultural legacies of this historic trade route, which saw its heaviest use between the 1820s and 1870s, remain just as distinct today. The Byway, which comprises a 188-mile portion of the trail, traverses one of the last strongholds of the nomadic Plains Indians and one of the first toeholds of Anglo-American pioneers who began homesteading along the Arkansas River in the 1860s. The Mountain Branch of the Santa Fe Trail traveled through the present-day city of Trinidad. It then crossed Raton Pass, a mountain gap used by Native Americans for centuries. The Byway's midpoint is Bent's Old Fort, once a trading post and cultural melting pot and now a National Historic Site.

Travelers on the Santa Fe Trail today enjoy the area for the variety of attractions and activities that it offers. The rich history of the area is reflected in many historic sites and museums along the Byway, and recreational sites offer enjoyment for the entire family. Fishing, camping, hunting, and hiking are all popular activities. John Martin Reservoir is the largest body of water in southeastern Colorado and provides a great deal of recreational opportunity for modern-day travelers of the Santa Fe Trail.

The Byway Story

The Santa Fe Trail Scenic and Historic Byway tells archaeological, cultural, historical, natural, recreational, and scenic stories that make it a unique and treasured Byway.

ARCHAEOLOGICAL

Early man has left signs of habitation along the Santa Fe Trail Scenic and Historic Byway in many forms, including rock art, Native American teepee rings and fire circles, and other evidence of prehistoric and settlement-era activities. Numerous rock art sites document continuous habitation of this region for over 5,000 years, covering Paleo-Indian, Archaid, Ceramic, and Protohistoric/Historic stages.

Southeastern Colorado has many sites that have both petroglyphs and pictographs. (Petroglyphs are images that are pecked into the rock, while pictographs are painted on to the rock.) These images speak of days long past, and part of the enjoyment of viewing rock art is hypothesizing about what the images may mean. Perhaps these symbols were religious in meaning, were used as calendars, or conveyed information about natural resources.

Visitors to the Santa Fe Scenic and Historic Byway will find sites where this rock art is located. Archaeological sites exist at Picket Wire Canyonlands, Picture Canyon, Comanche National Grassland, and Piñon Canyon. A 1997 archaeological survey documented more than 70 sites in the Timpas Creek (Comanche Grassland) area alone. Louden-Henritzie Archaeological Museum in Trinidad features exhibits on the area's geology, fossils, and archaeology.

CULTURAL

The culture of the Santa Fe Scenic and Historic Byway has been shaped by the many people who have traveled along the Santa Fe Trail. The Byway has signs of Mexican influence, as well as the impact of a variety of other people. The tradition of county fairs and local rodeos can be found all along this route, and community celebrations highlight some of the unique features of the area.

Southeastern Colorado is embedded with Mexican culture; the area was a Mexican territory longer than it has been a part of the United States. Even after the US acquired Mexico's northern provinces in 1848, the Santa Fe Trail served as a conduit for exchange between Spanish, Native American, and American cultures. Communities along the Byway continue to celebrate the diverse inhabitants through traditional celebrations, culturally representative architecture (such as adobe structures), religious folk art, and Hispanic culture at Trinidad's Baca House Museum (located in the Trinidad History Museum) and A. R. Mitchell Museum. Large murals depicting the Santa Fe Trail and Western history are painted on the exterior of commercial buildings as reminders of past and present cultural contributions.

Local community events highlight the area's rich traditions. The Santa Fe Trail saw many people moving from place to place, and this movement brought a variety of people and many new celebrations to the area located along the Byway. Local fairs and rodeos are held in Kiowa County, Bent County, and Crowley County, and they host parades and good old-fashioned fun. The Sand and Sage Roundup in Prowers County has a variety of events, including a rodeo, carnival, exhibits, and a host of other activities. Oktoberfest in Lamar celebrates in the Germanic tradition, with a parade, food, arts, crafts, and a street dance.

HISTORICAL

The Santa Fe Scenic and Historic Byway parallels the Santa Fe Trail, which served as a trade route between Missouri and the Mexican frontiers from 1821 to 1880. Traders, miners, military, and settlers all used this route in the settlement and exploration of the West. Even during the Civil War, the area saw action as Colorado volunteers fought against Confederate troops. With the coming of the railroad, the Santa Fe Trail entered a new phase of its history.

The Santa Fe Trail extended for 900 miles from Missouri to Santa Fe and was instrumental in carrying people and goods across the land. The Mountain Route of the Santa Fe Trail was traveled by caravans of traders, often journeying four horses abreast. Although the Mountain Route was 100 miles longer than the Cimarron Route and included the difficult climb over Raton Pass, the Mountain Route was preferred because water was more accessible and the area was less vulnerable to attacks from Native Americans.

Travel on the trail was beneficial but dangerous for those making the journey. In 1834, Charles and William Bent and Ceran St. Vrain, built a fort to protect trading activities between the Americans, Mexicans, and Native Americans. Visitors can visit Bent's fort today and see what fort life was like. Miners heading to California in search of gold often chose the shorter, although more dangerous, route of the Santa Fe Trail rather than the Oregon Trail.

After the railroad came through the area, the nature of the Santa Fe Trail changed, and in 1861, the Barlow-Sanderson stage line was established. This line provided a weekly schedule, and Trinidad was a major stop on this line. With America embroiled in the Civil War, the Colorado Territory also saw an increase in military traffic.

Visitors traveling the route today can discover the magic of the trail and retrace authentic steps taken by pioneers. Travelers of the trail today are able to recreate life along the Trail by viewing existing historic sites, including trading posts (Bent's Old Fort), stage stops, visible wagon ruts, graves, ruins of Trail-era ranches, and statues commemorating pioneers. Exhibits, interpretive displays, and living-history presentations that convey the history of the Trail are accessible to the public and can be explored at will.

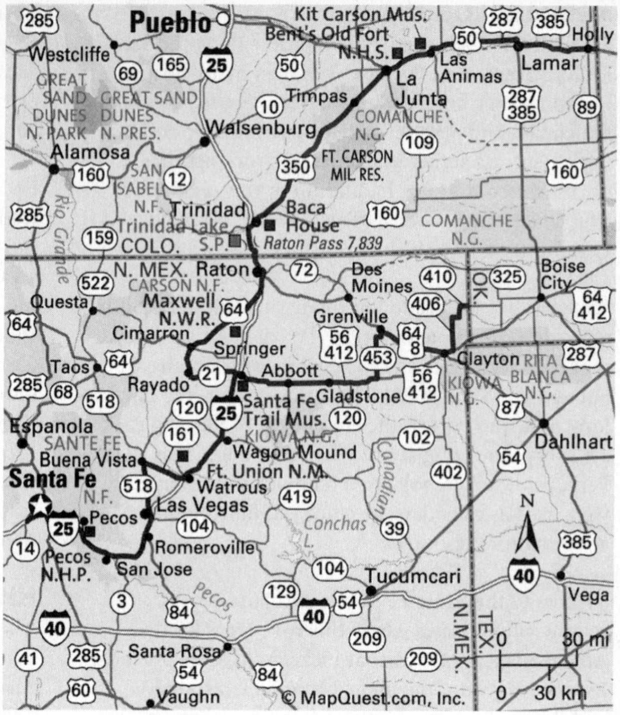

NATURAL

The Santa Fe Trail corridor provides an opportunity to discover an undisturbed, pristine landscape while observing the wide diversity of wildlife habitats. Southeastern Colorado varies from prime agricultural land to expanses of native grassland; four state wildlife areas in the corridor cover over 10,000 acres. Rivers have carved canyons and valleys, where striking geology and unusual rock formations can be found.

Wildlife consists of free-ranging antelope, mule deer, bighorn sheep, bobcats, foxes, coyotes, and mountain lions, as well as small mammals, amphibians, reptiles, fish, and birds. Comanche National Grassland alone provides habitat for approximately 275 species of birds, 60 species of mammals, 40 species of reptiles, 11 species of fish, and 9 species of amphibians.

The Comanche National Grassland offers an area of rich natural qualities. The features of this landscape vary from short and midgrass prairies to deep canyons and arroyos. Although it may be hard to imagine, this area was once the site of an ancient sea and today, fossils of pre-historic creatures of this sea have been found in the Comanche National Grassland. In addition to these fossils, there is a set of dinosaur tracks south of La Junta that is the longest set of tracks in North America.

RECREATIONAL

The Santa Fe Scenic and Historic Byway offers more than 30,000 acres of public land that supports a variety of recreational activities. Fishing, hunting, boating, golfing, four-wheeling, hiking, horseback riding, biking, wildlife viewing, and camping are all activities that you can enjoy along the Byway. Several warm-water lakes, state parks, and wildlife areas serve as multiple-use recreation areas. Picnic areas, trailheads, municipal parks, and golf courses are also found in communities and parks on the route.

The Arkansas and Timpas rivers follow the Byway for a good portion of the route, providing many opportunities to enjoy the riverbanks. In addition, the John Martin Reservoir is the largest body of water in Southeastern Colorado. The blue waters of the lake give you a chance to enjoy a fun day of swimming, picnicking, camping, boating, water-skiing, sailing, or windsurfing. Fishing is another popular activity both on the lake and in nearby rivers. A number of lakes and reservoirs located just off of the Byway provide additional opportunities to enjoy the recreational qualities of the area.

In addition to the many types of fish in the lakes and rivers, an abundance of additional wildlife are located along the Byway. Numerous state wildlife areas are situated on the Byway and give you a chance to view the wildlife of the area. Desert bighorn sheep, eagles, cranes, pelicans, lesser prairie chickens, and hummingbirds can often be spotted in the area. Hunters come to southeastern Colorado for prime hunting opportunities; in fact, Prowers County is known as the goose hunting capital of the nation and in December, hunters come from all over to participate in the annual Two Shot Celebrity Goose Hunt.

SCENIC

Scenic qualities along the Byway range from panoramic vistas of the Spanish Peaks, Fisher Peak, and Raton Pass to the verdant, irrigated croplands of Colorado's high plains. A sense of isolation is found on the expansive grasslands, one of the nation's disappearing resources. Because much of the Byway is virtually undeveloped, you can experience what traveling the Santa Fe Trail must have been like in the 1800s. Picturesque windmills and evidence of homesteads provide travelers with a glimpse of life as a settler. In addition, the Byway passes through communities that are scenic in their own right, from the Corazon de Trinidad National Historic District, with its period architecture and brick streets, to quaint rural farm towns with roadside stands selling locally grown produce.

Highlights

The Santa Fe Trail historical tour begins at Bent's Old Fort and follows the trail westward toward Trinidad. If you're beginning the tour from Trinidad, simply start at the bottom of the list and work your way up.

- **Bent's Old Fort:** This National Historical Site is a reconstruction of Bent's Fort, which was built in the 1830s. The fort played an important role as a trading post for trappers and the Plains Indians and also as a supply depot during the Mexican-American War.

- **Sierra Vista Overlook:** For Santa Fe Trail travelers heading south, the changing horizon from plains to mountains was a major milestone on their journey. One of their guiding landmarks was the distant Spanish Peaks, which came into view along this section of the trail. A short walk up the side of a bluff gives you an excellent view of the Rocky Mountains and surrounding prairie, much like what early travelers saw. To reach this overlook, drive southwest from La Junta on Highway 350 for 13 miles. Turn right (north) at Highway 71 for 1/2 mile, and then turn left (west) to the parking lot.

- **Trinidad History Museum:** This museum complex, operated by the Colorado Historical Society, houses five attractions in one location. Visitors to the site can visit the Santa Fe Trail Museum, the Baca House, the Bloom Mansion, the Historic Gardens, or the bookstore.

Top of the Rockies Scenic Byway

COLORADO

The cool mountain air and fresh scent of pine trees beckons you to the Top of the Rockies Scenic Byway. Traveling through two different national forests, thick stands of pine trees cover the mountain side. Towering peaks flank the highways, and open lowlands give you a rest from steep mountain passes. However, don't be fooled by these "lowlands," because Leadville, the hub of the Byway, is the highest incorporated community in the US, located 10,200 feet above sea level. Mount Elbert (14,433 feet) and Mount Massive (14,421 feet)—the highest and second highest mountains in Colorado—stand just outside of Leadville.

Quick Facts

Length: 75 miles.

Time to Allow: 2.5 hours to 1 day.

Best Time to Drive: Year-round; summer is the high season.

Byway Travel Information: Greater Leadville Area Chamber of Commerce: phone 719/486-3900; Byway local Web site: www.coloradobyways.org.

Special Considerations: The only part of this Byway that ever closes is the Vail Pass segment of I-70; bypass it by taking Highways 24 and 91, which take a little more time to travel. Due to the amount of snowfall along the Byway, use normal winter precautions when traveling this route. Wildfires are an ever-present danger in the dry summer months; follow posted signs regarding campfires and do not throw cigarettes out the car window. Abandoned mines are extremely dangerous–look and take pictures but do not explore. High altitudes bring increased sun exposure and reduced oxygen, so wear sunscreen and sunglasses and don't overexert yourself. Be prepared for cold mornings, even in August.

Restrictions: Highway 82, the Independence Pass Road between Twin Lakes and Aspen, is closed during the winter months at a point about 5 miles beyond the southwestern terminus of the Byway.

Bicycle/Pedestrian Facilities: Bicyclists and pedestrians share the road with cars. You'll find wide shoulders along some stretches of the road, especially around Leadville and the Twin Lakes area.

The colossal peaks of this area yielded huge fortunes in the 19th century as miners pulled millions of dollars of precious mineral from the ground. The most fortunate of them, Horace Tabor, became one of the titans of Colorado's silver industry. Leadville was the hub of activity during those silver mining days, with outlying areas acting as small mining towns and stopovers for travelers and miners alike.

While mining is still an integral part of the industry of the area, the town of Leadville is known more for its Victorian charm, colorful history, and historic buildings and churches. In addition, you'll find many activities and recreational opportunities along this 82-mile route that crosses the Continental Divide twice and traces the Arkansas River nearly to its source in the vicinity of Fremont Pass. Hiking, biking, skiing, and fishing are some of the most popular activities along the Byway.

THE BYWAY STORY

The Top of the Rockies tells historical, natural, recreational, and scenic stories that make it a unique and treasured Byway.

HISTORICAL

Mining shaped a way of life along the Top of the Rockies many years ago. The rich mines of the area led to the growth of communities such as Twin Lakes, Minturn, Leadville, and Redcliff. The military presence of the 10th Mountain Division at Camp Hale added another distinct chapter in the history of the Byway.

In 1860, the mountains and hills came alive as gold was discovered in California Gulch. Soon, silver was also discovered in the area, bringing individuals such as Horace Tabor, David May, J. J. and Margaret Brown, the Guggenheims, and the Boettchers. Fortunes were made, and communities soon developed to meet the needs of the growing mining populations. Many of these towns, such as Kokomo, Recen, and Robinson, are now nonexistent, having been destroyed by fires or other natural disasters. Other towns, such as Leadville and Twin Lakes, still retain a strong mining influence.

While mining brought many people to the area, when fortunes were harder to come by, many residents turned to farming, and thus the boomtowns remained lively communities. Leadville today maintains the Victorian charm and influence that kept people in town after the mining boom was over. Harrison Avenue boasts many historic structures, and the National Mining Museum relates the story of the importance of mining in the area and around the world. The wealth made in the nearby mines created well-to-do individuals, and the colorful stories of these individuals are still told today in the town. The Healy House and Dexter Cabin show what wealth did for individuals and allow you to see how they lived.

Mining was—and continues to be—one of the most important aspects of the area, but other factors contributed to its historical development. The 10th Mountain Division, which trained at Camp Hale near Ski Cooper, fought in the military campaign in Italy during World War II. Camp Hale was the training site of the Invisible Men on Skis. The troops used the high elevation, steep slopes, and winter conditions to train for mountain and winter warfare in the Apennine Mountains of Italy. The 10th Mountain Division did see action during the war, and a memorial to those who lost their lives in this campaign stands at the entrance to Ski Cooper.

NATURAL

The many impressive peaks along the Top of the Rockies Scenic Byway combined with the national forests in the area give the Byway a wealth of natural features. The Byway threads through three national forests—the Pike National Forest, the San Isabel National Forest, and White River National Forest—and one of the largest concentrations of congressionally designated Rare II Wildernesses. The area is so noteworthy that the Rocky Mountain Region of the US Forest Service has designated it a Center of Excellence. In all, six wilderness areas cover about 900 square miles. These primitive lands are being protected to ensure that future generations will be able to explore and experience this rugged and pristine wilderness.

The Mount Massive Wilderness Area covers 18,000 acres. Located in the San Isabel National Forest, this area is characterized by Mount Massive (14,421 feet), the second highest peak in Colorado. The processes of uplift, warping, buckling, and, to a lesser extent, glaciation, have given shape to the peaks in the Sawatch Mountain range and created many hidden mountain lakes. The Rocky Mountains and Continental Divide reach a higher point here than anywhere else between the Arctic Ocean and the Isthmus of Panama.

RECREATIONAL

Recreation along the Top of the Rockies is both diverse and abundant. During the winter and summer, you can enjoy a wide variety of recreational opportunities. The many lakes and streams provide rafting and fishing adventures, while the high Rocky Mountains lend themselves to camping, hiking, skiing, or mountain biking. Popular four-wheel drive vehicle trails take you off the beaten track to various destinations. Mount Massive Golf Course outside of Leadville claims the distinction of being the highest golf course on the continent.

The Arkansas and Colorado rivers give you a chance to enjoy rafting—from high water rapids to float trips, the area has something for everyone. These same rivers boast outstanding fishing. Twin Lakes and Turquoise Lake afford opportunities to fish, camp, and boat along the tranquil shores of the mountain lakes.

These lakes and rivers are set among and near some of the highest mountains in the Rocky Mountains. The Sawatch Mountain Range near Leadville has two peaks over 14,000 feet, and the Colorado and Continental Divide trails provide many opportunities for hiking. Numerous mountain biking trails are also in the area. Wilderness areas are the perfect place for extensive rugged outdoor adventure, such as backpacking, camping, picnicking, hunting, horseback riding, four-wheeling, and climbing. You can visit over 300 miles of hut-to-hut trails associated with the 10th Mountain Hut and Trail System, one of the most extensive back-country hut-to-hut systems in North America.

World-class skiing facilities along the Byway also make this one of the major recreational draws for the area. Both Copper Mountain Resort and Ski Cooper provide opportunities to ski. Other wintertime activities include backcountry skiing, cross-country skiing, and snowmobiling.

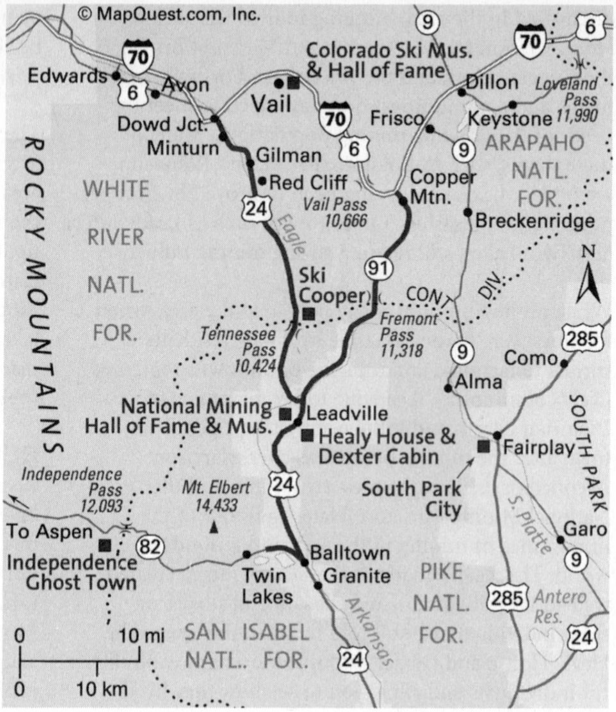

SCENIC

Driving the Top of the Rockies Byway is an adventure set among some of the highest country in Colorado. With Leadville located at just over 10,000 feet and Mount Elbert and Mount Massive both over 14,000, you are literally at the top of the Rocky Mountains. Both Tennessee Pass (10,424 feet) and Fremont Pass (11,318 feet) take you over the tops of these grand mountains, offering never-ending views of mountaintops and deep canyons. Cool air, even in the summer months, provides a perfect environment for exploring the many attractions along the Byway.

Every turn on Highway 91 and Highway 24 going to Leadville yields another view of a peak jutting into the sky. The forested mountainsides offer you a chance to witness the many shades of green that can be seen within the forests. Within each of the three national forests (Pike, San Isabel, and White River), woodland creatures, such as deer, may be spotted alongside the road. Clear mountain lakes and tumbling streams are easily accessible and seen from the road.

The open valley around Leadville is flanked on the west side by the Sawatch Mountain Range, with Mount Elbert (14,433 feet) and Mount Massive (14,421 feet) standing guard over the valley. Colorado's largest glacial lake, Twin Lakes, is set at the base of Twin Peaks and offers a peaceful and tranquil setting for the Byway traveler.

Highlights

The Top of the Rockies historical tour begins in the town of Dowd, which is about 5 miles west of Vail along Interstate 70. If you're beginning the tour from Leadville, simply start at the bottom of the list and work your way up.

- **Dowd and Minturn:** The Byway passes briefly through these small mountain communities, and then quickly gains elevation as it winds its way up and over rugged mountain passes. Be sure to bring a camera, because views from the road to the valleys below are incredible, especially in the fall.
- **Camp Hale Memorial and Historic Interpretive Site:** This site is located on the Byway near milepost 160 and features several plaques detailing the history of the 10th Mountain Division that trained here before serving in Europe in World War II.
- **National Mining Museum and Hall of Fame:** Located in Leadville, visitors can see displays of hundreds of fine specimens of gold, silver, ore, and minerals, including spectacular examples loaned from the Smithsonian Institute and the Harvard Mineralogical Museum.
- **Tabor Opera House:** When it opened in 1879, the Tabor Opera House was said to be the finest theater between St. Louis and San Francisco. This building is one of only a few Tabor-associated buildings still standing in Colorado.
- **Annunciation Church:** Started in 1879, this historic church in Leadville was dedicated on New Year's Day, 1880. This church's steeple has become a prominent landmark of this area. It houses an enormous bell that weighs more than 3,000 pounds.

Trail Ridge Road/ Beaver Meadow Road

COLORADO

An All-American Road

Sitting in a national park encompassed by national forests, the Trail Ridge Road/Beaver Meadow Road is arguably one of the most beautiful Byways in Colorado. The overarching characteristic of the Byway is its many overlooks, all of which bestow stirring vistas of 415 square miles of the towering (14,000+ feet) southern Rockies.

QUICK FACTS

Length: 53 miles.

Time to Allow: 2 hours or more.

Best Time to Drive: Open to through traffic Memorial Day to mid- or late October; closed by snow the rest of the year. High season includes June, July, and August, and the heaviest traffic is between 10 am and 4 pm.

Byway Travel Information: Rocky Mountain National Park Information Center: phone 970/586-1206; Byway local Web site: www.coloradobyways.org.

Special Considerations: You can't get fuel inside Rocky Mountain National Park, so you'll have to fill up in Estes Park or Grand Lake. Beware of vapor lock, a common occurrence for vehicles from low altitudes. Speed limits are generally 35 mph.

Restrictions: Rocky Mountain National Park is closed during the winter from mid- to late October until the Friday of Memorial Day weekend. Park entrance fees are required: $10 per carload for seven days, $5 per pedestrian, bicyclist, or motorcyclist for seven days; commercial bus fees vary.

Bicycle/Pedestrian Facilities: The road is narrow and has no shoulder or guardrail. At different points along the route, the drop-off is up to 2,000 vertical feet. Take extreme caution if biking this scenic road.

The clear atmosphere of this alpine tundra makes seeing the night sky from one of the overlooks incomparable. Constellations, planets, meteor showers, and phases of the moon seem brighter than ever and just beyond arm's reach.

Because this is such a protected area, elk, deer, mountain sheep, coyotes, moose, beavers, ptarmigans, marmots, pikas, eagles, and peregrine falcons can be seen more often than in other (unprotected) areas of Colorado and the nation. Also, the tender tundra wildflowers, which generally peak in July, are an exceptional treat.

The Byway Story

The Trail Ridge Road/Beaver Meadow Road tells historical, natural, recreational, and scenic stories that make it a unique and treasured Byway.

HISTORICAL

The first white men to see this area were French fur traders. In 1859, Joel Estes and his son, Milton, rode into the valley that now bears their name. A few others had settled in this rugged county by 1909 when Enos Mills, a naturalist, writer, and conservationist, began to campaign for preservation of the pristine area, part of which became the Rocky Mountain National Park in 1915.

NATURAL

One-third of the park is above the tree line, and the harsh, fragile alpine tundra predominates. The uniqueness of this area is a major reason why it has been set aside as a national park. Just below that, at the upper edges of the tree line, the trees are twisted, grotesque, and hug the ground. Here, more than one-quarter of the plants are also found in the Arctic.

Just below that, forests of Englemann spruce and subalpine fir take over in a subalpine ecosystem. Openings in these cool, dark forests expose wildflower gardens of rare beauty and luxuriance in which the blue Colorado columbine reigns. And in the foothills, open stands of ponderosa pine and juniper grow on the slopes facing the sun; on cooler north slopes grow Douglas fir.

RECREATIONAL

The recreational opportunities on this route are varied and excellent. For example, you can enjoy horseback riding, camping, fishing, rock climbing, and various winter activities.

Several campgrounds beckon, some of which are open year-round. The Rocky Mountain National Park maintains more than 260 miles of trails for private and commercial horse users. Hire horses and guides at two locations on the east side of the park or from a number of liveries outside the park boundaries during the summer season.

Four species of trout live in the mountain streams and lakes of Rocky Mountain National Park: German brown, rainbow, brook, and cutthroat trout. These cold waters may not produce large fish, but you do get to enjoy the superb mountain scenery as you fish. Rocky Mountain National Park also offers a variety of challenging ascents throughout the year for climbers. The Colorado Mountain School is the park's concessionaire, operating a climbing school and guide service.

Winter brings cross-country skiing in the lower valleys and winter mountaineering in the high country. Access roads from the east are kept open and provide you with a panorama of the high mountains.

SCENIC

The highest continuous road in the United States, this route affords an almost-too-rapid sequence of scenic overlooks as it skips along the roofs of some of the tallest Rockies (over 12,000 feet). From these wind-scoured peaks, you can gaze out to the dark masses of other Rockies, posed like hands of cards in the distance. The land adjacent to the Byway is otherworldly; the tundra's twisted, ground-creeping trees, crusted snow, and hard-faced boulders seem like they belong to a colder, more distant world.

Highlights

While visiting the Trail Ridge Road/Beaver Meadow Road, you can take a self-guided tour of the Byway. If you enter the park from the east (either the Fall River or Beaver Meadows entrance), start at the beginning and move down the list. If you are entering from the west (Grand Lake Entrance), begin at the bottom of the list and work your way up.

- **Rainbow Curve Overlook:** At 10,829 feet, this overlook is more than 2 vertical miles above sea level. At this elevation, every exposed tree is blasted by wind, ice, and grit into distinctive flag shapes. Tree branches here survive only on the downwind side of tree trunks. Higher still, trees survive only where the severely pruned shrubs are covered and protected by winter snowdrifts.

- **Forest Canyon Overlook:** Here, the erosive force of glacial ice is unmistakable. Although the ice did not reach as high as the overlook, it still lay more than 1,500 feet thick in a V-shaped stream valley. With the grinding of a giant rasp, the ice scoured the valley into the distinctive U shape of today.

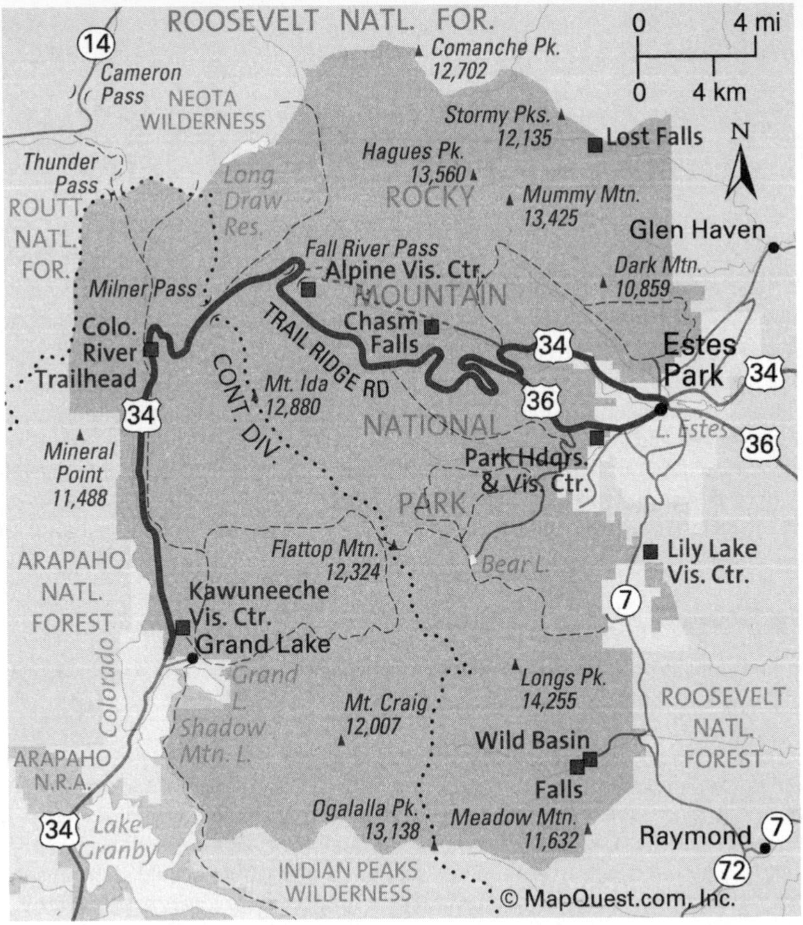

- **Rock Cut Overlook:** Here on the roof of the Rockies, the climate is rigorous. Severe weather can come at any time. Periods of drought may occur in both summer and winter, and winter blizzards are frequent. Temperatures remain below freezing all winter, and they frequently drop below freezing in summer. Wind speeds here can exceed 150 miles per hour in either summer or winter, and ultraviolet radiation is twice what it is at sea level. Sunlight is 50 percent more intense.

- **Fall River Pass and Alpine Visitor Center:** Besides the Visitor Center, there is a gift shop and a short trail to an overlook at 12,003 feet.

- **Milner Pass:** Here, Trail Ridge Road crosses the Continental Divide. At this point, waters enter either the Atlantic or Pacific drainages. The Rockies divide these two great watersheds, but the Continental Divide may be a mountaintop, a ridge, or a pass.

- From this point, a short trail leads past Poudre Lake, headwaters of the Cache La Poudre River, and up to Old Fall River Road. This road was the original road over the Continental Divide. The trail then connects with another trail leading to Mount Ida, at 1,288 feet. This is a 4 1/2-mile hike.

Lake Tahoe–Eastshore Drive

NEVADA

Called the most beautiful drive in America, the 72-mile Lake Tahoe–Eastshore Drive affords breathtaking views of spectacularly clear Lake Tahoe. The pristine alpine lake is surrounded by the snow-capped mountains of the Sierras. The Byway is mostly undeveloped, except for the fabulous recreational opportunities afforded by the lake, including the Zephyr Cove Resort, stables, campgrounds, the Tahoe Rim Trail, ski resorts, hotels and casinos, and fabulous golf courses. As part of the Pony Express trail and home to the historic sacred grounds of the Washo Indians, Lake Tahoe's eastern shore offers a wide variety of activities during every season. The Lake Tahoe–Eastshore Drive Byway is one of the most beautiful winter Byways in the country, with the draw of an alpine climate and the ever-crystalline lake. Throughout the year, visitors come from miles around to enjoy Lake Tahoe.

The Byway Story

The Lake Tahoe–Eastshore Drive tells cultural, historical, natural, recreational, and scenic stories that make it a unique and treasured Byway.

CULTURAL

Lake Tahoe is well known for its diverse and interesting culture of both recreation and arts. Events take place through the year that attract visitors for reasons ranging from high drama to downhill ski relays. During the summer months, artists gather at Lake Tahoe for exhibitions and workshops, making the area one of the best places to find cutting-edge and classic artwork. While Tahoe's art is a sight to behold, don't miss out on any of the many festivals that take place throughout the year. The festivals themselves are works of art.

Perhaps Lake Tahoe's best known summer festival is the Lake Tahoe Shakespeare Festival at Sand Harbor, which takes place every August. Imagine relaxing on a beautiful sand beach while enjoying your favorite Shakespearean drama. Enjoy the first-class performance near crystal blue waters, set against the stately backdrop of the Sierra Nevada, under a thousand glittering stars. The Lake Tahoe Shakespeare Festival has been voted the Best Summer Event and the Best Cultural Event at the lake. The theater was recently rebuilt and is magnificent. Bring a jacket, a blanket, and some edibles, and then sit back, relax, and enjoy high drama in one of the most stunning locations imaginable.

Lake Tahoe offers a variety of winter festivals as well. Winter begins early here with the Native American Festival and Snow Dance. During the Snow Dance, a two-day event held the first weekend in October, Native Americans dance in full regalia and pray for snow to ensure an abundantly snowy winter. Lake Tahoe also heralds the arrival of winter with other festivals such as the Northern Lights Winter Festival and Snow Fest. During Snow Fest, a ten-day festival with a huge variety of events, you can take part in ice-carving competitions, snow-sculpture contests, parades, and a polar bear swim in the still-frigid Lake Tahoe.

Quick Facts

Length: 28 miles.

Time to Allow: 1 hour.

Best Time to Drive: Year-round; high season is July through September and the last week of December.

Byway Travel Information: Tahoe Douglas Chamber of Commerce & Visitors Center: phone 775/588-4591; Byway travel and tourism Web site: www.tahoechamber.org.

Restrictions: There are occasional brief road closures during snowstorms.

Snow Fest's opening-night ceremonies feature activities such as a torchlight parade of skiers, fireworks, a bonfire, and music. Activities throughout the festival also include downhill finals, the largest cross-country ski races in the western US, and celebrity races. The closing weekend has included the nationally televised Incredible Snow Dog Challenge, which featured snow competitions of the canine variety, such as freestyle Frisbee, agility, search and rescue, and dog sledding.

HISTORICAL

Lake Tahoe was originally a peaceful, earthy place, connected to the rest of the world by narrow trails over high mountain passes. Native tribes would gather in the summer to fish, hunt, and harvest nuts and berries for the long winter spent in Nevada's high desert. The native tribes called their special place Da ow aga, meaning "the edge of the lake." It is believed that Tahoe got its name from the white settlers' mispronunciation of the first two syllables. Tahoe remains a gathering place for people hunting for the ultimate vacation.

While on an expedition in search of the mythical Buenaventura River in 1844, explorers Kit Carson and John C. Fremont instead stumbled on Lake Tahoe, letting out the secret that had long been kept from the outside world. Fremont's accurate accounts of his High Sierra travels led other curious explorers to the mountain lake. Soon after, gold and silver prospectors flocked to Lake Tahoe, but their explorations failed. However, in 1859, rich silver deposits in nearby Virginia City began a logging boom. While the Comstock Lode opened the area to big business, it nearly stripped the Lake Basin of its first growth of trees because its lumber was used for timber supports in the underground mines.

As more white men laid eyes on the natural treasure, word of the wondrous lake spread through the land. Among these proclaimers was humorist Mark Twain, who described the area as so wholesome and pure that "three months of camp life on Lake Tahoe would restore an Egyptian mummy to his pristine vigor and give him an appetite like an alligator." Stage stops over the Sierra exposed visitors to Tahoe's scenic beauty and tranquility. Many were lured to stay because they felt that they had found paradise.

Westerners began to develop Lake Tahoe's shore in the early 1900s as a summer retreat for San Francisco's elite. Plush hotels sprang up, and guests amused themselves at Lucky Baldwin's Tallac House and Casino, known today as the Tallac Historic Site at South Shore. Gambling was illegal on the California side of the lake, but enforcement was sporadic, and arrangements with cooperative authorities were routine. Raiding lawmen often found patrons playing nothing more than pinochle and canasta. By 1941, the Tahoe Tattle was reporting that Tahoe's number two industry was nightlife, a close second to the resorts. Each weekend, an estimated 3,000 people would flock to the bars, casinos, and dance halls and spend anywhere from 25 cents for a glass of beer to $50,000 for an expensive game.

A boom of another kind was soon occurring at Lake Tahoe. Using Nevada's advantageous tax laws as bait, an enterprising businessman named Norman Blitz convinced more than 80 of the nation's most rich and famous to make Lake Tahoe their home. This effort sparked the development of a thriving real estate and construction industry at the lake.

NATURAL

Lake Tahoe is a masterpiece of nature. Surrounded by mountains, Lake Tahoe is the highest lake in the United States, the third deepest lake in North America, and the tenth deepest lake in the world. The lake holds more than 39 trillion gallons of water: if it were to be drained, it would take 700 years to refill. Lake Tahoe is incredibly blue because the thin, clear mountain air allows the lake's pure, crystal-clear water to reflect the blue sky above. For this reason, the lake also appears a dramatic red during sunsets and reflects a somber, churning gray during storms. The spectacular shoreline is 71 miles long, 29 miles of which is on the Nevada side. Beautiful vegetation and numerous kinds of wildlife inhabit the area.

Lake Tahoe was created millions of years ago through the shifting of geological faults. Immense forces began the process with the tilting of the Sierra Nevada block. As a result, two parallel faults were developed. One margin created the Carson Range, and the other created the Sierra Nevada. About 2 million years ago, volcanic activity reshaped the entire landscape of the region. Lava formed a barrier across the basin's northeastern outlet, creating a natural dam and, eventually, Lake Tahoe. Next, vast glaciers formed in the surrounding mountains. These gradually moved down the V-shaped canyons on the western side of the lake. The massive glaciers scoured away any loose rock, and the canyons were reshaped into the wide, U-shaped valleys of Emerald Bay, Fallen Leaf Lake, and Cascade Lake.

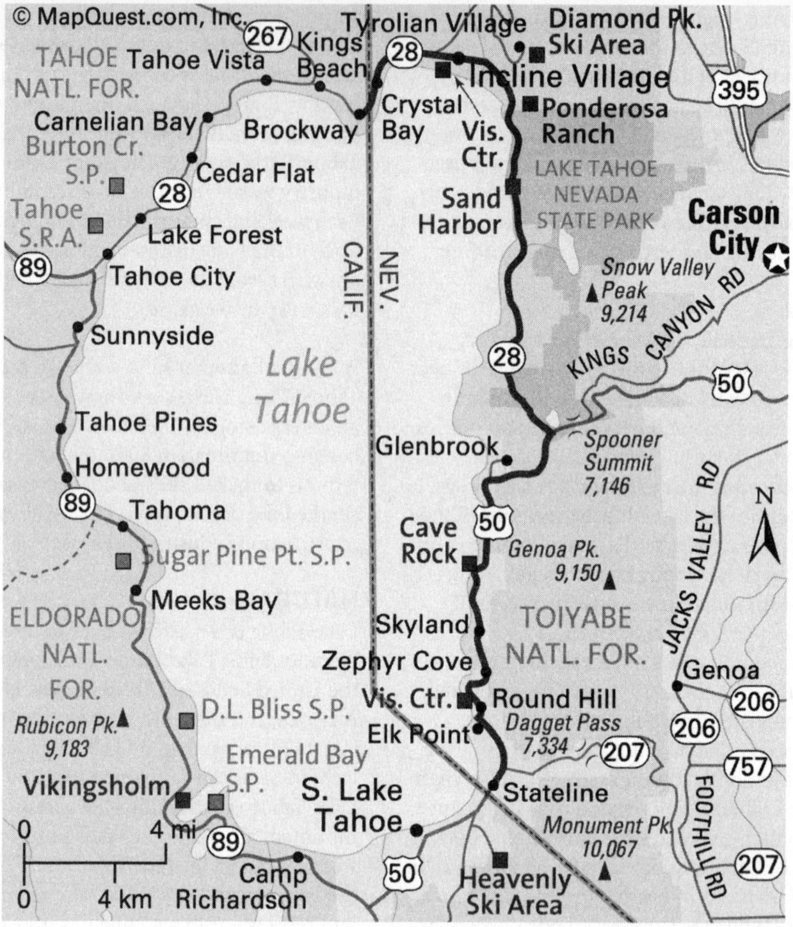

Lake Tahoe has a variety of unique plant and animal life that make hikes and walks an exciting experience. One particularly striking plant, a fairly common sight when the snow is melting, is the snowplant. This member of the wintergreen family is an asparagus-like plant that doesn't photosynthesize, but receives nourishment from the roots of neighboring plants and decaying organic matter. Despite its somewhat disturbing means of survival, the plant is extremely lovely, rare, and (fortunately) protected by law. Another beautiful flower is the crimson columbine, a well-known flower appreciated for its delicate features that grows in moist areas. The lupine is also easily recognized by the palmate leaf resembling the fingers of a hand and striking blue flowers.

While the Lake Tahoe area is full of a variety of animal life, from coyotes to bears, you will likely see various kinds of birds most often. The western tanager is a beautiful bird and one of the most colorful in the Lake Tahoe Basin, with a red head and a bright yellow body and black markings on its back, wings, and tail. Another common bird in the area is the mountain chickadee, the most common bird in the Tahoe Basin. This bird is small with a black cap, a black bib, and a white line over each eye. It is acrobatic and swings from branches as it hunts for insects and seeds; it also makes a distinctive three-note whistle.

RECREATIONAL

When it comes to winter activities, Lake Tahoe has it covered (literally). Tahoe has more snow (averaging about 400 inches per season), more variety, and more ways to play than just about any other place. Lake Tahoe has the largest concentration of ski resorts in North America, including six world-class resorts you won't want to miss. The terrain ranges from leisurely bowls to steep hills that make your heart thump. However, excellent skiing and snowboarding are not all that Lake Tahoe has to offer. Snowmobiling, snowshoe treks, snow tubing, and cross-country treks open up the millions of acres of national forest land waiting to be explored. Ice skating, sleigh rides, and sledding are fun activities close to the Byway. Lake Tahoe also hosts numerous special events all winter long. Snow Fest is a unique experience taking place in the beauty of the High Sierras, with 50 fun and diverse events. The events are not to be missed and include ice-carving competitions, snow-sculpture contests, parades, a polar bear swim in the frigid Lake Tahoe, and an opening night ceremony with a torchlight parade of skiers, fireworks display, a bonfire, and music.

If you prefer warmer weather, Lake Tahoe's links are second to none. Extra altitude makes even the worst golfer feel like a pro, and the breathtaking backdrops and outstanding course architecture will make bogeys seem a little less burdensome. The Lake Tahoe region boasts 12 courses accessible to all levels of play: Bijou Municipal, Glenbrook Golf Course, Lake Tahoe Golf Course, Incline Village Championship Course, The Mountain Course, Northstar-at-Tahoe Golf Course, Ponderosa Golf Course, Old Brockway Golf Course, Resort at Squaw Creek, Tahoe City Golf Course, Tahoe Donner Golf Course, and Tahoe Paradise Golf Course.

Surrounded by national forest lands, wilderness, and state parks, Lake Tahoe possesses some of the country's most spectacular scenery. With almost 300 miles of trails, hikers have plenty of room to roam. Backcountry buffs can trek up waterfall trails, hike along wildflower-carpeted meadows, or visit serene alpine lakes and stunning overlooks of Lake Tahoe. There are trails to suit every ability—flat, steep, and moderate. Looping its way around the lake, the Tahoe Rim Trail, a hiking and equestrian trail, offers 165 miles of trail, with elevations ranging from 6,300 feet to 9,400 feet. This trail is generally moderate in difficulty, with a 10 percent average grade, and provides views of Lake Tahoe, the high desert, and snow-capped peaks of the Sierra Nevada. Trailheads accessible along the Byway include Tahoe Meadows Trailhead to Tunnel Creek Road (Highway 431), Spooner Summit Trailhead (Highway 50), and Spooner Summit South to Kingsbury Grade. The Tunnel Creek Station Road Trail starts at Highway 28 across from Hidden Beach about 1 mile past Ponderosa Ranch (there's no sign, so look for the gate). This is a steep trail road, about 1 1/2 miles each way, located at the ruins of the western portal of the old log flume tunnel. There is limited parking along Highway 28. The Marlette Lake Trail starts near the Spooner Lake Picnic Area at the junction of Highway 28 and 50 at the green metal gate on the east side of Highway 28. This trail is about 5 miles each way to the lake and passes through mostly mild terrain.

A combination of one of the world's top single-track trails, spectacular views, and miles of open backcountry beckons bikers from around the world to the Lake Tahoe basin. The best-known Tahoe bike trail is the spectacular Flume Trail, carved out of the edge of a mountain some 2,000 feet above the lake's stunning east shore. The Flume Trail follows a precarious route dug out of the granite cliffs more than a century ago by laborers developing a water supply and lumber transport for the mines of the Comstock Lode. Today, the 14-mile Flume Trail offers a challenging ride with a 1,000-foot elevation gain and sweeping views, all within Nevada's Lake Tahoe State Park. The common starting point for this trail is Spooner Lake, which features parking and trail information. Located at the junction of Highways 28 and 50, Spooner Lake is a 15-minute drive south from Incline Village. Groves of aspen trees, towering peaks, old-growth pine, and high mountain lakes greet bikers along the Flume Trail. After a quick turn onto a small outlet creek, the trail suddenly clings to a slope overlooking the azure Lake Tahoe. The northern terminus of the trail can take the rider to either Sand Harbor or the Ponderosa Ranch. For the ambitious rider, a loop via Tunnel Creek Road, Red House, and Hobart Lake creates a 25-mile loop back to Marlette Lake, as well as a stunning downhill ride to Spooner.

SCENIC

Lake Tahoe has rightly been called the most beautiful drive in America. Many people find they don't have words to describe its exquisite beauty and often rely upon Mark Twain's well-worded acclaim and praise. After his first vision of the lake, Twain wrote, "The Lake burst upon us—a noble sheet of blue water uplifted six thousand three hundred feet above the level of the sea, and walled in by a rim of snow-clad mountain peaks that towered aloft full three thousand feet higher still! . . . As it lay there with the shadows of the mountains brilliantly photographed upon its still surface I thought it must surely be the fairest picture the whole Earth affords." He also wrote that "Down through the transparency of these great depths, the water was not merely transparent, but dazzlingly, brilliantly so. All objects seen through it had a bright, strong vividness, not only of outline, but of every minute detail, which they would not have had when seen simply through the same depth of atmosphere."

While it has been many years since Mark Twain visited Lake Tahoe, the startling beauty of the area has not diminished. Lake Tahoe still looks like a "beautiful relic of fairy-land forgotten and left asleep in the snowy Sierras when the little elves fled from their ancient haunts and quitted the Earth." Painters find their brushes inadequate to capture the deep-pines crowding the craggy cliffs, the crimson sunsets burnishing the skies, and the clear aquamarine waters reflecting the Sierra Nevada Range swathed in icy snow. Weather cooperates while visitors take in the splendor of their surroundings, and the sun shines an average of 307 days a year. The atmosphere "up here in the clouds is very pure and fine, bracing and delicious. And why shouldn't it be? It's the same the angels breathe." And while the pristine silence of the lake that Twain once enjoyed has been replaced by happy tourists, the majesty of Lake Tahoe still affords solitude and a purely heavenly ambience.

Highlights

To hit the highlights of the Lake Tahoe–Eastshore Drive, consider following this itinerary.

- You may want to begin traveling the Byway at the northern terminus at Crystal Bay along the California/Nevada border. There are several **casinos** in this area to enjoy.

- From here, the highway winds toward **Incline Village,** one of Tahoe's finest communities. A side trip up Mount Rose Highway, approximately 4 miles, leads to a lookout over the entire Tahoe Basin.

- Back on Highway 28, the **Ponderosa Ranch** is the location of TV's legendary *Bonanza* series that made Lake Tahoe famous worldwide. The Ponderosa offers Cartwright Ranch House tours, an Old West town with shops and memorabilia, summer hay-wagon breakfasts, and more.

- The Byway continues south down the east shore. One of Tahoe's most beautiful beaches, **Sand Harbor,** is located here in the Nevada Lake Tahoe State Park. Following the bouldered Nevada shore, the highway continues south through forests of pine and fir. Stop at **Spooner Lake** for wooded picnic areas and a walk along the water. Turn right at the intersection of Highway 50 and head south past historic **Glenbrook,** once a busy logging town and now an exclusive community and golf course.

- Your next landmark is **Cave Rock,** where the highway passes through 25 yards of solid stone. This is a holy spot for the native Washo Indians who put their deceased to rest in the cold waters below the outcropping. Farther along is **Zephyr Cove** with its beautiful old lodge, beach, and tour boats.

- The tour now returns you to South Lake Tahoe and the high-rise hotel/casinos in the **Stateline area;** a perfect place to stop at a restaurant or lounge, take in a show, or try your luck in the casinos.

Las Vegas Strip

NEVADA

An All-American Road

Often referred to as the Jewel of the Desert, Las Vegas has long been recognized as the entertainment vacation capital of the country, and the Las Vegas Strip—at the heart of this playland—sparkles like no other place on Earth. More than 31 million visitors from around the world are drawn to the lights of the Strip each year to experience its unique blend of exciting entertainment, scenic beauty, and lavishly landscaped resorts. An array of theme resorts can transport you to various exotic realms, from a medieval castle to a Parisian sidewalk café, a lakeside Italian village, or a pyramid in ancient Egypt.

The Las Vegas Strip hosts thousands of motorists a week; after you arrive on the Strip, however, you may be surprised to find that it's also a very enjoyable walking environment. The Strip is the only Byway that is more scenic at night than during the day. In fact, 365 days of the year, 24 hours a day, the Neon Trail offers a fascinating foray past spectacular resorts featuring a variety of visual delights. Whether it's pirates plundering, fiery volcanoes spouting, or tropical gardens luring the weary, the Las Vegas Strip offers a variety of fascinating visual experiences that enchant and mesmerize visitors of all ages. The many facets of this corridor make it truly a one-of-a-kind destination.

QUICK FACTS

Length: 4.5 miles.

Time to Allow: From half an hour to several hours.

Best Time to Drive: Las Vegas is warm year-round. The Strip is usually fairly crowded and congested. Nighttime is usually busier than daytime, and holidays are especially busy.

Byway Travel Information: Nevada Commission on Tourism: phone 775/687-4322.

Special Considerations: This is a pedestrian-rich environment, so be on the alert when driving. Consider driving the Byway once each direction. This way, you will be able to view all the sites that line both sides of the street and catch some that you may have missed.

Bicycle/Pedestrian Facilities: Sidewalks line the Strip and provide plenty of room for walking. Cyclists are welcome, but they must observe the same traffic laws as automobiles.

The Byway Story

The Las Vegas Strip tells cultural, historical, recreational, and scenic stories that make it a unique and treasured Byway.

CULTURAL

While Las Vegas is perhaps best known for its gaming culture—the popularity and influence of which have spread to cities all over the world—the Las Vegas Strip possesses many other outstanding cultural amenities. The diversity and virtuosity of the architecture of the hotels and resorts along the Strip are certainly worth noting. Some of the world's most talented architects have created complex fantasylands all along the Strip. Just a few of the more recent projects include reproductions of the streets of New York, a bayside Tuscany village, the canals of Venice, and a replica of the Eiffel Tower and the Arc de Triomphe.

Many of the resorts on the Las Vegas Strip also feature world-class art galleries full of paintings by world-renowned artists, such as Renoir, Monet, and Van Gogh. Other resorts hold galleries of other unique items, like antique automobiles or wax figures. The Guinness World of Records Museum offers an interesting array of the unusual, and the World of Coca-Cola Las Vegas features an interactive storytelling theater.

Various hotels on the Las Vegas Strip feature a variety of top-caliber theatrical and dance shows. Several hotels and casinos host world-class sporting events and concerts featuring top-name entertainers. And no matter where you go on the Strip, you are bound to run into the dazzling light displays that permeate the area. The magical re-creations found along the Byway are the symbols of our society's most fantastic dreams of luxury.

HISTORICAL

The Las Vegas Strip, world-renowned for its neon glitter, possesses an equally colorful historical past. The unique history of Las Vegas is undeniably entwined with the culture of gaming. Gambling was legalized in Nevada in 1931, and the first casino opened downtown that same year. Competition was intense, and casino builders soon were looking to land outside the city limits just south of downtown along Highway 91 (the Old Los Angeles Highway), which is now known as the Las Vegas Strip.

Most of the Las Vegas Strip is not really located within the Las Vegas city limits, but along a corridor of South Las Vegas Boulevard located in unincorporated Clark County. The area was sparsely developed until 1938, when the first resort property was built 4 miles south of downtown Las Vegas at the corner of San Francisco Avenue (now Sahara) and Highway 91 (South Las Vegas Boulevard). Reportedly, city officials had denied licenses to certain businessmen with questionable connections who had applied to build a casino downtown. Undaunted, they decided to build outside the city limits, just south of the downtown district.

In 1941, construction began on El Rancho Vegas resort at the corner of San Francisco Avenue and Highway 91. The original El Rancho Vegas introduced a new style of recreation and entertainment to the Nevada desert by combining lodging, gambling, restaurants, entertainment, shops, a travel agency, horseback riding, and swimming in one resort. El Rancho Vegas was followed a year later by the Last Frontier Resort Hotel & Casino. The well-known Little Church of the West was originally constructed in the resort's Frontier Village. Listed on the National Register of Historic Places, the small chapel has survived four moves on the Strip.

One of the Strip's more colorful (and infamous) characters, Ben "Bugsy" Siegel (reputed hit man for New York mobster Lucky Luciano), oversaw the construction of the fabulous Flamingo Hotel, the third major (and most extravagant) resort to be built on the Strip. Although Siegel met his unfortunate demise soon after the resort's 1946 opening, his prophecies for the future of Las Vegas came true. This new popular playground of Hollywood stars prospered, with the Flamingo setting the stage for the many luxurious resorts yet to be imagined.

As the 1950s began, only four major resorts stood along the Strip, but three more major players were about to hit the scene. The Desert Inn, the Sahara, and the Sands all arrived on the Strip in the early 1950s, further enhancing the Strip's image as a self-contained playground by featuring elaborate tennis courts, an 18-hole golf course, larger casinos, and fabulous showrooms with Broadway's and Hollywood's brightest stars. Las Vegas has continued to build on this legacy, developing newer and more elaborate resorts every year to make certain that Las Vegas retains the image of the most fabulous playground on Earth.

RECREATIONAL

The simplest and easiest recreation on the Strip is strolling and sightseeing along the Boulevard. Intriguing arrays of fantasylands in lush surroundings welcome you to the Strip. But the excitement only begins with sightseeing. From comfortable and plush hotels to exciting displays of lights and fountains, Las Vegas creates a dreamlike lifestyle with color, sound, and light all combined to make the experience on the Las Vegas Strip memorable.

For the more adventuresome, roller coasters featured at several hotels provide a ride that twists, loops, and turns to your delight. Other resorts provide 3-D ride films appealing to the senses of sight, sound, and motion. Many of these rides feature the latest technologies for extra thrills. Most of the resorts along the Strip offer displays of grandeur for every visitor to enjoy. Anyone driving the Byway can stop to see erupting volcanoes, dueling ships, dancing fountains, circus acts, and lush tropical gardens.

In addition to a variety of theatrical and dance shows, the resorts offer varied spectator sports, such as boxing matches. There isn't a resort on the Strip that doesn't offer visitors every amenity imaginable. World-class spas, pools, and exercise rooms are as enticing as the casinos. When you aren't searching for slot machines, you may choose to browse through the many stores and boutiques each resort has to offer. You will find everything from designer fashion to specialty candies to Las Vegas souvenirs. Whatever you choose to do, you can find it in Las Vegas.

SCENIC

As one of the most geographically isolated major cities in the continental United States, Las Vegas provides you with an extraordinary visual experience. The matchless Las Vegas Strip serves as the gateway to a host of memorable experiences that are distinctly Las Vegas. The Strip's incredible array of resorts are constructed around themes that transport visitors to different exotic realms, including a medieval castle, the Parisian Eiffel Tower, a lakeside Italian village, and a pyramid in ancient Egypt. Day or night, the Neon Trail provides a fascinating foray past spectacular resorts that offer a variety of visual delights to pedestrians and motorists alike.

Highlights

The Southern Las Vegas Strip Walking Tour begins at South Las Vegas Blvd and Russell Road, although you can go the opposite way by reading this list from the bottom up.

- The famous "Welcome to Fabulous Las Vegas" sign announces that you're on the right track. On the east side of the Strip, you see **The Little Church of the West,** the site of many celebrity weddings and a favorite place today to have the perfect wedding.

- Park the car at the free parking garage at **Mandalay Bay** (most of the large hotels offer plenty of covered free parking). Explore the tropical themed hotel, including a fun sand and surf beach. Mandalay Bay is one of the newest hotels on the Strip (built in 1999), and that makes it a popular attraction.

- From Mandalay Bay, you can walk north to **Luxor,** the great black glass pyramid. (If you prefer, hop on the free tram that takes you right to the front doors of Luxor—you may want to save your energy for later in the trip.) While at Luxor, don't miss the **King Tut Tomb exhibit**—an exact replica of the ancient Egyptian pharaoh's tomb. A rotating **IMAX** film experience is also a popular attraction here. This unique hotel is amazing and has one of the largest atriums in the world.

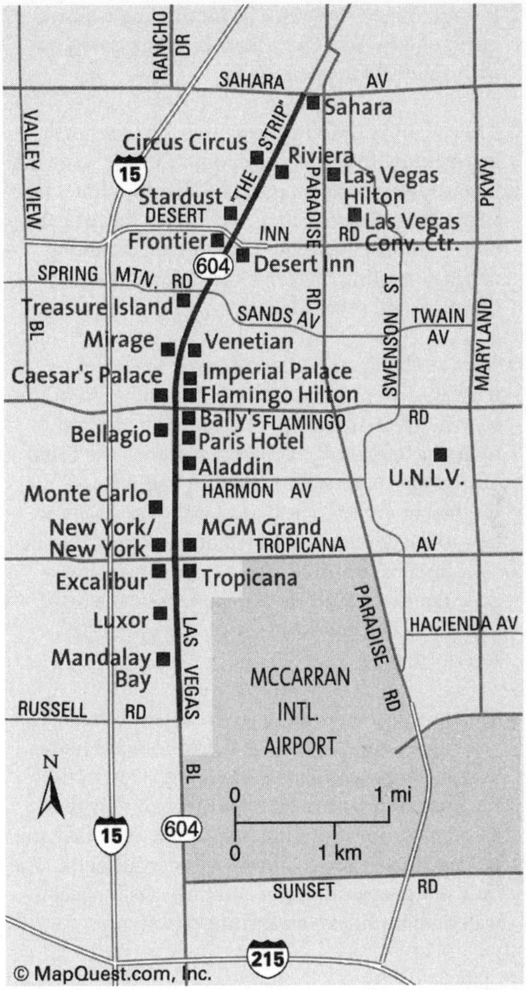

- After spending time at Luxor, hop on the tram that takes you over to **Excalibur.** This is the place for an exciting dinner and show. The majestic castle offers adventure at its **Fantasy Faire Midway**—an arena of games appropriate for everyone in the family.

- After spending time at the medieval castle, cross the over street walkway into 1930s- and '40s-inspired **New York-New York.** Billed as "the Greatest City in Las Vegas," New York-New York has attractions that are all themed to the New York life. Park Avenue shopping, a fast-paced Manhattan roller coaster, and Greenwich Village eateries help keep the theme intact.

- It's not time to stop yet. **The Monte Carlo,** just north of New York-New York, is just as classy, but with a purely European twist.

- After a jaunt to Monte Carlo, walk farther north, getting close to the halfway point. The big lake and fantastic fountains are part of **Bellagio,** a hotel that strives for utter perfection. Check out the art gallery here—it houses some fantastic pieces, including original paintings by Van Gogh, Monet, Renoir, Cezanne, and other masters.

- Now, at Flamingo Boulevard, cross the street to the east—over to **Paris.** This is the midpoint of the tour, and this area is full of areas to sit and rest or to grab a bite to eat. While at Paris, tour the **Eiffel Tower.** This is an exact replica, in half scale, of the original in France. The plans for the original were lent to the developers of the hotel so they could be as accurate as possible. There's also a two-thirds-scale replica of ***L'Arc de Triomphe*** near the hotel entrance—complete with Napoleon's victories inscribed on it.

- The next stop on this tour is the **MGM Grand.** This very large hotel strives to make visitors feel like stars. Elegance abounds at this hotel. Don't miss the **Lion Habitat** here: a walk-through tour that showcases some beautiful lions, some of which are descendants of Metro, the MGM marquee lion. The only thing separating you and the lions is a glass wall on both sides—an exciting experience.

- Just south of the MGM Grand is the famous **Tropicana,** home to the longest-running show on the Strip.

- After the Tropicana, cross the street again and take the tram from Excalibur to Mandalay Bay. At Mandalay Bay, get back in your car and cross the street to see the **Glass Pool Inn.** This motel was originally called The Mirage but sold the rights to its name to the much larger entity many years ago. The motel features an unusual above-ground pool with portal windows that has been featured in many movies.

- Finish off the tour of the Southern Las Vegas Strip by driving north back past the Tropicana and MGM Grand and beyond. The drive provides amazing views that you may have missed along the walk.

Pyramid Lake Scenic Byway

NEVADA

Pyramid Lake is a bright jewel in the arid Nevada landscape. Fish, animal, and plant life are sustained by its 300-foot-deep waters and by the fresh water flowing in the Truckee River. In addition to the cui-ui fish, the lake is known for the Lahontan cutthroat trout that the tribe manages through its fisheries program. The mountains surrounding the lake support deer, antelope, and bighorn sheep. The lake is also a resting place for a variety of migrating waterfowl. Anaho Island, a National Wildlife Refuge, is the breeding ground for the largest colony of American white pelicans. It is also home to a variety of other shorebirds. The tufa formations found at this lake are some of the lake's most distinctive natural features. These formations are calcium carbonate deposits formed by precipitation over hot springs. They include the Pyramid (which gives the lake its name) and the Needles.

The Byway Story

The Pyramid Lake Scenic Byway tells archaeological, cultural, historical, natural, recreational, and scenic stories that make it a unique and treasured Byway.

ARCHAEOLOGICAL

Since time immemorial, the Northern Paiute people were comprised of many bands that occupied northwestern Nevada and southeastern Oregon. By roaming in small, family-centered groups, these remarkable people developed an ingenious technology that made life possible in a high desert environment. One band centered its territory around Pyramid Lake and were called Kuyuidokado, or "cui-ui eaters." Cui-ui is an indigenous fish species found only in Pyramid Lake.

On display at the Pyramid Lake Visitors Center are tools and artifacts that reflect the ancient culture that was essential to these people's survival. Much of the collection has established a timeline for archaeologists in determining when these tools were used.

Quick Facts

Length: 37 miles.

Time to Allow: 2 hours to 1 day.

Best Time to Drive: Year-round; high season is July and August.

Special Considerations: Many of the road shoulders are sandy, and vehicles can get stuck easily. The best place to fill up with gasoline is in Wadsworth, near I-80.

CULTURAL

The Pyramid Lake Paiute Tribe is governed by ten tribal council members who are elected biannually in December and on staggered two-year terms. The majority of enrolled tribal members, numbering around 1,700 people, reside on the reservation, and approximately 12 percent of this membership reside in other areas throughout the western United States.

Given the strong cultural ties between the lake and the Paiute Tribe, the cultural attributes of the Byway are best described by the following speech given by a Tribal Chairman during Cui-Day in 1993:

"Welcome to our festival. This gathering was an annual time of celebration for our people, the Kuyuidokado, cui-ui eaters. It was in recognition of the renewal of life in the spring, which included the renewal of our lives as well. There was a time when the cui-ui run meant the continuation of our existence. If there was no cui-ui, a winter of hardship and great difficulty would follow for our people. The absence of a run would mean many of our people would not see the next spring. Our dependence on the land and our traditional way of life changed with the arrival of non-Indians. This change did not always come as a way of choice, but as a necessity. Our ability to live by our traditional way was no longer possible. This was the result of both the cultural and environmental changes brought by this new culture.

"There was a time when heavy snow in the mountains meant the river would flow and we could expect a good harvest of fish. But this pattern changed this century. Dams built on the river kept the snow water from reaching the Lake. And our cui-ui that used to follow the water up the river began to diminish. Feelings of despair replaced that feeling of anticipation in the spring.

"Our Tribe's repeat attempts to return the flow of the river to the Lake met with failure. Our contact with the non-Indian community was fraught with conflict. But today we welcome the non-Indian community to our celebration because we believe we can share the waters of Truckee [River] and [Pyramid] Lake in a way that would benefit all of our communities.

"There is no doubt that our Tribe's culture and society has changed over the years, and our past way of life will not be our future. But we will survive as a people, and the cui-ui will be part of our culture. Much as the eagle is the symbol of freedom for the people of the United States, the cui-ui represents life for our people. It is a sad statement that both of these animals are endangered. We as cultures must work together to see they survive."

HISTORICAL

Hundreds of years before white man traveled through Nevada, the Paiute Indians lived near Pyramid Lake, then called Coo-yu-ee Pah. According to a Paiute legend, the lake was also called Wano, meaning a conical basket turned upside down. This name stems from the legend of the Stone Mother, which says a grief-stricken mother cried so much over her sons, her tears filled her basket and overflowed to fill the entire lake.

The Paiute people have always lived near the lake. Their traditional culture was centered around the lake, and they were called Cui-ui Ticutta, or "cui-ui eaters." The lake was the center of the Paiute tribe's life. They depended on the cui-ui fish to survive. Unfortunately, in 1859, the Paiute Indian Reservation was formed, giving only a fraction of the land to the Paiute people. They continued to live as they had been and create a culture rich in history and family.

The present name of the lake was given by John C. Fremont on January 10, 1844. The first band of white explorers stumbled upon the lake after a difficult journey through the harsh desert that lasted several weeks. They pitched their camp near a striking 400-foot-high rock island outcropping. Fremont wrote in his journal on January 14, "We encamped on the shore, opposite a very remarkable rock in the lake, which attracted our attention for many miles. It rose, according to our estimate, 600 feet above the water, and, from the point we viewed it, presented a pretty exact outline of the great pyramid of Cheops. This striking feature suggested a name for the lake, and I called it Pyramid Lake." The explorers were also captivated by the stone needles, pinnacles, and steaming sulfur springs, which the Paiute people still hold sacred today.

NATURAL

The present-day vision of Pyramid Lake took millions of years to form. It is the remnant of an inland sea, Lake Lahontan, that covered over 8,000 square miles about 11 million years ago. Today, Pyramid Lake is 26 miles long, 4 to 11 miles wide, and 350 feet deep at its deepest point. It has been called the world's most beautiful desert lake and presents a range of colors from turquoise to emerald green to deep blue. Because Pyramid Lake used to be part of an inland sea, it is a very alkaline lake, the type found in semi-arid or arid environments. Visiting the lake is almost like going to the beach. Unlike the beach, however, Pyramid Lake has a number of interesting formations scattered around and throughout its waters. The lake is also home to a variety of wildlife that visitors usually don't see at the beach.

Tufa needs just the right kind of conditions to form, and Pyramid Lake is the world's largest producer of tufa rock. It forms when the following environment is present: a stable lake, a source of calcium, high water temperatures, and a stable bedrock or substrate. When all of these conditions are present, all that is necessary is a branch or rock around which the carbonate can form. Pyramid Lake demonstrates its age through the tufa formations. Changes in color and texture of the rock, as well as primary sill level changes, also indicate what kinds of weather Pyramid Lake has survived, including winds, droughts, floods, and glacial activity.

Other tufa formations attract attention, too. The primary area, the Needles, is located at the northwest end of the lake, in the hot springs area. This area of continuing geothermal activity contains more tufa depositions than anywhere else in the world. Other types of formations exist around the lake, such as the Stone Mother and her basket. The basket is actually a rounded, hollowed rock, but a legend exists about the Stone Mother that goes like this: In the ancient days, a mother had four sons. They could not get along and were forced to leave. Their mother, in terrible grief, sat in the middle of the desert and cried so many tears that they filled the lake. She was in such despair she just dropped her basket beside her, and then the mother and her basket turned to stone.

Anaho Island, located in Pyramid Lake, is a National Wildlife Refuge that is one of only eight nesting grounds for white pelicans in North America. As many as 9,500 pelicans nest on the island in the spring, so both the federal government and the Paiute Tribe carefully protect the island from intruding boats or visitors. The best place to view the pelicans is from the southeastern or southwestern shores with binoculars; the best time of year to see them is March through October. Numerous other types of birds, including double-crested cormorants, California gulls, blue herons, golden and bald eagles, rock wrens, owls, falcons, snowy egrets, and California quail, draw bird-watchers.

Because the nature of the lake is so well protected and preserved by the Paiute Tribe, an uncommon amount of wildlife lives undisturbed at Pyramid Lake. Not only do many birds live here, but also burros, big horn sheep, bobcats, wild horses, mountain lions, pronghorn antelope, coyotes, and jack rabbits. There are few spots in the county where visitors can see such a range of wildlife.

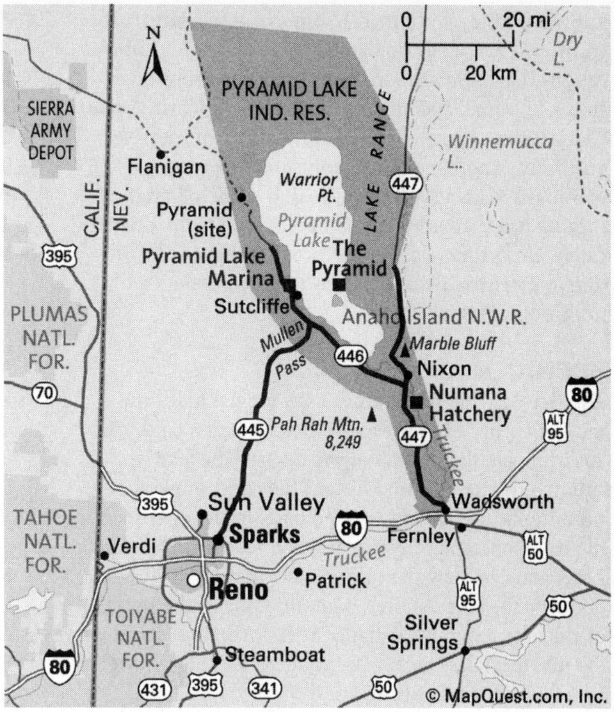

RECREATIONAL

Pyramid Lake offers all kinds of opportunities to enjoy the surrounding nature. You can hike, rock climb, ride horseback, backpack, and do so much more. And after a full day of activity, hot springs at the north end of the lake among the needle rocks allow you to relax while enjoying Pyramid Lake's famous tufa formations. The lake itself draws the most recreationists; it is a favorite of anglers, who throughout the history of the lake have gone from fishing as a means of survival to fishing as a business venture to fishing for sport.

Fishing at Pyramid Lake is an experience all its own. The water is unlike most lake water and a startling pastel blue. The surroundings are pure desert, with little vegetation. After some practice, many fishermen have discovered that the best way to catch fish in Pyramid Lake is from the top of a five-foot ladder or other tall object. The fish come into the shallows, and the added altitude gives anglers a better view, as well as a longer casting range. Be careful, though. While you can see the fish, the fish can also see you. Fish often roam the edges of the lake near a series of ledges or drop-offs. If you stand on a tall object and wear polarizing lens, you can actually see the fish take the fly ten feet away. Pyramid Lake has also been known for the size of its fish, especially the cutthroat trout. In 1925, a Paiute named Johnny Skimmerhorn caught the world's record cutthroat—a 41-pounder. In the '20s and '30s, photographs show celebrities like Clark Gable struggling to hold up a pair of massive cutthroat. Another photograph shows a group of Nevadans peeking out from behind a line of shimmering fish that stretches eight feet long from a day's catch. Unfortunately, the fish are no longer as large due to extensive fishing, but 5- to 10-pounders are not uncommon.

SCENIC

Travelers driving to Pyramid Lake for the first time may be surprised at the scenic beauty that a cold, blue lake offers in the middle of the desert. The lake is situated in a valley amid distant hills and snowcapped mountains. It is an unexpected oasis in the middle of the dry landscape of Nevada. Upon reaching Pyramid Lake, you can view the tufa rock formations that decorate the lake's shores, including one in the middle of the lake, a pyramid-shaped rock formation standing 400 feet tall. The lake was named for this feature by John C. Fremont in 1844.

A drive around Pyramid Lake offers an enchanting view of this remnant of an ancient inland sea that changes from green to turquoise to deep blue. The sunset casts a red glow on the lake and surrounding formations that you can behold at scenic turnouts. During the day, just the sight of the deep blue waters of Pyramid Lake is a refreshing experience for hot travelers.

Highlights

On this Pyramid Lake must-see tour, you can start in either Sparks or Wadsworth, because the driving directions given here start and end in the Reno/Sparks area.

- Start your trip by taking I-40 to West Wadsworth. Follow Highway 427 into town, and then drive north along Highway 447, following the course of the Truckee River. You can stop at the **Numana Hatchery Visitor Center** to learn about the area's natural history and the tribe's fisheries program or take a walk along the wetlands nature trail, where you experience the unique habitats of the river valley.

- As you continue to drive north, you will come over a rise and see the lake spread out before you. Just ahead is the **Scenic Byway Visitor Center and Tribal Museum.** From here, you can take a side trip north on Highway 447 into the town of **Nixon,** site of the Tribal Headquarters, and beyond to **Marble Bluff** and **Lake Winnemucca.**

- You can also head west on Highway 446 toward Sutcliffe. Highway 446 follows the west shore of **Pyramid Lake,** with plenty of beaches for swimming, fishing, or enjoying a picnic lunch. In **Sutcliffe,** you'll find the **Pyramid Lake Marina,** with a visitor center and museum, as well as stores and visitor services. North of Sutcliffe are more beaches, especially at **Pelican Point** and **Warrior Point.**

- Returning south from Sutcliffe, take Highway 445 south toward Sparks. As you drive up toward **Mullen Pass,** you can stop at the turnout on the left for a scenic vista of the lake. If you get a chance to visit here as the sun sets, the Pyramid, Anaho Island, and the slopes of the Lake Range may be bathed in a red glow, offering a dramatic counterpoint to the urban glitter awaiting you as you return to Reno.

Billy the Kid Trail

NEW MEXICO

The Lincoln County area surrounding the Billy the Kid Trail is rich in history. It has been home to Billy the Kid, the Lincoln County War, the Mescalero Apache tribe, Kit Carson, "Black Jack" Pershing, the Buffalo Soldiers, the world's richest quarter horse race, and Smokey Bear. The area is also rich in tradition, as well as in recreational opportunities.

The Byway Story

The Billy the Kid Trail tells archaeological, cultural, historical, natural, recreational, and scenic stories that make it a unique and treasured Byway.

ARCHAEOLOGICAL

A fingerprint, carbon-dated to be roughly 28,000 years old, was recently discovered in a cave 70 miles south of Ruidoso in the Tularosa Basin. It is the earliest known evidence of man's presence in North America. Members of the Paleo-Indian cultures converged in the area from 9000 BC to 6000 BC to hunt the woolly mammoth and now-extinct species of bison that roamed the area.

> **QUICK FACTS**
>
> **Length:** 84 miles.
>
> **Time to Allow:** 2 hours.
>
> **Best Time to Drive:** Summer and fall; high season is July and August.
>
> **Byway Travel Information:** Village of Ruidoso: phone 505/258-4343; Byway local Web site: www.zianet.com/billythekid.
>
> **Special Considerations:** The altitude along this Byway ranges from 6,500 to 7,000 feet above sea level. There are few, if any, seasonal limitations. All of the roadways are paved, and snow is cleared in the wintertime when there is significant accumulation.
>
> **Bicycle/Pedestrian Facilities:** Sidewalks and bicycle trails are available in some of the communities along the Byway. Some areas of the roadway also have shoulders for pedestrians.

CULTURAL

While many consider Santa Fe the cultural capital of New Mexico, Lincoln County is more than willing to rival this claim. Spectacular annual events showcase the cultural dynamics along the Billy the Kid Trail throughout the year: you can always find something brewing! From chuck wagon cookouts to arts festivals, from Blues festivals to community concerts, Lincoln County offers year-round cultural enjoyment.

Some of the best art in New Mexico can be found in Ruidoso. The Harris Poll has recognized the Ruidoso Art Festival, held each year in late July, as one of the most outstanding juried art shows in the Southwest. The cool pines create a beautiful mountain setting for spectacular art. Over 125 accomplished, professional artists display paintings, drawings, photography, glass, porcelain, woodwork, metalwork, jewelry, batik, pottery, weaving, fabric, leather, and sculpture.

If you have a kick for western cooking and music, be sure to catch the Lincoln County Cowboy Symposium. Held at Ruidoso Downs the second weekend of October, the

Symposium gathers the world's finest cowboy poets, musicians, chuck wagon cooks, and artisans.

For a better glimpse at the real West and American Indian cultures, be sure to see the Mescalero Apache Ceremonial Dances. Held during the first week of July, these ceremonial dances celebrate the Apache Spirit.

The cultural qualities of Lincoln County would be unfinished without mentioning the Spencer Theater for the Performing Arts. Opened in 1997, the Spencer Theater creates a year-round venue for world-class performances in theater, music, and dance. An aristocrat among theaters, the $22 million structure is splendid and elegant, yet intimate and welcoming.

HISTORICAL

The largely mysterious character of Billy the Kid and many other Old West icons lived in Lincoln County, giving the Byway the flair it has today. Henry McCarty, better known as Bonney or Billy the Kid, is the most well-known person from this area. His involvement in the Lincoln County War ensured that he would be remembered as one of the greatest stories of the Old West.

Billy the Kid is believed to have been born in New York City sometime in 1859 or 1860. His family moved to Indiana, and then to Wichita, Kansas. In 1874, his mother died, and Billy the Kid was placed in foster homes and worked washing dishes. He soon ran into trouble with the law and was sent to jail, only to escape through the chimney. Billy the Kid wandered from ranch to ranch, and eventually wound up in trouble with the law again when he killed a man at a saloon in Arizona.

When Billy the Kid returned to New Mexico, he and his gang of rustlers became embroiled with the feud going on between James Dolan, John Tunstall, and Alex McSween. The Kid started on Dolan's side, but when he was thrown in jail, he made a deal with Tunstall and became a part of the Regulators, a group that took the law into their own hands after some of their men had been killed.

After the Lincoln County War, Billy the Kid made his living by gambling and rustling cattle. He spent his time eluding the law, usually from Pat Garrett, whose job was to hunt for Billy the Kid. In December 1880, the Kid surrendered to Garrett and was put in jail in Lincoln County. On April 28, 1881, he made his escape to Fort Sumner, only to be followed in July by Garrett. Billy the Kid died in Pete Maxwell's bedroom at the hand of Garrett on July 14, 1881.

One small ferrotype is the only existing authentic photograph of Billy the Kid. Taken by an unknown itinerant photographer outside Beaver Smith's saloon in Old Fort Sumner in 1879, it reveals (as the Las Vegas Gazzette reported in 1880) a young man " … about 5 feet 8 or 9 inches tall, slightly built and lithe, weighing about 140; a frank open countenance, looking like a school boy, with the traditional silky fuzz on his upper lip; clear, blue eyes, with a roguish snap about them; light hair and complexion. He is, in all, quite a handsome looking fellow, the only imperfection being two prominent teeth, and he has agreeable and winning ways." The rumpled hat and layers of utilitarian clothing, especially the oversized, open-weave sweater, immediately clash with Hollywood's images of the outlaw. In the photo, he wears a gambler's pinkie ring on his left hand that means he may have cheated at cards. His colt pistol jaunts from his right hip—because the photo was accidentally reversed for many years, people thought the Kid was a lefty. Historians who examined the photo knew that the gun really was on his right hip by looking at the right-loading breech on his Winchester carbine. That's the only way Winchester manufactured them.

The Kid's real name, Henry McCarty, is rather ordinary, but his alias carries a lyrical quality that still gallops across the high plains of our imagination. Of all of America's outlaws, the name of Billy the Kid churns up powerful images and emotions that are forever linked to the Old West.

NATURAL

A drive along the Billy the Kid Trail not only provides Byway enthusiasts with glimpses into New Mexico's desperado past, but also offers grand views of the natural treasures afforded this region. From towering snowcapped peaks in the Lincoln National Forest to the river bottoms of the Rio Bonito and Rio Ruidoso rivers, the Billy the Kid Trail deals you a royal flush of nature's beauty.

The Lincoln National Forest is host to two prominent mountain ranges, the Sacramento Mountains to the south and the Capitan Mountains to the north. These ranges surround the Billy the Kid Trail and provide natural views guaranteed to beat the house. Each of these mountainous ranges holds towering peaks in an otherwise flat and arid region. Capitan Peak (10,083 feet) and Sierra Blanca (11,973 feet) provide stunning views and are solid bets for viewing wildlife.

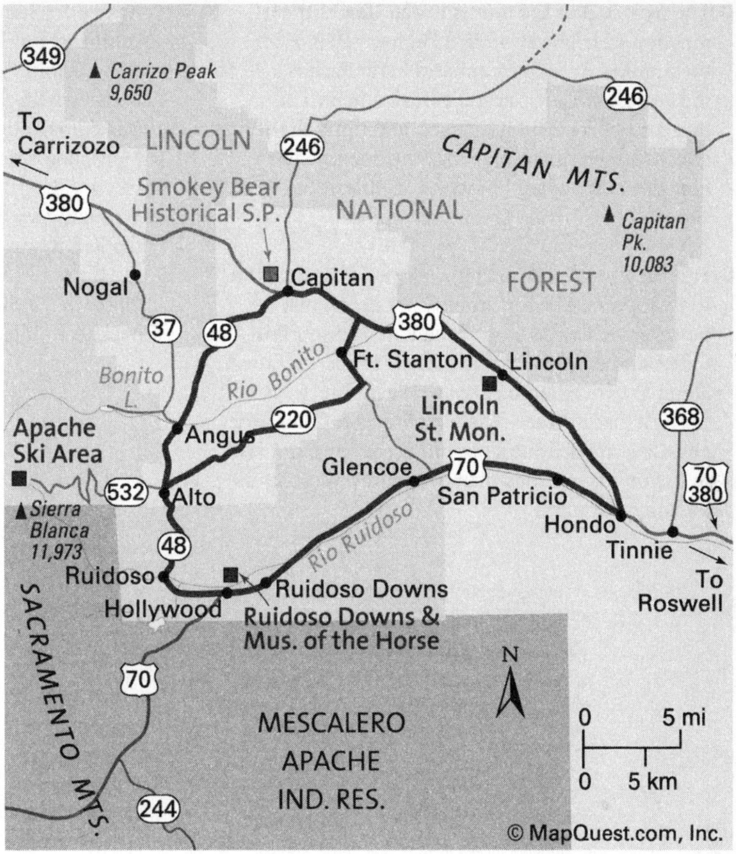

RECREATIONAL

The Billy the Kid Trail features many recreational opportunities through natural resources as well as man-made recreational features and cultural attractions. The historic district of Lincoln, the Museum of the Horse, Fort Stanton, the Spencer Theater for the Performing Arts, the Ruidoso Downs Race Track, the Smokey Bear Museum and State Park in Capitan, and Ski Apache all lend appeal to the area.

As wild as the West (and kids) can be, the Museum of the Horse is a place the whole family will enjoy. The hands-on displays let kids of all ages get a true feel for history. Visitors can climb in the saddle and sit in the starting gates just like real jockeys, or they can try on period Western clothing and brightly colored jockey silks. Practice your draw (with crayons, that is) at the special children's coloring area.

SCENIC

The Billy the Kid Trail travels through a region marked by exceptional natural beauty and diversity. From grassy plains to dense pine forests, the region is known for its stunning views and cool mountain climate. Teeming with fish and wildlife, this area beckons hunters, anglers, skiers, and photographers from around the country. Visually, it is breathtakingly different from the arid desert that surrounds it.

Highlights

Consider taking the following historic tour of Billy the Kid country.

- This tour of Billy the Kid country begins at the **Byway Visitor Center.** The center is located on Highway 70 in Ruidoso Downs. Spend time here viewing the exhibits and talking with the informative helpers at the center. A gift shop is available here, too.

- Right next door to the Visitors Center is the **Hubbard Museum of the American West.** Here, exhibits, artifacts, and fine art tell of the special history of the area.

- Heading west on Highway 70, you pass through the village of **Ruidoso,** and then turn north on Highway 48. Traveling about 26 miles along Highway 48, notice the beautiful Sierra Blanca to the west.

- The next stop of the tour is in **Capitan** at the junction of Highway 48 and Highway 380. Here, the **Smokey Bear Museum and State Park** is a must-see; Smokey is actually buried here. The museum offers exhibits, games, and films about fire safety. Of particular interest is the documentary film about the life of Smokey available at the Park Theater.

- Traveling southeast on Highway 380, **Fort Stanton** soon appears. The fort itself is not accessible; however, be sure to stop at the Fort Stanton Post Office and speak with Willie Mae Hobbs, an expert about the Fort Stanton area who can direct you to the best places to see. The **Fort Stanton Cemetery and Cave** are definite stops along the tour. If a visit to the cave is in order, plan to spend several hours or camp overnight.

- After Fort Stanton, along Highway 380, drive southeast until you arrive in the village of **Lincoln.** The Lincoln County War started here, and this is also where Billy the Kid made his last escape. Museums and markers are all over this village that looks almost exactly as it did in the 1850s.

- Wrapping up a visit in Lincoln, finish the Billy the Kid Byway by continuing down Highway 380 to Highway 70 in **Hondo.** Then, drive west on Highway 70 through San Patricio, Glencoe, and back to Ruidoso Downs.

El Camino Real

NEW MEXICO

One of the most important of the historic trails of New Mexico, El Camino Real is not only the first European road in what is now the United States, but for many years it was the longest road in North America. The northern portions of El Camino Real followed the Rio Grande Pueblo Indian Trail, which existed for centuries before the Spanish explorers arrived. The land area along El Camino Real has been a meeting ground of peoples and a haven of cultural diversity through the centuries.

El Camino Real follows the Rio Grande River from the US/Mexico border to Santa Fe. It traverses a land rich in history and culture. The scenic beauty of El Camino Real is as varied and colorful as its culture, history, and people. From the low-lying flatlands of the south to the soaring peaks of the northern mountains, the terrain climbs 10,000 feet in altitude, creating a landscape of dramatic contrasts.

QUICK FACTS

Length: 299 miles.

Time to Allow: 9 hours.

Best Time to Drive: Spring and fall.

Byway Travel Information: Albuquerque Chamber of Commerce: phone 505/842-9003.

Special Considerations: The weather in the Santa Fe area is warm in the summer but cold in the winter due to higher elevations. During the winter, there are frequent snowstorms. An especially dangerous area during a snowstorm is La Bajada, located south of Santa Fe en route to Albuquerque. Snowstorms usually occur from November through February, and mild winters are very infrequent. As you travel farther south and the elevation decreases, the temperature increases on a year-round trend. With the exception of possible bad weather conditions, the roads are open and in good condition all year.

Bicycle/Pedestrian Facilities: El Camino Real parallels Interstate 25. This allows access for pedestrians and bicycles in most areas of the Byway.

The Byway Story

El Camino Real tells archaeological, cultural, historical, natural, recreational, and scenic stories that make it a unique and treasured Byway.

ARCHAEOLOGICAL

Many archaeological attractions are found along El Camino Real in New Mexico. Kuana Pueblo was one of the Rio Grande Valley villages visited by Francisco Vasquez de Coronado in 1540. He called this region the Tiquex Province because its inhabitants spoke a common language, Tiwa. Abandoned before the 1680 Pueblo Revolt against Spanish rule, this large and important site, called the Coronado State Monument, has been excavated and partially restored.

The San Miguel mission in Santa Fe was established in the early 1600s. Records of its early history were destroyed during the Pueblo Revolt, but the adobe walls were left unharmed. In the early 1700s, the mission walls were reinforced with stone buttresses. An audio presentation is available for visitors.

Over 15,000 petroglyphs (rock drawings) have been carved into the lava rock that covers the mesa west of the Rio Grande. The earliest of these rock drawings were made by prehistoric inhabitants almost 3,000 years ago. Many others were added by Pueblo peoples, and more were added later by Spanish explorers and settlers. This gallery of ancient art is interpreted at Petroglyph National Monument.

CULTURAL

The cultural landscape along El Camino Real includes a rich variety of people and places. A number of American Indian Pueblos played a significant role in the history of El Camino Real, particularly in establishing trade routes before the arrival of the Spanish. Some Pueblos are open to the public year-round and encourage tourism and recreation. Others are open only by invitation during special events (such as feast day celebrations and dances). In addition, the cultural history of New Mexico and El Camino Real can be enjoyed at a number of museums throughout the Byway, including the Maxwell Museum of Anthropology in Albuquerque and the Geronimo Springs Museum in Truth or Consequences.

HISTORICAL

El Camino Real, also called the Royal Highway of the Interior Lands, linked New Mexico with New Spain (Mexico) in the Spanish colonial period (1598-1821), the Mexico national period (1821-1848), and the US Territorial period (1848-1912). El Camino Real ran from Mexico City to Chihuahua City, then crossed the desert to El Paso del Norte on what is now the US-Mexico border. After reaching El Paso del Norte, it more or less paralleled the Rio Grande (called Rio Bravo del Norte) as far as Santa Fe in northern New Mexico.

El Camino Real is one of the most important historic trails in New Mexico. The northern portions of El Camino Real followed the Rio Grande Pueblo Indian Trail, which existed for centuries before the Spanish explorers arrived. This route allowed the Pueblo Indians of New Mexico to have interregional trade with the pre-Columbian Indian civilizations of Mesoamerica. Throughout the Byway, you'll discover many historic places to visit.

NATURAL

The Lower Sonoran life zone covers much of the southern quarter of El Camino Real. At an altitude below 4,500 feet, these arid flatlands support cholla, prickly pear, creosote, and yucca, along with cottonwood, olive, and cedar trees. The Upper Sonoran life zone, ranging in elevation from 4,500 to 6,500 feet, encompasses the northern two-thirds of New Mexico. As in the Lower Sonoran, cacti and desert grasses thrive, but piñon and oak trees replace the yucca and creosote. In Santa Fe, the Transition zone (6,500 to 8,500 feet) consists of ponderosa pine, oak, juniper, spruce, and Douglas fir.

You'll find many natural features along El Camino Real, including the Sandia Mountains and other mountain ranges, many national forests, and several national wildlife refuges.

RECREATIONAL

El Camino Real provides a wealth of recreational sites and facilities for visitors to enjoy. From the Bosque del Apache and Caballo Lake in the south to Cochiti and Isleta lakes in the north, recreational sites lure many outdoor enthusiasts to the Land of Enchantment. Elephant Butte Lake State Park, the largest lake and park in New Mexico, hosts over a million visitors every year.

SCENIC

The scenic beauty of the Camino Real is as diverse and colorful as its culture, history, and people. From the low-lying flatlands of the south to the soaring peaks of the northern mountains, the terrain climbs 10,000 feet in altitude, creating a landscape of dramatic contrasts.

Highlights

This El Camino Real must-see tour begins in Santa Fe and continues south to Las Cruces. If you're traveling in the other direction, simply start at the bottom of the list and work your way up.

- The town of **Santa Fe** offers a bevy of sights, sounds, foods, and festivals. Stop for an hour or a week—you'll never tire of the offerings here.

- A visit to **Pecos National Historic Park** just south of Santa Fe is a great stop to learn about 10,000 years of history, including the ancient Pueblo of Pecos, two Spanish colonial missions, and the site of the Civil War battle of Glorieta Pass. Visits to nearby **Bandelier National Monument** and **Fort Union** are also fantastic adventures.

- Venturing south toward Albuquerque, be sure to stop at **Coronado State Park** near **Bernalillo.** Once in **Albuquerque,** stop in at **Petroglyph National Monument** before visiting this rich and diverse city.

- Shortly south of Albuquerque, stop at the **Isleta Pueblo.** Take time to examine the amazing art produced there—a treat best appreciated in person.

- A small side trip will bring a great afternoon at the **Salinas Pueblo Missions National Monument** in Abo. Passing into Soccorro County, the landscape flattens a little, and the Byway is surrounded by National Wildlife refuges, including **Bosque Del Apache** just south of San Antonio and Laborcita.

- Stop in the town of **Truth or Consequences** (T or C, for short), but visit **Fort Carig** first. And don't forget the **Geronimo Springs Museum** in downtown T or C.

- Back on El Camino Real, stop at **Elephant Butte State Park** in Elephant Butte, and then head south toward **Las Cruces.** On Interstate 10, head east toward Alamogordo, where a real treat awaits you at **White Sands National Monument.** Be sure to pick a day when missiles are not being tested, though: the highway is often closed during times of testing. Scheduling information is available by calling the monument. Spending an evening in Las Cruces is a perfect end to the exploration of El Camino Real.

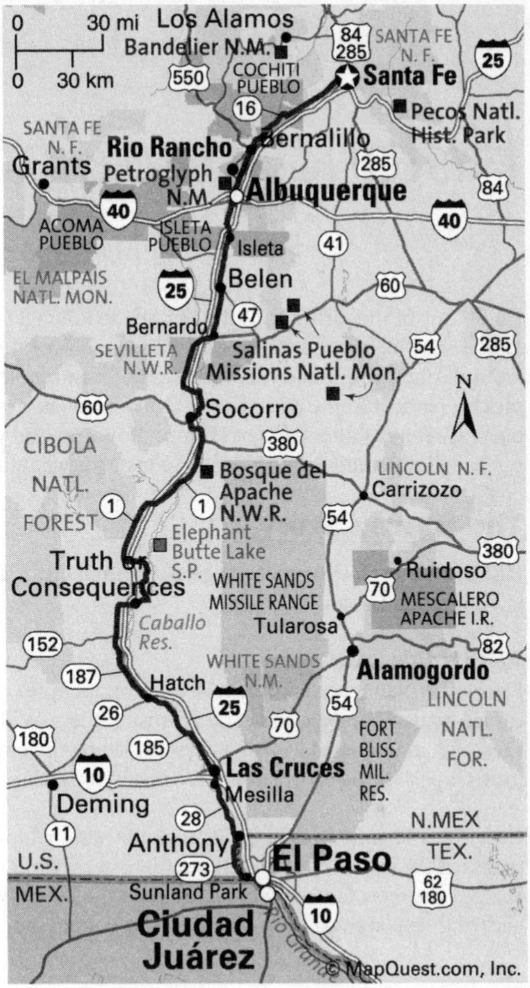

Historic Route 66

NEW MEXICO

Many of the early curiosities that made Route 66 intriguing to travelers have fallen victim to interstate highways, but you can still see much of the route's character if you leave the beaten path, both around Albuquerque and on other parts of Historic Route 66. On Albuquerque's eastern edge, you can pick up parts of Route 66 at Tijeras Canyon, where a serene and rural atmosphere allows you to leave the big city behind. Other parts of Historic Route 66 lead you to quaint and historic sites, enabling you to catch a glimpse into the past and get a taste for what life was like a few decades ago.

The Byway Story

Historic Route 66 tells archaeological, cultural, historical, natural, recreational, and scenic stories that make it a unique and treasured Byway.

ARCHAEOLOGICAL

Petroglyph National Monument along Albuquerque's West Mesa gives you the chance to see amazing images carved by native people and early Spanish settlers. With five volcanic cones, hundreds of archaeological sites, and an estimated 25,000 images carved by the native Pueblos and early Spanish settlers, the monument protects part of the early culture and history of the area for generations to come.

Covering a 17-mile stretch, the Petroglyph National Monument allows the past to come alive; images on the rocks tell the stories of natives and settlers in carvings of animals, people, spirals, stars, and geometric shapes. Perhaps the most famous symbol found at the Petroglyph National Monument is that of Kokopelli, the humpbacked flute player, which is still used as a symbol in modern Pueblo art.

Although no one knows the exact dates the carvings were made, archaeologists have compared the petroglyphs with other artwork of a known date. Some carvings are thought the have been created between AD 1300 and AD 1650; others are closer to 3,000 years old. The most recent are thought to have been created by Spanish settlers during the Spanish colonial period.

CULTURAL

Abandoned pueblos and museums featuring ancient artwork and dress provide Byway travelers with reminders of the early Native American and Spanish culture that thrived centuries before Europeans reached the continent. The Apache, the Navajo, and some nomadic tribes all inhabited the desert land—some lived in permanent mud-brick settlements near waterways that were called pueblos when first encountered by Spaniards. The word pueblo also refers to an Indian culture that is unique to the Southwest and not to a particular tribe. Although they share many common elements, each

Quick Facts

Length: 604 miles.

Time to Allow: 16 hours.

Best Time to Drive: Year-round; high seasons are summer and winter.

Byway Travel Information: New Mexico Route 66 Association: phone toll-free 800/766-4405; New Mexico Department of Tourism: phone toll-free 800/545-2070; Byway local Web site: www.rt66nm.org.

Special Considerations: In areas of higher altitude, sweaters and jackets are recommended, even in warmer months.

Bicycle/Pedestrian Facilities: Historic Route 66 sometimes parallels I-40, but parts of it are now the same road. In places where the two roads become one, biking is neither encouraged nor particularly safe.

pueblo has an independent government, and its own social order, religious practices, and language.

The Pueblo people are further distinguished by their unique art. Each tribe's jewelry, pottery, weavings, and other art have a different style. Black-on-black matte pottery, for example, is unique to the San Ildefonso pueblo. Geometric black and white pots are particular to the Acoma. Other non-Pueblo Indians, such as the Navaho and Apaches, are known for their unique and beautiful artwork as well: the Navajos for their weaving and silverwork; the Apaches for their basket weaving. All native artwork has influenced the architecture and art of the Southwest.

Many tribes have cultural centers, where contemporary artists' work can be viewed and purchased. Museums along the Byway also display ancient artifacts, such as pottery and dress, that brings past cultures a little closer. Visitors are also often allowed on tribal land to tour trading posts, cultural centers, and shops.

Spanish conquest is also much engrained in the early New Mexico's culture. Explorers from Spain in search of riches happened upon the New Mexico area in the early 1540s. Although they didn't find their sought-after gold, they did find thousands of potential Catholic converts: the native people of the area. By 1680, Spanish priests had set up more than 80 missions in the area. Although much of the colonization was peaceful, the Spanish culture and Catholic religion imposed on some tribes led to the Pueblo Revolt of 1680. Indians from all over the area overthrew the settlers, burned churches, and killed priests. The Spanish returned 12 years later and were more attuned to native cultures and religions.

Today's culture is a blend of the Spanish and Native American cultures: Catholicism and indigenous religions, along with festivals and architecture that reflect both cultures. Spanish and Native American art, architecture, and music meshed to create a blend that today is known simply as Southwestern. Mariachi music, pottery, and adobe buildings are cultural reflections of the Southwest that result from a fascinating mixture of many civilizations.

HISTORICAL

When incumbent governor A. T. Hannett lost the 1926 New Mexico gubernatorial election to Richard Dillon, he was infuriated over the loss and what he felt was a betrayal by his own party. So he exited with a flamboyant farewell gesture, sending orders to E. B. Bail, the district highway engineer, to assemble all road-building equipment north of Highway 60 and cut a new road between Santa Rosa and Moriarty before the year (and Hannett's term) ended. Historic Route 66 as we know it today was about to be created.

Prior to building Route 66, a road meandered northeast from Santa Rosa to Romeroville near Las Vegas and then joined Highway 85. From Santa Fe, it descended La Bajada Hill and continued south through Albuquerque to Los Lunas before heading west toward Gallup. The distance from Santa Rosa to Albuquerque during that time was 195 miles.

Hannett, in his 1964 book *Sagebrush Lawyer,* recounts that he conceived of the idea of a shorter route by laying a ruler on the map between Santa Rosa and Gallup and saying to a meeting of highway engineers, "Gentlemen, this will be our new highway." Of course, the idea was protested not only by chamber of commerce members in Santa Fe (who led a fight to enlarge and straighten the northern route), but also by delegations from the small towns along Highway 60, a highway that passed through Vaughn, Encino, Mountainair, and Socorro before heading north to Albuquerque. Business leaders in those towns knew that Highway 60 would have to compete with the new road, but Hannett prevailed, because the new shortcut would almost halve the distance from Santa Rosa to Albuquerque.

Plunging ahead, Bail, the district highway engineer, realized the near impossibility of the order. Assembling equipment and organizing road crews would take the rest of November, which meant that the actual construction of 69 miles had to be accomplished in just 31 days. The new cutoff would connect the road 7 miles west of Santa Rosa to an existing highway from Moriarty on into Duke City, reducing the distance from 195 miles to 114.

Bail's account of the adventure, first published in 1952 and later appended in *Sagebrush Lawyer,* credits the road crews with marshaling the motley collection of surplus World War I Caterpillars, tractors, and graders "in the late stages of dissolution." They did battle against the blowing snow and dense piñon forests. Irate citizens along the southern and northern routes, upset by the impact that reduced traffic would have on their vital tourist business, tried to sabotage the

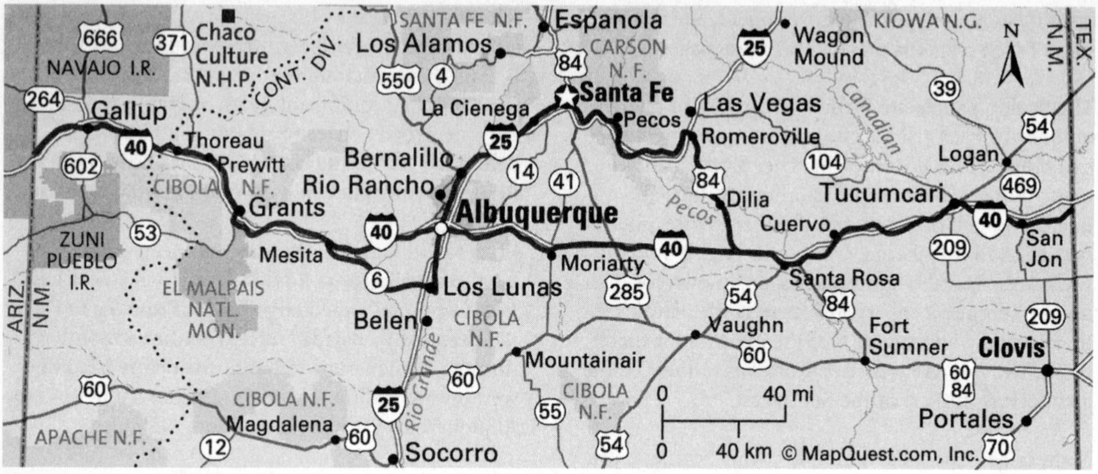

project. Workers found sugar in gas tanks and sand in their engines. Bail brought in blankets so that the men could sleep next to their equipment at night.

Ironically, no one troubled with the most logical way to put a hitch in the project—by fighting it with a lawsuit. Bail writes, "The one weapon which could have effectively stopped the work was, strangely enough, never used. We tore down fences and cut across pastures without let or hindrance. One property owner threatened us with the law and, so far as memory served, he was the only one in the entire 69 miles to indicate such resistance."

The road was not quite completed by the end of the year, so immediately after taking the oath of office on January 1, 1927, the new governor, Richard Dillon, dispatched an engineer from Santa Fe to halt the venture. However, inclement weather prevented his arrival at the job site before January 3. By then "Hannett's Joke" was complete, and cars drove across the new road. (Hannett denied that his method for accomplishing the project originated as a joke. "I was wide awake to the possibilities of a transcontinental road which would eventually attract a large amount of commercial and tourist trade," he said in *Sagebrush Lawyer.*)

Hannett, whose home base had been Gallup, moved to Albuquerque, practiced law from an office in the Sunshine Building, and wrote a daily column for the *Albuquerque Journal.* Although no monument credits him with the golden thread that helped Albuquerque develop into a metropolitan center, one of the city's streets is named Hannett.

NATURAL

The Historic Route 66 Scenic Byway is full of natural caves and geological formations. Located throughout the desert, these caves are in unspoiled condition and are open to visitors.

One of the most fascinating natural formations is La Ventana, a large natural arch in the sandstone bluffs on the east side of El Malpais Natural Monument and Conservation Area near Grants. Established in 1987, this monument preserves 114,277 acres, of which 109,260 acres are federal lands. El Malpais means "the badlands," but contrary to its name, this unique area holds many surprises. Volcanic features such as lava flows, cinder cones, pressure ridges, and complex lava tube systems dominate the landscape. Sandstone bluffs and mesas border the eastern side, providing access to vast wilderness.

Another famous and exciting place to visit in El Malpais is the Ice Cave and Bandara Volcano. Nicknamed the "Land of Fire and Ice," the two features offer contrasting phenomena: an ancient lava trail winding toward an ice cave on one fork and an erupted volcano on the other. In the ice cave, layers of blue-green ice are up to 20 feet thick and sit in part of a collapsed lava tube, and the temperature never rises above 31 degrees. The Bandara Volcano is 800 feet deep and erupted over 10,000 years ago, leaving a 23-mile lava flow.

RECREATIONAL

New Mexico is a land of diversity in culture, climate, and landscape. Evidence of this diversity is everywhere, making the area surrounding the Historic Route 66 the perfect place to find any type of recreation imaginable.

No trip to the area would be complete without dining in one of the authentic Mexican restaurants. Famous for its fiery-hot chili peppers, New Mexican cuisine is an adventure in itself. Mexican food is not all you will find in such a diverse area, however: traditional Native American, Asian, Greek, French, Middle Eastern, and every other conceivable cuisine is available, along with many vegetarian restaurants.

The climate of central New Mexico makes outdoor recreation possible year-round. Summers lend themselves to hiking, camping, biking, and fishing, while New Mexico's winters delight both downhill and cross-country skiers with trails and runs across the state.

The Sandia Mountains, located near Albuquerque, provide exciting recreational opportunities. Travelers enjoy hiking and biking beginner to advanced trails in the summer and skiing the 200 acres of terrain of the Sandia Peak Ski Area in the winter. The ski area's tramway whisks you and your skis or bike to the top of the mountain year-round—just one reason the Sandia Mountains are an excellent place for outdoor adventure.

The geography of the area is unlike any other place. Lush forests, clear lakes, and sporadic mountains break up the desert landscape. Natural caves and rock formations in El Malpais Natural Monument and Conservation Area are open for tourists to view. Erupted volcanoes, bat caves, and sandstone cliffs and mesas dot the beautiful area, providing a truly rare chance to see one of the world's most fascinating regions.

If urban entertainment is what you are looking for, New Mexico has that, too. You may want to catch a symphony, attend a hockey game, or shop in unique outdoor markets. The nightlife heats up as the temperatures cool down after dark. Dance clubs, bars, and live music venues around the larger cities come alive at night.

SCENIC

Route 66 is unique in that it embodies plains, grasslands, vistas, mountains, deserts, and virtually every kind of terrain available in New Mexico. The beautiful and varied desert landscape along the Byway, coupled with unique Southwestern architecture, provides an exceptionally scenic drive. The sunsets and sunrises on the Byway are spectacular, and you can see for miles in any direction in most places along the route.

Historic Route 66 is a truly exceptional visual experience. Orange rock dotted with green plantlife rests dramatically against a turquoise-blue sky in summer, creating a postcard-like desert scene. Yet, a few miles down the road, a forest surrounds a bright blue lake, with a waterfall cascading down the dark rock. You'll often find this contrast in this unique geological area: six of the seven life zones identified on Earth are found in New Mexico.

As you approach cities, you'll notice that the architecture of the cities also embodies Southwestern flavor. The stucco and brick buildings are often colorful and particular to the Art Deco style of the 1950s. This style is apparent in the downtown shops, outdoor markets, and residential areas. Even new construction keeps the traditional style alive with colorful buildings of stucco and landscape of cacti and yucca.

Highlights

Because Historic Route 66 is more than 600 miles long, the following must-see tour of the Byway is split into two sections: one starting west of Grants and heading westward into Gallup; the other starting east of Tucumcari and heading westward into Santa Rose.

WESTERN MUST-SEE TOUR

- The first stop along this section is just south of McCarty's, off of Exit 96. The **Acoma Sky Pueblo** offers a unique view worth seeing—a city atop a 400-foot mesa. The people of the Acoma Pueblo ask that visitors respect the posted warnings and signs and be respectful of residents. Always ask permission to take photos. Also, if you are fortunate to visit on a celebration day or during a dance, remember that dances are prayers and require concentration. Please do not talk to the dancers, walk on the dance plaza, or applaud when a dance ends.

- The next stop along Route 66 is **El Malpais National Monument** near Grants. The Monument can serve as a central post while visiting several other sites, including **La Ventana Natural Arch, Ice Cave and Bandera Volcano, Inscription Rock,** and **Historic Sands Motel.**

- North of Grants, **Bluewater Lake State Park** offers a relaxing afternoon of hiking and fishing. The **Casamero Pueblo Ruins** near County Road 19 offer a unique view of the area' s history. Casamero Pueblo was first recorded by an archaeologist in the mid 1960s. A portion of the site and many smaller sites were reported to have been vandalized prior to this time. Between 1966 and 1975, most of Casamero Pueblo was excavated by archaeologists. In 1976 and 1977, they stabilized the ruins to help prevent deterioration of the walls. Interpretive signs were placed at the site describing the cultural history of the Chacoan Anasazi and the features present at Casamero. The Bureau of Land Management restabilized Casamero Pueblo in 1986, replacing eroded mortar and loose stones. The Casamero Pueblo Ruins is fenced to keep livestock and vehicles from disturbing the site. A parking lot is provided along McKinley County Road 19 for visitors.

- The **Route 66 Drive-In** in Gallup makes a great stop for lunch in keeping with the theme of the drive. Don't forget the **Red Rock Museum** at **Red Rock State Park,** just east of Gallup. Also, while in Gallup, finish your trip along western Route 66 by inquiring about ongoing activities at the Gallup-McKinley County Chamber of Commerce on Montoya Street.

EASTERN MUST-SEE TOUR

- The modern Route 66 is essentially Interstate 40, although it detours slightly through Tucumcari and Santa Rosa. This section caused quite a lot of trouble back in the early days of Route 66, when the road was narrow and dangerous. This 40-mile stretch of road heading into Tucumcari was poorly maintained and was full of potholes. Driving long hours through this flat countryside often caused motorists to doze off; hitting an unexpected pothole would cause them to lose control. Many people died in collisions on this narrow road. In fact, some of the older residents in the area will tell you that there were "only six inches and a cigarette paper between you and death on 66." Today, I-40 is wider, safer, and well maintained.

- Once in Tucumcari, take exit 335 into town. Historic Route 66 continues along Tucumcari Boulevard. While in Tucumcari, you can easily spend the day shopping or visiting the **Blue Swallow Motel** (the oldest motel in town and one of the most famous along Route 66), **Mesalands Dinosaur Museum,** and **Tucumcari Historical Museum.**

- At the end of Tucumcari Boulevard, you can choose one of two routes. This tour takes you north on Route 54 toward Conchas home to **Conchas Lake State Park,** one of New Mexico's largest lakes. The park offers a wide variety of water activities, but onshore exploring offers the potential of finding ancient rock formations and Indian dwellings.

- As you drive south along State Highway 129 toward Newkirk, you'll notice mountains in the distance off to the north. They are home to the **Santa Fe Trail.** Route 66 later follows this trail from Romeroville to Pecos. As you rejoin Route 66 at Newkirk, you may want to take advantage of the rest stop found at the junction. The next nearest public facilities aren't until Santa Rosa.

- Heading farther east along I-40, you pass through **Cuervo,** and head on to **Santa Rosa,** where many activities await you. The **Route 66 Auto Museum** is a must-stop for anyone taking in the true spirit of Route 66. The more adventurous will most likely enjoy a dip at **Blue Hole,** an 81-foot deep clear, natural artesian spring famous for its scuba diving opportunities. A stop at nearby **Santa Rosa Lake State Park** and **Sumner Lake State Park** will give the recreationally minded plenty of choices.

Jemez Mountain Trail

NEW MEXICO

North of Albuquerque, at the unspoiled village of San Ysidro (at the junction of Highway 44 and Highway 4), quietly begins one of New Mexico's most spectacular scenic drives: the Jemez (pronounced HAY-mez or HAY-mus) Mountain Trail. San Ysidro, in the Upper Sonoran desert terrain, is a village where you can find the work of local artisans and view the restored Spanish adobe church.

Jemez Pueblo, about 5 miles from San Ysidro, is located at the gateway of the majestic Cañon de San Diego. There are over 3,000 tribal members, most of whom reside in a single Puebloan village known as walatowa—the Towa word meaning "this is the place." Enjoy traditional Jemez foods and arts and crafts available at roadside stands in the beautiful Red Rocks area. Jemez Pueblo also offers recreation areas where you can picnic, fish, and enjoy the great outdoors.

QUICK FACTS

Length: 132 miles.

Time to Allow: 3 hours.

Best Time to Drive: Spring and summer; summer is the high season.

Byway Travel Information: Jemez Springs Visitor Information: phone 505/829-9155.

Special Considerations: Highway 126 is not paved and is generally closed in the winter due to snow. Bicycles, pedestrians, and passenger vehicles are accommodated according to the various types of roadways. Different sections of the trail have various accessibility and safety issues. Highway 44 is traveled by heavy, high-speed traffic, usually at 65 mph. There are shoulders along the entire two-lane stretch of the highway, but it is not generally considered safe for pedestrians or bicycles. Highway 4 winds through the mountains and is traveled at lower speeds of around 35 mph. Highway 126 is maintained in the summer by the Forest Service and can accommodate all traffic except commercial truck traffic. Travelers should be aware of several fire precautions. Please be a responsible camper. Extinguish all fires completely and be aware of official fire hazard warnings. Call any US Forest Service Office for hazard updates.

Bicycle/Pedestrian Facilities: Highway 4 is used heavily by cyclists and pedestrians. The other roads making up this Byway are not safe for cyclists.

A leisurely day trip along the Byway takes you past fantastic geologic formations; ancient Indian ruins and Indian pueblos; and reminders of the area's logging, mining, and ranching heritage. Approximately 65 miles of the Byway wind through the Santa Fe National Forest, and 40 miles of this land is in the Jemez National Recreation Area, where you'll find many opportunities for hiking, fishing, camping, and, in the winter, cross-country skiing. The Jemez Mountains are also famous for natural hot springs.

This picturesque trail is also just a short jaunt from the city of Los Alamos and the Bandelier National Monument.

The Byway Story

The Jemez Mountain Trail tells cultural, historical, natural, recreational, and scenic stories that make it a unique and treasured Byway.

CULTURAL

The greater Santa Fe area is extremely culturally diverse due to strong Native American and Spanish influences.

The earliest inhabitants, the Pueblo Indians, greatly impacted the architecture and art that in turn impacted the architecture and art of the Spanish settlers who moved into the area. Today's Southwestern flavor is a blend of both colorful cultures. Of the 19 Native American communities located in New Mexico, eight are in the greater Santa Fe area. All eight are Pueblo Indian tribes, and their communities are referred to as pueblos. Many of these pueblos were established centuries ago—the Taos Pueblo, for example, is thought to have been continuously occupied for close to 1,000 years. Each pueblo has its own tribal government, traditions, and ceremonies and is a sovereign and separate entity. The pueblos typically welcome visitors, especially during specific dances and feast days that are open to the public.

A people of great faith, the early Spanish settlers arrived in 1607 with scores of Catholic priests. The gloriously well-preserved adobe mission churches that dot the greater Santa Fe landscape, along with Spanish-settled villages and Indian Pueblos, are a testament to the strong role of religion in this region. Just as the Spanish created houses of worship from an adobe mix of mud and straw, they built villages and towns in the same architectural fashion. The energy-efficient earthen structures fit into their high desert home in every way—keeping the heat in during the winter and out in the summer—while the low-slung, flat-roofed buildings blended naturally into the land.

Like adobe architecture, art forms practiced by early Spanish settlers were shaped largely from resources they found in their natural environment. Using native aspen and pine, paints derived from natural pigments, and other local materials, they created utilitarian goods and religious objects to adorn their homes and churches. At first, the work echoed the traditional artworks and motifs they had carried with them to the New World from Mexico and Spain. But in time, native artisans developed styles and techniques that were unique to New Mexico alone. Ranging from santos (carved images of saints), furniture, and textiles to works in tin, iron, silver, and straw, the art of the Spanish colonial era remains the art of many Santa Fe-area families who have practiced the traditional techniques for generations. Meanwhile, other contemporary area artists have carried the artistic legacy of their ancestors to new levels of excellence by working in more modern media, including sculpture, photography, painting, jewelry, and literature that reflect the ongoing evolution of Hispanic arts and culture. Today, their works are also collected and exhibited by museums, galleries, and private collectors worldwide, giving the art of New Mexicans a well-deserved place in the world of fine art.

HISTORICAL

Jemez State Monument and Bandelier National Monument are special places to discover more about the history of the Jemez Mountain Trail area. Both monuments have exhibits and self-guided tours. Ranger-guided tours are also given upon request. Currently, more than 500,000 people visit these monuments every year.

NATURAL

You'll find many natural wonders along the Jemez Mountain Trail. The Jemez Mountains are unique from the southern Rockies to the east in that the Jemez are of volcanic upbringing. In fact, the history of the Jemez goes back 1 million years to the eruption of a volcano many times the size of Mount St. Helens that created an area of mountains, mesas, and canyons the size of a small eastern state.

Dominating the western half of the Santa Fe National Forest, the Jemez Mountains resemble a wagon wheel on a topographic map. The hub is formed by the giant Valles Caldera (a crater formed by the volcano's violent explosion), and the spokes are formed by the mesas built of volcanic tuft. Elevations in the Jemez Mountains range from 6,000 feet to 11,000 feet at the top of Redondo Peak in the middle of the caldera. One of the unique legacies of the volcano are the Swiss cheese-like rock cliffs and strange cone-shaped tent rocks that decorate numerous canyons.

The volcanic history of the Jemez Mountains also gives it a colorful heritage. From the red rock country on its lower edges to the deep greens of the forests in its high country, the Jemez Mountains offer some of the greatest natural diversity on Earth. Fortunately, examples of most of it can be viewed or easily accessed from this Byway, the only paved highway that traverses these mountains.

As you travel past San Ysidro along the Jemez Mountain Trail, you pass the towering volcanic plug of Cabezon (meaning big head), which is famous in Navajo folklore. The volcano has a trail leading to its 8,000-foot summit. In addition, 1 mile north of the State Monument at Soda Dam is an unusual geological formation where, over thousands of years, minerals from a natural spring have created a dam that blocks the Jemez River. The river pours through a hole in the dam, forming a waterfall. Soda Dam has become one of the most popular swimming holes in the Jemez Mountains. Also along the Byway is Battleship Rock, a sheer cliff that rises suddenly above the river like the prow of a ship. A few miles past Battleship Rock is the parking lot for Spence Hot Springs, an accessible and scenic place for a long soak in hot mineral waters.

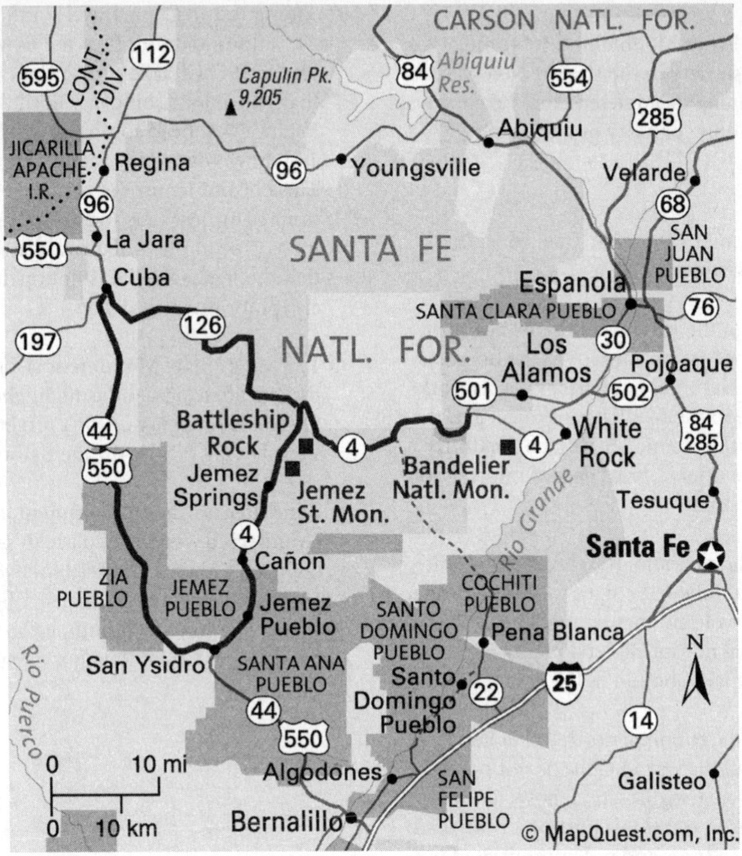

RECREATIONAL

The Jemez Mountain Trail offers all sorts of outdoor recreation. Travelers enjoy hiking trails of varying degrees of difficulty, biking trails, fishing, and several camping locations. The unique geological features also allow for outdoor adventures—you can visit caves and tunnels.

Hiking trails are for everyone. For the adventurous, Battleship Rock in the Jemez Mountains provides challenging terrain and an intriguing landscape—the trail is covered in shiny, black obsidian created from volcanic eruptions 5 million years ago. Families can enjoy the Las Conchas Trail, which provides an easy walk to picnic sites and beautiful Southwestern scenery.

If you enjoy biking, the Jemez Mountain Trail provides several trails for all skill levels. Advanced bikers may want to explore Guacamalla and Paliza Canyons, a steep terrain that offers excellent views of green meadows from the top.

Fishing fanatics can enjoy the calm waters located in the San Pedro Parks Wilderness, where cutthroat trout are found in large numbers. Close by, the Holy Ghost and Dragonfly reservoirs provide popular fishing and water recreation spots. Just a little farther down the Byway, you can catch warm-water fish, such as catfish, crappie, bass, bluegill, and perch at Cochiti Lake. Another fishing area is the Sandia Lakes Recreation Area, located on the Sandia Indian Reservation. Several ponds are stocked with trout and other varieties of fish.

If you wish to camp close by the Byway, the Santa Fe National Forest/Jemez National Recreation Area gives you a chance to camp out by rivers and hiking trails. Campgrounds along the Byway include Las Conchas and Jemez Falls (both close to the Jemez River), Redondo (the largest), and San Antonio (an excellent fishing spot offering handicapped-accessible sites).

SCENIC

In all seasons, the Jemez Mountains offer some of the most magnificent scenery in the state of New Mexico. Visitors enjoy escaping to a quieter, more relaxing way of life, even if it is only for a day or a weekend.

Highlights

As you travel the Jemez Mountain Trail, consider using the following itinerary.

- Your trip through the Jemez Mountains begins in **Los Alamos,** New Mexico, famous as the home of the **Los Alamos National Laboratory** for its work and historic role in the Manhattan Project and the development of the atomic bomb. The **Bradbury Science Museum** offers a great deal of information and fun for everyone.

- After a visit to the museum, travel east along State Highway 502 and follow the signs to **Valle Grande,** the remains of a volcano that erupted 1.4 million years ago. Natural hot springs and plenty of recreational opportunities abound in the area.

- After Valle Grande, continue north to Highway 126. This road, all the way to **Cuba,** is not paved but is well traveled. Use discretion, however, when deciding whether to travel this portion of the road: it may be rough in spots and not appropriate for passenger cars. A four-wheel-drive vehicle is recommended for better safety.

- After a rest in Cuba, travel south along Highway 44. A quick detour off of the Byway heading west on the 197 will take you to **Cabezon,** a ghost town that was a flourishing city until the 1940s. Back on Highway 44, head south through the national forest and down toward the many unique Indian Pueblos. The **Zia and Jemez Pueblos** have wonderful opportunities for learning and adventure. To find out more, stop at the **Walatowa Visitor's Center.** (Note that the Jemez Pueblo is not open to the public, except for on festival days.)

- The **Jemez State Monument** is a perfect getaway in the late afternoon and is highlighted by a dip in the **Spence Hot Springs.** Don't forget other wonderful sites that are farther off the Byway.

- **Bandelier National Monument,** near the **Rio Grande,** is a wonderful place to see the ruins of many cliff houses and pueblo-style dwellings of 13th-century Pueblo Indians. A little to the north of Los Alamos, in **Abiquiu,** a cluster of fantastic museums at **Ghost Ranch** is a trip not to be missed.

Santa Fe Trail

NEW MEXICO

Part of a multistate Byway; see also CO.

The Santa Fe Trail was the first of America's great trans-Mississippi routes. The trail, including the Mountain and Cimarron routes, traversed more than 1,200 miles from Franklin, Missouri, to Santa Fe, New Mexico. From 1821 to 1880, it was an important two-way avenue for commerce and cultural exchange among Spanish, Indian, and American cultures.

The area around the Santa Fe Trail boasts more than 20 historic districts and more than 30 individual sites that are recorded on the National Register of Historic Places. Most of these sites are directly related to the Santa Fe Trail.

QUICK FACTS

Length: 381 miles.

Time to Allow: 8 hours.

Best Time to Drive: Early spring through late fall.

Bicycle/Pedestrian Facilities: Sidewalks and bicycle trails are available in some of the communities along the Byway.

The Byway Story

The Santa Fe Trail tells archaeological, cultural, historical, natural, recreational, and scenic stories that make it a unique and treasured Byway.

ARCHAEOLOGICAL

The Santa Fe Trail offers many archaeological sites, including some that include early excavations. From 1915 to 1927, Pecos was the subject of one of the first organized excavations of a Southwestern ruin. Pioneer American archaeologist Alfred V. Kidder analyzed the stratigraphy (the sequence in which the archaeological remains of the pueblo were deposited). He noted changes in the artifacts, especially the pottery, from the lower, older layers of occupation through the upper, younger layers. Kidder used the relative ages of the pottery remains to establish relative dates of occupation at Pecos. Based on that information, he and his colleagues devised the Pecos Classification, a sequence of eight prehistoric cultural periods that applied to sites throughout the Southwest.

In 1965, Congress and the president authorized the establishment of Pecos National Monument. In the summer of 1966, National Park Service archaeologists began excavation of the church and convent; their findings not only cast new light on the history of the Southwest but also substantiated reports of 17th-century writers whose words had been held suspect.

Both the church and the convent were puzzling. The 17th-century ecclesiastics had described the church as being large, splendid, magnificent, and of unusual design, but the remaining adobe walls are of a church that had none of those characteristics. Other mission churches in New Mexico had obviously been much grander. Most historians had thought that the early accounts were exaggerated to gain added civil and religious support of missionary efforts in the remote and impoverished frontier province of New Mexico. However, it was discovered that the convent was much larger than those usually associated with a church of modest size.

In the summer of 1967, the project archaeologist discovered stone foundations resting on bedrock and fragments of burned adobe walls. Under and around the ruins of the known church, further excavations uncovered the foundations of an earlier church that was nearly 170 feet long, 90 feet wide at the transept, and 39 feet wide inside the nave. The building was typical of the fortress churches of Mexico. It had bastioned nave walls and subsidiary chapels in thick-walled, cruciform-like (that is, cross-shaped) arms near the sanctuary. Only 18 such structures were known in the Americas until the Pecos find, and none was north of Mexico City.

It is now clear that the large church and convent were constructed in the 1620s and later destroyed during the Pueblo Revolt of 1680. The convent was then reconstructed, and a new church was built following the Reconquest, probably in the early 1700s.

The archaeological survey now in progress is designed to locate small sites showing evidence of activities on which the Pecos livelihood was based. Evidence of agriculture field systems, including check dams, farming terraces, and overnight houses, has been uncovered. Rock art and hunting camps have also been identified, including Apache tipi ring sites that verify historical reports of Apache encampments for trade with the Pecos people. Some evidence suggests that the Pecos area may have been at least a marginal site for human occupation for several thousand years.

Recent excavations have uncovered two large semi-subterranean houses on the grassy flats south and west of monument headquarters. These pithouses, the first to be reported from the Upper Pecos River area, were built in the 9th century. They were probably part of a village that may have been occupied on a seasonal basis. The architecture is similar to that of both the Anasazi people of the Rio Grande Valley and the Mogollon of southern New Mexico.

CULTURAL

The Santa Fe Trail was the first trail of commerce between the Southwest and the United States. From 1821 to 1880, the Santa Fe Trail was an important two-way avenue for commerce and cultural exchange among Spanish, Native American, and American cultures. While traveling along the Byway, you can see evidence of this abounding culture in many of the events and activities.

HISTORICAL

The Santa Fe Trail was the first of America's great Trans-Mississippi routes. The trail, including the Mountain and Cimarron routes, crossed over 1,200 miles from Franklin, Missouri, to Santa Fe, New Mexico. The trail played a critical role in the westward expansion of the United States and fostered an exchange among Spanish, Native American, and American cultures. The Santa Fe Trail was the first international trade route, carrying needed materials from Missouri to northern Mexico and taking back silver, furs, mules, and wood to Missouri.

As early as the 1700s, Pueblo and Plains Indian trade fairs at Pecos and Taos introduced Spanish residents to native products. Yet trade between New Mexico and other settlements throughout the West was banned because New Mexico was a colony of Spain and could trade only with the mother country. Beginning in 1810 and succeeding in 1821, uprisings in Mexico gave New Mexico freedom to trade with anyone. November 16, 1821, is recognized as the start of legal international trade between New Mexico and the United States; this date also marks the beginning of the Santa Fe Trail.

The Santa Fe Trail passed through the territories and ranges of many Indian tribes, including the Pawnee, Arapaho, Cheyenne, Comanche, and the Kiowa, so Indian traders used it as a commercial route. After the Mexican War (1846-1848), the Jicarillas, Comanches, Kiowas, and other tribes became increasingly threatened by the traffic on the trail. With the American promise to the people of New Mexico to subdue the various Indian tribes, an intermittent war began that ended in the mid-1870s. The Indian tribes of New Mexico were then confined to reservations.

After the Mexican War (and with New Mexico a US Territory), the Santa Fe Trail became mainly a military road. It supplied goods to the large contingent of troops in the Southwest, and mercantile goods were still carried into New Mexico and Old Mexico. After the Civil War, railroads began laying tracks to the West. By 1879, the first locomotive reached Las Vegas, New Mexico, and in 1880, the railroad reached Lamy (basically the Santa Fe Depot), essentially ending wagon traffic across the 900 miles of plains.

Visitors to New Mexico can still see the most extensive remains of the trail. Historic sites and landmarks found along the trail include Raton Pass, Rabbit Ears, Cimarron, Rayado, Ocate Gap, Fort Union, McNees Crossing, Point of Rocks, the Rock Crossing of the Canadian, Wagon Mound, Watrous (La Junta), Las Vegas, Tecolote, San Miguel del Vado, San Jose del Vado, Pecos, and Santa Fe.

NATURAL

The Santa Fe Trail offers an array of flora and fauna. Vegetation ranges from small pockets of tall grass prairies to the buffalo and blue grama grass found on the short grass plains east of the Sangre de Cristo Mountains. South and east of Las Vegas, the trail enters the piñon pine and juniper vegetation zones as the elevation increases in the mountains. Antelopes, coyotes, elks, and bears are prevalent in the area. Bird life is profuse, including small mountain bluebirds, hawks, bald eagles, and golden eagles. Many species of reptiles also inhabit the area, including the famous prairie rattlesnake and the much larger and feared western diamondback rattlesnake.

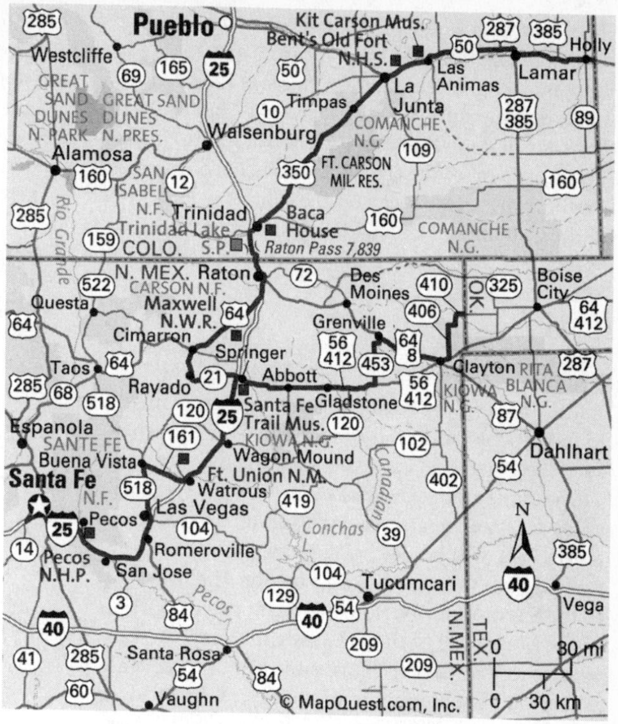

From its eastern-most point at Old Franklin, Missouri, the trail traveled west to Cimarron, Kansas, where it split into two routes. The original trail, the Cimarron Route, headed southwest across Colorado, Oklahoma, and New Mexico. The Mountain Route headed west into Colorado, and then went south to New Mexico across the rugged Raton Pass. The routes joined again at Watrous, New Mexico. Today, travelers can follow the trail through three national grasslands: Cimarron, Kiowa, and Comanche.

The Cimarron National Grassland near Elkhart, Kansas, contains 23 miles of the trail's Cimarron Route, the longest trail segment on public land. A 19-mile companion trail, a mowed swath across the prairie, parallels the actual trail route. It was constructed for non-motorized traffic. Two trailheads provide drinking water, rest room facilities, vehicle and trailer parking, stock unloading facilities, and ramps for mounting and dismounting horses. Point of Rocks, a large outcropping of rock that rises above the prairie, was visible for long distances from both directions along the trail, so it acted as a landmark and guide for travelers. The panoramic view of the Cimarron River Valley from Point of Rocks was excellent for seeing other travelers or game. Today, you can drive to the top to enjoy this view. A short distance east of Point of Rocks is Middle Springs, a small oasis on the prairie where water rises from an ever-flowing artesian spring. It was the only reliable watering spot for 30 miles each way along the trail. Today, the spring is home to tall trees and brushy undergrowth that attract migrating birds. However, during the Santa Fe Trail days, the spring was probably a treeless and muddy waterhole, trodden and stirred by buffalo, livestock, and trail travelers. This welcome resting spot along the trail now has a picnic area and walking trail for your enjoyment.

The winding ribbon of the Cimarron Route crosses the Kiowa National Grassland (part of the Kiowa and Rita Blanca National Grasslands) 15 miles north of Clayton, New Mexico, off Highway 406. Time, weather, and erosion have not erased the deep wagon ruts stretching across 2 miles of the Kiowa National Grassland. You can almost hear the rumble of freight wagons, the cracking of bullwhips, the thunder of buffalo, and the quiet conversations in Spanish and English by the campfires that took place here. You can also experience the stark isolation of prairie travel and glimpse the subtle prairie tapestry that was savored by countless trail travelers. You can step back in time and enjoy virtually the same prairie vistas and unspoiled beauty that travelers experienced more than 100 years ago. The trail across the Kiowa National Grassland lies between McNees Crossing and Turkey Creek, both resting and watering areas for weary travelers. Rabbit Ears Mountain and Round Mound can be seen looming to the west.

The Mountain Route of the trail coursed northwest after splitting from the main trail at Cimarron, Kansas. Along its length, the Mountain Route unraveled the Aubry Cutoff a few miles east of the Kansas/Colorado line, and the Granada-Fort Union Road just west of the state line. Segments of these two branches can be seen on the southern portion of the Comanche National Grassland; remnants of Springfield, and portions of the Granada-Fort Union Road can be seen near Kim.

As it continued its westward path, the Mountain Route curved to the north, tracing what is now Route 50. Here, the changing horizon from plains to mountains was a major milestone on the journey, surely causing great excitement among the travelers. The mountains may have also produced apprehension as travelers anticipated having to climb over rugged Raton Pass with heavily laden wagons. Today, trail travelers can turn south at La Junta on Highway 350 to the Sierra Vista Overlook on the northern portion of the Comanche National Grassland. Here, you can experience the same feelings as the early travelers did as you view the mountains to the west. You can also stop for a picnic at Timpas farther south on Highway 350 or continue on to Iron Spring, the first reliable water source after leaving the comforts of Bents Fort, which later became the site of a stage station. Good trail ruts can be found here today.

RECREATIONAL

You'll find many recreational activities along the Santa Fe Trail, including fishing, camping, skiing, mountain biking, and hiking. Several state parks and recreational areas are located in northeastern New Mexico. As a matter of fact, outdoor recreation is one of the top four reasons people visit New Mexico.

SCENIC

The Santa Fe Trail has some spectacular and rugged scenery. For example, amid the surrounding Fort Union Ranch at Fort Union National Monument, wagon ruts can be seen in the distance. These and other wagon ruts were worn into the landscape of northeastern New Mexico over 150 years ago. Nearby, travelers visit Fort La Junta (built in 1851) and the 1863 fort and supply depot.

There are also many different plants found along the Santa Fe Trail. For example, the flowering plants along the trail are the result of volcanic activity from long ago. Also, 6 miles of the Santa Fe National Forest embrace the trail between the villages of Glorieta (atop the 7,432-foot-high Glorieta Pass) and Canoncito. Stands of tall ponderosa pine, golden aspen, auburn scruboak, ubiquitous piñon pine (the state tree of New Mexico), and juniper are all found here.

Highlights

This Santa Fe Trail tour begins in Santa Fe and heads east over to Clayton, near the borders of Texas and Oklahoma. With a little backtracking, the trail goes north and enters Colorado over the Raton Pass. Full of scenic, natural, and historical treasures, the Byway offers numerous opportunities for both learning and recreation.

- Your first stop will be at Pecos National Historic Park, where you'll want to spend some time learning about the ruins of a 14th century Indian pueblo and two 17th century Franciscan missions that crown a fortress-like hill in the verdant Pecos River Valley.

- Your next stop should be in Las Vegas. No, not that Las Vegas. Las Vegas, New Mexico, has a fantastic wildlife refuge and is worth stopping at to explore the half-mile trail.

- Going north, still on I-25, you'll pass Buena Vista and come into Fort Union National Monument. The remains of this star-shaped fort are a fantastic sight.

- The Santa Fe Trail Museum should be your next stop as you approach the town of Springer, and the major highway junction. Enjoy the Kiowa National Grassland as you drive east to the border and the town of Clayton. While here, don't forget to stop and enjoy Clayton Lake State Park, a great place to camp for the evening.

- Next, leaving the Byway for a few miles, take Highway 64 up to Raton for a fun experience at the Sugarite Canyon State Park. Then, back on the Byway, hop on Highway 64 going south through Cimarron. This drive is fantastic and takes you through the Cimarron Canyon State Park. At this point, you may choose to head over to Taos and enjoy the museums and ghost towns there, or head back to Santa Fe.

Turquoise Trail

NEW MEXICO

Back roads often lead to glorious scenery and great discovery, and so it is with the Turquoise Trail. When you leave the freeway and venture onto the scenic and historic Turquoise Trail, you get a chance to see 15,000 square miles of central New Mexico from a bird's-eye view atop Sandia Crest, the magnificent summit of the Sandia Mountains that rises 10,678 feet. From here, you can venture into Sandia Crest Wilderness Area while hiking through aspen glades and across flowering meadows, coming upon one spectacular view after another.

You can also drive back in time by visiting the ghost mining towns of Golden, Madrid, and Cerrillos, towns that are now coming alive with arts, crafts, theater, music, museums, and restaurants. In addition, the Museum of Archaeology and Material Culture in Cedar Crest exhibits a 12,000-year timeline that tells the story of North America's earliest inhabitants and goes chronologically through history until the Battle of Wounded Knee in 1890.

All along the way, there is adventure and fun for everyone. To really discover the Land of Enchantment, travel the Turquoise Trail.

QUICK FACTS

Length: 61 miles.

Time to Allow: 3 hours.

Best Time to Drive: Year-round; high seasons are fall and spring.

Byway Travel Information: Turquoise Trail Association: phone toll-free 888/263-0003; Byway local Web site: www.turquoisetrail.org.

Special Considerations: If you're venturing into the mountains, take a coat or jacket.

Restrictions: Snow may cause a chain rule and/or four-wheel drive requirements to be in effect between October and March.

Bicycle/Pedestrian Facilities: There is an interpretive trail that you can hike at the Tijeras Pueblo near Tijeras. Also, keep an eye out for the Balsam Glade Picnic Ground, where unimproved Route 165 leads to a 1-mile trail to Sandia Cave.

The Byway Story

The Turquoise Trail tells archaeological, cultural, historic, natural, recreational, and scenic stories that make it a unique and treasured Byway.

ARCHAEOLOGICAL

Over thousands of years, many people have inhabited the area along the Turquoise Trail. Pottery shards, ancient mining quarries, and pueblos are just some of the evidence ancient inhabitants left behind. Prehistoric Indians relied on many features of the area for their economy, such as the rich deposits of turquoise and local lead, which were used for decoration and glazes in their pottery.

The Tijeras Pueblo, an archaeological site located near the ranger station of the Cibola National Forest, once housed several hundred people. These ancient people lived in the area over 600 years ago. The San Marcos Pueblo offers limited tours (by appointment) and serves as a research site that provides archaeological field experience for students at the University of New Mexico. Many adobe and masonry pueblo structures remain intact at the San

Marcos site, and estimates are that the pueblo had between 3,000 and 5,000 rooms. During the 1300s and mid-1400s, the pueblo was also a center for pottery making.

One of the oldest dwellings in the area may be Sandia Cave. Evidence surrounding the cave's earliest occupants remains controversial, but excavations from the cave suggest that people lived in the cave during three different time periods. Pre-Colombian Pueblo-style artifacts; hearths and tools of nomadic hunters; and Folsom spear points used on bison, giant sloths, and horses have all been found in the cave. These artifacts relate the story of a past people and indicate the way in which they lived.

The early pueblo inhabitants of the area surrounding what is known today as Cerrillos Hills Historic Park worked on many turquoise pits, quarries, lead (galena) mines, refining areas, workshops, hearths, and campsites. One of the largest mines is Mount Chalchihuitl. Most of the activity here occurred between AD 1375 and 1500, but grooved axes, mauls, picks, Indian pottery, and campfires are all that is left. The Mina del Tiro, which is thought to be one of the oldest lead mines in the North America, is located on private land nearby. These mines were critically important to the people in the area because they supplied valuable turquoise that allowed decoration of pottery, jewelry, and other items.

CULTURAL

New Mexico's vibrant history has permeated modern society and left cultural treasures throughout the area. Retaining the flavor of the Southwest, local artisans have saved several of the region's ghost towns and transformed them into artistic communities. Along the Byway, you will find shops and galleries filled with paintings, sculpture, pottery, leather goods, jewelry, furniture, beadwork, toys, art wear, and antiques. Some of the old company stores and houses have also been refurbished as restaurants and bed-and-breakfasts. You will likely want to plan extra time to peruse the cultural offerings of the Turquoise Trail.

HISTORICAL

New Mexico's rich mining legacy dates to before the first Spanish conquistadors began exploring the region. Native Americans were the first people who toiled to extract the gold, silver, lead, zinc, and turquoise from the surrounding hills. Indeed, the turquoise found near the Turquoise Trail is considered by some to be the finest in the world. Usually sky blue to light greenish blue, turquoise can also be white, dark blue, jade green, reddish brown, and even violet. In the early 1900s, Tiffany's of New York helped to popularize the shade known as "robins' egg blue."

When the Native Americans first began their mining efforts, the mineral deposits were in pure veins. Early digging implements included stone hammers, chisels, and files. After the minerals had been removed from the surrounding rock, the native miners would carry the ore and rock outside the mine in reed baskets or buckets made of hide. Spanish explorers estimated that native miners had removed 100,000 tons of rock, based on huge tailing piles and 400-year-old piñon trees growing from the piles.

Although some mining occurred during Spain's (and later Mexico's) ownership of the land, the majority of the mining appears to have been done during the territorial expansion of the United States. Mining communities and camps rapidly sprang up in the area to capitalize on the various minerals. Some died out or were absorbed into other communities, depending on the available riches.

Golden, New Mexico, began with humble beginnings during the 1825 gold rush, the first gold rush to occur west of the Mississippi. Here, two mining camps were created to mine placer gold (gold extracted from streams or rivers). In 1880, several mining companies moved into the area and renamed the two camps "Golden" to match their high hopes of developing profitable ventures. However, these hopes faded by 1884, and the population of Golden steadily decreased.

Another popular New Mexico mining community, Cerrillos, hit its peak in the 1880s, due in part to the arrival of the railroad. The early 1880s quickly expanded the local mines, with over 2,000 land claims filed on only a few square miles of land. Soon, Cerrillos swelled to accommodate 21 saloons and 4 hotels. Sadly, prosperity abandoned Cerrillos within the decade. Today, the Cerrillos Hills Historic Park and the immediately adjacent lands contain approximately 45 vertical or near-vertical shafts, with depths exceeding 6 feet.

Madrid, New Mexico, was founded in the oldest coal-mining region of the state and gradually grew to become the center of the coal-mining industry for the region. Under the direction of the superintendent of mines, Oscar Huber, Madrid became a model for other mining towns. Oscar believed that idleness was an enemy to a stable community. His radical views sharply changed mining towns by requiring the miners to participate in the community. Employees were to donate from 50 cents to $1 a month for community causes and were also required to participate in town events such as the Fourth of July celebrations and Christmas light displays. In fact, Madrid became famous for its Christmas light displays. Miners began to light up the winter sky with 150,000 Christmas lights, powered by 500,000 kilowatt hours of electricity. The power was provided by the company's own coal-fed generators. People from all over the state came to see the light displays and Madrid's annual pageant. The town's Christmas celebrations ended in 1941 with the start of World War II. Eventually, people began choosing natural gas in favor of coal, and the mines near Madrid closed in the early 1950s, causing the town to be abandoned.

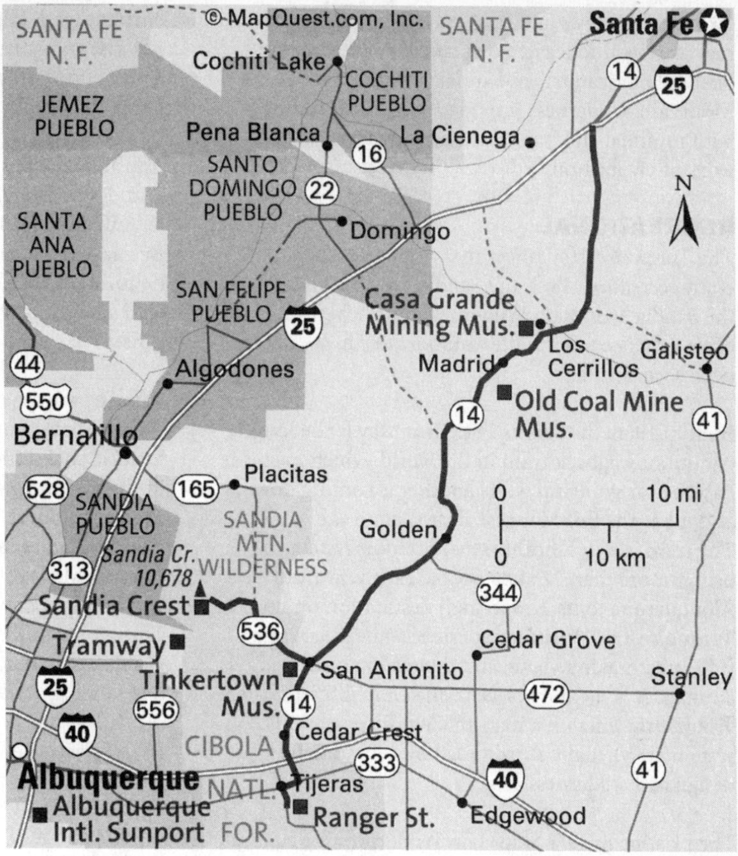

By the time early Native Americans began to settle these areas, these dikes were exposed and began to crack. This erosion process soon made the area famous for its rich supply of minerals, including gold, silver, lead, zinc, coal, and a wide assortment of turquoise. Today, fossil hunters sift through the outcroppings of shale, hoping to find one of the many fossils of prehistoric life hidden there.

NATURAL

Proud of its natural legacy, New Mexico has preserved many vibrant natural wonders that can be easily accessed along the Turquoise Trail. In the Byway's short length of 61 miles, you're whisked through forests and mountains that are home to a dazzling array of wildlife. Depending on the terrain, you can observe desert wildlife or woodland creatures. Many of these animals make their homes among the juniper, pine, and spruce-fir forests that grow along the Byway.

But the natural treasures found on the Turquoise Trail began forming millions of years before roads were constructed anywhere in the area. Twenty-four to 34 million years ago, the Cerrillos and Ortiz Mountains along the Turquoise Trail were dikes, or branches, of magma that solidified thousands of feet underground.

Part of the Byway travels into the Cibola National Forest. Here, the climate varies with elevation, which ranges from 5,000 to over 11,300 feet. Snow can be found in the timberline until June, and some of the higher elevations become very cold at night. During the late summer months, heavy thunderstorms occasionally rumble through higher elevations, dropping the temperature below zero.

The high points of a visit to the Turquoise Trail, however, are Sandia Peak and the Sandia Mountain Wilderness, which offer a view of the sublime. With far-reaching views and cool mountain breezes, you may not want to leave! Long considered sacred by Native American tribes, Sandia Peak and the Sandia Mountain Wilderness provide a welcomed respite with minimal effort for those seeking to escape the woes of civilization.

RECREATIONAL

The Turquoise Trail offers many opportunities to enjoy recreation. Both the Sandia Peak Tramway and the Sandia Mountain Wilderness hold adventure and offer a chance to view the outdoors like it has never been seen before.

Built in 1966, the Sandia Peak Tramway is the longest continuous jigback tram in the world, which means it has one car going up while another is coming down, and it has the third longest clear span in the world. The tram is a significant transportation system that brings more than 275,000 people each year from Albuquerque to its 2-mile-high destination on the Turquoise Trail. Visitors experience an exhilarating ride, breathtaking views, and interesting birds and animals. It is the only place in the United States where visitors traveling on a man-made transportation system are virtually surrounded by a nationally designated wilderness area.

The pristine Sandia Mountain Wilderness is a natural, scenic, and recreational wonder located adjacent to metropolitan Albuquerque. More than 100 miles of recreational trails in the wilderness area offer a wide variety of terrain. Included in the wilderness area are the Sandia Mountains and Sky Island, where a diverse and isolated ecosystem contains different life zones.

SCENIC

The Turquoise Trail offers some of the most spectacular scenic views in North America. The scenery on the Turquoise Trail is not only beautiful; it is also incredibly diverse. You can look more than a mile down at what was once the ocean floor millions of years ago, or you can enjoy pristine sights while driving through a variety of ecosystems. You can even look up above at the vastness of the universe as you watch billions upon billions of stars sparkle with no competition from city lights.

Not all of the scenic qualities of the Turquoise Trail are at the top of Sandia Crest, however. The Turquoise Trail offers many miles of unspoiled natural beauty. Its breathtaking scenery and unobstructed views enchant from Highway 14 mile 7 to mile 40. Mesas, deserts, and grasslands teem with wildlife and provide a home for horses, cattle, and even an occasional llama or ostrich.

A unique quality of this Byway is the weather. The arid desert climate makes the scenic drive possible in all four seasons. During the summer months on the Byway, you see fast-moving clouds and hundreds of lightning bolts electrifying the sky. In contrast to these wild storms, you may be inspired by the multicolored sunsets in a calm evening sky.

Some of the most enjoyable scenery found along the Byway is man-made. You can view tailings from historic coal mines, representing the only location in the nation where both anthracite and bituminous coal were found. They can also see giant artwork displayed adjacent to the road, the eclectic 1960s town of Madrid, and the Old West town of Cerrillos that inspired movies with its dusty, unpaved roads. The people in Madrid and Cerrillos and their highly visible cultural activities give the Byway some of its outstanding scenic qualities that visitors can enjoy.

Highlights

The best way to truly experience the unique nature of the Turquoise Trail is to stop at the small towns along the Byway and speak with the folks who live there. Here's a sampling of places you may want to stop.

- The first stop along the trail is at the **Sandia Ranger Station** on Highway 337. This marks the beginning of the Byway and a nice way to learn the early history of the area. Inquire about road conditions here, as well as special activities that may be planned.
- Between 1948 and 1976, excavations in this area turned up a great amount of archeological remains that helped scientists learn about the **Tijeras Pueblo,** a large tribe believed to exist between AD 1300 and 1600. Many skeletal remains, as well as other objects such as tools, jewelry, corn cobs, and arrow heads are on display at the Maxwell Museum of Anthropology at the University of New Mexico in Albuquerque. The pueblo itself includes 200 rooms, a dozen small buildings, and a kiva. After excavation was finished in the 1970s, the area was covered again with soil to preserve it. A self-guided tour of the area is available.

- Continuing north on 14 out of Tijeras, enjoy the scenery as the road turns from grassland to forest. Turn left on the 536 heading toward Sandia Peak. While at Sandia Peak, be sure to stop at the **Museum of Archaeology and Material Culture** and the **Tinkertown Museum.** Continue on up the windy road to the **Sandia Peak Tramway.** Take the tramway up the 2.7-mile climb and enjoy the view. After the tram, continue to the highpoint of the road and take a quick tour of the **Sandia Cave.** Don't forget your flashlight!

- Head back down 536 and turn left and continue north on 14. Continue up toward Madrid. Expect to spend some time here enjoying the uniqueness of the town by touring the **Old Coal Mine Museum** and the **Engine House Theatre.** Interesting to note is that this entire town, after being utterly deserted due to a mine shutdown, was advertised for sale in the *Wall Street Journal* in 1954 for a price of $250,000. No one took the offer, but the town has been revived since the 1970s by artisans. A visit here is a real treat.

- Just north of Madrid and before Cerillos, be on the lookout for a unique art display. Animal bones and glass are the tools of artist **Tammy Jean Lange.** No fees are charged here, but a donation box kindly makes a support request. A few miles up the road is **Cerillos,** a town of mostly dirt roads that is a hit for many a passerby. Thomas Edison is reported to have stayed here briefly while conducting studies with the area's minerals. The **Cerrillos Turquoise Mining Museum** run by Todd Brown is a special feature of the town. Be sure to ask him about the 28-room house that he and his wife built. Don't leave Cerillos without a stop at the **What Not Shop,** a gift shop selling mostly Indian jewelry and crafts.

- Five miles past Cerillos, look for signs pointing to the **Shona Sol Sculpture Garden,** a unique gallery of African sculpture. Finally, make a stop at the **J. W. Eaves Movie Ranch,** home to many famous movies, including *Silverado,* which was shot entirely on site. If you're lucky, the costume lady will show you her Emmy.

Dinosaur Diamond Prehistoric Highway

UTAH

Part of a multistate Byway; see also UT.

The Dinosaur Diamond Prehistoric Highway provides a unique and unparalleled opportunity to experience the thrilling story of dinosaurs and the science and history of discovery behind them. The route combines opportunities to see dinosaur bones still in the ground being excavated and to see dinosaur bones prepared by paleontologists for museums. Museums all along the Byway display both reconstructed skeletons and fleshed-out re-creations of dinosaurs found in the area. In between and sometimes overlapping the dinosaur sites are areas of major archaeological interest. This Byway was occupied by prehistoric Native Americans who saw the area's many rock cliffs as ideal surfaces for their petroglyphs and pictographs. Some of the finest examples and densest concentrations of this rock art in North America are located along or near the Byway.

QUICK FACTS

Length: 400 miles.

Time to Allow: 9 hours to several days.

Best Time to Drive: Year-round; high season is summer.

Byway Travel Information: Dinosaurland Travel Board: phone toll-free 800/477-5558; Byway local Web site: www.dinosaurdiamond.org.

Special Considerations: The mountain passes at Reservation Ridge on Highway 191 can be treacherous during winter storms. This road is rarely, if ever, officially closed, but sometimes a few hours' delay would be prudent.

Restrictions: Cleveland-Lloyd Dinosaur Quarry is at the end of 13 miles of gravel road that is accessible to sedans in all weather except deep snow; it is closed during the winter months. The Mill Canyon Dinosaur Trail and Copper Ridge Dinosaur Trackway are reached by a couple of miles of dirt road that is accessible to two-wheel-drive automobiles in good weather but are not advisable for the same vehicles in wet conditions. Dinosaur trackways are difficult if not impossible to see under snow cover.

Bicycle/Pedestrian Facilities: The Dinosaur Diamond Byway includes portions of the interstate (I-70) and various US highways. For this reason, bicycle and foot travel along the route may be prohibited and/or dangerous. However, numerous trails off the Byway delight visitors to the area. The Kokopelli Trail is designed and built for mountain bike travel between Moab and Fruita. Hiking for recreation, solitude, or sightseeing in the area of the Dinosaur Diamond is very popular, however, and you'll find many trails to follow.

Along the Byway, you'll find many opportunities to take a breather from the abundance of dinosaur sights and enjoy recreational opportunities. Hiking, camping, mountain biking, fishing, and many other activities can be enjoyed on the acres of public lands in the corridor. River rafting and kayaking suitable for all levels can be arranged on the Green, Yampa, and Colorado rivers. Horseback riding, llama-assisted pack trips, and even mule and goat pack trips can also be arranged through private operators in the area.

Along with unique red, gray, and green rock formations, you can enjoy forested mountain passes, canyons, cliffs, rivers, and plateaus along the Dinosaur Diamond Prehistoric Highway. Wide-open spaces and miles of unobstructed views are the reward for those who travel this Byway.

The Byway Story

The Dinosaur Diamond Prehistoric Highway tells archaeological, cultural, historical, natural, recreational, and scenic stories that make it a unique and treasured Byway.

ARCHAEOLOGICAL

The Dinosaur Diamond Prehistoric Highway showcases the archaeological qualities of about 1,000 years ago, when Native American cultures lived and hunted in the area. These cultures maintained their way of life in the desert, and today, remnants of this culture are found along the Byway. The best evidence of these ancient people is the abundance of petroglyphs and pictographs in the area. (Petroglyphs are pictures that are pecked into rock surfaces by using harder rocks, often made into tools; pictographs are pictures painted onto the rocks.)

Ancient Indian petroglyph panels show up on cliff sides and rock surfaces along the Byway, because the sheer rock cliffs and walls served as an ideal place to create this rock art. There are panels in both Utah and Colorado.

Hundreds of rock surfaces in the Moab area display rock art that was created by the Paleo-Indian Fremont and Anasazi cultures. The Golf Course Rock Art site near Moab Golf Course is a large area covered with human and animal figures. Within Arches National Park, Courthouse Wash has both petroglyphs and pictographs on a panel that is 19 feet high and 52 feet long. Also in Arches, Ute rock art may be seen at the Wolfe Ranch near the Delicate Arch Trailhead.

Between Wellington and Myton is Nine Mile Canyon, the greatest concentration of rock art in the world and the premier site of the archaic culture of the Fremont Indians. The canyon also has examples of dwellings that have been untouched for hundreds of years. Nine Mile Canyon is well preserved because of the dry climate and isolation from large population centers. Because of this preservation, the canyon is home to high-quality rock art that visitors can enjoy, with more than 1,000 sites catalogued to date.

Between Moab and Price are hundreds of additional panels at Thompson Springs, the mouth of Gray Canyon north of Green River, and all through the San Rafael Swell. There are further examples of rock art down in the canyon of the Price River east of Woodside. The Uinta Basin is rife with Fremont rock art in places like Dry Fork Canyon just northwest of Vernal and numerous significant sites in or near Dinosaur National Monument, such as McKee Springs, Cub Creek, and Jones Hole.

CULTURAL

Because of the isolating nature of living in the desert, many cultural events have sprung up to give people a reason to congregate and enjoy the splendid outdoors. Festivals and events honoring the heritage and natural features of the area give the Byway a cultural flair.

Eastern Utah has been and continues to be the home to many ranches and cattle. In celebration of this culture, rodeos are held periodically throughout the area. In Vernal, the Dinosaur Roundup Rodeo is one of the largest rodeos in the world. In Price, the Black Diamond Stampede Rodeo is held every year. In Vernal, Butch Cassidy Days celebrates the history of the area's most famous outlaws. The San Rafael Swell was a favorite hideout for Butch Cassidy and the Sundance Kid and their gang. The Outlaw Trail went from the wild country of Robber's Roost down by Hanksville, up through the San Rafael Swell and either Nine Mile Canyon or along the canyons of the Green River into the Uintah Basin. It then either continued along the Green or up and over the eastern Uintas to Brown's Park in the tri-state area of Wyoming, Colorado, and Utah. Matt Warner, a former outlaw in the gang, was elected marshal in Price for a number of years. Today, the Outlaw Trail Festival is held every summer in Vernal in honor of these famous outlaws. Josie Morris, an old friend of Cassidy's, built a small cabin in Cub Creek, part of Dinosaur National Monument. It is preserved and stabilized so that visitors can experience what it's like to rough it in the Old West.

Moab is known as the mountain bike capital of the world, but it is also home to many different festivals and celebrations. Every year in the early spring, participants from all over gather for the Jeep Safari. The slick red rock and warming temperatures in the desert at that time of the year make it a perfect location for extreme driving. If you have more traditional cultural events in mind, the Moab Film Festival showcases the work of independent filmmakers, and Moab hosts an outdoor music festival as well.

HISTORICAL

The high mountain desert of eastern Utah has drawn people to the area of the present-day Dinosaur Diamond Prehistoric Highway. Evidences of Native American cultures, such as the Fremont and Ute, can be seen in the rock art along the Byway. The Escalante-Dominguez Expedition, followed by scientific and paleontologic expeditions, undertook early exploration of the area, while Mormon settlers, miners, and immigrants from Europe settled in the area and created a unique and colorful history.

The first recorded venture of Europeans into the area was the Escalante-Dominguez Expedition in 1776. This expedition began in Santa Fe, New Mexico, and attempted to blaze a trail to California in order to access the missions located there; however, their journey was unsuccessful due to the barriers formed by the western Utah deserts. The expedition was led by Father Silvestre Velez de Escalante and Father Francisco Dominguez, accompanied by Captain Bernardo de Miera y Pacheco, a retired military engineer. They explored Canyon Pintado from Douglas Pass toward what is now Rangely, Colorado, crossed the Green River near Jensen, Utah, and traveled as far west as Spanish Fork before turning back south to return to Santa Fe.

While Escalante and Dominguez came to the area in search of another route west, others have been drawn to eastern Utah because of scientific exploration. Beginning with John C. Fremont in the early 1840s, reports of the majesty of the mountains, the roaring rivers, the expanse and austerity of the deserts, the abundance of game, and the clues to vast mineral resources have enticed adventurers to the intermountain west of the United States. John Wesley Powell, Clarence King, and Ferdinand V. Hayden led extensive geological surveys that helped quantify these resources. Their reports tempted paleontologists with a vast array of undescribed fossils, particularly dinosaurs and prehistoric mammals.

Settlement in the area inevitably brought about great changes to the landscape, such as mining. In the Uintah Basin, gilsonite was the first hydrocarbon to be mined, bringing a small narrow-gauge railroad (the Uintah Railroad) into the southeastern edge of the basin near Dragon. Although several attempts were made to build more railroads into the basin, none was successful. As a result, the Uintah Basin remains one of the largest areas of the US to be undeveloped by railroads. After World War II, petroleum development and phosphate mining became integral to the rural economy. The railroad from Grand Junction, Colorado, to Price, Utah, brought the development of the coal resources in Carbon and Emery counties. As a result of this mining industry, an influx of some 18 different ethnic groups from across southern and eastern Europe and Asia came to work in the mines. This economic development was a great boost to the area.

NATURAL

The area encompassed by this diamond-shaped Byway is the best place in the world to see dinosaurs in a variety of ways: models and bones on display in museums, bones still in the ground at the sites where they were discovered, bones currently being excavated by paleontologists, and trackways preserved in rocks.

Dinosaurs ruled the Earth long ago. Today, the bones and tracks of these extinct animals can be seen at various sites along the Byway. Many of these sites are located in their natural settings, which makes this Byway one of a kind. Actual dinosaur quarries, which are areas where dinosaur bones are excavated, are along the Byway. You may see dinosaur bones at Mill Canyon Dinosaur Trail or view dinosaur tracks at Copper Ridge Dinosaur Trackway Site, both near Moab. In the Vernal area, you can visit Red Fleet Reservoir State Park, where 190-million-year-old dinosaur tracks are preserved in stony sand dunes along the edge of the lake. Both the Cleveland-Lloyd Dinosaur Quarry near Price and Dinosaur National Monument near Vernal preserve the history of dinosaurs in their natural state.

The only two enclosed dinosaur quarries in America are located on the Dinosaur Diamond: one at Dinosaur National Monument and the other at the Cleveland-Lloyd Dinosaur Quarry. The bones discovered here in 1909 by Earl Douglass date from the Jurassic Period (about 145 million years ago) and were preserved in a riverbed that has been quarried for fossils. Portions of more than 300 individual dinosaurs have been recovered, making the site one of the most prolific dinosaur quarries in the world. The Cleveland-Lloyd Dinosaur Quarry National Natural Landmark has the densest concentration of Jurassic dinosaur bones in the world. The quarry is so dense because about 147 million years ago, dinosaurs were trapped in a muddy bog. Area ranchers found the jumbled remains of these bones, and the quarry has provided dinosaur mounts in more museums around the world than any other in existence. At this quarry, 44 complete Allosaurus specimens have been excavated; appropriately, Utah made the Allosaurus the state fossil in 1988. In nearby Price, dinosaur skeletons, tracks, and fossils are on display at the College of Eastern Utah Prehistory Museum. These exhibits invite visitors to learn more about the history of the area and the effect of the dinosaur on eastern Utah.

RECREATIONAL

River rafting is a popular sport to participate in along the Byway. Both calm-water and whitewater trips are available through companies out of Vernal, Moab, and Green River. The whitewater sections can be frightening even to experienced river runners during the high water levels of spring melt, yet some stretches of both the Green and Colorado rivers have flatwater that can be enjoyable in canoes. Grand scenery awaits around every bend in the river. In fact, the Green River in Desolation Canyon has cliffs higher than the Grand Canyon in Arizona.

Hiking opportunities are everywhere along the Byway. The terrain is varied, giving visitors a feel for the many aspects of the landscape along this route. In the mountains, numerous spectacular peaks and lakes are accessible to hikers. The Uinta Mountain Range, the largest east-west mountain range in the 48 contiguous United States, includes the highest point in Utah—Kings Peak—at 13,528 feet. The desert, particularly near Moab, is another popular place to hike and is an entirely different experience from alpine hiking. The red slickrock around Moab provides the perfect surface for hiking while looking for dinosaur trackways or arches. All of the national parks and monuments along the Byway are outstanding places for hiking and camping as well. Outfitters are available all along the Byway for visitors who want guides, horses, or even llamas to help with the load. Hunting and fishing are also popular recreational activities in the area.

Moab has world-famous mountain biking trails to challenge expert riders and lure beginners. The city has quickly become a mountain bikers' paradise, with trails traveling over many miles, often on slickrock. The Slickrock Bike Trail is located east of Moab in the Sand Flats Recreation Area. The Poison Spider Mesa Trail is another popular trail for both jeeps and bikes and is located on the Potash Road. This trail offers spectacular views of the area surrounding Moab and the Colorado River.

Winter sports are also popular along this Byway. Snowshoeing, cross-country skiing, snowmobiling, and ice fishing can be enjoyed in the high country, while hiking (without the summer heat) is a popular activity in the southern desert areas.

SCENIC

The Dinosaur Diamond Prehistoric Highway's many scenic views capture the expansive area of land surrounding the Byway. Wide vistas are normal in this desert country, with the horizon stretching on for miles. On hot summer days, the blue sky seems like an endless expanse, and sunsets—going on forever—are magnified because of the open sky. Vistas can include features that are more than 100 miles away.

Canyons with walls of red, green, beige, purple, gray, and white greet you. These scenes are intermingled with forested mountain passes and snowcapped mountains. As you travel winding roads out of canyons, sweeping views of the valleys below open up before you. Along the northern facet of the Dinosaur Diamond, the Uinta Mountains cut the skyline. Ancient faults and tectonics controlled the development of this maverick mountain range, creating the largest east-west-trending mountain range in the lower 48 states.

The Green River joins the Yampa River in Dinosaur National Monument at Steamboat Rock. The canyon it forms is spectacular whether viewed from the canyon rim or from the river edge. Farther downstream, the river cuts through Split Mountain and then the Gray Tertiary badlands of the Uinta and Green River formations of Desolation Canyon, the main drainage for the Book Cliffs. The Colorado River provides further scenic aspects, meandering through canyons of red rock. The green vegetation near the river contrasts nicely with the sheer red rock cliffs of the canyons, while snowcapped mountain ranges in the distance offer a break in the desert landscape.

The Energy Loop: Huntington and Eccles Canyons Scenic Byways

UTAH

Located in central Utah, the Energy Loop runs through the Manti-LaSal National Forest and offers a firsthand view of Utah's pristine backcountry. The Byway travels through a variety of landscapes that give you a natural perspective on the region, sprinkled with occasional remnants of days gone by.

Situated amid mountainous terrain and pine forests, the Energy Loop runs through Utah's beautiful backyard. Travelers come from miles away to fish the trout-filled waters along the route or to enjoy a picnic in the beautiful forest surroundings. You can also see signs of red rock country.

Deriving its name from the rich coal-mining history of the area, the Energy Loop combines two of Utah's byways: the Huntington Canyon Scenic Byway and the Eccles Canyon Scenic Byway. Along the Byway, you can see early Mormon settlements in Sanpete Valley or visit unique museums in the Byway communities. Towns from Scofield to Huntington revere the days when coal mining was the livelihood of so many of their ancestors. As you pass today's mines, note the harmony between the environment and industrial development.

Quick Facts

Length: 86 miles.

Time to Allow: 1.5 to 4 hours.

Best Time to Drive: Summer and fall; summer is the high season.

Byway Travel Information: Castle Country Travel Bureau: phone toll-free 800/842-0789; Byway local Web site: www.castlecountry.com/byways.htm.

Special Considerations: Because sections of this Byway climb to altitudes above 10,000 feet, dress warmly during all seasons.

Restrictions: Certain roads may be closed in winter due to heavy snowfall.

Bicycle/Pedestrian Facilities: Touring and mountain biking experiences are plentiful within minutes of the Byway. In addition, you'll find a variety of hiking and pedestrian trails along stretches of the Byway.

The Byway Story

The Energy Loop tells archaeological, cultural, historical, natural, recreational, and scenic stories that make it a unique and treasured Byway.

ARCHAEOLOGICAL

The Energy Loop and the surrounding areas in central Utah offer an archaeological menagerie for visitors of any knowledge level. As you pass places on the Byway, information kiosks offer stories and facts about the archaeological past of the area. Huntington Reservoir is especially notable for its excavation of the 27-foot mammoth skeleton that was found here in 1988. Other excavations in the area have yielded a short-faced bear, a giant ground sloth, a saber-toothed tiger, and a camel, all from an ice age long ago. Examples and casts of these archaeological finds can be seen in museums on and near the Byway, the most significant being the College of Eastern Utah Prehistoric Museum.

While the Energy Loop is most famous for the mammoth skeleton that was found at the Huntington Reservoir, other treasures await visitors as well. Museums in the area, like the Fairview Museum, the Museum of the San Rafael in Castle

Dale, and the College of Eastern Utah Prehistoric Museum, feature artifacts of human inhabitants from the recent past of the pioneers to the more distant past of the Fremont Indian culture. Near the Byway, you can travel through Nine Mile Canyon, a place that has more than 1,000 sites of pictographs and petroglyphs left on the rocks by an ancient people. (Petroglyphs are pictures that are pecked into rock surfaces using harder rocks, often made into tools; pictographs are pictures painted onto the rocks.)

You will also find a tribute to dinosaurs in many of the area museums. Not only have ice-age mammals been found; the area also holds an extensive dinosaur quarry. East of Huntington, the Cleveland-Lloyd Dinosaur Quarry is a place where 145-million-year-old bones and fossils from the Jurassic period are uncovered by paleontologists. The reconstructed skeletons and exhibits in the visitor center and area museums provide a vast amount of information on these creatures of the past. From millions of years ago to just hundreds of years ago, the Energy Loop and its surrounding areas have much to offer in the way of archaeological exploration.

CULTURAL

Unique cultures have been developing in this area for hundreds of years. Visitors who drive the Byway today can't help but notice buildings and artifacts that point to cultures of the past, yet coal mining and ranching are still very much a part of the lifestyles of the people who live along the Energy Loop now. From early native cultures to settlers from the East, all the cultures that have lived on the land around the Energy Loop have survived rugged territory and left a mark.

The cultural patchwork of the area begins with an ancient culture belonging to a people known as the Fremont Indians. These people moved into the area sometime between AD 300 and 500. Although they were a primitive people, they left behind artifacts of a rich culture in their rock art, baskets, and figurines. The Fremonts usually lived in pit houses made of wood and mud that were entered through an opening in the roof. The weapons and tools of this culture were much different than neighboring Indian cultures, indicating the unique existence of the Fremonts. By the time European settlers reached the area, the Fremont Indian culture had disappeared.

Settlers who came to the area in the early 1800s found an untamed wilderness with many resources. Ranchers found meadows with grass that was perfect for grazing livestock. The ranchers' way of life still continues today in the area. Coal was one of the most important resources found in the area, and as a result, coal-mining towns sprang up all around. The coal-mining culture was a society of hard-working men, women, and children who worked in and around the mines—often at the peril of their own lives. Their story can be found in places like the Scofield Cemetery and several deserted towns. Coal mining, power plants, and hydroelectric power harnessed in the reservoirs are all still present today. These all play a direct part in the name of this Byway—the Energy Loop.

HISTORICAL

Few areas in the United States can boast of undiscovered and diverse historical resources the way the area surrounding the Energy Loop can. Travelers along the route see a variety of important historical landmarks, including Native American history, Spanish exploration routes, and the early Mormon settlements that have grown into towns along the Byway. You are in for a diverse historical experience not likely to be matched as you experience the historic coal mining and railroad industries that have deep roots in the area, along with the unique small-town museums in the Byway communities.

NATURAL

The Energy Loop abounds with natural resources that make it the scenic and productive area that it is. All along the Byway, you see evidence of energy—harnessed or unharnessed—on the Energy Loop. Places like the Skyline Mine and the Huntington Power Plant bring natural fuels to the surface, while canyons and wildflowers bring scenic nature to the surface. With these natural qualities combined, the Wasatch Plateau is a thriving habitat for both wildlife and people.

Through ancient faultlines and geological uplifts, the canyons and valleys along the Byway present a unique topography and beautiful places to pass or stop at. Red rocks of sandstone line the walls of Huntington Canyon, while Eccles Canyon takes drivers through forested ridges and grassy meadows. Because of the thick forests of maple, aspen, and oak, the fall is a colorful time in the canyons of the Energy Loop. As the hundreds of shades of green turn to any number of shades between yellow and red, the Byway acquires a whole new splendor as it hosts a final celebration before the winter.

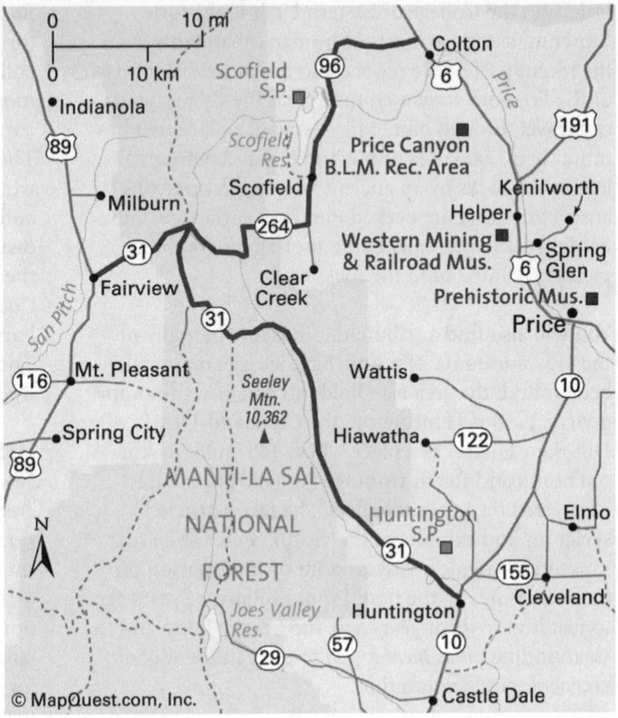

For the same reasons that this area is rich with prehistoric fossils, it is also rich with coal. The coal in this area was formed nearly 100 million years ago, when plants were covered by land or water. The plant matter was compressed by sediment and hardened into the carbon substance we call coal. Although you may not see any coal, its presence is one of the unique natural qualities of the Byway. The discovery of coal on the Byway was one of the original reasons this area was inhabited and is now appreciated and preserved.

As you drive the Byway, the natural splendor that surrounds the road is impossible to ignore. Streams rush by with trout hiding just near the banks. Mature forests of aspen and pine create a lush habitat for wildlife that lives on the Byway. You may catch a glimpse of a fox or a badger. The wetlands of the Fairview Lakes are the best place on the Byway to observe waterfowl or perhaps a bald eagle. The meadows, streams, and forests all combine to create the perfect habitat for creatures great and small. On the mountaintops, birds of prey circle near the clouds while chipmunks scurry through open fields. And in the spring and early summer, wildflowers dot the road and paint the ridgetops.

RECREATIONAL

All along the Byway, cars are pulled over, but the drivers are nowhere to be seen unless you check the river. Anglers come from all around to fish for the trout that swim in the waters of the Huntington Creek. Fly fishermen have their pick of cutthroat, brown, and rainbow trout when fishing the streams and rivers on the Byway. Fishing in the six reservoirs along the Byway is also a common recreational activity.

Hiking and biking are also activities worth trying along the Energy Loop. The rocks and cliffs of Huntington Canyon are an enticing invitation to explorers ready to hike along such diverse terrain. Tie Fork Canyon offers a hike among trees and wildflowers of every kind. Joes Valley is a stop that offers options for anglers and hikers. The valley is an excellent place for wildlife spotting or for enjoying the cool mountain air.

Wherever you end up stopping on the Byway, you'll come across several photo opportunities among the wildflowers and scenic overlooks. Capture a picnic or a hike on film. And even if fishing or boating are not options, stop to skip rocks at a reservoir or go wading in a mountain stream. Recreation creates itself in an area as beautiful as that of Huntington and Eccles canyons.

SCENIC

Wherever the starting point is on the Energy Loop, the road takes travelers through contrasting terrain that changes abruptly. The landscape of the Energy Loop is made up of different areas known as the San Rafael Swell and the Wasatch Plateau. As you drive through these areas, notice the interplay between vegetation and terrain as it creates a scenic view. In some places, mountains are covered in pine and aspen, creating lush, forested canyons. In others, the vegetation is sparse among the red rock formations along the plateaus. Drive the Energy Loop for more than one change of scenery.

Driving through the beautiful stands of mature trees of the Manti-LaSal National Forest, you will notice mountain streams and winding inclines. The shades of light and dark clash directly with the pine and the aspen on the mountaintops of Eccles Canyon.

The long grass in the meadows lines the banks of Huntington Creek, with some of the blades dipping down into the scurrying water below. In the distance, you may catch a glimpse of an old log cabin or, perhaps, a bluebird perched on an old fence. Grass and sagebrush appear among the aspen at the tops of the mountains, and a stop at Sanpete Overlook offers a view of the sprawling mountains and valleys beyond overshadowed by clouds.

Tucked away on the corners of the Energy Loop are small communities and historic mining towns. These present a break in the route and an opportunity to drive the streets of the communities to see buildings and cemeteries from days gone by. Many of the towns like Scofield and Fairview offer informational kiosks or museums for exploration. Driving down the streets of one of these quiet communities brings picturesque images.

The alluring wilderness begins to appear at the south end of the Byway in a swift transition from pine forested mountains to rocky, red cliffs. Unique yellow and red rock formations with holes, crevasses, and trees scattered throughout are the results of an erratic art form of nature. Some of the rocks appear in vertical slabs wedged together to form a cliff. Others have pockmarks so distinct that, from a distance, they could be mistaken for an archaic language. Scenic turnouts are irresistible for photographing a rock formation against the sky or a river rushing through the canyons.

The scenic qualities of the Energy Loop are diverse and breathtaking. The Byway stretches across the Wasatch Plateau, rising high through steep canyons and down into pristine valleys. As you follow the Byway route, you will be amazed at the constantly changing landscapes that make the drive pleasurable year-round. Castle Valley is located on the eastern side of the Byway at the edge of the dramatic San Rafael Swell near Huntington. This desert valley is gorgeous and in stark contrast with the forested canyons found between Huntington and Fairview.

The Byway makes its way up Huntington Canyon, over a high summit, and down into Fairview Canyon, where you are treated to extraordinary views of mountain slopes and the Sanpete Valley below. Streams, lakes, and reservoirs are abundant on the Byway. At the higher elevations where the Huntington and Eccles Canyons intersect, you'll see U-shaped glacial valleys with rounded peaks and cirques cut by ancient glaciers.

Highlights

Traveling from Fairview, this must-see tour suggests scenic vistas that will make your visit to the Energy Loop a fulfilling one. If you are beginning the tour in Huntington, start at the bottom of this list and work your way up.

- **Electric Lake and Burnout Canyon:** Beginning in Fairview, take Highway 31 approximately 10 miles to its junction with Highway 264. Follow 264 for about another 10 miles, and you will come upon a turnout and interpretive signs, along with a view of Burnout Canyon and Electric Lake. Electric Lake was constructed to provide power for the Huntington Power Plant. At the bottom of the lake lay old mines and kilns that were once part of the historic mining town of Connellsville.

- **Scofield:** Approximately 12 miles past the Electric Lake Overlook on Highway 264, you will meet with Highway 96. Travel north for 5 miles to the historic town of Scofield, once the largest town in all of Carbon County. On May 1, 1900, one of the worst mining accidents in US history claimed the lives of hundreds of miners. Visit the old cemetery to see the gravestones of the miners lost on that tragic day. A little farther north, Highway 96 runs beside Scofield State Park and Reservoir, which provides good fishing for trout.

- **Sanpete Valley Overlook:** Leave the Scofield area by heading south on Highway 96, following the road you came in on. Drive back to the junction of Highways 264 and 31 and follow 31 southeast toward the town of Huntington. Approximately 7 miles from the junction, you will find another turnout that shows an impressive view of the Sanpete Valley.

- **Joe's Valley Overlook:** Continue traveling south on Highway 31, and you will arrive at another scenic overlook in approximately 8 miles. This turnout provides interpretive signs and a view of Joe's Valley below, a popular recreation area for locals.

Flaming Gorge–Uintas Scenic Byway

UTAH

Quick Facts

Length: 82 miles.

Time to Allow: 3 hours.

Best Time to Drive: Year-round; high season is summer.

Byway Travel Information: Dinosaurland Travel Board: phone toll-free 800/ 477-5558.

Special Considerations: During the winter, extra care and caution will lengthen the time required to drive from one end of the Byway to the other–it will also lengthen your life span. Because the public lands along the Byway are managed under the Multiple Use Concept, you may have the opportunity to encounter a real western cattle drive along the roadway during the spring and fall months.

Restrictions: Sections of the mountain highway are occasionally closed due to extreme snowfall during the winter.

Bicycle/Pedestrian Facilities: A growing number of visitors experience this Byway and its surrounding area by utilizing bicycles, motorcycles, ATVs, and hiking trails. Although the Byway can be biked from end to end, stretches exist that require cautious travel. Hundreds of miles of designated trails are easily accessible from the Byway if you're interested in getting out of your vehicle and enjoying the backcountry. The Byway is fortunate to intersect several loop routes that are part of the state-designated Scenic Backways Program. Where appropriate (regarding traveler safety and environmental impact), these loops provide hikers, campers, and mountain bikers with recreational opportunities.

As one of the most aptly named landscapes in the country, Flaming Gorge provides the kind of scenic vistas that refuse to fit in the viewfinder of a camera and must be relived in your memory after you return home. Driving this Byway, you get to watch Flaming Gorge and the Uinta Mountains unfold from several different perspectives.

Outdoor recreation is the biggest attraction for travelers on this Byway. The Flaming Gorge Dam and National Recreation Area, created as a recreational destination, encompasses nearly half of the Byway. The Dinosaur National Monument and Dinosaur Quarry have been among the world's greatest sources for dinosaur skeletons and draw visitors from all over the world. This region has continued to gain popularity as an area where travelers can experience the essence of the West through the existence of world-class rock art and the folklore of early explorers, mountain men, outlaws, and cowboys.

The Byway Story

The Flaming Gorge–Uintas Scenic Byway tells archaeological, historical, natural, recreational, and scenic stories that make it a unique and treasured Byway.

ARCHAEOLOGICAL

Beyond its scenic beauty, Flaming Gorge Scenic Byway has pieces of stored ancient history within its grounds and cliff sides. Pictographs and petroglyphs are thought to have been left behind by the Fremont Indians many hundreds of years ago. (Petroglyphs are pictures that are pecked into rock surfaces by using harder rocks, often made into tools; pictographs are pictures painted onto the rocks.) They are evidence that Flaming Gorge has always been an inhabited spot. Ancient rock art can also be found near Dinosaur National Monument on one of the nature trails.

But ancient history goes back further on this Byway, and one of the main reasons people travel to this area is to see the largest quarry of Jurassic dinosaur skeletons in the country. Dinosaur National Monument is a must-see on the Flaming Gorge–Uintas Scenic Byway. Discovered in 1909, the quarry has yielded 11 dinosaur species that were found in the quarry, plus more than 1,600 bones. Here, you can see bones in and out of the quarry and all the places they have to go in between. The exhibits are fascinating, providing a close look at paleontology.

HISTORICAL

The route along the Flaming Gorge–Uintas Scenic Byway is rich in history and culture. The first European explorers were Fathers Dominguez and Escalante. Wesley Powell explored the Green River and named many of the Byway's geographic sites, including Flaming Gorge. General William H. Ashley explored the area and established several trading posts. He organized the first Mountain Man Rendezvous in 1825 near Manila.

The Byway parallels the Outlaw Trail that Butch Cassidy and members of the Wild Bunch used. Two turn-of-the-century homesteads on the Byway, Swett Ranch and Jarvies Ranch, are presently managed and interpreted by the Forest Service and Bureau of Land Management. The town of Vernal celebrates Outlaw Days with an outdoor theater depicting sagas of the Wild Bunch, a ride along the Outlaw trail, and other community events. The influence of the Mormon settlers is also evident in the Manila and Vernal areas.

NATURAL

The Flaming Gorge–Uintas Scenic Byway winds over the eastern flank of the Uinta Mountains and through the Flaming Gorge National Recreation Area, leading you through diverse plant communities that provide a great habitat for more than 390 species of birds, mammals, reptiles, amphibians, and fish. You'll have access to several developed viewing platforms, overlooks, displays, and signs that interpret the different wildlife species, and an outstanding number and variety of wildlife are available for viewing and photography, as well as for hunting and fishing. This Byway is one of the few areas in the US where visitors have the chance to see large herds of deer, elk, moose, and pronghorn antelopes on any given day throughout the year. The seasonal weather changes complement the wildlife migration patterns, which means that you may encounter Rocky Mountain bighorn sheep, river otters, yellow-bellied marmots, Kokanee salmon, red-tailed hawks, mountain bluebirds, golden eagles, bald eagles, and ospreys. Additionally, thousands of sandhill cranes migrate through the Vernal area in April and October each year.

This landscape is the basic setting for the real Jurassic Park, not only for dinosaurs but also for other prehistoric creatures, such as sharks, squids, and turtles. The Utah Field House of Natural History and Dinosaur Gardens serves as an orientation center for the Byway. Dinosaur National Monument features the largest working dinosaur quarry in the world; the world-class displays of dinosaurs and interpretive exhibits provide you with a greater appreciation for the geologic and prehistoric features found along the Byway.

RECREATIONAL

Flaming Gorge Reservoir is the most popular recreation spot in Utah. It offers highly developed facilities for camping, hiking, riding, skiing, snowmobiling, and other water-related opportunities on a year-round basis. The visitor centers, gift shops, restaurants, outfitters, guides, boat rentals, and other retailers work together as partners to make this a quality recreational experience. The businesses are set up to easily accommodate visitors for a week or even longer.

Three-hundred seventy-six shoreline miles surround Flaming Gorge Reservoir, creating an angler's paradise. World-record brown trout exceeding 30 pounds and lake trout over 50 pounds have been caught here. People from all over the world visit the Green River for premier blue-ribbon fly-fishing experiences. The nearby High Uintas Wilderness Area (Utah's largest), which offers hundreds of miles of hiking trails and numerous camping sites, also boasts of hundreds of high-elevation lakes that provide outstanding fishing opportunities.

In addition, some local outfitters offer a four-day Jurassic Journey for families with kids 6 to 12 years old. It includes Class II river rafting on the Green River, short hikes to dinosaur country, a visit to a museum, camping, cooking out, and children's activities that help parents vacation, too.

SCENIC

One of the most beautiful sights as you drive the Flaming Gorge–Uintas Scenic Byway is to watch the sun as it reflects off the water of the 91-mile Flaming Gorge reservoir. The most famous scenic view of the gorge, however, is of Red Canyon just below the Flaming Gorge Dam. The canyon walls on both sides of the water create an image of a lake clinging to the mountainsides. Half of the Byway follows Flaming Gorge as it curves into the Green River. The red plateaus sloping into Sheep Creek Bay look like abandoned sinking ships as the water laps at the edges.

The mountains that surround the gorge itself are densely forested, providing views of trees that carpet hillsides and scatter across ridges. Traveling through Ashley National Forest, the Byway gives you an excellent opportunity to enjoy the eastern edge of the Uinta mountain range, which is the only major east-west range in the United States. As Utah's tallest mountain range, the Uintas are an inviting sight as the peaks tower to the sky. The forest is home to wildlife and beautiful scenery consisting of red rocky mountains and majestic peaks. The crags and geological formations along the drive add immensely to the unique views that make Flaming Gorge memorable.

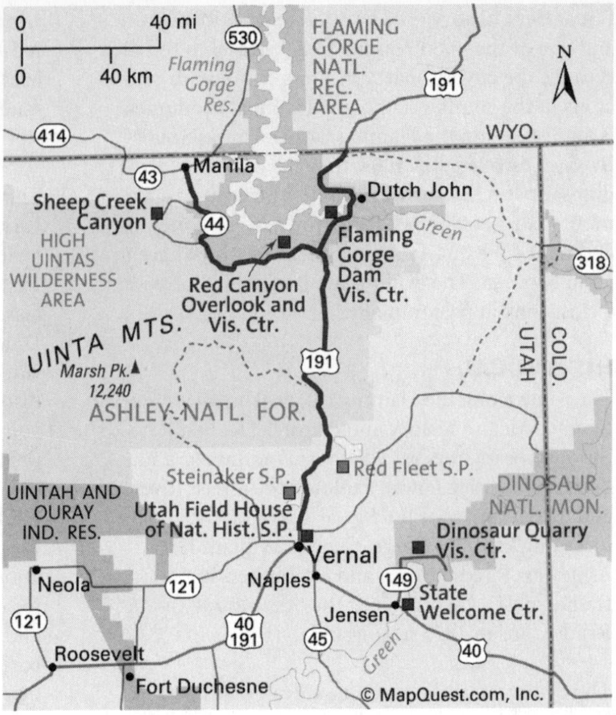

Highlights

While visiting the Flaming Gorge–Uintas Scenic Byway, you can take the following self-guided tour.

- Driving on the Byway from Vernal, you don't want to miss the **Utah Field House of Natural History and Dinosaur Gardens** on the north side of Main Street in the heart of Vernal. See 18 life-sized dinosaurs, as well as artifacts from the Fremont and Ute Indian cultures.

- If you have the time, take a short side trip, following Highway 40 and traveling 20 miles east of Vernal to visit the famous **Dinosaur National Monument.**

- If you're making a quick trip, continue on Highway 191 to the **Flaming Gorge Dam and Visitor Center,** 6 miles from the Greendale Junction (Highway 191 and Highway 44). There, you'll find picnic sites and other visitor facilities. Be sure to take the guided tour through the dam.

- Make a U-turn back on Highway 191 to travel west on Highway 44. If you have time for a longer visit, you could stop at the **Swett Ranch** and partake of pioneer history.

- Continue on your way to the **Red Canyon Overlook and Visitor Center in the Flaming Gorge National Recreation Area,** about 5 miles off of Highway 44. The caves and ledges of this scenic wonder offer glimpses into the ancient history of this area.

- If you have some extra time, continue on Highway 44 and turn left onto the **Sheep Creek Loop Drive** to see the **Ute Tower.**

A Journey Through Time Scenic Byway, Highway 12

UTAH

An All-American Road

QUICK FACTS

Length: 124 miles.

Time to Allow: 1 to 3 days.

Best Time to Drive: Spring is the best time of year to explore the lands surrounding Highway 12. High season comes during the summer, when travelers are visiting Bryce Canyon and Capitol Reef. Winter is the off-season, but many travelers find this area to be a winter wonderland, and the Byway is open and maintained year-round.

Byway Travel Information: Garfield County Travel Council: phone toll-free 800/444-6689; Byway travel and tourism Web site: www.brycecanyoncountry.com.

Special Considerations: Weather can change quickly; thunderstorms are common during the summer. Several stretches of this road are quite isolated and rugged, some with 12 percent grades. The road climbs to 8,000 feet as it crosses Boulder Mountain, rising and falling in steep switchbacks through Escalante Canyons and Boulder Mountain. You'll find several short tunnels in the Red Canyon area. The Aquarius Plateau/ Boulder Mountain segment receives heavy accumulations of winter snow and may be closed temporarily during heavy snowstorms. However, the road is plowed to allow year-round access.

Restrictions: The Hogsback is high and narrow and can be windy. High-profile vehicles should be prepared.

Bicycle/Pedestrian Facilities: Highway 12 offers a paved bicycle path that allows cyclists to pedal through Red Canyon. Other places along the Byway are suitable for cyclists, although places like the Hogsback have little shoulder space for bicycles.

As you drive the Byway that connects Bryce Canyon National Park and Capitol Reef National Park, you are treated to enticing views and stops, along with a kaleidoscope of color. Byway towns in between offer a flavor of a simple life in the middle of a fantastic wilderness. Historic stops and pullouts provide stories for curious Byway travelers. Ancient ruins and artwork can be found throughout the canyons and rock faces that line this Byway.

At nearly every turn, you have an opportunity to get out of the car and stretch. But stretching is only the beginning. Hiking, horseback riding, and traveling by ATV are irresistible activities that allow you to explore the back roads and trails of this wonderland of sculpted color.

The Byway Story

Highway 12 tells archaeological, cultural, historical, natural, recreational, and scenic stories that make it a unique and treasured Byway.

ARCHAEOLOGICAL

Driving this road through some of Utah's most unusual landscapes, the climate and the topography seem all too fantastic for human beings to dwell there. Nevertheless, evidence of ancient civilization is around every corner and within every crevasse of the canyons along Highway 12. The Anasazi, Fremont, and Utes all left their mark on the rugged and challenging land. Their occupation has been preserved in the sandstone of the plateaus and under the sands and soils of the valleys. A thousand years ago, these people made a home of this unique landscape and left evidence of their habitation for visitors, travelers, and archaeologists to see.

Not only was their survival in this wilderness commendable, but the structures that the Anasazi left behind astound travelers and archaeologists alike. As you drive along the base of cliffs and canyons on Highway 12, alcoves high in the rocks hold ancient stone granaries where this hunting and gathering culture would store the food they had collected. The granaries reside in grooves within the cliff side and consist of rocks stacked like bricks with a small hole in the center near the bottom of the structure. Today, we can only guess how the people of so long ago would have reached these heights.

Farther along the Byway, a remarkable display of an excavated Anasazi village is located on the Byway in the community of Boulder. The Anasazi Village State Park Visitor Center is located at the site of a village that once held 200 people. Walls of homes and structures of pit-houses are displayed there as examples of the way these people once lived. Only a few of the structures have been uncovered. The rest remain buried in the ground that surrounds the walkways that take visitors on a tour of the past. Signs of life from so many centuries ago captivate travelers.

One of the most riveting scenes on the Byway is an occasional glimpse of a petroglyph or pictograph. Some of the most impressive examples of this rock art can be seen at Capitol Reef as images of ancient people and animals line the red rock face of nearby Highway 24 and the Fremont River. Pictures and figures were etched on these stone walls all along the Byway and remain as a memorial to this vanished culture. Many of these pictures remain unknown and undiscovered, waiting to be found by an alert explorer. While hiking in the mountains of Highway 12, visitors are compelled to treat these drawings and carvings with an utmost solemnity. These pictures of the past are somehow related to us today, and to disturb them is to cause a breach in the connections of these two great periods.

CULTURAL

Embedded in the rocky precipices of Highway 12 is a conglomeration of cultures—past and present. Over the ages, travelers moving into the area built a home for themselves, incorporating ideas and methods of survival perfected by preceding cultures. The culture that permeates the Byway today is made up of people who hold a deep respect for their predecessors, and towns of the past are now a haven for both travelers and residents on the Byway. Find their heritage and their future in the many festivals and favorite spots all along the Byway.

The cultures of the Fremont Indians and the Anasazi vanished before any cultures surviving today could know them. However, their archaeological remains and artwork enable modern-day experts and visitors to speculate about what these people must have been like. These cultures had a belief system of legends and histories that explained the landforms that surrounded them. One thing is certain: the cultures of the Anasazi, Fremont, and Paiute revered the land of Highway 12 as a special land. Today's cultures feel the same way. Preserving the land and celebrating its natural beauty are common goals for the people who live in communities along the Byway.

Before there was a bridge between the cultures of the future and the past, there was a culture of growth and development. Mormon pioneers established communities over a century ago whose presence today has brought a new collection of stories and histories to tell the story of the Byway. The communities that visitors will observe display the classical elements of a Mormon settlement. People would gather in a town and spread their farms all around the town. This way, an agricultural people developed and preserved a sense of community. This strong sense of community still exists today, and you are invited to partake of it. Thus, influences of past cultures are a force that preserves the rural culture of today and passes its spirit onto the travelers who pass this way.

HISTORICAL

Visitors find a piece of history around every corner along the Journey Through Time. Before Highway 12 became a Scenic Byway, it was a passageway for native tribes, explorers, and pioneers. Their legacy is left behind in the names of prominent places like Powell Point and in places like the historic town of Escalante. Many of the sacred places of the Fremont and Anasazi have been lost and forgotten, but the history that these people left behind is archaeology now. Through the influences of the explorers and the pioneers, lands along the Byway reflect the history of the west to build upon an archaeological and geological history.

The first explorers were Spanish and claimed the land for Spain in 1776. The name of the town Escalante comes from one of the priests who was on the expedition, Silvestre Velez de Escalante. John Wesley Powell more thoroughly explored the land nearly 100 years later in 1869 on a treacherous journey where he lost several of his company. Nearby Lake Powell and Powell Point are now two landmarks that carry his name. By the time he explored the area, Mormon pioneers had already begun to inhabit the region in an attempt to make the desert bloom.

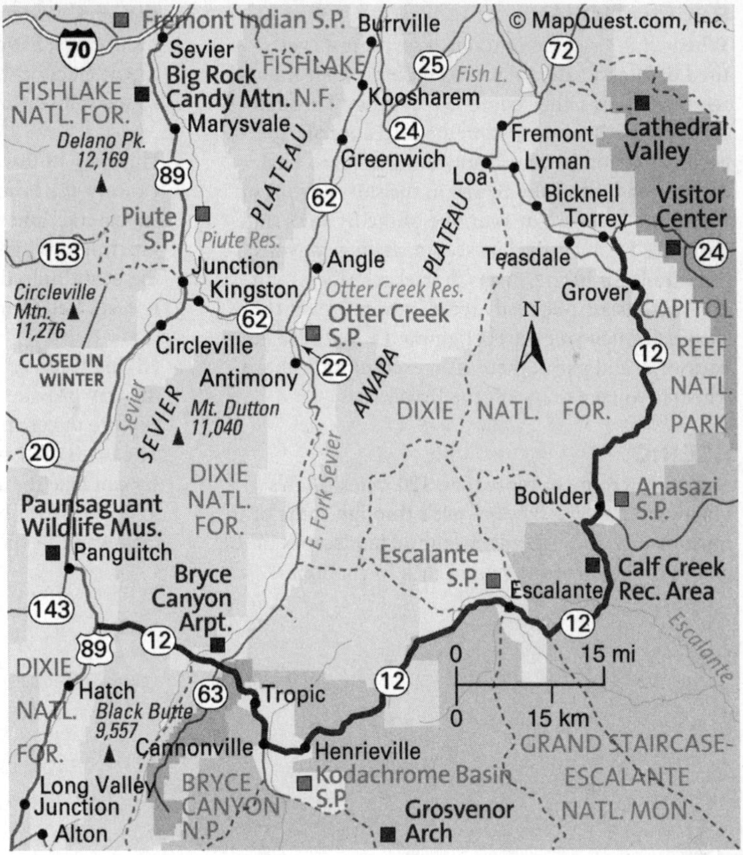

The town of Panguitch was the first place the pioneers attempted to settle. Because of conflicts with the native tribes, they abandoned the settlement until 1871. A string of other towns along the Byway retain a western town appearance with wood storefronts, stone walls, and old-fashioned architecture. In Tropic, visit Ebenezer Bryce's cabin. This rancher/farmer began to utilize the landscape at the mouth of what is now known as Bryce Canyon, one of Utah's most fantastic national parks. The town of Boulder was the last town on the Byway to receive mail by mule. This fertile mountainside is still covered with wooden pioneer fences and old-fashioned barns.

NATURAL

Landforms along the Highway 12 Scenic Byway inspire visitors with awe and curiosity for the powers of nature. Desertscapes have been preserved to become masterpieces of art that have been tempered with time. Their alluring shapes and curves have a story that begins millions of years ago. That story continues today with the thriving forests and wildlife that live along the Byway. Drive Highway 12 and tour a land carved by water and wind. Layers of rock stacked like giant pancakes pick at the imaginations of travelers. Why is the stone here so colorful? How can the rock formations maintain such unusual shapes? The answers are embedded in layers of color within plateaus and canyon walls that have been decorated with trees and wildlife.

Red Rock Canyon, Bryce Canyon, and Kodachrome Basin offer some of the strangest geological sites that travelers will ever see. The walls of Bryce Canyon are lined with singular, human-like pinnacles that protrude from the rock. So many of them in succession make the canyon look like a crowded stadium. The irregular shapes of the rocks in Bryce Canyon were formed when ancient rivers carved exposed layers of the Earth. The meandering of these rivers must have been erratic, for there are thousands of paths through the pinnacles at Bryce Canyon. Red Rock Canyon displays a range of orange and red colors in the rock. Take a hike to discover all the natural arches there. In Kodachrome Basin, evidence of another natural wonder from millions of years ago is in the strange pinnacles of stone. This used to be a geyser basin not unlike the kind found in Yellowstone National Park today. Geologists believe that the towers of stone there are actually fossilized geysers. Their vivid colors are evident from a distance.

RECREATIONAL

When Utah's visiting outdoor recreationists get tired of Utah's national parks and other well-known recreation areas, they come to A Journey Through Time Scenic Byway for supreme recreational experiences. Some of the most captivating hikes in Utah are located just off the Byway in the slot canyons of the Grand Staircase or near one of the Byway's state parks. Red Canyon and its accompanying canyons offer trails for hikers, bikers, horseback riders, and ATV enthusiasts. Be ready for an adventure on the slickrock when you travel Highway 12. With trails, backways, and paths, there is an exciting ride ahead whether you are on or off the Byway.

SCENIC

Spanning a route of more than 120 miles, Utah's Highway 12 Scenic Byway travels through some of the most diverse and ruggedly beautiful landscapes in the country. The surrounding red rock formations, slickrock canyons, pine and aspen forests, alpine mountains, national and state parks, and quaint rural towns all contribute in making Highway 12 a unique route well worth traveling.

Highway 12 travels from west to east through Garfield County, the home of three national parks, three state parks, and one national recreation area. At the junction of Highway 89, the Byway quickly bisects the beautiful red rock formations of Dixie National Forest's Red Canyon and continues eastward.

Hiking trails, campgrounds, and side roads along the way provide numerous opportunities to further explore the area. Highway 12 ends in Wayne County. The town of Torrey is near the junction, and travelers can take the short drive east along Highway 24 to Capitol Reef National Park, thus adding to the Highway 12 experience.

Logan Canyon Scenic Byway

UTAH

Beautiful mountains that tower over the city of Logan and the turquoise waters of Bear Lake captivate visitors and residents year-round. You'll be enchanted by inland seas, a dramatic landscape surrounding this Byway formed by great earthquakes and mountains that tower over the road on both sides. Driving the Logan Canyon Scenic Byway is like entering a new world where the mountains, trees, and river together reveal the undying patterns of nature.

The patterns of the canyon have become intertwined with the patterns of a culture. Once, the land was inhabited only by native tribes of Utah, but as trappers and pioneers entered the region, the land was forever changed. Today, the canyon is recognized as the gem of the surrounding communities. In the summer, the campgrounds are full and the echoes of chattering birds and wind through the trees can be heard throughout. In winter, the stillness of the snow-covered mountainsides lures travelers outdoors for a day of skiing.

Pioneers who made their way here to settle in Cache Valley were the first to make a road through the canyon. Through the determination of the past and the perseverance of today, the beauty of Logan Canyon is accessible as a National Scenic Byway.

QUICK FACTS

Length: 41 miles.

Time to Allow: 1 hour.

Best Time to Drive: Fall; summer is the high season.

Byway Travel Information: Bridgerland Travel Region: phone 435/752-2161.

Special Considerations: Logan Canyon Scenic Byway is a two-lane highway. Although the Byway has more passing zones on the upgrade than the downgrade, you'll find only five to eight passing zones.

Restrictions: Winter weather can be severe in Logan Canyon. The highway patrol may require that vehicles carry tire chains from November through March.

Bicycle/Pedestrian Facilities: Bicycle and pedestrian traffic through the canyon continues to increase as the population grows in Logan and surrounding communities. The Byway consists of roadway shoulders that provide the necessary facilities for bicycle and pedestrian traffic, although in some areas, the shoulders are mostly gravel. Several trail head and bike path entry points are located along the Byway, and several bicycle/pedestrian trails and paths run parallel to the roadway, including Logan River Trails.

The Byway Story

The Logan Canyon Scenic Byway tells cultural, historical, natural, recreational, and scenic stories that make it a unique and treasured Byway.

CULTURAL

From mountain men to mountain climbers, Logan Canyon has fostered a variety of cultures from its earliest days. As cultures have shifted and evolved over the last few centuries in this corner of northern Utah, memories of the past are still in place, which means you can experience a variety of cultural influences as you visit the Byway. Cultural influences of mountain men and tribal natives still surface from time to time in the now-modern cultures of agriculture and industry.

The Shoshone and Bannock tribes had been living in the areas near Cache Valley and Bear Lake for many years before their lands were forever changed by the coming of fur trappers and, later, settlers. Local tribes still gather to practice beautiful cultural dances and songs; their artwork can be seen in fairs and festivals all through the summer. Mountain men are also honored with festivals and activities.

The coming of the Mormon Pioneers made a significant impact on the culture of the area. Settlers from the Church of Jesus Christ of Latter Day Saints (LDS) developed an agricultural society that still thrives in Cache Valley. The Mormon pioneers also brought with them an appreciation for family and heritage that is still found along the Byway.

Today, because they live so close to a perfect wilderness, most everyone in Cache Valley and Bear Lake has a personal attachment to at least one aspect of Logan Canyon. From exploring nature trails to fishing and canoeing, the skills and pastimes of the first people in Logan Canyon remain with today's residents. Everyone has a niche, and everyone is equally convinced that the value of Logan Canyon is priceless.

You will be delighted as you encounter the cultures of today and celebrate the cultures of yesterday. Summer festivals and year-round information about people and places make every culture along the Byway accessible.

HISTORICAL

Although most of the places in Logan Canyon were named in the last 150 years, influences from an earlier past can still be found in places along the Byway. Guinavah-Malibu campground carries the Shoshone word for bird water, which was the earliest name for the Logan River. A mountain man named Jim Bridger gave his name to the region that encompasses the canyon known as Bridgerland. Cache Valley, at the west end of the canyon, was named for the caches that trappers made in the area to store their furs. As Mormon pioneers entered the area in mid-1800s, they established Temple Fork, where they procured the materials they would need to build their temple and tabernacle. And many of the names in the canyon came from the days of the Civilian Conservation Corps (CCC). As these men moved through the canyon, they left a trail of cabins, picnic areas, and campgrounds. Most notable of their achievements is the amphitheater at the Guinavah-Malibu campground.

Stories of highfalutin' families at Tony Grove or an 11-foot-tall bear named Ephraim can be found in places all along the way. These stories are told on Byway markers and at information centers. One of the best places to find out about Logan Canyon history is at Lady Bird Overlook at the mouth of the canyon in Logan, a location that carries history of its own. It was named for President Johnson's wife, Lady Bird Johnson, who initiated the highway beautification plan in the 1960s. At the overlook, you can discover the story of a 1,000-year-old tree and find out why one of the most beautiful spots on the Byway is called China Row.

Logan Canyon was in the land of the Shoshone and the Bannock. Later, Logan Canyon saw the days of the mountain man filled with rendezvous and trapping animals for their fur. When the Mormon pioneers came, the wild land of Logan Canyon was forever changed. Civilization came to the Byway to explore it and discover the wonders of the canyon in the same way that travelers do today. As you pass places along the way, you might be able to find the stories of Indian tribes, mountain men, pioneers, and farmers who all left their mark in different ways along the Logan Canyon Scenic Byway.

NATURAL

In Logan Canyon, where a wilderness waits at the doorstep of the Cache Valley community, nature is the one constant that draws people of every age and disposition. Whether they come for a hike in the mountains or to picnic by the riverside, the one unifying appeal is the natural atmosphere that thrives in Logan Canyon. From the moment you reach the mouth of the canyon, you feel an impulse to roll down the window and let the fresh canyon breeze—a mixture of pine, foliage, and the river—fill the car. The canyon is alive with wildflowers, shrubs, and trees of every kind.

Although the mountains seem high, they were once covered with the water of an inland sea called Lake Bonneville. Many of the rock formations that visitors enjoy in the canyon were caused by erosion from Lake Bonneville. Outcroppings, like the one called the China Wall, are simply ancient beaches where the sediment has become solid and provides a perfect place for activities like rock climbing. Just looking up at these mammoth walls of nature is a mesmerizing experience; knowing that they were once ancient beaches makes them even more exotic.

The enchanting Tony Grove Lake, formerly a glacier, is a favorite natural feature in the canyon. Covered with wildflowers in the spring, the shoreline of the lake is partly a mountainside and partly a forest of pine trees. Water has carved numerous caves through the limestone of the canyon, including Logan Cave and Ricks Spring. Other caves in Logan Canyon are not as well known, although backcountry hikers and rock climbers may have the opportunity to stumble across one of them.

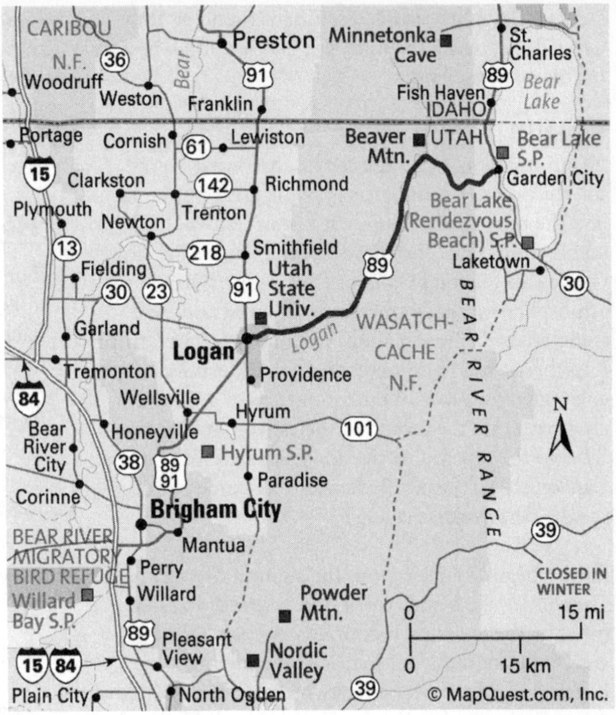

The Logan River is the heart of Logan Canyon, its rhythm changing with the seasons. During the spring, the river rages with snow melt runoff, reaching high velocities. In summer, the river slows, fed by delayed runoff from groundwater storage and augmented by the many springs and tributaries that flow into it. The river surface begins to freeze in the fall and by midwinter, the river forms ragged sheets of ice. When the weather is fair, visitors on the shores of Second Dam watch fish jumping and beavers swimming across the water to its dam. In the winter, deer step lightly on the mountainside and pause by the river for a drink. Through its seasons, the Logan River is central to the lives of local residents and wildlife.

RECREATIONAL

Logan Canyon recreation is one of the main reasons people come to Cache Valley to visit and to stay. After a short drive into the mountains, you'll find a garden of recreational opportunities—some relaxing and others extreme. From an early morning hike to rock climbing, Logan Canyon is the best place for miles around to unwind.

Logan Canyon's limestone outcroppings are calling for you to climb them. Rock climbers gather from spring through fall to challenge the million-year-old mountainsides. Most of the climbs are bolt-protected sport climbs and are in the 5.10 to 5.12 level of difficulty. In winter, climbers can be found making their way up a frozen waterfall. Another mountainside challenge is offered within the crisp winter air at Beaver Mountain, where skiers and snowboarders gather to test skills of balance and coordination.

Although they might be the most exciting of mountain sports, skiing and climbing aren't the only activities available in Logan Canyon. With 300 miles of hiking trails, Logan Canyon is also a hiker's paradise. Trails lead to every kind of destination, from an ancient juniper tree to a pristine mountain lake.

Runners and cyclists especially love the Logan River Trail starting at Red Bridge. On summer mornings, the air is cool and green leaves hang over the trail, creating a scenic place to exercise.

Roads available at Temple Fork and Right Hand Fork provide opportunities for ATVs and motorcyclists to enjoy the exciting back roads of the canyon. During the winter, trailers carrying snowmobiles can be seen entering Logan Canyon. They might be heading to Franklin Basin or the Sinks, where valleys between the trees offer the perfect place to traverse the snow.

When all the snow melts, water sports reach their height in Logan Canyon, whether you are boating or fishing. Logan Canyon is home to the Logan River and Bear Lake, where many travelers take boats and jet skis during the summer for an exhilarating run across its mesmerizing waters. Visitors can also fish for the Bonneville Cisco, which is only found in Bear Lake. The Logan River is famous for fly fishing, but anglers of every kind and age gather at Second and Third Dam to try their luck with a pole. A careful observer will be able to see groups of trout as they gather underneath a bridge nearby, but scuba divers at the east end of Bear Lake have the best view of the local fish. A more secluded setting is found at Tony Grove Lake, where the most popular activity—besides fishing—is canoeing.

SCENIC

Logan residents climb the canyon road year-round for recreation, a chance to enjoy the great outdoors, and the pure exhilaration that Logan Canyon scenery provides. They have favorite haunts like Tony Grove Lake, Second Dam, or China Row, where an atmosphere of shady trees, mossy banks, and clear water feeds the imagination. Visitors to Logan Canyon find themselves in an undiscovered wilderness, an enchanted forest, or in the mountains of a distant country. From the mouth of the canyon at First Dam to the captivating overlook at Bear Lake, Logan Canyon scenery draws audiences that come back to see the performance change.

As you begin your ascent to the summit of Logan Canyon Scenic Byway, you'll find yourself overshadowed by the towering mountains, the tops of which are 1 mile above the road. Just below the road, the Logan River flows over a rocky bed through a series of dams. Each dam has its own inviting qualities. Ducks swimming among cattails and reeds set a tranquil scene for anglers at Third Dam and Spring Hollow. A collection of shady picnic tables along the water's edge at Second Dam entices visitors for a lunchtime stop. Later on the drive, the mountains pull apart, revealing grassy meadows on either side of the Byway.

Evergreen pine and juniper intermingled with deciduous maples and aspen provide a contrast of color that makes Logan Canyon a superb road for seeing fall color. Strips of deep red run in the crevasses of the mountainsides where a cluster of maples is growing, making you wish that fall would linger in Logan Canyon. Perhaps one of the best times to enjoy the late fall is just after a rainstorm, when low-lying clouds float just above the road and every tree and leaf displays rich browns, oranges, and reds.

You may have trouble naming the most beautiful scenic highlight on the Byway or even pinpointing what makes the Byway beautiful. It's the way rocky precipices jut out of the mountainside; the way the mountainside slopes upward, taking a forest of trees with it; the way the trees become brilliant red in the fall; and the way the road winds through it all that make Logan Canyon Scenic Byway one of the most enchanting drives in the country.

Highlights

For your own Logan Canyon must-see tour, consider following this itinerary. Note that all mileages are taken from the Logan Ranger Station at the western mouth of the canyon.

- **Mile 2.5—Second Dam:** A favorite spot for local anglers.
- **Mile 5.0—Wind Caves:** This cave is high above the canyon. A 1.5-mile trail provides access. The cave is actually a triple arch formed by wind and water erosion.
- **Mile 12.0—Logan Cave:** This used to be a popular cave to explore, but because of vandalism in 1998, the Forest Service gated and locked the cave entrance. The upside is that by keeping people out of the cave, the native bat population will likely thrive.
- **Mile 15.4—Ricks Springs:** Despite its name, Ricks Spring is not really a spring; instead, it is a diversion of the Logan River, mixed with a little mountain snowmelt.
- **Mile 19.2—Tony Grove Lake Area:** This worthwhile side trip takes you up a winding road to beautiful Tony Grove Lake.
- **Mile 31.1—Bear Lake Overlook:** On a clear day, Bear Lake sparkles an unusually clear turquoise blue. A display explains the history and geology of the lake and surrounding area.

Nebo Loop Scenic Byway

UTAH

This Byway begins in the quiet community of Payson and ascends back and forth through a canyon of deep, fresh forest that turns to visual fire in the fall. The route continues alongside a cold, rocky creek that drops off into intermittent miniature waterfalls; fishers sit aside this creek in the cool of dusk and let their bait float, listening to a cricket symphony and the fading birds' sonata.

QUICK FACTS

Length: 37 miles.

Time to Allow: 1 hour.

Best Time to Drive: Summer through fall; summer is the high season.

Byway Travel Information: Mountainland Travel Region: phone 801/229-3800.

Special Considerations: Most of the route is somewhat narrow and winding. This means that you won't have much opportunity to pass slower vehicles, and speed limits average 30 mph. Plan to sit in the front seat of your vehicle if you are susceptible to carsickness. A 200-foot-long section of the route consists of hairpin curves, so you must slow to about 15 mph in order to get around the 90-degree turns safely.

Restrictions: Heavy snowfall in the winter necessitates the closure of the Nebo Loop Scenic Byway to passenger vehicles from October to the first of June each year. However, Utah State Park employees groom the road for winter use.

Bicycle/Pedestrian Facilities: This Byway is a popular destination for both road and mountain bikers. The route offers 214 miles of paved and dirt roads, 103 miles of hiking and biking trails, and 71,270 roadless acres for visitors to enjoy. Although a formal bicycle lane has not been designated and the shoulder isn't very wide in most places, cyclists frequently ride the 37-mile loop.

By degrees, the landscape changes into a high-mountain wilderness. Only fields of crisp, bright wildflowers interrupt the thick stands of aspen. Incredibly high overlooks show the Wasatch Mountains sitting loosely below you like a pile of ribbon. From these overlooks, you can also see the Byway's namesake, 11,877-foot Mount Nebo.

This area is so well liked that more than 1 million people visit annually, and a good percentage of them reserve campsites a year in advance to ensure that they get a good spot to relax for a few days. During the summer, most people like to fish at the glass-smooth lakes, such as Payson, or hike on the many trails, such as Loafer Mountain Trail.

The Byway Story

The Nebo Loop Scenic Byway tells archaeological, cultural, historical, natural, recreational, and scenic stories that make it a unique and treasured Byway.

ARCHAEOLOGICAL

Archaeological sites in the area show that this valley had one of the largest Native American populations in the Great Basin. In fact, if you had gone to the Byway's Utah Valley Overlook in about AD 1500, you would have seen smoke curling up from several large villages. This Byway now retains two archaeological sites, both of which are associated with Native Americans.

The first, the Nephi Mounds, was an agricultural site used by the Fremont Indians around AD 1300. The Nephi Mounds archaeological site is agriculture in nature, as opposed to most of the mounds in the United States, which are ritualistic or artistic in nature. As one of the primary sites for the Fremont Indian farming, Nephi Mounds was discovered by modern peoples when a farmer uncovered Indian relics in his field.

The second is Walker Flat, a favorite camping spot of the Ute Indians, who liked to spend their summers in these mountains. Walker Flat is also where the Walker War broke out between the Utes and Mormon settlers. The historic Peteeneet Academy displays information about Ute Chief Walker and his followers, the protagonists of the Walker War.

CULTURAL

Settled by Mormon Pioneers in 1850, the area surrounding the Byway took on the culture of the farmer and the frontiersman, with pieces of the native cultures mixed in. Although towns like Payson and Nephi were established nearby, Mount Nebo and its surrounding landscape were preserved even after a road ran through these backwoods areas; to destroy some of nature's finest work is beyond the culture that still remains on the Nebo Loop today. Proud of their pioneer and native heritage and the legacy of the Nebo Loop, the residents of Payson, Nephi, and surrounding communities enjoy the rivers, lakes, and forests nearby to their fullest extent.

The Byway covers two counties, and as you continue south, the communities become smaller and life becomes simpler. The city now known as Payson was once called Peteetneet, named for Chief Peteetneet of the Ute Tribe. Peteetneet, which means "little waters," is now the name of the Academy that exhibits art and museum pieces. Visitors stop at the Peteetneet Academy on their way to the natural wonders of the Nebo Loop. And like any communities with traditions, the Byway communities host unique festivals throughout the year. Over Labor Day weekend, for example, Payson hosts the Golden Onion Days celebration.

As you drive the Byway, you may want to follow the examples of the local residents and grab your tent and a fishing pole to camp your way along the Nebo Loop. Stop by some of the orchards along the way that have been a main supply of food and income for Nebo's communities for nearly two centuries. By stopping at small communities along the way, you get to see what's in store beyond Mount Nebo.

HISTORICAL

The road that became the Nebo Loop had been used for centuries by Native Americans and, later, by explorers and sawmill companies. The road was then built by the Civilian Conservation Corps (CCC) and enhanced by the addition of recreational facilities.

People have inhabited the Byway and its surrounding areas for unrecorded amounts of time. The elusive Fremont Indians made their home here before the Utes, who played a part as settlers arrived in Utah. The Walker War, one of two significant wars between Utah Utes and the Mormon settlers, took place on the northern end of the Byway.

Important explorers, such as Dominques and Escalante (1776), Jedediah Smith (1826), and John C. Fremont (1843), investigated the area and found it attractive. Mountain man Daniel Potts, who came in 1827, said of the Utah Valley, "This is a most beautiful country." The Mormon Battalion also used the road in 1848 on their way back from California and the Mexican War, and the 49ers used it to go west for gold.

Early white settlement is marked by places such as Pete Winward Reservoir. Payson farmers built the Reservoir between 1890 and 1907 with horse teams and drags and named it after the city's first water master. Later, in the mid-1930s, the CCC made significant contributions to the development of the Byway and its components. For example, they built Dry Lake, which was ingeniously filled with water from a canal that was more than a mile away. More importantly, the CCC's rockwork allowed both the paved Byway road and the stream to occupy the narrow space that it does.

The old Loafer Ski Area and the Maple Dell Scout Camp demonstrate the longtime popularity of this Byway for recreation. The Loafer Ski Area was a popular place to relax from 1947 to the mid-1950s. The old slope, whose concrete slab foundations you can still see, had a 930-foot-long towrope and a 284-foot elevation drop. The ski area was rudimentarily furnished: a simple shelter, a toilet, and an outdoor picnic area. The Maple Dell Scout Camp has produced vivid memories for Utah scouts since 1947. Continual improvements have been made at the camp; one of the most notable was construction of a large lodge in 1960, which was made possible by the donations of Mr. Clyde, then the governor of Utah and president of the Boy Scout Council. Later, a dance hall, cottages, and a swimming pool filled with water from a nearby icy spring were added.

By preserving the Nebo Loop as it is today, visitors are able to see this beautiful wilderness as it was 100 or 200 years ago. Its more recent history is preserved in its museums and exhibits and in structures and buildings all along the Byway.

NATURAL

Named for the tallest peak on the Wasatch mountain range, the Nebo Loop Scenic Byway travels through a variety of terrains and a multitude of natural treasures. From lakes to forests to rocky overlooks, the Nebo Loop displays some of Utah's most beautiful natural settings.

The Byway takes you into the Wasatch mountain range, where you overlook the Utah Valley. The range was formed from great movements of the Earth's crust and an uplift of sedimentary layers; today, Mount Nebo reaches the height of 11,877 feet above sea level. Viewing the topography from the Byway gives you a sense of Utah's place in the Rocky Mountains.

Some favorite places for travelers on the Byway are Payson Lakes Recreation Area and Devil's Kitchen. Climbing the Byway toward the lakes, you'll pass Payson Creek running through the forest. When you reach the peaceful lakes, you'll find them to be a mountain retreat perfect for fishing, picnicking, or just enjoying the serenity of the gently lapping waters. The Devil's Kitchen has been compared to Bryce Canyon: red rock and strange pillars of rock called hoodoos decorate this part of the Byway. This is where Utah's sandstone sculptures begin.

The Byway travels through the Uinta National Forest full of cottonwoods, maples, pines, and aspen. The forest springs up on either side of the road, shading it with millions of leaves. You may also notice the change in plant life as you ascend the Byway—views of sagebrush are soon overtaken by pine and spruce trees. Among the trees live elk, deer, and bobcats. On a very rare occasion, a bear or a cougar comes into view, but these creatures spend time in the most secluded places of the Mount Nebo Wilderness Area.

From lush forests to sandstone basins, the Nebo Loop offers a compact view of some of Utah's unique terrains. Be sure to explore realms of the Nebo Loop Scenic Byway—all created by nature.

RECREATIONAL

All the typical outdoor recreational activities can be done here, and some activities, like hunting and horseback riding, that are rarely allowed in other urban forests are allowed here. Nebo Loop is also a popular area for watching wildlife; specific viewpoints have been designated for observing deer, elk, moose, and bears.

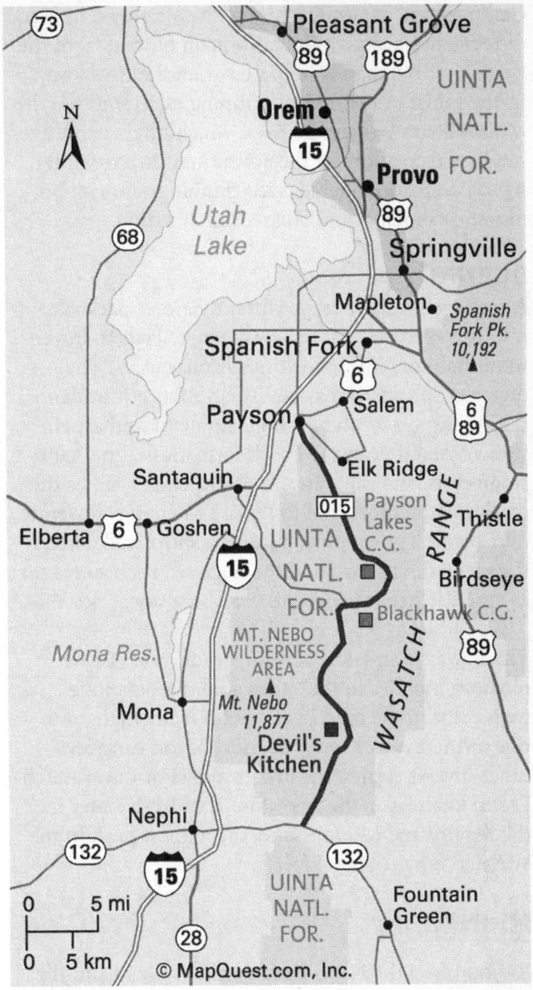

Because the Byway is so popular, reservations must be made at least a year in advance for Blackhawk and Payson Lakes campgrounds; the typical weekend occupancy rate is 95 percent during the camping season. Payson Lake is the most popular campground because it offers swimming, canoeing, hiking, fishing, a fully accessible nature trail, and fishing piers for people with disabilities. Blackhawk Campground has the only horse transfer station for people with disabilities in the region that is within an hour of urban populations. Few scenic Byways offer so much recreation while showing so little evidence of use.

Although the Byway attracts more than 1 million visitors each year, the design of the facilities makes them almost fade into the woods, keeping them fairly invisible to the scenic driver. Payson Lakes

Campground illustrates this fact by offering a myriad of recreational activities that remain hidden from the Byway, yet the road is only a few hundred feet away. In the midst of the typical camping experiences is the Mount Nebo Wilderness Area, which offers primitive, roadless recreation for the adventurer. In the winter, Byway recreation includes ice climbing, snowmobiling, snowshoeing, and cross-country skiing.

SCENIC

A rare spectrum of crisp, vibrant views is packed into this relatively short Byway, where jagged, frozen mountains are infused with vigorous colors. The diversity spreads across the Byway's flat bottomlands, mid-elevation scrub oak, high alpine fir and aspen, snow-covered peaks, red rock formations, gray sandstone cliffs, and salt flats. Devil's Kitchen typifies this diversity: the short trail to Devil's Kitchen is towered over by dark green pine, but just a short walk later, the green disappears, and the huge red rock spires that are the Kitchen jab into the deep blue sky.

The Byway is an essay in color: wildflowers paint blossom mosaics in the spring and trees explode with color in the fall. If you get up really high, onto one of the Byway's many overlooks, you can view other diverse scenes: the urban sprawl of the Wasatch Front; Utah Lake, the largest body of fresh water in the region; and Mount Nebo, the highest peak in the Wasatch range (11,994 feet).

Highlights

As you travel the Nebo Loop Scenic Byway from the Payson end, consider following this itinerary. If you're starting at the other end, simply read this list from the bottom and work your way up.

- **Mile 0—Peteetneet Academy.** The school was built in 1901 by well-known architect Richard C. Watkins and consists of a three-story building with a bell tower and red sandstone accent on red brick walls. Peteetneet is still used for classes in the fine arts and public meetings and events.

- **Mile 0.8—Maple Dell Scout Camp.** Since 1947, this camp has given scouts a chance to take in vivid scenery and participate in outdoor recreation. In 1960, a large lodge was constructed, along with a dance hall, cottages, and a swimming pool.

- **Miles 7.0 and 7.1—Payson Lakes Day Use Area, Fisherman Entrance.** Payson Lakes has trailer camping and handicapped-accessible sites and features a shoreline nature trail, two beaches, and a universal access pier.

- **Mile 10.2—Blackhawk Campground.** This popular Forest Service campground has group and individual campsites as well as a horse camping facility. The area accommodates equestrian users by featuring tie racks, double-wide camping spurs, and easy access to the trails.

- **Mile 11.5—Beaver Dam Overlook.**

- **Mile 16.2—Santaquin Overlook.**

- **Mile 17.3—Bald Mountain Overlook.**

- **Mile 18.0—Utah Lake Overlook.**

- **Mile 21.9—Nebo Bench Trail (trail head sign).**

- **Mile 22.5—Mount Nebo Overlook.** Much of the geologic base of Mount Nebo is derived from the Oquirrh formation, which includes quartzite, limestone, and sandstone. The multiple advances and retreats of mountain glaciers formed cirque-shaped basins predominantly found in Bald Mountain and Mount Nebo. Many legends are associated with Mount Nebo and its Native American history.

- **Mile 26.6—Devil's Kitchen.** Devil's Kitchen Geologic Area is one of the highlights of the Byway. Eroded layers of red-tinted river gravel and silt form spires and sharp ridges. Visitors viewing this unique feature will marvel at its brilliant contrast to the surrounding mountain greenery. There is a rest room and a handicapped-accessible picnic area.

- **Mile 28.0—Salt Creek Overlook.**

- **Mile 35.2—Junction with Highway 132.** Here you come to the end of the Byway. Nephi is about 10 miles west.

Arizona

This rapidly growing state has more than tripled its population since 1940. Its irrigated farms grow citrus fruits, cotton, vegetables, and grain on lush green lands that contrast sharply with the surrounding desert. It also produces 60 percent of the nation's copper.

Population: 5,130,632
Area: 113,642 square miles
Elevation: 70-12,633 feet
Peak: Humphreys Peak (Coconino County)
Entered Union: February 14, 1912 (48th state)
Capital: Phoenix
Motto: God Enriches
Nickname: Grand Canyon State
Flower: Saguaro (sah-WAH-ro) Cactus Blossom
Bird: Cactus Wren
Tree: Palo Verde
Time Zone: Mountain
Web site: www.arizonaguide.com
Fun Fact:
- Among all the states, Arizona has the largest percentage of its land set aside and designated as Native American lands.

In winter, the areas around Phoenix, Tucson, and Yuma offer sunshine, relaxation, and informal Western living. Air-conditioning and swimming pools make year-round living pleasant. In summer, the northern mountains, cool forests, spectacular canyons, trout streams, and lakes offer a variety of vacation activities, including hunting and fishing camps, ghost and mining towns, meadows filled with wildflowers, intriguing ancient Native American villages, cliff dwellings, and dude ranches.

Francisco Vasquez de Coronado crossed the area in 1540 on his ill-fated search for the nonexistent gold of Cibola. Grizzled prospectors panned for gold in mountain streams and hit pay dirt. The missions built by Father Kino and his successors date back as far as 1692. Irrigation ditches, built by the Hohokam people hundreds of years earlier, have been incorporated into modern systems.

The state has 23 reservations and one of the largest Native American populations in the United States. More than half of that population is Navajo. Craft specialties include basketry, pottery, weaving, jewelry, and kachina dolls.

Arizona is a state of contrasts. It has modern and prehistoric civilizations, mountains, deserts, and modern agriculture. Arizona offers fascinating adventures for everyone.

When to Go/Climate

We recommend visiting Arizona in the spring or fall, when the temperatures are milder and the heavy tourist traffic is over.

AVERAGE HIGH/LOW TEMPERATURES (° F)

Flagstaff

Jan 42/15	**May** 67/33	**Sept** 74/41
Feb 45/18	**June** 78/41	**Oct** 63/31
Mar 49/21	**July** 82/51	**Nov** 51/22
Apr 58/27	**Aug** 79/49	**Dec** 43/16

Phoenix

Jan 66/49	**May** 94/64	**Sept** 98/73
Feb 71/45	**June** 104/73	**Oct** 88/61
Mar 76/49	**July** 106/81	**Nov** 75/49
Apr 85/55	**Aug** 104/79	**Dec** 66/42

Calendar Highlights

January

Fiesta Bowl *(Tempe). ASU Sun Devil Stadium. Phone 480/350-0900.* College football game.

Native American Festival *(Litchfield Park). Phone West Valley Fine Arts Council 623/935-6384.* Approximately 100 Native American craft vendors. Native American dancing and other authentic entertainment.

February

Arabian Horse Show *(Scottsdale). WestWorld. Phone 480/515-1500.* The largest Arabian horse show in the world. More than 2,000 champion horses. Barn parties and more than 300 commercial vendors.

Arizona Renaissance Festival *(Apache Junction). Phone 520/463-2700.* Hundreds of participants enjoy music, theater, crafts exhibits, and games. Concessions. Jousting tournament at King's Jousting Arena.

Chrysler Classic of Tucson *(Tucson). Omni Tucson National Golf Resort & Spa and The Gallery Golf Club. Phone toll-free 800/882-7660.* $3-million tournament featuring top pros.

Winter Fest *(Flagstaff). Phone 800/842-7293.* Features art contest and exhibit, theater performances, workshops, sled dog and other races, and games; Winterfaire with arts and crafts; entertainment.

March

Spring Festival of the Arts *(Tempe). Downtown. Phone Mill Avenue Merchants Association 480/967-4877.* Artists' exhibits, food, entertainment, family activities.

September

Sedona Jazz on the Rocks *(Sedona). Phone 520/282-1985.* More than 5,000 people attend this outdoor jazz festival, featuring internationally renowned artists.

Southwestern Navajo Nation Fair *(Dilkon). Navajo Nation Fairgrounds. Phone 520/657-3376.* Navajo traditional song and dance; Inter-tribal powwow; All-Indian Rodeo; parade, concerts, exhibits.

October

Arizona State Fair *(Phoenix). State Fairgrounds. Phone 602/252-6771.*

December

Tostitos Fiesta Bowl Block Party *(Tempe). Phone 480/784-4444.* Includes games, rides, entertainment, pep rally, fireworks, and food.

Parks and Recreation

Water-related activities, hiking, riding, various other sports, picnicking, camping, and visitor centers are available at all parks. There is a $5/car day-use fee at state parks; $45 and $75 annual day-use permits are available. Camping costs $10-$16/day. Arizona also has nine state historic parks ($3-$6; guided tours additional fee). For further information, contact Arizona State Parks, Public Information Officer, 1300 W Washington, Phoenix 85007; phone 602/542-1996.

FISHING AND HUNTING

Both are excellent in a number of sections of the state. Nonresident fishing licenses: one-day (except Colorado River), $12.50; five-day, $26; four-month, $37.50; general, $51.50; Colorado River, all species, $42.50; trout stamp, $49.50. Urban fishing (for 14 lakes in six cities), $16. Inquire for fees to fish on Native American reservations. Nonresident hunting licenses: three-day small game, $38; general, $85.50. Tags cost from $50.50 for turkey to $3,755 for buffalo. Permits for most big-game species are available by drawing only. Combination nonresident licenses (fishing and hunting), $177.50 (includes a trout stamp). Fees subject to change. For updated information, contact the Arizona Game & Fish Department, 2222 W Greenway Rd, Phoenix 85023; phone 602/942-3000.

Driving Information

Safety belts are mandatory for all persons in the front seat of a vehicle. Children under 4 years or under 40 pounds in weight must be in approved safety seats anywhere in the vehicle. For further information, phone 602/223-2000.

INTERSTATE HIGHWAY SYSTEM

Use the following list as a guide to access interstate highways in Arizona. Always consult a map to confirm driving routes.

Highway Number	Cities/Towns within 10 Miles
Interstate 8	Casa Grande, Gila Bend, Yuma.
Interstate 10	Casa Grande, Chandler, Glendale, Litchfield Park, Mesa, Phoenix, Scottsdale, Tempe, Tucson, Willcox.
Interstate 17	Cottonwood, Flagstaff, Glendale, Phoenix, Scottsdale, Sedona, Tempe.
Interstate 19	Nogales, Tucson.
Interstate 40	Flagstaff, Holbrook, Kingman, Seligman, Williams, Winslow.

Additional Visitor Information

Arizona Highways is an excellent monthly magazine; to obtain a copy, contact 2039 W Lewis Ave, Phoenix 85009. Several informative booklets may be obtained from the Arizona Office of Tourism, 2702 N 3rd St, Suite 4015, Phoenix 85004; phone 602/230-7733 or toll-free 888/520-3434.

YOU'VE SEEN THE GRAND CANYON—NOW WHAT?

This loop drive, a side trip for visitors to the South Rim of Grand Canyon National Park, combines scenic beauty with archeological, historical, geologic, and scientific sites. It can be done in one full day or divided into a day and a half with an overnight stop in Flagstaff.

From Grand Canyon Village, head south on Hwy 64/Hwy 180, turning southeast on Hwy 180 at Valle for a slow but beautiful drive through the San Francisco Mountains. Those interested in the history of the area, including prehistoric peoples and more recent American Indians, will want to stop at the Museum of Northern Arizona (3101 N Ft. Valley Rd, Flagstaff). Then continue along Hwy 180 to the turnoff to Lowell Observatory (1400 W Mars Hill Rd, Flagstaff), which has been the site of many important astronomical discoveries since its founding in 1894. Guided tours of the facilities are offered, and there's a public observatory. Kids especially like the interactive displays in the exhibit hall and the Pluto Walk, a trip through the solar system.

You are now on the north edge of Flagstaff, and the city is a good spot to spend the night. Flagstaff's top attractions include Riordan Mansion State Historic Park, where you'll step back into the early 20th century to the rustic elegance of the home of two wealthy brothers, Tim and Mike Riordan, who were very successful in the timber industry. Actually two homes in one large log building, the mansion is somewhat unique among historic homes in that it contains practically all of its original furnishings–the exact pieces bought by the Riordan brothers and their wives (also two siblings) in 1904. The mansion was constructed and then furnished in American Arts and Crafts style, also called Craftsman, a style of furniture that was simple, well made, and durable.

From Flagstaff, go east on I-40, and take the turnoff to Walnut Canyon National Monument to see dozens of small cliff dwellings built by the Sinagua people some 800 years ago. You'll explore the monument on two trails. One is a fairly easy walk along a mesa-top; the other is a bit more strenuous but provides a much closer look at the cliff dwellings as it drops about 400 feet into Walnut Canyon.

Leaving the monument, head back toward Flagstaff on I-40 and go north on Hwy 89 to the Sunset Crater Volcano/Wupatki national monuments loop road, where you'll find an extinct volcano, fields of lava rock, and ruins of prehistoric stone pueblos. Wupatki National Monument's main attraction is Wupatki Pueblo, a

100-room dwelling, three stories high in places, built in the 12th century by the Sinaguans. This handsome apartment house was constructed of red sandstone slabs, blocks of pale beige limestone, and chunks of brown basalt, cemented together with clay. Nearby, Sunset Crater Volcano National Monument offers an intimate look at a dormant volcano, with its rugged landscape of jet black basalt, twisted into myriad shapes ranging from humorous to grotesque. Sunset Crater's primary eruption was in the winter of 1064-1065, and archeologists continue to speculate as to how this tremendous event affected the people who lived in this area at the time, primarily the Sinagua at nearby Wupatki and Walnut Canyon.

After rejoining US 89, continue north into the Navajo Reservation and the community of Cameron, with the historic but still operating Cameron Trading Post, which sells museum-quality items as well as more affordable rugs, baskets, jewelry, and other Native American crafts. From Cameron, head west on Hwy 64 back into the national park. **(Approximately 215 miles)**

Bisbee (F-5)

See also Douglas, Sierra Vista, Tombstone

Founded 1880
Population 6,090
Elevation 5,400 ft
Area Code 520
Zip 85603
Information Greater Bisbee Chamber of Commerce, 7 Main St, Box BA; phone 520/432-5421
Web site www.bisbeearizona.com

Nestled in the foothills of the Mule Mountains of southeastern Arizona, Bisbee once was a tough mining town known as "Queen of the Copper Camps." Today, Bisbee is rich in architecture and culture with many art galleries, period hotels, and bed-and-breakfasts.

What to See and Do

Bisbee Mining and Historical Museum. *5 Copper Queen Plz, Bisbee. Phone 520/432-7071. www.bisbeemuseum.org.* Housed in the 1897 office building of the Copper Queen Consolidated Mining Company. Depicts early development of this urban center through displays on mining, minerals, social history, and period offices; historical photographs. Shattuck Memorial Research Library. (Daily 10 am-4 pm; closed Jan 1, Thanksgiving, Dec 25) 207B Youngblood Hill. Also operates Muheim Heritage House (early 1900s). (Fri-Tues) **$$**

Bisbee Restoration Association & Historical Museum. *37 Main St, Bisbee. Phone 520/432-4106.* Local historical and pioneer artifacts; Native American relics. (Mon-Sat; closed holidays) **DONATION**

Mine tours. *118 Arizona St, Bisbee. On Hwy 80 near Old Bisbee. Phone 520/432-2071.* Tours include

Lavender Pit. *37 Main St, Bisbee. Phone 520/432-2071.* A 340-acre open-pit copper mine, now inactive. Approximately one-hour van tour of surface mine and historic district (daily 9 am, 10:30 am, noon, 2 pm, 3:30 pm; closed Thanksgiving, Dec 25). Lavender Viewpoint (daily; free). **$$$**

Queen Mine. *118 Arizona St, Bisbee. Phone 520/432-2071.* Approximately one-hour guided tour on mine train; takes visitors 1,800 feet into mine tunnel. Mine temperature 47° F-49° F; jacket recommended. Underground tour (daily 9 am, 10:30 am, noon, 2 pm, 3:30 pm; closed Thanksgiving, Dec 25). **$$**

Limited-Service Hotel

★★ COPPER QUEEN HOTEL. *11 Howell Ave, Bisbee (85603). Phone 520/432-2216; fax 520/432-4298. www.copperqueen.com.* Built in 1902. 48 rooms, 4 story. Check-in 2 pm, check-out 11 am. Restaurant, bar. Outdoor pool. **$**

Specialty Lodging

The following lodging establishment is approved by Mobil Travel Guide but, due to its unique and individualized nature has not been given a traditional Mobil Star rating. Included in this listing you may find bed-and-breakfasts, limited-service inns, guest ranches, and other unique hotel properties.

CALUMET AND ARIZONA GUEST HOUSE. *608 Powell St, Bisbee (85603). Phone 520/432-4815. www.calumetaz.com.* 6 rooms, 2 story. Pets accepted. Complimentary full breakfast. Check-out 10:30 am. **$**

Bullhead City (B-1)

See also Kingman; Laughlin, NV

Founded 1946
Population 21,951
Elevation 540 ft
Area Code 928
Information Chamber of Commerce, 1251 Hwy 95, 86429; phone 928/754-4121
Web site www.bullheadcity.com

Bullhead City was established in 1945 as a construction camp for Davis Dam, a reclamation facility located 3 miles to the north. The name is derived from its proximity to Bullhead Rock, now largely concealed by the waters of Lake Mojave. Bullhead City is across the Colorado River from Laughlin, Nevada (see) and its casinos.

What to See and Do

Davis Dam and Power Plant. *Bullhead City. 4 miles N on Colorado River. Phone 928/754-3626.* Dam (200 feet high, 1,600 feet long) impounds Lake Mohave, which has a surface area of 28,500 acres and reaches 67 miles upstream to Hoover Dam. Self-guided tour through the power plant (daily). **FREE**

Fishing, camping. *Bullhead City. Phone 928/754-3245.* Trout, bass, bluegill, crappie, and catfish. Campsites, picnic grounds at Katherine Landing, 5 miles north, a part of the Lake Mead National Recreation Area (see NEVADA).

Limited-Service Hotels

★ BEST WESTERN BULLHEAD CITY INN. *1126 Hwy 95, Bullhead City (86429). Phone 928/754-3000; toll-free 800/780-7234; fax 928/754-5234. www.bestwestern.com.* 88 rooms, 2 story. Pets accepted; fee. Complimentary continental breakfast. Check-in 2 pm, check-out noon. Outdoor pool, whirlpool. **$**

★ ★ LAKE MOHAVE RESORT. *2960 E Katherine Spur Rd (86430). Phone 928/754-3245; fax 928/754-1125. www.sevencrown.com.* 49 rooms, 2 story. Pets accepted, some restrictions; fee. Check-out 11 am. Restaurant, bar. **$**

Restaurant

★ EL ENCANTO. *1884 S Hwy 95, Bullhead City (86442). Phone 928/754-5100.* Mexican menu. Lunch, dinner. Closed holidays. Bar. Children's menu. Outdoor seating. **$**

Canyon de Chelly National Monument (A-5)

See also Ganado

Web site www.nps.gov/cach

In the NE corner of the state at Chinle.

The smooth red sandstone walls of the canyon extend straight up as much as 1,000 feet from the nearly flat sand bottom. When William of Normandy defeated the English at the Battle of Hastings in 1066, the Pueblo had already built apartment houses in these walls. Many ruins are still here.

The Navajo came long after the original tenants had abandoned these structures. In 1864, Kit Carson's men drove nearly all the Navajo out of the area, marching them on foot 300 miles to the Bosque Redondo in eastern New Mexico. Since 1868, Navajo have returned to farming, cultivating the orchards, and grazing their sheep in the canyon. In 1931, Canyon de Chelly (pronounced "de-SHAY") and its tributaries, Canyon del Muerto and Monument Canyon, were designated a national monument.

There are more than 60 major ruins, some dating from circa A.D. 300, in these canyons. White House, Antelope House, and Mummy Cave are among the most picturesque. Most ruins are inaccessible but can be seen from either the canyon bottom or from the road along the top of the precipitous walls. Two spectacular, 16-mile rim drives can be made by car in any season. Lookout points, sometimes a short distance from the road, are clearly marked. The only self-guided trail (2 1/2 miles round-trip) leads to the canyon floor and White House ruin from White House Overlook. Other hikes can be made only with a National Park Service permit and an authorized Navajo guide (fee). Only four-wheel drive vehicles are allowed in the canyons; each vehicle must be accompanied by an authorized Navajo guide (fee) and requires a National Park Service permit obtainable from a ranger at the visitor center.

The visitor center has an archaeological museum and rest rooms. (Daily; free) Rim drive guides and White House Trail guides are available at the visitor center bookstore. Picnic areas and campgrounds (free).

What to See and Do

★ Canyon Tours. *Hwy 191 and RR 7, 3 mi E, Chinle. Phone 928/674-5841; toll-free 800/679-2473.* Offered by Thunderbird Lodge (see LIMITED-SERVICE HOTELS). Lodge personnel conduct jeep tours into the canyons; half-day (daily) and full-day (Apr-Oct, daily) trips. **$$$$**

Limited-Service Hotels

★ ★ BEST WESTERN CANYON DE CHELLY INN. *100 Main St (Rte 7), Chinle (86503). Phone 928/674-5874; toll-free 800/327-0354; fax 928/674-3715.*

www.bestwestern.com. 99 rooms. Pets accepted; fee. Check-out 11 am. Restaurant. Indoor pool. **$**

★ ★ THUNDERBIRD LODGE. *Hwy 191 and Rte 7, Chinle (86503). Phone 928/674-5841; toll-free 800/679-2473; fax 928/674-5844. www.tbirdlodge.com.* This is the only lodging located within the monument. 72 rooms. Check-out 11 am. Restaurant. Airport transportation available. **$**

Carefree (D-3)

See also Chandler, Mesa, Phoenix, Scottsdale, Tempe

Population 2,927
Elevation 2,389 ft
Area Code 480
Zip 85377
Information Carefree/Cave Creek Chamber of Commerce, 748 Easy St, Marywood Plaza, Box 734; phone 480/488-3381
Web site www.carefree.org

The immense Tonto National Forest (see PAYSON) stretches to the north and east; the Ranger District office for the forest's Cave Creek District is located here. Located in the center of town is the largest and most accurate sundial in the Western Hemisphere.

Special Events

Carefree Fine Art and Wine Festivals. *Downtown, Easy and Ho Hum sts, Carefree. Phone 480/837-5637. www.thunderbirdartists.com.* At each of these pleasant outdoor festivals, held three times a year, more than 150 booths feature the work of nationally recognized artists. You'll find a wide range of mediums—from paintings and pottery to sculptures and stained glass—in all price ranges. In the wine pavilion, host to Arizona's largest wine-tasting event, visitors can sample vintages from around the world. The popular festivals draw more than 180,000 art lovers each year. (Late Oct, early Nov, mid-Jan, early Mar: Fri-Sun 10 am-5 pm) **$**

Fiesta Days. *Memorial Arena, Carefree. Phone 480/488-4043.* PRCA rodeo, parade. Usually the first weekend in Apr.

Full-Service Resort

★ ★ ★ ★ THE BOULDERS RESORT AND GOLDEN DOOR SPA. *34631 N Tom Darlington Dr, Carefree (85377). Phone 480/488-9009; toll-free 800/553-1717; fax 480/488-4118. www.wyndham.com.* Nestled in the foothills of the Sonoran Desert near Scottsdale, The Boulders Resort and Golden Door Spa is a most unusual place, with a flair for the dramatic. Mimicking the natural landscape in its architecture, it teases the eye as it blends perfectly with the surrounding rock outcroppings, ancient boulders, and saguaro cactus plants. The adobe casitas make wonderful homes and are distinguished by overstuffed leather chairs, exposed beams, and Mexican tiles, while one-, two-, and three-bedroom Pueblo Villas are ideal for families traveling together or for those on longer visits. The resort boasts a first-rate tennis facility and two 18-hole championship golf courses. The Golden Door Spa, an outpost of the famous California spa, is simply divine. A cavalcade of flavors is discovered at the five restaurants, from Mexican and Spanish to Southwestern and continental. 215 rooms, 2 story. Pets accepted, some restrictions; fee. Check-in 4 pm, check-out noon. High-speed Internet access. Restaurants (public by reservation), bar. Children's activity center. Fitness room, spa. Three outdoor pools, whirlpool. Golf, 36 holes. Tennis. Business center. **$$$$**

Spa

★ ★ ★ GOLDEN DOOR SPA AT THE BOULDERS. *34631 N Tom Darlington Dr, Carefree (85377). Phone 480/595-3500; toll-free 800/553-1717. www.wyndham.com.* Golden Door Spa, a branch of the original California spa, is the jewel in the crown at this luxurious resort. Founded in 1958, the first Golden Door was inspired by the Honjin Inns of Japan, where water and massage therapies soothed both body and mind. Long considered the mother of the spa movement, the Golden Door remains at the forefront of the industry. Blending Asian, European, and Native American philosophies of healing, the Golden Door Spa at The Boulders is a perfect complement to the serenity of the Arizona desert.

The 33,000-square-foot facility is a veritable temple of well-being with 26 treatment rooms, a movement studio, and even a meditation labyrinth inspired by Hopi medicine wheels. Keeping fit is a central component of the Golden Door experience, and the comprehensive fitness center filled with state-of-the-art cardiovascular equipment is just the beginning. Personal assessments help you uncover your strengths and weaknesses, while guided nature hikes and rock-climbing excursions go beyond the ordinary to help you attain your goals. Yoga, tai chi, Pilates, spinning, and kickboxing are just some of the group classes available at the movement studio.

Three Vichy showers complete with heated tile floors, Swiss showers, and a Watsu area provide a nirvana for aqua therapy, and all the spa treatments begin with a Golden Door ritual, a soothing and refreshing shower. Head-to-toe pampering is available, from 12 kinds of stress-reducing massages to nourishing facials and body wraps. Many treatments are a nod to the region's Native American history. Ancient Ayurvedic principles are revived in the mystical treatments of bindi balancing, where crushed herbs exfoliate and light oils moisturize your skin, and shirodhara, which begins with massaging warm oil into your scalp and concludes with a mini facial massage and a heated hand and foot treatment.

Restaurant

★★★ THE LATILLA ROOM. *34631 N Tom Darlington Dr, Carefree (85377). Phone 480/488-9009; toll-free 800/553-1717; fax 480/595-3552. www.wyndham.com/boulders.* Regional American fare is served with understated elegance at the Boulders Resort's Latilla Room, a glass-walled space tucked into the Sonoran Desert and surrounded by 12-million-year-old granite boulder formations. The menu here is a zesty blend of Louisiana Creole and Arizona Southwestern fare, which means that dishes pack a serious punch of flavor. Timid palates need not apply. The rustic, cozy dining room is decorated with Native American weavings, and, as its name suggests, the main room's ceiling is crafted from Ocotillo branches (called latilla, which means "little sticks" in Spanish). The outdoor patio, warmed by a blazing fire, is an ideal spot to have a drink before or after dinner—or simply to soak up the views at twilight. Southwestern menu. (See also THE BOULDERS RESORT.) Dinner, Sun brunch (Dec-May). Bar. Children's menu. Casual attire. Reservations recommended. Outdoor seating. **$$$**

Casa Grande (D-3)

See also Florence, Gila Bend, Phoenix

Population 25,224
Elevation 1,405 ft
Area Code 520
Zip 85222
Information Chamber of Commerce, 575 N Marshall St; phone 520/836-2125 or toll-free 800/916-1515
Web site www.casagrandechamber.org

Named for the Hohokam ruins 20 miles northeast of town, Casa Grande is situated in an agricultural and industrial area.

What to See and Do

Casa Grande Valley Historical Society & Museum. *110 W Florence Blvd, Casa Grande. Phone 520/836-2223. www.cgvhs.org.* Exhibits tracing Casa Grande Valley growth from prehistoric times to the present with an emphasis on farm, ranch, mining, and domestic life. Gift shop. (Sept-May, Mon-Sat 1-5 pm; closed summer, holidays) **$**

Factory outlet stores. *Casa Grande.* Two different outlet malls: Factory Stores of America, 440 N Camino Mercado, phone 602/986-7616; and Tanger Factory Outlet Center, 2300 E Tanger Dr, phone 520/836-9663.

Picacho Peak State Park. *15520 Picacho Peak Rd, Picacho. 24 miles SE off I-10, Picacho Peak exit. Phone 520/466-3183. www.pr.state.az.us/Parks/parkhtml/picacho.html.* This 3,400-acre park includes a sheer-sided peak rising 1,500 feet above the desert floor, which was a landmark for early travelers. The only Civil War battle in Arizona was fought near here. Colorful spring wildflowers; desert nature study. Hiking, picnicking (shelter). Interpretive center programs (seasonal). (Daily 8 am-10 pm)

Special Event

O'Odham Tash-Casa Grande's Indian Days. *1201 Pinal Ave, Casa Grande. Phone 520/836-4723.* Rodeo, parades, ceremonial dances, arts and crafts, chicken scratch dance and bands; Native American foods, barbecue. Reservations advised. Mid-Feb.

Limited-Service Hotel

★★ HARRAH'S AK-CHIN CASINO RESORT. *15406 N Maricopa Rd, Maricopa (85239). Phone 480/802-5000; toll-free 800/427-7247; fax 480/802-3009. www.harrahs.com.* 146 rooms. Check-in 4 pm, check-out noon. Restaurant, bar. Fitness room. Outdoor pool, whirlpool. Casino. **$**

Casa Grande Ruins National Monument (D-3)

See also Casa Grande, Chandler, Florence, Phoenix

33 miles SE of Chandler on Hwy 87, 1 mile N of Coolidge.

The Hohokam people existed in the Salt and Gila river valleys for hundreds of years before abandoning the region sometime before 1450. They built irrigation canals in order to grow beans, corn, squash, and cotton. Casa Grande (Big House) was built during the 14th century. Casa Grande was constructed of caliche-bearing soil (a crust of calcium carbonate on stony soil) and is four stories high (although the first story was filled in with dirt). The top story probably provided an excellent view of the surrounding country and may have been used for astronomical observations. After being occupied for some 100 years, Casa Grande was abandoned. Father Kino, the Jesuit missionary and explorer, sighted and named it Big House in 1694 Casa Grande is the only structure of its type and size in southern Arizona. It is covered by a large protective roof. There is a museum with archaeological exhibits (daily); self-guided tours. Contact Superintendent, 1100 Ruins Dr, Coolidge 85228; phone 520/723-3172.

Chandler (D-3)

See also Mesa, Phoenix, Scottsdale, Tempe

Population 176,581
Elevation 1,213 ft
Area Code 480
Information Chandler Chamber of Commerce, 25 S Arizona Pl, 85225; phone 480/963-4571 or toll-free 800/963-4571
Web site www.chandleraz.org

Cotton, citrus fruits, pecans, and sugar beets are grown in the surrounding area. A growing number of high-technology companies have facilities here including Intel, Motorola, and Microchip Technologies.

What to See and Do

Casa Paloma. *7131 W Ray Rd, Chandler. Phone 602/284-4346.* Shoppers often dismiss strip centers with a big ho-hum, but they give this one a big thumbs-up. The Rolex street clock outside the Coffin & Trout jewelry store hints at why: above-average shops—35 in all—in a stylish setting. Some of the retail names you know, such as Ann Taylor and Sur La Table. Others you probably don't: Red Rock Trading Post sells fine Indian jewelry, for example. After shopping, pamper yourself at Rolf's Salon and Spa or dine at one of seven restaurants. (Daily; closed Dec 25)

Chandler Center for the Arts. *250 N Arizona Ave, Chandler. Phone 480/732-2680. www.chandlercenter.org.* The arts-minded city of Chandler shines the spotlight on both national and local talent at this 64,000-square-foot performance center known for its superb acoustics. The London City Opera, Jay Leno, Anne Murray, Rita Moreno, Bob Newhart, and the Phoenix Boys Choir are among those who have helped the center earn its reputation for staging shows that bring audiences to their feet. The main auditorium seats 1,550 but can be subdivided into three separate halls holding 1,000, 350, and 250 people, respectively.

Devil's Claw Course at Whirlwind Golf Club at Wildhorse Pass. *5692 West North Loop Rd, Chandler. Phone toll-free 866/564-7667.* For information, see www.whirlwindgolf.com.

Gila River Arts & Crafts Center. *Sacaton. 15 miles S via Hwy 93 at junction I-10 (exit 175), on Gila River Indian Reservation. Phone 480/963-3981. www.gilaindiancenter.com.* Gallery featuring the works of outstanding Native American artists and artisans from more than 30 tribes. Restaurant features Native American food. Museum preserves cultural heritage of Pima and Maricopa tribes. Gila Heritage Park features five Native American villages. (Daily 8 am-5 pm; closed holidays) **FREE**

Gila River Casino. *5550 W Wild Horse Pass, Chandler. Phone toll-free 800/946-4452. www.wingilariver.com.* With nearly 170,000 square feet of gaming action, this casino offers lots of options when you're ready to take some risks in hopes of going home a winner. The card room is decked out with 50 poker tables; the bingo hall, 1,500 seats; and the 24-hour live keno section, 36 seats. Or do some arm-pulling at any of the 500 slot machines. If you're lucky, one or more may cough up some coins just for you.

Whirlwood Golf Club at Wildhorse Pass-Cattail Course. *5692 West North Loop Rd, Chandler. Phone toll-free 866/564-7667.* For information, see www.whirlwindgolf.com.

Special Events

ASA Amateur Softball National Tournament. *Snedigar Sportsplex, Chandler. Phone 480/782-2727.* Sept.

Chandler Jazz Festival. *Downtown. Phone 480/786-4424. www.chandlerjazz.com.* Each year, downtown Chandler transforms itself into New Orleans's Bourbon Street for a lively salute to jazz. But this festival showcases the modern version, not the traditional one that rings through the Crescent City. So the 20-plus bands that perform play mostly swing music featuring the sweet sounds of the piano, saxophone, trumpet, and upright bass. The event attracts about 6,000 jazz lovers, and the beat goes on for three days at a price that can't be beat. Early May. **FREE**

Chandler Ostrich Festival. *Tumbleweed Park, 2250 S McQueen Rd, Chandler. Phone 480/963-0571.* Features ostrich racing, food, entertainment, arts and crafts, carnival with rides and other amusements, petting zoo, and pony rides. Early Mar. **$**

Limited-Service Hotels

★ FAIRFIELD INN. *7425 W Chandler Blvd, Chandler (85226). Phone 480/940-0099; toll-free 800-228-2800; fax 480/940-7336. www.marriott.com.* 66 rooms, 3 story. Complimentary continental breakfast. Check-in 3 pm, check-out noon. Pool, whirlpool. **$**

★ ★ WYNDHAM GARDEN HOTEL. *7475 W Chandler Blvd, Chandler (85226). Phone 480/961-4444; toll-free 800/889-8846; fax 480/940-0269. www.wyndham.com.* 178 rooms, 4 story. Check-in 3 pm, check-out noon. Restaurant, bar. Fitness room. Pool, whirlpool. **$**

Full-Service Resort

★ ★ ★ SHERATON SAN MARCOS GOLF RESORT AND CONFERENCE CENTER. *One San Marcos Pl, Chandler (85225). Phone 480/812-0900; toll-free 800/528-8071; fax 480/963-6777. www.sanmarcosresort.com.* Located just minutes from Phoenix, this historic resort marries both business and pleasure into a desert oasis. Golf, tennis, and horseback riding are available on site, with great shopping and excursions close by, insuring that there's something for everyone. 307 rooms, 4 story. Pets accepted, some restrictions; fee. Check-in 3 pm, check-out noon. Restaurant, bar. Fitness room. Pool, children's pool, whirlpool. Golf. Tennis. Business center. **$**

Restaurants

★ ★ C-FU GOURMET. *2051 W Warner, Chandler (85224). Phone 480/899-3888; fax 602/899-1388. www.cfugourmet.com.* Chinese menu. Dinner. Bar. Casual attire. Reservations recommended. **$$**

★ ★ ★ KAI. *5594 Wild Horse Pass Blvd, Chandler (85070). Phone 602/458-8005. www.starwood.com/wildhorsepass.* Tucson-based chef Janos Wilder has been active in preserving Native American agricultural seeds. And in his restaurant Kai, which translates to "seed" in the Pima tongue, he uses plenty of them. Lodged in the Sheraton Wild Horse Pass resort south of Phoenix on Gila River tribal land, the sophisticated eatery showcases locally grown produce and a surprisingly rich Arizona-made olive oil in recipes that merge contemporary tastes and time-honored Native American techniques. The results, expertly prepared by chef de cuisine Sandy Garcia, include lobster tail, corn and avocado atop fry bread, and rack of lamb sauced with a mole made from Native American seeds. In fair weather, request a table on the terrace, which takes in romantic views over the undeveloped desert and distant mountains. Southwestern menu. Dinner. Closed Sun-Mon. Bar. Casual attire. Outdoor seating. **$$$**

Chiricahua National Monument (E-5)

See also Willcox

Web site www.nps.gov/chir.

32 miles SE of Willcox on Hwy 186, then 3 miles E on Hwy 181.

This national monument features 20 square miles of picturesque natural rock sculptures and deep twisting canyons.

The Chiricahua (Cheer-a-CAH-wah) Apaches hunted in the Chiricahua Mountain range. Cochise, Geronimo, "Big Foot" Massai, and other well-known Apaches undoubtedly found their way into this region during the 1870s and 1880s. A visitor center, 2 miles from the entrance, has geological, zoological, and historical displays. (Daily)

At Massai Point Overlook, geologic exhibits explain the volcanic origin of the monument. The road up Bonita Canyon leads to a number of other outlook points; there are also 20 miles of excellent day-use trails to points of special interest.

Picnicking and camping sites are located within the national monument. There is a 26-foot limit on trailers. Contact Superintendent, HCR #2, Box 6500, Willcox 85643. (Daily 8 am-4:30 pm)

Clifton (D-5)

See also Safford

Settled 1872
Population 2,596
Elevation 3,468 ft
Area Code 520
Zip 85533

The scenic Coronado Trail (Hwy 666) begins here and continues north 90 miles to Alpine. The Apache National Forest (see SHOW LOW) stretches north and east of Clifton; the Clifton Ranger District office of the Apache-Sitgreaves National Forest is located here.

What to See and Do

Old Jail & Locomotive. *Hwy 191, Clifton. Phone 520/824-3560.* This jail was blasted out of mountainside, first occupied by the man who built it.

Cottonwood (C-3)

See also Flagstaff, Prescott, Sedona

Population 9,179
Elevation 3,314 ft
Area Code 928
Zip 86326
Information Chamber of Commerce, 1010 S Main St; phone 928/634-7593
Web site www.cottonwoodarizona.com

This town is in the beautiful Verde Valley, an area offering many opportunities for exploration.

What to See and Do

Dead Horse Ranch State Park. *675 Dead Horse Ranch Rd, Cottonwood. At Verde River, N of town on 10th St. Phone 928/634-5283. www.go-arizona.com/Dead-Horse-Ranch-State-Park.* This 320-acre park offers fishing; nature trails, hiking, picnicking (shelter), camping (dump station). Visitor center. (Daily from 8 am)

Fort Verde State Historic Park. *125 E Hollomon, Camp Verde. 15 miles SE on Hwy 279/260. Phone 928/567-3275. www.pr.state.az.us/parks/parkhtml/fortverde.html.* Four original buildings of a US Army fort, a major base during the campaigns of 1865-1890; museum; two furnished officers' quarters; post doctor's quarters; military artifacts. Picnicking. (Daily 8 am-5 pm; closed Dec 25)

Jerome. *8 miles W on Hwy 89A. Phone 928/634-2900 (Chamber of Commerce). www.azjerome.com.* 3,200-5,200 feet almost straight up. Historic old copper-mining town with cobblestone streets and renovated structures now housing gift, jewelry, antique, and pottery shops; art galleries; restaurants; and hotels. Views of Verde Valley and the Mogollon Rim. Also in Jerome is

> **Jerome State Historic Park.** *Douglas Rd. Off Hwy 89A. Phone 928/634-5381. www.pr.state.az.us/parks/parkhtml/jerome.html.* The Douglas Memorial Mining Museum depicts the history of Jerome and of mining in Arizona; it's housed in

the former house of "Rawhide" Jimmy Douglas (fee). Picnicking. No overnight facilities. (Daily 8 am-5 pm; closed Dec 25)

Tuzigoot National Monument. *1 Tuzigoot Rd, Clarkdale. 2 miles NW via N Main St, follow signs. Phone 928/634-5564.* Excavated pueblo occupied from AD 1000-1450. Visitor center, museum with artifacts of Sinagua culture. (Daily) **$$**

Verde Canyon Railroad. *300 N Broadway, Clarkdale. 2 miles NW via Hwy 89A. Phone 928/639-0010; toll-free 800/320-0718. www.verdecanyonrr.com.* This scenic excursion train takes passengers through the Verde Canyon on a four-hour round-trip from Clarkdale to Perkinsville. Panoramic views of the rugged high-desert area, the Verde River, and Native American ruins. Some open-air viewing cars. Starlight rides (summer). (Daily, schedule varies; closed Jan 1, Thanksgiving, Dec 25) **$$$$**

Special Events

Fort Verde Days. *Fort Verde State Historic Park, 125 E Hollomon St, Camp Verde. Phone 602/542-4174 (information); toll-free 800/285-3703.* Parade, dancing, barbecue, historical reenactments, arts and crafts, live entertainment. Second weekend in Oct.

Paseo de Casas. *Jerome. Phone 928/634-5477.* Tours of unique old homes and old public buildings. Paseo de Casas also includes an art exhibition by local artists and a photographic display from the historical society. Third weekend in May. **$**

Verde Valley Fair. *Fairgrounds, 800 E Cherry St, Cottonwood. Phone 928/634-3290. www.verdevalleyfair.com.* This annual fair features live music, arts and crafts, racing and swimming swines, novelty shows, food, and contests. First weekend in May. **$**

Limited-Service Hotels

★★ BEST WESTERN COTTONWOOD INN. *993 S Main St, Cottonwood (86326). Phone 928/634-5575; toll-free 800/377-6414; fax 928/634-5576. www.cottonwoodinn-az.com.* 77 rooms, 2 story. Complimentary continental breakfast. Check-in 2 pm, check-out 11 am. Outdoor pool, whirlpool. **$**

★★ QUALITY INN. *301 W Hwy 89A, Cottonwood (86326). Phone 928/634-4207; toll-free 800/228-5151; fax 928/634-5764. www.qualityinn-az.com.* 52 rooms, 2 story. Complimentary continental breakfast. Check-out 11 am. Restaurant, bar. Pool, whirlpool. **$**

Douglas (F-5)

See also Bisbee

Founded 1901
Population 14,312
Elevation 3,990 ft
Area Code 520
Zip 85607
Information Chamber of Commerce, 1125 Pan American; phone 520/364-2477

Located on the Mexican border, this diversified manufacturing town is a warm, sunny place abounding in Western hospitality. A Ranger District office of the Coronado National Forest (see TUCSON) is located here.

Special Events

Cinco de Mayo. Mexican independence festival. Early May.

Cochise County Fair & College Rodeo. *Cochise County Fairgrounds, 3677 N Leslie Canyon Rd, Douglas. Phone 520/364-3819; toll-free 888/315-9999. www.explorecochise.com.* Third weekend in Sept.

Douglas Fiestas. Mid-Sept.

Horse races. *Cochise County Fairgrounds, 3677 N Leslie Canyon Rd, Douglas. Phone 520/364-7701.* Mid-Apr-mid-Sept.

Flagstaff (B-3)

See also Cottonwood, Sedona, Williams, Winslow

Settled 1876
Population 52,894
Elevation 6,910 ft
Area Code 928
Information Chamber of Commerce, 101 W Rte 66, 86001; phone 928/774-4505
Web site www.flagstaff.az.gov

In 1876, the Boston Party, a group of men who had been lured west, made camp in a mountain valley on the Fourth of July. They stripped a pine tree of its branches and hung a flag at its top. Afterward, the tree was used as a marker for travelers who referred to the place as the spring by the flag staff. In 1882, Flagstaff became a railroad town when the Atlantic and Pacific Railroad (now the Santa Fe) was built.

Flagstaff, home of Northern Arizona University (1899), is an educational and cultural center. Tourism is Flagstaff's main industry; the city is a good place to see the Navajo country, Oak Creek Canyon, the Grand Canyon (see), and Humphreys Peak (12,670 feet), the tallest mountain in Arizona. Tall pine forests of great beauty abound in the surrounding area. A Ranger District Office of the Coconino National Forest is located here.

What to See and Do

Arizona Historical Society Pioneer Museum. *2340 N Fort Valley Rd, Flagstaff. 2 1/2 miles NW on Fort Valley Rd (US 180). Phone 928/774-6272.* This museum highlights the history of Flagstaff and northern Arizona. There are changing exhibits throughout the year. (Mon-Sat; closed holidays) **FREE**

Arizona Snowbowl Ski & Summer Resort. *6355 Hwy 180, Flagstaff. 7 miles NW off Hwy 180 at Snowbowl Rd in Coconino National Forest. Phone 928/779-1951. www.arizonasnowbowl.com.* The 50-acre resort has two triple, two double chairlifts; patrol, school, rentals; restaurants, bars, lounge; lodges. Thirty-two trails, longest run more than 2 miles; vertical drop 2,300 feet. (Mid-Dec-mid-Apr, daily) Skyride (Memorial Day-Labor Day; fee) takes riders to 11,500 feet. **$$$$**

Coconino National Forest. *2323 E Greenlaw Ln, Flagstaff. Phone 928/527-3600. www.fs.fed.us/r3/coconino.* This national forest surrounds the city of Flagstaff and the community of Sedona (see). Outstanding scenic areas include Humphreys Peak, Arizona's highest point; parts of the Mogollon Rim and the Verde River Valley; the red rock country of Sedona and Oak Creek Canyon, where Zane Grey wrote Call of the Canyon; the San Francisco Peaks; seven wilderness areas; the eastern portions of Sycamore Canyon and Kendrick wilderness areas and the northern portion of Mazatzal Wilderness area; extinct volcanoes; high country lakes. Fishing; hunting on almost 2 million acres, winter sports, picnicking, camping (fee).

Lowell Observatory. *1400 Mars Hill Rd, Flagstaff. 1 mile W on Mars Hill Rd, off Santa Fe Ave. Phone 928/774-3358. www.lowell.edu.* Established by Percival Lowell in 1894; the planet Pluto was discovered from this observatory in 1930. Guided tours; slide presentations; telescope viewing (seasonal). Museum, gift shop. Telescope domes are unheated; appropriate clothing advised. (Nov-Mar: daily noon-5 pm; Apr-Oct: daily 9 am-5 pm; evening program hours vary, call for information; closed holidays) **$**

Mormon Lake Ski Center. *4825 S Lake Mary Rd (Mormon Lake Ranger Station), Flagstaff. From Flagstaff, take Lake Mary Rd (Forest Highway 3) S 20 miles to the Forest Rd 90 intersection. Turn W and drive 8 miles to the Mormon Lake Village. The Ski Touring Center is on the right. Phone 928/774-1147.* Terrain includes snowy meadows; huge stands of pine, oak, and aspen; old logging roads; and turn-of-the-century railroad grades. School. Has 21 miles of marked, groomed trails; 7,200-foot elevation; restaurant, bar; motel, cabins. Rentals, ski shop. Guided tours, moonlight tours on full moon weekends. (Daily 9 am-5 pm) **$**

Museum of Northern Arizona. *3101 N Fort Valley Rd, Flagstaff. 3 miles NW on Hwy 180. Phone 928/774-5213..www.musnaz.org.* Exhibits on the archaeology, geology, biology, paleontology, and fine arts of the Colorado Plateau; offers Hispanic, Hopi, Navajo, Zuni, and Pai exhibits and summer marketplaces, revealing the region's artistic traditions, native cultures, and natural sciences. (Daily 9 am-5 pm; closed Jan 1, Thanksgiving, Dec 25) **$**

Oak Creek Canyon. *Slide Rock State Park, 6871 N Hwy 89A, Sedona. 14 miles S. Phone 928/203-0624 (visitor center). www.oakcreekcanyon.net.* This spectacular gorge may look familiar to you; it's a favorite location for western movies. The northern end of the road starts with a lookout point atop the walls and descends nearly 2,000 feet to the stream bed. The creek has excellent trout fishing. At the southern mouth of the canyon is Sedona (see), a resort town.

Riordan Mansion State Historic Park. *409 Riordan Rd, Flagstaff. W on I-40, exit Flagstaff/Grand Canyon, then N on Milton Rd; turn right at sign past second light. Located next to Northern Arizona University. Phone 928/779-4395. www.pr.state.az.us/parks/parkhtml/riordan.html.* This 6-acre park features an Arts and Crafts-style mansion built in 1904 by Michael and Timothy Riordan. The brothers played a significant role in the development of Flagstaff and northern Arizona. Original artifacts, handcrafted furniture, mementos. Picnic area; no overnight facilities. Guided tours (reservations recommended). (May-Oct:

daily 8:30 am-5 pm; Nov-Apr: daily 10:30 am-5 pm; closed Dec 25) **$$$**

Walnut Canyon National Monument. *Walnut Canyon Rd, Flagstaff. 7 miles E on I-40 (Hwy 66), 3 miles off exit 204. Phone 520/526-3367. www.nps.gov/waca.* A spectacular, rugged 400-foot-deep canyon with 300 small cliff dwellings dating back to around AD 1100. The dwellings are well-preserved because they are under protective ledges in the canyon's limestone walls. There are two self-guided trails and an educational museum in the visitor center. Picnic grounds. (Daily; closed December 25) **$**

Special Events

Coconino County Fair. *I-17, Coconino County Fairgrounds/Race Track-Fort Tuthill County Park, Flagstaff. I-17, exit 337 Phone 928/774-5139.* This annual fair in Coconino County features livestock auctions, contests, entertainment, fine arts, and food. Labor Day weekend.

Flagstaff Festival of the Arts. *Northern Arizona University campus, SW edge of city. Phone 928/774-7750; toll-free 800/266-7740.* Symphonic/pops concerts, chamber music; theater; dance; art exhibits; poetry; film classics. July-early Aug.

Hopi Artists' Exhibition. *Museum of Northern Arizona, 3101 N Fort Valley Rd, Flagstaff. Phone 928/774-5213. www.musnaz.org.* Late June-early July.

Navajo Artists' Exhibition. *Museum of Northern Arizona, 3101 N Fort Valley Rd, Flagstaff. Phone 928/774-5213. www.musnaz.org.* Last weekend in July-first weekend in Aug.

Winter Festival. *Phone 520/774-4505.* Features art contest and exhibit; theater performances; workshops; sled dog and other races, games; Winterfaire, with arts and crafts; entertainment. Feb.

Zuni Artists' Exhibition. *Museum of Northern Arizona, 3101 N Fort Valley Rd, Flagstaff. Phone 928/774-5213. www.musnaz.org.* Five days beginning the Sat before Memorial Day.

Limited-Service Hotels

★ BEST WESTERN PONY SOLDIER INN & SUITES. *3030 E Rte 66, Flagstaff (86004). Phone 928/526-2388; toll-free 800/356-4143; fax 928/527-8329. www.bestwestern.com.* 92 rooms, 2 story. Complimentary continental breakfast. Check-in 2 pm, check-out 11 am. Indoor pool. **$**

★★ EMBASSY SUITES. *706 S Milton Rd, Flagstaff (86001). Phone 928/774-4333; toll-free 800/774-4333; fax 928/774-0216. www.embassysuites.com.* Within walking distance of historic Flagstaff, this hotel offers a complimentary made-to-order breakfast each morning. 119 rooms, 3 story, all suites. Pets accepted, some restrictions; fee. Complimentary full breakfast. Check-out noon. Fitness room. Pool, whirlpool. **$**

★ FAIRFIELD INN. *2005 S Milton Rd, Flagstaff (86001). Phone 928/773-1300; toll-free 800/574-6395; fax 928/773-1462. www.fairfieldinn.com.* 134 rooms, 3 story. Complimentary continental breakfast. Check-in 3 pm, check-out noon. Pool. **$**

★ HAMPTON INN. *2400 S Beulah Blvd, Flagstaff (86001). Phone 520/913-0900; toll-free 800/426-7866; fax 520/913-0800. www.hampton.com.* 126 rooms, 5 story. Complimentary continental breakfast. Check-out noon. Fitness room. Indoor pool, whirlpool. **$**

★★ HOLIDAY INN. *2320 E Lucky Ln, Flagstaff (86004). Phone 928/714-1000; toll-free 800/533-2754; fax 928/779-2610. www.holiday-inn.com/flagstaffaz.* 157 rooms, 5 story. Pets accepted; fee. Check-in 3 pm, check-out noon. Restaurant, bar. Fitness room. Indoor pool, whirlpool. Airport transportation available. **$**

★★ LITTLE AMERICA HOTEL. *2515 E Butler Ave, Flagstaff (86004). Phone 928/779-2741; toll-free 800/352-4386; fax 928/779-7983. www.littleamerica.com.* Located on 500 acres of beautiful ponderosa pine forest, this hotel offers luxurious amenities with access to all the cultural and natural riches of northern Arizona. Private hiking trails and complimentary hors d'oeuvres served nightly are sure to delight guests. 256 rooms, 2 story. Check-in 4 pm, check-out 1 pm. Restaurant, bar. Fitness room. Pool, whirlpool. **$**

Full-Service Inn

★★★ **INN AT 410 BED & BREAKFAST.** *410 N Leroux St, Flagstaff (86001). Phone 928/774-0088; toll-free 800/774-2008; fax 928/774-6354. www.inn410.com.* Known as the place with the personal touch, this charming 1894 Craftsman home offers fresh-baked cookies in the evenings. 9 rooms, 2 story. Complimentary full breakfast. Check-in 4-6 pm, check-out 11 am. **$**

Restaurants

★★ **COTTAGE PLACE.** *126 W Cottage Ave, Flagstaff (86001). Phone 928/774-8431. www.cottageplace.com.* Intimate dining in a 1909 cottage. American menu. Dinner. Closed Mon. Children's menu. **$$**

★ **KACHINA DOWNTOWN.** *522 E Rte 66, Flagstaff (86001). Phone 928/779-1944; fax 928/773-7826.* Mexican menu. Lunch, dinner. Closed some holidays. Bar. Children's menu. **$**

★★ **MAMMA LUISA.** *2710 N Steves Blvd, Flagstaff (86004). Phone 928/526-6809.* Italian menu. Dinner. Closed Thanksgiving, Dec 25. Children's menu. **$$**

Florence (D-3)

See also Casa Grande

Population 17,054
Elevation 1,490 ft
Area Code 520
Zip 85232
Information Chamber of Commerce, Box 929, phone 520/868-9433 or toll-free 800/437-9433; or the Pinal County Visitor Center, PO Box 967, phone 520/868-4331
Web site www.florenceaz.org

Set in the desert amid multicolored mountains, the seat of Pinal County is the fifth oldest pioneer settlement in the state. Florence has many early houses still standing, making the town something of a living relic of pioneer days.

What to See and Do

McFarland State Historic Park. *Ruggles Ave and Main St, Florence. Phone 520/868-5216. www.pr.state.az.us/Parks/parkhtml/mcfarland.html.* (1878) The first of three courthouses built here; restored adobe building with interpretive center, displays of early Arizona and US legal history, and the personal collections of Governor Ernest McFarland, also a US Senator and state supreme court justice. (Thurs-Mon 8 am-5 pm; closed Dec 25) **$**

Pinal County Historical Society Museum. *715 S Main St, Florence. Phone 520/868-4382.* Exhibits depict early life in the area. (Wed-Sat 11 am-4 pm, Sun noon-4 pm; closed holidays, also mid-July-Aug) **DONATION**

Special Event

Junior Parada. *291 N Bailey St, Florence. Phone 520/868-9433. www.florenceaz.org.* Three-day celebration features parade and rodeo. Sat of Thanksgiving weekend.

Fountain Hills (D-3)

See also Scottsdale

What to See and Do

Fort McDowell Casino. *Fort McDowell Rd and Beeline Hwy (Hwy 87), Fountain Hills. 2 miles N of Shea Blvd. Phone toll-free 800/843-3678. www.fortmcdowellcasino.com.* With 148,000 square feet of 'round-the-clock gaming action, this casino is big. Its operator, the Yavapai Nation Indian tribe, also thinks big—as in the state's largest card room; a 1,400-seat bingo hall with jackpots as high as $50,000; a keno lounge with million-dollar payouts; and 475 slot machines that keep the decibel level high night and day. Spend some of your winnings (hey, think positive) in one of four restaurants or at the lounge, which offers live entertainment daily. Only those 18 and older can come and play. (Daily) **FREE**

Full-Service Hotels

★★★ **COPPERWYND RESORT AND CLUB.** *13225 N Eagle Ridge Dr, Fountain Hill (85268). Phone 480/333-1900; toll-free 877/707-7760; fax 480/333-1901. www.copperwynd.com.* 40 rooms. Check-in 3 pm, check-out 11 am. Restaurant, bar. Children's activity center. Fitness room, spa. Outdoor pool, whirlpool. Tennis. **$$$**

★★★ **INN AT EAGLE MOUNTAIN.** *9800 N Summer Hill Blvd, Fountain Hill (85268). Phone*

602/816-3000; toll-free 800/992-8083; fax 602/816-3090. www.innateaglemountain.com. Located on the 18th fairway with views of Red Mountain. 42 rooms, 2 story. Check-in 3 pm, check-out 11 am. Restaurant. Outdoor pool, whirlpool. **$**

Ganado (B-5)

See also Canyon de Chelly National Monument, Window Rock

Population 1,505
Elevation 6,386 ft
Area Code 928
Zip 86505

What to See and Do

Hubbell Trading Post National Historic Site. *Hwy 264, Ganado. 1 mile W on Hwy 264. Phone 928/755-3475 (visitor information). www.nps.gov/hutr.* The oldest continuously operating trading post (1878) on the Navajo Reservation; named for founder John Lorenzo Hubbell, who began trading with the Navajo in 1876. Construction of the present-day post began in 1883. The visitor center houses exhibits; Navajo weavers and a silversmith can be observed at work; tours of the Hubbell house, containing paintings, Navajo rugs, and Native American arts and crafts; self-guided tour of the grounds (ranger-conducted programs in summer). (Summer hours: daily 8 am-6 pm; winter hours: daily 8 am-5 pm; closed Jan 1, Thanksgiving, Dec 25) **FREE**

Glendale (D-3)

See also Litchfield Park, Mesa, Phoenix, Scottsdale, Tempe

Founded 1892
Population 218,812
Elevation 1,150 ft
Area Code 623
Information Chamber of Commerce, 7105 N 59th Ave, Box 249, 85311; phone 623/937-4754 or toll-free 800/437-8669
Web site www.ci.glendale.az.us

Located just west of Phoenix in the beautiful and scenic Valley of the Sun, Glendale shares all of the urban advantages of the area. Luke Air Force Base is located here.

What to See and Do

Arizona's Antique Capital. *Glendale. Phone 623/930-4500; toll-free 877/800-2601. pnilz.pni.com/cities/glendale/.* Shopping area in downtown Glendale includes antique stores, specialty shops, and candy factory. (Most stores open Mon-Sat)

Bo's Funky Stuff. *5605 W Glendale Ave, Glendale. Phone 623/842-0220.* No run-of-the-mill antique store, this offbeat emporium proves the old adage that one man's junk is another man's treasure. Two side-by-side rooms are crammed with old advertising signs, housewares, and '50s furniture—all of it fun, and all of it funky. Sure, some items are pure kitsch, but some are one-of-a-kind collectibles. Prices range from under a dollar to several thousand. (Sept-May: daily noon-5 pm; June-Aug: Thurs-Sun noon-5 pm)

Cerreta Candy Company. *5345 W Glendale Ave, Glendale. Phone 623/930-1000. www.cerreta.com.* Attractions don't get any sweeter than this—just ask almost anyone under 4 feet tall. In its old-fashioned factory, the Cerreta family has been cooking up mouthwatering confections for more than 30 years, and locals eat 'em up. Guided tours are offered at 10 am and 1 pm Monday through Friday, but only a waist-high partition separates workers from lookers, so you can watch and drool anytime. In the candy store, you can pick and choose from all the individually wrapped, bite-size treats. (Mon-Sat; closed holidays) **FREE**

Waterworld Safari. *4243 W Pinnacle Peak Rd, Glendale (85301). Phone 623/581-1947.* Despite its desert location, there's no water shortage at this wildly fun aquatic playland with an African theme. Ride the big ones at the Serengeti Surf wave pool, zoom down the Cobra and Black Mamba slides, squeeze into an inner tube and float down the Zambezi River, play with the little ones in Jungle Jim's wading pool, and much more. What better way to stay all wet behind the ears in Arizona's dry heat? (Late May-early Sept: Mon-Thurs 10 am-8 pm, Fri-Sat to 9 pm, Sun 11 am-7 pm) **$$$$**

Limited-Service Hotels

★ **HAMPTON INN.** *8408 W Paradise Ln, Peoria (85382). Phone 623/486-9918; toll-free 800/426-7866; fax 623/486-4842. www.hamptoninn.com.* 112 rooms, 5 story. Complimentary continental breakfast. Check-in 3 pm, check-out noon. Fitness room. Outdoor pool, whirlpool. **$**

★ **LA QUINTA INN.** *16321 N 83rd Ave, Peoria (85382). Phone 623/487-1900; toll-free 800/687-6667; fax 623/487-1919. www.laquinta.com.* 113 rooms, 5 story. Pets accepted, some restrictions. Complimentary continental breakfast. Check-in 3 pm, check-out noon. Fitness room. Outdoor pool, whirlpool. **$**

Globe (D-4)

See also San Carlos

Settled 1876
Population 7,486
Elevation 3,509 ft
Area Code 928
Zip 85501
Information Greater Globe-Miami Chamber of Commerce, 1360 N Broad St, Box 2539, 85502; phone 928/425-4495 or toll-free 800/804-5623
Web site www.globemiamichamber.com

A silver strike settled Globe, but copper made the town what it is today. One of the original copper mines, Old Dominion, is no longer worked; however, other mines are still in operation. Cattle ranching also contributes to the economy. A Ranger District office for the Tonto National Forest (see PAYSON) is located here.

What to See and Do

Besh-Ba-Gowah Indian Ruins. *150 N Pine St, Globe. From the end of S Broad St, turn right across the bridge and continue on Jess Hayes Rd. Phone 928/425-0320.* Ruins of a village inhabited by the Salado from 1255-1400. More than 200 rooms. Visitor center, museum, 15-minute video presentation, ethnobotany garden. (Daily 9 am-5 pm; closed Jan 1, Thanksgiving, Dec 25) **$**

Boyce Thompson Southwestern Arboretum. *37615 Hwy 60, Superior. 28 miles W on Hwy 60; 3 miles W of Superior. Phone 928/689-2723 (office). ag.arizona.edu/BTA.* Large collection of plants from arid parts of world added to native flora in high Sonoran Desert setting at foot of Picketpost Mountain; labeled plants in 39-acre garden. Picnicking. Book store. Visitor center features biological and historical displays. (Daily 8 am-5 pm; closed Dec 25) **$$**

Gila County Historical Museum. *1330 N Broad St, Globe. 1 mile N on Hwy 60. Phone 928/425-7385.* Exhibit of artifacts of Gila County, including those of the Apache. From 1914 until the 1960s, the museum building was used as a fire and rescue station for the old Dominion Mine. (Mon-Fri 10 am-4 pm, Sat 11 am-3 pm; closed holidays) **DONATION**

Special Events

Apache Days. *Gila County Historical Museum, 1330 N Broad St, Globe. Phone 928/425-7385.* Street fair where Native Americans from different tribes congregate. Includes Native American arts, crats, food, and clothing. Fourth Sat in Oct. **FREE**

Gila County Fair. *Hwys 60 and 70, Globe. Phone 928/425-5924.* Four days in mid-Sept.

Goodyear

What to See and Do

Estrella Mountain Ranch Golf Club. *11800 S Golf Club Dr, Goodyear. For information, phone toll-free 866/564-7667, or see www.estrellamountainranch.com/golf.*

Grand Canyon National Park (A-2)

See also Flagstaff, Williams

Web site www.nps.gov/grca

Approximately 50 miles N on Hwy 180 (Hwy 64) to the South Rim.

Look out over the great expanse of the Grand Canyon, and the awe-inspiring vistas reveal a spectacular desert landscape. Rocks in this great chasm change colors from sunrise to sunset and hide an ecosystem of wildlife, including at least 287 different species of birds, 76 kinds of mammals, 35 types of reptiles, and 6 breeds of amphibians.

Millions of visitors pay this 6 million-year-old creation a visit each year, although it wasn't always considered the treasure it is today. In 1540, when the first European, Spanish explorer de Cardenas, discovered the area, his party was unable to cross and soon left. In 1875, American Lieutenant Joseph Ives said the region was "altogether valueless. Ours has been the first and will doubtless be the last party of whites to visit this profitless locality."

It took the nation's presidents to deem this land worthy of public attention and preservation. The area known as the Grand Canyon was first set aside as a forest reserve in 1893 by President Benjamin Harrison. Theodore Roosevelt took the process further, establishing Grand Canyon National Monument in 1908. In 1919, it became a national park, enlarged in 1975 with the Grand Canyon National Park Enlargement Act.

No superlative is sufficient to describe the park. Facts and figures highlight the sweeping grandeur of the terrain. The entire park is 1,904 square miles in size, with 277 miles of the Colorado River running through it. At its widest point, the north and south rims are 18 miles across, with average elevations of 8,000 feet and 7,000 feet, respectively. The canyon averages a depth of 1 mile. At its base, 2 billion-year-old rocks are exposed.

Visitors to the canyon come to hike its trails, travel down it by mule or over it by plane, camp at the rim or the base, and raft the river. Many simply visit the North Rim or the more popular South Rim to take in the views and visit area attractions.

The South Rim (see), open all year, has the greater number of services, including day and overnight mule trips through Xanterra Parks & Resorts; horseback riding through Apache Stables (located outside the park), phone 928/638-2891; and air tours (both fixed-wing and helicopter) through several local companies.

In addition to these tours, there are a variety of museums and facilities on the South Rim. The Kolb Studio in the Village Historic District at the Bright Angel Trailhead features art displays and a bookstore. It was once the home and business of the Kolb brothers, who were pioneering photographers here. The Yavapai Observation Station, 1 mile east of Market Plaza, contains temporary exhibits about the fossil record at Grand Canyon. Several information centers are located on the South Rim, as are restaurants, concessions, and gift shops.

The North Rim (see), blocked by heavy snows in winter, is open from mid-May to mid-Oct. Although there are few dining facilities and gift shops, the visitor center contains park information, a bookstore and exhibits, and offers interpretive programs. Due to the higher elevation, mule trips from the North Rim do not go to the river. Trips range in length from one hour to a full day. For more information, contact Grand Canyon Trail Rides at 435/679-8665.

For the hardier souls who elect to venture onto the backcountry trails, it's best to plan in advance and to avoid the busy summer season. Fall and spring are the best times to visit. Do not plan to hike to the base and back up in one day. Changing elevations and temperatures can exhaust hikers quickly. It's best to camp in the canyon overnight (plan on an additional night if hiking from the North Rim). Fifteen main trails provide access to the inner canyon. Make reservations for camping or lodging facilities early.

Rafting the Colorado River through Grand Canyon National Park also requires reservations far in advance of your intended visit. Trips vary in length from 3 to

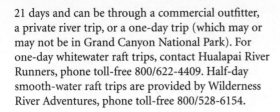

21 days and can be through a commercial outfitter, a private river trip, or a one-day trip (which may or may not be in Grand Canyon National Park). For one-day whitewater raft trips, contact Hualapai River Runners, phone toll-free 800/622-4409. Half-day smooth-water raft trips are provided by Wilderness River Adventures, phone toll-free 800/528-6154.

However you elect to experience the Grand Canyon, national park services make your visit more comfortable and rewarding. There are rest rooms throughout the park, a free shuttle bus system, restaurants and grocery stores, lodging, and camping (within the park at Mather Campground and in Trailer Village, phone 303/297-2757).

Pets must be leashed and are not allowed on trails below the rim. For further information, contact Trip Planner, Grand Canyon National Park, PO Box 129, Grand Canyon 86023. Per vehicle **$$$$**

North Rim (Grand Canyon National Park)

What to See and Do

Camping. *North Rim (Grand Canyon National Park). Phone toll-free 800/365-2267.* Campsites, trailer parking space at North Rim Campground (seven-day limit; no hookups). Call for camping reservations. **$$$$**

Drive to Cape Royal *About 23 miles from Bright Angel Point over paved road.* There are several good viewpoints along the way. Many think the view from here is better than from the South Rim. Archaeology and geology talks are given in summer and fall.

Limited-Service Hotel

★★ **GRAND CANYON LODGE.** *Hwy 67, Grand Canyon (86052). Phone 928/638-2611; fax 928/638-2554. www.grandcanyonnorthrim.com.* View of canyon. 201 rooms. Closed mid-Oct-mid-May. Check-in 4 pm, check-out 11 am. Restaurant, bar. **$**

Restaurants

★★ **ARIZONA ROOM.** *West Rim Dr, Grand Canyon Village (86023). Phone 303/297-2757.* An upscale dining room known for its prime steaks and magnificent canyon views. American menu. Lunch, dinner. **$$**

★★ **GRAND CANYON LODGE.** *Hwy 67, Grand Canyon (86052). Phone 928/638-2611.* Featuring spectacular views of the North Rim as a backdrop to the dining experience. American menu. Breakfast, lunch, dinner. **$**

★ **JACOB LAKE INN.** *Hwy 89A and SR 67, Jacob Lake (86022). About 44 miles from North Rim. Phone 928/643-7232. www.jacoblake.com.* Featuring distinctive regional cuisine in a country setting. American menu. Lunch, dinner. Closed Jan 1, Dec 25. **$**

South Rim (Grand Canyon National Park)

What to See and Do

Camping. *1 Main St, South Rim (Grand Canyon National Park). Phone toll-free 800/365-CAMP.* Sites (no hookups) at Mather Campground (fee); reservations can be made through BIOSPHERICS. **$$$$**

Drives to viewpoints. *1 Main St, South Rim (Grand Canyon National Park).* There are West Rim and East Rim drives out from Grand Canyon Village; each is rewarding. Grandview Point and Desert View on the East Rim Drive are especially magnificent. West Rim Drive is closed to private vehicles early Apr-early Oct. Free shuttle buses serve the West Rim and Village area during this period.

Evening programs. *1 Main St, South Rim (Grand Canyon National Park).* Every night all year by Park Service ranger-naturalist in an outdoor amphitheater;

inside the Shrine of the Ages Building during the colder months; daytime talks given all year at Yavapai Observation Station and at the visitor center. **FREE**

Grand Canyon IMAX Theatre. *Hwys 64 and 180, Grand Canyon. 1 mile S of park entrance. Phone 928/638-2203.* Large screen film (35 minutes) highlighting features of the Grand Canyon. (Mar-Oct: 8:30 am-8:30 pm; Nov-Feb: 10:30 am-6:30 pm; movie is shown hourly on the half hour) **$$**

Guided river trips. *1 Main St, South Rim (Grand Canyon National Park).* Reservations should be made well in advance.

Hiking. *South Rim (Grand Canyon National Park).* Six trails (1/4 mile to 10 miles); some are self-guided.

Hiking down into the canyon. *1 Main St, South Rim (Grand Canyon National Park).* Not recommended except for those in good physical condition, because the heat and the 4,500-foot climb back are exhausting. Consult Backcountry Office staff before attempting this hike. (Caution: Always carry sufficient water and food; neither is available along the trails.) Reservations and fees are required for camping below the rim; by mail from Backcountry Office, PO Box 129, Grand Canyon 86023, or in person at Backcountry, located adjacent to Maswik Lodge.

Kaibab National Forest. *200 E Railroad Ave, Williams (Coconino County). The Ranger District office for the Tusayan District is located in Tusayan, 4 miles S of the park. Phone 928/635-4707; toll-free 800/863-0546. www.fs.fed.us/r3/kai.* More than 1 1/2 million acres; one area surrounds Williams and includes Sycamore Canyon and Kendrick Mountain wilderness areas and part of National Historic Route 66. A second area is 42 miles north on Hwy 180 (Hwy 64) near the South Rim of the Grand Canyon; a third area lies north of the Grand Canyon (outstanding views of the canyon from seldom-visited vista points in this area) and includes Kanab Creek and Saddle Mountain wilderness areas, the Kaibab Plateau, and the North Rim Parkway National Scenic Byway. The forest is home to a variety of wildlife unique to this area, including mule deer and the Kaibab squirrel. Fishing (trout); hunting, picnicking, camping (fee). Also in forest are

Mule trips into the canyon. *1 Main St, South Rim (Grand Canyon National Park). Phone 303/297-2757. www.grandcanyonlodges.com.* Easier than walking and quite safe; a number of trips are scheduled, all with guides. There are some limitations. Trips take one, two, or three days. Reservations should be made several months in advance (preferably one year prior).

Scenic flights over the canyon. *1 Main St, South Rim (Grand Canyon National Park).* Many operators offer air tours of the Grand Canyon, flights depart from many different airports. For a partial list of companies, contact the Grand Canyon Chamber of Commerce, PO Box 3007, Grand Canyon 86023.

Tusayan Museum. *Desert View Rd, South Rim (Grand Canyon National Park). 22 miles E of Grand Canyon Village, 3 miles W of Desert View.* Exhibits on prehistoric man in the Southwest. Excavated pueblo ruin (circa 1185) nearby. (Daily 9 am-5 pm, weather permitting). Ranger-led tours (daily 11 am-1:30 pm) **FREE**

Yavapai Observation Station. *On the South Rim, 1 mile E of Grand Canyon Village.* The station features a small museum, scenic views, geological exhibits, and a bookstore. (Daily 8 am-7 pm) **FREE**

Limited-Service Hotels

★★ BEST WESTERN GRAND CANYON SQUIRE INN. *Hwy 64, Grand Canyon (86023). Phone 928/638-2681; toll-free 800/622-6966; fax 928/638-2782. www.bestwestern.com.* 250 rooms, 3 story. Check-out noon. Restaurant, bar. Fitness room. Pool, whirlpool. Cowboy museum. **$$**

★★ BRIGHT ANGEL LODGE. *PO Box 699, Grand Canyon (86023). Phone 928/638-2631; fax 928/638-9247. www.grandcanyonlodges.com.* 89 rooms. Check-out 11 am. Restaurant, bar. Some canyon-side rooms. Canyon tour service. **$**

★ KACHINA LODGE. *1 Main St, Grand Canyon (86023). Phone 928/638-2631; fax 928/638-9247. www.grandcanyonlodges.com.* 49 rooms, 2 story. Check-out 11 am. **$**

★★ QUALITY INN. *Hwy 64, Grand Canyon (86023). Phone 928/638-2673; toll-free 800/221-2222; fax 928/638-9537. www.grandcanyonqualityinn.com.* 232 rooms, 3 story. Check-out 11 am. Restaurant. Pool, whirlpool. **$**

★ THUNDERBIRD LODGE. *1 Main St, Grand Canyon (86023). Phone 928/638-2631; fax 928/638-9247. www.grandcanyonlodges.com.* Some canyon-side rooms. Canyon tour service. 55 rooms, 2 story. Check-out 11 am. **$**

★ ★ YAVAPAI LODGE. *1 Main St, Grand Canyon (86023). Phone 928/638-2631; fax 928/638-9247. www.grandcanyonlodges.com.* 358 rooms, 2 story. Check-out 11 am. Cafeteria-style restaurant. **$**

Full-Service Hotels

★ ★ ★ EL TOVAR. *1 Main St, Grand Canyon (86023). Phone 928/638-2631; fax 928/638-9247. www.grandcanyonlodges.com.* The premier lodging facility at the Grand Canyon, El Tovar Hotel—named in honor of the Spanish explorer Don Pedro de Tovar, who reported the existence of the Grand Canyon to fellow explorers—opened its doors in 1905 and was dubbed "the most expensively constructed and appointed log house in America." Just 20 feet from the edge of the Canyon's South Rim, the building is a little Swiss, vaguely Scandinavian, and charmingly rustic. Upon entering, guests are greeted by a roaring fire, striking paintings of the Canyon, copper statues depicting the American West, and a bustling peacefulness that ensures a remarkable stay. The hotel features a fine dining room, lounge, and a gift shop highlighting Native American artisans. With so much to do right at your doorstep—hiking, mule rides, train excursions, interpretive walks, cultural activities—El Tovar offers the best of the Grand Canyon, combining turn-of-the-century lodge ambience with the highest standard of service on the Canyon's edge. Advance reservations are recommended, especially for the summer season, which is usually booked up a year in advance. 78 rooms, 4 story. Check-out 11 am. Restaurant, bar. **$**

★ ★ GRAND HOTEL. *Grand Canyon National Park, Tusayan. Phone 928/638-3333; toll-free 888/252-5151; fax 928/638-3131. www.visitgrandcanyon.com.* 121 rooms. Check-in 3 pm, check-out 11 am. Restaurant, bar. **$$**

Restaurants

★ ★ ★ EL TOVAR DINING ROOM. *1 Main St, South Rim (86023). Phone 928/638-2631.* Located 20 feet from the South Rim of the Grand Canyon, the El Tovar Dining Room—in the spectacularly rustic and historic El Tovar Hotel (see)—is considered the premier dining establishment at the Grand Canyon. It provides a memorable experience thanks to the spicy regional cuisine and spectacular Canyon views. The atmosphere is casually elegant with native stone fireplaces, Oregon pine vaulted ceilings, Native American artwork, and Mission-style accents. Diners can select from a well-rounded menu that blends regional flavors and contemporary techniques and offers many vegetarian options. The menu is unique and the wine list extensive. Southwestern menu. Breakfast, lunch, dinner. Children's menu. Reservations recommended. **$$**

★ STEAKHOUSE AT THE GRAND CANYON. *Hwy 64 and Hwy 180, Grand Canyon (86023). Phone 928/638-2780; fax 520/638-0331.* Covered wagon in front yard. Steak, barbecue menu. Dinner. Bar. Children's menu. Hayrides, stagecoach rides Mar-Oct. **$$**

Greer (C-5)

See also McNary, Pinetop, Springerville

Population 125
Elevation 8,380 ft
Area Code 520
Zip 85927
Web site www.greerarizona.com

Within the Apache-Sitgreaves National Forests, this town is 18 miles southwest of Springerville (see) on Hwy 273. Cross-country and downhill skiing are available nearby from December to March; fishing, hunting, backpacking, bicycling, and camping are popular at other times of year.

Holbrook (C-4)

See also Hopi Indian Reservation, Navajo Indian Reservation, Winslow

Population 4,917
Elevation 5,083 ft
Area Code 928
Zip 86025
Information Chamber of Commerce, 100 E Arizona St; phone 928/524-6558 or toll-free 800/524-2449
Web site www.ci.holbrook.az.us

What to See and Do

Navajo County Historical Museum. *100 E Arizona, Holbrook. In Old County Courthouse. Phone 928/524-6558.* Exhibits on Navajo, Apache, Hopi, and Hispanic culture; petrified forest; local history; dinosaurs. (May-Sept: Mon-Sat; rest of year: Mon-Fri; closed holidays) **DONATION**

Special Events

Navajo County Fair and Rodeo. *County Fairgrounds, 402 E Hopi Dr, Holbrook. Phone 928/524-6407.* Mid-Sept.

Old West Celebration. *100 E Arizona St, Holbrook. Phone 928/524-6558.* Second week in June.

Limited-Service Hotels

★★ BEST WESTERN ARIZONIAN INN. *2508 Navajo Blvd, Holbrook (86025). Phone 928/524-2611; toll-free 877/280-7300; fax 928/524-2253. www.bestwestern.com.* 70 rooms, 2 story. Pets accepted, some restrictions; fee. Check-out 11 am. Restaurant. Outdoor pool. **$**

★ HOLIDAY INN EXPRESS. *1308 Navajo Blvd, Holbrook (86025). Phone 928/524-1466; fax 928/524-1788. www.holiday-inn.com.* 59 rooms, 2 story. Pets accepted; fee. Complimentary continental breakfast. Check-out 11 am. Indoor pool, whirlpool. **$**

Restaurant

★★ MESA ITALIANA. *2318 N Navajo Blvd, Holbrook (86025). Phone 928/524-6696; fax 928/524-3130.* Italian menu. Lunch, dinner. Closed Mon. Bar. Children's menu. **$$**

Hopi Indian Reservation (B-4)

See also Canyon de Chelly National Monument, Holbrook, Kayenta, Page

Web site www.hopi.nsn.us

Completely surrounded by the Navajo Indian Reservation (see) is the 1 1/2 million-acre Hopi Indian Reservation. The Hopi are pueblo people of Shoshonean ancestry who have lived here for more than 1,000 years. The Hopi have a complex religious system. Excellent farmers, they also herd sheep, as well as craft pottery, silver jewelry, kachina dolls, and baskets. They live in some of the most intriguing towns on the North American continent.

Both the Navajo and Hopi are singers and dancers—each in their own style. The Hopi are most famous for their Snake Dance, which may not be viewed by visitors, but there are dozens of other beautiful ceremonies that visitors are allowed to watch. However, the photographing, recording, or sketching of any events on the reservation is prohibited.

All major roads leading into and across the Navajo and Hopi Reservations are paved. Do not venture off the main highways.

The Hopi towns are located, for the most part, on three mesas. On the first mesa is Walpi, founded around 1680, one of the most beautiful Hopi pueblos. It is built on the tip of a narrow, steep-walled mesa, along with its companion villages, Sichomovi and Hano, which are inhabited by the Tewa and the Hano. Hanoans speak a Tewa language as well as Hopi. You can drive to Sichomovi and walk along a narrow connecting mesa to Walpi. Only passenger cars are allowed on the mesa; no RVs or trailers. Individuals of Walpi and First Mesa Villages offer Hopi pottery and kachina dolls for sale; inquire locally.

The second mesa has three towns: Mishongnovi, Shipaulovi, and Shongopovi, each fascinating in its own way. The Hopi Cultural Center, located on the second mesa, includes a museum and craft shops (daily), a restaurant serving both Hopi and American food, and a motel; reservations (phone 520/734-2421) for May-August should be made at least three months in advance. Near the Cultural Center is a primitive campground (free).

The third mesa has Oraibi, the oldest Hopi town, and its three offshoots, Bacabi, Kyakotsmovi, and Hotevilla, a town of considerable interest. A restaurant, a small motel, and tent and trailer sites can be found at Keams Canyon. There are not many places to stay, so plan your trip carefully.

Kayenta (A-4)

See also Hopi Indian Reservation, Navajo Indian Reservation

Population 4,922
Elevation 5,641 ft
Area Code 928
Zip 86033
Web site www.kayentatownship.com

Located in the spectacular Monument Valley, Kayenta's (Kay-en-TAY) surrounding area offers some of the most memorable sightseeing in the state; the great tinted monoliths are spectacular.

What to See and Do

Crawley's Monument Valley Tours, Inc. *PO Box 187, Kayenta. Phone 928/697-3734. www.crawleytours.com.* Guided tours in backcountry vehicles to Monument Valley, Mystery Valley, and Hunt's Mesa. Half- and full-day rates; sunset tours are also available. (Daily) **$$$$**

Guided tours. Available through Bennett Tours, phone 800/862-8270; Daniel's Guided Tours, phone 800/596-8427; Totem Pole Tours, phone 800/345-8687; Goulding's Monument Valley Lodge, phone 801/727-3231. Fees and schedules vary.

Monument Valley Navajo Tribal Park. *PO Box 360289, Monument Valley. The visitor center is located 4 miles SE of Hwy 163. Phone 801/727-3353.* Self-guided tours of the valley (road conditions vary, inquire locally). Camping (at Park Headquarters only; fee). Note: Visitors should not photograph the Navajo people, their homes, or their possessions without asking permission. Visitor center and park (May-Sept: 8 am-7 pm; Oct-Apr: 8 am-5 pm; closed Jan 1, Dec 25) **$**

Limited-Service Hotels

★ ★ GOULDING'S LODGE. *1000 Main, Monument Valley (84536). Phone 435/727-3231; fax 435/727-3344. www.gouldings.com.* One building is an old trading post; now a museum. John Wayne movies filmed here. 19 rooms, 2 story. Pets accepted. Check-out 11 am. Restaurant. Indoor pool. **$**

★ ★ HOLIDAY INN. *Jct Hwys 160 and 163, Kayenta (86033). Phone 928/697-3221; toll-free 800/465-4329; fax 928/697-3349. www.holiday-inn.com.* 162 rooms, 2 story. Check-out noon. Restaurant. Pool, children's pool. **$**

Kingman (B-1)

See also Bullhead City, Lake Havasu City

Population 20,069
Elevation 3,341 ft
Area Code 928
Zip 86401
Information Chamber of Commerce, 333 W Andy Devine, Box 1150, 86402; phone 928/753-6106
Web site www.kingmantourism.org

Kingman is the seat of Mohave County. It lies at the junction of two transcontinental highways, I-40 reaching from the East to the West coast, and Hwy 93 from Fairbanks, Alaska, to Guatemala, Mexico. It is a convenient stop on the way to the Grand Canyon, Las Vegas, or Los Angeles. Nearby are Lakes Mead, Mohave, and Havasu, with year-round swimming, waterskiing, fishing, and boating. To the south are the beautiful Hualapai Mountains. This city lies at the heart of historic Route 66 and was once a rich silver and gold mining area; several ghost towns are nearby.

What to See and Do

Bonelli House. *430 E Spring St, Kingman. Phone 928/753-1413.* (1894) One of the earliest permanent structures in the city. Restored and furnished with many original pieces. (Thurs-Mon 1-4 pm; closed major holidays) **FREE**

Mohave Museum of History and Art. *400 W Beale St, Kingman. 1/4 mile E of I-40, Beale St/Las Vegas exit. Phone 928/753-3195. www.ctaz.com/~mocohist/museum.* Exhibits trace local and state history; portrait collection of US presidents and first ladies; Andy Devine display; turquoise display; rebuilt 1926 pipe organ; Native American displays. Local artists' gallery. (Daily; closed holidays) **$**

Oatman. *Kingman. 28 miles SW, located on old Hwy 66. Phone 928/768-6222.* In the 1930s, this was the last stop in Arizona before entering the Mojave Desert in California. Created in 1906 as a tent camp, it flourished as a gold mining center until 1942, when Congress declared that gold mining was no longer essential to the war effort. The ghost town has been kept as authentic as possible; several motion pictures have been filmed here. Wild burros abound, many roaming streets that are lined with historic buildings, former mine sites, old town jail, old and modern hotels, museum, turquoise and antique shops. Gunfights staged on weekends. Contact the Oatman Chamber of Commerce. **FREE**

Powerhouse Visitor Center. *120 W Rte 66, Kingman. Phone 928/753-6106; toll-free 866/427-7866. www.kingmantourism.org.* Renovated power generating station (1907). Houses Historic Route 66 Association of Arizona, Tourist Information Center, Carlos Elmer Memorial Photo Gallery, model railroad shop, gift shop, deli. (Mar-Nov: daily 9 am-6 pm; Dec-Feb: daily 9 am-5 pm; closed holidays) **FREE**

Special Events

Andy Devine Days & PRCA Rodeo. *Mohave County Fairgrounds, 2600 Fairgrounds Blvd, Kingman. Phone 928/715-4003.* Sports tournaments, parade, other events. Two days in late Sept.

Mohave County Fair. *Mohave County Fairgrounds, 2600 Fairgrounds Blvd, Kingman. Phone 928/753-2636.* Annual event featuring a carnival, livestock auctions, 4-H competition, and food. First weekend after Labor Day.

Limited-Service Hotels

★ BEST WESTERN A WAYFARER'S INN. *2815 E Andy Devine Ave, Kingman (86041). Phone 928/753-6271; toll-free 800/548-5695; fax 928/753-9608. www.bestwestern.com.* 101 rooms, 2 story. Pets accepted, some restrictions; fee. Check-out noon. Pool. **$**

★ QUALITY INN. *1400 E Andy Devine Ave, Kingman (86401). Phone 928/753-4747; toll-free 800/869-3252; fax 928/753-5175. www.qualityinn.com.* 98 rooms, 2 story. Pets accepted; fee. Complimentary continental breakfast. Check-out noon. Fitness room. Pool, whirlpool. **$**

Lake Havasu City (C-1)

See also Kingman, Parker, Needles

Founded 1964
Population 41,938
Elevation 600 ft
Area Code 928
Zip 86403
Information Lake Havasu Tourism Bureau, 314 London Bridge Rd; phone 928/855-4115 or toll-free 800/242-8278
Web site www.golakehavasu.com

Lake Havasu City Fun Fact

- The original London Bridge was shipped stone by stone and reconstructed in Lake Havasu City.

This is the center of a year-round resort area on the shores of 45-mile-long Lake Havasu. London Bridge, imported from England and reassembled here as part of a recreational area, was designed by John Rennie and built from 1824-1831; it spanned the Thames River in London until 1968. It now connects the mainland city with a 3-square-mile island that has a marina, golf course, tennis courts, campgrounds, and other recreational facilities.

What to See and Do

Lake Havasu State Park. *699 London Bridge Rd, Lake Havasu City. Off Hwy 95 and Industrial Blvd. Phone 928/855-2784. www.pr.state.az.us/Parks/parkhtml/havasu.html.* There are 13,000 acres along 23 miles of shoreline. Windsor Beach Unit, 2 miles north on old US 95 (London Bridge Rd), has swimming, fishing, boating (ramps), hiking, and camping (dump station); phone 928/855-2784. Cattail Cove Unit, 15 miles south and 1/2 mile west of Hwy 95, has swimming, fishing, boating (ramps), and camping (including some water-access sites; fee); phone 928/855-1223. (Sunrise-10 pm)

London Bridge Resort & English Village. *1477 Queens Bay, Lake Havasu City. Phone 928/855-0888; toll-free 800/624-7939. www.londonbridgeresort.com.* English-style village on 21 acres; home of the world-famous London Bridge. Specialty shops, restaurants, boat rides, nine-hole golf course, accommodations. Village (daily).

Sightseeing. *Phone 928/680-6151.* Outback Off-Road Adventures, phone 928/680-6151; Lake Havasu Boat Tours, phone 928/855-7979; Bluewater Jet Boat Tours, phone 928/855-7171; Dixie Bell Boat Tours, phone 928/453-6776; London Jet Boat Tours, phone 888/505-3545. **$$$$**

Topock Gorge. *10 miles N on the lake (accessible only by boat), S boundary of Havasu National Wildlife Refuge.* Scenic steep volcanic banks along the Colorado River. Migratory birds winter here; herons, cormorants, and egrets nest in April and May. Fishing; picnicking. **FREE**

Limited-Service Hotel

★★ **HOLIDAY INN.** *245 London Bridge Rd, Lake Havasu (85204). Phone 928/855-4071; toll-free 888/428-2465; fax 928/855-2379. www.holiday-inn.com.* 162 rooms, 4 story. Pets accepted; fee. Check-out noon. Restaurant, bar. Pool. **$**

Restaurant

★★ **SHUGRUE'S.** *1425 McCulloch Blvd, Lake Havasu City (86403). Phone 928/453-1400; fax 928/453-3577. www.shugrues.com.* Seafood, steak menu. Lunch, dinner. Closed Dec 25. Bar. Children's menu. **$$**

Litchfield Park

See also Glendale, Mesa, Phoenix, Scottsdale, Tempe

Population 3,810
Elevation 1,027 ft
Area Code 623
Zip 85340
Information Southwest Valley Chamber of Commerce, 289 N Litchfield Rd, Goodyear 85338; phone 623/932-2260.
Web site www.litchfield-park.org

In 1916, the Goodyear Tire and Rubber Company purchased and leased two tracts of land to grow Egyptian cotton. One tract was west of the Agua Fria River and was, for a short time, referred to as the Agua Fria Ranch. In 1926, the name was changed to Litchfield in honor of Paul W. Litchfield, vice president of the company.

What to See and Do

Duncan Family Farms. *17203 W Indian School Rd, Goodyear. 5 miles S in Goodyear; off of Cotton Ln. Phone 623/853-9880.* Two-thousand-acre working fruit and vegetable farm allows guests to pick their own organic produce. Petting zoo; farm play yard with "kittie kattle train," swings, giant maze. Country market and bakery. Seasonal festivals. (Fri-Sun; closed holidays) **FREE**

Wildlife World Zoo. *16501 W Northern Ave, Litchfield Park. Phone 623/935-9453. www.wildlifeworld.com.* White tigers. African lions. Dromedary camels. White rhinos. Go wild on these 55 acres and feast your eyes on Arizona's largest collection of exotic animals—about 1,300, representing nearly 320 species. But do more than just hoof it from one exhibit to the next. Get a bird's-eye view from high above on a brand-new sky ride. Feed giraffes, lemurs, and touracos. Take a safari through Africa on a train, ride a pontoon through the Australian Outback, and much more. (Daily 9 am-5 pm) **$$$**

Special Events

Billy Moore Days. *Coldwater Park, Avondale. E of Dysart Rd between Riley and Western Ave. Phone 623/932-2260.* Carnival, entertainment, parade, other events. Mid-Oct.

Goodyear Rodeo Days. *Estrella Mountain Regional Park, 14805 W Vineyard Ave, Goodyear. Phone 623/932-2260.* Includes entertainment, family games, dancing. Late Feb.

West Valley Invitational Native American Arts Festival. *The West Valley Fine Arts Council, 387 Wigwam Blvd, Litchfield Park. Phone 623/935-6384. www.wvfac.org/2003/seasonframe.html.* Approximately 100 Native American craft vendors. Native American dancing and other authentic entertainment. Mid-Jan. Weekend pass **$$**.

Limited-Service Hotel

★ **HOLIDAY INN EXPRESS.** *1313 N Litchfield Rd, Goodyear (85338). Phone 623/535-1313; fax 623/535-0950. www.holiday-inn.com.* 90 rooms,

3 story. Pets accepted, some restrictions; fee. Complimentary continental breakfast. Check-out noon. Fitness room. Pool, whirlpool. **$**

Full-Service Resort

★★★ **THE WIGWAM RESORT AND GOLF CLUB.** *300 Wigwam E Blvd, Litchfield Park (85340). Phone 623/935-3811; toll-free 888/382-8610; fax 623/856-1016. www.starwood.com.* Once a private club for executives of the Goodyear Tire Company, The Wigwam Resort is one of Arizona's finest. Located in the village of Litchfield Park, it is only 20 minutes from downtown Phoenix. The rooms and suites highlight authentic regional design. Whitewashed wood furniture, slate floors, Mexican ceramic tiles, and traditional Southwestern colors distinguish the accommodations. Comfortable and spacious, the rooms could convince some guests to remain within, yet the tempting array of outdoor pursuits lures visitors from their hideaways. Three award-winning golf courses, nine tennis courts, two pools with a waterslide, and a fitness center with spa keep adults satisfied, while Camp Pow Wow puts smiles on the faces of the youngest guests. Five restaurants and bars have something for everyone, from continental cuisine and live entertainment to regional dishes in a traditional Southwestern kitchen. 331 rooms, 2 story. Pets accepted, some restrictions; fee. Check-in 4 pm, check-out noon. Restaurants, bars. Children's activity center. Fitness room. Two outdoor pools, two whirlpools. Airport transportation available. Business center. **$$$**

Restaurant

★★★ **ARIZONA KITCHEN.** *300 Wigwam E Blvd, Litchfield Park (85340). Phone 623/935-3811; toll-free 888/382-8610; fax 623/856-1016. www.wigwamresort.com.* Given Arizona Kitchen's adobe fireplace, red brick floors, wood-beamed ceilings, and stunning exhibition kitchen featuring a mesquite wood-fired hearth and grill, seekers of authentic Arizona cuisine and atmosphere should feel quite rewarded after an evening here. Located just 20 minutes from Phoenix in the historic Wigwam Resort (see), this perpetually packed Southwestern restaurant is a showcase for the fiery culinary techniques and flavors of the region. Using herbs grown just steps from the door, the kitchen pays homage to local ingredients with signature dishes like smoked corn chowder, grilled sirloin of buffalo with sweet potato pudding, and mesquite-dusted Chilean sea bass. If you're searching for a place to feast on terrific, authentic Arizona-style fare, look no further. This is the real thing. Southwestern menu. Dinner. Closed Sun-Mon. Bar. Casual attire. Reservations recommended. Outdoor seating. **$$$**

Marble Canyon (A-3)

See also Page

Population 150
Elevation 3,580 ft
Area Code 928
Zip 86036

What to See and Do

Marble Canyon. *Phone toll-free 800/433-2543.* Part of Grand Canyon National Park (see).

River-running trips. *Hwy 180, Grand Canyon. Phone 928/638-7888.* Multiday trips on the Colorado River. For a list of commercial operators, contact Grand Canyon National Park, PO Box 129, Grand Canyon 86023.

Limited-Service Hotel

★ **CLIFF DWELLERS LODGE.** *Hwy 89A, Marble Canyon (85321). Phone 928/355-2228; toll-free 800/433-2543; fax 928/355-2271. www.leesferry.com.* 20 rooms. Check-out 11 am. Restaurant. **$**

McNary (C-5)

See also Greer, Pinetop, Show Low, Springerville

Population 349
Elevation 7,316 ft
Area Code 928
Zip 85930

McNary is in the northeastern section of the Fort Apache Indian Reservation. "Hon-dah" is Apache for "be my guest," and visitors find a warm welcome here. The White Mountain Apaches have a number of recreation areas on their reservation. Trout fishing, exploring, and camping are available. For further information, contact White Mountain Recreation Enterprise, Game & Fish Department, Box 220, Whiteriver 85941; phone 928/338-4385.

What to See and Do

Hawley Lake. *White Mountain Apache Indian Reservation, McNary. 12 miles E on Hwy 260, then 11 miles S on Hwy 473. Phone 928/335-7511.* With an elevation of 8,200 feet, Hawley Lake is one of the highest lakes in Arizona. Summer activities include fishing, hiking, camping, and cabin rentals. Ice fishing is a popular winter activity.

Sunrise Park Resort. *Fort Apache Indian Reservation, Hwy 273, Greer. 20 miles E on Hwy 260, then S on Hwy 273. Phone 928/735-7669; toll-free 800/772-7669. www.sunriseskipark.com.* Resort has two quad, four triple, double chairlift, three rope tows; patrol, school, rentals; cafeteria, restaurants, bars. Sixty-five runs. Also snowboarding. (Nov-mid-Apr, daily) Summer activities include swimming, fishing, canoeing, hiking, horseback riding, and tennis. Camping. **$$$$**

Mesa (D-3)

See also Casa Grande, Chandler, Glendale, Litchfield Park, Phoenix, Scottsdale, Tempe

Founded 1878
Population 396,375
Elevation 1,241 ft
Information Convention & Visitors Bureau, 120 N Center, 85201; phone 480/827-4700 or toll-free 800/283-6372
Web site www.mesacvb.com

Mesa, Spanish for "table," sits atop a plateau overlooking the Valley of the Sun and is one of the state's largest and fastest-growing cities. Mesa offers year-round golf, tennis, hiking, and water sports. It also provides easy access to other Arizona and Southwest attractions.

What to See and Do

Arizona Museum for Youth. *35 N Robson St, Mesa. Phone 480/644-2467. www.arizonamuseumforyouth.com.* Fine arts museum with changing hands-on exhibits for children. (Memorial Day-Labor Day: Tues-Sun 9 am-5 pm; Labor Day-Memorial Day: Tues-Fri 1-5 pm, Sat-Sun 9 am-5 pm; closed major holidays) **$**

Arizona Temple Visitors' Center. *525 E Main St, Mesa. Phone 480/964-7164. www.lds.org/placestovisit.* Murals; 10-foot replica of Thorvaldsen's Christus statue; history of prehistoric irrigation; films; dioramas; information. Temple gardens (site of a concert series) have a large variety of trees, cacti, and shrubs collected from all over the world; extensive light display during the Christmas season. The Church of Jesus Christ of Latter-day Saints (Mormon) Arizona Temple (not open to the public) is located just south of the visitors' center (tours) (Daily 9 am-9 pm). **FREE**

Boyce Thompson Southwestern Arboretum. *37615 Hwy 60, Superior. 28 miles W on Hwy 60; 3 miles W of Superior. Phone 928/689-2723 (office). ag.arizona.edu/bta.* Large collection of plants from arid parts of the world added to native flora in a high Sonoran Desert setting at the foot of Picketpost Mountain; labeled plants in a 39-acre garden. Picnicking. Bookstore. Visitor center features biological and historical displays. (Daily 8 am-5 pm; closed Dec 25) **$$**

Dolly Steamboat Cruises. *Canyon Lake Marina, 16802 NE Hwy 88, Mesa. Phone 480/827-9144; fax 480/671-0483. www.dollysteamboat.com.* Narrated tours and twilight dinner cruises of Canyon Lake, following the original path of the Salt River. (Nature Cruise: daily at noon, 2 pm by reservation only, arrangements can be made for 10 am or 4 pm; Twilight Dinner Cruise: weekends, call for schedule; closed Thanksgiving, Dec 25) **$$$$**

Factory Stores of America. *2050 S Roslyn Pl, Mesa. SE Corner of Power and Baseline Rds. Superstition Springs Freeway exit 188 (Power Rd). Phone 480/984-0697.* If you can't get your fill of good deals, check out all the bargains just waiting for you and your shopping bags at this factory outlet mall. The price is usually right at any of its 25 stores, which include All-Star Music, Book Warehouse, Casual Corner Outlet, Factory Brand Shoes, KB Toy Liquidators, Assonate, and Wallet Works. (Mon-Sat 10 am-8 pm, Sun 11 am-5 pm)

Lost Dutchman State Park. *6109 N Apache Trail, Apache Junction. 14 miles E via Hwy 60/89 to Apache Junction, then 5 miles NE via Hwy 88 (Apache Trail Hwy). Phone 480/982-4485. www.pr.state.az.us/Parks/parkhtml/dutchman.html.* A 300-acre park in the Superstition Mountains area. Hiking, picnicking (shelter), improved camping (dump station). Interpretive trails and access to nearby forest service wilderness area. (Daily sunrise-10 pm; closed Dec 25)

Mesa Southwest Museum. *53 N MacDonald St, Mesa. One block N of Main St in downtown Mesa. Take Hwy 60 or 202 to Country Club Dr, go to Main St, and proceed 1/2 mile E to MacDonald. Phone 480/644-2230. www.ci.mesa.az.us/swmuseum.* At this natural history museum, you'll have only one thing on your mind: the Southwest, from the past to the present. You'll learn about the dinosaurs that once walked this very land and the Native Americans who lived off of it. You'll also see art of the ancient Americas, a replica of a Spanish mission, territorial jail cells from the Old West, and much more, as you explore this 80,000-square-foot regional resource. At the Adventure Center, interactive exhibits stimulate the young and curious. (Tues-Sat 10 am-5 pm, Sun 1-5 pm; closed holidays) **$$**

River tubing. *Salt River Recreation Inc. Tonto National Forest, 1320 N Bush Hwy, Mesa. 15 miles NE in Tonto National Forest (see PAYSON): E on Hwy 60 to Power Rd, then N to junction Usery Pass Hwy. Phone 480/984-3305. www.saltrivertubing.com.* Fee includes tube rental, parking, and shuttle bus service to various points on the Salt River. (Early May-Sept, daily 9 am-7 pm) **$$$**

Special Events

Arizona Renaissance Festival & Artisan Marketplace. *12601 E Hwy 60, Apache Junction. Near the foothills of the Superstition Mountains on Hwy 60, E of Apache Junction, just E of Gold Canyon Golf Resort. Phone 520/463-2600. www.royalfaires.com/arizona/arf_main.htm.* This annual festival features 12 performances stages, street performers, jousting, rides, food, and arts and crafts. Weekends Feb-late Mar. **$$$$**

Chicago Cubs Spring Training. *Hohokam Park, 1235 N Center St, Mesa. Phone 480/964-4467 (recording). www.cactus-league.com/cubs.html.* Chicago Cubs baseball spring training, exhibition games. Early Mar-early Apr. **$$$$**

Mesa Territorial Day Festival. *Sirrine House, 160 N Center, Mesa. Phone 480/644-2760. www.ci.mesa.az.us/swmuseum/shevents.asp.* Come celebrate Arizona's birthday in Old West style. The Mesa Territorial Day Festival features Western arts and crafts, music, food, games and activities, and historical re-enactments. Second Sat in Feb.

Limited-Service Hotels

★★ BEST WESTERN DOBSON RANCH INN & RESORT. *1666 S Dobson Rd, Mesa (85202). Phone 480/831-7000; toll-free 800/528-1356; fax 480/831-7000. www.dobsonranchinn.com.* 213 rooms, 2 story. Pets accepted. Complimentary full breakfast. Check-in 2 pm, check-out noon. Restaurant, bar. Fitness room. Pool, whirlpool. **$**

★ BEST WESTERN SUPERSTITION SPRINGS INN. *1342 S Power Rd, Mesa (85206). Phone 480/641-1164; toll-free 800/780-7234; fax 480/641-7253. www.bestwestern.com.* 59 rooms, 2 story. Pets accepted; fee. Complimentary continental breakfast. Check-in 2 pm, check-out 11 am. Fitness room. Pool, whirlpool. **$**

★ LA QUINTA INN. *6530 E Superstition Springs Blvd, Mesa (85206). Phone 480/654-1970; fax 480/654-1973. www.laquinta.com.* 113 rooms, 6 story. Pets accepted, some restrictions. Complimentary continental breakfast. Check-in 2 pm, check-out noon. Fitness room. Pool, whirlpool. **$**

Full-Service Hotel

★★★ HILTON PHOENIX EAST/MESA. *1011 W Holmes Ave, Mesa (85210). Phone 602/833-5555; toll-free 800/544-5266; fax 602/649-1886. www.mesapavilion.hilton.com.* 314 rooms, 8 story. Check-in 3 pm, check-out noon. Restaurant, bar. Fitness room. Pool. Business center. **$**

Full-Service Resorts

★★★ ARIZONA GOLF RESORT & CONFERENCE CENTER. *425 S Power Rd, Mesa (85206). Phone 480/832-3202; toll-free 800/528-8282; fax 480/981-0151. www.azgolfresort.com.* Tropical palms and beautiful lakes are the setting at this 150-acre golf resort. Guest suites, designed in clusters, have BBQs and heated spas. 187 rooms, 2 story. Pets accepted. Check-in 3 pm, check-out noon. Restaurant, bar. Fitness room. Pool. Golf. Tennis. **$**

★★★ GOLD CANYON GOLF RESORT. *6100 S Kings Ranch Rd, Gold Canyon (85218). Phone 480/982-9090; toll-free 800/624-6445; fax 480/830-5211. www.gcgr.com.* Whether taking in beautiful sunsets or hitting the driving range, guests at this golf resort will experience attentive service. In the foothills of the Superstition Mountains on 3,300 acres. 101 rooms, 1 story. Pets accepted; fee. Check-in 4 pm, check-out 11 am. Restaurant, bar. Pool, whirlpool. Golf, 36 holes. Tennis. **$**

Restaurants

★ ★ **LANDMARK.** *809 W Main St, Mesa (85201). Phone 480/962-4652; fax 480/962-1124. www.lmrk .com.* Former Mormon church (circa 1905). American menu. Lunch, dinner. Closed July 4, Thanksgiving, Dec 25. Children's menu. Casual attire. **$$**

★ ★ **MICHAEL MONTI'S MESA GRILL.** *1233 S Alma School Rd, Mesa (85210). Phone 480/844-1918; fax 480/834-5317. www.montis.com.* American menu. Lunch, dinner. Closed Dec 25. Bar. Children's menu. Casual attire. Outdoor seating. **$$**

Montezuma Castle National Monument (C-3)

See also Cottonwood, Flagstaff

Web site www.nps.gov/moca

20 miles SE of Cottonwood on Hwy 260, then N and E off I-17.

This five-story, 20-room structure was built by Native Americans more than 800 years ago and is one of the most remarkable cliff dwellings in the United States. Perched under a protective cliff, which rises 150 feet, the dwelling is 70 feet straight up from the talus.

Visitors are not permitted to enter the castle, but a self-guided trail offers a good view of the structure and of other ruins in the immediate area. Castle "A," a second ruin, is nearby. Montezuma Well, about 11 miles northeast, is a 470-foot-wide limestone sinkhole, with a lake 55 feet deep. Around the rim are well-preserved cliff dwellings. An irrigation system, built by the first inhabitants, leads from the spring. Limited picnicking; no camping. The Castle Visitor Center and a self-guided trail are both accessible to wheelchairs. (Sept-May: daily 8 am-5 pm; May-Sept: daily 8 am-7 pm) Contact the Chief Ranger, Box 219, Camp Verde 86322; phone 520/567-3322. **$**

Navajo Indian Reservation (A-4)

See also Holbrook, Kayenta, Page, Winslow

Web site www.explorenavajo.com.

The Navajo Nation is the largest Native American tribe and reservation in the United States. The reservation covers more than 25,000 square miles within three states: the larger portion in northeastern Arizona and the rest in New Mexico and Utah.

More than 400 years ago, the Navajo people (the Dineh) moved into the arid southwestern region of the United States and carved out a way of life that was in harmony with the natural beauty of present-day Arizona, New Mexico, and Utah. In the 1800s, this harmonious life was interrupted by westward-moving settlers and the marauding cavalry. For the Navajo, this conflict resulted in their forced removal from their ancestral land and the "Long Walk" to Fort Sumner, New Mexico. This forced removal of the Navajo was judged a failure; in 1868, they were allowed to return to their homeland.

Coal, oil, and uranium have been discovered on the reservation. The income from these, which is handled democratically by the tribe, has helped improve its economic and educational situation.

The Navajo continue to practice many of their ancient ceremonies, including the Navajo Fire Dance and the Yei-bi-chei (winter) and Enemy Way Dances (summer). Many ceremonies are associated with curing the sick and are primarily religious in nature. Visitors must obtain permission to view these events; photography, recording, and sketching are prohibited.

Most of the traders on the reservation are friendly and helpful. Do not hesitate to ask them when and where the dances take place. Navajo tribal rangers, who patrol tribal parks, also are extremely helpful and can answer almost any question that may arise.

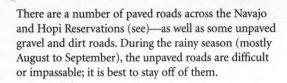

There are a number of paved roads across the Navajo and Hopi Reservations (see)—as well as some unpaved gravel and dirt roads. During the rainy season (mostly August to September), the unpaved roads are difficult or impassable; it is best to stay off of them.

Some of the most spectacular areas in Navajoland are Canyon de Chelly National Monument (see); Navajo National Monument (see); Monument Valley Navajo Tribal Park, north of Kayenta (see); Four Corners Monument; and Rainbow Bridge National Monument in Utah (see). Hubbell Trading Post National Historic Site is in Ganado (see).

Accommodations on the reservation are limited; reservations are recommended months in advance. For information, contact the Navajoland Tourism Department, Box 663, Window Rock, AZ 86515.

Navajo National Monument (A-4)

See also Kayenta

Web site www.nps.gov/nava

19 miles SW of Kayenta on Hwy 163, then 9 miles N on paved road Hwy 564 to visitor center.

This monument comprises three scattered areas totaling 600 acres and is surrounded by the Navajo Nation. Each area is the location of a large and remarkable prehistoric cliff dwelling. Two of the ruins are accessible by guided tour.

Headquarters for the monument and the visitor center are near Betatakin, the most accessible of the three cliff dwellings. Guided tours, limited to 25 people (Betatakin tour), are arranged on a first-come, first-served basis (May-Sept; tours sometimes possible earlier in spring and late in fall; phone for schedule). Hiking distance is 5 miles round-trip including a steep 700-foot trail and takes five to six hours. Because of hot temperatures, high elevations, and rugged terrain, this tour is recommended only for those in good physical condition. Betatakin may also be viewed from the Sandal Trail overlook—a 1/2-mile, one-way, self-guided trail. (Daily)

The largest and best preserved ruin, Keet Seel (Memorial Day-Labor Day, phone for schedule), is 8 1/2 miles one-way by foot or horseback from headquarters. A permit is required either way, and reservations can be made up to two months in advance. Primitive campground available for overnight hikers. The horseback trip takes all day; horses should be reserved when making reservations (fee for horses and for guide; no children under 12 without previous riding experience).

The visitor center has a museum and film program. There are picnic tables, a campground, and a craft shop at the headquarters area. (Daily; closed Jan 1, Thanksgiving, Dec 25) Contact the Superintendent, HC-71, Box 3, Tonalea 86044-9704; phone 928/672-2367.

Nogales (F-4)

See also Patagonia, Tucson

Founded 1880
Population 20,878
Elevation 3,869 ft
Area Code 520
Zip 85621
Information Nogales-Santa Cruz County Chamber of Commerce, 123 W Kino Park Pl; phone 520/287-3685
Web site www.nogaleschamber.com

This is a pleasant city and port of entry directly across the border from Nogales, Mexico. (For Border Crossing Regulations, see MAKING THE MOST OF YOUR TRIP.) A Ranger District office of the Coronado National Forest (see TUCSON) is located here.

What to See and Do

Pimeria Alta Historical Society Museum. *136 N Grand Ave, Nogales. In former City Hall. Phone 520/287-4621. www.dakotacom.net/~museum/about.htm.* History of southern Arizona and northern Sonora, from AD 1000-present. Photo collection; library; archives; self-guided walking tours. (Mon-Sat 8 am-5 pm; closed holidays) **FREE**

Tubac Presidio State Historic Park. *Tubac. 20 miles N off I-19. Phone 520/398-2252. www.pr.state.az.us/parks/parkhtml/tubac.html.* This was the site of Arizona's first European settlement, where a presidio (military post) was built in 1752. The park features Spanish colonial and territorial ruins and a museum with exhibits and an underground view of the remains of the presidio's main building. (Daily 8 am-5 pm; closed Dec 25) **$**

Full-Service Resort

★★★ RIO RICO RESORT AND COUNTRY CLUB. *1069 Camino Caralampi, Rio Rico (85648). Phone 520/281-1901; toll-free 800/288-4746; fax 520/281-7132. www.rioricoresort.com.* Go back in time at this picturesque resort with its very own ghost town on a mesa top with a scenic view. 180 rooms, 3 story. Pets accepted, some restrictions; fee. Check-in 4 pm, check-out noon. Restaurant, two bars. Fitness room. Outdoor pool, whirlpool. Golf (Robert Trent Jones, Sr., designer), 18 holes. Tennis. Airport transportation available. Business center. **$**

Restaurant

★ MR C'S. *282 W View Point Dr, Nogales (85621). Phone 520/281-9000; fax 520/281-1220.* Seafood, steak menu. Lunch, dinner. Closed Sun; Jan 1, Dec 25. Bar. Children's menu. Casual attire. **$$**

Organ Pipe Cactus National Monument (E-2)

Web site www.nps.gov/orpi

Park entrance 15 miles S of Ajo on Hwy 85; visitor center 35 miles S of Ajo on Hwy 85.

This 516-square-mile Sonoran desert area on the Mexican border is Arizona's largest national monument. The organ pipe cactus grows as high as 20 feet and has 30 or more arms, which resemble organ pipes. The plant blooms in May and June. Blossoms, usually at branch tips, are white with pink or lavender touches. During February and March, depending on the rainfall, parts of the area may be covered with Mexican goldpoppy, magenta owl clover, blue lupine, and bright orange mallow. Mesquite, saguaro, several species of cholla, barrel cacti, paloverde trees, creosote bush, ocotillo, and other desert plants thrive here.

There are two graded scenic drives, both self-guided: the 53-mile Puerto Blanco and the 21-mile Ajo Mountain drives. There is a 208-site campground near headquarters (May-mid-Jan, 30-day limit; mid-Jan-Apr, 14-day limit; 35-foot RV limit; fee), no reservations; groceries (5 miles). Information service and exhibits are at the visitor center (daily). Contact the Superintendent, Rte 1, Box 100, Ajo 85321; phone 520/387-6849.

Specialty Lodging

The following lodging establishment is approved by Mobil Travel Guide but, due to its unique and individualized nature has not been given a traditional Mobil Star rating. Included in this listing you may find bed-and-breakfasts, limited-service inns, guest ranches, and other unique hotel properties.

GUEST HOUSE INN. *700 Guest House Rd, Ajo (85321). Phone 520/387-6133; fax 520/387-3995. www.guesthouseinn.biz.* Former executive guest house built in 1925; stately dining room. 4 rooms. Complimentary full breakfast. Check-in 2 pm, check-out 11 am. **$**

Page (A-3)

See also Marble Canyon, Navajo Indian Reservation

Population 6,809
Elevation 4,000 ft
Area Code 520
Zip 86040
Information Page/Lake Powell Chamber of Commerce, 644 N Navajo, Tower Plaza, Box 727; phone 520/645-2741 or toll-free 888/261-7243.
Web site www.cityofpage.org

Page is at the east end of the Glen Canyon Dam, on the Colorado River. The dam, 710 feet high, forms Lake Powell, a part of the Glen Canyon National Recreation Area. The lake, 186 miles long with 1,900 miles of shoreline, is the second-largest man-made lake in the United States.

The dam was built for the Bureau of Reclamation for water storage and the generation of electric power. The lake is named for John Wesley Powell, the intrepid and brilliant geologist who lost an arm at the Battle of Shiloh, led an expedition down the Colorado in 1869, and was later director of the US Geological Survey.

What to See and Do

Boat trips on Lake Powell. *Wahweap Lodge & Marina, 100 Lake Shore Dr, Page. 6 miles N on Hwy 89. Phone 928/645-2433; toll-free 800/528-6154.* One-hour to one-day trips; some include Rainbow Bridge National Monument. Houseboat and powerboat rentals. Reservations advised.

Glen Canyon National Recreation Area. *Hwy 89, Page. Phone 928/608-6404 (Carl Hayden Visitor Center). www.nps.gov/glca.* More than 1 million acres, including Lake Powell. Campfire program (Memorial Day-Labor Day). Swimming, water-skiing, fishing, boating (ramps, marina); hiking, picnicking, restaurants, lodge, camping. Developed areas in Utah include Bullfrog, Hite, Halls Crossing, and Dangling Rope (accessible by boat only); many of these areas have ranger stations, marinas, boat rentals and trips, supplies, camping, and lodging. Lees Ferry on the Colorado River (approximately 15 miles downstream from the dam, but a 45-mile drive southwest from Page) has a launch ramp and camping. Visitor center on canyon rim, adjacent to Glen Canyon Bridge on Hwy 89, has historical exhibits. Ranger station, 7 miles north of the dam at Wahweap. Guided tours (summer). (Daily; closed Jan 1, Dec 25)

John Wesley Powell Memorial Museum. *6 N Lake Powell Blvd, Page. Phone 928/645-9496; toll-free 888/597-6873. www.powellmuseum.org.* Fluorescent rock collection, Native American artifacts; books, videos; replica of Powell's boat. (Mon-Fri 9 am-5 pm) **$**

Rainbow Bridge National Monument. *Box 1507, Page. Approximately 60 miles NE in Utah, NW of Navajo Mountain. Phone 928/608-6404. www.nps.gov/rabr.* (See UTAH)

Scenic flights over the area. *Page Airport in Classic Helicopter Building, 1/2 mile NE on Hwy 89. Phone 928/645-2494.* Trips vary from 30 minutes to more than two hours. For fee information, contact Scenic Air, Box 1385. (Daily; closed Jan 1, Thanksgiving, Dec 25)

Wilderness River Adventures. *2040 E Frontage Rd, Page. Phone 928/645-3296; toll-free 800/992-8022. whitewater-rafting.gordonsguide.com/wildernessriveradventures/index.cfm.* Specializes in multi-day trips on the Colorado River in Glen Canyon in raftlike neoprene boats. Reservations are required. (Apr-Oct) **$$$$**

Limited-Service Hotels

★ BEST WESTERN PAGE INN. *207 N Lake Powell Blvd, Page (86040). Phone 928/645-2451; toll-free 800/637-9183; fax 928/645-9552. www.bestwestern.com.* 90 rooms, 3 story. Pets accepted; fee. Complimentary continental breakfast. Check-out 11 am. Pool, whirlpool. Airport transportation available. **$**

★★ QUALITY INN. *287 N Lake Powell Blvd, Page (86040). Phone 928/645-8851; fax 928/645-2523.* 130 rooms, 3 story. Pets accepted, some restrictions. Check-out 11 am. Restaurant, bar. Pool. **$**

★★ WAHWEAP LODGE. *100 Lakeshore Dr, Page (86040). Phone 928/645-2433; toll-free 800/528-6154; fax 928/645-1031. www.visitlakepowell.com.* Located on beautiful Lake Powell, this homey lodge has a spectacular atmosphere. Guest rooms include lake or resort views to enjoy. 350 rooms, 2 story. Pets accepted. Check-out 11 am. Restaurant, bar. Fitness room. Two pools, whirlpool. Airport transportation available. **$**

Restaurant

★★ BELLA NAPOLI. *810 N Navajo Dr, Page (86040). Phone 928/645-2706; fax 928/645-2554.* Italian menu. Dinner. **$$**

★ KEN'S OLD WEST. *718 Vista, Page (86040). Phone 928/645-5160; fax 928/645-3349.* Steak menu. Dinner. Closed Jan 1, Thanksgiving, Dec 25. Bar. Children's menu. Reservations recommended. Outdoor seating. **$$$**

Paradise Valley

Web site www.ci.paradise-valley.az.us

Full-Service Inn

★★★ THE HERMOSA INN. *5532 N Palo Cristi Rd, Paradise Valley (85253). Phone 602/955-8614; toll-free 800/241-1210; fax 602/955-8299. www.hermosainn*

.com. Accommodations range from spacious villas to cozy adobe casitas. Sitting on a half-acre marked by gracious olive and mesquite trees, towering palms, and brilliant flowers, this inn occasionally gets ghostly visits from its original owner. 35 rooms, 1 story. Pets accepted. Complimentary continental breakfast. Check-in 3 pm, check-out noon. Restaurant, bar. Outdoor pool, whirlpool. Tennis. **$$**

Full-Service Resort

★★★ SANCTUARY ON CAMELBACK MOUNTAIN *5700 E McDonald Dr, Paradise Valley (85253). Phone 480/948-2100; fax 480/483-7314. www.sanctuaryaz.com.* The Sanctuary on Camelback Mountain is the very essence of desert chic. Perched high above the Valley, this sleek resort is a haven of tranquility and a hot spot for a stylish clientele. The mountainside casitas boast luxurious privacy and are fitted with creature comforts such as Frette linens and candlelight turndown service. The spa is a major draw with its Asian-inspired interiors and relaxing, innovative treatments. Four pools, including the signature sleek infinity pool, provide a welcome respite from the heat. Tennis courts and a fitness facility are also available, yet "less is more" is the mantra at this hideout. Elements restaurant's fresh American cuisine is punctuated with Asian flavors, and its hip look matches the cutting-edge cooking. 98 rooms, 1 story. Pets accepted. Check-in 4 pm, check-out noon. Four indoor pools, whirlpool. Business center. **$$$**

Spa

★★★ THE SANCTUARY SPA AT SANCTUARY CAMELBACK MOUNTAIN. *5700 E McDonald Dr, Paradise Valley (85253). Phone 480/607-2330; toll-free 800/259-4171. www.sanctuaryaz.com.* Most people visit the Sanctuary for blissful quiet time and reflection. Four pools, including Arizona's largest infinity-edge pool, add scenic diversions, but it is the spa that commands the attention of most guests. As you enter the Sanctuary Spa, the energy and spirit of the Far East instantly calm you. Composed of a fitness center, a 25-yard lap pool, a Watsu pool, ten treatment rooms, and a meditation area with a reflecting pool, this spa is certain to soothe with its exotic approach to beauty and well-being. Body treatments such as the seaweed roll and the ume plum roll are renowned for their stimulating and detoxifying benefits. Give your circulation a jump-start with the aspara treatment, which uses marine water with sage, lavender, and essential oils to improve blood flow and energy. A Japanese spring recognized for rejuvenating skin is the inspiration behind the onsen longevity treatment. The yuzu contouring glaze is a wonderfully relaxing treatment where algae and Japanese yuzu are massaged into the skin to restore its youthfulness. The luxurious Sumatra coconut body polish calms and comforts sensitive skin, while the bamboo lemongrass scrub is ideal for dehydrated skin.

In keeping with the spa's exotic appeal, the facials—from the dragonfly and sacred rain to the porcelain and spring mist—tackle dry, sensitive, sun-damaged, or tired skin in an inspired manner. Should you prefer to indulge in a treatment while relishing the privacy of your guest room, be sure to book one of the fabulous in-room ceremonies. Many of these treatments, such as the prana footbath with massage and the mandi susu, an ancient Indonesian cleansing ritual for dry skin, evoke the mysticism and magic of the East. Succumb to the tension-reducing pleasures of the wild lime blossom scalp and body massage or indulge in more than a dozen other types of massage. From nutritional consultations and acupuncture to stress reduction classes and dream interpretations, The Sanctuary Spa can help you achieve much-deserved tranquility.

Restaurants

★★★ LON'S. *5532 N Palo Cristi Rd, Paradise Valley (85253). Phone 602/955-7878; fax 602/955-7893. www.lons.com.* Built by Southwestern artist Lon Megargee in the 1930s, Hermosa Inn's adobe design and rustic furnishings provide the right setting for some of the best comfort food in Phoenix. Fresh fruits, vegetables and herbs from the chef's onsite garden make up the seasonal specials. Contemporary American menu. Lunch Mon-Sat, dinner, Sun brunch. Closed some holidays. Bar. Children's menu. Casual attire. Reservations recommended. Outdoor seating. **$$$**

★★★ ELEMENTS. *5700 E McDonald Rd, Paradise Valley (85253). Phone 480/607-2300; fax 480/948-1739. www.elementsrestaurant.com.* American menu. Breakfast, lunch, dinner. Bar. Casual attire. Outdoor seating. **$$$**

Parker (C-1)

See also Lake Havasu City

Founded 1908
Population 3,140
Elevation 413 ft
Area Code 520
Zip 85344
Information Chamber of Commerce, 1217 California Ave; phone 520/669-2174
Web site www.ci.parker.az.us

Parker is located on the east bank of the Colorado River, about 16 miles south of Parker Dam (320 feet high, 856 feet long), which forms Lake Havasu. Popular recreational activities in the area include fishing, frogging, boating, jet and water skiing, hunting, golfing, rock hunting, and camping. The town has become the trade center for surrounding communities and the Colorado Indian Reservation.

What to See and Do

Buckskin Mountain State Park. *5476 Hwy 95, Parker. Approximately 12 miles NE on Hwy 95. Phone 928/667-3231. www.pr.state.az.us/Parks/parkhtml/buckskin.html.* On 1,676 acres. Scenic bluffs overlooking the Colorado River. Swimming, fishing, boating (ramp, marina); nature trails, hiking, picnicking (shelter), concession, camping (electric hookups, dump station), riverside cabanas (fee). River Island Unit has boating (ramp); picnicking (shelter), camping (water hook-ups). (Daily) 1/2 mile N of main unit.

Colorado River Indian Tribes Museum. *Rodeo Dr, Parker. Phone 928/669-9211.* Museum contains exhibits that interpret the history of the four Colorado River Tribes: Mohave, Chemehuevi, Navajo, and Hopi. Authentic Native American arts and crafts for sale. Bluewater Casino is open 24 hours; slots, poker, bingo. Operated by the Colorado River Indian Tribes. (Mon-Fri; closed holidays) **$**

La Paz County Park. *7350 Riverside Dr, Parker. 8 miles N on Hwy 95. Phone 928/667-2069. www.co.la-paz.az.us/parks/lapaz_county_park.htm.* A 540-acre park with 4,000 feet of Colorado River beach frontage. Swimming, water-skiing, fishing, boating (ramps); tennis court, golf course, driving range, picnicking (shelter), playground, camping (electric hookups, dump station). Fee for some activities. **$**

Parker Dam & Power Plant. *Parker. 17 miles N via Hwy 95, Riverside Dr exit. Phone 760/663-3712.* One of the deepest dams in the world, 65 percent of its structural height of 320 feet is below the riverbed. Only 85 feet of the dam is visible, while another 62 feet of its superstructure rises above the roadway, across the top of the dam. (Daily)

Special Events

Holiday Lighted Boat Parade. *Parker River.* Decorated boats parade on the 11-mile strip to a selected site for trophy presentation; viewing from both sides of the Parker River. Late Nov.

La Paz County Fair. *Fairgrounds at Four Corners, 13991 2nd Ave, Parker. Phone 928/669-2179.* Carnival, livestock auction, Farm Olympics, entertainment. Mid-Mar.

Parker 400 Off Road Race. *1217 S California Ave, Parker. Phone 928/669-2174.* Three Arizona loops. Four hundred miles of desert racing. Late Jan.

Parker Enduro-Aquasports Weekend. *One Park Dr, Parker. Phone 928/855-2208.* Longest and oldest boat racing event in the country. May.

Limited-Service Hotel

★ KOFA INN. *1700 S California Ave, Parker (85344). Phone 928/669-2101; toll-free 800/742-6072; fax 928/669-6902.* 41 rooms, 2 story. Check-out noon. Pool. **$**

Patagonia (F-4)

See also Nogales, Sierra Vista

Population 881
Elevation 4,057 ft
Area Code 520
Zip 85624
Information Information/Visitors Center, Horse of a Different Color Emporium, Box 241; phone 520/394-0060 or toll-free 888/794-0060

A small cattle town with a distinct mining flavor, Patagonia is surrounded by beautiful mountains and Hollywood-style Western scenery.

What to See and Do

Patagonia Lake State Park. *400 Patagonia Lake Rd, Patagonia. 8 miles S on Hwy 82, then 4 miles N on Patagonia Lake Rd. Phone 520/287-6965. www.pr.state.az.us/parks/parkhtml/patagonia.html.* A 265-acre park with a lake. Swimming beach, fishing, boating (ramp, rentals, marina); hiking, picnicking, concession, ramadas, camping (dump station). (Daily 8 am-10 pm)

Patagonia-Sonoita Creek Preserve. *150 Salero Canyon Rd, Patagonia. W along Hwy 82, then W on 4th Ave, turn S on Pennsylvania, cross the creek, and go about 1 mile to the entrance. Phone 520/394-2400.* The 1,350 protected acres extend downstream along Sonoita Creek for approximately 2 miles. Bordered by willows, cottonwoods, and ash, it provides a perfect sanctuary for more than 300 species of birds. There is also a wide array of fish and butterflies here. Tour of the preserve (Sat 9 am). (Oct-Mar: Wed-Sun 7:30 am-4 pm; Apr-Sept: Wed-Sun 6:30 am-4 pm) **$**

Full-Service Resort

★ ★ TUBAC GOLF RESORT. *1 Otero Rd, Tubac (85646). Phone 520/398-2211; toll-free 800/848-7893; fax 520/398-9261. www.tubacgolfresort.com.* 46 rooms. Check-in 3 pm, check-out noon. Restaurant, bar. Outdoor pool. Golf, 18 holes. Tennis. **$$**

Payson (C-4)

See also Phoenix

Founded 1882
Population 13,620
Elevation 5,330 ft
Area Code 520
Zip 85541
Information Chamber of Commerce, Box 1380, 85547; phone 520/474-4515 or toll-free 800/6-PAYSON
Web site www.ci.payson.az.us

Payson, in the heart of the Tonto National Forest, provides many outdoor recreational activities in a mild climate.

What to See and Do

Tonto National Forest. *PO Box 5348, 2324 E McDowell Rd, Payson. Phone 602/225-5200. www.fs.fed.us/r3/tonto/indexy.html.* This area includes almost 3 million acres of desert and mountain landscape. Six lakes along the Salt and Verde rivers offer opportunities for fishing, boating, hiking, and camping. Seven wilderness areas are located within the forest's boundaries, providing hiking and bridle trails. The forest also features Tonto Natural Bridge, the largest natural travertine bridge in the world. Scenic attractions include the Apache Trail, Four Peaks, the Mogollon Rim, and Sonoran Desert country.

Wilderness Aware. *PO Box 1550, Buena Vista. Phone 719/395-2112; toll-free 800/462-7238. www.inaraft.com.* One- to five-day whitewater rafting trips through the Salt River Canyon. (Mar-May)

Special Events

Old-Time Fiddler's Contest & Festival. *1000 W Country Club Dr, New Rodeo Grounds, Payson. Phone 928/474-3398.* Fiddling contest, storytellers, Irish step-dancers, entertainment, food, arts and crafts, and fiddle-making demonstrations. Late Sept.

World's Oldest Continuous PRCA Rodeo. *Multi-Event Center, Payson. Phone 928/474-4515; toll-free 800/672-9766.* The rodeo features calf roping, bull riding, and barrel racing. Third weekend in Aug. **$$$**

Limited-Service Hotel

★ ★ BEST WESTERN PAYSON INN. *801 N Beeline Hwy, Payson (85541). Phone 928/474-3241; toll-free 800/247-9477; fax 928/472-6564. www.bestwestern.com.* 99 rooms, 2 story. Pets accepted; fee. Complimentary continental breakfast. Check-out 11 am. Restaurant, bar. Pool, whirlpool. **$**

Peoria

Web site www.peoriaaz.com

What to See and Do

Lake Pleasant Regional Park. *The main park entrance is located 2 miles N of State Rte 74, off Castle Hot Springs Rd. Phone 602/372-7460.*

www.maricopa.gov/parks/lake_pleasant. So what if Arizona is landlocked? Hitch your motorboat, sailboat, or jet ski to the back of your car, pack up the fishing tackle and water skis, and go coastal 30 miles north of Phoenix at this manmade reservoir with 114 miles of sun-drenched shoreline. The park has campgrounds for RVs and tents, boat ramps, plenty of picnic tables with grills, and an overlook and visitors' center where you can learn more about the lake—and those bass you'll want to bait. (Daily) Overlook and visitor center (weekends). **$$**

Restaurant

★ ★ LE RHONE. *9401 W Thunderbird Rd, Peoria (85381). Phone 623/933-0151; fax 623/933-7187.* French menu. Dinner. Closed Mon; Jan 1. Bar. Casual attire. **$$**

Petrified Forest National Park (C-5)

See also Holbrook

Web site www.nps.gov/pefo

North entrance: 25 miles E of Holbrook on I-40; south entrance: 19 miles E of Holbrook on US 180.

These 93,532 acres include one of the most spectacular displays of petrified wood in the world. The trees of the original forest may have grown in upland areas and then washed down onto a floodplain by rivers. Subsequently, the trees were buried under sediment and volcanic ash, causing the organic wood to be filled gradually with mineral compounds, especially quartz. The grain, now multicolored by the compounds, is still visible in some specimens.

The visitor center is located at the entrance off I-40. The Rainbow Forest Museum (off US 180) depicts the paleontology and geology of the Triassic Era (daily; closed Dec 25). Service stations and cafeteria at the north entrance; snacks only at south entrance. Prehistoric Pueblo inhabitants left countless petroglyphs of animals, figures, and symbols carved on sandstone throughout the park.

The park contains a portion of the Painted Desert, a colorful area extending 200 miles along the north bank of the Little Colorado River. This highly eroded area of mesas, pinnacles, washes, and canyons is part of the Chinle formation, a soft shale, clay, and sandstone stratum of the Triassic age. The sunlight and clouds passing over this spectacular scenery create an effect of constant, kaleidoscopic change. There are very good viewpoints along the park road.

Picnicking facilities at Rainbow Forest and at Chinle Point on the rim of the Painted Desert; no campgrounds. Important: It is forbidden to take even the smallest piece of petrified wood or any other object from the park. Nearby curio shops sell wood taken from areas outside the park. (Daily; closed Dec 25) Contact the Superintendent, Box 2217, Petrified Forest National Park 86028; phone 520/524-6228.

Phoenix (D-3)

See also Casa Grande, Chandler, Glendale, Litchfield Park, Mesa, Payson, Wickenburg

Settled 1864
Population 1,321,045
Elevation 1,090 ft
Area Code 602
Information Greater Phoenix Convention & Visitors Bureau, One Arizona Center, 400 E Van Buren St, Suite 600, 85004; phone 602/254-6500
Web site www.visitphoenix.com
Suburbs Glendale, Mesa, Scottsdale, Tempe

The capital of Arizona lies on flat desert, surrounded by mountains and green irrigated fields of cotton, lettuce, melons, and alfalfa and groves of oranges, grapefruit, lemons, and olives. It is a resort area as well as an industrial area. It is also the home of Grand Canyon University (1949). The sun shines practically every day. Most rain falls in December, with some precipitation in summer. There is swimming, fishing, boating, horseback riding, golf, and tennis. Phoenix, like Tucson, is a health center, known for its warm temperatures and low humidity. As a vacation spot, it is both sophisticated and informal.

Additional Visitor Information

Phoenix Metro Magazine, available at newsstands, has up-to-date information on cultural events and articles of interest to visitors.

The Greater Phoenix Convention & Visitors Bureau has helpful information for visitors; contact them at

One Arizona Center, 400 E Van Buren St, Suite 600, 85004; phone 602/254-6500; visitor information, phone 602/252-5588.

Public Transportation

Buses (Valley Metro Transit System), phone 602/253-5000

Airport Phoenix International Airport

Information Phone 602/273-3300

Web site http://phoenix.gov/aviation

Lost and Found Phone 602/273-3307

Airlines Aeromexico, Air Canada, Alaska Airlines, Aloha Airlines, America West, American, ATA, Arizona Express, British Airways, Continental, Delta, Frontier, Great Lakes Aviation, Hawaiian Airlines, Lufthansa, Midwest Airlines, Northwest, Southwest, Sun Country, United, US Airways

What to See and Do

Antique Gallery/Central Antiques. *5037 N Central Ave, Phoenix. Phone 602/241-1174 (Antique Gallery). www.antiquegalleryaz.com.* As you browse through these two appealing galleries, sister stores in the same upscale shopping center, you'll be oohing and ahhing every step of the way. In 30,000 square feet of retail space, about 150 dealers showcase heirloom-quality antiques. No collectibles, no kitsch. We're talking period furniture, American and English silver, European porcelain, and much more. Even if the prices top your budget, you'll be glad you stopped in for a look-see. (Mon-Sat 10 am-5:30 pm, Sun noon-5 pm; closed major holidays)

Arizona Diamondbacks (MLB). *Bank One Ballpark, 401 E Jefferson, Phoenix. Phone 602/462-6000. arizona.diamondbacks.mlb.com.* Professional baseball team.

Arizona Mining and Mineral Museum. *1502 W Washington, Phoenix. Phone 602/255-3791. www.admmr.state.az.us/musgen.htm.* Collections of minerals, ores, gems; petrified wood; mining exhibits. Maintained by the Arizona Department of Mines and Mineral Resources. (Mon-Fri 8 am-5 pm, Sat 11 am-4 pm; closed holidays) **$**

★ **Arizona Science Center.** *600 E Washington St, Phoenix. Phone 602/716-2000. www.azscience.org.* People of all ages tote their curiosity to this cavernous learning center and have a field day getting smarter. More than 300 hands-on exhibits give the serious and mysterious world of science a fun twist and help teach inquiring minds about topics ranging from geology and weather to healing and information technology. See the universe up close in a planetarium and stare wide-eyed at science films in a theater with a five-story screen. (Daily 10 am-5 pm; closed Thanksgiving, Dec 25) **$$**

Arizona State Capitol Museum. *1700 W Washington St, Phoenix. Phone 602/542-4581. www.dlapr.lib.az.us/museum/capitol.htm.* Built in 1899, this stately building first served as the capitol for the territorial government, then as the state capitol beginning in 1912, when Arizona was admitted to the Union. In need of more space, the state moved to adjacent office buildings in the 1970s, and this original structure has operated as a museum since its restoration in 1981. Wander through its history-filled halls and you'll see offices with period furniture and the House and Senate chambers exactly as they looked in early statehood. Don't miss the mosaic Arizona state seal on the rotunda floor and Winged Victory, a 16-foot zinc weather vane standing tall atop the capitol's copper dome. Guided tours are offered daily at 10 am and 2 pm. A landscaped area includes a variety of native trees, shrubs, and cacti. Museum (Mon-Fri 8 am-5 pm, Sat 10 am-3 pm) **FREE**

Biltmore Fashion Park. *2502 E Camelback Rd, Phoenix. Phone 602/955-1963. www.shopbiltmore.com.* If you have expensive taste, take your designer pocketbook here for high-end shopping in a low-key, relaxed outdoor setting. The more than 40 stores include A-list retailers such as Cartier, Christofle, Escada, Gucci, and Saks Fifth Avenue and a few less pricey options—Banana Republic, Chico's, Macy's, and Talbots among them. The merchants line a red-brick walkway that's colorfully landscaped and dotted with soothing water fountains. Dine in one of several restaurants, some with alfresco seating perfect for fashionista watching. (Mon-Wed, Sat 10 am-6 pm; Thurs-Fri 10 am-8 pm; Sun noon-6 pm; closed Thanksgiving, Dec 25)

Camelback Mountain. *E McDonald at Tatum Blvd, Phoenix. Trailheads at Echo Canyon Pkwy, south of McDonald Dr; and Cholla Ln, east of 64th St. Phone 602/262-8318. www.ci.phoenix.az.us/PARKS/hikecmlb.html.* Its distinctive hump makes this mountain a very visible local landmark—and a very popular spot for hiking and toning those thighs. Go and enjoy its trails, which wind through desert flora and fauna, but don't be overzealous: the two strenuous summit trails, 1.2 and 1.5 miles one way, gain more than 1,200 feet in elevation and aren't for the out of shape. Two shorter ones at the base provide much easier trekking, with elevation gains of only 100 and 200 feet. (Daily dawn-dusk)

Celebrity Theatre. *440 N 32nd St, Phoenix. Phone 602/267-1600. www.celebritytheatre.com.* The stargazing's stellar in the wide-open Arizona desert, but you can get front-row views of shining stars without ever leaving the busy streets of Phoenix. Some of the entertainment industry's biggest names bring their music and comedy to this theater. And even though the venue holds more than 2,000, no seat is more than 75 feet from center stage, a guarantee that you'll like what you see. Plus, the stage revolves, so you see a show from all angles.

Char's Has the Blues. *4631 N 7th Ave, Phoenix. Phone 602/230-0205. www.charshastheblues.com.* At this small, nothing-fancy joint, bands sing the blues every night. *New Times,* the weekly alternative newspaper in Phoenix, named Char's the city's best blues club for 11 consecutive years. A diverse crowd spans all ages. (Daily, doors open at 7 pm; closed Dec 24-25) **$$**

Desert Botanical Garden. *Papago Park, 1201 N Galvin Pkwy, Phoenix. Phone 480/941-1217. www.dbg.org.* When some people think desert, they think ugly—real ugly. But these mistaken souls would have a change of heart if they ever meandered along the peaceful trails of this 150-acre botanical oasis, home to one of the world's foremost collections of desert plants. Thousands of the beauties line the one-third mile main trail, including more than half the world's cactus, century plant, and aloe species. Shorter trails that branch off the main one offer insight into desert landscaping and gardening, desert wildflowers, the uses of plants by people, and more. You can stroll the serene grounds on your own, but you'll learn so much more about the lay of the land on a guided tour. On cool days, enjoy a relaxing lunch in the outdoor café, surrounded by all the greenery. From February through June, on Friday evenings, Music in the Gardens features performances by local bands, many of them jazz groups. Talk about a hot and sassy way to get the weekend started. (Oct-Apr: daily 8 am-8 pm; May-Sept: 7 am-8 pm; closed July 4, Dec 25) **$$**

Dog racing. *Phoenix Greyhound Park. 3801 E Washington St, Phoenix. For information, phone 602/273-7181, or see www.phoenixgreyhoundpark.com.* (Daily)

Encanto Park and Recreation Area. *2605 N 15th Ave, Phoenix. Phone 602/261-8993.* Pack up the family and head to this 222-acre park for lots of fun in the sun just minutes from downtown. Active kids with energy to burn can fish in a small lake, feed ducks in a pond, ride in boats, frolic on playground equipment, cool off in the swimming pool, hop aboard a train and eight other rides geared toward 2- to 10-year-olds at the Enchanted Island amusement park (phone 602/254-1200) (Wed-Sun; $$), and more. Two public golf courses (18 holes and 9 holes; $$-$$$$) appeal to the older crowd. (Daily) **FREE**

★ **The Heard Museum.** *2301 N Central Ave, Phoenix. Phone 602/252-8848 (recording). www.heard.org.* At this stellar museum, which has won international accolades, immerse yourself in the cultures and art of Native Americans of the Southwest. The 130,000-square-foot attraction has nearly 30,000 square feet of exhibit space in 10 galleries (and a working-artist studio)—all packed with must-sees that attract nearly 250,000 visitors each year. Its collection of 32,000 works of art and ethnographic objects includes 3,600 pieces of contemporary Native American fine art, 437 historic Hopi katsina dolls, more than 500 pieces of important Navajo and Zuni jewelry, and 90 prize-winning documented Navajo textiles. As part of its year-round education program, the Heard also offers artist demonstrations, music and dance performances, and many classes and workshops. An 8,500-square-foot branch location in north Scottsdale (34505 N Scottsdale Rd; phone 480/488-9817) features changing exhibitions by Native American artists. (Daily 9:30 am-5 pm; closed holidays) **$$**

Heritage Square. *Heritage & Science Park, 115 N Sixth St, Phoenix. Phone 602/262-5071. www.ci.phoenix.az.us/parks/heritage.html.* Heritage Square is one of three sites that make up Heritage & Science Park; the other two sites are the Arizona Science Center and Phoenix Museum of History. Historic Heritage Park has eight turn-of-the-century houses, including the restored 1895 Victorian Rosson House (docent-guided tours: Wed-Sat 10 am-3:30 pm, Sun noon-3:30 pm; closed mid-Aug-Labor Day; fee) and Arizona Doll & Toy Museum (The Stevens House)(Tues-Sat 10 am-4 pm, Sun noon-4 pm; closed early Aug-Labor Day; fee). Also open-air Lath House Pavilion. (Daily) **FREE**

MercBar. *Camelback Esplanade, 2525 E Camelback Rd, Phoenix. Phone 602/508-9449.* The beautiful people who come to this ultrachic bar to see and be seen know the drink of choice: the martini, which the Merc shakes up in 13 different ways. Its various takes on this classic cocktail rate among the best in the Valley—as well they should at $9 to $10 a glass. Patrons savor the pricey drinks in their best attire; this is not the place to dress down. Dark wood and leather seating give this hotspot a sophisticated, worldly look that clashes with casual. (Mon-Fri from 4 pm, Sat-Sun from 6 pm)

Mr. Lucky's. *3660 NW Grand Ave, Phoenix. Phone 602/246-0686. www.mrluckys.com.* Cowboys and cowgirls have been slippin' into their boots and slidin' over to this old-fashioned country dance hall for serious two-steppin' to live music since 1966. Come join in the foot-shufflin' even if you're a city slicker frettin' about steppin' on toes; instructors will teach you all the right moves. Try the live bull-riding in the parking lot, too. Bring the kids on Friday night for mutton-bustin' (sheep-riding) at 7:30, just before the kids' talent show. (Wed-Sat) Wed and Thurs no cover charge. **$**

★ **Mystery Castle.** *800 E Mineral Rd, Phoenix. Seven miles S via Central Ave, E on Baseline Rd, S on 7th St, then E on Mineral Rd. Phone 602/268-1581.* Some dads build dreamy playhouses for their little girls, but Boyce Luther Gulley fashioned an 18-room castle with 13 fireplaces for his daughter Mary Lou. It's how Gulley marked time between 1930 and 1945 after being diagnosed with tuberculosis and abandoning his family in Washington State to try beating his disease in barren Arizona. Mary Lou learned about her dad's labor of love after his death in the 1940s and has been keeping up appearances there ever since. If you're lucky, the lady of the house will lead your tour herself, as she often does. Architectural Digest it's not. Quirky best describes what you'll see in this unconventional, imaginative desert manor made of native stone and found objects and furnished with Southwestern antiques. (Oct-June, Thurs-Sun 11 am-4 pm) **$**

Papago Park. *Galvan Pkwy and Van Buren St, Phoenix. Phone 602/256-3220. phoenix.gov/PARKS/hikepapa.html.* This 1,200-acre park with sandstone buttes is flatter than many others in the area, so it doesn't offer serious fitness buffs strenuous hiking. But the terrain appeals to novice hikers and mountain-bikers, who like to pedal its 10 miles of trails. And because it's close to the Phoenix Zoo, families often come to enjoy its many picnic areas and fishing lagoon. The golf course lures duffers. All park visitors get good views of the city, especially at sunset from the Hole-in-the-Rock Archaeological Site, a naturally eroded rock formation. (Daily 6 am-11 pm) **FREE**

★ **Phoenix Art Museum.** *1625 N Central Ave, Phoenix. Phone 602/257-1222 (recording). www.phxart.org.* At more than 160,000 square feet, this spectacle of color is one of the largest art museums in the Southwest. Its collection spans the centuries and exceeds 17,000 works, about 1,000 on display at any given time in several galleries divided into three main sections: Art of Asia; Art of the Americas and Europe to 1900; and Art of Our Time: 1900 to the Present. Major traveling exhibits also hang here. Every third Sunday of each month, the museum sponsors Family Sundays for children ages 5-12 and the adults in their lives who want to encourage their creative development. The participatory fun includes imaginative art projects and self-guided explorations of the galleries. (Tues-Wed, Fri-Sun 10 am-5 pm; Thurs 10 am-9 pm; closed major holidays) Free admission Thurs. **$$**

Phoenix Coyotes (NHL). *Glendale Arena, 6520 N 91st Ave, Glendale. At the intersection of Loop 101 and Glendale Ave. Phone 480/563-7825. www.phoenixcoyotes.com/index.php.* Professional hockey team.

Phoenix International Raceway. *7602 S 115th Ave, Avondale. Phone 602/252-2227. www.phoenixintlraceway.com.* If you've seen *Days of Thunder,* starring Tom Cruise, you've seen this high-octane attraction on the big screen. On six weekends spread throughout the year, big-name drivers fire up their souped-up engines and go for speedy spins on its 1-mile track. The NASCAR Weekend in late fall generates the most sparks, with more than 100,000 fans lapping up all the fast-forward action, which features the Winston Cup Series, the Busch Series, and the Craftsman Truck Series. Other events that zoom into town and onto the track include the Rolex Grand American Sports Car Series and the IRL Indy Car Series. No other speedway in Arizona opens its greasy pits to so many different classes of cars. IRL also hosts plenty of non-racing events—a large Fourth of July celebration, festivals, arts and crafts fairs, and one of the Southwest's largest chili cook-offs. **$$$$**

Phoenix Mercury (WNBA). *America West Arena, 201 E Jefferson St, Phoenix. Phone 602/252-9622 (tickets). www.wnba.com/mercury.* Women's professional basketball team.

Phoenix Mountains Preserve. *16th St and Greenway Rd, Phoenix. Phone 602/262-6861. www.ci.phoenix.az.us/parks/hikephx.html.* Located in both the northern and southern parts of the city, the parks offer more than 7,000 acres of unique desert mountain recreational activities. Hiking, horseback riding, and picnicking. (Daily 5 am-11 pm) **FREE** Located here are

Echo Canyon. *Camelback Mountain, E McDonald and Tatum Blvd, Phoenix. Phone 602/256-3220.* Hiking.

North Mountain Recreation Area. *Phoenix. Phone 602/262-7901.* Hiking on mountain trails. Picnicking (shelter).

South Mountain. *10919 S Central, Phoenix. Phone 602/262-6111. www.ci.phoenix.az.us/PARKS/hikesoth.html.* Offers 16,000 acres in a rugged mountain range. Hiking trails, park drives to scenic overlooks, picnicking (shelter).

Squaw Peak Park. *Phoenix. 9 miles NE. Phone 602/262-7901. www.ci.phoenix.az.us/parks/hikephx.html.* When you want to get your heart pumping, go trailblazing on this craggy pinnacle. When you do, you'll probably have plenty of company, and it will soon become apparent why. Besides a calorie-busting workout, this vertical climb delivers views that may take your breath away as much as the hiking does. The demanding, 1.2-mile trek up the Summit Trail will test you every step of the way. For an easier go, opt for the Circumference Trail. (Daily)

Phoenix Museum of History. *Heritage & Science Park, 105 N 5th St, Phoenix. Phone 602/253-2734. www.pmoh.org.* More than 2,000 years of Arizona history; changing exhibits. (Tues-Sat 10 am-5 pm; closed holidays) Wed free 2-5 pm. **$**

Phoenix Suns (NBA). *America West Arena, 201 E Jefferson, Phoenix. Phone 602/379-7867. www.nba.com/suns.* Professional basketball team.

Phoenix Zoo. *Papago Park, 455 N Galvin Pkwy, Phoenix. Phone 602/273-1341. www.phoenixzoo.org.* Now that the Arabian oryx—the flagship species at this animal attraction—have moved into a new home at the zoo, visitors get even better views of these desert bighorn sheep. You don't want to butt heads with them, of course, but you'll be glad to get good glimpses of them. In all, you'll see more than 400 mammals, 500 birds, and 500 reptiles and amphibians. (Sept-May: daily 9 am-5 pm; June-Aug: daily 7 am-4 pm; closed Dec 25) **$$$** Opposite the zoo is

Hall of Flame Firefighting Museum. *Papago Park, 6101 E Van Buren St, Phoenix. Phone 602/275-3473. www.hallofflame.org.* So many kids dream of someday sliding down a firehouse pole, climbing aboard a bright red firetruck, and rushing off to battle a three-alarm blaze. So it's no wonder that this smokin' museum, believed to be the largest of its kind in the world, brings big, wide smiles to kids' faces. Its five galleries are packed with more than 100 pieces of awe-inspiring firefighting equipment, from antique, hand-drawn pumps dating as far back as the 1700s to snazzy, motorized fire engines. (Mon-Sat 9 am-5 pm, Sun noon-4 pm; closed Jan 1, Thanksgiving, Dec 25) **$$**

Pioneer Living History Museum. *3901 W Pioneer Rd, Phoenix. Phone 623/465-1052. www.pioneer-arizona.com.* Escape the freeways of modern-day Phoenix and experience city life as pioneers in the Old West knew it, sans cars. On these 90 acres celebrating the 1800s, you can belly up to the bar in the saloon, check out the chiseling in the blacksmith shop, eye the vintage fashions in the dress store, say a little prayer in the community church, and more. While in town, mind your manners: say howdy to the manly cowboys and tip your hat to the lovely Victorian ladies. (Mid-Sept-May: Wed-Sun 9 am-5 pm; late June-mid-Sept: Fri-Sun 9 am-2 pm) **$$**

Pueblo Grande Museum and Archaeological Park. *4619 E Washington St, Phoenix. Approximately 1 mile NE of Sky Harbor International Airport. Phone 602/495-0901; toll-free 877/706-4408. www.ci.phoenix.az.us/parks/pueblo.html.* At the ruins of a Hohokam village, you can revisit the past and learn how these prehistoric people lived in Arizona 1,500 years ago. You'll see an old platform mound that the Hohokam probably used for ceremonies or as an administrative center, an excavated ball court, reproductions of adobe homes, and irrigation canals used for farming. Make the rounds of this 102-acre park on your own, or take a guided tour on Saturday at 11 am or 1 pm, on Sunday at 1:30 pm. (Mon-Sat 9 am-4:45 pm, Sun 1-4:45 pm; closed major holidays) Free admission Sun. **$**

Roadrunner Park Farmers' Market. *3501 Cactus Rd, Phoenix. Phone 623/848-1234.* On Saturday mornings, up to 5,000 people shop at this outdoor market to stock up on fresh produce grown in the Arizona desert. As many as 60 vendors sell melons, onions, peppers, squash, tomatoes, and other fresh-from-the-farm crops (though a few peddle arts and crafts, instead). The same association that operates this food fest also runs seven smaller ones in the area, including two downtown at Heritage Square (Thurs, 10 am-2 pm, Oct-May) and Patriot Square (Wed, 10 am-2 pm, Oct-Apr). (Sat 8 am-noon; closed Jan 1, Dec 25) **FREE**

The Shops at Arizona Center. *400 E Van Buren, Phoenix. Van Buren St between 3rd and 5th sts. Phone 602/271-4000. www.arizonacenter.com.* Tucked behind two downtown office buildings—One Arizona Center and Two Arizona Center—sits this parklike plaza for your entertainment pleasure. Even though the plaza is attractively landscaped with palm trees, gardens, and pools, you may not notice it from the street, but you'd be wise to look for it. While you're there, you can shop at about 15 stores and kiosks, including Copper Square Clothing Company, where nothing sells for more than $12.99. Who can resist a good bargain? The hungry break bread in seven restaurants, while revelers whoop it up in four nightclubs. The more sedate sit back, relax, and take in the latest Hollywood flicks at a 24-screen theater. (Daily; closed Jan 1, Thanksgiving, Dec 25)

Thoroughbred horse racing. *Turf Paradise. 1501 W Bell Rd, Phoenix. 10 miles N on I-17 to Bell Rd exit. Phone 602/942-1101. www.turfparadise.com.* (Late Sept-early May: Mon-Tues, Fri-Sun; closed holidays) **$**

Vans Skatepark. *9617 N Metro Pkwy W, Suite 2129, Phoenix. Phone 602/944-2204. www.vans.com/skatepark.org/phoenix.html.* If you or your family members like to skateboard or go in-line skating, this is the place to spin your wheels in Phoenix. The riding areas and obstacles include a street course with birch ramps and a wooden bowl with swimming-pool tiles and coping. The park accommodates all skill levels, so don't worry if you're not up for a challenge. Three days a week, it also offers sessions for BMX bikers. (Mon-Thurs 10 am-10 pm, Fri 10 am-midnight, Sat-Sun 10 am-9:45 pm)

Special Events

Arizona Opera. *225 E Adams St, Phoenix. Phone 602/266-7464. www.azopera.com.* The high notes of arias have been ringing across the Arizona wilderness for more than 25 years, prompting many a bravo. So if the passionate music of opera lights your fire, you'll likely be drawn to the Phoenix Symphony Hall, where this company produces five operas each season in both Phoenix and Tucson. Oct-Mar, Fri-Sun.

Arizona State Fair. *1826 W McDowell Rd, Phoenix. Phone 602/252-6771. www.azstatefair.com.* This annual event attracts big, big crowds—and with good reason. It's fun and entertaining, and has everything you'd expect at a good ol' state fair: a busy midway packed with exciting rides and games; high-decibel concerts, some featuring marquis names such as country crooners Mark Chesnutt, Joe Diffie, and Tracy Lawrence; gooey cotton candy and other carnival fare; animal and 4-H exhibits; all-Indian rodeo action; cooking contests guaranteed to whet any appetite, and much, much more. Mid-late Oct.

Arizona Theatre Company. *Herberger Theater Center, 502 W Roosevelt, Phoenix. Phone 602/256-6899. www.aztheatreco.org.* Professional regional company performs both classic and contemporary works. Oct-May. **$$$$**

Cowboy Artists of America Sale and Exhibition. *Phoenix Art Museum, 1625 N Central Ave, Phoenix. Phone 602/257-1880. www.phxart.org/cowboys37.html.* Members of Cowboy Artists of America—a select group of 20-plus who produce fine Western American art—are considered the most prestigious in this genre. At this annual event, they offer more than 100 of their new, never-before-viewed works for sale, but not at Old West prices. Indeed, some of the art commands six figures. Whoa! But don't worry if that's way more bucks than you can wrangle. All the paintings, drawings, and sculptures, remain on exhibit for several weeks before buyers claim them, so you can appreciate these colorful pieces without having to pony up a cattle baron's pay. Late Oct-mid-Nov.

Firecracker Sports Festival. *Rose Mofford, Papago, and Desert West Complexes, Phoenix. Phone 602/262-6483.* About 140 teams from throughout Arizona come to play ball during this annual event, the state's largest and longest-running softball tournament. The action features adult slow pitch and youth (girls) fast pitch in up to 13 divisions (based on age, sex, and skill level of players). The Ross Mofford Sports Complex hosts the opening-night party and colorful fireworks display that launch the tourney each year, but three other venues also host all the pitching, hitting, and fielding. Last weekend in June.

Indian Fair and Market. *The Heard Museum, 2301 N Central Ave, Phoenix. Phone 602/252-8840. www.heard .org/fair.php.* Native American artisans, demonstrations, dances, native foods. First weekend in Mar. **$$**

The New Works Festival. *Phoenix Theatre's Little Theatre, 100 E McDowell Rd, Phoenix. Phone 602/ 254-2151. www.newplays.net.* Want to see plays and musicals staged in their early phases? This festival does just that, as actors perform works-in-progress with "books in hand," and with minimal set decorations. Ultimately, some of those put to the test get further developed and fine-tuned, then get produced as part of Phoenix Theatre's regular season. But you can brag you saw them first. Mid-July-early Aug. **$$**

The Phoenix Symphony. *Symphony Hall, 225 E Adams St, Phoenix. Phone 602/495-1999 (box office); toll-free 800/776-9080. www.phoenixsymphony.org.* Annual programming includes classics, chamber orchestra, symphonic pops, and family and holiday events. May.

Tostitos Fiesta Bowl. *ASU Sun Devil Stadium, 5th St and College Ave, Tempe. Phone 480/350-0900. www. tostitosfiestabowl.com.* College football classic game. Early Jan.

Yaqui Indian Holy Week Ceremonials. *Yaqui Temple and Ceremonial Grounds, Guadalupe. Phone 602/ 883-2838.* Fri evenings prior to Easter, beginning the first Fri after Ash Wednesday.

Limited-Service Hotels

★ ★ DOUBLETREE GUEST SUITES PHOENIX GATEWAY CENTER. *320 N 44th St, Phoenix (85008). Phone 602/225-0500; toll-free 800/800-3098; fax 602/231-0561. www.doubletree.com.* Enjoy the convenience of this hotel's location, just 2 miles north of Sky Harbor Airport and minutes from shopping, sporting events, and casinos. 242 rooms, 6 story, all suites. Complimentary full breakfast. Check-in 3 pm, check-out noon. High-speed Internet access. Restaurant, bar. Fitness room. Pool, whirlpool. Airport transportation available. Business center. **$**

★ ★ EMBASSY SUITES HOTEL PHOENIX-NORTH. *2577 W Greenway Rd, Phoenix (85023). Phone 602/375-1777; toll-free 800/527-7715; fax 602/993-5963. www.embassysuites.com.* In northwest Phoenix, this hotel is conveniently located near sporting events, shopping, and much more. 314 rooms, 3 story, all suites. Complimentary full breakfast. Check-in 3 pm, check-out noon. Restaurant, bar. Fitness room. Outdoor pool, children's pool, whirlpool. Tennis. **$**

★ ★ EMBASSY SUITES PHOENIX-BILTMORE. *2630 E Camelback Rd, Phoenix (85016). Phone 602/955-3992; toll-free 800/362-2779; fax 602/955-6479. www.embassysuites.com.* Waterfalls cascade and Koi fish splash as guests enter the lobby of this hotel tucked in Phoenix's most renowned residential area. 232 rooms, 5 story, all suites. Pets accepted; fee. Complimentary full breakfast. Check-in 3 pm, check-out 1 pm. Wireless Internet access. Restaurant, bar. Fitness room. Pool, whirlpool. **$**

★ ★ HILTON PHOENIX AIRPORT. *2435 S 47th St, Phoenix (85034). Phone 480/894-1600; toll-free 800/445-8667; fax 480/921-7844. www.hilton.com.* 255 rooms, 4 story. Check-in 3 pm, check-out noon. Restaurant, bar. Fitness room. Pool, whirlpool. Airport transportation available. Business center. **$**

Full-Service Hotel

★ ★ ★ ★ THE RITZ-CARLTON, PHOENIX. *2401 E Camelback, Phoenix (85016). Phone 602/ 468-0700; fax 602/468-0793. www.ritzcarlton.com.* The Ritz-Carlton is the premier address in Phoenix. Not far from the airport, the hotel is located in the city's Camelback Corridor, known for its shopping, dining, and businesses, and all of Phoenix is within reach from here. All accommodations are graciously styled with classic décor. Discerning travelers appreciate the views of the skyline or the Squaw Peak Mountain Range. A fitness center keeps guests in tiptop shape, and the outdoor pool is a splendid spot for reflection and relaxation. Winning accolades for its high levels of personal service, the hotel consistently exceeds guests' expectations. Dining is always a pleasure, whether in the comfort and privacy of a guest room or in the vibrant setting of Bistro 24 (see also BISTRO 24). Festive and stylish, the restaurant is commended for its modern take on French classics. 281 rooms, 11 story. Check-in 3 pm, check-out noon. Restaurant, bar. Fitness room, spa. Outdoor pool. Airport transportation available. Business center. **$$$**

Full-Service Resorts

★★★ ARIZONA BILTMORE RESORT AND SPA. *2400 E Missouri Rd, Phoenix (85016). Phone 602/955-6600; fax 602/381-7600. www.arizonabiltmore.com.* Earning the moniker "the Jewel of the Desert," the venerated Arizona Biltmore Resort and Spa opened to great fanfare in 1929. This resort bears the distinction of being the only existing hotel touched by the hands of Frank Lloyd Wright. The architect's influence is also evident in the private spaces, where Mission-style furnishings, neutral tones, and unique lamps honor the 1930s heritage. Eight pools keep the warm rays of the Arizona sun at bay; golfers have their choice of more than 30 courses in the valley, in addition to the resort's adjacent course; and tennis players are well cared for with 18 courts. From desert Jeep and Grand Canyon tours to horseback riding and hot-air ballooning, this resort truly has something for everyone. Native American wisdom is employed at the 22,000-square-foot spa, while Southwestern, French, and Asian flavors tempt diners in the four restaurants. 738 rooms, 4 story. Pets accepted. Check-in 4 pm, check-out noon. Restaurant, bar. Children's activity center. Fitness room, spa. Eight outdoor pools, whirlpool. Tennis **$$$**

★★★ JW MARRIOTT DESERT RIDGE RESORT AND SPA. *5350 E Marriott Dr, Phoenix (85054). Phone 480/293-5000; toll-free 888/236-2427; fax 480/293-3600. www.jwdesertridgeresort.com.* The JW Marriott Desert Ridge Resort and Spa offers guests the total resort experience. Set against the striking backdrop of the Sonoran Desert, this Phoenix resort has it all, with 4 acres that include sun-kissed pools, two 18-hole golf courses designed by Arnold Palmer and Tom Fazio, an eight-court tennis center, miles of hiking trails, the educational and enjoyable Desert Botanical Garden, and the renowned Revive Spa. Ten restaurants allow visitors to taste the flavors of Hawaii, Tuscany, and the Southwest, among others, in a variety of casually elegant settings. Dramatic and distinctive, the commodious rooms and suites look to the elements of fire, water, earth, and sky for inspiration. 950 rooms, 5 story. Check-in 4 pm, check-out noon. Restaurant, bar. Children's activity center. Fitness room, spa. Five outdoor pools, whirlpool. Golf. Tennis. Business center. **$$**

★★★ POINTE HILTON SQUAW PEAK RESORT. *7677 N 16th St, Phoenix (85020). Phone 602/997-2626; toll-free 800-445-8667; fax 602/997-2391. www.pointehilton.com.* Families will love this all-suite desert resort with 8 acres of pool area, mountain views and creative kids' programs. At the base of the 300-acre Squaw Peak mountain preserve, there are plenty of outdoor activities in a Spanish Mediterranean-style setting. 563 rooms, 4 story. Check-in 4 pm, check-out noon. High-speed Internet access. Restaurants, bars. Children's activity center. Fitness room, spa. Pool, children's pool, whirlpools. Tennis. Airport transportation available. Business center. **$**

★★★ POINTE HILTON TAPATIO CLIFFS RESORT. *11111 N 7th St, Phoenix (85020). Phone 602/866-7500; toll-free 800-445-8667; fax 602/993-0276. www.pointehilton.com.* Architectural wonder terraces the slopes of the Phoenix North Mountain Preserve. The highlight of the property is a 40-foot waterfall and open-air bar/restaurant pavilion. 585 rooms, 6 story. Check-in 4 pm, check-out noon. High-speed Internet access. Restaurant, bar. Children's activity center. Fitness room, spa. Pool, whirlpool. Golf. Tennis. Airport transportation available. Business center. **$**

★★★ POINTE SOUTH MOUNTAIN RESORT. *7777 S Pointe Pkwy, Phoenix (85044). Phone 602/438-9000; toll-free 877/800-4888; fax 602/431-6535. www.pointesouthmtn.com.* With 700 acres of breathtaking landscape, this resort has fun for all. Don't miss the tin slide and cowboy poetry at Rustler's Rooste. 640 rooms, 5 story. Check-in 4 pm, check-out noon. Restaurant, bar. Children's activity center. Fitness room, spa. Seven outdoor pools, children's pool, seven whirlpools. Golf. Tennis. Business center. **$$**

★★★ ROYAL PALMS RESORT AND SPA. *5200 E Camelback Rd, Phoenix (85018). Phone 602/840-3610; toll-free 800/652-6011; fax 602/840-6927. www.royalpalmsresortandspa.com.* Royal Palms Hotel and Spa is an intriguing and intimate hideaway. Constructed in the late 1920s as a private mansion, this hotel brings a bit of the

Mediterranean to the Sonoran desert. Graceful palm trees reign over the entrance to this convenient, yet secluded, place halfway between the Biltmore area and downtown Scottsdale. The casitas and guest rooms are light-filled and extraordinary. Rich details, jewel tones, and unique accents create a wondrous ambience. Fireplaces, balconies, and patios complete the experience. Great care is paid to the grounds, where fragrant blossoms, stone walkways, and well-tended courtyards are de rigueur. Set against a backdrop of the Camelback Mountains, the pool is dreamy, and the spa induces a trancelike state with its wonderful offerings. The Bar and Cigar Room are ideal for lingering, but the pièce de résistance is T. Cook's (see also T. COOK'S), where the rustic elegance is a perfect setting for the award-winning cuisine. 117 rooms, 2 story. Pets accepted. Check-in 3 pm, check-out noon. Restaurant, bar. Fitness room, spa. Outdoor pool, whirlpool. Business center. **$$$**

★ ★ ★ SHERATON WILD HORSE PASS RESORT AND SPA. *5594 W Wild Horse Pass, Phoenix (85070). Phone 602/225-0100; fax 602/225-0300. www.wildhorsepassresort.com.* 500 rooms. Pets accepted; fee. Check-in 3 pm, check-out noon. High-speed Internet access. Restaurants, bars. Children's activity center. Fitness room, spa. Pools, children's pool, two whirlpools. Golf. Tennis. Business center. **$$$**

★ ★ THE LEGACY GOLF RESORT. *6808 S 32nd St, Phoenix (85042). Phone 602/305-5500; toll-free 888/828-3673; fax 602/305-5501. www.legacygolfresort.com.* 328 rooms, 2 story. Check-out 11 am. Restaurant, bar. Fitness room. Pool, whirlpool. Golf, 18 holes. Tennis. **$$**

Specialty Lodging

The following lodging establishment is approved by Mobil Travel Guide but, due to its unique and individualized nature has not been given a traditional Mobil Star rating. Included in this listing you may find bed-and-breakfasts, limited-service inns, guest ranches, and other unique hotel properties.

MARICOPA MANOR BED & BREAKFAST. *15 W Pasadena Ave, Phoenix (85013). Phone 602/274-6302; toll-free 800/292-6403; fax 602/266-3904. www.maricopamanor.com.* This historic Spanish-style bed-and-breakfast, built in 1928, provides a quiet oasis within a large city. Its staff caters to a guest's every need. Have the Breakfast in a Basket delivered each morning for an intimate in-room dining experience. 6 rooms, 1 story. Complimentary continental breakfast. Check-in 4-6 pm, check-out 11 am. Pool, whirlpool. Restored Spanish mission-style mansion (1928). **$**

Spas

★ ★ ★ ★ ALVADORA, SPA AT ROYAL PALMS. *5200 E Camelback Rd, Phoenix (85018). Phone 602/977-6400; toll-free 800/672-6011. www.royalpalmsresortandspa.com.* True to the spirit of the resort (see ROYAL PALMS RESORT AND SPA), Alvadora echoes the Mediterranean style in its architecture and spirit. Inspired by that region's native flowers, herbs, and oils, this spa brings the outdoors in through its open-air design and plant-inspired therapies. The healing properties of water are a focal point here; whether you soak in a bath of grape seeds and herbs or seawater and algae, or float in the Watsu pool as you are massaged and stretched, you will relish the Acqua Dolce rituals. The European-influenced therapies seduce with their exotic names and soothing qualities. Skin is properly pampered with treatments such as the royal body polish, the orange blossom body buff, and the lavender and aloe quench. Indulge in the fango mud wrap, a traditional therapy that uses volcanic mud from Italy's northern regions to purify and cleanse skin. The facials also pay special tribute to Italy with offerings such as the vino therapy facial, which uses grape leaf extract for its superior moisturizing benefits, and the citrus grove facial, which employs the oil of bitter oranges to combat the signs of aging.

A paraffin manicure or pedicure or a refreshing eucalyptus pedicure at the full-service salon is a perfect gift for your hands or feet. To stay lean and strong during your visit to the Arizona countryside, take advantage of the 24-hour fitness center and enjoy personalized training sessions or private yoga, tai chi, meditation, and mat Pilates classes.

★ ★ ★ REVIVE SPA AT JW MARRIOTT DESERT RIDGE RESORT. *5350 E Marriott Dr, Phoenix (85054). Phone 480/293-3700; toll-free 866/738-4834. www.desertridgeresort.com.* Let the gentle spirit of the desert wash over you at Revive Spa.

In the lobby, directly over the main water structure, an open skylight shines two stories above. Flowing waters throughout the spa enhance the soothing ambience. The serenity and beauty of the desert are the true inspirations here, where outside celestial showers for men and women, private balconies—ideal for outdoor massages—and a rooftop garden with a flowing water feature entice guests.

Indigenous botanicals influence most of Revive's body treatments. Wrap yourself in an exceedingly comfortable robe and succumb to one of the nine different massages available to calm weary souls and tired muscles. The healing skin therapy banishes blemishes, while the sensitive anticapillary facial was designed for those with rosacea. The herbal enzyme peel uncovers younger-looking skin, as does the antioxidant elements facial, which uses a blend of vitamins, minerals, flora extracts, and spirulina desert algae. Avocado-lime and desert sun renewal treatments nourish and hydrate, while mesquite clay and desert algae body wraps detoxify and purify. Prickly pear and lime-salt body scrubs are other appetizing ways to achieve softer skin.

Recharge with a workout in the spacious and well-equipped fitness center. In addition to cardio machines and free weights, this facility offers several classes, including tai chi, water fitness, golf conditioning, flexibility, yoga, and mat Pilates. Swim laps in the Olympic-sized pool, or relax outside on the landscaped deck or in a private cabana. After your workout, dine on calorie-conscious meals and delicious treats at Revive's Spa Bistro. This charming eatery also features a juice bar with fruit smoothies, fresh-squeezed specialties, and protein drinks.

Restaurants

★★★ **AVANTI OF PHOENIX.** *2728 E Thomas Rd, Phoenix (85016). Phone 602/956-0900; fax 602/468-1913. www.avanti-az.com.* A stark Art Deco interior of black and white is the backdrop for this romantic restaurant. Fresh pasta with rich sauces is the mainstay here. Italian menu. Lunch, dinner. Closed July 4, Dec 25. Bar. Casual attire. Valet parking. Outdoor seating. **$$**

★ **BABY KAY'S CAJUN KITCHEN.** *2119 E Camelback Rd, Phoenix (85016). Phone 602/955-0011; fax 602/955-2288. www.babykays.com.* Cajun menu. Lunch, dinner. Closed Thanksgiving, Dec 25. Bar. Outdoor seating. **$$**

★★★ **BISTRO 24.** *2401 E Camelback Rd, Phoenix (85016). Phone 602/952-2424; fax 602/468-0793. www.ritzcarlton.com.* A classic bistro, complete with wicker chairs and soft lighting, this popular new restaurant is all that it promises to be. Entrées are hearty and succulent, yet unassuming, served by debonair waiters. A great spot for a nightcap or light bite. American menu. Breakfast, lunch, dinner, Sun brunch. Bar. Children's menu. Reservations recommended. Valet parking. Outdoor seating. **$$**

★ **CHOMPIE'S.** *3202 E Greenway Rd, Phoenix (85032). Phone 602/971-8010; fax 602/971-2343. www.chompies.com.* Kosher deli menu. Breakfast, lunch, dinner. Children's menu. Casual attire. Outdoor seating. **$**

★★★ **CHRISTOPHER'S FERMIER BRASSERIE.** *2584 E Camelback Rd, Phoenix (85016). Phone 602/522-2344; fax 602/468-0314. www.fermier.com.* Chef Christopher Gross has created a winning combination of casual French bistro ambience, attentive service, and wonderful cuisine. Save room for the irresistable desserts. French menu. Lunch, dinner. Closed holidays. Reservations recommended. **$$**

★★ **COMPASS.** *122 N 2nd St, Phoenix (85004). Phone 602/440-3166; fax 602/440-3132. www.hyatt.com.* American menu. Lunch, dinner, Sun brunch. Bar. Children's menu. Casual attire. Reservations recommended. Valet parking. **$$$**

★★★ **DIFFERENT POINTE OF VIEW.** *11111 N 7th St, Phoenix (85020). Phone 602/863-0912; fax 602/866-6358. www.hilton.com.* Innovative American cuisine is the result of the chef's flair for mixing fresh-from-the-garden herbs and vegetables with wild game and hearty meats. A spectacular view of the city accompanies the chic menu. French, Mediterranean menu. Dinner. Closed Sun-Mon (mid-June-Oct). Bar. Children's menu. Casual attire. Reservations recommended. Valet parking. Outdoor seating. **$$$**

★★ **FISH MARKET.** *1720 E Camelback Rd, Phoenix (85016). Phone 602/277-3474; toll-free 800/230-3474; fax 602/277-2543. www.thefishmarket.com.* Retail fish market. Seafood menu. Lunch, dinner. Closed Thanksgiving, Dec 25. Bar. Children's menu. Casual attire. Outdoor seating. **$$**

★ ★ ★ **GREEKFEST.** *1940 E Camelback Rd, Phoenix (85016). Phone 602/265-2990; fax 602/265-3036. www.thegreekfest.com.* A merry, family atmosphere and authentic décor transport guests to the Mediterranean for a feast of Greek foods. Lunch, dinner. Closed Sun; Jan 1, Dec 25. Bar. Casual attire. **$$**

★ ★ **HAVANA CAFE.** *4225 E Camelback Rd, Phoenix (85018). Phone 602/952-1991.* Cuban menu. Dinner. Closed holidays. Bar. Casual attire. Outdoor seating. **$$**

★ ★ ★ **LA FONTANELLA.** *4231 E Indian School Rd, Phoenix (85018). Phone 602/955-1213; fax 602/955-1491. www.lafontanella.com.* A local favorite, this fine restaurant is renowned for its warm atmosphere and elaborate dishes. Italian menu. Dinner. Closed Dec 25; two weeks in July. Bar. Casual attire. Reservations recommended. **$$$**

★ ★ **LOMBARDI'S.** *455 N 3rd St, Phoenix (85004). Phone 602/257-8323; fax 602/257-0591. www.lombardisrestaurants.com.* Italian menu. Lunch, dinner. Closed holidays. Bar. Casual attire. Outdoor seating. **$$**

★ ★ **MONTI'S.** *12025 N 19th Ave, Phoenix (85029). Phone 602/997-5844; fax 602/997-0060.* Steak menu. Dinner. Closed Dec 25. Bar. Children's menu. Casual attire. Outdoor seating. **$$**

★ ★ **PIZZERIA BIANCO.** *623 E Adams St, Phoenix (85004). Phone 602/258-8300.* This casual restaurant specializing in wood-fired pizzas makes its own dough and mozzarella. Lunch, dinner. Closed Mon; also the last week of Aug and the first two weeks of Sept. Italian menu. Bar. Casual attire. Reservations recommended. **$$**

★ ★ **PRONTO RISTORANTE.** *3950 E Campbell, Phoenix (85018). Phone 602/956-4049; fax 602/956-4460. www.prontoristorante.com.* Italian menu. Dinner. Closed Sun; Thanksgiving, Dec 25. Bar. Casual attire. Dinner theater Fri, Sat. **$$**

★ ★ **RUSTLER'S ROOSTE.** *7777 S Pointe Pkwy, Phoenix (85044). Phone 602/431-6474; fax 602/431-6529. www.rustlersrooste.com.* Steak menu. Dinner. Bar. Children's menu. Casual attire. Valet parking. Outdoor seating. **$$**

★ ★ ★ **RUTH'S CHRIS STEAK HOUSE.** *2201 E Camelback Rd, Phoenix (85016). Phone 602/957-9600; fax 602/224-1948. www.ruthschris.com.* Steak menu. Dinner. Closed Thanksgiving, Dec 25. Bar. Reservations recommended. Valet parking. Outdoor seating. **$$$**

★ ★ **STEAMERS SEAFOOD AND RAW BAR.** *2576 E Camelback Rd, Phoenix (85016). Phone 602/956-3631; fax 602/957-7847.* Seafood menu. Lunch, dinner. Closed Thanksgiving, Dec 25. Bar. Children's menu. Valet parking. Outdoor seating. **$$$**

★ ★ ★ **T. COOK'S.** *5200 E Camelback Rd, Phoenix (85018). Phone 602/808-0766; fax 602/808-3115. www.royalpalmsresortandspa.com.* Tucked away in the Royal Palms Hotel and Spa (see) is a jewel of a restaurant, stylishly decorated with deep cherry wood, hand-painted Italian frescos, and artisan-carved and painted wooden shelves. The menu has a decidedly Mediterranean slant and includes dishes inspired by Spain, Tuscany, and the south of France, accented with Arizona's regional flair. Ingredients are organic whenever possible, and the kitchen has a knack for preparing simple yet elegant plates that easily inspire love at first bite. For those who enjoy a stogie and whiskey as well as a terrific meal, T. Cook's Cigar Room is luxuriously appointed with deep red, custom-made leather upholstery and antique lamps, making it the perfect place to unwind after a long day. Mediterranean menu. Breakfast, lunch, dinner, Sun brunch. Bar. Casual attire. Reservations recommended. Valet parking. Outdoor seating. **$$**

★ ★ ★ **TARBELL'S.** *3213 E Camelback Rd, Phoenix (85018). Phone 602/955-8100; fax 602/955-8181. www.tarbells.com.* This restaurant maintains a friendly, neighborhood charm with a sophisticated yet relaxed atmosphere. Fresh, seasonal dishes of refined comfort food are whisked from the open-view kitchen to guests' tables by attentive, well-trained servers. American menu. Dinner. Closed holidays. Bar. Casual attire. **$$$**

★★ TOMASO'S. *3225 E Camelback Rd, Phoenix (85016). Phone 602/956-0836; fax 602/956-0842.* Italian cuisine, made of the finest ingredients, keeps guests coming back to this upscale restaurant. The pace is leisurely, the atmosphere relaxed. Italian menu. Lunch, dinner. Closed Super Bowl Sun. Bar. Casual attire. Reservations recommended. **$$**

★★ TOP OF THE MARKET. *1720 E Camelback Rd, Phoenix (85016). Phone 602/277-3474; toll-free 800/230-3474; fax 602/227-2543. www.thefishmarket.com.* Seafood menu. Lunch, dinner. Closed Thanksgiving, Dec 25. Bar. Children's menu. Reservations recommended. **$$**

★ TUCCHETTI. *2135 E Camelback Rd, Phoenix (85016). Phone 602/957-0222; fax 602/381-1950. www.tucchetti.com.* Italian menu. Lunch, dinner. Closed Thanksgiving, Dec 25. Bar. Children's menu. Outdoor seating. **$**

★★★ VINCENT GUERITHAULT ON CAMELBACK. *3930 E Camelback Rd, Phoenix (85018). Phone 602/224-0225; fax 602/956-5400. www.vincentsoncamelback.com.* This intimate restaurant, which fearlessly combines hearty Southwest flavors with elegant French cuisine, spawned Phoenix's culinary reputation. The flawless waitstaff and enduring menu continue to impress diners. American menu. Lunch, dinner. Closed holidays; also Sun-Mon (June-Sept). Bar. Casual attire. Reservations recommended. Valet parking. **$$$**

★★★ WRIGHT'S. *2400 Missouri Rd, Phoenix (85016). Phone 602/954-6600; fax 602/381-7600. www.arizonabiltmore.com.* A homage to the celebrated Frank Lloyd Wright, the dining room reflects the architect's penchant for stark angles and contrasts. Innovative cuisine is served for dinner and the unparalleled Sunday brunch. Be sure to sample one of the delectable chocolate desserts! Contemporary Mediterranean menu. Dinner, Sun brunch. Casual attire. Valet parking. **$$$**

★★ ZEN 32. *3160 E Camelback Rd, Phoenix (85016). Phone 602/954-8700; fax 602/667-9510. www.zen32.com.* Japanese menu. Lunch, dinner. Casual attire. **$$**

Pinetop (C-5)

See also Greer, McNary, Show Low

Population 3,582
Elevation 6,959 ft
Area Code 520
Zip 85935
Information Pinetop-Lakeside Chamber of Commerce, 102-C W White Mountain Blvd, PO Box 4220; phone 520/367-4290
Web site www.pinetoplakesidechamber.com

Trout fishing, horseback riding, hiking, biking, and golfing are popular summer activities here; skiing and snowmobiling draw many winter visitors.

Limited-Service Hotel

★ BEST WESTERN INN OF PINETOP. *404 S White Mount Blvd, Pinetop (85935). Phone 928/367-6667; toll-free 800/780-7234; fax 928/367-6672. www.bestwestern.com.* 41 rooms, 2 story. Complimentary continental breakfast. Check-out 11 am. **$**

Pipe Spring National Monument (A-2)

See also Kanab, UT

Web site www.nps.gov/pisp

14 miles W of Fredonia on a spur off Hwy 389.

Located on the Kaibab-Paiute Indian Reservation, the focal point of this monument is a beautifully built sandstone Mormon fort, dating to 1870. Several years earlier, Brigham Young had ordered the exploration of this region north of the Grand Canyon. According to legend, rifleman William "Gunlock Bill" Hamblin gave the place its name by shooting the bottom out of a smoking pipe at 50 paces.

The fort, actually a fortified ranchhouse, was built under the direction of Bishop Anson P. Winsor to protect the families caring for the church's cattle. Cattle drives, headed for the railroad in Cedar City, Utah, began here.

Guide service (daily); living history demonstrations (June-Sept). Kaibab Paiute Campground (fee), 1/2 mile N of access road to visitor center. Area closed Jan 1, Thanksgiving, Dec 25. Contact the Superintendent, HC 65, Box 5, Fredonia 86022; phone 928/643-7105. **$**

Prescott (C-3)

See also Cottonwood

Founded 1864
Population 33,938
Elevation 5,368 ft
Area Code 928
Information Chamber of Commerce, 117 W Goodwin St, PO Box 1147, 86302; phone 928/445-2000 or toll-free 800/266-7534
Web site www.prescott.org

When President Lincoln established the territory of Arizona, Prescott became the capital. In 1867, the capital was moved to Tucson and then back to Prescott in 1877. After much wrangling, it was finally moved to Phoenix in 1889.

Tourism and manufacturing are now Prescott's principal occupations. The climate is mild during summer and winter. The Prescott National Forest surrounds the city; its headquarters are located here.

What to See and Do

Arcosanti. *HC 74, Box 4136, Prescott. 36 miles SE on Hwy 69 to Cordes Jct, then 2 miles E on unnumbered road (follow signs or inquire locally for directions). Phone 928/632-7135. www.arcosanti.org.* Architectural project by Paolo Soleri and the Cosanti Foundation. This prototype town is being constructed as a functioning example of "arcology," a fusion of architecture and ecology. Guided tours ($-$$). (Daily; closed holidays) **DONATION**

Prescott National Forest. *344 S Cortez St, Prescott. 20 miles NE on Hwy 89A or 1 mile SW on Hwy 89. Phone 928/445-1762. gorp.away.com/gorp/resource/US_National_Forest/az_presc.htm.* Minerals and varied vegetation abound in this forest of more than 1 million acres. Within the forest are Juniper Mesa, Apache Creek, Granite Mountain, Castle Creek, Woodchute, and Cedar Bench wilderness areas, and parts of Sycamore Canyon and Pine Mountain wilderness areas. Fishing (Granite Basin, Lynx lakes); hunting, picnicking, camping.

Sharlot Hall Museum. *415 W Gurley St, Prescott. Phone 928/445-3122. www.sharlot.org.* Period houses include the Territorial Governor's Mansion (1864), restored in 1929 by poet-historian Sharlot Hall; Fort Misery (1864); William Bashford house (1877); and John C. Frémont house (1875). Period furnishings. Museum, library, and archives. Also on the grounds are the grave of Pauline Weaver; rose and herb garden; pioneer schoolhouse. All buildings (May-Sept: Mon-Sat 10 am-5pm, Sun 1-5 pm; Oct-Apr: Mon-Sat 10 am-4 pm; closed Jan 1, Thanksgiving, Dec 25). **$**

Smoki Museum. *147 N Arizona St, Prescott. Phone 928/445-1230. www.smokimuseum.org.* Native American artifacts, ancient and modern. (Apr-Dec: Mon-Sat 10 am-4 pm, Sun 1-4 pm; Jan-Mar: Fri-Sat, Mon 10 am-4 pm, Sun 1-4 pm) **$$**

Special Events

Bluegrass Festival. *Courthouse Plaza, 130 N Cortez St, Prescott. Phone 928/445-2000.* Mid-June.

Phippen Museum Fine Art Show & Sale. *Courthouse Plaza, 130 N Cortez St, Prescott. Phone 928/778-1385. www.phippenartmuseum.org/events/pms03.html.* More than 50 artists. Memorial Day weekend. **FREE**

Prescott Frontier Days Rodeo. *Prescott. Phone 928/445-3103; toll-free 800/358-1888 or 866/407-6336 (tickets). www.worldsoldestrodeo.com.* Spend a day or two or three at the "world's oldest rodeo." Festivities and events are held throughout the city. There is also a parade and laser show. Late June-July 4. **$$$**

Territorial Prescott Days. *Courthouse Plaza, 130 N Cortez St, Prescott. Phone 928/445-0204.* This citywide celebration features an art show, craft demonstrations, old-fashioned contests, and home tours. Early June.

Limited-Service Hotels

★ **DAYS INN.** *7875 E Hwy 69, Prescott Valley (86314). Phone 928/772-8600; fax 928/772-0942. www.daysinn.com.* 59 rooms, 2 story. Pets accepted; fee.

Complimentary continental breakfast. Check-out 11 am. Pool, whirlpool. **$**

★ ★ FOREST VILLAS HOTEL. *3645 Lee Cir, Prescott (86301). Phone 928/717-1200; toll-free 800/223-3449; fax 928/717-1400. www.forestvillas.com.* This hotel has flowing fountains and a panoramic view of the Prescott Mountains. Wine and champagne are served nightly in the elegant Mediterranean-style lobby, which features oversized chairs and crystal chandeliers. 76 rooms, 2 story. Complimentary continental breakfast. Check-in 3 pm, check-out 11 am. Pool, whirlpool. **$**

★ ★ HASSAYAMPA INN. *122 E Gurley St, Prescott (86301). Phone 928/778-9434; toll-free 800/322-1927; fax 928/445-8590. www.hassayampainn.com.* On the National Register of Historic Places. 68 rooms, 4 story. Complimentary full breakfast. Check-in 3 pm, check-out noon. Restaurant, bar. **$**

Specialty Lodging

The following lodging establishment is approved by Mobil Travel Guide but, due to its unique and individualized nature has not been given a traditional Mobil Star rating. Included in this listing you may find bed-and-breakfasts, limited-service inns, guest ranches, and other unique hotel properties.

PLEASANT STREET INN BED & BREAKFAST. *142 S Pleasant St, Prescott (86303). Phone 928/445-4774; toll-free 877/226-7128; fax 928/777-8696. www.pleasantstreetinn-bb.com.* Built in 1906; Victorian décor. 6 rooms, 2 story. Complimentary full breakfast. Check-in 2-5 pm, check-out 11 am. **$**

Restaurants

★ ★ GURLEY STREET GRILL. *230 W Gurley St, Prescott (86301). Phone 928/445-3388; fax 928/445-8412.* American menu. Dinner. Closed Dec 25. Bar. Children's menu. Casual attire. Outdoor seating. **$$**

★ ★ MURPHY'S. *201 N Cortez, Prescott (86301). Phone 928/445-4044; fax 928/778-4844. www.murphysrestaurants.com.* Restored mercantile building (circa 1890). Memorabilia from turn-of-the-century on display. American, seafood, steak menu. Dinner. Closed day after Labor Day, Dec 25. Bar. Children's menu. Casual attire. **$$$**

★ PINE CONE INN. *1245 White Spar Rd, Prescott (86303). Phone 928/445-2970.* American menu. Dinner. Closed Dec 24-26. Bar. Children's menu. Casual attire. **$$**

Safford (D-5)

See also Clifton, Willcox

Founded 1874
Population 9,232
Elevation 2,920 ft
Area Code 928
Zip 85546
Information Graham County Chamber of Commerce, 1111 Thatcher Blvd; phone 928/428-2511
Web site www.graham-chamber.com

Safford is a marketplace for cotton, alfalfa, grain, vegetables, and fruit produced on 35,000 acres irrigated by waters from the Gila River. It is the trade center for a wide area. Nearby is Aravaipa Canyon, a designated primitive area. A Ranger District office for the Coronado National Forest (see TUCSON) is located here.

What to See and Do

Roper Lake State Park. *101 E Roper Lake Rd, Safford. Located off Hwy 191, 6 miles S of Safford. Phone 928/428-6760. www.pr.state.az.us/parks/parkhtml/roper.html.* This 320-acre park includes a small artificial lake, a swimming beach, and natural hot springs with tubs for public use; fishing (dock), boat launch (no gas-powered motors); nature trails, hiking, picnicking (shelter), camping, tent and trailer sites (hook-ups, dump station). Fishing dock accessible to the disabled. Dankworth Unit, 6 miles S, is a day-use area with fishing and picnicking. (Daily 6 am-10 pm)

The Swift Trail. *504 S 5th Ave, Safford. Phone 928/428-4150.* Hwy 366 snakes its way 36 miles SW from Safford to the high elevations of the Pinaleño Mountains in Coronado National Forest; splendid view from the top, where Mount Graham towers 10,713 feet. There are five developed campgrounds (mid-Apr-mid-Nov, weather permitting); trout fishing at Riggs Flat Lake and in the streams. The upper elevations of Hwy 366 are closed mid-Nov-mid-Apr.

Special Events

Cinco de Mayo Bash. *311 S Central Ave, Safford. Phone 928/428-4920.* Mexican-American commemoration of Cinco de Mayo (May 5th), date of Mexican independence from Europe. Entertainment, dancing, world's longest tequila shot chain, games. First weekend in May.

Graham County Fair. *527 E Armory Rd, Safford. Phone 928/428-7180. www.grahamcounty.casinocity .com.* Horse racing, quarter horse racing, race book. The complex also hosts the annual rodeo, Old Time Fiddlers Contest, and other events. Mid-Oct.

Pioneer Days. Commemorates Mormon settlement. Late July.

Limited-Service Hotel

★ COMFORT INN. *1578 W Thatcher Blvd, Safford (85546). Phone 928/428-5851; fax 928/428-4968. www. choicehotels.com.* 44 rooms, 2 story. Pets accepted, some restrictions; fee. Complimentary continental breakfast. Check-in 11 am, check-out 11 am. Outdoor pool. **$**

Saguaro National Park (E-4)

See also Tucson

Web site www.nps.gov/sagu

Rincon Mountain District: 17 miles E of Tucson via Broadway and Old Spanish Trail. Tucson Mountain District: 16 miles W of Tucson via Speedway and Gates Pass Rd.

The saguaro (sah-WAH-ro) cactus may grow as high as 50 feet and live to be 200 years old. The fluted columns, spined with sharp, tough needles, sometimes branch into fantastic shapes. During the rainy season, large saguaros can absorb enough water to sustain themselves during the dry season.

The saguaro's waxy, white blossoms (Arizona's state flower), which open at night and close the following afternoon, bloom in May and June; the red fruit ripens in July. The Tohono O'Odham eat this fruit fresh and dried; they also use it to make jellies, jams, and wines.

Wildlife is abundant. Gila woodpeckers and gilded flickers drill nest holes in the saguaro trunks. Once vacated, these holes become home to many other species of birds, including the tiny elf owl. Peccaries (piglike mammals), coyotes, mule deer, and other animals are often seen. Yuccas, agaves, prickly pears, mesquite, paloverde trees, and many other desert plants grow here.

The Rincon Mountain District offers nature trails, guided nature walks (winter), 8-mile self-guided drive (fee), mountain hiking, bridle trails, picnicking (no water), back-country camping. Visitor center with museum and orientation film.

The Tucson Mountain District offers nature trails, a 6-mile self-guided drive, and hiking and bridle trails. Five picnic areas (no water). Visitor center; exhibits, slide program (daily). Contact the Superintendent, 3693 S Old Spanish Trail, Tucson 85730. **FREE**

San Carlos (D-4)

See also Globe

Population 2,918
Elevation 2,635 ft
Area Code 520
Zip 85550
Information San Carlos Recreation & Wildlife Department, PO Box 97; phone 520/475-2343

The San Carlos Apache Indian Reservation covers almost 2 million acres ranging from desert to pine forests. Many lakes, rivers, and ponds offer fishing (fee) year-round for trout, bass, and catfish. Hunting for small game, large game, and waterfowl is also year-round. Camping (fee). Apache guides may be hired to lead visitors into the wilderness portions of the reservation. Sunrise ceremonial dances are held from time to time.

Scottsdale (D-3)

See also Chandler, Glendale, Litchfield Park, Mesa, Phoenix, Tempe

Population 202,705
Elevation 1,250 ft
Area Code 602/480
Information Chamber of Commerce, 7343 Scottsdale Mall, 85251; phone 480/945-8481 or toll-free 800/877-1117
Web site www.scottsdalecvb.com

Scottsdale is a popular resort destination located on the eastern border of Phoenix. It is renowned for outstanding art galleries, excellent shopping and dining, lush golf courses, abundant recreational activities, and Western and Native American heritage.

What to See and Do

Antique Trove. *2020 N Scottsdale Rd, Scottsdale. Phone 480/947-6074. www.antiquetrove.com.* If you have a soft spot for all things old, you'll be hard pressed to leave this treasure-packed store empty-handed. In a 25,000-square-foot showroom, 150 dealers have packed stall after stall with anything and everything from the good ol' days. Mosey down one aisle after the other, and you'll likely find vintage mink jackets, colonial rockers from the 1940s, claw-foot bathtubs, and so much more. Prices range from $1 to several thousand. (Daily)

Arizona Wine Company. *2515 N Scottsdale Rd, #15, Scottsdale. Phone 480/423-9305. www.azwineco.com.* This unassuming store in a strip shopping center happens to stock one of the more varied wine selections in the Valley, often at better prices than its competitors. That's reason enough to wander its aisles, but here's another incentive: any of its friendly, knowledgeable wine consultants will gladly help you make just the right picks—taking the fear factor out of the buying experience. If you're in a sampling mood, pull up a seat at the wine bar. (Mon-Tues 10 am-6 pm, Wed-Sat 10 am-10 pm, Sun noon-10 pm) **FREE**

Casino Arizona at Salt River. *524 N 92nd St, Scottsdale. Phone 480/850-7777. www.casinoaz.com.* The Salt River Pima-Maricopa Indian Community hit the jackpot when it opened the betting at this casino in a prime location off the 101 Freeway on the Valley's east side. All the gamblers throwing down their chips prompted the tribe to up the ante and open a second location just a few miles north, off the same freeway (9700 E Indian Bend Rd). The original funhouse is larger and a notch more upscale with five restaurants—the best being the elegant Cholla Prime Steakhouse—and four lounges, including a 250-seat cabaret-style showroom that rocks with name entertainers. Cards, keno, slot machines, and other games of chance remain the real draws, though. Each casino restricts play to those 21 and older. (Daily)

Cooking with Class. *14202 N Scottsdale Rd, Suite 100, Scottsdale. Phone 480/607-7474. www.cookingwithclass.com.* With the classes at this cooking school, add variety and zing to the meals you prepare at home, which should keep your family coming back for seconds. Vegetarian Italian, Santa Fe Supper, Sweet and Savory Crepes, and Easy Gourmet Appetizers are among the many options. Some classes are taught by demonstration, with instructors showing how to whip up savory dishes. In others, you and your fellow cooks-in-training do the chopping and sautéing, or whatever skills a recipe calls for.

Cosanti Foundation. *6433 Doubletree Ranch Rd, Scottsdale. 1 mile W off N Scottsdale Rd. Phone 480/948-6145. www.arcosanti.org/expCosanti/main.html.* Earth-formed concrete structures and studios by Italian architect Paolo Soleri; constructed by Soleri's students. Soleri windbells made in crafts areas. Self-guided tours daily. Guided tours by reservation only. (Daily 9 am-5 pm; closed holidays) **FREE**

Desert Course at The Phoenician. *6000 E Camelback Rd, Scottsdale. For information, phone toll-free 866/564-7667, or see www.thephoenician.com.* Golf.

Grayhawk Golf Club. *8620 E Thompson Peak Pkwy, Scottsdale. Phone 480/502-1800. www.grayhawk.com.* Grayhawk has two courses: Talon (designed by David Graham and Gary Panks) and Raptor (designed by Tom Fazio). Both are nice, but Talon deserves more attention. Built in the Sonoran Desert, the course features many shots over desert brush or sand, with some water worked in for good measure. The course is good enough to host international-caliber tournaments such as the World Championship of Golf. If your game needs work, schedule some time at the Kostis McCord Learning Center, whose instructors include the two CBS commentators. **$$$$**

Gray Line sightseeing tours. *1243 S 7th St # 2, Phoenix. Phone 602/495-9100; toll-free 800/732-0327. www.graylinearizona.com.* Sightseeing tours, package tours, and charter services.

Hot Air Expeditions. *Cave Creek and Jomax rds, Scottsdale. Phone 480/502-6999. www.hotairexpeditions.com.* See this beautiful desert region from on high, in a hot-air balloon. For up to an hour, float above this barren land for gorgeous 360-degree views. You'll likely catch glimpses of its animal life—jack-rabbits, quails, roadrunners, coyote, maybe even deer and javelina—and descend close to its trees, cacti, and other plants. The trip ends with a champagne breakfast or hors d'oeuvres on the desert floor.

Ironwood Course at The Westin Kierland Golf Resort & Spa. *15636 Clubgate Dr, Scottsdale. For information, phone toll-free 866/564-7667, or see www.kierlandgolf.com.* Golf.

Kierland Commons. *Scottsdale Rd and Greenway Pkwy, Scottsdale. Phone 480/951-1100. www.kierlandcommons.com/index.shtml.* This 38-acre urban village bills itself as "today's version of yesterday," given its Main Street feel and pedestrian-friendly layout. Its well-landscaped streets are lined with offices and more than 50 upscale specialty retailers, including Agata Boutique, Chocolates by Bernard Callebaut, Crate and Barrel, Optical Shop of Aspen, Smith and Hawken, and Z Gallerie. Among its dining options are Morton's Steak House, News Cafe, and P.F. Chang's China Bistro. Do hang out here if you like hangin' with the trendy crowd. (Mon-Sat 10 am-9 pm, Sun noon-6 pm; closed Easter, Thanksgiving, Dec 25)

Legend Trail Golf Club. *9462 E Legendary Ln, Scottsdale. For information, phone toll-free 866/564-7667, or see www.legendtrailgc.com.*

Martini Ranch. *7295 E Stetson Dr, Scottsdale. Phone 480/970-0500.* As the name implies, the martini gets preferential treatment at this 10,000-square-foot people magnet conveniently located in Old Town Scottsdale. The suave drink comes in about 30 variations, so take your pick. Every night, the lusty cocktails share center stage with live music from the hottest local and regional bands. If the beat doesn't move you, you can tune it out and tune into major sporting events on the large television screens, or play billiards. (Wed-Sun) **$$**

McCormick-Stillman Railroad Park. *7301 E Indian Bend Rd, Scottsdale. Phone 480/312-2312. www.therailroadpark.com.* Watch your little ones smile as they climb on the fast track and loop this 30-acre city park aboard the Paradise and Pacific Railroad, a miniature reproduction of a Colorado narrow-gauge railroad. After circling on the choo-choo, they'll want to head over to the 1950s carousel for a bumpier ride, then to one of two well-equipped playgrounds. Be sure to tour the Roald Amundsen Pullman Car, used by four US presidents: Herbert Hoover, Franklin Roosevelt, Harry Truman, and Dwight Eisenhower. (Daily; closed Thanksgiving, Dec 25) Fee ($) for rides.

Mesquite Course at The Westin Kierland Golf Resort & Spa. *15636 Clubgate Dr, Scottsdale. For information, phone toll-free 866/564-7667, or see www.kierlandgolf.com.* Golf.

Monument Course at Troon North Golf Club. *10320 E Dynamite Blvd, Scottsdale. For information, phone toll-free 866/564-7667, or see www.troonnorthgolf.com.*

North Course at Talking Stick Golf Club. *9998 E Indian Bend Rd, Scottsdale. For information, phone toll-free 866/564-7667, or see www.talkingstickgolfclub.com.*

Oasis Course at The Phoenician. *6000 E Camelback Rd, Scottsdale. For information, phone toll-free 866/564-7667, or see www.thephoenician.com.* Golf.

★ Out of Africa Wildlife Park. *9736 N Fort McDowell Rd, Scottsdale. Phone 480/837-7779. www.outofafricapark.com.* You'll be glued to your seat as you watch tigers chase their human caretakers into a pool and then frolic with them. The Tiger Splash is the most popular of nine daily, unrehearsed shows that feature wild animals from around the world, but mostly Africa. Bears, cougars, leopards, lions, pythons, wolves, and other wondrous creatures also interact with one another and the park's staff. A few even interact with the trustiest of visitors. Between shows, wander numerous trails to view the animals living in natural habitats. (Tues-Sun) **$$$**

Phoenician-Canyon Course. *6000 E Camelback Rd, Scottsdale. For information, phone toll-free 866/564-7667, or see www.thephoenician.com.* Golf.

Pinnacle Course at Troon North Golf Club. *10320 E Dynamite Blvd, Scottsdale. For information, phone toll-free 866/564-7667, or see www.troonnorthgolf.com.*

Rawhide Wild West Town. *23023 N Scottsdale Rd, Scottsdale. Phone 480/502-5600. www.rawhide.com.* Gallop into the Old West at Arizona's largest Western-themed attraction, a 160-acre spread packed with cowpoke fun 1880s style. Roam the range on the stagecoach or train, test your aim in the shooting gallery, hang tight on the mechanical bull, pan for gold, go horseback riding, and take in the shows—from stuntmen throwing punches and squaring off in gunfights to performances by Native American and Mexican dancers. The Steakhouse serves up mesquite-grilled steaks, just the way ranch hands ate 'em. For added fun, browse through the 15 shops. (Daily; closed Dec 25) Fee ($) for some attractions.

Sanctuary. *7340 E Shoeman Ln, Scottsdale. Phone 480/970-5000. www.sanctuaryclub.com.* For the well-dressed and hip, this 16,000-square-foot party house is one of the places to escape to after dark. Patrons pack themselves into five lavishly decorated lounges with differing themes. To add even more spark to the high-caliber action, bartenders light martinis with blowtorches. Flashing lasers have the same effect on the large dance floor, where an elaborate sound system blasts Top 40 tracks. (Wed, Fri, Sat) **$$**

Scottsdale Center for the Arts. *7380 E 2nd St, Scottsdale. Phone 480/994-2787. www.scottsdalearts.org.* Offers theater, dance; classical, jazz and popular music; lectures; outdoor festivals and concerts. Sculpture garden; art exhibits (daily; closed holidays). **$$$**

Scottsdale Fashion Square. *7014-590 E Camelback Rd, Scottsdale. Phone 480/994-8048. www.westcor.com.* The largest shopping destination in the Southwest features more than 225 retailers, meaning that you're likely to find something you gotta have. Just remember, this multilevel shoppers' mecca sells variety, not surprises. Most tenants are familiar names such as Dillard's, Macy's, Neiman Marcus, Nordstrom, and Robinsons-May. But Louis Vuitton, Sephora, Tiffany & Co., and 37 others don't have stores anywhere else in Arizona. Ten restaurants, a food court, and two theater complexes round out the mall's inventory. (Daily; closed Jan 1, Thanksgiving, Dec 25)

Sur La Table. *7122 E Greenway Pkwy, Suite 100, Scottsdale. Phone 480/998-0519. www.surlatable.com.* In the 1970s, Seattle spawned this clearinghouse for hard-to-find kitchen gear, and it soon became known as a source for cookware, small appliances, cutlery, kitchen tools, linens, tableware, gadgets, and specialty foods. Sur La Table has since expanded to include cooking classes ($$$$), chef demonstrations, and cookbook author signings, as well as a catalog and online presence. Cooking connoisseurs discover such finds as cool oven mitts, zest graters, copper whisks, onion soup bowls, and inspired TV dinner trays. (Daily)

★ **Taliesin West.** *12621 N Frank Lloyd Wright Blvd, Scottsdale. Phone 480/860-2700. www.franklloydwright.org.* Take a guided tour of this amazing compound and see Frank Lloyd Wright's architectural genius at work, and his passion for "organic architecture." In the late 1930s, Wright and his apprentices literally built this winter camp out of the Sonoran desert, using rocks and sand they gathered from the rugged terrain. In true Wright fashion, the architect designed the various buildings with terraces, gardens, and walkways that link the outdoors with the indoors. To help ensure Wright's legacy lives on, Taliesin West still functions as a school for 20-plus architectural students who subscribe to his philosophies about the craft he loved and mastered. (Daily) **$$$$**

Talking Stick Golf Club-South Course. *9998 E Indian Bend Rd, Scottsdale. For information, phone toll-free 866/564-7667, or see www.talkingstickgolfclub.com.*

Tournament Players Club of Scottsdale. *17020 N Hayden Rd, Scottsdale. Phone 480/585-4334; toll-free 866/217-3161. www.tpc.com.* Follow in the footsteps of Tiger Woods, Vijay Singh, and other big-name golfers and swing into action on the TPC's greens, home of the Phoenix Open, the best-attended event on the PGA Tour each year. The club has two options: the Stadium Course (the one the pros shoot) and the Desert Course, both open for daily-fee play. Are you ready to compare your game to Tiger's, hole by hole? **$$$$**

Westin Kierland Golf Resort & Spa-Acacia Course. *15636 Clubgate Dr, Scottsdale. For information, phone toll-free 866/564-7667, or see www.kierlandgolf.com.*

WestWorld of Scottsdale. *16601 N Pima Rd, Scottsdale. Phone 480/312-6802. www.scottsdaleaz.gov/westworld.* A 360-acre recreation park, equestrian center, and event facility at the base of the McDowell Mountains. Hosts concerts, sports competitions, special events. (Daily)

Wild West Jeep Tours. *7343 Scottsdale Mall, Scottsdale. Phone 480/922-0144. www.wildwestjeeptours.com.* Four-hour guided desert tour. Explore an ancient ruin. (Daily) **$$$$**

Special Events

Arabian Horse Show. *WestWorld, 16601 N Pima Rd, Scottsdale. Phone 480/515-1500. www.scottsdaleshow.com.* Arabian horse owners come from all over the world to show their horses. Two weeks in mid-Feb.

ArtWalk. *Along Main St and Marshall Way in downtown Scottsdale. Phone 480/990-3939. www.scottsdalegalleries.com.* Locals brag that Scottsdale has more art galleries per capita than most any other US city. To get a good taste of this thriving scene, stroll the downtown streets during ArtWalk, a weekly Thursday night tradition for more than 20 years. For two hours, galleries host special exhibits, demonstrations, and meet-the-artist receptions, complete with wine, champagne, and tasty hors d'oeuvres. You'll almost feel like an insider yourself, not a potential buyer. Thurs evenings. **FREE**

Parada del Sol & Rodeo. *Phone 480/990-3179 (parade). www.scottsdalejaycees.com/home.htm.* This annual festival is sponsored by the Scottsdale Jaycees. It includes a parade, a rodeo, and live music. Mid-Feb.

San Francisco Giants Spring Training. *Scottsdale Stadium, 7408 E Osborn Rd, Scottsdale. Phone 480/990-2886. www.cactus-league.com/giants.html.* San Francisco Giants baseball spring training, exhibition games. Early Mar-early Apr.

Scottsdale Culinary Festival. *7375 E Sixth Ave, Suite 9, Scottsdale. Events held at various locations throughout Scottsdale. Phone 480/945-7193. www.scottsdaleculinaryfestival.org.* If you appreciate mouthwatering cuisine, then savor some of the tastiest dishes imaginable at this hot culinary adventure that mixes the Southwest's best chefs with food lovers from the Valley and way beyond. Choose from any of nine individual events ranging from casual to black-tie-only. In most cases, wine and music spice up the menu to set just the right mood. Proceeds benefit area charities. Mid-Mar and mid-Apr.

The Tradition at Superstition Mountain. *Superstition Mountain Golf & Country Club, 3976 S Ponderosa Dr, Superstition Mountain. Phone toll-free 877/983-3300. www.superstitionmountain.com.* Senior PGA Tour golf tournament. Early Apr.

Limited-Service Hotels

★ ★ CHAPARRAL SUITES RESORT. *5001 N Scottsdale Rd, Scottsdale (85250). Phone 480/949-1414; toll-free 800/528-1456; fax 480/947-2675. www.chaparralsuites.com.* 311 rooms, 4 story, all suites. Pets accepted, some restrictions; fee. Complimentary full breakfast. Check-in 3 pm, check-out noon. High-speed Internet access. Restaurant, bar. Fitness room. Two pools, whirlpool. Tennis. Airport transportation available. Business center. **$$**

★ COUNTRY INN & SUITES BY CARLSON. *10801 N 89th Pl, Scottsdale (85260). Phone 480/314-1200; toll-free 800/456-4000; fax 480/314-7367. www.countryinns.com.* 91 rooms, 3 story. Pets accepted, some restrictions; fee. Complimentary continental breakfast. Check-in 3 pm, check-out noon. Fitness room. Outdoor pool, children's pool, whirlpool. **$**

★ GAINEY SUITES. *7300 E Gainey Suites Dr, Scottsdale (85258). Phone 480/922-6969; toll-free 800/970-4666; fax 480/922-1689. www.gaineysuiteshotel.com.* 162 rooms, 3 story, all suites. Complimentary continental breakfast. Check-in 3 pm, check-out noon. High-speed Internet access. Fitness room. Pool, whirlpool. Business center. **$**

★ HAMPTON INN. *4415 N Civic Center Plaza, Scottsdale (85251). Phone 480/941-9400; fax 480/675-5240. www.hamptoninnoldtown.com.* 135 rooms, 5 story. Pets accepted; fee. Complimentary continental breakfast. Check-in 3 pm, check-out noon. Pool. **$**

★ ★ HILTON GARDEN INN. *7324 E Indian School Rd, Scottsdale (85251). Phone 480/481-0400; toll-free 877/782-9444; fax 480/481-0800. www.scottsdale.gardeninn.com.* Conveniently situated near Old Town Scottsdale, major shopping centers, and numerous restaurants, this modern hotel is designed for the business traveler. In addition to a host of amenities, it offers attractive public areas and large, well-furnished guest rooms. 199 rooms, 7 story. Check-in 3 pm, check-out noon. High-speed Internet access. Restaurant, bar. Fitness room. Pool, whirlpool. Business center. **$$**

★ LA QUINTA INN. *8888 E Shea Blvd, Scottsdale (85260). Phone 480/614-5300; fax 480/614-5333. www.laquinta.com.* 140 rooms, 3 story. Pets accepted. Complimentary continental breakfast. Check-in 2 pm, check-out noon. Fitness room. Outdoor pool, whirlpool. **$**

★ SUMMERFIELD SUITES. *4245 N Drinkwater Blvd, Scottsdale (85251). Phone 480/946-7700; toll-free 800/833-4353; fax 480/946-7711. www.wyndham.com.*

This all-suite property has numerous amenities that make it an ideal location for families and extended-stay guests. 163 rooms, 3 story, all suites. Pet accepted; fee. Complimentary full breakfast. Check-in 4 pm, check-out noon. Fitness room. Pool, whirlpool. **$**

Full-Service Hotels

★★★ JAMES HOTEL. *7353 E Indian School Rd, Scottsdale (85251). Phone 480/994-9203; toll-free 866/505-2637; fax 480/308-1200. www.jameshotel.com.* 194 rooms. Check-in 3 pm, check-out noon. Restaurant, bar. **$**

★★★ MARRIOTT SCOTTSDALE AT MCDOWELL MOUNTAIN. *16770 N Perimeter Dr, Scottsdale (85260). Phone 480/502-3836; toll-free 800/288-6127; fax 480/502-0653. www.marriottscottsdale.com.* This all-suites hotel is located in north Scottsdale. The colorful, attractive public areas and well-furnished guest rooms are designed for both families and the business traveler. Some rooms have views of the TPC-Scottsdale golf course. 270 rooms, 5 story, all suites. Check-in 4 pm, check-out noon. Restaurant, bar. Fitness room. Pool, whirlpool. Golf. Business center. **$**

★★★ MARRIOTT SUITES SCOTTSDALE OLD TOWN. *7325 E 3rd Ave, Scottsdale (85251). Phone 480/945-1550; toll-free 800/228-9290; fax 480/874-6095. www.marriott.com.* Having everything for the business traveler, the suites at this hotel come fully loaded with the latest in office amenities, as well as plenty of recreational facilities to help wind down from the day. 251 rooms, 7 story, all suites. Check-in 4 pm, check-out noon. High-speed Internet access. Restaurant, bar. Fitness room. Pool, whirlpool. Airport transportation available. Business center. **$**

Full-Service Resorts

★★★ THE FAIRMONT SCOTTSDALE PRINCESS. *7575 E Princess Dr, Scottsdale (85255). Phone 480/585-4848; fax 480/585-0086. www.fairmont.com.* The Fairmont Scottsdale Princess is a cosmopolitan oasis snuggled on 450 lush acres overlooking Scottsdale and the majestic McDowell Mountains. The pink Spanish Colonial buildings are just the beginning at this comprehensive resort, where recreational opportunities are plentiful. Two championship golf courses, one of which hosts the PGA Tour's Phoenix Open; seven tennis courts; and an extensive fitness center please the active minded, while the Willow Stream Spa soothes the weary with its serene design and balancing principles. Four pools cool guests, and adults and children alike are tickled pink by the aquatic recreation area complete with two waterslides. The rooms and suites are a blend of Mediterranean design interspersed with Southwestern accents. Spacious and comfortable, the accommodations have fantastic views. Diners traverse the world at the six restaurants and bars, where dishes hailing from the Italian Riviera, Mexico, and the American heartland delight guests. 650 rooms, 4 story. Check-in 4 pm, check-out noon. Restaurant, bar. Children's activity center. Fitness room, spa. Three pools, whirlpool. Golf, 36 holes. Tennis. Business center. **$$$$**

★★★★ FOUR SEASONS RESORT SCOTTSDALE AT TROON NORTH. *10600 E Crescent Moon Dr, Scottsdale (85255). Phone 480/515-5700; toll-free 800/332-3442; fax 480/515-5599. www.fourseasons.com.* The Four Seasons Resort Scottsdale at Troon North basks in the abundant golden sunshine synonymous with the Southwest. Blending with the natural surroundings, this two-story resort rests within a 40-acre nature preserve. The rooms and suites are housed in 25 casitas clustered around the grounds. Native American pottery and textiles add local flavor and set a sense of place in the rooms, where fireplaces warm the interiors and windows frame expansive views of the stunning desert. Extra luxuries like plunge pools, alfresco garden showers, and outdoor kiva fireplaces characterize the gracious suites. Influenced by the location, the spa offers desert nectar facials and moonlight massages, and the landscaped pool deck provides a pleasurable place for relaxation. Three restaurants reflect the resort's casually elegant attitude in their ambience and menu. A veritable mecca for golfers, the resort grants priority tee times at Troon North's two courses, considered among the best in the world. 210 rooms, 2 story. Pets accepted, some restrictions. Check-in 4 pm, check-out noon. Restaurant, bar. Children's activity center. Fitness room, spa. Outdoor pool, children's pool, whirlpool. Golf. Tennis. Business center. **$$$**

★★★ HILTON SCOTTSDALE RESORT AND VILLAS. *6333 N Scottsdale Rd, Scottsdale (85250). Phone 480/948-7750; toll-free 800/528-3119; fax 480/948-2232. www.scottsdaleresort.hilton.com.* Conveniently located near major shopping areas, restaurants, and attractions, this resort offers standard guest rooms as well as one- and two-bedroom villas with full kitchens, fireplaces, and washers and dryers. 185 rooms, 3 story. Check-in 4 pm, check-out noon. Three restaurants, three bars. Fitness room, spa. Two pools, children's pool, whirlpool. Business center. **$**

★★★ HYATT REGENCY SCOTTSDALE RESORT AT GAINEY RANCH. *7500 E Doubletree Ranch Rd, Scottsdale (85258). Phone 480/991-3388; toll-free 800/233-1234; fax 480/483-5511. www.scottsdale.hyatt.com.* The Hyatt Regency Scottsdale Resort at Gainey Ranch enjoys a truly spectacular setting. Set against the backdrop of the McDowell Mountai ns, the resort is nestled on 560 acres filled with shimmering pools, trickling fountains, and cascading waterfalls. Neutral tones and regional furnishings create serene havens in the rooms and suites. This is a desert playground for the whole family, with exceptional recreational facilities. The resort is committed to preserving the integrity of its home, from the innovative environmental conservation techniques to the cultural programming on the Southwest's indigenous people. A wide variety of restaurants take guests on a culinary journey, and in the case of Ristorante Sandolo, a gondola ride. Diners can feast on Northern Italian specialties, continental cuisine, and Southwestern dishes in refined or casual settings. 500 rooms, 4 story. Check-in 3 pm, check-out noon. Restaurant, bar. Children's activity center. Fitness room, spa. Beach. Outdoor pool, children's pool, whirlpool. Golf, 27 holes. Tennis. Business center. **$$**

★★★ MARRIOTT CAMELBACK INN RESORT GOLF CLUB & SPA. *5402 E Lincoln Dr, Scottsdale (85253). Phone 480/948-1700; toll-free 800/242-2635; fax 480/951-8469. www.camelbackinn.com.* Since the 1930s, the Camelback Inn has appealed to travelers seeking the very best in the American Southwest. This special hideaway, reminiscent of a hacienda, is situated on 125 acres in Arizona's beautiful Sonoran Desert. Supremely comfortable, the rooms and suites share the distinctive charms of the region while providing modern luxuries. To further indulge guests, the suites even offer private pools. Outdoor enthusiasts explore the region on horseback, enjoy the thrill of whitewater rafting, or marvel at the view from above in a hot-air balloon, while tennis courts, three heated pools, and a comprehensive fitness center keep guests occupied closer to home. Set at the base of Mummy Mountain, the spa is a peaceful retreat. All cravings are satisfied here, with a total of seven dining venues ranging from quick and casual to more formal settings ideal for lingering over sensational meals. 453 rooms, 2 story. Pets accepted, some restrictions; fee. Check-in 4 pm, check-out 11 am. Restaurant, bar. Children's activity center. Fitness room, spa. Three pools, whirlpool. Golf, 36 holes. Tennis. Business center. **$$$**

★★★ MILLENNIUM RESORT SCOTTSDALE, MCCORMICK RANCH. *7401 N Scottsdale Rd, Scottsdale (85253). Phone 480/948-5050; toll-free 800/243-1332; fax 480/948-9113. www.millennium-hotels.com/scottsdale.* At Scottsdale's single lakeside resort, enjoy a day on the lake with paddleboats or sailing, complimentary for resort guests only. 128 rooms, 3 story. Check-in 3 pm, check-out noon. Restaurant, bar. Fitness room. Pool, whirlpool. Tennis. Business center. **$**

★★★ ORANGE TREE GOLF RESORT. *10601 N 56th St, Scottsdale (85254). Phone 480/948-6100; toll-free 800/228-0386; fax 480/483-6074. www.orangetree.com.* A luscious landscape and a championship 18-hole golf course set the stage for this desert resort that was once an orange orchard. Spacious and cozy suites have French doors that open onto private terraces. 160 rooms, 2 story. Check-in 4 pm, check-out 11 am. Restaurant, bar. Children's activity center. Fitness room, spa. Outdoor pool, children's pool, whirlpool. Golf, 18 holes. **$$**

★★★★ THE PHOENICIAN. *6000 E Camelback Rd, Scottsdale (85251). Phone 480/941-8200; toll-free 800/888-8234; fax 480/947-4311. www.thephoenician.com.* The world-class Phoenician rests at the base of Camelback Mountain in Scottsdale's Valley of the Sun. This patrician resort almost defies belief. Home to an $8 million art collection, this resort embodies sophistication in the desert and stands out for its European panache. Aubusson tapestries and antiques in the lobby impart a continental feeling, yet the expansive, unobstructed views of the striking desert firmly root visitors in the Southwest. The rooms and suites are elegantly appointed, and meticulous attention to detail is a hallmark of this resort. Every imaginable recreational opportunity is available here, including desert hikes. Swimmers can take a dip in one of the many pools and enjoy the thrill of the 165-foot water-slide. The impressive spa nurtures the spirit, while the fabulous restaurants feed the soul and garner praise from gourmets. 654 rooms, 6 story. Pets accepted. Check-in 4 pm, check-out noon. Restaurants, bar. Children's activity center. Fitness room, spa. Outdoor pool, children's pool, whirlpool. Golf. Tennis. Airport transportation available. Business center. **$$$**

★ ★ ★ RADISSON RESORT & SPA SCOTTSDALE. *7171 N Scottsdale Rd, Scottsdale (85253). Phone 480/991-3800; toll-free 800/333-3333; fax 480/948-1381. www.radisson.com.* A perfect retreat for business or pleasure, this desert resort is located in Scottsdale's cultural district. 318 rooms, 2 story. Pets accepted, fee. Check-in 3 pm, check-out 1 pm. Restaurant, bar. Children's activity center. Fitness room, spa. Eight pools, children's pool, whirlpool. Tennis. Business center. **$$**

★ ★ ★ RENAISSANCE SCOTTSDALE RESORT. *6160 N Scottsdale Rd, Scottsdale (85253). Phone 480/991-1414; toll-free 800/468-3571; fax 480/951-3350. www.renaissancehotels.com.* Nestled in the famous Camelback Mountain, this 25-acre oasis is beautifully intimate. Whether shopping at the Borgata, shaping up with Splash Aerobics, or chowing down at a private Western-style dinner, guests enjoy the Southwestern flair. 171 rooms, 3 story. Pets accepted, some restrictions. Check-in 3 pm, check-out noon. High-speed Internet access. Restaurant, bar. Pools, whirlpool. Tennis. **$**

★ ★ ★ SUNBURST RESORT. *4925 N Scottsdale Rd, Scottsdale (85251). Phone 480/945-7666; toll-free 800/528-7867; fax 480/946-4056. www.sunburstresort.com.* A Mediterranean-like escape in the middle of the Southwestern desert describes the garden courtyard and the sandy pool area. Near many PGA golf courses and shopping. 204 rooms, 2 story. Check-in 3 pm, check-out noon. Restaurant, bar. Fitness room, spa. Pool, children's pool, whirlpool. Business center. **$$**

★ ★ ★ THE WESTIN KIERLAND RESORT AND SPA. *6902 E Greenway Pkwy, Scottsdale (85254). Phone 480/624-1000; toll-free 800/937-8461; fax 480/624-1001. www.westin.com/kierlandresort.* The Westin Kierland Resort and Spa shares a typical Southwestern look and feel with its guests. The spacious rooms and suites are enhanced with soothing earth tones and regional furnishings, and the Agave Spa looks to the traditional therapies used by Native Americans for inspiration. Golf, tennis, and multiple pools (including a flowing river pool with landscaped waterfall), beach, and volleyball court, compete for attention, and the eight dining outlets ensure that all cravings are satisfied. Located in northeast Phoenix, this resort is adjacent to the 38-acre Kierland Commons, where specialty boutiques and restaurants attract serious shoppers and diners. 735 rooms. Pets accepted; fee. Check-in 4 pm, check-out noon. Restaurant, bar. Children's activity center. Fitness room, spa. Beach. Outdoor pool, children's pool, whirlpool. Golf. Tennis. **$$$**

Spas

★ ★ ★ THE CENTRE FOR WELL-BEING AT THE PHOENICIAN. *6000 E Camelback Rd, Scottsdale (85251). Phone 480/423-2452; toll-free 800/843-2392. www.centreforwellbeing.com.* The Centre for Well-Being is the jewel in the crown at The Phoenician, nestled at the base of Camelback Mountain. Comprising a fitness center and a spa dedicated to health, rejuvenation, and relaxation, this full-service facility lures athletic-minded guests, sybarites, and first-time spa-goers. On the day of your spa treatment, enjoy complimentary use of the well-equipped fitness center, where conditioning assessments, body-composition analyses, stretching sessions, and personal training are available. To improve your strength, coordination, and cardiovascular health, work one-on-one with a yoga instructor or hike with an experienced guide. Spirituality is a large component of the experience at this spa, and the meditation atrium is a tranquil area perfect for reconnecting with yourself. Learn visualization, stress-reduction, and energy-balancing techniques in a private meditation session.

With an appealing array of options, The Centre for Well-Being offers a full range of spa services to meet guests' individual needs. Fifteen types of massage are available, from favorites such as Swedish and sports to newer therapies such as lymphatic drainage and craniosacral, which employs light touch along the spine and head to relieve stress. The neuromuscular treatment offers spot relief for injuries, while jin shin jyutsu utilizes a series of holding techniques to alleviate tension blocked in the body.

Customized for specific complexions, the facials achieve luminous, healthier-looking skin with soothing aloe vera, nourishing vitamin C, cooling masks, and antiaging Retinol. Rest your body and eliminate its impurities with a serenity seaweed scrub and wrap or a thermal moor mud wrap. The rosemary soothing soufflé wrap, complete with a foot exfoliation and a face and scalp massage, re-energizes your spirit, while the vanilla-rose sugar glow smoothes and moisturizes rough skin. Tired legs and feet appreciate the invigorating scrubs and massages that are part of a "Barefoot in the Lemongrass" treatment and a salt and peppermint foot therapy.

★★★★ SPA AT FOUR SEASONS RESORT SCOTTSDALE AT TROON NORTH. *10600 E Crescent Moon Dr, Scottsdale (85262). Phone 480/513-5145; toll-free 888/207-9696. www.fourseasons.com.* Serenity and relaxation are guaranteed at this 12,000-square-foot spa. Let your tensions go with a Swedish, deep tissue, aromatherapy, shiatsu, hydrotherapy, or reflexology massage, or take Massage 101, where you learn the tricks of the trade to bring home as a special souvenir. The resort's signature moonlight massage is one of the best ways to bid farewell to a wonderfully rewarding day, and all the massages are available in the privacy of your room or balcony. Other signature treatments include hot stone massages, desert nectar facials, and aromatherapy treatments that alternate seasonally.

Surround yourself with the luxurious pampering of a willow herbal and chamomile aromatherapy body wrap or repair your skin with a revitalizing vitamin facial or a purifying back treatment. Many of the treatments showcase ingredients indigenous to the region, such as the saguaro blossom body polish. From green tea to milk and honey, natural ingredients are used to cleanse, nourish, and refresh your skin. Half-day and full-day packages are available to take advantage of several treatments, and a full-service salon is on hand to beautify you from head to toe.

The fitness center draws exercise buffs with its weight-training and cardiovascular equipment. Working out not only recharges, but also entertains here, where audiovisual equipment and wireless headsets accompany each machine. Personal trainers are available for individualized instruction and programs.

★★★ WILLOW STREAM-THE SPA AT THE FAIRMONT SCOTTSDALE PRINCESS. *7575 E Princess Dr, Scottsdale (85255). Phone 480/585-2732; toll-free 800/908-9540. www.fairmont.com.* Framed by the McDowell Mountains with the Sonoran Desert stretching beyond, The Fairmont Scottsdale Princess is blessed with one of the most picturesque settings in Scottsdale's renowned Valley of the Sun. There's something for everyone at this comprehensive resort, where two 18-hole golf courses, seven tennis courts, and five pools are just the beginning. If you would prefer to while away your stay at the spa, the Fairmont's Willow Stream was created with you in mind. With its waterfall treatment room and rooftop adult pool, it's easy to understand why Willow Stream is one of the leading resort spas. It is a complete experience, and spa-goers often incorporate the philosophy behind it into their daily lives after they visit. The fitness center is state-of-the-art and offers cutting-edge classes, while the spa cuisine makes healthy dining a pleasure. Be sure to try the refreshing prickly pear lemonade. The spa's clean, simple design appeals to both men and women, yet separate facilities are provided to ensure comfort and privacy. The outside treatment rooms are worth every penny as the soothing sounds of waterfalls gently lull you into a Zenlike trance.

Inspired by the hidden oasis of the same name in the Grand Canyon, the Havasupai body oasis treatment combines warm eucalyptus footbaths and herbal baths with the healing power of the waterfalls. Skin parched from the Arizona sun will drink in the moisturizing benefits of the aloe body wrap and aloe-eucalyptus scrub. The royal Sonoran body polish buffs and comforts skin with luscious cream and soothing chamomile. Several treatments, including the body experience—which blends a mud wrap with a healing waters bath, a light massage, and aromatherapy—are Willow Stream signatures. From massages and mineral baths to European kurs, the spa's serenity and high attention to detail appeal to seasoned spa-goers and beginners alike. In addition to hair care services, the Thomas Salon keeps fingers and toes pretty with five types of manicures and six types of pedicures.

Restaurants

★★★★ ACACIA. *10600 E Crescent Moon Dr, Scottsdale (85255). Phone 480/515-5700; toll-free*

800/332-3442; fax 480/513-5300. www.fourseasons.com. If you happen to find yourself nibbling on artistic, up-to-the-minute American fare under a vast, dark sky carpeted with stars, faced with stunning views of the McDowell Mountains and with the twinkle of city lights around you, chances are you are at The Four Seasons Resort Scottsdale at Troon North (see), dining at its flagship eatery, Acacia. Decked out in glossy wood floors, wood-beamed ceilings, and serene earth tones, the restaurant is warmed with light from wrought-iron alabaster chandeliers and a two-way fireplace the size of a small home. Acacia is one of the most beautiful places to sink into for an evening of dining and atmosphere. Entrées are divided among steaks and chops (USDA Prime and certified Angus), seafood, and poultry. Signatures include five-spiced tuna with soy sauce, wasabi, and pickled ginger; and grilled, dry-rubbed, double-cut lamb chops, making Acacia a perfect place for all sorts of eaters and appetites. Steak menu. Dinner. Bar. Children's menu. Casual attire. Outdoor seating. **$$$**

★ ★ CANTINA DEL PEDREGAL. *34631 N Scottsdale Rd, Scottsdale (85202). Phone 480/488-0715; toll-free 800/553-1717. www.wyndham.com.* Mexican menu. Lunch, dinner. Closed Thanksgiving, Dec 25. Bar. Children's menu. Casual attire. Reservations recommended. Outdoor seating. **$$$**

★ ★ CHAPARRAL DINING ROOM. *5402 E Lincoln Dr, Scottsdale (85253). Phone 480/948-1700; fax 480/905-7948. www.camelbackinn.com.* This Scottsdale landmark sports excellent views of Camelback Mountain, creating a breathtaking ambience. American menu. Dinner. Bar. Casual attire. Reservations recommended. Valet parking. **$$$**

★ ★ CHART HOUSE. *7255 McCormick Pkwy, Scottsdale (85258). Phone 480/951-2250; fax 480/951-1733. www.scottsdalecharthouse.com.* Seafood menu. Dinner. Bar. Closed holidays. Children's menu. Casual attire. Outdoor seating. **$**

★ CHOMPIE'S. *9301 E Shea Blvd, Scottsdale (85260). Phone 480/860-0475; fax 480/860-8422. www.chompies.com.* Located in the Mercado del Rancho shopping area, Chompie's serves fresh-made bagels, bialys, and stacked-high sandwiches. They say that people drive an hour to pick up what locals agree are the best bagels in town. Kosher deli menu. Breakfast, lunch, dinner. Closed holidays. Bar. Children's menu. Casual attire. Outdoor seating. **$**

★ ★ CREW. *34505 N Scottsdale Rd, Suite 32, Scottsdale (85262). Phone 480/488-8840; fax 480/488-6830. www.creweats.com.* American menu. Dinner. Closed Thanksgiving, Dec 25. Bar. Children's menu. Casual attire. Outdoor seating. **$$**

★ ★ ★ DESEO. *6902 E Greenway Pkwy, Scottsdale (85254). Phone 480/624-1015; toll-free 800/937-8461; fax 480/624-1001. www.kierlandresort.com.* An open display kitchen is the focal point of this restaurant located in Scottsdale's Westin Kirkland Resort (see). Rich gold and rust tones dominate the dining room, while ceviche is the highlight of the menu. Nuevo Latino menu. Dinner. Closed Sun. Bar. Children's menu. Casual attire. Reservations recommended. Outdoor seating. **$$**

★ ★ DON AND CHARLIE'S AMERICAN RIB AND CHOP HOUSE. *7501 E Camelback Rd, Scottsdale (85251). Phone 480/990-0900; fax 480/947-3464. www.donandcharlies.com.* American menu. Dinner. Closed Thanksgiving. Bar. Children's menu. Casual attire. **$$$**

★ ★ DRIFT. *4341 N 75th St, Scottsdale (85251). Phone 480/949-8454; fax 480/949-8457. www.driftlounge.com.* Polynesian menu. Dinner. Bar. Casual attire. Outdoor seating. **$$**

★ ★ EL CHORRO LODGE. *5550 E Lincoln Dr, Scottsdale (85253). Phone 480/948-5170; fax 480/483-2283. www.elchorro.com.* American menu. Dinner. Bar. Casual attire. Valet parking. Outdoor seating. **$$$**

★ ★ ★ EVERETT'S STEAKHOUSE & BLUES BAR. *20701 N Scottsdale Rd, Scottsdale (85255). Phone 480/515-5891; fax 480/568-0298.* A live blues band livens things up on weekends at this casual steakhouse located in the Grayhawk Plaza shopping center. An exhibition kitchen keeps hungry diners entertained before their cuts of prime beef arrive at the table. Steak menu. Dinner. Bar. Children's menu. Casual attire. Outdoor seating. **$$$**

★ ★ ★ ★ GOLDEN SWAN. *7500 E Doubletree Rd, Scottsdale (85258). Phone 480/483-5572; fax 480/483-5550. www.scottsdale.hyatt.com.* Modern, upscale Southwestern fare is the culinary theme at The Golden Swan, a stone-floored, desert-toned dining room set in the Hyatt Regency Scottsdale Resort (see). The kitchen is known for adding spark to the plate with the heat of the region's indigenous chilies, barbecue sauces, and spices; free-range chicken baked in Arizona red rock clay and grilled Pacific salmon with mesquite-honey barbecue sauce are signatures. The food here is fantastic, which is part of the explanation behind the restaurant's unstoppable popularity. With its movie-set views of the lake and gazebo, it is not surprising to learn that the restaurant boasts four or five marriage proposals per week. If you have room in your schedule on a Sunday, make a point of getting to the Sunday Chef's Brunch. It includes belt-busting numbers of selections: salads, shellfish, sushi, pastas, breakfast pastries, fresh-baked breads, and hand-carved meats, and the added bonus of ordering your meal in the kitchen directly from the chef. International menu. Dinner, Sun brunch. Bar. Casual attire. Reservations recommended. Valet parking. Outdoor seating. **$$$**

★★★ **HAPA.** *6204 N Scottsdale Rd, Scottsdale (85253). Phone 480/998-8220; fax 480/998-2355. www.restauranthapa.com.* Hapa is Hawaiian slang for "half" and refers to the Asian-American ancestry of chef James McDevitt. With his wife Stacey creating splendid desserts, like warm chocolate cake with mango sauce, the Pacific Rim menu is interesting from start to finish. Asian, American menu. Dinner. Closed Sun; holidays; also two weeks in summer. Bar. Casual attire. Reservations recommended. Outdoor seating. **$$$**

★★★ **L'ECOLE.** *8100 E Camelback Rd, Scottsdale (85251). Phone 480/990-7639; fax 480/990-3773. www.scichefs.com.* You can be sure that the food is top-of-the-line at this training ground for the Scottsdale Culinary Institute. The student-operated restaurant is set in a lovely dining room that is booked weeks in advance. Diners also enjoy the patio setting with its colorful awnings. French menu. Lunch, dinner. Closed Sat-Sun. Reservations recommended. **$$**

★★★ **LA HACIENDA.** *7575 E Princess Dr, Scottsdale (85255). Phone 480/585-4848; fax 480/585-2742. www.fairmont.com.* In a turn-of-the-century Mexican ranch house on the lush grounds of the Fairmont Scottsdale Princess, a notable southwestern resort and spa (see), La Hacienda offers traditional Mexican specialties. Signatures like filete a la parrilla—grilled filet mignon with corn, poblano salsa, and cascabel glaze—and cochinillo asado—a barbacoa-style suckling pig that is spit-roasted and stuffed with homemade chorizo sausage and carved tableside—are prepared with care and the technique of generations past. Strolling mariachis, flagstone flooring, wood-beamed ceilings, hurricane lamps, tapestry-upholstered seating, assorted artifacts from Mexico, and magnificent views make this an alluring spot to dine and watch the sun go down. Like any respectable authentic Mexican eatery, La Hacienda makes killer margaritas, served with crisp, golden tortilla chips to keep you thirsting for more. Mexican menu. Dinner. Closed Wed; also Mon-Tues in summer. Bar. Children's menu. Casual attire. Reservations recommended. Valet parking. Outdoor seating. **$$$**

★★★ **MANCUSO'S.** *6166 N Scottsdale Rd, Scottsdale (85253). Phone 480/948-9988; fax 480/948-6011. www.mancusosrestaurant.com.* Delicate piano music sets the mood at this polished Italian restaurant, which reflects the richness of the Renaissance period. Guests sip cappuccinos in the espresso bar after dinner. Italian menu. Dinner. Closed Dec 25. Bar. Valet parking. **$$**

★★ **MARCO POLO SUPPER CLUB.** *8608 E Shea Blvd, Scottsdale (85260). Phone 480/483-1900; fax 480/483-9752. www.marcopolosupperclub.com.* American menu. Dinner. Bar. Reservations recommended. Valet parking. Outdoor seating. **$$$**

★★★ **MARIA'S WHEN IN NAPLES.** *7000 E Shea Blvd, Scottsdale (85254). Phone 480/991-6887; fax 480/483-3818. www.mariaswheninnaples.com.* At this local favorite, handmade pasta and fresh sauces are served in a casually elegant atmosphere. A local favorite. Italian menu. Dinner. Closed holidays. Bar. Casual attire. Outdoor seating. **$$**

★★★ **MARQUESA.** *7575 E Princess Dr, Scottsdale (85255). Phone 480/585-4848; fax 480/585-2742. www.fairmont.com.* Marquesa is one of those restaurants that can be habit forming. Lucky for you, in terms of addictions, this one is not detrimental to your health but actually has health benefits. Marquesa features the wonderful foods of the Mediterranean Riviera. The kitchen stays true to the peasant dishes of Italy, France, and Spain but also offers a selection of more innovative creations, which means that classic dishes like bouillabaisse and paella share menu space with more extravagant dishes like duck and squab with pistachio, caramelized pears, turnip gratin, and fruit reduction. The soothing dining room is all atmosphere—appointed with wildflowers, brocade tapestries, rich leather, magnificent paintings, and antiques from the 16th and 17th centuries. Dining under the stars with a bird's-eye view of the McDowell Mountains is made possible in chilly weather thanks to a stone fireplace. Mediterranean menu. Dinner, Sun brunch. Closed Mon-Tues; also mid-June-mid-Sept. Bar. Children's menu. Casual attire. Reservations recommended. Valet parking. Outdoor seating. **$$$**

★ ★ ★ ★ **MARY ELAINE'S.** *6000 E Camelback Rd, Scottsdale (85251). Phone 480/423-2444; fax 480/947-4311. www.thephoenician.com.* Never mind the extraordinary prices: this bastion of luxury is worth the price tag. The impeccable service staff will anticipate your every need, whether it's a stool on which to rest your handbag or guidance navigating the impressive wine list. Seafood is the specialty, with heavenly choices including pan-seared New Zealand John Dory, Sea of Cortez scallops, and roasted American red snapper. French menu. Dinner. Closed Sun-Mon; also the month of July. Bar. Jacket required. Reservations recommended. Valet parking. **$$$$**

★ ★ ★ **MICHAEL'S.** *8700 E Pinnacle Peak Rd, Scottsdale (85255). Phone 480/515-2575; fax 480/515-1451. www.michaelsrestaurant.com.* This namesake restaurant of Michael DeMaria is in The Citadel resort in the Sonoran Desert. Signature features are a demonstration cooking studio and a chef's table with kitchen views. The bright dining room is a great space to showcase contemporary American cuisine. American menu. Lunch, dinner. Closed some holidays. Bar. Casual attire. Reservations recommended. Outdoor seating. **$$**

★ ★ ★ **PALM COURT.** *7700 E McCormick Pkwy, Scottsdale (85258). Phone 480/596-7700; fax 480/596-7427. www.thescottsdaleresort.com.* This candlelit restaurant maintains the classic traditions of fine dining with lavish fare prepared tableside in a dazzling production. Dapper, tuxedo-clad waiters serve decadent mainstays. American menu. Breakfast, lunch, dinner, Sun brunch. Bar. Children's menu. Jacket required (dinner). Reservations recommended. Valet parking. **$$**

★ **PISCHKE'S PARADISE.** *7217 E 1st St, Scottsdale (85251). Phone 480/481-0067. www.pischkesparadise.com.* American menu. Dinner. Closed holidays. Bar. Casual attire. Outdoor seating. **$$**

★ **QUILTED BEAR.** *6316 N Scottsdale Rd, Scottsdale (85253). Phone 480/948-7760; fax 480/948-2749. www.quiltedbearaz.com.* American menu. Breakfast, lunch, dinner. Bar. Children's menu. Casual attire. Outdoor seating. **$$**

★ ★ **RANCHO PINOT GRILL.** *6208 N Scottsdale Blvd, Scottsdale (85253). Phone 480/367-8030; fax 480/443-7616. www.ranchopinot.com.* California menu. Dinner. Closed Sun-Mon; also the first two weeks of July. Bar. Casual attire. Reservations recommended. **$$$**

★ ★ ★ **RAZZ'S RESTAURANT & BAR.** *10315 N Scottsdale Rd at Shea, Scottsdale (85253). Phone 480/905-1308; fax 480/607-6698. www.razzsrestaurant.com.* Chef Razz Kamnitzer is the Wolfgang Puck of the Southwest, setting the pace for innovative cuisine in Scottsdale. His dazzling, unpredictable menu combines edible flowers and fresh herbs and vegetables from his own garden with familiar dishes from around the world. With rustic flagstone flooring and bright skylights, the small, cozy dining room is an inviting space in which to enjoy Kamnitzer's creations. Eclectic/International menu. Dinner. Closed Sun-Mon; holidays; also early June-Labor Day. Bar. Casual attire. Reservations recommended. Outdoor seating. **$$$**

★ ★ ★ **REMINGTON'S.** *7200 N Scottsdale Rd, Scottsdale (85253). Phone 480/951-5101; fax 480/951-5108. www.scottsdaleplaza.com.* A handpainted skyscape creates a unique indoor ambience, or enjoy patio dining with a fantastic view of Camelback Mountain. Located in the Scottsdale Plaza Hotel. American menu. Lunch, dinner. Bar. Casual attire. Outdoor seating. **$$$**

★ ★ ★ **ROARING FORK.** *4800 N Scottsdale Rd, Scottsdale (85251). Phone 480/947-0795; fax 480/994-1102. www.roaringfork.com.* One of the founders of Southwestern cuisine, chef Robert McGrath turns out Western American cooking at this rustic yet refined dining room filled with exposed brick and blond wood. The adjacent J-Bar is a fun place to congregate for a drink. American menu. Dinner. Closed Sun; holidays. Bar. Children's menu. Casual attire. Reservations recommended. Valet parking Fri-Sat. Outdoor seating. **$$**

★ ★ ★ RUTH'S CHRIS STEAK HOUSE. *7001 N Scottsdale Rd, Scottsdale (85253). Phone 480/991-5988; fax 480/991-6850. www.ruthschris.com.* White tablecloths and finely dressed waiters create an atmosphere of elegance at this cosmopolitan steakhouse. Dinner. Closed Thanksgiving, Dec 25. Bar. Casual attire. Reservations recommended. Outdoor seating. **$$$**

★ ★ SALT CELLAR. *550 N Hayden Rd, Scottsdale (85257). Phone 480/947-1963; fax 480/941-0929. www.saltcellarrestaurant.com.* Seafood menu. Dinner. Closed Dec 25. Bar. Children's menu. Casual attire. **$$**

★ ★ SUSHI ON SHEA. *7000 E Shea Blvd, Scottsdale (85254). Phone 480/483-7799; fax 480/483-7779. www.sushionshea.com.* Japanese menu. Dinner. Closed holidays. Bar. Children's menu. Casual attire. **$$$**

★ ★ ★ THE TERRACE DINING ROOM. *6000 E Camelback Rd, Scottsdale (85251). Phone 480/423-2530; fax 480/423-2640. www.thephoenician.com.* Inside or outside, The Terrace Dining Room is a majestic and breathtaking (not to mention very tasty) place to dine. The glowing indoor space is lined with picture windows, floral murals, and creamy Frette-topped tables, while the stunning outdoor terrace is enveloped in picturesque views of the Phoenician's croquet fields, and the resort's beautifully landscaped grounds, including a turquoise pool inlaid with mother of pearl. To add to the visual pleasure, The Terrace's new American menu of pastas, fish, poultry, and steaks cut at the in-house butcher shop is impeccably prepared using the finest products. A live orchestra plays nightly to make every evening an enchanted one. Try to pry yourself out of bed if you are there on a Sunday for their fabulous feast commonly known as brunch. (See also THE PHOENICIAN.) Mediterranean menu. Breakfast, lunch, dinner, Sun brunch. Bar. Children's menu. Casual attire. Reservations recommended. Valet parking. Outdoor seating. **$$$**

★ ★ VIC'S AT PINNACLE PEAK. *8711 E Pinnacle Peak Rd, Scottsdale (85255). Phone 480/998-2222; fax 480/585-6635. www.vics-restaurant.com.* American menu. Lunch, dinner. Bar. Casual attire. Outdoor seating. **$$$**

Sedona (C-3)

See also Cottonwood, Flagstaff

Founded 1902
Population 10,192
Elevation 4,400 ft
Area Code 928
Information Sedona-Oak Creek Canyon Chamber of Commerce, PO Box 478, 86339; phone 928/282-7722 or toll-free 800/288-7336
Web site www.sedonachamber.com

Known worldwide for the beauty of the red rocks surrounding the town, Sedona has grown from a pioneer settlement into a favorite film location. This is a resort area with numerous outdoor activities, including hiking, fishing, and biking, that can be enjoyed all year. Also an art and shopping destination, Sedona boasts Tlaquepaque (T-lock-ay-POCK-ay), a 4 1/2-acre area of gardens, courtyards, fountains, galleries, shops, and restaurants. A Ranger District office of the Coconino National Forest is here.

What to See and Do

Chapel of the Holy Cross. *780 Chapel Rd, Sedona. 2 1/2 miles S on Hwy 179. Phone 928/282-4069. www.diocesephoenix.org/parish/st_john_vianney_sed/chapel.htm.* Chapel perched between two pinnacles of uniquely colored red sandstone. Open to all for prayer and meditation. (Daily 9 am-5 pm; closed holidays) **FREE**

Oak Creek Canyon. *Sedona. Phone 928/282-2085. www.oakcreekcanyon.net.* A beautiful drive along a spectacular fishing stream, north toward Flagstaff (see). In the canyon is

> **Slide Rock State Park.** *6871 N Hwy 89A, Sedona. 7 miles N on Hwy 89A. Phone 928/282-3034. www.pr.state.az.us/parks/parkhtml/sliderock.html.* A 43-acre day-use park on Oak Creek. Swimming, natural sandstone waterslide, fishing; hiking, picnicking. Concessions. (Summer: daily 8 am-7 pm; winter: daily 8 am-5 pm; fall and spring: daily 8 am-6 pm) **$$**

Red Rock Jeep tours. *270 N Hwy 89A, Sedona. Phone 928/282-6826; toll-free 800/848-7728. www.redrockjeep.com.* Two-hour backcountry trips. (Daily) Other tours also available. **$$$$**

Sedona Cultural Park. *PO Box 2515, 50 Cultural Park Pl, Sedona. Off Hwy 89A. Phone 928/282-0747; toll-free 800/780-2787. www.sedonaculturalpark.org.* A 5-acre park that is home to the Georgia Frontiere Performing Arts Pavilion (seating 1,200-5,500), plus nature trails, picnic areas, and splendid views of the surrounding red rock country. Performing arts season (May-Oct) features classical, jazz, country, and popular music, plus live theater and an outdoor cinema. (Daily) **$$$$**

Tlaquepaque. *336 Hwy 179, Sedona. On Hwy 179. Phone 928/282-4838. www.tlaq.com.* Consists of 40 art galleries and stores set in a Spanish-style courtyard; cafés. (Daily at 10 am; closed holidays) **FREE**

Special Events

Red Rock Fantasy of Lights. *160 Portal Ln, Sedona. Phone 928/282-1777; toll-free 800/418-6499. www.redrockfantasy.com.* An annual event featuring kids' activities, concerts, carriage rides, and special events. Late Nov-mid-Jan. **$$**

Sedona Film Festival. *Sedona Cultural Park, 50 Cultural Park Pl, Sedona. Phone 928/282-0747; toll-free 800/780-2787. www.sedonafilmfestival.com.* Features independent films and film workshops. First full weekend in Mar. **$$$$**

Sedona Jazz on the Rocks. *Suite 9, 1487 W Hwy 89A, Sedona. Phone 928/282-1985. www.sedonajazz.com.* Late Sept. **$$$$**

Limited-Service Hotels

★ BEST WESTERN ARROYO ROBLE HOTEL & CREEKSIDE VILLAS. *400 N Hwy 89A, Sedona (86336). Phone 928/282-4001; toll-free 800/773-3662; fax 928/282-4001. www.bestwesternsedona.com.* Views of red sandstone buttes. 66 rooms, 5 story. Complimentary continental breakfast. Check-out 11 am. Fitness room. Indoor pool, outdoor pool. Tennis. **$**

★ BEST WESTERN INN OF SEDONA. *1200 W Hwy 89A, Sedona (86336). Phone 928/282-3072; toll-free 800/292-6344; fax 928/282-7218. www.innofsedona.com.* 110 rooms, 3 story. Pets accepted; fee. Complimentary continental breakfast. Check-out 11 am. Fitness room. Pool, whirlpool. Airport transportation available. **$**

★ HAMPTON INN. *1800 W Hwy 89A, Sedona (86336). Phone 928/282-4700; fax 928/282-0004. www.sedonahamptoninn.com.* 56 rooms, 2 story. Complimentary continental breakfast. Check-out noon. Pool, whirlpool. **$**

★ ★ SEDONA REAL INN. *95 Arroyo Pinon Dr, Sedona (86336). Phone 928/282-1414; toll-free 800/353-1239; fax 928/282-0900. www.sedonareal.com.* Resort-like amenities are included in this all-suite inn. Surrounded by the majestic red rocks and near the Grand Canyon, you will find spacious rooms with separate sitting areas along with personal attention. 47 rooms, 2 story, all suites. Complimentary continental breakfast. Check-out 11 am. Fitness room. Pool, whirlpool. **$**

Full-Service Hotel

★ ★ ★ HILTON SEDONA RESORT AND SPA. *90 Ridge Trail Dr, Sedona (86351). Phone 928/284-4040; fax 928/284-0170. www.hiltonsedona.com.* 219 rooms, 3 story, all suites. Pets accepted; fee. Check-out noon. Restaurant, bar. Children's activity center. Fitness room, spa. Pool, children's pool, whirlpool. Golf, 18 holes. Tennis. **$**

Full-Service Resorts

★ ★ ★ AMARA CREEKSIDE RESORT. *310 N Hwy 89A, Sedona (86336). Phone 928/282-4828; fax 928/282-4825. www.amararesort.com.* 100 rooms. Check-in 4 pm, check-out noon. Restaurant, bar. **$$**

★ ★ ★ ENCHANTMENT RESORT. *525 Boynton Canyon Rd, Sedona (86336). Phone 520/282-2900; toll-free 800/826-4180; fax 520/282-9249. www.enchantmentresort.com.* Travelers check out of the world when checking in at Enchantment Resort, where Sedona's rugged natural beauty revives the spirit and soothes the soul. Scenery is paramount at this resort, nestled within the spectacular Boynton Canyon. Whether they're dining with 180-degree views or enjoying the sights from private decks, guests are treated to unforgettable vistas. This resort is full of Southwestern character, from the Native American furnishings and decorative accents in the accommodations to the regional kick of the sensational dining. Tennis, croquet, swimming, and pitch-and-putt golf are just some of the activities available for adults, while Camp Coyote entertains young guests with arts and crafts and special programs. Sybarites head straight for the Mii Amo Spa, a destination unto itself with 16 casitas for the total spa experience. Often considered one of the best spas in the country, this facility is guaranteed to recharge and rejuvenate. 236 rooms. Check-in 4 pm, check-out noon. Restaurants, bar. Children's activity center. Fitness room, spa. Indoor pool, outdoor pool, whirlpool. Tennis. Business center. **$$$**

★★★ L'AUBERGE DE SEDONA. *301 L'Auberge Ln, Sedona (86336). Phone 928/282-1661; toll-free 800/272-6777; fax 928/282-1064. www.lauberge.com.* L'Auberge brings French country charm to Sedona. This one-of-a-kind establishment feels secreted away, providing just the right mood for romantic retreats. Cottages with creek or garden views, an inviting lodge, and the four-bedroom Creekside Lodge with its luxurious honeymoon suite showcase the uniquely appealing accommodations. Views of the Red Rock Canyon and Magenta Cliffs make for a scenic backdrop. Gourmet dining is an integral part of the experience here. L'Auberge Restaurant is noted for its fine French food, special five-course tasting menu, and award-winning wine list. In warmer months, the restaurant serves its food outdoors at the lovely Terrace on the Creek. 26 rooms, 2 story. Check-out 11 am. Restaurant, bar. Pool, whirlpool. Airport transportation available. **$$**

★★ LOS ABRIGADOS RESORT AND SPA. *160 Portal Ln, Sedona (86336). Phone 928/282-1777; toll-free 800/521-3131; fax 928/282-0199. www.ilxresorts.com.* Spanish-style stucco and tile-roofed buildings set among the buttes of Oak Creek Canyon. 172 rooms, 2 story. Check-in 4 pm, check-out noon. Restaurant, bar. Fitness room. Two pools, whirlpool. Tennis. **$$**

★★★ ORCHARD'S INN AT L'AUBERGE DE SEDONA. *254 Hwy 89A, Sedona (86336). Phone 928/282-1661; toll-free 877/367-2269; fax 928/282-2885. www.lauberge.com.* 41 rooms. Check-in 3 pm, check-out noon. Restaurant, bar. **$$**

★★ RADISSON POCO DIABLO RESORT. *1752 S Hwy 179, Sedona (86336). Phone 928/282-7333; toll-free 800/333-3333; fax 928/282-2090. www.radisson.com.* Views of Red Rock mountains. 137 rooms, 2 story. Check-out 11 am. Restaurant, bar. Fitness room. Pool, whirlpool. Golf, 9-hole, par-3. Tennis. **$**

Full-Service Inn

★★★ CANYON VILLA BED AND BREAKFAST INN. *125 Canyon Circle Dr, Sedona (86351). Phone 928/284-1226; toll-free 800/453-1166; fax 928/284-2114. www.canyonvilla.com.* The Canyon Villa Bed and Breakfast Inn opens its arms to travelers longing for the comforts of home. All guests feel like family here, where the warm, friendly innkeepers personally welcome each visitor. Charming and intimate, the inn mesmerizes its guests with staggering views of Sedona's renowned red rock formations. Nearly all of the guest rooms frame unparalleled vistas, with French doors opening onto private patios or decks for even better viewing. English country meets the American Southwest in the interiors. Four-poster beds and floral patterns add a romantic touch, while Indian rugs and iron furnishings reflect a regional flavor. No alarm clocks are necessary here, where the wonderful aroma of freshly baked cinnamon buns gently coaxes guests from deep slumber. Every delicious morsel of the inn's gourmet breakfast is savored, and the gracious poolside hors d'oeuvre service offers visitors a chance to make new friends. 11 rooms, 2 story. Children over 11 years only. Complimentary full breakfast. Check-in 3 pm, check-out 11 am. Outdoor pool. **$$$**

Specialty Lodgings

The following lodging establishment is approved by Mobil Travel Guide but, due to its unique and individualized nature has not been given a traditional Mobil Star rating. Included in this listing you may find bed-and-breakfasts, limited-service inns, guest ranches, and other unique hotel properties.

A TOUCH OF SEDONA BED AND BREAKFAST. *595 Jordan Rd, Sedona (86336). Phone 928/282-6462; toll-free 800/600-6462; fax 928/282-1534. www.touchsedona.com.* 5 rooms. Complimentary full breakfast. Check-in 4-6 pm, check-out 11 am. **$**

ADOBE VILLAGE GRAHAM INN. *150 Canyon Circle Dr, Sedona (86351). Phone 928/284-1425; toll-free 800/228-1425; fax 928/284-0767. www.sedonasfinest.com.* Bake bread in your own private casita with a king bed and a waterfall shower! The beautifully landscaped pool and courtyard are delightful. 11 rooms, 2 story. Complimentary full breakfast. Check-in 3-6 pm, check-out 11 am. Pool, whirlpool. Business center. **$$$**

ALMA DE SEDONA INN. *50 Hozoni Dr, Sedona (86336). Phone 928/282-2737; toll-free 800/923-2282; fax 928/203-4141. www.almadesedona.com.* 12 rooms. Check-in 3 pm, check-out 11 am. **$$**

APPLE ORCHARD INN. *656 Jordan Rd, Sedona (86336). Phone 928/282-5328; toll-free 800/663-6968; fax 928/204-0044. www.appleorchardbb.com.* Personal service awaits guests at this inn that has a charming Southwestern atmosphere. It has easily accessible hiking trails with spectacular views of Wilson Mountain and Steamboat Rock. 6 rooms, 2 story. Children over 12 years only. Complimentary full breakfast. Check-in 3-6 pm, check-out 11 am. Pool, whirlpool. **$$**

CASA SEDONA BED AND BREAKFAST. *55 Hozoni Dr, Sedona (86336). Phone 928/282-2938; toll-free 800/525-3756; fax 928/282-2259. www.casasedona.com.* Each room has a view of Red Rocks. 16 rooms, 2 story. Children over 12 years only. Complimentary full breakfast. Check-in 3-6 pm, check-out 11 am. Whirlpool. **$$$**

EL PORTAL SEDONA. *95 Portal Ln, Sedona (86336). Phone toll-free 800/313-0017; fax 928/282-1941. www.innsedona.com.* 12 rooms, all suites. Check-in 2 pm, check-out 11 am. **$$$**

THE INN ON OAK CREEK. *556 Hwy 179, Sedona (86336). Phone 928/282-7896; toll-free 800/499-7896; fax 928/282-0696. www.theinnonoakcreek.com.* This former art gallery turned inn is as exquisite as the view. Family designed and built, it sits on Oak Creek, near Indian reservations and fantastic shopping. A professional cooking staff prepares different breakfasts and hors d'oeuvres daily. 13 rooms, 2 story. Children over 10 years only. Complimentary full breakfast. Check-in 3-6 pm, check-out 11 am. **$$$**

THE LODGE AT SEDONA. *125 Kallof Pl, Sedona (86336). Phone 928/204-1942; toll-free 800/619-4467; fax 928/204-2128. www.lodgeatsedona.com.* Two hours south of the Grand Canyon, this lodge is situated on 2 1/2 wooded acres with rustic timber and red sandstone decor. A labyrinth of rocks on a clearing of red earth creates a quiet place to meditate. 14 rooms, 2 story. Complimentary full breakfast. Check-in 4-8 pm, check-out 11 am. **$$$**

SOUTHWEST INN AT SEDONA. *3250 W Hwy 89A, Sedona (86336). Phone 928/282-3344; toll-free 800/483-7422; fax 928/282-0267. www.swinn.com.* This Santa Fe-style inn offers the best of Sedona with all the amenities of home. Relax with a breathtaking view from your room or soak in the beautifully landscaped pool. 28 rooms, 2 story. Complimentary continental breakfast. Check-in 3–9 pm, check-out 11 am. Fitness room. Pool, whirlpool. **$$**

TERRITORIAL HOUSE BED AND BREAKFAST. *65 Piki Dr, Sedona (86336). Phone 928/204-2737; toll-free 800/801-2737; fax 928/204-2230. www.territorialhousebb.com.* The Old West comes alive with the sounds of the wild, and with tastefully decorated rooms reminiscent of the old Western movies. Deliciously hearty breakfasts and late-day snacks are just parts of the hospitality guests find here. 4 rooms, 2 story. Complimentary full breakfast. Check-in 4-6 pm, check-out 11 am. **$**

Restaurants

★★ COWBOY CLUB. *241 N Hwy 89A, Sedona (86336). Phone 928/282-4200; fax 928/204-5985. www.cowboyclub.com.* Lunch, dinner. Closed Thanksgiving, Dec 25. Bar. Children's menu. **$$$**

★★★ HEARTLINE CAFE. *1610 W Hwy 89A, Sedona (86336). Phone 928/282-0785; fax 928/204-9206. www.heartlinecafe.com.* This intimate and cozy restaurant in a cottage surrounded by an English garden showcases unique daily specials. Eclectic menu. Lunch, dinner. Bar. Children's menu. Outdoor seating. **$$**

★ **HIDEAWAY.** *179 Country Sq, Sedona (86336). Phone 928/282-4204; fax 928/282-7583. www.sedona.net/hideaway.* The outdoor dining area here overlooks Oak Creek and the Red Rock Mountains. Italian menu. Lunch, dinner. Closed Thanksgiving, Dec 24-25. Bar. Outdoor seating. **$**

★★★ **L'AUBERGE.** *301 L'Auberge Ln, Sedona (86339). Phone 928/282-1667; fax 928/282-2885. www.lauberge.com.* Overlooking Oak Creek, the dining room is decorated with imported fabrics and fine china. French menu. Breakfast, lunch, dinner, Sun brunch. Bar. Children's menu. Jacket (dinner). Outdoor seating. **$$**

★★★ **PIETRO'S.** *2445 W Hwy 89A # 3, Sedona (86336). Phone 928/282-2525. www.pietrossedona.com.* This charming little café has a cozy bar, wine cellar, and enclosed patio. The menu features simple, but elegant, northern Italian cuisine. Guests can try the early-bird menu, which offers six entrée selections. Italian menu. Dinner. Closed Dec 25. Bar. **$$$**

★★★ **RENÉ AT TLAQUEPAQUE.** *Hwy 179, Sedona (86336). Phone 928/282-9225; fax 928/282-5629. www.rene-sedona.com.* French, American menu. Lunch, dinner. Closed Dec 25. Bar. Outdoor seating. **$$$**

★★★ **SHUGRUE'S HILLSIDE GRILL.** *671 Hwy 179, Sedona (86336). Phone 928/282-5300; fax 928/282-7379. www.shugrues.com.* American menu. Lunch, dinner. Closed Dec 25. Bar. Children's menu. Outdoor seating. **$$$**

★ **WILD TOUCAN.** *2081 W Hwy 89A, Sedona (86340). Phone 928/284-1604; fax 928/284-0517. www.wildtoucan.com.* Lunch, dinner. Closed Thanksgiving, Dec 25. Bar. Children's menu. **$$**

★★★ **YAVAPAI.** *525 Boynton Canyon Rd, Sedona (86336). Phone 928/204-6000; fax 928/282-1370. www.enchantmentresort.com.* At this fine-dining restaurant, guests watch the breathtaking Boynton Canyon through large windows that provide a 180-degree view. Guests can enjoy the sunset while dining on the terrace. American menu. Breakfast, lunch, dinner, Sun brunch. Children's menu. Casual attire. Outdoor seating. **$$$**

Seligman (B-2)

See also Flagstaff, Williams

Population 456
Elevation 5,242 ft
Area Code 928
Zip 86337
Information Chamber of Commerce, Box 65, 86337; phone 928/422-3939

What to See and Do

Grand Canyon Caverns. *Old Rte 66, mile marker 115, Peach Springs. 25 miles W on Rte 66. Phone 928/422-3223. www.gccaverns.com.* Includes the 18,000-square-foot "Chapel of Ages" and other rooms and tunnels; 3/4-mile trail; temperature 56° F. Elevator takes visitors 210 feet underground; 50-minute guided tours. Motel, restaurant; Western-style cookouts (May-Sept). (Summer: daily 8 am-6 pm; winter: 10 am-5 pm; closed Dec 25; tours depart every half hour) Golden Age Passport accepted. **$$$**

Sells (E-3)

See also Tucson

Population 2,799
Elevation 2,360 ft
Area Code 520
Zip 85634
Information Tohono O'Odham Nation Executive Office, Box 837; phone 520/383-2028

This is the headquarters of the Tohono O'Odham Indian Reservation (almost 3 million acres). The Papagos farm, raise cattle, and craft pottery and baskets. The main road (Hwy 86) passes through the reservation, and side roads lead to other villages. The older houses are made of saguaro ribs plastered with mud. More recently, burnt adobe (mud brick) construction and conventional housing have been adopted.

What to See and Do

Kitt Peak National Observatory. *Tohono O'Odham Reservation, Sells. Approximately 36 miles NE on Hwy 86, then 12 miles S on Hwy 386, in the Quinlan*

Mountains of the Sonoran Desert (elevation 6,882 feet). Phone 520/318-8726. www.noao.edu/kpno. (National Optical Astronomy Observatories) Site of world's largest collection of ground-based optical telescopes; 36-, 50-, 84-, and 158-inch stellar telescopes; world's largest solar telescope (60 inches). Visitor center (daily 9 am-3:45 pm) with exhibits. Tours (daily 10 am, 11:30 am, 1:30 pm). Observatory (daily; closed holidays). **DONATION**

Show Low (C-5)

See also McNary, Pinetop

Population 7,695
Elevation 6,347 ft
Area Code 928
Zip 85901
Information Show Low Regional Chamber of Commerce, 951 W Deuce of Clubs, PO Box 1083, 85902; phone 928/537-2326 or toll-free 888-SHOW-LOW
Web site www.ci.show-low.az.us

This town, astride the Mogollon Rim on Hwy 60, is a good stop for the golf enthusiast, angler, photographer, or nature lover.

What to See and Do

Apache-Sitgreaves National Forests. *309 S Mountain Ave, Show Low. Phone 928/333-4301; toll-free 800/280-2267 (reservations). www.fs.fed.us/r3/asnf.* Combined into one administrative unit, these two forests (see SPRINGERVILLE) encompass more than 2 million acres of diverse terrain. The Sitgreaves Forest (Hwy 260) is named for Captain Lorenzo Sitgreaves, conductor of the first scientific expedition across the state in the 1850s; part of the General George Cook military trail is here. Fishing; hunting, self-guided nature hikes, picnicking, camping (dump station; fee). Sat evening programs in summer.

Fishing. *915 W Deuce of Clubs, Show Low. Phone 928/537-2326.* **Rainbow Lake.** *8 miles SE on Hwy 260.* **Show Low Lake.** *4 miles SE off Hwy 260.* **Fool Hollow Lake.** *3 miles NW.* Many other lakes in the area. Boat rentals at some lakes.

Hunting. *915 W Deuce of Clubs, Show Low. Phone 928/537-2326.* Elk, deer, turkeys, bears, mountain lions, bighorn sheep, and antelopes.

Limited-Service Hotels

★★ BEST WESTERN PAINT PONY LODGE. *581 W Deuce of Clubs Ave, Show Low (85901). Phone 928/537-5773; fax 928/537-5766. www.bestwestern.com.* 50 rooms, 2 story. Pets accepted; fee. Complimentary continental breakfast. Check-out 11 am. Restaurant, bar. Airport transportation available. **$**

★★ DAYS INN. *PO Box 2437, Show Low (85902). Phone 928/537-4356; fax 928/537-8692. www.daysinn.com.* 122 rooms, 2 story. Pets accepted; fee. Complimentary full breakfast. Check-out noon. Restaurant. Pool. Airport transportation available. **$**

Sierra Vista (F-4)

See also Bisbee, Patagonia

Population 37,775
Elevation 4,623 ft
Area Code 520
Zip 85635
Information Chamber of Commerce, 21 E Wilcox; phone 520/458-6940
Web site www.visitsierravista.com

What to See and Do

Coronado National Forest. *300 W Congress St, Sierra Vista. Phone 520/670-4552. www.fs.fed.us/r3/coronado.* (See TUCSON) One of the larger sections of the forest lies to the south and west of Fort Huachuca Military Reservation. Picnicking, camping (fee). Parker Canyon Lake offers boating, fishing, and camping (fee). A Ranger District office is located in Sierra Vista.

Coronado National Memorial. *4101 E Montezuma Canyon Rd, Sierra Vista. 16 miles S via Hwy 92 to S Coronado Memorial Dr. Phone 520/366-5515. www.nps.gov/coro.* Commanding view of part of Coronado's route through the Southwest in 1540-1542. Hiking trails, picnic grounds. Visitor center (daily 9 am-5 pm; closed Jan 1, Dec 25). Grounds (daily 8 am-5 pm; closed Jan 1, Dec 25). **FREE**

Fort Huachuca. *Hwy 90, Sierra Vista. Phone 520/538-7111. huachuca-www.army.mil.* Founded by the US Army in 1877 to protect settlers and travelers from hostile Apache raids, the fort is now the home of the US Army Intelligence Center, the Information Systems Command, and the Electronic Proving Ground. A historical museum is on the "Old Post," Boyd and Grierson avenues (Mon-Fri 9 am-4 pm, Sat-Sun 1-4 pm; closed Jan 1, Thanksgiving, Dec 25). The historic Old Post area (1885-1895) is typical of frontier post construction and is home to the post's ceremonial cavalry unit; open to public. Directions and visitor's pass at main gate, just west of Sierra Vista. Bronze statue of buffalo soldier. **DONATION**

Specialty Lodging

The following lodging establishment is approved by Mobil Travel Guide but, due to its unique and individualized nature has not been given a traditional Mobil Star rating. Included in this listing you may find bed-and-breakfasts, limited-service inns, guest ranches, and other unique hotel properties.

RAMSEY CANYON INN. *29 E Ramsey Canyon Rd, Hereford (85615). Phone 520/378-3010; fax 520/378-1480. www.ramseycanyoninn.com.* Situated on a winding mountain stream, in a wooded canyon, this is a hummingbird haven. More than 10 species visit the inn's feeders during the year. 9 rooms. Children under 16 years cottages only. Complimentary full breakfast. Check-in 3 pm, check-out 11 am. **$$**

Restaurant

★★ MESQUITE TREE. *Hwy 92 S and Carr Canyon Rd, Sierra Vista (85635). Phone 520/378-2758; fax 520/378-3003. www.mesquitetreerestaurant.com.* Steak menu. Dinner. Closed Mon; Thanksgiving, Dec 25. Bar. Children's menu. Outdoor seating. **$$**

Springerville (C-5)

See also Greer, McNary

Population 1,972
Elevation 6,968 ft
Area Code 928
Zip 85938
Information Round Valley Chamber of Commerce, 318 E Main St, PO Box 31; phone 928/333-2123
Web site www.springerville.com

The headquarters for the Apache-Sitgreaves National Forests is located here.

What to See and Do

Apache-Sitgreaves National Forests. *309 S Mountain Ave, Springerville. Phone 928/333-4301.* Combined into one administrative unit, these two forests (see SHOW LOW) encompass more than 2 million acres of diverse terrain. The Apache Forest (on Hwy 180/666) features the Mount Baldy, Escudilla, and Bear Wallow wilderness areas and Blue Range Primitive Area, which are accessible only by foot or horseback, and the Coronado Trail (Hwy 666), the route followed by the explorer in 1540. Lake and stream fishing; big-game hunting, picnicking, camping (fee charged in some campgrounds).

Lyman Lake State Park. *Hwy 191, Saint Johns. Phone 928/337-4441. www.pr.state.az.us/Parks/parkhtml/lyman.html.* There are 1,180 acres bordering a 1,500-acre reservoir near headwaters of the Little Colorado River; high desert, juniper country. Swimming, waterskiing, fishing (walleye, trout, channel and blue catfish), boating (ramps); hiking, picnicking (shelter), tent and trailer sites (dump station). (Daily 7 am-10 pm)

Madonna of the Trail. *S Mountain and Hwy 60, Springerville. Phone 928/333-2123.* Erected in 1927, the statue is one of 12 identical monuments placed in states along the National Old Trails Highway to commemorate pioneer women who trekked west.

Sunset Crater Volcano National Monument (B-3)

See also Flagstaff

Web site www.nps.gov/sucr

15 miles N of Flagstaff on Hwy 89, then 2 miles E on Sunset Crater/Wupatki Loop Rd.

Between the growing seasons of 1064 and 1065, violent volcanic eruptions built a large cone-shaped mountain of cinders and ash called a cinder cone volcano. Around the base of the cinder cone, lava flowed from cracks, creating the Bonito Lava Flow on the west side of the cone and the Kana'a Lava Flow on the east side. The approximate date of the initial eruption was determined by examining tree rings of timber found in the remains of Native American pueblos at Wupatki National Monument (see).

This cinder cone, now called Sunset Crater, stands about 1,000 feet above the surrounding terrain. Mineral deposits around the rim stained the cinders, giving the summit a perpetual sunset hue, thus the name Sunset Crater. Along the Lava Flow Trail at the base of the cone, visitors will find "squeeze-ups" and other geologic features related to lava flows.

Park rangers are on duty all year. Do not attempt to drive off the roads; the cinders are soft, and the surrounding landscape is very fragile. The US Forest Service maintains a campground (May-mid-September; fee) opposite the visitor center. Guided tours and naturalist activities are offered during the summer. Visitor center (daily; closed December 25). A 20-mile paved road leads to Wupatki National Monument (see). Phone 520/556-7042. **$$**

Tempe (D-3)

See also Chandler, Glendale, Litchfield Park, Mesa, Phoenix, Scottsdale

Founded 1871
Population 158,625
Elevation 1,160 ft
Area Code 480
Information Chamber of Commerce, 909 E Apache Blvd, PO Box 28500, 85285; phone 480/967-7891
Web site www.tempecvb.com

Founded as a trading post by the father of former Senator Carl Hayden, this city is now the site of Arizona State University, the state's oldest institution of higher learning.

What to See and Do

Arizona Cardinals (NFL). *ASU Sun Devil Stadium, 5th St and College Ave, Tempe. Phone 480/965-2381 (tickets); toll-free 800/999-1402. www.azcardinals.com.* Professional football team.

Arizona Historical Society Museum. *Papago Park, 1300 N College Ave, Tempe. Phone 480/939-0292. www.arizonahistoricalsociety.org.* Wander through this regional museum to learn more about 20th-century life in the Salt River Valley. The 28,000 items in its collection include about 14,000 pieces in a country store and 2,800 stage props and sets from the 37-year run of the Wallace and Ladmo Show on KPHO Television. Another exhibit focuses on the many ways World War II transformed Arizona. (Tues-Sat 10 am-4 pm, Sun noon-4 pm) **$**

Arizona Mills. *5000 S Arizona Mills Cir, Tempe. Phone 480/491-7300. www.arizonamills.com.* Shoppers on the prowl for bargains flock to this indoor outlet mall, which looks as nice as any regular mall. More than 150 stores offer tempting markdowns, with some of the best buys at headliners such as Kenneth Cole New York, Last Call From Neiman Marcus, OFF 5TH-Saks Fifth Avenue Outlet, and Off Rodeo Dr. Beverly Hills. Shopping diversions include a large food court, five restaurants, a 24-screen cinema, and an IMAX theater. (Daily)

Arizona State University. *University Dr and Mill Ave, Tempe. In town center on Hwy 60/80/89. Phone 480/965-4980 (tours). www.asu.edu.* (1885) (52,000 students) Divided into 13 colleges. Included on the 700-acre main campus are several museums and collections featuring meteorites; anthropology and geology exhibits; the Charles Trumbull Hayden Library, the Walter Cronkite School of Journalism, and the Daniel Noble Science and Engineering Library. Also on campus are

Grady Gammage Memorial Auditorium. *Mill and Apache Blvd, Tempe. Phone 480/965-4050 (tours). www.asu.edu/tour/main/ggma.html.* (1964) Last major work designed by Frank Lloyd Wright. Guided tours (Mon-Fri). **FREE**

Nelson Fine Arts Center. *Tempe. Phone 480/965-2787. asuartmuseum.asu.edu/index.html.* Exhibits of American paintings and sculpture; Latin American art; comprehensive print collection; American crockery and ceramics. Tours available. (Tues (school year) 10 am-9 pm; Tues (summer) 10 am-5 pm; Wed-Sat 10 am-5 pm) **FREE**

Bandersnatch Brew Pub. *125 E Fifth St, Tempe. Phone 480/966-4438. www.bandersnatch-pub.com.* Fresh-brewed beer and tasty Italian food keep the tables hoppin' at this friendly, decidedly casual drinking hole just blocks from Arizona State University. But the cozy pub isn't a hangout for the young and restless exclusively; the eclectic crowd includes stout-hearted ale lovers of all ages who like to tip a few, especially in the large outdoor beer garden. Bring your laptop and take advantage of the DSL hookups and wireless connections. (Daily; closed Easter, Thanksgiving, Dec 25)

Big Surf. *1500 N McClintock, Tempe. Phone 480/947-2477.* Surfer dudes can't hang on ocean beaches in the Valley of the Sun, of course, but your family can go splish-splashing at America's original water park, a 20-acre desert oasis with a Polynesian theme. Lather on the sunscreen, and then ride some big ones in the wave pool, whoosh down 16 slippery water slides, and more. What better way to keep your cool on a sizzling hot day in the desert? (June-mid-Aug, daily; late May and mid-late Aug, weekends; closed rest of year) **$$$$**

Niels Petersen House Museum. *1414 W Southern Ave, Tempe. Phone 480/350-5151.* Built in 1892 and remodeled in the 1930s. Restoration retains characteristics of both the Victorian era and the 1930s. Half-hour, docent-guided tours available. (Tues-Thurs, Sat 10 am-2 pm) **FREE**

Phoenix Rock Gym. *1353 E University, Tempe. Phone 480/921-8322. www.phoenixrockgym.com.* At Arizona's largest climbing gym, 30-foot-high walls of varying difficulty await fitness buffs who want to claw their way to the top indoors instead of outdoors. The gym also welcomes novices eager to develop rock-hard muscles. For safety's sake, first-timers receive some brief video training and a hands-on orientation before they do any scaling. Rule number one: hold on tight. Gear is available to rent. (Daily; closed Jan 1, Thanksgiving, Dec 25) **$$$**

Tempe Bicycle Program. *20 E 6th St, 3rd floor, Tempe. Phone 480/350-2775. www.tempe.gov/bikeprogram.* For a change of pace, two-wheel your way around Tempe. This bicycle friendly city has more than 150 miles of bikeways along its streets and through its parks. For your convenience, most major destinations provide bicycle racks, some particularly eye-catching ones designed by local artists. If you get tired and want to hitch a ride, city buses are also equipped with racks. Several bicycle shops offer rentals for as little as $15 per day—and they also have free bikeway maps to keep you on the right path.

Tempe Historical Museum. *809 E Southern Ave, Tempe. Phone 480/350-5100. www.tempe.gov/museum/default.asp.* Exhibits relate the history of Tempe from the prehistoric Hohokam to the present, with artifacts, videos, and interactive exhibits. Research library; gift shop. (Mon-Thurs, Sat 10 am-5 pm, Sun 1-5 pm; closed holidays) **FREE**

Tempe Improvisation Comedy Theatre. *930 E University Dr, Tempe. Phone 480/921-9877. www.tempeimprov.com.* If you need a few laughs, take a seat here and listen to some of the country's best stand-up comedians say the darnedest things. Unless you're a real sourpuss, these foolish folks will surely crack you up with their zaniness. An optional dinner precedes the 8 pm shows. (Thurs-Sun; major holidays) **$$$$**

Special Events

Anaheim Angels Spring Training. *Tempe Diablo Stadium, 2200 W Alameda Dr, Tempe. Phone 602/438-9300; toll-free 888/994-2567. cactus-league.com/angels.html.* Anaheim Angels baseball spring training, exhibition games. Early Mar-early Apr.

Spring Festival of the Arts. *804 St. Germanine St, Tempe. Phone 480/965-2278.* Last weekend in Mar.

Tempe Festival of the Arts. *Mill Ave, Tempe. Downtown. Phone 480/967-4877. www.millavenue.org/tfa.htm.* When a three-day event attracts nearly a quarter-million people, you know that it belongs at the top of your to-do list, too. For this blast of a street party, Mill Avenue in downtown Tempe closes to traffic so that fun-loving people of all ages can have a good time milling around. They buy handmade goods from more than 500 artisans, chow down on tasty food from around the world, quench their thirst with ice-cold beer and other beverages, and rock to live bands amped up on multiple stages. In an area just for them, youngsters make their own fun creating crafts and taking part in activities designed to make any kid smile. The best news: this party gets crankin' twice a year, in spring and fall. Late Mar and early Dec.

Tostitos Fiesta Bowl. *ASU Sun Devil Stadium, 5th St and College Ave, Tempe. Phone 480/350-0900. www.tostitosfiestabowl.com.* College football game. Early Jan.

Tostitos Fiesta Bowl Block Party. *Tempe Beach Park and Mill Ave, Tempe. Phone 480/350-0900. www.tostitosfiestabowl.com/events/block.html.* Includes games, rides, entertainment, pep rally, fireworks, food. Dec 31.

Limited-Service Hotels

★ COUNTRY INN & SUITES. *1660 W Elliot, Tempe (85284). Phone 480/345-8585; toll-free 800/*

456-4000; fax 480/345-7461. www.countryinns.com. 138 rooms, 3 story. Pets accepted; fee. Complimentary continental breakfast. Check-in 3 pm, check-out noon. High-speed Internet access. Pool, children's pool, whirlpool. Airport transportation available. **$**

★ ★ EMBASSY SUITES. *4400 S Rural Rd, Tempe (85282). Phone 480/897-7444; toll-free 800/362-2779; fax 480/897-6112. www.embassysuitestempe.com.* This hotel is only 3 miles from Arizona State University. 224 rooms, 3 story, all suites. Complimentary full breakfast. Check-in 3 pm, check-out 1 pm. Restaurant, bar. Fitness room. Pool, whirlpool. Airport transportation available. **$**

★ HOLIDAY INN EXPRESS. *5300 S Priest Dr, Tempe (85283). Phone 480/820-7500; toll-free 800/465-4329; fax 480/730-6626. www.hiexpress.com/tempeaz.* 160 rooms, 4 story. Pets accepted, some restrictions; fee. Complimentary continental breakfast. Check-in 2 pm, check-out noon. High-speed Internet access. Fitness room. Pool, whirlpool. Airport transportation available. **$**

Full-Service Hotels

★ ★ SHERATON PHOENIX AIRPORT HOTEL TEMPE. *1600 S 52nd St, Tempe (85281). Phone 480/967-6600; toll-free 800/346-3049; fax 480/966-2392. www.sheraton.com/phoenixairport.* 210 rooms, 4 story. Pets accepted, some restrictions; fee. Check-in 3 pm, check-out noon. Restaurant, bar. Fitness room. Pool, whirlpool. Airport transportation available. Business center. **$**

★ ★ TEMPE MISSION PALMS HOTEL. *60 E 5th St, Tempe (85281). Phone 480/894-1400; toll-free 800/547-8705; fax 480/968-7677. www.missionpalms .com.* This southwestern-style hotel is located in Old Town Tempe, within walking distance of the Sun Devil Stadium. 303 rooms, 4 story. Check-in 4 pm, check-out noon. High-speed Internet access. Restaurant, bar. Fitness room. Pool, whirlpool. Tennis. Airport transportation available. Business center. **$$**

Full-Service Resorts

★ ★ FIESTA INN RESORT. *2100 S Priest Dr, Tempe (85282). Phone 480/967-1441; toll-free 800/501-7590; fax 480/967-0224. www.fiestainnresort.com.* Frank Lloyd Wright's design influence is evident from the landscape and lobby to the guest rooms at this beautiful inn. 271 rooms, 3 story. Check-in 2 pm, check-out 11 am. Restaurant, bar. Fitness room. Pool, whirlpool. Tennis. Airport transportation available. Business center. **$**

★ ★ ★ THE WYNDHAM BUTTES RESORT. *2000 Westcourt Way, Tempe (85282). Phone 602/225-9000; toll-free 800/996-3426; fax 602/438-8622. www.wyndham.com.* Large resort, with a heliport, built into the mountainside. 353 rooms, 5 story. Check-in 3 pm, check-out noon. Restaurant, bar. Fitness room, spa. Outdoor pool, children's pool, whirlpool. Tennis. Business center. **$$**

Restaurants

★ ★ BYBLOS. *3332 S Mill Ave, Tempe (85282). Phone 480/894-1945; fax 480/829-8022. www.amdest .com/az/tempe/br/byblos.html.* Mediterranean menu. Lunch, dinner. Closed Mon; Jan 1, Dec 25; also three weeks in July. Belly dancing the last Sun of the month. Bar. Casual attire. **$$**

★ ★ HOUSE OF TRICKS. *114 E 7th St, Tempe (85281). Phone 480/968-1114; fax 480/968-0080. www. houseoftricks.com.* Restored cottage (1918); hardwood and tile floors, stone fireplace. American menu. Lunch, dinner. Closed Sun; holidays; also the first two weeks in Aug. Bar. Children's menu. Casual attire. Outdoor seating. **$$**

★ MACAYO DEPOT CANTINA. *300 S Ash Ave, Tempe (85281). Phone 480/966-6677; fax 480/894-9196. www.macayo.com.* Old Mexican-style cantina located in a converted train station. Mexican menu. Lunch, dinner, late-night. Bar. Children's menu. Casual attire. Outdoor seating. **$**

★ ★ MARCELLO'S PASTA GRILL. *1701 E Warner Rd, Tempe (85284). Phone 480/831-0800; fax 480/831-5745. www.marcellospastagrill.com.* Italian menu. Dinner. Closed holidays. Bar. Children's menu. Casual attire. Outdoor seating. **$$**

★ **SIAMESE CAT.** *5034 S Price Rd, Tempe (85282). Phone 480/820-0406. www.thesiamesecat.com.* Thai menu. Dinner. Closed holidays. Casual attire. **$**

Tombstone (E-5)

See also Bisbee

Founded 1879
Population 1,504
Elevation 4,540 ft
Area Code 520
Zip 85638
Information Tombstone Chamber of Commerce, PO Box 995; 888/457-3929.
Web site www.tombstone.org

Shortly after Ed Schieffelin discovered silver, Tombstone became a rough-and-tumble town with saloons, bawdyhouses, and lots of gunfighting. Tombstone's most famous battle was that of the O.K. Corral, between the Earps and the Clantons in 1881. Later, water rose in the mines and could not be pumped out; fires and other catastrophes occurred, but Tombstone was "the town too tough to die." Now a health and winter resort, it is also a museum of Arizona frontier life. In 1962, the town was designated a National Historic Landmark by the US Department of the Interior.

What to See and Do

Bird Cage Theatre. *517 E Allen, Tombstone. Phone 520/457-3421; toll-free 800/457-3423. www.tombstoneaz.net.* Formerly a frontier cabaret (1880s), this landmark has seen many of the West's most famous characters. In its heyday, it was known as "the wildest and wickedest nightspot between Basin Street and the Barbary Coast." The upstairs "cages," where feathered girls plied their trade, inspired the refrain "only a bird in a gilded cage." Original fixtures and furnishings. (Daily) **$$**

Boothill Graveyard. *Tombstone. NW on Hwy 80 W. Phone 520/457-9344.* About 250 marked graves, some with unusual epitaphs, many of famous characters. **FREE**

Crystal Palace Saloon. *420 Allen St, Tombstone. Phone 520/457-3611. www.crystalpalacesaloon.com.* Restored. Dancing Fri-Sun evenings. (Daily)

O.K. Corral. *308 Allen St E, Tombstone. Phone 520/457-3456. www.ok-corral.com.* Restored stagecoach office and buildings surrounding the gunfight site; life-size figures; Fly's Photography Gallery (adjacent) has early photos. (Daily 9 am-5 pm; closed Dec 25) **$$$**

Rose Tree Inn Museum. *116 S 4th St, Tombstone. Phone 520/457-3326.* Largest rose bush in the world, spreading over 8,000 square feet; blooms in April. The museum is housed in an 1880 boarding house (the oldest house in town); original furniture, documents. (Daily 9 am-5 pm; closed Dec 25) **$**

St. Paul's Episcopal Church. *19 N 3rd St, Tombstone. 3rd and Safford sts. Phone 520/432-5402. www.1882.org.* (1882) Oldest Protestant church still in use in the state; original fixtures. Services 10:30 am every Sun.

Tombstone Courthouse State Historic Park. *219 E Toughnut St, Tombstone. Off Hwy 80. Phone 520/457-3311. www.pr.state.az.us/Parks/parkhtml/tombstone.html.* Victorian building (1882) houses exhibits that recall Tombstone in the turbulent 1880s. Tombstone and Cochise County history. (Daily 8 am-5 pm; closed Dec 25)

Tombstone Epitaph Museum. *9 S 5th St, Tombstone. Phone 520/457-2211. www.tombstone-epitaph.com.* The oldest continuously published newspaper in Arizona, founded in 1880; it is now a monthly journal of Western history. Office houses a collection of early printing equipment. (Daily 9:30 am-5 pm) **FREE**

Tombstone Historama. *308 Allen St E, Tombstone. Adjacent to the O.K. Corral. Phone 520/457-3456.* Electronic diorama and film narrated by Vincent Price tell the story of Tombstone. (Daily 9 am-5 pm; hourly showings; closed Dec 25) **$$**

Special Events

Helldorado. *Phone 520/457-3197.* Three days of Old West re-enactments of Tombstone events of the 1880s. Third full weekend in Oct.

Territorial Days. *4th and Fremont sts, Tombstone. Phone 520/457-9317.* Commemorates formal founding of the town. Fire-hose cart races and other events typical of a celebration in Arizona's early days. Second weekend in Mar.

Wild West Days and Rendezvous of Gunfighters. *O.K. Corral, 308 Allen St E, Tombstone. Phone 520/457-9465.*

Gunfights and Saloons

Begin exploring "The Town Too Tough to Die" on Toughnut Street. At the corner of Third and Toughnut, explore the gorgeous Cochise County Courthouse, now a museum and state historic park. Built in 1882, it's a beautiful testament to Victorian Neoclassical architecture; check out the town gallows in the courtyard, and browse the book shop. To the west a few steps, Victoria's B&B Wedding Chapel (on Toughnut between Second and Third) is located in an 1880s home. To the east one block, the Rose Tree Inn Museum at Fourth and Toughnut occupies another 1880s home; inside its courtyard is a century-old rose tree that blooms every April and covers an 8,000-square-foot space. At Fifth and Toughnut streets, Nellie Cashman's is the oldest restaurant in town, specializing in homemade pies.

Now follow Third Street north one block to Allen Street, essentially the main drag of historic Tombstone. Stop in between Third and Fourth streets on Allen, where the Historama offers a 30-minute presentation (narrated by Vincent Price) that tells the town story in film and animated figures. Next door, see life-size figures in the O.K. Corral, the alleged site of the legendary gunfight between the Earp and Clanton brothers and Doc Holliday. (Actually, it took place on nearby Fremont Street.) Across the street, Tombstone Art Gallery offers works by local artisans and crafters.

On the corner of Allen and Fifth streets, the Crystal Palace Saloon has been restored to its 1879 glory, looking every bit the lusty watering hole and gambling den of legend. On the block of Allen between Fifth and Sixth streets, the Prickly Pear Museum is chock-full of military history; on Allen at Sixth, find the famous old Bird Cage Theater Museum. The Pioneer Home Museum, between Eighth and Ninth streets, continues telling the rowdy-days story.

From Fifth and Allen, walk north a half-block to the Tombstone Epitaph Museum to see an 1880s printing press and newsroom equipment and buy a copy of the 1881 Epitaph report of the O.K. Corral shoot-out. Continue walking north of Fifth, crossing Fremont Street and turning left onto Safford Street. Walk west on Safford three blocks to Second and Safford, where the two-story adobe called Buford House B&B occupies an 1880s home bearing a National Historic Landmark plaque.

This annual event showcases different gunfight re-enactment groups from throughout the United States. Activities include costume contests and a parade. Labor Day weekend.

Wyatt Earp Days. *O.K. Corral, 108 W Allen St E, Tombstone. Phone 520/457-3434.* This annual festival is held in honor of the famous lawman. The festivities include a barbecue, gunfights, street entertainment, dances, and a chili cook-off. There are also fiddlers' contests. Memorial Day weekend.

Restaurants

★ LONGHORN. *501 E Allen St, Tombstone (85638). Phone 520/457-3405; fax 520/457-3803. www.bignosekates.com.* American menu. Breakfast, lunch, dinner. Closed Thanksgiving, Dec 25. Casual attire. **$**

★ NELLIE CASHMAN'S. *117 S 5th St, Tombstone (85638). Phone 520/457-2212.* In historic adobe building (1879); established in 1882 by Nellie Cashman, "the angel of Tombstone," at height of silver boom. American menu. Breakfast, lunch, dinner. Casual attire. Outdoor seating. **$$**

Tucson (E-4)

See also Nogales, Sells

Founded 1775
Population 486,669
Elevation 2,386 ft
Area Code 520
Information Metropolitan Tucson Convention & Visitors Bureau, 110 S Church Ave, #7199, 85701; phone 520/624-1817
Web site www.visittucson.org

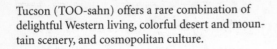

Tucson (TOO-sahn) offers a rare combination of delightful Western living, colorful desert and mountain scenery, and cosmopolitan culture.

It is one of several US cities that developed under four flags. The Spanish standard flew first over the Presidio of Tucson, built to withstand Apache attacks in 1776. Later, Tucson flew the flags of Mexico, the Confederate States and, finally, the United States.

Today, Tucson is a resort area, an educational and copper center, a cotton and cattle market, headquarters for the Coronado National Forest, and a place of business for several large industries. Health-seekers, under proper medical advice, nearly always find relief. The city's shops, restaurants, resorts, and points of interest are varied and numerous.

What to See and Do

Arizona Historical Society Fort Lowell Museum. *2900 N Craycroft Rd, Tucson. In Fort Lowell County Park, N end of Craycroft Rd. Phone 520/885-3832. www.oflna.org/fort_lowell_museum/ftlowell.htm.* Reconstruction of commanding officer's quarters. Exhibits, period furniture. (Wed-Sat 10 am-4 pm; closed holidays) **FREE**

Arizona Historical Society Fremont House Museum. *151 S Granada Ave, Tucson. In the Tucson Community Center Complex, downtown. Phone 520/622-0956.* (Circa 1880) Adobe house restored and furnished in period style. Once occupied by John C. Frémont's daughter, Elizabeth, when he was territorial governor (1878-1881). Special programs all year, including slide shows on Arizona history (Sat; free) and walking tours of historic sites (Nov-Mar, Sat; fee; registration in advance). Museum (Wed-Sat 10 am-4 pm). **$**

Arizona Historical Society Museum, Library, and Archives. *949 E 2nd St, Tucson. Phone 520/628-5774.* Exhibits depicting state history from the Spanish colonial period to present; Arizona mining hall; photography gallery. Research library (Mon-Sat) contains collections on Western history; manuscripts. (Mon-Sat, also Sun afternoons; closed holidays) **DONATION**

Catalina State Park. *11570 N Oracle Rd, Tucson. 9 miles N on Hwy 77. Phone 520/628-5798. www.desertusa.com/azcatalina/azcatalina.html.* A 5,500-acre desert park with a vast array of plants and wildlife; bird area (nearly 170 species). Nature and horseback riding trails, hiking, trail access to adjacent Coronado National Forest; picnicking, camping (dump station). **$**

Colossal Cave Mountain Park. *16721 E Old Spanish Trail Rd, Vail, CO. 19 miles SE on I-10 to Vail, exit 279, then follow the signs for 7 miles N. Phone 520/647-7275. www.colossalcave.com.* Inside the cave, fossilized marine life provides evidence of an ocean that once covered the Arizona desert. 70° F year-round. Forty-five-minute to one-hour guided tours. Other activities in the park include horseback riding trails, hayrides, stagecoach rides, and wildlife. (Mid-Mar-mid-Sept: Mon-Sat 8 am-6 pm, Sun and holidays 8 am-7 pm; mid-Sept-mid-Mar: Mon-Sat 9 am-5 pm, Sun and holidays 9 am-6 pm) **$$**

Columbia University's Biosphere 2 Center. *32540 S Biosphere Rd, Tucson. 35 miles N on Hwy 89 to Hwy 77 milepost 96.5, then 1/2 mile N to Biosphere 2 Rd. Phone 520/896-6220. www.bio2.edu.* An ambitious attempt to learn more about our planet's ecosystems began in September 1991 with the first of a series of missions in this 3 1/2-acre, glass-enclosed, self-sustaining model of Earth. Isolated from the outside, a rotating crew of researchers rely entirely on the air, water, and food generated and recycled within the structure. It contains over 3,500 species of plants and animals in multiple ecosystems, including a tropical rain forest with an 85-foot-high mountain. Visitors are permitted within the biospherian living areas of the enclosure. They may also view the interior from outside as well as enjoy many other exhibits located throughout the campus. Because of variance in research schedule, the biospherian crew may not always be present. Walking tours (wear comfortable shoes) include multimedia introduction to Biosphere 2. Visitor center, observatory, gift shop, restaurant. (Daily 8:30 am-5 pm; closed Dec 25) **$$$**

Coronado National Forest. *300 W Congress St, Tucson. Phone 520/670-4552. www.fs.fed.us/r3/coronado.* Mount Lemmon Recreation Area, part of this forest (almost 2 million acres), offers fishing, bird-watching, hiking, horseback riding, picnicking, skiing, and camping (fee). Madera Canyon offers recreation facilities and a lodge. Peña Blanca Lake and Recreation Area (see NOGALES) and the Chiricahua Wilderness area in the southeast corner of the state are part of the 12 areas that make up the forest. The Santa Catalina Ranger District, located in Tucson (phone 520/749-

8700), has its headquarters at Sabino Canyon, 12 miles northeast on Sabino Canyon Rd; a 1/4-mile nature trail begins at the headquarters, as does a shuttle ride almost 4 miles into Sabino Canyon (fee). Northeast, east, and south of the city.

Gray Line bus tours. *181 W Broadway Blvd, Tucson. Phone 520/622-8811; toll-free 800/276-1528. www.graylinearizona.com.* This popular tour company offers sightseeing tours, package tours, and charter services in the Tucson area.

Greyhound racing. *Tucson Greyhound Park. 2601 S 3rd Ave, Tucson. Phone 520/884-7576; toll-free 800/777-7275. www.tucdogtrak.com.* Pari-mutuel wagering. (Daily 9:30 am-midnight; call for schedule and off-track betting locations)

International Wildlife Museum. *4800 W Gates Pass Rd, Tucson. On Speedway 5 miles W of I-10. Phone 520/617-1439. www.thewildlifemuseum.org.* Includes hundreds of wildlife exhibits from around the world; hands-on, interactive computer displays; videos; café. (Mon-Fri 9 am-5 pm, Sat-Sun 9 am-6 pm; closed Thanksgiving, Dec 25) **$$**

The Lodge at Ventana Canyon-Canyon Course. *6200 N Clubhouse Ln, Tucson. For information, phone toll-free 866/564-7667, or see www.ventanacanyonclub.com.* Golf.

Mountain Course at The Lodge at Ventana Canyon. *6200 N Clubhouse Ln, Tucson. For information, phone toll-free 866/564-7667, or see www.ventanacanyonclub.com.* Golf.

Mount Lemmon Ski Valley. *10300 Ski Run Rd, Mount Lemmon. 35 miles NE via Mt Lemmon Hwy. Phone 520/576-1321 (information). www.fs.fed.us/r3/coronado/scrd/rec/skiing/skivalley.htm.* Double chairlift, two tows; patrol, school, rentals; snack bar, restaurant. Twenty-one runs, longest run 1 mile; vertical drop 900 feet. (Late Dec-mid-Apr, daily) Chairlift operates the rest of the year (daily; fee). Nature trails. **$$$$**

Old Town Artisans. *201 N Court Ave, Tucson. Phone 520/623-6024. www.oldtownartisans.com.* Restored adobe buildings (circa 1850s) in the historic El Presidio neighborhood are a marketplace for handcrafted Southwestern and Latin American art. Courtyard café. Shops (Sept-May: Mon-Sat 9:30 am-5:30 pm, Sun 11 am-5 pm; June-Aug: Mon-Sat 10 am-4 pm, Sun 11 am-4 pm; closed holidays). The Modern Hand Gallery (Mon-Sat 10 am-5 pm, Sun noon-5 pm; closed holidays)

Pima Air & Space Museum. *6000 E Valencia Rd, Tucson. Phone 520/574-0462. www.pimaair.org/pasmhome.shtml.* Aviation history exhibits with an outstanding collection of more than 250 aircraft, both military and civilian. Walking tours. (Daily 9 am-5 pm; closed Thanksgiving, Dec 25) **$$**

Reid Park Zoo. *Tucson. Off of Randolph Way, just N of 22nd St. Phone 520/791-4022 (recording). www.tucsonzoo.org.* Picnicking; zoo; rose garden; outdoor performance center. (Daily 9 am-4 pm; closed Dec 25) **$**

Titan Missile Museum. *1580 W Duval Mine Rd, Green Valley. Approximately 20 miles S via I-19, exit 69 (Duval Mine Rd), then W, past La Canada, turn right and follow signs. Phone 520/625-7736. www.pimaair.org/titanmm/titanhome.shtml.* Deactivated Titan II missile on display; memorabilia, models, rocket engine that powered the missile, support vehicles, UH1F helicopter, various exhibits. A one-hour guided tour begins with a briefing and includes a visit down into the missile silo (may be strenuous; comfortable walking shoes required in the missile silo). The silo may also be viewed from a glass observation area located at the museum level. (Nov-Apr: daily 9 am-5 pm; May-Oct: Wed-Sun 9 am-5 pm; closed Thanksgiving, Dec 25) **$$**

Tohono Chul Park. *7366 N Paseo del Norte, Tucson. Ina and Oracle rds. Phone 520/575-8468. www.tohonochulpark.org.* A 37-acre preserve with more than 400 species of arid climate plants; nature trails; demonstration garden; geology wall; recirculating stream; ethnobotanical garden. Many varieties of wild birds visit the park. Exhibits, galleries, tea room, and gift shops in restored adobe house. Walking tours. (Daily 8 am-5 pm; buildings closed holidays) **$**

Tucson Botanical Gardens. *2150 N Alvernon Way, Tucson. Phone 520/326-9686. www.tucsonbotanical.org.* Gardens include Mediterranean and landscaping plants; native wildflowers; tropical greenhouse; xeriscape/solar demonstration garden. Tours, botanical classes; special events. Picnic area (free). (Daily 8:30 am-4:30 pm; closed holidays) **$**

Tucson Mountain Park. *1204 W Silverlake Rd, Tucson. 12 miles W, via Hwy 86 (Ajo Way) about 6 miles to Kinney Rd, turn right. Phone 520/883-4200.* More than 18,000 acres of saguaro cactus and mountain scenery. Picnic facilities. Gilbert Ray Campground (electric hookups, dump station; fee). Also here is

Arizona-Sonora Desert Museum. *2021 N Kinney Rd, Tucson. Phone 520/883-2702. www.desertmuseum.org.* Live desert creatures: mountain lions, beavers, bighorn sheep, birds, tarantulas, prairie dogs, snakes, otters, and many others. Nature trails through labeled desert botanical gardens. Underground earth sciences center with limestone caves; geological, mineral, and mining exhibits. Orientation room provides information on natural history of deserts. (Oct-Feb: 8:30 am-5 pm; Mar-Sept: 7:30 am-5 pm) **$$$**

★ **Tucson Museum of Art.** *140 N Main Ave, Tucson. Phone 520/624-2333. www.tucsonarts.com.* Housed in six renovated buildings within the boundaries of El Presidio Historic District (circa 1800). Pre-Columbian, Spanish colonial, and Western artifacts; decorative arts and paintings; art of the Americas; contemporary art and crafts; changing exhibits. Mexican heritage museum; historic presidio room; 6,000-volume art resource library; art school. (Mon-Sat 10 am-4 pm, Sun noon-4 pm; closed holidays) Free admission Sun. **$**

University of Arizona. *Campbell Ave and 6th St, Tucson. Phone 520/621-5130. www.arizona.edu.* (1885) (35,000 students) The 343-acre campus is beautifully landscaped, with handsome buildings. Visitor center, located at University Boulevard and Cherry Avenue, has campus maps and information on attractions and activities. Tours (Mon-Sat). On campus are

Arizona State Museum. *1013 E University Blvd, Tucson. Phone 520/621-6302. www.statemuseum.arizona.edu.* Exhibits on the Native American cultures of Arizona and the Southwest from 10,000 years ago to the present. (Mon-Fri 8 am-5 pm; closed holidays) **$**

Center for Creative Photography. *University of Arizona, 1030 N Olive Rd, Tucson. S of pedestrian underpass on Speedway Blvd, 1 block E of Park Ave. Phone 520/621-7968. www.library.arizona.edu/branches/ccp/home/home.html.* Archives, museum, and research center include archives of Ansel Adams and Richard Avedon, collection of works by more than 2,000 photographers; changing exhibits. Gallery (Mon-Fri 9 am-5 pm, Sat-Sun noon-5 pm; closed holidays) **FREE**

Flandrau Science Center & Planetarium. *University of Arizona, 1601 E University Blvd, Tucson. Phone 520/621-7827. www.flandrau.org.* Interactive, hands-on science exhibits (Mon-Wed 9 am-5 pm; Thurs-Sat 9 am-5 pm, 7-9 pm; Sun 1-5 pm; closed holidays); planetarium shows (limited hours). Nightly telescope viewing (mid-Aug-mid-May: Wed-Sat 6:40-10 pm; mid-May-mid-Aug: Wed-Sat 7:30-10 pm). **$$**

Mineral Museum. *University of Arizona, N Cherry Ave and E University Blvd, Tucson. Basement of Flandrau Science Center. Phone 520/621-4227. www.geo.arizona.edu/minmus.* Rocks, minerals, gemstones, and cuttings; paleontological materials. Meteorite exhibit. (Mon-Sat 9 am-5 pm, Sun 1-5 pm; closed holidays) **$**

Museum of Art. *University of Arizona, N Park Ave and E Speedway Blvd, Tucson. Phone 520/621-7567. artmuseum.arizona.edu.* Art museum (free) with extensive collection, including Renaissance, baroque, and contemporary art; changing exhibits. (Tues-Fri 9 am-5 pm, Sat-Sun noon-4 pm; closed holidays) Music building and theater, in which plays are produced by students. Inquire locally for programs. **FREE**

Special Events

Arizona Opera. *Tucson Convention Center, 260 S Church Ave, Tucson. Phone 520/293-4336 (office). www.azopera.com.* The high notes of arias have been ringing across the Arizona wilderness for more than 25 years, prompting many a bravo. So if the passionate music of opera lights your fire, you'll likely be drawn to the Tucson Convention Center, where this company produces five operas each season. Oct-Mar: Fri-Sun. **$$$$**

Arizona Theatre Company. *The Temple of Music and Art, 330 S Scott Ave, Tucson. Phone 520/622-2823. www.aztheatreco.org.* The State Theatre of Arizona performs both classic and contemporary works. Evening performances Tues-Sun; matinees Wed, Sat-Sun. Sept-May. **$$$$**

Baseball. *Hi Corbett Field. Tucson Electric Park, 2500 E Ajo Way, Tucson. Phone 520/434-1111.* Colorado Rockies, Chicago White Sox, and Arizona Diamondbacks baseball spring training, exhibition games; late Feb-late Mar. Also the home of the Arizona Diamondbacks' minor league team, the Tucson Sidewinders; Apr-Sept.

Chrysler Classic of Tucson. *Omni Tucson National Golf Resort & Spa, 2727 W Club Dr, Tucson. Phone 520/297-2271. www.tucsonopen.pgatour.com/*

tournaments/r001/charity.html. This $3-million tournament features top pros. Late Feb-early Mar.

Fiesta del Presidio. *Tucson Museum of Art Plaza, 140 N Main Ave, Tucson. Phone 520/624-2333.* Low-rider car show, dancing, Mexican fiesta events, costumes, food.

Gem & Mineral Show. *Tucson Convention Center, 260 S Church Ave, Tucson. Phone 520/322-5773; toll-free 800/638-8350. www.tgms.org.* Displays of minerals; jewelry; lapidary skills; Smithsonian Institution collection. Mid-Feb.

Tucson Meet Yourself Festival. *El Presidio Park, Tucson. Between the Old County Courthouse and City Hall. Phone 520/882-3060. www.tucsonfestival.org/TucsonMeetYourself.html.* Commemorates Tucson's cultural and historic heritage with a torchlight pageant, Native American dances, children's parade, Mexican fiesta, frontier encampment, and other events. Oct.

Tucson Symphony Orchestra. *Tucson Symphony Center, 2175 N 6th Ave, Tucson. Phone 520/882-8585 (box office). www.tucsonsymphony.org/index.html.* Sept-May.

Limited-Service Hotels

★ BEST WESTERN CONTINENTAL INN. *8425 N Cracker Barrel Rd, Marana (85743). Phone 520/579-1099; toll-free 800/937-8376; fax 520/579-6938. www.bestwestern.com.* 65 rooms. Complimentary continental breakfast. Check-in 2 pm, check-out 11 am. Fitness room. Outdoor pool, whirlpool. **$**

★ ★ BEST WESTERN ROYAL SUN INN AND SUITES. *1015 N Stone Ave, Tucson (85705). Phone 520/622-8871; toll-free 800/545-8858; fax 520/623-2267. www.bestwestern.com.* 79 rooms, 2 story. Check-in 2 pm, check-out noon. Restaurant, bar. Pool, whirlpool. **$**

★ ★ CLARION HOTEL AIRPORT. *6801 S Tucson Blvd, Tucson (85706). Phone 520/746-3932; toll-free 800/526-0550; fax 520/889-9934. www.choicehotels.com.* 190 rooms, 2 story. Complimentary full breakfast. Check-in 2 pm, check-out noon. Restaurant, bar. Fitness room. Pool, whirlpool. Airport transportation available. Business center. **$**

★ CLARION HOTEL RANDOLPH PARK. *102 N Alvernon Way, Tucson (85711). Phone 520/795-0330; fax 520/326-2111.* 174 rooms, 3 story. Pets accepted. Complimentary full breakfast. Check-in 3 pm, check-out noon. Fitness room. Pool, children's pool. Business center. **$**

★ COUNTRY INN & SUITES BY CARLSON. *7411 N Oracle Rd, Tucson (85704). Phone 520/575-9255; toll-free 800/456-4000; fax 520/575-8671. www.countryinns.com.* 156 rooms, 3 story. Complimentary continental breakfast. Check-in 3 pm, check-out noon. Pool, whirlpool. Airport transportation available. **$**

★ ★ COURTYARD BY MARRIOTT. *2505 E Executive Dr, Tucson (85706). Phone 520/573-0000; toll-free 800/321-2211; fax 520/573-0470. www.marriott.com.* 165 rooms, 3 story. Check-in 3 pm, check-out noon. Restaurant, bar. Fitness room. Pool, whirlpool. Airport transportation available. **$**

★ ★ DOUBLETREE HOTEL. *445 S Alvernon Way, Tucson (85711). Phone 520/881-4200; fax 520/323-5225. www.doubletreehotels.com.* Ten minutes from downtown and the airport. Directly across the street is the expansive Reid Park. 302 rooms, 9 story. Pets accepted; fee. Check-in 3 pm, check-out noon. Restaurant, bar. Fitness room. Pool, whirlpool. Tennis. Business center. **$**

★ ★ EMBASSY SUITES. *5335 E Broadway, Tucson (85711). Phone 520/745-2700; fax 520/790-9232. www.embassysuites.com.* 142 rooms, 3 story, all suites. Complimentary full breakfast. Check-in 3 pm, check-out noon. Pool, whirlpool. **$**

★ ★ EMBASSY SUITES AIRPORT. *7051 S Tucson Blvd, Tucson (85706). Phone 520/573-0700; toll-free 800/362-2779; fax 520/741-9645. www.embassysuites.com.* 204 rooms, 3 story, all suites. Pets accepted, some restrictions. Complimentary full breakfast. Check-in 3 pm, check-out 1 pm. Restaurant, bar. Fitness room. Pool, whirlpool. Airport transportation available. **$$**

★ ★ **FOUR POINTS BY SHERATON.** *1900 E Speedway Blvd, Tucson (85719). Phone 520/327-7341; fax 520/327-0276. www.fourpoints.com.* 151 rooms, 7 story. Check-in 3 pm, check-out noon. Restaurant, bar. Pool, whirlpool. **$**

★ **HAMPTON INN.** *6971 S Tucson Blvd, Tucson (85706). Phone 520/889-5789; fax 520/889-4002. www.hamptoninn.com.* 129 rooms, 4 story. Complimentary continental breakfast. Check-in 3 pm, check-out noon. Pool, whirlpool. Airport transportation available. **$**

★ ★ **RADISSON CITY CENTER TUCSON.** *181 W Broadway Blvd, Tucson (85701). Phone 520/624-8711; fax 520/624-9963. www.radisson.com.* 309 rooms, 12 story. Pets accepted, some restrictions; fee. Check-in 3 pm, check-out noon. Restaurant, bar. Fitness room. Outdoor pool. Airport transportation available. **$**

★ ★ **SHERATON TUCSON HOTEL AND SUITES.** *5151 E Grant Rd, Tucson (85712). Phone 520/323-6262; toll-free 800/257-7275; fax 520/325-2989. www.sheraton.com.* 216 rooms, 4 story. Pets accepted; fee. Complimentary continental breakfast. Check-in 3 pm, check-out noon. Restaurant, bar. Fitness room. Outdoor pool. **$**

★ **WINDMILL SUITES AT ST. PHILLIPS PLAZA.** *4250 N Campbell Ave, Tucson (85718). Phone 520/577-0007; toll-free 800/547-4747; fax 520/577-0045. www.windmillinns.com.* 122 rooms, 3 story, all suites. Pets accepted. Complimentary continental breakfast. Check-in 4 pm, check-out 11 am. Outdoor pool, whirlpool. **$**

Full-Service Hotel

★ ★ ★ **MARRIOTT TUCSON UNIVERSITY PARK.** *880 E 2nd St, Tucson (85719). Phone 520/792-4100; fax 520/882-4100. www.marriott.com.* Just off of the University of Arizona's campus, this hotel provides the comfort and convenience demanded by business and leisure travelers alike. 267 rooms, 9 story. Check-in 3 pm, check-out noon. Restaurant, bar. Fitness room. Outdoor pool, whirlpool. Business center. **$**

Full-Service Resorts

★ ★ ★ **ARIZONA INN.** *2200 E Elm St, Tucson (85719). Phone 520/325-1541; toll-free 800/933-1093; fax 520/881-5830. www.arizonainn.com.* This family-owned inn was built in 1930 and features quiet comfort in adobe-style buildings (1930) on 15 acres of landscaped lawns and gardens. Guest rooms are individually decorated. 101 rooms, 2 story. Check-in 3 pm, check-out noon. Restaurant. Fitness room. Pool. Tennis. **$$**

★ ★ ★ **THE GOLF VILLAS.** *10950 N La Canada, Tucson (85737). Phone 520/498-0098; toll-free 888/388-0098; fax 520/498-5150. www.thegolfvillas.com.* Luxury one-, two-, and three-bedroom villas afford golf course views. Guests have use of an extensive array of recreational facilities at El Conquistador Country Club across the street. 79 rooms, 2 story. Pets accepted; fee. Check-in 3 pm, check-out noon. Fitness room. Pool. Business center. **$$**

★ ★ ★ **HILTON TUCSON EL CONQUISTADOR GOLF & TENNIS RESORT.** *10000 N Oracle Rd, Tucson (85737). Phone 520/544-5000; toll-free 800/325-7832; fax 520/544-1228. www.hiltonelconquistador.com.* This resort and country club lures visitors with its extensive golf and tennis facilities, including 45 holes and 31 lighted courts, but just gazing at the sunsets and spectacular Santa Catalina Mountain views is therapeutic. The grounds, 2,000 feet below the Pusch Ridge cliffs, feature 45,000 square feet of meeting space. 428 rooms. Pets accepted. Check-in 3 pm, check-out noon. Five restaurants; bars. Children's activity center. Fitness room, spa. Six outdoor pools, children's pool, four whirlpools. Golf (Greg Nash and Jeff Hardely, designers), 45 holes. Tennis. Business center. **$$**

★ ★ ★ **LODGE AT VENTANA CANYON RESORT.** *6200 N Clubhouse Ln, Tucson (85750). Phone 520/577-1400; toll-free 800/828-5701; fax 520/577-4065. wyndhamventanacanyon.com.* The Lodge at Ventana Canyon is a desert paradise. Nestled in the foothills of the Santa Catalina Mountains on a 600-acre desert preserve, the Lodge is a peaceful getaway for tennis players, golfers, and those in pursuit of nothing more challenging than a day at the pool.

Two 18-hole Tom Fazio-designed golf courses wind their way through the stunning landscape of wild brush and giant saguaros. The 12 hard-surface tennis courts are perfect for a match, and the Dennis Ralston Tennis Camp helps guests master their serves or perfect their backhands. Whether horseback riding through the canyon or lounging by the Olympic-size pool, visitors reap the rewards of this idyllic setting. Mission-style furniture, fully stocked kitchens, and even old-fashioned freestanding bathtubs create a sense of luxurious comfort in the guest accommodations. Regional cuisine is highlighted at Hearthstone Restaurant, and dining under the stars at Sabino Terrace is a romantic treat. 50 rooms, 2 story. Check-in 4 pm, check-out noon. Restaurant, bar. Fitness room. Outdoor pool, children's pool, whirlpool. Golf, 36 holes. Tennis. **$$$$**

★★★ **LOEWS VENTANA CANYON RESORT.** *7000 N Resort Dr, Tucson (85750). Phone 520/299-2020; toll-free 800/235-6397; fax 520/299-6832. www.loewshotels.com.* Loews Ventana Canyon Resort is a lush oasis in the Sonoran Desert. Set on 93 acres near Tucson, this splendid resort caters to a sophisticated clientele seeking the finest accommodations, fresh cuisine, and world-class amenities. Drenched in glorious sunlight, the grounds exude tranquility and are perfect for activities like guided hikes and biking excursions. The award-winning designs of Tom Fazio beckon golfers, eight tennis courts call out to players, and two pools cool off guests in superb style. Visitors preferring hydrotherapy to hot-air ballooning take advantage of the spa's complete services. The guest rooms are furnished in a luxurious continental style, and many rooms feature fireplaces. Five restaurants and lounges offer a taste of everything in a variety of settings, from poolside cafés to refined dining rooms. Ventana Room grabs the attention of epicureans with its artfully presented, elegant cuisine. 398 rooms, 4 story. Pets accepted. Check-in 3 pm, check-out noon. Four restaurants, bars. Children's activity center. Fitness room, spa. Outdoor pool, whirlpool. Golf, 36 holes. Tennis. Business center. **$$**

★★★ **OMNI TUCSON NATIONAL GOLF RESORT & SPA.** *2727 W Club Dr, Tucson (85742). Phone 520/297-2271; toll-free 800/843-6664; fax 520/297-7544. www.omnihotels.com.* Breathtaking views, championship golf, and first-class service make the Omni Tucson National Golf Resort & Spa a favorite of leisure travelers. Just outside Tucson, the resort enjoys a peaceful location in the Sonoran Desert. Golf is the centerpiece here, where the 27-hole course is the home of the annual PGA Tucson Open; however, all guests are well taken care of with two pools, a comprehensive fitness center, and tennis, basketball, and sand volleyball courts, as well as a 13,000-square-foot spa featuring the finest therapies and treatments. The rich colors of the Southwest dictate a soothing ambience in the guest rooms. These comfortable retreats are enhanced by expansive views of the verdant golf course or majestic mountains. Some accommodations feature full kitchens, but with four grills, lounges, and restaurants turning out delicious meals, most guests leave the cooking to the resort's talented professionals. 167 rooms, 2 story. Pets accepted; fee. Check-in 4 pm, check-out noon. Restaurants, bars. Fitness room, spa. Two outdoor pools, two whirlpools. Golf (Robert Bruce Harris, designer), 27 holes. Tennis. **$$**

★★★ **THE WESTIN LA PALOMA RESORT AND SPA.** *3800 E Sunrise Dr, Tucson (85718). Phone 520/742-6000; toll-free 800/937-8461; fax 520/577-5878. www.westin.com/lapaloma.* The Westin La Paloma Resort and Spa brings European elegance to the desert. This sophisticated resort shows off a Continental flair in its public and private spaces. The rooms and suites are luxuriously appointed and are considered the most spacious in the Tucson area. The Westin is a superb destination for golfers, with the La Paloma Country Club and its acclaimed 27-hole Jack Nicklaus-designed course adjoining the resort. Tennis is another popular pursuit, and aquatic fun is to be had in the three shimmering pools and 177-foot waterslide. The Elizabeth Arden Red Door Spa is on hand to primp and pamper guests, while five restaurants and bars cater to many moods. 487 rooms, 3 story. Pets accepted. Check-in 4 pm, check-out noon. Five restaurants, bars. Children's activity center. Fitness room, spa. Three outdoor pools, children's pool, whirlpool. Golf. Tennis. Business center. **$$**

★★★ **WESTWARD LOOK RESORT.** *245 E Ina Rd, Tucson (85704). Phone 520/297-1151; toll-free 800/722-2500; fax 520/297-9023. www.westwardlook.com.* Nestled at the base of the Santa Catalina Mountains and overlooking the city of Tucson, the Westward Look Resort is like a breath of fresh air. This resort proudly displays its Southwestern heritage, with the original 1912 homestead serving as a guiding force. From the spicy flavors of traditional dishes and furnishings typical of the region to the spa treatments that harness the healing powers of mud, stones, and herbs from the Sonoran Desert, the Westward Look is the very essence of the Arizona desert. Set on 80 acres filled with giant cacti and blooming wildflowers, this resort invites its guests to enjoy peace and quiet, along with horseback riding, on-site tennis, and nearby golf. 246 rooms, 2 story. Pets accepted; fee. Check-in 4 pm, check-out noon. Restaurant, bar. Fitness room, spa. Three pools, whirlpool. Tennis. Business center. **$**

Specialty Lodgings

The following lodging establishments are approved by Mobil Travel Guide, but due to their unique and individualized nature have not been given a traditional Mobil Star rating. Included in this listing you may find bed-and-breakfasts, limited-service inns, guest ranches, and other unique hotel properties.

ADOBE ROSE INN BED AND BREAKFAST. *940 N Olsen Ave, Tucson (85719). Phone 520/318-4644; toll-free 800/328-4122; fax 520/325-0055. www.aroseinn.com.* 7 rooms, 2 story. Children over 10 years only. Complimentary full breakfast. Check-in 3-6 pm, check-out 11 am. Pool, whirlpool. **$**

CASA ALEGRE BED AND BREAKFAST INN. *316 E Speedway Blvd, Tucson (85705). Phone 520/628-1800; toll-free 800/628-5654; fax 520/792-1880. www.casaalegreinn.com.* 4 rooms, 1 story. Complimentary full breakfast. Check-in 4-6 pm, check-out 11 am. Pool, whirlpool. **$**

CATALINA PARK INN. *309 E 1st St, Tucson (85705). Phone 520/792-4541; toll-free 800/792-4885. www.catalinaparkinn.com.* Built in 1927, the house is detailed with Mexican mahogany; and unique antiques. 6 rooms, 2 story. Closed mid June-Aug. Children over 10 years only. Complimentary full breakfast. Check-in 4-6 pm, check-out 11 am. **$**

SUNCATCHER BED AND BREAKFAST TUCSON DESERT RETREAT. *105 N Avenida Javalina, Tucson (85748). Phone 520/885-0883; toll-free 877/775-8355; fax 520/885-0883. www.thesuncatcher.com.* Guests looking for gracious hospitality in a serene desert setting find their desires fulfilled at this charming bed-and-breakfast. Gourmet breakfasts and beautiful rooms await in this architecturally stunning home on 4 unspoiled acres. 4 rooms, 1 story. Complimentary full breakfast. Check-in 3 pm, check-out noon. Outdoor pool. **$**

TANQUE VERDE GUEST RANCH. *14301 E Speedway Blvd, Tucson (85748). Phone 520/296-6275; toll-free 800/234-3833; fax 520/721-9426. www.tanqueverderanch.com.* Guests have the opportunity to explore the uniqueness of the Sonoran desert. This ranch offers rooms and suites that include gorgeous views. 94 rooms, 1 story. Complimentary full breakfast. Check-in 2 pm, check-out noon. High-speed Internet access. Restaurant. Children's activity center. Fitness room. Indoor pool, children's pool. Tennis. Airport transportation available. **$$**

WHITE STALLION RANCH. *9251 W Twin Peaks Rd, Tucson (85743). Phone 520/297-0252; toll-free 888/977-2624; fax 520/744-2786. www.wsranch.* Guests are sure to enjoy the Southwest-ranch-style rooms. This ranch, on 3,000 acres, is located 17 miles from Tucson. 41 rooms. Closed June-Aug. Complimentary full breakfast. Check-in 2 pm, check-out 11 am. Restaurant, bar. Outdoor pool, whirlpool. Tennis. Airport transportation available. **$$$**

Spa

★★★★ THE SPA AT OMNI TUCSON NATIONAL. *2727 West Club Dr, Tucson (85742). Phone 520/575-7559; toll-free 800/528-4856. www.tucsonnational.com.* The Omni Tucson National Golf Resort & Spa enjoys a tranquil and picturesque setting in the foothills of the Santa Catalina Mountains. This resort is a fitness lover's dream, with two heated outdoor pools, four tennis courts, sand volleyball, basketball courts, and a state-of-the-art fitness center. Guided power walks led by the resort's conditioning experts provide a scenic change of pace. Daily group classes at the gym include yoga, tai chi, stretch, and even golf stretch. One-on-one sessions with a personal trainer include mindful strengthening, which harnesses the power of your body weight to develop and tone your physique; stress management to help you battle anxiety; and golf conditioning, where you learn exercises and stretches to improve your game and your flexibility. The Greco-Roman ambience of the fitness center inspires you to go the extra mile.

After a challenging round of golf or an intense workout, unwind at the luxurious 13,000-square-foot spa. Private men's and women's lounges and locker rooms are equipped with saunas, steam rooms, and Jacuzzis, offering the perfect spots to relax pre- and post-treatment. Roman-style ceiling tiles add artistic touches to the treatment rooms, while the spa's dragonfly motif—a centuries-old symbol of balance and clarity—serves as an ever-present reminder of nature's ability to help you refocus your life.

Whether you have half an hour or an entire day, this spa has something to offer you. In 25 minutes, the tension reliever massage works its magic on the spot where you are most tense, while the business facial cleanses, tones, exfoliates, and hydrates in just under 30 minutes. Other types of facials include aromatherapy, deep-cleansing, antiaging, and deluxe hydration. Body masks smooth rough skin with a variety of ingredients, including seaweed, desert rose clay, rich mud from the Dead Sea, shea butter, and aspara, a plant that grows by the beach and is recognized for its calming properties. From Swedish, deep tissue, desert stone, and aromatherapy to reflexology, prenatal, and duet massages, you are certain to discover a favorite method of muscle relaxation.

Restaurants

★★ CAFE POCA COSA. *88 E Broadway, Tucson (85701). Phone 520/622-6400.* Mexican menu. Dinner. Closed Sun; holidays. Bar. Casual attire. Outdoor seating. **$$**

★★ CAPRICCIO. *4825 N 1st Ave, Tucson (85718). Phone 520/887-2333; fax 520/887-0385.* Italian menu. Dinner. Closed Sun; Jan 1, Thanksgiving, Dec 25; also Mon (mid-May-Aug). **$$**

★★ CHAD'S STEAKHOUSE. *3001 N Swan, Tucson (85712). Phone 520/881-1802.* Steak menu. Dinner. Closed Thanksgiving, Dec 25. Bar. Children's menu. Casual attire. **$$**

★★ CITY GRILL. *6464 E Tanque Verde, Tucson (85715). Phone 520/733-1111; fax 520/733-1933. www.metrorestaurants.com.* American menu. Dinner. Closed holidays. Bar. Children's menu. Casual attire. Outdoor seating. **$$**

★ DELECTABLES. *533 N 4th Ave, Tucson (85705). Phone 520/884-9289; fax 520/628-7948. www.delectables.com.* American menu. Dinner. Closed holidays. Bar. Children's menu. Casual attire. Outdoor seating. **$**

★★★ EVANGELOS SCORDATO'S. *4405 W Speedway Blvd, Tucson (85745). Phone 520/792-3055; fax 520/792-9808.* Two-time recipient of the Golden Plate award, Evangelos is the place to get your favorite Italian veal dish and enjoy a beautiful view of the Tucson Mountains. Italian menu. Dinner. Closed Sun-Mon (June-Aug); July 4, Thanksgiving, Dec 25. Bar. Children's menu. Casual attire. Outdoor seating. **$$**

★★★ FUEGO. *6958 E Tanque Verde Rd, Tucson (85715). Phone 520/886-1745; fax 520/886-6084. www.fuegorestaurant.com.* Southwestern menu. Dinner. Closed holidays. Bar. Children's menu. Casual attire. Outdoor seating. **$$**

★★★ THE GOLD ROOM. *245 E Ina Rd, Tucson (85704). Phone 520/297-1151; toll-free 800/722-2500; fax 520/742-2540. www.westwardlook.com.* Set high in the foothills overlooking Tucson, The Gold Room features both regional Southwestern fare and traditional American cuisine, combining the simplicity of steaks and seafood with more intricate and robust dishes that reflect the region's local color. Native produce—assorted chilies, beans, squash, and the like—are cultivated in the chef's on-site garden and are winningly blended into entrées like mesquite-grilled buffalo sirloin with chipotle maple glaze and mesquite-grilled lamb, ostrich, and venison with green chile mashed potatoes. Wraparound windows afford spectacular views of the mountains and desert. A jazz brunch on Sundays features a weekly changing menu of inspired regional dishes like blue corn pancakes with prickly pear syrup and Sonoran Caesar salad with smoked duck. Southwestern menu. Breakfast, lunch, dinner, Sun brunch. Children's menu. Casual attire. Valet parking. Outdoor seating. **$$$**

★★★ THE GRILL AT HACIENDA DEL SOL. *5601 N Hacienda del Sol Rd, Tucson (85718). Phone 520/529-3500; fax 502/299-5554. www.haciendadelsol.com.* Rustic Spanish colonial architecture, fine pottery, and Mexican art adorn this beautifully restored Tucson landmark. Several tables afford diners spectacular valley views, and the award-winning New American cuisine is complemented by a superlative wine list and excellent service. The creative menu, which includes dishes like roasted tomato and basil soup with garlic and chevre croustade, makes this one of Tucson's favorite dining destinations. Contemporary American menu. Dinner, Sun brunch. Bar. Children's menu. Casual attire. Outdoor seating. **$$$**

★ ★ ★ **JANOS RESTAURANT.** *3770 E Sunrise Dr, Tucson (85718). Phone 520/615-6100; fax 520/615-3334. www.janos.com.* The legendary Janos Wilder presides over this French-inspired Southwestern masterpiece 30 minutes northeast of town on the grounds of the Westin La Paloma Resort & Spa (see). Diners are surrounded by original artwork and romatic décor, and enjoy a view overlooking the Tucson valley. Features both tasting and à la carte menus, which are constantly changing and are inspired by diverse influences from around the world. Southwestern menu. Dinner. Closed Sun; Jan 1, Dec 25. Casual attire. Outdoor seating. **$$$**

★ ★ ★ **KINGFISHER.** *2564 E Grant, Tucson (85716). Phone 520/323-7739; fax 520/795-7810. www.kingfisherbarandgrill.com.* A full-service raw oyster bar with 15 varieties of oysters is a prominent aspect of this restaurant. American, seafood menu. Dinner. Closed holidays. Bar. Children's menu. Casual attire. **$$**

★ ★ **LA FUENTE.** *1749 N Oracle Rd, Tucson (85705). Phone 520/623-8659; fax 520/623-6188.* Mexican menu. Dinner. Closed holidays. Children's menu. **$$**

★ **LA PLACITA CAFE.** *2950 N Swan Rd, Tucson (85712). Phone 520/881-1150; fax 520/881-3922.* Sonoran décor; turn-of-the-century Tucson prints, raised-hearth tile fireplace, serape drapes. Mexican menu. Dinner. Closed Jan 1, Thanksgiving, Dec 25. Outdoor seating. **$**

★ ★ ★ **MCMAHON'S PRIME STEAKHOUSE.** *2959 N Swan Rd, Tucson (85712). Phone 520/327-7463; fax 520/327-2999. www.metrorestaurants.com.* Steak menu. Lunch, dinner. Closed July 4. Bar. Children's menu. Casual attire. Valet parking (dinner). Outdoor seating. **$$$**

★ ★ ★ **OLIVE TREE.** *7000 E Tanque Verde Rd, Tucson (85715). Phone 520/298-1845; fax 520/298-1846.* This local favorite serves the freshest Greek food in town. Greek menu. Dinner. Closed Mon (June-Sept); also holidays. Bar. Children's menu. Outdoor seating. **$$$**

★ **PINNACLE PEAK.** *6541 E Tanque Verde Rd, Tucson (85715). Phone 520/296-0911; fax 520/298-3614.* Steak menu. Dinner. Closed Thanksgiving, Dec 25. Bar. Children's menu. **$$**

★ ★ **PRESIDIO GRILL.** *3352 E Speedway, Tucson (85716). Phone 520/327-4667; fax 520/323-2037. www.dotucson.com.* American menu. Dinner. Closed holidays. Bar. Children's menu. Casual attire. **$$**

★ **SERI MELAKA.** *6133 E Broadway, Tucson (85711). Phone 520/747-7811; fax 520/790-2707. www.serimelaka.com.* Chinese, Malaysian menu. Dinner. Casual attire. **$$$**

★ ★ ★ **SOLEIL.** *3001 E Skyline Dr, Tucson (85718). Phone 520/299-3345; fax 520/232-0815.* Mediterranean menu. Dinner. Closed Mon. Casual attire. **$$$**

★ **TOHONO CHUL TEA ROOM.** *7366 N Paseo del Norte, Tucson (85704). Phone 520/797-1222; fax 520/797-7598. www.tohonochulpark.org.* Adobe house in a park dedicated to arid flora and landscape. Southwestern menu. Breakfast, lunch. Closed holidays. Children's menu. Casual attire. Outdoor seating. **$$**

★ ★ ★ ★ **THE VENTANA ROOM.** *7000 N Resort Dr, Tucson (85750). Phone 520/299-2020; fax 520/299-6832. www.loewshotels.com.* Intimate and romantic, The Ventana Room offers the perfect balance of rustic charm and upscale elegance. The airy, windowed restaurant is appointed with tall floral arrangements, wine cases, a dramatic front entryway with striking, angled doors, and tables lit with candles of different heights. The restaurant's upper-tier fireplace is open on both sides for warm and cozy dining, and the glass-enclosed room, with southern exposure, offers panoramic views of the lights of Tucson or the Catalina Mountains. The meticulously prepared continental menu stays true to regional ingredients and features wild cuts of game as well as a wide variety of seafood and locally farmed poultry, veal, and lamb, each prepared in harmony with the seasons. For those who love cheese after dinner, the restaurant offers more than 50 imported and domestic cheeses, including several varieties that are made and aged in-house. Eclectic/International menu. Dinner. Closed Sun-Mon; also Tues in summer. Bar. Children's menu. Casual attire. Valet parking. **$$$**

Tumacacori National Historical Park

See also Nogales, Patagonia, Tucson

Web site www.nps.gov/tuma

Exit 29 on I-19, 48 miles S of Tucson, 18 miles N of Nogales.

Father Kino, a Jesuit missionary, visited the Pima village of Tumacacori in 1691. Work began on the present historic mission church in 1800. It was completed in 1822 but was abandoned in 1848. There is a beautiful patio garden and a museum with fine dioramas (daily; closed Thanksgiving, Dec 25). Self-guided trail; guided tours (Dec-April, daily; advance notice needed rest of year). There is a fiesta held on the first weekend in December with entertainment, music, and food. Contact the Superintendent, PO Box 67, Tumacacori 85640; phone 520/398-2341. **$$**

Full-Service Resort

★★ TUBAC GOLF RESORT. *1 Otero Rd, Tubac (85646). Phone 520/398-2211; toll-free 800/848-7893; fax 520/398-9261. www.tubacgolfresort.com.* 46 rooms. Check-out noon. Restaurant, bar. Pool. Golf. Tennis. **$$**

Walnut Canyon National Monument (B-3)

See Flagstaff

Wickenburg (C-2)

See also Phoenix

Founded 1863
Population 5,082
Elevation 2,070 ft
Area Code 928
Information Chamber of Commerce, Santa Fe Depot, 216 N Frontier St, 85390; phone 928/684-5479 or toll-free 928/684-0977
Web site www.wickenburgchamber.com

Wickenburg was first settled by early Hispanic families who established ranches in the area and traded with the local Native Americans. The town was relatively unpopulated until a Prussian named Henry Wickenburg picked up a rock to throw at a stubborn burro and stumbled onto the richest gold find in Arizona, the Vulture Mine. His find began a $30-million boom and the birth of a town. Today, Wickenburg is the oldest town north of Tucson and is well-known for its area dude ranches.

What to See and Do

Desert Caballeros Western Museum. *21 N Frontier St, Wickenburg. Phone 928/684-2272. www.westernmuseum.org.* This museum houses a Western art gallery, diorama room, street scene (circa 1915), period rooms, mineral display, and Native American exhibit. (Mon-Sat 10 am-5 pm, Sun noon-4 pm; closed holidays) **$**

Frontier Street. *Wickenburg. Phone 928/684-5479.* Preserved in early 1900s style. Train depot (houses the Chamber of Commerce), brick Hassayampa building (former hotel) and many other historic buildings.

The Jail Tree. *Tegner and Wickenburg Way, Wickenburg. Phone 928/684-5479.* This tree was used from 1863 to 1890 (until the first jail was built) to chain rowdy prisoners. Friends and relatives visited the prisoners and brought picnic lunches. Escapes were unknown.

Little Red Schoolhouse. *245 N Tegner St, Wickenburg. Four blocks N of Wickenburg Way on Tegner. Phone 928/684-5479.* This pioneer schoolhouse is on the National Register of Historic Places.

Old 761 Santa Fe Steam Locomotive. *Apache and Tegner, Wickenburg. Behind Town Hall. Phone*

928/684-5479. This engine and tender ran the track between Chicago and the West.

Special Events

Bluegrass Music Festival. *Bowman Rodeo Grounds, Wickenburg. Phone 928/684-5479.* Four-Corner States Championship. Contests include mandolin, violin, guitar, and banjo. Second full weekend in Nov. **$$**

Gold Rush Days. *Wickenburg. Events held throughout town. Phone 928/684-5479.* Bonanza days are revived during this large festival, with a chance to pan for gold and keep all you find. Rodeo, contests, food, parade. Second full weekend in Feb. **$$**

Septiembre Fiesta. *Community Center, Wickenburg. Phone 928/684-5479.* A celebration of Hispanic heritage featuring exhibits, arts and crafts, food, dancers, and mariachi bands. First Sat in Sept.

Limited-Service Hotel

★ BEST WESTERN RANCHO GRANDE. *293 E Wickenburg Way, Wickenburg (85390). Phone 928/684-5445; toll-free 800/528-1234; fax 928/684-7380. www.bwranchogrande.com.* 80 rooms, 2 story. Pets accepted. Check-out noon. Pool, whirlpool. Tennis. Airport transportation available. **$**

Specialty Lodgings

The following lodging establishments are approved by Mobil Travel Guide, but due to their unique and individualized nature have not been given a traditional Mobil Star rating. Included in this listing you may find bed-and-breakfasts, limited-service inns, guest ranches, and other unique hotel properties.

FLYING E RANCH. *2801 W Wickenburg Way, Wickenburg (85390). Phone 928/684-2690; toll-free 888/684-2650; fax 928/684-5304. www.flyingeranch.com.* On a 20,000-acre cattle ranch in the shadow of Vulture Peak. 17 rooms. Closed Mar-Oct. Family-style meals. Breakfast cookouts, chuckwagon dinners. Check-in varies, check-out 11 am. Fitness room. Pool. Tennis. No credit cards accepted. **$$**

RANCHO DE LOS CABALLEROS. *1551 S Vulture Mine Rd, Wickenburg (85390). Phone 928/684-5484; toll-free 800/684-5030; fax 928/684-2267. www.sunc.com.* Experience the Old West at this historic guest ranch and golf club. Visit ghost towns and gold mines, ride in a rodeo, and dine by campfire. 79 rooms. Closed mid-May-mid-Oct. Check-in 4 pm, check-out 1 pm. Restaurant, bar. Children's activity center. Pool. Golf. Tennis. Airport transportation available. **$$$$**

Willcox (E-5)

See also Safford

Population 3,733
Elevation 4,200 ft
Area Code 520
Zip 85643
Information Chamber of Commerce, Cochise Information Center, 1500 N Circle I Rd; phone 520/384-2272 or toll-free 800/200-2272
Web site www.willcoxchamber.com

What to See and Do

Amerind Foundation. *PO Box 400, 2100 N Amerind Rd, Dragoon. Approximately 1 mile SW via I-10, exit 318 on Dragoon Rd. Phone 520/586-3666. www.amerind.org.* Amerind (short for American Indian) Museum contains one of the finest collections of archaeological and ethnological artifacts in the country. Displayed in the art gallery are paintings by Anglo and Native American artists. Picnic area, museum shop. (Oct-May: daily 10 am-4 pm; June-Sept: Wed-Sun 10 am-4 pm; closed holidays) **$**

Cochise Information Center. *1500 N Circle I Rd, Willcox. 1 mile N via Circle I Rd just off Fort Grant Rd, exit from I-10. Phone 520/384-2272; toll-free 800/200-2272.* (Daily; closed Jan 1, Thanksgiving, Dec 25) **FREE**

Cochise Stronghold. *Coronada National Forest, 1500 N Circle I Rd, Willcox. SW via I-10 to Hwy 191 S, then W on Ironwood Rd. Phone 520/364-3468.* This rugged canyon once sheltered Chiricahua Apache; unique rock formations provided protection and vantage points. Camping, picnicking; nature, hiking, horseback, and history trails. (Daily)

Fort Bowie National Historic Site. *Apache Pass Rd, Willcox. 22 miles SE on Hwy 186, then 6 miles NE on graded road leading E into Apache Pass and 2 miles to trailhead, then walk 1 1/2 miles on foot trail to the fort ruins. Phone 520/847-2500. www.nps.gov/fobo.* Visitors pass ruins of Butterfield Stage Station, post cemetery, Apache Spring, and the first Fort Bowie on the way to ruins of the second Fort Bowie. Visitor center (daily 8 am-4:30 pm; closed Dec 25). Carry water in summer, and beware of flash floods and rattlesnakes. Do not climb on ruins or disturb any of the site's features. **FREE**

The Rex Allen Arizona Cowboy Museum and Cowboy Hall of Fame. *150 N Railroad Ave, Willcox. Phone 520/384-4583; toll-free 877/234-4111.* Museum dedicated to Willcox native Rex Allen, the "last of the Silver Screen Cowboys." Details his life from ranch life in Willcox to radio, TV, and movie days. Also special exhibits on pioneer settlers and ranchers. The Cowboy Hall of Fame pays tribute to real cattle industry heroes. (Daily; closed Jan 1, Thanksgiving, Dec 25) **$**

Special Events

Rex Allen Days. *Rex Allen Arizona Cowboy Museum and Cowboy Hall of Fame, 150 N Railroad Ave, Willcox. Phone 520/384-2272. www.rexallendays.com.* PRCA Rodeo, concert by Rex Allen, Jr., parade, country fair, Western dances, softball tournament. First weekend in Oct.

Wings Over Willcox/Sandhill Crane Celebration. *1500 N Circle I Rd, Willcox. Phone 520/384-2272; toll-free 800/200-2272. www.wingsoverwillcox.com.* Tours of bird-watching areas, trade shows, seminars, workshops. Third weekend in Jan.

Limited-Service Hotel

★★ **BEST WESTERN PLAZA INN.** *1100 W Rex Allen Dr, Willcox (85643). Phone 520/384-3556; toll-free 800/262-2645; fax 520/384-2679. www.bestwestern.com.* 91 rooms, 2 story. Pets accepted; fee. Complimentary full breakfast. Check-in 2 pm, check-out noon. Restaurant, bar. Outdoor pool. **$**

Williams (B-3)

See also Flagstaff, Seligman

Settled 1880
Population 2,842
Elevation 6,750 ft
Area Code 928
Zip 86046
Information Williams-Grand Canyon Chamber of Commerce, 200 W Railroad Ave; phone 928/635-4061
Web site www.williamschamber.com

This town lies at the foot of Bill Williams Mountain (named for an early trapper and guide) and is the principal entrance to the Grand Canyon (see). It is a resort town in the midst of Kaibab National Forest, which has its headquarters here. There are seven small fishing lakes in the surrounding area.

What to See and Do

★ **Grand Canyon Railway.** *233 N Grand Canyon Blvd, Williams. Phone toll-free 800/843-8724. www.thetrain.com.* First operated by the Santa Fe Railroad in 1901 as an alternative to the stagecoach, this restored line carries passengers northward aboard authentically refurbished steam locomotives and coaches. Full-day round trips include a 3 1/2-hour layover at the canyon. At Williams depot, there is a museum of railroad history. Railway (closed Jan 1, Dec 25). **$$$$**

Kaibab National Forest. *200 E Railroad Ave, Williams (Coconino County). The Ranger District office for the Tusayan District is located in Tusayan, 4 miles S of the park. Phone 928/635-4707; toll-free 800/863-0546. www.fs.fed.us/r3/kai.* More than 1 1/2 million acres; one area surrounds Williams and includes Sycamore Canyon and Kendrick Mountain wilderness areas and part of National Historic Route 66. A second area is 42 miles north on Highway 180 (Highway 64) near the South Rim of the Grand Canyon; a third area lies north of the Grand Canyon (outstanding views of the canyon from seldom-visited vista points in this area) and includes Kanab Creek and Saddle Mountain wilderness areas, the Kaibab Plateau, and the North Rim Parkway National Scenic Byway. The forest is home to a variety of wildlife unique to this area, including mule deer and the Kaibab squirrel. Fishing (trout); hunting, picnicking, camping (fee). Also in the forest is

> **Williams Ski Area.** *PO Box 953, Williams (Coconino County). 4th St, 2 miles S, right on gravel road, on the N slopes of Bill Williams Mountain. Phone 928/635-9330. www.williamsskiarea.com.* Pomalift, rope tow; patrol, school, rentals; snack bar. Vertical drop 600 feet. (Mid-Dec-Easter: Mon, Thurs-Sun) Sledding slopes and cross-country trails nearby. **$$$$**

Special Events

Bill Williams Rendezvous Days. *Buckskinner's Park, Williams (Coconino County).* Black powder shoot, carnival, street dances, pioneer arts and crafts. Memorial Day weekend.

Labor Day Rodeo. *200 W Railroad, Williams (Coconino Co). Phone 928/635-4061.* Professional rodeo and Western celebration. Labor Day weekend.

Limited-Service Hotels

★ BEST WESTERN INN OF WILLIAMS. *2600 W Rte 66, Williams (86046). Phone 928/635-4400; toll-free 800/635-4445; fax 928/635-4488. www.bestwestern.com.* 79 rooms, 2 story. Complimentary full breakfast. Check-out noon. Bar. Pool, whirlpool. **$**

★ ★ FRAY MARCOS HOTEL. *235 N Grand Canyon Blvd, Williams (86046). Phone 928/635-4010; toll-free 800/843-8724; fax 928/635-2180. www.thetrain.com.* 297 rooms, 2 story. Check-out 11 am. Restaurant, bar. **$**

★ ★ GRAND CANYON RAILWAY & RESORT. *233 N Grand Canyon Blvd, Williams (86046). Phone toll-free 800/843-8724. www.thetrain.com.* 196 rooms. Check-in 3 pm, check-out 11 am. Restaurant, bar. **$**

★ ★ HOLIDAY INN. *950 N Grand Canyon Blvd, Williams (86046). Phone 928/635-4114; toll-free 800/465-4329; fax 928/635-2700. www.holiday-inn.com.* 120 rooms, 2 story. Pets accepted. Check-out 11 am. Restaurant, bar. Indoor pool, whirlpool. **$**

★ ★ MOUNTAINSIDE INN. *642 E Rte 66, Williams (86046). Phone 928/635-4431; fax 928/635-2292. www.mtnsideinn.com.* 96 rooms, 2 story. Pets accepted; fee. Check-out noon. Restaurant, bar. Pool, whirlpool. **$**

Specialty Lodging

The following lodging establishment is approved by Mobil Travel Guide but, due to its unique and individualized nature has not been given a traditional Mobil Star rating. Included in this listing you may find bed-and-breakfasts, limited-service inns, guest ranches, and other unique hotel properties.

TERRY RANCH BED AND BREAKFAST. *701 Quarterhorse Rd, Williams (86046). Phone 928/635-4171; toll-free 800/210-5908; fax 928/635-2488. www.terryranchbnb.com.* Country Victorian log house. 4 rooms. Complimentary full breakfast. Check-in 4-6 pm, check-out 10 am. **$**

Restaurant

★ ROD'S STEAK HOUSE. *301 E Bill Williams Ave, Williams (86046). Phone 928/635-2671; fax 928/635-9557. www.rods-steakhouse.com.* Steak menu. Lunch, dinner. Closed Thanksgiving, Dec 24-25. Bar. Children's menu. **$$**

Window Rock (B-5)

See also Ganado

Population 3,059
Elevation 6,880 ft
Area Code 928
Information Navajoland Tourism Department, PO Box 663; phone 928/871-6436 or toll-free 928/871-7371

This is the headquarters of the Navajo Nation. The 88-member tribal council, democratically elected, meets in an octagonal council building; tribal officials conduct tribal business from Window Rock.

Behind the town is a natural bridge that looks like a window. It is in the midst of a colorful group of sandstone formations called "the Window Rock."

What to See and Do

Canyon de Chelly National Monument. *Hwy 191, Window Rock. In the NE corner of the state at Chinle. Phone 928/674-5500. www.nps.gov/cach.* (See Canyon de Chelly National Monument)

Guided tours of Navajoland. *Phone 928/871-6436.* Various organizations and individuals offer walking and driving tours of the area. Fees and tours vary; phone for information.

Hozhoni Tours. *PO Box 1995, Kayenta. Phone 520/697-8198. www.hol-biz.com/hozhonitours.*

Roland's Navajo Land Tours. *N Hwy 163 Milepost 394, Window Rock. Phone 928/697-8198.*

Stanley Perry, Step-On Tours. *PO Box 2381, Window Rock. Phone 520/871-2484 (after 7 pm).*

Navajo Nation Museum. *Navajo Arts & Crafts Enterprise Center, Hwy 264 and Loop Rd, Window Rock. E of junction Hwy 264 and Indian Rte 12. Phone 928/871-6675.* Established in 1961 to preserve Navajo history, art, culture, and natural history; permanent and temporary exhibits. Literature and Navajo information available. (Mon 8 am-5 pm, Tues-Fri 8 am-8 pm, Sat 9 am-5 pm; closed tribal and other holidays) **DONATION**

Navajo Nation Zoological and Botanical Park. *Tse Bonito Tribal Park, Window Rock. E of junction Hwy 264 and Indian Rte 12, on Hwy 264. Phone 928/871-6573.* Features a representative collection of animals and plants of historical or cultural importance to the Navajo people. (Daily 8 am-5 pm; closed Jan 1, Dec 25) **FREE**

St. Michael's. *Window Rock. S of Hwy 264, and 4 miles W of Window Rock. Phone 928/871-4172.* This Catholic mission, established in 1898, has done much for the education and health of the tribe. The original mission building now serves as a museum depicting the history of the area. Gift shop. (Memorial Day-Labor Day, daily) **FREE**

Special Events

Navajo Nation Fair. *Navajo Nation Fairgrounds, Window Rock. N of I-40. Phone 928/871-6478. www.navajonationfair.com.* Navajo traditional song and dance; intertribal powwow; all-Indian rodeo; parade, concerts, and exhibits. Early Sept. **$**

Powwow and PRCA Rodeo. *Navajo Nations Fairgrounds, Window Rock. N of I-40. Phone 928/871-6478.* Rodeo, carnival, fireworks, and entertainment. July 4.

Winslow (B-4)

See also Flagstaff, Holbrook, Hopi Indian Reservation, Navajo Indian Reservation

Founded 1880
Population 9,520
Elevation 4,880 ft
Area Code 928
Zip 86047
Information Chamber of Commerce, 300 W North Rd, PO Box 460; phone 928/289-2434 or 928/289-2435
Web site www.winslowarizona.com

A railroad town, Winslow is also a trade center and convenient stopping point in the midst of a colorful and intriguing area; a miniature painted desert lies to the northeast. The Apache-Sitgreaves National Forests, with the world's largest stand of ponderosa pine, lie about 25 miles to the south.

What to See and Do

Homolovi Ruins State Park. *HCR 63, Box 5, Winslow. 3 miles E on I-40, then 1 mile N on Hwy 87. Phone 928/289-4106. www.pr.state.az.us/parks/parkhtml/homolovi.html.* This park contains six major Anasazi ruins dating from AD 1250-1450. The Arizona State Museum conducts occasional excavations in June and July. The park also has trails, a visitor center, and interpretive programs. (Daily; closed Dec 25)

Meteor Crater. *I-40 and exit 233, Winslow. 20 miles W on I-40, then 5 miles S on Meteor Crater Rd. Phone 928/289-2362; toll-free 800/289-5898. www.meteorcrater.com.* Crater is 1 mile from rim to rim and 560 feet deep. The world's best-preserved meteorite crater was used as a training site for astronauts. Museum, lecture; Astronaut Wall of Fame; telescope on highest point of the crater's rim offers excellent view of surrounding area. (Mid-May-mid-Sept: 6 am-6 pm; mid-Sept-mid-May: 8 am-5 pm) **$$$**

Old Trails Museum. *212 N Kinsley Ave, Winslow. Phone 928/289-5861.* Operated by the Navajo County Historical Society; exhibits and displays of local history, Native American artifacts, and early Americana. (Apr-Oct: Tues-Sat; rest of year: Tues, Thurs, and Sat; closed holidays) **FREE**

Limited-Service Hotel

★★ BEST WESTERN ADOBE INN. *1701 N Park Dr, Winslow (86047). Phone 928/289-4638; fax 928/289-5514. www.bestwestern.com.* 72 rooms, 2 story. Pets accepted; fee. Check-out 11 am. Restaurant, bar. Indoor pool, whirlpool. **$**

Wupatki National Monument (B-3)

See also Flagstaff

Web site www.nps.gov/wupa.

35 miles N of Flagstaff on Hwy 89.

The nearly 2,600 archaeological sites of the Sinagua and Anasazi cultures were occupied between AD 1100–1250. The largest of them, Wupatki Pueblo, was three stories high, with about 100 rooms. The eruption of nearby Sunset Crater (see) spread volcanic ash over an 800-square-mile area and, for a time, made this an active farming center.

The half-mile ruins trail is self-guided; books are available at its starting point. The visitor center and main ruin are open daily (closed December 25). Rangers on duty. Wupatki National Monument and Sunset Crater Volcano National Monument (see) are located on a 35-mile paved loop off of Hwy 89. Nearest camping at Bonito Campground (May-Oct; phone 520/526-0866). Contact the Superintendent, Flagstaff Area National Monuments, 6400 Hwy 89, Flagstaff 86004; phone 520/526-1157. **$$**

Yuma (E-1)

Founded 1849
Population 77,515
Elevation 138 ft
Area Code 928
Information Convention & Visitors Bureau, 377 Main St, PO Box 11059, 85366; 928/783-0071
Web site www.visityuma.com

Hernando de Alarcion, working with the Coronado Expedition, passed this point on the Colorado River in 1540. Father Kino came into the area in 1699. Padre Francisco Tomas Garces established a mission in 1780, which was destroyed a year later. The Yuma Crossing, where the Colorado River narrows between the Yuma Territorial Prison and Fort Yuma (one of Arizona's oldest military posts), was made a historic landmark in recognition of its long service as a river crossing for many peoples.

Yuma's air-conditioned stopping places are a great comfort to motorists crossing the desert. If the scenery looks familiar, it may be because movie producers have used the dunes and desert for location shots.

Irrigation from the Colorado River makes it profitable to raise cattle, alfalfa, cotton, melons, lettuce, citrus fruits, and other crops here. A Marine Corps Air Station and an army proving ground are adjacent to the town.

What to See and Do

Arizona Historical Society Sanguinetti House
240 Madison Ave, Yuma. Phone 928/782-1841. Former home of E. F. Sanguinetti, pioneer merchant; now a division of the Arizona Historical Society. Artifacts from Arizona Territory, including documents, photographs, furniture, and clothing. Gardens and exotic birds surround museum. Historical library open by appointment. (Tues-Sat 10 am-4 pm; closed holidays) **FREE**

Fort Yuma-Quechan Museum. *488 S Maiden Ln, Yuma. Phone 619/572-0661.* Part of one of the oldest military posts (1855) associated with the Arizona Territory; offered protection to settlers and secured the Yuma Crossing. Fort Yuma is headquarters for the Quechan Tribe. Museum houses tribal relics of southwestern Colorado River Yuman groups. (Mon-Fri 8 am-5 pm, Sat 10 am-4 pm; closed holidays) **$**

Imperial National Wildlife Refuge. *100 Red Cloud Mine Rd, Yuma. N on Hwy 95 for 25 miles. Turn W on Martinez Lake Rd for 13 miles and follow signs to visitor center. Phone 928/783-3371. southwest.fws.gov/refuges/arizona/imperial.html.* Bird-watching; photography. Fishing; hunting, hiking. Interpretive center/office (Apr-mid-Nov: Mon-Fri 7:30-4 pm; rest of year: Mon-Fri 7:30 am-4 pm, Sat-Sun 9 am-4 pm). **FREE**

Yuma River Tours. *1920 Arizona Ave, Yuma. Phone 928/783-4400. www.yumarivertours.com.* Narrated historical tours on the Colorado River; half- and full-day trips. Sunset dinner cruises. Also jeep tours to sand dunes. (Mon-Fri; fees vary)

Yuma Territorial Prison State Historic Park. *1 Prison Hill Rd, Yuma. Off I-8, Giss Pkwy exit. Phone 928/783-4771. www.pr.state.az.us/Parks/parkhtml/yuma.html.* Remains of 1876 prison; museum, original cell blocks. Southwest artifacts and prison relics. Gift shop; picnic area. (Daily 8 am-5 pm; closed Dec 24-25)

Yuma Valley Railway. *980 S Palm Ave, Yuma. Levee at 8th St. Phone 928/783-3456.* Tracks run 12 miles through fields along the Colorado River levee and Morelos Dam. Two-hour trips; dinner trips. (Nov-Mar, Sat-Sun; Apr-May, Oct, Sat only; June by appointment only; closed July-Sept) **$$$**

Special Events

Midnight at the Oasis Festival. *The Ray Kroc Complex, Desert Sun Stadium, 3500 S Avenue A, Yuma. Phone 928/343-1715.* This annual event features classic cars and concerts. First full weekend in Mar.

Yuma County Fair. *2520 E 32nd St, Yuma. Phone 928/726-4420.* Five days in early Apr.

Limited-Service Hotels

★★ QUALITY INN. *711 E 32nd St, Yuma (85365). Phone 928/726-4721; toll-free 800/835-1132; fax 928/344-0452. www.travelodge.com.* 80 rooms, 2 story. Pets accepted, some restrictions; fee. Complimentary full breakfast. Check-in 2 pm, check-out noon. Restaurant, bar. Outdoor pool. **$**

★★ SHILO INN. *1550 S Castle Dome Ave, Yuma (85365). Phone 928/782-9511; toll-free 800/222-2244; fax 928/783-1538. www.shiloinns.com.* 134 rooms, 4 story. Pets accepted. Complimentary full breakfast. Check-in 2 pm, check-out noon. Restaurant, bar. Fitness room. Outdoor pool, whirlpool. Airport transportation available. **$**

Restaurants

★ THE CROSSING. *2690 S 4th Ave, Yuma (85364). Phone 928/726-5551; fax 928/726-6064.* American menu. Lunch, dinner. Children's menu. Casual attire. Outdoor seating. **$$**

★ HUNTER STEAKHOUSE. *2355 S 4th Ave, Yuma (85364). Phone 928/782-3637; fax 928/329-8129.* Steak menu. Lunch, dinner. Closed Dec 25. Bar. Children's menu. Casual attire. **$$**

Side Trips

After exploring the Phoenix area, head over to California to check out one of the most interesting national parks in the United States: Joshua Tree. The park preserves sections of two deserts, the Mojave and the Colorado, with terrain ranging from mountains to desert flats. The temperature also ranges from sweltering in the summer to freezing in the winter. This is a fine example of extremes.

Joshua Tree National Park, CA

5 hours, 300 miles from Phoenix, AZ

Web site www.nps.gov/jotr

Entrances: 25 miles E of Indio on I-10 or S of Joshua Tree, Yucca Valley, and Twentynine Palms on Hwy 62.

Covering more than 1,236 square miles, this park preserves a section of two deserts: the Mojave and the Colorado. Particularly notable are the variety and richness of desert vegetation. The park shelters many species of desert plants. The Joshua tree, which gives the park its name, was christened thus by the Mormons because of its upstretched "arms." A member of the Lily family, this giant yucca attains heights of more than 40 feet. The area consists of a series of block mountains ranging in altitude from 1,000 to 5,800 feet and separated by desert flats. The summer gets very hot, and the temperature drops below freezing in the winter. Water is available only at the Black Rock Canyon Visitor Center/Campground,

Cottonwood Campground, the Indian Cove Ranger Station, and the Twentynine Palms Visitor Center. Pets are permitted on leash only; pets are not allowed on trails. Guided tours and campfire programs (Feb-May and Oct-Dec). Picnicking is permitted in designated areas and campgrounds, but no fires may be built outside the campgrounds. For additional information, contact 74485 National Park Dr, Twentynine Palms 92277; phone 760/367-5500.

What to See and Do

Camping. *74485 National Monument Dr, Joshua Tree National Park. Phone toll-free 800/365-2267.* Restricted to nine campgrounds with limited facilities; bring your own firewood and water. Thirty-day limit, July-Sept; 14-day limit the rest of the year. Cottonwood, Black Rock Canyon, and Indian Cove Campgrounds (fee); other campgrounds free. Group camping at Cottonwood, Indian Cove, and Sheep Pass. Campgrounds are operated on a first-come, first-served basis except for Indian Cove, Sheep Pass, and Black Rock Canyon.

Hidden Valley Nature Trail. *74485 National Park Dr, Joshua Tree National Park.* One-mile loop; access from picnic area across Hidden Valley Campground. Valley enclosed by wall of rocks.

Keys View. *74485 National Park Dr, Joshua Tree National Park.* (5,185 feet) Sweeping view of Coachella valley, desert, and mountain. A paved path leads off the main road.

Lost Palms Canyon. *74485 National Park Dr, Joshua Tree National Park.* Eight-mile round-trip hike. Reached by 4-mile trail from Cottonwood Spring. Shelters the largest group of palms (120) in the park. Day use only.

Oasis Visitor Center. *74485 National Park Dr, Joshua Tree National Park. Park headquarters, just N of park at Twentynine Palms entrance.* Exhibits; self-guided nature trail through the Oasis of Mara, discovered by a government survey party in 1855. (Daily)

Stands of Joshua trees. *74485 National Park Dr, Joshua Tree National Park.* In Queen and Lost Horse valleys.

Special Event

Pioneer Days. *Twentynine Palms. Phone 760/367-3445.* Carnival, parade, rodeo, food, and games. Third weekend in Oct.

Limited-Service Hotel

★ BEST WESTERN GARDEN INN & SUITES. *71487 Twentynine Palms Hwy, Twentynine Palms (92277). Phone 760/367-9141; fax 760/367-2584. www.bestwestern.com.* 84 rooms, 2 story. Pets accepted; fee. Complimentary continental breakfast. Check-out 11 am. Fitness room. Outdoor pool, whirlpool. **$**

Specialty Lodging

The following lodging establishment is approved by Mobil Travel Guide but, due to its unique and individualized nature has not been given a traditional Mobil Star rating. Included in this listing you may find bed-and-breakfasts, limited-service inns, guest ranches, and other unique hotel properties.

JOSHUA TREE INN. *61259 Twentynine Palms Hwy, Joshua Tree (92252). Phone 760/366-1188; fax 760/366-3805. www.jtinn.com.* 10 rooms. Complimentary continental breakfast. Check-in 3 pm, check-out 11 am. Outdoor pool. **$**

Colorado

Population: 4,301,261
Area: 104,100 square miles
Elevation: 3,350–14,433 feet
Peak: Mount Elbert (Lake County)
Entered Union: August 1, 1876 (38th state)
Capital: Denver
Motto: Nothing without Providence
Nicknames: Centennial State, Silver State
Flower: Rocky Mountain Columbine
Bird: Lark Bunting
Tree: Colorado Blue Spruce
Fair: August in Pueblo
Time Zone: Mountain
Web site: www.colorado.com

From the eastern plains westward through the highest Rockies, Colorado's terrain is diverse, fascinating, and spectacularly beautiful. The highest state in the Union, with an average elevation of 6,800 feet and with 53 peaks above 14,000 feet, Colorado attracts sports enthusiasts and vacationers as well as high-technology research and business.

When gold was discovered near present-day Denver in 1858, an avalanche of settlers poured into the state; when silver was discovered soon afterward, a new flood came. Mining camps, usually crude tent cities clinging to the rugged slopes of the Rockies, contributed to Colorado's colorful, robust history. Some of these mines still operate, but most of the early mining camps are ghost towns today. Thousands of newcomers arrive yearly, drawn to Colorado's Rockies by the skiing, hunting, fishing, and magnificent scenery.

Throughout the state there are deep gorges, rainbow-colored canyons, mysterious mesas, and other strange and beautiful landmass variations carved by ancient glaciers and eons of erosion by wind, rain, and water. Great mountains of shifting sand lie trapped by the Sangre de Cristo Mountains in Great Sand Dunes National Monument (see also); fossils 140 million years old lie in the quarries of Dinosaur National Monument (see also).

Spaniards penetrated the area by the mid-1500s. American exploration of the area first took place in 1806, three years after a good portion of the region became American property through the Louisiana Purchase. The leader of the party was Lieutenant Zebulon M. Pike, for whom Pikes Peak is named. Pike pronounced the 14,110-foot mountain unclimbable. Today, one may drive to the top on a good gravel highway (first 5 miles paved). Colorado became a territory in 1861 and earned its "Centennial State" nickname by becoming a state in 1876, 100 years after the signing of the Declaration of Independence.

Colorado produces more tin, molybdenum, uranium, granite, sandstone, and basalt than any other state. The mountain area also ranks high in production of coal, gold, and silver; the state as a whole has vast deposits of brick clay and oil. Its extensively irrigated plateaus and plains are good grazing lands for stock and rich producers of potatoes, wheat, corn, sugar beets, cauliflower, fruit, and flowers.

When to Go/Climate

Most of Colorado falls in a semiarid climate zone. Springs are short; summers are dry. Winters are surprisingly mild along the Front Range, but annual snowfall in the mountains often exceeds 20 feet.

AVERAGE HIGH/LOW TEMPERATURES (° F)

Colorado Springs

Jan 41/16	**May** 69/42	**Sept** 74/47
Feb 45/19	**June** 79/51	**Oct** 64/36
Mar 50/25	**July** 84/57	**Nov** 51/25
Apr 60/33	**Aug** 81/55	**Dec** 42/17

Calendar Highlights

JANUARY

National Western Livestock Show, Horse Show & Rodeo *(Denver). National Western Complex and Coliseum. Phone 303/297-1166.*

Winterskol Carnival *(Aspen). Phone 970/925-1940.* Parade, fireworks, skiing, and ice skating.

MAY

Bolder Boulder *(Boulder). Phone 303/444-7223.* Ten-kilometer race. Includes a citizens race and world-class heats.

JUNE

FIBArk River International Whitewater Boat Race *(Salida). Phone 719/539-2068.* 26-mile kayak race. Other events include slalom, raft, foot, and bicycle races.

Colorado Stampede *(Grand Junction). Phone 970/245-7723.* Rodeo.

AUGUST

Pikes Peak Marathon *(Colorado Springs). Phone 719/473-2625.* Footrace on Barr's Trail from cog depot to the top of Pikes Peak and back.

Jazz *(Telluride). Town Park and local nightclubs. Phone 800/525-3455.* Mainstream jazz with international flavors, performed in various locales throughout the city.

Boulder County Fair & Rodeo *(Longmont). Fairgrounds. Phone 303/441-3927.*

Colorado State Fair *(Pueblo). Fairgrounds, Prairie Ave. Phone toll-free 800/876-4567.* PRCA rodeo, grandstand and amphitheater entertainment, livestock and agricultural displays, industrial and high technology displays, arts and crafts, and a carnival.

SEPTEMBER

Vintage Auto Race & Concours d'Elegance *(Steamboat Springs). Mt Werner Circle and downtown. Phone 970/879-3120.* Vintage auto racing, exhibition of restored vintage automobiles, and an art show of works by automotive artists.

Telluride Airmen's Rendezvous & Hang Gliding Festival *(Telluride). Pilots phone 970/728-5793.* Pilots converge on Telluride for a week of hang gliding and paragliding. Climax is the World Aerobatic Hang Gliding Championship in Town Park.

Denver

Jan 43/16	**May** 71/44	**Sept** 77/48
Feb 47/20	**June** 81/52	**Oct** 66/36
Mar 52/26	**July** 88/59	**Nov** 53/25
Apr 62/35	**Aug** 86/57	**Dec** 45/17

Parks and Recreation

Water-related activities, hiking, riding, various other sports, picnicking, and visitor centers, as well as camping, are available in many of Colorado's parks. Interpretive and watchable wildlife programs are available as well. A parks pass is required, good for driver and passengers; annual pass, $50; one-day pass, $3-$6/car. Passes are available at self-service dispensers at all state parks and park offices. Camping is available in most parks. Reservations can be made by phoning 303/470-1144 or toll-free 800/678-2267 from 8 am to 4:30 pm, Mon-Fri. Reservations cost $7 and a campground fee of $6-$16 is charged, depending on the services offered. Electrical hookups are $5-$8 per night.

Fishing, camping, and picnicking are possible in most parks. For further information or a free Colorado State Parks Guide, contact Colorado State Parks, 1313 Sherman #618, Denver 80203; phone 303/866-3437; parks.states.co.us.

FISHING AND HUNTING

Nonresident fishing licenses: annual $40.25; five-day, $18.25; one-day, $5.25; additional one-day stamp, $5; second-rod stamp, $4. Many varieties of trout can be found in Colorado: rainbow and brown in most streams, lakes, and western Colorado River, brook in all mountain streams, and cutthroat in most mountain lakes. Mackinaw can be found in many lakes and reservoirs. Kokanee salmon are also found in many reservoirs.

Nonresident hunting licenses: elk, $250.25; deer, $150.25; small game, $40.25. For information about regulations, write to the Division of Wildlife, 6060 Broadway, Denver 80216; or phone 303/297-1192.

Driving Information

Safety belts are mandatory for all persons in the front seat of a vehicle. Children under 4 years and under 40 pounds in weight must be in approved safety seats anywhere in the vehicle. Phone 303/239-4500 for more information.

INTERSTATE HIGHWAY SYSTEM

The following alphabetical listing of Colorado towns in this book shows that these cities are within 10 miles of the indicated interstate highways. Check a highway map for the nearest exit.

Highway Number	Cities/Towns within 10 Miles
Interstate 25	Colorado Springs, Denver, Englewood, Fort Collins, Lakewood, Longmont, Loveland, Manitou Springs, Pueblo, Trinidad, Walsenburg.
Interstate 70	Breckenridge, Burlington, Central City, Denver, Dillon, Evergreen, Georgetown, Glenwood Springs, Golden, Grand Junction, Idaho Springs, Lakewood, Limon, Vail.
Interstate 76	Denver, Fort Morgan, Sterling.

Additional Visitor Information

Colorado Outdoors magazine is published six times a year by the State Department of Wildlife, 6060 Broadway, Denver 80216; phone 303/297-1192. *Colorado, Official State Vacation Guide* is available from the Colorado Travel & Tourism Authority, PO Box 3524, Englewood 80155; phone toll-free 800/COLORADO. A pamphlet on guest ranches is available from the Colorado Dude & Guest Ranch Association, PO Box 2120, Granby 80446; phone 970/724-3653.

Seven welcome centers in Colorado provide brochures and travel information. They are located at I-70 westbound in Burlington, I-70 eastbound in Fruita, Hwy 40 eastbound in Dinosaur, I-25 northbound in Trinidad, Hwy 160/666 northbound in Cortez, Hwy 50 westbound in Lamar, and I-76 westbound in Julesburg.

Gold mining towns abound in Colorado, as they do in many Western states. Although not all towns can be reached by passenger cars, Colorado has developed the jeep tour to great advantage. Information about ghost towns and jeep trips is listed under Breckenridge, Gunnison, Ouray, Salida, and Silverton.

COLORADO'S GOLD MINES

The San Juan Skyway is a spectacular scenic 236-mile loop out of Durango that ranges over five mountain passes as it wanders through the San Juan Mountains. From Durango, head west on Hwy 160 to Hesperus, where you can take a side trip into La Plata Canyon to see mining ruins and a few ghost towns. Continuing west, you'll pass Mesa Verde National Park and come to Hwy 145 shortly before Cortez. Head north to the town of Dolores and the Anasazi Heritage Center, which features a large display of artifacts, most more than 1,000 years old. The road now follows the Dolores River, a favorite of trout anglers, and climbs the 10,222-foot Lizard Head Pass, named for the imposing rock spire looming overhead. Descending from the pass, take a short side trip into Telluride, a historic mining town and ski resort nestled in a beautiful box canyon. Follow the San Miguel River valley to Hwy 62, and turn north to cross the 8,970-foot Dallas Divide. After the historic railroad town of Ridgway and Ridgway State Park, where you might stop for a swim or picnic, turn south on Hwy 550 and drive to Ouray, a picturesque old mining town. Continue over the 11,008-foot Red Mountain Pass; there is a monument here dedicated to snowplow operators who died while trying to keep the road open during winter storms. Next stop is Silverton, a small mining town and the northern terminus of the Durango and Silverton Narrow Gauge Railroad. South of Silverton is the 10,910-foot Molas Divide, after which the road almost parallels the rails as they follow the Animas River back to Durango. This tour can be done in one long day by those who want to see only the mountain scenery, but is better over two or three days, with stops at Mesa Verde National Park and the historic towns along the way. **(Approximately 236 miles)**

Alamosa (E-3)

See also Monte Vista

Founded 1878
Population 7,960
Elevation 7,544 ft
Area Code 719
Zip 81101
Information Alamosa County Chamber of Commerce, Cole Park; phone 719/589-3681 or toll-free 800/BLU-SKYS
Web site www.alamosa.org

The settlers who came to the center of the vast San Luis Valley were pleased to find a protected area on the Rio Grande shaded by cottonwood trees and named their new home Alamosa, Spanish for "cottonwood." The little town quickly became a rail, agricultural, mining, and educational center. A Ranger District office of the Rio Grande National Forest (see SOUTH FORK) is located in La Jara, 14 miles south on Hwy 285.

What to See and Do

Cole Park. *On Rio Grande River, 425 4th St, Alamosa. Phone 719/589-3681.* Old Denver and Rio Grande Western narrow-gauge trains on display. Chamber of Commerce located in old train station. Tennis, bicycle trails, picnicking, playgrounds. **FREE**

Cumbres & Toltec Scenic Railroad, Colorado Limited. *500 S Terrace Ave, Antonito. 28 miles S. Phone 719/376-5483; toll-free 888/286-2737.* Round-trip excursion to Osier on an 1880s narrow-gauge steam railroad. Route passes through backwoods country and mountain scenery, including the Phantom Canyon and the Toltec Gorge. Warm clothing is advised due to sudden weather changes. (Memorial Day-mid-Oct, daily) Also trips to Chama, New Mexico, via the New Mexico Express with van return. Reservations advised. **$$$$**

Fort Garland Museum. *29477 Hwy 159, Fort Garland. 25 miles E off Hwy 160 at Fort Garland. Phone 719/379-3512.* Army post (1858-1883) where Kit Carson held his last command. Restored officers' quarters; collection of Hispanic folk art. (Apr-Oct: daily 9 am-5 pm; rest of year: Thurs-Mon 8 am-4 pm) **$**

Special Events

Early Iron Festival. *Cole Park, 425 4th St, Alamosa. Phone 719/589-6077; toll-free 877/589-0774.* This annual auto show attracts lovers of antique cars and hot rods. Labor Day weekend.

Sunshine Festival. *Cole Park, 425 5th St, Alamosa. Phone 719/589-6077.* Arts, crafts, food booths, bands, horse rides, parade, pancake breakfast, contests. First full weekend in June.

Limited-Service Hotels

★★ BEST WESTERN ALAMOSA INN. *1919 Main St, Alamosa (81101). Phone 719/589-2567; toll-free 800/459-5123; fax 719/589-8998. www.bestwestern.com/alamosainn.* 53 rooms, 2 story. Pets accepted, some restrictions; fee. Complimentary continental breakfast. Check-in 2 pm, check-out 11 am. Restaurant, bar. Indoor pool, whirlpool. Airport transportation available. **$**

★★ HOLIDAY INN. *333 Santa Fe Ave, Alamosa (81101). Phone 719/589-5833; toll-free 800/669-1658; fax 719/589-4412. www.holiday-inn.com.* 126 rooms, 2 story. Pets accepted; fee. Check-in 3 pm, check-out noon. Restaurant, bar. Indoor pool, whirlpool. Airport transportation available. Business center. **$**

Restaurant

★ TRUE GRITS STEAKHOUSE. *100 Santa Fe Ave, Alamosa (81101). Phone 719/589-9954.* John Wayne memorabilia. Steak menu. Lunch, dinner. Closed Thanksgiving, Dec 25. Bar. Children's menu. Casual attire. **$$**

Aspen (C-2)

See also Snowmass Village

Settled 1879
Population 5,914
Elevation 7,908 ft
Area Code 970
Zip 81611
Information Aspen Chamber Resort Association, 425 Rio Grande Place; phone 970/925-1940 or toll-free 800/26-ASPEN
Web site www.aspenchamber.org

Aspen's first white settlers put down stakes in 1878 in pursuit of silver and enjoyed early prosperity that fizzled after the silver market crashed in 1893. By World War I, most of the local mining operations had gone bust, and Aspen deteriorated toward ghost town status, bottoming out in population at 700 residents. But in 1946, the town's fortunes reversed course when developer Walter Paepcke founded the Aspen Skiing Company with the vision of a cerebral, arts-oriented community. In 1950, Aspen hosted the alpine skiing world championship and another boom commenced—this one based on bringing tourists in rather than taking minerals out. Today, Aspen is home to some of the most expensive real estate in the world and draws in the rich and famous en masse with immaculate ski slopes, trendy shopping and nightlife, and an air of historic luxury that outclasses its rival ski resorts in Colorado.

Aspen Fun Fact

- The world's largest silver nugget (1,840 pounds) was found near Aspen in 1894.

What to See and Do

Ashcroft Ghost Town. *Castle Creek Rd, Aspen. 10 miles S in Castle Creek Valley. Phone 970/925-3721.* Partially restored ghost town and mining camp features 1880s buildings and a hotel. Guided tours (mid-June-early Sept: daily 11 am, 1 pm and 3 pm). Self-guided tours available daily. **$**

Aspen Highlands. *0076 Boomerang Rd, Aspen. 1 1/2 miles SW on Maroon Creek Rd, in White River National Forest (see GLENWOOD SPRINGS). Phone 970/925-1220; toll-free 800/525-6200. www.onthesnow .com/CO/24.* Three quads, one triple chairlift; patrol, school, rentals, snowmaking; three restaurants, bar. One hundred twelve runs; longest run 3 1/2 miles; vertical drop 3,635 feet. Snowboarding. Shuttle bus service to and from Aspen. Half-day rates. (Mid-Dec-early Apr, daily) **$$$$**

Aspen Mountain. *601 E Dean, Aspen. Phone 970/ 925-1220; toll-free 800/525-6200. www.skiaspen.com.* Three quad, four double chairlifts; gondola; patrol, school, snowmaking; restaurants, bars. Seventy-six runs; longest run 3 miles; vertical drop 3,267 feet. (Dec-mid-Apr, daily) Shuttle bus service to Buttermilk, Aspen Highlands, and Snowmass. **$$$$**

Blazing Adventures. *407 E Hyman Ave, Aspen. Phone 970/923-4544; toll-free 800/282-7238. www. blazingadventures.com.* Half-day, full-day, and overnight river rafting trips on the Arkansas, Roaring Fork, Colorado, and Gunnison rivers. Trips range from scenic floats for beginners to exciting runs for experienced rafters. Whitewater rafting (May-Oct; reservations required) Transportation to site. Bicycle, jeep, and hiking tours are also available. **$$$$**

Buttermilk Mountain. *806 W Hallam, Aspen. 2 miles W on Hwy 82. Phone 970/925-1220; toll-free 800/ 525-6200. www.skiresortsguide.com/stats.cfm/co09.htm.* Quad, five double chairlifts, surface lift; patrol, school, rentals, snowmaking; cafeteria, restaurants, bar, nursery. Forty-three runs; longest run 3 miles; vertical drop 2,030 feet. Snowboarding. (Mid-Dec-early Apr: daily 9 am-3:30 pm) Shuttle bus service from Ajax and Snowmass. **$$$$**

HeritageAspen. *620 W Bleeker St, Aspen. Phone 970/925-3721; toll-free 800/925-3721. www. aspenhistory.org.* The exhibits here depict Aspen area history. (Early June-Sept and mid-Dec-mid-Apr: Tues-Fri; rest of year: by appointment; closed Dec 25)

Independence Pass. *Hwy 82 from Hwy 24 to Aspen. Phone 970/925-3445.* A route to be shunned if you are afraid of heights, Hwy 82 through Independence Pass is, nevertheless, a spectacular visual treat, not to mention an adrenaline rush. The winding, cliff-hanging road between Hwy 24 and Aspen is among the nation's highest, reaching 12,095 feet at its rocky summit. It offers beautiful vistas of Colorado's majestic forests and snow-covered peaks at every hair-raising turn. Stop at the top for the views and a short trail hike. The pass is closed between Nov and May.

Recreation. *Aspen.* Swimming, fishing, river rafting; hunting (deer, elk), hiking, climbing, horseback riding, golf, tennis, ice skating, camping, pack trips, kayaking, hang-gliding, paragliding, sailplaning, and ballooning. There are 1,000 miles of trout streams and 25 lakes within a 20-mile radius of Aspen, plus many more in the surrounding mountains. More than ten public campgrounds. Contact the Aspen Chamber Resort Association for details.

Snowmass. *12 miles NW (see SNOWMASS VILLAGE). www.skiaspen.com.*

Special Events

Aspen Music Festival. *2 Music School Rd, Aspen. Phone 970/925-3254. www.aspenmusicfestival.com.* Held in several locations, including Aspen Music Tent, Wheeler Opera House, and Harris Concert Hall. Symphonies, chamber music concerts, opera, and jazz. June-Aug.

Aspen Theater in the Park. *Suite 103, Rio Grande Ball Field, Aspen. The theater tent is located on the NE corner of the Rio Grande Ball Field. Phone 970/925-9313. www.aspentip.org.* Performances nightly and afternoons. June-Aug. **$$$$**

Winterskol Carnival. *Throughout the city. Phone 970/925-1940.* Also known as the Festival of Snow, this annual four-day event features a parade, torchlit ski procession, contests, and more. Mid-Jan.

Limited-Service Hotels

★ASPEN MOUNTAIN LODGE. *311 W Main St, Aspen (81611). Phone 970/925-7650; toll-free 800/362-7736; fax 970/925-5744. www.aspenmountainlodge.com.* A massive river rock fireplace dominates the large lobby of this homey lodge within walking distance of downtown and on the shuttle bus route to the slopes. The guest rooms, which face an open courtyard, have refrigerators and TVs with VCRs. Some have private balconies and jetted tubs as well. 38 rooms, 4 story. Closed late Apr-late May. Pets accepted, some restrictions; fee. Complimentary continental breakfast. Check-in 4 pm, check-out 11 am. Outdoor pool, whirlpool. **$$**

★ HOTEL ASPEN. *110 W Main St, Aspen (81611). Phone 970/925-3441; toll-free 800/527-7369; fax 970/920-1379. www.aspen.com/ha.* 45 rooms, 3 story. Pets accepted; fee. Complimentary continental breakfast. Check-in 4 pm, check-out 11 am. Pool, whirlpool. **$$**

★ LIMELITE LODGE. *228 E Cooper St, Aspen (81611). Phone 970/925-3025; toll-free 800/433-0832; fax 970/925-5120. www.aspen.com/limelite.* 63 rooms, 3 story. Pets accepted. Complimentary continental breakfast. Check-out 11 am. Two pools, whirlpool. **$**

★ MOLLY GIBSON LODGE. *101 W Main St, Aspen (81611). Phone 970/925-3434; toll-free 800/356-6559; fax 970/925-2582. www.mollygibson.com.* 58 rooms, 2 story. Complimentary continental breakfast. Check-in 3 pm, check-out 10 am. Bar. Fitness room. Pool, whirlpool. Airport transportation available. Business center. **$**

Full-Service Hotels

★ ★ ★ HOTEL JEROME. *330 E Main St, Aspen (81611). Phone 970/920-1000; toll-free 800/331-7213; fax 970/925-2784. www.hoteljerome.com.* Built to rival the Ritz in Paris, the Hotel Jerome has been an Aspen landmark since 1889. Located in the heart of downtown, this historic hotel is within walking distance of the town's boutiques and restaurants, yet only minutes from the slopes (with complimentary transportation a nice bonus). Guests feel cosseted here; the concierge meets every demand, and the ski concierge assists with rentals, tickets, and insight on the trails. The boutique-style rooms are magnificent, reflecting the hotel's Victorian heritage with carved armoires and beautiful beds. Every amenity is supplied here, and after a long day of skiing or hiking, guests appreciate the extra touches. The dashing J Bar, a popular watering hole since the 1890s, is still one of the hottest places in town. 91 rooms, 4 story. Pets accepted, some restrictions; fee. Check-in 4 pm, check-out 11 am. Restaurant, bar. Fitness room. Pool, whirlpool. Airport transportation available. **$$$$**

★ ★ ★ ★ ★ THE LITTLE NELL. *675 E Durant Ave, Aspen (81611). Phone 970/920-4600; toll-free 800/525-6200; fax 970/920-4670. www.thelittlenell.com.* Tucked away at the base of a mountain, The Little Nell provides its guests with a perfect location either to hit the slopes for a day of skiing or to pound the streets in search of Aspen's latest fashions. Offering unparalleled luxury, it captures the essence of an elegant private hideaway while maintaining the services usually associated with larger resorts. Romantic in winter, The Little Nell delights visitors throughout the year with its European savoir faire and breathtaking views. The rooms and suites are heavenly cocoons with fireplaces, overstuffed furniture, and luxurious bathrooms. Some suites feature vaulted ceilings showcasing glorious mountainside views, while others overlook the charming former mining town. A well-equipped fitness center challenges guests to vigorous workouts, while the outdoor pool and Jacuzzi soothe tired muscles. The Little Nell's Montagna (see) is one of the hottest tables in town with its inventive reinterpretation of American cuisine. *Secret Inspector's Notes: Lively crowds and frequent celebrity sightings (even Antonio Banderas) make the après-ski scene at The Little Nell's Garden Bar and Hotel Lounge Bar worthy destinations even if you're not a guest at the hotel.* 92 rooms, 4 story. Closed late Apr-mid-May. Pets accepted. Check-in 4 pm, check-out noon. Restaurant, bar. Fitness room. Outdoor pool, children's pool, whirlpool. Airport transportation available. Business center. **$$$$**

★★★★ THE ST. REGIS, ASPEN. *315 E Dean St, Aspen (81611). Phone 970/920-3300; toll-free 888/454-9005; fax 970/925-8998. www.stregisaspen.com.* The St. Regis radiates luxury in its superb location at the base of Aspen Mountain. From its elegant interpretation of Western style to its white-glove service, this hotel is the very definition of refinement. Memorable skiing is guaranteed here, with a terrific location between the gondola and lift, gracious shuttles from door to door, and easy transportation to nearby Aspen Highlands, Buttermilk Mountain, and Snowmass. Aspen's picture-perfect vistas attract hikers, while its clear streams appeal to anglers. The sparkling outdoor pool and accompanying lounge are ideal for whiling away warm afternoons. Well-heeled guests succumb to the sumptuous accommodations, where overstuffed leather chairs and stunning appointments create cocoonlike shelters. Guests beat a path to Olives (see), where renowned chef Todd English creates his inspired dishes from the Mediterranean. Live entertainment is enjoyed in the Lobby Lounge, and Whiskey Rocks is a hip gathering place, perfect after a long day spent in the great outdoors. *Secret Inspector's Notes: The St. Regis Aspen is the place to stay for guests who want to be treated well. The staff is incredibly warm, welcoming, and accommodating. Everything at this hotel oozes with luxury; whether you're skiing or not, you feel like a VIP amidst Aspen's mountain beauty.* 257 rooms, 6 story. Closed late Oct-mid-Nov. Pets accepted; fee. Check-in 3 pm, check-out noon. Restaurant, bar. Fitness room. Outdoor pool, children's pool, whirlpool. Business center. **$$$**

Full-Servce Resort

★★★ ASPEN MEADOWS. *845 Meadows Rd, Aspen (81611). Phone 970/925-4240; toll-free 800/452-4240; fax 970/925-7790. www.dolce.com.* Six buildings are nestled into this 40-acre mountain retreat, host to leaders from around the world since 1949. 98 rooms. Check-in 4 pm, check-out 11 am. Restaurant. Fitness room. Outdoor pool, whirlpool. Tennis. Airport transportation available. Business center. **$$$**

Full-Service Inn

★★★ HOTEL LENADO. *200 S Aspen St, Aspen (81611). Phone 970/925-6246; toll-free 800/321-3457; fax 970/925-3840. www.hotellenado.com.* Located in the heart of Aspen, this hotel offers personalized touches and is a comfortable year-round retreat. Four-poster beds adorn each room. 19 rooms, 3 story. Pets accepted, some restrictions. Complimentary full breakfast (in season), continental breakfast (off-season). Check-in 4 pm, check-out noon. Bar. Whirlpool. **$$$$**

Specialty Lodgings

The following lodging establishments are approved by Mobil Travel Guide, but due to their unique and individualized nature have not been given a traditional Mobil Star rating. Included in this listing you may find bed-and-breakfasts, limited-service inns, guest ranches, and other unique hotel properties.

HEARTHSTONE HOUSE. *134 E Hyman Ave, Aspen (81611). Phone 970/925-7632.* 15 rooms. Check-in 3 pm, check-out 11 am. **$$**

THE INDEPENDENCE SQUARE. *404 S Galena, Aspen (81611). Phone 970/920-2313; toll-free 800/633-0336. www.indysquare.com.* 28 rooms. Check-in 3 pm, check-out 11 am. **$$**

INNSBRUCK INN. *233 W Main St, Aspen (81611). Phone 970/925-2980; fax 970/925-6960. www.preferredlodging.com.* 30 rooms, 2 story. Pets accepted; fee. Complimentary continental breakfast. Check-in 3 pm, check-out 11 am. Pool, whirlpool. **$**

Restaurants

★ ★ **AJAX TAVERN.** *685 E Durant, Aspen (81611). Phone 970/920-9333. www.ajaxtavern.com.* At the foot of the gondola, this restaurant features a seasonal Italian, seafood menu. Lunch, dinner. Closed mid-Apr-mid-May. Bar. Casual attire. Valet parking. Outdoor seating. **$$$**

★ **BOOGIE'S DINER.** *534 E Cooper Ave, Aspen (81611). Phone 970/925-6610; fax 970/920-1560. www.boogiesaspen.com.* American menu. Lunch, dinner. Closed mid-Apr-mid-June. Bar. Children's menu. Casual attire. **$$**

★ ★ **CANTINA.** *411 E Main St, Aspen (81611). Phone 970/925-3663.* Mexican menu. Lunch, dinner. Bar. Children's menu. Casual attire. Outdoor dining. **$$**

★ ★ ★ **JIMMY'S AN AMERICAN RESTAURANT.** *205 S Mill St, Aspen (81611). Phone 970/925-6020; fax 970/925-6048.* American menu. Dinner. Closed Thanksgiving, Dec 25. Bar. Children's menu. Casual attire. Outdoor seating. **$$$**

★ ★ **LA COCINA.** *308 E Hopkins, Aspen (81611). Phone 970/925-9714.* Mexican menu. Dinner. Closed Dec 25; also mid-Apr-mid June. Bar. Children's menu. Outdoor seating. **$**

★ ★ **L'HOSTARIA.** *620 E Hyman Ave, Aspen (81611). Phone 970/925-9022; fax 970/925-5868. www.lhostaria.com.* Italian menu. Dinner. Closed mid-Apr-mid May. Bar. Children's menu. Casual attire. Reservations recommended. Outdoor seating. **$$**

★ ★ ★ **MATSUHISA.** *303 E Main St, Aspen (81611). Phone 970/544-6628; fax 970/544-6630.* This outpost of Nobu Matsuhisa's LA sushi-shrine is every bit as good as the original; amazing given that it is 9,000 feet above sea level. Creative dishes reflect a thoughtful mind, and the service is arguably among the best in town. Japanese menu. Dinner. Bar. Casual attire. **$$$$**

★ ★ **MEZZALUNA.** *624 E Cooper Ave, Aspen (81611). Phone 970/925-5882; fax 970/925-3423. www.mezzalunaaspen.com.* Italian menu. Lunch, dinner. Casual attire. **$$$**

★ ★ ★ ★ **MONTAGNA.** *675 E Durant Ave, Aspen (81611). Phone 970/920-6313; fax 970/920-4670. www.thelittlenell.com.* The Little Nell (see) is one of the most picturesque spots in Aspen, filled with guests who are often as stunning to look at as the breathtaking views of the mountains. It's no surprise, then, that The Little Nell's contemporary American restaurant, Montagna, is a coveted dining spot. With its glossy, buttery walls, rustic wood, iron chandeliers, and deep picture windows, the restaurant has the feeling of chic Swiss chalet. The food is perfect for satiating post-ski hunger pangs, and the staff will graciously accommodate any special requests. The wine service is especially attentive and is sensitive to the high-altitude effects of alcohol. Montagna has the ability to be simultaneously casual and elegant, proving itself equally appropriate for a family gathering or a romantic meal. *Secret Inspector's Notes: Breakfast at Montagna is a worthy treat. Even a simple fruit plate shines with the decadent touch of chocolate chip banana bread. Lunch at the très French café before the doors to Montagna is a culinary delight, its filling fare presented with witty creativity and cocktails mixed with flawless precision. Dinner may not be the strong point of this charming dining destination, but it is well worth a visit at any point throughout the day.* American menu. Dinner, Sun brunch. Closed late Apr-mid-May. Bar. Children's menu. Casual attire. Valet parking. Outdoor seating. **$$$$**

★ ★ **MOTHERLODE.** *314 E Hyman Ave, Aspen (81611). Phone 970/925-7700; fax 970/925-7197. www.motherloderestaurant.com.* Italian, seafood menu. Dinner. Closed mid-Apr-June. Bar. Casual attire. Outdoor seating. **$$**

★ ★ ★ **OLIVES.** *315 E Dean St, Aspen (81611). Phone 970/920-7356; toll-free 888/920-7356. www.stregisaspen.com.* Located in the St. Regis hotel (see) and featuring famed Boston chef Todd English's Mediterranean-influenced cuisine, this casually elegant restaurant is alive with warm woods, rich fabrics, and an open kitchen. Stellar entrées include pecorino-stuffed lamb ribs with mushroom bordelaise and creamy polenta. Mediterranean menu. Lunch, dinner. Children's menu. **$$$**

★ ★ **PACIFICA.** *307 S Mill St, Aspen (81611). Phone 970/920-9775; fax 970/920-9773.* American, seafood menu. Lunch, dinner. Bar. Children's menu. Outdoor seating. **$$**

★ ★ ★ PINE CREEK COOKHOUSE. *12500 Castle Creek Rd, Aspen (81611). Phone 970/925-1044; fax 970/925-7939. www.pinecreekcookhouse.com.* Unique dining in a cabin located in a scenic valley in the Elk Mountains (elevation 9,800 feet); overlooks Castle Creek. American menu. Lunch, dinner. Closed mid-Apr-mid-June, mid-Sept-mid-Nov. Bar. Casual attire. Reservations recommended. Outdoor seating. **$$$**

★ ★ ★ PIÑON'S. *105 S Mill St, Aspen (81611). Phone 970/920-2021.* If you find yourself having dinner at Piñon's, make a point of stopping for a moment between sumptuous bites of the restaurant's wonderfully prepared American fare to express your thanks to the person at your table responsible for making your reservation. Sincere gratitude is required because a place at a table at Piñon's is one of the most sought-after seats in Aspen. Hidden away on the second floor of a shop in downtown Aspen, the restaurant is light, contemporary, and decorated in a tropical theme. The service is warm; the innovative, seasonal menu approachable; and the music upbeat and festive, perfect for lively conversation of the personal or business variety. *Secret Inspector's Notes: Piñon's has a fantastic energy with lively guests and a cheerful staff. It may not run as smoothly as one would expect, but both the food and the scene make for a fun evening with family or friends.* American menu. Dinner. Closed early Apr-early June, Oct-Nov. Bar. Casual attire. **$$$**

★ ★ ★ RESTAURANT CONUNDRUM. *325 E Main St, Aspen (81611). Phone 970/925-9969; fax 970/925-7808.* Restaurant Conundrum is perfect for many things. People-watching is one, as the dining room is often filled with Aspen's most hip and glamorous diners. Atmosphere is another, since the serene russet, gold, and sage-colored dining room appointed with a warm, leafy fabric makes the room feel like a clear, sunny autumn day. And then there's the food, which is the most perfect part of Restaurant Conundrum. Flavorful, stylish, appealing, delicious, and wow are words that come to mind when describing the menu here. Straightforward technique is deftly put to use, bringing ingredients like Colorado lamb chops, Atlantic salmon, and range-fed steaks to thrilling life on the plate and on the tongue. *Secret Inspector's Notes: There is nothing difficult about Conundrum. The service is welcoming, the menu arranged to satisfy each diner's personal preferences, and the lobster bisque dreamy to the last drop. With the restaurant's upbeat atmosphere and intensely flavorful food, you'll have few complaints after enjoying a carefully chosen bottle of wine and an aptly recommended combination of plate elements.* Steak menu. Dinner. Closed mid-Apr-May. Bar. Casual attire. Reservations recommended. Outdoor seating. **$$$**

★ ★ ★ SYZYGY. *520 E Hyman Ave, Aspen (81611). Phone 970/925-3700; fax 970/925-5593.* This restaurant features a dimly lit, romantic setting. Guests can enjoy their dinner and watch for celebrities, too. American menu. Dinner. Closed mid-Apr-May. Bar. Children's menu. Casual attire. **$$$**

★ ★ TAKAH SUSHI. *420 E Hyman Ave, Aspen (81611). Phone 970/925-8588; fax 970/925-4255. www.takahsushi.com.* Japanese, sushi menu. Dinner. Closed Thanksgiving; mid Apr-May, late Oct-late Nov. Bar. Casual attire. **$$**

★ ★ UTE CITY BAR & GRILL. *501 E Hyman Ave, Aspen (81611). Phone 970/920-4699; fax 970/544-9463.* American menu. Lunch, dinner. Bar. Originally a bank (1890). Murals. **$$$**

★ ★ WIENERSTUBE. *633 E Hyman Ave, Aspen (81611). Phone 970/925-3357; fax 970/925-2572.* Austrian menu. Breakfast, lunch. Closed Mon. Bar. Children's menu. Outdoor seating. **$$**

Avon (B-2)

Web site www.avon.org

Full-Service Resorts

★ ★ ★ PARK HYATT BEAVER CREEK RESORT AND SPA. *50 E Thomas Pl, Avon (81620). Phone 970/949-1234; fax 970/949-4164. www.hyatt.beavercreek.com.* Snuggled at the base of the Gore Mountains in the heart of the Beaver Creek Village, the ski-in/ski-out Park Hyatt Beaver Creek Resort and Spa is an alpine paradise. Three of the West's best ski resorts, Beaver Creek, Bachelor Gulch, and Arrowhead, are accessed from the hotel, and Vail is only 10 miles away. Skiers of all levels are accommodated, and the resort's Performance Skiing Program helps guests improve their levels within days. This year-round resort delights visitors in any season, however, with championship golf, the Allegria Spa, and a host of other activities. Five restaurants cover all the bases, with family dining places and romantic après-ski bars. From the giant chandelier crafted of antlers and the massive stone fireplaces to the pine furnishings in the guest rooms, this resort is Western-country style at its best. 274 rooms, 6 story. Check-in 4 pm, check-out noon. Restaurant, bar. Children's activity center. Fitness room, spa. Outdoor pool, children's pool, whirlpools. Golf. Tennis. Business center. **$$$**

★★★ THE PINES LODGE. *141 Scott Hill Rd, Avon (81620). Phone 970/845-7900; toll-free 800/859-8242; fax 970/845-7809.* Perched above the Beaver Creek Resort and golf course, this hotel, condo, and townhouse complex has splendid views and a warm, mountain décor of pine, tapestries, and wildflowers. 60 rooms, 4 story. Complimentary continental breakfast. Check-in 4 pm, check-out 10 am. Restaurant. Fitness room. Outdoor pool, whirlpool. **$$$**

★★★★ THE RITZ-CARLTON BACHELOR GULCH. *0130 Daybreak Ridge, Avon (81620). Phone 970/748-6200; toll-free 800/241-3333; fax 970/748-6300. www.ritzcarlton.com.* Rugged meets refined at The Ritz-Carlton, Bachelor Gulch. From the doorman who greets you with a ten-gallon hat and sweeping capelike coat to the rustic great room, this resort captures the spirit of the Old West while incorporating the polished style that is synonymous with Ritz-Carlton hotels. Located at the base of the mountain at Beaver Creek, this resort offers a true alpine getaway. The rooms and suites are comfortably stylish. Leather club chairs and stone fireplaces highlight the rustic elegance of the resort. The public spaces proudly show off their Western roots with rough-hewn exposed beams, iron chandeliers, and twig furnishings. Attentive and friendly, the service at The Ritz-Carlton is exemplary. 237 rooms, 8 story. Pets accepted. Check-in 3 pm, check-out noon. Restaurant, bar. Fitness room, spa. Outdoor pool. Business center. **$$$$**

Specialty Lodging

The following lodging establishment is approved by Mobil Travel Guide, but due to its unique and individualized nature has not been given a traditional Mobil Star rating. Included in this listing you may find bed-and-breakfasts, limited-service inns, guest ranches, and other unique hotel properties.

WEST BEAVER CREEK LODGE. *220 W Beaver Creek Blvd, Avon (81620). Phone toll-free 888/795-1061; fax 970/949-9091. www.wbclodge.com.* This cozy B&B, within walking distance to shops, restaurants, and Nottingham Park, is a budget-friendly alternative to the area's tony resorts. All rooms feature rustic beamed ceilings; larger rooms and condos are available for families and groups. In the common Great Room, you'll find books, board games, videos, and afternoon snacks. Door-to-door shuttles to Beaver Creek and Vail, onsite ski storage, and discounted lift tickets and equipment rentals make this lodge a natural choice for ski enthusiasts. 9 rooms. Complimentary full breakfast. Check-in 2 pm, check-out 11 am. **$$**

Spas

★★★ ALLEGRIA SPA AT PARK HYATT BEAVER CREEK. *136 E Thomas Pl, Avon (81620). Phone 970/748-7500; toll-free 888/591-1234. www.allegriaspa.com.* The Allegria Spa offers a blend of local-flavored and Eastern-inspired therapies. Unwind and rejuvenate in the spa's sanctuary, where aged copper fountains and a crackling fireplace create a haven for quiet time and reflection. The spa menu offers an alluring mix of treatments and services. Aromatherapy, enzyme, and vitamin C are a few of the 11 types of facials available. A three-layer hydration facial is a lifesaver to skin stressed by the high altitude. Let a therapist work wonders on your sore muscles with a Swedish, shiatsu, deep tissue, sports, or hot stone massage. Asian foot and scalp, barefoot, and Thai massages are delightful as well.

The three feng shui-inspired body treatments awaken your senses and create a positive energy flow. These themed treatments incorporate gentle exfoliation, a nourishing body wrap, and a rewarding massage into one blissful experience. The body scrubs take their inspiration from the garden, with a wild berry and honey scrub, sweet orange and citrus salt glow, and ginger-peach polish rendering supple skin. The lavender, lemon, and Japanese mint hot oil wraps are luxurious ways to calm your soul and battle parched skin. Pamper your hands with a signature manicure, or treat your feet to a honey-ginger, cucumber-mint, or hot stone and mineral pedicure. Create a new look or enhance your natural beauty with a makeup application or the various hair care services offered at the spa.

Fitness plays an important role at this resort and spa. Enjoy spectacular views of the Rocky Mountains while you work out in the fitness center. In addition to various machines and free weights, you can take advantage of nutritional and body-composition analyses or participate in Pilates, yoga, spinning, aerobics, and sports conditioning classes. Or take your fitness regime outdoors with a guided snowshoe journey or hike.

★★★★ THE BACHELOR GULCH SPA AT THE RITZ-CARLTON. *0130 Daybreak Ridge, Avon (81620). Phone 970/343-1138; toll-free 800/576-5582. www.ritzcarlton.com.* Restful and soothing, The Bachelor Gulch Spa captures the essence of its alpine surroundings with the polished rock, stout wood, and flowing water in its interiors. The rock grotto with a lazy river hot tub is a defining feature, and the fitness rooms frame majestic mountain views. The beauty of the outdoors is harnessed here, from the peaceful atmosphere to the treatments that utilize ingredients indigenous to the region. Alpine berries, Douglas fir, and blue spruce sap are just some of the natural components of the exceptional signature treatments. Special attention is paid to skin parched by the high-altitude setting, and treatments like the boot and glove relief and fun-in-the-mud nourish and cleanse skin.

With the roaring rapids massage, the healing power of hydrotherapy cures whatever ails you. Tired muscles beg for the X-stream sports mineral wrap, where essential oils and heated wraps coax the knots out of any weekend warrior. Take a few years off with one of the sensational facials, including the invigorating collagen infusion treatment or the luxurious Champagne therapy. Relax with a four-hands massage, where two therapists pamper you, or succumb to the pleasures of heated river stones.

Restaurants

★★★ BEANO'S CABIN. *PO Box 915, Avon (81620). Phone 970/949-9090; fax 970/845-5769.* This restaurant is located amid the aspen trees on Beaver Creek Mountain. Access by horse-drawn wagon, van, or horseback; with reservations, guests can enjoy a winter moonlit sleigh ride to the restaurant. American menu. Dinner, summer brunch. Closed Mon-Tues in summer; also mid-Apr-May. Bar. Children's menu. Reservations recommended. Outdoor seating. **$$$$**

★★★ GROUSE MOUNTAIN GRILL. *141 Scott Hill Rd, Avon (81620). Phone 970/949-0600; fax 970/949-1221.* American menu. Dinner. Closed Easter; mid-Apr-mid-May. Bar. Casual attire. Free valet parking. Outdoor seating. **$$$**

Beaver Creek

Full-Service Hotel

★★★ BEAVER CREEK LODGE. *26 Avondale Ln, Beaver Creek (81620). Phone 970/845-9800; fax 970/845-8242. www.beavercreeklodge.net.* At the base of the Beaver Creek Resort, this lodge is close to the Centennial and Strawberry Park chairlifts. Each two-room suite offers Southwest-inspired décor. 77 rooms, 6 story, all suites. Closed mid-Apr-mid-May, late Oct-early Nov. Check-in 3 pm, check-out noon. Restaurant. Fitness room. Outdoor pool, whirlpool. **$$**

Full-Service Resort

★★★ THE CHARTER AT BEAVER CREEK. *120 Offerson Rd, Beaver Creek (81620). Phone 970/949-6660; toll-free 800/525-6660; fax 970/949-4489. www.thecharter.com.* 64 rooms, 6 story. Check-in 4 pm, check-out 11 am. Restaurant, bar. Children's activity center. Fitness room. Indoor pool, outdoor pool, children's pool, whirlpool. **$$**

Full-Service Inn

★★★ THE INN AT BEAVER CREEK. *10 Elk Track Ln, Avon (81620). Phone 970/845-7800; toll-free 800/859-8242; fax 970/845-5279. www.innatbeavercreek.com.* This ideal ski-in/ski-out location near the Strawberry Park Express chairlift is also within walking distance of Beaver Creek Resort shops and eateries. The rooms and suites have mountain lodge décor. 45 rooms,

4 story. Complimentary continental breakfast. Check-out 10 am. Bar. Fitness room. Pool, whirlpool. **$$$**

Restaurants

★★★★ MIRABELLE AT BEAVER CREEK. *55 Village Rd, Beaver Creek (81657). Phone 970/949-7728; fax 970/845-9578. www.mirabelle1.com.* Set in a charming cottage in the mountains, Mirabelle at Beaver Creek appears to have dropped out of a fairy tale. The cottage, which dates to the 19th century, is perfect for quiet, intimate dining. Each of the restaurant's spacious, bright rooms is cozy and warm, while the outdoor porch, lined with colorful potted flowers, makes for ideal alfresco dining. A meal at Mirabelle is as magical as the surroundings. The kitchen offers sophisticated Belgian-tinged French food prepared with a modern sensibility. Signature dishes include Colorado lamb chops "My Grand Daddy Style" and roasted elk medallions with fruit compote. House-made ice creams are a special treat, so save room for several scoops if at all possible. French menu. Dinner. Closed Sun; also May, Nov. Bar. Children's menu. Casual attire. Outdoor seating. **$$$**

★★★ SPLENDIDO AT THE CHATEAU. *17 Chateau Ln, Beaver Creek (81620). Phone 970/845-8808; fax 970/845-8961. www.splendidobeavercreek.com.* Special occasions draw many locals to this elegantly appointed, picturesque, chalet-style dining room tucked into the hills of Beaver Creek. Other guests come for the wonderful live piano, offered nightly. But truth be told, the food is Splendido's biggest draw, and for good reason. The menu is upscale and eclectic, merging ingredients from around the world with those of Colorado's native soil. Flavors balance, sauces glisten, and the mouth is treated to a magnificent meal. You'll be hard pressed to find a dish here that does not impress even the most discerning diner. The menu changes nightly, but seasonal signatures have included dishes like sesame-crusted Atlantic salmon with coconut basmati rice and cilantro-lemongrass sauce and grilled elk loin with braised elk osso buco. American menu. Dinner. Closed mid-Apr-mid-June, mid-Oct-mid-Nov. Bar. Children's menu. Reservations recommended. Valet parking. **$$$**

Black Canyon of the Gunnison National Monument (D-1)

See also Montrose

Web site www.nps.gov/blca

15 miles NE of Montrose via Hwy 50, Hwy 347.

Within this monument, 12 of the most spectacular miles of the rugged gorge of the Gunnison River slice down to a maximum depth of 2,660 feet. At one point, the river channel is only 40 feet wide. The narrowest width between the north and south rims at the top is 1,100 feet. The combination of dark, weathered rock and lack of sunlight due to the narrowness of the canyon give the monument its name.

Piñon trees, some more than 800 years old, add to the spectacular scenery, along with numerous mule deer. There are scenic drives along south rim (road plowed to Gunnison Point in winter) and north rim (approximately May to October). There are also hiking areas and concessions (June-Labor Day). The visitor center is located at Gunnison Point on the south rim. A descent into the canyon requires a free hiking permit from the visitor center. Cross-country skiing is open in winter from Gunnison Point to High Point. Interpretive programs are offered (summer only). Contact the Superintendent, 102 Elk Creek, Gunnison 81230; phone 970/641-2337. Per vehicle **$**

Black Hawk

What to See and Do

Black Hawk Casino by Hyatt. *111 Richman St, Black Hawk. 1 mile N of Central City, 30 miles W of Denver on Hwy 119. Phone 303/567-1234.* Once a boom-to-bust mining town, Black Hawk is experiencing a new rush of fortune-seekers with the 1990 introduction of limited-stakes gambling in Colorado. Of the 25 casinos that have taken up residence in Black Hawk and nearby Central City, the 55,000-square-foot Black Hawk by Hyatt is by far the largest and most elaborate. Boasting 1,332 slot machines and video poker terminals, 22 poker and blackjack game tables, and three restaurants, the property is centered around a 5,000-square-foot circular lounge with seven-story, two-sided fireplaces; a circular bar; and a stage for live entertainment. Other fees vary by game. (Daily 8-2 am) **FREE**

Boulder (B-3)

See also Denver, Longmont, Lyons

Settled 1858
Population 94,673
Elevation 5,344 ft
Area Code 303
Information Convention & Visitors Bureau, 2440 Pearl St, 80302; phone 303/442-2911 or toll-free 800/444-0447
Web site www.bouldercvb.com

This is the only city in the United States that obtains part of its water supply from a city-owned glacier, Arapaho Glacier, 28 miles west. Boulder's location at the head of a rich agricultural valley and the base of the Rocky Mountains gives it an ideal year-round climate. The city's unique greenbelt system serves as both a buffer to preserve its picturesque setting and as an extensive park system for outdoor enthusiasts.

Considered the technical and scientific center of Colorado, Boulder is home to the laboratories of the National Institute of Standards and Technology, the National Center for Atmospheric Research, and many private high-tech companies.

Like many cities in Colorado, Boulder enjoys a wealth of cultural activity, including a symphony, music and dance festivals, and outdoor performances of Shakespeare on summer evenings.

A Ranger District office of the Roosevelt National Forest (see ESTES PARK) is located in Boulder.

What to See and Do

Boulder Creek Path. *From 55th St and Pearl Pkwy to Boulder Canyon. Path parallels Arapahoe Ave. Phone 303/413-7200.* A nature and exercise trail that runs some 16 miles through the city and into the adjacent mountains, with no street crossings, leading past a sculpture garden, restored steam locomotive, and several city parks. (Daily) **FREE**

Boulder History Museum. *Harbeck Bergheim House, 1206 Euclid Ave, Boulder. Phone 303/449-3464. www.boulderhistorymuseum.org.* Collections of Boulder history from 1858 to the present including 20,000 artifacts, 111,000 photographs, and 486,000 documents; permanent and rotating interpretive exhibits; and educational programs. (Tues-Fri 10 am-4 pm, Sat-Sun noon-4 pm) **$**

Boulder Museum of Contemporary Art. *1750 13th St, Boulder. Phone 303/443-2122. www.bmoca.org.* Exhibits of contemporary and regional painting, sculpture, and other media; experimental performance series (Thurs, fee); changing exhibits with local, domestic, and international artists. Lectures, workshops, and special events. (Wed-Fri noon-6 pm, Sat 9 am-4 pm, Sun noon-4 pm; closed holidays) **$**

Boulder Reservoir. *5100 51st St, Boulder. 2 miles N on Hwy 119. Phone 303/441-3461.* Swimming (Memorial Day-Labor Day, daily), water-skiing, fishing, boating (daily; get permit for power boat at main gate), rentals; picnicking. (Daily) **$**

Celestial Seasonings Factory Tour. *4600 Sleepytime Dr, Boulder. Phone 303/581-1202. www.celestialseasonings.com.* A tour of the Celestial Seasonings factory in Boulder is a visual, olfactory, and taste delight—and it's free to boot. The 45-minute tour takes visitors through the company's art gallery of original paintings from tea boxes, into the beautiful gardens that produce the herbs and botanicals used in the teas, through the sinus-clearing Mint Room, and into the production area, where 8 million tea bags are made every day. You even have the opportunity to be among the first to sample some of the company's newest blends. Children must be over 5 to enter the factory. [Mon-Sat 10 am-3 pm, Sun 11 am-3 pm (tours on the hour); closed holidays] **FREE**

Eldora Mountain Resort. *2861 Eldora Ski Rd #140, Nederland. 21 miles W on Hwy 119. Phone 303/440-8700; toll-free 800/444-0447. www.eldora.com.* Two quad, two triple, four double chairlifts; four surface lifts; patrol, school, rentals, snowmaking; cafeteria, bar, nursery. Fifty-three runs; longest run 3 miles; vertical drop 1,400 feet. (Mid-Nov-early Apr) Cross-country skiing (27 miles). **$$$$**

Leanin' Tree Museum of Western Art. *6055 Longbow Dr, Boulder. Phone 303/530-1442; toll-free 800/777-8716. www.leanintreemuseum.com.* Museum displaying the original works of art used in many of the greeting cards produced by Leanin' Tree, a major greeting card publisher. The museum also features the private collection of paintings and sculptures from Edward P. Trumble, the chairman and founder of Leanin' Tree Inc. (Mon-Fri 8 am-4:30 pm, Sat-Sun 10 am-4 pm; closed holidays) **FREE**

National Center for Atmospheric Research. *1850 Table Mesa Dr, Boulder. Phone 303/497-1174 (recording). www.ncar.ucar.edu/ncar.* Designed by I. M. Pei. Exhibits on global warming, weather, the sun, aviation hazards, and supercomputing. Also a 400-acre nature preserve on site. Guided tours. Visitor center (Mon-Fri 8 am-5 pm; Sat-Sun, holidays 9 am-4 pm). **FREE**

Pearl Street Mall. *900 to 1500 Pearl St, Boulder. Phone 303/449-3774.* At Pearl Street Mall, locals and visitors gather to enjoy the unique character—and some of the unique characters—of Boulder. Open year-round, this open-air retail and restaurant district is particularly appealing in the summer with its brick walkways, Victorian storefronts, lush landscaping, and parade of colorful personalities. Offering four blocks of mostly upscale restaurants, galleries, bars, and boutiques, the mall beckons visitors to conclude a day of shopping with a meal, al fresco, at one of its many European-style cafés while taking in the impromptu performances of street musicians, jugglers, artists, and mimes.

University of Colorado. *914 Broadway St, Boulder. Phone 303/492-1411. www.colorado.edu.* (1876) (25,000 students) Tours of campus. On the 786-acre campus, the distinctive native sandstone and red-tile buildings include Old Main, Norlin Library, and

Fiske Planetarium and Science Center. *Regent Dr, Boulder. Phone 303/492-5001 (recording).* Programs using a new computerized control system giving a three-dimensional effect; science classes for all ages, special events (fees). Lobby exhibits. Laser shows. **$$$**

Macky Auditorium Concert Hall. *17th St and University Ave, Boulder. Phone 303/492-6309. www.colorado.edu/macky.* This 2,047-seat auditorium hosts the Artist Series, guest artists, and the Boulder Philharmonic Orchestra. Concerts during the academic year.

Sommers-Bausch Observatory. *2475 Kittridge Loop Dr, Boulder. Phone 303/492-6732 (day). lyra.colorado.edu/sbo.* Stargazing. (Weather permitting, school year; closed school holidays) Reservations required Fri. **FREE**

University of Colorado Museum. *Henderson Building, 15th St and Broadway St, Boulder. Phone 303/492-6892. cumuseum.colorado.edu.* Displays relics and artifacts of early human life in the area, plus regional geological, zoological, and botanical collections. Changing exhibits. (Mon-Fri 9 am-5 pm, Sat 9 am-4 pm, Sun 10 am-4 pm; closed school holidays) **$**

Special Events

Bolder Boulder 10K Race. *First National Bank of Colorado, 30th and Diagonal, Boulder. Phone 303/444-7223. www.bolderboulder.com.* Whether you are one of the 45,000 racers or among the 100,000 spectators, just being in Boulder on Memorial Day is a chance to be part one of the largest road races in the world. The popular 10K Bolder Boulder race through town and the surrounding neighborhoods draws participants of all abilities, from professional runners vying for a prize purse to casual walkers enjoying the race-day festivities and camaraderie. Live music and entertainment along the route add to the enjoyment of this family-centered celebration. Races begin at 7 am, awards at 2:30 pm. **$**

Boulder Bach Festival. *Grusin Concert Hall, University of Colorado, Boulder. Phone 303/494-3159. www.boulderbachfest.org.* Concerts of the music of Johann Sebastian Bach. Late Jan.

Colorado Music Festival. *Chautauqua Auditorium, 1525 Spruce St, Boulder. Phone 303/449-1397; toll-free 866/464-2626 (tickets). www.coloradomusicfest.org.* Classical music concerts featuring the CMF Chamber Orchestra, lectures. Eight weeks in June-Aug.

Colorado Shakespeare Festival. *Mary Rippon Outdoor Theatre, University of Colorado, Boulder. Phone 303/492-7355. www.coloradoshakes.org.* Three Shakespeare plays in repertory. June-Aug.

Kinetic Conveyance Sculpture Challenge. *Boulder Reservoir, Boulder. Phone 303/444-5600.* People-powered sculpture race across land, mud, and water. Early May.

Limited-Service Hotels

★ ★ COURTYARD BY MARRIOTT. *4710 Pearl E Cir, Boulder (80301). Phone 303/440-4700; fax 303/440-8975. www.courtyard.com.* 161 rooms, 3 story. Check-in 3 pm, check-out noon. Restaurant, bar. Fitness room. Indoor pool, whirlpool. Airport transportation available. **$**

★ HAMPTON INN. *912 W Dillon Rd, Louisville (80027). Phone 303/666-7700; toll-free 800/426-7866; fax 303/666-7374. www.stonebridgecompanies.com.* 80 rooms, 3 story. Complimentary continental breakfast. Check-out 11 am. Fitness room. Indoor pool, whirlpool. Airport transportation available. Business center. **$**

★ QUALITY INN & SUITES. *2020 Arapahoe Ave, Boulder (80302). Phone 303/449-7550; fax 303/449-1082. www.qualityinnboulder.com.* 40 rooms. Check-in 3 pm, check-out noon. **$**

Full-Service Hotels

★ ★ ★ HOTEL BOULDERADO. *2115 13th St, Boulder (80302). Phone 303/442-4344; toll-free 800/433-4344; fax 303/442-4378. www.boulderado.com.* Boulder was a sleepy little town of 11,000 back in 1905, when the city fathers decided they could move things along by providing the "comfort of a first-class hotel." Thus was born the Hotel Boulderado, in which men worked 24 hours a day stoking the huge coal furnace to keep the hotel evenly heated, and where rooms went for $1 per night. Today there is central heating and the rooms are a bit more expensive, but the hotel is still first-class—and it has been restored to its 1909 grandeur. The lobby's stained-glass ceiling, cantilevered cherry staircase, plush velvet furniture, and overhead fans create a sensation of stepping back in time. The old Otis elevator is the same one that took traveling salesmen up to the fifth floor, where they were allotted space to display their wares. Don't miss the large safe behind the reception desk; it once held the valuables of such rich and famous guests as Ethel Barrymore, Billy Sunday, and Bat Masterson. The Boulderado is still the only hotel in downtown Boulder. 160 rooms, 5 story. Check-out 11 am. Restaurant, bar. Business center. **$$**

★ ★ ★ MILLENNIUM HARVEST HOUSE BOULDER. *1345 28th St, Boulder (80302). Phone 303/443-3850; toll-free 800/545-6285; fax 303/443-1480.* The hotel's sprawling 16 acres are what set it apart in this town of outdoor enthusiasts. The Millennium Harvest House wisely utilizes the acreage for 14 tennis courts (four under what it calls a "tennis bubble," allowing guests to play regardless of weather), plus tents and gazebos for various functions. The Millennium also sits along the Boulder Creek Path, a popular 13-mile path used for jogging, biking, and hiking. 277 rooms, 5 story. Check-in 3 pm, check-out noon. Restaurant, bar. Fitness room. Indoor pool, outdoor pool, children's pool, whirlpool. Business center. **$**

★ ★ ★ ST. JULIEN HOTEL & SPA. *900 Walnut St, Boulder (80302). Phone toll-free 877/465-3741.* 200 rooms. Check-in 3 pm, check-out noon. Restaurant, bar. **$$**

Full-Service Inn

★ ★ ★ ALPS BOULDER CANYON INN. *38619 Boulder Canyon Dr, Boulder (80302). Phone 303/444-5445; toll-free 800/414-2577; fax 303/444-5522. www.alpsinn.com.* If you can find it, you're in for a treat. Tucked away in a mountainside along the curve of a road, the Alps is a cross between a luxurious country inn and a cozy bed-and-breakfast. Once a stagecoach stop, then a bordello, then a stopping place for miners traveling to and from county mining districts, the Alps now caters to Boulder visitors who want to stay ten minutes outside the city in a place that feels like it's a million miles away. The rooms, each with private bath and wood-burning fireplace, have mountain views and sitting areas, and some have claw-foot tubs or double Jacuzzis. Common areas are a combination of the great north woods and a turn-of-the-century mountain lodge. The breakfast room is where most guests love to congregate, conversing over endless cups of coffee and a choice of two entrées, such as French toast or eggs Benedict. If breakfast doesn't fill you up, wait a bit: you'll be served afternoon tea, then evening desserts. 12 rooms, 2 story. Children over 12 years only. Complimentary full breakfast. Check-in 4-9 pm, check-out 11 am. **$**

Specialty Lodging

The following lodging establishment is approved by Mobil Travel Guide, but due to its unique and individualized nature has not been given a traditional Mobil Star rating. Included in this listing you may find bed-and-breakfasts, limited-service inns, guest ranches, and other unique hotel properties.

BRIAR ROSE BED & BREAKFAST. *2151 Arapahoe Ave, Boulder (80302). Phone 303/442-3007; fax 303/786-8440. www.briarrosebb.com.* A lovely, airy feel greets guests at this Victorian-style 1896 home. Cozy rooms lay claim to authenticity ("Now remember," host Robert Weisenbach will tell guests who are not used to such things, "this is a *wood-burning* fireplace and you must open the flue"). There is also an extended-stay suite with a full kitchen that is rented by the week or the month. A highlight of any stay is the inn's afternoon tea tray, with herbal and black teas, iced tea, lemonade, cider, and the Briar Rose Bed & Breakfast's special shortbread cookies. 9 rooms, 2 story. Children over 6 years only. Complimentary continental breakfast. Check-in 3-9 pm, check-out noon. **$$**

Restaurants

★ ★ ANTICA ROMA CAFFE. *1308 Pearl St, Boulder (80302). Phone 303/442-0378; fax 303/449-3876. www.anticaroma.com.* Italian menu. Lunch, dinner. Closed Dec 25. Bar. Children's menu. Outdoor seating. **$$**

★ ★ EUROPEAN CAFE. *2460 Arapahoe, Boulder (80302). Phone 303/938-8250; fax 303/444-8770.* American, French menu. Lunch, dinner. Closed Sun; Memorial Day, July 4, Labor Day. Casual attire. **$$**

★ ★ ★ ★ FLAGSTAFF HOUSE RESTAURANT. *1138 Flagstaff Rd, Boulder (80302). Phone 303/442-4640; fax 303/442-8924. www.flagstaffhouse.com.* From its perch on Flagstaff Mountain, the Flagstaff House Restaurant is easily one of the most amazing spots to watch the sun drift down the horizon in an orange haze. But try to tear your eyes away from the view to check out what's on your plate: it's worth a look and then some. The wine list is massive (the restaurant has a 20,000-bottle wine cellar), so enlist the assistance of the attentive sommelier for guidance. The upscale and inspired menu changes daily and is impressive in style and substance. Classic plates like beef Wellington dressed up with black truffle sauce share menu space with more modern, global dishes like Hawaiian ono with ginger, scallions, and soft-shell crabs. The restaurant is owned by the Monette family, which means that dining here is a delight from start to finish, as you are pampered with refined service and homegrown hospitality. If you can, plan on arriving early and have a seat at the stunning mahogany bar for a pre-dinner cocktail. American menu. Dinner. Closed holidays. Bar. Valet parking. **$$$**

★ ★ FULL MOON GRILL. *2525 Arapahoe Ave, Boulder (80302). Phone 303/938-8800; fax 303/938-5926. www.fullmoongrill.com.* Northern Italian menu. Lunch, dinner. Closed holidays. Bar. Outdoor seating. **$$**

★ ★ ★ THE GREENBRIAR INN. *8735 N Foothills Hwy (US 36), Boulder (80302). Phone 303/440-7979; fax 303/449-2054. www.greenbriarinn.com.* This restaurant offers a gourmet getaway in a mountainside setting. American menu. Dinner, Sun brunch. Closed Mon; Jan 1. Bar. Outdoor seating. **$$$**

★ ★ ★ JOHN'S RESTAURANT. *2328 Pearl St, Boulder (80302). Phone 303/444-5232. www.johnsrestaurantboulder.com.* When you walk into tiny John's Restaurant, you get the feeling that you're walking into someone's home. That's because this century-old cottage used to be just that. Today, it's a charming, 52-seat restaurant with lace curtains and white tablecloths, an intimate place where marriage proposals, anniversaries, and family gatherings are celebrated in equal abundance. In the spring and summer, windows open to courtyards filled with bright flowers. American menu. Dinner. Closed Sun-Mon; July 4, Dec 25. **$$$**

★ ★ LAUDISIO. *2785 Iris, Boulder (80304). Phone 303/442-1300; fax 303/442-6617. www.laudisio.com.* It's easy to overlook Laudisio, housed as it is in a strip mall outside of downtown Boulder. But if you want a taste of Italy, just open its door. First comes the smell of buttery garlic; next is the whimsical drawing of a chef looking at you and raising a glass in your honor. And then there's the wine list—Italian wines, only Italian wines (with a tip of the hat to French Champagnes), more than 300 of them—the largest selection of Italian wines in Colorado, in fact. One of the two terra-cotta dining rooms features an open kitchen. Italian menu. Lunch, dinner. Closed holidays. Bar. Outdoor seating. **$$$**

★ ★ THE MEDITERRANEAN. *1002 Walnut St, Boulder (80302). Phone 303/444-5335; fax 303/444-6451. www.themedboulder.com.* At this restaurant in the heart of Boulder, an after-work crowd of young professionals can be found on the lush outdoor patio having glasses of wine and eating tapas. Inside are bright flowers and a clean, spacious feel. Mediterranean menu. Lunch, dinner. Closed holidays. Bar. Children's menu. Outdoor seating. **$$**

★ ★ ★ Q'S. *2115 13th St, Boulder (80302). Phone 303/442-4880; fax 303/442-4378.* If you dine out often enough, you may find, on occasion, that menu items seem recycled and tired. But this is not the case at Q's, a cozy, welcoming, bistro-style restaurant in the Hotel Boulderado (see). At Q's, bold, contemporary American cuisine is created with spark, style, creativity, and a healthy dose of culinary passion. Digging into the region's best local ingredients, the kitchen offers a spectacular selection of seafood, meat, game, and produce. The international wine collection is eclectic and includes small barrel and boutique selections as well as a proprietor's reserve list. The service is delightful and efficient, making dining here a complete pleasure. American menu. Breakfast, lunch, dinner, Sat-Sun brunch. Bar. **$$$**

★ ★ RHUMBA. *950 Pearl St, Boulder (80302). Phone 303/442-7771; fax 303/448-1185. www.rhumbarestaurant.com.* If nothing else, come to Rhumba to experience a list of 40+ rums. But there are plenty of other reasons to visit this Boulder hotspot, a place to see and be seen in a colorful, casual setting. The servers are young and friendly, the music is energetic but not overpowering, and the island theme is prevalent from the avant-garde *Time* magazine cover of Che Guevara to the rotating overhead fans. If you're in town on a Sunday, don't miss the live music, always Latin or Brazilian, when the windows are thrown open and people come downtown to dance in the street to the beat. Caribbean menu. Lunch, dinner. Children's menu. **$$**

★ ROYAL PEACOCK. *5290 Arapahoe Ave, Boulder (80303). Phone 303/447-1409; fax 303/447-0781.* The Royal Peacock is a mainstay of the Boulder scene. Hidden away in a shopping mall on the outskirts of town, the good news is that there's plenty of easy parking. The better news is that it's owned and operated by Shanti Awatramani and his family, who know how to cook up authentic samosas and chicken makhani with a side of piping hot sikander roti. Never mind if you don't understand; Shanti will explain it so your mouth will water, and your taste buds will be forever grateful. While you're waiting for your food to arrive, spend some time looking at the framed batik prints on the walls to help get yourself in the mood. East Indian menu. Lunch, dinner. Outdoor seating. **$$**

★ ★ ★ TRIO'S. *1155 Canyon Blvd, Boulder (80302). Phone 303/442-8400; fax 303/442-8730. www.triosgrille.com.* Contemporary American menu. Lunch, dinner, Sun brunch. Closed holidays. Bar. **$$$**

Breckenridge (B-3)

See also Dillon, Fairplay

Settled 1859
Population 2,408
Elevation 9,602 ft
Area Code 970
Zip 80424
Information Breckenridge Resort Chamber, 311 S Ridge St, phone 970/453-2913; or Guest Services and Activities Center, 137 S Main St, phone 970/453-5579
Web site www.breckenridge.com

Born as a mining camp when gold was discovered along the Blue River in 1859, modern Breckenridge wears its rough-and-tumble past like a badge. With 350 historic structures, the town is the largest historic district in Colorado. The population peaked at near 10,000 in the 1880s but dwindled to less than 400 in 1960, the year before the town's ski resort opened. The downslide ended, and Breckenridge, thanks to its proximity to Denver, now sees more than 1 million skier-visits annually. Located on four interconnected mountains named Peaks 7, 8, 9, and 10, the ski terrain is revered by skiers but is especially popular with snowboarders. Modern Breckenridge may be a step down the luxury ladder from Vail and Aspen, but it is more affordable—and rowdier—than its ritzier peers.

What to See and Do

Breckenridge Ski Area. *Ski Hill Rd, Breckenridge. 1 mile W off Hwy 9. Phone 970/453-5000; toll-free 800/789-7669 or 800/221-1091 (lodging information* *and reservations). www.breckenridge.snow.com.* Six high-speed quad, triple, seven double chairlifts; five surface lifts, six carpet lifts; school, rentals, snowmaking; four cafeterias, five restaurants on mountain, picnic area; four nurseries (from 2 months old). One hundred twelve runs on three interconnected mountains; longest run 3 miles; vertical drop 3,398 feet. Ski (mid-Nov-early May, daily). Cross-country skiing (23 kilometers), heliskiing, ice skating, snowboarding, sleigh rides. Shuttle bus service. Multiday, half-day, and off-season rates. Chairlift and alpine slide operate in summer (mid-June-mid-Sept). **$$$$**

Ghost towns. *Lincoln City, Swandyke, Dyersville, others.* Some can be reached only by jeep or on horseback; inquire locally.

Summit County Biking Tour. *PO Box 4452, Dillon. www.summitbiketours.com.* The Summit County region in northwest Colorado is a mountain biker's dream with its diverse terrain, spectacular scenery, and Wild West heritage. Hundreds of miles of wilderness roads and trails, many left over from the days when miners crisscrossed the land in search of gold and silver, draw cyclists into an unforgettable exploration of Colorado's high country. A good place to begin is Breckenridge, which is traversed by numerous trails through densely forested valleys, along sparkling lake and riverfronts, and into the peaks of the Continental Divide. A ride over the Argentine Pass, at an elevation of more than 13,207 feet, is the ultimate conquest for experienced bikers. Those who enjoy the thrill without the work can opt to ride a ski lift up the mountain for some awe-inspiring views of the Ten Mile Range, followed by a breathtaking, one-way plunge back to the valley below. Check out area visitor centers, bike shops, and ski resorts for tips and trail maps. (Mar-Nov)

Summit Historical Society walking tours. *Activity Center in Blue River Plaza, 137 S Main St, Breckenridge. Phone 970/453-9022. www.summithistorical.org.* Through the historic district; also tours to abandoned mines, gold panning, and assay demonstrations. (Late June-Aug: Tues-Sat 10 am) **$**

Special Events

Backstage Theatre. *121 S Ridge St, Breckenridge. Phone 970/453-0199. www.backstagetheatre.org.* Melodramas, musicals, comedies. July-Labor Day, mid-Dec-Mar. **$$$$**

Breckenridge Music Festival. *150 W Adams, Breckenridge. Phone 970/453-9142. www.breckenridgemusicfestival.com.* Some of the best classical music in the country is showcased at one of the most beautiful spots on Earth—Breckenridge, Colorado—during the annual Breckenridge Festival of Music. This eight-week summer celebration includes regular full orchestra performances by Breckenridge's own, highly acclaimed National Repertory Orchestra. Performances are held at Riverwalk Center in the heart of downtown Breckenridge. The center is an 800-seat, tented amphitheater opening in back to allow lawn seating for an additional 1,500-2,000 symphony lovers who come to picnic and enjoy music under the stars. Most concerts begin at 7:30 pm. Late Jun-mid Aug.

International Snow Sculpture Championships. *Breckenridge. Phone 970/453-2913.* Sixteen teams from around the world create works of art from 12-foot-tall, 20-ton blocks of artificial snow. Late Jan-early Feb.

No Man's Land Day Celebration. *Breckenridge. Phone 970/453-6018.* Celebrates the time when Colorado became a state of the Union, while the Breckenridge area was mistakenly forgotten in historic treaties. This area became part of Colorado and the US at a later date. Celebration features emphasis on Breckenridge life in the 1880s; parade, dance, games. Second weekend in Aug.

Ullr Fest & World Cup Freestyle. *Breckenridge. Phone 970/453-6018.* Honors the Norse god of snow. Parades, fireworks, Nordic night, and ski competition. Seven days in late Jan.

Full-Service Resorts

★★★ BEAVER RUN RESORT AND CONFERENCE CENTER. *620 Village Rd, Breckenridge (80424). Phone 970/453-6000; toll-free 800/288-1282; fax 970/453-2454. www.beaverrun.com.* The largest self-contained resort in the area, this picturesque property nestled in the mountains is popular with families in both winter and summer. 567 rooms, 8 story. Check-out 11 am. Restaurant, bar. Fitness room. Indoor pool, outdoor pool, whirlpool. Tennis. Business center. **$$**

★ ★ ★ GREAT DIVIDE LODGE. *550 Village Rd, Breckenridge (80424). Phone 970/453-4500; toll-free 800/321-8444; fax 970/453-0212. www.greatdividelodge.com.* Located just 50 yards from the base of Peak 9 and two blocks from Main Street, this lodge is excellent for winter or summer vacationing. 208 rooms, 10 story. Check-out 10 am. Restaurant, bar. Fitness room. Indoor pool, whirlpool. Airport transportation available. **$$**

★ ★ ★ LODGE AND SPA AT BRECKENRIDGE. *112 Overlook Dr, Breckenridge (80424). Phone 970/453-9300; toll-free 800/736-1607; fax 970/453-0625. www.thelodgeatbreck.com.* With exposed wood beams and richly colored fabrics, the décor of this small, full-service spa is sophisticatedly rustic. 47 rooms, 4 story. Pets accepted; fee. Check-out 11 am. Restaurant, bar. Fitness room. Indoor pool, whirlpool. Business center. **$**

Full-Service Inn

★ ★ ★ ALLAIRE TIMBERS INN. *9511 Hwy 9, Breckenridge (80424). Phone 970/453-7530; toll-free 800/624-4904; fax 970/453-8699. www.allairetimbers.com.* The log cabin construction of this charming bed-and-breakfast at the south end of Main Street is made from local pine. Innkeepers Jack and Kathy Gumph welcome guests with hearty homemade breakfasts, afternoon snacks, and warm hospitality. 10 rooms, 2 story. Children over 13 years only. Complimentary full breakfast. Check-in 3-7 pm, check-out 11 am. **$$**

Specialty Lodgings

The following lodging establishments are approved by Mobil Travel Guide, but due to their unique and individualized nature have not been given a traditional Mobil Star rating. Included in this listing you may find bed-and-breakfasts, limited-service inns, guest ranches, and other unique hotel properties.

BED & BREAKFAST ON NORTH MAIN ST. *303 N Main St, Breckenridge (80424). Phone 970/453-2975; toll-free 800/795-2975; fax 970/453-5258. www.breckenridge-inn.com.* Innkeepers Fred Kinat and Diane Jaynes welcome guests to one of the three historic inns that compose this bed-and-breakfast. The individually decorated rooms are pleasant. 12 rooms. Closed three weeks in May, last week in Oct, first two weeks in Nov. No children allowed. Complimentary full breakfast. Check-in by appointment, check-out 11 am. **$**

HUNT PLACER INN. *275 Ski Hill Rd, Breckenridge (80424). Phone 970/453-7573; toll-free 800/472-1430; fax 970/453-2335. www.huntplacerinn.com.* Individually designed rooms with mountain views and hearty, homemade breakfasts distinguish this romantic, chalet-style bed-and-breakfast located just blocks from Main Street. 8 rooms, 3 story. Children over 12 years only. Complimentary full breakfast. Check-in 4-6 pm, check-out 11 am. **$**

Restaurants

★ BRECKENRIDGE BREWERY. *600 S Main St, Breckenridge (80424). Phone 970/453-1550; fax 970/453-0928. www.breckenridgebrewery.com.* American menu. Lunch, dinner. Closed Dec 25. Bar. Children's menu. Outdoor seating. **$$**

★ BRIAR ROSE. *109 E Lincoln St, Breckenridge (80424). Phone 970/453-9948; fax 970/453-2630.* Victorian décor; on the site of an old mining boarding house. American menu. Dinner. Bar. Children's menu. **$$$**

★ ★ CAFE ALPINE. *106 E Adams, Breckenridge (80424). Phone 970/453-8218; fax 970/453-6936. www.cafealpine.com.* Cozy, informal dining in three rooms. American menu. Lunch, dinner. Bar. Children's menu. Outdoor seating. **$$**

★ ★ HEARTHSTONE. *130 S Ridge St, Breckenridge (80424). Phone 970/453-1148; fax 970/453-0247. www.stormrestaurants.com.* In a Victorian house (1886). American menu. Lunch, dinner. Bar. Children's menu. Outdoor seating. **$$$**

★ ★ HORSESHOE 2. *115 S Main, Breckenridge (80424). Phone 970/453-7463; fax 970/453-6223.* A former miners' supply store (1880). American menu. Lunch, dinner. Bar. Children's menu. Casual attire. Outdoor seating. **$$$**

★ MI CASA MEXICAN CANTINA. *600 S Park St, Breckenridge (80424). Phone 970/453-2071; fax*

970/453-0249. www.stormrestaurants.com. Mexican menu. Lunch, dinner. Bar. Children's menu. Outdoor seating. **$$**

★★★ PIERRE'S RIVERWALK CAFE. *137 S Main, Breckenridge (80424). Phone 970/453-0989.* French menu. Lunch, dinner. Closed Dec 25; also May, Oct, and the first two weeks of Nov. Bar. Outdoor seating. **$$$**

★★ SALT CREEK. *110 E Lincoln Ave, Breckenridge (80424). Phone 970/453-4949; fax 970/453-7945.* Steak menu. Lunch, dinner. Bar. Children's menu. Casual attire. Outdoor seating. **$$$**

★★ ST. BERNARD INN. *103 S Main St, Breckenridge (80424). Phone 970/453-2572. www.thestbernard.com.* In a historic mercantile building. Old mining memorabilia. Northern Italian menu. Dinner. Closed May. Bar. Children's menu. **$$**

★★ SWAN MOUNTAIN INN. *16172 Hwy 9, Breckenridge (80424). Phone 970/453-7903. www.swanmountaininn.com.* American menu. Breakfast, lunch, dinner. Bar. Children's menu. Outdoor seating. **$$**

★★ TOP OF THE WORLD. *112 Overlook Dr, Breckenridge (80424). Phone 970/453-9300; fax 970/453-0625. www.colorado.net/thelodge.* American menu. Dinner. Bar. Children's menu. Casual attire. **$$**

Broomfield

See also Leadville, Salida

What to See and Do

FlatIron Crossing. *1 W FlatIron Cir, Broomfield. 15 miles N of Denver and 9 miles S of Boulder, on Hwy 36 at West or East FlatIron Cir exit. Phone 720/887-7467. www.flatironcrossing.com.* This architecturally innovative, 1.5 million-square-foot retail and entertainment complex located between Denver and Boulder was designed to reflect the natural flatirons, canyons, and prairies of its surroundings. The result is a one-of-a-kind visual and shopping experience. At the heart of the center, home to more than 200 stores, is a 240,000-square-foot outdoor "Village" with numerous restaurants for both indoor and outdoor dining. Anchored by Nordstrom, Dillard's, Lord & Taylor, and Foley's, the mall includes a number of art and sports specialty shops, as well as two movie complexes. (Daily; closed Easter, Dec 25)

Full-Service Resort

★★★ OMNI INTERLOCKEN RESORT. *500 Interlocken Blvd, Broomfield (80021). Phone 303/438-6600; toll-free 800/843-6664; fax 303/438-7224. www.omnihotels.com.* Metropolitan Denver is home to the wonderful Omni Interlocken Resort. Situated midway between Denver and Boulder in the area's technology corridor, the resort is part of the Interlocken Advanced Technology Park. Sharing space with leading businesses and the FlatIron Crossings shopping center, this all-season resort is a premier recreational destination. Set against the backdrop of the Rocky Mountains, the 300-acre property has something for everyone. Golfers needing to brush up on their game head for the L. A. W.s Academy of Golf for its celebrated instruction before hitting the three 9-hole courses. The well-equipped fitness center and pool keep guests active, while the full-service spa attends to every need. Indigenous Colorado materials are used throughout the resort, enhancing the local flavor of the design. The guest rooms are comfortably elegant and include 21st-century amenities like WebTV and high-speed Internet connections. Three restaurants run the gamut from traditional to pub style. 390 rooms, 11 story. Pets accepted; fee. Check-out noon. Restaurant, bar. Children's activity center. Fitness room, spa. Pool, whirlpool. Golf. Business center. **$**

Buena Vista (C-3)

Founded 1879
Population 2,195
Elevation 7,955 ft
Area Code 719
Zip 81211
Information Chamber of Commerce, 343 S US 24, Box 2021; phone 719/395-6612
Web site www.buenavistacolorado.org

Lying at the eastern edge of the Collegiate Range and the central Colorado mountain region, Buena Vista is a natural point of departure for treks into the mountains. Within 20 miles are 12 peaks with elevations above 14,000 feet, four rivers, and more than 500 mountain lakes and streams.

What to See and Do

Arkansas River Tours. *126 S Main St, Buena Vista. Phone 719/942-4362; toll-free 800/321-4352. www.arkansasrivertours.com.* The upper Arkansas River in south-central Colorado offers some of the nation's most beautiful and challenging rafting experiences. With its long, placid stretches of scenic wilderness punctuated by hair-raising plunges through dramatic whitewater canyons, it accommodates all levels of river-rafting thrill-seekers. Experienced rafters won't want to miss an adrenaline-pumping ride through the magnificent Royal George Canyon. Families, on the other hand, will love a scenic float through the gently rolling Cottonwood Rapid. Arkansas River Tours is one of several rafting outfitters along Highway 50 offering a variety of outings, from 1/4-day trips to multiple-day high-adventure expeditions. (Daily; weather permitting) **$$$$**

Bill Dvorak's Kayak & Rafting Expeditions. *17921 Hwy 285, Nathrop. Phone 719/539-6851; toll-free 800/824-3795. www.dvorakexpeditions.com.* Half-day to 12-day trips on the Arkansas, Colorado, Dolores, Green, Gunnison, North Platte, Rio Chama, Rio Grande, and San Miguel rivers. Guided fishing trips; kayak instruction. (Mid-Apr-early Oct) **$$$$**

Hiking, camping, mountain biking, snowmobiling, and cross-country skiing. *Buena Vista. Phone 719/395-8001.* Equipment rentals, supplies, maps, and information on trails and routes may be obtained from Trailhead Ventures.

Noah's Ark Whitewater Rafting Company. *23910 Hwy 285 S, Buena Vista. Phone 719/395-2158. www.noahsark.com.* Half-day to three-day trips on the Arkansas River. (Mid-May-late Aug) **$$$$**

St. Elmo ghost town. *County Rd 162, St. Elmo. Take Hwy 24 to County Rd 162 and follow for 19 miles. Phone 719/395-6612 (Chamber of Commerce).* The abandoned remains of a once-thriving Colorado mining town stand as melancholy testimony to fortunes made and lost. A visit to one of these ghostly ruins is a trip back in time, filled with enticing secrets that only the imagination can unlock. All it takes is a flexible schedule, a four-wheel drive vehicle, sturdy shoes, and a sense of adventure. Among the most accessible and best-preserved ghost towns is St. Elmo, just west of Buena Vista in the south-central part of the state. With 24 original buildings still standing, it entices visitors to take a walk along its wood-plank sidewalks and contemplate, in the silence, what it must have been like in the high-spirited gold frenzy days of the late 1800s. Just outside St. Elmo are the abandoned ruins of the Mary Murphy gold mine. Those with four-wheel-drive vehicles can traverse the rocky terrain to the mine for a closer look. Caution is advised!

Wilderness Aware. *12600 Hwy 24/285, Buena Vista. Phone 719/395-2112; toll-free 800/462-7238. www.inaraft.com.* Half-day to ten-day river rafting trips on the Arkansas, Colorado, Dolores, North Platte, and Gunnison rivers. (May-Sept) **$$$$**

Limited-Service Hotel

★BEST WESTERN VISTA INN. *733 Hwy 24 N, Buena Vista (81211). Phone 719/395-8009; toll-free 800/809-3495; fax 719/395-6025. www.bestwestern.com.* 41 rooms, 2 story. Pets accepted, some restrictions; fee. Check-in 2 pm, check-out 11 am. Three hot springs whirlpools. **$**

Restaurants

★★ BUFFALO BAR & GRILL. *710 Hwy 24 N, Buena Vista (81211). Phone 719/395-6472.* American menu. Dinner. Closed Sun. Bar. Children's menu. **$$**

★ CASA DEL SOL. *333 Hwy 24 N, Buena Vista (81211). Phone 719/395-8810.* In 1880 miner's cabin. Mexican menu. Lunch, dinner. Closed late May-Labor Day. Children's menu. Casual attire. Outdoor seating. **$**

Burlington (C-6)

Population 3,678
Elevation 4,160 ft
Area Code 719
Zip 80807
Information Chamber of Commerce, 415 15th St, PO Box 62; phone 719/346-8070
Web site www.burlingtoncolo.com

What to See and Do

Bonny Lake State Park. *30010 County Rd 3, Idalia. 23 miles N on Hwy 385. Phone 970/354-7306. parks.state*

.co.us. A 2,000-acre lake has swimming, water-skiing, fishing, and boating (with ramps), plus picnicking, concession, and camping. (Daily) **$**

Kit Carson County Carousel. *Fairgrounds, Colorado Ave and 15th St, Burlington. www.burlingtoncolo.com/carousel.htm.* Built in 1905, this restored carousel houses a 1912 Wurlitzer Monster Military Band organ. A quarter will get you a tour and a ride. (Memorial Day-Labor Day: daily 1-8 pm) **$**

Old Town. *420 S 14th St, Burlington. Phone 719/346-7382. www.burlingtoncolo.com/oldtown.htm.* This historical village with 20 buildings reflects Colorado prairie heritage. Also cancan shows, gunfights, and melodramas (summer); two-day hoedown (Labor Day weekend). Tours. (Memorial Day-Labor Day: Mon-Sat 9 am-5 pm, Sun noon-5 pm; closed holidays) **$**

Special Events

Kit Carson County Fair & Rodeo. *Fairgrounds, Burlington. Phone 719/346-5566.* Early Aug.

Little Britches Rodeo. *Fairgrounds, Colorado Springs. Phone 719/389-0333.* Late May.

Limited-Service Hotel

★ BEST VALUE INN-BURLINGTON. *1901 Rose Ave, Burlington (80807). Phone 719/346-5333; toll-free 800/362-0464; fax 719/346-9536.* 29 rooms, 2 story. Check-out 10:30 am. Pool. **$**

Cañon City (D-3)

See also Colorado Springs, Cripple Creek, Pueblo

Founded 1859
Population 15,431
Elevation 5,332 ft
Area Code 719
Zip 81212
Information Chamber of Commerce, 403 Royal Gorge Blvd, PO Bin 749; phone 719/275-2331 or toll-free 800/876-7922
Web site www.canoncitychamber.com

Lieutenant Zebulon Pike, in 1807, was one of the first white men to camp on this site, which was long a favored spot of the Ute Indians. Cañon (pronounced Canyon) City is located at the mouth of the Royal Gorge, ringed by mountains. The poet Joaquin Miller, as town judge, mayor, and minister during the early gold-mining days, once proposed renaming the town Oreodelphia, but the horrified miners protested that they could neither spell nor pronounce it. Legend has it that the same earthy logic prevailed when, in 1868, Cañon City was offered either the state penitentiary or the state university. The miners chose the former, pointing out that it was likely to be the better attended institution. A Ranger District office of the San Isabel National Forest (see PUEBLO) is located in Cañon City; phone 719/269-8500.

What to See and Do

Buckskin Joe Frontier Town & Railway. *1193 Fremont County Rd 3A, Cañon City. 8 miles W via Hwy 50, 1 mile S to Royal Gorge. Phone 719/275-5149. www.buckskinjoes.com.* Old West theme park includes old Western town with 30 authentic buildings; restaurant and saloon. Other activities here are daily gunfights, horse-drawn trolley ride, magic shows, and entertainment. Also 3-mile, 30-minute train ride to the rim of Royal Gorge. Railway (Mar-Oct: daily 8 am-7 pm, Nov-Dec: weekends). Park (May-Sept: daily 9 am-6:30 pm). **$$$$**

Cañon City Municipal Museum. *612 Royal Gorge Blvd, Cañon City. Phone 719/276-5279.* The complex includes outdoor buildings; Rudd Cabin, a pioneer log cabin constructed in 1860, and Stone House, built in 1881. Second-floor Municipal Building galleries display minerals and rocks, artifacts from settlement of the Fremont County region, and guns. (Early May-Labor Day, Tues-Sun; rest of year, Tues-Sat; closed holidays) **$**

Colorado Territorial Prison Museum and Park. *201 N 1st St, Cañon City. Phone 719/269-3015. www.prisonmuseum.org.* Housed in a women's prison facility (1935), this museum and resource center displays exhibits and memorabilia of the Colorado prison system. Picnicking is permitted on the grounds. Adjacent is an active medium-security prison. (Memorial Day-Labor Day: daily 8:30 am-6 pm; early May-Memorial Day, Labor Day-mid-Oct: daily 10 am-5 pm; mid-Oct-Apr: Fri-Sun 10 am-5 pm; closed holidays) **$$**

Fremont Center for the Arts. *505 Macon Ave, Cañon City. Phone 719/275-2790. www.fremontarts.org.* Community art center features visual art exhibits and cultural programs. (Tues-Sat; closed holidays) **$**

Rafting. *Cañon City. Phone toll-free 800/876-7922.* There are many rafting companies in the area. For information, contact the Cañon City Chamber of Commerce.

Royal Gorge. *4218 County Rd 3A, Cañon City. 8 miles W on Hwy 50, then 4 miles SW. Phone 719/275-7507; toll-free 888/333-5597. www.royalgorgebridge.com.* This is a magnificent canyon with cliffs rising more than 1,000 feet above the Arkansas River. The Royal Gorge Suspension Bridge, 1,053 feet above the river, is the highest in the world (recreational vehicles larger than small van or small camper are not permitted on the bridge). The Royal Gorge Incline Railway, the world's steepest, takes passengers 1,550 feet to the bottom of the canyon. A 2,200-foot aerial tramway glides across the spectacular canyon. Theater; entertainment gazebo; petting zoo; restaurants; gift shops. (Daily 10 am-4:30 pm)

Royal Gorge Route. *401 Water St, Cañon City. Phone 303/569-2403; toll-free 888/724-5748. www.royalgorgeroute.com.* Travel by train through the Royal Gorge on two-hour round-trips departing from Cañon City. (Summer, daily; call for schedule) **$$$$**

Special Events

Blossom & Music Festival. *Depot Park, Cañon City. Phone 719/275-2331.* This celebration of springtime features arts and crafts, a parade, and a carnival. First weekend in May.

Royal Gorge Rodeo. *1436 S 4th St, Cañon City. Phone 719/275-0118.* First weekend in May.

Limited-Service Hotel

★★ BEST WESTERN ROYAL GORGE. *1925 Fremont Dr, Cañon City (81212). Phone 719/275-3377; toll-free 800/231-7317; fax 719/275-3931. www.bestwestern.com.* 67 rooms, 2 story. Pets accepted, some restrictions; fee. Check-out 11 am. Restaurant, bar. Pool, whirlpool. **$**

Restaurants

★★ LE PETIT CHABLIS. *512 Royal Gorge Blvd, Cañon City (81212). Phone 719/269-3333.* A local favorite serving authentic country French cuisine. Lunch, dinner. Closed Sun-Mon. **$**

★★ MERLINO'S BELVEDERE. *1330 Elm Ave, Cañon City (81212). Phone 719/275-5558; toll-free 800/625-2526; fax 719/275-8980. www.belvedererestaurant.com.* American, Italian menu. Dinner. Closed Thanksgiving, Dec 25. Bar. Children's menu. **$$**

Central City (B-3)

See also Denver, Georgetown, Golden, Idaho Springs

Settled 1859
Population 515
Elevation 8,496 ft
Area Code 303
Zip 80427

Perched along steep Gregory Gulch, Central City's precarious location did not prevent it from becoming known as "the richest square mile on earth" when the first important discovery of gold in Colorado was made here in 1859. More than $75 million worth of metals and minerals have come from Central City and neighboring settlements.

What to See and Do

Central City Opera House. *124 Eureka St, Central City. 35 miles W of Denver, 1 mile W of Blackhawk on Hwy 279. Phone 303/292-6700; toll-free 800/851-8175. new.centralcityopera.org.* Established at the site of Colorado's first major gold strike, Central City gained prominence in the 1860s as the financial and cultural center of the state. Although it's now a center for gambling, Central City preserves the riches of its cultural past in the form of a beautiful Opera House. Designed by Denver architect Robert S. Roeschlaub, this lavish 1878 Historic Landmark building hosts an annual summer opera festival (June-Aug) that draws audiences from around the world to experience its historic charm and acoustic perfection. Tours (fee). Fees vary for performances.

Gilpin County Historical Society Museum. *228 E High St, Central City. Phone 303/582-5283. www.coloradomuseums.org/historym.htm.* Exhibits, housed in an early schoolhouse (1870) under continuing restoration, re-create early gold-mining life in Gilpin County; replicas of a Victorian house and period shops with authentic furnishings; collection of antique dolls; personal effects of a sheriff gunned down in 1896. (Memorial Day-Labor Day: daily 11 am-4 pm; or by appointment) **$** Also maintained by the Historical Society is

The Thomas House Museum. *209 Eureka St, Central City. Phone 303/582-5283. www.coloradomuseums .org/thomasho.htm.* (1874) On display are the belongings of one family who lived in this house. (Memorial Day-Labor Day: Fri-Mon 11 am-4 pm; rest of year: by appointment) **$**

Gold Belt Loop. *W of Colorado Springs, starting at Hwy 67 between Hwys 24 and 50.* Remnants of the glorious, raucous gold rush days can still be found scattered throughout the Colorado landscape. The unexpected discovery of an abandoned mine shaft, rail track, mining camp, or prospector's shack conjures visions of those who were willing to risk it all in the Colorado wilderness for the promise of fame and fortune. Take the time to explore all or part of the Gold Belt Loop, a designated backcountry byway west of Colorado Springs that connects some of the state's most scenic roadway with some of its most historic locales. A good starting point is Cripple Creek or Victor, both located on Hwy 67. These former boomtowns grew up around the most prolific gold mine in the country. Today, they continue to lure fortune seekers with their thriving casino businesses. For a more family-friendly 1800s mining town experience, visit charming Leadville, located northwest of Cripple Creek at the headwaters of the Arkansas River. With 70 square blocks of restored Victorian buildings, its former saloons, boardinghouses, banks, and theaters now house antique stores, restaurants, hotels, and specialty shops. A designated Historic National Landmark District and the home of the National Mining Hall of Fame Museum, Leadville is a great base from which to explore the surrounding mining district as well as its numerous outdoor recreation offerings, including skiing, hiking, mountain biking, horseback riding, rock climbing, hunting, and fishing.

Site of first gold lode discovery in Colorado. *Boundary of Central City and Black Hawk.* Granite monument marks spot where John H. Gregory first found gold on May 6, 1859.

Special Events

Central City Music Festival. *Central City.* Three days of great sounds. Late Aug.

Colorado National Monument (C-1)

See also Grand Junction

5 miles W of Grand Junction, off Hwy 340.

Wind, water, a 10-mile fault, and untold eons have combined to produce spectacular erosional forms. In the 32-square-mile monument, deep canyons with sheer walls form amphitheaters for towering monoliths, rounded domes, and other geological features. Wildlife includes deer, foxes, coyotes, porcupines, and a growing herd of desert bighorn sheep. Rim Rock Drive, accessible from either Fruita or Grand Junction, is a spectacular 23-mile road along the canyon rims. There are picnicking and camping facilities within the monument (all year; fee for camping). The Saddlehorn Visitor Center has geology and natural history exhibits (daily). Interpretive programs are offered in summer. Hiking and cross-country skiing trails are open in season. For detailed information, contact the Superintendent, Fruita, CO 81521; phone 970/858-3617. Per vehicle **$**

Colorado Springs (C-4)

See also Cañon City, Cripple Creek, Manitou Springs

Founded 1871
Population 360,890
Elevation 6,035 ft
Area Code 719
Information Convention & Visitor Bureau, 515 S Cascade, Suite 104, 80903; phone 719/635-7506 or toll-free 800/368-4748
Web site www.coloradosprings-travel.com

Colorado Springs, at the foot of Pikes Peak, is surrounded by areas containing fantastic rock formations. It was founded by General William J. Palmer and the Denver and Rio Grande Railroad as a summer playground and health resort. The headquarters of Pike National Forest is Colorado Springs.

What to See and Do

Broadmoor-Cheyenne Mountain Area. *1 Lake Ave, Colorado Springs. 4 miles S on Nevada Ave, then W on Lake Ave to the Broadmoor Hotel.* Located here are

Broadmoor-Cheyenne Mountain Highway. *Colorado Springs.* Zig-zags up the east face of Cheyenne Mountain; view of plains to the east. Round-trip to Shrine of the Sun (see) is 6 miles. (Daily; weather permitting) Toll (includes zoo, Shrine of the Sun) **$$$**

Cheyenne Mountain Zoological Park. *4250 Cheyenne Mountain Zoo Rd, Colorado Springs. From I-25, take exit 138, the Circle Dr exit, and drive W to the Broadmoor Hotel. Turn right at the hotel and follow the signs. Phone 719/633-9925 (recording). www.cmzoo.org.* This little gem located on the side of the Cheyenne Mountains in Colorado Springs is known for the diversity of its animal collection and the beauty of its setting. Six hundred fifty animals, including many endangered species, make their home here. The most popular exhibits are the monkey house, the birds of prey, and a herd of giraffe that welcome feedings from visitors. Admission includes access to the Will Rogers Shrine of the Sun, from which you can marvel at the spectacular panoramic view of the Colorado Springs and Pikes Peak regions. (Memorial Day-Labor Day: daily 9 am-6 pm; Labor Day-Memorial Day: daily 9 am-5 pm; early closing Thanksgiving, Dec 24-25) **$$$**

El Pomar Carriage Museum. *16 Lake Circle, Colorado Springs. Phone 719/577-5710. www.elpomar.org/founder2.html.* Collection of fine carriages, vehicles, Western articles of 1890s. (Mon-Sat 10 am-5 pm, Sun 1-5 pm; closed Jan 1, Thanksgiving, Dec 25) **FREE**

Shrine of the Sun. *4250 Cheyenne Mountain Zoo Rd, Colorado Springs. Phone 719/578-5367. www.cmzoo.org/shrine.html.* Memorial to Will Rogers, an American entertainer who was killed in a plane crash in 1935. Built of Colorado gray-pink granite and steel. Contains Rogers memorabilia. Fee for visit is included in zoo admission price. (Memorial Day-Labor Day: daily 9 am-5 pm; Labor Day-Memorial Day: daily 9 am-4 pm; closed Jan 1, Thanksgiving, Dec 25)

Colorado Springs Fine Arts Center. *30 W Dale St, Colorado Springs. Phone 719/634-5581. www.csfineartscenter.org.* Permanent collections include Native American and Hispanic art, Guatemalan textiles, 19th- and 20th-century American Western paintings, graphics, and sculpture by Charles M. Russell and other American artists. Changing exhibits; painting and sculpture classes; repertory theater performances; films. Free admission on Saturdays. (Tues-Sat 9 am-5 pm, Sun 1-5 pm; closed holidays) **$**

Colorado Springs Pioneers Museum. *Former El Paso County Courthouse, 215 S Tejon St, Colorado Springs. Phone 719/385-5990. www.cspm.org.* Exhibits portray the history of the Pikes Peak region. (Tues-Sat 10 am-5 pm, Sun 1-5 pm (May-Oct); closed holidays) **FREE**

Flying W Ranch. *3330 Chuckwagon Rd, Colorado Springs. 8 miles NW on 30th St, 2 miles W of I-25 on Garden of the Gods Rd. Phone 719/598-4000; toll-free 800/232-3599. www.flyingw.com.* A working cattle and horse ranch with chuckwagon suppers and Western stage show. More than 12 restored buildings with period furniture. Reservations required. (Mid-May-Sept: daily; rest of year: Fri-Sat; closed Dec 25-Feb) **$$$$**

★ **Garden of the Gods.** *1805 N 30th St, Colorado Springs. Hwy 24 W from I-25 to Ridge Rd exit, or W from I-25 on Garden of the Gods Rd, left of 30th St at Gateway Rd. Phone 719/634-6666. www.gardenofthegods.com.* This 1,350-acre park at the base of Pike's Peak is a showcase of geological wonders. It's best known for its outstanding red sandstone formations, which include the famous Balanced Rock and Kissing Camels. A hiker's delight, the park offers 8 miles of well-groomed trails that provide easy access to its geological treasures, plants, and wildlife. Other favorite activities include horseback riding and rock climbing (by permit only). Try to plan a visit at sunrise or sunset, when you'll get a true understanding of where the name "Garden of the Gods" came from. Visitors center (summer, 8 am-8 pm; winter, 9 am-5 pm; closed Jan 1, Thanksgiving, Dec 25) **FREE** In the park is

Garden of the Gods Trading Post. *324 Beckers Ln, Manitou Springs. Near Balanced Rock, at S end of park. Phone 719/685-9045; toll-free 800/874-4515. www.co-trading-post.com.* Established in 1900. Southwestern art gallery displays contemporary Native American jewelry, Santa Clara pottery, Hopi kachinas. Gift shop. (Summer, 8 am-8 pm; winter, 9 am-5:30 pm) **FREE**

Gray Line bus tours. *3704 W Colorado Ave, Colorado Springs. Phone 719/633-1747; toll-free 800/345-8197. www.coloradograyline.com.* Tours include Royal Gorge, the Air Force Academy, Garden of the Gods, and Pikes Peak. **$$$$**

Lake George (Eleven Mile State Park) ice fishing. *4229 Hwy Rd 92, Lake George. 38 miles W of Colorado Springs. Phone 719/748-3401.* The fish are biting year-round in Colorado, and the Lake George Eleven Mile

Exploring the Saratoga of the West

Nestled at the foot of Pikes Peak, a mere 7 miles west of downtown Colorado Springs, Manitou Springs is one of the state's definitive-and most accessible-mountain communities. A walking tour of Manitou Avenue, a bustling boulevard rife with artists' studios, restaurants, and boutiques that is one of the country's largest historic districts, is a good place to begin. Start at Memorial Park on the town's east side (Manitou and Deer Path avenues), which is surrounded by ample parking and centered around Seven Minute Springs, one of ten named mineral springs in the area that are renowned for their cool, drinkable water. (As a result, Manitou has been called "The Saratoga of the West.") From the park, walk west two blocks on Manitou Avenue to the Canon Avenue intersection. This is the central business district, and most of the restaurants and galleries are within a three-block radius. One can't-miss establishment is Arcade Amusements (930 Manitou Avenue), one of the West's oldest amusement arcades, featuring an array of antique coin-operated games. The downtown area is also ground zero for the Manitou Art Project, an annually rotating installation of 20 outdoor sculptures. Just west of the Canon-Manitou intersection is the Jerome Wheeler Town Clock, a landmark named for its eponymous donor, the onetime president of Macy's Department Stores who brought his ailing wife to the area in the 19th century. Continuing west on Manitou Avenue, it's a short walk to Ruxton Avenue, which will be on the left. Head southwest on Ruxton to the Miramont Castle (9 Capitol Hill Avenue, immediately adjacent to Ruxton), one of the architectural gems of Manitou Springs. Built as a home for a Catholic priest in 1895, the castle features English Tudor and Byzantine motifs in its eclectic design. After touring Miramont Castle, you might want to continue up Ruxton Avenue on a steep, 3/4-mile hike to the Manitou & Pikes Peak Railway Depot (515 Ruxton Avenue), the departure point for a rail trip to the pinnacle of Pikes Peak (open daily in the summertime). However, Miramont is also a good place to backtrack to your car for a drive to Manitou Springs attractions that are less accessible by foot, such as the railway, the Cliff Dwellings Museum, and the Cave of the Winds.

Reservoir at Eleven Mile State Park is one of the best spots to experience the unique appeal of ice fishing. Offering 3,400 surface acres, the reservoir is fully stocked with hungry kokanee salmon, carp, trout, and northern pike. A number of local outfitters, such as 11 Mile Sports, Inc. (phone toll-free 877/725-3172) can supply the necessary equipment as well as a guide. (Daily) **$$**

Magic Town. *2418 W Colorado Ave, Colorado Springs. Phone 719/471-9391; toll-free 800/731-3908. www.michaelgarman.com/magic_town.* Theatrical sculpture, created by sculptor Michael Garman, is a combination of miniature cityscapes and characters together with theater techniques. Gift shop. (Daily 10 am-5:30 pm) **$$**

May Natural History Museum. *710 Rock Creek Canyon Rd, Colorado Springs. 9 miles SW on Hwy 115. Phone 719/576-0450; toll-free 800/666-3841. www.maymuseum-camp-rvpark.com.* Collection of more than 8,000 invertebrates from the tropics. Also here is the Museum of Space Exploration with hundreds of models and NASA space photos and movies. (May-Oct, daily; rest or year, by appointment) Campground (fee). **$**

McAllister House Museum. *423 N Cascade Ave, Colorado Springs. Phone 719/635-7925. www.oldcolo.com/~mcallister.* (1873) Six-room, Gothic-style cottage; Victorian furnishings. Carriage house. Guided tours. (Sept-Apr: Thurs-Sat 10 am-4 pm; May-Aug: Wed-Sat noon-4 pm) **$$**

Museum of the American Numismatic Association. *818 N Cascade Ave, Colorado Springs. Phone 719/632-2646; toll-free 800/367-9723. www.money.org/moneymus.html.* Displays and research collections of coins, tokens, medals, paper money; changing exhibits; library. (Mon-Fri 9 am-4 pm, Sat 10 am-4 pm, Mon by appointment; closed holidays) **FREE**

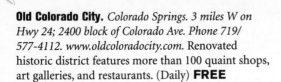

Old Colorado City. *Colorado Springs. 3 miles W on Hwy 24; 2400 block of Colorado Ave. Phone 719/577-4112. www.oldcoloradocity.com.* Renovated historic district features more than 100 quaint shops, art galleries, and restaurants. (Daily) **FREE**

Palmer Park. *Colorado Springs. On Maizeland Rd off N Academy Blvd. Phone 719/578-6640.* Magnificent views from scenic roads and trails among its 710 acres on Austin Bluffs. Picnic areas. **FREE**

Peterson Air & Space Museum. *150 E Ent Ave, 21st Space Wing/MU, Peterson Air Force Base. Main gate off Hwy 24. Phone 719/556-4915. www.petemuseum.org.* Display of 17 historic aircraft from WWI to present, plus exhibits on the history of the Air Force base; uniforms; models; satellites. (Open on restricted basis, call for times) **FREE**

Pike National Forest. *1920 Valley Dr, Pueblo. Phone 719/545-8737.* The more than 1,100,000 acres north and west of town via Hwy 24 include world-famous Pikes Peak; picnic grounds, campgrounds (fee); Wilkerson Pass (9,507 feet), 45 miles W on Hwy 24, with visitor information center (Memorial Day-Labor Day); Lost Creek Wilderness, NW of Lake George; Mount Evans Wilderness, NW of Bailey. Contact the Supervisor, 1920 Valley Dr, Pueblo 81008. There is also a Ranger District office in Colorado Springs at 601 S Weber; phone 719/636-1602. **FREE**

★ **Pikes Peak.** *Colorado Springs. 10 miles W on Hwy 24 to Cascade, then 19 miles on toll road to summit. Phone 719/684-9383.* (14,110 feet) Toll road climbs 7,309 feet. (Daily; weather permitting) Closed during annual Hill Climb in July (see SPECIAL EVENTS). **$$$** Here is

> **Cog railway.** *515 Ruxton Ave, Manitou Springs. 5 miles W on Hwy 24. Phone 719/685-5401. www.cograilway.com.* Up to eight trips daily (May-Oct, inquire for schedule). Reservations required. **$$$$**

Pikes Peak Auto Hill Climb Educational Museum. *135 Manitou Ave, Colorado Springs. Phone 719/685-4400.* More than two dozen race cars plus numerous exhibits on the Pikes Peak race, considered America's second-oldest auto race. (Daily, shorter hours in winter; closed holidays) **$**

Pikes Peak ghost town. *400 S 21st St, Colorado Springs. Hwy 24 W. Phone 719/634-0696.* Authentic Old West town under one roof in an 1899 railroad building. Includes antique-furnished buildings such as a general store, livery, jail, saloon, and re-created Victorian home. Also horseless carriages and buggies and a 1903 Cadillac. Old-time nickelodeons, player pianos, arcade "movies", and shooting gallery. (Daily) **$$$**

Pro Rodeo Hall of Fame and Museum of the American Cowboy. *101 Pro Rodeo Dr, Colorado Springs. I-25 exit 147 Rockrimmon Blvd. Phone 719/528-4764. www.prorodeo.org/hof.* Traces the rodeo lifestyle and its development over more than 100 years. Multimedia presentation documents rodeo's evolution from its origins in 19th-century ranch work to its present status as a major spectator sport. More than 90 exhibits of historic and modern cowboy and rodeo gear; changing Western art exhibits. The outdoor exhibits include live rodeo animals and a replica rodeo arena. (Daily 9 am-5 pm; closed holidays) **$$$**

Rock Ledge Ranch Historic Site. *3202 Chambers Way, Colorado Springs. 4 miles W via I-25, Garden of the Gods exit to 30th St, S to Gateway Rd at E entrance of Garden of the Gods. Phone 719/578-6777.* A living history program demonstrating everyday life in the region; 1868 homestead, 1895 working ranch, 1907 Orchard House. Braille nature trail. (June-Labor Day: Wed-Sun 10 am-5 pm; Labor Day-Dec: Sat 10 am-4 pm, Sun noon-4 pm) **$**

Seven Falls. *2850 S Cheyenne Canyon Rd, Colorado Springs. 7 miles SW on Cheyenne Blvd in South Cheyenne Canyon. Phone 719/632-0765. www.sevenfalls.com.* Only completely lighted canyon and waterfall in the world. Best seen from Eagle's Nest, reached by mountain elevator. Native American dance interpretations (summer, daily). Night lighting (summer). **$**

US Air Force Academy. *2160 Vickers Dr, Suite G, Colorado Springs. N on I-25 exit 150 B (South Gate) or 156 B (North Gate). Phone 719/472-0102; toll-free 800/955-4438. www.usafa.af.mil.* (1955) (4,200 cadets.) On 18,500 acres at foot of Rampart Range of Rocky Mountains where cadets undergo four-year academic, military, and physical training. Striking, modern cadet chapel (daily; closed for private services; Sunday service open to public). Cadet Wing marches to lunch may be watched from wall near Chapel (academic year). Planetarium programs for public (free). Visitor center has self-guided tour brochures, theater, and exhibits on cadet life and academy history (daily 5:30 am-6 pm; closed Jan 1, Thanksgiving, Dec 25). **FREE**

US Olympic Complex and Visitor Center. *One Olympic Plaza, Colorado Springs. 2 blocks N of Platte Ave (Hwy 24 E), at Union Blvd. Phone 719/866-4618; toll-free 888/659-8687. www.olympic-usa.org.* National headquarters of the US Olympic Committee, 15 national sports governing bodies, and Olympic Training Center, where more than 15,000 athletes train each year. Guided tours include film and walking tour of training center. Tours depart each hour. (Mon-Sat 9 am-4 pm) **FREE**

Van Briggle Art Pottery Company Tour. *600 S 21st St, Colorado Springs. At Cimarron St. Phone 719/633-7729; toll-free 800/847-6341. www.vanbriggle.com.* Exhibitions of "throwing potter's wheel." Self-guided tours (Mon-Sat 8:30 am-4 pm); showroom (8:30 am-5 pm). **FREE**

World Figure Skating Hall of Fame and Museum. *20 First St, Colorado Springs. Off Lake Ave. Phone 719/635-5200. www.usfsa.org.* Exhibits on history of figure skating; art, memorabilia, library, skate gallery, video collection. (Mon-Fri 10 am-4 pm; Nov-Apr: Sat 10 am-4 pm; May-Oct: Sat 10 am-5 pm; closed holidays) **$**

Special Events

Colorado Springs Balloon Classic. *Memorial Park, Colorado Springs. Off Pikes Peak Ave between Hancock and Union sts. Phone 719/471-4833. www.balloonclassic.com.* An annual event featuring more than 100 balloons and entertainment. Labor Day weekend. **FREE**

Greyhound racing. *Post Time Greyhound Park. 3701 N Nevada Ave, Colorado Springs. E of I-25 between Garden of the Gods and Fillmore. Phone 719/632-1391. www.wembleyco.com/post_time_greyhound_park.shtml.* Pari-mutuel and simulcast wagering. Apr-late Sept. **$**

Motor sports. *Pikes Peak International Raceway. 16650 Midway Ranch Rd, Fountain. S on I-25. Phone 719/382-7223; toll-free 800/511-7747. www.ppir.com.* May-Sept. **$$$$**

Pikes Peak International Hill Climb. *Suite 105, 3630 Sinton Rd, Colorado Springs. Last 12 miles of Pikes Peak Hwy. Phone 719/685-4400. www.ppihc.com.* The "Race to the Clouds" has been a part of Colorado Springs' July 4 celebration for more than 80 years. Spectators of all ages marvel at the fine skill and sheer gutsiness of those who dare speed their racecars, trucks, and motorcycles along the final 12.4 miles of Pikes Peak Highway, a gravel route with 156 turns and a 5,000-foot rise in elevation. Vehicles can reach more than 130 mph on straightaways, and there isn't a guardrail in sight. Spectators need to be on the mountain at the crack of dawn to catch the action. Those who don't take advantage of the overnight parking the evening before the race can arrive as early as 4 am to stake out a good spot. The road closes to additional spectators at 8 am, so plan to spend the day here. Those who park above the start line won't be able to leave until late afternoon when the race is over—otherwise, they could become part of the race. The best views are above the tree line, so dress warmly. Late June. **$$$$**

Pikes Peak Marathon. *Race starts at Memorial Park in Colorado Springs and ends at Ruxton and Manitou aves in Manitou Springs. Phone 719/473-2625. www.pikespeakmarathon.org.* Come watch this 26.2-mile footrace from cog depot to summit and back. Late Aug.

Pikes Peak or Bust Rodeo. *Colorado Springs World Arena, 3185 Venetucci Blvd, Colorado Springs. Phone 719/635-3547. www.pikespeakorbustrodeo.org.* Bareback riding, bull riding, calf roping, steer wrestling, and more. Mid-Aug.

Limited-Service Hotels

★★ THE ANTLERS ADAM'S MARK HOTEL. *4 S Cascade, Colorado Springs (80903). Phone 719/473-5600; toll-free 800/627-6275; fax 719/389-0259. www.adamsmark.com.* Though no longer housed in the original, historic building that opened in 1883 and was destroyed by fire, this modern rendition attempts to re-create the hospitable feel of the original. There is much to do in the area, and many rooms have views of the main attraction, Pikes Peak. 298 rooms, 13 story. Check-out noon. Restaurant, bar. Fitness room. Indoor pool, whirlpool. **$**

★★ DOUBLETREE HOTEL. *1775 E Cheyenne Mt Blvd, Colorado Springs (80906). Phone 719/576-8900; fax 719/576-4450. www.doubletree.com.* This contemporary hotel is situated at the base of the mountains in Colorado Springs, with access to many of the recreational activities in the area. 299 rooms, 5 story. Pets accepted; fee. Check-out noon. Restaurant, bar. Fitness room. Indoor pool, whirlpool. Airport transportation available. **$**

★ DRURY INN. *8155 N Academy Blvd, Colorado Springs (80920). Phone 719/598-2500; toll-free 800/325-8300; fax 719/598-2500. www.drury-inn.com.* 118 rooms, 4 story. Pets accepted, some restrictions. Complimentary continental breakfast. Check-out noon. Fitness room. Indoor pool, outdoor pool, whirlpool. **$**

★ ★ EMBASSY SUITES. *7290 Commerce Center Dr, Colorado Springs (80919). Phone 719/599-9100; fax 719/599-4644. www.embassysuites.com.* Located in the northwest end of the city, this hotel has good views of the Rocky Mountains. 207 rooms, 4 story, all suites. Complimentary full breakfast. Check-out noon. Restaurant, bar. Fitness room. Indoor pool, whirlpool. **$**

★ FAIRFIELD INN. *2725 Geyser Dr, Colorado Springs (80906). Phone 719/576-1717; fax 719/576-4747. www.fairfieldinn.com.* 85 rooms, 3 story. Complimentary continental breakfast. Check-out noon. Fitness room. Indoor pool, whirlpool. **$**

★ HOLIDAY INN EXPRESS. *1815 Aeroplaza Dr, Colorado Springs (80916). Phone 719/591-6000; toll-free 800/465-4329; fax 719/591-6100. www.holiday-inn.com.* 94 rooms, 4 story. Complimentary continental breakfast. Check-out noon. Fitness room. Airport transportation available. Business center. **$**

★ ★ RADISSON INN COLORADO SPRINGS NORTH. *8110 North Academy Blvd, Colorado Springs (80920). Phone 719/598-5770; fax 719/598-3434. www.radisson.com.* This hotel is the closest option to the US Air Force Academy. 200 rooms, 4 story. Pets accepted, some restrictions; fee. Check-out noon. Restaurant, bar. Fitness room. Indoor pool, whirlpool. Airport transportation available. **$**

Full-Service Hotel

★ ★ ★ SHERATON COLORADO SPRINGS HOTEL. *2886 S Cir Dr, Colorado Springs (80905). Phone 719/576-5900; toll-free 800/981-4012; fax 719/576-7695. www.sheraton.com.* This hotel is near the airport, Pikes Peak, the US Airforce Academy, and the Olympic training facility. 500 rooms, 4 story. Check-out 11 am. Restaurant, bar. Fitness room. Indoor pool, children's pool, whirlpool. Tennis. Airport transportation available. Business center. **$**

Full Service Resort

★ ★ ★ ★ ★ THE BROADMOOR. *1 Lake Ave, Colorado Springs (80906). Phone 719/634-7711; toll-free 800/634-7711; fax 719/577-5700. www.broadmoor.com.* Located at the foot of the Rocky Mountains and surrounded by the sparkling beauty of Cheyenne Lake, The Broadmoor has been one of America's favorite resorts since 1918. This paradise for outdoor enthusiasts is close to Colorado Springs, yet feels a million miles away with its verdant fields carpeted in brilliant wildflowers, perfectly manicured golf courses, and opulent accommodations. This all-season resort is grand in scale, and the accommodations are at once lavish and comfortable. The Broadmoor's myriad recreational opportunities include tennis, golf on three championship courses, horseback riding through old mining claims, fly fishing in pristine streams, and hot air ballooning over the Colorado countryside. Incorporating indigenous botanicals, pure spring water, and natural elements, the spa offers a variety of soothing treatments. Others seek a different kind of therapy in the resort's unique shops, while 11 restaurants and bars cater to all moods. 700 rooms, 3 story. Check-in 4 pm, check-out noon. Restaurant, bar. Children's activity center. Fitness room, spa. One indoor pool, three outdoor pools, children's pool, whirlpool. Golf. Tennis. Airport transportation available. Business center. **$$$**

Full-Service Inn

★ ★ ★ CHEYENNE CAÑON INN. *2030 W Cheyenne Blvd, Colorado Springs (80906). Phone 719/633-0625; fax 719/633-8826. www.cheyennecanoninn.com.* Built in 1921 for Colorado Spring's elite, this resort was originally an upscale bordello and gambling hall. This restored Mission-style mansion, with spectacular views of the mountains and Cheyenne Cañon and warm, professional service, is an exceptional find. 10 rooms, 2 story. Complimentary full breakfast. Whirlpool. **$**

Specialty Lodgings

The following lodging establishments are approved by Mobil Travel Guide, but due to their unique and individualized nature have not been given a traditional Mobil Star rating. Included in this listing you may find bed-and-breakfasts, limited-service inns, guest ranches, and other unique hotel properties.

HOLDEN HOUSE 1902 BED & BREAKFAST. *1102 W Pikes Peak Ave, Colorado Springs (80904). Phone 719/471-3980; toll-free 888/565-3980; fax 719/471-4740. www.holdenhouse.com.* Located in a historic house and carriage house dating to 1902, this inn has modern guest rooms with Victorian charm. Two purebred Siamese cats stand guard. 5 rooms, 2 story. No children allowed. Complimentary full breakfast. Check-in 4-6 pm, check-out 11 am. **$**

LOST VALLEY RANCH. *29555 Goose Creek Rd, Sedalia (80135). Phone 303/647-2311; fax 303/647-2315. www.lostvalleyranch.com.* Set upon 40,000 acres of the Pike National Forest, this dude ranch is a perfect getaway spot for corporate retreats or family vacations. Homesteaded in 1883. 24 rooms. Check-in Sun 2 pm, check-out Sun 10 am. Children's activity center. Pool, whirlpools. Tennis. **$$$**

OLD TOWN GUEST HOUSE. *115 S 26th St, Colorado Springs (80904). Phone 719/632-9194; toll-free 888/375-4210; fax 719/632-9026. www.oldtown-guesthouse.com.* Built in 1997, this bed-and-breakfast has all the amenities of a modern hotel, including an elevator, but it is located in the heart of Old Colorado City. 8 rooms, 3 story. Complimentary full breakfast. Check-in 4-6 pm, check-out 11 am. Fitness room. **$**

Restaurants

★ ★ ★ CHARLES COURT. *1 Lake Ave, Colorado Springs (80906). Phone 719/577-5774; toll-free 800/634-7711; fax 719/577-5738. www.broadmoor.com.* One of nine restaurants at the luxurious Broadmoor Hotel, Charles Court offers progressive American fare in a relaxed, open, airy, and contemporary setting. In warm weather, alfresco dining with lakeside views can't be beat. The American-style menu features fresh, seasonal ingredients and borrows influences from Asia, Italy, and Mexico. While there are global accents on the menu, the kitchen also offers a selection of regional Rocky Mountain fare, such as Colorado rack of lamb and the signature Charles Court Game Grill. The restaurant's wine list boasts more than 800 selections from America, France, Italy, Germany, Australia, and New Zealand. For special occasions, head inside to the kitchen for dinner. At the Chef's Table in the kitchen (four guests minimum), you can sit down and have the chef cook the multicourse meal of your choosing. American menu. Breakfast, dinner. Bar. Jacket required. Valet parking. **$$$**

★ ★ EDELWEISS. *34 E Ramona Ave, Colorado Springs (80906). Phone 719/633-2220; fax 719/471-8413. www.restauranteur.com/edelweiss.* Former schoolhouse (1890). German menu. Lunch, dinner. Closed Dec 25. Bar. Outdoor seating. **$$**

★ GIUSEPPE'S OLD DEPOT. *10 S Sierra Madre, Colorado Springs (80903). Phone 719/635-3111; fax 719/444-0857. www.giuseppes-depot.com.* In a historic railroad depot (1887); railroad memorabilia on display. American, Italian menu. Lunch, dinner. Closed Thanksgiving, Dec 25. Bar. Children's menu. Outdoor seating. **$$**

★ ★ HATCH COVER. *252 E Cheyenne Mountain Blvd, Colorado Springs (80906). Phone 719/576-5223; fax 719/576-3557.* Aquariums. American menu. Lunch, dinner. Bar. **$$$**

★ LA CREPERIE. *204 N Tejon, Colorado Springs (80903). Phone 719/632-0984. www.restauranteur.com/lacreperie.* Former streetcar horse stable (1892). French menu. Lunch, dinner. Closed holidays. **$$**

★ ★ LA PETITE MAISON. *1015 W Colorado Ave, Colorado Springs (80904). Phone 719/632-4887; fax 719/632-0343. www.restauranteur.com/maison.* In a renovated house (1894). French menu. Dinner. Closed Sun-Mon; Jan 1, July 4, Dec 24-25. **$$$**

★★ **MACKENZIE'S CHOP HOUSE.** *128 S Tejon, Colorado Springs (80903). Phone 719/635-3536; fax 719/635-1225. www.mackenzieschophouse.com.* Built in 1890. American menu. Lunch, dinner. Closed Dec 25. Bar. Outdoor seating. **$$$**

★ **MAGGIE MAE'S.** *2405 E Pikes Peak Ave, Colorado Springs (80909). Phone 719/475-1623; fax 719/475-8593.* Mexican, American menu. Breakfast, lunch, dinner. Closed Dec 25. Bar. Children's menu. **$**

★ **OLD CHICAGO.** *7115 Commerce Center Dr, Colorado Springs (80919). Phone 719/593-7678; fax 719/593-2914. www.oldchicago.com.* Italian, American menu. Lunch, dinner. Closed Thanksgiving, Dec 25. Bar. Children's menu. **$$**

★ **OLD CHICAGO PASTA & PIZZA.** *118 N Tejon, Colorado Springs (80903). Phone 719/634-8812; fax 719/634-0629.* Italian menu. Lunch, dinner. Closed Thanksgiving, Dec 25. Bar. Children's menu. Outdoor seating. **$**

★★★★ **PENROSE ROOM.** *1 Lake Ave, Colorado Springs (80906). Phone 719/634-7711; fax 719/577-5700. www.broadmoor.com.* With panoramic views of the city lights and surrounding mountains, dinner at the Penrose Room is a visually thrilling event. The glamorous room, appointed with glittering crystal chandeliers, vintage carpets, tufted armchairs, and luxurious linen tabletops, is steeped in old-world charm. The Penrose Room, which opened its doors in 1918, transports you back to a time when women wore long gloves to dinner and men checked their top hats at the door. But the thrills are not limited to the sense of sight; your sense of taste is also in for a treat. The menu is French contemporary and includes Francophile favorites such as escargots, Coquilles St. Jacques, foie gras terrine, and Chateaubriand of beef (carved tableside), in addition to more modern global fare like Colorado lamb chop with a clover blossom honey glaze. Don't worry about calories here; a big band plays nightly, so you can revive the waltz or the foxtrot on the spacious dance floor to work off your decadent dinner. French Menu. Dinner. Bar. Jacket required. **$$$$**

Copper Mountain

See Dillon

Cortez (E-1)

Settled 1890
Population 7,977
Information Cortez/Mesa Verde Visitor Info Bureau, PO Box HH; phone 970/565-8227 or toll-free 800/253-1616
Web site www.cortezchamber.org

Originally a trading center for sheep and cattle ranchers whose spreads dot the plains to the south, Cortez now accommodates travelers visiting Mesa Verde National Park (see) and oil workers whose business takes them to the nearby Aneth Oil Field. The semidesert area 38 miles southwest of Cortez is the only spot in the nation where one can stand in four states (Colorado, Utah, Arizona, New Mexico) and two Native American nations (Navajo and Ute) at one time; a simple marker located approximately 100 yards from the Four Corners Highway (Hwy 160) indicates the exact place where these areas meet. There are many opportunities for hunting and fishing in the Dolores River valley.

What to See and Do

Anasazi Heritage Center and Escalante. *27501 Hwy 184, Dolores. 8 miles N on Hwy 145, then 2 miles NW on Hwy 184. Phone 970/882-5600. www.co.blm.gov/ahc/index.htm.* Museum of exhibits, artifacts, and documents from excavations on public lands in southwest Colorado, including the Dolores Archaeological Program. Represents the Northern San Juan Anasazi Tradition (AD 1 to 1300). Within 1/2 mile of the center are the Dominguez and Escalante sites—the latter discovered by a Franciscan friar in 1776. Excavations revealed kivas and other structures, pottery, and ceremonial artifacts. (Mar-Oct: daily 9 am-5 pm; Nov-Feb: daily 9 am-4 pm; closed Jan 1, Thanksgiving, Dec 25) **$**

Hovenweep National Monument. *McElmo Rte, Cortez. 20 miles NW on Hwy 666 to Pleasant View; follow signs 5 miles W on County Rd BB, then 20 miles S on County 10. Phone 970/562-4282. www.nps.gov/hove.* Monument consists of six units of prehistoric ruins; the best preserved is at Square Tower, which includes the remains of pueblos and towers. Self-guided trail, park ranger on duty; visitor area (daily 8 am-5 pm). **$$$**

Lowry Pueblo. *County Rd CC, Cortez. 21 miles NW on Hwy 666 to Pleasant View, then 9 miles W on County Rd CC. Phone 970/247-4874.* Constructed by the Anasazi (circa 1075). Forty excavated rooms including one great and seven smaller kivas. The Lowry Pueblo is part of the Canyons of the Ancients National Monument. Picnic facilities. No camping. (Daily, weather and road conditions permitting) **FREE**

Ute Mountain Tribal Park. *Hwy 666, Cortez. Phone 970/749-1452. www.utemountainute.com/tribalpark.htm.* The Ute Mountain Tribe developed this 125,000-acre park on their tribal lands, opening hundreds of largely unexplored 800-year-old Anasazi ruins to the public. Tours begin at the Ute Mountain Visitor Center/Museum, 19 miles S via Hwy 666 (daily); reservations required. Backpacking trips in summer. Primitive camping available. **$$$$**

Special Events

Montezuma County Fair. *30100 Hwy 160, Cortez. Phone 970/565-3123. www.co.montezuma.co.us.* First week in Aug.

Ute Mountain Rodeo. *Montezuma County Fairgrounds, Cortez. Phone 970/565-4485.* Early-mid June.

Limited-Service Hotels

★ BEST WESTERN TURQUOISE INN & SUITES. *535 E Main St, Cortez (81321). Phone 970/565-3778; toll-free 800/547-3376; fax 970/565-3439. www.cortezbestwestern.com.* 77 rooms, 2 story. Pets accepted; fee. Complimentary continental breakfast. Check-in 3 pm, check-out 11 am. Outdoor pool, whirlpool. Airport transportation available. **$**

★ HOLIDAY INN EXPRESS. *2121 E Main St, Cortez (81321). Phone 970/565-6000; toll-free 800/626-5652; fax 970/565-3438. www.coloradoholiday.com.* 100 rooms, 3 story. Pets accepted, some restrictions. Complimentary continental breakfast. Check-in 3 pm, check-out 11 am. Fitness room. Indoor pool, whirlpool. Airport transportation available. **$**

Restaurant

★★ HOMESTEADERS. *45 E Main St, Cortez (81321). Phone 970/565-6253; fax 970/564-9217.* Southwestern menu. Breakfast, lunch, dinner. Closed holidays; also Sun Nov-Apr. Bar. Children's menu. Casual attire. **$$**

Craig (A-2)

See also Steamboat Springs

Population 9,189
Elevation 6,186 ft
Area Code 970
Zip 81625
Information Greater Craig Area Chamber of Commerce, 360 E Victory Way; phone 970/824-5689 or toll-free 800/864-4405
Web site www.craig-chamber.com

Craig is known for excellent big-game hunting for elk, deer, and antelope, and bass fishing in Elkhead Reservoir. The Yampa River area draws float-boaters, hikers, and wildlife photographers in summer and cross-country skiers and snowmobilers in winter.

What to See and Do

Marcia. *Craig City Park, 341 E Victory Way, Craig. Hwy 40. Phone 970/824-5689.* Private, luxury Pullman railroad car of David Moffat that is listed on the National Register of Historic Places. The car was named after his daughter. Tours are available through the Moffat County Visitors Center. **FREE**

Museum of Northwest Colorado. *590 Yampa Ave, Craig. Located in the former Colorado State Armory, center of town. Phone 970/824-6360. www.museumnwco.org.* Local history, Native American artifacts; wildlife photography. Cowboy and gunfighter collection. Also the Edwin C. Johnson Collection (Johnson was governor of Colorado and a US senator). (Mon-Sat 9 am-5 pm) **DONATION**

Save Our Sandrocks Nature Trail. *900 Alta Vista Dr, Craig. Phone 970/824-6673.* This sloped, 3/4-mile trail provides a view of Native American petroglyphs on the sandrocks. Trail guide is available at the Cooperative Extension Office, 200 W Victory Way. (May-Nov) **FREE**

Limited-Service Hotel

★★ HOLIDAY INN. *300 S Hwy 13, Craig (81625). Phone 970/824-4000; toll-free 800/465-4329; fax 970/824-3950. www.holiday-inn.com.* 152 rooms,

2 story. Pets accepted, some restrictions; fee. Check-in 4 pm, check-out 11 am. Restaurant. Fitness room. Outdoor pool, whirlpool. **$**

Crested Butte (C-2)

See also Gunnison

Founded 1880
Population 1,529
Elevation 8,908 ft
Area Code 970
Zip 81224
Information Crested Butte Vacations, 500 Gothic Road, PO Box A, Mount Crested Butte 81225; toll-free 800/544-8448
Web site www.crestedbutteresort.com

Crested Butte is a remarkably picturesque mining town in the midst of magnificent mountain country. Inquire locally for information on horseback pack trips to Aspen (see) through the West Elk Wilderness. Guided fishing trips are available on the more than 1,000 miles of streams and rivers within a two-hour drive of Crested Butte.

What to See and Do

Crested Butte Mountain Resort Ski Area. *12 Snowmass Rd, Crested Butte. 3 miles N on county road in Gunnison National Forest (see). Phone toll-free 800/810-7669. www.skicb.com.* Three high-speed quad, three triple, three double chairlifts, four surface lifts, two magic carpets; patrol, school, rentals, snowmaking; cafeteria, restaurant, bar, nursery. Eighty-five runs; longest run 2 1/2 miles; vertical drop 3,062 feet. Multiday, half-day rates. (Late Nov-mid-Apr, daily) Nineteen miles of groomed cross-country trails, 100 miles of wilderness trails; snowmobiling, sleigh rides. **$$$$**

Specialty Lodging

The following lodging establishment is approved by Mobil Travel Guide, but due to its unique and individualized nature has not been given a traditional Mobil Star rating. Included in this listing you may find bed-and-breakfasts, limited-service inns, guest ranches, and other unique hotel properties.

THE NORDIC INN. *14 Treasury Rd, Crested Butte (80216). Phone 970/349-5542; toll-free 800/542-7669; fax 970/349-6487. www.nordicinncb.com.* 27 rooms, 2 story. Closed May. Complimentary continental breakfast. Check-out 11 am. Whirlpool. **$**

Restaurants

★ DONITA'S CANTINA. *330 Elk Ave, Crested Butte (81224). Phone 970/349-6674; fax 970/349-6817.* Former hotel (1881) with original pressed-tin ceiling. Mexican menu. Dinner. Bar. Children's menu. Casual attire. **$$**

★★ LE BOSQUET. *6th and Belleview, Crested Butte (81224). Phone 970/349-5808; fax 970/349-5677.* French menu. Dinner. Closed mid-Apr-mid-May. Bar. Outdoor seating. **$$**

Cripple Creek (C-4)

See also Cañon City, Colorado Springs, Manitou Springs

Settled 1891
Population 1,115
Elevation 9,494 ft
Area Code 719
Zip 80813
Information Chamber of Commerce, PO Box 650; phone 719/689-2169 or toll-free 800/526-8777
Web site www.cripple-creek.co.us

Long considered worthless by mining experts despite frequent reports of gold, the "$300 million cow pasture" was finally developed by tenderfeet, who did their prospecting with pitchforks.

At its height, Cripple Creek and the surrounding area produced as much as $25 million in gold in a single year (at $20 per ounce). Few "Wild West" towns experienced a more colorful past. Jack Johnson and Jack Dempsey both worked here, the latter once fighting a long, bloody battle for $50. Texas Guinan, the speakeasy hostess, started her career here. In 1900, the town had a population of more than 25,000 with more than 500 gold mines in operation. Today, only a handful of people live in the shadow of 10,400-foot Mount Pisgah. The town has been designated a National Historic Mining District. The present buildings were built after a great fire in 1896 destroyed the old town.

What to See and Do

Cripple Creek Casinos. *Cripple Creek. 48-mile drive from Colorado Springs. Take Hwy 24 W, Colorado Hwy 67 S. Phone toll-free 800/235-2922. www.cripple-creek .co.us.* Historic Cripple Creek has managed to preserve some of its Old West charm despite the frenzied arrival of legalized gambling in the 1990s. More family friendly than the big casino center of Black Hawk, Cripple Creek nevertheless has nearly 20 limited-stakes ($5 bet limit) casinos along its Victorian storefront main street area. The massive Imperial Palace Hotel (123 N 3rd St, 800/235-2922) built in 1896, offers a multi-tiered gambling parlor with antique décor—and a good night's sleep in one of its lovely, turn-of-the-century hotel rooms. For a more Vegas-style experience, check out the glitzy, noisy Double Eagle Hotel & Casino (422 E Bennett Ave, 800/711-7234), with more than 600 slot machines, poker, and blackjack tables under a vaulted stained-glass ceiling. A modern, 158-room hotel is attached. Both establishments include restaurants or buffets and offer live entertainment. (Daily) **FREE**

Cripple Creek District Museum. *5th and Bennett, Cripple Creek. Located in the former Midland-Terminal Railroad Depot. Phone 719/689-2634. www.cripple-creek .org.* Artifacts of Cripple Creek's glory; pioneer relics, mining and railroad displays; Victorian furnishings. Heritage Art Gallery and Assay Office. Extensive activities for research. Gift shop. (June-Sept: daily 10 am-5 pm; Oct-May: Fri-Sun 11 am-4 pm) **$**

Cripple Creek-Victor Narrow Gauge Railroad. *520 Carr St, Cripple Creek. On Hwy 67. Phone 719/689-2640.* An authentic locomotive and coaches depart from Cripple Creek District Museum. Four-mile round-trip past many historic mines. (Late May-early Oct: daily, departs every 45 minutes) **$$$**

Imperial Casino Hotel. *123 N 3rd St, Cripple Creek. Phone 719/689-7777. www.imperialcasinohotel.com.* (see HOTELS) This hotel was constructed shortly after the town's great fire. (1896) **$$$**

Mollie Kathleen Gold Mine. *Hwy 67, Cripple Creek. 1 mile N on Hwy 67. Phone 719/689-2466; toll-free 888/291-5689. www.goldminetours.com.* Descend 1,000 feet on a one-hour guided tour through a gold mine. (Apr-Oct: daily; tours depart every ten minutes) **$$$**

Victor. *5 miles S on Hwy 67, on the SW side of Pikes Peak. Phone 719/689-2284. www.tellercountyrdc.com/ victorchamber.htm.* Victor, the "city of mines," actually does have streets paved with gold (low-grade ore was used to surface streets in the early days).

Special Events

Donkey Derby Days. *City Park and Bennett, Cripple Creek. Phone 719/689-3315.* Donkey races. Last full weekend in June.

Veteran's Memorial Rally. *City Park, Cripple Creek. Phone 719/487-8005.* Four-day event honoring veterans. Mid-Aug.

Limited-Service Hotels

★ ★ DOUBLE EAGLE HOTEL & CASINO. *442 E Bennett Ave, Cripple Creek (80813). Phone 719/689-5000; toll-free 800/711-7234; fax 719/689-5050. www. decasino.com.* 157 rooms, 5 story. Complimentary full breakfast. Check-out 11 am. Restaurant. **$**

★ HOLIDAY INN EXPRESS. *601 E Galena Ave, Cripple Creek (80813). Phone 719/689-2600; toll-free 800/445-3607; fax 719/689-3426. www.holidayinncc .com.* 67 rooms, 3 story. Complimentary continental breakfast. Check-out 11 am. **$**

★ ★ IMPERIAL CASINO HOTEL. *123 N 3rd St, Cripple Creek (80813). Phone 719/689-7777; toll-free 800/235-2922; fax 719/689-1008. www. imperialcasinohotel.com.* Built in 1896. Victorian décor; antiques. Gold Bar Room Theatre. 29 rooms, 3 story. Check-out 11 am. Restaurant, bar. **$**

Specialty Lodging

The following lodging establishment is approved by Mobil Travel Guide, but due to its unique and individualized nature has not been given a traditional Mobil Star rating. Included in this listing you may find bed-and-breakfasts, limited-service inns, guest ranches, and other unique hotel properties.

VICTOR HOTEL. *4th St and Victor Ave, Victor (80860). Phone 719/689-3553; toll-free 800/713-4595; fax 719/689-4197. www.victorhotel.com.* 20 rooms, 4 story. Complimentary continental breakfast. Check-in noon, check-out 11 am. Restaurant. **$**

Restaurant

★★ **STRATTON DINING ROOM.** *123 N 3rd St, Cripple Creek (80813). Phone 719/689-7777; fax 719/689-1008.* Authentic Old West Victorian décor. Breakfast, lunch, dinner. Bar. Valet parking. **$$**

Delta (C-1)

See also Montrose

Settled 1880
Population 6,400
Elevation 4,953 ft
Area Code 970
Zip 81416
Information Chamber of Commerce, 301 Main St; phone 970/874-8616
Web site www.deltaco.org

Situated in Colorado's largest fruit-growing area, Delta annually produces millions of dollars worth of apples, peaches, and cherries. For information on Gunnison National Forest (see GUNNISON), Uncompahgre National Forest (see NORWOOD), and Grand Mesa National Forest (see GRAND JUNCTION), write the Supervisor, 2250 US 50 in Delta.

What to See and Do

Crawford State Park. *4050 Hwy 92, Crawford. 20 miles E to Hotchkiss, then 11 miles S on Hwy 92. Phone 970/921-5721. parks.state.co.us.* Swimming, water-skiing, fishing, boating (ramps); winter sports, picnicking, camping. (Daily) **$**

Sweitzer State Park. *1735 E Road, Delta. 3 miles SE off Hwy 50. Phone 970/874-4258. parks.state.co.us.* Swimming, water-skiing, fishing, boating (ramps); picnicking, bird-watching. (Daily) **$**

Special Events

Deltarado Days. *Delta Area Chamber of Commerce, 301 Main St, Delta. Phone 970/874-8616.* Delta Round-Up Club. Parade, barbecue, craft booths, games, square dancing, PRCA Rodeo. Last weekend in July.

Limited-Service Hotels

★★ **BEST WESTERN SUNDANCE.** *903 Main St, Delta (81416). Phone 970/874-9781; toll-free 800/626-1994; fax 970/874-5440. www.bestwesternsundance.com.* 41 rooms, 2 story. Pets accepted, some restrictions; fee. Complimentary full breakfast. Check-out 11 am. Restaurant, bar. Fitness room. Pool, whirlpool. **$**

★ **COMFORT INN.** *180 Gunnison River Dr, Delta (81416). Phone 970/874-1000; toll-free 800/228-5150; fax 970/874-4154. www.comfortinn.com.* 47 rooms, 2 story. Pets accepted; fee. Complimentary continental breakfast. Check-in 2 pm, check-out 11 am. Whirlpool. **$**

Denver (B-4)

See also Boulder, Central City

Settled 1858
Population 544,636
Elevation 5,280 ft
Area Code 303
Information Denver Metro Convention & Visitors Bureau, 1555 California St, Suite 300, 80202; phone 303/892-1112 or toll-free 800/233-6837
Web site www.denver.org
Suburbs: Boulder, Central City, Englewood, Evergreen, Golden, Idaho Springs, Lakewood (See individual alphabetical listings.)

The Mile High City, capital of Colorado, began as a settlement of gold seekers, many of them unsuccessful. In its early years, Denver almost lost out to several booming mountain mining centers in becoming the state's major city. In 1858, the community consisted of some 60 raffish cabins, plus Colorado's first saloon. With the onset of the silver rush in the 1870s, Denver came into its own. By 1890, the population had topped 100,000. Nourished by the wealth that poured in from the rich mines in the Rockies, Denver rapidly became Colorado's economic and cultural center. It boomed again after World War II and in the 1990s; there were a few financial busts along the way as well.

Today, with the Great Plains sweeping away to the east, the foothills of the Rocky Mountains immediately to the west, and a dry, mild climate, Denver is a growing city with 2.5 million people in the metropolitan area. A building boom in the 1990s resulted in a new airport, a downtown baseball park surrounded by a lively nightlife district dubbed LoDo ("lower downtown"), new football and basketball/hockey stadiums, and a redeveloped river valley just west of downtown with an aquarium, amusement park, and shopping district. Once economically hitched to the ebb and flow of the market for Colorado's natural resources, Denver now boasts one of the most diverse economies in the US and is entrenched as a hub for the cable and telecom industries.

Parks have long been a point of civic pride in Denver, and the Denver Mountain Park System is a unique land-management arrangement in the Rocky Mountain foothills (beyond the city limits). It covers 13,448 acres, scattered over 380 square miles. The chain begins 15 miles west of the city at Red Rocks Park (the site of a renowned musical venue) and extends to Summit Lake (perched 12,740 feet above sea level), 60 miles to the west.

Public Transportation

Buses (Regional Transportation District), phone 303/299-6000.

Airport Information

For additional accommodations, see DENVER INTERNATIONAL AIRPORT AREA, which follows DENVER.

Denver Fun Fact

- Denver lays claim to the invention of the cheeseburger. The trademark for the name Cheeseburger was awarded to Louis Ballast in 1935.

What to See and Do

16th Street Mall. *16th St, Denver. Between Market St and Broadway. Phone 303/534-6161.* This tree-lined pedestrian promenade of red-and-gray granite runs through the center of Denver's downtown shopping district; outdoor cafés, shops, restaurants, hotels, fountains, and plazas line its mile-long walk. European-built shuttle buses offer transportation from either end of the promenade. Along the mall are

Tabor Center. *1201 16th St, Denver. Between Arapahoe and Larimer sts. Phone 303/572-6868. www.taborcenter.com.* Tabor Center is a sophisticated urban shopping, dining, and lodging center in the heart of downtown Denver's retail district. Though smaller than outlying malls, Tabor Center nevertheless provides a full array of name-brand men's and women's apparel, gift and jewelry stores, a food court, and three full-service restaurants: The Cheesecake Factory, Big Bowl, and ESPN Zone. The center recently underwent a $26 million renovation. (Mon-Sat 10 am-7 pm; closed Jan 1, Dec 25)

Antique Row. *400-2000 S Broadway, Denver. www.antiques-internet.com/colorado/antiquerow.* Denver's largest concentration of antique dealers can be found along a 14-block stretch of South Broadway. More than 400 shops sell everything old, from books to music, vintage Western wear to museum-quality furniture. Take the light rail to Broadway and I-25 to begin your antiquing tour. Most dealers are located between the 400 and 2000 blocks of South Broadway and 25 and 27 blocks of East Dakota Avenue. (Daily)

Arvada Center for the Arts & Humanities. *6901 Wadsworth Blvd, Arvada. Phone 303/431-3080. www.arvadacenter.org.* Performing arts center with concerts, plays, classes, demonstrations, art galleries, banquet hall. Amphitheater seats 1,200 (June-early Sept). Historical museum with old cabin and pioneer artifacts. Museum and gallery (Mon-Fri 9 am-6 pm, Sat 9 am-5 pm, Sun 1-5 pm). **FREE**

★ **Brown Palace Hotel.** *321 17th St, Denver. One block from the 16th St pedestrian mall. Phone 303/297-3111; toll-free 800/321-2599. www.brownpalace.com.* Located in the heart of downtown Denver, this stunning landmark hotel has played gracious host to presidents, princesses, and countless celebrities in the 110 years since it was built by noted Colorado architect Frank E. Edbrooke. With its unique triangle shape and nine-story atrium lobby, it is worth a visit, if only to experience the sheer opulence of its interior details and lush décor. For a real taste of turn-of-the-century elegance, stay for afternoon tea, served daily from noon to 4 pm in the atrium lobby. Reservations are recommended.

Byers-Evans House Museum. *1310 Bannock St, Denver. Phone 303/620-4933.* Restored Victorian house featuring the history of two noted Colorado pioneer families. Guided tours available. (Tues-Sun 11 am-3 pm; closed holidays) **$**

Chatfield State Park. *11500 N Roxborough Park Rd, Littleton. 1 mile S of C-470 on Wadsworth St, near Littleton. Phone 303/791-7275. parks.state.co.us.* Swimming beach, bathhouse, water-skiing, fishing, boating (rentals, dock), marina; hiking, biking, bridle trails; picnicking, snack bar, camping (electrical hookups, dump station). Nature center; interpretive programs. (Daily) **$**

Cherry Creek State Park. *4201 S Parker Rd, Aurora. 1 mile S of I-225 on Parker Rd (Hwy 83), near south Denver. Phone 303/699-3860. www.parks.state.co.us.* Swimming, bathhouse, water-skiing, fishing, boating (ramps, rentals); horseback riding, picnicking (shelters), concession, camping. Model airplane field, shooting range. (Daily) **$**

Civic Center. *100 W 14th Ave Pkwy, Denver. W of Capitol Complex.* Includes

Denver Art Museum. *100 W 14th Ave Pkwy, Denver. S side of Civic Center. Phone 720/865-5000. www.denverartmuseum.org.* Houses collection of art objects representing almost every culture and period, including a fine collection of Native American arts; changing exhibits. (Tues-Sat 10 am-5 pm, Sun noon-5 pm; closed holidays) Free admission Sat for Colorado residents. **$$**

Denver City and County Buildings. *100 W 14th Ave Pkwy, Denver. W side of Civic Center. Phone 303/866-2604.* Courts, municipal council, and administrative offices.

Denver Public Library. *10 W 14th Ave Pkwy, Denver. Phone 720/865-1111. www.denver.lib.co.us.* First phase of new library opened in 1995; it encompasses the old library. Largest public library in Rocky Mountain region with nearly 4 million items; outstanding Western History collection, Patent Depository Library, genealogy collections, and branch library system. Programs, exhibits. (Mon-Tues 10 am-9 pm, Thurs-Sat 10 am-5:30 pm, Sun 1-5 pm; closed holidays) **FREE**

Greek Theater. *100 W 14th Ave Pkwy, Denver. S side of Civic Center.* Outdoor amphitheater, summer folk dancing.

Colorado's Ocean Journey. *Qwest Park, 700 Water St, Denver. Located in the Central Platte Valley on the NE corner of I-25 and 23rd Ave. Phone 303/561-4450; toll-free 888/561-4450. www.oceanjourney.org.* This world-class, 106,500-square-foot aquarium brings visitors face to face with more than 300 species of fish, birds, mammals, and invertebrates from around the world. Exhibits follow the re-creation of water's journey from river to ocean, showcasing the varied and often exotic variety of habitats and creatures found along the way. Several areas encourage hands-on encounters between visitors and animals, including the Critters Up Close demonstrations, the Tide Pool Treasures touchable tide pool display, and the Parade of Rays pool stocked with pettable stingrays. Additional attractions include the Seafoam Fun Zone play area for young children and the "AquaPod" virtual aquatic adventure ride. Upon your arrival, check out the daily presentation notice for times and locations of special exhibits. (Late May-early Sept: daily 10 am-6 pm; early Sept-late May: daily 10 am-5 pm, hours are subject to change without notice). **$$$**

Colorado Avalanche (NHL). *Pepsi Center, 1000 Chopper Cir, Denver. Phone 303/405-1100. www.coloradoavalanche.com.* Professional hockey team.

Colorado Bug Tours. *Denver. Phone toll-free 888/528-5285.* Auto tours in a classic Volkswagen convertible.

Colorado History Tours. *Phone 303/866-4686.* Two-hour guided walking tours; three-hour guided step-on bus tours. Reservations required; ten people minimum. Prices and schedules vary.

Colorado Rapids (MLS). *Invesco Field at Mile High, 1701 Bryant St, Denver. Phone 720/258-3888; toll-free 800/844-7777. www.coloradorapids.com.* Professional soccer team. Tours (fee) (Thurs-Sat 10 am-2 pm, every 30 minutes).

Colorado Rockies (MLB). *Coors Field, 2001 Blake St, Denver. Phone 303/292-0200; toll-free 800/388-7625 (tickets). colorado.rockies.mlb.com.* Professional baseball team. Tours of Coors Field available; call for fees and schedule.

Comanche Crossing Museum. *56060 E Colfax Ave, Strasburg. 30 miles E. Phone 303/622-4322.* Memorabilia of the completion of the transcontinental railway, artifacts pertaining to area history; two buildings with period rooms; restored schoolhouse (circa 1891); Strasburg Union Pacific Depot; caboose, wood-vaned windmill (circa 1880), and homestead on landscaped grounds. (May-Aug: daily 1-4 pm) **DONATION**

Denver Botanic Gardens. *1005 York St, Denver. Phone 720/865-3500. www.botanicgardens.org.* This tropical paradise in the middle of the Rockies is home to more than 15,000 plant species from around the world. Located ten minutes east of downtown Denver, the Denver Botanic Gardens beckons visitors to explore its 23 acres of beautiful outdoor and indoor displays. The Conservatory, with more than 850 tropical and subtropical plants in an enclosed rain forest setting, is a soothing retreat for midwinter guests. A newer exhibit is the 20-x-40-foot Cloud Forest Tree covered with hundreds of orchids and rare tropical plants. Other gardens include alpine, herb, Japanese, shade, and wildflower displays. Children particularly enjoy navigating the mazes in the Secret Path garden and climbing the resident banyan tree. (Mid-Sept: daily 9 am-5 pm; May-mid-Sept: Sat-Tues 9 am-8 pm, Wed-Fri 9 am-5 pm; closed Thanksgiving) **$$**

Denver Broncos (NFL). *Invesco Field at Mile High, 1701 Bryant St, Denver. Phone 303/433-7466. www.denverbroncos.com.* Professional football team. Tours available; call for fees and schedule.

Denver Firefighters Museum. *1326 Tremont Pl, Denver. Phone 303/892-1436. www.denverfirefightersmuseum.org.* Housed in Fire House No. 1; maintains the atmosphere of a working firehouse; firefighting equipment from the mid-1800s. (Mon-Sat 10 am-4 pm; closed holidays) **$**

Denver Museum of Nature and Science. *2001 Colorado Blvd, Denver. In City Park. Phone 303/322-7009; toll-free 800/925-2250. www.dmns.org.* Ninety habitat exhibits from four continents displayed against natural backgrounds; Prehistoric Journey exhibit displays dinosaurs in re-created environments; earth sciences lab; gems and minerals; Native American collection. (Daily 9 am-5 pm; closed Dec 25) **$$** Combination tickets available for

Charles C. Gates Planetarium. *2001 Colorado Blvd, Denver. Phone 303/322-7009 (schedule and fees). www.dmns.org/planetarium.* Contains a Minolta Series IV star projector; presents a variety of star and laser light shows daily. The Phipps IMAX Theater has an immense motion picture system projecting images on screen 4 1/2 stories tall and 6 1/2 stories wide. Daily showings. **$$**

Hall of Life. *2001 Colorado Blvd, Denver. Phone 303/322-7009.* Health education center has permanent exhibits on genetics, fitness, nutrition, and the five senses. Classes and workshops (fee). (Daily)

Denver Nuggets (NBA). *Pepsi Center, 1000 Chopper Cir, Denver. Phone 303/405-1212. www.nba.com/nuggets.* Professional basketball team. Tours available; call 303/405-8556 for information.

Denver Performing Arts Complex. *950 13th St, Denver. Phone 303/640-2862. www.artscomplex.com.* One of the most innovative and comprehensive performing arts centers in the country. With the addition of the Temple Hoyne Buell Theatre, the complex is the largest art center under one roof in the nation. The complex also contains shops and restaurants.

Auditorium Theatre. *Phone 303/640-2862.* (1908) Past host to grand opera, political conventions, minstrel shows, revivalist meetings, and military maneuvers; now hosts touring Broadway productions and the Colorado Ballet. Home of Colorado Contemporary Dance.

Boettcher Concert Hall. *Phone 303/640-2862.* The first fully "surround" symphonic hall in the US; all of its 2,630 seats are within 75 feet of the stage. Home of the Colorado Symphony Orchestra (Sept-early June) and Opera Colorado with performances "in the round" (May).

The Galleria. A walkway covered by an 80-foot-high arched glass canopy. It connects all the theaters in the complex.

The Helen Bonfils Theatre Complex. *Phone 303/893-4000 (tours).* Home of the Denver Center Theatre Company. Contains three theaters: the Stage, seating 547 in a circle around a thrust platform; the Space, a theater-in-the-round seating 450; and the Source, a small theater presenting plays by American playwrights. Also contains the Frank Ricketson Theatre, a 195-seat theater available for rental for community activities, classes, and festivals.

Temple Hoyne Buell Theatre. *Phone 303/640-2862.* The most recent addition to the complex. The 2,800-seat theater has a glass facade and Colorado sandstone walls. It is host to Opera Colorado and Broadway plays and home of the Colorado Ballet.

★ Denver Zoo. *City Park, 2300 Steele St, Denver. Phone 303/376-4800. www.denverzoo.org.* Among Colorado's most popular city attractions is the Denver Zoo. Located in City Park just east of downtown, this 80-acre zoological wonderland is home to more than 4,000 animals representing 700 species. Founded in 1896, the zoo has evolved into one of the nation's premier animal exhibits, noted for its beautiful grounds, innovative combination of outdoor and enclosed habitats, and world-class conservation and breeding programs. Don't miss the Primate Panorama, a 7-acre showcase of rare monkeys and apes. Visit the 22,000-square-foot, glass-enclosed Tropical Discovery and feel what it's like to walk into a tropical rain forest complete with caves, cliffs, waterfalls, and some of the zoo's most exotic (and dangerous!) creatures. Equally popular is the Northern Shores Arctic wildlife habitat, which provides a nose-to-nose underwater look at swimming polar bears and sea lions. Be sure to check out the feeding schedule posted just inside the zoo's entrance. During the evenings throughout December, millions of sparkling lights and holiday music transform the zoo as part of the traditional "Wonderlights" festival. (Apr-Sept: daily 9 am-6 pm; Oct-Mar: daily 10 am-5 pm) **$$$**

Forney Transportation Museum. *4303 Brighton Blvd, Denver. Phone 303/297-1113. www.forneymuseum.com.* The museum's collection houses more than 300 antique cars, carriages, cycles, sleighs, steam locomotives and coaches; many with costumed figures. One of the most notable permanent exhibits is that of Union Pacific "Big Boy" locomotive X4005, which was involved in a horiffic crash in 1953, but has been restored and sits on the museum's grounds. The "Gold Bug" Kissel automobile owned by Amelia Earhart and Crown Prince Aly Khan's Rolls Royce are also here. If it has wheels, chances are the Forney Museum has something like it! (Mon-Sat 9 am-5 pm) **$$**

Four Mile Historic Park. *715 S Forest St, Denver. Located east of Colorado Boulevard between Cherry Creek Dr S and Alameda. Phone 303/399-1859. www.fourmilehistoricpark.org.* Take a stroll through Denver history at Four Mile Historic Park. Once a stage stop, this 14-acre living history museum encompasses the oldest house still standing in Denver (circa 1859), plus other outbuildings and farm equipment from the late 1800s. Guides in period costume reenact life on a farmstead. It's a great place for a picnic. Kids particularly enjoy chasing the chickens, visiting with the draft horses, and riding on a real stagecoach (weekends only). (Apr-Sept: Wed-Fri noon-4 pm, Sat-Sun 10 am-4 pm; Oct-Mar: Sat-Sun noon-4 pm) **$**

Gray Line bus tours. *5855 E 56th Ave, Commerce City. Phone 303/289-2841; toll-free 800/348-6877. www.coloradograyline.com.* Call or visit Web site for schedule and tour information.

Hyland Hills Adventure Golf. *9650 N Sheridan Blvd, Westminster. Phone 303/650-7587. www.hylandhills.org/adventuregolf.html.* It's miniature golf on a mega scale. Located 15 minutes north of downtown Denver, Hyland Hills Adventure Golf puts your putting skills and your imagination to the test with 54 stunningly landscaped holes in a fantasy setting of cliffs, caves, and waterfalls. (Closed during winter months) **$$**

★ Hyland Hills Water World. *88th Ave and Pecos St, Federal Heights. 15 minutes N of downtown Denver. Phone 303/427-7873. www.waterworldcolorado.com.* Ranked among the nation's largest water parks, this 64-acre aquatic extravaganza is not a place for the faint of heart, but it's a great spot for the young at heart and a terrific good time for all ages. One admission fee provides unlimited access to 40 amusement and water thrill rides. Water World's beautifully landscaped grounds include a wave pool the size of a football field, 16 water slides, nine inner-tube rides, and a splash pool for tots. Older kids won't want to miss the Lost River of the Pharaohs, a whitewater rafting trip through a mummy-filled pyramid and down a spiraling slide. Younger visitors will enjoy Voyage to the Center of the Earth, a gentler ride featuring close encounters with animatronic dinosaurs. Hours vary according to season and weather, so be sure to call ahead. (Late May-early Sept: daily 10 am-6 pm) **$$$$**

Larimer Square. *Larimer and 14th sts, Denver. Phone 303/534-2367. www.larimersquare.com.* Restoration of the first street in Denver, this collection of shops, galleries, nightclubs, and restaurants is set among Victorian courtyards, gaslights, arcades, and buildings; carriage rides around square. (Daily)

Molly Brown House Museum. *1340 Pennsylvania St, Denver. Phone 303/832-4092. www.mollybrown.org.* The Molly Brown House Museum stands as an enduring tribute to one of Denver's most prominent architects, William Lang, and one of its most colorful characters, Margaret "Molly" Brown. A spectacular example of Colorado Victorian design, the fully restored 1880s sandstone and lava stone mansion now serves as a museum, filled with many of the lavish furnishings and personal possessions of its most famous occupant. Anyone interested in the story of the Titanic and the heroics of its "Unsinkable" survivor should take a moment to step back in time and enjoy a tour of her home. (Sept-May: Tues-Sat open 10 am, last tour at 3:30 pm; Sun open noon, last tour at 3:30 pm. June-Aug: Mon-Sat open 9:30 am, last tour at 4 pm; Sun open noon, last tour at 3:45 pm) **$$**

Park system. *2300 15th St #150, Denver. Phone 303/964-2500.* More than 200 parks within the city provide approximately 4,400 acres of facilities for boating, fishing, and other sports. The system includes six golf courses. There are also 27 mountain parks within 72 miles of the city, covering 13,448 acres of land in the Rocky Mountain foothills. Parks of special interest are

Cheesman Park. *1177 Race St, Denver. E 8th Ave and Franklin St. Phone 303/322-0066.* This park has excellent views of nearby mountain peaks with aid of dial and pointers. Congress Park swimming pool (fee) is adjacent. Located between Cheesman and Congress parks is the Denver Botanic Gardens (fee), with the Boettcher Memorial Conservatory.

City Park. *Colorado Blvd and York St, Denver. Runs between 17th and 26th aves. Phone 303/331-4113.* Contains the Denver Museum of Nature and Science (see), an 18-hole golf course, and the Denver Zoo (see). Animals in natural habitats; primates, felines, and giraffes; aviary, children's zoo, miniature railroad. (Daily) Children under 16 must be accompanied by adult at zoo. **$$$**

★ **Red Rocks Park.** (see MORRISON)

Washington Park. *Runs between S Downing and S Franklin sts, E Louisiana and E Virginia aves. Phone 303/698-4930.* This 165-acre park features a large recreation center with indoor pool (fee). Floral displays include a replica of George Washington's gardens at Mount Vernon.

Pearce-McAllister Cottage. *1880 N Gaylord St, Denver. Phone 303/322-1053.* (1899) Dutch Colonial Revival house contains original furnishings. Guided tours give insight into upper middle-class lifestyle of the 1920s. Second floor houses Denver Museum of Dolls, Toys, and Miniatures. (Tues-Sat 10 am-4 pm, Sun 1-4 pm) **$**

Pint's Pub Brewery and Freehouse. *211 W 13th Ave, Denver. Phone 303/534-7543. www.pintspub.com.* Just south of Civic Center Park on 13th and Broadway, Pint's Pub and Brewery brings a bit of old England to downtown Denver. Bright, lively, and distinctively British, this traditional brewpub offers a wide variety of handcrafted ales on tap, many found nowhere else in the US, plus what they claim is the largest selection of single malt whiskeys in the country. Sit down to an order of fish and chips or sheepherder's stew to go with your brew selection and make a night of it. Look for the red English-style phone booth and British flag at the front entrance. (Mon-Sat 11 am-11 pm, Sun 11 am-8 pm)

Sakura Square. *1255 19th St, Denver. Lawrence to Larimer sts. Phone 303/295-0305.* Denver's Japanese Cultural and Trade Center features Asian restaurants, shops, businesses; authentic Japanese gardens. Site of a famed Buddhist Temple.

Six Flags Elitch Gardens. *2000 Elitch Cir, Denver. Phone 303/595-4386. www.sixflags.com/parks/elitchgardens/home.asp.* If you're into adrenaline overload, then Six Flags Elitch Gardens is your kind of place. This granddaddy of amusement parks in downtown Denver features more than 45 rides sure to satisfy even the most experienced coasterhead. The park is best known for its extreme roller coaster rides; other favorites include a 22-story freefall in the Tower of Doom, Disaster Canyon whitewater rafting, and the new Flying Coaster, which simulates the experience of flying. Six Flags includes a kiddie park for younger children, the popular Island Kingdom water park, and live entertainment nightly. (June-Aug 10 am-10 pm; limited and weekend hours May and Sept) **$$$$**

Ski Train. *555 17th St, Denver. Phone 303/296-4754. www.skitrain.com.* A ride on the Ski Train from Denver to Winter Park has long been a favorite day trip for skiers, hikers, bikers, and family vacationers. Operating weekends year-round, the train takes its passengers on a spectacular wilderness ride through the Rockies and then drops them off at the front entrance of beautiful Winter Park Resort. Tickets are for round-trip, same-day rides only, reservations are highly recommended to assure a seat. (Sat-Sun, winter; June-Aug, Sat) **$$$$**

State Capitol. *200 E Colfax Ave, Denver. Phone 303/866-2604.* This magnificent edifice overlooking Civic Center Park is a glorious reminder of Denver's opulent past. Today, it serves as Colorado's legislative center. Designed by architect Elijah Myers in the classical Corinthian style, it was 18 years in the making before its official dedication in 1908. The building is renowned for its exquisite interior details and use of native materials such as gray granite, white marble, pink Colorado onyx, and, of course, the gold that covers its dome. Tours include a climb to the dome, 272 feet up, for a spectacular view of the surrounding mountains. Make sure that the kids find the special marker on the steps outside noting that they are, indeed, a mile high. (Mon-Fri 7 am-5:30 pm, some Sat in summer) **FREE** Also here is

The Children's Museum of Denver. *2121 Children's Museum Dr, Denver. Off I-25, exit 211. Phone 303/433-7444. www.cmdenver.org.* This 24,000-square-foot, two-story hands-on environment allows children to learn and explore the world around them. Exhibits include a room with thousands of plastic balls; Kidslope, a year-round ski slope; science center; and a grocery store. (Mon-Fri 9 am-4 pm, Sat-Sun 10 am-5 pm; closed holidays) Children's Museum Theater (weekends) and special events. **$$**

Colorado History Museum. *1300 Broadway, Denver (80203). Phone 303/866-3682.* Permanent and rotating exhibits on people and history of Colorado. Dioramas, full-scale mining equipment, Native American artifacts, photographs; sodhouse. Headquarters of the Colorado Historical Society. (Mon-Sat 10 am-4:30 pm, Sun noon-4:30 pm; closed Jan 1, Thanksgiving, Dec 25) **$**

University of Denver. *S University Blvd and E Evans Ave. Phone 303/871-2711. www.du.edu.* (1864) (8,500 students) Handsome 125-acre main campus with Penrose Library, Harper Humanities Gardens, Shwayder Art Building, Seely G. Mudd Building (science), William T. Driscoll University Center, and historic buildings dating from the 1800s. The 33-acre Park Hill campus at Montview Boulevard and Quebec Street is the site of the University of Denver Law School (Lowell Thomas Law Building) and the Lamont School of Music (Houston Fine Arts Center; for schedule phone 303/871-6400). Campus tours. The university maintains

Chamberlin Observatory. *2930 E Warren Ave, Denver. Observatory Park. Phone 303/871-5172. www.du.edu/~rstencel/Chamberlin.* Houses a 20-inch aperture Clark-Saegmuller refractor in use since 1894; lectures. Tours (Tues and Thurs; closed holidays, Christmas week; reservations required). **$**

Special Events

Cherry Creek Arts Festival. *In Denver's Cherry Creek North, on Second and Third aves between Clayton and Steele sts. www.cherryarts.org.* Features works by 200 national artists; culinary, visual, and performing arts. July 4 weekend.

Denver Film Festival. *Starz FilmCenter at the Tivoli, 900 Auraria Pkwy, Denver. Phone 303/595-3456. www.denverfilm.org.* Movie junkies will get more than their fill of flicks at the ten-day Denver International Film Festival in October. Showcasing 175 films while playing host to many of their stars, the festival includes international feature releases, independent fiction and documentaries, experimental productions, and children's programs. All films are shown at the Starz FilmCenter at the Tivoli. It's best to order tickets ahead of time, as many of the features sell out. Oct. **$$**

Denver Lights and Parade of Lights. *Downtown Denver, starting at Civic Center Park in front of the City and County Building. Phone 303/478-7878. www.denverparadeoflights.com.* From early December through January, downtown Denver is ablaze with what is very possibly the largest holiday light show in the world. Locals and tourists alike drift down to Civic Center Park after dark to view the incredible rainbow display covering the buildings. A spectacular Parade of Lights that winds for 2 miles through Denver's downtown kicks off the holiday season.

Furry Scurry. *Washington Park, Louisiana Ave and Downing St, Denver. Phone 303/964-2522. www.ddfl.org/furryscurry.htm.* The Furry Scurry is a 2-mile walk and fun run through Denver's Washington Park. Featuring a 2.6-mile jogging trail, several picnic areas, large flower gardens, and two lakes, the park is the perfect spot for an outdoor-loving family to spend the day. The race is a fundraiser for the Denver Dumb Friends League, and most participants bring their dogs as racing companions. The event typically attracts more than 6,000 two- and four-legged participants and raises $400,000 for the league. Early May. **$**

Greyhound racing. *Mile High Greyhound Park, 6200 Dahlia St, Commerce City. 7 miles NE at junction I-270 and Vasquez Blvd. Phone 303/288-1591.* Pari-mutuels. Mid-June-mid-Feb, nightly Tues-Sat; matinee racing Mon, Fri-Sat. Satellite "off-track" betting all year.

The International at Castle Pines Golf Club. *1000 Hummingbird Ln, Castle Rock. 29 miles south of Denver. Phone 303/688-6000. www.golfntl.com.* The International is a week-long, world-class golf event that attracts some of the top professional golfers. The Jack Nicklaus-designed course is renowned for the beauty of its pine-strewn mountain setting and the challenge of its terrain. The tournament begins in earnest on Thursday, but spectators are welcome to watch practice rounds as well as the junior and pro-am tournaments held earlier in the week. One week in August. **$$$$**

National Western Livestock Show, Horse Show, & Rodeo. *National Western Complex, 4655 Humboldt St, Denver. Located E of I-25 on I-70. Phone 303/297-1166; toll-free 888/551-5004 (tickets). www.nationalwestern.com.* If you are in Denver in the middle of January, you'd better hang onto your Stetson, because that's when the National Western Stock Show and Rodeo comes to town, along with 600,000 rootin' tootin' exhibitors and spectators. Billed as the largest livestock exhibition in the world, this two-week extravaganza is packed with nonstop shows and demonstrations, from sheep shearing to steer wrestling. Daily rodeos showcase the horse and bull-riding skills of some of the best riders in the country before cheering, sellout crowds in the National Western Complex. Other favorites include barrel races, show-horse contests, a junior rodeo (where some of the riders are 3 years old!), Wild West shows, and the colorful Mexican Rodeo Extravaganza. Take a break from the action and tour the exhibition hall for demonstrations in wool spinning and goat milking, or walk the grounds to see what a yak looks like up close. Mid-Jan. **$$**

Limited-Service Hotels

★ COMFORT INN DOWNTOWN. *401 17th St, Denver (80202). Phone 303/296-0400; fax 303/312-5941. www.comfortinn.com.* Clean, comfortable, and pet-friendly, with a bountiful complimentary continental breakfast and high-speed Internet access in every guest room, this Comfort Inn offers a rare bonus: access to the facilities of its next-door neighbor, the Mobil Four-Star Brown Palace Hotel. This includes a spectacular health club, laundry service, and dining at all of the Brown Palace's restaurants (with a 15 percent discount). And when the Brown Palace upgrades, the Comfort Inn has been known to tag along. Witness the "bookmark" TV feature, which allows guests to take advantage of pay-per-view, pause a movie in the middle to go for dinner, and then pick up where they left off, at no additional cost. 231 rooms, 22 story. Complimentary continental breakfast. Check-in 3 pm, check-out noon. High-Speed Internet access. Restaurant, bar. Fitness room. **$$**

★★ FOUR POINTS DENVER CHERRY CREEK. *600 S Colorado Blvd, Denver (80246). Phone 303/757-3341; toll-free 800/359-7234; fax 303/756-6670.* 210 rooms. Complimentary continental breakfast. Check-in 3 pm, check-out noon. Restaurant, bar. **$**

★★ HOLIDAY INN. *10 E 120th Ave, Northglenn (80233). Phone 303/452-4100; fax 303/457-1741. www.holiday-inn.com.* 235 rooms, 6 story. Pets accepted; fee. Check-out noon. Restaurant, bar. Fitness room. Indoor pool, whirlpool. **$**

★★ OXFORD HOTEL. *1600 17th St, Denver (80202). Phone 303/628-5400; toll-free 800/228-5838; fax 303/628-5413. www.theoxfordhotel.com.* Built in 1891 and located next to Union Station, this luxurious restored hotel has become a landmark in Denver, touted as the city's "oldest grand hotel." Centrally located, it is near many attractions, including Coors Field, the 16th Street Mall, Larimer Square, and many shops and galleries. 80 rooms, 5 story. Complimentary continental breakfast. Check-out 1 pm. Restaurant, bar. Fitness room, spa. Whirlpool. **$$**

Full-Service Hotels

★★★★ THE BROWN PALACE HOTEL. *321 17th St, Denver (80202). Phone 303/297-3111; toll-free 800/321-2599; fax 303/312-5900. www.brownpalace.com.* This historical landmark has been hosting visitors since 1892, and many presidents, monarchs, and celebrities have graced its halls. In the lobby, a magnificent stained-glass ceiling tops off six levels of cast-iron balconies. Victorian and Art Deco decor. The award-winning Palace Arms restaurant (see also PALACE ARMS) features signature favorites like rack of lamb and pan-roasted veal. Cigar aficionados flock to the library ambience of the Churchill Bar, while the Ship Tavern appeals to lovers of the sea. Ellygnton's Sunday brunch is legendary. 241 rooms, 10 story. Check-in 3 pm, check-out noon. Restaurant, bar. Fitness room. Business center. **$$$**

★ ★ ★ HOTEL MONACO DENVER. *1717 Champa St, Denver (80202). Phone 303/296-1717; toll-free 800/397-5380; fax 303/296-1818. www.monaco-denver.com.* Just how much fun can sophistication be? To find out, check in to the Hotel Monaco. When you enter the lobby, you'll feel like you're in an elegant, somewhat exotic living room—did they mean to call it the Hotel Morocco?—with cushy couches, recessed bookshelves, and potted palms. Then you look up and see that you're sitting under what the Monaco's designer calls a Russian Circus Tent. The domed ceiling is all about wide stripes and diamonds, blues and golds, a theme that carries through to the subtly striped wall coverings in the halls and meeting rooms, the softly colored guest room doors, and the stripes-on-wood chests of drawers. Yet the plush duvet covers, bathroom phones, 24-hour room service, terrycloth shower curtains, and automatic turndown service remind you that the Monaco is as serious about service as it is about fun. Even your dog will think so when he is presented with his own bowl and a bag of gourmet treats. Don't forget to buy a yo-yo from your mini-bar. 189 rooms, 7 story. Pets accepted. Check-out noon. Restaurant, bar. Fitness room. Business center. **$$**

★ ★ ★ HOTEL TEATRO. *1100 14th St, Denver (80202). Phone 303/228-1100; toll-free 888/727-1200; fax 303/228-1101. www.hotelteatro.com.* This downtown boutique hotel is located in a historic landmark building adjacent to the theater district, across the street from the Denver Center for the Performing Arts. If you want someone to draw you an aromatherapy bath with your turndown service, this is the hotel for you. The Teatro prides itself on the extras it offers its guests, and the automatic bath is just one. An in-room laser printer and fax machine is another; a full-size Krups coffeemaker is one more. How about customizing your own mini-bar when you check in? If you don't want the temptation of chips or Twizzlers, ask for fresh fruit and mineral water instead (and it will be waiting for you the next time you check in, too). Guest rooms include niceties like down comforters, Frette linens, Aveda bath products, and Starbucks coffee. The hotel even has Range Rovers to transport you around the downtown area. The hotel's two American restaurants, one casual and one more upscale, are operated by acclaimed chef Kevin Taylor, who also provides 24-hour room service. And don't think you're the only one who will be pampered here. The Teatro is so pet-friendly that not only does it not charge a deposit for Fido, but the hotel will provide a customized doggie dish with his name on it and present him with a bowl of Fiji water to lap. 111 rooms, 9 story. Pets accepted, some restrictions. Check-in 3 pm, check-out noon. Restaurant, bar. Children's activity center. Fitness room. **$$$**

★ ★ ★ HYATT REGENCY DENVER. *1750 Welton St, Denver (80202). Phone 303/295-1234; fax 303/292-2472. www.denver.regency.hyatt.com.* The beautiful lobby of this centrally located hotel boasts a 20-foot sandstone fireplace and cozy seating areas with touches of mahogany, granite, and wrought iron, a tip of the hat to the Rocky Mountains. The hotel's restaurant is called 1876, which is the year Colorado became a state. But that's where the antiquity ends. The Hyatt is all about step-to-it service and modern conveniences, even providing guests with rooftop tennis courts surrounded by a jogging track, plus an indoor swimming pool and a health club with free weights, exercise cycles, treadmills, and stair climbers. 511 rooms, 26 story. Check-out noon. Restaurant, bar. Fitness room. Indoor pool. Tennis. Business center. **$**

★ ★ ★ LOEWS DENVER HOTEL. *4150 E Mississippi Ave, Denver (80246). Phone 303/782-9300; fax 303/758-6542. www.loewshotels.com.* The Pet Room Service menu, replete with veterinarian-approved items for dogs and cats, is just one of the amenities in the hotel's "Loews Loves Pets" program, which includes dog and cat beds in different sizes, leashes and collars, pet-walking and sitting services, toys, and pet videos. The hotel seems to love kids just as much, offering Frisbees, backpacks, and games for kids of all ages and a plethora of amenities for the littlest ones, from baby tubs and electric bottle warmers to tub faucet guards, rattles, and invisible outlet plugs. For mom and dad, there's a menu of "comfort items" like chenille throws, different sleeping pillows, and CDs and a player. 183 rooms, 11 story. Check-out 11 am. Restaurant, bar. Fitness room. Business center. **$$**

★ ★ ★ LUNA HOTEL. *1612 Wazee St, Denver (80202). Phone 303/572-3300; fax 303/623-0773. www.lodoinn.com.* 20 rooms. Check-in 3 pm, check-out noon. Restaurant, bar. Fitness center. Business center. **$$**

★★★ **THE MAGNOLIA HOTEL.** *818 17th St, Denver (80202). Phone 303/607-9000; toll-free 888/915-1110; fax 303/607-0101. www.themagnoliahotel.com.* Many visitors to Denver make the Magnolia their home for extended stays, and it's easy to see why. Set back from busy 17th Street, its double-door entrance framed by potted evergreens, the Magnolia says "cozy" from the wingback chairs in its lobby to the full-size kitchens in its suites. Access to a snazzy health club is included with your stay—state-of-the-art machines set in a hexagonal pattern, lit with a bluish light "to simulate the outdoors." A men's and women's steam room is tucked into each changing room. For a few dollars more, guests can use the Magnolia Club, which offers wireless Internet access, a nightly cocktail reception, and late-night cookies and milk. Just the thing after a day of high-powered business meetings. 244 rooms, 10 story. Pets accepted. Complimentary continental breakfast. Check-out 11 am. Airport transportation available. Business center. **$$**

★★★ **MARRIOTT DENVER CITY CENTER.** *1701 California St, Denver (80202). Phone 303/297-1300; fax 303/298-7474. www.marriott.com.* A better health club in an urban hotel may not exist. Bench press, free weights, treadmills, stair climbers, recumbent and upright bicycles, rowing machines, a personal trainer, massages, body treatments...and, of course, a swimming pool and whirlpool. And you may need the workout facilities after you've put in a long day of business. This hotel has the facilities for that, too. There is high-speed Internet access in every guest room, wireless Internet access in the lobby, and a business center if you need it. Located in downtown Denver, this property is within walking distance of Coors Field, and several restaurants and shops. 614 rooms, 19 story. Pets accepted. Check-out noon. Restaurant, bar. Fitness room. Indoor pool, whirlpool. Business center. **$$**

★★★ **RENAISSANCE DENVER HOTEL.** *3801 Quebec St, Denver (80207). Phone 303/399-7500; fax 303/321-1966. www.renaissancehotels.com.* This atrium hotel boasts breathtaking Rocky Mountain views. With indoor and outdoor swimming pools, a well-equipped fitness center, an on-site restaurant providing room service, and large guest rooms that include standard amenities plus mini-refrigerators, the Renaissance Denver is a good choice for families looking for a full-service hotel while trying to stay within a budget. The sights and attractions of downtown Denver are about a ten-minute drive away. 422 rooms, 12 story. Check-in 2 pm, check-out noon. Restaurant, bar. Fitness room. Indoor pool, outdoor pool, whirlpool. Airport transportation available. Business center. **$**

★★★ **THE WESTIN TABOR CENTER.** *1672 Lawrence St, Denver (80202). Phone 303/572-9100; fax 303/572-7288. www.westin.com/taborcenter.* The Starbucks in the lobby might be enough for some. Others may like the whirlpool, the sauna, the outstanding fitness center (with a personal flat-screen TV on each piece of cardio equipment), or the indoor half-basketball court. And the Westin's in-room high-speed Internet access and business center make this hotel a good choice for those who want to work as well as work out or play. Centrally located to downtown Denver and adjacent to the 16th Street Mall, this hotel boasts some of the largest guest rooms in the city, many with views of the Rocky Mountains. The Westin's signature Heavenly Beds ensure a good night's sleep. 430 rooms, 19 story. Pets accepted; fee. Check-out 1 pm. Restaurant, bar. Fitness room. Business center. Indoor pool, outdoor pool, whirlpool. **$$**

★★★ **THE WESTIN WESTMINSTER.** *10600 Westminster Blvd, Westminster (80020). Phone 303/410-5000; fax 303/410-5005. www.westin.com.* 369 rooms, 14 story. Pets accepted; fee. Check-out noon. Restaurant, bar. Children's activity center. Fitness room. Indoor pool, whirlpool. Business center. **$**

Full-Service Inn

★★★ **HISTORIC CASTLE MARNE INN.** *1572 Race St, Denver (80206). Phone 303/331-0621; toll-free 800/926-2763; fax 303/331-0623. www.castlemarne.com.* This lovely bed-and-breakfast, which does indeed resemble a castle, was built in 1889 by well-known Denver architect William Lang. It is on the National Register of Historic Structures and is as beautiful inside as outside: period antiques, family heirlooms, hand-rubbed wood, stained-glass windows, and personal warmth from the proprietors that translates into well-cared-for guests. The Marne has nine rooms of varying sizes, some with whirlpools for one or two, one with an 18-foot cathedral ceiling, and others with beds with feather ticks or pedestal sinks and claw-foot tubs. Melissa Feher-Peiker serves her guests afternoon tea in the parlor (or, weather permitting, in the garden) and will even serve a private candlelight dinner if you make reservations. 9 rooms, 3 story. Complimentary full breakfast. Check-in 4 pm, check-out 11 am. Business center. **$**

Specialty Lodgings

The following lodging establishments are approved by Mobil Travel Guide, but due to their unique and individualized nature have not been given a traditional Mobil Star rating. Included in this listing you may find bed-and-breakfasts, limited-service inns, guest ranches, and other unique hotel properties.

CAPITOL HILL MANSION BED & BREAKFAST. *1207 Pennsylvania St, Denver (80203). Phone 303/839-5221; toll-free 800/839-9329; fax 303/839-9046. www.capitolhillmansion.com.* With its ruby sandstone exterior and dramatic entrance, this 1891 mansion offers a romantic getaway for couples. Rooms feature fresh flowers, soft lighting, and antique furniture. Be sure to have the owners arrange a horse-drawn carriage ride. 8 rooms, 3 story. Complimentary full breakfast. Check-in 4:30-8 pm, check-out 11 am. **$**

HAUS BERLIN BED & BREAKFAST. *1651 Emerson St, Denver (80218). Phone 303/837-9527; toll-free 800/659-0253. www.hausberlinbandb.com.* This inn was built in 1892 and features original art and many antiques. Listed on the National Register of Historic Places, it is conveniently located five minutes from downtown. This elegant property is a favorite with business travelers. 4 rooms, 3 story. Complimentary full breakfast. Check-in 4-8 pm, check-out 11 am. **$**

THE LUMBER BARON INN. *2555 W 37th Ave, Denver (80211). Phone 303/477-8205; toll-free 800/697-6552; fax 303/477-0269. www.lumberbaron .com.* This place is *big*—and there are only five guest rooms. The ground floor consists of a parlor, huge dining room, kitchen, and entertainment room with a 61-inch TV. The entire third floor is a big old ballroom. Doesn't every B&B have one? The Lumber Baron Inn was built in 1890 by an immigrant who made his considerable fortune in, yes, lumber, and each room of this mansion consists of a different wood—cherry, sycamore, oak, maple, poplar, and walnut. Each of the guest rooms has a different theme, but they all have ceilings covered with wallpaper that replicates old Victorian prints, created especially for the inn. Rooms also have separate showers and whirlpool tubs. And that third-floor ballroom, with its 20-foot vaulted ceiling, small kitchen and own bathroom? It's used for anything from a romantic dinner for two to the weekly murder mystery dinners hosted by the inn. 5 rooms, 3 story. Complimentary full breakfast. Check-in 4 pm, check-out 11 am. **$$**

QUEEN ANNE BED AND BREAKFAST. *2147-2151 Tremont Pl, Denver (80205). Phone 303/296-6666; toll-free 800/432-4667; fax 303/296-2151. www.queenannebnb.com.* Built in the 1800s, this bed-and-breakfast faces the Benedict Fountain Park in the Clement Historic District of downtown Denver. Four of the two-room gallery suites are named for famous painters and display samples of their work. The Aspen Room is spectacular, with a mural of an aspen forest that covers both the walls and the ceiling that rises to the top of the Victorian turret. 14 rooms, 3 story. Complimentary full breakfast. Check-in 3 pm, check-out noon. **$**

Restaurants

★ ANNIE'S CAFÉ. *4012 E 8th Ave, Denver (80220). Phone 303/355-8197.* If you're looking for pure fun with your French toast, look no further. Annie's, which serves breakfast all day, boasts an authentic, old-fashioned soda fountain where you can get real root beer floats and even egg creams. Sit in a vinyl booth at a Formica table, listen to oldies on the sound system, and savor the sights of walls covered with old movie posters and vintage toys. And when was the last time you had a jar of peanut butter sitting on your table along with ketchup and mustard? American menu. Breakfast, lunch, dinner. Closed holidays. Bar. Children's menu. **$**

★★ BABY DOE'S MATCHLESS MINE. *2520 W 23rd Ave, Denver (80211). Phone 303/433-3386; fax 303/433-2041.* Replica of Matchless Mine in Leadville; memorabilia of era. American menu. Lunch, dinner, Sun brunch. Closed Mon, Children's menu. **$$**

★★ BAROLO GRILL. *3030 E 6th Ave, Denver (80206). Phone 303/393-1040; fax 303/333-9240.* Northern Italian menu. Dinner. Closed Sun-Mon; holidays. Bar. Children's menu. Free valet parking. Outdoor seating. **$$**

★★ BENNY'S. *301 E 7th Ave, Denver (80203). Phone 303/894-0788; fax 303/839-5488. www.bennysrestaurant.com.* Mexican menu. Lunch, dinner. Closed Thanksgiving, Dec 25. Bar. Casual attire. Outdoor seating. **$**

★ BRITTANY HILL. *9350 Grant, Thornton (80229). 11 miles north of Denver. Phone 303/451-5151; fax 303/451-1013.* American menu. Lunch, dinner, Sun brunch. Bar. Patio deck. **$$**

★★★ BROKER. *821 17th St, Denver (80202). Phone 303/292-5065; fax 303/292-2652. www.brokerrestaurant.com.* Built inside a former turn-of-the-century bank vault, the restaurant's trademark is its free bowls of steamed shrimp for every diner. American menu. Lunch, dinner. Closed Dec 25. Bar. **$$$**

★★ BUCKHORN EXCHANGE. *1000 Osage St, Denver (80204). Phone 303/534-9505; fax 303/534-2814. www.buckhorn.com.* The Buckhorn Exchange, Denver's oldest (and most famous) restaurant, is part dining establishment, part saloon, and part museum, built in 1893. It's worth a visit, if only to marvel at the collection of more than 500 wall-mounted big-game hunting trophies, as well as photos and artifacts from the many dignitaries who have dined here. Its casual Western charm has been honed through 100 years of continuous service. Take the opportunity to sample buffalo sausage, fried alligator tail, or marinated rattlesnake before digging into one of Buckhorn's famous steaks. On weekends, live music and dancing liven up the Lounge. Lunch, dinner. Closed holidays. Bar. Outdoor seating. **$$$**

★★ COOS BAY BISTRO. *2076 S University Blvd, Denver (80210). Phone 303/744-3591; fax 303/744-6246. www.coosbaybistro.com.* French, Italian menu. Lunch, dinner. Closed holidays. Bar. Outdoor seating. **$$**

★★ DENVER CHOPHOUSE & BREWERY. *1735 19th St, Denver (80202). Phone 303/296-0800; fax 303/296-2800. www.chophouse.com.* Historic warehouse converted into a restaurant; microbrewery. American menu. Lunch, dinner. Bar. Outdoor seating. **$$**

★ EMPRESS SEAFOOD. *2825 W Alameda Ave, Denver (80219). Phone 303/922-2822; fax 303/922-2810.* Chinese menu. Lunch, dinner. Bar. **$**

★★ FOURTH STORY RESTAURANT & BAR. *2955 E 1st Ave, Denver (80206). Phone 303/322-1824; fax 303/399-2279. www.fourthstory.com.* In this light-filled restaurant, you can take your pick of what to digest: soup, pasta, roasted sea bass, or the latest best-seller. The Fourth Story is, indeed, the fourth story of Denver's famous Tattered Cover bookstore, and not only are you welcome to peruse while you eat, but you can leave the books at your table and the servers will reshelve them after you leave. The restaurant itself is filled with bookshelves; grab the latest biography, political discourse, cookbook, or volume of poems, and if you decide to purchase it, it can be added to your lunch or dinner tab. Depending on what day you're visiting, you might run into a monthly tea tasting or wine dinner, a jazz brunch or a food writer book signing. This is a haven for bookies of the literary kind. American menu. Lunch, dinner, Sun brunch. Closed holidays. Bar. Children's menu. **$$**

★★★ HIGHLANDS GARDEN CAFE. *3927 W 32nd Ave, Denver (80212). Phone 303/458-5920; fax 303/477-6695.* Take two side-by-side circa 1890 Victorian houses, join them, renovate, and surround them with lush foliage and flower gardens and you'll have this unique Denver mainstay. The "eclectic American" menu takes advantage of seasonal ingredients. The main dining room is all exposed brick, polished hardwood floors, and crisp white tablecloths, but other rooms have a different ambience; the French Country Room, for instance, is painted white and has double French doors leading out to the gardens. American menu. Lunch, dinner, Sun brunch. Closed Mon; holidays. Outdoor seating. **$$$**

★★ IL FORNAIO. *1631 Wazee St, Denver (80202). Phone 303/573-5050. www.ilfornaio.com.* Italian menu. Lunch, dinner. Closed July 4, Thanksgiving, Dec 25. Bar. Children's menu. Valet parking. Outdoor seating. **$$**

★★★ IMPERIAL CHINESE. *431 S Broadway, Denver (80209). Phone 303/698-2800; fax 303/698-2820. www.imperialchinese.com.* Chinese menu. Lunch, dinner. Closed July 4, Thanksgiving, Dec 25. Bar. Casual attire. **$$**

★★ INDIA'S RESTAURANT. *3333 S Tamarac, Denver (80231). Phone 303/755-4284; fax 303/752-9814. www.indiasrestaurant.com.* Northern Indian menu. Lunch, dinner. Bar. **$$**

★ JAPON RESTAURANT. *1028 S Gaylord St, Denver (80209). Phone 303/744-0330; fax 303/715-0336. www.japonsushi.com.* Japanese menu. Lunch, dinner. Closed July 4, Thanksgiving, Dec 25. **$$**

★ JAX FISH HOUSE. *1539 17th St, Denver (80202). Phone 303/292-5767; fax 303/292-0530. www.jaxfishhousedenver.com.* Seafood menu. Dinner. Closed holidays. Bar. Children's menu. **$$**

★ LAS DELICIAS. *439 E 19th Ave, Denver (80203). Phone 303/839-5675; fax 303/839-5859.* This popular, family-run Mexican restaurant is shaped like a rectangle—an entire block long and about as wide as a pair of maracas. Its popularity is a testament to the no-frills ethnic restaurant that serves up great, authentic meals. Food is brought by servers who bustle with efficiency, particularly amazing at lunch when the crowds are greatest. Regulars swear by the breakfast burrito, served Friday through Sunday. The restaurant has a trio of musicians who rotate among Las Delicias' four locations. Breakfast, lunch, dinner. Closed Thanksgiving, Dec 25. **$**

★★ LE CENTRAL. *112 E 8th Ave, Denver (80203). Phone 303/863-8094; fax 303/863-0219. www.lecentral.com.* French menu. Lunch, dinner, Sat and Sun brunch. Closed Dec 25. Bar. Casual attire. **$**

★★ MEL'S RESTAURANT AND BAR. *235 Fillmore, Denver (80206). Phone 303/333-3979; fax 303/355-7005. www.melsbarandgrill.com.* Set in a tony area of art galleries and handcrafted jewelry, where art glass and funky clothing compete for window space, Mel's is a surprisingly calm oasis for shoppers and non-shoppers alike. It is bright and cheery with a polished bistro look. Seating can be on zebra-striped chairs pushed up to linen-lined tables, or you can opt for one of the restaurant's cozy alcoves. In nice weather, the windows open out to patio seating and a parade of always-interesting shoppers. American menu. Lunch, dinner. Closed Easter, Thanksgiving, Dec 25. Bar. Outdoor seating. **$$$**

★★★ MORTON'S OF CHICAGO. *1710 Wynkoop St, Denver (80202). Phone 303/825-3353; fax 303/825-1248. www.mortons.com.* One of the few places left where one can light up a cigar without interference, this national chain fits right into the upscale Denver meat-and-potatoes scene. The martinis are top-notch (as is the beef, naturally). Steak menu. Menu recited. Dinner. Closed holidays. Bar. Valet parking. **$$$**

★★★ PALACE ARMS. *321 17th St, Denver (80202). Phone 303/297-3111; fax 303/297-3928. www.brownpalace.com.* The Palace Arms opened its doors in 1892. Granted, 111 years is a long time to carry on culinary excellence, but the task is achieved gracefully and winningly here. This century-old restaurant is a treasure of history and gastronomy. Located in the Brown Palace Hotel (see), the majestic Palace Arms dining room has a unique western charisma, with rich wood, brocade-upholstered seating, and 17th-century antiques. Just as refined as the atmosphere is the delicious contemporary French cuisine, prepared with regional accents and served with impeccable care. The Palace Arms offers guests a rare opportunity to dine in historically opulent surroundings on a menu of magnificent fare. American menu. Dinner. Closed holidays. Jacket required. Reservations recommended. Valet parking. **$$$**

★ POTAGER. *1109 Ogden St, Denver (80218). Phone 303/832-5788. www.coloradocuisine.com.*

French-American menu. Dinner. Closed Sun-Mon; holidays. Outdoor seating. **$$**

★★ REDFISH. *1701 Wynkoop, Denver (80202). Phone 303/595-0443; fax 303/595-8858. www.redfishamerica.com.* Cajun menu. Lunch, dinner. Closed Sun; holidays. **$$**

★★★★ RESTAURANT KEVIN TAYLOR. *1106 14th St, Denver (80202). Phone 303/820-2600; fax 303/893-1293.* Frequently hailed as one of Denver's best, Restaurant Kevin Taylor is the flagship eatery of the chic Hotel Teatro, located in the heart of Denver (see HOTEL TEATRO). Parisian elegance is achieved with earth-toned walls, stunning floral arrangements, alabaster chandeliers, Versailles mirrors, original artwork, and striped silk-covered chairs. The menu is inspired by France, with an emphasis on local, seasonal ingredients that, thanks to chef-owner Kevin Taylor, dazzle the taste buds. A tasting menu and à la carte selections are available. The wine list includes 900 bottles. Dinner. Closed Sun; holidays. **$$$**

★ ROCKY MOUNTAIN DINER. *800 18th St, Denver (80202). Phone 303/293-8383. www.rockymountaindiner.com.* Lunch, dinner. Closed holidays. Bar. Children's menu. Outdoor seating. **$$**

★★★ STRINGS. *1700 Humboldt St, Denver (80218). Phone 303/831-7310; fax 303/860-8812. www.stringsrestaurant.com.* This casual restaurant attracts celebrities for power lunching. The presentation can be jaw-droppingly good. Lunch, dinner. Closed holidays. Bar. Children's menu. Valet parking. Outdoor seating. **$$$**

★★★ TANTE LOUISE. *4900 E Colfax Ave, Denver (80220). Phone 303/355-4488; fax 303/321-6312. www.tantelouise.com.* If you have a romantic evening in Denver planned, there's little reason to dine anywhere other than Tante Louise. This country inn-style restaurant, equipped with a blazing fire and vintage wall coverings, is the ideal spot for soft, intimate conversations and long, luxurious dinners. Even if you are not in love with your dinner companion when you get there, the mood here is so perfect that you'll leave enamored, if not with each other, then at least with the food and the tranquil, charming setting. The artistic cuisine at Tante Louise features playful and surprising twists on classic French dishes prepared with impressive local ingredients. To match the ambience and the cuisine, the wine list boasts an incredible selection of 600 domestic and imported wines and sparkling wines, perfect for keeping the romance going. French menu. Dinner. Closed Sun. Bar. Valet parking. Outdoor seating. **$$$**

★★ THREE SONS. *2915 W 44th Ave, Denver (80211). Phone 303/455-4366; fax 303/433-2664.* Only Lissa, a bottled water from Italy, is used at this Italian restaurant, which gives you an idea of how seriously they take their mission. Small shelves protruding from the walls hold olive oil bottles and dried flowers, and crystal wineglasses on crisp white tablecloths stand ready to be filled with the restaurant's latest Italian vintage. Of course, you can always order a white Burgundy from France or a Pinot Grigio from California—but what better to go with your chicken cacciatore than a good Chianti? Lunch, dinner. Closed Mon; holidays. Bar. Children's menu. **$$**

★★ TOMMY TSUNAMI'S. *1432 Market St, Denver (80202). Phone 303/534-5050; fax 303/534-3030. www.tommytsunamis.com.* Pan-Asian menu. Lunch, dinner. Closed Thanksgiving, Dec 25. Bar. Outdoor seating. **$$**

★ TRINITY GRILLE. *1801 Broadway, Denver (80202). Phone 303/293-2288; fax 303/293-3817. www.trinitygrille.com.* American menu. Lunch, dinner. Closed Sun; holidays. Bar. **$$**

★★★ TUSCANY. *4150 E Mississippi Ave, Denver (80246). Phone 303/782-9300; fax 303/758-6542.* Within the walls of the Loews Hotel (see) is one of Denver's top Italian restaurants, where executive chef John P. Mertes supervises the creation of all sorts of regional wonders. Northern Italian menu. Breakfast, lunch, dinner, Sun brunch. Bar. Children's menu. Reservations recommended. Valet parking. Outdoor seating. **$$**

★ WAZEE SUPPER CLUB. *1600 15th St, Denver (80202). Phone 303/623-9518. www.wazeesupperclub.com.* American menu. Lunch, dinner. Closed Jan 1, Dec 25. Bar. **$$**

★★★ WELLSHIRE INN. *3333 S Colorado Blvd, Denver (80222). Phone 303/759-3333; fax 303/759-3487. www.wellshireinn.com.* Flowers and latticework in rose, cobalt blue, and gold adorn the china atop the crisp white tablecloths at the Wellshire Inn. You won't see the pattern anywhere else; it was created exclusively for the Wellshire and based on the splendor of England's Tudor period, a theme that is richly executed in this elegant restaurant. Built in 1926 as a clubhouse for the exclusive Wellshire Country Club, the castle-like building fell into disrepair until the late 1970s, when it underwent a painstaking renovation by new owners. Today it boasts four intimate dining rooms. The elegance is not without whimsy: stained-glass windows, intimate seating nooks, high beamed ceilings, and a pair of century-old hand-painted windows share space with a Victorian croquet set, an antique leather hat box, and weathered signs from ancient taverns. American menu. Breakfast, lunch, dinner, Sun brunch. Closed Jan 1, Memorial Day, Labor Day. Bar. Outdoor seating. **$$$**

★ WYNKOOP BREWING COMPANY. *1634 18th St, Denver (80202). Phone 303/297-2700; fax 303/297-2958. www.wynkoop.com.* In the J. S. Brown Mercantile Building (1899). American menu. Dinner. Closed Thanksgiving, Dec 25. Bar. Outdoor seating. **$$**

★ ZAIDY'S DELI. *121 Adams St, Denver (80206). Phone 303/333-5336; fax 303/333-4118. www.zaidysdeli .com.* There's nothing elegant about Zaidy's. There's nothing even remotely classy about it. In fact, if you're looking for something that even comes close to calm, you might want to look elsewhere. But if you're looking for a typical Jewish deli, with a reputation for the best deli food in all of Grand County, treat yourself to this commotion. Try to find a parking spot—good luck—and then sit down at a comfy booth, listen to servers ask the regulars about their kids, their parents, their vacation, or their doctor's appointment, and watch them carry a dozen plates up their arms for four different tables without a single written reminder of what goes where. Try real—not canned—corned beef hash for breakfast, chicken soup and a kosher hot dog for lunch, and a brisket plate for dinner. When was the last time you had a box lunch complete with cole slaw, pickle, and a cookie? Breakfast, lunch, dinner. Kosher. Closed Thanksgiving, Rosh Hashanah, Yom Kippur. Bar. Children's menu. Outdoor seating. **$**

Denver International Airport Area (B-4)

See also Denver

Information 303/342-2000 or 800/AIR2DEN
Web site www.flydenver.com
Lost and Found 303/342-4062
Airlines Air Canada, Air Tran Airways, Alaska Airlines, America West, American Airlines, ATA, British Airways, Continental Airlines, Delta Air Lines, Frontier Airlines, Great Lakes Aviation, jetBlue Airways, Lufthansa, Mexicana, Midwest Express, Northwest Airlines, Spirit Airlines, United Airlines, US Airways

Limited-Service Hotel

★ ★ DOUBLETREE HOTEL. *13696 E Iliff Pl, Aurora (80014). Phone 303/337-2800; toll-free 800/ 528-0444; fax 303/337-9691. www.doubletree.com.* 248 rooms, 6 story. Check-out noon. Restaurant, bar. Fitness room. Indoor pool. Business center. **$**

★ HAMPTON INN. *1500 S Abilene St, Aurora (80012). Phone 303/369-8400; toll-free 800/426-7866; fax 303/369-0324. www.hampton-inn.com.* 132 rooms, 4 story. Complimentary continental breakfast. Check-out noon. Pool. **$**

Restaurant

★ LA CUEVA. *9742 E Colfax Ave, Aurora (80010). Phone 303/367-1422; fax 303/367-4071. www.lacueva .net.* Mexican menu. Lunch, dinner. Closed Jan 1, Thanksgiving, Dec 25. Bar. Casual attire. **$$**

Dillon (B-3)

See also Breckenridge, Copper Mountain, Georgetown, Keystone, Leadville, Vail

Population 802
Elevation 8,858 ft
Area Code 970
Zip 80435
Information Summit County Chamber of Commerce, PO Box 214, Frisco 80443; toll-free 800/530-3099
Web site www.summitnet.com

The entire town was moved in the early 1960s to make way for Dillon Lake, a reservoir for the Denver water system. The new Dillon, a modern, planned community, has become a popular resort area in the midst of wonderful mountain scenery. Ranger District offices of the Green Mountain Reservoir (see KREMMLING) and the White River National Forest, Arapaho division, (see GLENWOOD SPRINGS) are located in Dillon.

What to See and Do

Arapaho National Forest. *1311 S College Ave, Fort Collins. N, S, and E via Hwy 6, Hwy 9. Phone 970/498-2770.* Campgrounds, picnic grounds, and winter sports areas on more than 1 million acres. Of special interest are Lake Dillon, Arapaho National Recreation Area with five reservoirs, and Mount Evans Wilderness Area with the 14,264-foot-high Mount Evans, which has the highest auto road in the US.

Copper Mountain Resort Ski Area. *I-70 and Hwy 91, Dillon. 9 miles SW. Phone 970/968-2882; toll-free 800/458-8386. www.coppercolorado.com.* Six-person, four high-speed quad, five triple, five double chairlifts; six surface lifts; patrol, school, rentals, snowmaking; cafeteria, restaurants, bar, nursery. One hundred twenty-six runs; longest run approximately 3 miles; vertical drop 2,601 feet. (Nov-Apr, daily) Cross-country skiing. Half-day rates. Athletic club. Summer activities include boating, sailing, rafting; hiking, bicycling, horseback riding, golf; jeep tours. Chairlift also operates to the summit of the mountain (late June-Sept, daily). **$$$$**

Lake Dillon. *680 Blue River Pkwy, Silverthorne. Just S of town in the Arapaho National Forest, on 3,300 acres. Phone 970/468-5400.* Fishing, boating, rafting (ramps, rentals, marinas); hiking, picnicking, camping. Jeep tours (fee). (Daily) **FREE**

Silverthorne Factory Stores. *PO Box 1547, 309-M Rainbow Dr, Silverthorne. 2 miles N to I-70, exit 205. Phone 970/468-5780; toll-free 866/746-7686. www.silverthornefactorystores.com.* Mall contains more than 45 outlet stores. (Mon-Sat 10 am-8 pm, Sun 10 am-6 pm)

Special Event

Mountain Community Fair. *Blue River Park, Silverthorne. Phone 970/513-8081. www.mountaincommunityfair.com.* Second weekend in July. **$$**

Limited-Service Hotels

★ BEST WESTERN PTARMIGAN LODGE. *652 Lake Dillon Dr, Dillon (80435). Phone 970/468-2341; toll-free 800/842-5939; fax 970/468-6465. www.bestwestern.com.* 69 rooms, 2 story. Pets accepted; fee. Complimentary continental breakfast. Check-out 11 am. Bar. Whirlpool. **$**

★ DAYS INN. *580 Silverthorne Ln, Silverthorne (80498). Phone 970/468-8661; toll-free 800/520-4267; fax 970/468-1421. www.daysinn.com.* 73 rooms, 4 story. Pets accepted. Complimentary continental breakfast. Check-out 11 am. Children's pool, whirlpool. **$**

★★ FOUR POINTS BY SHERATON. *560 Silverthorne Ln, Silverthorne (80498). Phone 970/468-6200; toll-free 888/625-5144; fax 970/468-7829. www.starwood.com.* 160 rooms, 6 story. Complimentary continental breakfast. Check-out 10 am. Restaurant, bar. Pool, whirlpool. **$**

★★ HOLIDAY INN. *1129 N Summit Blvd, Frisco (80443). Phone 970/668-5000; toll-free 800/782-7669; fax 970/668-0718. www.holiday-inn.com.* 217 rooms, 6 story. Check-out 11 am. Restaurant, bar. Fitness room. Indoor pool, whirlpool. **$**

Full-Service Resorts

★★★ COPPER MOUNTAIN RESORT. *509 Copper Rd, Copper Mountain (80443). Phone 970/968-2882; toll-free 800/458-8386; fax 970/968-6227. www.ski-copper.com.* Guests flock to this resort for one reason—it's all about the slopes. Extensive grounds on 250 acres. 560 rooms, 7 story. Check-in 4 pm, check-out 11 am. Restaurant, bar. Children's activity center. Fitness room. Indoor pool, whirlpool. Golf. Tennis. Business center. **$**

★★★ **KEYSTONE LODGE.** *22101 Hwy 6, Keystone (80435). Phone 970/496-4500; fax 970/496-4215.* Just a little over an hour from Denver, Keystone Lodge is a perfect Rocky Mountain getaway. This resort entices with its variety of activities, comfortable accommodations, and enjoyable dining. The guest rooms and suites are the picture of mountain chic, with large windows framing unforgettable views of snowcapped peaks and the Snake River. From the flavors of France's Normandy coast at Champeaux to the juicy bites at Bighorn Steakhouse, dining is superb here. Guests are never at a loss for something to do, with ice skating, BMW driving tours, nearby skiing and golf, and a complete fitness center. After an action-packed day, the Avanyu Spa offers a full range of ways to soothe tired muscles. 152 rooms, 5 story. Check-out 11 am. Pool, whirlpool. **$$$**

Specialty Lodgings

The following lodging establishments are approved by Mobil Travel Guide, but due to their unique and individualized nature have not been given a traditional Mobil Star rating. Included in this listing you may find bed-and-breakfasts, limited-service inns, guest ranches, and other unique hotel properties.

CREEKSIDE INN. *51 W Main St, Frisco (80443). Phone 970/668-5607; toll-free 800/668-7320; fax 970/668-8635. www.creeksideinn-frisco.com.* This inn provides a quiet getaway for nature lovers. Afternoon tea and refreshments are included with your stay. View of mountains; Ten Mile Creek at edge of backyard. 7 rooms, 2 story. Complimentary full breakfast. Check-in 4-7 pm, check-out 11 am. Whirlpool. **$**

SKI TIP LODGE. *764 Montezuma Rd, Keystone (80435). Phone 970/496-4950; fax 970/496-4940.* 11 rooms, 2 story. Complimentary full breakfast. Restaurant, bar. Whirlpool. Tennis. **$**

Dinosaur National Monument (A-1)

Web site www.nps.gov/dino

88 miles W of Craig on Hwy 40 to monument headquarters.

This 325-square-mile monument in the northwest corner of the state holds one of the largest concentrations of fossilized Jurassic-era dinosaur bones in the world. Visitors can get a close-up view of a quarry wall containing at least 1,500 fossil bones dating back 150 million years. The wall, enclosed in an information-packed Dinosaur Quarry visitors center, was once part of an ancient riverbed. The monument itself, spanning more than 300 square miles on the Colorado/Utah border, is distinguished by its ruggedly beautiful landscape of high plateaus and river-carved canyons. Access to the Colorado backcountry section, a land of fantastic, deeply eroded canyons of the Green and Yampa rivers, is via the Harpers Corner Road, starting at monument headquarters on Hwy 40, 2 miles east of Dinosaur. At Harpers Corner, the end of this 32-mile surfaced road, a 1-mile foot trail leads to a promontory overlooking the Green and Yampa rivers.

The entrance to the Dinosaur Quarry section in Utah is at the junction of Hwy 40 and Hwy 149 in Jensen, Utah, 13 miles east of Vernal. Seven miles north on Hwy 149 is the Dinosaur Quarry; 4 to 5 miles farther is the Green River campground. No lodgings are available other than at campgrounds.

The visitor centers and one quarry-section campground are open all year; the remainder are often closed by snow approximately mid-November to mid-April.

What to See and Do

Camping, picnicking. *4545 Hwy 40, Dinosaur National Monument.* Green River campground near Dinosaur Quarry in Utah (Memorial Day-Labor Day; fee); Lodore and Echo Park (fee), Deerlodge campgrounds in Colorado; Harpers Corner has picnic facilities.

Dinosaur Quarry. *11625 E 1500 S, Jensen. 7 miles N of Jensen, UT, on Hwy 149. Phone 970/374-3000.*

www.nps.gov/dino. Remarkable fossil deposit; exhibit of 150-million-year-old dinosaur remains; preparation laboratory on display. (Early June-early Sept: daily 8 am-7 pm; rest of the year: daily 8 am-4:30 pm; closed Jan 1, Thanksgiving, Dec 25) **$$$**

Fishing. *4545 Hwy 40, Dinosaur National Monument.* Utah or Colorado license required.

Monument Headquarters and Information Center. *4545 Hwy 40, Dinosaur National Monument. Phone 970/374-3000 (headquarters). www.nps.gov/dino.* At park entrance in Colorado. Display panels; audio-visual program, talks. (June-Labor Day: daily 8 am-6 pm; rest of year: Mon-Fri 8 am-4:30 pm; closed holidays) **FREE**

Other activities. *4545 Hwy 40, Dinosaur National Monument.* Self-guided nature trails (all year), evening campfire programs, guided nature walks, children's programs, dinosaur talks (summer). Backpacking on marked trails; obtain permit at visitor centers.

River rafting. *Dinosaur National Park.* Permit must be obtained in advance from National Park Service. Guided trips from various concessionaires. Obtain list at visitor centers or from the superintendent.

Durango (E-1)

See also Cortez

Founded 1880
Population 13,922
Elevation 6,523 ft
Area Code 970
Zip 81301
Information Durango Area Chamber Resort Association, 111 S Camino Del Rio, PO Box 2587; phone 970/247-0312, toll-free 800/525-8855, or 800/GO-DURANGO
Web site www.durango.org

Will Rogers once said of Durango, "It's out of the way and glad of it." For more than 100 years, this small Western city has profited from its "out of the way" location at the base of the San Juan Mountains. Durango has been the gateway to Colorado's riches for Native Americans, fur traders, miners, prospectors, ranchers, and engineers. Founded by the Denver & Rio Grande Railroad, Durango was a rowdy community during its early days. The notorious Stockton-Eskridge gang once engaged local vigilantes in an hour-long gun battle in the main street. A local expedition to New Mexico to "dig up Aztecs" in 1885 was supplied with "5 cases of chewing tobacco, 3 cases of beer, 10 gallons of heavy liquids, 4 burro-loads of the stuff that busted Parliament, 7 reels of fuse, a box of soap, 2 boxes of cigars, a fish line, 20 pairs of rubber boots, 200 loaves of bread, a can of lard, and one pound of bacon." In the 1890s, the Durango Herald-Democrat was noted for the stinging, often profane, wit of pioneer editor "Dave" Day, who once had 42 libel suits pending against him. Headquarters of San Juan National Forest is in Durango, as well as a District Ranger office for the forest.

What to See and Do

Big-game hunting (in season). *Durango.* Vallecito Lake Resort Area. San Juan National Forest. Also on Bureau of Land Management.

Diamond Circle Theatre. *Strater Hotel, 699 Main Ave, Durango. Phone 970/247-3400; toll-free 877/325-3400. www.diamondcirclemelodrama.com.* Professional turn-of-the-century melodrama and vaudeville performances (June-Sept, nightly; closed Sun). Advance reservations advised. **$$$$**

★ **Durango & Silverton Narrow Gauge Railroad.** *479 Main Ave, Durango. Depot. Phone 970/247-2733; toll-free 888/872-4607. www.durangotrain.com.* This historic Narrow Gauge Railroad, in operation since 1881, links Durango in southwest Colorado with the Victorian-era mining town of Silverton, 45 miles away. A journey on this coal-fired, steam-powered locomotive up the Animas River and through the mountainous wilderness of the San Juan National Forest gives you the chance to relive history while taking in some of the most breathtaking scenery Colorado has to offer. Round-trip travel takes approximately nine hours. Same-day travelers may opt to return by bus; others can stay overnight in historic Silverton (see also SILVERTON) with a return train ride the next day. During the winter season, the train makes a shorter, round-trip journey to and from Cascade Canyon. Wheelchair accessible cars are available; reservations for all riders are highly recommended. For details, check with the passenger agent. (May-Oct; shorter routes during the winter months) **$$$$** Also located here is

Durango & Silverton Narrow Gauge Railroad Museum. *479 Main Ave, Durango. Phone 970/247-2733; toll-free 888/872-4607. www.durangotrain.com.* Museum in conjunction with Durango & Silverton Narrow Gauge Railroad that contains exhibits on steam trains, historic photos, railroad art, and restored railroad cars and a locomotive that can be entered. (Hours correspond to the train depot hours) **$**

Fishing. *Durango.* Lemon Dam, *12 miles NE on Florida Rd.* Vallecito Lake, *18 miles NE on Florida Rd.* Also Pine, Animas, Dolores rivers.

Purgatory Resort. *1 Skier Pl, Durango. 25 miles N on Hwy 550, in San Juan National Forest. Phone 970/247-9000; toll-free 800/982-6103. www.ski-purg.com.* Quad, three triple, five double chairlifts; patrol, school, rentals; five restaurants, five bars, nursery, lodge, specialty stores. Seventy runs; longest run 2 miles; vertical drop 2,029 feet. (Late Nov-early Apr) Cross-country skiing. Multiday, half-day rates. Chairlift and alpine slide also operate mid-June-Labor Day (daily; fee); other summer activities. **$$$$**

San Juan National Forest. *15 Burnett Ct, Durango. N on Hwy 550; E and W on Hwy 160. Phone 970/247-4874.* This forest of nearly 2 million acres includes the Weminuche Wilderness, Colorado's largest designated wilderness, with several peaks topping 14,000 feet, as well as the South San Juan and Lizard Head wildernesses. The Colorado Trail begins in Durango and traverses the backcountry all the way to Denver. Recreation includes fishing in high mountain lakes and streams, boating, whitewater rafting; hiking, biking, camping, and four-wheel driving. The San Juan Skyway is a 232-mile auto loop through many of these scenic areas. (Daily)

Southern Ute Indian Cultural Museum. *Southern Ute Indian Reservation, Ignacio. 23 miles SE via Hwy 160 and Hwy 172. Phone 970/563-9583. www.southernutemuseum.org.* Historical museum contains archival photos, turn-of-the-century Ute clothing, tools, and accessories. Multimedia presentation. Gift shop. (Daily, call for exhibit hours; closed holidays)

Special Events

Durango Cowboy Gathering. *Stater Hotel, 699 Main Ave, Durango. Phone 970/385-8904. www.durangocowboygathering.org.* First weekend in Oct. **$$$$**

Iron Horse Bicycle Classic. *346 S Camino Del Rio, Durango. Phone 970/259-4621. www.ironhorsebicycleclassic.com.* Bicyles race the Silverton narrow-gauge train in this 47-mile race. Late May.

Snowdown Winter Carnival. *PO Box 1, Durango. Phone 970/247-8163. www.snowdown.org.* Winter festival with entertainment, contests, food, and more. Late Jan-early Feb.

Limited-Service Hotels

★ BEST WESTERN DURANGO INN AND SUITES. *21382 US Hwy 160 Durango (81301). Phone 970/247-3251; toll-free 800/547-9090; fax 970/385-4835. www.durangoinn.com.* 71 rooms, 2 story. Check-in 2 pm, check-out 11 am. Restaurant, bar. Indoor pool, children's pool, whirlpool. **$**

★★ BEST WESTERN LODGE AT DURANGO MOUNTAIN. *49617 Hwy 550 N, Durango (81301). Phone 970/247-9669; toll-free 800/637-7727; fax 970/247-9681. www.bestwestern.com.* 32 rooms, 2 story. Pets accepted; fee. Complimentary continental breakfast. Check-in 3 pm, check-out 11 am. Restaurant. Fitness room. Indoor pool, whirlpool. **$**

★ DAYS INN. *1700 County Rd 203, Durango (81301). Phone 970/259-1430; toll-free 866/338-1116; fax 970/259-5741. www.daysinndurango.com.* 94 rooms, 3 story. Pets accepted, some restrictions. Complimentary continental breakfast. Check-in 2 pm, check-out 11 am. Fitness room, spa. Indoor pool, whirlpool. **$**

★★ DOUBLETREE HOTEL. *501 Camino Del Rio, Durango (81301). Phone 970/259-6580; fax 970/259-4398. www.doubletree.com.* Overlooking the magnificent Animas River, this hotel is just two blocks from the historic Durango & Silverton Railroad and the downtown entertainment center. 159 rooms, 3 story. Pets accepted, some restrictions; fee. Check-in 3 pm, check-out noon. Restaurant, bar. Fitness room. Indoor pool, whirlpool. Airport transportation available. **$**

★ ★ **STRATER HOTEL.** *699 Main Ave, Durango (81301). Phone 970/247-4431; toll-free 800/247-4431; fax 970/259-2208. www.strater.com.* Henry H. Strater built this Victorian hotel in 1887 when he was just 20 years old. Restored to its original grandeur, the guest rooms are all impeccably adorned with period pieces and modern-day amenities. Visit one of the most famous ragtime piano bars, "The Diamond Belle Saloon"; it's like going back in time. 93 rooms, 4 story. Complimentary full breakfast. Check-in 4 pm, check-out 11 am. Restaurant, bar. Whirlpool. **$**

Full-Service Resort

★ ★ ★ **TAMARRON RESORT.** *40292 Hwy 550 N, Durango (81301). Phone 970/259-2000; toll-free 800/678-1000; fax 970/382-7822. www.lodgeattamarron .com.* Pine trees surround this scenic resort, located on a 750-acre site in the San Juan Mountains. 210 rooms, 4 story. Pets accepted; fee. Check-in 4 pm, check-out 11 am. Restaurant, bar. Children's activity center. Fitness room, spa. Indoor pool, outdoor pool, whirlpool. Golf. Airport transportation available. **$**

Full-Service Inn

★ ★ ★ **APPLE ORCHARD INN.** *7758 County Rd 203, Durango (81301). Phone 970/247-0751; toll-free 800/426-0751; fax 970/385-6976. www.appleorhcardinn .com.* 10 rooms, 2 story. Complimentary full breakfast. Check-in 4-7 pm, check-out 11 am. **$$**

Specialty Lodgings

The following lodging establishments are approved by Mobil Travel Guide, but due to their unique and individualized nature have not been given a traditional Mobil Star rating. Included in this listing you may find bed-and-breakfasts, limited-service inns, guest ranches, and other unique hotel properties.

COLORADO TRAILS RANCH. *12161 County Rd 240, Durango (81301). Phone 970/247-5055; toll-free 800/323-3833; fax 970/385-7372. www.coloradotrails .com.* On 450 acres adjacent to San Juan National Forest. 15 rooms. Closed Oct-May. Check-in 3 pm, check-out 9 am. Restaurant. Children's activity center. Outdoor pool, whirlpool. Airport transportation available. **$$**

COUNTRY SUNSHINE BED & BREAKFAST. *35130 Hwy 550 N, Durango (81301). Phone 970/ 247-2853; toll-free 800/383-2853; fax 970/247-1203. www.countrysunshine.com.* 6 rooms, 2 story. Complimentary continental breakfast. Check-in 4-6 pm, check-out 10:30 am. Whirlpool. **$**

GENERAL PALMER HOTEL. *567 Main Ave, Durango (81301). Phone 970/247-4747; toll-free 800/ 523-3358; fax 970/247-1332. www.generalpalmerhotel .com.* 39 rooms. Check-in 2 pm, check-out noon. **$$**

JARVIS SUITE HOTEL. *125 W 10th St, Durango (81301). Phone 970/259-6190; toll-free 800/824-1024; fax 970/259-6190. www.durangohotel.com.* Restored historic hotel (1888). 21 rooms, 3 story. Complimentary continental breakfast. Check-in 3 pm, check-out 11 am. Whirlpool. **$**

LAKE MANCOS RANCH. *42688 County Rd N, Mancos (81328). Phone 970/533-7900; toll-free 800/ 325-9462; fax 970/533-7858. www.lakemancosranch.com.* 17 rooms. Closed mid-Oct-May. Check-in 2 pm, check-out 10 am. Restaurant. Children's activity center. Pool, whirlpool. Airport transportation available. **$$**

LELAND HOUSE BED & BREAKFAST SUITES. *721 E 2nd Ave, Durango (81301). Phone 970/385-1920; toll-free 800/664-1920; fax 970/385-1967. www.leland-house.com.* Restored apartment building (1927); many antiques. 10 rooms, 2 story. Pets accepted, some restrictions; fee. Complimentary full breakfast. Check-in 3 pm, check-out 11 am. **$$**

LIGHTNER CREEK INN. *999 County Rd 207, Durango (81301). Phone 970/259-1226; toll-free 800/268-9804; fax 970/259-9526. www.lightnercreekinn .com.* This inn, built in 1903, resembles a French country manor and offers finely decorated rooms. A mountain getaway located only five minutes from downtown and fine dining. 10 rooms, 2 story. Children over 6 years only. Check-in 4 pm, check-out 11 am. **$$**

NEW ROCHESTER HOTEL. *726 E 2nd Ave, Durango (81301). Phone 970/385-1920; toll-free 800/664-1920; fax 970/385-1967. www.rochesterhotel .com.* Built in 1892, this hotel offers guest rooms named after historic figures from the Old West. 15 rooms, 2 story. Pets accepted, some restrictions; fee. Complimentary continental breakfast. Check-in 3 pm, check-out 11 am. **$$**

TALL TIMBER RESORT. *1 Silverton Star Rte, Durango (80901). Phone 970/259-4813. www.talltimberresort.com.* Accessible exclusively by train or helicopter, Tall Timber Resort is the perfect getaway for alpine Robinson Crusoes. This unique resort rests on 180 private acres rimmed by the San Juan National Forest. There are no televisions, radios, or telephones to distract visitors from the majestic beauty of Tall Timber's crashing waterfalls, majestic evergreens, and mesmerizing canyons. The spirit of the Old West is revived, from the still-visible mining spurs to the Silverton train, the last scheduled narrow-gauge train in the United States. Only 30 guests are treated to this singular experience at one time. The resort's two-story, ski condo-like accommodations feature simple, rustic décor with stone fireplaces and faux wood paneling, while the casual ease in Tall Timber's dining room permeates its way into the kitchen's basic cooking. Tall Timber lures the entire family with its variety of leisurely pursuits, from trout fishing and trail hiking to helicopter touring and streamside napping. *Secret Inspector's Notes: Tall Timber is a great getaway if you are looking to escape from it all but are not seeking opulent luxury or pretentious service. It is far from "the real world," a spot to become one with nature in the incredible setting. The quality of the food, however, may drive you to a fast-food drive-through at the conclusion of your trip.* 10 rooms, 2 story. Closed late Oct-May. Check-in 3 pm, check-out noon. Indoor pool, whirlpool. **$$$$**

WIT'S END GUEST RANCH AND RESORT. *254 County Rd 500, Bayfield (81122). Phone 970/884-4113; toll-free 800/236-9483; fax 970/884-3261. www.witsendranch.com.* In a valley on 550 acres; all cabins are adjacent to a river or pond. 19 rooms, 2 story. Check-in noon, check-out 10 am. Restaurant, bar. Children's activity center. Spa. Outdoor pool, whirlpool. Airport transportation available. **$$$$**

Restaurants

★★ ARIANO'S ITALIAN RESTAURANT. *150 E College Dr, Durango (81301). Phone 970/247-8146.* Turn-of-the-century building originally a saloon and brothel. Northern Italian menu. Dinner. Closed Thanksgiving, Dec 25. Bar. Children's menu. Casual attire. **$$**

★ CARVER BREWING CO. *1022 Main Ave, Durango (81301). Phone 970/259-2545; fax 970/385-7268.* American, Southwestern menu. Breakfast, lunch, dinner. Closed Jan 1, Thanksgiving, Dec 25. Bar. Children's menu. Casual attire. **$**

★★ FRANCISCO'S. *619 Main Ave, Durango (81301). Phone 970/247-4098; fax 970/247-1373.* Mexican, American menu. Lunch, dinner. Bar. Children's menu. Casual attire. **$$**

★★ PALACE. *505 Main Ave, Durango (81301). Phone 970/247-2018; fax 970/247-0231. www.palacerestaurants.com.* American menu. Lunch, dinner. Closed Dec 25; Sun Nov-May. Bar. Casual attire. Outdoor seating. **$$**

★★RED SNAPPER. *144 E 9th St, Durango (81301). Phone 970/259-3417; fax 970/259-3441. www.frontier.net/~theredsnapper.* Turn-of-the-century building (1904). Seafood, steak menu. Dinner. Closed Thanksgiving, Dec 25. Bar. Children's menu. Casual attire. **$$**

Edwards

See also Vail

Limited-Service Hotel

★★ THE INN AND SUITES AT RIVERWALK. *27 Main St, Edwards (81632). Phone 970/926-0606; toll-free 888/926-0606; fax 970/926-0616. www.innandsuitesatriverwalk.com.* 59 rooms. Check-in 3 pm, check-out 11 am. Two restaurants, bar. **$**

Full-Service Resort

★★★ LODGE AND SPA AT CORDILLERA. *2205 Cordillera Way, Edwards (81632). Phone 970/926-2200; toll-free 800/877-3529; fax 970/926-2486. www.cordillera-vail.com.* The French-chateau architecture and beautiful mountaintop location make this one of the most exclusive resorts in the Vail/Beaver Creek area. Part of a community that includes private homes and a golf club, this resort treats its guests to unparalleled intimacy. A lovely country style dominates the accommodations, where wood-burning or gas fireplaces add warmth and breathtaking mountain views set a sense of place. Award-winning golf and a full-service spa are at the doorstep, and world-class skiing is just down the road. Four restaurants garner praise from critics and gourmets, from the nightly works of art at Restaurant Picasso (see) to the American dishes with a Western slant at the Timber Hearth Grille. Steaks and seafood are delicious at Chaparral, while the Grouse-on-the-Green, whose interiors were constructed in Ireland, is a true taste of the Emerald Isle. 56 rooms, 3 story. Check-in 4 pm, check-out noon. Restaurant, bar. Fitness room. Indoor pool, outdoor pool, whirlpool. Golf. Tennis. Business center. **$$**

Englewood (B-4)

See also Denver, Lakewood

Population 31,727
Elevation 5,369 ft
Area Code 303
Information Greater Englewood Chamber of Commerce, 770 W Hampden Ave, #110, 80110; phone 303/789-4473; or the South Metro Denver Chamber of Commerce, 7901 S Park Plaza #110, Littleton 80120; phone 303/795-0142
Web site www.ci.englewood.co.us

Englewood is located in Denver's south metro area, which is home to the Denver Technological Center.

What to See and Do

Castle Rock Factory Shops. *5050 Factory Shops Blvd, Castle Rock. Approximately 24 miles S on I-25, exit 184. Phone 303/688-4494.* More than 40 outlet stores; food court. (Daily)

The Museum of Outdoor Arts. *Suite 2-230, 1000 Englewood Pkwy, Englewood. 1 mile S on S Broadway, then 4 miles E on E Arapahoe Rd, then N on Greenwood Plaza Blvd. Phone 303/806-0444. www.moaonline.org.* Outdoor sculpture garden on 400 acres. Guided tours available (fee). Lunchtime summer performance series (Wed). (Daily; closed holidays) **FREE** The museum includes

Fiddler's Green Amphitheater. *6350 Greenwood Plaza Blvd, Greenwood Village (80111). Phone 303/220-7000. www.hob.com/venues/concerts/fiddlers.* Fiddler's Green Amphitheatre is located 15 minutes south of downtown Denver. The parklike setting is an inviting venue for a wide variety of musical performances during the summer months, from up-and-comers to marquee names, classical orchestras to rock and roll, single acts to all-day festivals. Come early to enjoy the mountain sunset. Bring a blanket or tarp (no lawn chairs are allowed), a picnic dinner, and the kids. Or reserve an indoor seat, purchase dinner from one of the many vendors, and watch the acts up close. More than 16,000 patrons regularly pack the park for shows. (June-Aug)

Limited-Service Hotels

★★ **EMBASSY SUITES.** *10250 E Costilla Ave, Englewood (80112). Phone 303/792-0433; toll-free 800/654-4810; fax 303/792-0432. www.embassysuites.com.* Located in the south Denver Metro Denver Tech Center area, this hotel is convenient for business travelers. 236 rooms, 9 story, all suites. Complimentary full breakfast. Check-out noon. Restaurant, bar. Fitness room. Indoor pool, whirlpool. **$**

★ **HAMPTON INN.** *9231 E Arapahoe Rd, Englewood (80112). Phone 303/792-9999; fax 303/790-4360. www.hamptoninn.com.* 150 rooms, 5 story. Pets accepted; fee. Complimentary continental breakfast. Check-in 3 pm, check-out noon. Fitness room. Pool. **$**

Full-Service Hotel

★★★ **SHERATON DENVER TECH CENTER HOTEL.** *7007 S Clinton, Greenwood Village (80112). Phone 303/799-6200; fax 303/799-4828. www.sheraton.com.* The spacious guest rooms at this hotel suit the needs of both business and leisure travelers. Nearby attractions include the Denver Musuem of Natural History, the Denver Zoo, and the Coors Brewery. Complimentary shuttle service is provided within a 5-mile radius. 266 rooms, 10 story. Check-in 3 pm, check-out noon. Restaurant, bar. Fitness room. Pool, whirlpool. Airport transportation available. Business center. **$**

Full-Service Resort

★★★ **INVERNESS HOTEL AND GOLF CLUB.** *200 Inverness Drive W, Englewood (80112). Phone 303/799-5800; fax 303/799-5874. www.invernesshotel.com.* A terrific choice for corporate retreats, this hotel and conference center has more than 60,000 square feet of function space and is well suited to productive meetings with naturally lit board rooms, "fatigue-free" chairs, built-in audiovisual equipment, and more. 302 rooms, 5 story. Check-out noon. Restaurant, bar. Fitness room. Indoor pool, outdoor pool, whirlpool. Golf. Tennis. Airport transportation available. Business center. **$$**

Estes Park (B-3)

See also Fort Collins, Granby, Grand Lake, Loveland, Lyons

Settled 1875
Population 5,413
Elevation 7,522 ft
Area Code 970
Zip 80517
Information Information Center at the Chamber of Commerce, 500 Big Thompson Ave, PO Box 3050; phone 970/586-4431 or toll-free 800/443-7837
Web site www.estesparkresort.com

Estes Park occupies an enviable swath of land at the eastern edge of the Rockies. Many claim that Estes Park, with its panoramic views and bountiful recreational opportunities, offers the quintessential Colorado experience. History certainly would support this assertion. The area has been a vacation destination for thousands—yes, thousands—of years. Archaeological evidence indicates that American Indians were drawn here to escape the summer heat. Situated 7,500 feet above sea level, the town's elevation does manage to keep summertime temperatures comfortably cool, but it also brings an average of 63 inches of snow during the winter months. The snowfall draws hordes of skiers and snowboarders to the area, with a season that typically lasts from November until April. During the warmer months, Estes Park becomes even more crowded. The area's landscape—dominated by craggy peaks and cut by serpentine, glacier-fed streams—lends itself to outdoor activities like camping, hiking, fly fishing, horseback riding, kayaking, and rock climbing. Estes Park serves as the gateway to one of our most popular national treasures, Rocky Mountain National Park. The park's headquarters are located on the western side of town, just off Highway 36. Drive west on 36, connecting to Trail Ridge Road, and within an hour you'll ascend to the alpine environment of Fall River Pass at an elevation of 11,796 feet. The great outdoors is not all that Estes Park has to offer; the downtown area features an array of shops, restaurants, and accommodations, including The Stanley Hotel, a beautiful facility constructed nearly 100 years ago in the neoclassical Georgian style. While staying at this hotel in 1973, Stephen King wrote much of the horror novel *The Shining*, which was later adapted into a film starring Jack Nicholson.

What to See and Do

Aerial Tramway. *420 Riverside Dr, Estes Park. Two blocks S of Elkhorn St. Phone 970/756-6921.* Two cabins, suspended from steel cables, move up or down Prospect Mountain at 1,400 feet per minute. During the trip you get a supurb view of the Continental Divide; if you wish, pack a lunch and enjoy the picnic facilities at the 8,896-foot summit. (There's a snack bar if you fail to plan ahead.) (Mid-May-mid-Sept, daily)

Big Thompson Canyon. *Estes Park. E on Hwy 34.* One of the most beautiful canyon drives in the state.

Enos Mills Original Cabin. *6760 Hwy 7, Estes Park. 8 miles S. Phone 970/586-4706.* (1885) On this family-owned 200-acre nature preserve stands the cabin of Enos Mills, regarded as the "Father of Rocky Mountain National Park." In the shadow of Longs Peak, the cabin contains photos, notes, and documents of the famed naturalist. Nature guide (fee) and self-guided nature trails. (Memorial Day-Labor Day: daily 11 am-5 pm; rest of year: by appointment) **FREE**

Estes Park Area Historical Museum. *200 Fourth St, Estes Park. Just W of the Stanley Park Fairgrounds and across from the lake. Phone 970/586-6256. www.estesnet.com/Museum.* Three facilities including a building that served as headquarters of Rocky Mountain National Park from 1915 to 1923. Exhibits on history of the park, the town, and surrounding area. Gallery (May-Oct: Mon-Sat 10 am-5 pm, Sun 1-5 pm; Nov-Apr: Fri-Sat 10 am-5 pm, Sun 1-5 pm) **$**

Estes Park Ride-a-Kart. *2250 Big Thompson Ave, Estes Park. 1 mile E on Hwy 34. Phone 970/586-6495. www.rideakart.com.* Go-karts, bumper boats and cars, mini-golf, and a mini-train in a miniature Western town. Separate fees. (Memorial Day-Labor Day: Mon-Fri 9:30 am-10 pm; May, Sept: Mon-Fri 11 am-6 pm, Sat-Sun 11 am-7 pm) **$$**

Fishing, boating, hiking, horseback riding, mountain climbing. *Hwys 34 and 36, Estes Park.* Fishing for trout in local lakes and streams. Fishing license needed. Boating on Lake Estes; motors, boats for rent; permit required for private boats; docks (mid-May-early Sept, daily). More than 1,500 mountain-trained horses and ponies are used for breakfast rides, pack trips. The National Park Service conducts guided hikes in Rocky Mountain National Park (see); climbers attempt Longs Peak (14,255 feet). Certified guides also available in town.

Fun City Amusement Park. *455 Prospect Village Dr, Estes Park. Phone 970/586-2070. www.funcityofestes.com.* Bumper cars (fee); 15-lane giant slide and spiral slide (fee); arcade; miniature golf; two 18-hole golf courses; go-karts. (Mid-May-mid-Sept, daily)

Roosevelt National Forest. *240 W Prospect Rd, Fort Collins. Surrounds town on north, east and south. Phone 970/498-1100. www.fs.fed.us/r2/arnf.* More than 780,000 acres of icy streams, mountains, and beautiful scenery. Trout fishing; hiking trails, winter sports area, picnicking, camping. Of special interest are the Cache la Poudre River, five wilderness areas, and the Peak to Peak Scenic Byway. For information, contact the Visitor Center, 1311 S College, Fort Collins 80526. **FREE**

Special Events

Estes Park Music Festival. *Performance Park Pavilion, Estes Park. Phone 970/586-9203.* Chamber, symphonic, and choral concerts. Early June-late Aug.

Horse shows. *Estes Park.* Weekends in June-Sept.

Longs Peak Scottish-Irish Highland Festival. *Estes Park. Phone 970/586-6308. www.scotfest.com.* Athletic and dance competitions, arts and crafts shows, magic shows, folk dancing. Weekend after Labor Day.

Rooftop Rodeo. *Stanley Park Fairgrounds, Estes Park. Phone 970/586-6104. www.estesnet.com/events/rooftoprodeo.htm.* Rodeo parade, nightly dances, kids jamboree, saddle bronc riding, steer wrestling, bull riding. Five days in mid-July. **$$$**

Limited-Service Hotels

★ BEST WESTERN SILVER SADDLE. *1260 Big Thompson Ave, Estes Park (80517). Phone 970/586-4476; fax 970/586-5530. www.bestwestern.com.* 55 rooms, 1 story. Complimentary continental breakfast. Check-out 10 am. Pool, whirlpool. **$**

★ BOULDER BROOK ON FALL RIVER. *1900 Fall River Rd, Estes Park (80517). Phone 970/586-0910; toll-free 800/238-0910; fax 970/586-8067. www.estespark.com/boulderbrook.* Fall asleep listening to the Fall River gurgle outside your back door or watch it from the "Spa Room." Fishing is widely available in the lake, river, stream, or creek. 16 rooms, 2 story. Check-in 2:30 pm, check-out 10 am. Airport transportation available. **$**

★ COMFORT INN. *1450 Big Thompson Ave, Estes Park (80517). Phone 970/586-2358; fax 970/586-4473. www.comfortinn.com.* 75 rooms, 2 story. Closed Nov-Apr. Complimentary continental breakfast. Check-out 10:30 am. Pool, whirlpool. **$**

★ ★ HOLIDAY INN. *101 S St. Vrain, Estes Park (80517). Phone 970/586-2332; toll-free 800/803-7837; fax 970/586-2038. www.holiday-inn.com.* 150 rooms, 4 story. Check-out 11 am. Restaurant, bar. Fitness room. Indoor pool, whirlpool. Airport transportation available. **$**

★ PONDEROSA LODGE. *1820 Fall River Rd, Estes Park (80517). Phone 970/586-4233; toll-free 800/628-0512. www.estes-park.com/ponderosa.* 23 rooms, 2 story. Check-in 2 pm, check-out 10 am. **$**

★ SUNNYSIDE KNOLL RESORT. *1675 Fall River Rd, Estes Park (80517). Phone 970/586-5759; toll-free 800/586-5212. www.sunnysideknoll.com.* This property is located in Fall River Valley, just a few miles from downtown Estes Park and Rocky Mountain National Park. The resort caters to couples and persons wishing to "get away from it all." 17 rooms. Children over 12 years only. Check-in 2 pm, check-out 11 am. Pool, whirlpool. **$**

Full-Service Hotel

★ ★ ★ STANLEY HOTEL. *333 Wonderview Hotel, Estes Park (80517). Phone 970/586-3371; toll-free 800/976-1377; fax 970/586-3673. www.stanleyhotel.com.* The property that inspired Stephen King's novel

The Shining is located less than two hours northwest of Denver in the Rocky Mountains. Built in 1909 by automaker F. O. Stanley, this hotel has 35 acres of sprawling grounds. 162 rooms, 4 story. Check-in 4 pm, check-out 11 am. Restaurant, bar. Pool. Tennis. **$**

Specialty Lodgings

The following lodging establishments are approved by Mobil Travel Guide, but due to their unique and individualized nature have not been given a traditional Mobil Star rating. Included in this listing you may find bed-and-breakfasts, limited-service inns, guest ranches, and other unique hotel properties.

ASPEN LODGE RANCH. *6120 Hwy 7, Estes Park (80517). Phone 970/586-8133; toll-free 800/332-6867.* 59 rooms. Check-in 4 pm, check-out 11 am. Restaurant (open to the public by reservation), bar. Children's activity center. Fitness room. Pool, whirlpool. Tennis. Airport transportation available. Business center. **$$**

ROMANTIC RIVERSONG INN. *1765 Lower Broadview Rd, Estes Park (80517). Phone 970/586-4666; fax 970/577-0699. www.romanticriversong.com.* Built in 1928; decorated with a blend of antique and modern country furnishings. A gurgling trout stream, gazebo, and pond add to the charm of this bed-and-breakfast (all rooms are named after wildflowers). Located on 27 acres to adjacent Rocky Mountain National Park, the property offers breathtaking views. 16 rooms, 2 story. Children over 12 years only. Complimentary full breakfast. Check-in 4-7 pm, check-out noon. Airport transportation available. **$$**

Restaurants

★ ★ ★ BLACK CANYON INN. *800 MacGregor Ave, Estes Park (80517). Phone 970/586-9344. www.estespark.com/blackcanyon.* Built in 1927 of rough-cut logs. American menu. Lunch, dinner. Closed Mon. Bar. Children's menu. **$$**

★ ★ ★ FAWN BROOK INN. *Hwy 7 Business Loop, AllensPark (80510). Phone 303/747-2556.* American menu. Dinner. Closed Mon. Bar. Children's menu. **$$**

★ MAMA ROSE'S. *338 E Elkhorn Ave, Estes Park (80517). Phone 970/586-3330.* Victorian décor; large fireplace. Italian menu. Breakfast, dinner. Closed holidays; Jan-Feb; also Mon-Wed (winter). Bar. Children's menu. Outdoor seating. **$$**

★ ★ NICKY'S. *1350 Fall River Rd, Estes Park (80517). Phone 970/586-5376. www.nickysresort.com.* American menu. Breakfast, lunch, dinner. Bar. Children's menu. Outdoor seating. **$$**

Evergreen (B-3)

See also Central City, Denver, Golden, Idaho Springs

Population 9,216
Elevation 7,040 ft
Area Code 303
Zip 80439
Information Evergreen Area Chamber of Commerce, 29029 Upper Bear Creek Rd #202, PO Box 97; phone 303/674-3412
Web site www.evergreenchamber.org

What to See and Do

Hiwan Homestead Museum. *4208 S Timbervale Dr, Evergreen. Phone 303/674-6262.* Restored 17-room log lodge (1880); Native American artifacts, changing exhibits. (Sept-May: Tues-Sun noon-5 pm; June-Aug: Tues-Sun 11 am-5 pm; closed holidays) **FREE**

International Bell Museum. *30213 Upper Bear Creek Rd, Evergreen. Off Hwy 74. Phone 303/674-3422.* More than 5,000 bells of widely varying sizes and ages, many historic, artistic, or unusual. (Memorial Day-Labor Day, Tues-Sun) **$$**

Special Events

Mountain Rendezvous. *4208 S Timbervale Dr, Evergreen. Phone 303/674-6262. At Hiwan Homestead Museum (see).* Craft and trapping demonstrations by mountain men; food, entertainment, and old-fashioned games. First Sat in Aug.

Rodeo Weekend. *Evergreen. Phone 303/298-0220.* Rodeo, parade. Father's Day weekend.

Specialty Lodging

The following lodging establishment is approved by Mobil Travel Guide, but due to its unique and individualized nature has not been given a traditional Mobil Star rating. Included in this listing you may find bed-and-breakfasts, limited-service inns, guest ranches, and other unique hotel properties.

THE HIGHLAND HAVEN CREEKSIDE INN. *4395 Independence Trail, Evergreen (80439). Phone 303/674-3577; toll-free 800/459-2406; fax 303/674-9088. www.highlandhaven.com.* This inn on Bear Creek is located only a short walk away from the main street in town, where guests can enjoy shopping in local galleries and stores. It is perfect for a romantic getaway. 16 rooms, 2 story. Complimentary full breakfast. Check-in 3 pm, check-out 11 am. **$**

Fairplay (C-3)

See also Breckenridge, Buena Vista

Settled 1859
Population 610
Elevation 9,920 ft
Area Code 719
Zip 80440
Information Town Clerk, 400 Front St, PO Box 267; phone 719/836-2622

This broad valley, known for many years as South Park, was called "Bayou Salado" or "Salt Creek" by early French trappers. The Ute prized the valley for summer trapping and as a hunting ground. In 1859, gold was discovered and several towns, including Fairplay, sprang up overnight. Now the county seat, Fairplay was founded with the slogan, "In this camp we will have fair play; no man can have more ground than he can work." Within the valley, which is larger than the state of Rhode Island, nearly every kind of recreational opportunity is available to visitors.

What to See and Do

Monument to Prunes, a Burro. *7th and Front St, Fairplay. Phone 719/836-2622.* In memory of a faithful burro named Prunes who packed supplies to every mine in Fairplay for more than 60 years.

Pike National Forest. *601 S Weber St, Fairplay. Phone 719/553-1400. www.fs.fed.us/r2/psicc.* (See COLORADO SPRINGS) Camping. A Ranger District office is located at the junction of Hwy 285 and Hwy 9. (Daily) **FREE**

South Park City Museum. *100 4th St, Fairplay. Phone 719/836-2387. www.southparkcity.org/index.htm.* Restoration of a mining town including 42 original buildings, 60,000 artifacts (circa 1860-1900); exhibits on trading, mining, and social aspects of the era. (Memorial Day-Labor Day: daily 9 am-7 pm; Labor Day-mid-Oct: daily 9 am-5 pm; rest of year, by appointment) **$$**

South Park Historical Foundation, Inc. *100 4th St, Fairplay. Phone 719/836-2387.* More than 30 historic buildings are included in this painstaking restoration of a 19th-century Colorado boomtown. (Memorial Day-Labor Day: daily 9 am-7 pm; Labor Day-mid-Oct: daily 9 am-5 pm; rest of year, by appointment)

Special Event

Fairplay Burro Race. *Fairplay. Phone 719/836-2233.* For one weekend of the year, the normally quiet little town of Fairplay becomes the site of Colorado's most uproarious athletic event: the annual Pack Burro Race. Held the last Sunday in July, the festival draws 15,000 participants and spectators to see which team of runner and burro will be the first to complete a 29-mile race to the top of Mosquito Pass and back—together. The greatest challenge for the contestants is not the steep and treacherous course, but the tendency of the burros to go their own way. Food booths, crafts, music, and a parade are all part of the festivities. Last Sun in July. **FREE**

Florissant Fossil Beds National Monument (C-4)

See also Colorado Springs, Cripple Creek, Manitou Springs

22 miles W of Manitou Springs on Hwy 24.

Florissant Fossil Beds National Monument consists of 6,000 acres once partially covered by a prehistoric lake. Thirty-five million years ago, ash and mud flows from volcanoes in the area buried a forest of redwoods, filling the lake and fossilizing its living organisms. Insects, seeds, and leaves of the Eocene Epoch are preserved in perfect detail, along with remarkable samples of standing petrified sequoia stumps. On the grounds are nature trails, picnic areas, and a restored 19th-century homestead. Guided tours are available. The visitor center is 2 miles south on Teller County Road 1 (daily; closed January 1, Thanksgiving, December 25). Contact the Superintendent, PO Box 185, Florissant 80816; phone 719/748-3253. **$$**

Fort Collins (A-4)

See also Estes Park, Greeley, Loveland

Settled 1864
Population 118,652
Elevation 5,003 ft
Area Code 970
Information Fort Collins Convention & Visitors Bureau, 3745 E Prospect Rd, Suite 200; phone 970/491-3388
Web site www.ftcollins.com

A favorite camping ground for pioneers, Fort Collins is now an educational, recreational, and industrial community. Headquarters for the Roosevelt National Forest (see ESTES PARK) and the Arapaho National Forest (see DILLON) are located in Fort Collins.

What to See and Do

Anheuser-Busch Brewery Tour. *2351 Busch Dr, Fort Collins. Take I-25 to Mountain Vista Dr (exit 271) and turn right onto Busch Dr. Phone 970/490-4691. www.budweisertours.com.* A tour of the Anheuser-Busch Brewery in Fort Collins is bound to leave an impression—any operation that can produce 2.6 million cans of beer daily is worthy of note. The presentation includes an overview of the company's history (which dates back to the mid-1800s), a walking tour of the brewing and control rooms, and a visit with the famous Budweiser Clydesdales, housed with their Dalmatian companions in picturesque historic-landmark stables on the beautiful Busch estate. Those of legal drinking age can enjoy complimentary tastings at the end of the tour. (Oct-May: Thurs-Mon 10 am-4 pm; June-Aug: daily 9:30 am-5 pm; Sept: daily 10 am-4 pm) **FREE**

Colorado State University. *Fort Collins. Main entrance at W Laurel and Howes sts, W of College Ave. Phone 970/491-1101. welcome.colostate.edu.* (1870) (24,500 students) Land-grant institution with an 833-acre campus. Pingree Park at 9,500 feet, adjacent to Rocky Mountain National Park, is the summer campus for natural resource science education and forestry.

Discovery Science Center. *703 E Prospect Rd, Fort Collins. Phone 970/472-3990. www.dcsm.org.* Hands-on science and technology museum features more than 100 educational exhibits. (Tues-Sat 10 am-5 pm, Sun noon-5 pm; closed holidays) **$$**

Fort Collins Museum. *Library Park, 200 Mathews St, Fort Collins. Phone 970/221-6738. www.ci.fort-collins.co.us/museum.* Exhibits include a model of the city's namesake, the army post Fort Collins; a fine collection of Folsom points and Native American beadwork; display of historic household, farm, and business items; and three historic cabins. (Tues-Sat 10 am-5 pm, Sun noon-5 pm; closed holidays) **FREE**

Lincoln Center. *417 W Magnolia, Fort Collins. Phone 970/221-6733.* Includes a theater for the performing arts, concert hall, sculpture garden, art gallery, and display areas with changing exhibits. (Daily)

Lory State Park. *708 Lodgepole Dr, Bellvue. 9 miles NW. Phone 970/493-1623.* Approximately 2,500 acres. Nearby is Horsetooth Reservoir. Water-skiing, boating (ramps, rentals); nature trails, hiking, stables, picnicking. (Daily) **$**

Scenic circle drives. Eleven colorful drives, from 50 to 200 miles, including trip through beautiful Poudre Canyon and Cameron Pass (10,285 feet) in Roosevelt National Forest (see ESTES PARK). Inquire at Fort Collins Convention & Visitors Bureau.

Limited-Service Hotels

★ BEST WESTERN KIVA INN. *1638 E Mulberry St, Fort Collins (80524). Phone 970/484-2444; toll-free 888/299-5482; fax 970/221-0967. www.bestwestern.com.* 62 rooms, 2 story. Complimentary continental breakfast. Check-in 1 pm, check-out 11 am. Fitness room. Pool, whirlpool. **$**

★ BEST WESTERN UNIVERSITY INN. *914 S College Ave, Fort Collins (80524). Phone 970/484-1984; fax 970/484-1987. www.bestwestern.com.* 75 rooms, 2 story. Pets accepted, some restrictions; fee. Complimentary continental breakfast. Check-in 3 pm, check-out 11 am. Fitness room. Pool, whirlpool. **$**

★★ **RAMADA INN.** *3836 E Mulberry St, Fort Collins (80524). Phone 970/484-4660; fax 970/484-2326.* 198 rooms, 4 story. Pets accepted, some restrictions; fee. Check-in 4 pm, check-out noon. Restaurant, bar. Fitness room. Indoor pool, children's pool, whirlpool. **$**

Full-Service Hotel

★★★ **MARRIOTT FORT COLLINS.** *350 E Horsetooth Rd, Fort Collins (80525). Phone 970/226-5200; toll-free 800/548-2635; fax 970/282-0561. www.marriott.com.* Located just 3 miles from Colorado State University, the Marriott is a great place to stay during parents' weekend. 256 rooms, 6 story. Pets accepted, some restrictions; fee. Check-in 4 pm, check-out noon. Restaurant, bar. Fitness room. Indoor pool, outdoor pool, whirlpool. Business center. **$**

Specialty Lodging

The following lodging establishment is approved by Mobil Travel Guide, but due to its unique and individualized nature has not been given a traditional Mobil Star rating. Included in this listing you may find bed-and-breakfasts, limited-service inns, guest ranches, and other unique hotel properties.

PORTER HOUSE B&B INN. *530 Main St, Windsor (80550). Phone 970/686-5793; toll-free 888/686-5793; fax 970/686-7046. www.bbonline.com/co/porterhouse.* Built in 1898. 4 rooms. Children over 12 years only. Complimentary full breakfast. Check-in 4-6 pm, check-out 11 am. Whirlpool. Airport transportation available. **$**

Fort Morgan (B-4)

See also Sterling

Population 11,034
Elevation 4,330 ft
Area Code 970
Zip 80701
Information Fort Morgan Area Chamber of Commerce, 300 Main St, PO Box 971; phone 970/867-6702 or toll-free 800/354-8660
Web site www.fortmorganchamber.com

What to See and Do

Fort Morgan Museum. *414 Main St, Fort Morgan. Phone 970/867-6331. www.ftmorganmus.org.* Permanent and changing exhibits depict the history of northeast Colorado. Pamphlet for self-guided walking tour of historic downtown. (Mon-Fri 10 am-5 pm, Sat 11 am-5 pm; Tues-Thurs eves 6-8 pm) **FREE**

Jackson Lake State Park. *26363 County Rd 3, Orchard. I-76 W to Hwy 39, 7 1/4 miles N to County Y5, then 2 1/2 miles W to County Rd 3. Phone 970/645-2551. parks.state.co.us.* Swimming, water-skiing, fishing, boating (rentals, ramps); picnicking (shelters), concession, groceries, camping, wildlife watching. (Daily) **$**

Special Events

Colorado Rodeo. *Brush. 10 miles E. Phone 806/244-3822. www.brushcolo.com/rodeo.htm.* World's largest amateur rodeo. Weekend in early July.

Festival in the Park. *1600 N Main St, Fort Morgan. Phone 970/867-3808.* Arts, crafts, parade, pancake breakfast. Third weekend in July.

Glenn Miller Festival. *400 Main St, Fort Morgan. Phone 970/867-6702.* Big band music. Third weekend in June.

Limited-Service Hotel

★ **BEST WESTERN PARK TERRACE INN.** *725 Main, Fort Morgan (80701). Phone 970/867-8256; toll-free 888/593-5793; fax 970/867-8257. www.bestwestern.com.* 24 rooms, 2 story. Pets accepted; fee. Check-out 11 am. Pool, whirlpool. **$**

Frisco (B-3)

Restaurants

★★ **BLUE SPRUCE INN.** *20 Main St, Frisco (80443). Phone 970/668-5900; fax 970/668-8574. www.thebluespruce.com.* American menu. Dinner. Bar. **$$**

★★ **MATTEO'S.** *106 3rd Ave, Frisco (80433). Phone 970/668-3773.* Notable for its New York-style pizza and great sandwiches. A local favorite. Italian menu. Lunch, dinner. **$**

Georgetown (B-3)

See also Central City, Dillon, Golden, Idaho Springs, Winter Park

Founded 1859
Population 1,088
Elevation 8,512 ft
Area Code 303
Zip 80444
Information Town of Georgetown Visitor Information, PO Box 426; phone 303/569-2555
Web site www.georgetowncolorado.com

Georgetown is named for George Griffith, who discovered gold in this valley in 1859 and opened up the area to other gold seekers. The area around Georgetown has produced almost $200 million worth of gold, silver, copper, lead, and zinc. Numerous 19th-century structures remain standing. Georgetown's famous Hotel de Paris was run by a Frenchman, Louis Dupuy, who, though charming, was very cavalier to any guest who did not please him.

What to See and Do

Hamill House Museum. *305 Argentine St, Georgetown. Phone 303/569-2840. www.historicgeorgetown.org/houses/hamill.htm.* (1867) Early Gothic Revival house acquired by William A. Hamill, Colorado silver magnate and state senator; period furnishings. Partially restored carriage house and office. (Late May-Sept, daily; rest of year, by appointment) **$$**

Hotel de Paris Museum. *409 6th St, Georgetown. Phone 303/569-2311. www.hoteldeparismuseum.org.* (1875) Internationally known hostelry built and operated by Louis Dupuy; elaborately decorated; original furnishings; courtyard. (Memorial Day-Labor Day: daily 10 am-4:30 pm; May, Sept-Dec: Sat-Sun noon-4 pm) **$**

Loveland Ski Area. *Loveland Pass, Georgetown. 12 miles W on I-70, exit 216. Phone 303/569-3203; toll-free 800/225-5683. www.skiloveland.com.* Quad, two triple, five double chairlifts, Pomalift, Mighty-mite; patrol, school, rentals, snowmaking; cafeteria, restaurants, bars, nursery. Sixty runs; longest run 1 1/2 miles; vertical drop 2,410 feet. Lifts (Mid-Oct-mid-May: Mon-Fri 9 am-4 pm, Sat-Sun 8:30 am-4 pm) **$$$$**

Special Event

Georgetown Christmas Market. *Georgetown. 45 miles W of Denver on I-70. Phone 303/569-2840. www.georgetowncolorado.com.* For a delightful old-fashioned Christmas experience, visit the pretty little Victorian hamlet of Georgetown during the first two weekends in December. The streets and shops come alive with holiday lights, music, dancing, and strolling carolers. Old Kris Kringle is on hand to hear the wishes of young believers, while Mom and Dad will enjoy browsing through the European-style open market for food and handcrafted gifts from around the world. Early Dec.

Specialty Lodging

The following lodging establishment is approved by Mobil Travel Guide, but due to its unique and individualized nature has not been given a traditional Mobil Star rating. Included in this listing you may find bed-and-breakfasts, limited-service inns, guest ranches, and other unique hotel properties.

NORTH FORK. *55395 Hwy 285, Shawnee (80475). Phone 303/838-9873; toll-free 800/843-7895; fax 303/838-1549.* On the South Platte River. 6 rooms. Closed mid-Sept-mid-May. Check-in 3 pm, check-out 10 am. Restaurant. Children's activity center. Pool, whirlpool. Airport transportation available. **$$**

Restaurant

★ HAPPY COOKER. *412 6th St, Georgetown (80444). Phone 303/569-3166; fax 303/569-0429.* American menu. Breakfast, lunch. Closed Thanksgiving, Dec 25. Children's menu. Outdoor seating. **$**

Glenwood Springs (B-2)

See also Aspen, Snowmass Village

Settled 1885
Population 7,736
Elevation 5,763 ft
Area Code 970
Zip 81601
Information Chamber Resort Association, 1102 Grand Ave; phone 970/945-6589 or toll-free 888/4-GLENWOOD
Web site www.glenscape.com

Doc Holliday, the famous gunman, died here in 1887. His marker bears the wry inscription, "He died in bed."

Today, Glenwood Springs is a popular year-round health spa resort where visitors may both ski and swim in a single day. The town is the gateway to White River National Forest. Aspen and Vail (see both) are less than an hour's drive. Excellent game and fishing country surrounds Glenwood Springs, and camping areas are sprinkled throughout the region.

What to See and Do

Glenwood Hot Springs Pool. *Hot Springs Lodge and Pool, 415 6th St, Glenwood Springs. I-70 W, exit 116. Phone 970/945-6571; toll-free 800/537-7946. www.hotspringspool.com.* For centuries, visitors have traveled to the hot springs in Colorado to soak in their soothing and, many say, healing mineral-rich waters. Today, those same legendary springs feed the world's largest hot spring pool. Located between Aspen and Vail on the forested banks of the Colorado River, historic Glenwood Hot Springs Lodge and Pool is a great mini-escape for visitors just stopping through, as well as for those looking for a unique resort getaway. The main pool, more than two blocks long, circulates 3.5 million gallons of naturally heated, spring-fed water each day. The complex includes lap lanes, a shallow play area, diving area, two water slides (summer only), and a therapy pool. The nearby town of Glenwood Springs offers museums, art galleries, specialty shops, and restaurants in a relaxed, western-style setting. (Late May-early Sept: daily 7:30 am-10 pm; early Sept-late May: daily 9 am-10 pm) **$$$$**

Scenic drives. *Glenwood Springs. On Hwy 133, visit Redstone, Marble, and Maroon peaks. I-70 provides access to Lookout Mountain and Glenwood Canyon.* Beautiful Hanging Lake and Bridal Veil Falls are a 2-mile hike from the road. The marble quarries in the Crystal River Valley are the source of stones for the Lincoln Memorial in Washington, DC, and the Tomb of the Unknown Soldier in Arlington National Cemetery.

Sunlight Mountain Resort. *10901 County Rd 117, Glenwood Springs. 10 miles SW via County 117. Phone 970/945-7491; toll-free 800/445-7931. www.sunlightmtn.com.* Triple, two double chairlifts; surface tow; patrol, school, rentals; cafeteria, bar, nursery. 67 runs; longest run 2 1/2 miles; vertical drop 2,010 feet. Snowmobiling Half-day rates. (Late Nov-early Apr, daily) Also cross-country touring center, 10 miles. **$$$$**

White River National Forest. *N, W, E, and S of town. Phone 970/945-2521. www.fs.fed.us/r2/whiteriver.* More than 2,500,000 acres in the heart of the Colorado Rocky Mountains. Recreation at 70 developed sites with boat ramps, picnicking, campgrounds (fee), and observation points; Holy Cross, Flat Tops, Eagles Nest, Maroon Bells-Snowmass, Raggeds, Collegiate Peaks, and Hunter-Frying Pan wildernesses (check with local ranger for information before entering wildernesses or any backcountry areas). Many streams and lakes with trout fishing; large deer and elk populations; Dillon, Green Mountain, and Ruedi reservoirs. Winter sports at 11 ski areas. Contact the Supervisor's Office, Old Federal Building, 9th and Grand, PO Box 948.

Special Events

Garfield County Fair & Rodeo. *Garfield County Fairgrounds, 1001 Railroad Ave, Rifle. Phone 970/625-2514.* Mid-Aug.

Strawberry Days Festival. *Sayre Park, Glenwood Springs. Phone 970/945-6589. www.strawberrydaysfestival.com.* Arts and crafts fair, rodeo, parade. Third weekend in June.

Limited-Service Hotels

★ BEST WESTERN ANTLERS. *171 W Sixth St, Glenwood Springs (81601). Phone 970/945-8535; toll-free 800/626-0609; fax 970/945-9388. www.bestwestern.com.* 100 rooms, 2 story. Complimentary continental breakfast. Check-in 2 pm, check-out 11 am. Outdoor pool, whirlpool. **$**

★ HOT SPRINGS LODGE. *415 E 6th St, Glenwood Springs (81602). Phone 970/945-6571; toll-free 800/537-7946; fax 970/947-2950. www.hotspringspool.com.* Vacationers from all around the world come to visit this property's hot springs pool, the world's largest. The pool area features two waterslides, an 18-hole miniature golf course, and a snack bar and deli. The adjacent athletic club, offering exercise equipment, racquetball courts, and aerobics classes, as well as massages and facials, is available to hotel guests for a small fee. Room rates include unlimited free access to the pool. 107 rooms. Complimentary continental breakfast. Check-in 4 pm, check-out noon. Outdoor pool. Airport transportation available. **$**

Restaurants

★★ FLORINDO'S. *721 Grand Ave, Glenwood Springs (81601). Phone 970/945-1245; fax 970/876-2024.* Italian menu. Dinner. Bar. Children's menu. Casual attire. **$$**

★ LOS DESPERADOS. *55 Mel Rey Rd, Glenwood Springs (81601). Phone 970/945-6878.* Mexican menu. Lunch, dinner. Bar. Children's menu. Casual attire. Outdoor seating. **$**

★★ RIVER'S RESTAURANT. *2525 S Grand Ave, Glenwood Springs (81601). Phone 970/928-8813; fax 970/928-8814. www.theriversrestaurant.com.* American menu. Dinner, Sun brunch. Closed Dec 25. Bar. Children's menu. Casual attire. Outdoor seating. **$$**

Golden (B-3)

See also Central City, Denver, Evergreen, Georgetown, Idaho Springs

Founded 1859
Population 17,159
Information Greater Golden Chamber of Commerce, PO Box 1035, 80402; phone 303/279-3113 or toll-free 800/590-3113
Web site www.ci.golden.co.us

Once a rival of Denver, Golden was capital of the Colorado Territory from 1862 to 1867.

What to See and Do

Armory Building. *13th and Arapahoe sts, Golden. Phone 303/270-3113.* This is the largest cobblestone building in the US (circa 1913). Approximately 3,000 wagon loads of cobblestones were used in the construction. The rocks are from Clear Creek and the quartz from Golden Gate Canyon.

Astor House Hotel Museum. *822 12th St, Golden. Phone 303/278-3557. www.astorhousemuseum.org.* (1867) The first stone hotel west of the Mississippi. Period furnishings. Self-guided and guided tours (reservations required). Victorian gift shop. (Tues-Sat 10 am-4:30 pm; closed holidays) **$**

Colorado Railroad Museum. *17155 W 44th Ave, Golden. Phone 303/279-4591; toll-free 800/365-6263. www.crrm.org.* An 1880s-style railroad depot houses memorabilia and an operating model railroad. More than 50 historic locomotives and cars from Colorado railroads displayed outside. (Daily 9 am-5 pm; closed Thanksgiving, Dec 25) **$$**

Colorado School of Mines. *1500 Illinois St, Golden. Main entrance at 19th and Elm sts. Phone 303/273-3000; toll-free 800/446-9488. www.mines.edu.* (1874) (3,150 students) World-renowned institution devoted exclusively to education of mineral, energy, and material engineers and applied scientists. Tours of campus. On campus are

> **Edgar Mine.** *365 8th Ave, Idaho Springs. Located in Idaho Springs (see). Phone 303/567-2911.* Experimental mine operated by Colorado School of Mines, state government, and by manufacturers for equipment testing. (Mon-Fri, by appointment) **$$$**
>
> **Geology Museum.** *16th and Maple sts, Golden. Phone 303/273-3823. www.mines.edu/academic/geology/museum.* Mineral and mining history exhibits. (Mon-Sat 9 am-4 pm, Sun 1-4 pm; closed holidays) **FREE**

★ Coors Brewery Tour. *12th and Ford sts, Golden. 15 miles W of downtown Denver. Phone 303/277-2337 (tour info). www.coors.com.* For a fun, free factory tour, visit Coors Brewing Company in Golden and see how this favorite Colorado brew is made. The 40-minute walking tour reviews the malting, brewing, and packaging processes at the nation's third largest brewer. The tour ends with a free sampling in the hospitality room—proper ID required. Visitors under 18 must be accompanied by an adult. (Mon-Sat 10 am-4 pm) **FREE**

Golden Gate Canyon State Park. *3873 Hwy 46, Golden. 2 miles N via Hwy 93, then left on Golden Gate Canyon Rd and continue W for 15 miles. Phone 303/582-3707. parks.state.co.us.* On 12,000 acres. Nature and hiking trails, cross-country skiing, snowshoeing, biking, horseback riding, ice skating, picnicking, camping (dump station, electrical hook-ups). Visitor center. Panorama Point Overlook provides a 100-mile view of the Continental Divide. (Daily) **$**

Golden Pioneer Museum. *923 10th St, Golden. Phone 303/278-7151. www.goldenpioneermuseum.com.* Houses more than 4,000 items dating from Golden's territorial capital days; including household articles, clothing, furniture; mining, military, and ranching equipment; unique Native American doll collection. (Mon-Sat 10 am-4:30 pm; Memorial Day-Labor Day: Sun 11 am-5 pm) **$**

Heritage Square. *18301 W Colfax Ave, Golden. 1 mile S of 6th Ave on Hwy 40. Phone 303/279-2789. www.heritagesquare.info.* Located 15 minutes from downtown Denver in the foothills of Golden, Heritage Square family entertainment park is reminiscent of an 1870s Colorado mining town with its Old West streetscapes and Victorian facades. In addition to specialty shops, restaurants, museums, and theater, there are amusement rides for the younger children, a water slide, a 70-foot bungee tower, go-karts, and a miniature golf course. Heritage Square is also home to Colorado's longest, 1/2-mile Alpine slide. The slide is particularly popular with teenagers, or anyone else who enjoys the feeling of plunging down a mountainside track on a small fiberglass sled with wheels. The sleds do have handbrakes, so moms and dads can go a little slower. (Winter: Mon-Sat 10 am-5 pm, Sun noon-5 pm; summer: Mon-Sat 10 am-8 pm, Sun noon-8 pm)

Lariat Trail. *Golden. Also known as Lookout Mountain Rd, the trail begins W of 6th Ave at 19th St. Phone toll-free 800/590-3113.* Leads to Denver Mountain Parks. Lookout Mountain, 5 miles W off Hwy 6, is the nearest peak. At the summit is

Buffalo Bill Grave and Museum. *987-1/2 Lookout Mountain Rd, Golden. Phone 303/526-0747. www.buffalobill.org.* Lookout Mountain, 30 minutes west of downtown Denver, is the final resting place of the man who virtually defined for the world the spirit of the Wild West. A born adventurer, William F. "Buffalo Bill" Cody's life included stints as a cattle driver, fur trapper, gold miner, Pony Express rider, and scout for the US cavalry. He became world famous with his traveling "Buffalo Bill's Wild West Show." At the Buffalo Bill Grave and Museum, Cody still draws crowds who come to see the museum's western artifacts collection, take advantage of the beautiful hilltop vistas, and pay homage to this most legendary of Western heroes. (May-Oct: daily 9 am-5 pm; Nov-Apr: Tues-Sun 9 am-4 pm; closed Dec 25) **$**

Rocky Mountain Quilt Museum. *1111 Washington Ave, Golden. Phone 303/277-0377. www.rmqm.org.* Houses more than 250 quilts. Ten exhibits each year. (Mon-Sat 10 am-4 pm; closed holidays) **$**

USGS National Earthquake Information Center. *1711 Illinois St, Golden. Phone 303/273-8500. www.earthquake.usgs.gov.* (Mon-Fri, by appointment; closed holidays) **FREE**

Special Event

Buffalo Bill Days. *Golden.* Parade, golf tournament. July.

Limited-Service Hotels

★ LA QUINTA INN. *3301 Youngfield Service Rd, Golden (80401). Phone 303/279-5565; toll-free 800/687-6667; fax 303/279-5841. www.laquinta.com.* 129 rooms, 3 story. Pets accepted. Complimentary continental breakfast. Check-out noon. Pool. **$**

★ ★ TABLE MOUNTAIN INN. *1310 Washington Ave, Golden (80401). Phone 303/277-9898; toll-free 800/762-9898; fax 303/271-0298. www.tablemountaininn.com.* 32 rooms, 2 story. Check-out 11 am. Restaurant, bar. Airport transportation available. **$**

Full-Service Hotel

★ ★ ★ MARRIOTT DENVER WEST. *1717 Denver West Blvd, Golden (80401). Phone 303/279-9100; fax 303/271-0205. www.marriott.com.* 307 rooms, 6 story. Check-out noon. Restaurant, bar. Fitness room. Indoor/outdoor pool, whirlpool. **$**

Restaurants

★ ★ CHART HOUSE. *25908 Genesee Trail Rd, Golden (80401). Phone 303/526-9813; fax 303/526-0753.* American menu. Dinner. Bar. Children's menu. **$$**

★ ★ SIMMS LANDING. *11911 W 6th Ave, Golden (80401). Phone 303/237-0465; fax 303/237-6993. www.simmslanding.com.* American menu. Lunch, dinner, Sun brunch. Closed Dec 25. Children's menu. Valet parking. Outdoor seating. **$$**

★ ★ TABLE MOUNTAIN INN. *1310 Washington Ave, Golden (80401). Phone 303/216-8020; fax 303/271-0298. www.tablemountaininn.com.* Southwestern menu. Breakfast, lunch, dinner, Sun brunch. Bar. Children's menu. Outdoor seating. **$$**

Granby (B-3)

See also Estes Park, Grand Lake, Kremmling, Winter Park

Population 1,525
Elevation 7,939 ft
Area Code 970
Zip 80446
Information Greater Granby Area Chamber of Commerce, PO Box 35; 970/887-2311 or 800/325-1661
Web site www.granbychamber.com

Immediately northeast of Granby is the Arapaho National Recreation Area, developed by the Department of Interior as part of the Colorado-Big Thompson Reclamation Project. There is swimming and mineral bathing at Hot Sulphur Springs. Several national forests, lakes, and big-game hunting grounds are within easy reach. Two ski areas are nearby (see WINTER PARK) and a Ranger District Office of the Arapaho National Forest (see DILLION) is located in Granby.

What to See and Do

Arapaho National Recreation Area. *9 Ten Mile Dr, Granby. 6 miles NE on Hwy 34. Phone 970/887-4100.* The area includes Shadow Mountain, Willow Creek, Monarch, Grand, and Granby lakes. Boating, fishing; hunting, camping (fee), picnicking, horseback riding. (Daily) **$$**

Grand County Historical Association. *5950 County Rd 5, Hot Sulphur Springs. 10 miles W via Hwy 40. Phone 970/725-3939. www.grandcountymuseum.com.* The association has three museums that have exhibits depicting the history of skiing, ranching, and Rocky Mountain railroads; archaeological finds; reconstructed old buildings, wagons, and tools. Cozens Ranch Museum (Winter: Tues-Sat 11 am-4 pm, Sun noon-4 pm; summer: Tues-Sat 10 am-5 pm, Sun 1-5 pm). Grand County Museum Complex (Winter: Wed-Sat 11 am-4 pm; summer: Tues-Sun 9 am-5 pm). **$**

SilverCreek Ski Area. *1000 Village Rd, Granby. 3 miles SE on Hwy 40. Phone 970/887-3384; toll-free 888/283-7458.* Two triple, double chairlifts; Pomalift; patrol, school, rentals, snowmaking; concession, cafeteria, bar, nursery, day-lodge. 22 runs; longest run 6,100 feet; vertical drop 1,000 feet. (Dec-mid-Apr) Snowboarding, sleigh rides. Health club. **$$$$**

Full-Service Resort

★ INN AT SILVERCREEK. *62927 Hwy 40, Silver Creek (80451). Phone 970/887-2131; toll-free 800/927-4386; fax 970/887-4083. www.silvercreeklodging.com.* 342 rooms, 3 story. Pets accepted, some restrictions; fee. Check-in 4 pm, check-out 11 am. Bar. Fitness room. Pool, whirlpool. Tennis. **$**

Specialty Lodgings

The following lodging establishments are approved by Mobil Travel Guide, but due to their unique and individualized nature have not been given a traditional Mobil Star rating. Included in this listing you may find bed-and-breakfasts, limited-service inns, guest ranches, and other unique hotel properties.

C LAZY U RANCH. *3640 Hwy 125, Granby (80446). Phone 970/887-3344; fax 970/887-3917. www.clazyu.com.* Since the 1940s, C Lazy U Ranch has been offering families a taste of life on a Western ranch. Situated less than 100 miles west of Denver, the ranch enjoys the beautiful Colorado countryside as its backdrop. Visitors come here to return to a simpler time; outside distractions are eliminated with the banishment of televisions and telephones in all accommodations. The guest rooms are decorated with a distinctively Western décor, and nearly all have fireplaces. The rustic design of the Main Lodge belies the sophisticated cooking featured within. Meals are served family style, and afterward, visitors are encouraged to join the fireside sing-a-long. During winter months, snowshoeing, cross-country skiing, sleigh rides, and nearby downhill skiing are popular activities, while hiking, biking, and swimming are pursued during warmer months. The horsemanship program is the centerpiece of the ranch, however, and guests are matched with one horse for the duration of their stay. 44 rooms. Closed Apr-May, Oct-mid-Dec. Check-in 3 pm, check-out 10 am. Restaurant (guests only), bar. Children's activity center. Fitness room. Pool, whirlpool. Tennis. No credit cards accepted. **$$$**

DROWSY WATER RANCH. *County Rd 219, Granby (80446). Phone 970/725-3456; toll-free 800/845-2292; fax 970/725-3611. www.drowsywater.com.* 17 rooms. Closed mid-Sept-May. Check-in 2:30 pm, check-out 11 am. Children's activity center. Pool, whirlpool. **$$**

Restaurants

★ LONGBRANCH & SCHATZI'S PIZZA. *165 E Agate Ave, Granby (80446). Phone 970/887-2209.* Eclectic, American menu. Lunch, dinner. Closed Thanksgiving, Dec 25; also mid-Apr-mid-May and mid-Oct-mid-Nov. Bar. Children's menu. **$$**

★ PAUL'S CREEKSIDE GRILL. *62927 Hwy 40, Granby (80451). Phone 970/887-2484.* American menu. Breakfast, lunch, dinner. Bar. Children's menu. Casual attire. Outdoor seating. **$**

Grand Junction (C-1)

Settled 1881
Population 41,986
Elevation 4,597 ft
Area Code 970
Information Visitor & Convention Bureau, 740 Horizon Dr, 81506; phone 970/244-1480 or toll-free 800/962-2547
Web site www.visitgrandjunction.com

Grand Junction's name stems from its location at the junction of the Colorado (formerly the Grand) and Gunnison rivers. The altitude and warm climate combine to provide a rich agricultural area, which produces peaches, pears, and grapes for the local wine industry. The city serves as a trade and tourist center for western Colorado and eastern Utah as well as a gateway to two national parks, six national forests, and 7 million acres of public land. Fishing, hunting, boating, and hiking may all be enjoyed in the nearby lakes and mountain streams.

What to See and Do

Adventure Bound River Expeditions. *2392 H Rd, Grand Junction. Phone 970/245-5428; toll-free 800/423-4668. www.raft-colorado.com.* Two- to five-day whitewater rafting trips on the Colorado, Green, and Yampa rivers. **$$$$**

Colorado River. *E Of Palisade. 15 miles E, off I-70 exit 47. Phone 970/464-0548.* Swimming, fishing; picnicking, camping. Grocery nearby.

Cross Orchards Historic Farm. *3073 F Rd, Grand Junction. Phone 970/434-9814. www.wcmuseum.org/crossorchards.htm.* Operated 1896-1923 by owners of Red Cross shoe company. Living history farm with historically costumed guides interprets the social and agricultural heritage of western Colorado. Restored buildings and equipment on display; narrow gauge railroad exhibit and country store. Demonstrations, special events. (Mid-Apr-mid-Oct: Tues-Sat 9 am-3 pm) **$**

Dinosaur Hill. *Fruita. 5 miles W, 1 1/2 miles S of Fruita on Hwy 340. Phone 970/858-7282; toll-free 888/488-3466. www.dinosaurjourney.com.* Self-guided walking trail interprets quarry of paleontological excavations. (Daily sunrise to sunset) **FREE**

★ Grand Mesa National Forest. *Delta. Approximately 40 miles E via I-70 and Hwy 65. Phone 970/874-6600.* This 346,221-acre alpine forest includes a flat-top, basalt-capped tableland at 10,500 feet. There are more than 300 alpine lakes and reservoirs, many with trout; boat rentals are available. The mesa is also a big-game hunting area, with horses available for rent. There are excellent areas for cross-country skiing, snowmobiling, picnicking, and camping (fee at some campgrounds); there is also a lodge and housekeeping cabins. From the rim of Lands End, the westernmost spot on Grand Mesa, there is a spectacular view of much of western Colorado. Also located within the forest is Powderhorn Ski Resort and the Crag Crest National Recreational Trail. Ranger District offices are located in Grand Junction and Collbran and for Uncompaghre Forest to the southwest as well. Forest Supervisor, 2250 Hwy 50 (81416).

Highline Lake. *1800 11 8/10 Rd, Grand Junction. 18 miles NW on I-70 to Loma, then 6 miles N on Hwy 139. Phone 970/858-7208.* Swimming, water-skiing, fishing, boat ramps, shelters; waterfowl hunting, picnicking, camping.

Museum of Western Colorado. *462 Ute Ave, Grand Junction. Phone 970/242-0971; toll-free 888/480-3466. www.wcmuseum.org.* Features exhibits on regional, social, and natural history of the Western Slope; collection of small weapons; wildlife exhibits. (Tues-Sat 10 am-3 pm) Tours by appointment. **$**

Powderhorn Ski Resort. *4828 Powderhorn Rd, Mesa. 20 miles E via I-70, exit 49. E on Hwy 65. Phone 970/268-5700; toll-free 800/241-6997. www.powderhorn.com.* Quad, two double chairlifts; surface lift; patrol, school, rentals, snowmaking; snack bar, restaurants, bar, day-lodge. Twenty-nine runs; longest run 2 miles; vertical drop 1,650 feet. Half-day rates. (Mid-Dec-mid-Apr, daily) Cross-country trails (7 miles), snowboarding, snowmobiling, sleigh rides.

Summer activities include fishing, rafting trips, biking, horseback riding, Western cookouts. **$$$$**

Rabbit Valley Trail through Time. *2815 H Rd, Grand Junction. 30 miles W on I-70, 2 miles from UT border. Phone 970/244-3000.* A 1 1/2 mile self-guided walking trail through a paleontologically significant area. Fossilized flora and fauna from the Jurassic Age. No pets allowed. (Daily) **FREE**

Riggs Hill. *S Broadway and Meadows Way, Grand Junction. Phone 970/241-9210.* A 3/4 mile, self-guided walking trail in an area where bones of the Brachiosaurus dinosaur were discovered in 1900. (Daily) **FREE**

Special Events

Colorado Mountain Winefest. *2785 Hwy 50, Grand Junction. Phone 970/256-1531. www.coloradowinefest.com.* Wine tastings, outdoor events. Late Sept. **$**

Colorado Stampede. *Grand Junction.* Rodeo. Third week in June.

Limited-Service Hotels

★ ★ ADAM'S MARK. *743 Horizon Dr, Grand Junction (81506). Phone 970/241-8888; fax 970/242-7266. www.adamsmark.com.* 273 rooms, 8 story. Check-in 3 pm, check-out noon. Restaurant, bar. Fitness room. Outdoor pool, whirlpool. Tennis. Airport transportation available. **$**

★ BEST WESTERN SANDMAN MOTEL. *708 Horizon Dr, Grand Junction (81506). Phone 970/243-4150; toll-free 800/780-7234; fax 970/243-1828. www.bestwestern.com.* 80 rooms, 2 story. Check-in 3 pm, check-out 11 am. Pool, whirlpool. Airport transportation available. **$**

★ ★ GRAND VISTA HOTEL. *2790 Crossroads Blvd, Grand Junction (81506). Phone 970/241-8411; toll-free 800/800-7796; fax 970/241-1077. www.grandvistahotel.com.* 158 rooms, 6 story. Pets accepted, some restrictions; fee. Check-in 3 pm, check-out noon. Restaurant, bar. Indoor pool, whirlpool. Airport transportation available. **$**

★ ★ HOLIDAY INN. *755 Horizon Dr, Grand Junction (81506). Phone 970/243-6790; toll-free 888/489-9796; fax 970/243-6790. www.holiday-inn.com.* 292 rooms. Pets accepted. Check-in 4 pm, check-out 11 am. Restaurant, bar. Fitness room. Indoor, outdoor pool, children's pool, whirlpool. Airport transportation available. **$**

Restaurants

★ ★ FAR EAST RESTAURANT. *1530 North Ave, Grand Junction (81501). Phone 970/242-8131; fax 970/242-8170.* Chinese, American menu. Lunch, dinner. Closed holidays. Bar. Children's menu. **$**

★ STARVIN' ARVIN'S. *752 Horizon Dr, Grand Junction (81506). Phone 970/241-0430.* Casual atmosphere; antique photographs. American menu. Breakfast, lunch, dinner. Closed Thanksgiving, Dec 25. Bar. Children's menu. **$**

★ ★ WINERY RESTAURANT. *642 Main St, Grand Junction (81501). Phone 970/242-4100; fax 970/242-3618. www.wineryrestaurant.com.* Restored 1890s building. American menu. Dinner. Closed Dec 25. Bar. **$$**

Grand Lake (B-3)

See also Estes Park, Granby, Rocky Mountain National Park

Population 447
Elevation 8,380 ft
Area Code 970
Zip 80447
Information Grand Lake Area Chamber of Commerce, PO Box 57; phone 970/627-3402 or toll-free 800/531-1019
Web site www.grandlakechamber.com

Grand Lake is on the northern shore of the largest glacial lake in Colorado, source of the Colorado River. The Ute shunned the vicinity because, according to legend, mists rising from the lake were the spirits of women and children killed when Cheyenne and Arapahoe attacked a Ute village on the shore.

As one of the state's oldest resort villages, Grand Lake boasts the world's highest yacht club, a full range of water recreation, and horseback riding and pack trips on mountain trails. Grand Lake is at the terminus of Trail Ridge Road at the west entrance to Rocky Mountain National Park.

What to See and Do

Hiking, fishing, boating, horseback riding. *Grand Lake. Phone 970/627-3220 (Gala Marina).* Boat rentals available from Gala Marina. Horseback riding can be scheduled with Winding River Resort. Other outdoor activities abound in summer at Grand Lake, Shadow Mountain Lake, and Lake Granby.

Snowmobiling and cross-country skiing. *Grand Lake.* Back areas of Arapaho National Forest (see DILLON), portion of Trail Ridge Rd, and local trails around Grand Lake, Shadow Mountain, and Granby Lakes. Inquire locally for details. (Nov-May)

Special Events

Buffalo Barbecue & Western Week Celebration. *Grand Lake. Phone 970/627-3402.* Parade, food; Spirit Lake Mountain Man rendezvous. Third week in July.

Lipton Cup Sailing Regatta. *Grand Lake. Phone 970/627-3402.* Early Aug.

Rocky Mountain Repertory Theatre. *Community Building, Town Square, Grand Lake. At W entrance of Rocky Mountain National Park. Phone 970/627-3421 (box office). www.rkymtnhi.com.* Three musicals change nightly, Mon-Sat. Reservations advised. Late June-late Aug.

Winter Carnival. *Grand Lake. Phone toll-free 800/531-1019. www.grandlakechamber.com.* Ice skating, snowmobiling, snow sculptures, ice-fishing derby, ice-golf tournament. Last weekend in Jan.

Limited-Service Hotel

★ BEST VALUE INN. *613 Grand Ave, Grand Lake (80447). Phone 970/627-8101; toll-free 888/315-2378; fax 970/627-3771. www.bestvalueinn.com.* 20 rooms, 2 story. Check-out 10 am. Whirlpool. **$**

Specialty Lodging

The following lodging establishment is approved by Mobil Travel Guide, but due to its unique and individualized nature has not been given a traditional Mobil Star rating. Included in this listing you may find bed-and-breakfasts, limited-service inns, guest ranches, and other unique hotel properties.

SPIRIT MOUNTAIN RANCH. *3863 County Rd 41, Grand Lake (80447). Phone 970/887-3551. www.fcinet.com/spirit.* 4 rooms, 2 story. Children over 10 years only. Complimentary full breakfast. Check-in 4 pm, check-out 11 am. Whirlpool. **$**

Restaurants

★★★ CAROLINE'S CUISINE. *9921 Hwy 34 #27, Grand Lake (80447). Phone 970/627-9404; fax 970/627-9424. www.sodaspringsranch.com.* Large windows offer views of either the mountain or the hills. French, American menu. Dinner. Closed two weeks in Apr and two weeks in Nov. Bar. Children's menu. Outdoor seating. **$$**

★ E. G.'S GARDEN GRILL. *1000 Grand Ave, Grand Lake (80447). Phone 970/627-8404; fax 970/627-0118. www.egscountryinn.com.* American menu. Lunch, dinner. Closed Dec 25. Bar. Children's menu. Outdoor seating. **$$**

★★ GRAND LAKE LODGE RESTAURANT. *15500 Hwy 34, Grand Lake (80447). Phone 970/627-3967.* Steak menu. Breakfast, lunch, dinner. Closed mid-Sept-May. Bar. Children's menu. Casual attire. Outdoor seating. **$$**

Great Sand Dunes National Monument (D-3)

Web site www.nps.gov/grsa

35 miles NE of Alamosa, reached by Hwy 160 and Hwy 150 from the S or from Hwy 17 and County Six Mile Ln from the W. Phone 719/378-2312. www.nps.gov/grsa/.

Boasting the tallest sand dunes in North America, the 33-square-mile Great Sand Dunes National Monument and Preserve is a fun and fascinating place to visit. The kids will love running and rolling on the sides of sand mountains, some rising over 700 feet. The park is a geological and botanical showcase and a hiker's delight with its alpine lakes and tundras, groves of ancient spruce and pine, grasslands and wetlands, and diversity of wildlife. Kite flying is a favorite activity here, as is, of course, building sand castles. Monument (daily). Visitor center (daily; closed Jan 1, Dec 25).

What to See and Do

Great Sand Dunes Four-Wheel Drive Tour. *5400 Hwy 150, Great Sand Dunes National Monument. Phone 719/378-2222.* A 12-mile, two-hour round-trip tour through the Great Sand Dunes National Monument; spectacular scenery; stops for short hikes on dunes. (May-Oct, daily) Five-person minimum. For information, contact Great Sand Dunes Oasis, Mosca 81146. **$$$$**

Greeley (A-4)

See also Fort Collins, Loveland

Founded 1870
Population 76,930
Elevation 4,664 ft
Area Code 970
Zip 80631
Information Greeley Convention & Visitors Bureau, 902 7th Ave; phone 970/352-3566 or toll-free 800/449-3866
Web site www.greeleycvb.com

Horace Greeley conceived of "Union Colony" as a Utopian agricultural settlement similar to the successful experiment at Oneida, New York. The town was founded by Nathan Meeker, agricultural editor of Greeley's New York Tribune. Thanks to irrigation, the region today is rich and fertile and sustains a thriving community. Greeley is the seat of Weld County. A Ranger District office of the Roosevelt National Forest (see ESTES PARK) is located in Greeley.

What to See and Do

Centennial Village. *1475 A St, Greeley. Phone 970/350-9220.* Restored buildings show the growth of Greeley and Weld County from 1860 to 1920; period furnishings; tours, lectures, special events. (Apr-Oct, Tues-Sun) **$$**

Fort Vasquez. *13412 Hwy 85, Greeley. 18 miles S on Hwy 85 near Platteville. Phone 970/785-2832.* Reconstructed adobe fur trading post of the 1830s contains exhibits of Colorado's fur trading and trapping industries, the Plains Indians, and archaeology of the fort. (Wed-Sat, Sun afternoons; Memorial Day-Labor Day, Sun afternoons) **FREE**

Meeker Home. *1324 9th Ave, Greeley. Phone 970/350-9220.* (1870) The house of city founder Nathan Meeker contains many of his belongings, as well as other historical mementos. (Apr-Oct, Tues-Sat; closed holidays) **$$**

Municipal Museum. *919 7th St, Greeley. Phone 970/350-9220.* County history archives, pioneer life exhibits; library; tours. (Tues-Sat; closed holidays) **FREE**

University of Northern Colorado. *501 20th St, Greeley. Phone 970/351-1890.* (1889) (10,500 students) On the 236-acre campus are

James A. Michener Library. *1400 22nd Ave, Greeley. Phone 970/351-1890.* Colorado's largest university library. Collection includes materials owned by Michener while writing the book Centennial.

Mariani Art Gallery. *1819 8th Ave, Greeley. Phone 970/351-4890.* Features faculty, student, and special exhibitions. Multipurpose University Center. **FREE**

Special Events

Greeley Independence Stampede. *600 N 14th Ave, Greeley. Phone 970/356-2855; toll-free 800/982-2855. www.greeleystampede.org.* For one week each summer, the Old West meets the New West at the Greeley Independence Stampede, a spirited, week-long town celebration culminating in the "World's Largest 4th of July Rodeo." In addition to classic rodeo events, the Stampede features nightly stage shows including country & western and classic rock concerts by top-name entertainers, a bull-riding and -fighting event, a kids' rodeo, and the ever-popular demolition derby. The midway carnival is open daily. Fees vary per event. Late June-early July.

Weld County Fair. *501 N 14th St, Greeley. Phone 970/356-4000.* First week in Aug.

Limited-Service Hotel

★★ BEST WESTERN REGENCY HOTEL. *701 8th St, Greeley (80631). Phone 970/353-8444; toll-free 800/780-7234; fax 970/353-4269. www.bestwestern.com.* 148 rooms, 3 story. Pets accepted, some restrictions;

fee. Complimentary continental breakfast. Check-out 11 am. Restaurant, bar. Indoor pool. **$**

Specialty Lodging

The following lodging establishment is approved by Mobil Travel Guide, but due to its unique and individualized nature has not been given a traditional Mobil Star rating. Included in this listing you may find bed-and-breakfasts, limited-service inns, guest ranches, and other unique hotel properties.

SOD BUSTER INN. *1221 9th Ave, Greeley (80631). Phone 970/592-1221; toll-free 888/300-1221. www.sodbusterinn.com.* 10 rooms, 2 story. Check-in 4 pm, check-out 11 am. High-speed Internet access. **$**

Gunnison (C-2)

See also Crested Butte

Settled 1874
Population 5,409
Elevation 7,703 ft
Information Gunnison Country Chamber of Commerce, 500 E Tomichi Ave, Box 36; phone 970/641-1501
Web site www.visitgunnison.com

With 2,000 miles of trout-fishing streams and Colorado's largest lake within easy driving range, Gunnison has long been noted as an excellent fishing center.

What to See and Do

Alpine Tunnel. *500 E Tomichi Ave, Gunnison. 36 miles NE via Hwy 50, County 765, 3 miles E of Pitkin on dirt road.* Completed by Denver, South Park & Pacific Railroad in 1881 and abandoned in 1910, this railroad tunnel, 11,523 feet above sea level, is 1,771 feet long. (July-Oct)

Cumberland Pass. *Chamber of Commerce, 500 E Tomichi Ave, Gunnison. 36 miles NE via Hwy 50, County 765.* (12,200 feet) Gravel road linking the towns of Pitkin and Tincup. (July-Oct)

Curecanti National Recreation Area. *102 Elk Creek, Gunnison. 5 miles W on Hwy 50. Phone 970/641-0406.* Named for the Ute Chief Curicata, who roamed and hunted in this territory. This area along the Gunnison River drainage includes Blue Mesa, Morrow Point, and Crystal reservoirs. Elk Creek Marinas, Inc., offers boat tours on Morrow Point Lake (Memorial Day-Labor Day, daily); phone 970/641-0402 for reservations. Blue Mesa Lake has water-skiing, windsurfing, fishing, boating (ramps, rentals); picnicking, camping (fee). The Elk Creek visitor center is 16 miles W (mid-Apr-Oct, daily). **FREE**

Gunnison National Forest. *216 N Colorado St, Gunnison. N, E, and S on Hwy 50. Phone 970/641-0471.* Forest contains 27 peaks more than 12,000 feet high within 1,662,839 acres of magnificent mountain scenery. Activities include fishing; hiking, picnicking, camping. A four-wheeling and a winter sports area is nearby (see CRESTED BUTTE). Also within the forest are West Elk Wilderness and portions of the Maroon Bells-Snowmass, Collegiate Peaks, La Garita, and Raggeds wilderness areas.

Gunnison Pioneer Museum. *S Adams and Tomico Hwy 50, Gunnison. E edge of town on Hwy 50. Phone 970/641-4530.* County and area history; pioneer items, narrow-gauge railroad, 1905 school house. (Memorial Day-Labor Day, Sun afternoons) **$$**

Old mining town of Tincup. *500 E Tomichi Ave, Gunnison. 40 miles NE on County Rd 765. Phone 970/641-1501.* Inquire locally about other mining towns; "20-Circle Tour" ghost town maps provided free at the visitor center, 500 E Tomichi Ave (Hwy 50).

Taylor Park Reservoir. *216 N Colorado St, Gunnison. 10 miles N on Hwy 135 to Almont, then 22 miles NE on County Rd 742 (Hwy 59) in Gunnison National Forest. Phone 970/641-2922.* Road runs through 20-mile canyon of Taylor River. Fishing, boating; hunting, camping (fee). (Memorial Day-Sept, daily) **FREE**

Tincup, Colorado. *Drive E from Gunnison on Hwy 50 to Parlin, N on Quartz Creek Rd to Pitkin, N on Cumberland Pass Rd to Tincup—also accessible from Taylor Canyon east of Almont and from Cottonwood Pass west of Buena Vista.* For a trip back in time, drive north from Pitkin over the beautiful Cumberland Pass and into the fascinating little town of Tincup. Once a notorious rough-and-tumble mining community known for gambling, brothels, saloons, and shootouts, Tincup is now a sleepy near-ghost town that has preserved a piece of its heritage in a collection of rustic buildings restored to their original 1850s condition. An exploration of the town and surroundings reveals a number of ruins from Tincup's lawless past, including the graves of its earliest inhabitants and abandoned mines. Don't miss a chance to eat at the restored Frenchy's Café, known for its rustic charm and hearty, home-cooked meals. **FREE**

Western State College of Colorado. *909 Escalante Dr, Gunnison. Between N Adams and N Colorado sts. Phone 970/943-2103.* (1901) (2,500 students) In the college library is the Jensen Western Colorado Room containing a collection of books and materials relating to western Colorado history and culture.

Special Events

Cattlemen's Days, Rodeo, and County Fair. *Gunnison.* Third full weekend in July.

Limited-Service Hotels

★★ BEST WESTERN TOMICHI VILLAGE. *41883 E Hwy 50, Gunnison (81230). Phone 970/641-1131; toll-free 800/641-1131; fax 970/641-9554. www.bestwestern.com/tomichivillageinn.* 49 rooms, 2 story. Check-in 3 pm, check-out 11 am. Restaurant. Fitness room. Indoor pool, whirlpool. Airport transportation available. **$**

★ HOLIDAY INN EXPRESS. *400 E Tomichi Ave, Hwy 50, Gunnison (81230). Phone 970/641-1288; toll-free 800/486-6476; fax 970/641-1332. www.holiday-inn.com.* 54 rooms, 2 story. Complimentary continental breakfast. Check-in 3 pm, check-out noon. Fitness room. Indoor pool, whirlpool. Airport transportation available. **$**

Specialty Lodgings

The following lodging establishments are approved by Mobil Travel Guide, but due to their unique and individualized nature have not been given a traditional Mobil Star rating. Included in this listing you may find bed-and-breakfasts, limited-service inns, guest ranches, and other unique hotel properties.

HARMEL'S RANCH RESORT. *Box 944m, Almont (81210). Phone 970/641-1740; toll-free 800/235-3402; fax 970/641-1944.* 300 acres on the Taylor River. 37 rooms. Closed Nov-mid-May. Complimentary full breakfast. Check-in 2 pm, check-out 10 am. Restaurant, bar. Children's activity center. Pool, whirlpool. Airport transportation available. **$$$**

POWDERHORN GUEST RANCH. *1525 County Rd 27, Powderhorn (81243). Phone 970/641-0220; fax 970/642-1399.* Family-oriented ranch in a remote area along Cebolla Creek. 14 rooms. Closed late Sept-May. Check-in 2 pm, check-out noon. Pool, whirlpool. Airport transportation available. **$$**

Restaurant

★★★ TROUGH. *Hwy 50, Gunnison (81230). Phone 970/641-3724.* American menu. Dinner. Closed Easter, Thanksgiving, Dec 25. Bar. Children's menu. Casual attire. **$$**

Idaho Springs (B-3)

See also Central City, Denver, Dillon, Evergreen, Georgetown, Golden, Winter Park

Settled 1859
Population 1,889
Elevation 7,524 ft
Area Code 303
Zip 80452
Information Visitors Center, PO Box 97; phone 303/567-4382 or toll-free 800/685-7785
Web site www.idahospringschamber.com

Idaho Springs, the site of Colorado's earliest gold strikes (1859), is today a tourist resort as well as the urban center for more than 200 mines, from which uranium, molybdenum, tungsten, zinc, lead, and gold are pulled from the earth. The town is named for the famous hot springs, first known and used by the Ute; bathing in the springs is still considered beneficial. The world's longest mining tunnel (5 miles) once ran from Idaho Springs through a mountain to Central City (see); only a portion remains (not open to visitors). The road to Mount Evans (elevation 14,260 feet) is the highest paved driving road in North America. A Ranger District office of the Arapaho National Forest (see DILLON) is located in Idaho Springs.

What to See and Do

Argo Town, USA. *2350 Riverside Dr, Idaho Springs. Phone 303/567-2421.* Reproduction of a Western mining town, including shops and Argo Gold Mill. This mill was first operated in 1913 to support mines intersected by the "mighty Argo" Tunnel; today it offers guided tours that unfold the history of the mill and the story of mining. Clear Creek Mining and Milling Museum illustrates the role of mining in the past. Double Eagle Gold Mine is an authentic and truly representative gold mine with direct access from the Argo Gold Mill. (Daily) **$$$**

Colorado School of Mines-Edgar Mine. *365 8th Ave, Idaho Springs. Phone 303/567-2911.* Experimental mine operated by students, also by government for training and by manufacturers for equipment testing; one-hour guided tours hourly (mid-June-mid-Aug, Tues-Sat; rest of year, by appointment). **$$**

Jackson Monument. *Colorado Blvd and Miner St, Idaho Springs. Hwy 103 in front of Clear Creek Secondary School. Phone toll-free 800/685-7785.* George J. Jackson made the first major gold discovery in Colorado here on Jan 1, 1859. **FREE**

Phoenix Gold Mine. *834 Country Rd 136, Idaho Springs. Approximately 2 1/2 miles SW via Stanley Rd to Trail Creek Rd. Phone 303/567-0422; toll-free 800/685-7785.* The only working gold mine in the state that is open to the public. (Daily; closed Dec 25) **$$$**

St. Mary's Glacier. *12 miles NW via I-70, Fall River Rd to Alice, a ghost town.* Park car approximately 1 mile NW of Alice, then proceed 1/2 mile on foot.

Special Event

Gold Rush Days. *Idaho Springs.* Parades, picnic, foot races, mining contests, arts and crafts. Aug.

Specialty Lodging

The following lodging establishment is approved by Mobil Travel Guide, but due to its unique and individualized nature has not been given a traditional Mobil Star rating. Included in this listing you may find bed-and-breakfasts, limited-service inns, guest ranches, and other unique hotel properties.

ST. MARY'S GLACIER BED AND BREAKFAST. *336 Crest Dr, Idaho Springs (80452). Phone 303/567-4084.* Looking to ski in July? Visit North America's highest bed-and-breakfast, where the snow stays year-round! Only an hour from Denver, this log retreat borders the Arapaho National Forest. Romantic guest rooms feature hand-sewn quilts and many have private decks with spectacular views. 7 rooms, 3 story. Pets accepted, some restrictions; fee. Complimentary full breakfast. Check-in 4-7 pm, check-out 11 am. **$**

Keystone

See also Dillon

What to See and Do

Keystone Resort Ski Area. *1254 Soda Ridge Rd, Dillon. Phone toll-free 800/222-0188.* Four ski mountains. Patrol, school, rentals. Snowmaking at Keystone, North Peak, and The Outback. Cafeteria, restaurant, bar, nursery, lodge. (Late Oct-early May) Cross-country skiing, night skiing, ice skating, snowmobiling, sleigh rides. Shuttle bus service. Combination and half-day ski rates; package plans. Summer activities include boating and rafting, gondola rides; golf, tennis, horseback riding, bicycling, and jeep riding. **$$$$** The four ski mountains here are

Arapahoe Basin. *Hwy 6, Dillon. Phone 970/468-0718; toll-free 888/272-7246. www.arapahoebasin.com.* Two triple, three double chairlifts. Sixty-nine runs; longest run 1 1/2 miles; vertical drop 2,257 feet. (Nov-early July; dates are tentative and may change) **$$$$**

Keystone Mountain. *Hwy 6, Keystone.* Six-passenger gondola; two triple, eight double, four quad, two high-speed chairlifts; four surface lifts. Fifty-three runs; longest run 3 miles; vertical drop 2,340 feet. (Late Oct-early May) Night skiing on 13 runs (mid-Nov-early Apr). **$$$$**

North Peak. *Keystone.* High-speed gondola; quad and triple chairlifts. Nineteen runs; longest run 2 1/2 miles; vertical drop 1,620 feet. (Mid-Nov-late Apr) **$$$$**

The Outback. *Keystone.* High-speed quad chairlift. Seventeen runs; longest run 2 1/2 miles, vertical drop 1,520 feet. (Mid-Nov-late Apr) **$$$$**

Restaurant

★★★ SKI TIP LODGE. *764 Montezuma Rd, Keystone (80435). Phone 970/468-4202; fax 970/496-4940. www.skitiplodge.com.* For more than 50 years, this charming bed-and-breakfast has been serving American regional cuisine. Dinner. Bar. Children's menu. **$$$**

Kremmling (B-3)

See also Granby

Population 1,578
Elevation 7,360 ft
Area Code 970
Zip 80459
Web site www.kremmlingchamber.com

A Ranger District office of the Arapaho National Forest (see DILLON) is located in Kremmling.

What to See and Do

Green Mountain Reservoir. *680 Blue River Pkwy, Silverthorne. 16 miles S on Hwy 9. Phone 970/468-5400.* Water-skiing, fishing, boating (ramps); picnicking, groceries, camping (fee). Contact Dillon Ranger District, Box 620, Silverthorne 80498. (Daily)

Specialty Lodging

The following lodging establishment is approved by Mobil Travel Guide, but due to its unique and individualized nature has not been given a traditional Mobil Star rating. Included in this listing you may find bed-and-breakfasts, limited-service inns, guest ranches, and other unique hotel properties.

LATIGO RANCH. *201 County Rd 1911, Kremmling (80459). Phone 970/724-9008; toll-free 800/227-9655. www.latigotrails.com.* 10 rooms. Closed Apr-May, mid-Nov-mid-Dec. Check-in 2 pm, check-out 4 pm. Restaurant. Children's activity center. Pool, whirlpool. Airport transportation available. **$$**

La Junta (D-5)

Settled 1875
Population 7,568
Elevation 4,066 ft
Area Code 719
Zip 81050
Information Chamber of Commerce, 110 Santa Fe Ave; phone 719/384-7411
Web site www.lajuntachamber.com

La Junta (la HUN-ta, Spanish for "the Junction") is at a junction of the old Navajo and Santa Fe trails. The town is known for its Koshare Indian Dancers, a group of Explorer Scouts who perform authentic Native American dances here and throughout the country.

This is the center of an irrigated farming area, producing melons and commercial vegetables. Cattle auctions are held throughout the year. The Holbrook Lake area has become a popular recreational center.

What to See and Do

Bent's Old Fort National Historic Site. *35110 Hwy 194 E, La Junta. 8 miles NE on Hwy 109 and 194 E. Phone 719/838-5010.* The fort has been reconstructed as accurately as possible to its appearance in 1845-1846; the furnishings are antique and reproductions. The original structure, located on the Mountain Branch of the Santa Fe Trail, was built as a privately owned frontier trading post (circa 1833). The old fort played a central role in the "opening of the west." For 16 years, until its abandonment in 1849, the fort was an important frontier hub of American trade and served as a rendezvous for trappers, Native Americans, and Hispanic traders on the Santa Fe Trail. It also served as the center of Army operations to protect the traders using the Santa Fe Trail. Self-guided tour. Summer "living history" programs. (Daily; closed Jan 1, Thanksgiving, Dec 25) **$**

Koshare Indian Kiva Museum. *115 W 18th St, La Junta. Phone 719/384-4411.* Housed in a domed building, a copy of ceremonial kivas in the Southwest, the museum features Native American baskets, arrowheads, paintings, and carvings, as well as paintings by Southwestern artists. (Daily; closed holidays) **$**

Otero Museum. *218 Anderson, La Junta. Phone 719/384-7500.* History of Otero County and surrounding areas. Santa Fe Railroad history; artifacts. (June-Sept, Mon-Sat) **FREE**

Special Events

Arkansas Valley Fair and Exposition. *Rocky Ford Fairgrounds. 105 N Main St, Rocky Ford. Phone 719/254-7483.* Colorado's oldest continuous fair. Highlight is "watermelon day," when every visitor receives free watermelon. One week late in Aug.

Early Settlers Day. *La Junta.* Fiddlers contest, crafts, parade. Sat after Labor Day.

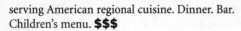

Koshare Indian Dances. *Kiva Museum, 115 W 18th St, La Junta. Phone 719/384-4411.* Dances by a nationally famous Boy Scout troop. Sat evenings. Late June-early Aug.

Koshare Winter Night Ceremonial. *Kiva Museum, 115 W 18th St, La Junta. Phone 719/384-4111.* Nightly performances. Week of Dec 25 and first weekend in Jan.

Limited-Service Hotel

★★ BEST WESTERN BENT'S FORT INN. *10950 Hwy 50, Las Animas (81054). Phone 719/456-0011; fax 719/456-2550. www.bestwestern.com.* 38 rooms, 2 story. Pets accepted. Complimentary full breakfast. Check-out 11 am. Restaurant, bar. Pool. Airport transportation available. **$**

Restaurant

★ CHIARAMONTE'S. *27696 Harris Rd, La Junta (81050). Phone 719/384-8909; fax 719/853-6619.* American menu. Lunch, dinner. Closed holidays. Bar. **$$**

Lake City

Population 375
Elevation 8,671 ft
Area Code 970
Zip 81235
Information Chamber of Commerce, PO Box 430; phone 970/944-2527 or toll-free 800/569-1874
Web site www.lakecityco.com

Lake City teemed with gold seekers in the 1870s. Now empty cabins and entire ghost towns dot the hills above the town. Among Lake City's 75 historic homes and buildings are the first church and bank on the Western Slope. Lake San Cristobal and the Lake Fork of the Gunnison River offer excellent fishing.

In the winter of 1873-1874, Alferd Packer led a group of gold prospectors into the San Juan Mountains above Lake City. Emerging from the mountains in the spring, only Packer survived, claiming his companions had abandoned him. For the next ten years, Packer was a fugitive. However, in 1883, he was convicted of murder and cannibalism. The victims' gravesites are located on the south edge of town.

What to See and Do

Alpine Triangle Recreation Area. *216 N Colorado St, Lake City. S and W of town; access by the Alpine Loop National Backcountry Byway (four-wheel drive necessary in some places). Phone 970/641-0471.* Approximately 250,000 acres administered by Bureau of Land Management and the US Forest Service for primitive and motorized recreation, mining, grazing, and watershed protection. The area has five peaks that are more than 14,000 feet high; excellent backpacking and fishing; habitat for deer, elk, mountain sheep, black bear. Many historical mining tramways, stamp mills, and ghost towns are scattered throughout the area. Mill Creek Campground (14 miles SW) has a picnic area and 22 tent and trailer sites with water (Memorial Day-Oct, daily, weather permitting; fee for camping). Lake San Cristobal (3 miles south of town), the second-largest natural lake in the state, was formed by the Slumgullion earthflow 700 years ago. Williams Creek (10 miles southwest) has picnic areas and 21 tent and trailer sites with water (Memorial Day-Oct, daily; fee for camping). Southwest of town is the site where Alferd Packer murdered and mutilated five prospectors in the winter of 1873-1874.

Hinsdale County Historical Society Tours. *130 Silver St, Lake City. Phone 970/944-2050.* Weekly guided walking tours, about two hours long, to historic homes, the local cemetery, and "ghostly" sites. (Mid-June-Labor Day; call for specific dates and times) **$$**

Hinsdale County Museum. *130 Silver St, Lake City. Phone 970/944-2050.* This small museum has exhibits on the trial of the notorious cannibal Alferd Packer and the area's silver-mining history, plus a furnished 1870s-era Victorian home. (Mid-June-Labor Day: daily; hours vary rest of year) **$**

Special Events

Alferd Packer Barbeque Cookoff. *Lake City.* Late May.

Ghost Town Narration Tours. *Lake City.* Aug.

Limited-Service Hotel

★★ MELODY C. CRYSTAL LODGE. *PO Box 246, Lake City (81235). Phone 970/944-2201; toll-free 800/984-1234; fax 970/944-2503. www.crystallodge*

.net. Surrounded by the San Juan Mountains. 28 rooms, 2 story. Pets accepted, some restrictions; fee. Check-in noon, check-out 10 am. Restaurant. Whirlpool. **$**

Lakewood (B-4)

See also Denver, Englewood, Golden

Population 144,126
Elevation 5,450 ft
Area Code 303
Information West Chamber Serving Jefferson County, PO Box 280748, 80228-0748; phone 303/233-5555
Web site www.ci.lakewood.co.us

This suburban community west of Denver was once dotted with farms and fruit orchards and with the summer houses of wealthy Denver residents.

What to See and Do

Bear Creek Lake Park. *15600 W Morrison Rd, Lakewood. 1/4 mile E of Hwy 470. Phone 303/697-6159.* Approximately 2,600 acres. Water-skiing school, fishing, boating (10 hp limit, rentals, marina); hiking, bicycle trails, picnicking, camping (no electricity). Archery. View of downtown Denver from Mount Carbon. (Daily; closed Jan 1, Thanksgiving, Dec 25) **$**

Colorado Mills. *14500 W Colfax Ave, Lakewood. Phone 303/384-3000. www.coloradomills.com.* Just ten minutes from downtown Denver, the brand-new, 1.2 million-square-foot Colorado Mills brings a vast array of value-oriented stores, restaurants, and entertainment venues together in an exciting, state-of-the-art retail and entertainment complex. Shoppers can choose from more than 200 retailers, anchored by a Neiman Marcus clearance center, Off 5th Saks Fifth Avenue, Eddie Bauer Outlet, and Off Broadway Shoe Warehouse. Movie theaters, restaurants, an interactive play area for young children, and a 40,000 square-foot ESPN X Games Skatepark for older kids form the core of the entertainment center. (Daily)

Crown Hill Park. *W 26th Ave and Kipling St (Hwy 391), Lakewood. Phone 303/271-5925.* This 168-acre nature preserve includes Crown Hill Lake and a wildlife pond. Fishing; hiking, bicycle, bridle trails. (Daily) **FREE**

Lakewood's Heritage Center. *797 S Wadsworth Blvd (Hwy 121), Lakewood. Just S of Alameda Blvd (Hwy 26). Phone 303/987-7850.* Nature, art, and historical exhibits in 127-acre park. Turn-of-the-century farm; one-room schoolhouse; vintage farm machinery; Barn Gallery with permanent and changing exhibits, interpretive displays. Lectures, workshops; visitor center. (Tues-Sun) **$$**

Limited-Service Hotels

★ HAMPTON INN. *3605 S Wadsworth Blvd, Lakewood (80235). Phone 303/989-6900; toll-free 800/426-7866; fax 303/985-4730. www.hamptoninn.com.* 150 rooms, 4 story. Complimentary continental breakfast. Check-out noon. Fitness room. Pool. **$**

★ ★ HOLIDAY INN. *7390 W Hampden Ave, Lakewood (80227). Phone 303/980-9200; toll-free 800/465-4329; fax 303/980-6423. www.holiday-inn.com.* 190 rooms, 6 story. Pets accepted, some restrictions; fee. Check-out noon. Restaurant, bar. Fitness room. Pool, whirlpool. **$**

Full-Service Hotel

★ ★ ★ SHERATON DENVER WEST HOTEL. *360 Union Blvd, Lakewood (80228). Phone 303/987-2000; toll-free 800/525-3966; fax 303/969-0263. www.sheraton.com.* 242 rooms, 12 story. Check-out 1 pm. Restaurant, bar. Fitness room. Indoor pool, whirlpool. Business center. **$$**

Restaurants

★ ★ ★ 240 UNION. *240 Union, Lakewood (80228). Phone 303/989-3562; fax 303/989-3565. www.240union.com.* Continental menu. Lunch, dinner. Closed holidays. Bar. Children's menu. Outdoor dining. **$$**

★ CASA BONITA OF DENVER. *6715 W Colfax Ave, Lakewood (80214). Phone 303/232-5115; fax 303/232-7801. www.casabonitadenver.com.* Mexican, American menu. Lunch, dinner. Closed Thanksgiving, Dec 25. Children's menu. **$**

★ **DARDANO'S.** *11968 W Jewell Ave, Lakewood (80228). Phone 303/988-1991. www.dardanosrestaurant.com.* Italian, American menu. Lunch, dinner. Closed Mon; Thanksgiving, Dec 24-25. Bar. Children's menu. **$$**

★ ★ ★ **THE FORT.** *19192 Hwy 8, Morrison (80465). Phone 303/697-4771; fax 303/697-9310. www.thefort.com.* In an accurate adobe recreation of the historic Bent's Fort, Sam Arnold's popular, kitschy restaurant, southwest of Denver, has been serving the food of the early West for more than 30 years. Southwestern menu. Dinner. Closed Dec 25. Bar. Children's menu. Outdoor dining. **$$$**

★ ★ **GRADY'S AMERICAN GRILL.** *5140 S Wadsworth Blvd, Lakewood (80123). Phone 303/973-5140; fax 303/973-4129.* Three dining areas on two levels. American menu. Lunch, dinner. Closed Thanksgiving, Dec 25. Bar. Children's menu. Outdoor seating. **$$**

Lamar (D-5)

Population 8,869
Elevation 3,622 ft
Area Code 719
Zip 81052
Information Chamber of Commerce, 109A E Beech St; phone 719/336-4379

What to See and Do

Big Timbers Museum. *7517 Hwy 50, Lamar. Phone 719/336-2472.* Named for the giant cottonwoods on the banks of the Arkansas River. Museum with newspapers, art, drawings, artifacts of area history. (Daily, afternoons; closed holidays) **FREE**

Limited-Service Hotel

★ ★ **BEST WESTERN COW PALACE INN.** *1301 N Main St, Lamar (81052). Phone 719/336-7753; toll-free 800/678-0344; fax 719/336-9598. www.bestwestern.com.* 95 rooms, 2 story. Pets accepted. Check-out 11 am. Restaurant, bar. Indoor pool, whirlpool. Airport transportation available. **$**

Restaurant

★ ★ **BLACKWELL STATION.** *1301 S Main St, Lamar (81052). Phone 719/336-7575.* Featuring authentic local cuisine and prime aged steaks. American menu. Lunch, dinner. **$$**

Leadville (C-3)

See also Buena Vista, Dillon, Vail

Settled 1860
Population 2,821
Elevation 10,430 ft
Area Code 719
Zip 80461
Information Greater Leadville Area Chamber of Commerce, 809 Harrison Ave, PO Box 861; phone 719/486-3900 or toll-free 888/264-5344
Web site www.leadvilleusa.com

Located just below the timberline, Leadville's high altitude contributes to its reputation for excellent skiing, cool summers, and beautiful fall colors. First a rich gold camp, then an even richer silver camp, the town boasts a lusty, brawling past in which millionaires were made and destroyed in a single day; a barrel of whiskey could net $1,500; tents pitched on the main street were advertised as "the best hotel in town;" and thousands of dollars could be—and were—lost on the turn of a card in the town's iniquitous saloons and smoky gambling halls.

Leadville's lively history is intertwined with the lives of Horace Tabor and his two wives, Augusta and Elizabeth Doe, whose rags-to-riches-to-rags story is the basis of the American opera *The Ballad of Baby Doe.* The famed "unsinkable" Molly Brown made her fortune here, as did David May, Charles Boettcher, Charles Dow, and Meyer Guggenheim.

Until 1950, Leadville was a decaying mining town. However, a burst of civic enthusiasm rejuvenated it in the following years. Today it is filled with attractions that date back to the town's glory days, including several museums and a Victorian downtown area.

A Ranger District office of the San Isabel National Forest (see PUEBLO) is located in Leadville.

What to See and Do

Earth Runs Silver. *809 Harrison Ave, Leadville. Phone 719/486-3900; toll-free 800/933-9301.* Video presentation featuring Leadville's legendary mining camp with music and narration. (Daily; closed Jan 1, Thanksgiving, Dec 25) **$$**

Healy House-Dexter Cabin. *912 Harrison Ave, Leadville. Phone 719/486-0487.* The restored Healy House, built in 1878, contains many fine Victorian-era furnishings. Dexter Cabin, built by early mining millionaire James V. Dexter, appears on the outside to be an ordinary two-room miner's cabin; built as a place to entertain wealthy gentlemen, the cabin's interior is surprisingly luxurious. (Memorial Day-Labor Day, daily) **$$**

Heritage Museum and Gallery. *9th St and Harrison Ave, Leadville. Phone 719/486-1878.* Diorama and displays depict local history; scale-model replica of Ice Palace, Victorian costumes, memorabilia of mining days. Changing exhibits of American art. (Mid-May-Oct, daily) **$$**

Leadville, Colorado & Southern Railroad Train Tour. *326 E 7th St, Leadville. Phone 719/486-3936.* Departs from the old depot for 23-mile round-trip scenic ride following the headwaters of the Arkansas River through the Rocky Mountains. (Memorial Day-Oct, daily) **$$$$**

Leadville National Fish Hatchery. *2844 Hwy 300, Leadville. 7 miles SW via Hwy 24, Hwy 300. Phone 719/486-0189.* The original hatchery building constructed in 1889 is still in use. Approximately 45 tons of brook, lake, brown, and cutthroat trout are produced here annually. Hiking and ski-touring trails are nearby. (Daily) **FREE**

The Matchless Mine. *Leadville. 1 1/4 miles E on E 7th St. Phone 719/486-1899.* When H. A. W. Tabor died in 1899, his last words to his wife, Baby Doe, were "Hold on to the Matchless," which had produced as much as $100,000 a month in its bonanza days. Faithful to his wish and ever hopeful, the once fabulously rich Baby Doe lived on in poverty in the little cabin next to the mine for 36 years; in it, she was found frozen to death in 1935. The cabin is now a museum. (June-Labor Day, daily) **$$**

National Mining Hall of Fame and Museum. *120 W 9th St, Leadville. Phone 719/486-1229.* History and technology exhibits of the mining industry. Hall of Fame dedicated to those who have made significant contributions to the industry. (May-Oct, daily; rest of year, Mon-Fri; closed winter holidays) **$$**

Ski Cooper. *Hwy 24, Leadville. Summit of Tennessee Pass, 10 miles N on Hwy 24. Phone 719/486-3684. www.skicooper.com.* Triple, double chairlift; Pomalift, T-bar; patrol, school, rentals; snowcat tours; cafeteria, nursery. Twenty-six runs; longest run 1 1/2 miles; vertical drop 1,200 feet. Groomed cross-country skiing (15 miles). (Late Nov-early Apr, daily) **$$$$**

★ **Tabor Opera House.** *308 Harrison Ave, Leadville. Phone 719/486-8409.* (1879) Now a museum, this theater was elegantly furnished when constructed. At the time, Leadville had a population of 30,000. The theater was host to the Metropolitan Opera, the Chicago Symphony, and most of the famous actors and actresses of the period. Their pictures line the corridors. Many of the original furnishings, much of the scenery, and the dressing areas are still in use and on display. The Tabor box, where many dignitaries were Tabor's guests, is part of the theater tour. Summer shows (inquire locally). Self-guided tours (Memorial Day-Sept, daily) **$$**

Special Events

Boom Days & Burro Race. *Leadville.* First full weekend in Aug.

Crystal Carnival. *Leadville.* First weekend in Mar.

Victorian Christmas & Home Tour. *Leadville.* First Sat in Dec.

Limited-Service Hotel

★★ **DELAWARE HOTEL.** *700 Harrison Ave, Leadville (80461). Phone 719/486-1418; toll-free 800/748-2004; fax 719/486-2214. www.delawarehotel.com.* Historic hotel (1886); Victorian lobby. 36 rooms, 3 story. Complimentary continental breakfast. Check-in 2 pm, check-out 11 am. Restaurant. Whirlpool. **$**

Specialty Lodgings

The following lodging establishments are approved by Mobil Travel Guide, but due to their unique and individualized nature have not been given a traditional Mobil Star rating. Included in this listing you may find bed-and-breakfasts, limited-service inns, guest ranches, and other unique hotel properties.

ICE PALACE INN BED & BREAKFAST. *813 Spruce St, Leadville (80461). Phone 719/486-8272; toll-free 800/754-2840; fax 719/486-0345. www.icepalaceinn.com.* Built in 1879. 5 rooms, 2 story. Complimentary full breakfast. Check-in 4 pm, check-out 11 am. Whirlpool. **$**

THE LEADVILLE COUNTRY INN. *127 E 8th St, Leadville (80461). Phone 719/486-2354; toll-free 800/748-2354. www.leadvillebednbreakfast.com.* This stately 15-room Victorian mansion was built in the 1800s and has been an inn since 1999. 9 rooms, 3 story. Complimentary full breakfast. Check-in 4 pm, check-out 11 am. **$$**

Restaurants

★ HIGH COUNTRY. *115 Harrison Ave, Leadville (80461). Phone 719/486-3992.* Three dining areas. Mounted wildlife. American menu. Lunch, dinner. Closed holidays. Bar. Children's menu. Casual attire. Outdoor seating. **$**

★★★ TENNESSEE PASS COOKHOUSE. *1892 Hwy 25, Leadville (80461). Phone 719/486-8114. www.tennesseepass.com.* This skiing-oriented dining room serves one prix fixe meal nightly with entrées ordered 24 hours in advance. American menu. Lunch, dinner. Reservations recommended. **$$$**

Limon (C-5)

Population 2,071
Elevation 5,365 ft
Area Code 719
Zip 80828
Web site www.limonchamber.com

Limited-Service Hotel

★ BEST WESTERN LIMON INN. *925 T Ave, Limon (80828). Phone 719/775-0277; fax 719/775-2921. www.bestwestern.com.* 47 rooms, 2 story. Pets accepted; fee. Complimentary continental breakfast. Check-out 11 am. Indoor pool. **$**

Specialty Lodging

The following lodging establishment is approved by Mobil Travel Guide, but due to its unique and individualized nature has not been given a traditional Mobil Star rating. Included in this listing you may find bed-and-breakfasts, limited-service inns, guest ranches, and other unique hotel properties.

MIDWEST COUNTRY INN. *795 Main St, Limon (80828). Phone 719/775-2373; toll-free 888/610-6683; fax 719/775-8808.* 32 rooms, 2 story. Check-in anytime, check-out 10 am. **$**

Restaurant

★ FIRESIDE JUNCTION. *2295 9th St, Limon (80828). Phone 719/775-2396; fax 719/775-2398.* Mexican, American menu. Breakfast, lunch, dinner. Closed Dec 24-25. Bar. Children's menu. **$$**

Littleton (B-4)

Restaurants

★ COUNTY LINE SMOKEHOUSE & GRILL. *8351 Southpark Ln, Littleton (80120). Phone 303/797-3727; fax 303/795-1576.* Barbecue menu. Lunch, dinner. Closed Thanksgiving, Dec 24-25. Bar. Children's menu. **$**

★★★ Z' TEJAS GRILL. *8345 S Park Meadows Center Dr, Littleton (80124). Phone 303/768-8191; fax 303/768-8185. www.ztejas.com.* Jalapeños and habañeros spice up the food at this casual, friendly Mexican grill. Southwestern menu. Lunch, dinner, Sat and Sun brunch. Closed Thanksgiving, Dec 25. Bar. Children's menu. **$$**

Longmont (B-4)

See also Boulder, Denver, Loveland, Lyons

Founded 1870
Population 71,093
Elevation 4,979 ft
Area Code 303
Information Chamber of Commerce, 528 Main St, 80501; phone 303/776-5295
Web site www.longmontchamber.org

What to See and Do

Longmont Museum. *400 Quail Rd, Longmont. Phone 303/651-8374.* Changing and special exhibits on art, history, space, and science; permanent exhibits on the history of Longmont and the St. Vrain Valley. (Tues-Sat, Sun afternoons) **FREE**

Special Events

Boulder County Fair and Rodeo. *Fairgrounds, Longmont. Phone 303/441-3927.* Nine days in early Aug.

Rhythm on the River. *St. Vrain Greenway, Roger's Grove, Longmont. Phone 303/776-6050.* Sept.

Full-Service Hotel

★★ RAINTREE PLAZA HOTEL & CONFERENCE CENTER. *1900 Ken Pratt Blvd, Longmont (80501). Phone 303/776-2000; toll-free 800/843-8240; fax 303/678-7361. www.raintreeplaza.com.* 211 rooms, 2 story. Pets accepted; fee. Complimentary continental breakfast. Check-out noon. Restaurant, bar. Fitness room. Pool. Airport transportation available. **$**

Loveland (B-4)

See also Estes Park, Fort Collins, Greeley, Longmont, Lyons, Rocky Mountain National Park

Founded 1877
Population 50,608
Elevation 4,982 ft
Area Code 970
Information Visitor Center/Chamber of Commerce, 5400 Stone Creek Circle, 80538; phone 970/667-5728 or toll-free 800/258-1278
Web site www.loveland.org

In recent years, more than 300,000 valentines have been remailed annually by the Loveland post office, stamped in red with the "Sweetheart Town's" cachet, a different valentine verse each year.

What to See and Do

Boyd Lake State Park. *3720 N Country Rd, Loveland. 1 mile E on Hwy 34, then 2 miles N. Phone 970/669-1739.* Swimming, water-skiing, fishing, boating (ramps, rentals); picnicking (shelters, showers), camping (dump station). (Daily) **$$**

Special Events

Dog racing. *Cloverleaf Kennel Club, 4 miles E at junction Hwy 34, I-25. 2577 NW Frontage Rd, Loveland. Phone 970/667-6211.* Races nightly. Matinees Mon, Wed, Sat, and Sun. Pari-mutuel betting. No minors. Mar-June.

Larimer County Fair and Rodeo. *700 S Railroad Ave, Loveland.* Mid-Aug.

Specialty Lodgings

The following lodging establishments are approved by Mobil Travel Guide, but due to their unique and individualized nature have not been given a traditional Mobil Star rating. Included in this listing you may find bed-and-breakfasts, limited-service inns, guest ranches, and other unique hotel properties.

CATTAIL CREEK INN BED & BREAKFAST. *2665 Abarr Dr, Loveland (80538). Phone 970/667-7600; toll-free 800/572-2466; fax 970/667-8968. www.cattailcreekinn.com.* Located on the Cattail Creek Golf Course, this luxury inn offers views of Lake Loveland and the Rocky Mountains. The open guest rooms have cherry woodwork and ceiling fans. Delicious breakfasts include dishes like Belgian pecan waffles with sautéed peaches. 8 rooms, 2 story. Children over 14 years only. Complimentary full breakfast. Check-in 4-9 pm, check-out 11 am. **$**

SYLVAN DALE GUEST RANCH. *2939 N County Rd 31 D, Loveland (80538). Phone 970/667-3915; toll-free 877/667-3999; fax 970/635-9336. www.sylvandale.com.* Owned and operated by the Jessup family, this dude ranch was established in the 1920s and is proud to still be a working cattle and horse ranch. Located in a river valley at the mouth of Colorado's

Big Thompson Canyon, the ranch has more than 3,000 acres to enjoy, with elevations ranging from 5,325 feet to 7,500 feet at "Cow Camp." 23 rooms, 2 story. Complimentary full breakfast. Check-in 3 pm, check-out 11 am. Restaurant (public by reservation). Children's activity center. Pool. Tennis. Airport transportation available. Business center. **$**

Restaurant

★ ★ **CACTUS GRILL NORTH.** *281-A E 29th St, Loveland (80538). Phone 970/663-1550.* Southwestern menu. Lunch, dinner. Closed Dec 25. Bar. Children's menu. Outdoor seating. **$$**

Lyons (B-4)

See also Boulder, Estes Park, Longmont, Loveland, Rocky Mountain National Park

Population 1,585
Elevation 5,360 ft
Area Code 303
Zip 80540
Information Chamber of Commerce, PO Box 426; 303/823-5215. The visitor center at 4th and Broadway is staffed Memorial Day-Labor Day, daily; phone 303/823-6640
Web site www.lyons-colorado.com

Special Event

Good Old Days Celebration. *350 Broadway Ave, Lyons. Phone 303/823-5215.* Midway, parade, flea market, craft fair, food. Last weekend in June.

Specialty Lodging

The following lodging establishment is approved by Mobil Travel Guide, but due to its unique and individualized nature has not been given a traditional Mobil Star rating. Included in this listing you may find bed-and-breakfasts, limited-service inns, guest ranches, and other unique hotel properties.

PEACEFUL VALLEY RANCH. *475 Peaceful Valley Rd, Lyons (80540). Phone 303/747-2881; toll-free 800/955-6343; fax 303/747-2167. www.peacefulvalley.com.* Mountain setting on 300 acres. 52 rooms. Check-in 2-4 pm, check-out 10 am. Restaurant. Children's activity center. Indoor pool, children's pool, whirlpool. Airport transportation available. Business center. **$$**

Restaurants

★ **ANDREA'S GERMAN CUISINE.** *216 E Main St, Lyons (80540). Phone 303/823-5000; fax 303/823-0860.* German menu. Breakfast, lunch, dinner. Closed Wed; Dec 25. Bar. **$$**

★ ★ ★ **BLACK BEAR INN.** *42 E Main St, Lyons (80540). Phone 303/823-6812; fax 303/823-5953. www.blackbearinn.com.* Since 1977, owners Hand and Annalies Wyppler have welcomed guests to their cozy Alpine-style restaurant just outside of Lyons. American menu. Lunch, dinner. Closed Mon-Tues; also Jan-mid-Feb. Bar. Outdoor seating. **$$$**

★ ★ ★ **LA CHAUMIERE.** *Hwy 36, Lyons (80540). Phone 303/823-6521.* French menu. Dinner. Closed Mon. Children's menu. **$$**

Manitou Springs (C-4)

See also Colorado Springs, Cripple Creek, Florissant Fossil Beds National Monument

Founded 1872
Population 4,980
Elevation 6,320 ft
Area Code 719
Zip 80829
Information Chamber of Commerce, 354 Manitou Ave; phone 719/685-5089 or toll-free 800/642-2567
Web site www.manitousprings.org

Manitou Springs's many mineral springs, familiar to the Native Americans, gave nearby Colorado Springs its name. The natives, attributing supernatural powers to the waters (Manitou is a Native American word for "Great Spirit"), once marked off the surrounding area as a sanctuary. Today, the town is a National Historic District and a popular tourist resort.

What to See and Do

Cave of the Winds. *W Hwy 24, Manitou Springs. From Manitou Ave and Hwy 24, go 6 miles W on Hwy 24 to Cave of the Winds Rd; turn right and continue 1/2 mile to visitor center. Phone 719/685-5444.* Fascinating 45-minute guided tour through underground passageways filled with beautiful stalactites, stalagmites, and flowstone formations created millions of years ago. Tours leave every 15 minutes (daily). Light jacket and comfortable shoes recommended. Laser light show in canyon (May-Sept, Fri, Sat evenings; rest of year, daily) is 15 stories high and is accompanied by music. (May-Sept, daily) **$$$$**

Iron Springs Chateau. *444 Ruxton Ave, Manitou Springs. Phone 719/685-5104.* Melodrama dinner theater featuring a traditional "olio" show. Named for the mineral-rich water beneath the ground. (Mon-Sat) **$$$$**

Manitou Cliff Dwellings Museum. *Hwy 24 W, Manitou Springs. Phone 719/685-5242.* Outdoor Native American preserve; architecture of the cliff-dwelling natives, AD 1100-1300. Native American dancing (June-Aug). Museum (Mar-Nov, daily). **$$$**

Miramont Castle Museum. *9 Capitol Hill Ave, Manitou Springs. Phone 719/685-1011.* A 46-room, four-story Victorian house (circa 1895) featuring nine styles of architecture, miniatures and doll collection, tea room, soda fountain, gardens. (Tues-Sun; closed Easter, Thanksgiving, Dec 25) **$$**

Pikes Peak Cog Railway. *515 Ruxton Ave, Manitou Springs. Phone 719/685-5401.* (See COLORADO SPRINGS)

Limited-Service Hotel

★ BEST VALUE INN. *481 Manitou Ave, Manitou Springs (80829). Phone 719/685-5492; fax 719/685-4143. www.villamotel.com.* 47 rooms, 2 story. Check-out 11 am. Pool, whirlpool. **$**

Full-Service Hotel

★★★ THE CLIFF HOUSE OF PIKES PEAK. *306 Canon Ave, Manitou Springs (80829). Phone 719/685-3000; toll-free 888/212-7000; fax 719/685-3913. www.thecliffhouse.com.* 200 rooms. Check-in 3 pm, check-out noon. Restaurant, bar. **$$$**

Specialty Lodgings

The following lodging establishments are approved by Mobil Travel Guide, but due to their unique and individualized nature have not been given a traditional Mobil Star rating. Included in this listing you may find bed-and-breakfasts, limited-service inns, guest ranches, and other unique hotel properties.

BLACK BEAR INN OF PIKES PEAK. *5250 Pikes Peak Hwy, Cascade (80809). Phone 719/684-0151; toll-free 877/732-5232. www.blackbearinnpikespeak.com.* View of mountains. 9 rooms, 2 story. Children over 10 years only. Complimentary full breakfast. Check-in 4-6 pm, check-out 10:30 am. Whirlpool. **$**

EASTHOLME IN THE ROCKIES. *4445 Haggerman Ave, Cascade (80809). Phone 719/684-9901; toll-free 800/672-9901. www.eastholme.com.* Originally a hotel built in 1885. 8 rooms, 3 story. Complimentary full breakfast. Check-in 4 pm, check-out 11 am. **$**

RED CRAGS BED & BREAKFAST INN. *302 El Paso Blvd, Manitou Springs (80829). Phone 719/685-1920; toll-free 800/721-2248; fax 719/685-1073. www.redcrags.com.* Mansion (1870) originally built as a clinic. On a bluff with a view of Pikes Peak, Garden of the Gods. 8 rooms, 4 story. Children over 10 years only. Complimentary full breakfast. Check-in 4-6 pm, check-out 11 am. Whirlpool. **$**

ROCKLEDGE COUNTRY INN. *328 El Paso Blvd, Manitou Springs (80829). Phone 719/685-4515; toll-free 888/685-4515; fax 719/685-1031. www.rockledgeinn.com.* 5 rooms. Check-in 3 pm, check-out 11 am. **$$$**

Restaurants

★★★ BRIARHURST MANOR. *404 Manitou Ave, Manitou Springs (80829). Phone 719/685-1864; fax 719/685-9638. www.briarhurst.com.* Located in a Tudor manor house built in 1876 by the founder of Manitou Springs, William Bell, this elegant fine-dining restaurant has been under the control of chef/owner Sigi Krauss since 1975. Home-grown fresh vegetables and herbs. American menu. Dinner. Bar. Children's menu. Outdoor seating. **$$$**

★★★ CRAFTWOOD INN. *404 El Paso Blvd, Manitou Springs (80829). Phone 719/685-9000; fax 719/685-9088. www.craftwood.com.* This romantic restaurant is located in a Tudor manor house. Built in 1912 on 1 1/2 acres of landscaped gardens; view of Pikes Peak. American menu. Dinner. Closed Jan 1, Dec 25. Bar. Outdoor seating. **$$$**

★★ MISSION BELL INN. *178 Crystal Park Rd, Manitou Springs (80829). Phone 719/685-9089; fax 719/685-9317. www.missionbellinn.com.* Mexican menu. Dinner. Closed Jan 1, Thanksgiving, Dec 25; also Mon Oct-May. Outdoor seating. **$$**

★★ STAGE COACH. *702 Manitou Ave, Manitou Springs (80829). Phone 719/685-9400; fax 719/685-1216. www.stagecoachinn.com.* Historic log stage stop built in 1881. Steak menu. Dinner. Closed Jan 1, Dec 25. Bar. Children's menu. Outdoor seating. **$$**

Mesa Verde National Park (E-1)

See also Cortez, Durango

Web site www.nps.gov/meve

8 miles E of Cortez, 36 miles W of Durango, on Hwy 160 to park entrance, then 15 miles S to visitor center.

In the far southwest corner of Colorado exists the largest—and arguably the most fascinating—archaeological preserve in the nation. Mesa Verde National Park, with 52,000 acres encompassing 4,000 known archaeological sites, is a treasure trove of ancestral Pueblo cultural artifacts, including the magnificent, mysterious Anasazi cliff dwellings. Constructed in the 13th century, these huge, elaborate stone villages built into the canyon walls are spellbinding. To fully appreciate their significance, first take a walk through the park's Chapin Mesa Museum for a historical overview. A visit to the actual sites can be physically challenging but is well worth the effort. Several of the sites can be explored year-round, free of charge; others require tickets for ranger-guided tours in summer months only. Tour tickets can be purchased at the park's Far View Visitor Center. (Daily)

What to See and Do

Cliff Dwelling Tours. *Administration Bldg 15, Mesa Verde National Park. Phone 970/529-4461.* The cliff dwellings can be entered only while rangers are on duty. During the summer, five cliff dwellings may be visited at specific hours; during the winter there are trips to Spruce Tree House only, weather permitting. Obtain daily tickets for Cliff Palace, Balcony House, and Long House tours at Far View Visitor Center. Balcony House tours are limited to 50 persons; Cliff Palace tours are limited to the first 60; and Long House tours are limited to 40 persons. The cliff dwellings that are open to the public are

Balcony House. *Administration Building 15, Mesa Verde National Park. On Cliff Palace Loop Rd, 25-minute drive from visitor center. Phone 970/529-4461.* Noted for ladder and tunnel features; accessible only by a 32-foot-long ladder. Ranger-guided mid-May to mid-Oct. **$**

Cliff Palace. *Administration Building 15, Mesa Verde National Park. On Cliff Palace Loop Rd, 20-minute drive from the visitor center. Phone 970/529-4461.* First major dwelling to be discovered (1888). More than 200 living rooms, 23 kivas, numerous storage rooms. Guided tours in summer, fall, and spring; closed winter. **$**

Long and Step Houses and Badger House Community. *Administration Building 15, Mesa Verde National Park. On Wetherill Mesa, 12 miles from visitor center. Phone 970/529-4461.* Ranger-conducted (Long) and self-guided (Step) trips (Memorial Day-Labor Day); inquire at visitor center or museum for details.

Spruce Tree House. *Administration Building 15, Mesa Verde National Park. In canyon behind museum. Phone 970/529-4461.* Best preserved in Mesa Verde; contains 114 living rooms and eight ceremonial rooms, called kivas. Self-guided tour to site in summer; ranger-guided rest of year.

★ Far View Visitor Center. *Administration Building 15, Mesa Verde National Park. 15 miles S of park entrance. Phone 970/529-4461.* All visitors are recommended to stop at the center first. (May-Sept, daily)

Mesa Top Loop and Cliff Palace Loop. *Administration Building 15, Mesa Verde National Park. Enter at crossroads near museum. Phone 970/529-4461.* Two 6-mile, self-guided loops afford visits to ten excavated mesa-top sites illustrating 700 years of architectural development; views of 20 to 30 cliff dwellings from canyon rim vantage points. (Daily; closed during heavy snowfalls)

Museum. *Administration Building 15, Mesa Verde National Park. Park headquarters, 21 miles S of park entrance. Phone 970/529-4461.* Exhibits tell the story of the Mesa Verde people: their arts, crafts, industries. (Daily) **FREE**

Park Point Fire Lookout. *Administration Building 15, Mesa Verde National Park. Halfway between park entrance and headquarters. Phone 970/529-4461.* Elevation, 8,572 feet. Spectacular views of the entire Four Corners area of Colorado, Arizona, New Mexico, and Utah. Access road closed in winter.

Picnic areas. *Administration Bldg 15, Mesa Verde National Park. Phone 970/529-4461.* One at headquarters and one on each loop of Mesa Top Loop Rd.

Limited-Service Hotel

★★ FAR VIEW LODGE IN MESA VERDE. *1 Navajo Hill, Mile 15, Mesa Verde National Park (81328). Phone 970/529-4421; fax 970/533-7831.* View of canyon. 150 rooms, 2 story. Closed late Oct-mid-Apr. Pets accepted, some restrictions; fee. Check-out 11 am. Restaurant, bar. **$**

Minturn

Specialty Lodging

The following lodging establishment is approved by Mobil Travel Guide, but due to its unique and individualized nature has not been given a traditional Mobil Star rating. Included in this listing you may find bed-and-breakfasts, limited-service inns, guest ranches, and other unique hotel properties.

THE MINTURN INN. *442 Main St, Minturn (81645). Phone 970/827-9647; fax 970/827-5590.* 10 rooms. Check-in 3 pm, check-out noon. **$$**

Restaurants

★ CHILI WILLY'S. *101 Main St, Minturn (81645). Phone 970/827-5887; fax 970/926-0886. www.chiliwilly.com.* Rustic décor; casual atmosphere. Tex-Mex menu. Lunch, dinner. Closed Thanksgiving, Dec 25. Bar. Children's menu. Outdoor seating. **$$**

★ MINTURN COUNTRY CLUB. *131 Main St, Minturn (81645). Phone 970/827-4114.* American menu. Dinner. Closed Dec 25. Children's menu. **$$$**

Monte Vista (E-3)

See also Alamosa, South Fork

Population 4,529
Elevation 7,663 ft
Area Code 719
Zip 81144
Information Monte Vista Chamber of Commerce, 1035 Park Ave; phone 719/852-2731 or toll-free 800/562-7085
Web site www.monte-vista.org

Located in the heart of the high-altitude San Luis Valley, Monte Vista means "mountain view" in Spanish.

What to See and Do

Historical Society Headquarters. *110 Jefferson St, Monte Vista.* In 1875 library; information about history of Monte Vista. (Apr-Dec, Mon-Fri afternoons) **FREE**

Monte Vista National Wildlife Refuge. *9383 El Rancho Ln, Monte Vista. 6 miles S via Hwy 15. Phone 719/589-4021.* Created as a nesting, migration, and wintering habitat for waterfowl and other migratory birds. Marked visitor tour road. **FREE**

Special Events

Monte Vista Crane Festival. *Ski-Hi Park, 2345 Sherman Ave, Monte Vista. Phone 719/852-3552.* Tours of refuge to view cranes and other wildlife. Arts, crafts, workshops. Mid-Mar.

San Luis Valley Fair. *Ski-Hi Park, 2345 Sherman Ave, Monte Vista. Phone 719/589-2271.* Mid-Aug.

Ski-Hi Stampede. *Ski-Hi Park, 835 1st Ave, Monte Vista. Phone 719/852-2055.* Rodeo, carnival, arts and crafts show, street parade, barbecue, Western dances. Last weekend in July.

Limited-Service Hotels

★★ BEST WESTERN MOVIE MANOR. *2830 W Hwy 160, Monte Vista (81144). Phone 719/852-5921; toll-free 800/771-9468; fax 719/852-0122. www.bestwestern.com.* Drive-in movies visible from rooms; speakers in most rooms. 60 rooms, 2 story. Pets accepted, some restrictions; fee. Check-in noon, check-out 11 am. Restaurant, bar. **$**

★ **COMFORT INN.** *1519 Grand Ave, Monte Vista (81144). Phone 719/852-0612; fax 719/852-3585. www.comfortinn.com.* 44 rooms, 2 story. Pets accepted. Complimentary continental breakfast. Check-in noon, check-out 11 am. Indoor pool, whirlpool. **$**

Montrose (D-1)

See also Black Canyon of the Gunnison National Monument, Delta, Ouray

Founded 1882
Population 12,344
Elevation 5,806 ft
Area Code 970
Zip 81401
Information Montrose Chamber of Commerce, 1519 E Main St; 970/249-5000 or 800/923-5515
Web site www.montrosechamber.com

Montrose is a trading center for a rich mining, agricultural, and recreational area in the Uncompahgre Valley, irrigated by diversion of the waters of the Gunnison River to the Uncompahgre. It is headquarters for the operation and maintenance of all generating and transmission facilities of the Colorado River Storage Project stemming from the Power Operations Center. Several fishing areas are nearby, including the Gunnison River east of town and Buckhorn Lakes southeast. A Ranger District office of the Uncompahgre National Forest (see NORWOOD) is located in Montrose.

What to See and Do

Black Canyon of the Gunnison National Monument. *102 Elk Creek, Montrose. 12 miles NE via Hwy 50, Hwy 347. Phone 970/249-1914. www.nps.gov/blca.* (see)

Montrose County Historical Museum. *In Depot Building, 21 N Rio Grande, Montrose. Phone 970/249-2085.* Collections of antique farm machinery; archaeological artifacts; pioneer cabin with family items; tool collection; early electrical equipment; Montrose newspapers 1896-1940. (May-Sept, daily) **$**

Ridgway State Park. *28555 Hwy 550, Ridgway. 20 miles S on Hwy 550. Phone 970/626-5822.* This 2,320-acre park includes four recreational areas and a reservoir. Swimming, water-skiing, scuba diving, sailing, sailboarding, boating (marina); hiking, bicycling, cross-country skiing, sledding, picnicking, playground, improved camping, laundry, concession. (Daily) **$**

Scenic Drive. *Owl Creek Pass, Montrose. Drive 23 miles S on Hwy 550 to the left-hand turnoff for Owl Creek Pass, marked by a US Forest Service sign, then E 7 miles along Cow Creek to Debbie's Park.* In this meadow, Debbie Reynolds was filmed in the wild west breakfast scene in *How the West Was Won.* The next 8 miles, climb to the crest of Owl Creek Pass at 10,114 feet. Fifteen miles from the pass is Silver Jack Reservoir, an area with good fishing and scenic hiking trails. About 20 miles N, the road joins Hwy 50 at Cimarron. The road is not recommended for large trucks or RVs and may be impassable in inclement weather.

Ute Indian Museum and Ouray Memorial Park. *17253 Chipeta Dr, Montrose. 3 miles S on Hwy 550. Phone 970/249-3098.* On home grounds of Chief Ouray and his wife, Chipeta. History of the Utes in artifacts and objects of 19th- and early 20th-century Ute craftsmanship, clothing, dioramas, photographs. Self-guided tours. (Daily; Nov-May, Mon-Sat) **$$**

Limited-Service Hotel

★★ **BEST WESTERN RED ARROW.** *1702 E Main St, Montrose (81402). Phone 970/249-9641; toll-free 800/468-9323; fax 970/249-8380. www.bestwestern.com/redarrow.* 62 rooms, 2 story. Pets accepted; fee. Check-out 11 am. Restaurant. Fitness room. Pool, whirlpool. Airport transportation available. Business center. **$**

Restaurants

★★ **GLENN EYRIE RESTAURANT.** *2351 S Townsend Ave, Montrose (81401). Phone 970/249-9263; fax 970/240-6002.* American menu. Lunch, dinner. Closed Sun-Mon; Jan 1, July 4, Dec 25. Bar. Children's menu. Casual attire. **$$**

★ **WHOLE ENCHILADA.** *44 S Grand Ave, Montrose (81401). Phone 970/249-1881.* Mexican menu. Lunch, dinner. Closed Sun. Bar. Casual attire. Outdoor seating. **$**

Morrison

Web site www.town.morrison.co.us

What to See and Do

Red Rocks Park and Amphitheater. *16352 County Rd #93, Morrison. Phone 303/640-2637. www.redrocksonline.com.* Red Rocks Amphitheater is located in the majestic 816-acre Red Rocks Park, 15 miles west of Denver. Once the playground of dinosaurs, the naturally created open-air arena is formed by two 300-foot sandstone monoliths that serve as stadium walls. During the summer months, the 8,000-seat amphitheater, with its perfect acoustical conditions, awe-inspiring beauty, and panoramic view of Denver, serves as a stunning stage for performers ranging from chart-topping rock bands to world-renowned symphony orchestras. Call for schedules and to reserve tickets. Performance price varies. **FREE**

Nederland

Restaurant

★★ BLACK FOREST RESTAURANT. *24 Big Springs Dr, Central City (80466). Phone 303/279-2333; fax 303/258-3005.* German, seafood, steak menu. Lunch, dinner. Bar. Casual attire. **$$**

Norwood (D-1)

See also Telluride

Population 438
Elevation 7,006 ft
Area Code 970
Zip 81423
Web site www.norwoodcolorado.com

Near the edge of the Uncompahgre National Forest, this ranching community sits atop Wright's Mesa. This mesa and surrounding national forests contain a wide variety of wildlife that makes this one of the most popular hunting areas in Colorado.

What to See and Do

Miramonte Lake. *USFS Rd 610, Norwood. 18 miles SW.* Fishing, boating, windsurfing. Fishing also in San Miguel River, Gurley Lake, Ground Hog Reservoir, and nearby streams and mountain lakes. Inquire locally for information and permits.

Uncompahgre National Forest. *1150 Forest St, Norwood. N, E and S of town. Phone 970/327-4261.* More than 940,000 acres of alpine forest ranging in elevation from 7,500 to 14,000 feet, with many peaks higher than 13,000 feet. Fishing; hunting, hiking, picnicking, camping (fee at some campgrounds). Four-wheel drive areas. Snowmobiling, cross-country skiing. Within the forest are Big Blue and Mount Sneffles wilderness areas and portions of Lizard Head Wilderness Area. Also within the forest is a portion of the San Juan Skyway.

Special Event

San Miguel Basin Fair and Rodeo. *Fairgrounds, 1120 Summit, Norwood. Phone 970/327-4393.* Fair and rodeo. Last full weekend in July.

Ouray (D-2)

See also Montrose, Silverton

Settled 1876
Population 813
Elevation 7,811 ft
Area Code 970
Zip 81427
Information Ouray Chamber Resort Association, PO Box 145; phone 970/325-4746 or toll-free 800/228-1876
Web site www.ouraycolorado.com

The average 19th-century traveler found the gold and silver mines around Ouray of greater interest than the town's setting. In the 20th century, with the mining boom days over, Ouray's location in a natural basin surrounded by majestic 12,000- to 14,000-foot peaks of the San Juan Mountains has finally gained the appreciation of the visitor. Ouray, named for a Ute chief, is reached by the magnificent Million Dollar Highway section of the San Juan Skyway, which was blasted from sheer cliff walls high above the Uncompahgre River.

What to See and Do

Bachelor-Syracuse Mine Tour. *1222 County Rd 14, Ouray (81427). 1 mile N via Hwy 550, Dexter Creek Rd exit. Phone 970/325-0220.* Mine in continuous operation since 1884. Guided tour aboard a mine train, advances 3,350 feet horizontally into Gold Hill (mine temperature 47° F). Within the mine, visitors see mining equipment, visit work areas, and learn how explosives are used. Gold panning. Outdoor café. (Late May-Sept, daily; closed July 4) **$$$$**

Bear Creek Falls. *1230 Main, Box 145, Ouray. 3 miles S on Hwy 550. Phone 970/325-4746.* Road crosses a bridge over 227-foot falls; an observation point is nearby.

Box Cañon Falls Park. *Ouray. 1/2 mile S on Hwy 550. Phone 970/325-4464.* Canyon Creek has cut a natural canyon 20 feet wide, 400 feet deep. View of thundering falls from floor of canyon is reached by stairs and suspended bridge. Picnic tables are available in beautiful settings. Children must be accompanied by an adult. (Daily)

Fishing. *Ouray.* In lakes and streams. Hunting, riding, biking, hiking in surrounding mountains. Ski course with rope tow at edge of town; designed for children and beginners (free).

Hot Springs Pool. *Ouray City Park, 1200 Main, Phone 970/325-4638.* Outdoor, million-gallon pool fed by natural mineral hot springs; sulphur-free. Bathhouse; spa. (Daily) **$$**

Jeep trips. *710 Main, Ouray. Phone 970/325-4746.* Guides take visitors to ghost towns, mountain passes, and mines, many above the timberline; some full-day trips. (Mid-May-mid-Oct, daily) Also jeep rentals. **$$$$**

Ouray County Historical Museum. *420 6th Ave, Ouray. Phone 970/325-4576.* Former hospital constructed in 1887 now houses artifacts; mining, ranching, and Ute relics. (Daily) **$$**

Special Events

Artists' Alpine Holiday & Festival. *476 Main St, Ouray. Phone 970/626-3611.* National exhibit, competition in all media. One week in mid-Aug.

Imogene Pass Mountain Marathon. *100 5th St, Ouray. Phone 970/255-1002.* The 18-mile course starts at Ouray's 7,800-foot elevation, crosses over Imogene Pass (13,114 feet), and ends at Main St, Telluride (8,800 feet). Race route follows old mining trail. Sat after Labor Day.

Ouray County Fair & Rodeo. *Hwy 550 at 62, Ouray. 12 miles N in Ridgway.* Labor Day weekend.

Limited-Service Hotels

★ BOX CANYON LODGE & HOT SPRING. *45 Third Ave, Ouray (81427). Phone 970/325-4981; toll-free 800/327-5080; fax 970/325-0223. www.boxcanyonouray.com.* At the mouth of the canyon; scenic view. 38 rooms, 2 story. Check-in 3 pm, check-out 11 am. Outdoor pool, whirlpool. **$**

★ COMFORT INN. *191 5th Ave, Ouray (81427). Phone 970/325-7203; toll-free 800/438-5713; fax 970/325-4840. www.ouraycomfortinn.com.* Mountain views. 33 rooms, 2 story. Pets accepted. Complimentary continental breakfast. Check-in 2 pm, check-out 11 am. Whirlpool. **$**

Full-Service Inn

★★★ ST. ELMO HOTEL. *426 Main St, Ouray (81427). Phone 970/325-4951; fax 970/325-0348. www.stelmohotel.com.* The guest rooms at this restored 1898 hotel are individually decorated in Victorian style and feature period antiques. Guests can enjoy a wine and cheese social hour every afternoon in the parlor. 9 rooms, 2 story. Complimentary continental breakfast. Check-in 2 pm, check-out 11 am. Restaurant. Whirlpool. **$**

Specialty Lodgings

The following lodging establishments are approved by Mobil Travel Guide, but due to their unique and individualized nature have not been given a traditional Mobil Star rating. Included in this listing you may find bed-and-breakfasts, limited-service inns, guest ranches, and other unique hotel properties.

CHINA CLIPPER BED BREAKFAST INN. *525 2nd St, Ouray (81427). Phone 970/325-0565; toll-free 800/315-0565; fax 970/325-4190. www.chinaclipperinn.com.* No matter what the season, this property offers a relaxing experience. Each guest room has a view of the magnificent San Juan Mountains. Winter guests receive half-price coupons to the nearby million-gallon, natural Hot Springs Pool. 12 rooms, 2 story. Children over 15 years only. Complimentary continental breakfast. Check-in 2-7 pm, check-out 10:30 am. Whirlpool. **$**

DAMN YANKEE COUNTRY INN. *100 6th Ave, Ouray (81427). Phone 970/325-4219; toll-free 800/845-7512; fax 970/325-4339. www.damnyankeeinn.com.* This inn, complete with natural hot springs pool, is located in the San Juan Mountains. Rooms are furnished with ceiling fans, two-person whirlpools, and remote-controlled gas fireplaces. 10 rooms, 3 story. Children over 16 years only. Complimentary continental breakfast. Check-in 3-6 pm, check-out 11 am. Whirlpool. **$**

Restaurants

★★BON TON. *426 Main St, Ouray (81427). Phone 970/325-4951; fax 970/325-0348. www.stelmohotel.com.* Built in 1898. American, Italian menu. Dinner. Closed Dec 25. Bar. Children's menu. Casual attire. Outdoor seating. **$$$**

★BUEN TIEMPO. *515 Main St, Ouray (81427). Phone 970/325-4544; fax 970/325-0348. www.stelmohotel.com.* In 1891 building; originally a hotel. Mexican menu. Lunch, dinner. Closed Dec 25. Bar. Children's menu. Casual attire. Outdoor seating. **$$**

★CECILIA'S. *630 Main St, Ouray (81427). Phone 970/325-4223; fax 970/325-4208.* In vintage movie theater. American menu. Breakfast, lunch, dinner. Closed mid-Oct-mid-May. Children's menu. Casual attire. **$$**

Pagosa Springs (E-2)

Founded 1880
Population 1,207
Elevation 7,105 ft
Area Code 970
Zip 81147
Information Pagosa Springs Chamber of Commerce, 402 San Juan St, PO Box 787; phone 970/264-2360 or toll-free 800/252-2204
Web site www.pagosa-springs.com

These remarkable mineral springs (153° F) are used for bathing and to heat houses and buildings. Deer and elk hunting are popular activities. The town is surrounded by the San Juan National Forest (see DURANGO). A Ranger District office of the forest is located in Pagosa Springs.

What to See and Do

Chimney Rock Archaeological Area. *180 N Pagosa Blvd, Pagosa Springs. SE via Hwy 151. Phone 970/883-5359.* Area features twin pinnacles, held sacred by the Anasazi; Fire Tower, which offers a spectacular view of ruins; and Great House, which sits atop a mesa accessible only by a steep-walled narrow causeway. Guided tours only (four scheduled tours daily). **$$**

Fred Harman Art Museum. *2560 W Hwy 160, Pagosa Springs. 2 miles W on Hwy 160, across from junction Piedra Rd. Phone 970/731-5785.* Displays of original paintings by Fred Harman, Western artist and comic illustrator best remembered for his famous Red Ryder and Little Beaver comic strip. Also rodeo, movie, and Western memorabilia. (Late May-early Oct, daily; rest of year, Mon-Fri; closed July 4) **$$**

Navajo State Park. *Arboles, 1526 County Rd 982, Arboles. 17 miles W on Hwy 160, then 18 miles S on Hwy 151. Phone 970/883-2208.* Water-skiing, fishing, boating (ramps, rentals); picnicking (shelters), groceries, restaurant, camping (dump station). Visitor center. (Daily) **$**

Rocky Mountain Wildlife Park. *4821 Hwy 84, Pagosa Springs. 5 miles S on Hwy 84. Phone 970/264-4515.* Zoo exhibits animals indigenous to the area; wildlife museum; wildlife photography displays. (May-Nov, daily; rest of year, Mon-Tues, Thurs-Sat afternoons) **$$**

Wolf Creek Pass. *PO Box 2800, Pagosa Springs. 20 miles NE of Hwy 160 and Hwy 84. Phone 970/264-5639.* (10,857 feet) Scenic drive across the Continental Divide. The eastern approach is through the Rio Grande National Forest (see SOUTH FORK), the western approach through the San Juan National Forest (see DURANGO). Best time to drive through is Sept; spectacular views of aspens changing color. Drive takes approximately one hour. Nearby are

Treasure Mountain. *Pagosa Springs.* Begin at top of Wolf Creek Pass, just east of summit marked where Continental Divide Trail winds southward and connects with Treasure Mountain Trail. Legend states that in 1790, 300 men mined 5 million dollars in gold and melted it into bars, but were forced to leave it behind. The gold has never been found.

Wolf Creek Ski Area. *PO Box 2800, Pagosa Springs. 20 miles NE of Hwy 160 and Hwy 84. Phone 970/264-5629 (snow conditions and off-season).* Two triple, two double chairlifts; Pomalift; patrol, school, rentals; cafeteria, restaurant, bar, day lodge. Fifty runs; longest run 2 miles; vertical drop 1,425 feet. Shuttle bus service. (Early Nov-Apr, daily) **$$$$**

Special Event

Winter Fest. *Chamber of Commerce, 800 Goodnight Ave, Pagosa Springs. Phone 970/264-2360.* Winter carnival, individual and team events for all ages. Early Feb.

Limited-Service Hotel

★ ★ BEST VALUE HIGH COUNTRY LODGE. *3821 E Hwy 160, Pagosa Springs (81147). Phone 800/862-3707; toll-free 800/862-3707; fax 970/264-4185. www.highcountrylodge.com.* 35 rooms, 2 story. Pets accepted; fee. Complimentary continental breakfast. Check-in 2:30 pm, check-out 11 am. Restaurant. Whirlpool. **$**

Full-Service Resort

★★PAGOSA LODGE. *3505 W Hwy 160, Pagosa Springs (81147). Phone 970/731-4141; toll-free 800/523-7704; fax 970/731-4343. www.pagosalodge.com.* 101 rooms, 3 story. Check-in 4 pm, check-out 11 am. Restaurant, bar. Indoor pool, whirlpool. Airport transportation available. **$**

Restaurant

★ ★ TEQUILA'S. *439 San Juan St, Pagosa Springs (81157). Phone 970/264-2175; fax 970/264-6149.* Mexican menu. Lunch, dinner. Children's menu. Casual attire. Outdoor seating. **$**

Palisade (C-1)

Web site www.palisadecoc.com

Special Events

Colorado Mountain Winefest. *319 Main St, Palisade. 12 miles E of Grand Junction, exit 42 or 44 off of I-70. Phone 970/464-7458. www.coloradowinefest.com.* For a taste of Colorado's softer side, plan a visit to the Western Slopes region east of Grand Junction, where numerous wineries have established themselves on the gentle hills between Grand Rapids and Glenwood Springs. At the heart of Colorado's wine country is the charming valley town of Palisade, home of the annual Colorado Mountain Winefest. This colorful weekend harvest celebration in mid-September begins on a Friday with elaborate harvest banquets served at several area restaurants. The next morning, riders embark on a 25-mile bicycle tour thorough the region while winemakers and wine lovers converge for the lively Festival in the Park. As wineries from throughout Colorado present their favorite vintages for sampling, festivalgoers enjoy food, music, contests, demonstrations, and a chance to try their hand (or toes) at grape-stomping. The festival concludes with a wine-tasting tour of the Grand Valley vineyards. Many of the larger wineries are open for tours year-round. For a listing of local wineries and tour hours, contact the Palisades Chamber of Commerce. Mid-Sept, Fri-Sun. **$$$$**

Pueblo (D-4)

See also Cañon City, Colorado Springs

Settled 1842
Population 102,121
Elevation 4,695 ft
Area Code 719
Information Chamber of Commerce, PO Box 697, 81002; phone 719/542-1704; or the Pueblo Visitors Information Center, 302 N Santa Fe Ave, 81003. The Visitors Information Center is open daily.
Web site www.pueblo.org

Pueblo began as a crossroad for Native Americans, Spaniards, and fur traders. When the Rio Grande Railroad reached here in 1872, Pueblo was the leading center for steel and coal production west of the Mississippi. Today, Pueblo is a major transportation and industrial center; more than half of all goods manufactured in Colorado are produced in Pueblo.

What to See and Do

City parks. *Pueblo.* Approximately 700 acres of parks within city. Two of the largest are

City Park. *Pueblo Blvd and Goodnight Ave, Pueblo. Phone 719/542-1704.* Swimming pool (Memorial Day-Labor Day, daily; fee), children's fishing; 9-hole, 18-hole golf and driving range (fee); tennis, picnicking, zoo (fee); herds of wildlife, children's farm, Eco Center, Rainforest. Historical carousel area (Memorial Day-Labor Day, daily; fee). Thirty-five-mile river trail system. Park (daily). **FREE**

Mineral Palace Park. *1500 N Santa Fe, Pueblo. Phone 719/566-1745.* Swimming pool (fee), children's fishing; picnicking. Rose garden, greenhouse. Pueblo Art Guild Gallery with local artists exhibits (Sat-Sun; closed Dec-Feb). **FREE**

El Pueblo Museum. *324 W First St, Pueblo. Phone 719/583-0453.* Full-size replica of Old Fort Pueblo, which served as a base for fur traders and other settlers from 1842-1855. Exhibits on the Anasazi, steel and ore production, and narrow-gauge railroads. (Daily; closed Thanksgiving, Dec 25) **$$**

Fred E. Weisbrod Aircraft Museum. *Pueblo Memorial Airport, 31001 Magnuson Ave, Pueblo. Phone 719/948-3355.* Outdoor museum features static aircraft display. Adjacent is the B-24 Aircraft Memorial Museum, with indoor displays of the history of the B-24 bomber. Guided tours. (Daily; closed holidays) **$$**

Lake Isabel. *Pueblo. 43 miles SW via I-25, Hwy 165 or 32 miles SW on Hwy 76.* This 310-acre recreation area offers fishing, boating (no motors), picnicking, and camping. No swimming is permitted.

Lake Pueblo State Park. *640 Pueblo Reservoir Rd, Pueblo. 6 miles W via Hwy 96 or Hwy 50 W. Phone 719/561-9320.* Swimming, water-skiing, boating; hiking, camping (dump station). (Daily) **$**

Rosemount Victorian House Museum. *419 W 14th St, Pueblo. Phone 719/545-5290.* This 37-room mansion contains original Victorian furnishings and the McClelland Collection of world curiosities. (Tues-Sun; closed holidays; also Jan) **$$$**

Sangre de Cristo Arts and Conference Center. *210 N Santa Fe Ave, Pueblo. Phone 719/295-7200.* Four art galleries include the Francis King Collection of Western Art on permanent display; changing art exhibits; children's museum, workshops, dance studios, theater; gift shop. (Mon-Sat; closed holidays) **$**

San Isabel National Forest. *2840 Kachina Dr, Pueblo. NW and W via Hwy 50. Phone 719/545-8737.* On 1,109,782 acres. Three sections of forest lie adjacent to this highway with picnicking, camping, and two winter sports areas: Monarch and Ski Cooper. In the southern part of the forest is the Spanish Peaks National Natural Landmark. Collegiate Peaks, Mount Massive, and Holy Cross Wilderness areas are also within the forest, as well as four wilderness study areas. Colorado's highest peak, Mount Elbert (14,433 feet), is within the forest south of Leadville (see). Also in the forest is

The Greenway and Nature Center of Pueblo. *5200 Nature Center Rd, Pueblo. 5 miles W via Hwy 50. Phone 719/549-2414.* Small reptile exhibit and Raptor Center, special nature programs (by appointment). Also 36 miles of hiking and biking trails (rentals). Café. (Tues-Sun; closed Jan 1, Thanksgiving, Dec 25)

University of Southern Colorado. *2200 Bonforte Blvd, Pueblo. Phone 719/549-2461.* (1975) (4,000 students) Developed from Pueblo Junior College established in 1933. Chemistry Building has Geological Museum with mineral, rock, and fossil exhibits, maps (academic year, Mon-Fri; closed holidays; free). Campus tours (Mon-Fri, by appointment), contact Admissions Office, Administration Building.

Special Events

Colorado State Fair. *Fairgrounds, 1001 Beulah Ave, Pueblo. Phone 719/561-8484; toll-free 800/444-3247.* PRCA rodeo, grandstand and amphitheater entertainment, livestock and agricultural displays, industrial and high technology displays, home arts, fine arts and crafts, carnival. Aug-Sept.

Pueblo Greyhound Park. *3215 Lake Ave, Pueblo. S on I-25. Phone 719/566-0370.* Pari-mutuel betting. Satellite betting Apr-Sept. Live racing Oct-Mar.

Limited-Service Hotels

★★ **BEST WESTERN INN AT PUEBLO WEST.** *201 S McCulloch Blvd, Pueblo West (81007). Phone 719/547-2111; toll-free 800/448-1972; fax 719/547-0385. www.bestwestern.com/innatpueblow.* 79 rooms, 2 story. Pets accepted; fee. Check-out 11 am. Restaurant. Fitness room. Pool. **$**

★ **DAYS INN.** *4201 N Elizabeth, Pueblo (81008). Phone 719/543-8031; fax 719/546-1317. www.daysinn.com.* 58 rooms, 2 story. Complimentary continental breakfast. Check-out 11 am. Fitness room. Indoor pool, whirlpool. **$**

★★ **HOLIDAY INN.** *4001 N Elizabeth St, Pueblo (81008). Phone 719/543-8050; fax 719/545-2271. www.holiday-inn.com.* 193 rooms, 2 story. Check-out 11 am. Restaurant, bar. Fitness room. Indoor pool, whirlpool. Airport transportation available. Business center. **$**

Full-Service Hotel

★★★ **MARRIOTT PUEBLO CONVENTION CENTER.** *110 W First St, Pueblo (81003). Phone 719/542-3200; fax 719/542-3226. www.marriott.com.* 164 rooms, 7 story. Check-in 3 pm, check-out noon. Restaurant, bar. Fitness room. Indoor pool, whirlpool. Business center. **$$**

Full-Service Inn

★★★ **ABRIENDO INN.** *300 W Abriendo Ave, Pueblo (81004). Phone 719/544-2703; fax 719/542-6544.* Built in 1906. 10 rooms, 3 story. Children over 6 years only. Complimentary full breakfast. Check-in 3:30-9 pm, check-out 11 am. **$**

Restaurants

★★ **CAFE DEL RIO.** *5200 Nature Center Rd, Pueblo (81003). Phone 719/549-2029; fax 719/549-2547.* Scenic view of Arkansas river; adobe building built by volunteers. Southwestern menu. Lunch, dinner, Sun brunch. Closed Mon. Children's menu. Outdoor seating. **$$**

★★ **GAETANO'S.** *910 Hwy 50 W, Pueblo City (81008). Phone 719/546-0949; fax 719/546-1636.* Italian, American menu. Lunch, dinner. Closed Sun; Jan 1, Dec 25. Bar. Children's menu. Casual attire. Outdoor seating. **$$**

★★ **LA MELA DI ANGELO.** *123 N Main St, Pueblo (81003). Phone 719/253-7700.* Serving family-style regional Italian cuisine. Lunch, dinner. **$**

★★★ **LA RENAISSANCE.** *217 E Routt Ave, Pueblo (81004). Phone 719/543-6367; fax 719/543-6374.* Church built in 1886; garden room. French menu. Dinner. Closed Sun; holidays. Bar. **$$**

★★ **PATTI'S RESTAURANT.** *241 S Santa Fe, Pueblo (81003). Phone 719/543-2371. www.pattisonline.com.* The oldest continually running restaurant in Pueblo, Patti's has been a local favorite for more than 65 years. American menu. Breakfast, lunch, dinner. Closed Mon-Tues. **$**

Rocky Mountain National Park (B-3)

See also Estes Park, Granby, Grand Lake, Loveland, Lyons

Web site www.nps.gov/romo

Park headquarters is 3 miles W of Estes Park on Hwy 36; western entrance at Grand Lake.

More than 100 years ago, Joel Estes built a cabin on Fish Creek, one of the higher sections of north-central Colorado. Although the Estes family moved away, more settlers soon followed, and the area became known as Estes Park. Described by Albert Bierstadt, one of the great 19th-century landscape artists of the West, as America's finest composition for the painter, the land west of where Estes settled was set aside as Rocky Mountain National Park in 1915.

Straddling the Continental Divide, with valleys 8,000 feet in elevation and 114 named peaks more than 10,000 feet high, the 415-square-mile park contains a staggering profusion of peaks, upland meadows, sheer canyons, glacial streams, and lakes. Dominating the scene is Longs Peak, with its east face towering 14,255 feet above sea level. The park's forests and meadows provide sanctuary for more than 750 varieties of wildflowers, more than 260 species of birds, and such indigenous mammals as deer, wapiti (American elk), bighorn sheep, beaver, and other animals. There are five campgrounds, two of which take reservations from May to early Sept (fee; write to Destinet, 9450 Carroll Park Dr, San Diego CA, 92121-2256; phone 800/365-2267). Some attractions are not accessible during the winter months. $10 per car per week; Golden Eagle Passports are accepted (see MAKING THE MOST OF YOUR TRIP). Contact the Superintendent, Rocky Mountain National Park, Estes Park 80517-8397; phone 970/586-1206.

What to See and Do

Bear Lake Road. *Rocky Mountain National Park.* Scenic drive (plowed in winter months) into high mountain basin is rimmed with precipitous 12,000- to 14,000-foot peaks. At end of the road, the self-guided nature trail circles Bear Lake. Other trails lead to higher lakes, gorges, glaciers. Bus service (summer).

★ **Headquarters Building.** *Just outside the E entrance station on Hwy 36 approach. Rocky Mountain National Park.* Information (publications sales, maps); program on park (daily); guided walks and illustrated evening programs (summer only; daily).

Moraine Park Museum. *1 mile inside the park from the Beaver Meadows entrance. Rocky Mountain National Park.* Exhibits, information, publications sales, maps. (May-Sept, daily)

Never Summer Ranch. *10 miles N of the Grand Lake entrance on Trail Ridge Rd. Rocky Mountain National Park. Phone 970/627-3471.* Historic pioneer homestead and preserved 1920s dude ranch. (Weather permitting, mid-June-Labor Day, daily)

Trail Ridge Road. *Between Grand Lake and Estes Park in Rocky Mountain National Park. Phone 970/586-1363. www.coloradobyways.org.* Among the most scenic drives in Colorado is the Trail Ridge Road between Grand Lake and Estes Park. Winding through 53 miles of beautiful alpine forest and tundra in the heart of Rocky Mountain National Park, the road reaches an elevation of 12,183 feet to offer stunning vistas of the southern Rockies. In mid-July, wildflowers blanket the tundra, while elk, deer, mountain sheep, and moose are often seen along the route. The drive without stopping takes approximately two hours, but the experience would be lost without stops to take in the views or explore the numerous hiking paths along the way.

Salida (C-3)

See also Buena Vista

Founded 1880
Population 5,504
Elevation 7,036 ft
Area Code 719
Zip 81201
Information Heart of the Rockies Chamber of Commerce, 406 W US 50; phone 719/539-2068
Web site www.salidachamber.org

On the eastern slope of the Rocky Mountains, Salida is a town surrounded by San Isabel National Forest (see PUEBLO). A pleasant climate (thus Salida's nickname "the banana belt") makes Salida ideal for recreational activities throughout the year, including river rafting, fishing, mountain biking, hiking, and hunting.

What to See and Do

The Angel of Shavano. *Salida.* Every spring the snow melts on the 14,239-foot slopes of Mount Shavano leaving an outline called "The Angel."

Arkansas Headwaters State Recreation Area. *307 W Sackett, Salida. Hwys 24, 285, and 50. Phone 719/539-7289.* An area of 5,000 acres, with an outstanding waterway that cuts its way through rugged canyons for 148 miles, from Leadville to Pueblo. One of the world's premier waterways for kayaking and white-water rafting; fishing, boating (ramps); hiking, bridle trails; picnicking, camping. Interpretive programs. (Daily) **$**

Jeep tours. *Chamber of Commerce, 406 W Rainbow Blvd, Salida.* To mountainous areas inaccessible by car, over trails, old railroad beds. Outfitters offer half-hour, half-day, and full-day trail rides; fishing, hunting, photography, and pack trips. Contact Chamber of Commerce for details.

Monarch Ski & Snowboard Area. *1 Powder Pl, Monarch. 18 miles W on Hwy 50 at Monarch Pass (11,312 feet). Phone 719/539-3573 (lodge); toll-free 888/996-7669 (ski administration) or 800/228-7943 (recorded information).* Four double chairlifts; patrol, school, rentals; cafeteria, restaurant, bar, nursery. Fifty-four runs; longest run 2 miles; vertical drop 1,160 feet. Multiday, half-day rates. (Mid-Nov-mid-Apr, daily) Cross-country skiing. **$$$$**

Mountain Spirit Winery. *201 F St, Salida. 13 miles W of Salida on Hwy 50. Phone 719/539-1175.* Family-operated boutique winery. Five acres with apple orchard, homestead. Tours, tastings (Memorial Day-Labor Day, weekends). **FREE**

Mount Shavano Fish Hatchery. *Salida. 1/2 mile W on Hwy 291, Hwy 50. Phone 719/539-6877.* State-operated hatchery. (Daily)

Salida Museum. *Hwy 50 at I St, Salida. Phone 719/539-7483.* Museum features mineral display, Native American artifacts, early pioneer household display, mining and railroad display. (Late May-early Sept, daily) **$$**

Tenderfoot Drive. *Salida. W on Hwy 291.* Spiral drive encircling Mount Tenderfoot. Views of the surrounding mountain area and the upper Arkansas Valley.

Special Events

Artwalk. *Downtown Historic District, 406 W Rainbow Blvd, Salida.* Local artisans, craftspeople, and entertainers display artwork. Last weekend in June.

Chaffee County Fair. *10165 County Rd 120, Poncha Springs. Phone 719/539-6151.* Five days beginning the last weekend in July.

Christmas Mountain USA. *406 W Rainbow Blvd, Salida. Phone 719/539-2068.* Three-day season opener; more than 3,500 lights outline a 700-foot Christmas tree on Tenderfoot Mountain; parade. Day after Thanksgiving.

FIBArk River International Whitewater Boat Race. *240 N F St, Salida. Phone 719/539-7997.* International experts compete in a 26-mile kayak race. Other events include slalom, raft, foot, and bicycle races. Father's Day weekend.

Specialty Lodging

The following lodging establishment is approved by Mobil Travel Guide, but due to its unique and individualized nature has not been given a traditional Mobil Star rating. Included in this listing you may find bed-and-breakfasts, limited-service inns, guest ranches, and other unique hotel properties.

TUDOR ROSE BED & BREAKFAST. *6720 County Rd 104, Salida (81201). Phone 719/539-2002; toll-free 800/379-0889; fax 719/530-0345. www.thetudorrose.com.* 6 rooms, 3 story. Children over 10 years only. Complimentary full breakfast. Check-in 4 pm, check-out 11 am. Whirlpool. **$**

Restaurants

★★ COUNTRY BOUNTY. *413 W Rainbow Blvd, Salida (81201). Phone 719/539-3546; fax 719/539-6792. www.countrybounty.net.* American menu. Breakfast, lunch, dinner. Closed Thanksgiving, Dec 24-25. Children's menu. Casual attire. **$**

★ WINDMILL. *720 E Rainbow Blvd, Salida (81201). Phone 719/539-3594; fax 719/539-3479.* American menu. Lunch, dinner. Closed Thanksgiving, Dec 25. Bar. Children's menu. Casual attire. **$**

Silverton (E-1)

See also Durango, Ouray

Settled 1874
Population 531
Elevation 9,318 ft
Area Code 970
Zip 81433
Information Silverton Chamber of Commerce, 414 Greene St; phone 970/387-5654 or toll-free 800/752-4494
Web site www.silverton.org

"The mining town that never quit" sits in the San Juan Mountains with other communities that provide reminders of Colorado's mining history; the last mine in Silverton closed in 1991. Tourists have now discovered the natural beauty, historic ghost towns, and many recreational opportunities of the area.

What to See and Do

Circle Jeep Tour. *414 Greene St, Silverton. Phone 970/387-5654; toll-free 800/752-4494.* Mapped Jeep route with historical information to many mines and ghost towns. **$**

Old Hundred Gold Mine Tour. *721 County Rd 4 A, Silverton. 5 miles E via Hwy 110. Phone 970/387-5444; toll-free 800/872-3009.* Guided one-hour tour of underground mine offers view of mining equipment, crystal pockets, veins; learn about methods of hardrock mining. (Memorial Day-Sept, daily). **$$$$**

Red Mountain Pass. *Hwy 550 between Ouray and Silverton.* Traveling through the towering San Juan Mountains, the 23-mile stretch of Hwy 550 between Ouray and Silverton passes through some of Colorado's wildest country. Traversing numerous gorges, past cascading falls and tunnels, the road rises to 11,075 feet to cross the Red Mountain Pass, a favorite spot for hikers, rock climbers, mountain bikers, and backcountry ski enthusiasts. Abandoned log cabins and mining equipment still visible from the roadside are evidence of the region's history. Weather permitting.

San Juan County Historical Society Museum. *1315 Snowden, Silverton. 5 miles E via Hwy 110. Phone 970/387-5838.* Located in an old three-story jail. Mining and railroad artifacts from Silverton's early days. (Memorial Day-mid-Oct, daily) **$$**

Special Events

Brass Band Festival. *Phone toll-free 800/752-4497.* Mid-Aug.

Hardrockers Holiday. *Phone toll-free 800/752-4497.* Mining skills competition. Mid-Aug.

Iron Horse Bicycle Classic. *346 S Camino Del Rio, Durango. Phone 970/259-4621.* Bicycles race the Silverton narrow-gauge train. Late May.

Silverton Jubilee Folk Music Festival. *Silverton. Phone 970/387-5737.* Late June.

Full-Service Inn

★★ **WYMAN HOTEL.** *1371 Greene St, Silverton (81433). Phone 970/387-5372; toll-free 800/609-7845; fax 970/387-5745. www.silverton.org/wymanhotel.* Built in 1902. Victorian furnishings. 17 rooms, 2 story. Closed late Mar-early May, mid-Oct-mid-Dec. Pets accepted, some restrictions; fee. Complimentary continental breakfast. Check-in 3-8 pm, check-out 11 am. Restaurant. **$**

Specialty Lodging

The following lodging establishment is approved by Mobil Travel Guide, but due to its unique and individualized nature has not been given a traditional Mobil Star rating. Included in this listing you may find bed-and-breakfasts, limited-service inns, guest ranches, and other unique hotel properties.

ALMA HOUSE BED AND BREAKFAST. *220 E 10th St, Silverton (81433). Phone 970/387-5336; toll-free 800/267-5336; fax 970/387-5974.* Built in 1898. Victorian furnishings. 9 rooms, 2 story. Check-in 3 pm, check-out 11 am. Whirlpool. **$**

Snowmass Village (C-2)

See also Aspen, Glenwood Springs

Population 1,822
Elevation 8,604 ft
Area Code 970
Zip 81615
Information Snowmass Resort Association, 38 Village Square, PO Box 5566; phone 970/923-2000 or toll-free 800/766-9627
Web site www.snowmassvillage.com

All facilities of Snowmass Village are available to guests of the accommodations listed below. Year-round: nearly 50 outdoor heated pools and hot tubs, saunas. Children's and teen programs; sitter list. Convention facilities. More than 20 restaurants in village; bars. Free shuttle bus throughout village; local airport transportation. Summer: fishing (license, equipment available). Rafting, hiking, horseback riding, 18-hole golf, tennis (fees for all); jeep and bicycle tours; hot-air balloon rides. Winter: skiing (beginner-to-expert runs), instruction; cross-country skiing, barbecue sleigh rides, dogsled tours, guided snowshoe tours; swimming, indoor tennis.

What to See and Do

Bicycle trips and Jeep trips. *105 Snowmass Village Mall, Snowmass Village. Phone 970/923-4544.* Throughout the Snowmass/Aspen area. Transportation and equipment provided. (June-Sept) **$$$$**

Krabloonik Husky Kennels. *4250 Divide Rd, Snowmass Village. 5 miles SW of Hwy 82. Phone 970/923-3953.*

Half-day dog-sled trips by reservation (Dec-Apr). Kennel tours (mid-June-Sept, Mon-Sat). **$$$$**

River rafting. *Snowmass Whitewater. 70 Snowmass Village Mall, Snowmass Village. Phone 970/923-4544.* Half-day, full-day, and overnight trips on the Arkansas, Roaring Fork, Colorado, Gunnison, and Dolores rivers. Trips range from scenic floats for beginners to exciting runs for experienced rafters. (May-Oct daily, depending on snow melt) Transportation to site. **$$$$**

Snowmass Ski Area. *40 Carriage Way, Snowmass Village. Phone 970/923-1220. www.aspensnowmass .com.* Seven quad, two triple, six double chairlifts; two platter pulls; patrol, school, rentals, snowmaking; restaurants, bar, nursery. Eighty-three runs; longest run 5 miles, vertical drop 4,406 feet. Cross-country skiing (50 miles). Shuttle bus service from Aspen. (Late Nov-mid-Apr, daily) **$$$$**

Limited-Service Hotels

★ ★ STONEBRIDGE INN. *P O Box 5008, Snowmass Village (81615). Phone 970/923-2420; toll-free 800/213-3214; fax 970/923-5889. www. stonebridgeinn.com.* 92 rooms, 7 story. Closed mid-Apr-May. Complimentary continental breakfast. Check-in 4 pm, check-out 10 am. Restaurant. Fitness room. Outdoor pool, children's pool, whirlpool. Airport transportation available. **$$**

★ ★ WILDWOOD LODGE. *40 Elbert Ln, Snowmass Village (81615). Phone 970/923-3550; toll-free 800/445-1642; fax 970/923-4844. www. wildwood-lodge.com.* 140 rooms, 3 story. Closed early Apr-May. Pets accepted, some restrictions. Complimentary continental breakfast. Check-in 4 pm, check-out 11 am. Restaurant. Children's activity center. Outdoor pool, children's pool, whirlpool. Airport transportation available. **$$**

Full-Service Resorts

★ ★ ★ SILVERTREE HOTEL SNOWMASS VILLAGE. *100 Elbert Ln, Snowmass Village (81615). Phone 970/923-3520; toll-free 800/837-4255; fax 970/923-5792. www.silvertreehotel.com.* This year-round mountain resort provides skiing right from the hotel with over 5,000 acres of ski area. Summer brings balloon rides, hiking and jazz concerts. 260 rooms, 7 story. Pets accepted, some restrictions. Check-out 11 am. Restaurant. Children's activity center. Fitness room. Outdoor pool, children's pool, whirlpool. Airport transportation available. Business center. **$$$**

★ ★ ★ SNOWMASS CLUB. *0239 Snowmass Club Cir, Snowmass Village (81615). Phone 970/923-5600; toll-free 800/525-0710; fax 970/923-6944. www. snowmassclub.com.* This year-round resort is located in the Elk Mountain range area. 55 rooms, 4 story. Check-in 4 pm, check-out 10 am. Restaurant. Children's activity center. Fitness room, spa. Two outdoor pools, children's pool, whirlpool. Golf. Tennis. Airport transportation available. Business center. **$$$$**

Restaurants

★ ★ ★ KRABLOONIK. *4250 Divide Rd, Snowmass Village (81615). Phone 970/923-3953; fax 970/923-0246. www.krabloonik.com.* This casual, elegant restaurant has a rustic décor and panoramic views of the mountains. American, seafood menu. Lunch, dinner. Closed mid-Apr-May, Oct-Thanksgiving. Children's menu. Casual attire. Reservations recommended. **$$$**

★ ★ ★ SAGE. *239 Snowmass Cir, Snowmass Village (81615). Phone 970/923-0923; fax 970/923-6944.* In the summer, the patio offers unobstructed views of Mount Daly. Contemporary American menu. Breakfast, lunch, dinner. Bar. Children's menu. Valet parking. Outdoor seating. **$$$**

★ ★ TOWER. *45 Village Sq, Snowmass Village (81615). Phone 970/923-4650; fax 970/923-4651.* Casual mountain-lodge décor; view of mountains. American, seafood menu. Lunch, dinner. Bar. Children's menu. Outdoor seating. **$$**

South Fork (D-2)

See also Monte Vista

Population 604
Elevation 8,200 ft
Area Code 719
Zip 81154
Information South Fork Visitors Center, PO Box 1030; phone 719/873-5512 or toll-free 800/571-0881
Web site www.southfork.org

Located at Wolf Creek Pass along Hwy 160 in the heart of the San Juan Mountains, this resort community is popular for skiing, snowmobiling, biking, camping, hiking, fishing, and rafting, and for the Jeep trails in the surrounding area. The Silver Thread National Scenic Byway, a 75-mile drive, begins here and travels through the spectacular scenery of the Continental Divide, ending at Lake City (see).

What to See and Do

Rio Grande National Forest. *1803 Hwy 160 W, South Fork. Phone 719/852-5941.* This rugged forest surrounding the San Luis Valley includes Wolf Creek Pass (10,850 feet) (see PAGOSA SPRINGS). Within the forest is the rugged Sangre de Cristo backcountry and parts of Weminuche, South San Juan, and La Garita wildernesses. Fishing, boating; hunting, hiking, downhill and cross-country skiing, snowmobiling, picnicking, camping. In the forest is

Creede. *South Fork. 22 miles NW on Hwy 149.* (Pop 653) Frontier mining town.

Special Events

Creede Repertory Theater. *124 N Main St, Creede. 21 miles NW on Hwy 149 in Creede. Phone 719/658-2540.* Classic and modern comedies, drama, musicals. Advance reservations suggested. Nightly Tues-Sun; also Wed and Fri afternoons; children's matinee Sat in Aug. Early June-Labor Day.

Logger Days Festival. *South Fork.* Logging competition, crafts, food, music. Third weekend in July.

Steamboat Springs (A-2)

See also Craig

Settled 1875
Population 9,815
Elevation 6,695 ft
Area Code 970
Zip 80477
Information Steamboat Springs Chamber Resort Association, PO Box 774408; phone 970/879-0880 or toll-free 800/922-2722
Web site www.steamboat.com

Before the Ute retreated into Utah, Steamboat Springs was originally their summer home. The area's first white settlers were ranchers. Coal mining also became a very viable industry. Skiing and Norwegian-style ski-jumping came to this area with the arrival of the Norseman Carl Howelsen in 1913, becoming two of the most popular winter sports in the area. Ten national ski-jumping records have been set on Steamboat Springs's Howelsen Hill; the area has produced 47 winter Olympians, which has helped earn it the name of "Ski Town USA." Summer activities include camping, fishing, hot-air ballooning, horseback riding, hiking, bicycling, river rafting, canoeing, and llama trekking. One of the largest elk herds in North America ranges near the town. There are more than 100 natural hot springs in the area. The headquarters and access routes to Routt National Forest are in or near Steamboat Springs.

What to See and Do

Howelsen Hill Ski Complex. *245 Howelsen Pkwy, Steamboat Springs. Off Hwy 40 on River Rd via 5th St bridge. Phone 970/879-4300.* International ski/jump complex includes a double chairlift, Pomalift, rope tow, five ski jumping hills; patrol; ice skating, snowboarding. Evening skiing available. (Dec-Mar, daily) Also summer activities. **$$$$**

Routt National Forest. *925 Weiss Dr, Steamboat Springs. Phone 970/879-1722.* More than 1 million acres include the 139,898-acre Mount Zirkel Wilderness and 38,870 acres of the 235,230-acre Flat Tops Wilderness. Fishing; hunting, winter sports area, hiking, picnicking, camping.

Scenic drives. *Steamboat Springs.* The following drives are accessible in summer and are well-maintained paved and gravel-surfaced roads. Impressive view of the valley and Howelsen Ski Complex. **Fish Creek Falls** (283 feet) 3 miles E. Picnic area. **Buffalo Pass** (10,180 feet) 15 miles NE. Impressive road atop Continental Divide leading to formerly inaccessible trout-filled lakes. **Rabbit Ears Pass** (9,680 feet) 22 miles SE. Additional information available at information centers.

Steamboat. *2305 Mount Werner Cir, Steamboat Springs. 3 miles E on Hwy 40. Phone 970/879-6111; toll-free 800/922-2722. www.steamboat.com.* High-speed gondola; four high-speed quad (two covered), quad, six triple, seven double chairlifts; two surface tows; patrol, school, rentals, snowmaking; cafeterias, restaurants, bars, nursery. One hundred forty-two runs; longest run more than 3 miles; vertical drop 3,668 feet. Snowboarding. Cross-country skiing (14 miles). Multiday, half-day rates. (Late Nov-early Apr, daily) Gondola also operates mid-June-mid-Sept (daily; fee). **$$$$**

Steamboat Health & Recreation Association. *136 Lincoln Ave, Steamboat Springs. E end of town. Phone 970/879-1828.* Three hot pools fed by 103° F mineral water; lap pool, saunas, exercise classes, massage, weight room, tennis courts (summer). (Daily) **$$$** Also here is

Hot Slide Hydrotube. *136 Lincoln Ave, Steamboat Springs. Phone 970/879-1828.* Tube slide with 350 feet of hot water. (Daily) **$$$**

Steamboat Lake State Park. *61855 Routt County Rd 129, Steamboat Springs. 26 miles N on County 129. Phone 970/879-3922.* Swimming, water-skiing, fishing, boating (ramps); picnicking, camping. (Daily) **$**

Strawberry Park Natural Hot Springs. *44200 County Rd 36, Steamboat Springs. 7 miles NE. Phone 970/879-0342.* Mineral springs feed four pools; water cooled from 160° F to 105° F. Changing area; picnicking, camping, cabins. (Daily)

Tread of Pioneers Museum. *800 Oak St, Steamboat Springs. Phone 970/879-2214.* Victorian house with period rooms and furnishings. Pioneer and cattle-ranching artifacts, Native American displays, permanent ski exhibit tracing the evolution of skiing. (Fall/spring, Tues-Sat; summer/winter, Mon-Sat) **$$**

Special Events

Cowboy Roundup Days. *Steamboat Springs.* Rodeos, parade, entertainment. July 4 weekend.

Mustang Round-Up. *Steamboat Springs.* Mid-June.

Rainbow Weekend. *Steamboat Springs.* Balloon rally, arts and crafts fair, concerts, rodeo. Mid-July.

Winter Carnival. *Steamboat Springs.* Snow and ski competitions, parade. Early Feb.

Limited-Service Hotels

★★ BEST WESTERN PTARMIGAN INN. *2304 Apres Ski Way, Steamboat Springs (80477). Phone 970/879-1730; toll-free 800/538-7519; fax 970/879-6044. www.steamboat-lodging.com.* View of Mount Werner, valley. 77 rooms, 4 story. Closed early Apr-late May. Pets accepted, some restrictions; fee. Check-in 4 pm, check-out 10 am. Restaurant, bar. Outdoor pool, whirlpool. **$**

★ FAIRFIELD INN BY MARRIOTT. *3200 S Lincoln Ave, Steamboat Springs (80477). Phone 970/870-9000; toll-free 800/228-2800; fax 970/870-9191.* 66 rooms. Check-in 3 pm, check-out noon. **$**

★ HAMPTON INN & SUITES. *725 S Lincoln Ave, Steamboat Springs (80487). Phone 970/871-8900; fax 970/871-9444. www.hamptoninn.com.* 40 rooms. Check-in 3 pm, check-out noon. **$**

Full-Service Hotels

★★★ SHERATON STEAMBOAT SPRINGS RESORT AND CONFERENCE CENTER. *2200 Village Inn Court, Steamboat Springs (80477). Phone 970/879-2220; toll-free 800/848-8877; fax 970/879-7686. www.steamboat-sheraton.* 317 rooms, 8 story. Closed mid-Apr-May, fall season. Check-in 4 pm, check-out 11 am. Restaurant, bar. Children's activity center. Fitness room, spa. Outdoor pool, children's pool, whirlpool. Golf. **$$**

★★★ THE STEAMBOAT GRAND RESORT HOTEL. *2300 Mount Werner Cir, Steamboat Springs (80487). Phone 970/871-5500; toll-free 877/367-2269; fax 970/871-5501. www.steamboatgrand.com.* 327 rooms. Check-in 3 pm, check-out noon. Restaurant, bar. **$$$**

Specialty Lodgings

The following lodging establishments are approved by Mobil Travel Guide, but due to their unique and individualized nature have not been given a traditional Mobil Star rating. Included in this listing you may find bed-and-breakfasts, limited-service inns, guest ranches, and other unique hotel properties.

THE HOME RANCH. *54880 County Rd 129, Clark (80428). Phone 970/879-1780; fax 970/879-1795.* Appropriately named, The Home Ranch makes everyone feel at home. Situated in the Elk River Valley with the majestic Rocky Mountains in the distance, the ranch is only 18 miles from the famed ski resort of Steamboat Springs. This natural paradise offers visitors an authentic guest ranch experience. Activities are plentiful, with more than 12 miles of snow-covered trails for snowshoeing and cross-country skiing in winter and mountain biking and hiking in summer. Horsemanship is the focus here, with cattle-working and stockmanship lessons offered in addition to general riding. Eight cabins provide a secluded visit, while the rooms in the main lodge are convenient to the pool and dining room. Chef Clyde Nelson's culinary skills are highly praised, and the family-style meals are memorable. After dinner, guests listen to the sounds of the Ranch Hand Band, visit rodeos, or simply retire to the comfort of their Western-style rooms. 8 rooms. Closed late Oct-mid-Dec, late Mar-late May. Check-in 4 pm, check-out 10 am. Restaurant. Children's activity center. Outdoor pool, whirlpool. Airport transportation available. **$$$**

VISTA VERDE GUEST AND SKI RANCH. *31100 Seedhouse Rd, Steamboat Springs (80428). Phone 970/879-3858; toll-free 800/526-7433; fax 970/879-1413. www.vistaverde.com.* Situated on 500 acres in the Rocky Mountains, this wonderful ranch encourages guests to unwind while exploring the Old West. Private cabins and lodge rooms are decorated with a distinctive regional flair; the accommodations even feature furnishings handcrafted by the ranch's very own woodworker. Visitors are tempted by an array of on-property activities, from backcountry skiing and sleigh rides to fly fishing, hot-air ballooning, and hiking. Off the property, visitors enjoy dogsledding, whitewater rafting, and a host of other thrilling adventures. Naturally, horseback riding is the most popular activity at the ranch, and instruction is available for both children and adults. After a long day on the range, guests feast on gourmet meals at the lodge or on the sundeck while discussing the day's accomplishments with newly discovered friends. 12 rooms, 2 story. Closed late Sept-late Dec, late Mar-early June. Restaurant. Children's activity center. Fitness room. Airport transportation available. **$$$**

Restaurants

★ ★ ANTARES. *57 1/2 8th St, Steamboat Springs (80477). Phone 970/879-9939; fax 970/879-0718.* 1909 building has Victorian-era furnishings; Victrola, large picture windows, stone fireplace. New American menu. Dinner. Closed Thanksgiving; also Apr 15-June 1. Bar. Children's menu. Casual attire. **$$$**

★ ★ ★ L'APOGEE. *911 Lincoln Ave, Steamboat Springs (80487). Phone 970/879-1919; fax 970/879-2746. www.lapogee.com.* American menu. Dinner. Bar. Children's menu. Casual attire. Outdoor seating. **$$$**

★ ★ LA MONTANA. *2500 Village Dr, Steamboat Springs (80477). Phone 970/879-5800; fax 970/879-5373. www.la-montana.com.* Southwestern, Mexican menu. Dinner. Closed Thanksgiving; also Apr 15-June 1. Bar. Children's menu. Casual attire. Outdoor seating. **$$**

★ ★ ORE HOUSE AT THE PINE GROVE. *1465 Pine Grove Rd, Steamboat Springs (80477). Phone 970/879-1190; fax 970/879-0479. www.orehouseatthepinegrove.com.* American menu. Dinner. Closed Apr 15-May 15. Bar. Children's menu. Casual attire. Outdoor seating. **$$$**

★ THE TUGBOAT GRILL & PUB. *1860 Mt Werner Rd, Steamboat Springs (80487). Phone 970/879-7070.* American menu. Lunch, dinner. Closed mid-Apr-June 1. Bar. Children's menu. Casual attire. Outdoor seating. **$**

★ WINONA'S DELI-BAKERY. *617 Lincoln Ave, Steamboat Springs (80477). Phone 970/879-2483; fax 970/879-3277.* American menu. Breakfast, lunch. Closed Thanksgiving, Dec 25. Children's menu. Casual attire. Outdoor seating. **$**

Sterling (A-5)

See also Fort Morgan

Population 11,360
Elevation 3,939 ft
Area Code 970
Zip 80751
Information Logan County Chamber of Commerce, 109 N Front St, PO Box 1683; phone 970/522-5070 or toll-free 800/544-8609
Web site www.sterlingcolo.com

What to See and Do

Outdoor sculptures. *Sterling.* Sterling is known as the "City of Living Trees" because of the unique carved trees found throughout town. A self-guided tour map shows where to find the 16 sculpted trees created by a local sculptor. Call the Logan County Chamber of Commerce for more information.

Overland Trail Museum. *21053 County Rd 26 1/2, Sterling. Just off I-76. Phone 970/522-3895.* Village of seven buildings. Collections of Native American artifacts, cattle brands, farm machinery; archaeological and paleontological exhibits, one-room schoolhouse, fire engine, children's displays; local historical items; park and picnic area. (Apr-Oct, daily; rest of year, Tues-Sat) **FREE**

Limited-Service Hotels

★ BEST WESTERN SUNDOWNER. *Overland Trail St, Sterling (80751). Phone 970/522-6265; toll-free 800/780-7234; fax 970/522-6265. www.bestwestern.com.* 30 rooms. Pets accepted, some restrictions; fee. Complimentary continental breakfast. Check-out 11 am. Fitness room. Pool, whirlpool. **$**

★ ★ RAMADA INN. *22246 E Hwy 6, Sterling (80751). Phone 970/522-2625; toll-free 800/835-7275; fax 970/522-1321. www.ramada.com.* 100 rooms, 2 story. Pets accepted, some restrictions; fee. Check-out noon. Restaurant, bar. Fitness room. Indoor pool, whirlpool. **$**

Specialty Lodging

The following lodging establishment is approved by Mobil Travel Guide, but due to its unique and individualized nature has not been given a traditional Mobil Star rating. Included in this listing you may find bed-and-breakfasts, limited-service inns, guest ranches, and other unique hotel properties.

ELK ECHO RANCH. *47490 Weld County Rd 155, Stoneham (80754). Phone 970/735-2426; fax 970/735-2427. www.wapiti.net/co/eer.htm.* This 5,200-square-foot log bed-and-breakfast offers guest rooms with a quiet atmosphere. Guests can enjoy watching 500 head of elk and a small buffalo herd from the deck, or take advantage of the complimentary tour, which includes a guest photo. 4 rooms, 3 story. Complimentary full breakfast. Check-in 4 pm, check-out 11 am. **$**

Restaurant

★ T. J. BUMMER'S. *203 Broadway, Sterling (80751). Phone 970/522-8397; fax 970/521-9554.* American menu. Breakfast, lunch, dinner. Closed holidays. Children's menu. **$$**

Telluride (D-2)

See also Norwood

Settled 1878
Population 2,221
Elevation 8,800 ft
Area Code 970
Zip 81435
Information Telluride Visitor Services, 666 W Colorado Ave, Box 653; phone 970/728-4431 or toll-free 888/605-2578
Web site www.telluride.com

Gray granite and red sandstone mountains surround this mining town named for the tellurium ore containing precious metals found in the area. Telluride, proud of its bonanza past, has not changed its façade. Because of its remoteness and small size, Telluride remains uncrowded and retains its history. Summer activities include fly-fishing, mountain biking, river rafting, hiking, Jeep trips, horseback riding, and camping, as well as many annual events and festivals from May to October.

What to See and Do

Bear Creek Trail. *S end of Pine St, Telluride.* A 2-mile canyon walk with view of tiered waterfall. (May-Oct)

Bridal Veil Falls. *Telluride. 2 1/2 miles E on Hwy 145.* Highest waterfall in Colorado. Structure at top of falls was once a hydroelectric power plant, which served the Smuggler-Union Mine operations. It has been recently renovated and now provides auxiliary electric power to Telluride.

Telluride Gondola. *Aspen and San Juan, Telluride.* Four gondola terminals: Station Telluride, Oak St; Station St. Sophia, on the ski mountain; stations Mount Village and Village Parking in Mount Village. Passengers are transported from downtown Telluride, over ski mountain, and to Mount Village. (Early June-early Oct and late Nov-mid-Apr, daily) **FREE**

Telluride Historical Museum. *201 W Gregory Ave, Telluride. Phone 970/728-3344. www.telluridemuseum.com.* Built in 1893 as the community hospital, this historic building houses artifacts, historic photos, and exhibits that show what Telluride was like in its Wild West days. (Tues-Sat noon-5 pm) **$**

Telluride Ski Resort. *565 Mt Village Blvd, Telluride. Phone toll-free 800/801-4832. www.telski.com.* Three-stage gondola; four quad, two triple, two double chairlifts; one surface lift; patrol, school, rentals; restaurants, nursery. Sixty-six runs; longest run 3 miles; vertical drop 3,522 feet. (Thanksgiving-early Apr, daily) Cross-country skiing, heliskiing, ice skating, snowmobiling, sleigh rides. Shuttle bus service and two in-town chairlifts. **$$$$**

Special Events

Balloon Rally. *Telluride.* Early June.

Chamber Music Festival. *110 N Oak St, Telluride. Phone 970/728-6769.* Mid-Aug.

Jazz Celebration. *Town Park, Telluride.* Early Aug.

Mountain Film Festival. *207 W Columbia Ave, Telluride. Phone 970/728-4401.* Labor Day weekend.

Telluride Airmen's Rendezvous & Hang Gliding Festival. *Telluride.* Mid-Sept.

Telluride Bluegrass Festival. *Telluride. Phone toll-free 800/624-2422. www.bluegrass.com.* For four days each June, thousands of music lovers flock to Telluride for what many agree is the nation's premier bluegrass festival. A tradition for more than 30 years, the festival draws some of the nation's top bluegrass and folk performers who pluck their stuff for the adoring throngs at Town Park. Spontaneous jams continue throughout the day and into the wee hours of the night at local eating and drinking spots. The festival includes amateur competitions and workshops. It is a favorite destination for campers wishing to experience the natural beauty of Telluride's mountain setting and the high-spirited fun of the festival. Mid-June. **$$$$**

Full-Service Hotel

★★★ COLUMBIA HOTEL. *300 W San Juan Ave, Telluride (81435). Phone 970/728-0660; toll-free 800/201-9505; fax 970/728-9249. www.columbiatelluride.com.* 21 rooms, 4 story. Pets accepted, some restrictions; fee. Check-out 11 am. Restaurant, bar. Fitness room. **$$**

Full-Service Resort

★★★ WYNDHAM PEAKS RESORT & GOLDEN DOOR SPA. *136 Country Club Dr, Telluride (81435). Phone 970/728-6800; toll-free 800/789-2220; fax 970/728-6175. www.thepeaksresort.com.* Nestled atop the mountain in Telluride, the Wyndham Peaks Resort is a skier's heaven with ski-in/ski-out access and a ski valet who warms and tunes equipment, yet this resort is a year-round paradise with exceptional golf and a world-class spa. The guest rooms and suites are cocoons of luxury, with superior amenities and striking views of the San Juan Mountains. This resort is the perfect home for outdoor enthusiasts who like to rough it up a bit outdoors, yet live it up indoors. The centerpiece of this first-class resort is the Golden Door Spa, an outpost of the legendary California destination spa. Restorative treatments and an oxygen bar to help combat the effects of the high altitude are among the highlights. 174 rooms, 6 story. Closed mid-Apr-mid-May, mid-Oct-mid-Nov. Pets accepted; fee. Check-in 4 pm, check-out noon. Restaurant, bar. Children's activity center. Fitness room, spa. Indoor pool, outdoor pool, children's pool, whirlpool. Golf. Tennis. Airport transportation available. Business center. **$$$**

Full-Service Inn

★★★ NEW SHERIDAN HOTEL. *231 W Colorado Ave, Telluride (81435). Phone 970/728-4351; toll-free 800/200-1891; fax 970/728-5024. www.newsheridan.com.* Built in 1891, this hotel is located in the heart of Telluride. Many of the elegant guest rooms feature mountain views and separate sitting rooms. Warm up with a hearty gourmet breakfast and then relax in the afternoon with a complimentary glass of Pine Ridge wine at the New Sheridan Bar. 26 rooms, 3 story. Closed mid-Apr-mid-May. Complimentary continental breakfast. Check-in 2 pm, check-out 11 am. Restaurant. Fitness room. Whirlpool. **$$**

Specialty Lodging

The following lodging establishment is approved by Mobil Travel Guide, but due to its unique and individualized nature has not been given a traditional Mobil Star rating. Included in this listing you may find bed-and-breakfasts, limited-service inns, guest ranches, and other unique hotel properties.

THE SAN SOPHIA INN AND CONDOMINIUMS. *330 W Pacific Ave, Telluride (81435). Phone 970/728-3001; toll-free 800/537-4781; fax 970/728-6226. www.sansophia.com.* Modern frame structure built in Victorian style with octagon tower observatory; bay windows; library, sitting room. Interiors blend Victorian and modern Southwest design; stained and etched glass, period furnishings. Mountain views. 16 rooms, 2 story. Closed Apr, Nov. Children over 9 years only. Complimentary full breakfast. Check-in 3 pm, check-out 11 am. Whirlpool. **$**

Restaurants

★★★ **ALLRED'S.** *2 Coonskin Ridge, Telluride (81435). Phone 970/728-7474.* American menu. Dinner. Closed mid-Apr-mid-June, late Sept-mid-Dec. Bar. Children's menu. Casual attire. Reservations recommended. **$$$**

★★★ **COSMOPOLITAN.** *300 W San Juan, Telluride (81435). Phone 970/728-1292; fax 970/728-9249. www.cosmotelluride.com.* French, American menu. Dinner. Closed mid-Apr-mid-May and the last week in Oct. Bar. Children's menu. Casual attire. Reservations recommended. **$$**

★★ **FLORADORA.** *103 W Colorado Ave, Telluride (81435). Phone 970/728-3888; fax 970/728-4846.* Stained-glass windows, Tiffany-style lamps. Southwestern, American menu. Lunch, dinner. Bar. Children's menu. **$$**

Trinidad (E-4)

See also Walesenburg

Settled 1859
Population 9,078
Elevation 6,025 ft
Area Code 719
Zip 81082
Information Trinidad-Las Animas County Chamber of Commerce, 309 Nevada Ave; phone 719/846-9285
Web site www.trinidadco.com

Bat Masterson was marshal and Kit Carson was a frequent visitor to Trinidad when it was a busy trading post along the Santa Fe Trail. Today the town specializes in small manufacturing and distribution, ranching, farming, and tourism. It is the seat of Las Animas County.

What to See and Do

A. R. Mitchell Memorial Museum of Western Art. *150 E Main St, Trinidad. Phone 719/846-4224.* Features Western paintings by Arthur Roy Mitchell, Harvey Dunn, Harold von Schmidt, and other famous artists; Western and Native American artifacts; Hispanic religious folk art. Housed in a 1906 former department store with original tin ceiling, wood floors, horseshoe-shaped mezzanine. (Apr-Sept, Mon-Sat; also by appointment; closed holidays) **FREE**

Trinidad History Museum. *300 E Main St, Trinidad. On the historic Santa Fe Trail. Phone 719/846-7217.* Colorado Historical Society administers this museum complex. The Baca House (1870) is a restored 9-room, 2-story adobe house purchased by a wealthy Hispanic sheep rancher. The Bloom House (1882) is a restored Victorian mansion and garden built by cattleman and banker Frank C. Bloom. The Santa Fe Museum is also here. Guided tours (Memorial Day-Sept, daily; rest of year, by appointment) **$$**

Trinidad Lake State Park. *32610 State Hwy 12, Trinidad. 3 miles W on Hwy 12. Phone 719/846-6951.* A 2,300-acre park with a 900-acre lake. Water-skiing, fishing, boating (ramps); nature trails, mountain biking, picnicking, playground, camping (electrical hookups, showers, dump station). Interpretive programs (Memorial Day-Labor Day, Fri, Sat, holidays). (Daily) **$**

Limited-Service Hotel

★★ **HOLIDAY INN.** *3125 Toupal Dr, Trinidad (81082). Phone 719/846-4491; fax 719/846-2440. www.holiday-inn.com.* 113 rooms, 2 story. Pets accepted. Check-out noon. Restaurant, bar. Fitness room. Indoor pool, whirlpool. **$**

Restaurants

★★ **CHEF LIU'S CHINESE RESTAURANT.** *1423 Santa Fe Trail, Trinidad (81082). Phone 719/846-3333; fax 719/846-6688.* Chinese menu. Dinner. Closed Thanksgiving; also Mon Thanksgiving-Mar. Bar. **$**

★ MAIN BAKERY CAFE. *121 W Main St, Trinidad (81082). Phone 719/846-8779. www.mainstreetbakery .net.* Serving modern American cuisine in a family setting. Breakfast, lunch. **$**

★ NANA & NANO MONTELEONE'S DELI & PASTA HOUSE. *418 E Main St, Trinidad (81082). Phone 719/846-2696.* A local favorite known for its homemade sausages and authentic Italian cuisine. Lunch, dinner. Closed Sun-Mon. **$**

Vail (B-3)

See also Beaver Creek, Dillon, Edwards, Leadville

Population 4,531
Elevation 8,160 ft
Information Vail Valley Tourism & Convention Bureau, 100 E Meadow Dr; phone 970/476-1000 or toll-free 800/525-3875
Web site www.vail.com

Before the chairlifts opened, Native Americans frequented the area occupied by present-day Vail, but never permanently settled there. That all changed with the arrival of skiers by the thousands beginning in 1962. Built from the ground up to resemble a Bavarian village, Vail today is the world's largest single-mountain ski resort and a prototype for ski towns the world over. Known for having vast and varied terrain for every skill level of skier or snowboarder, Vail often tops "Best Ski Resorts in the US" lists and gets rave reviews for its legendary powder. And summer has emerged as a prime recreation season on Vail Mountain, with mountain biking the sport of choice. Today, ski conglomerate Vail Resorts owns numerous ski resorts in Colorado, including Beaver Creek, Breckenridge, and Arapahoe Basin; many passes work at all the properties.

What to See and Do

Beaver Creek/Arrowhead Resort. *137 Benchmark Rd, Avon. 10 miles W on I-70, exit 167, then 3 miles S. Phone 970/949-5750. www.beavercreek.com.* Six quad, three triple, four double chairlifts; patrol, rentals, snowmaking; cafeteria, restaurants, bar, nursery. Longest run 2 3/4 miles; vertical drop 4,040 ft. (Late Nov-mid-Apr, daily) Cross-country trails and rentals (Nov-Apr), ice skating, snowmobiling, sleigh rides. Chairlift rides (July-Aug, daily; Sept, weekends). **$$$$**

Colorado Ski Museum & Ski Hall of Fame. *In Vail Village Transportation Center, 231 S Frontage Rd E, Vail. Phone 970/476-1876; toll-free 800/950-7410. www. skimuseum.net.* Skiing artifacts and photographs tracing the history of skiing in Colorado for more than 120 years. (Memorial Day-late Sept and late Nov-mid Apr, Tues-Sun; closed holidays) **$**

Gerald R. Ford Amphitheater Vilar Pavilion/Betty Ford Alpine Gardens. *Ford Park and the Betty Ford Alpine Gardens, Vail. Phone 970/476-0103; toll-free 888/883-8245. www.vvf.com/ford_amph.cfm.* The Gerald R. Ford Amphitheater Vilar Pavilion is an open-air stadium that gives music lovers of all ages the chance to enjoy a wide variety of shows while sitting under Vail's crystal-clear, starlit skies. Surrounded by the Betty Ford Alpine Gardens, a public botanical garden with more than 500 varieties of wildflowers and alpine plants, the amphitheater combines natural beauty with top-quality entertainment. Performances throughout the summer normally include classical music, rock and roll, jazz, ballet, contemporary dance, and children's theater. (June-Aug) **$$$$**

Vail Ski Resort. *137 Benchmark Rd, Avon. In town on I-70, exit 176. Phone 970/476-9090. www.vail.com.* Gondola; 14 high-speed quad, seven fixed-grip quad, three triple, five double chairlifts; ten surface lifts; patrol, school, rentals, snowmaking; cafeterias, restaurants, bars, nursery. Longest run 4 miles; vertical drop 3,450 feet. (Late Nov-mid-Apr, daily) Cross-country trails, rentals (Nov-Apr; fee), ice skating, snowmobiling, sleigh rides. Gondola and Vista Bahn (June-Aug, daily; May and Sept, weekends; fee). **$$$$**

Special Event

Taste of Vail. *Various venues, Vail. Phone toll-free 888/311-5665. www.tasteofvail.com.* Several wine tastings combine with unique competitions and cooking seminars at this upscale festival. Go to a picnic on top of a mountain, sample premium desserts, or watch the annual Vail Bartender Cocktail Mix-Off. Listen to winemakers talk about their craft—and then taste the fruits of their labor! Also, watch for such exclusives as expert chefs in Japanese cuisine explaining how to pair wine with food and how to please umami, the recently identified fifth taste bud. If you want a relaxing, truly unique food festival, choose Taste of Vail. Early Apr.

Limited-Service Hotels

★ ★ **BEST WESTERN THE FABULOUS VAILGLO LODGE.** *701 W Lionshead Cir, Vail (81658). Phone 970/476-5506; toll-free 800/541-9423; fax 970/476-3926. www.bestwestern.com.* 34 rooms, 4 story. Complimentary continental breakfast. Check-out noon. Pool, whirlpool. **$**

★ **CHATEAU AT VAIL.** *13 Vail Rd, Vail (81657). Phone 970/476-5631; toll-free 800/451-9840; fax 970/477-7457. www.chateauvail.com.* 120 rooms, 4 story. Check-in 4 pm, check-out 10 am. Restaurant, bar. Pool, whirlpool. Golf. Tennis. **$$**

★ ★ **HOTEL GASTHOF GRAMSHAMMER.** *231 E Gore Creek Dr, Vail (81657). Phone 970/476-5626; toll-free 800/610-7374; fax 970/476-8816. www.pepis .com.* 40 rooms, 4 story. Closed late Apr-late May. Complimentary continental breakfast. Check-in 3 pm, check-out 11 am. Restaurant, bar. Fitness room. **$$$**

★ ★ **MOUNTAIN LODGE & SPA.** *352 E Meadow Dr, Vail (81657). Phone 970/476-0700; toll-free 800/822-4754; fax 970/476-6451. www. vailmountainlodge-spa.com.* 38 rooms, 3 story. Complimentary continental breakfast. Check-out 11 am. Restaurant, bar. Fitness room, spa. Indoor pool, whirlpool. **$$$$**

★ **SITZMARK LODGE.** *183 Gore Creek Dr, Vail (81657). Phone 970/476-5001; toll-free 888/476-5001; fax 970/476-8702.* 35 rooms, 3 story. Complimentary continental breakfast (winter). Check-in 4 pm, check-out 11 am. Outdoor pool, whirlpool. **$$**

★ **VAIL'S MOUNTAIN HAUS.** *292 E Meadow Dr, Vail (81657). Phone 970/476-2434; toll-free 800/237-0922; fax 970/476-3007. www.mountainhaus.com.* 72 rooms, 5 story. Check-out 10 am. Bar. Fitness room. Pool, whirlpool. **$**

Full-Service Resorts

★ ★ **LION SQUARE LODGE.** *660 W Lionshead Pl, Vail (81657). Phone 970/476-2281; toll-free 800/525-5788; fax 970/476-7423. www.lionsquare.com.* 108 rooms, 7 story. Check-out 10 am. Restaurant. Children's activity center. Outdoor pool, whirlpool. **$$**

★ ★ ★ **THE LODGE AT VAIL.** *174 E Gore Creek Dr, Vail (81657). Phone 970/476-5011; fax 970/476-7425. www.vail.net/thelodge.* The Lodge at Vail is perfectly located in the heart of the pedestrian village, at the base of Vail Mountain. Skiers need to take only a few steps to the lift, while shoppers and diners walk out to enjoy the village's boutiques and cafés. Visitors reap the rewards of this Eden for outdoor enthusiasts. Summer adventures include whitewater rafting, golf, fishing, hot-air ballooning, and horseback riding, while winter is all about snowshoeing, skiing and snowboarding on the renowned slopes, and a host of other wintertime activities. Four whirlpools, one sauna, and an outdoor pool soothe weary muscles. Two restaurants satisfy hearty appetites, while Mickey's Piano Bar entertains. Individually decorated, the guest rooms are a perfect blend of European grace and Western aplomb. The Lodge marries the charm of an Alpine inn with the amenities of a world-class resort. 124 rooms, 2 story. Check-in 4 pm, check-out 11 am. Restaurant, bar. Fitness room. Outdoor pool, children's pool, whirlpool. **$$$**

★ ★ ★ **MARRIOTT VAIL MOUNTAIN RESORT.** *715 W Lionshead Cir, Vail (81657). Phone 970/476-4444; toll-free 888/236-2427; fax 970/479-6996. www.marriott.com.* The guest rooms range from a well-appointed standard to the Timberland Suite that has magnificent views of Vail Mountain. 350 rooms, 6 story. Check-in 4 pm, check-out 11 am. Restaurant, bar. Fitness room, spa. Indoor pool, outdoor pool, whirlpool. Tennis. Business center. **$$**

★ ★ ★ **SONNENALP RESORT OF VAIL.** *Twenty Vail Rd, Vail (81657). Phone 970/476-5656; toll-free 800/654-8312; fax 970/476-1639. www. sonnenalp.com.* Family-owned and -operated, Sonnenalp Resort of Vail carries on the tradition of Europe's finest lodgings. Recalling the Bavarian countryside in its architecture, this charming, all-suite property retains an unparalleled intimacy. Just steps from Vail Village and the ski lift, this luxurious alpine chalet is a natural choice for winter sports lovers, yet it is an ideal vacation spot throughout the year with an inviting array of multi-seasonal recreational activities. Five restaurants celebrate the cuisines of Europe and the American Southwest, and a spa is on hand to induce total relaxation. Sonnenalp's residential ambience extends to the library, where curling up with a good book is de rigueur. 88 rooms, 4 story. Check-in 4 pm, check-out 11 am. High-speed Internet access. Restaurants, bar. Fitness room. Indoor/outdoor pool, whirlpools. Business center. **$$**

★ ★ ★ VAIL CASCADE RESORT & SPA. *1300 Westhaven Dr, Vail (81657). Phone 970/476-7111; toll-free 800/420-2424; fax 970/479-7020. www.vailcascade.com.* Located on Gore Creek at the base of Vail Mountain, this European-style alpine village contains a combination of standard guest accommodations, condominiums, and private residences. Highlights include the Aria Spa & Club (the largest athletic facility in the Vail Valley) and the upscale Chap's Grill and Chophouse, as well as a shopping arcade, two movie theaters, and a beauty shop. The heated pools are great for lounging, and the 50,000 square feet of meeting space enable the resort to accommodate large groups. With the slopes being the major draw here, the resort offers equipment rentals and a ski concierge. Guest rooms in either the main lodge or the Terrace Wing have refrigerators and walk-out balconies for enjoying the mountain views. Live entertainment at the Fireside Bar encourages mingling, and Camp Cascade keeps kids entertained throughout the day. 292 rooms, 4 story. Check-out noon. Restaurant, bar. Children's activity center. Fitness room, spa. Two pools, five whirlpools (two indoor). Tennis. Ski in/ski out. Business center. **$$$**

Full-Service Inn

★ ★ ★ CHRISTIANA AT VAIL. *356 E Hanson Ranch Rd, Vail (81657). Phone 970/476-5641; fax 970/476-0470. www.christiania.com.* Bavarian-style inn. 22 rooms, 3 story. Complimentary continental breakfast. Check-in 4 pm, check-out 11 am. Pool. **$$**

Specialty Lodgings

The following lodging establishments are approved by Mobil Travel Guide, but due to their unique and individualized nature have not been given a traditional Mobil Star rating. Included in this listing you may find bed-and-breakfasts, limited-service inns, guest ranches, and other unique hotel properties.

GALATYN LODGE. *365 Vail Valley Dr, Vail (81657). Phone 970/479-2419; toll-free 800/943-7322; fax 970/479-0102. www.galatyn.com.* 15 rooms. Check-in 3 pm, check-out noon. **$$**

SAVORY INN. *2405 Elliott Rd, Vail (81657). Phone 970/476-1304; fax 970/476-0433. www.vail.net/blackbear.* On the banks of Gore Creek. 12 rooms, 2 story. Closed mid-Apr-mid-May. Complimentary full breakfast. Check-in 3-7 pm, check-out 11 am. Whirlpool. **$**

Restaurants

★ ALPENROSE. *100 E Meadow Dr, Vail (81657). Phone 970/476-3194; fax 970/476-5184.* German menu. Lunch, dinner. Closed Tues; also mid-Apr-late May and mid-Oct-mid-Nov. Bar. Outdoor seating. **$$**

★ BLU'S. *193 E Gore Creek Dr, Vail (81657). Phone 970/476-3113; fax 970/476-4319.* American, eclectic menu. Breakfast, lunch, dinner. Bar. Children's menu. Casual attire. Outdoor seating. **$$**

★ ★ GOLDEN EAGLE INN. *118 Beaver Creek Pl, Vail (81620). Phone 970/949-1940; fax 970/949-6085.* American menu. Lunch, dinner. Bar. Children's menu. Casual attire. Outdoor seating. **$$$**

★ ★ LANCELOT INN. *201 E Gore Creek Dr, Vail (81657). Phone 970/476-5828; fax 970/476-4746. www.lancelotinn.com.* Overlooks a landscaped creek. American menu. Lunch (summer), dinner. Closed May. Bar. Children's menu. Outdoor seating. **$$**

★ ★ ★ LEFT BANK. *183 Gore Creek Dr, Vail (81657). Phone 970/476-3696.* As the name suggests, this restaurant serves classic French cuisine with a friendly, casual elegance, right in the heart of the Village. Dinner. Closed Wed; Memorial Day, Dec 25; also mid-Apr-mid-June, Oct-mid-Nov. Bar. Casual attire. **$$$**

★★ MONTAUK SEAFOOD GRILL. *549 W Lionshead Mall, Vail (81657). Phone 970/476-2601. www.montaukseafoodgrill.com.* Seafood menu. Dinner. Closed Thanksgiving. Bar. Outdoor seating. **$$**

★★★ RESTAURANT PICASSO. *2205 Cordillera Way, Edwards (81632). Phone 970/926-2200; fax 970/926-2486. www.cordillera-vail.com.* French menu. Dinner. Bar. Valet parking. Outdoor seating. **$$$**

★★★ SWEET BASIL. *193 E Gore Creek Dr, Vail (81657). Phone 970/476-0125; fax 970/476-0137. www.sweetbasil-vail.com.* Eclectic, international menu. Lunch, dinner. Bar. Casual attire. Reservations recommended. Outdoor seating. **$$$**

★★ THE TYROLEAN. *400 E Meadow Dr, Vail (81657). Phone 970/476-2204; fax 970/476-3652. www.tyrolean.net.* Three level dining area. Large logging sled chandelier. American menu. Dinner. Closed late Apr-May. Bar. Children's menu. Outdoor seating. **$$$**

★★★ THE WILDFLOWER. *174 Gore Creek Dr, Vail (81657). Phone 970/476-5011; fax 970/476-7425. www.vail.net/thelodge.* If you're searching for a memorable dining experience—something more than just a night out—then make it over to The Wildflower, a beautiful restaurant that, as you might expect from its name, feels like spring in full bloom. Filled with baskets of wildflowers and massive floral arrangements, the room boasts wonderful views and tables lined with country-style Laura Ashley linens. You'll find a delicious and innovative selection of seafood, poultry, and game (Nebraska ostrich, anyone?) that is accented with global flavors like lemongrass, curry, and chilies and incorporates local fruits and vegetables, including herbs grown in The Wildflower's garden. An extensive, thoughtful, and reasonably priced wine list concentrates on Italy and matches the distinctive global menu. Dinner. Closed Mon in winter. Casual attire. Valet parking. Outdoor seating. **$$$**

Walsenburg (D-4)

See also Trinidad

Founded 1873
Population 4,182
Elevation 6,182 ft
Area Code 719
Zip 81089
Information Walsenburg Chamber of Commerce, 400 Main St, Railroad Depot; phone 719/738-1065

Named after a German pioneer merchant, the present town was originally the small Spanish village of La Plaza de los Leones.

What to See and Do

Francisco Fort Museum. *La Veta. 16 miles SW on Hwy 160 and Hwy 12. Phone 719/742-5501.* Original adobe trading fort (1862) now contains exhibits of pioneer cattle ranching and commercial mining. The site also has a saloon, blacksmith shop, one-room schoolhouse, and collection of Native American artifacts. (Late May-early Oct, Wed-Sun) **$$**

Lathrop State Park. *70 County Rd 502, Walsenburg. 3 miles W on Hwy 160. Phone 719/738-2376.* Swimming, water-skiing, fishing, boating (ramps); golf, picnicking (shelters), camping (dump station). Visitor center. (Daily) **$**

Walsenburg Mining Museum. *Old County Jail Building, 400 Main St, Walsenburg. Phone 719/738-1992.* Exhibits on the history of coal mining in Huerfano County, the Trinidad coal fields, and Raton basin. (May-Sept, Mon-Sat; rest of year, by appointment) **$**

Limited-Service Hotel

★★ BEST WESTERN RAMBLER. *I-25, exit 52, Walsenburg (81089). Phone 719/738-1121; fax 719/738-1093. www.bestwestern.com.* 35 rooms. Pets accepted, some restrictions. Check-out 11 am. Restaurant. Pool. **$**

Restaurant

★ ★ IRON HORSE. *503 W 7th St, Walsenburg (81089). Phone 719/738-9966.* Three dining rooms in a turn-of-the-century armory. American menu. Lunch, dinner. Closed Thanksgiving, Dec 24-25; also three weeks in Feb. Bar. **$$**

Winter Park (B-3)

See also Central City, Georgetown, Granby, Idaho Springs

Population 662
Elevation 9,040 ft
Area Code 970
Zip 80482
Information Winter Park/Fraser Valley Chamber of Commerce, PO Box 3236; phone toll-free 800/903-7275
Web site www.winterpark-info.com

Winter Park is part of the unique Denver Mountain Park System, located on the western slope of Berthoud Pass in the Arapaho National Forest (see DILLON).

What to See and Do

Winter Park Resort. *677 Winter Park Dr, Winter Park. 1 mile SE off Hwy 40. Phone 970/726-5514. www.skiwinterpark.com.* Eight high-speed quad, five triple, seven double chairlifts; patrol, school, rentals, snowmaking; cafeterias, restaurants, bars. NASTAR and coin-operated race courses. (Mid-Nov-mid-Apr, daily) The five interconnected mountain areas include Winter Park, Mary Jane, and Vasquez Ridge. One hundred thirty-four runs; longest run 5 miles; vertical drop 2,610 feet. Half-day rates. Chairlift and alpine slide also operate late June-mid-Sept (daily). Bicycle rentals, miniature golf (summer, fee). **$$$$** Within the resort is

> **The Children's Center.** *677 Winter Park Dr, Winter Park. Phone 970/726-5514.* An all-inclusive ski center for children (inquire about ages) with children's ski slopes, rentals, school, and day care (winter); human maze, 18-hole Frisbee golf, indoor/outdoor climbing wall (summer). **$$$$**

Limited-Service Hotel

★ ★ THE VINTAGE RESORT. *100 Winter Park Dr, Winter Park (80482). Phone 970/726-8801; toll-free 800/472-7017; fax 970/726-9230. www.vintagehotel.com.* Traveling with Fido? He'll love it here, where you'll be greeted by Tipper, the resident pooch. For a $25 fee, your dog can stay as long as you do. Another plus, this one for humans, is that The Vintage is located at the base of Winter Park resort, has a shuttle that goes to the lifts in the mornings, and has both standard hotel rooms and rooms with kitchenettes. Après-ski, if you're feeling brave, there are a couple of things to try: the resort's heated outdoor pool and the restaurant's deep-fried Twinkie. 170 rooms, 5 story. Pets accepted; fee. Check-out 11 am. Restaurant, bar. Fitness room. Pool, whirlpool. **$**

Full-Service Resort

★ ★ IRON HORSE RESORT. *101 Iron Horse Way, Winter Park (80482). Phone 970/726-8851; toll-free 800/621-8190; fax 970/726-2321. www.ironhorse-resort.com.* 130 rooms, 5 story. Check-in 4 pm, check-out 10 am. Restaurant, bar. Fitness room. Indoor/outdoor pool, whirlpool. Business center. **$**

Specialty Lodgings

The following lodging establishments are approved by Mobil Travel Guide, but due to their unique and individualized nature have not been given a traditional Mobil Star rating. Included in this listing you may find bed-and-breakfasts, limited-service inns, guest ranches, and other unique hotel properties.

CREEKSIDE B & B. *156 High Seasons Way, Winter Park (80482). Phone 970/726-8422.* 6 rooms, 2 story. Complimentary continental breakfast. Check-in 2 pm, check-out noon. Whirlpool. **$$**

GASTHAUS EICHLER HOTEL. *78786 Hwy 40, Winter Park (80482). Phone 970/726-4244; toll-free 800/543-3899; fax 970/726-5175.* Well-positioned on Hwy 40 as you drive into town, this hotel changed hands in 2003, and the owners set to work on immediate upgrades. They include whirlpool tubs in every room, bathrobes in every closet, bottled water on every dresser, and plush duvets on every bed. In the hallway is a glass cabinet overflowing with board games for guests to use after a long day of winter skiing or summer hiking. The two restaurants—the casual/fine dining Dezeley and the more casual Fondue Stube—are now run by owner Rene Weder, former executive chef of Denver's Palace Arms. 16 rooms. Check-out 10 am. Restaurant, bar. **$**

GRAND VICTORIAN AT WINTER PARK. *78542 Fraser Valley Pkwy, Winter Park (80482). Phone 970/726-5881; toll-free 800/205-1170; fax 970/726-5602.* Victorian architectural style. 10 rooms, 3 story. Closed May. Children over 12 years only. Complimentary full breakfast. Check-in 4 pm, check-out 11 am. **$$**

Restaurants

★ ★ DENO'S MOUNTAIN BISTRO. *78911 Hwy 40, Winter Park (80482).* When you walk in the door of this funky place, you find yourself in a sports bar, but take two steps down and this "bistro" turns into a dining room. Along the walls are booths with shining copper tables, and in the center of the room are tables with white linen tablecloths topped with white paper. Draped above are evergreen boughs interwoven with tiny white lights. The menu? A little red pepper hummus and roasted mixed Greek olives, a bit of grilled New York strip steak and sesame crusted seared ahi tuna. But the biggest surprise at this place of revelry, popular among the less-than-quiet post-skiing crowd, is Deno's wine list, which has received Wine Spectator magazine's Award of Excellence every year since 1991. It's not uncommon to see a $110 bottle of 1984 Napa Valley Raymond Reserve on a table next to a couple of plates of buffalo wings. American menu. Lunch, dinner. Bar. Children's menu. Casual attire. Outdoor seating. **$**

★ ★ DEZELEY'S. *78786 Hwy 40, Winter Park (80482). Phone 970/726-5133; fax 970/726-5175.* Schnitzels and strudels are here in force, but that's not all you'll find on the menu at this casual-upscale dining room at the Gasthaus Eichler hotel. The hotel changed hands in 2003, and the restaurants are now under the watchful supervision of owner Rene Weder, former executive chef of Denver's Palace Arms. In addition to German/Swiss fare, you'll find entrées such as grilled buffalo tournedos and basil-seared salmon, attentively served in a lovely white-tablecloth restaurant. If you're looking for a vast selection of imported beers or European wines by the glass, look no further. German, American menu. Breakfast, lunch, dinner. Bar. Children's menu. Casual attire. Outdoor seating. **$$**

★ ★ ★ DINING ROOM AT SUNSPOT. *Winter Park Ski Resort, Winter Park (80482). Phone 970/726-1446.* This restaurant, the upscale dining room at the Winter Park ski resort, sits perched on a mountaintop at 10,700 feet and can be reached only by chairlift. If you are a skier, you have it made; if you aren't a skier, Sunspot is reason enough to become one. The restaurant has the intentional feel of a mountain lodge, semi-rustic but warm, built with logs from Grand County. It is a glorious, almost heavenly setting, and those who built it knew how to take full advantage of its magic. Sunspot has windows that are 8 feet high, so customers can eat lunch or dinner with magnificent views of the Continental Divide. American menu. Lunch, dinner. Closed May-Oct. Bar. Children's menu. Reservations recommended. **$$$**

★ ★ GASTHAUS EICHLER. *78786 Hwy 40, Winter Park (80482). Phone 970/726-5133; fax 970/726-5175. www.gasthauseichler.com.* German, American menu. Breakfast, lunch, dinner. Bar. Children's menu. Casual attire. Outdoor seating. **$$**

★ ★ RANDI'S IRISH SALOON. *78521 Hwy 40, Winter Park (80482). Phone 970/726-1186.* Chalet-style building with fireplace, early American furnishings; patio has rock garden and fountain. Irish menu. Breakfast, lunch, dinner. Bar. Children's menu. Outdoor seating. **$**

Nevada

Famous for gambling and glamorous nightlife, Nevada also has a rich history and tradition, magnificent scenery, and some of the wildest desert country on the continent.

Population: 1,998,257
Area: 110,567 square miles
Elevation: 470-13,143 feet
Peak: Boundary Peak (Esmeralda County)
Entered Union: October 31, 1864 (36th state)
Capital: Carson City
Motto: All for Our Country
Nickname: Silver State
Flower: Sagebrush
Bird: Mountain Bluebird
Tree: Piñon and Bristlecone Pine
Fair: August, in Reno
Time Zone: Pacific
Web site: www.travelnevada.com
Fun Fact:

- Nevada is the largest gold-producing state in the nation. It is second in the world behind South Africa.

Tourism is still the lifeblood of Nevada, with some 42 million visitors a year coming for vacation or conventions. Because of its central location and lack of inventory tax on goods bound out of state, Nevada is becoming increasingly important as a warehousing center for the western states.

Gambling (Nevadans call it "gaming") was first legalized in the Depression year of 1931, the same year residency requirements for obtaining a divorce were relaxed. Gaming is strictly controlled and regulated in Nevada, and casinos offer each bettor a fair chance to win. Taxes derived from the casinos account for nearly half of the state's revenue.

Most Nevadans feel that it is preferable to license, tax, and regulate gambling strictly than to tolerate the evils of bribery and corruption that inevitably accompany illegal gambling activities. While the state enforces numerous regulations, such as those barring criminals and prohibiting cheating, it does not control the odds on the various games.

Although Nevada has little rainfall and few rivers, water sports are popular on a few large lakes, both natural and man-made. These include Lakes Tahoe, Mead, and Lahontan; Pyramid Lake; and Walker Lake.

Mining and ranching have always been important facets of Nevada's economy. Sheep raising became important when millions of sheep were needed to feed the hungry miners working Nevada's Comstock Lode and California's Mother Lode.

Most of these sheepherders were Basque. Although today's sheepherder is more likely of Peruvian or Mexican descent, the Basques are still an important influence in the state.

Because of Nevada's arid land, cattle have to roam over a wide area; therefore, ranches average more than 2,000 acres in size. Most Nevada beef cattle are shipped to California or to the Midwest for fattening prior to marketing.

Known for its precious metals, Nevada produces more than $2.6 billion worth of gold and silver a year. Eerie ghost towns still hint at the romantic early days of fabulous gold and silver strikes that made millionaires overnight and generated some of the wildest history in the world. In the southern part of the state, the deserted mining camps of Rhyolite, Berlin, Belmont, Goodsprings, and Searchlight, to name a few, still delight explorers. Industrial metals and minerals also have an impact on the economy.

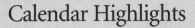

Calendar Highlights

JANUARY

National Cowboy Poetry Gathering *(Elko). Phone 775/738-7508.* Working cowpersons participate in storytelling verse. Demonstrations; country music.

MAY

Laughlin Riverdays *(Laughlin). Contact Laughlin Chamber of Commerce, phone 800/227-5245.* World's longest line dance, carnival, and golf tournament.

JUNE

Fallon Air Show *(Fallon). Fallon Naval Air Station. Phone 775/423-2544.* Military exhibition flying, civilian aerobatics, and aircraft displays; Blue Angels Demonstration Team.

Helldorado Days *(Las Vegas). Phone 702/870-1221.* Rodeos, parades, carnival, street dance, and chili cook-off; Western theme throughout.

Kit Carson Rendezvous *(Carson City). Contact the Carson City Convention & Visitors Bureau, phone 775/687-7410 or toll-free 800/638-2321; www.carson-city.org.* Mountain man encampment, Civil War camp, Native-American village with competition dancing, music, arts and crafts, and food vendors.

Winnemucca Basque Festival *(Elko). Phone 775/623-5071.* Contests in weightlifting, sheephooking, and other skills of mountaineers; dancing, feast.

AUGUST

Nevada State Fair *(Reno). Fairgrounds. Phone 775/688-5767.* Exhibits, entertainment, rides, games, and more.

SEPTEMBER

National Championship Air Races *(Reno). Stead Air Field. Phone 775/972-6663.* The world's longest-running air race, featuring four race classes: Unlimited, Formula One, AT-6, and Biplane. Skywriting, aerobatics, and displays.

OCTOBER

Invensys Classic *(Las Vegas).* PGA golf tournament with more than $4.5 million in prize money.

DECEMBER

National Finals Rodeo *(Las Vegas). Thomas and Mack Center. Phone 702/895-3900.* Nation's richest professional rodeo, featuring 15 finalists in seven rodeo disciplines.

The fur traders of the 1820s and 1830s, Jedediah Smith, Peter Ogden, and Joseph Walker and the Frémont expeditions, guided by Kit Carson in 1848, were the first to report on the area that is now Nevada.

The Mormons established a trading post in 1851. Now called Genoa, this was Nevada's first non-Indian settlement. Gold was found along the Carson River in Dayton Valley in May of 1850. A decade later, the fabulous Comstock Lode (silver and gold ore) was discovered. The gold rush was on, and Virginia City mushroomed into a town of 20,000. Formerly a part of Utah and New Mexico Territory, ceded by Mexico in 1848, Nevada became a territory in 1861 and a state in 1864. Before Europeans arrived, Nevada was the home of the Paiute, the Shoshone, and the Washoe, and even earlier, the Basketmakers.

Note: It is illegal to pick many types of wildflowers in Nevada, as well as to gather rocks. Tossing away lighted cigarette butts is also illegal in this dry land.

When to Go/Climate

Temperatures vary greatly in Nevada—from scorching desert days in Death Valley to bone-chilling night freezes in the Sierra Nevada. The entire state is arid. You may want to avoid visiting Nevada in the hot summer months of June, July, and August, when daytime temperatures can remain above 100 degrees in many parts of the state.

AVERAGE HIGH/LOW TEMPERATURES (° F)

Elko

Jan 37/13	**May** 69/37	**Sept** 78/39
Feb 43/20	**June** 80/47	**Oct** 66/30
Mar 50/25	**July** 91/50	**Nov** 49/23
Apr 60/30	**Aug** 89/49	**Dec** 37/14

Las Vegas

Jan 57/34	**May** 88/60	**Sept** 95/66
Feb 63/39	**June** 100/69	**Oct** 82/54
Mar 69/44	**July** 106/76	**Nov** 67/43
Apr 78/51	**Aug** 103/74	**Dec** 58/34

Parks and Recreation

Water-related activities, hiking, riding, various other sports, picnicking, and visitor centers, as well as camping, are available in many of Nevada's parks. "Roughing it" may be necessary in remote areas. Camping on a first-come, first-served basis; $3-$9 per night. Boat launching $2-$6, except Lake Tahoe (covers all fees, including boat launching). Inquire locally about road conditions for areas off paved highways. Carry drinking water in remote areas. Pets on leash only. For detailed information, contact the Nevada Division of State Parks, 1300 S Curry St, Carson City 89703-5202; phone 775/687-4384.

FISHING AND HUNTING

Nevada's streams and lakes abound with trout, bass, mountain whitefish, and catfish. Most fishing areas are open year-round. Some exceptions exist; inquire locally. Nonresident license: $51 for one year or $12 for one day. Special-use stamp ($3) for Lake Mead, Lake Mohave, and the Colorado River; $10 annual trout stamp required to take or possess trout.

There is an abundance of wildlife—mule deer, quail, ducks, geese, and partridges. Deer-hunting season lasts four to five weeks from the first two weekends in October; the season varies in some counties. Nonresident hunting license: $111 plus $155 for deer tag and processing. Deer hunting with bow and arrow: nonresidents $111 for license and $200 for deer tag and processing. Archery hunts are usually held from August 8 to September 4, prior to rifle season.

For a digest of fishing and hunting regulations, write to the Nevada Division of Wildlife, PO Box 10678, Reno 89520; phone 775/688-1500; www.ndow.org.

Driving Information

Safety belts are mandatory for all persons anywhere in a vehicle. Children under 5 years and under 40 pounds in weight must be in approved safety seats anywhere in a vehicle. For further information, phone toll-free 877/368-7828.

INTERSTATE HIGHWAY SYSTEM

Use the following list as a guide to access interstate highways in Nevada. Always consult a map to confirm driving routes.

Highway Number	Cities/Towns within 10 Miles
Interstate 15	Las Vegas, Overton.
Interstate 80	Battle Mountain, Elko, Lovelock, Reno, Winnemucca.

Additional Visitor Information

Nevada Magazine, an illustrated bimonthly magazine, and Nevada's Events Guide (free) may be obtained by contacting the Nevada Commission on Tourism, 401 N Carson St, Carson City 89701; phone 775/687-4322 or toll-free 800/NEVADA-8; www.travelnevada.com.

For information about the Lake Mead area, write to the Public Affairs Officer, Lake Mead National Recreation Area, 601 Nevada Hwy, Boulder City 89005; phone 702/293-8907; www.nps.gov/lame.

Information about camping, fishing and hunting, water sports, gambling, ghost towns, mining, agriculture, and the state capitol and museum may be obtained from the Commission on Tourism (see above).

SCENIC NEVADA

This tour from Reno, which can be accomplished over one or two days, combines the scenic beauty and recreational opportunities of Lake Tahoe with historic sites from Nevada's mining days. From Reno, go south on Hwy 395 to Hwy 431 (the Mount Rose Scenic Byway), which heads west and southwest as it climbs to an 8,911-foot pass and then drops down to Lake Tahoe, providing splendid panoramic views of the lake. Continue on Hwy 431 to Hwy 28 and Incline Village, a good base from which to enjoy the beach, swimming, fishing, and the spectacular views at Lake Tahoe Nevada State Park. The sandy beach at the park's Sand Harbor section is delightful but also very popular; those looking for more solitude can opt for Memorial Point and Hidden Beach, less-frequented areas of the state park. Those visiting from late July through August might want to experience the Lake Tahoe Shakespeare Festival, with shows at an outdoor theater at Sand Harbor. Also in Incline Village is the Ponderosa Ranch, a western theme park where the popular television series Bonanza was filmed from 1959 to 1973. Tours of the ranch house film set are given, and the ranch also includes an Old West town with a working blacksmith shop, a saloon, a church, historic wagons and automobiles, a petting farm, pony rides, and staged gunfights.

From Incline Village, continue south on Hwy 28 along Lake Tahoe's eastern shore, and then take Hwy 50 east to Carson City. Part of the Lake Tahoe Scenic Byway, this route offers panoramic views of the lake and nearby mountains. Carson City, Nevada's capital, is roughly the halfway point of this tour and is a good spot to spend the night. Founded in 1858, Carson City features numerous historic sites, including the handsome State Capitol, built in 1871, with a dome of silver. Attractions also include the 1864 Bowers Mansion, built of granite and furnished with many original pieces; the Warren Engine Company No. 1 Fire Museum, where you'll see a variety of historic firefighting equipment; and the Nevada State Railroad Museum, with three steam locomotives and numerous freight and passenger cars.

Carson City is an especially family-friendly city, with lots of activities and attractions for children. There are several fun exhibits for kids at the Nevada State Museum, such as a full-size replica of a ghost town and an underground mine tunnel. Preteens especially enjoy the Children's Museum of Northern Nevada, which boasts numerous interactive exhibits, including Musical Hands, in which a motion detector helps children "conduct" an orchestra; a small-scale grocery store; and a Show Box that produces body prints. The Children's Museum also has a fire engine that kids can climb on and the huge walk-on piano from the 1988 Tom Hanks movie *Big*.

Now head northeast on Hwy 50 to Hwy 341, which you follow north to picturesque Virginia City, a historic mining town that had its heyday in the 1870s. Beautifully restored, Virginia City today offers a glimpse into its opulent and sometimes wicked past with historic buildings, a mine, and a working steam train. To see the epitome of 19th-century extravagance, stop at The Castle, an 1868 Victorian mansion known for its marble fireplaces, crystal chandeliers, and silver doorknobs. Other attractions include Piper's Opera House, which hosted the major stars of the late 1800s, and the Mackay Mansion, built in 1860 as the headquarters of mining magnate John Mackay. Western history is highlighted at The Way It Was Museum and The Wild West Museum. Those interested in Virginia City's seamier side won't want to miss the Nevada Gambling Museum, with antique slot machines, cheating devices, and other gambling memorabilia; and the Bullette Red Light Museum, which features a mock bordello with Oriental art and vintage erotica, as well as a reproduction of a 19th-century doctor's office with antique medical equipment. Tours are offered at the Choller, an 1860s gold and silver mine, and steam train rides through the historic mining district are offered by the Virginia & Truckee Railroad. To return to Reno, take Hwy 341 north to Hwy 395 north. **(Approximately 100 miles)**

Austin (C-3)

See also Battle Mountain

Settled 1862
Population 350
Elevation 6,525 ft
Area Code 775
Zip 89310
Information Austin Chamber of Commerce, PO Box 212; phone 775/964-2200
Web site www.bigsmokyvalley.com

Austin was the mother town of central and eastern Nevada mining. For a time its strike did not attract hordes because of the phenomenal character of the Comstock Lode in booming Virginia City. By 1867, however, the number of ore-reduction mills had increased to 11, and 6,000 claims had been filed.

Many of its old buildings have deteriorated and fallen down, but Austin firmly denies that it is a ghost town. Rather, it is a relic of Nevada's greatest days of fame and glory, looking toward a future of renewed mining activity made possible through improved methods for using low-grade ore.

A Ranger District office of the Toiyabe National Forest (see RENO) is located here.

What to See and Do

Berlin-Ichthyosaur State Park. *50 miles SW via Hwy 50, then 30 miles S on Hwy 361 to Gabbs, then 22 miles E on Hwy 844, in Toiyabe National Forest. Phone 775/964-2440.* Approximately 1,070 acres. Fossilized remains of marine reptiles, some up to 50 feet long, with fish-shaped bodies and long, narrow snouts. The ghost town of Berlin is also here. Hiking and nature trails, picnicking, camping facilities (fee, dump station). (Daily) **$$**

Hickison Petroglyph Recreation Site. *24 miles E on Hwy 50. Phone 775/635-4000.* Native American drawings carved in stone (circa 1000 BC-AD 1500); near former Pony Express trail. Picnicking, camping; no drinking water available. (Daily) **FREE**

The Lander County Courthouse. *Austin.* Oldest county courthouse in the state and one of the plainest. Its sturdy construction, without frills, suited the early residents.

Mountain biking. *610 SW Main St, Austin. Phone 775/964-1212.* Many miles of biking trails through central Nevada's varied terrain. Brochure describing designated trails available from Chamber of Commerce or Tyrannosaurus Rix Mountain Bike & Specialties.

Other old buildings. *610 SW Main St, Austin. Phone 775/964-1133.* Stores, churches, hotels, and saloons. Stokes Castle is a century-old, three-story stone building that can be seen for miles.

The Reese River Reveille. *Austin.* Published from May 16, 1863, to 1993; complete files are preserved.

Battle Mountain (B-3)

See also Austin

Settled 1868
Population 2,871
Elevation 4,512 ft
Area Code 775
Zip 89820
Web site www.battlemountain.org

Limited-Service Hotel

★ **COMFORT INN.** *521 E Front St, Battle Mountain (89820). Phone 775/635-5880; toll-free 800/228-5150; fax 775/635-5788. www.comfortinn.com.* 72 rooms, 3 story. Pets accepted; fee. Complimentary continental breakfast. Check-out 11 am. Pool, whirlpool. **$**

Boulder City (F-5)

See also Henderson, Lake Mead National Recreation Area, Las Vegas

Founded 1931
Population 14,966
Elevation 2,500 ft
Area Code 702
Information Boulder City Chamber of Commerce, 1305 Arizona St; phone 702/293-2034
Web site www.ci.boulder-city.nv.us

Boulder City owes its birth to the construction of the mighty Hoover Dam, which spans the Colorado River. A movie on the project can be seen daily at the Hoover Dam Museum (phone 702/294-1988).

This is a well-planned model city built by the federal government to house personnel and serve as headquarters for Reclamation, Park Service, and Bureau of Mines forces operating in the area. It also serves as a gateway to the Lake Mead National Recreation Area.

What to See and Do

Bootleg Canyon. *Take Hwy 93/95 east to Boulder City, where the freeway portion ends. Turn left on Yucca St and go 2 miles to the trailhead parking lot.* Thirty-six miles of trails, most built along the slopes of an ancient volcano cone, challenge cyclists in this desert setting. Some of the paths take pedal pushers on cross-country routes; others take them downhill, sometimes at steep angles. Some are suitable for the less serious cyclists, but most require the skills of intermediate to expert riders.

Special Events

Art in the Park. *Bicentennial and Escalante parks, Boulder Hwy and Colorado St, Boulder City. Phone 702/294-1611. www.artinthepark.org.* This annual event which benefits the Boulder City Hospital features fine arts and crafts and handmade crafts. First full weekend in Oct.

Boulder Damboree. *Central Park, 5th St and Ave B, Boulder City. Phone 702/293-9256.* July 4.

Limited-Service Hotel

★ SUPER 8. *704 Nevada Hwy, Boulder City (89005). Phone 702/294-8888; toll-free 800/800-8000; fax 702/293-4344. www.super8.com.* 114 rooms, 3 story. Pets accepted; fee. Check-in 3 pm, check-out noon. Restaurant, bar. Indoor pool, whirlpool. Airport transportation available. **$**

Caliente (D-5)

See also Las Vegas, Overton

Population 1,123
Elevation 4,395 ft
Area Code 775
Zip 89008
Information Chamber of Commerce, PO Box 553; phone 775/726-3129
Web site www.lincolncountynevada.com

This is a ranch and recreation center situated in a fertile valley.

What to See and Do

Beaver Dam. *6 miles N on Hwy 93, then 28 miles E on improved gravel road. Phone 775/728-4460.* (Check conditions locally; trailers over 24 feet not recommended.) More than 2,200 acres set amid pine forests and lofty cliffs. Fishing; hiking, picnicking, camping. (Apr-Oct)

Cathedral Gorge. *Hwy 93 and State Park Rd, Panaca. 14 miles N on Hwy 93. Phone 775/728-4460.* This 1,633-acre park is a long, narrow valley cut into tan bentonite clay formations. Peculiar erosion has created unique patterns, fluting the gorge walls and forming isolated towers that resemble cathedral spires. Hiking, picnicking, camping facilities.

Echo Canyon. *25 miles N on Hwy 93, then 4 miles E on Hwy 322, then 10 miles SE on Hwy 323. Phone 775/728-4460.* A 920-acre park. Swimming, fishing on 65-acre reservoir (daily), boat launching; picnicking, camping (dump station).

Spring Valley. *26 miles N on Hwy 93 to Pioche, then 18 miles E on Hwy 322. Phone 775/728-4460.* A 1,630-acre park. Boating and fishing on Eagle Valley Reservoir; picnicking, camping (dump station). (Daily)

Special Events

Lincoln County Fair and Rodeo. *Hwy 93 and Hwy 322, Pioche. Phone 775/962-5103.* Mid-Aug.

Lincoln County Homecoming. *Memorial Park, Caliente. Phone 775/726-3129.* Barbecue, celebrity auction, art show. Memorial Day weekend.

Meadow Valley Western Days. *Rodeo Grounds on Rowan Dr, Caliente. Phone 775/726-3129.* Hayrides, rodeo, talent show. Third weekend in Sept.

Carson City (C-1)

See also Incline Village, Reno, Stateline, Virginia City

Founded 1858
Population 52,457
Elevation 4,687 ft
Area Code 775
Zip 89701
Information Carson City Convention and Visitors Bureau, 1900 S Carson St, Suite 200; phone 775/687-7410 or toll-free 800/638-2321
Web site www.carson-city.org

State capital and a county itself, Carson City is situated near the edge of the forested eastern slope of the Sierra Nevada in Eagle Valley. It was first called Eagle Ranch and later renamed for Kit Carson. It became the social center for nearby settlements and shared Wild West notoriety in the silver stampede days of the last century. Fitzsimmons knocked out Corbett here in 1897. Movies of the event (the first of their kind) grossed $1 million.

A Ranger District office of the Toiyabe National Forest (see RENO) is located here.

What to See and Do

Bowers Mansion. *4005 Old Hwy 395, Washoe Valley. 10 miles N. Phone 775/849-0201.* (1864) The Bowers, Nevada's first millionaires, built this $200,000 granite house with the profits from a gold and silver mine. Their resources were soon depleted, leaving them penniless and forcing Mrs. Bower to become the "Washoe seeress," telling fortunes for a living. Half-hour guided tours of 16 rooms with many original furnishings. (Memorial Day-Labor Day, daily 11 am-4:30 pm; May, Sept-Oct, weekends). Swimming pool (Memorial Day-Labor Day; fee) and picnicking in adjacent park. **$**

Children's Museum of Northern Nevada. *813 N Carson St, Carson City. Phone 775/884-2226. www.cmnn.org.* This excellent kids' museum provides 8,000 square feet of education and playground-style fun in the former Carson City Civic Center. Wee World, a play area for toddlers, is among the permanent exhibits here, alongside a mini grocery store, an arts and crafts station, and a walk-in kaleidoscope. The facility also houses three fitting collections: minerals, antique rocking horses, and model trains. (Tues-Sun 10 am-4:30 pm; open Mon holidays; closed Jan 1, Dec 25) **$**

State Capitol. *101 N Carson St, Carson City. Carson and Musser sts. Phone 775/684-5700.* (1871) Large Classical Revival structure with Doric columns and a silver dome. Houses portraits of past Nevada governors. Self-guided tours. (Daily 8 am-5 pm) Near the capitol are

Nevada State Museum. *600 N Carson St, Carson City. Phone 775/687-4810. dmla.clan.lib.nv.us/docs/museums/cc/carson.htm.* Former US Mint. Exhibits of Nevada's natural history and anthropology; life-size displays of Nevada ghost town, Native American camp with artifacts and walk-through "Devonian sea." A 300-foot mine tunnel with displays runs beneath the building. (Daily 8:30 am-4:30 pm; closed Jan 1, Thanksgiving, Dec 25) **$**

Nevada State Railroad Museum. *2180 S Carson St, Carson City. At Fairview Dr. Phone 775/687-6953. www.nsrm-friends.org.* This museum houses more than 600 pieces of railroad equipment. It also exhibits 50 freight and passenger cars, as well as five steam locomotives that once belonged to the Virginia and Truckee railroad. Houses pictorial history gallery and artifacts of the famed Bonanza Road. Motor car rides (summer weekends; fee) and steam-engine rides (summer holidays and some weekends; fee). Museum (daily 8:30 am-4:30 pm; closed Jan 1, Thanksgiving, and Dec 25). **$**

State Library Building. *100 N Stewart, Carson City. Phone 775/684-3360. dmla.clan.lib.nv.us/docs/nsla.* Files of Nevada newspapers and books about the state. (Mon-Fri 8 am-5 pm; closed holidays) **FREE**

Warren Engine Company No. 1 Fire Museum. *777 S Stewart St, Carson City. Phone 775/887-2210.* Currier and Ives series "The Life of a Fireman," old photographs, antique fire-fighting equipment, state's first fire truck (restored), 1863 Hunneman handpumper,

Mining and Money in Carson City

Home to Nevada's largest historical homes district and the State Capitol, a walking tour of Carson City offers a good viewpoint for investigating the heady days of the Old West's 19th-century mining boom. The legendary Comstock Lode, one of the era's richest silver strikes, was discovered in nearby Virginia City in 1859, creating the need for a US Mint in the area. As a result, Carson City was home to a US Mint from 1870 to 1895, pressing more than $50 million in coinage during that span. A half-century after it closed, the Mint building became the Nevada State Museum (600 North Carson Street), a good starting point for a tour of Carson City on foot. The museum mixes natural and cultural history in a collection of archaeological finds, dioramas, Indian baskets, and an antique-and operational-coin press. From the Nevada State Museum, it's only two blocks north on Carson Street to the Children's Museum of Northern Nevada (813 North Carson Street), the area's best attraction for kids. Backtracking south on Carson Street, you'll pass through Carson City's primary casino district in the vicinity of Spear and Telegraph streets. The casinos house the majority of the restaurants in downtown Carson City, so this is a good opportunity to grab a bite to eat. Continuing south on Carson Street for three blocks, the quarried sandstone Nevada State Capitol (just east of the intersection of Carson and Second streets) is the cornerstone of a beautifully landscaped plaza that is also home to the state's Supreme Court, Legislative Building, and Library and Archives Building (where Nevada Historic Marker Guides are available on the second floor). Just southeast of the Capitol plaza on Stewart Street is the Warren Engine Company No. 1 Museum (777 South Stewart Street), with exhibits, photographs, and memorabilia detailing the oldest continuously operating firefighting company in the West. From here, it is a just block north on Stewart Street to Fifth Street; take Fifth west to Nevada Street and walk three blocks north to King Street, on which you'll want to go west once again. At 449 West King Street is the Brewery Arts Center, a showcase for the work of local artists in the former Carson Brewing Company building, which was built in 1864 and is currently on the National Historic Register. The Arts Center is in the heart of Carson City's most historic neighborhood. A good way to cap the walking tour is to follow the Kit Carson Trail to get a peek at the city's "Talking Houses" by continuing west on King Street, turning right on Mountain Street, and going north to Robinson Street. At the Mountain-Robinson intersection are a pair of notable mansions: the Governor's Mansion and the Bliss Mansion. On the short walk back east on Robinson Street to the Nevada State Museum, you'll pass several more historic structures. (For information on the self-guided walking tour of the entire 2 1/2-mile Kit Carson Trail, contact the Carson City Convention and Visitors Bureau.)

1847 four-wheel cart. Children under 18 must be accompanied by an adult. **FREE**

Special Events

Kit Carson Rendezvous. *Mills Park and Hwy 50 E, Carson City. Phone 775/687-7410.* Mountain man encampment, Civil War camp, Native American village with competition dancing, music, arts and crafts and food vendors. Second weekend in June.

Nevada Day Celebration. *Carson St and Hwy 50 E, Carson City. Phone 775/882-2600; toll-free 866/683-2948. www.nevadaday.com.* Commemorates Nevada's admission to the Union. Grand Ball, parades, exhibits. Four days in late Oct.

Limited-Service Hotel

★ PARK INN. *917 N Carson St, Carson City (89701). Phone 775/882-7744; toll-free 800/626-0793; fax 775/887-0321. www.parkhtls.com.* 62 rooms, 3 story. Check-out 11 am. **$**

Restaurants

★ ★ ADELE'S. *1112 N Carson St, Carson City (89701). Phone 775/882-3353; fax 775/882-0437.* Comstock Victorian décor in Second Empire house. American menu. Lunch, dinner. Closed Sun; also week of Dec 31-mid-Jan. **$$**

★ ★ CARSON NUGGET STEAK HOUSE. *507 N Carson St, Carson City (89701). Phone 775/882-1626; fax 775/883-1106. www.nevada-events.net/rest_steakhouses.shtml.* Steak menu. Dinner. Bar open 24 hours. Children's menu. Valet parking. **$$**

★ SILVANA'S. *1301 N Carson St, Carson City (89701). Phone 775/883-5100.* Italian menu. Dinner. Closed Sun-Mon; Dec 25. Bar. **$$**

Elko (B-4)

Settled circa 1870
Population 16,708
Elevation 5,067 ft
Area Code 775
Zip 89801
Information Elko Chamber of Commerce, 1405 Idaho St; phone 775/738-7135 or toll-free 800/428-7143
Web site www.elkonevada.com

On the Humboldt River, Elko is the center of a large ranching area. Originally a stopping point for wagon trains headed for the West Coast, its main sources of revenue today are tourism, ranching, gold mining, gaming, and a large service industry.

What to See and Do

Humboldt-Toiyabe National Forest. *Idaho St, Elko. 10 miles W on I-80, then W on Hwy 27. Phone 775/331-6444.* At 6.3 million acres, this is the largest national forest in the lower 48 states. It extends across Nevada from the California border in a scattershot pattern, comprising ten ranger districts that encompass four distinct ecologies: meadows, mountains, deserts, and canyons. Just northwest of the Reno city limits, Peavine Mountain is crisscrossed by a number of old mining roads now reserved for hikers and mountain bikers. Other Humboldt-Toiyabe highlights include scenic Lamoille Canyon and the Ruby Mountains, southeast of Elko; the rugged, isolated Toiyabe Range, near the geographical center of Nevada; and, well southeast of Reno on the California-Nevada border, Boundary Peak, the state's highest point at 13,143 feet. Beyond hikers and bikers, off-road vehicles, snowmobiles, and campers flock to various areas in the vast forest. **FREE**

Licensed casinos, nightclubs. *Idaho St, Elko. Phone 775/738-2111.*

Northeastern Nevada Museum. *1515 Idaho St, Elko. Phone 775/738-3418.* Three galleries feature art, historical, Native American, and nature exhibits of area. Pioneer vehicles and original 1860 pony express cabin on grounds. (Daily; closed Jan 1, Thanksgiving, Dec 25) **$$**

Special Events

County Fair and Livestock Show. *13th and Cedar sts, Elko. Phone 775/738-7135.* Horse racing. Four days on Labor Day weekend.

Cowboy Poetry Gathering. *501 Railroad St, Elko. Phone 775/738-7135.* Working cowpersons participate in storytelling verse. Demonstrations; music. Last full week in Jan.

National Basque Festival. *Basque House at Golf Course Rd and Cedar St, Elko. Phone 775/738-7135.* Contests in weightlifting, sheephooking, other skills of mountaineers; dancing, feast. Weekend early in July.

Limited-Service Hotels

★ ★ HIGH DESERT INN. *3015 E Idaho St, Elko (89801). Phone 775/738-8425; toll-free 888/394-8303; fax 775/753-7906.* 170 rooms, 4 story. Pets accepted, some restrictions; fee. Check-out noon. Restaurant, bar. Fitness room. Indoor pool, whirlpool. Airport transportation available. **$**

★ ★ RED LION. *2065 E Idaho St, Elko (89801). Phone 775/738-2111; toll-free 800/545-0044; fax 775/753-9859.* 223 rooms, 3 story. Pets accepted, some restrictions; fee. Check-out noon. Restaurant, bar. Pool. Airport transportation available. Casino. **$**

Ely (C-4)

Settled 1868
Population 4,041
Elevation 6,427 ft
Area Code 775
Zip 89301
Information White Pine Chamber of Commerce, 636 Aultman St; phone 775/289-8877
Web site www.whitepinechamber.com

Although founded in 1868 as a silver mining camp, Ely's growth began in 1906 with the arrival of the Nevada Northern Railroad, which facilitated the development, in 1907, of large-scale copper mining. Gold and silver are still mined in Ely. The seat of White Pine County, it is the shopping and recreational center of a vast ranching and mining area. The city is surrounded by mountains that offer deer hunting, trout fishing, and winter skiing. High elevation provides a cool, sunny climate.

A Ranger District office of the Humboldt National Forest (see ELKO) is located here.

What to See and Do

Cave Lake State Park. *33 Cathedral Gorge Rd, Panaca. 8 miles S on Hwy 93, then 7 miles E on Success Summit Rd, Hwy 486. Phone 775/728-4467.* A 1,240-acre area; 32-acre reservoir provides swimming, fishing (trout), boating; picnicking, camping (dump station, showers). (Daily; access may be restricted in winter)

Nevada Northern Railway Museum. *1100 Ave A, Ely. Phone 775/289-2085.* Located in the historic Nevada Northern Railway Depot (1906). **$$$$**

Ward Charcoal Ovens State Historic Park. *Hwy 6/50/93 and Cave Valley Rd, Ely. 7 miles SE on Hwy 6/50/93, then 11 miles W on Cave Valley Rd, a gravel road. Phone 775/728-4467.* Six stone beehive charcoal ovens used during the 1870 mining boom. Hunting in season. Picnicking.

White Pine Public Museum. *2000 Aultman St, Ely. Phone 775/289-4710.* 1905 stagecoach, early-day relics and mementos, mineral display. (Daily) **FREE**

Special Events

Auto races. *Hwy 318 Lund to Hiko, Ely. Phone 775/289-8877.* Open road auto races. Phone 775/289-8877. Third weekend in May and Sept.

Pony Express Days. *Hwy 50 and Pony Express Trail, Ely. Phone 775/289-8877.* Pari-mutuel betting. Phone 775/289-8877. Last two weekends in Aug.

White Pine County Fair. *McGill Hwy and Fairview Ln, Ely. www.289-8877.* Third weekend in Aug.

Limited-Service Hotel

★★ RAMADA INN & COPPER QUEEN CASINO. *805 E 7th St, Ely (89301). Phone 702/289-4884; toll-free 800/851-9526; fax 702/289-1480. www.ramada.com.* 65 rooms, 2 story. Complimentary continental breakfast. Check-out noon. Restaurant, bar. Indoor pool, whirlpool. Airport transportation available. Casino. **$**

Fallon (C-2)

Population 7,536
Elevation 3,963 ft
Area Code 775
Zip 89406
Information Fallon Chamber of Commerce, 65 S Maine St, Ste C; phone 775/423-2544
Web site www.fallonchamber.com

What to See and Do

Lahontan State Recreation Area. *16799 Lahontan Dr, Silver Springs. 18 miles W on Hwy 50. Phone 775/867-3500.* Approximately 30,000 acres with a 16-mile-long reservoir. Water sports, fishing, boating (launching, ramps); picnicking, camping (dump station).

Special Events

All Indian Rodeo. *65 S Maine St, Fallon. Phone 775/423-2544.* Rodeo events, parade, powwow, Native American dances, arts, games. Third weekend in July.

Fallon Air Show. *Fallon Naval Air Station, 4755 Pasture Rd, Fallon. Phone 775/426-2880. www.fallon.navy.mil.* Military exhibition flying, civilian aerobatics, aircraft displays; Blue Angels Demonstration Team. Ground events and static displays of vintage and modern aircraft. Late spring-early summer.

Limited-Service Hotels

★ COMFORT INN. *1830 W Williams Ave, Fallon (89406). Phone 775/423-5554; toll-free 888/691-6388; fax 775/423-0663. www.bestinn.com.* 82 rooms, 2 story. Complimentary continental breakfast. Check-out noon. Indoor pool. **$**

★ **SUPER 8.** *855 W Williams Ave, Fallon (89406). Phone 775/423-6031; fax 775/423-6282.* 75 rooms, 2 story. Pets accepted, some restrictions; fee. Check-out 11 am. Restaurant, bar. Casino. **$**

Gardnerville (C-1)

See also Carson City, Stateline

Population 3,357
Elevation 4,746 ft
Area Code 775
Zip 89410
Information Carson Valley Chamber of Commerce & Visitors Authority, 1513 Hwy 395 N; phone 775/782-8144 or toll-free 800/727-7677
Web site www.carsonvalleynv.org

Gardnerville lies just southeast of Minden, seat of Douglas County. The two are considered contiguous towns.

What to See and Do

Mormon Station State Historic Park. *Genoa Ln and Foothill Rd, Genoa. 4 miles N via Hwy 395, then 4 miles W on Hwy 57. Phone 775/782-2590.* Fort/stockade. Museum exhibits relics of the early pioneer days and the first white settlement in state. Also picnicking, tables, grills. (Mid-May-mid-Oct, daily)

Special Events

Carson Valley Days. *Hwy 395, Gardnerville. Phone 775/782-8144.* Parade, arts and crafts, rodeo, sport tournaments. Second weekend in June.

Carson Valley Fine Arts & Crafts Street Celebration. *Esmeralda Street, Gardnerville. Phone 775/782-8144.* Street celebration with hundreds of crafters, treasures, entertainment, and food. Sept.

Full-Service Hotel

★★ **CARSON VALLEY INN HOTEL CASINO.** *1627 US 395 N, Minden (89423). Phone 775/782-9711; toll-free 800/321-6983; fax 775/782-4772. www.cvinn.com.* Located just minutes from Lake Tahoe, this full-service family resort offers a wide array of gaming, convention, and recreation services. 153 rooms, 4 story. Check-out noon. Restaurant, bar. Children's activity center. Casino. **$**

Great Basin National Park (C-5)

Web site www.nps.gov/grba

5 miles W of Baker on Hwy 488. Established as a national park in 1986, Great Basin includes Lehman Caves (formerly Lehman Caves National Monument), Wheeler Peak (elevation 13,063 feet), the park's only glacier, and Lexington Arch, a natural limestone arch more than six stories tall. The park consists of 77,092 acres of diverse scenic, ecologic, and geologic attractions. Of particular interest in the park is Lehman Caves, a large limestone solution cavern. The cave contains numerous limestone formations, including shields and helictites. Temperature in the cave is 50° F; jackets are recommended. The 12-mile Wheeler Peak Scenic Drive reaches to the 10,000-foot elevation mark of Wheeler Peak. From there, you can hike to the summit. Backcountry hiking and camping are permitted. The Lexington Arch is located at the south end of the park. Camping is allowed at three campgrounds located along the Wheeler Peak Scenic Drive: the Wheeler Peak Campground, the Upper Lehman Creek Campground, and the Lower Lehman Campground. Baker Creek Campground is located approximately 5 miles from park headquarters. Picnic facilities are available near park headquarters. Park headquarters and the Visitor Center are located at Lehman Caves (daily; closed Jan 1, Thanksgiving, Dec 25; extended hours in summer). Also here is a souvenir and snack shop (early Apr-mid-Oct; daily). For further information, contact the Superintendent, Great Basin National Park, Baker 89311.

Hawthorne (C-2)

Population 3,311
Elevation 4,320 ft
Area Code 775
Zip 89415
Information Chamber of Commerce, 932 E St, PO Box 1635; phone 775/945-5896

Hawthorne, seat of Mineral County, is a truly Western desert town on a broad plain rimmed by beautiful mountains where gold has been mined. The area is inviting to people who like to explore the "old" Nevada.

What to See and Do

Walker Lake. *Hwy 95 and Walker Lake, Hawthorne. 12 miles N on Hwy 95. Phone 775/885-6000.* Named for the trapper and scout Joseph Walker, this is a remnant of ancient Lake Lahontan. It is 15 miles long and 5 miles wide. Fishing is good for cutthroat trout in these alkaline and saline waters; swimming, water skiing, boating (landing). Camping sites. The US Bureau of Land Management maintains one recreational area: Sportsman's Beach (boat launching; camping; free). Also here is

Walker Lake State Recreation Area. *Hwy 95 and Walker Lake, Hawthorne. Phone 775/885-6000.* Approximately 280 acres. Swimming, fishing, boating (launching ramp); picnicking, shade structures. **FREE**

Henderson (F-4)

See also Boulder City, Lake Mead National Recreation Area, Las Vegas

Settled 1942
Population 175,381
Elevation 1,960 ft
Area Code 702
Zip 89015
Information Henderson Chamber of Commerce, 590 S Boulder Hwy; phone 702/565-8951
Web site www.hendersonchamber.com

The industrial center of Nevada, Henderson is on level desert terrain, midway between Boulder City (see) and Las Vegas (see). It was originally created to provide housing for the employees of a wartime magnesium plant. The fastest growing city in Nevada, it has become the third-largest city in the state.

What to See and Do

Clark County Heritage Museum. *1830 S Boulder Hwy, Henderson. Phone 702/455-7955. www.co.clark.nv.us.* This museum tells the southern Nevada story—from the beginning 10,000 years ago to all the dice-throwing today. History unfolds as you explore the many exhibits in this informative and comprehensive museum. You'll see replicas of Native American dwellings, historic homes and businesses from the early 20th century, a ghost town, vintage automobiles, a 1932 train depot, old photos of the Strip when gaming first rolled into town, and more. A detailed timeline charts the region's evolution from prehistoric times. (Daily 9 am-4:30 pm; closed Jan 1, Thanksgiving, Dec 25) **$**

Ethel M. Chocolates Factory & Cactus Garden. *2 Cactus Garden Dr, Henderson. Phone 702/458-8864; toll-free 888/627-0990. www.ethelm.com.* Expect your mouth to water when you take the self-guided tour of this factory, where everything from chewy caramels to crunchy nut clusters roll off the assembly line. Bite into some delectable free samples, and then stop by the gift shop to buy your favorites to take home. After you get your fill of the sweet stuff, burn off all those extra calories meandering through the 2.5-acre garden packed with hundreds of different cacti and other desert flora. (Daily 8:30 am-7 pm; closed major holidays) **FREE**

The Galleria at Sunset. *1300 W Sunset Rd, Henderson. Phone 702/434-0202. www.galleriaatsunset.com.* Tourists fill the expensive fashion malls on The Strip, but you'll find mostly locals in the 140 shops and restaurants at the Galleria, a 1 million-square-foot shoppers' delight. The five big draws are Dillard's, JCPenney, Mervyn's, Robinsons May, and Galyan's, an 85,000-square-foot sporting goods store with a free rock climbing wall. But plenty of smaller retailers are sandwiched between these big department stores, including familiar names such as Gordon's Jewelers, Lane Bryant, Miller's Outpost, Radio Shack, and Wicks n' Sticks. (Mon-Sat 10 am-9 pm, Sun 11 am-6 pm; closed Thanksgiving, Dec 25) **FREE**

MonteLago Village. *1600 Lake Las Vegas, Henderson. Phone toll-free 888/593-8060. www.montelagovillage.com.* Less than 20 miles from The Strip, on the shores of Lake Las Vegas, escape to a charming new development reminiscent of a centuries-old seaside village on the Italian Mediterranean. Ultimately, about 35 unique shops and restaurants will line the cobblestone streets of MonteLago, which borders the recently opened Ritz-Carlton Las Vegas. About one-third of the retailers have already started welcoming patrons, offering everything from fine art and custom-made jewelry to women's apparel and handcrafted home furnishings. If gambling fever strikes you while you're exploring the village, place your bets in MonteLago's own European-style casino. (Shop hours vary)

Reflection Bay Golf Club. *75 MonteLago Blvd, Henderson. Phone 702/740-4653. www.lakelasvegas.com.* Designed by golf great Jack Nicklaus, Reflection Bay was the first in a trio of courses at the Lake Las Vegas development about 20 miles from The Strip (Nicklaus and Tom Weiskopf planned the others, with another from Tom Fazio yet to come). The public, par-72 resort course follows the rugged desert contours with the final holes along the shore of the 320-acre man-made Lake Las Vegas. Interesting, and frustrating, water features including waterfalls, arroyo-meets-grass flora, and maddening bunkers make the course memorable. The Mediterranean-style clubhouse with patio dining under a colonnade goes a long way to making you feel better about your game. (Winter 7 am-dusk, summer 6:30 am-dusk) **$$$$**

Rio Secco Golf Club. *2851 Grand Hills Dr, Henderson. Phone toll-free 800/470-4622. www.rio-seco-golf-club.com.* Rio Secco is an expensive course, but its variety makes it well worth playing. The course is essentially divided into thirds, with six holes in small canyons, six on plateaus with views of the local skyline, and six reminiscent of the Nevada desert. The course is more than 7,300 yards long, so be prepared to swing for the fences. Number 9 is a long par-five with bunkers surrounding the green. Make the turn facing the city and count yourself lucky if you've played 8 and 9 (back-to-back par-fives measuring 1,150 yards combined) at one or two over. **$$$$**

Ron Lee's World of Clowns. *330 Carousel Pkwy, Henderson. Phone 702/434-1700.* If clowns make you chuckle (as well they should), taking the self-guided tour of this factory may leave you downright giddy. The shop makes impressive, sometimes intricate, clown figurines for Disney and other top-name entertainment companies, and visitors can watch them being made. You'll also want to eyeball a delightful display of clown memorabilia, take a spin on the carousel, and wander through the gift shop to pick up some figurines of your own. (Mon-Fri 8:30 am-4:30 pm, Sat 10 am-4 pm) **FREE**

Whiskey Bar. *2300 Paseo Verde Pkwy, Henderson. At Green Valley Ranch Station. Phone 702/617-7560.* Yes, owner Rande Gerber is married to supermodel Cindy Crawford, but he's a celebrity in his own right, having opened the wildly popular Sky Bar in Los Angeles and the Whiskey Bar in New York. At this Las Vegas offshoot of the latter, patrons can relax and chitchat in a cozy bar area with sofas, chairs, and a large fireplace. But the party crowd gathers in a separate room that's more of a nightclub, with loud music and plenty of action on the dance floor. Outside, Whiskey Beach has a pool, café, and amphitheater used for live concerts. You're way off The Strip at this hotspot, but you still get splendid views of it. (Daily 4 pm-4 am)

Special Event

Heritage Days. *590 S Boulder Hwy, Henderson. Phone 702/565-8951.* This annual festival is one of the largest in Henderson. It lasts nine days and features food, a carnival, an appraisal fair, and more. Late Apr.

Limited-Service Hotel

★★ SUNSET STATION HOTEL. *1301 W Sunset Rd, Henderson (89014). Phone 702/547-7716; toll-free 888/319-4655; fax 702/547-7744. www.sunsetstation.com.* 460 rooms, 20 story. Check-in 3 pm, check-out noon. Restaurants, bars. Fitness room. Outdoor pool, children's pool. Casino. Airport transportation available. **$**

Full-Service Resorts

★★★ GREEN VALLEY RANCH RESORT & SPA. *2300 Paseo Verde Pkwy, Henderson (89052). Phone 702/617-7777; toll-free 866/782-9487; fax 702/617-7778. www.greenvalleyranchresort.com.* Close enough to the action, yet just far enough away, the peaceful Green Valley Ranch Resort & Spa rests on 8 perfectly manicured acres overlooking the Las Vegas Strip. This first-rate resort treats its guests to the best of both worlds with an intimate hideaway feel and a complete range of services. The accommodations echo the property's elegant European influence and are inviting havens from the hustle and bustle of this entertainment capital. From the six restaurants specializing in cuisines from around the world to the fabulous casino, this resort is a world unto its own. The Dolphin Court Grand Spa is the jewel in the crown, with a mesmerizing array of treatments, including 20 different kinds of massage therapies. 201 rooms. Pets accepted, some restrictions. Check-in 3 pm, check-out 11 am. High-speed Internet access. Six restaurants, four bars. Outdoor pool, children's pool, whirlpool. Beach. Tennis. Casino. Airport transportation available. Business center. **$$**

★★★ HYATT REGENCY LAKE LAS VEGAS RESORT. *101 Montelago Blvd, Henderson (89011). Phone 800/55h-yatt; toll-free 800/55-HYATT; fax 702/567-6067. www.hyatt.com.* The Hyatt Regency Lake Las Vegas Resort takes guests on a magic carpet ride to seductive and mystical Morocco. Located in the heart of the Nevada desert on the white-sand shores of Lake Las Vegas, this 2,600-acre resort captures Morocco's exotic and sensuous essence. While the Hyatt Regency is a destination of its own, this romantic resort is also a perfect base for rolling the dice in Sin City or exploring the nearby Hoover Dam, Lake Mead, and Red Rock Canyon. Guests can even helicopter to the Grand Canyon, only an hour away. North African touches, including hand-painted armoires and headboards, give the accommodations a unique flavor. The restaurants and lounges span the world for their influences, while the plentiful diversions at the Hyatt include two championship golf courses, a fabulous fitness center and spa, and an exciting casino. 496 rooms, 6 story. Check-out noon. Restaurant, bar. Fitness room, spa. Pool, whirlpool. Golf. Business center. **$**

★★★★ THE RITZ-CARLTON, LAKE LAS VEGAS. *1610 Lake Las Vegas Pkwy, Henderson (89011). Phone 702/567-4700; fax 702/567-4777.* Supreme elegance reigns 17 miles southeast of the Las Vegas Strip at The Ritz-Carlton, Lake Las Vegas. This palatial lakeside resort transports visitors to northern Italy with its romantic Mediterranean-style architecture, Pontevecchio Bridge, and regal interiors. The rooms and suites are lavishly decorated with polished wood furnishings and luxurious fabrics, while white-glove service ensures that all guests are pampered to the highest degree. Shuttle service is available between the resort and the Strip, but with 36 holes of Tom Weiskopf- and Jack Nicklaus-designed golf, a lavish European-style spa, and one of the area's best restaurants, Medici Café and Terrace, many guests find themselves leaving the glittering lights behind for the relaxed pace and smart elegance found here. 200 rooms. Check-in 3 pm, check-out noon. Restaurant, bar. **$$$**

Restaurant

★ RAINBOW CLUB. *122 Water St, Henderson (89015). Phone 702/565-9777; fax 702/565-4809. www.rainbowclubcasino.com.* Breakfast, lunch, dinner, late-night. Bar. Casual attire. **$**

Incline Village (C-1)

See also Carson City, Stateline

Population 9,952
Elevation 6,360 ft
Area Code 775
Zip 89451
Information Lake Tahoe Incline Village/Crystal Bay Visitors Bureau, 969 Tahoe Blvd; phone 775/832-1606 or toll-free 800/GO-TAHOE
Web site www.gotahoe.com

What to See and Do

Diamond Peak Ski Resort. *1210 Ski Way, Incline Village. Junction Hwy 28 and Country Club Dr. Phone 775/832-1177 (information). www.diamondpeak.com.* Three quads, three double chairlifts; patrol, school, rentals, snowmaking; cafeteria, bar, lodge. Thirty runs; longest run approximately 2 1/2 miles; vertical drop 1,840 feet. (Mid-Dec-mid-Apr, daily) **$$$$**

Lake Tahoe Nevada State Park. *2005 Hwy 28, Incline Village. Phone 775/831-0494. parks.nv.gov.* Approximately 14,200 acres on the eastern shore of beautiful Lake Tahoe consisting of five management areas. Gently sloping sandy beach, swimming, fishing, boating (ramp); hiking, mountain biking, cross-country skiing. Picnic tables, stoves. No camping. (Daily)

Ponderosa Ranch Western Studio and Theme Park. *100 Ponderosa Ranch Rd, Incline Village. Off Hwy 28 on the N shore of Lake Tahoe. Phone 775/831-0691. www.ponderosaranch.com.* The location for the long-running television western *Bonanza*, the Ponderosa Ranch blends authentic pioneer history with its Hollywood counterpart, the end result being a tad kitschy but educational and fun. Visitors can explore the real history via a re-creation of an 1870s "Wild West" town, with historic structures relocated to the ranch over the years and an actual wagon recovered from the infamous Donner party who perished in the Sierra Nevada in 1846. On the *Bonanza* side, fans of Ben Cartwright and company will get their fill of behind-the-scenes trivia at the Ranch House, through a video presentation and a look at the show's primary soundstage. Other diversions include live entertainment (running the gamut from music to magic to trick roping), a Western-themed photo studio, chuck-wagon breakfasts (for an additional fee), a shooting gallery, and demonstrations by a frontier blacksmith. (Mid-Apr-Oct: daily 9:30 am-6 pm) **$$$**

Special Events

Lake Tahoe Chautauqua. *Sand Harbor State Park, Hwy 28, Incline Village. Phone toll-free 800/468-2463 (tickets). www.tahoehistoryfestivals.com.* One of the last remnants of the Chautauqua movement (which began in New York in the 1870s), this annual two-day event features costumed speakers who portray historical characters. Held at Sand Harbor, past Lake Tahoe Chautauquas have had such themes as the American Revolution and Lewis and Clark. The proceedings are interactive: The audience is encouraged to wear period clothing and ask questions of the speakers. Late June.

Lake Tahoe Shakespeare Festival. *Sand Harbor State Park, Hwy 28, Incline Village. Phone 775/832-1616; toll-free 800/747-4697. www.laketahoeshakespeare.com.* After a humble beginning in 1972, this has grown into one of the premiere Shakespeare festivals in the West. The troupe performs nightly from mid-July to late August, staging a pair of the Bard's works each season in a natural amphitheater on the water's eastern edge at Sand Harbor. A food court serves tasty fare from several outstanding local eateries, as well as beer and wine. Mid-July-late Aug.

Lake Tahoe Winter Games Festival. *Diamond Peak Ski Resort, 1210 Ski Way, Incline Village. Phone 775/832-1177.* Early Mar.

Limited-Service Hotels

★ ★ CAL NEVA. *2 Stateline Rd, Crystal Bay (89402). Phone 775/832-4000; toll-free 800/225-6382; fax 775/831-9007. www.calnevaresort.com.* First opened in 1926, this intimate lakeside resort continues to maintain an air of nostalgic elegance. It doesn't hurt that Frank Sinatra owned the place from 1960 to 1963, or that socialites and celebrities gambled and caroused here in the early days. (The main lodge was rebuilt after it burned to the ground in 1937, and the resort deteriorated after Sinatra's ownership, only to be restored to its grandeur in the 1980s.) Today, Cal Neva is a hotspot for weddings and honeymoons, with a glitzy casino, a top-notch health spa, breathtaking views of Lake Tahoe, and cabins and chalets complementing the rooms in the main lodge. The Circle Bar in the lobby is a work of art, encircled by woodcarvings and topped by an ornate glass dome. 200 rooms, 9 story. Check-out noon. Restaurant, bar. Fitness room. Pool, whirlpool. Tennis. **$**

★ ★ TAHOE BILTMORE HOTEL AND CASINO. *5 Hwy 28, Crystal Bay (89402). Phone 775/831-0660; toll-free 800/245-8667; fax 775/833-6715. www.tahoebiltmore.com.* One of the top gaming destinations in the North Lake Tahoe area, the Tahoe Biltmore has a casino with plenty of jackpots and a comp club, as well as two restaurants, a lobby bar, and a shopping arcade. The proximity to both ski slopes (with a free shuttle stopping at the resort) and Lake Tahoe is a big draw. 92 rooms, 4 story. Complimentary full breakfast. Check-out 11 am. Restaurant, bar. Pool. **$**

Full-Service Resort

★ ★ ★ HYATT REGENCY LAKE TAHOE RESORT & CASINO. *1111 Country Club Dr Incline Village (89450). Phone 775/832-1234; fax 775/831-7508. www.hyatt.com.* This resort is a top pick for rustic, luxury accommodations on the North Shore of Lake Tahoe. Although it's not located on a ski mountain, the resort makes every effort to help you get to and enjoy the sites around the lake, including snow skiing, snowmobiling, hiking, tennis, golf, and water sports. Spa services are offered through the fitness center. The hotel itself houses a small but charmingly old-style casino, a private hotel beach, and a destination restaurant with arguably one of the best dining views of the lake. Three additional restaurants in the main resort building, Ciao Mein (an Italian and Asian bistro), Sierra Grill (American), and Cutthroat Saloon (Western saloon), round out the dining options. 449 rooms, 12 story. Check-out 11 am. Restaurant, bar. Children's activity center. Pool, whirlpool. Business center. Casino. **$$**

Restaurant

★ LAS PANCHITAS. *930 Tahoe Blvd, Incline Center, Incline Village (89451). Phone 775/831-4048.* Mexican menu. Lunch, dinner. Closed Thanksgiving, Dec 25. Bar. Outdoor seating. **$**

Lake Mead National Recreation Area (F-5)

See also Boulder City, Overton

Web site www.nps.gov/lame

Alan Bible Visitor Center off Hwy 93 near Boulder City, roughly 30 miles from Las Vegas. Vast Lake Mead, formed with the 1935 completion of the Hoover Dam, is, after the Bellagio Fountains, Las Vegas's key water attraction. Visitors popularly make the 30-mile trek from town to fish (for trout, bass or bluegill) and boat. Several marinas around the lake and on neighboring Lake Mojave offer rentals of every form of aquatic transportation from kayaks to houseboats which sleep up to 14 people (because of the great demand for the latter authorities suggest you reserve a houseboat six months prior to your visit). Despite the lake's allure, almost 90 percent of the federally managed park is on land. Road trippers, especially hikers, gain views to plateaus, desert basins, steep canyons, rainbow-hued rocks and wildlife including bighorn sheep in the recreation area surrounding the lake which marks the convergence of three of the nation's four desert ecosystems, the Mojave, Great Basin and Sonoran Deserts. (Open 24 hours; visitors center 8:30 am-4:30 pm)

What to See and Do

Davis Dam. *Hwy 95 and Davis Dam, Bullhead. Phone 702/293-8431.* (See BULLHEAD CITY, AZ)

★ **Hoover Dam.** *Hwy 93, Boulder City. 30 miles SE of Las Vegas on Hwy 93 at the Nevada-Arizona border. Phone 702/293-8421. www.usbr.gov/lc/hooverdam.* It took 6.6 million tons of concrete—enough to pave a highway between New York and San Francsico—to stop the mighty Colorado River at Hoover Dam, completed in 1935 and now a National Historic Landmark. To get a sense of the magnitude of the 726-foot high dam and Lake Mead, the reservoir it created, drive over the dam into Arizona. For a more thorough investigation, backtrack to the visitor's center where admission allows you to roam artifact-filled exhibit halls with guides strategically placed to offer commentary. Among highlights, a 15-minute film tells the perilous story of the dam's construction in Black Canyon. An elevator plunges 500 feet down the canyon wall, depositing passengers in a tunnel that leads to the power plant and its eight enormous generators. A photo opp stop, the observation deck takes in both sides of the dam, including Lake Mead and the Colorado River. (Daily 9 am-5 pm; closed Thanksgiving, Dec 25) **$$**

Lake Mead Cruises. *Lake Mead Marina, 480 Lakeshore Rd, Boulder City. 7 miles E of Boulder City on Lakeshore Dr. Phone 702/293-6180. www.lakemeadcruises.com.* A 90-minute sightseeing cruise to Hoover Dam on the paddlewheelers *Desert Princess* or *Desert Princess Too.* Breakfast and dinner cruises available. (Daily; closed Dec 25) **$$$$**

Swimming, fishing, boating, camping, hiking. *601 Nevada Hwy, Boulder City. Phone 702/293-8906.* Developed areas in Nevada: Boulder Beach on Lake Mead, 6 miles NE of Boulder City; Las Vegas Bay, 10 miles NE of Henderson; Callville Bay, 24 miles NE of Henderson; Overton Beach, 9 miles S of Overton; Echo Bay, 23 miles S of Overton; Cottonwood Cove, 14 miles E of Searchlight. Developed areas in Arizona: Willow Beach on Lake Mohave, 18 miles S of Hoover Dam (no camping); Temple Bar on Lake Mead, 50 miles E of Hoover Dam; Katherine on Lake Mohave, 3 miles N of Davis Dam (campgrounds, stores, restaurants, motels, marinas, boat ramps in these areas). (All these sites, except Willow Beach and Overton Beach, have campgrounds, $10/site/night; stores, restaurants, marinas, and boat ramps.)

Lake Tahoe (C-1)

(See South Lake Tahoe; also Lake Tahoe Area Side Trip)

Las Vegas (E-4)

See also Boulder City, Caliente, Henderson

Settled 1905
Population 478,434
Elevation 2,020 ft
Area Code 702
Information Las Vegas Convention/Visitors Authority, Convention Center, 3150 Paradise Rd, 89109; phone 702/892-7575
Web site www.lasvegas24hours.com

Mention Las Vegas, and one word comes to mind immediately: casinos. After all, this city that never sleeps is home to "the Strip," that famous boulevard lined with some of the world's finest gambling parlors, all of them packed with slot machines, blackjack tables, and most every other game of chance on which risk-takers can place bets. And plenty do just that—every day of the year. More than 35 million visitors rolled into town in 2002, and 89 percent of them tried to beat the house and pocket some cash.

That doesn't mean visitors hoping to win big park themselves in the casinos 24/7. On average, they spend only about four hours a day gambling. They can easily fill up the rest of their time with other exciting activities in this city that bills itself as the Entertainment Capital of the World.

Many of the Strip's luxury hotels take visitors on memorable journeys to other magical places, including New York, Egypt, France, Greece, Rome, and the Tropics. Even though you're on the edge of the Mojave Desert, you can hop into a gondola for a leisurely ride on a Venetian canal, see the sights from high atop the Eiffel Tower, explore King Tut's tomb, and walk through a tank of killer sharks (well, sort of). The hotels also dazzle crowds with glitzy, sophisticated stage shows that aren't just about scantily clad showgirls anymore. Think Celine Dion, Cirque du Soleil, and Blue Man Group. The city hosts some of the world's most-hyped sporting events as well, especially prize fights. And the Vegas dining scene, long scoffed at for its cheap all-you-can-eat buffets, has heated up in recent years with the arrival of high-end restaurants operated by celebrity chefs from culinary hotspots such as Los Angeles and New York City. In addition, there's a multitude of new shopping malls featuring designer boutiques, as well as decadent spas and fun-packed family attractions.

With all this modern-day development, it's hard to believe that this is the same isolated desert region that Spanish explorers first discovered back in the early 1800s, when they sought a route along the Spanish Trail to Los Angeles. Here in the Las Vegas Valley, they found an abundance of wild grasses and water, which made their long treks west easier and less harsh. A few decades later, in the 1850s, Mormons introduced mining in the region, and then the railroad steamed into town in 1905 with the completion of the main railway linking southern California to Salt Lake City. Again, because of its abundant water supply, Las Vegas was deemed a good resting place for passengers and a good spot for refueling. When the state legalized gambling in 1931, however, the city soon went off in a new direction, ultimately establishing itself as the gaming mecca it is today with all those first-class hotels, casinos, and attractions now operating on or near the Strip.

Of course, that's all manufactured fun. For a natural high, escape into the great outdoors. An easy drive away from all those one-armed bandits, you'll find numerous scenic getaways in the mountains, canyons, and valleys that surround the city. Enjoy spectacular sightseeing and a wide range of recreational activities—from hiking, swimming, fishing, biking, and boating to horseback riding, rock climbing, camping, and whitewater rafting. This combination of man-made and natural draws makes Las Vegas a royal flush for visitors.

Las Vegas Fun Facts

- In 1931, the Pair-O-Dice Club was the first casino to open on Highway 91, the future Las Vegas Strip.
- The Strip is 3 miles long.
- Las Vegas telephone officials admitted that from 1961 to 1963, they had leased 25 lines to the FBI. These lines led from the local FBI office to concealed listening devices in various hotels including the Desert Inn, Stardust, Fremont, Sands, Dunes and Riviera.
- At any time of the day or night in Vegas a person can hire an attorney, have carpets cleaned, pick up dry cleaning, shop for groceries, get married, and get divorced.
- In 2002, it was stated that at the intersection of Tropicana and the Strip there are 12,000 hotel rooms divvied up between four hotels–MGM Grand, New York-New York, Excalibur, and Tropicana.

Public Transportation

Buses Citizens Area Transit (CAT), phone 702/455-4481.

Airport **Las Vegas McCarran International Airport (LAS).**

Information Phone 702/261-5211

Web site www.mccarran.com

Lost and Found Phone 702/261-5134

Airlines Aeromexico, Air Canada, Air Trans Airways, Alaska Airlines, Allegiant Air, Allegro, Aloha Airlines, America West, American, ATA, Aviacsa, Champion Air, Continental, Delta, Frontier, Hawaiian Airlines, HMY Airways, JAL, jetBlue, jetsgo, Mexicana, Midwest, Northwest, Southwest, Spirit, Sun Country, United, US Airways, Skywest

What to See and Do

The Adventuredome. *Circus Circus Hotel & Casino, 2880 Las Vegas Blvd S, Las Vegas. Phone 702/794-3939. www.adventuredome.com.* Even the intense summer heat can't put a damper on the fun at this 5-acre thrill center, the country's largest indoor theme park. Dare to board more than 15 exciting rides, including the Canyon Blaster, a double-loop, double-corkscrew roller coaster; and the wet and wild Rim Runner, which climaxes with a slide down a 60-foot waterfall. Some of the tamer rides keep the kiddies happy, especially Miner Mike, a junior roller coaster. A carnival midway and clown shows add to the good time. (Mon-Thurs 10 am-6 pm; Fri-Sat to midnight; Sun to 8 pm) **$$$**

Air Play. *Tropicana Hotel & Casino, 3801 Las Vegas Blvd S, Las Vegas. Phone 702/739-2222. www.tropicanalv.com.* Step inside the doors to the casino to watch a performance by acrobats, aerialists, jugglers, singers, and more. The 20-minute show takes place just under the famous Tiffany glass ceiling on a stage that was set up atop a bank of slot machines. The show has four dancers and a male and female singer who perform a variety of music that changes at every performance. (Daily at 3 pm, 5 pm, 7:30 pm, and 9:30 pm) **FREE**

***A New Day . . .* by Celine Dion at the Coliseum at Caesars Palace.** *3570 Las Vegas Blvd S, Las Vegas. Phone 702/866-1400. www.celinedion.com.* Proving her box office might, songstress Celine Dion had an entire theater built for her in Las Vegas at Caesars Palace (see), a 4,000-seat circular affair modeled on Rome's Coliseum where she performs nightly in A New Day. . . In choosing a director, Dion went straight to the top, getting Franco Dragone, the creative genius behind French Canada's Cirque du Soleil, which puts on several Las Vegas shows, to stage the mega-production in which Dion is backed by a cast of 70 dancers, musicians, and "artists." (Wed-Sun 8:30 pm) **$$$$**

Antique Sample Shoppes. *6115 W Tropicana Ave, Las Vegas. Phone 702/368-1170. www.antiquesample.com/lv/lvhome.htm.* At Nevada's largest antiques and collectibles mall, more than 200 dealers sell everything from affordable knickknacks and fine china to handsome, high-quality antique furniture with four- and five-figure price tags. Wear comfortable walking shoes, because the crowded showroom floor covers 40,000 expansive square feet. Munch on scones, sausage rolls, sandwiches, salads, and more in the cozy English tearoom, which serves a proper British high tea every afternoon. (Mon-Sat 10 am-7 pm, Sun noon-7 pm)

Art Encounter. *3979 Spring Mountain Rd, Las Vegas. Phone 702/227-0220; toll-free 800/395-2996. www.artencounter.com.* Whatever your taste in art, you're likely to find something that appeals to you inside this 8,000-square-foot gallery of immense creativity. More than 100 artists display oils, watercolors, jewelry, pottery, sculpture, and more in a wide variety of styles. Even if you don't buy a thing, you'll be awed by all the color and imaginative thinking you encounter as you wander the aisles. Most of the artists call Nevada home, although some out-of-state ones also sell their work here. (Tues-Fri 10 am-6 pm, Sat and Mon noon-5 pm; closed major holidays)

Baby's. *Hard Rock Hotel Casino, 4455 Paradise Rd, Las Vegas. Phone 702/693-5555. www.babyslasvegas.com.* This is the sort of dance club to which the uninitiated need guidance. Which is precisely why Baby's hides behind an unmarked door two floors beneath the Hard Rock Hotel (see) and often hits up out-of-towners for higher cover charges. Its resulting mystique has kept the dance club on the cutting edge, a late night spot to groove to trip-hop and house tunes in somewhat retro digs. (Wed-Sat 10:30 pm-4:30 am) **$$**

Badlands Golf Club. *9119 Alta Dr, Las Vegas. Phone toll-free 800/470-4622.* Badlands is one in an increasing trend of golf courses with three sets of nine holes, offering different combinations of courses. Named Diablo, Desperado and Outlaw, the three nines at Badlands are markedly different. The Outlaw course is more forgiving than the other two, which are are the usual tournament 18. The course was designed by former PGA'ers Chi Chi Rodriguez and Johnny Miller. **$$$$**

Bali Hai Golf Club. *5150 Las Vegas Blvd S, Las Vegas. Phone toll-free 800/470-4622.* Opened in 2000, Bali Hai takes a South Pacific theme to a beautiful end. The white sand bunkers complement the traditional architecture of the clubhouse, which contains Cili, an exclusive Vegas eatery. The signature hole is the 16th, a par-three with an island green. It wouldn't be so bad if those having a drink on the nearby patio weren't watching as you try to hit the target. Like many other Vegas courses, this one's cost is steep, usually fetching about $250 for 18 holes. **$$$$**

The Beach. *365 Convention Center Dr, Las Vegas. Phone 702/731-1925. www.beachlv.com.* Every night of the week, the party-hearty crowd rides the surf to this happening nightclub with a beach theme for fun that leans toward the rowdy. The lively patrons—mostly young singles (21+)—keep the multiple bars hopping, do Jell-O body shots to loosen up, shake their booties on two dance floors, and do a whole lot of serious flirting. A cabana and sports bar stay open 24 hours, so the drinks flow all day long as well. (Dance club open Mon-Thurs 10 pm-4 am, Fri-Sun 10 pm-6 am) **$$** for men; **FREE FOR WOMEN**

Bellagio Casino. *Bellagio Las Vegas, 3600 Las Vegas Blvd S, Las Vegas. Phone 702/693-7111. www.bellagiolasvegas.com.* Where other Vegas casinos cram in the tables and pour on the flash, Bellagio makes a more soothing pitch for risking your money. Tables are well spaced, colors run the soft brown gamut from tan to gold, and slot machines sing at less annoying volume levels. (Daily, 24 hours)

Bellagio Conservatory and Botanical Gardens. *Bellagio Las Vegas, 3600 Las Vegas Blvd S, Las Vegas. Phone 702/693-7111. www.bellagiolasvegas.com.* When you want a peaceful escape from all the bustle on the Strip, take a leisurely stroll through the 90,000-square-foot conservatory at the Bellagio (see). With its thousands of gorgeous plants and colorful blooms, this serene setting has a calming effect. Don't come expecting to see desert foliage; rather, be prepared to feast your eyes on orchids and other exotics that are painstakingly maintained by 100 horticulturists. (Daily, 24 hours) **FREE**

Bellagio Gallery of Fine Art. *Bellagio Las Vegas, 3600 Las Vegas Blvd S, Las Vegas. Phone 702/693-7111. www.bellagiolasvegas.com.* A refined retreat amid the Sin City madness, the Bellagio Gallery of Fine Art mounts rotating exhibitions organized by a New York gallery on subjects ranging from Faberge eggs to Calder mobiles. A featured exhibit in 2003 was "Andy Warhol: The Celebrity Portraits," a look at Warhol's silkscreens of the famous with an audio tour taped by Liza Minnelli, whose portrait also appears in the exhibit. The gallery's fine shop stocks arty souvenirs. (Daily 9 am-9 pm) **$$$**

Belz Factory Outlet World. *7400 Las Vegas Blvd S, Las Vegas. Phone 702/896-5599.* Two and a half miles from the tony shops of the Strip lies the local king of off-price retailing, Belz Factory Outlet World. Where you can get Saks Fifth Avenue in the heart of the Strip, you can get Off 5th Saks Fifth Avenue, the department store's discount operation, at Belz. The mall now boasts 155 shops and two food courts with plans to expand. Top-drawer draws include Tommy Hilfiger, Calvin Klein, and Bose. (Mon-Sat 10 am-9 pm, Sun 10 am-6 pm)

Blue Man Group: Live at Luxor. *Luxor Hotel and Casino, 3900 Las Vegas Blvd S, Las Vegas. Phone 702/262-4400. www.luxor.com.* Wordless performing artists Blue Man Group make you laugh while they tweak your expectations. Riffing on modern art and the advertising culture, among other themes, three enigmatic bald, blue-faced men create music, paintings, and general mayhem in vaudevillian stunts that involve props like Captain Crunch cereal, toilet paper rolls, and plastic plumbing tubes. A three-story-high drum wall was created just for the Vegas performance (versus tours in cities like Chicago and New York). This is a see-it-to-believe-it show that tickles all brows, both high and low. (Nightly at 7 and 10 pm) **$$$$**

Bonnie Springs Old Nevada. *1 Gunfighter Ln, Blue Diamond (89004). 20 miles W via W Charleston Blvd. Phone 702/875-4191. www.bonniesprings.com.* You can do more than imagine what life was like in the Wild West in the 1880s. Experience those days firsthand at this replica of a mining town from that era, built on a 115-acre ranch. Everything you've seen in old Western movies comes to life here—stagecoaches, saloons, a Boot Hill cemetery, simulated gunfights, a melodrama, and even a public hanging (staged, of course). Bring the family for this wild and fun walk down Memory Lane. (Summer: daily 10:30 am-6 pm; winter: daily 10:30 am-5 pm) **$$**

Boulevard Mall. *3528 S Maryland Pkwy, Las Vegas. Phone 702/732-8949. www.blvdmall.com.* More than

150 stores make Boulevard Mall one of the biggest in town. It specializes in moderately priced retailers, a divergence from the largely upscale shops on The Strip. Anchor tenants include Macy's, Sears, JCPenney, and Dillard's. A range of national retailers such as American Eagle Outfitters, Gymboree, Victoria's Secret, and Gap join them. Food offerings tend to be fast. (Mon-Sat 10 am-9 pm, Sun 11 am-6 pm; closed Jan 1, Thanksgiving, Dec 25)

Boxing at Caesars Palace. *Caesars Palace, 3570 Las Vegas Blvd S, Las Vegas. Phone 702/731-7110; toll-free 877/427-7243. www.parkplace.com/caesars/lasvegas.* Nowhere is the sport of boxing cheered more vigorously than in Las Vegas, where bouts are often sponsored by Caesars Palace (even when the match takes place at another area, such as the UNLV's Thomas & Mack Center). Key title match-ups range from featherweight to heavyweight. Major boxing event weekends tend to flood Las Vegas with Saturday night visitors, making both beds and tickets hard to come by without advance planning.

Broadacres Swap Meet. *2930 Las Vegas Blvd N, North Las Vegas. Phone 702/642-3777.* A cross-section of people shop at Nevada's largest outdoor swap meet, but they all share one thing in common: they're on the prowl for bargains—and, boy, they've come to the right place for good deals. Up to 1,000 vendors hawk new, old, and off-the-wall merchandise that's priced to sell. As you wander through the various stalls, you'll be reminded of this old saying: one man's trash is another man's treasure. (Fri 6:30 am-12:30 pm, Sat-Sun 6:30 am-2 pm) **$**

Casino Legends Hall of Fame Museum. *Tropicana Hotel & Casino, 3801 Las Vegas Blvd S, Las Vegas. Phone 702/739-5444. www.tropicanalv.com.* Though the name sounds like an ode to backroom high rollers, the Casino Legends Hall of Fame zests things up by showcasing entertainers, filmed-in-Vegas movies, and notorious gangsters. There's a vast chip collection from every casino that's ever existed here. But it's the human legends that make Casino Legends detour-worthy. Frank Sinatra and fellow Rat Pack pals join casino operator Benny Binion and mobster Bugsy Siegel in the hall highlighted by clips of "Viva Las Vegas" and casino implosions. (Daily 9 am-9 pm) **$$**

Castaways Bowling Center. *Castaways Hotel, 2800 E Fremont St, Las Vegas. Phone 702/385-9123. bowling.castaways-lv.com.* Most people come to Vegas hoping to roll the dice and strike it rich in the casinos, but bowlers come to this house of pins hoping to get on a roll and score lots of strikes. And they have plenty of room to do so: with 106 lanes, Castaways is the largest bowling alley in the United States, one reason it hosts major professional tournaments every year. On-site childcare is provided daily for children ages 2-9, 10 am-midnight. (Daily, 24 hours) **$**

Club Utopia. *3765 Las Vegas Blvd S, Las Vegas. Phone 702/740-4646. www.clubutopia.net.* Three bars and three VIP rooms spread over two levels at this high-energy dance club where color-driven space-age interiors are boosted by gelled lighting and a 32,000-watt sound system. Two prized perches include red padded pod chairs and backlit translucent dancing platforms. If you're looking for the rave scene in Las Vegas, look here, a popular spot for promoter's parties. (Fri 10 pm-4 am, Sat 10 pm-6 am) **$$**

Coney Island Emporium. *New York-New York Hotel and Casino, 3790 Las Vegas Blvd S, Las Vegas. Phone 702/736-4100. www.nynyhotelcasino.com.* If you want to score big points with your kids, take them to this 32,000-square-foot fun palace inside the New York-New York Hotel and Casino (see). They'll be all smiles as they excitedly play more than 20 midway-style games and more than 200 coin-operated arcade games for the chance to win typical carnival prizes. They can also test their aim in laser tag, get rowdy in bumper cars (they're bright yellow just like the cabs in the Big Apple), pretend they're daring racecar drivers in Daytona-style driving stimulators, and hold on tight on a fast-paced roller coaster. Prices for games and rides start at 25 cents. (Sun-Thurs 8 am-midnight, Fri-Sat 8-2 am) **FREE**

Cottonwood Valley. *On State Rte 160, at about mile marker 17.* Pedal your way across the desert in one of the most popular cycling areas in the Las Vegas Valley. Several trails snake their way through this rugged but beautiful terrain, so take your pick and get moving. Trail maps are available at kiosks in the area.

Creative Cooking School. *7385 W Sahara Ave, Las Vegas. In the Monte Cristo Plaza, 4 miles W of Las Vegas Blvd. Phone 702/562-3900. www.creativecookingschool.com.* Boosting Las Vegas's growing reputation for cuisine, chef-author Catherine Margles opened the city's first cooking school, Creative Cooking. Classes are divided between shorter two- to three-hour demonstration classes, in which students watch an instructor, and longer hands-on affairs of four to five hours. Thirty-minute meals, French basics, and knife skills typify the range of instruction available here. While most of the courses are designed for avid or improving amateurs, Creative Cooking also offers children's classes. **$$$$**

Danny Gans Show. *The Mirage Hotel and Casino, 3400 Las Vegas Blvd S, Las Vegas. Phone toll-free 800/214-4267. www.dannygansshow.com.* One minute you might be listening to Eric Clapton or Janet Jackson; the next, Frank Sinatra or Dean Martin. When you take a seat at one of Danny Gans' performances, which routinely sell out, you'll hear up to 100 of your favorite vocalists croon familiar tunes. This singer-impressionist never disappoints an audience with his dead-on mimicking, making his award-winning show one of the hottest on the Strip. Talented folks like Gans give the word "copycat" a good name. (Tues-Thurs, Sat-Sun 8 pm) **$$$$**

Derek Daly Performance Driving Academy. *7055 Speedway Blvd, Las Vegas. 15 miles NE of The Strip. Phone 702/643-2126; toll-free 888/463-3735. www.derekdaly.com.* Do you long to be the next Jeff Gordon? Or do you just want to know what it's really like to gun an engine around a track, reaching speeds in excess of 100 mph? Enroll in one of the classes at this academy and learn the ins and outs of living life full-throttle as a racecar driver. Half-day and full-day classes cover the basics; three- and four-day ones are much more intense. You'll be burnin' rubber in the same type of Formula One or BMW cars the pros do. **$$$$**

Desert Fox Tours. *7564 Placid St, Las Vegas. Phone 702/361-0676. www.vegashummertours.com.* If you're the adventurous type, go off-road in a Hummer—the all-terrain vehicle tough enough for the US military—and see the desert in all its rugged glory. Various tours last from three to six hours and take the rough-minded to Red Rock National Conservation Area (see WEST OF THE STRIP), the Valley of Fire (see WEST OF THE STRIP), or a gold mine and ghost town. Just remember to fasten your seat belt; you're in for a bumpy (but exciting) ride. **$$$$**

Desert Passage. *Aladdin Resort & Casino, 3663 Las Vegas Blvd S, Las Vegas. Phone 702/866-0710. www.desertpassage.com.* Among the largest shopping centers on the Strip, Aladdin's Desert Passage models a North African bazaar with Moroccan archways, mosaic tiles, fountain courtyards, and stucco walls. The circular center tallies over 130 shops and 14 restaurants, most more affordable than those at the designer-driven Forum Shops. Key tenants include cookware specialist Sur La Table, beauty supplier Sephora, trendsetter North Beach Leather, and outdoor outfitter Eddie Bauer. Direct from New Orleans, Commander's Palace restores the shop-weary lunch set. (Sun-Thurs 10 am-11 pm, Fri-Sat 10 am-midnight)

Desert Pines Golf Club. *3415 E Bonanza Rd, Las Vegas. Phone toll-free 800/470-4622.* Desert Pines strives to make itself as much like courses in the American South as it can, emulating the seaside designs found in the Carolinas. Pine trees line most of the narrow fairways, and several ponds can increase a score in short order. The Desert Pines golf center is comprehensive, even offering target areas shaped like famous holes such as the 17th island green at Sawgrass and the 2nd hole at Pinehurst. **$$$$**

Dylan's Dance Hall and Saloon. *4660 S Boulder Hwy, Las Vegas. Phone 702/451-4006.* Avid country-western music fans hit the large dance floor at this old favorite for some serious boot-scootin'—to live music on some nights, to a DJ on others. True, Dylan's is nowhere near as slick as the hotspots on the Strip, but its regulars will tell you that it's every bit as much fun. And it's no sweat if you're new to line dancing and swing; instructors teach newbies all the right moves from 7-9 pm each night. If you get tired of shuffling those feet, take a break and shoot some pool. (Daily 7 pm-3 am)

Eiffel Tower Experience. *Paris Las Vegas, 3655 Las Vegas Blvd S, Las Vegas. Phone 702/946-7000. www.parislasvegas.com.* The City of Light immigrates to Las Vegas in the form of a 50-story half-scale replica of the Eiffel Tower. A glass elevator whisks tourists to 460 feet for panoramic views of the mountain-ringed valley by day and the neon canyon by night. The 11th-floor restaurant Eiffel Tower serves the fine French food of native Frenchman (and longtime Chicago chef) Jean Joho. (Daily 10 am-1 am) **$$**

Elvis-A-Rama Museum. *3401 Industrial Rd, Las Vegas. Phone 702/309-7200. www.elvisarama.com.* Viva Elvis Presley! The star of *Viva Las Vegas,* who came to spend his fading years playing Vegas showrooms, is immortalized at Elvis-A-Rama. The strip mall-lodged exhibit tucked behind the Fashion Show Mall (see NORTH STRIP) enshrines the singer's life and music in memorabilia ranging from his blue-suede-shoes era to his rhinestone-jumpsuit era. The museum is the brainchild of Chris Davidson, owner of the largest private Elvis-related goods collection. The 2,000-piece collection features three of the King's cars, including his 1955 concert tour limo, as well as a speedboat, a guitar, an army uniform, personal letters, and half a million dollars in gems. Supplementing the exhibits, a roster of Elvis impersonators perform daily. Most performances are included with the price of admission, although evening concerts require a separate ticket. (Daily 10 am-7 pm) **$$**

Fantastic Indoor Swap Meet. *1717 S Decatur Blvd, Las Vegas. Phone 702/877-0087. www.fantasticswap.com.* Locals flock to this giant indoor swap meet, Nevada's largest, in search of bargains—and they find plenty of good deals. In all, about 700 air-conditioned shops packed with merchandise fill the 153,000-square-foot market. Automobile accessories, Beanie Babies, crystal, perfumes, rugs, toys—you name it, you can buy it here. Best of all, you'll have money left over for those one-armed bandits back on The Strip. (Fri-Sun 10 am-6 pm) **$**

Fashion Show Mall. *3200 Las Vegas Blvd S, Las Vegas. Phone 702/369-8382. www.thefashionshow.com.* Most of the nation's major department stores anchor the vast two-story Fashion Show Mall, including Nordstrom, Neiman Marcus, Lord & Taylor, Saks Fifth Avenue, and Macy's, as well as regionals like Dillard's and Robinsons-May. Among novelties in the 150 or so tenants, Boblbee from Sweden sells design-forward custom made backpacks, Stefanel offers Italian casualwear, France-based Jacadi deals in charming children's clothing, and San Francisco Music Box Company imports music boxes from Italy. Just south of the Strip hotels, the Fashion Show competes for customers with the many hotel malls in the area, meaning you'll often find it uncrowded, or at least tourist free. (Mon-Fri 10 am-9 pm, Sat 10 am-7 pm, Sun noon-6 pm)

Flamingo Wildlife Habitat. *Flamingo Las Vegas, 3555 Las Vegas Blvd S, Las Vegas. Phone 702/733-3111. www.flamingolasvegas.com.* Meander through this 1 1/2-acre birdhouse and you'll see hundreds of feathery creatures making themselves at home in the desert—although their manmade habitat is very lush and green. You'll see Chilean flamingos, crowned cranes, swans, African penguins, pheasants, quail, and more. Visitors flock to this attraction at 8:30 am and 3 pm in particular, when caretakers feed the hungry penguins and share lots of details about the crowd-pleasing waddlers. (Daily, 24 hours) **FREE**

Floyd Lamb State Park. *9200 Tule Springs Rd, Las Vegas. 10 miles N via Hwy 95. Phone 702/486-5413. parks.nv.gov/fl.htm.* Once called Tule Springs, this pleasant 2,000-acre park has four small fishing lakes, so come with your pole and some fresh bait. It also has tree-shaded picnic areas with tables and grills, a walking/bicycle path for those who want to get some exercise, volleyball courts, and horseshoe pits if you're in a pitching mood. No overnight camping. **$**

Flyaway Indoor Skydiving. *200 Convention Center Dr, Las Vegas. Phone 702/731-4768; toll-free 877/545-8093. www.flyawayindoorskydiving.com.* This is America's first vertical wind tunnel that stimulates the freefall experience of skydiving. The column of air is 12 feet across and up to 22 feet high, with vertical airspeeds of up to 120 mph. Your experience begins with a 20-minute training class and a 15-minute equipment preparation and concludes with a 3-minute flight session. (Daily 10 am-7 pm) **$$$$**

Folies Bergère. *Tropicana Hotel & Casino, 3801 Las Vegas Blvd S, Las Vegas. Phone 702/739-2411. www.tropicanalv.com.* This daring cabaret show debuted on the Strip in 1959 and has been packing in audiences ever since, making it Sin City's longest-running production show. It's all about beautiful, shapely women in revealing costumes performing sexy dance numbers. In other words, it's all about that adult Vegas tradition—scantily clad showgirls seductively strutting their stuff. The 90-minute extravaganza also features vocalists, acrobats, adagio artists, and a juggler. All-ages shows (no nudity) are held Mon, Wed, Thurs, and Sat at 7:30 pm. **$$$$**

The Forum Shops at Caesars Palace. *Caesars Palace, 3500 Las Vegas Blvd S, Las Vegas. Phone 702/893-4800. www.forumshops.com.* With piazzas, fountains, and an ever-changing (painted) sky overhead, The Forum Shops evoke an ancient Roman street in keeping with landlord Caesars Palace (see). Time your visit to catch one of the hourly shows at the Festival Fountain, where the statues of Bacchus, Venus, Apollo, and Mars come to life in an animatronic bacchanal (there's also a similar show at the other end of the mall involving Atlas). Stores scale toward luxury retailers like Bvlgari, Escada, Gucci, and Fendi but also include crowd pleasers like Gap, FAO Schwarz, and Niketown.

Several good restaurants, including Spago and Chinois, both from Wolfgang Puck, warrant a visit even for those who tend to shy away from shopping. (Sun-Thurs 10 am-11 pm, Fri-Sat 10 am-midnight)

Fountains of Bellagio. *Bellagio Las Vegas, 3600 Las Vegas Blvd S, Las Vegas. Phone 702/693-7111. www.bellagiolasvegas.com.* A Busby Berkeley chorus line with water cannons subbing for gams, the Fountains of the Bellagio perform daily to a roster of tunes ranging from campy to operatic. The razzle-dazzle really roils after dark, when 4,500 lights dramatize the 1,000-nozzle, 27-million-gallon performances. Crowds tend to stake out spots along the wall ringing the hotel-fronting lake several minutes before every evening show. But if you're a hotel guest, you can catch it on the TV's Bellagio channel. (Mon-Fri 3 pm-midnight; Sat-Sun noon-midnight)

★ **Fremont Street Experience.** *425 Fremont St, Las Vegas. Phone 702/678-5600. www.vegasexperience.com.* Old downtown Las Vegas aimed to compete with Strip neon via the Fremont Street Experience, a light and sound show broadcast on a 90-foot-high canopy over a four-block stretch of Fremont Street installed in 1995. And the $70 million gamble paid off. Embedded with 2.1 million lights and 218 speakers, the overhead show synchronizes music and colored-light-derived images in each six-minute show. Only the hottest hands in the 10 casinos that border the thoroughfare (also sponsors of the Experience) can resist filing outside for the on-the-hour shows. Each computerized performance per night is different, keying off various musical styles from calypso to disco to country western. (Hourly shows dusk to midnight) **FREE**

Gamblers General Store. *800 Main St, Las Vegas. Phone 702/382-9903. www.gamblersgeneralstore.com.* Take the casino action home with you courtesy of Gamblers General Store, an emporium for the wagering addicted. Wares range from portable poker chip sets and playing cards to roulette wheels, slot machines and raffle drums—all shippable, fortunately. Did the tables teach you an expensive lesson? Bone up for a return visit through the store's library of gaming books and videos. (Daily 9 am-5 pm; closed holidays)

GameWorks Las Vegas. *3785 Las Vegas Blvd S, Las Vegas. Phone 702/432-4263. www.gameworks.com.* An arcade of casino dimensions, GameWorks combines the talents of director Steven Spielberg with game specialist Sega in a chain of game rooms catering to both kids and adults. Over 300 video and virtual reality games as well as a 75-foot climbing wall entertain the clan, while the adults-only bar offers pool tables and live music. The kitchen serves casual fare should you require mid-game refueling. (Sun-Thurs 10 am-midnight; Fri-Sat 10-2 am)

Ghost Bar. *The Palms Casino Resort, 4321 W Flamingo Rd, Las Vegas. Phone 702/938-2666. www.n9negroup.com.* Perched atop the trendy Palms, with an outdoor 55th-floor terrace, the groovy Ghost Bar benefits from its half-mile-off-the Strip locale, offering 360-degree views of the neon-lit Las Vegas Boulevard. Having had a guest appearance on MTV's "The Real World," filmed at the hotel, Ghost Bar draws more than its share of the young and the beautiful who somehow manage to remain looking so under the ghostly blue and green lighting while draped over custom-designed mod furniture. (Nightly from 8 pm) **$$$$**

Gilley's Saloon. *Frontier Hotel and Casino, 3120 Las Vegas Blvd S, Las Vegas. Phone 702/794-8200. www.frontierlv.com/gilleys.htm.* In the movie *Urban Cowboy*, Hollywood made the Texas honky-tonk called Gilley's a household name. Now, when on the Strip, you can slip on your boots and jeans and pretend you're John Travolta or Debra Winger at the 9,000-square-foot Vegas version of the Texas original. Do some two-stepping or line dancing, chug an ice-cold beer or two, ride the mechanical bull like a pro, chow down on mouthwatering barbecue, and just have a heckuva good time being a fun-loving cowpoke for a few rollicking hours. On some nights, country-western stars perform live. (Opens daily at 4 pm, closing times vary)

Grand Canal Shoppes at the Venetian. *The Venetian Resort and Casino, 3355 Las Vegas Blvd S, Las Vegas. Phone 702/414-1000. www.venetian.com.* A 1,200-foot-long replica of the Grand Canal bisects the Grand Canal Shoppes, making this one of the Strip's more elegant retail emporiums. Venetian bridges, arches, and arcades dress up the mall. International luxury purveyors like Burberry, Jimmy Choo, and Wolford make a strong showing here. Try Il Prato or Ripa de Monte for Venetian paper goods, carnival, masks and Murano glass. When you're ready to drop, there's a food court and a number of full-service restaurants, many with patio seating. (Sun-Fri 10 am-11 pm, Sat 10 am-midnight)

Guggenheim Hermitage Museum. *The Venetian Resort and Casino, 3355 Las Vegas Blvd S, Las Vegas. Phone 702/414-2440. www.guggenheimlasvegas.org.* A venue for rotating exhibitions, the Guggenheim Hermitage is actually managed by a trio of museums, including the New York Guggenheim, Russia's Hermitage, and the Kunsthistorisches Museum in Vienna. Its open-ended, long-running show "Art Through the Ages" features 40 paintings that take a sweeping look at art history, from the 15th-century's Jan Van Eyck through the popular French Impressionist period to the Expressionism of Jackson Pollock. Hot Dutch architect Rem Koohaas designed the showcase and broke ground with its design by using textured industrial metal walls in place of the velvet used at the Hermitage, providing a modern counterpoint to the baroque trimmings of the Venetian (see). (Daily 9:30 am-8:30 pm) **$$$**

Guinness World Records Museum. *2780 Las Vegas Blvd S, Las Vegas. Phone 702/792-0640. www.guinnessmuseum.com.* Most everyone has heard of the Guinness Book of World Records, which sometimes grabs headlines by documenting the wacky things people do to make a name for themselves. Through its exhibits, this 5,000-square-foot museum brings to life some of those off-the-wall feats. For example, Las Vegas resident Louise J. Greenfarb has collected nearly 30,000 magnets, more than 7,000 of which are on display here. You may also shake your head at a tribute to the most tattooed lady and a bizarre collection of air-sickness bags from hundreds of airlines. Odd, odd, odd, but oodles of fun. (Daily 9 am-5 pm) **$$**

Hard Rock Memorabilia Tour. *Hard Rock Hotel Casino, 4455 Paradise Rd, Las Vegas. Phone 702/693-5058; toll-free 800/473-7625. www.hardrockhotel.com.* This is the largest exhibition of rock memorabilia ever assembled in one place. Shuttles depart from the Harley-Davidson Café, Fashion Show Mall, and Caesars Palace between 10 am and 7 pm daily, and maps of the exhibits are available at the concierge desk. **FREE**

Houdini Museum. *The Venetian Resort and Casino, 3355 Las Vegas Blvd S, Las Vegas. Phone toll-free 888/283-6423.* If master magician Houdini fascinates you, so will this museum. It features all types of Houdini memorabilia collected by Geno Munari, a diehard collector of all things Houdini. You'll see newspaper clippings, handcuffs and other various props the magician used to perform his escape tricks, letters he wrote to family and friends, and more. A tour guide gives insight into the man who grabbed everyone's attention with his daring stunts, so bring your questions. (Sun-Thurs 9 am-11 pm, Fri-Sat 9 am-midnight) **$**

Imperial Palace Auto Collection. *Imperial Palace Hotel & Casino, 3535 Las Vegas Blvd, Las Vegas. Phone 702/794-3174. www.imperialpalace.com/auto.php.* Part museum, part sales floor, and all Vegas, the Auto Collection housed on the fifth floor of the parking lot at Imperial Palace behind the casino (yes, it's a trek) showcases vintage cars, most for ogling, many for sale. Still, it's a nice daytime diversion from the Strip's casinos and shops, drawing a million visitors annually. Models range from historic autos to muscle cars, with a few late-model luxury brands thrown in. Since some do sell, the 170-plus-car exhibit changes frequently, but examples like the 1962 red Alfa Romeo Spider, the 1954 Chevy Bel Air convertible, and the 1929 Duesenberg sedan generally wow the crowds. In addition to the autos and the occasional antiques and collectibles auction held here, look to the collection for vintage car parts and jukeboxes. (Daily 9:30 am-9:30 pm) **$$$**

King Tut's Tomb and Museum. *Luxor Resort and Casino, 3900 Las Vegas Blvd S, Las Vegas. Phone 702/262-4555. www.luxor.com.* Even though you're in the Desert Southwest, a visit to this museum will transport you back in time thousands of years to ancient Egypt. On the 15-minute self-guided audio tour (available in several languages), you'll explore an exact replica of King Tutankhamun's tomb, the only full-scale one outside of Egypt. You'll see hundreds of reproductions of tremendous treasures found in the original—the guardian statues, the king's sarcophagus, baskets, pottery, vases, and so much more that will have your eyeballs popping. (Sun-Thurs 9 am-11 pm, Fri-Sat to midnight) **$**

Lake Mohave. *10000 Cottonwood Cove Rd, Cottonwood Cove. Phone 702/297-1464. www.nps.gov/lame/visit/lakemojave/.* This lake near the Nevada-Arizona border offers all the fun you want and expect in a water attraction. If you don't own your own boat, rent anything from a personal watercraft to a houseboat that sleeps 14 at Cottonwood Cove or Katherine's Landing, two lakefront areas that also have lodging facilities and RV campgrounds with hookups (fee). For hiking information, stop by the Alan Bible Visitor Center

(Hwy 93 and Lakeshore Scenic Dr). Plan on hoofing it in the cooler months (Nov-Mar); the temperature soars too high in summer for extended walks in the desert terrain. (Daily, 24 hours) **FREE**

Lance Burton: Master Magician. *Monte Carlo Resort and Casino, Las Vegas Blvd S, Las Vegas. Phone toll-free 877/386-8224. www.lanceburton.com.* Don't believe everything you see—especially not at this dazzling, tantalizing show inside the Lance Burton Theatre at the Monte Carlo Resort and Casino (see). Since 1996, this world-champion magician has been mesmerizing audiences five nights a week with impressive illusions that defy logic. Smoke effects, pyrotechnics, and even a live bird named Elvis help add pizzazz to this entertaining, 90-minute spectacle. And it's family friendly, so bring the kids. In fact, to perform his sleight-of-hand tricks, Burton often enlists the help of wide-eyed youngsters on stage. (Tues-Sat evenings) **$$$$**

Laser Quest. *7361 W Lake Mead Blvd, Las Vegas. Phone 702/243-8881. www.laserquest.com.* If you want to see your kids beaming, pack them into the car and shoot over to this futuristic laser adventure. People of all ages play the action-packed game by snaking through labyrinths and using laser pistols to take their best shots and tag other players wearing vests with laser-sensitive targets. Shots can even be ricocheted off mirrored reflecting paper hanging from the walls. (Tues-Thurs 2-10 pm, Fri 2-11 pm, Sat noon-11 pm, Sun noon-6 pm) **$$**

Las Vegas 51s. *850 Las Vegas Blvd N, Las Vegas. Phone 702/386-7200. www.lv51s.com.* Come early April each year, the 51s come out swinging, in hopes of winning ballgames in the AAA Pacific Coast League. A farm team of Major League Baseball's Los Angeles Dodgers, the 51s play at Cashman Field, which seats 9,000-plus fans. The team plays ball through early September, when the season ends.

Las Vegas Art Museum. *Sahara West Library/Fine Arts Museum, 9600 W Sahara Ave, Las Vegas. Phone 702/360-8000. www.lasvegasartmuseum.org.* An affiliate of Washington, DC's Smithsonian, the Las Vegas Art Museum serves primarily as a venue for traveling shows, including those mounted by the Smithsonian's traveling exhibition service. Other exhibits, sometimes locally curated by affiliates of the Guggenheim Hermitage in town, change roughly every two months, often showcasing modern or contemporary works. (Tues-Sat 10 am-5 pm, Sun 1-5 pm) **$**

Las Vegas Convention Center. *3150 Paradise Rd, Las Vegas. S of town. Phone 702/892-0711. www.lasvegas24hours.com.* The largest single-level convention center in the country; a 3.2-million-square foot facility. The center is operated by the Las Vegas Convention & Visitors Authority.

Las Vegas Harley-Davidson/Buell. *2605 S Eastern Ave, Las Vegas. Phone 702/431-8500; toll-free 877/571-7174. www.lvhd.com.* With its 104,000-square-foot facility, this Harley dealership ranks as the world's largest. Either buy one of its flashy two-wheelers as a pricey souvenir to drive at home, or rent one (**$$$$**) to see this desert region in style. If none of the Harleys rev you up, maybe one of the Buell or Ducati bikes will. If you need a lift to the showroom, the dealership offers shuttle service from some area hotels. (Mon-Fri 9 am-7 pm, Sat 9 am-6 pm, Sun 10 am-5 pm; closed major holidays)

Las Vegas Mini Gran Prix. *1401 N Rainbow Blvd, Las Vegas. Phone 702/259-7000. www.lvmgp.com.* If you have a lead foot when you get behind the wheel of a car, then you'll want to shift into high gear and high-tail it to this speed lover's paradise. Three of its tracks feature go-carts, sprint carts, and Gran Prix cars, so take your pick, start your engine, and zoom off. The smallest of drivers maneuver kiddie carts around the fourth track. After you finish your fast-paced laps, keep your adrenaline pumping in the large arcade and on the amusement rides, including a roller coaster and a 90-foot slide. (Sun-Thurs 10 am-10 pm; Fri-Sat to 11 pm; closed Dec 25) **$**

Las Vegas Motor Speedway. *7000 Las Vegas Blvd N, Las Vegas. Phone toll-free 800/644-4444. www.lvms.com.* If it has wheels, it's raced at the popular Las Vegas Motor Speedway, home to 12 tracks suitable for everything from go-carts to NASCAR events. More than 4 million cubic yards of dirt were moved in northeast Las Vegas to create the 1,500-acre complex constructed of 42,000 tons of asphalt racing surface, or roughly 17 roadway miles. Competitive events occur most weekends and include short-track programs as well as motocross, dragway, and marquee races like NASCAR Winston Cup races. In addition to watching the action, fans can get in on it at driving schools that operate at the Speedway, including the popular Richard Petty Driving Experience and CART Driving 101.

Las Vegas Natural History Museum. *900 Las Vegas Blvd N, Las Vegas. Phone 702/384-3466. www.lvnhm*

.org. From ancient dinosaurs to modern day bighorn sheep, Nevada's state mammal, the Las Vegas Natural History Museum surveys a range of animals both extinct and thriving that represent environments as diverse as Arctic and African. Though most of the museum is devoted to animal taxidermy, the Marine Life gallery showcases live sharks, stingrays, and eels in a 3,000-gallon reef tank (popular shark feedings take place several times weekly at 2 pm). (Daily 9 am-4 pm; closed Thanksgiving, Dec 25) **$$**

Las Vegas Ski and Snowboard Resort. *Hwy 156, Las Vegas. Take Hwy 95 N to Hwy 156, then go W on Hwy 156 for 17 miles. Phone 702/385-2754. www.skilasvegas .com.* If you tire of all the gaming action and glitzy shows on the Strip in winter, you can easily hit the snowy slopes for some skiing and snowboarding fun. Choose from eight different ski runs at this alpine resort, just 45 minutes from the city in the Spring Mountain Range, in Mount Charleston's Lee Canyon. A halfpipe and terrain park challenge snowboarders. (Thanksgiving-Easter, daily; Sun-Fri 9 am-4 pm, Sat 9 am-10 pm) **$$$$**

Las Vegas Soaring Center. *23600 S Las Vegas Blvd, Jean. 30 miles S. Phone 702/874-1010; toll-free 888/874-1010. www.lasvegassoaring.com.* In an experience that gives meaning to the phrase "the winds beneath my wings," go soaring high in the sky above the desert in a towplane or sailplane. Forget expensive jet fuel when nature's drafts can do the job on their own in a ride like no other. Are you up for the thrill? (Daily 10 am-dusk) **$$$$**

Las Vegas Sports Park. *1400 N Rampart Blvd, Las Vegas. Phone 702/233-3600.* Even though you're in the middle of the hot desert, you can still lace up a pair of ice skates and go for a cool spin around the frozen rink at this park. Practice your figure 8s, hone some of your hockey moves, or just have some fun living life on the edge of your blades. If you're a baseball fan, you may want to watch some of the league action on the three softball fields or step up to the plate in one of the batting cages and hit a few balls yourself. You can also roller skate or play basketball, volleyball, or indoor soccer here. Fees vary by activity. (Mon-Sat 9 am-10 pm, Sun 9 am-5 pm)

Le Boulevard District. *Paris Las Vegas, 3655 Las Vegas Blvd S, Las Vegas. Phone toll-free 888/266-5687. www. paris-lv.com.* Go on a French-style spending spree in this 31,500-square-foot shopping district that transports you overseas to the City of Light. The cobblestone streets and winding alleyways will make you feel like you're in gay Paris, as will the shops themselves. For example, buy French wines, cheese, pâtés, and other gourmet foods at La Cave. Choose from designer handbags, French perfumes, trendy jewelry, and more at La Vogue. Wander through Les Elements for the type of tasteful home and garden items popular in Provence.

Left of Center Art Gallery and Studio. *2207 W Gowan, North Las Vegas. Phone 702/647-7378.* In a nothing-fancy building in an industrial area, local and national artists from culturally diverse backgrounds display artwork that typically touches on social issues. Explore the 3,600-square-foot gallery and you'll see all types of colorful, creative pieces—fine art, folk art, sculpture, and much more. Resident artists present workshops and gallery talks and teach classes. (Tues-Fri 1-6 pm, Sat 10 am-2 pm) **FREE**

Liberace Museum. *1775 E Tropicana Ave, Las Vegas. Phone 702/798-5595. www.liberace.org.* The flamboyance of late pianist Liberace shines on eternally at the Liberace Museum. From cars to capes, rhinestoned pianos to Russian antiques, all the glitz that made "Mr. Showman" who he was is enshrined in this kitschy collection. Now that Las Vegas has upscaled to the tasteful level with fine restaurants, top-notch spas, and groundbreaking shows, this tour recalls the good ol' tacky days when Liberace pulled up in a convertible Rolls painted red, white, and blue to play one of 39 pianos (18 shown here), including one festooned entirely in mini-mirror tiles, while wearing a 200-pound Neptune costume by the light of a rococo candelabra. In addition to costumes and a piano-shaped watch, Liberace's personal effects include fine French and Russian furnishings in a re-creation of his Palm Springs boudoir. Piped-in music and a gallery of Liberace photographs round out the trip down memory lane. (Mon-Sat 10 am-5 pm, Sun noon-4 pm; closed Jan 1, Thanksgiving, Dec 25) **$$$**

Lion Habitat. *MGM Grand, 3799 Las Vegas Blvd S, Las Vegas. Phone 702/891-1111. www.mgmgrand.com.* MGM's mascot lions lounge by day near the casino floor in a skylit habitat surrounded by waterfalls, Acacia trees, and a pond. For close encounters, pass through it via a see-through tunnel as the lions pad above and below. Feline expert Keith Evans trucks up to six big cats daily to the Strip from his ranch 12 miles away. (Daily 11 am-11 pm) **FREE**

Madame Tussaud's Las Vegas. *The Venetian Resort and Casino, 3377 Las Vegas Blvd S, Las Vegas. Phone 702/862-7800. www.venetian.com/attractions/madame_tussauds.cfm.* Jon Bon Jovi. Cher. Sean Connery. Gloria Estefan. Harrison Ford. Mick Jagger. Madonna. Barbara Streisand. In Vegas, the stargazing doesn't get any brighter than at Madame Tussaud's. Of course, the 100-plus celebrities you'll eyeball here are of the wax kind—meaning they don't walk, talk, or breathe. They just look good and look like the Real McCoys. Don't leave without having your picture taken with your favorites. Your family and friends back home need never know the real story. (Daily 9:30 am-11 pm) **$$$$**

Manhattan Express. *New York-New York Hotel & Casino, 3790 Las Vegas Blvd S, Las Vegas. Phone 702/740-6969. www.nynyhotelcasino.com.* Looping around the faux Big Apple skyline, New York-New York's Manhattan Express roller coaster looks tame enough from street level. But buckled into one of its yellow cab cars, it's a streaker, climbing 16 stories, dropping 12, and reaching 67 miles per hour through somersaults, barrel rolls, and a twisting dive dubbed a "heartline"—not for the faint of heart. (Daily 10 am-11 pm) **$$**

Masquerade Show in the Sky. *Rio All-Suite Hotel and Casino, 3700 W Flamingo Rd, Las Vegas. Phone 702/777-7777; toll-free 888/746-7153. www.playrio.com.* This unique and exciting show is modeled after Brazil's Carnivale. The show features state-of-the-art floats suspended from the ceiling that parade above the casino floor. Performers wear exotic masks and colorful costumes. Audience members can take part in the parade and ride a float and wear a costume **($$)**. (Thurs-Mon at 3 pm, 4 pm, 5 pm, 6:30 pm, 7:30 pm, 8:30 pm, and 9:30 pm) **FREE**

Mount Charleston Recreation Area. *15 miles NW on Hwy 95, then 21 miles W on Hwy 157, which leads to Toiyabe National Forest (see RENO).* Picnicking, camping (fee).

***Mystere* by Cirque du Soleil.** *Treasure Island at the Mirage, 3300 Las Vegas Blvd S, Las Vegas. Phone 702/796-9999. www.treasureisland.com.* Quebec's nouveau-circus company Cirque du Soleil maintains permanent residence at Treasure Island (see) with "Mystere," or mystery. Cirque combs the world for astonishing acts, training them to combine physical wonder with theatrical flourish. Aerialists, trampoline-launched acrobats, strength acts, and daring bungee jumpers share the stage, sometimes all at once, in a sensory stimulating show amplified by original music and dramatic lighting. (Wed-Sun 7:30 and 10:30 pm; closed Mon-Tues) **$$$$**

Neon Museum. *3rd and Fremont sts, Las Vegas. Phone 702/387-6366. www.neonmuseum.org.* In an effort to preserve the outrageous neon signs for which the city is famed, Las Vegas' Neon Museum currently consists of ten vintage ads, refurbished and remounted in two outdoor "galleries." Neon touting Dot's Flowers (from 1949), the Nevada Motel (1950), the Red Barn bar's martini glass (1960) and Anderson Dairy's delivery boy (1956) almost seem quaint beside today's more elaborately evolved wattage. Guided tours ($). (Daily, 24 hours) **FREE**

Neonopolis. *450 Fremont St, Las Vegas. Phone 702/477-0470. www.neonopolis.com.* This three-story, 200,000-square-foot entertainment complex has upped the ante on non-gaming activities for the family in the heart of downtown, near the Fremont Street Experience. Take in one of the latest Hollywood flicks at the 14-screen Crown Theatre multiplex or dine in one of the casual restaurants, including Jillian's, an all-in-one fun center with video games, billiards, and a bowling alley, as well as fast-food outlets. And with a name like Neonopolis, you'd expect to see some cool neon signs here, and you will indeed. (Sun-Thurs 11 am-9 pm, Fri-Sat 11 am-10 pm)

Nevada State Museum and Historical Society. *Lorenzi Park, 700 Twin Lakes Dr, Las Vegas. Phone 702/486-5205. www.dmla.clan.lib.nv.us/docs/museums/lv/vegas.htm.* The Nevada State Museum and Historical Society delivers a mix of natural and human history. Prehistory galleries mount a reconstructed Columbian mammoth and Pacific horse as well as an ichthyosaur fossil. Regional coverage includes gangster Bugsy Siegel's involvement in the Flamingo hotel. Though the museum primarily draws school groups, its sylvan lakeside setting in Lorenzi Park boosts the incentive to visit. (Daily 9 am-5 pm; closed Jan 1, Thanksgiving, Dec 25) **$**

Nevada Test Site History Center. *2621 Losee Rd, North Las Vegas. Phone 702/295-1198.* At this center, learn more about what role this site played in strengthening the country's defense and increase your overall knowledge of the US nuclear testing program, from 1950 to the present. You'll see exhibits on Camp Desert Rock, experiments done to try building a nuclear rocket for manned flight to Mars, and other interesting topics. (Mon-Fri noon-4 pm) **FREE**

***Nevada Yesterdays* on KNPR 89.5 FM.** *Las Vegas. Phone 702/387-6366. www.kpnr.org.* Looking for the story behind the glitz? Listen to Frank Wright, a local historian whose "Nevada Yesterdays" weekly programs range from topics like the failed efforts to unionize workers at Hoover Dam to Las Vegas' embrace of Prohibition in 1919 and its later legalization of gambling in 1931. The public radio station's web site maintains an archive of Wrights essays, which make fine preparatory listening prior to any visit. (Fri 5:36 am, 6:36 am, 6:29 pm, Sun 6:35 am)

***O* by Cirque du Soleil.** *Bellagio Las Vegas, 3600 Las Vegas Blvd S, Las Vegas. Phone 702/796-9999. www.bellagiolasvegas.com.* The inventive French Canadian troop Cirque du Soleil takes their acrobatic choreography to the pool in "O," a play on the French word "eau," meaning water. In a theater built specifically for the aquatic show, an on-stage 1.5-million-gallon pool takes a variety of forms from deep plunge to shallow puddle as performers vault into it, dance on it, and of course swim in it. Circus standards like trapeze artists, contortionists, and clowns reinvent their tricks, uniquely adapting to the depths where they join a smiling school of synchronized swimmers. Cirque's signature haunting soundtrack and surreal references rivet audiences from junior to senior. (Fri-Tues 7:30 and 10:30 pm; closed Wed-Thurs) **$$$$**

Painted Desert Golf Club. *5555 Painted Mirage Rd, Las Vegas. Phone toll-free 800/470-4622.* Painted Desert is one of the older desert-style golf courses in Vegas, and it makes a deliberate effort to be playable to almost everyone, even on a bad day. A source of pride for those who live near the course, it is meticulously maintained, the greens kept straight and true and nary an unrepaired ball mark in sight. Eight of the nine par-fours measure less than 400 yards, so if your approach shots are good, you have a nice chance of making some birdies while enjoying the course's namesake feature. **$$$$**

Penn and Teller. *Rio All-Suite Hotel and Casino, 3700 W Flamingo Rd, Las Vegas. Phone toll-free 888/746-7784. www.pennandteller.com.* For 85 minutes of pure entertainment, these two funnymen mix magic with comedy inside the Samba Theatre at the Rio All-Suite Hotel and Casino (see). Their amazing illusions will mystify you—unless, of course, this irreverent duo tells you how they did them, as they're prone to do, just for the fun of it. Throughout the show, you'll either be gasping in amazement or laughing at all the antics of this talented pair. (Wed-Mon, 9 pm) **$$$$**

Pink E's. *3695 W Flamingo Rd, Las Vegas. Phone 702/252-4666.* This restaurant and bar appeals to those who like to mix their partying with recreation. Competitive-minded patrons play pool, darts, ping-pong, and shuffleboard when they're not eating, listening to live bands, or laughing at comedy shows. But you're in Vegas, so expect a little unexpected flair: most of the pool tables are lined with pink felt instead of the traditional green, which is quite a surprise to first-timers. (Daily 24 hours)

★ Red Rock Canyon National Conservation Area. *HCR 33, Box 5500, Las Vegas. From Las Vegas Blvd (the Strip), go W on Charleston Blvd for 17 miles to Red Rock Scenic Dr. Phone 702/515-5340. www.redrockcanyon.blm.gov.* As the days wear on in Vegas and the trilling of slot machines wears you down, head to the red rocks that form the western view from Strip hotel windows. Though only 10 miles from town limits, Red Rock Canyon couldn't be more dissimilar from the Neon Gulch. The 13-mile drive through the conservation area on a one-way road takes you to its most entertaining features, including several trailhead stops for day hikes and an almost certain photo opp with the assertive wild burros who thrive here. Thirty miles of Mojave desert trails take hikers deep into the petrified sand dunes, past ancient pictographs and mysterious waterfalls. Difficulty varies but there's something here for everyone from the Sunday stroller to the intermediate scrambler and advanced climber. Bureau of Land Management rangers often lead interpretive walks; call for details. (Winter 6 am-5 pm, spring and fall to 7 pm, summer to 8 pm; visitors center, winter 8 am-4:30 pm, summer to 5:30 pm) **$$**

Red Rooster Antique Mall. *307 W Charleston Blvd, Las Vegas. Phone 702/382-5253.* Housed in a former soda pop bottling plant, Red Rooster Antique Mall lets space to 50 antiques and collectible dealers who spread their wares over 25,000 square feet. Goods constantly change, but aficionados check the warehouse-sized space frequently for old signs, vintage Vegas memorabilia, and 50's modern furniture. The oldest antique mall in town encourages extended rummaging and advises browsers to "bring your lunch." (Mon-Sat 10 am-6 pm, Sun 11 am-5 pm; closed Jan 1, Thanksgiving, Dec 25)

Rhodes Ranch Golf Club. *20 Rhodes Ranch Pkwy, Las Vegas. Phone 702/740-4114. www.rhodesranch.com.* Tucked into the southwest corner of the Las Vegas valley, the Ted Robinson-designed Rhodes Ranch course centers a 1500-acre planned community. Open to the public, the well-groomed 162-acre course spreads over multiple elevations with city, plateau and mountain views plus ample oases-in-the-desert water features. Course management claims three of Robinson's best par-threes. (Winter 6:30 am-dusk, summer 5:30 am-dusk) **$$$$**

Royal Links Golf Club. *5995 E Vegas Valley Dr, Las Vegas. Phone toll-free 800/470-4622.* One thing that is at a premium in Las Vegas golf is variety. To that end, Royal Links does its best to create the atmosphere of a traditional Scottish or Irish golf links. Each hole was inspired by one on which the British Open is contested each year. Hole designs were taken from Royal Troon, Prestwick, and Royal Birkdale, among others. **$$$$**

rumjungle. *Mandalay Bay Resort and Casino, 3950 Las Vegas Blvd S, Las Vegas. Phone 702/632-7408. www.mandalaybay.com.* One of the hottest scenes in Las Vegas, rumjungle pours on the eye candy, from platform-top dancing girls to gushing waterfalls. Until 9 pm weekdays and 11 pm on weekends, the nightspot opens as an eatery, dishing global island fare with loads of sharable, martini-friendly finger foods. After hours, the place turns full-on nightclub with a blend of house and Latin music. (Sun-Wed 5 pm-2 am, Thurs-Sat 5 pm-4 am)

Scandia Family Fun Center. *2900 Sirius Ave, Las Vegas. Phone 702/364-0700.* Kids can't help but have a good ol' time when they walk through the front doors of this 5-acre, up-to-par fun center. Three miniature golf courses, batting cages, bumper boats, a go-cart track, and an arcade can keep even the most hyper youngsters occupied, and smiling, for hours. Grown-ups get into the swing of things here as well. (Daily 10-1 am) **$$$$**

Scenic Airlines. *2705 Airport Dr, Las Vegas (89032). Phone 702/638-3300; toll-free 800/634-6801. scenicairlines.com.* Board one of this company's twin-engine planes for a bird's-eye view of the glorious Grand Canyon. More than 20 different tours are offered, ranging from one hour to three days of sightseeing. Depending on which tour you choose, you'll also see other popular natural attractions, such as Bryce Canyon, the Hoover Dam, Lake Mead, Monument Valley, and the Valley of Fire. On some tours, you'll also spend some time exploring on foot or in a boat. **$$$$**

The Secret Garden of Siegfried & Roy. *The Mirage Hotel and Casino, 3400 Las Vegas Blvd S, Las Vegas. Phone 702/791-7111. www.themirage.com.* The 50 or so animals that live in this lush garden are best described as rare and exotic. Besides the stunningly beautiful Royal white tigers that are synonymous with Siegfried & Roy, you'll see an Asian elephant, a black panther, heterozygous tigers, a snow leopard, white lions, and more wild creatures. Also visit the 2.5-million-gallon Dolphin Habitat, where Atlantic bottlenose dolphins will charm you with their playfulness. (Mon-Tues, Thurs-Fri 11 am-5 pm; Sat-Sun 10 am-5 pm; Dolphin Habitat open until 7 pm; closed Wed)

Seven. *3724 Las Vegas Blvd S, Las Vegas. Phone 702/739-7744.* Seven attracts the chic and hip looking for a memorable night out that stretches into the morning, via a popular after-hours party. The setting is distinctive, with tiger-print booths, a sunken dance floor, and the less-than-subtle Pink Room. But you already know this if you saw *Ocean's Eleven*; some of the hit movie's scenes were shot at this hotspot. (Mon-Wed 11 pm-2 am, Thurs-Sat 11 pm-8 am)

Shadow Creek Golf Club. *5400 Losee Rd, North Las Vegas. Phone toll-free 800/470-4622.* Probably the most exclusive course in Las Vegas is Shadow Creek, where a tee time will cost you $500 and you stand a better chance of playing behind a celebrity like George Clooney or Michael Jordan than you do of shooting a low score. The course's views of the surrounding mountains are breathtaking, and there are rarely many golfers brave enough to foot the bill for a round, so you can take your time. **$$$$**

★ **Shark Reef at Mandalay Bay.** *Mandalay Bay Resort and Casino, 3950 Las Vegas Blvd S, Las Vegas. Phone 702/632-7777. www.mandalaybay.com/entertainment/shark/.* See some of the sea's most dangerous predators in 14 exhibits at this 90,560-square-foot aquarium that takes you on an amazing journey through an ancient temple being claimed by the ocean. Among the more than 2,500 animals are 15 species of sharks, water-monitor lizards (cousins to the Komodo dragon), piranhas, rare golden crocodiles, sea jellies, and other scary creatures from the ocean's depths. At the Touch Pool, prove your bravado and put your hands in water rife with juvenile bamboo sharks, Southern stingrays, sea stars, sea urchins, and horseshoe crabs. **$$$**

Siena Golf Club. *10575 Siena Monte Ave, Las Vegas. Phone toll-free 800/470-4622.* To say that Siena has a lot of bunkers would be like saying that Shaquille O'Neal is of above-average height. The sand is nearly omnipresent, but it's only a problem on the back nine, which features doglegs and blind shots that stand in contrast to the long, straight holes of the front side. Siena is more of a risk-reward course than it is a course for playing target golf. You could go for an adventurous shot in many places, but by the end of the day, the sand traps may have you thinking twice before you play such brazen golf. **$$$$**

Sirens of TI. *3300 Las Vegas Blvd S, Las Vegas. Phone 702/894-7111. www.treasureisland.com.* It used to be that sailors of the HMS *Britannia* challenged pirates offloading their stolen booty from the Hispaniola in this animatronic spectacle staged outside Treasure Island at the Mirage (see). The show has recently been updated, bringing new innovations in lighting and pyrotechnics and adding a sexy new twist: Sirens of TI. These women battle it out with the renegade pirates in a more "adult" interpretation of this popular attraction. Join the crowds that cluster around the ships well before showtime for best viewing. (Daily at 6, 8, and 10 pm)

Southern Nevada Zoological-Botanical Park. *1775 N Rancho Dr, Las Vegas. Phone 702/647-4685. www.lasvegaszoo.org.* Given its 3-acre site, this city zoo isn't one of the larger ones in the United States. Even so, families still go ape over its more than 150 species of animals and plants. Its two major distinctions: it's home to the last family of Barbary Apes in this country, and it displays oh-so-rare Bali Mynah birds. The rest of the animal attractions include endangered cats, chimpanzees, eagles, emus, ostriches, venomous reptiles native to southern Nevada, and wallabies. Endangered cycads and rare bamboos grab the attention of botany fans. Half-day and full-day eco-desert tours are also available. (Daily 9 am-5 pm) **$$**

Speed-The Ride. *NASCAR Café, Sahara Hotel & Casino, 2535 Las Vegas Blvd S, Las Vegas. Phone 702/737-2111.* This 70-mph thrill ride begins inside the NASCAR Café and propels you over its first hill with electromagnetic force. It then travels through a loop, shoots up a 222-foot tower, stalls, and then drops backward down the same track. (Sun-Thurs 11 am-midnight, Fri-Sat to 1 am) **$$**

Sports Book at the Mirage Hotel and Casino. *The Mirage Hotel and Casino, 3400 Las Vegas Blvd S, Las Vegas. Phone 702/791-7111. www.mirage.com.* Most casinos have one, but sports books are shrinking in newer hotels, carving a scant 5,000 square feet out of the casino. The Mirage (see) boasts a 10,000-square-foot sports betting palace. If there's a sport that can be bet on, it's on the busy tote boards and televisions here, easily accounting for the visual confusion of neophytes. If you don't understand the odds, ask the window clerks. Sports bookies have dreamed up myriad ways to bet: not just who wins, who loses, and the point spread, but who wins the coin toss, what the halftime score will be, and who will score more points today, an individual NBA star or the Green Bay Packers. Big events, including the Super Bowl, the Kentucky Derby, and the NBA Finals, are predictably jammed. But niche sports like NCAA basketball and World Cup soccer draw sizable contingents to the book as well, making seats scarce. (Daily, 24 hours)

Sports Hall of Fame. *Las Vegas Club Casino and Hotel, 18 E Fremont St, Las Vegas. Phone 702/385-1664. www.vegasclubcasino.net.* Hardcore sports fans won't want to miss a visit to this championship attraction, which is packed with memorabilia connected to some of the sports world's biggest names. The all-star collection includes Michael Jordan's autographed University of North Carolina basketball jersey; an autographed picture of the 1976 Super Bowl champs, the Oakland Raiders; ten autographed NFL footballs; prized photos of boxing greats such as Muhammad Ali and Joe Louis; and many more noteworthy items worth cheering about. The hotel showcases all the memorabilia in the long hallways that connect its two towers. (Daily, 24 hours) **FREE**

Spring Mountain Ranch State Park. *8000 W Blue Diamond Rd, Blue Diamond. Approximately 18 miles W on W Charleston Blvd. Phone 702/875-4141. parks.nv.gov.* Visitor center at main ranch house (daily 10 am-4 pm; closed Jan 1, Thanksgiving, Dec 25) has brochures with self-guided tours of the park and interpretive trails. Guided tours of ranch buildings (Mon-Fri at noon, 1 pm, 2pm; Sat-Sun at noon, 1 pm, 2 pm, 3 pm). Picnicking (daily). **$$**

Stallion Mountain Country Club. *5500 E Flamingo Rd, Las Vegas. Phone toll-free 800/470-4622.* A private 54-hole facility, Stallion Mountain follows the lead of several other courses in the area and gives its three tracks the names Secretariat, Man O' War, and Citation, after the legendary Triple Crown winning thoroughbreds. Secretariat is the course to play if you have to choose just one. It plays at the foot of Sunrise Mountain, and each hole has a name that suggests something about the track's layout (names include Forced Carry and Entrapment). A fairly difficult, pricey course. Be prepared to part with both cash and golf balls. **$$$$**

Star Trek: The Experience. *3000 Paradise Rd, Las Vegas. Phone 702/697-8717. www.startrekexp.com.* If you can't talk Trekkie, take a pass. But if the phrase "Beam me up, Scotty!" brings a chortle, you just might enjoy this sci-fi immersion. It begins by beaming you onto the bridge of the famed Starship *Enterprise* to start your "Voyage through Space." The 22-minute tour Turbo-lifts you to the Shuttlebay to board a four-minute sound-and-motion simulator ride through space, the highlight of the journey. Disembark at the History of the Future Museum filled with props and costumes from the various Star Trek series. Quark's, the canteen based on the café aboard *Deep Space Nine,* tickles Trekkies with "hamborgers" and glop on a stick. (Daily 11 am-11 pm) **$$$$**

★ **The Strip.** *Las Vegas Blvd, Las Vegas. S of town. Phone 702/735-1616.* Las Vegas's biggest attraction, with dazzling casinos, roulette wheels, luxurious hotels, glamorous chorus lines, and top entertainers. Some shows are free; some require buying food or drink. Make reservations.

Stratosphere Tower Thrill Rides. *Stratosphere Hotel and Casino, 2900 Las Vegas Blvd S, Las Vegas. Phone toll-free 800/998-6937. www.stratospherehotel.com/las_vegas_attractions/index.html.* High atop the 1,149-foot-tall Stratosphere Tower, two thrill rides are guaranteed to get your adrenaline pumping—if you dare to ride them. High Roller, billed as the world's highest roller coaster, darts all around the outside of the tower's pod, making more than a few hair-raising vertical drops. As Big Shot takes them straight up another 160 feet into the air, riders experience 4 Gs of force before being dropped back down to the launching pad. After all, what goes up must come down. While in the tower, you can also dine and do some shopping. (Sun-Thurs 10-1 am, Fri-Sat 10-2 am) **$**

Sundance Helicopter Tours. *5596 Haven St, Las Vegas. Phone toll-free 800/653-1881. www.helicoptour.com.* Take a seat in one of Sundance's whirlybirds for a breathtaking, bird's-eye view of the majestic Grand Canyon. On some of the more expensive tours, you'll descend below the canyon rim and even land for a scenic boat ride along the Colorado River, followed by a picnic lunch and champagne toasts. For a lot less money, you can fly over the Strip to see the city's trump card from high above the nonstop action. Call for a tour schedule. **$$$$**

Sunset Park. *2601 E Sunset Rd, Las Vegas. Near Las Vegas McCarran International Airport. Phone 702/455-8200. www.accessclarkcounty.com/parks.* When you feel like getting out of those windowless casinos and into the Great Outdoors for some sports or recreation with the family, consider heading to this 320-acre park. Shoot some hoops on one of the basketball courts, get buff on the fitness course, throw Frisbees, shoot horseshoes or a round of disk golf, go swimming, play tennis or volleyball, take a long walk, play with Fido in the dog park, or reel in some of the catfish and trout in the lake. Be sure to pack something tasty to eat, because the park has ample picnic facilities for when the munchies strike. Picnic areas can be reserved for parties for a fee. (Daily 7 am-11 pm) **FREE**

Tournament Players Club at The Canyons. *9851 Canyon Run Dr, Las Vegas. Phone toll-free 800/470-4622. www.tpc.com/daily/the_canyons/.* Co-designed by PGA legend Raymond Floyd, the Canyons features short fairways and rough that's consistent but tough. The course hosts the Las Vegas Senior Classic on the PGA's Champion's Tour each year. There are fairway bunkers on many holes to penalize golfers for hitting errant tee shots, and the greens make it challenging to get your approach shots close enough to have consistent birdie opportunities. It's a difficult course, but one not to miss. **$$$$**

Tropicana Bird Show. *Tropics Lounge, Tropicana Hotel & Casino, 3801 Las Vegas Blvd S, Las Vegas. Phone 702/739-2222; toll-free 888/826-8767. www.tropicanalv.com.* Three shows daily feature animal trainer Tianna Carroll and her fine-feathered cast of talented birds. The birds sing, dance, ride bicycles, fly through hoops on command, and even juggle. Lively audience participation is encouraged. (Fri-Wed at 11 am, 12:30 pm, and 2 pm) **FREE**

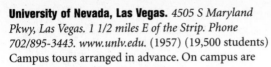

University of Nevada, Las Vegas. *4505 S Maryland Pkwy, Las Vegas. 1 1/2 miles E of the Strip. Phone 702/895-3443. www.unlv.edu.* (1957) (19,500 students) Campus tours arranged in advance. On campus are

Artemus W. Ham Concert Hall. *4505 S Maryland Pkwy, Las Vegas. Phone 702/895-2787 (box office).* A 1,900-seat theater featuring yearly Charles Vanda Master Series of symphony, opera, and ballet. Jazz and popular music concerts also performed here.

Donna Beam Fine Art Gallery. *Alta Ham Fine Arts Building, Las Vegas. Phone 702/895-3893. www.unlv.edu.* Exhibits by professional artists, faculty, students; emphasis on contemporary art. (Mon-Fri 9 am-5 pm, Sat 10 am-2 pm; closed holidays) **FREE**

The Flashlight. A 38-foot-tall steel sculpture by Claes Oldenburg and Coosje von Bruggen.

Judy Bayley Theatre. *4505 S Maryland Pkwy, Las Vegas. Phone 702/895-2787 (box office). www.unlv.edu.* Varied theatrical performances all year.

Marjorie Barrick Museum of Natural History. *4505 S Maryland Pkwy, Las Vegas. Phone 702/895-3381.* Exhibits of the biology, geology, and archaeology of the Las Vegas area, including live desert animals. (Mon-Fri 8 am-4:45 pm, Sat 10 am-2 pm; closed holidays) **FREE**

Thomas & Mack Center. *4505 S Maryland Pkwy, Las Vegas. Phone 702/895-3761. www.thomasandmack.com.* This 18,500-seat events center features concerts, ice shows, rodeos, and sporting events.

UNLV Sports. *Las Vegas. Phone 702/739-3267. unlvrebels.ocsn.com.* A perennial contender in the NCAA's basketball tourney each March, the UNLV's Runnin' Rebels basketball team (see THOMAS & MACK CENTER) is the one the locals cheer, the oldest team in a town that lacks deep roots (in fact it's the only one called "Runnin' Rebels"; all the school's other teams are just Rebels). Football games (Sam Boyd Stadium, 7000 E Russell Rd) come with all the pageantry from marching bands to tailgating parties. (Basketball Nov-Mar; football Aug-Nov)

Xeriscape. *4505 Maryland Pkwy, Las Vegas. Located at the entrance to the Barrick Museum of Natural History, on the UNLV campus. Phone 702/895-3392. www.unlv.edu/facilities/landscape/history.html.* This 1 1/2-acre garden proves that a landscape featuring desert plants can be a real eye-pleaser, despite what many people might think. You'll get lost in the serene setting as you wander the many paved pathways and cross over the wooden bridges scattered across the grounds. Plenty of benches make it easy to sit for a spell and rest or take in the botanical beauty all around you. Many of the plants are indigenous to North America's four desert regions, while others were introduced from Australia, the Mediterranean, Mexico, and South America. (Daily 8 am-5 pm) **FREE**

V Bar. *The Venetian Resort and Casino, 3355 Las Vegas Blvd S, Las Vegas. Phone 702/414-3200. www.venetian.com.* For a hip lounge with the kind of cool minimalism rarely seen in Vegas (imported, in fact, by the team behind LA's trendy Sunset Room), drop into V Bar at the Venetian (see). Leather daybeds here have cushioned the derrieres of bona fide celebrities like George Clooney and Brad Pitt. Local singles, the more scantily clad the better, make an exception and travel to the Strip just to sit and sip here. DJs spin everything from hip-hop to 1980s new wave. (Daily 6 pm-4 am)

Valentino's Zoot Suit Connection. *906 S 6th St, Las Vegas. Phone 702/383-9555.* Fans of vintage clothing, many from abroad, make the trek to Valentino's for the good-quality selection of threads from the 1940s and 50s. In addition to the eponymous zoot suits, Valentino's stocks glamorous cocktail dresses, men's fedoras and women's pumps—perfect hit-the-town costumes. This is no Salvation Army; expect to pony up plenty of cash for mint-condition apparel. (Mon-Sat 11 am-5 pm)

Via Bellagio. *Bellagio Las Vegas, 3600 Las Vegas Blvd S, Las Vegas. Phone 702/693-7111. www.bellagio.com.* The skylit Via Bellagio provides fittingly luxe surrounds for high-end designer shops, with emphasis on Italian firms like Giorgio Armani, Moschino, Gucci, and Prada. Chanel, Yves Saint Laurent, and Hermes compose a strong French contingent. Both Tiffany and Fred Leighton deal baubles to high rollers. Don't fear the price tags. For architecture alone, the sunny Via warrants a stroll. (Daily 10 am-7 pm)

Wet 'n Wild Las Vegas. (Closed Sept 2004) *2601 Las Vegas Blvd, Las Vegas. Phone 702/765-9700. www.wetnwildlv.com.* Primed to cool the kiddies in the desert dog days, the conveniently located Wet 'n Wild pumps nearly 2 million gallons of water through chutes, flumes, slides, a lazy river, and wave pool. Some features, including seven-story plummets, are restricted to teens and adults.

For the littlest, there's a pirate ship-cum-playground over the shallowest of pools. Rafts, tubes, and lockers are available for rent. (May-Sept, open daily at 10 am; closed Oct-mid-Apr) **$$$$**

Wynn Collection of Fine Art. *3145 Las Vegas Blvd S, Las Vegas. Phone 702/733-4100.* While he readies his latest casino resort, Strip developer and art collector Steve Wynn, the mastermind behind the Bellagio, displays 13 of his paintings in what's left of the razed Desert Inn. If the quantity of works sounds paltry, consider the quality of artists here: Picasso, Manet, Matisse, Cezanne, Van Gogh, Warhol. Wynn himself supplies the narration on the audio tour, offering keen insights as well as a self-deprecating story about posing for Andy Warhol (the image appears in this collection). The star of the show, "La Reve," a portrait of a woman dreaming by Picasso, is Wynn's inspiration for the resort he is currently building on this property, also to be called La Reve. (Wed-Sun 10 am-5 pm) **$$**

Special Events

Invensys Classic (Las Vegas Invitational). *Tournament Players Club at Summerlin, 1700 Village Center Cir, Las Vegas. Phone 702/242-3000. www.pgatour.com/tournaments/r047/index.html.* A top Professional Golfer's Association tournament, autumn's annual Las Vegas Invitational (now known as the Invensys Classic) draws the pro tour's elite to Sin City. Host of the PGA event since 1992, the Tournament Players Club at Summerlin was designed by architect Bobby Weed with input from player/consultant Fuzzy Zoeller. In addition to offering elevation changes and a variety of challenges, the course was built to accommodate spectators with natural amphitheaters and clear sightlines to the tees. Oct. **$$$$**

National Finals Rodeo. *Thomas & Mack Center, University of Las Vegas, 4505 S Maryland Pkwy, Las Vegas. Phone 719/593-8840. sports.espn.go.com/prorodeo/index.* For 10 days in December, the Old West rides into Las Vegas, rounding up glory in the American mythic arenas of bull riding, calf roping, and barrel racing. Only the top 15 money winners per event annually on the Professional Rodeo Cowboys Association competitive circuit earn the right to rodeo here, competing for millions in prize money, not to mention the champion belt buckles. For a novelty act, this rodeo is one of the most sought-after tickets in Vegas (several web-based brokers hawk tickets well in advance). Among related affairs, the rodeo also produces a Miss Rodeo contest, a horse and bull sale, and a cowboy Christmas gift show. Ten days in early Dec.

UNLV Performing Arts Center. *University of Nevada Las Vegas, 4505 S Maryland Pkwy, Las Vegas. Phone 702/895-3801. pac.nevada.edu.* Touring performers as diverse as Herbie Hancock, Yo-Yo Ma, the Shanghai Ballet, Regina Carter, and Andre Watts play at the Performing Arts Center found on the University of Nevada Las Vegas campus. In addition to classical musicians, jazz players, and world dance troops, the center stages lectures by visiting authors like John Irving and journalists such as Cokie Roberts. The UNLV departments of theater and performing arts also mount shows on the several stages here. **$$$$**

World Series of Poker. *Binion's Horseshoe Hotel & Casino, 128 E Fremont St, Las Vegas. Phone 702/382-1600. www.binions.com.* Since 1970, the Binion Horseshoe (see) has been hosting this high-stakes tournament for serious poker players. Through the years, however, the number of competitors has increased dramatically, from fewer than 100 in the early days to more than 7,000 in recent years. The prize money has climbed proportionately, to nearly $20 million, about $2 million of which the champion pocketed in 2003. A wide variety of games are played, and anyone age 21 or older can enter the competition, which continues for five suspenseful, nerve-wracking weeks. (Apr-May)

Limited-Service Hotels

★★ BARBARY COAST HOTEL & CASINO. *3595 S Las Vegas Blvd, Las Vegas (89109). Phone 702/737-7111; fax 702/894-9954. www.barbarycoastcasino.com.* 300 rooms. Check-in 3 pm, check-out noon. Restaurant, bar. Casino. **$**

★★ CLARION HOTEL & SUITES. *325 E Flamingo Rd, Las Vegas (89109). Phone 702/732-9100; toll-free 877/224-2287; fax 702/731-9784. www.choicehotels.com.* 150 rooms, 3 story. Check-in 3 pm, check-out noon. Restaurant, bar. Fitness room. Outdoor pool. Airport transportation available. **$**

★★ COURTYARD BY MARRIOTT. *3275 Paradise Rd, Las Vegas (89109). Phone 702/791-3600; 800/321-2211; fax 702/796-7981. www.marriott.com.* 149 rooms, 3 story. Check-in 3 pm, check-out noon.

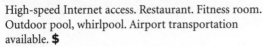

High-speed Internet access. Restaurant. Fitness room. Outdoor pool, whirlpool. Airport transportation available. **$**

★★ EMBASSY SUITES HOTEL LAS VEGAS. *4315 Swenson St, Las Vegas (89119). Phone 702/795-2800; fax 702/795-1520. www.embassysuites.com.* 65 rooms, all suites. Check-in 3 pm, check-out noon. Restaurant, bar. **$$**

★ FAIRFIELD INN. *3850 Paradise Rd, Las Vegas (89109). Phone 702/791-0899; toll-free 800/228-2800; fax 702/791-2705. www.marriott.com.* 129 rooms, 4 story. Check-in 3 pm, check-out noon. Outdoor pool. **$**

★★ FIESTA RANCHO STATION CASINO HOTEL. *2400 N Rancho Dr, Las Vegas (89130). Phone 702/631-7000; toll-free 800/678-2846; fax 702/221-6510. www.fiestacasino.com.* 100 rooms, 5 story. Check-in 3 pm, check-out noon. High-speed Internet access. Three restaurants, two bars. Pool. Airport transportation available. Casino. Near North Las Vegas Airport. Casino. **$**

★★ FITZGERALDS CASINO. *301 Fremont St, Las Vegas (89101). Phone 702/388-2400; toll-free 800/274-5825; fax 702/388-2181. www.fitzgeralds.com.* If the name doesn't give away the Irish theme, the hotel's entrance does: a giant leprechaun, pot of gold, and rainbow greet guests ready to place their bets. The theme extends to the restaurants, including Limericks Steakhouse and the Shamrock Café. At 34 stories, the hotel is the tallest in the downtown area, so many of its guest rooms offer splendid views of the Valley and the surrounding mountains. The 42,000-square-foot casino has nearly 1,000 slot machines and 23 table games. 638 rooms, 34 story. Check-out noon. Restaurant, bar. Casino. **$**

★★ FLAMINGO LAS VEGAS. *3555 Las Vegas Blvd S, Las Vegas (89109). Phone 702/733-3111; toll-free 800/308-8899; fax 702/733-3353. www.flamingolasvegas.com.* This large, self-contained casino resort predates the recent explosion of mega-hotels on the Strip while bridging the old and new Vegas charm. Amenities include a water sports area and the new Radio City Music Hall Review, featuring the Rockettes. 3,655 rooms, 28 story. Pets accepted, some restrictions. Check-in 3 pm, check-out noon. Restaurant, bar. Fitness room, spa. Outdoor pool. Tennis. Business center. Casino. **$**

★ LA QUINTA INN. *3970 Paradise Rd, Las Vegas (89109). Phone 702/796-9000; fax 702/796-3537. www.laquinta.com.* 251 rooms, 3 story. Pets accepted, some restrictions. Complimentary continental breakfast. Check-in 3 pm, check-out noon. Pool. Airport transportation available. **$**

★★ LAS VEGAS CLUB HOTEL AND CASINO. *18 E Fremont St, Las Vegas (89109). Phone 702/385-1664; toll-free 800/634-6532; fax 702/385-5193. www.vegasclubcasino.net.* Sports fanatics can score big at this smaller hotel, and not just in the casino, which is known for its "liberal" blackjack rules and its 900-plus slot machines. The hotel features restaurants with sports themes and a Sports Hall of Fame with memorabilia that any sports fan has to love. Walk outside the front door and you're at the entrance to downtown's Fremont Street Experience, a Vegas-style pedestrian mall with a glitzy sound and light show. 410 rooms, 16 story. Check-in 3 pm, check-out noon. Restaurants, bars. Casino. **$**

★★ MAIN STREET STATION. *200 N Main St, Las Vegas (89101). Phone 702/387-1896; toll-free 800/465-0711; fax 702/388-4421. www.mainstreetcasino.com* Despite its 28,000-square-foot game area, this Victorian-era property is more than just an award-winning casino. It is also home to downtown's only microbrewery and an antique collection that includes Buffalo Bill Cody's private rail car. 406 rooms, 15 story. Check-in 4 pm, check-out noon. Restaurants, bars. Business center. Casino. **$**

★★ ORLEANS HOTEL AND CASINO. *4500 W Tropicana Ave, Las Vegas (89103). Phone 702/365-7111; fax 702/365-7505. www.orleanscasino.com.* 1,426 rooms. Check-in 3 pm, check-out noon. Restaurant, bar. Casino. **$$**

★★ PALACE STATION HOTEL. *2411 W Sahara Ave, Las Vegas (89102). Phone 702/367-2411; fax 702/367-2478. www.palacestation.com.* 1,021 rooms. Check-in 3 pm, check-out 11 am. Restaurant, bar. Casino. **$**

★★ SAHARA HOTEL & CASINO. *2535 Las Vegas Blvd S, Las Vegas (89109). Phone 702/737-2654; toll-free 888/696-2121; fax 702/791-2027. www.saharavegas.com.* The architecture says that you've packed your bags and gone to Morocco, but step into the spacious 85,000-square-foot casino and you know that you're in Vegas. Everything else about this hotel is big, too—it has 1,720 rooms decorated in a Moroccan motif and a 5,000-square-foot pool with private cabanas and a gazebo-covered spa. Be sure to check out the thrill rides inside the hotel's NASCAR Cafe. 1,720 rooms, 27 story. Check-in 3 pm, check-out noon. Restaurant, bar. Outdoor pool, children's pool. Business center. Casino. **$**

★★ SAM'S TOWN HOTEL AND GAMBLING HALL. *5111 Boulder Hwy, Las Vegas (89122). Phone 702/456-7777; toll-free 800/897-8696; fax 702/454-8107. www.samstownlv.com.* Old West meets Las Vegas. Sound impossible? Just visit this western-style casino hotel, which features a 25,000-square-foot atrium with a nightly laser show and a 56-lane bowling center. Visitors can buy their 10-gallon hats at the Western Emporium, attached to the casino, and join in the nightly Sunset Stampede. Old West décor; atrium. 648 rooms, 9 story. Check-out noon. Restaurant. Pool, whirlpool. Casino. Bowling center. **$**

★★ SANTA FE STATION HOTEL. *4949 N Rancho Dr, Las Vegas (89130). Phone 702/658-4900; toll-free 866/767-7771; fax 702/658-4919. www.stationcasinos.com.* This hotel serves up more than a few surprises. For starters, it's several miles northwest of the Strip and most of its competition. Also, it's small, with just 200 rooms. And some of its amenities aren't the norm, either—specifically, its ice skating rink and bowling alley. Of course, it does have that Vegas mainstay, a casino packed with slot machines and table games. As the name implies, the décor is distinctively Southwestern. 200 rooms, 5 story. Check-in 3 pm, check-out noon. Restaurants, bars. Pool, whirlpool. Casino. **$**

★★ SILVERTON HOTEL CASINO. *3333 Blue Diamond Rd, Las Vegas (89139). Phone 702/263-7777; toll-free 800/588-7711; fax 702/896-5635. www.silvertoncasino.com.* 300 rooms, 4 story. Check-in 3 pm, check-out noon. Restaurants, bars. Pool, children's pool, whirlpool. Casino. **$**

Full-Service Hotels

★★★ ALADDIN RESORT AND CASINO. *3667 Las Vegas Blvd S, Las Vegas (89109). Phone 702/736-0111; toll-free 800/207-6900; fax 702/785-5557. www.aladdincasino.com.* 2,600 rooms. Check-in 3 pm, check-out 11 am. Restaurants, bars. Two outdoor pools. Casino. **$$$**

★★★ ALEXIS PARK RESORT. *375 E Harmon Ave, Las Vegas (89109). Phone 702/796-3300; fax 702/796-4334. www.alexispark.com.* Clean, quiet, all-suite Alexis Park lacks a casino, an omission that bolsters its tranquil appeal. Two-story residence-style suites include a dining area and gas fireplace with one bedroom per floor, making this resort a good choice for families and longer stays. An on-site convention center encourages business affairs, while the freeform swimming pool, shallow children's pool, and full-service spa provide resort amenities. To get in on the gaming action, the Strip casinos and attractions are just several blocks away. 500 rooms, 2 story, all suites. Check-in 3 pm, check-out 11 am. Restaurant, bar. Outdoor pool, children's pool. Business center. **$$**

★★★ BALLY'S LAS VEGAS. *3645 Las Vegas Blvd, Las Vegas (89109). Phone 702/967-4111; toll-free 888/742-9248; fax 702/967-4405. www.ballyslv.com.* A neon-lit tunnel ushers you from the heart of the Strip into Bally's, offering good value in a prime location. At over 500 square feet, the recently renovated rooms are spacious and comfortable. The palm-fringed pool and spa, though small here, are musts for any Strip address. But what marquees Bally's is its showroom, where the showgirl-driven *Jubilee* is frequently named best of its kind by locals. While Bally's is old Las Vegas, it shares ownership, and a connecting walkway, with Paris Las Vegas (see), one of The Strip's newest and showiest comers, convenient for its many shopping and dining options. 2,832 rooms, 26 story. Check-out 11 am. Restaurant, bar. Fitness room. Outdoor pool, children's pool. Tennis. Casino. **$**

★★★★ BELLAGIO. *3600 Las Vegas Blvd S, Las Vegas (89109). Phone 702/693-7111; toll-free 888/*

742-9248; fax 702/967-4405. www.bellagiolasvegas.com. The Bellagio Las Vegas is a visual masterpiece. From its bold designs and world-class artwork to its acclaimed entertainment and award-winning cuisine, the Bellagio delights the senses. The lobby draws attention with its dazzling bursts of color from the 2,000 hand-blown glass flowers by renowned artist Dale Chihuly. The rooms delightfully combine European élan with American comfort. A fantastic casino is only the beginning at this all-encompassing resort, which hosts an impressive swimming pool and fountain area, an arcade of fine shopping, and a Conservatory and Botanical Gardens under its roof. Discriminating diners will applaud the culinary works of art created in the resort's many fine dining establishments (see AQUA, LE CIRQUE, JASMINE, OLIVES, PICASSO, PRIME, and SHINTARO). Figuring largely in the Bellagio experience is its 8-acre lake, where mesmerizing fountains perform to a symphony of sounds and lights every half-hour or so. The Bellagio is also home to Cirque du Soleil's *O*, a heart-stopping aquatic performance that is simply not to be missed. *Secret Inspector's Notes: The Bellagio wins decadent, opulent hotel awards year after year and continues to impress visitors and guests alike. Be aware, however, that a hotel with this many rooms often struggles to take care of its many guests in a style of service that a smaller hotel is able to provide.* 3,005 rooms, 36 story. No children allowed. Check-in 3 pm, check-out noon. High-speed Internet access. Wireless Internet access. Restaurants, bars. Fitness room, spa. Pool, whirlpool. Airport transportation available. Business center. Casino. **$$**

★ ★ ★ **CAESARS PALACE.** *3570 Las Vegas Blvd S, Las Vegas (89109). Phone 702/731-7110; toll-free 800/634-6001; fax 702/731-7172. www.caesars.com.* The Roman-themed Caesars was the Strip's first mega-resort when it opened in 1966. And though little lasts long in Vegas, Caesars still reigns, constantly growing, and challenging competitors to keep up. To its Italian facade, Caesars recently added a replica of Rome's Coliseum in which singer Celine Dion entertains. The hotel's swimming deck, modeled on Pompeii, trims three pools in marble statues. The confusing layout of the casino floor is an open play to keep you in house. But there's plenty to recommend it, including 808 and Bradley Ogden restaurants, as well as the high-end Forum Shops (see). Standard guest quarters include a couch as well as a marble bathroom. 2,500 rooms, 32 story. Check-in 5 pm, check-out noon. High-speed Internet access. Wireless Internet access. Restaurant, bar. Fitness room, spa. Three pools, whirlpool. Airport transportation available. Business center. Casino. **$$**

★ ★ ★ **CROWNE PLAZA.** *4255 S Paradise Rd, Las Vegas (89109). Phone 702/369-4400; toll-free 800/227-6963; fax 702/369-3770. www.crowneplaza.com.* Conveniently located near the Las Vegas Strip and the convention center, this non-gaming hotel offers a bit of peace and quiet for its guests. The lobby boasts an impressive glass atrium and working waterfall, and guests can escape the heat of the desert sun with a swim in the outdoor pool. 201 rooms, 6 story, all suites. Check-in 3 pm, check-out noon. Restaurant, bar. Outdoor pool, children's pool. Business center. **$**

★ ★ ★ ★ **FOUR SEASONS HOTEL LAS VEGAS.** *3960 Las Vegas Blvd S, Las Vegas (89119). Phone 702/632-5000; toll-free 800/634-6405; fax 702/632-5195. www.fourseasons.com.* The Four Seasons Hotel is a palatial refuge in glittering Las Vegas. Located on the southern tip of the famous strip, the Four Seasons remains close to the attractions of this dynamic city while providing a welcome respite from the hustle and bustle. This non-gaming hotel occupies the 35th through 39th floors of the Mandalay Bay Resort tower (see), yet it is distinctively Four Seasons with its sumptuous décor and inimitable service. Guests surrender to the plush furnishings in the stylish rooms, and floor-to-ceiling windows showcase exhilarating views of the strip's neon lights or the stark beauty of the Nevada desert. Steak lovers rejoice at Charlie Palmer Steak, while the sun-filled Verandah (see) offers a casual dining alternative. The glorious pool is a lush oasis with its swaying palm trees and attentive poolside service. Lucky visitors retreat to the sublime spa, where JAMU Asian techniques soothe the weary. 424 rooms, 5 story. Pets accepted, some restrictions. Check-in 3 pm, check-out noon. High-speed Internet access. Wireless Internet access. Restaurant, bar. Fitness room. Outdoor pool, children's pool. Airport transportation available. Business center. **$$$**

★ ★ ★ **GOLDEN NUGGET HOTEL AND CASINO.** *129 E Fremont St, Las Vegas (89101). Phone 702/385-7111; toll-free 800/846-5336; fax 702/386-6970. www.goldennugget.com.* Downtown Las Vegas's star hotel, the Golden Nugget is run by MGM Mirage, meaning that you get the same Strip-style amenities—including a cabana-ringed pool with a mist-cooled deck, fitness center, and full-service spa—at discount prices. Everything is cheaper downtown, including the gambling minimums, but the Nugget upholds elegant standards with a marble-trimmed lobby just off raucous Fremont Street. Among entertainment options, the International Beer Bar pours 40 foreign brands, and Zax serves an eclectic sushi-to-tostada menu through dinner, drinking, and dancing into the wee hours. 1,907 rooms, 22 story. Check-in 3 pm, check-out noon. Restaurants, bars. Fitness room, spa. Pools, whirlpool. Business center. Casino. **$**

★ ★ ★ **HARD ROCK HOTEL CASINO.** *4455 Paradise Rd, Las Vegas (89109). Phone 702/693-5000, toll-free 800/473-7625; fax 702/693-5010. www.hardrockhotel.com.* Rock-and-rollers play and stay at the Hard Rock, and so do their fans. A youthful party atmosphere prevails in the memorabilia-strewn complex run by the founder of the Hard Rock Café chain. About a mile off the Strip, Hard Rock generates its own fun, particularly when a big act is booked at The Joint concert hall. Then the swim-up blackjack tables by the pool, where rock music is piped underwater, get hot, and the lines for Nobu (see), the celebrated sushi spot, lengthen. Hip room décor features French doors that open to neon-lit Strip views (preferred over mountain views). 646 rooms, 11 story. Check-in 3 pm, check-out noon. Restaurants, bars. Fitness room, spa. Pool. Airport transportation available. Casino. **$$**

★ ★ ★ **HARRAH'S HOTEL AND CASINO LAS VEGAS.** *3475 Las Vegas Blvd S, Las Vegas (89109). Phone 702/369-5000; fax 702/369-6014. www.harrahs.com.* The gaming powerhouse Harrah's runs this Strip hotel, where the emphasis, as you might expect, is on the casino. Bolstering the hotel and casino's carnival theme décor, an outdoor plaza showcases entertainers, trinket vendors, and snack booths. Spacious but rather bland rooms are lodged in a 35-story tower behind the gaming floor, although guests spend most of their time at the many tables, Olympic-size swimming pool, boutique spa, or 8 eateries. Popular entertainer Clint Holmes rules the showroom here with song and dance. 2,673 rooms, 35 story. Check-in 4 pm, check-out noon. Restaurants, bars. Fitness room, spa. Outdoor pool. Casino. **$**

★ ★ ★ **LAS VEGAS HILTON.** *3000 Paradise Rd, Las Vegas (89109). Phone 702/732-5111; toll-free 800/732-7117; fax 702/794-7117. www.lvhilton.com.* Play craps, get a massage, book a meeting, or enjoy the food and entertainment at this popular Las Vegas destination adjacent to the Convention Center. Set upon 80 lushly landscaped acres, this 30-story hotel has several venues for fun beyond the casino, including the Race and Sports SuperBook, a "high-tech wonderland for the sports enthusiast," and a 1,600-seat theater. 3,174 rooms, 30 story. Check-in 3 pm, check-out noon. High-speed Internet access. Wireless Internet access. Restaurant, bars. Fitness room, spa. Pool, children's pool, whirlpool. Tennis. Business center. Airport transportation available. Casino. **$$**

★ ★ ★ **LUXOR HOTEL AND CASINO.** *3900 Las Vegas Blvd S, Las Vegas (89119). Phone 702/262-4444; toll-free 888/288-1000; fax 702/262-4977. www.luxor.com.* A 30-story glass pyramid in the desert, the thoroughly thematic Luxor emulates ancient Egypt, from its sphinx figurehead outdoors to gold-costumed employees within. Elevators travel the pyramid's incline to deposit guests at room hallways that overlook the world's largest atrium. Five pools, a fitness center, and a spa provide recreation, while an IMAX theater, two-story game room for the kids, and a museum devoted to King Tut entertain. The inventive performance artists Blue Man Group (see) headline Luxor's stage options. 4,400 rooms, 30 story. Check-in 3 pm, check-out 11 am. Restaurant, bar. Fitness room, spa. Outdoor pool, children's pool. Business center. Casino. **$**

★ ★ ★ **MANDALAY BAY RESORT AND CASINO.** *3950 Las Vegas Blvd S, Las Vegas (89119). Phone 702/632-7777; toll-free 877/632-7000; fax 702/632-7234. www.mandalaybay.com.* Even in over-the-top Las Vegas, Mandalay Bay exceeds expectations. This all-encompassing resort captures the spirit of the tropics with its 11-acre sandy beach and three pools with lazy river ride. The stylish accommodations flaunt a tropical flavor, and the casino is a paradise of lush foliage and flowing water, yet this resort is perhaps best known for its mystifying Shark Reef (see). This facility goes far beyond the ordinary aquarium and takes the entire family on an unforgettable adventure. In true Vegas style, this resort has it all, including a 30,000-square-foot spa and terrific shopping. Thirteen restaurants offer a taste of the world, while an astounding variety of entertainment options include everything from live music to Broadway-style shows. 3,215 rooms, 36 story. Check-in 3 pm, check-out 11 am. Restaurant, bar. Fitness room, spa. Beach. Outdoor pool, children's pool, whirlpool. Casino. **$**

★ ★ ★ MARRIOTT SUITES LAS VEGAS. *325 Convention Center Dr, Las Vegas (89109). Phone 702/650-2000; toll-free 800/228-9290; fax 702/650-9466. www.marriott.com.* 270 rooms, 17 story, all suites. Check-in 4 pm, check-out noon. Restaurant, bar. Fitness room. Pool, whirlpool. Airport transportation available. Business center. **$**

★ ★ ★ MGM GRAND HOTEL AND CASINO. *3799 Las Vegas Blvd S, Las Vegas (89109). Phone 702/891-1111; toll-free 877/880-0880; fax 702/891-1030. www.mgmgrand.com.* The largest hotel on the Strip, the MGM Grand virtually pulses with Las Vegas energy. If you've come for nonstop thrills, check in here, where the attractions work well to keep you out of your comfortable room. In the casino, a glassed-in lion habitat with waterfalls showcases a wild pride. The outdoor pool includes a current-fed lazy river, and the spa specializes in cutting-edge treatments. MGM eateries Coyote Café, NobHill, and Craftsteak (see) are thought to be some of the best in the city. Big-name headliners like Cher and David Copperfield often play the MGM, and the French act Le Femme updates the showgirl revue. The party crowd crows for the dance club Studio 54 and the lounge Tabu. 5,018 rooms, 29 story. Check-in 3 pm, check-out 11 am. High-speed Internet access. Wireless Internet access. Restaurants, bars. Children's activity center. Fitness room, spa. Pool, children's pool, whirlpool. Airport transportation available. Business center. Casino. **$$**

★ ★ ★ MIRAGE HOTEL AND CASINO. *3400 Las Vegas Blvd S, Las Vegas (89109). Phone 702/791-7111; toll-free 800/374-9000; fax 702/791-7446. www.mgm-mirage.com.* The Strip-side volcano—which erupts every 15 minutes at night—marks the Mirage and its exotic theme. Tropical fish tanks back the registration desks, the route to room elevators passes through a cascade of jungle foliage, and a lavish pool deck is ringed by towering palms. Among Mirage's many eateries, Renoir (see) is one of town's tops for fine dining, while the Brazilian-style Samba (see) makes a celebration of meat-eating. One of Vegas' most popular shows—impersonator Danny Gans (see)—plays the Mirage. Rooms, recently and smartly renovated, include spacious, marble-trimmed baths. 3,044 rooms, 30 story. Check-in 2 pm, check-out noon. High-speed Internet access. Wireless Internet access. Restaurant, bar. Fitness room, spa. Pool, children's pool, whirlpool. Airport transportation available. Business center. Casino. **$$**

★ ★ ★ MONTE CARLO RESORT & CASINO. *3770 Las Vegas Blvd S, Las Vegas (89109). Phone 702/730-7777; toll-free 800/311-8999; fax 702/730-7250. www.montecarlo.com.* Modeled on the sophisticated European republic of Monaco, this Strip resort is relatively toned down in comparison to its neighbor Bellagio. Its quiet opulence, replete with marble floors underfoot and chandeliers above, is its chief asset and a significant contrast to the party-hearty set. But the Monte Carlo couldn't claim a piece of Strip real estate without its considerable amenities: four pools, including a lazy river and a wave pool; a spa; and eateries. Standard rooms are bright and attractively furnished in cherry wood and Italian marble and granite. Crowd-pleasing magician Lance Burton (see) is the house entertainer. 3,002 rooms, 32 story. Check-in 3 pm, check-out noon. Restaurant. Fitness room, spa. Pools. Tennis. Business center. Casino. **$**

★ ★ ★ NEW YORK-NEW YORK HOTEL & CASINO. *3790 Las Vegas Blvd S, Las Vegas (89109). Phone 702/740-6969; toll-free 800/693-6763; fax 702/740-6920. www.nynyhotelcasino.com.* A hotel with a Manhattan skyline façade, New York-New York does a cheerful imitation of the Big Apple. Its main-floor casino models Central Park with trees, bridges, and brooks. Coney Island (see), New York-New York's upper-level midway, beckons with carnival games and the thrilling Manhattan Express roller-coaster. In perhaps a New York tradition the hotel didn't intend, standard rooms can feel cramped. Not that guests spend much time there, preferring the pool, a fairly straightforward affair relative to its Strip competitors. Among the many eateries, Il Fornaio (see) does fine Italian. Wisecracking comedian Rita Rudner in the theater is a must-see. 2,033 rooms, 45 story. Check-in 3 pm, check-out noon. High-speed Internet access. Wireless Internet access. Restaurants, bars. Fitness room, spa. Pool, whirlpool. Airport transportation available. Business center. Casino. **$$**

★ ★ ★ THE PALMS LAS VEGAS. *4321 W Flamingo Rd, Las Vegas (89103). Phone 702/942-7777; toll-free 866/942-7770; fax 702/942-7001. www.palms.com.* Hipsters flock to The Palms for its seductive spirit and fabulous people-watching. From the Ghost Bar located 50 stories above the city to sultry dance clubs and outdoor nightclubs, the night and the clientele are always young at this Vegas hotspot. If the party scene isn't enough entertainment, the 95,000-square-foot casino gets the heart racing with slot machines, lively poker and blackjack games, and many other gaming opportunities. Standard accommodations are inviting with earth tones and luxuriously comfortable beds, but this hotel is known for its wild 1960s-style bachelor and bachelorette suites, MTV's *Real World* residence, and even suites tailored to the oversize specifications of NBA basketball players. Seven different restaurants span the globe for culinary inspiration. 430 rooms. Check-in 3 pm, check-out 11 am. Restaurant, bar. Casino. **$$$**

★ ★ ★ PARIS LAS VEGAS. *3645 Las Vegas Blvd S, Las Vegas (89109). Phone 702/946-7000; toll-free 877/796-2096; fax 702/946-4405. www.parislasvegas.com.* A half-scale model of the Eiffel Tower landmarks Paris Las Vegas, an ode to French savoir faire, complete with a copy of the Arc de Triomphe and costumed landscape painters fronting the Strip-side pavilion. Its charms continue inside, where three legs of the Eiffel rest in the casino and a cobblestone street wends its way through the shopping arcade. Rooms underscore the theme with French fabrics and custom furniture. Request a Strip view to see the dancing Bellagio fountains across the street. Most of the restaurants here are French, including the charming Mon Ami Gabi, which features outdoor dining on a Las Vegas Boulevard terrace that offers prime people-watching. 2,916 rooms, 30 story. Check-in 3 pm, check-out 11 am. Restaurants, bar. Fitness room. Outdoor pool, children's pool. Business center. Casino. **$**

★ ★ ★ RIO ALL-SUITE HOTEL AND CASINO. *3700 W Flamingo Rd, Las Vegas (89103). Phone 702/777-7777; toll-free 888/684-3746; fax 702/777-2360. www.playrio.com.* The all-suite Rio furnishes spacious, comfortable rooms with sitting areas supplementing its bed-and-bath arrangement. Off the Strip, its rooms offer expansive views of the Strip and the mountains beyond through floor-to-ceiling windows. Rio's Brazilian theme accounts for the carnival that parades above the casino floor seven times a day and the sand entries into Rio's four pools. Among attractions that draw guests as well as visitors, modern magicians Penn & Teller star in the showroom, and Rosemary's restaurant is acclaimed by local gourmets. 2,500 rooms, 41 story, all suites. Check-in 4 pm, check-out noon. Restaurant, bar. Outdoor pool, children's pool. Casino. **$**

★ ★ ★ ST. TROPEZ ALL SUITE HOTEL. *455 E Harmon Ave, Las Vegas (89109). Phone 702/369-5400; toll-free 800/666-5400; fax 702/369-1150. www.sttropezlasvegas.com.* Ideal for Las Vegas visitors who like the climate and excitement of the city but not the endless clanging of slot machines, the St. Tropez is a low-key respite off the Strip by a mile. Arrayed around the landscaped pool, standard suites combine both living and sleeping quarters in one spacious room. Complimentary breakfast is included in the room rate. For midnight duffers, the resort operates a 24-hour driving range. The closest casino to this nongaming hotel is the Hard Rock Hotel (see) across the street. 149 rooms, 2 story, all suites. Complimentary continental breakfast. Check-in 3 pm, check-out noon. Outdoor pool, children's pool. Airport transportation available. **$**

★ ★ ★ THE VENETIAN RESORT HOTEL CASINO. *3355 Las Vegas Blvd S, Las Vegas (89109). Phone 702/414-1000; toll-free 877/283-6423; fax 702/414-4805. www.venetian.com.* From the masterfully re-created Venetian landmark buildings to the frescoed ceilings and gilded details, the Venetian Resort Hotel Casino faithfully re-creates the splendor that is Venice in the heart of the Las Vegas strip. Guests amble down the winding alleys and glide past ornate architecture in gondolas in this perfect reproduction of the golden island that has inspired countless artists for centuries. Inside, the Venetian is glamorous and refined. This all-suite property ensures the comfort of its guests in its spacious and luxurious accommodations. After winning a hand in the casino, head for the upscale boutiques displaying world-famous brands alongside signature Murano glass and carnival masks. Some of the biggest names in American cuisine operate award-winning restaurants here (see LUTECE), while the Venetian's Guggenheim and Madame Tussaud's Wax Museum (see) always delight. Guests soak away their sins at the Canyon Ranch Spa Club, the only outpost of the famous destination spa. *Secret Inspector's Notes: Rooms at the Venetian make guests feel like they, too, can live like kings or queens in their own palace. Opulent décor and ample square footage in the rooms make this hotel incredibly enjoyable, while the shopping downstairs can make significant improvements to any wardrobe. Avoid the oddly laid-out pool area, though, which feels more like a city sidewalk than an Italian escape.* 4,049 rooms, 35 story. Check-in 3 pm, check-out noon. High-speed Internet access. Wireless Internet access. Restaurant, bar. Fitness room, spa. Outdoor pool, children's pool, whirlpool. Airport transportation available. Business center. Casino. **$$**

★ ★ ★ TREASURE ISLAND. *3300 Las Vegas Blvd S, Las Vegas (89109). Phone 702/894-7111; toll-free 800/288-7206; fax 702/894-7446. www.treasureisland .com.* An MGM Mirage casino hotel, Treasure Island's South Seas pirate theme makes it appealing to travelers with children. Nightly, the sinking of a British frigate in Buccaneer Bay outside the hotel draws gawkers to Treasure Island, as does Cirque du Soleil's show "Mystère," (see) staged here. For guests, there's a tropical pool deck with tiki accents and outdoor dining. Done in beige and gold hues, the guest rooms provide a tranquil respite from the hyper-theming. 2,679 rooms, 36 story. Check-in 3 pm, check-out noon. High-speed Internet access. Wireless Internet access. Restaurants, bars. Fitness room, spa. Pool, children's pool, whirlpool. Airport transportation available. Business center. Casino. **$$**

★ ★ ★ THE WESTIN CASUARINA HOTEL & SPA. *160 E Flamingo Rd, Las Vegas (89109). Phone 702/836-9775; fax 702/836-9776.* Deluxe accommodations, business amenities, a large casino, and an ideal location near the Strip, convention center, and other area attractions make The Westin Casuarina Hotel & Spa an ideal destination for both corporate and leisure travelers. This hotel caters to the modern traveler in both its look and feel, and the rooms and suites show off a stylish contemporary design. Westin signature amenities, including the comfortable Heavenly Bed and soothing Heavenly Bath, are among the many perks of a visit to this hotel, and comprehensive business services and a full-service fitness center are notable. All-day dining is available, and the hotel's own Starbucks is a boon to those who need a java jolt. 825 rooms. Check-in 3 pm, check-out 11 am. Restaurant, bar. **$$**

Full-Service Resort

★ ★ ★ JW MARRIOTT LAS VEGAS RESORT. *221 N Rampart Blvd, Las Vegas (89145). Phone 702/869-7777; toll-free 877/869-7777; fax 702/869-7339. www.marriott.com.* Fifteen minutes from the Strip, the JW Marriott Las Vegas Resort offers a tranquil alternative to the neon lights. Set on 50 acres of lush tropical gardens against the backdrop of the Red Rock Mountains, this resort brings the essence of Europe to the Nevada desert. The guest rooms are at once lavish and comfortable. Luxurious details, such as marble-paved entries, premium bedding, and oversized bathrooms, make a lasting impression. The shimmering pool is an inviting spot to enjoy the warm weather, while eight championship courses lure golfers away from their lounge chairs. After a hard day on the course or a rigorous afternoon spent at the pool, the deluxe European-style spa is the perfect retreat, while those who prefer blackjack to body treatments head for the resort's casino. Reflecting the sophistication of the property, the grand promenade entices guests with its alluring array of dining establishments and shops. 536 rooms, 6 story. Check-in 3 pm, check-out noon. High-speed Internet access. Restaurant, bar. Fitness room, spa. Outdoor pool. **$$$$**

Spas

★ ★ ★ ★ CANYON RANCH SPACLUB AT THE VENETIAN. *3355 Las Vegas Blvd S, Las Vegas (89109). Phone 702/414-3600; toll-free 877/220-2688. www.canyonranch.com.* For years, Canyon Ranch has been the gold standard in the spa industry, known for its innovative approach to healthy living. Canyon

Ranch takes a practical and inviting approach to health through fitness, proper nutrition, and stress management. Guests leave the spa feeling refreshed and revitalized, with a healthy new lifestyle as the ultimate souvenir. This Canyon Ranch SpaClub brings the essence of the original Canyon Ranches in Tucson and the Berkshires to guests at The Venetian, allowing them to devote a few hours, a day, or even a weekend to their well-being.

Fitness is a major component of the Canyon Ranch lifestyle, and this SpaClub is no exception. This 65,000-square-foot facility has the largest fitness center on the Las Vegas Strip. In an exercise rut? You'll have no problem jump-starting your routine with cutting-edge fitness classes, state-of-the-art equipment, and even a 40-foot rock-climbing wall. After a vigorous workout, reward yourself with one of the spa's massages or body treatments. From facials that nourish and hydrate and body wraps that slim and detoxify to scrubs that exfoliate and polish, the therapies cover all the bases—from head to toe. Traditionalists might opt for a Swedish or stone massage, while the more adventurous are lured by tempting treatments such as the lulur ritual or the rasul ceremony, performed in the mystical Middle Eastern-inspired room. A full-service salon caters to your complete beauty needs with hair care, nail enhancements, pedicures, and makeup applications.

★★★★ **SPA BELLAGIO.** *3600 Las Begas Blvd S, Las Vegas (89109). Phone 702/693-7472; toll-free 888/987-6667. www.bellagio.com.* This Roman-style spa is the height of luxury, even in over-the-top Las Vegas. The facility boasts a redwood sauna, a eucalyptus steam room, heated whirlpools, and cold plunge pools in addition to its comprehensive fitness center, full-service salon, and treatment rooms. The staff attends to your every whim, and little touches go a long way. You certainly will feel spoiled as you sip a latte from the hotel's Bernadaud china, served on a tiny tray that fits perfectly into the armrest of your pedicure chair. The well-equipped fitness center is a boon to visitors, especially with gourmet restaurants tempting taste buds at every turn.

The spa entices with a variety of massages, including Swedish, lemon-ginger stone, and deluxe scalp massages. Some are available in the privacy of your room or, in season, in a cabana. Hot toe voodoo can be added to any massage and is a wonderfully relaxing treatment in which warm stones are placed between your toes to re-energize you. For the three cool eyes massage therapy enhancement, chilled aquamarine, amethyst, or citrine stones rest over chamomile-filled eye compresses to help reduce swelling. The lemon-ginger scrub is another fantastic extra.

Facials target common problems, such as sun damage, dehydration, wrinkles, rosacea, and loss of elasticity. Eye and lip treatments can be added to facials to boost these often neglected areas. Active foaming body wraps, seaweed body peels, fleurs garden aromatherapy wraps, aromatic moor mud wraps, and Vichy body exfoliations restore a glow to lifeless skin while lulling you to sleep with their relaxing techniques and heady scents. Hydrotherapy services that allow the new you to shine through include thalasso seaweed baths, revitalizing mineral baths, and aromatic moor mud baths.

★★★★ **THE SPA AT FOUR SEASONS HOTEL LAS VEGAS.** *3960 Las Vegas Blvd S, Las Vegas (89119). Phone 702/632-5302; toll-free 877/632-5000. www.fourseasons.com.* Relaxation is the mantra at the Four Seasons, especially at its Asian-inspired spa. Sharing the beauty of Indonesia with guests, silks and decorative objects call to mind this alluring place, while Javanese and Balinese treatments encourage spa-goers to indulge. Kuan Yin, the Buddhist goddess of compassion, greets everyone who enters the spa and serves as a constant reminder of the spa's guiding principles. Most of the treatments here incorporate the essence of Bali. JAMU Asian rituals, which blend exotic ingredients with ancient wisdom to promote well-being, are a centerpiece of this spa.

Relax as the royals would with the Javanese lulur ritual, inspired by treatments originating in the palaces of Central Java. During this experience, your skin is exfoliated and nourished with a heady mix of turmeric, rice, and jasmine. The Bali spice ritual employs native spices, including clove and ginger, to revitalize and increase circulation, while the Bali sea and flower ritual uses hand-sifted sea salts and native flowers to soothe skin. The volcanic earth ritual cools and relaxes body and mind with a mask of volcanic clay, followed by a soak in a citrus-scented bath. Prepare yourself for 80 minutes of pure heaven if you opt for the wonderful JAMU massage, which blends Hindu, Chinese, and European styles and techniques with essential oils to work out every last kink. Balinese foot washes, aromatherapy scalp massages, and reflexology can be savored on their own or added to any massage for extra enjoyment.

From facials that cleanse, plump, and hydrate to body treatments that relax and revive, this spa offers a comprehensive list of options. Traditionalists adore the herbal wraps, seaweed body wraps, salt glows, Champagne mud wraps, and purifying or European facials, while those seeking a more unique experience book mini versions of JAMU rituals like the Bali sea or spice rub, royal rub, and Java lava treatment.

Restaurants

★ ★ ★ ALIZÉ. *4321 W Flamingo Rd, Las Vegas (89103). Phone 702/951-7000; fax 702/951-7002. www.alizelv.com.* In a casino selling spiked snowcones by the pool and housing a tattoo parlor, Alizé imports class. Acclaimed Las Vegas chef Andre Rochat, of longstanding favorite Andre's French Restaurant, runs this destination eatery on the top floor of the Palms, providing meal-stopping panoramas of the Strip. His signature French fare—highlighted by seared venison with quince chutney, filet under green peppercorn and cognac cream, and sautéed Dover sole—is complemented by a 1,000-varietal wine cellar in the middle of the room. A second cellar of Champagnes, cognacs, and the like lines the hallway leading into the dining room. French menu. **$$$$**

★ ★ ALL AMERICAN BAR & GRILL. *3700 W Flamingo Rd, Las Vegas (89103). Phone 702/777-7923.* Amid the casino action at the Rio hotel (see), All American Bar & Grille offers something for all Americans, from casual dining to more elaborate fare. The sports bar section serves up pints and burgers—including one gonzo version built for two—along with ESPN on the tube. Behind it, the grill room proves a cozy dining space warmed by a fire with generous booths and woody good looks. The menu leans carnivorous, proffering steaks, lamb, and ribs grilled over mesquite wood. Ample chicken, fish, and shellfish choices placate those with less hearty appetites. American menu. Lunch, dinner. Bar. Casual attire. **$$**

★ ★ AMERICA. *3790 Las Vegas Boulevard S, Las Vegas (89109). Phone 702/740-6541. www.nynyhotelcasino.com.* The casual, 24-hour diner of the New York-New York Hotel & Casino (see) takes its name from the 90-by-20-foot 3-D map of the States unfurled in the center of the restaurant. The menu follows theme with an eclectic roster of regional dishes from New York pizza to Maryland crabcakes, Tex-Mex nachos, and California sushi rolls. Wash it all down with a beverage from the similarly well-traveled beer and wine list. Vintage posters and postcards on the wall amplify the retro vibe. American menu. Breakfast, lunch, dinner, late-night. **$$**

★ ★ ANTONIO'S. *3700 W Flamingo Rd, Las Vegas (89103). Phone 702/252-7737.* If you are looking for romantic ambience, the Rio (see) might have your answer. Featuring one of the finest dining rooms in Vegas, Antonio's kitchen turns out fabulous specialties. Let the super-friendly waitstaff take care of you as you admire the marble and glass dome-ceiling surroundings. Italian menu. Dinner. Bar. Casual attire. Reservations recommended. Valet parking. **$$$**

★ ★ ★ ★ AQUA. *3600 Las Vegas Blvd S, Las Vegas (89109). Phone 702/693-7223; toll-free 888/987-6667; fax 702/693-6512. www.bellagiolasvegas.com.* After strolling through the Bellagio Hotel's Conservatory & Botanical Gardens (see BELLAGIO LAS VEGAS) on the way to dinner, guests find a luxurious, contemporary dining room bathed in blond wood, creamy neutral tones, and golden light. The menu here is in the care of a talented group of chef-creators, trained and transported from the original Aqua in San Francisco. The kitchen is passionate about the sea; delicious dishes tend to concentrate on the creatures of the deep blue ocean jazzed up with California ingredients. The menu is extensive and offers à la carte selections in addition to a pair of five-course tasting menus, one vegetarian and one seasonal. The wine list focuses on American producers and contains some gems from small vineyards as well; you'll find lots of fish-friendly options. *Secret Inspector's Notes: The signature lobster pot pie is worth every penny. Fresh lobster bathed in a creamy sauce accompanied by wilted spinach and tender mushrooms is a divine creation.* American menu. Dinner, late-night. Bar. Jacket required. Reservations recommended. Valet parking. **$$$$**

★ ★ ★ AQUAKNOX. *3355 S Las Vegas Blvd, Las Vegas (89109). Phone 702/414-3776. www.venetian.com.* The Venetian's restaurant row offers an eatery to satisfy every culinary craving, with AquaKnox, sibling to the popular Dallas eatery, positioned to please seafood-seeking diners. Beginning with a raw bar inventoried in oysters and stone crab claws, menu choices range from standard grilled fish to contemporary sauced versions. Despite the frequency of high-end luxuries—caviar with accoutrements, grilled lobster—AquaKnox plays the urban sophisticate without snobbery. Running water courses over the walk-in wine cellar, and an exhibition kitchen provides a bustling focal point for the sleek dining room. American menu, steak menu. Lunch, dinner, late-night. Bar. Casual attire. **$$$**

★★ **ASIA.** *3475 Las Vegas Blvd S, Las Vegas (89109). Phone 702/369-5000; toll-free 800/392-9002. www.harrahs.com.* Harrah's explores the Orient with the appropriately named Asia, proffering an array of pan-Asian dishes. From Japan to India, the full range of eastern cultures earns berths on the catch-all menu. Choices range from Thai-style spiced shrimp to Szechwan eggplant, with upscale specials such as abalone making occasional appearances. The décor is upscale and the experience unhurried, although Asia can be a good choice for those looking for a satisfying bite between blackjack hands. Asian menu. Dinner. Closed Wed-Thurs. Bar. Casual attire. Reservations recommended. **$$$**

★★★★ **AUREOLE.** *3950 Las Vegas Blvd, Las Vegas (89119). Phone 702/632-7401; toll-free 877/632-7401; fax 702/632-7425. www.aureolerestaurant.com.* A branch of chef Charlie Palmer's New York original, Aureole wows patrons with its centerpiece four-story wine tower. Be sure to order a bottle just to see the catsuit-clad climber, suspended by ropes, locate your vintage. Its 12,000 bottles complement Palmer's seasonal contemporary American cuisine typified by dishes like Peking duck with foie gras ravioli and roast pheasant with sweet potato gnocchi. The modern, but romantic, room with encircling booths sets the stage for event dining at Mandalay Bay. Progressive American menu. Dinner. Bar. Jacket required. Reservations recommended. Valet parking. **$$$**

★★ **BLUE AGAVE.** *4321 W Flamingo Rd, Las Vegas (89103). Phone 702/951-7000. www.thepalmslasvegas.com.* Fittingly named for the plant from which tequila is made, Blue Agave celebrates the spirit with more than 150 varieties behind the bar, the bases of infinite margarita possibilities. These are dispensed from a crowd-drawing circular bar romanced by star-shaped light fixtures overhead. Don't sip without supping from the menu featuring fresh oysters, steamed clams, ceviche, and roast lobster. The chile bar refers to the bar's many sauce and salsa options. Look for Blue Agave within Garduño's (see), its New Mexican sister. Mexican menu. Bar. **$$$**

★★★★ **BRADLEY OGDEN.** *3570 Las Vegas Blvd, Las Vegas (89109). Phone 702/731-7731; toll-free 877/427-7143.* Many celebrity chefs opened up shop in Las Vegas, but only California's Bradley Ogden actually moved there, ensuring that his Caesars Palace restaurant got the attention to detail that diners associate with his culinary chops. The result: Bradley Ogden won 2004 best restaurant of the year from the prestigious James Beard Society. Ogden's contemporary American food focuses on farm-fresh ingredients and treats them sparely, cooking clean, carefully spiced, modern meals. Start with the Maytag blue cheese soufflé or the quartet of oysters, each in a unique vinaigrette, and then move on to the seared diver scallops or the wood-grilled lamb chops, saving room for American artisanal cheeses. The atmosphere, like the food, is refined but unpretentious, although routinely packed before and after Celine Dion performs across the casino. American menu. Dinner. Bar. Business casual attire. Reservations recommended. Valet parking. **$$$**

★ **THE BUFFET AT BELLAGIO.** *3600 Las Vegas Blvd S, Las Vegas (89109). Phone 702/693-8111. www.bellagiolasvegas.com.* Even at a classy hotel like the Bellagio (see), the hordes must be fed. Ergo the buffet, a crowd-feeding staple at every Strip and off-Strip casino hotel. But like everything else at the Bellagio, the buffet redefines the standard. Amid the sprawling choices, you'll find mounds of jumbo cocktail shrimp, Japanese sushi rolls, cheese boards, carving stations, made-to-order dishes, and ethnic fare from China to Italy. Prices are higher than at rival spreads, but so is the quality. To make the best of it, go very hungry. American menu. Breakfast, lunch, dinner. Bar. Children's menu. Casual attire. **$$**

★★ **BUZIO'S.** *3700 W Flamingo Rd, Las Vegas (89103). Phone 702/777-7923.* Named for an area in Brazil famed for its beaches, Buzio's in the Rio hotel (see) does its culinary part to exotically transport you from the desert locale by specializing in seafood. Oysters, clams, and shrimp in various combinations star in the opening act, followed by chowders, fish, and shellfish entrées. Choices range from seafood shack standards like steamed lobster to more contemporary preparations such as wasabi-crusted ahi. Sizeable steaks and ethnic-inspired noodle dishes, such as Thai curry, stray far enough from theme to entice landlubbers. In keeping with its shoreline inspiration, Buzio's spies the Rio's pools and beach through picture windows. American menu. Lunch, dinner. Bar. Casual attire. Outdoor seating. **$$$**

★ ★ ★ **CHINOIS.** *3500 Las Vegas Blvd S, Las Vegas (89109). Phone 702/737-9700; fax 702/737-9710. www.wolfgangpuck.com.* A spin-off of chef Wolfgang Puck's acclaimed Chinois on Main in Santa Monica, California, Las Vegas's Chinois features similar Asian fusion fare in the Forum Shops at Caesars Palace (see). The spare, artifact-decorated shop-level café, specializing in pan-Asian fare often lightened California style to please western palettes, is a well-located lunch spot. The broad-ranging menu includes sushi and sashimi, dim sum, wok-fried meat and vegetable recipes such as kung pao chicken, and Asian noodle dishes like pad Thai. Asian menu. Lunch, dinner. Bar. Children's menu. Casual attire. Valet parking. **$$$**

★ ★ ★ **COMMANDER'S PALACE.** *3663 S Las Vegas Blvd, Las Vegas (89109). Phone 702/731-7731. www.commanderspalace.com.* Straight from the Garden District of New Orleans comes this Commander's Palace clone lodged in the Aladdin (see). Unlike many a Sin City spin-off, the Las Vegas Commander's imported and kept several of the people behind the original's success, chiefly manager Brad Brennan of the famed Brennan restaurant clan, which owns Commander's. With palms in the corners, tufted silk on the ceiling, and linen topping the tables, the restaurant evokes the gracious style of the Crescent City, while its pecan-crusted fish, turtle soup, and bread pudding send your tastebuds south. There's even a Dixieland jazz brunch on Sundays. Cajun/Creole menu. Breakfast, lunch, dinner, late-night. Bar. Casual attire. Outdoor seating. **$$$**

★ ★ **COYOTE CAFE.** *3799 Las Vegas Blvd S, Las Vegas (89109). Phone 702/891-7777; fax 702/891-7333. www.coyotecafe.com.* Celebrated chef Mark Miller runs this spin-off of his Santa Fe original just off the casino floor in the MGM Grand (see). It couldn't be a better place for a break from the slots. Despite his status, Miller's food is highly approachable, beginning with his zesty homemade salsas and potent margaritas. Mexican standards like quesadillas, tacos, and enchiladas gain a Southwestern accent in blue corn tortillas and New Mexican chiles. Additional seafood choices and burgers ensure that there's something for everyone on the menu. Drop into the lively, casual café or make a reservation to dine in the adjacent Grill Room, which serves more upscale versions of Miller's fare. Southwestern menu. Breakfast, lunch, dinner. Casual attire. Valet parking. **$$$**

★ ★ ★ **CRAFTSTEAK.** *3799 S Las Vegas Blvd, Las Vegas (89109). Phone 702/736-2100. www.mgmgrand.com.* After earning the James Beard Society's 2002 best new restaurant award for Craft in New York, chef Tom Colicchio spun off a Vegas version, Craftsteak, in the MGM Grand (see). With an emphasis on top-shelf ingredients from boutique farms and artisinal producers, the á la carte menu spans fish, shellfish, poultry, veal, lamb, and pork as well as steak. A raw bar, generous salads, and a roster of veggies supplement the mains. Many dishes are served in small skillets or pots that facilitate sharing. The handsome room features generous circular booths and open sightlines for spotting the celebrities who frequently dine here. American menu. Dinner. Bar. Casual attire. Reservations recommended. **$$$$**

★ ★ ★ **DELMONICO STEAKHOUSE.** *3355 S Las Vegas Blvd, Las Vegas (89109). Phone 702/414-3737. www.emerils.com.* Exuberant New Orleans chef Emeril Lagasse, famed showman of the Food Network, runs this meat-centric dining room in the Venetian (see), a sequel to the Crescent City original. Luxe appointments—a baby grand piano, French doors, and linen-clothed tables—make a seductive affair of the indulgence. All the steakhouse standards make the menu, along with specialties such as Creole marinated rack of lamb, chateaubriand for two, and charred sirloin. Southern takes on seafood bear Emeril's signature "Bam!" level of spice. Steak menu. Dinner. Bar. Casual attire. Reservations recommended. **$$$**

★ ★ **DRAI'S OF LAS VEGAS.** *3595 Las Vegas Blvd S, Las Vegas (89109). Phone 702/737-0555; fax 702/737-5557. www.draislasvegas.com.* Named after former movie producer Victor Drai, this restaurant brings the glamour of Hollywood to Las Vegas. Complete with leopard skin overstuffed chairs, this restaurant offers Provencal cuisine without the heavy ingredients. French menu. Dinner. Bar. Valet parking. **$$$**

★ ★ **ELEMENTS.** *3667 S Las Vegas Blvd, Las Vegas (89109). Phone 702/785-5555. www.aladdincasino.com.* For all the exoticism of the Aladdin (see), its upscale restaurant Elements goes back to basics. Inspired by the elements of air, water, fire, and earth, the contemporary restaurant keys in on prime flavor complements and doesn't overload dishes with complicating and competing ingredients. Consequently, the fine foie gras is sweetened by apples, spicy ahi tuna tempered by sweet potato, and veal enriched with Marsala sauce. For even simpler preparations, opt for the sushi and sashimi bar. Harmony also reigns in the dining room as well, which is centered by a water wall and trimmed in wood and stone. International menu. Dinner, late-night. Bar. Casual attire. **$$$**

★ ★ THE EMBERS. *3535 S Las Vegas Blvd, Las Vegas (89109). Phone 702/794-3261; toll-free 888/777-7664; fax 702/794-3353. www.imperialpalace.com.* The steakhouse of the Imperial Palace Hotel and Casino, The Embers simulates fine dining for budget-minded Las Vegas visitors, providing the refined atmosphere without the correspondingly steep prices. Steaks and choice meats such as milk-fed veal, rack of lamb, and prime rib dominate the menu, although some creative seafood (macadamia nut orange roughy) and poultry (Long Island duck roast) makes an appearance. Candlelight and oil paintings set a gracious tone for dinner, after which the affordable-by-steakhouse-standards tab is a welcome surprise. Steak menu. Dinner. Closed Mon-Tues. Bar. Casual attire. **$$**

★ ★ ★ EMERIL'S NEW ORLEANS. *3799 Las Vegas Blvd S, Las Vegas (89109). Phone 702/891-7374; fax 702/891-7338. www.emerils.com.* Big Easy big-timer Emeril Lagasse runs this Louisiana kitchen at the MGM Grand (see). Wrought-iron gates, a stone courtyard, and French doors aim to evoke historic New Orleans. But the star, of course, is the bold food for which the gregarious chef of Food Network fame is renowned. Creole-spiced lobster, pecan-roasted redfish, and cedar plank steak typify Emeril's big flavors, while a raw bar and po' boys wave the regional flag. Finish off with the rave-worthy banana cream pie. Cajun/Creole menu. Lunch, dinner. Bar. Casual attire. Reservations recommended. Valet parking. **$$**

★ ★ ★ EMPRESS COURT. *3570 Las Vegas Blvd S, Las Vegas (89109). Phone 702/731-7731. www.caesars.com.* Native Hong Kong chefs distinguish themselves at Empress Court, frequently cited in local dining polls for authentic Chinese cuisine. Overlooking the Roman pool deck at Caesars Palace (see), Empress Court prepares a range of dishes from the Asian larder, including recipes from Malaysia, Thailand, and Indonesia, as well as China. Fresh and saltwater tanks stock cod, crab, and lobster. To splurge, opt for the multicourse, fixed-price meals made for two. Quality china, rare fare such as abalone, and the attention of knowledgeable servers justify the upmarket prices. Chinese menu. Dinner. Closed Mon-Tues. Bar. Jacket required. Reservations recommended. Valet parking. **$$$**

★ ★ FASOLINI'S PIZZA CAFE. *222 S Decatur Blvd, Las Vegas (89107). Phone 702/877-0071; fax 702/877-7144.* It's in a strip mall on the west side of town, well off the Strip, with minimal atmosphere save for movie posters on the walls. Still, locals rave about Fasolini's, a lunchtime favorite for authentic Italian-style pizza. Run by the Fasolini family, the café serves pies with a light and crispy crust and original toppings such as homemade sausage and roast peppers. Classics like lasagna, clam linguine, and garlic chicken as well as desserts—applause for the cannoli—round out the offerings. Italian menu. Dinner. Closed Sun; Jan 1, Easter, Dec 25. Children's menu. **$$**

★ ★ FERRARO'S. *5900 W Flamingo Rd, Las Vegas (89103). Phone 702/364-5300; fax 702/871-2721. www.ferraroslasvegas.com.* In a city where famous out-of-town chefs commonly slap their names on spin-offs and then abdicate the kitchen, Ferraro's is an indigenous delight. Owner Gino Ferraro has nurtured the west side's success on the strength of his hearty family recipes. Crowd-pleasing Italian classics like veal scalloppine, gnocchi (listed on the menu as actress "Julia Roberts' favorite"), lamb chops, and osso buco distinguish the kitchen. Roman columns, subtle lighting, and the Wine Spectator-awarded cellar housed in glass generate intimacy. Italian menu. Dinner. Bar. Children's menu. Casual attire. **$$$**

★ ★ FIORE STEAKHOUSE. *3700 W Flamingo Rd, Las Vegas (89103). Phone 702/777-7923.* Celebrating a win at the tables? Newfound high-roller status? Toast your good fortune at Fiore in the Rio hotel (see), which revels in the good life. The food is meat-focused—specialties include steaks grilled over olive and mesquite wood—but not to the exclusion of lighter, Mediterranean-inspired choices, either from the raw bar or from the seafood list, which includes lobster bisque, sea bass with clams, and cured salmon. Linger over a cognac or port from the dessert menu on the cigar-friendly terrace after paying a visit to the walk-in humidor. American menu. Dinner. Bar. Casual attire. **$$$**

★ ★ GOLDEN STEER STEAK HOUSE. *308 W Sahara Ave, Las Vegas (89109). Phone 702/384-4470.*

Steak menu. Dinner. Bar. Children's menu. Casual attire. Valet parking. **$$$**

★★ HAMADA OF JAPAN. *365 E Flamingo Rd, Las Vegas (89119). Phone 702/733-3005; fax 702/733-7708. www.hamadaofjapan.com.* Hamada of Japan owners June and Jay Hamada virtually dominate Japanese food in Las Vegas, with hotel outposts in the Flamingo, the JW Marriott, Stratosphere, and the MGM, as well as this original location on Flamingo Road. Their high volume garners Hamada some of the freshest fish on the market in sushi preparations, from domestic (California roll) to traditional (sea urchin). In the Teppan Room, Benihana-style chefs prepare steaks, shrimp, and chicken using flashing knives, to the the delight of diners. If you can get it in Japan, you can get it here, from teriyaki preparations to fondue-style shabu-shabu, tempura, and noodles. Japanese menu. Lunch, dinner. Bar. Casual attire. Valet parking. **$$$**

★★ IL FORNAIO. *3790 Las Vegas Blvd S #13, Las Vegas (89109). Phone 702/650-6500; fax 702/740-2449. www.ilfornaio.com.* For flavor and fun in a casino restaurant, it's hard to beat Il Fornaio. Surrounded by the New York-New York's version of Central Park, including a stream diners must bridge to get to the restaurant, Il Fornaio earns high marks for atmosphere. Bilingual waiters with lovely Italian accents port baskets of crusty homemade bread that alone warrants repeat trips ("il fornaio" means "the baker"). Authenticity rules the cooking in wood-fired pizzas, house-made pastas, and rotisserie meats. In all, a great place to carbo-load before undertaking a casino marathon. Italian menu. Dinner. Bar. Casual attire. Valet parking. **$$$**

★★★ ISIS. *3900 S Las Vegas Blvd, Las Vegas (89119). Phone 702/262-4772.* American menu. Dinner. Closed Tues-Wed. Bar. Casual attire. Reservations recommended. **$$$**

★★★ JASMINE. *3600 S Las Vegas Blvd, Las Vegas (89109). Phone 702/693-8111. www.bellagiolasvegas.com.* If you're familiar with the dining scene in Hong Kong, you may know chef Philip Lo, who is credited with creating nouveau Chinese. He is the talent behind the elegant Jasmine in the equally elegant Bellagio (see). There's nothing Asian about the design. Instead, the room features grand chandeliers, pastel chintz, and swagged windows that overlook the famed Bellagio fountains. Reserve a table to experience Lo's fresh and light hand with seemingly familiar Cantonese, Szechwan, and Hunan preparations. All are elevated by ingredient luxuries, as in Maine lobster dumplings, sautéed and wok-fried Alaskan giant clam, and garlic beef tenderloin. Chinese menu. Dinner, late-night. Bar. Casual attire. Reservations recommended. **$$$**

★★★ LE CIRQUE. *3600 Las Vegas Blvd S, Las Vegas (89109). Phone 702/693-8100; toll-free 888/987-6667; fax 702/693-8106. www.lecirque.com.* The hallowed temple of cuisine for New York's financial elite has made it to Las Vegas. Restaurateur and charmer Sirio Maccioni, the face and creative force behind the Gotham power scene, brought a branch to the Bellagio (see). Like its New York City sibling, this Le Cirque is a shining jewel of a restaurant, awash in bold colors and warm fabrics, with a bright, silk-tented ceiling that brings a festive big-top feel to the intimate dining room. The three-course prix fixe menu features rustic French fare that includes something for everyone: snails, fish, lamb, beef, and game, as well as salads and pasta. In signature Maccioni style, each dish is prepared with precision and delivered with care. Caviar service is available for those seeking extreme luxury, and the wine list boasts several stellar choices. French menu. Dinner, late-night. Bar. Jacket required. Reservations recommended. Valet parking. **$$$**

★★★ LILLIE LANGTRY'S. *129 E Fremont St, Las Vegas (89101). Phone 702/385-7111. www.goldennugget.com.* Presenting Cantonese and Szechwan favorites and mesquite-grilled steaks in a soft and surreal atmosphere. Specialties include Mongolian beef and stir-fried lobster. Chinese menu. Dinner. Bar. Casual attire. Reservations recommended. Valet parking. **$$$**

★★★ LUTECE. *3355 Las Vegas Blvd S, Las Vegas (89109). Phone 702/414-2220; fax 702/414-2221. www.lutece.com.* Lutece is located in the luxurious Venetian (see). In this bright setting, the kitchen turns out an exciting selection of updated classic French recipes. You'll find high-end seasonal ingredients and a gentle flirtation with global flavors that brighten both the plate and the palate. This is a restaurant that will satisfy foodies and more conservative eaters alike. Divided into Appetizers, Caviar, Soup, Fish & Shellfish, and Meat & Poultry, the menu is like a classic navy blue pinstripe suit paired with a fun, bright tie: classic, with a sexy edge. Diners can choose from à la carte selections or a five-course tasting menu. The dessert list is impressive as well and includes three varieties of soufflé and a cheese course, among other lip-licking alternatives. *Secret Inspector's Notes: Dining at Lutece can be disappointing at times. Although it is still a classic and continues to offer a lovely dining experience, it may not always hold up to guests' expectations of excellence and grandeur.* French menu. Dinner, late-night. Bar. Business casual attire. Reservations recommended. Valet parking. Outdoor seating. **$$$**

★ ★ **MARRAKECH.** *3900 Paradise Rd, Las Vegas (89109). Phone 702/737-5611; fax 702/737-4603. www.marrakech-lv.com.* Middle Eastern menu. Dinner. Closed Dec 25. Bar. Casual attire. **$$$**

★ ★ **MAYFLOWER CUISINIER.** *4750 W Sahara Ave, Las Vegas (89102). Phone 702/870-8432; fax 702/259-8493. www.mayflowercuisinier.com.* Enlightened Chinese stars at Mayflower Cuisinier, a west side favorite among locals. Chef Ming See Woo improves on classics like Peking duck and Hong Kong chow mein by using fresh ingredients and banning gummy sauces. Much of her cooking mingles cultures in creative dishes like seafood ravioli, ginger-basil seafood, and ginger-scallion pesto vegetables. Desserts, however, are wholly Western, including Black Forest cake and creme brulée. An art-filled room and attentive servers further distinguish Mayflower meals. Chinese menu. Dinner. Closed Sun; holidays. Bar. Outdoor seating. **$$**

★ ★ ★ **MICHAEL'S.** *3595 S Las Vegas Blvd, Las Vegas (89109). Phone 702/737-7111. www.barbarycoastcasino.com.* Classics meet Victorian frill at Michael's, a longstanding Las Vegas gourmand housed in the Barbary Coast casino. Lace tablecloths, crystal chandeliers, marble floors, and a domed stained-glass ceiling strike a formal note in the intimate 50-seater. Reserve in advance such for meals-with-flourish as chateaubriand, Dover sole, veal Florentine, and flaming desserts including bananas Foster, crepes Suzette, and cherries jubilee. With just two seatings nightly—at 6 and 9 pm—Michael's offers a slow-paced option amid the frenzy of the Strip. French, American menu. Dinner, late-night. Bar. Casual attire. Reservations recommended. **$$$$**

★ ★ ★ **NOBHILL.** *3799 S Las Vegas Blvd, Las Vegas (89109). Phone 877/736-2100. www.mgmgrand.com.* Chef Michael Mina of San Francisco and the Bellagio teamed with hot designer Tony Chi to create a snug City-by-the-Bay-inspired eatery in Sin City's MGM Grand (see). Named for the ritzy San Fran enclave, NobHill conjures culinary California with fresh-baked sourdough bread, organic produce, natural meats, locally caught sand dabs, and a heaping raw bar. Don't miss the whipped potatoes, which come in a chorus of flavors from leek to cheese. You won't find any Golden Gate images in Chi's sophisticated design. Glass-walled booths oppose the bar, which dispenses the rave-worthy house Cable Car martini. American menu. Dinner, late-night. Bar. Casual attire. Reservations recommended. **$$$**

★ ★ ★ **NOBU.** *4455 Paradise Rd, Las Vegas (89109). Phone 702/693-5090; fax 702/693-5091. www.hardrockhotel.com.* The Zenlike décor of Nobu at the Hard Rock Hotel (see)—bamboo-lined walls, seaweed-toned banquettes—brings a serene sense of peace to the otherwise frenetic pace of dining out in Las Vegas. This is a beautiful place to settle in for an evening. As at its sister restaurant in New York City's Tribeca, the quality of the sushi here is fantastic. Whether eaten as sashimi or sushi or tucked into fat, flavor-packed maki (rolls), the silky fish virtually melts in your mouth. Folks who shiver at the word sushi need not miss out on celebrity chef Nobu Matsuhisa's magnificent culinary talent (although you should at least try Nobu's sushi before swearing off of it based on fear alone). In addition to raw fish, the menu includes soup, kushiyaki (skewers of fish, chicken, vegetables, or beef), ceviches, salads, noodle bowls, teriyaki plates, and tempura, as well as a selection of hot entrées. An omakase (chef's choice) menu is also available for truly inspired (and adventurous) dining. *Secret Inspector's Notes: Pass on the omakase; it often features dishes that do not truly reflect the chef's talents. Instead, request that the waitstaff point out some of the menu's highlights, focusing on a variety of dishes that can be shared at the table.* Japanese menu. Dinner. Bar. Jacket required. Reservations recommended. Valet parking. **$$**

★ ★ **OLIVES.** *3600 S Las Vegas Blvd, Las Vegas (89117). Phone 702/693-7223. www.bellagio.com.* Boston-based celebrity chef Todd English brings his famed Mediterranean fare to the Bellagio (see) in Olives. The setting couldn't be better suited, and if you choose to wait for a much-in-demand terrace table overlooking the hotel's lake, exercise extreme patience. But whether you sit outside or in, the fare at Olives delights, from the marinated olives that show up complimentary to signature flatbread pizzas and rotisserie meats. Creative salad and sandwich preparations make this a good place to refuel after a shopping spree along the Via Bellagio. American menu. Lunch, dinner, late-night. Bar. Casual attire. Outdoor seating. **$$$**

★ ★ ORTANIQUE. *3655 Las Vegas Blvd S, Las Vegas (89109). Phone 702/967-7999. www.parislasvegas.com.* A trip to the French Caribbean in the all-things-French Paris Las Vegas (see), Ortanique conjures the culinary tropics. Chef Cindy Hutson spins off a Vegas version of her Miami hotspot, preparing sun-kissed dishes like curried crab cakes, "rasta pasta" with jerk shrimp, Jamaican-spiced ahi, and Caribbean bouillabaisse. A half-dozen meat dishes forego the exotic to court more conservative carnivores. Jazz, steel drum, and reggae music keep the island beat. Look for Ortanique in the walkway en route to Bally's next door. French-Caribbean menu. Dinner. **$$**

★ ★ OSTERIA DEL CIRCO. *3600 S Las Vegas Blvd, Las Vegas (89117). Phone 702/693-7223.* Though billed as the casual cousin to its neighbor and sibling Le Cirque, Circo is hardly less sophisticated. Its harlequin patterns and jewel tones reference the circus, and the windows frame ringside views of the Bellagio's dancing fountains (see BELLAGIO LAS VEGAS). But the food is quite serious, focusing on Italian cuisine rather than Le Cirque's French fare. Pastas are house-made, pizzas and often fish are wood-fired, and everything comes artfully arranged on the plate. Reservations are essential on most nights, particularly for diners seeking a table before the Cirque du Soleil O show across the casino at Bellagio. Italian menu. Lunch, dinner. Bar. Casual attire. **$$**

★ ★ ★ THE PALM. *3500 Las Vegas Blvd S, Suite A, Las Vegas (89109). Phone 702/732-7256; fax 702/732-0229. www.thepalm.com.* A destination eatery in the Forum Shops at Caesars Palace (see), the Palm steakhouse is a branch of the New York power eatery. The woody surroundings lend a clubby feel to the dining room that specializes in healthy portions of meat supplemented by à la carte veggies and potatoes. Lunches of salads, pastas, and the house burger make this a more affordable midday option. Local notables like mayor Oscar Goodman and tennis pro Andre Agassi have been spotted dining here, as have many others; celebrity cartoon caricatures festoon the Palm's walls. Steak menu. Lunch, dinner; late-night. Bar. Business casual attire. Reservations recommended. **$$**

★ ★ PEARL. *3799 Las Vegas Blvd S, Las Vegas (89109). Phone 702/736-2100. www.mgmgrand.com.* Asians are the high rollers of Las Vegas to whom every casino worthy of the Strip caters with an Asian restaurant. Pearl goes far beyond formula in presenting updated takes on Cantonese and Shanghai cooking in a smart, contemporary room from hip designer Tony Chi. Seafood and meat choices divide the menu, where East leans somewhat West in dishes like vegetable cannelloni with black bean sauce, Asian bouillabaisse, and wok-fried venison. Order tea to take advantage of the tea trolley that arrives tableside to brew you a perfect cup from a menu of Asiatic blends. Chinese menu. Dinner. **$$$**

★ ★ ★ PEGASUS. *375 E Harmon Ave, Las Vegas (89109). Phone 702/796-3353; fax 702/796-4334.* Located half a mile off the Strip at the Alexis Park Resort (see), Pegasus brings formal dining to the lush Mediterranean hotel grounds. The service is notably attentive and the atmosphere romantic, with cozy booths, hand-blown glass chandeliers, piano music, and views of the landscape. The restaurant's menu merges French and Italian cooking in fish, chicken, and meat dishes. Jackets are required, and reservations are strongly suggested, making Pegasus a special-occasion candidate. Mediterrean menu. Dinner. Bar. Jacket required. Valet parking. **$$**

★ PHARAOH'S PHEAST. *3900 S Las Vegas Blvd, Las Vegas (89119). Phone 702/262-4772. www.luxor.com.* Catering to the mass of Luxor hotel guests and gamblers, Pharaoh's Pheast lays out a buffet suitable for Tutankhamen himself. Amid the Egypt-inspired room, a vast bank of kitchen-side serving stations lays out options highlighted by a 30-foot salad bar, homemade pizzas, carved-to-order meats, and made-to-order omelets. Save room for a trip through the enticing dessert section, which offers sugarless versions for those watching their waistlines. The all-you-can-eat prices are quite reasonable, ranging from about $10 per person at breakfast to around $17 at dinner. American menu. Breakfast, lunch, dinner. Bar. Casual attire. **$$**

★★★★ **PICASSO.** *3600 Las Vegas Blvd S, Las Vegas (89109). Phone 702/693-7223; toll-free 888/987-6667; fax 702/693-8546. www.bellagiolasvegas.com.* The Bellagio (see) is home to some of the finest restaurants in Las Vegas. Le Cirque, Olives, Aqua, and Prime Steakhouse are all inside. But Picasso stands out among them. It offers exquisite food in a serene space, and it's one of those two-for-one experiences. If you're trying to decide between visiting a museum and having an elegant and inspired meal, you can do both at Picasso. The master painter's original works adorn the walls of this beautiful, cozy, country-style room with soaring wood-beamed ceilings, sage-toned upholstery, and a stunning view of the lake. The menu is also artwork. The kitchen uses French technique as a canvas for layering Spanish and Mediterranean flavor. (You can opt for a four-course tasting menu or a chef's degustation option as well.) To match the museum-worthy food, you'll be offered a rare and magnificent selection of international wines. If the weather is warm, you can also dine al fresco by the lake—nature's art. *Secret Inspector's Notes: Avoid the highly regarded seafood sausage if it is on the menu. It's not as flavorful as one would expect. Be sure to request a table near the window so that you can enjoy the water show on the lake every 20 to 30 minutes throughout your meal.* French, Spanish menu. Dinner, late-night. Closed Mon. Bar. Jacket required. Reservations recommended. Valet parking. Outdoor seating. **$$$**

★★ **PIETRO'S.** *3801 S Las Vegas Blvd, Las Vegas (89109). Phone 702/739-2341. www.tropicanalv.com.* For old-fashioned restaurant razzle-dazzle distinct from contemporary Vegas interpretations, cop a table at Pietro's. The namesake is Pietro Musetto, who garnered a following of fans at the now-vanished Dunes and several Tropicana restaurants before this one. They come to see the friendly Pietro, of course, but more importantly to watch the tableside preparations of steak Diane and flaming crepes. Classics like lobster bisque and chateaubriand also anchor the menu. The tuxedoed waiters and deluxe table settings keep it classy. French, American menu. Dinner. **$$$**

★★ **PINOT BRASSERIE.** *3355 S Las Vegas Blvd, Las Vegas (89109). Phone 702/414-3737. www.patinagroup.com.* Chef Joachim Splichal, famed for Patina in LA and Pinot restaurants throughout California, runs the very French Pinot Brasserie in the otherwise very Italian Venetian Resort (see). Brass rails, crimson and mirrored walls, and wood ceilings do the design end of evoking Paris. The kitchen does the rest, with foie gras and apples, roast rabbit, and coq au vin. There's also an oyster bar complete with items popular in Europe, such as periwinkles. If you're looking for savory fare in a romantic but not stifling setting, decant this Pinot. American menu. Breakfast, lunch, dinner. Bar. Casual attire. **$$**

★★ **POSTRIO.** *3355 S Las Vegas Blvd, Las Vegas (89109). Phone 702/414-3737; fax 702/796-1112. www.wolfgangpuck.com.* Adding to his already considerable Las Vegas portfolio, chef Wolfgang Puck backs this branch of his acclaimed San Francisco restaurant Postrio, located in the Venetian Resort (see). Like sibling Spago, Postrio blends Cal-Ital influences in a hard-to-choose-from menu that includes wood-fired pizzas, homemade pastas, grilled steaks, and seafood luxuries like a lobster club sandwich and raw bar oysters. Look for it among the Grand Canal shops, where patio dining offers a peek at the human parade in the Venetian carnival-themed mall, while a more formal dining room within shelters you from it. American menu. Lunch, dinner. Bar. Casual attire. **$$$**

★★★ **PRIME.** *3600 Las Vegas Blvd S, Las Vegas (89109). Phone 702/693-7223; fax 702/693-9127. www.bellagiolasvegas.com.* Famed New York fusion chef Jean-Georges Vongerichten opened his first and only steakhouse with the stylish Prime. Located in the Bellagio (see) with waterside views of the dancing fountains, Prime serves superior cuts of beef, veal, and lamb with a range of sauces, from standard béarnaise to very Vongerichten tamarind. Ample fish and chicken selections and creative appetizers entice lighter appetites. Elegant surrounds, including Baccarat crystal chandeliers and velvet draperies, distract from the expense-account prices. Steak menu. Dinner, late-night. Bar. Jacket required. Reservations recommended. Outdoor seating. **$$$**

★★★★ **RENOIR.** *3400 Las Vegas Blvd S, Las Vegas (89109). Phone 702/791-7223; fax 702/791-7437. www.mgm-mirage.com.* As you might expect from the restaurant's name, the works of French impressionist Pierre-Auguste Renoir are among the original works of art on display at Renoir, the Mirage Hotel's (see) opulent restaurant featuring contemporary French cuisine. Swathed in ornate silks and vintage tapestries, the room has an old-world elegance that is accented further by its dark-wood moldings and vintage brocade banquettes. Wear something neutral, or you are bound to clash with the room's elaborate design. The dining room is one of the most opulent and luxurious in Las Vegas, and it's worth taking in the plush surroundings with the fewest possible distractions. Fortunately, the food is as impressive as the décor. Inventive, modern French dishes focus on ingredients, revealing that the kitchen is of the "less is more" school of thought. Restraint pays off. Plates shine in their simplicity and make dinner at Renoir a winning experience. *Secret Inspector's Notes: The service at Renoir is as commendable as the food, if not more so. A well-trained army of staff attentively cater to each guest's needs and wants.* French menu. Dinner. Closed Sun-Mon. Bar. Jacket required. Reservations recommended. Valet parking. **$$$**

★ ★ SACRED SEA. *3900 Las Vegas Blvd S, Las Vegas (89119). Phone 702/262-4756; fax 702/262-4717. www.luxor.com.* The all-things-Egyptian Luxor (see) hosts Sacred Sea, which pays tribute to the bounty of Egypt's Nile River with a seafood-focused menu. Don't worry; the fish themselves aren't Nile caught. Instead, there's New Zealand mussels, Alaskan king and Maryland soft-shell crab, plus lobster from a live tank. In the indulgent spirit of the pharaohs, a list of feasts centers the menu: surf-and-turf staples like filet mignon and lobster tail. Scallop-shaped blue banquettes and murals of the great river underscore the theme. Steak, seafood menu. Dinner. Closed Wed-Thurs. Bar. Casual attire. Valet parking. **$$$**

★ SAM WOO BBQ. *4215 Spring Mountain Rd, Las Vegas (89102). Phone 702/368-7628; fax 702/368-7568.* Chinese menu. Lunch, dinner, late-night. Casual attire. **$**

★ ★ SAMBA BRAZILIAN STEAKHOUSE. *3400 Las Vegas Blvd S, Las Vegas (89109). Phone 702/791-7111; toll-free 800/456-4564. www.themirage.com.* In keeping with the Mirage's exotic theme, Samba, just off the gaming floor, imports the Brazilian rodizio tradition. The lively restaurant specializes in endless portions of marinated meat, skewered, slow-roasted, and then carved on your plate tableside. Servers roam the floor proffering cuts of baby back ribs, bacon-wrapped turkey, flank steak, sirloin, and chicken. Diners turn a table indicator to green to request more, or red to say "Basta!" Side dishes of beans and plantains accompany the meats. To best enjoy the feast, bring a band of caipirinha-drinking friends. South American menu. Dinner. Reservations recommended. **$$$**

★ ★ SHALIMAR. *3900 Paradise Rd, Las Vegas (89109). Phone 702/796-0302; fax 702/796-6480.* Indian menu. Dinner. Bar. Casual attire. **$$**

★ ★ SHANGHAI LILLY. *3950 Las Vegas Blvd S, Las Vegas (89119). Phone 702/632-7409; toll-free 877/632-7800. www.mandalaybay.com.* Shanghai Lilly's upscale Chinese cuisine dished up on Limoges china strikes a refined note in the often party-hearty Mandalay Bay Resort (see). Despite its location near the gaming floor, the elegant restaurant designed by the celebrated Tony Chi does its best to conjure tranquility. A water wall leads guests into the dining room, where three-story ceilings create a grand stage, while sheer curtain-draped booths serve those seeking intimacy. Cantonese, Szechwan, and Hong Kong specialties feature authentic indulgences like braised shark's fin, abalone with sea cucumber, lobster sashimi, and Peking duck. Dinner. **$$**

★ ★ ★ SHINTARO. *3600 Las Vegas Blvd S, Las Vegas (89109). Phone 702/693-7223. www.bellagiolasvegas.com.* Though primarily aimed at the Bellagio's high-rolling Asian gamblers, Shintaro warrants the attention of anyone serious about eastern food. The pan-Asian offerings lean toward Japanese, with sushi, tempura, and teriyaki. There's a Vegas-appropriate entertainment element to it all. Request a spot at the teppan yaki table for a ringside seat of the chefs as they cook a multicourse meal for you. And don't miss the vivid display of live jellyfish floating in a wall tank behind the sushi bar. Japanese menu. Dinner. Bar. Jacket required. Reservations recommended. Outdoor seating. **$$$**

★ ★ ★ SMITH & WOLLENSKY. *3767 Las Vegas Boulevard S, Las Vegas (89109). Phone 702/862-4100; fax 702/933-3931. www.smithandwollensky.com.* This Las Vegas outpost of the growing Manhattan-based chain re-creates the atmosphere of the original, right down to the chalkboards listing daily specials. Steak menu. Dinner. Bar. Casual attire. Valet parking. **$$$**

★ SPICE MARKET BUFFET. *3667 Las Vegas Blvd S, Las Vegas. Phone 702/785-5555. www.aladdincasino.com.* A local's favorite for buffet dining on the Strip, Spice Market Buffet in the Aladdin does its culinary part in transmitting the casino's One Thousand and One Nights theme. The serving tables here include Middle Eastern specialties such as tabbouleh, hummus, olives, and lamb shish kebab. Less adventurous palates will be pleased by the vast array of Mexican, Chinese, and Italian stations, plus prime rib and mounds of cold shrimp. The popular pastry selections include homemade chocolate chip cookies and made-to-order dessert crepes. Breakfast, lunch, dinner, Sun brunch. **$$**

★ STAGE DELI. *3500 Las Vegas Blvd S, Las Vegas (89109). Phone 702/893-4045; fax 702/893-1241. www.arkrestaurants.com.* American, deli menu. Dinner. Bar. Children's menu. Casual attire. Valet parking. **$**

★ ★ THE STEAK HOUSE. *2880 Las Vegas Blvd S, Las Vegas (89114). Phone 702/734-0410; fax 702/794-3874.* If you're not put off by seeking fine dining amid the carnival atmosphere of Circus Circus (see), The Steak House rewards your lack of pretension with high quality at reasonable prices. The 21-day-aged cuts of beef—New York strips, sirloins, porterhouses, and filets—are displayed amid the wood-paneled dining room and then charcoal-broiled in an exhibition kitchen. Portions are large, and many of the sides—potato, vegetable, and salad—that other meateries list á la carte are included in the price of a steak. Normally open only for dinner, a Champagne brunch each Sunday offers three early to midday seatings. Steak menu. Dinner, Sun brunch. Bar. Valet parking. **$$$**

★ ★ THE STEAKHOUSE AT CAMELOT. *3850 Las Vegas Blvd S, Las Vegas (89109). Phone 702/597-7449. www.excalibur.com.* Camelot serves gourmet dishes in a romantic setting. A cigar room, wine cellar, fireplace, and open kitchen are some of the classic elements found here. Steak menu. Dinner. Closed Mon-Tues. Bar. Casual attire. Valet parking. **$$$**

★ ★ TILLERMAN. *2245 E Flamingo Rd, Las Vegas (89109). Phone 702/731-4036; fax 702/731-1560. www.tillerman.com.* Serious seafood, fresh and simply prepared, has been served for years at this perennial favorite. American menu. Dinner. Closed holidays. Valet parking. Outdoor seating. **$$$**

★ ★ ★ TOP OF THE WORLD. *2000 Las Vegas Blvd S, Las Vegas (89104). Phone 702/380-7711. www.stratlv.com.* In a town of few casino windows and even fewer restaurant views, Top of the World atop the Stratosphere Hotel Tower stands out. The circular room revolves once every 90 minutes, offering 360-degree nighttime views of Vegas by neon. Few scenery-centric restaurants push the culinary envelope, and Top of the World is no exception, although it does a nice job with steaks and continental classics like lobster bisque. A mini Stratosphere in chocolate is a must for dessert, serving two. American menu. Dinner. Bar. Reservations recommended. Valet parking. **$$$**

★ ★ ★ VALENTINO. *3355 S Las Vegas Blvd, Las Vegas (89109). Phone 702/414-3737; fax 702/414-3099. www.valentinolv.com.* LA restaurateur Piero Selvaggio's signature restaurant, Valentino, is a Vegas replica of his Angeleno original. Authentic Italian complemented by a vast 24,000-bottle wine cellar distinguishes the Venetian Resort (see) fine-dinery. Chef Luciano Pellegrini hails from Italy, where he learned to create the savory, rustic fare that makes the intimate Valentino a worthy destination. The bilingual menu includes classic á la carte choices such as carpaccio and lasagna, as well as several seasonal five-course tasting menus that delve into delicacies like quail paired with foie gras and oysters accented with caviar. Italian menu. Dinner, late-night. Bar. Casual attire. Reservations recommended. **$$$$**

★ ★ ★ THE VERANDAH. *3960 Las Vegas Blvd S, Las Vegas (89119). Phone 702/632-5195.* The Strip's classiest hotel, the Four Seasons (see), houses its classiest dining patio, The Verandah. Overlooking the palm-flanked pool, The Verandah serves as the hotel's all-day restaurant, serving breakfast, lunch, dinner, and afternoon tea casually but stylishly. Selections are eclectic but generally high-end and include ahi sashimi, crab napoleon, seared salmon, and beef tenderloin with foie gras sauce. All sorts of Vegas visitors would be happy here, from foodies, served by a degustation menu, to children who get their own cart. American menu. Breakfast, lunch, dinner. Bar. Casual attire. Outdoor seating. **$$$**

★ ★ VIVA MERCADOS. *6182 W Flamingo Rd, Las Vegas (89103). Phone 702/871-8826; fax 702/871-6915. www.vivamercados.com.* Mexican menu. Lunch, dinner. Closed Sun; holidays. Bar. Children's menu. Casual attire. Reservations recommended. **$**

★ ★ VOODOO CAFE. *3700 W Flamingo Rd, Las Vegas (89103). Phone 702/777-7923.* Dine on the darker side of New Orleans at VooDoo Café on the 50th floor of the Rio hotel (see). Spooky black walls, cryptic symbols, and ornate chandeliers and sconces aim to evoke a witchy den, while the panorama beyond the windows constantly reminds you that this is the viva Las Vegas version. Fans of Cajun, Creole, and Southern cooking will find a satisfying if somewhat spice-shy menu. An observation deck off the lounge warrants a visit over either aperitifs or digestifs. American menu. Dinner. Bar. Casual attire. **$$**

★ WOLFGANG PUCK CAFE. *3799 Las Vegas Blvd S, Las Vegas (89109). Phone 702/895-9653; fax 702/895-7571. www.mgmgrand.com.* The first celebrity chef to hit the big numbers in Vegas, LA's Wolfgang Puck does a casual version of his signature Spago cuisine at the Wolfgang Puck Café in the casino at MGM Grand (see). The menu globe-trots in crowd-pleasing style, from east-meets-west fare such as spicy shrimp spring rolls and vegetable potstickers to Mexican tortilla soup and Italian bruschetta and pizzas. Colorful broken mosaic tiles and a lively open kitchen make the café right at home amid the slot machine stands and dice rollers. Breakfast, lunch, dinner. Bar. **$$**

★ XINH-XINH. *220 W Sahara Ave, Las Vegas (89102). Phone 702/471-1572.* Vietnamese menu. Dinner. Bar. Casual attire. **$$**

★ ★ YOLIE'S BRAZILIAN STEAKHOUSE. *3900 Paradise Rd, Las Vegas (89109). Phone 702/794-0700; fax 704/794-0459. www.yoliesbraziliansteakhouse.com.* Steak menu. Dinner. Bar. Reservations recommended. Outdoor seating. **$$$**

Laughlin (F-5)

See also Bullhead City, AZ; Kingman, AZ

Population 7,076
Elevation 520 ft
Area Code 702
Zip 89029
Information Laughlin Chamber of Commerce, PO Box 77777; toll-free 800/227-5245
Web site www.visitlaughlin.com

This resort community offers a pleasant change of pace from the dazzle of Las Vegas. In many ways, it resembles Las Vegas in its earlier days. Many hotels and casinos line the Colorado River; some provide ferry service to and from parking facilities on the Arizona side. But Laughlin offers other diversions as well; water sports such as fishing, waterskiing, and swimming in nearby Lake Mohave are popular.

Special Event

Laughlin River Days. *Hwy 95 and Colorado River, Laughlin. Phone 702/298-2214. www.superstockracing.com.* APBA Powerboat racing on a 1 1/2-mile course. Early June.

Limited-Service Hotels

★ ★ DON LAUGHLIN'S RIVERSIDE HOTEL. *1650 Casino Dr, Laughlin (89029). Phone 702/298-2535; toll-free 800/227-3849; fax 702/298-2695. www.riversideresort.com.* 1,404 rooms, 28 story. Pets accepted, some restrictions; fee. Check-in 3 pm, check-out 11 am. Restaurant, bar. Outdoor pool. Airport transportation available. Business center. Casino. Movie theaters. **$**

★ ★ RIVER PALMS. *2700 S Casino Dr, Laughlin (89029). Phone 702/298-2242; toll-free 800/835-7903; fax 702/298-2196. www.rvrpalm.com.* 1,003 rooms, 25 story. Check-in 3 pm, check-out 11 am. Restaurant, bar. Fitness room, spa. Outdoor pool, whirlpool. Airport transportation available. **$**

Full-Service Hotels

★ ★ ★ FLAMINGO LAUGHLIN. *1900 S Casino Dr, Laughlin (89029). Phone 702/298-5111; toll-free 800/258-7469; fax 702/298-5177. www.laughlinflamingo.com.* The largest resort on the Colorado River, this enormous property offers activities for every member of the family. Visitors will enjoy the 350-seat showroom, 3,000-seat outdoor amphitheater, and 60,000-square-foot casino. 1,912 rooms, 18 story. Check-in 3 pm, check-out 11 am. Restaurant, bar. Fitness room, spa. Outdoor pool. Tennis. Airport transportation available. Casino. **$**

★ ★ ★ GOLDEN NUGGET. *2300 S Casino Dr, Laughlin (89028). Phone 702/298-7222; toll-free 800/950-7700; fax 702/298-7122. www.gnlaughlin.com.* A jungle in the middle of the desert best describes this "tropical paradise" casino on the Colorado River. The rain forest-inspired lobby, tropical-themed guest rooms, and Tarzan's Night Club complete the illusion. 300 rooms, 4 story. Check-in 3 pm, check-out noon. Restaurant, bar. Outdoor pool. Airport transportation available. Casino. **$**

Lovelock (B-2)

Settled early 1840s
Population 2,003
Elevation 3,977 ft
Area Code 775
Zip 89419
Information Pershing County Chamber of Commerce, 25 W Marzen Lane, PO Box 821; phone 775/273-7213

The 49ers stopped in Lovelock Valley on their way west. There was plenty of feed for weary oxen and horses because beavers had dammed the Humboldt River, thus providing a steady water supply. The travelers mended their wagons and made other preparations for the 36-hour dash across the dreaded 40-mile desert to Hot Springs.

A deep layer of rich, black loam, left in the Lovelock Valley as the waters of an ancient lake receded, spreads over more than 40,000 acres. This soil, irrigated from the Rye Patch Reservoir, supports rich farms and productive ranches. Lovelock, the seat of Pershing County, was named for an early settler, George Lovelock, across whose ranch the original Central Pacific Railroad was built. Ore mines, mineral deposits, and a seed-processing plant in the area contribute to the growth of modern Lovelock.

What to See and Do

Courthouse Park. *1127 Central Ave, Lovelock. Phone 775 2737213.* The only round courthouse still in use. Shaded picnic grounds; swimming pool. (May-Aug, daily) **$**

Rye Patch State Recreation Area. *2505 Rye Patch Reservoir Rd, Lovelock. 23 miles N on I-80. Phone 775/538-7321.* Approximately 27,500 acres on 200,000-acre reservoir; swimming, waterskiing, fishing, boating (launching ramps); picnicking, camping (dump station).

Special Event

Frontier Days. *Courthouse Park, 1127 Central Ave, Lovelock. Phone 775/273-7213.* Parade, races, rodeo. Late July or early Aug.

Lunar Crater (D-4)

See also Ely, Tonopah

Near Hwy 6 between Tonopah and Ely.

This is a vast field of cinder cones and frozen lava. The crater is a steep-walled pit, 400 feet deep and 3/4-mile in diameter, created by volcanic action about 1,000 years ago. The earth exploded violently, heaving cinders, lava, and rocks the size of city blocks high into the air. Awed by the remains, pioneers named the pit Lunar Crater.

Primm (F-4)

See also Las Vegas

What to See and Do

Fashion Outlets of Las Vegas. *Primm. Take 1-15 S to exit 1. The mall is on the E side of the freeway. Phone 702/874-1400. www.fashionoutletlasvegas.com.* At most of the swanky hotels on the Strip, you can buy designer goods at high-end shops and boutiques. But you can save more than a few bucks on the same type of fashionable goods at this outlet mall, about 30 miles south of all the gaming action. Brooks Brothers, Burberry, Calvin Klein, Coach, Escada, Kenneth Cole New York, Last Call from Neiman-Marcus, Polo Ralph Lauren Factory Store, and Versace are among the nearly 100 retailers that entice bargain hunters with their marvelous markdowns. If you don't have a car, the mall offers daily shuttle service ($12.99 round-trip) from the MGM Grand Hotel and Casino. (Mon-Sat 10 am-9 pm, Sun 10 am-8 pm; closed Thanksgiving, Dec 25) **FREE**

Full-Service Resort

★★★ PRIMM VALLEY RESORT & CASINO. *31900 S Las Vegas Blvd, Primm (89019). Phone 702/386-7867.* Just 35 miles from Las Vegas, Primm Valley Resort & Casino has all the action of Sin City but with a gentler pace and a family-friendly attitude. This full-service resort welcomes guests with a country club setting and elegant accommodations. The 46,000-square-foot casino allows players to take a chance on a variety of games, and the top-notch entertainment and special events at Buffalo Bill's keep guests tapping their toes and clapping their hands. Shopping is a major attraction here, with the Fashion Outlets of Las Vegas just steps away via a resort connector. The rooms and suites reflect the resort's casual elegance, and after a full day of rolling the dice or hitting the stores, guests relish the many comforts of the stylish digs. 624 rooms. Check-in 3 pm, check-out noon. Restaurant, bar. Casino. **$$$**

Pyramid Lake (B-1)

See also Reno

36 miles N of Reno on Hwy 445.

Surrounded by rainbow-tinted, eroded hills, this lake is a remnant of prehistoric Lake Lahontan, which once covered 8,400 square miles in western Nevada and northeastern California. The largest natural lake in the state, Pyramid is about 30 miles long and 7 to 9 miles wide, with deep-blue sparkling waters. It is fed by scant water from the diverted Truckee River and by brief floods in other streams. Since the Newlands Irrigation Project deprives it of water, its level is receding. General John C. Frémont gave the lake its name when he visited the area in 1844, apparently taking it from the tufa (porous rock) islands that jut up from the water. One, 475 feet high, is said by Native Americans to be a basket inverted over an erring woman. Though turned to stone, her "breath" (wisps of steam from a hot spring) can still be seen. Another island is called Stone Mother and Basket. At the north end is a cluster of sharp spires known as the Needles. Anahoe Island, in the lake, is a sanctuary and breeding ground for more than 10,000 huge white pelicans. An air of mystery surrounds the area, bred by the murmuring waves, the spires and domes with their wisps of steam, and the ever-changing tints of the folded, eroded hills. At nearby Astor Pass, railroad excavations uncovered a horse skull and fragmentary remains of an elephant, bison, and camel, all believed to have lived on the lakeshore in prehistoric times. Pyramid Lake abounds with Lahonton cutthroat trout; it is one of the top trophy trout lakes in the United States. All rights belong to the Native Americans. For information about roads, fishing, and boat permits, contact the Sutcliffe Ranger Station or Pyramid Lake Fisheries, Star Rte, Sutcliffe 89510; phone 775/476-0500. Camping, boating, and fishing at Pyramid Lake are considered by many to be the best in the state. Day use $5-$10. Visitor centers, located in the hatcheries at Sutcliffe and between Nixon and Wadsworth, describe the land, lake, and people through photographs and displays (daily).

Reno (C-1)

See also Carson City, Incline Village, Virginia City

Founded 1868
Population 180,480
Elevation 4,498 ft
Area Code 775
Information Chamber of Commerce, 1 E First St, 16th Floor, 89501 775/337-3030. For information on cultural events, contact the Sierra Arts Foundation, 200 Flint St, 89501; phone 775/329-2787
Web site www.reno-sparkschamber.org

Reno, "the biggest little city in the world," renowned as a gambling and vacation center, is an important distribution and merchandising area, the home of the University of Nevada-Reno, and a residential city. Between the steep slopes of the Sierra and the low eastern hills, Reno spills across the Truckee Meadows. The neon lights of the nightclubs, gambling casinos, and bars give it a glitter that belies its quiet acres of fine houses, churches, and schools. The surrounding area is popular for sailing, boating, horseback riding, and deer and duck hunting.

Reno was known as Lake's Crossing and was an overland travelers' camping place even before the gold rush. It grew with the exploitation of the Comstock Lode and became a city in May 1868, with a public auction of real estate by a railway agent. Within a month there were 100 houses. A railroad official named the town in honor of a Union officer of the Civil War, General Jesse Lee Reno. In 1871 it became the seat of Washoe County.

Many Nevadans resent Reno's reputation as a divorce capital. They point out that many more couples are married than divorced at the Washoe County Courthouse. A six-month divorce law had been on the books since 1861, before Nevada became a state. The six-week law became effective in the 1930s.

What to See and Do

Animal Ark. *Reno. Take Hwy 395 N to exit 78, turn right on Red Rock Rd and drive 11.5 miles, turn right on Deerlodge and drive 1 mile to 1265. Phone 775/970-3111. www.animalark.org.* Tucked amidst the forested hills north of Reno, Animal Ark is not a zoo, but a sanctuary for animals that cannot be returned to the wild—many were disabled or orphaned, and others were unwanted exotic pets. The residents include big cats (tigers, snow leopards, and cougars), gray wolves, black bears, and a few reptiles and birds. Each has a name and is presented as an "ambassador" for its species. (Apr-Oct, Tues-Sun 10 am-4:30 pm; open Mon holidays) **$$**

Blue Lamp. *125 W 3rd St, Reno. Phone 775/329-6969.* A crowded, casual space laden with big couches and velvet art, this hip nightspot in downtown Reno has a vibe that's more San Francisco than northern Nevada. The stage here hosts live music, mainly jazz and rock, and DJs also hold court on regular theme nights.

Downtown Reno shopping district. *Reno.* Reno's neon-laden city center is not made up entirely of casinos and hotels. The downtown Riverwalk along the Truckee's banks (on Virginia, Sierra, First, and Second streets) is loaded with hip coffee shops and art galleries, and also is home to a number of chic eateries, eclectic boutiques, antique stores, salons, and theaters.

Foley's Irish Pub. *2780 S Virginia St, Reno. Phone 775/829-8500. www.ripkord.com/foleys.* Authentically Irish and a favorite after-work hangout south of downtown Reno, Foley's is an agreeable place to sip on a pint and have a conversation. The food is good (the menu offers a nice mix of Irish standards and American pub grub), the bartenders are friendly, and there are both TVs for sports and video poker machines.

Great Basin Adventure. *Rancho San Rafael Regional Park, 1502 Washington St, Reno. Phone 775/785-4319. www.maycenter.com.* Part of the Wilbur D. May Center in Rancho San Rafael Regional Park, Great Basin Adventure consists of several kids' attractions designed to educate and entertain simultaneously. At Wilbur's Farm, pint-sized visitors can take a pony ride or explore the 1.5-acre petting zoo. Guests can pan for gold at a replica mine building, with faux mine shafts that double as slides and displays on minerals and the area's mining history. Also onsite are the Discovery Room, a small "please touch" natural history museum with daily special events (storytelling, arts and crafts, and other kids' activities); a log flume ride on a man-made river (a great opportunity to cool off in the summer); and a colorful playground with swings and slides shaped like dinosaurs. (Tues-Sat 10 am-5 pm, Sun noon-5 pm) **$**

Humboldt-Toiyabe National Forest. *1200 Franklin Way, Sparks. 10 miles W on I-80, then W on Hwy 27. Phone 775/331-6444. www.fs.fed.us/htnf.* At 6.3 million acres, this is the largest national forest in the lower 48 states. It extends across Nevada from the California border in a scattershot pattern, comprising ten ranger districts that encompass four distinct ecologies: meadows, mountains, deserts, and canyons. Just northwest of the Reno city limits, Peavine Mountain is crisscrossed by a number of old mining roads now reserved for hikers and mountain bikers. Other Humboldt-Toiyabe highlights include scenic Lamoille Canyon and the Ruby Mountains, southeast of Elko; the rugged, isolated Toiyabe Range, near the geographical center of Nevada; and, well southeast of Reno on the California-Nevada border, Boundary Peak, the state's highest point at 13,143 feet. Beyond hikers and bikers, off-road vehicles, snowmobiles, and campers flock to various areas in the vast forest. **FREE**

Meadowood Mall. *5515 Meadowood Mall Cir, Reno. Phone 775/825-3955.* The most contemporary and posh shopping center in the region, Reno's Meadowood Mall is actually the city's most-visited tourist attraction. The more than 100 stores under the mall's roof include anchors Macy's, JCPenney, and Sears, alongside a massive sporting goods store—Copeland's. There are also specialty stores like Brookstone and Victoria's Secret, and a number of restaurants.

Mount Rose Ski Area. *22222 Mt Rose Hwy, Reno. 12 miles NE on Hwy 431. Phone 775/849-0704; toll-free 800/754-7673 (except in NV). www.mtrose.com.* Of all the ski resorts in the Reno-Tahoe area, Mount Rose has the highest base elevation (a precipitous 8,260 feet above sea level), making it the best bet for late-season skiing. Six lifts, including a six-person, high-speed chairlift, take skiers and snowboarders to the 9,700-foot summit, to 1,000 acres of terrain nearly evenly split among skill levels (30% beginner, 30% intermediate, and 40% advanced) and a pair of snowboarding parks. Located northwest of Lake Tahoe, Mount Rose is also known for its excellent "first-timer" program for beginners. There are no on-mountain accommodations. (Mid-Nov-mid-Apr, daily) **$$$$**

National Automobile Museum (The Harrah Collection). *10 Lake St S, Reno. At the corner of Lake and Mill. Phone 775/333-9300. www.automuseum.org.* The brainchild of car collector and gaming titan Bill Harrah, this excellent facility covers more than a century of automotive history in fascinating detail. Four galleries house the museum's collection of more than 200 cars: The first details the late 19th and early 20th century (complete with a blacksmith's shop, the garage of the day); the second covers 1914 to 1931; the third, 1932 to 1954; and the fourth, 1954 to modern day. Also in the fourth gallery, the Masterpiece Circle Gallery accommodates temporary themed exhibits on subjects ranging from Porsches to pickup trucks. The oldest car in the museum dates from 1892, and there are a number of collector's trophies (such as the 1949 Mercury Coupe driven by James Dean in Rebel Without a Cause) and one-of-a-kind oddities (the steam-powered 1977 Steamin' Demon). (Mon-Sat 9:30 am-5:30 pm, Sun 10 am-4 pm; closed Thanksgiving, Dec 25) **$$**

Nevada Museum of Art. *160 W Liberty St, Reno. Phone 775/329-3333. www.nevadaart.org.* The only nationally accredited art museum in the entire state, the Nevada Museum of Art would be a top-notch facility no matter where it was located. Perhaps the most distinctive architectural specimen in all of artsy Reno, the curved, sweeping structure is a work of art in and of itself: modern (it opened in 2003) and monolithic (60,000 square feet), evoking the image of the legendary Black Rock of the Nevada desert. The collection housed within is equally impressive, broken into five different themes: contemporary art, contemporary landscape photography (one of the best of its kind anywhere), regional art, American art from 1900 to 1945, and the E. L. Weigand Collection, American art with a "work ethic" theme. The museum also plays host to several temporary exhibitions every year, and has a café, a store, and an art school on site. (Tues-Wed, Fri-Sun 11 am-6 pm, Thurs 11 am-8 pm; closed major holidays) **$$**

★ **Reno Arch.** *Virginia St, downtown, Reno.* In 1926, Reno commemorated the completion of the first transcontinental highway in North America—which ran through the city en route to San Francisco—with an arch that traverses Virginia Street downtown. Three years later, locals adopted the tagline "The Biggest Little City in the World" and added it to the landmark. The arch has since been replaced twice—in 1964 and in 1987—but remains one of the most photographed structures in the US. The original arch was scrapped, but the 1964 arch found a new home across town at the National Automobile Museum (see).

Reno-Sparks Theater Coalition. *528 W First St, Reno. Phone 775/786-2278. www.theatercoalition.org.* Consisting of more than 20 separate companies in the Reno-Sparks area, this organization is a cooperative effort to market a varied slate of theater, dance, and other performing arts. Member troupes range from the avant-garde to the kid-friendly, and the Coalition puts together an up-to-date events schedule for all of them.

Scruples Bar and Grill. *91 W Plumb St, Reno. Phone 775/322-7171.* Nondescript on the exterior (it's tucked away in a strip mall), Scruples is cozier on the inside, just a good neighborhood bar, with rock on the jukebox and patio seating. It's a good bet for late night burgers and fries, and also the best place to watch a ballgame, especially those involving teams from the University of Nevada, Reno.

Sierra Nevada Bus Tours. *2050 Glendale Ave, Sparks. Phone 775/331-1147; toll-free 800/822-6009.* To Virginia City, Ponderosa Ranch, Lake Tahoe, and other nearby points.

Sierra Safari Zoo. *10200 N Virginia St, Reno. 8 miles N of downtown. Phone 775/677-1101. www.sierrasafarizoo.com.* The largest zoo in Nevada (but a fairly average one in national terms), Sierra Safari is home to 150 representatives of more than 40 species. The majority of the animals were selected for the rugged Reno climate, including a Siberian tiger and a number of other felines, but there are also tropical birds, a few reptiles, and a number of primates. A petting zoo and a picnic area are on site. (Apr-Oct, daily 10 am-5 pm) **$**

University of Nevada, Reno. *1664 N Virginia St, Reno. 9th and Virginia sts. Phone 775/784-4700 (tours). www.unr.edu.* (1874) (12,000 students) The campus covers 200 acres on a plateau overlooking the Truckee Meadows, in the shadow of the Sierra Nevada Mountains. Opened in Elko, it was moved to Reno and reopened in 1885. Tours of campus. On campus are

Fleischmann Planetarium and Science Center. *1650 N Virginia St, Reno. Phone 775/784-4811. planetarium.unr.nevada.edu.* This facility projects public star shows on the inside of its 30-foot dome. The museum here houses all four of the meteorites that have landed in Nevada (including a massive specimen that weighs more than a ton) and scales rigged to reflect the gravity on Jupiter or a neutron star. On cloudless Friday nights, guests can peer through telescopes with members of the Astronomical Society of Nevada. (Mon-Fri 8 am-8 pm, Sat-Sun 11 am-8 pm) **$$**

Nevada Historical Society Museum. *1650 N Virginia St, Reno. Phone 775/688-1190. dmla.clan.lib.nv.us/docs/museums/reno/his-soc.htm.* Founded in 1904, this is Nevada's oldest museum and one of its best. On permanent display is "Nevada: Prisms and Perspectives," which examines the Silver State's five biggest historical stories: the Native American perspective, the mining boom, the neon-lit story of gaming, transportation, and the "Federal Presence"—as the federal government owns 87 percent of Nevada's land. A store, changing exhibit gallery, and library are also on site. Galleries (Mon-Sat 10 am-5 pm; closed holidays) **$**

W. M. Keck Earth Sciences and Engineering Museum. *Mackay School of Mines Building, 9th and Virginia sts, Reno. Phone 775/784-6987. mines.unr.edu/museum.* Located in the Mackay School of Mines Building, the Keck Museum focuses on the state's mining history. The collection of specimens originated from Nevada's most renowned mining districts—the Comstock Lode, Tonopah, and Goldfield—but exotic minerals from all over the world share the space. Rounding out the museum are displays of fossils, vintage mining equipment, and a collection of fine silver donated by the family of mining tycoon John Mackay. (Mon-Fri 9 am-4 pm; closed holidays) **FREE**

Special Events

Artown Festival. *Throughout the city. Phone 775/322-1538. www.artown.org.* Held annually in July (with a newer holiday counterpart in November and December), Reno's Artown Festival is a month-long extravaganza that includes more than 200 events and exhibitions and 1,000 artists in all. (That makes it the largest arts festival in the US, and one that has won its fair share of national acclaim since it launched in 1996.) The artists span the disciplines of ballet, opera, theater, film, and the visual arts—there are flamenco dancers, comedy troupes, and internationally known performers of all stripes, not to mention the myriad gallery openings and historical tours. Multiple downtown venues host various aspects of the festival: Wingfield Park is the setting of an outdoor film every week, Rollin' on the River is a weekly concert series. Mondays are family nights, with entertainment ranging from science experiments to storytelling. July.

Best of the West Rib Cook-off. *John Ascuaga's Nugget Casino Resort, 1100 Nugget Ave, Sparks. Phone 775/356-3300; toll-free 800/648-1177. www.janugget.com/events/ribcookoff.cfm.* Rack after gargantuan rack of baby-back ribs, slathered in sweet-hot sauce, lure nearly 300,000 barbecue fanatics to John Ascuaga's Nugget in Sparks every Labor Day weekend. In recent years, about 150,000 pounds of ribs have been consumed by the masses at this five-day event. (For those who are counting, that makes it the largest such event in the whole nation.) If you can pull yourself away from the addictive barbecue, there is also a lineup of live entertainment on numerous outdoor stages (ranging from rock to blues to zydeco), vendors hocking crafts and ribs at booths, and even karaoke. The "Best of the West" moniker is no joke: Just two dozen of the West's most revered barbecue pros (all invited) compete for the first-prize trophy and the judges are also culinary notables. The winner is presented with a pig-shaped check at the awards ceremony. Labor Day weekend.

Eldorado's Great BBQ, Brew, and Blues. *4th and Virginia sts, Reno. Outside and inside of Eldorado Hotel and Casino. Phone 775/786-5700; toll-free 800/648-5966. www.eldoradoreno.com.* Held over the last weekend every June by the Eldorado Hotel and Casino, this street fair focuses on the three staples in its name: tangy barbecue, ice-cold beer, and a pair of stages featuring nonstop blues. The participating breweries hail from Nevada, California, and Oregon, and only those 21 years old and over are admitted. Last weekend in June.

Eldorado Great Italian Festival. *4th and Virginia sts, Reno. Outside and inside the Eldorado Hotel and Casino. Phone 775/786-5700; toll-free 800/648-5966. www.eldoradoreno.com.* Red, white, and green streamers and flags blanket Virginia Street for two days in early October. The food runs the Italian gamut, from pasta, calamari, and risotto to gelato and, of course, vino. Put on by the Eldorado Hotel and Casino, the event includes several buffets, a farmers' market, and live entertainment, but the contests are the real attractions: a spaghetti sauce cook-off, a gelato-eating contest for kids, and the big event, the grape-stomping competition. Early Oct.

Hot August Nights. *1425 E Greg St, Sparks. Outside of Reno-Sparks Convention Center. Phone 775/356-1956. www.hotaugustnights.net.* Held over a weekend in early August, this retro event pays homage to the 1950s and '60s. Highlights include a series of concerts by nostalgia acts (past performers have included Chuck Berry, the Turtles, and Jan and Dean) and a classic car parade. There are street dances and sock hops, and casinos get in on the action by awarding a classic car or two to a few lucky winners. Early Aug.

National Championship Air Races. *Reno/Stead Airport, 4895 Texas Ave, Reno. Phone 775/972-6663. www.airrace.org.* Races (classes include Biplane, Formula One, Unlimited, Jet, Sport, and T-6), demonstrations, and fly-bys. Four days in mid-Sept. **$$$$**

Nevada Opera. *Pioneer Center for the Performing Arts, 100 S Virginia St, Reno. Phone 775/786-4046. www.nevadaopera.com.* Founded in 1967 and surviving a tumultuous financial era in the late 1990s, the Nevada Opera stages several noteworthy operas each year in its fall/spring calendar. Recent productions have included Madame Butterfly and Carmen. While the group tours the entire state, its Reno home is the Pioneer Center for the Performing Arts. **$$$$**

Nevada State Fair. *1350 N Wells Ave, Reno. Phone 775/688-5767 (tickets). www.nevadastatefair.org.* A Reno area tradition since 1874, the Nevada State Fair is held annually in late August, with rodeo events, livestock competitions, and a carnival midway. Beyond the expected fair diversions, the event also includes a kid-oriented science festival, an aerial motorcycle stunt show, and contests for the best homemade pies, cookies, and salsa. Late Aug.

Reno Basque Festival. *Wingfield Park, Reno. Phone 775/787-30309.* Basques from northern Spain and southern France immigrated to Nevada's Great Basin in the early 20th century to herd sheep, and they have been a visible part of the Reno community ever since. Held over a weekend in late July, the Reno Basque Festival started in 1959 with the goal of preserving Basque culture in the US. Today, it's one of the largest events of its kind in the country, kicked off by a parade that snakes around downtown before coming to a stop at Wingfield Park along the Truckee River. From there, the festival takes over, with food, dancing, singing, and athletic competitions. Basque cuisine available for the sampling includes sheepherder bread, Basque beans, lamb stew, and other hearty staples, and there's also a market. Crowds gather for the traditional games: soka tira (a Basque tug-of-war), woodcutting, and weightlifting. Late July.

Reno Film Festival. *Reno Film Festival Office, 528 W First St, Reno. Phone 775/334-6707. www.renofilmfestival.com.* Drawing a handful of celebrities to downtown Reno every November, this film festival consists of Hollywood productions, independent features, world premieres, and retrospective revivals. Screenings are shown at various downtown venues (i.e., casinos, museums, and theaters), and there are also a number of film-related workshops, demonstrations, and lectures. Early Nov.

Reno Jazz Festival. *University of Nevada, Reno. Phone 775/784-6847 (tickets).* Held on the University of Nevada at Reno campus since 1963, this three-day event is one of the biggest of its kind, drawing hundreds of school bands (junior high to college) from Nevada, California, Oregon, Idaho, and Washington. The top bands and soloists play at a concluding encore performance, and the first two nights are highlighted by sets from nationally known jazz names. Late Apr. **$$$$**

Reno Philharmonic Orchestra. *Pioneer Center for the Performing Arts, 925 Riverside Dr #3, Reno. Phone 775/323-6393. www.renophilharmonic.com.* Reno's symphony orchestra plays a September-to-April "Master Classics Series" (as well as a July 4th pops concert) at a number of venues in town, with Pioneer Center for the Performing Arts serving as its home stage. The orchestra plays works from composers such as Mozart, Beethoven, Copland, and Gershwin. "Preview from the Podium" is a free one-hour lecture given immediately before each concert. **$$$$**

Reno Rodeo. *Reno Livestock Events Center, 1350 N Wells Ave, Reno. Phone 775/329-3877; toll-free 800/225-2277 (tickets). www.renorodeo.com.* Known as the "Wildest, Richest Rodeo in the West"—with a total purse in excess of $1 million—the Reno Rodeo has been a big event since its inaugural year, 1919. The rodeo is one of the largest PRCA (Professional Rodeo Cowboys Association) events in the US and features bull riding, barrel racing, and roping events. Late June. **$$**

Sparks Hometowne Farmers' Market. *Victorian Square, downtown, Sparks. Phone 775/353-2291.* Every

Thursday evening between June and August, Victorian Square in downtown Sparks comes alive with foods that will tempt even the most finicky tastes. Over 100 vendors furnish both fresh ingredients and finished meals, everything from rhubarb to pastries to tacos. Beyond the seemingly endless supply of good food, there is a nightly 6 pm cooking demonstration, a kids' area, and home and garden vendors.

Limited-Service Hotels

★ ★ BEST WESTERN AIRPORT PLAZA HOTEL. *1981 Terminal Way, Reno (89502). Phone 775/348-6370; toll-free 800/648-3525; fax 775/348-9722. www.bestwestern.com.* 270 rooms, 3 story. Check-out noon. Restaurant, bar. Fitness room. Pool, whirlpool. Airport transportation available. Business center. Casino. **$**

★ ★ FITZGERALD'S CASINO HOTEL. *255 N Virginia St, Reno (89501). Phone 775/785-3300; toll-free 800/535-5825; fax 775/786-3686. www.fitzgeralds .com.* 351 rooms, 16 story. Check-out 11 am. Restaurant, bar. Casino. **$**

★ LA QUINTA INN. *4001 Market St, Reno (89502). Phone 775/348-6100; fax 775/348-8794. www.laquinta .com.* 130 rooms, 2 story. Pets accepted, some restrictions. Complimentary continental breakfast. Check-out noon. Pool. Airport transportation available. **$**

Full-Service Hotels

★ ★ ★ ATLANTIS CASINO RESORT. *3800 S Virginia St, Reno (89502). Phone 775/825-4700; toll-free 800/723-6500; fax 775/826-7860. www. atlantiscasino.com.* What began as a 142-room hotel in the early 1970s underwent a significant facelift in the 1990s. Now Atlantis, located about 3 miles south of downtown, is among Reno's top resorts, with several smoke-free gaming areas in the glass-enclosed casinos, a top-notch business center, and a dizzying array of rooms. Two highlights: the Sky Terrace restaurant, with sushi and oyster bars, and an excellent spa, featuring Ahava, Aveda, and Dermalogica products. 973 rooms, 27 story. Pets accepted, some restrictions; fee. Check-out 11 am. Restaurant, bar. Spa. Pool, whirlpool. Airport transportation available. Casino. **$**

★ ★ ★ ELDORADO HOTEL AND CASINO. *345 N Virginia St, Reno (89505). Phone 775/786-5700; toll-free 800/648-5966; fax 775/348-9269. www. eldoradoreno.com.* Of the casinos in downtown Reno, Eldorado is the one that attracts the youngest and hippest crowd, based primarily on its myriad nightspots: a microbrewery with live rock and blues, a martini/piano bar, and BuBinga, a popular dance club with DJs and live bands. Eldorado has some of the best-looking hotel rooms in town, airy and sunny with light tones, and the impressive "Fountain of Fortune" in the mezzanine plaza, a Baroque marvel adorned with dozens of ornate marble statues. The casino features 2,000 slots, boasts the best poker room in town, and is known for its generous comps, earned through Club Eldorado. Among the ten restaurants are eateries specializing in Chinese and Italian, as well as a seafood buffet. 817 rooms, 26 story. Check-out noon. Restaurant, bar. Pool, whirlpool. Airport transportation available. Casino. **$**

★ ★ ★ HARRAH'S HOTEL RENO. *PO Box 10, Reno (89520). Phone 775/786-3232; fax 775/788-2815. www.harrahs.com.* In the heart of downtown (right next to the Reno Arch), Harrah's Reno is one of the glitziest casinos in the city, a distinction it's held since opening in the early 1960s. The casino is immense and diverse, featuring 1,300 slot machines, table games of all kinds, and a sports book. Accommodations come in the form of nearly 1,000 sleek hotel rooms, ranging in style from standard rooms to skyline suites. There are seven restaurants, including the renowned Steak House at Harrah's Reno. Non-gamers can spend the day at Xtreme Park, a small amusement park featuring the hair-raising, 145-foot Xtreme Machine, which vaults passengers skyward at speeds up to 100 miles per hour. And entertainers work the crowd onstage at Sammy's Showroom, named after Sammy Davis, Jr., who performed here 40 times. 952 rooms, 26 story. Pets accepted, some restrictions. Check-out noon. Restaurant, bar. Pool, whirlpool. Airport transportation available. Business center. Casino. **$**

★ ★ ★ HILTON RENO. *2500 E Second St, Reno (89595). Phone 702/789-2000; toll-free 800/648-5080; fax 702/789-1678. www.hilton.com.* With a 40,000-square-foot Fun Quest Center and a recreational vehicle park, this casino resort is for the whole family. Other activities available include hang gliding, bungee jumping, sky diving, bowling, a health and fitness center, aquatic driving range, an indoor golf and sports center, six restaurants, a comedy club and swimming pool. 2,000 rooms, 27 story. Check-out 11 am. Restaurant, bar. Fitness room. Pool, whirlpool. Airport transportation available. Business center. Casino. **$**

★ ★ ★ JOHN ASCUAGA' S NUGGET. *1100 Nugget Ave, Sparks (89431). Phone 775/356-3300; toll-free 800/648-1177; fax 775/356-4258. www.janugget.com.* An anchor in downtown Sparks, the Nugget has been one of the top resorts in the Reno area since opening in 1955. It's a few miles outside of the hubbub in downtown Reno, but right on the doorstep of Victorian Square, the site of numerous special events. (The Nugget itself hosts one of these big fiestas: the Best of the West Rib Cook-off.) The casino is loaded with all of the standards—slots, table games, a poker room, and a sports book. If food is your game, there are eight restaurants to choose from including a Basque restaurant and a longstanding steakhouse. The Celebrity Showroom is the place to go for fabulous entertainment. The hotel itself is a landmark, with a pair of 29-story towers flanking the casino—1,600 rooms in all—and a slate of amenities that includes everything from an arcade to a wedding chapel. 1,407 rooms, 29 story. Check-out 11 am. Restaurants, bars. Fitness room. Indoor pool, outdoor pool, whirlpool. Airport transportation available. Business center. Casino. **$**

★ ★ ★ PEPPERMILL HOTEL AND CASINO RENO. *2707 S Virginia St, Reno (89502). Phone 775/826-2121; toll-free 800/648-6992; fax 775/689-7127. www.peppermillcasino.com.* Consistently ranked near the top of the lists for best and hippest casinos in the city (and the country, for that matter), Peppermill's flagship resort, renovated for a tab of $300 million in 2000-2001, is a fixture in the entertainment district near the airport, about 2 miles south of downtown. The slick property features 1,100 rooms, 2,000 slot machines, the full spectrum of table gaming, poker, sports betting, and nightly live entertainment in the swanky Cabaret and the more intimate Piano Lounge. Among the amenities, the pool—replete with a man-made waterfall—stands out, as do the seven restaurants. The dozen themed nightspots are a prime lure; the highlights are the aquarium-laden Fish Bar and the domed, effects-laden ultra lounge at Romanza, one of the hippest, see-and-be-seen nightclubs in town. 1,070 rooms, 16 story. Check-out noon. Restaurant, bar. Fitness room. Outdoor pool, whirlpool. Airport transportation available. Casino. **$**

★ ★ ★ SIENA HOTEL SPA CASINO. *1 S Lake St, Reno (89505). Phone 775/337-6260; toll-free 877/743-6233. www.sienareno.com.* The Siena Hotel Spa Casino brings the romance of the Tuscan countryside to Reno. Located along the banks of the Truckee River, this comprehensive resort is at once restful and thrilling. A 23,000-square-foot casino invites gaming, while a full-service spa with a complete range of services caters to overworked individuals. Designed to resemble a Tuscan village, the resort carries the country Italian theme through to its delightful and soothing guest accommodations. Three dining establishments keep diners on their toes. Lexie's on the River shows off water views, although its exhibition kitchen captures the attention of many diners. Contrada Café satisfies hunger throughout the day with its informal fare, and Enoteca is an oenophile's fantasy with its extensive wine list, and excellent food and wine pairings. 214 rooms, 9 story. Check-out noon. Restaurants, bars. Fitness room, spa. Business center. Casino. **$**

★ ★ ★ SILVER LEGACY RESORT CASINO RENO. *407 N Virginia St, Reno (89501). Phone 775/329-4777; toll-free 800/687-7733; fax 775/325-7474. www.silverlegacyresort.com.* A large and relatively new (1995) casino hotel in downtown Reno, the Silver Legacy sports a Victorian theme, under an enormous steel and brass dome and behind a façade designed to resemble 1890s storefronts. Beyond the gaming—2,000 slots, table games, a sports book, and a keno lounge—there is a comedy club and a rum bar with dueling pianos. The showroom attracts big-name entertainers. 1,720 rooms, 38 story. Check-out 11 am. Restaurant, bar. Pool, whirlpool. Airport transportation available. **$**

Restaurants

★ ★ BRICKS RESTAURANT AND WINE BAR. *1695 S Virginia St, Reno (89502). Phone 775/786-2277; fax 775/786-3377.* American menu. Lunch, dinner. Closed Sun; holidays. Bar. **$$**

★★ **FAMOUS MURPHY'S.** *3127 S Virginia St, Reno (89502). Phone 775/827-4111; fax 775/824-2599. www.famousmurphys.com.* Seafood, steak menu. Lunch, dinner. Closed Sun. Bar. Children's menu. **$$**

★★ **PALAIS DE JADE.** *960 W Moana Ln #107, Reno (89509). Phone 775/827-5233.* Chinese menu. Lunch, dinner. Closed holidays. Bar. **$$**

★★ **RAPSCALLION.** *1555 S Wells Ave, Reno (89502). Phone 775/323-1211; fax 775/323-6096. www.rapscallion.com.* Seafood menu. Dinner, Sun brunch. Closed Thanksgiving, Dec 25. Bar. Outdoor seating. **$$**

★★ **WASHOE GRILL.** *4201 W 4th St, Reno (89503). Phone 775/786-1323.* Seafood, steak menu. Dinner. Closed Thanksgiving. Bar. **$$$**

South Lake Tahoe (C-1)

What to See and Do

Factory Stores at the Y. *Hwys 50 and 89, South Lake Tahoe. Phone 530/573-5545. www.tahoefactorystores.com.* Named for a location at the intersection of Highways 50 and 89, this small group of South Lake Tahoe factory stores draws vacationers exhausted from a few days on the slopes. Among the manufacturer-owned tenants are retailers of clothing (Adidas, Big Dog, Izod), luggage (Samsonite), and sweets (Rocky Mountain Chocolate Factory). (Daily 9 am-6 pm)

Special Event

Valhalla Winter Microbrew Festival. *Horizon Casino, 50 Hwy 50, South Lake Tahoe. Phone 530/542-4166. www.valhalla-tallac.com.* Held at the Horizon Casino, this annual February fundraiser for the Valhalla Arts and Music Festival gives attendees the chance to sample 120 microbrews from Nevada and northern California. Admission includes a souvenir glass and unlimited samples. Beyond the array of handcrafted suds, there is also a live jazz and blues concert. Mid-Feb.

Sparks (C-1)

See also Reno

What to See and Do

Sparks Heritage Museum. *820 Victorian Ave, Sparks. Phone 775/355-1144.* Sparks is nicknamed "Rail City," making it fitting for this museum to focus on local railroad history. Housed in a former courthouse, the museum's exhibits detail Sparks' progression from a train depot to a mining hub to a municipality of 80,000 people. Highlights include a vintage model train set and a pump-powered antique player piano. (Tues-Fri 11 am-4 pm, Sat-Sun 1-4 pm) **DONATION**

Wild Island Family Adventure Park. *250 Wild Island Ct, Sparks. Just off I-80 at the Sparks Blvd exit. Phone 775/359-2927. www.wildisland.com.* Primarily known as a summer water park, Wild Island is now a year-round facility with the 2003 addition of Coconut Bowl, a state-of-the-art 20-lane bowling alley ($ per game), and the surprisingly chic Smokin Marlin Grill. The water park ($$$$) is the region's biggest, with a wave pool, tubing river, and myriad slides. Rounding out the sprawling fun center are a pair 18-hole miniature golf courses ($$), a three-story interactive play area, an arcade, and a roller coaster. (Hours vary by attraction and season)

Stateline (C-1)

See also Carson City, Gardnerville, Incline Village

Population 1,215
Elevation 6,360 ft
Area Code 775
Zip 89449

This area is best known for its famous high-rise casino/hotels, cabarets, and fine dining, but as an integral part of Tahoe's "south shore," it is also appreciated for its spectacular natural beauty. Alpine beaches and Sierra forests afford visitors an endless variety of year-round recreation. There are several excellent public golf courses in the area.

Limited-Service Hotels

★ **HORIZON CASINO RESORT.** *50 Hwy 50, Stateline (89449). Phone 775/588-6211; toll-free 800/648-3322; fax 775/588-1344. www.horizoncasino.com.* 539 rooms, 15 story. Check-out noon. Restaurant, bar. Fitness room. Pool, whirlpool. Casino. **$**

★★ **LAKESIDE INN AND CASINO.** *Hwy 50 at Kingsbury Grade, Stateline (89449). Phone 775/588-7777; toll-free 800/624-7980; fax 775/588-4092.*

www.lakesideinn.com. 124 rooms, 2 story. Check-out noon. Restaurant, bar. Pool. Casino. **$**

Full-Service Hotels

★ ★ ★ **CAESARS TAHOE.** *55 Hwy 50, Stateline (89449). Phone 775/588-3515; toll-free 888/829-7630; fax 775/586-4694. www.caesars.com.* One of four Caesars' properties in the US, this is the ultimate high-roller's property in northern Nevada, located just a stone's throw from Lake Tahoe. While smaller than its peers in downtown Reno, the hotel has a more elegant, exclusive vibe, and features six restaurants, a shopping arcade, and a yacht that takes guests on lake cruises. 440 rooms, 15 story. Check-out noon. Restaurant, bar. Fitness room. Indoor pool, whirlpool. Tennis. Business center. Casino. **$**

★ ★ ★ **HARRAH'S LAKE TAHOE.** *Hwy 50, Stateline (89449). Phone 775/588-6611; toll-free 800/648-3773; fax 775/586-6552. www.harrahstahoe.com.* This property offers 18,000 square feet of function space and plenty of recreation options for leisure visitors. Shop at the Galleria, swim in the glass-domed pool, tan on the sun deck, or do the obvious at the casino. 532 rooms, 18 story. Pets accepted, some restrictions; fee. Check-out noon. Restaurant, bar. Fitness room. Indoor pool, whirlpool. Casino. **$**

★ ★ ★ **HARVEY'S LAKE TAHOE.** *Stateline Ave (Hwy 50), Stateline (89449). Phone 775/588-2411; toll-free 800/427-2789; fax 775/588-6643. www.harveys.com.* Tahoe's first gaming establishment (1944), most rooms at this property have a view of Lake Tahoe or the Sierra Nevada mountains. There is plenty of entertainment from the casino alone, however, should guests care to look for other activities, they are sure to be pleased. 740 rooms, 19 story. Check-out noon. Restaurant, bar. Fitness room. Pool, whirlpool. Airport transportation available. Business center. Casino. **$**

Restaurants

★ ★ **CHART HOUSE.** *392 Kingsbury Grade, Stateline (89449). Phone 775/588-6276; fax 775/588-4562. www.chart-house.com.* American menu. Dinner. Bar. Children's menu. Outdoor seating. **$$$**

★ ★ ★ **FRIDAY'S STATION STEAK & SEAFOOD GRILL.** *Hwy 50, Stateline (89449). Phone 775/588-6611. www.harrahs.com/our_casinos/tah/dining.* The view of the lake from this restaurant, located on the 18th floor, is truly breathtaking. Seafood, steak menu. Dinner. Bar. **$$$**

★ ★ ★ **LEWELLYN'S.** *Hwy 50, Stateline (89449). Phone 775/588-2411; fax 775/586-6876.* High atop Harveys on the 19th floor, Llewellyn's offers a spectacular view of Lake Tahoe and an innovative menu with a beautiful presentation. International menu. Dinner. Bar. Valet parking. **$$$**

★ ★ ★ **SAGE ROOM.** *Hwy 50, Stateline (89449). Phone 775/588-2411; fax 775/586-6854.* Since 1947, the Sage Room Steak House has been world renowned for its old western ambiance and fine cuisine. Dine among the works of Russell and Remington while enjoying traditional Steak House dining highlighted by tableside flambe service. Top off your meal with the Sage Room's famous Bananas Foster. Continental, American menu. Dinner. Bar. Valet parking. **$$$**

★ ★ ★ **SUMMIT.** *Hwy 50, Stateline (89449). Phone 775/588-6611; fax 775/586-6643. www.harrahs.com/our_casinos/tah/dining/.* Located on the 16th and 17th floors of Harrah's, this restaurant has stunning views of the lake and mountains. American menu. Dinner. Bar. Valet parking. **$$$$**

Tonopah (D-3)

Settled 1900
Population 2,627
Elevation 6,030 ft
Area Code 775
Zip 89049
Information Chamber of Commerce, 301 Brougher St, PO Box 869; phone 775/482-3859
Web site www.tonopahnevada.com

Founded by prospector Jim Butler in 1900 and named by his wife, Tonopah was a high-spirited but unusually orderly camp in its early days. "Tono" is a shrub of the greasewood family, the roots of which can be eaten; "pah" means water in the Shoshone language. There are a couple of gold mines and a silver mine in the vicinity. The Tonopah Test Range is approximately 35 miles east. A Ranger District office of the Toiyabe

National Forest (see RENO) is located here, as well as a detached area office of the Bureau of Land Management.

What to See and Do

Central Nevada Museum. *1900 Logan Field Rd, Tonopah. Phone 775/482-9676.* Historical, mining, and gem displays. (Daily; closed Dec 25) **DONATION**

Rock Collecting. *520 McCulloch (Mining Museum & Park), Tonopah. Phone 775/482-9274.* Historic mining park. Rich variety of minerals. (Daily)

Limited-Service Hotels

★ BEST WESTERN HI-DESERT INN. *120 Main St, Tonopah (89049). Phone 775/482-3511; toll-free 877/286-2208; fax 775/482-3300. www.bestwestern.com.* 62 rooms, 2 story. Pets accepted, some restrictions. Complimentary full breakfast. Check-in 3 pm, check-out 11 am. Pool, whirlpool. **$**

★★ STATION HOUSE HOTEL AND CASINO. *1137 S Main St, Tonopah (89049). Phone 775/482-9777; toll-free 866/611-9777; fax 775/482-5807.* 78 rooms, 2 story. Pets accepted. Check-in 11 am, check-out noon. Restaurant, bar. Fitness room. Casino. **$**

Valley of Fire State Park (E-5)

Web site parks.nv.gov/vf.htm

51 miles NE of Las Vegas via I-15, exit 75.

Red sandstone carved and sanded by geological upheaval, wind, and rain left behind a gallery of natural sculptures forming beehives, domes, arches and even pachyderms that populate the dramatic Valley of Fire, Nevada's oldest and largest state park. With photo ops at every turn, hikes among the colorful outcroppings bear witness to the rainbow-stripped rocks as well as the ancient Basket Maker and Anasazi people who left behind their art in 3,000-year-old petroglyphs. Spring blooms in the not-so-barren Mojave make that season one of the most picturesque. Where Red Rock Canyon serves those who want only a temporary breather from town tables, Valley of Fire, a good hour's drive from Las Vegas, best suits those with more time and outdoor interest. (Daily 8:30 am-4:30 pm) **$**

What to See and Do

Lost City Museum of Archaeology. *721 S Moapa Valley Blvd, Overton. 1 mile S on Hwy 169. Phone 702/397-2193. www.comnett.net/lostcity.* At this museum, also called Pueblo Grande de Nevada, step back in time thousands of years ago to learn more about the Anasazi and the valley's other ancient inhabitants. Impressive Anasazi artifacts fill the museum's original wing, which opened in 1935. Another wing features exhibits about early man, the Paiute, and the area's geology. You can also wander around an archeological site, a Pueblo foundation excavated in the 1930s. (Daily 8:30 am-4:30 pm; closed Jan 1, Thanksgiving, Dec 25) **$**

Virginia City (C-1)

See also Carson City, Reno

Settled 1859
Population 750
Elevation 6,220 ft
Area Code 775
Zip 89440
Information Chamber of Commerce, South C Street, PO Box 464; phone 775/847-0311
Web site www.virginiacity-nv.org

Nevada's most famous mining town, Virginia City once had a population of about 35,000 people and was one of the richest cities in North America. Its dazzling career coincided with the life of the Comstock Lode, which yielded more than $1 billion worth of silver and gold. In the 1870s, Virginia City had four banks, six churches, 110 saloons, an opera house, numerous theaters, and the only elevator between Chicago and San Francisco. Great fortunes, including those of Hearst and Mackay, were founded here.

Virginia City is perched on the side of Mount Davidson, where a diagonal slit marks the Comstock Lode. The site is beautiful and the air is so clear that the blue and purple masses of the Stillwater Range can be seen 120 miles away. Nearer are the green fields and cottonwoods along the Carson River and the white sands of Forty Mile Desert. Gold was found in this area in 1848, but the big silver strike was made in 1859.

Visitors can tour mines and old mansions, some of which have been restored (Easter week, Memorial Day-October, daily); visit several museums and saloons (daily); stroll through the local shops; and ride on the steam-powered V&T Railroad (May-Sept).

What to See and Do

The Castle. *70 South B St, Virginia City. Phone 775/847-0275.* (1868) Built by Robert N. Graves, a mine superintendent of the Empire Mine, the building was patterned after a castle in Normandy, France. It was once referred to as the "house of silver doorknobs." Filled with international riches and original furnishings. (Memorial Day weekend-Oct; daily) **$$**

Special Events

Camel Races. *Arena at Sutton and E sts, Virginia City. Phone 775/847-0311.* Early Sept.

Winnemucca (B-2)

Settled circa 1850
Population 7,174
Elevation 4,299 ft
Area Code 775
Zip 89445
Information Humboldt County Chamber of Commerce, 30 W Winnemucca Blvd; phone 775/623-2225
Web site www.winnemucca.nv.us

Originally called French Ford, the town was renamed for the last great chief of the Paiutes, who ruled the area. Winnemucca was first settled by a Frenchman who set up a trading post. Many Basques live here. A Ranger District office of the Humboldt National Forest (see ELKO) is located here.

What to See and Do

Humboldt Museum. *175 W Jungo Rd, Winnemucca. Jungo Rd and Maple Ave. Phone 775/623-2912.* Historical museum features Native American artifacts; bottles; pioneers' home items, tools, utensils; local history; antique auto display; old country store. (Mon-Fri, also Sat afternoons; closed holidays) **DONATION**

Limited-Service Hotels

★ BEST WESTERN GOLD COUNTRY INN. *921 W Winnemucca Blvd, Winnemucca (89445). Phone 775/623-6999; toll-free 800/346-5306; fax 775/623-9190. www.bestwestern.com.* 71 rooms, 2 story. Pets accepted; fee. Check-out noon. Pool. Airport transportation available. **$**

★ DAYS INN. *511 W Winnemucca Blvd, Winnemucca (89445). Phone 775/623-3661; toll-free 800/548-0531; fax 775/623-4234. www.daysinn.com.* 50 rooms, 2 story. Pets accepted, some restrictions; fee. Check-out noon. Pool. **$**

★ ★ RED LION. *741 W Winnemucca Blvd, Winnemucca (89445). Phone 775/623-2565; toll-free 800/633-6435; fax 775/623-2527.* 105 rooms, 2 story. Pets accepted. Check-out noon. Restaurant, bar. Pool. Airport transportation available. Casino. **$**

Restaurant

★ ORMACHEA'S. *180 Melarky St, Winnemucca (89445). Phone 775/623-3455; fax 775/623-5208.* Basque, American menu. Dinner. Closed Mon; some holidays. Bar. Children's menu. **$$**

Yerington (C-1)

Population 2,883
Elevation 4,384 ft
Information Mason Valley Chamber of Commerce, 227 S Main St; phone 775/463-2245
Web site www.masonvalleychamber.com

The town was once named Pizen Switch, presumably because of the bad whiskey being sold in a saloon. Wovoka, the Paiute messiah, grew up in this area. In 1889, Wovoka claimed to have had a vision in which he was instructed to teach a new dance that would oust the white intruders and restore to the Native Americans their lands and old way of life.

In 1894, the citizens saw the economic value of being on the route of the Carson and Colorado Railway. They decided to rename their town after the man with the power to decide the route—Henry Marvin Yerington. The railroad never did come to Yerington, instead established at nearby Wabuska.

What to See and Do

Fort Churchill State Historic Park. *10000 Hwy 95A, Yerington. Phone 775/577-2345.* This post was established when the rush to the Comstock began as protection against the Paiutes. It was garrisoned from 1860-1869. Adobe walls of the old buildings exist in a state of arrested decay. The visitor center has displays. Picnicking, trails, and camping facilities on 1,232 acres. **$$$**

Lyon County Museum. *215 S Main, Yerington. Phone 775/463-6576.* Complex includes a general store, natural history building, blacksmith shop, schoolhouse. (Thurs-Sun; closed Thanksgiving, Dec 25) **FREE**

Side Trips

Following the bright lights and late nights in the casinos in Nevada, a trip to connect with nature just might refresh your soul. Within a few hours, you could be sitting by Yosemite Falls at Yosemite National Park, checking out lava at Lava Beds National Monument, or wading in the water at Lake Tahoe, all of which are in California.

Death Valley National Park, CA

3 1/2 hours, 141 miles from Las Vegas, NV

Web site www.nps.gov/deva

70 miles E of Lone Pine on Hwy 190. Phone 760/786-2331.

Here, approximately 300 miles northeast of Los Angeles, are more than 5,200 square miles of rugged desert, peaks, and depressions—an unusual and colorful geography. The park is one vast geological museum, revealing secrets of ages gone by. Millions of years ago, this was part of the Pacific Ocean; then violent uplifts of the earth occurred, creating mountain ranges and draining water to the west. Today, 200 square miles of the valley are at or below sea level. The lowest point on the continent (282 feet below sea level) is here; Telescope Peak, at 11,049 feet, towers directly above it. The valley itself is about 140 miles long and 4-16 miles wide. The average rainfall is less than two inches a year. From October to May, the climate is very pleasant. In summer, it's extremely hot; a maximum temperature of 134° F in the shade has been recorded. If considered altogether, this is the lowest, hottest, and driest area in North America.

Death Valley was named in 1849 when a party of gold hunters took a shortcut here and were stranded for several weeks awaiting help. The discovery and subsequent mining of borax, hauled out by the famous 20-mule teams, led to development of the valley as a tourist attraction.

The visitor center at Furnace Creek is open daily. Guided walks, evening programs and talks (Nov-Apr). Golden Age, Golden Eagle, Golden Access passports (see MAKING THE MOST OF YOUR TRIP) are accepted. Per vehicle $$.

Note: Venturing off paved roads in this area in the summer months can be very dangerous. Carefully obey all National Park Service signs and regulations. Make sure that your vehicle has plenty of gas and oil. Carry water when you explore this park, especially in hot weather.

What to See and Do

20-Mule-Team Canyon. *Lone Pine. Phone 760/786-2331.* Viewed from a twisting road on which RVs and trailers are not allowed. (This is an unpaved, one-way road; watch carefully for the entrance sign.)

Artist's Palette. A particularly scenic auto drive (9 miles one way), with spectacular colors. Because of difficult roads, RVs and trailers are advised not to drive here.

Badwater. *Lone Pine. Phone 760/786-2331.* At 279 feet below sea level, near the lowest spot on the North American continent; look for the sea level sign.

Camping. *Death Valley National Park. Phone 760/786-2331.* Developed and primitive camping in the area; limited hookups. It is suggested that campers check with the visitor center for important information on camping facilities and road conditions. (Daily) **FREE**

Charcoal kilns. *Death Valley National Park. Phone 760/786-2331.* Beehive-shaped stone structures, formerly used to make charcoal for nearby mines. Note: The last mile of the access road is unpaved.

Dante's View. *Death Valley National Park. Phone 760/786-2331.* (5,475 feet) View of Death Valley with a steep drop to 279 feet below sea level at Badwater.

Devil's Golf Course. *Death Valley National Park. Phone 760/786-2331.* Vast beds of rugged salt crystals.

Golden Canyon. *Death Valley National Park. Phone 760/786-2331.* Offers a display of color ranging from deep red to rich gold. A 1-mile trail provides access.

Natural Bridge. *Death Valley National Park. Phone 760/786-2331.* A bridge spanning a rugged canyon in the Black Mountains; 1-mile walking trail.

Rhyolite Ghost Town. *Death Valley National Park. Phone 760/786-2331. www.nps.gov/deva/rhyolite.htm.* This was the largest town in the mining history of Death Valley in the early 1900s; 5,000-10,000 people lived here then. The town bloomed from 1905 to 1910; by 1911, it was a ghost town. One structure still left standing from that era is the "bottle house," constructed of 12,000-50,000 beer and liquor bottles (depending on who does the estimating).

Sand dunes. *Death Valley National Park. Phone 760/786-2331.* Sand blown by the wind into dunes 5 to 100 feet high.

Scotty's Castle. *Death Valley National Park. Phone 760/786-2331. www.nps.gov/deva/scottys1.htm.* A desert mansion (circa 1922-1931), designed and built to be viewed as a work of art, as well as a house. The furnishings are typical of the period; many were especially designed and hand crafted for this house. Living history tours are led by costumed interpreters. (Daily 9 am-5 pm) **$$$**

Telescope Peak. *Death Valley National Park. Phone 760/786-2331.* Highest point in the Panamint Range (11,049 feet). Although there is a 14-mile round-trip hiking trail, it is inaccessible in the winter months.

Ubehebe Crater. *Death Valley National Park. Phone 760/786-2331.* Colorful crater left by a volcanic steam explosion.

Visitor Center. *At Furnace Creek. Hwy 190, Death Valley. Phone 760/786-2331.* It is recommended that visitors stop here first on for an orientation film, day-trip suggestions, help in organizing sightseeing routes, and important information on camping areas and road conditions.

Zabriskie Point. *Death Valley National Park. Phone 760/786-2331.* View of Death Valley and the Panamint Range from the rugged badlands of the Black Mountains.

Limited-Service Hotels

★ ★ CARRIAGE INN. *901 N China Lake Blvd, Ridgecrest (93555). Phone 760/446-7910; toll-free 800/772-8527; fax 760/446-6408. www.carriageinn.biz.* Offering a mix of luxury suites and poolside cabanas in a full-service hotel environment. 162 rooms, 1 story. **$**

★ ★ HERITAGE INN AND SUITES. *1050 N Norma St, Ridgecrest (93555). Phone 760/446-6543; toll-free 800/843-0693; fax 760/446-3139.* This large, well-appointed hotel is geared toward business travelers and tourists. 169 rooms, 2 story, all suites. Restaurant. **$**

★ ★ STOVEPIPE WELLS VILLAGE. *CA 190, Death Valley (92328). Phone 760/786-2387; fax 760/786-2389. www.stovepipewells.com.* Panoramic view of the mountains, desert, and dunes. 83 rooms. Pets accepted; fee. Check-out 11 am. Restaurant, bar. Pool. Landing strip. **$**

Full-Service Inn

★ ★ ★ FURNACE CREEK INN. *CA 190, Death Valley (92328). Phone 760/786-2345; fax 760/786-2307. www.furnacecreekresort.com.* This elegant and charming inn is part of a larger property that includes a resort. It features the lowest golf course in the world, which seems like an oasis in these dead and desert surroundings. 66 rooms, 4 story. Check-out noon. Restaurant, bar. Fitness room. Outdoor pool. Tennis. **$$$**

Restaurants

★ THE 19TH HOLE. *Hwy 190, Furnace Creek (92328). Phone 760/786-2345. www.furnacecreekresort .com.* Located on a site overlooking the world's lowest golf course (214 feet below sea level), this establishment also offers drive-through service for golf carts. American menu. Lunch, dinner. **$**

★ CHARLIE'S PUB & GRILL. *901 N China Lake Blvd, Ridgecrest (93555). Phone toll-free 800/772-8527. www.carriageinn.biz.* Serving family-style food in a unique décor of aircrew memorabilia donated from squadrons around the world. American menu. Lunch, dinner. **$**

★ FARRIS RESTAURANT. *1050 N Norma St, Ridgecrest (93555). Phone toll-free 800/843-0693.* A favorite dining spot for locals, the Farris Restaurant offers regional American cuisine in a comfortable atmosphere. American menu. Lunch, dinner. **$**

★★★ INN DINING ROOM. *CA 190, Death Valley National Park (92328). Phone 760/786-2361. www.furnacecreekresort.com.* When you are in Death Valley, visit this inn for delicious food. Try their steak while enjoying the 1930s décor under beamed ceilings. American menu. Breakfast, lunch (Oct-May), dinner. Bar. Jacket required. Valet parking. **$$$**

Lake Tahoe Area, CA

1 1/2 hours, 51 miles from Reno, NV

Web site www.visitinglaketahoe.com

Lake Tahoe is one of the most magnificent mountain lakes in the world, with an area of about 200 square miles, an altitude of approximately 6,230 feet, and a maximum depth of more than 1,600 feet. Mostly in California, partly in Nevada, it is circled by paved highways edged with campgrounds, lodges, motels, and resorts. The lake, with some fine beaches, is surrounded by forests of ponderosa, Jeffrey and sugar pine, white fir, juniper, cedar, aspen, dogwood, and cottonwood, as well as a splendid assortment of wildflowers.

The Sierra Nevada, here composed mostly of hard granite, is a range built by a series of roughly parallel block faults along its eastern side, which have tipped the mountainous area to the west, with the eastern side much steeper than the western. Lake Tahoe lies in a trough between the Sierra proper and the Carson Range, similarly formed and generally regarded as a part of the Sierra, to its east.

There are spectacular views of the lake from many points on the surrounding highways. Eagle Creek, one of the thousands of mountain streams that feed the lake, cascades 1,500 feet over Eagle Falls into Emerald Bay at the southwestern part of the lake. Smaller mountain lakes are scattered around the Tahoe area; accessibility varies. Tahoe and El Dorado National Forests stretch north and west of the lake, offering many recreational facilities.

Public and commercial swimming (there are 29 public beaches), boating, and fishing facilities are plentiful. In winter, the area is a mecca for skiers. There is legalized gambling on the Nevada side.

Note: Accommodations around Lake Tahoe are listed under South Lake Tahoe, Tahoe City, and Tahoe Vista. In this area, many motels have higher rates in summer and during special events and holidays. Reservations are recommended.

What to See and Do

Alpine Meadows Ski Area. *2600 Alpine Meadows Rd, Lake Tahoe Area. 6 miles NW of Tahoe City off Hwy 89. Phone 530/583-4232. www.skialpine.com.* Best known for its varied terrain—Skiing magazine labeled it a mountain with "a mild side and a wild side"—Alpine Meadows consists of 2,000 acres split between six bowls, steep chutes, and wide-open glades (25% beginner, 40% intermediate, and 35% advanced). The resort—13 miles south of I-80 at Truckee—features 14 lifts, a pair of snowboarding-oriented terrain parks, and a 600-foot superpipe for serious carvers. The nearest accommodations are in Tahoe City. (Mid-Nov-late May: daily) **$$$$**

D. L. Bliss State Park. *Hwy 89, Tahoma. 17 miles S of Tahoe City on Hwy 89. Phone 530/525-7277. www. parks.ca.gov.* Named for a local lumber and railroad baron of the early 1900s, D. L. Bliss State Park is on the western shore of Lake Tahoe and is home to a popular campground, a few trails, and good water access for swimmers and anglers. The park also boasts one of the lake's most sublime vistas: Rubicon

Point affords views 100 feet down into Tahoe's blue depths. Also noteworthy is Balancing Rock Nature Trail, a half-mile jaunt to a 130-ton granite monolith positioned atop a much thinner pedestal. **$**

Desolation Wilderness Area. *Eldorado National Forest, 100 Forni Rd, Placerville. Phone 530/622-5061. www.fs.fed.us/r5/eldorado/wild/deso.* Once known as Devil's Valley, Desolation is known for a natural beauty that rivals Yosemite's, but without the roads and, by extension, traffic. The granite peaks and 130 alpine lakes in this 64,000-acre wilderness southwest of Lake Tahoe still attract their fair share of backpackers and anglers, but the fact that travel is limited to horseback or foot helps keep the volume down. Glaciers were responsible for carving and polishing the rock here—1,000-foot-thick sheets of ice covered the entire area 200,000 years ago. The rocky ground supports limited tree cover and vegetation, but the animal life—including mule deer, black bears, porcupines, badgers, and coyotes—is diverse. The lakes and streams have sustaining populations of rainbow and brook trout, making fishing a big draw. Backpackers and hikers operate under daily quotas; reservations are required.

Emerald Bay State Park. *Hwy 89, Tahoe City. 22 miles S of Tahoe City on Hwy 89. Phone 530/525-7232. www.parks.ca.gov.* Home to the Scandinavian-style castle known as Vikingsholm (see), Emerald Bay State Park is, true to its name, one of the crown jewels of California's state park system. Centered on the glacially-carved inlet of its name, the park is surrounded by granite peaks and cliffs on the west side of Lake Tahoe. The park is home to the only island in the entire lake, Fanette Island, a lone chunk of granite that survived the glacial period. Below the lake's surface is another noteworthy aspect: Underwater Park, a scuba-diving hotspot, thanks to the presence of numerous shipwrecks dating from the late 1800s, the heyday of the long-gone Emerald Bay Resort. There are also several nature trails, a 70-site campground, and a beach with swimming access. **$**

Grover Hot Springs State Park. *3415 Hot Springs Rd, Lake Tahoe Area. 29 miles S of South Lake Tahoe on Hwy 89. Phone 530/694-2248. www.parks.ca.gov.* This California state park sits where the Sierra Nevada and the Great Basin meet, a pine-clad valley surrounded on three sides by majestic peaks. Six mineral springs feed a concrete pool with a water temperature in excess of 100° F. The hot springs are hot year-round, soothing hikers, anglers, and campers in the summer and cross-country skiers and snowshoers in the winter. (Daily)

Heavenly Ski Resort. *3860 Saddle Rd, South Lake Tahoe. 1 mile E of Hwy 50. Phone 775/586-7000; toll-free 800/243-2836. www.skiheavenly.com.* One of the crown jewels of Vail Resorts' portfolio of ski meccas, Heavenly straddles the Nevada-California border just south of Lake Tahoe and has a distinct ski area on each side of the line. In California, Heavenly West offers 18 lifts that take skiers and snowboarders to trails that have the state's longest vertical drop—3,500 feet—and a snowboarding half pipe. On the Nevada side of the mountain, Heavenly North has 11 lifts, a snowboard cross-trail, and a terrain park. In both states, the snow is revered and plentiful: 300 inches is the average annual snowfall, bolstered by one of the biggest snowmaking operations in the world. A redeveloped village opened in 2002, featuring a bevy of eateries, nightspots, shops, and hotel rooms, not to mention a movie multiplex and an ice skating rink. **$$$$**

Kirkwood Mountain Resort. *1501 Kirkwood Meadows Dr, Lake Tahoe Area. 30 miles S off Hwy 88. Phone 209/258-6000; toll-free 877/547-5966 (snow conditions). www.kirkwood.com.* This beautiful resort is less crowded than some of the slopes closer in and has varied terrain among its 2,300 acres (15% beginner, 50% intermediate, and 35% advanced). It's also quite high, with a base of 7,800 feet and a vertical rise that adds another 2,000. There are 12 lifts in all, plus a halfpipe and a snowboard park that blasts loud music. Kirkwood also has about 12 miles of groomed cross-country trails, a 15-mile snowshoe trail system, and a wide range of on-mountain accommodations. (Mid-Nov-mid-May, daily) **$$$$**

Lake Tahoe Cruises. *900 Ski Run Blvd, Lake Tahoe Area. Phone 530/541-3364. www.laketahoecruises.com.* This long-standing operation offers a full slate of cruises—breakfast, brunch, lunch, dinner/dance, and sightseeing. The fleet includes a pair of Mississippi River-style paddlewheelers used for the scheduled cruises: the 151-foot M.S. *Dixie II,* ported in Zephyr Cove, and the *Tahoe Queen,* based out of South Lake Tahoe. The former offers lake cruises year-round; the latter becomes a ski shuttle/charter vessel during winter. Cruises depart daily, and reservations are required. **$$$$**

Lake Tahoe Historical Society Museum. *3058 Lake Tahoe Blvd (Hwy 50), Lake Tahoe Area. Phone 530/541-5458.* The highlights at this South Lake Tahoe museum are a scale model of the SS *Tahoe*—a legendary steamship that was intentionally sunk in 1940—the Lake Tahoe Basin's oldest building (1859). Among the black-and-white photos and rusty pioneer implements, you'll also find a fine collection of Washoe basketry. A few blocks west in Bijou Community Park is the museum's narrow-gauge railroad exhibit. (Late June-Labor Day, Tues-Sat afternoons; rest of year, weekends) **$**

Ponderosa Ranch Western Studio and Theme Park. *100 Ponderosa Ranch Rd, Incline Village. Off Hwy 28 on the N shore of Lake Tahoe, in Incline Village, NV. Phone 775/831-0691. www.ponderosaranch.com.* The location for the long-running television western *Bonanza,* the Ponderosa Ranch blends authentic pioneer history with its Hollywood counterpart, the end result being a tad kitschy but educational and fun. Visitors can explore the real history via a re-creation of an 1870s "Wild West" town, with historic structures relocated to the ranch over the years and an actual wagon recovered from the infamous Donner party who perished in the Sierra Nevada in 1846. On the *Bonanza* side, fans of Ben Cartwright and company will get their fill of behind-the-scenes trivia at the Ranch House, through a video presentation and a look at the show's primary soundstage. Other diversions include live entertainment (running the gamut from music to magic to trick roping), a Western-themed photo studio, chuckwagon breakfasts (for an additional fee), a shooting gallery, and demonstrations by a frontier blacksmith. (Mid-Apr-Oct, daily 9:30 am-6 pm) **$$$**

Riding. *Camp Richardson Corral, 4 Emerald Bay Rd, Lake Tahoe Area. Phone 530/541-3113.* One- and two-hour rides, breakfast and steak rides (May-Oct, daily); sleigh rides (Dec-Mar). Contact PO Box 8335, South Lake Tahoe 96158. **$$$$**

Sierra at Tahoe. *1111 Sierra at Tahoe Rd, Lake Tahoe Area. 12 miles W of South Lake Tahoe on Hwy 50. Phone 530/659-7453. www.sierraattahoe.com.* Founded in 1968, Sierra at Tahoe is a big but low-key resort. Its 2,000 acres are set against a 2,212-foot rise, with 25% beginner, 50% intermediate, and 25% expert slopes. A favorite of snowboarders, the resort features two terrain parks, two halfpipes, and a superpipe. There is also a popular tubing hill, but no on-mountain lodging. Shuttle bus service is available. (Nov-Apr, daily) **$$$$**

Squaw Valley USA. *1960 Squaw Valley Rd, Lake Tahoe Area. 7 miles NW of Tahoe City off Hwy 89. Phone 530/583-6985. www.squaw.com.* Five high-speed quads, eight triple, eight double chairlifts, aerial cable car, gondola, five surface lifts; patrol, school, rentals; snack bars, cafeterias, restaurants, bars. Longest run 3.2 miles; vertical drop 2,850 feet. (Mid-Nov-mid-May, daily) Cross-country skiing (25 miles); rentals (mid-Nov-late-May, daily). Aerial cable car also operates year-round (daily and evenings). **$$$$**

Tahoe State Recreation Area. *Sugar Pine Point State Park, Tahoe City. On Hwy 28. Phone 530/583-3074 (general information).* Cross-country skiing. Camping (fee). Pine Lodge is refurbished turn-of-century summer home (Ehrman Mansion), tours (July-Labor Day). Pier, picnicking, camping.

Tallac Historic Site. *Emerald Bay Rd at Fallen Leaf Rd, 3 miles NW of South Lake Tahoe. Phone 530/541-5227. tahoe.ceres.ca.gov/usfs/tallac.html.* "Old Tahoe" is preserved in the form of this National Forest Service site, composed of three grand estates that give a good sense of what a Lake Tahoe getaway was like a century ago. Two of the estates date from the Roaring Twenties. Today, the Baldwin estate houses a museum, and the Heller estate, also known as Valhalla, serves as a community center and performing arts venue. The Tevis-Pope estate, which is the oldest of the three (1894), offers tours and living history presentations. All three properties sit on a 1/4-mile of lakefront near Emerald Bay and the ruins of the long-abandoned Tallac Resort, once known as the "greatest casino in America." The site is also the former domain of the native Washoe people, and trails and exhibits examine their lifestyle. Visitor center (daily 8 am-5:30 pm, Fri until 7 pm). Museum (Wed-Mon 11 am-3 pm). **$**

US Forest Service Visitor Center. *870 Emerald Bay Rd. On Hwy 89, 3 miles NW of South Lake Tahoe. Phone 530/573-2600.* Information, campfire programs, guided nature walks and self-guided trails. Visitors look into Taylor Creek from the Stream Profile Chamber; exhibits explain role of stream to Lake Clarity. (Memorial Day-Oct) **FREE**

Valhalla Boathouse Theatre. *Tallac Historic Site, Hwys 50 and 89, Lake Tahoe Area. Phone 530/542-4166; toll-free 888/631-9153.* Dating back to the 1880s, this former boathouse predates the neighboring historic structures at the Tallac Historic Site. After a long period of neglect, it was restored and converted into a charming 200-seat theater that now serves as a cultural focal point for South Lake Tahoe. During the summer, events take place here nearly every night, predominately plays, concerts, and films.

Vikingsholm. *10 miles S of Tahoe City on Hwy 89. Phone 530/525-7277. www.vikingsholm.com.* Nestled amidst the cedars at the base of granite cliffs in Emerald Bay State Park is "Lake Tahoe's Hidden Castle," Vikingsholm. The surrounding land was the site of one of the lake's first summer homes (1863), but the Scandinavian-style castle dates from 1929. Then-landowner Lorna Knight commissioned her nephew, a Swedish architect, to design the place, taking cues from Norwegian churches, Swedish castles, and more common wooden homes in both countries. Note that visitors must hike a steep 1-mile trail from the parking lot to get to Vikingsholm's doors. Parking is limited. (Mid-June-late Sept: daily 10 am-4 pm) **$**

Special Events

American Century Investments Celebrity Golf Championship. *Edgewood Tahoe Golf Course, 1156 Ski Run Blvd, Lake Tahoe Area. Phone 530/544-5050.* More than 70 sports and entertainment celebrities compete for a $500,000 purse. July.

Great Gatsby Festival. *Tallac Historic Site, Hwys 50 and 89, Lake Tahoe Area. Phone 530/544-5227.* The Tallac Historic Site turns back the clock to the roaring twenties for a weekend every August with this living history event; period costumes (i.e., flapper dresses, boiler hats) are encouraged. The atmosphere matches the F. Scott Fitzgerald classic for which the event is named, with an array of old-fashioned events: an antique car show, a croquet competition, big band concerts, and even a pie-eating contest. Aug.

Kokanee Salmon Festival. *Taylor Creek, Lake Tahoe. Phone 530/573-2674.* At the height of Kokanee spawning season, Taylor Creek near the southern shore of Lake Tahoe is rife with these landlocked salmon, all migrating upstream to mate. The festival celebrates this natural phenomenon at the National Forest Service visitor center. Rangers are on hand to explain the ecology of the fish and detail these annual mating rituals—which start in September and continue through October. There is also musical entertainment, competitive trail runs, and games for kids. Late Sept-Oct.

Lake Tahoe Music Festival. *PO Box 62, Tahoe City. Throughout the city. Phone 530/583-3101. www.tahoemusic.org.* This highly regarded concert series has been a Lake Tahoe tradition since 1982. The festival tends to focus on classical and choral music—a 2003 highlight was a performance by the Vienna Boys Choir—but the calendar doesn't begin and end with symphonies and waltzes. It also includes an eclectic slate of performers, practitioners of everything from bluegrass to jazz to poetry. Special events include opening and closing galas, as well as an art auction. The performances take place during July and August at multiple venues in the Tahoe area (including Squaw Valley, Donner Lake, and the campus of Sierra Nevada College). The festival also has a relatively new educational component called the Academy Program, by which professional performers-in-residence tutor young artists. July-Aug.

Lassen Volcanic National Park, CA

4 1/2 hours, 165 miles from Reno, NV

Web site www.nps.gov/lavo

44 miles E of Redding via Hwy 44; 51 miles E of Red Bluff via Hwy 36, 89.

This 165-square-mile park was created to preserve the area including 10,457-foot Lassen Peak, a volcano last active in 1921. Lassen Park, in the southernmost part of the Cascade Range, contains glacial lakes, virgin forests, mountain meadows, and snow-fed streams. Hydrothermal features, the Devastated Area, and Chaos Jumbles can be seen from Lassen Park Road. Boiling mud pots and fumaroles (steam vents) can be seen a short distance off the road at Sulphur Works. At Butte Lake, colorful masses of lava and volcanic ash blend with the forests, meadows, and streams. The peak is named for Peter Lassen, a Danish pioneer who used it as a landmark in guiding immigrant trains into the northern Sacramento Valley.

After being denuded in 1915 by a mudflow and a hot blast, the Devastated Area is slowly being reclaimed by small trees and flowers. The Chaos Crags, a group of lava plugs, were formed some 1,100 years ago. Bumpass Hell, a colorful area of mud pots, boiling pools, and steam vents, is a 3-mile round-trip hike from Lassen Park Road. Clouds of steam and sulfurous gases pour from vents in the thermal areas. Nearby is Lake Helen, named for Helen Tanner Brodt, the first white woman to climb Lassen Peak, in 1864. At the northwest entrance is a visitor center (late June-Labor Day, daily) where you can find information about the park's human, natural, and geological history. There are guided walks during the summer; self-guided nature trails; and evening talks at some campgrounds. Camping (fee) is available at eight campgrounds; there's a two-week limit except at Lost Creek and Summit Lake campgrounds, which impose a seven-day limit; check at a ranger station for regulations.

Lassen Park Road is usually open mid-June-mid-Oct, weather permitting. The Sulphur Works entrance to the south and the Manzanita Lake entrance to the northwest are open during the winter months for winter sports.

There are facilities for the disabled, including the visitor center, comfort station, and amphitheater at Manzanita Lake.

Lava Beds National Monument, CA

6 1/2 hours, 220 miles from Reno, NV

Web site www.nps.gov/labe

30 miles SW of Tulelake, off Hwy 139.

Seventy-two square miles of volcanic formations are preserved here in the extreme northeastern part of the state. Centuries ago, rivers of molten lava flowed here. In cooling, they formed a strange and fantastic region. Cinder cones dot the landscape, one rising 476 feet from its base. Winding trenches mark the collapsed roofs of lava tubes, an indicator of the 380 caves beneath the surface. Throughout the area are masses of lava hardened into weird shapes. Spatter cones may be seen where vents in the lava formed vertical tubelike channels, some only 3 feet in diameter but reaching downward 100 feet.

Outstanding caves include Sentinel Cave, named for a lava formation in its passageway; Catacombs Cave, with passageways resembling Rome's catacombs; and Skull Cave, with a broad entry cavern reaching approximately 80 feet in diameter. (The name comes from the many skulls of mountain sheep that were found here.) The National Park Service provides ladders and trails in the 24 caves that are easily accessible to the public.

One of the most costly Native American campaigns in history took place in this rugged, otherworldly setting. The Modoc War of 1872-1873 saw a small band of Native Americans revolt against reservation life and fight a series of battles with US troops. Although they were obliged to care for their families and live off the country, the Modocs held off an army almost ten times their number for more than five months.

There is a campground at Indian Well (fee, water available mid-May-Labor Day), and there are picnic areas at Fleener Chimneys and Captain Jacks Stronghold (no water). Guided walks, audiovisual programs, cave trips, and campfire programs are held daily, mid-June-Labor Day. Park headquarters has a visitor center (daily). No gasoline is available in the park, so fill your gas tank before entering. Golden Eagle, Golden Age, and Golden Access passports accepted (see MAKING THE MOST OF YOUR TRIP). Per vehicle $2-$5.

Yosemite National Park, CA

4 1/2 hours, 180 miles from Reno, NV

Web site www.nps.gov/yose

67 miles NE of Merced on Hwy 140; 62 miles N of Fresno on Hwy 41; 13 miles W of Lee Vining on Hwy 120.

John Muir, the naturalist who was instrumental in the founding of this national park, wrote that here are "the most songful streams in the world, the noblest forests, the loftiest granite domes, the deepest ice sculptured canyons." More than 3 million people visit Yosemite year-round, and most agree with Muir. An area of 1,169 square miles, it is a park of lofty waterfalls, sheer cliffs, high wilderness country, alpine meadows, lakes, snowfields, trails, streams, and river beaches. There are magnificent waterfalls during spring and early summer. Yosemite's granite domes are unsurpassed in number and diversity. The entrance fee is $20 per vehicle. Routes to Yosemite

National Park involve some travel over steep grades, which may extend driving times. The portion of Tioga Pass (Hwy 120) that travels over Tioga Pass to Lee Vining/Hwy 395 is closed in winter. Hwy 120 is open year-round to Crane Flat, where the Big Oak Flat Road continues into Yosemite Valley.

For general park information, contact the Public Information Office, PO Box 577, Yosemite National Park; phone 209/372-0200. For lodging information, contact Yosemite Concession Services, Yosemite National Park; phone 559/252-4848. For recorded camping information, phone 209/372-0200. Camping reservations are taken by NPRS, the National Park Reservation System for Yosemite Valley (phone toll-free 800/436-7275) and other campgrounds.

What to See and Do

Boating. *Yosemite National Park.* No motors permitted.

Campfire programs. *Yosemite National Park.* At several campgrounds; in summer, naturalists present nightly programs on park-related topics and provide tips on how to enjoy the park. Evening programs are offered all year in the Valley only.

Camping. *Yosemite National Park.* Limited to 30 days in a calendar year; May-mid-Sept, camping is limited to seven days in Yosemite Valley, in the rest of the park to 14 days. Campsites in the Valley campgrounds, Hodgdon Meadow, Crane Flat, Wawona, and half of Tuolumne Meadows campgrounds may be reserved through NPRS. Other park campgrounds are on a first-come, first-served basis. Winter camping in the Valley, Hodgdon Meadow, and Wawona only.

Fishing. *Yosemite National Park.* California fishing regulations pertain to all waters. State license, inland waters stamp, and trout stamp are required. Special regulations for Yosemite Valley also apply.

Glacier Point. *Yosemite National Park.* Offers one of the best panoramic views in Yosemite. From here the crest of the Sierra Nevada can be viewed, as well as Yosemite Valley 3,214 feet below. Across the valley are Yosemite Falls, Royal Arches, North Dome, Basket Dome, Mount Watkins, and Washington Column; up the Merced Canyon are Vernal and Nevada falls; Half Dome, Grizzly Peak, Liberty Cap, and the towering peaks along the Sierran crest and the Clark Range mark the skyline. (Road closed in winter)

Hiking and backpacking. *Yosemite National Park. Phone 209/372-0740.* On 840 miles of maintained trails. Wilderness permits are required for all overnight backcountry trips. Advance reservations for permits may be made up to 24 weeks in advance.

Pioneer Yosemite History Center. *Yosemite National Park.* A few miles from Mariposa Grove in Wawona. Has a covered bridge, historic buildings, wagons, and other exhibits. Living history program in summer.

Swimming. *Yosemite National Park.* Prohibited at Hetch Hetchy Reservoir and in some areas of the Tuolumne River watershed. Swimming pools are maintained at Camp Curry, Yosemite Lodge, and Wawona.

The Giant Sequoias. *Yosemite National Park.* Located principally in three groves. Mariposa Grove is near the south entrance to the park; toured on foot or by 50-passenger trams (May-early Oct; fee). Merced and Tuolumne groves are near Crane Flat, northwest of Yosemite Valley. The Grizzly Giant in Mariposa Grove is estimated to be 2,700 years old and is 209 feet high and 34.7 feet in diameter at its base.

The High Country. *Yosemite National Park. Phone 559/253-5674.* Tioga Road (closed in winter) crosses the park and provides the threshold to a vast wilderness accessible via horseback or on foot to mountain peaks, passes, and lakes. Tuolumne Meadows is the major trailhead for this activity; one of the most beautiful and largest of the subalpine meadows in the High Sierra, 55 miles from Yosemite Valley by way of Big Oak Flat and Tioga roads. Organized group horse and hiking trips start from Tuolumne Meadows (except winter), follow the High Sierra Loop, and fan out to mountain lakes and peaks. Each night's stop is at a High Sierra Camp; the pace allows plenty of time to explore at each camp.

The Nature Center at Happy Isles. *Yosemite National Park. E end of Yosemite Valley.* Exhibits on ecology and natural history. (Summer, daily)

Visitor Center. *At Park Headquarters in Yosemite Valley. Yosemite National Park. Phone 209/372-0265.* Orientation slide program on Yosemite (daily). Exhibits on geology and ecology; naturalist-conducted walks and evening programs offered throughout the year on varying seasonal schedules. Native American cultural demonstrators (summer, daily).

The Indian Cultural Museum. *Yosemite National Park.* Located in the building west of the Valley visitor center, the museum portrays the cultural history of the Yosemite Native Americans. Consult Yosemite Guide for hours.

Indian Village (Ahwahnee). *Yosemite National Park.* This reconstructed Miwok-Paiute Village is behind the visitor center and has a self-guided trail.

Yosemite Fine Arts Museum. *Yosemite National Park.* The gallery features contemporary art exhibits and the Yosemite Centennial. Consult Yosemite Guide for hours.

Walks and hikes. *Yosemite National Park.* Conducted all year in the Valley and, during summer, at Glacier Point, Mariposa Grove, Tuolumne Meadows, Wawona, White Wolf, and Crane Flat.

Waterfalls. *Yosemite National Park.* Reaching their greatest proportions in mid-May, they may, in dry years, dwindle to trickles or disappear completely by late summer. The Upper Yosemite Fall drops 1,430 feet; the lower fall drops 320 feet. With the middle Cascade they have a combined height of 2,425 feet and are the fifth-highest waterfall in the world. Others are Ribbon Fall, 1,612 feet; Vernal Fall, 317 feet; Bridalveil Fall, 620 feet; Nevada Fall, 594 feet; and Illilouette Fall, 370 feet.

Winter sports. *Yosemite National Park. Phone 209/372-1000 for snow conditions. Centered around the Badger Pass Ski Area, 23 miles from Yosemite Valley on Glacier Point Road.* One triple, three double chairlifts, cable tow; patrol, rentals; snack stand, sun deck, nursery (minimum age three years); instruction (over four years). (Mid-Dec-mid-Apr, daily, weather permitting) cross-country skiing. Ice skating (fee) in Yosemite Valley; scheduled competitions. Naturalists conduct snowshoe tours (fee) in the Badger Pass area. **$$$$**

Yosemite Mountain-Sugar Pine Railroad. *Yosemite National Park. 4 miles S of south park entrance on Hwy 41. Phone 559/683-7273. www.ymsprr.com.* Four-mile historic narrow-gauge steam train excursion through scenic Sierra National Forest. Picnic area. Museum; gift shops. Logger steam train (mid-May-Sept, daily; early May and Oct, weekends). Jenny Railcars (Mar-Oct, daily). Evening steam train, outdoor barbecue, live entertainment (late May-early Oct, Sat evenings; reservations advised). **$$$$**

Yosemite Valley. *Yosemite National Park.* Surrounded by sheer walls, waterfalls, towering domes, and peaks. One of the most spectacular views is from Tunnel View, looking up the Valley to Clouds Rest. El Capitan (7,569 feet) on the left, Bridalveil Falls on the right. The east end of the Valley, beyond Camp Curry, is closed to automobiles, but is accessible by foot, bicycle, and, in summer, shuttle bus (free); special placards permit the disabled to drive in a restricted area when the route is drivable. The placards are available at visitor centers and entrance stations.

Limited-Service Hotels

★ ★ **CEDAR LODGE.** *9966 Hwy 140, El Portal (95318). Phone 209/379-2612; toll-free 800/321-5261; fax 209/379-2712. www.yosemite-motels.com/cedarlodge.* 211 rooms, 2 story. Check-out 11 am. Bar. Indoor pool, outdoor pool, whirlpool. **$**

★ ★ **GROVELAND HOTEL AT YOSEMITE NATIONAL PARK.** *P O Box 481, Groveland (95321). Phone 209/962-4000; toll-free 800/273-3314; fax 209/962-6674. www.groveland.com.* Built in 1849; European antiques. 17 rooms. Pets accepted. Complimentary full breakfast. Check-in 2 pm, check-out noon. Restaurant, bar. **$$**

★ ★ **PINES RESORT.** *54449 Rd 432, Bass Lake (93604). Phone 559/642-3121; toll-free 800/350-7463; fax 559/642-3902. www.basslake.com.* 104 rooms, 2 story. Complimentary continental breakfast. Check-in 3 pm, check-out 11 am. Restaurant, bar. Outdoor pool, whirlpool. Tennis. **$$**

★ ★ **WAWONA HOTEL.** *Yosemite National Park, Wawona (95389). Phone 209/375-6556; fax 209/375-6601. www.yosemitepark.com.* Historic summer hotel. 104 rooms, 2 story. Weekends only Jan-Mar. Check-in 4 pm, check-out 11 am. Restaurant. Outdoor pool. Golf. Tennis. Airport transportation available. **$**

★ ★ **YOSEMITE LODGE.** *Hwy 41/140, Yosemite National Park (95389). Phone 559/252-4848; fax 209/372-1414. www.yosemitepark.com.* 245 rooms,

2 story. Check-in 5 pm, check-out 10 am. Restaurant, bar. Outdoor pool. **$**

★ ★ YOSEMITE VIEW LODGE. *11136 Hwy 140, El Portal (95318). Phone 209/379-2681; toll-free 800/321-5261; fax 209/379-2704. www.yosemite-motels.com.* 279 rooms, 3 story. Pets accepted, some restrictions; fee. Check-in 3 pm, check-out 11 am. Restaurant, bar. Indoor pool, outdoor pool, whirlpool. **$$**

Full-Service Resorts

★ ★ ★ THE AHWAHNEE. *Yosemite Valley, Yosemite National Park (95389). Phone 559/372-1407; fax 559/456-0542. www.yosemitepark.com.* 123 rooms, 6 story. Check-in 5 pm, check-out noon. Restaurant, bar. Outdoor pool. Tennis. **$$$$**

★ ★ ★ TENAYA LODGE AT YOSEMITE. *1122 Hwy 41, Fish Camp (93623). Phone 559/683-6555; toll-free 888/514-2167; fax 559/683-8684. www.tenayalodge.com.* 244 rooms, 4 story. Check-in 3 pm, check-out 11 am. Restaurant, bar. Children's activity center. Fitness room, spa. Indoor pool, outdoor pool, whirlpool. Business center. On river; water sports. June-Sept Western jamboree cookouts, wagon rides. **$$**

Specialty Lodging

The following lodging establishment is approved by Mobil Travel Guide, but due to its unique and individualized nature has not been given a traditional Mobil Star rating. Included in this listing you may find bed-and-breakfasts, limited-service inns, guest ranches, and other unique hotel properties.

THE HOMESTEAD. *4110 Rd 600, Ahwahnee (93601). Phone 559/683-0495; toll-free 800/483-0495; fax 559/683-8165. www.homesteadcottages.com.* 4 rooms. Complimentary continental breakfast. Check-in 3 pm, check-out 11 am. **$$**

Restaurants

★ ★ CHARLES STREET DINNER HOUSE. *5043 Charles St, Mariposa (95338). Phone 209/966-2366. www.charlesstreetdinnerhouse.com.* 19th-century house. American, California menu. Dinner. Closed Mon-Tues; Thanksgiving, Dec 24-25. Children's menu. **$$**

★ ★ NARROW GAUGE INN. *48571 Hwy 41, Fish Camp (93623). Phone 559/683-7720. www.narrowgaugeinn.com.* Located in historic Fish Camp, this restaurant offers unique local cuisine in a rustic environment filled with antiques and a nightly fire in the fireplace. American menu. Dinner. **$$**

★ ★ THE VICTORIAN ROOM. *18767 Main St, Groveland (95321). Phone 209/962-4000; toll-free 800/273-3314; fax 209/962-6674. www.groveland.com.* Victorian décor. California menu. Dinner. Bar. Children's menu. Outdoor seating. **$$**

New Mexico

Fray Marcos de Niza first saw what is now New Mexico in May, 1539. From a nearby mesa he viewed the Zuni pueblo of Hawikíúh, not far from the present Gallup. He returned to Mexico with tales of cities of gold which so impressed the Viceroy that in 1540 he dispatched Francisco Coronado with an army and Fray Marcos as his guide. They found no gold and very little of anything else. Coronado returned home two years later a broken man.

Population: 1,819,046
Area: 121,593 square miles
Elevation: 2,817-13,161 feet
Peak: Wheeler Peak (Taos County)
Entered Union: January 6, 1912 (47th state)
Capital: Santa Fe
Motto: It Grows as It Goes
Nickname: Land of Enchantment
Flower: Yucca
Bird: Chaparral (roadrunner)
Tree: Piñon
Fair: September in Albuquerque
Time Zone: Mountain
Web site: www.newmexico.org
Fun Facts: One out of four workers in New Mexico work directly for the federal government.

While others came to New Mexico before him for a variety of purposes, Don Juan de Oñate established the first settlement in 1598. Don Pedro de Peralta founded Santa Fe as the capital in 1609. Spanish villages were settled all along the Rio Grande until 1680, when the Pueblo, with Apache help, drove the Spaniards out of New Mexico in the famous Pueblo Revolt.

Twelve years later, Don Diego de Vargas reconquered the province with little resistance. The territory grew and prospered, though not entirely without conflict, since the Spanish were determined to maintain control at any cost. They forbade trade with the French of Louisiana, their nearest neighbors and rivals.

In 1810 Napoleon overran Spain; in 1821 Mexico won its independence and formed a republic. The following year, William Becknell of Missouri brought the first wagons across the plains and blazed what was later called the Santa Fe Trail. After the Mexican War of 1846, New Mexico became a US territory, joining the Union in 1912.

New Mexico is a land of contrasts. Traces of prehistoric Folsom Man and Sandia Man, whose ancestors may have trekked across the Bering Strait land bridge from Asia, have been found here. Working in the midst of antiquity, scientists at Los Alamos opened up the new atomic world.

Southern New Mexico has fascinating desert country and cool, green, high forests popular with campers, anglers, and vacationers. In the north, it also has desert lands, but most of this area is high mountain country with clear streams and snow, which sometimes stays all year. Spanish-speaking farmers mix with Native Americans and urban Americans in the plazas of Santa Fe and Albuquerque.

Where sheep and cattle were once the only industry, extractive industries—of which oil and uranium are a part—now yield nearly $5 billion a year.

NATIVE AMERICANS IN NEW MEXICO

Native Americans occupied New Mexico for centuries before the arrival of Europeans. The exploring Spaniards called them Pueblo Indians because their tightly clustered communities were not unlike Spanish pueblos, or villages. The Apache and Navajo, who arrived in New Mexico after the Pueblo people, were seminomadic wanderers. The Navajo eventually adopted many of the Pueblo ways, although their society is less structured and more individualistic than the Pueblo. The main Navajo

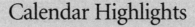

Calendar Highlights

January

New Year's Celebration *(Albuquerque). Taos Pueblo. Contact Albuquerque Convention Center, phone 505/768-4575.* Turtle dance.

April

Trinity Site Tour *(Alamogordo). Phone 505/437-6120 or toll-free 800/826-0294.* Visit the site of the first A-bomb explosion; only time the site is open to the public.

June

New Mexico Arts & Crafts Fair *(Albuquerque). Fairgrounds. Phone 505/884-9043.* Exhibits and demonstrations by craftsworkers representing Spanish, Native American, and other North American cultures. Concerts in Popejoy Hall on the University of New Mexico campus.

July

Taos Pueblo Pow Wow *(Taos). Taos Pueblo. Phone 505/758-1028.* Intertribal dancers from throughout US, Canada, and Mexico participate; competition.

August

Fiesta at Santo Domingo Pueblo *(Santa Fe). Phone 505/465-2214.* Corn dance. This fiesta is probably the largest and most famous of the Rio Grande pueblo fiestas.

Indian Market *(Santa Fe). Santa Fe Plaza. Phone 505/983-5220 or toll-free 800/777-CITY.* One of largest juried displays of Native-American art in the country. Dances. Make reservations at lodgings well in advance.

Inter-Tribal Indian Ceremonial *(Gallup). Red Rock State Park. Phone 505/863-3896 or toll-free 800/233-4528.* A major Native American festival; more than 50 tribes from the US, Canada, and Mexico participate in parades, rodeos, games, contests, dances, art and crafts sales.

September

Enchanted Circle Century Bike Tour *(Red River). Contact Chamber of Commerce, phone 505/754-2366 or toll-free 800/348-6444.* Nearly 1,000 cyclists participate in a 100-mile tour around the Enchanted Circle (Red River, Angel Fire, Taos, Questa).

New Mexico State Fair *(Albuquerque). Phone 505/265-1791.* Horseracing, rodeo, midway; entertainment.

Santa Fe Fiesta *(Santa Fe). Sweeney Center. Phone 505/955-6200 or toll-free 800/777-2489.* This ancient folk festival, dating to 1712, features historical pageantry, religious observances, arts and crafts shows, street dancing. Celebrates the reconquest of Santa Fe by Don Diego de Vargas in 1692. Make reservations well in advance.

Southern New Mexico State Fair & Rodeo *(Las Cruces). Phone 505/524-8612.*

December

Christmas Festivals *(Acoma Pueblo). San Estevan del Rey Mission, Old Acoma. Contact Tourist Visitation Center, phone 505/740-4966 or toll-free 800/747-0181.* Dances, luminarias.

Red Rock Balloon Rally *(Gallup). Contact Convention & Visitors Bureau, phone 505/863-3841 or toll-free 800/242-4282.*

reservation straddles New Mexico and Arizona (see SHIPROCK). The Apache, living closer to the Plains Indians, remained more nomadic.

The 19 Pueblo groups have close-knit communal societies and cultures, even though they speak 6 different languages. Their pueblos are unique places to visit. In centuries-old dwellings, craftspeople make and sell a variety of wares. The religious ceremonies, which include many dances and songs, are quite striking and not to be missed. While some pueblos are adamantly uninterested in tourists, others are trying to find a way to preserve those aspects of their ancient culture they most value, while taking advantage of what is most beneficial to them in non-Native American culture and ways.

Tourists are welcome at all reservations in New Mexico on most days, although there are various restrictions. Since the religious ceremonies are sacred, photography is generally prohibited. This may also be true of certain sacred areas of the pueblo (in a few cases, the entire pueblo). Sometimes permission to photograph or draw is needed, and fees may be required. The ancient culture and traditions of these people hold great meaning; visitors should be as respectful of them as they would be of their own. Questions should be directed to the pueblo governor or representative at the tribal office.

More can be learned about New Mexico's Native Americans and their origins at the many museums and sites in Santa Fe (see), the visitor center at Bandelier National Monument (see), and the Indian Pueblo Cultural Center (see ALBUQUERQUE). For further information, contact the Office of Indian Affairs, 228 E Palace Ave, Santa Fe 87501; phone 505/827-6440.

When to Go/Climate

Extreme variations in elevation and terrain make New Mexico's weather unpredictable and exciting. One minute the sun may be shining, and the next could bring a cold, wind-whipping thunderstorm. Mountain temperatures can be freezing in winter; summers in the desert are hot and dry.

AVERAGE HIGH/LOW TEMPERATURES (° F)

Albuquerque

Jan 47/22	**May** 80/49	**Sept** 82/55
Feb 54/26	**June** 90/58	**Oct** 71/43
Mar 61/32	**July** 93/64	**Nov** 57/31
Apr 71/40	**Aug** 89/63	**Dec** 48/23

Roswell

Jan 54/25	**May** 85/55	**Sept** 86/59
Feb 60/29	**June** 94/62	**Oct** 77/47
Mar 68/36	**July** 95/67	**Nov** 66/35
Apr 77/45	**Aug** 92/65	**Dec** 56/26

Parks and Recreation

Water-related activities, hiking, riding, various other sports, picnicking, camping and visitor centers are available in many of New Mexico's parks. Most parks are open all year. Day-use fee per vehicle is $4 at most parks. Camping: $8-$10/day; electrical hookups $4 (where available); sewage hookups $4. Limit 14 consecutive days during any 20-day period; pets on leash only. Annual entrance passes and camping permits are available. For further information, contact the New Mexico State Park and Recreation Division, PO Box 1147, Santa Fe 87504-1147; phone 888/667-2757.

FISHING AND HUNTING

New Mexico, with six of the seven life zones found on the North American continent, has a large number of wildlife species, among them four varieties of deer, as well as mountain lion, bear, elk, Rocky Mountain and Desert Bighorn sheep, oryx, antelope, javelina, Barbary sheep, ibex, wild turkey, goose, duck, quail, pheasant, and squirrel. There is good fishing for trout in mountain streams and lakes; bass, bluegill, crappie, walleye, and catfish can also be found in many of the warmer waters.

Nonresident fishing license (includes trout stamp): annual $40; 5-day $17; 1-day $9. Nonresident hunting license: deer $190-$310; bear $160; cougar $210; elk $281-$756; antelope $192; turkey $75. (Fees include $1 vendor fee.)

Hunting and fishing regulations are complex and vary from year to year. For detailed information, contact the New Mexico Game and Fish Department, Villagra Building, 408 Galisteo, Santa Fe 87503; phone 800/862-9310.

Driving Information

Safety belts are mandatory for all persons in the front seat of a vehicle. Children under 11 years must be in approved passenger restraints anywhere in the vehicle. Children ages 5-10 may use regulation seat belts. Children ages 1-4 may use regulation seat belts in the back seat; however, in the front seat they must use approved safety seats. Babies under age 1 must be in approved safety seats. For more information, phone 505/827-0427.

INTERSTATE HIGHWAY SYSTEM

The following alphabetical listing of New Mexico towns in this book shows that these cities are within 10 miles of the indicated interstate highways. Check a highway map for the nearest exit.

Highway Number	Cities/Towns within 10 Miles
Interstate 10	Deming, Las Cruces,
Interstate 25	Albuquerque, Las Cruces, Las Vegas, Raton, Santa Fe, Socorro, Truth or Consequences.
Interstate 40	Albuquerque, Gallup, Grants, Santa Rosa, Tucumcari.

Additional Visitor Information

For free information, contact the New Mexico Department of Tourism, Lamy Building, Room 751, 491 Old Santa Fe Trail, Santa Fe 87503; phone 505/827-7400 or toll-free 800/733-6396. *New Mexico,* a colorful, illustrated magazine, is published monthly; to order, contact New Mexico Magazine at the Lew Wallace Building, 495 Old Santa Fe Trail, Santa Fe 87501; phone 505/827-7447 or toll-free 800/435-0715.

There are several welcome centers in New Mexico; visitors who stop by will find information and brochures helpful when planning stops at points of interest. They are located in Anthony (24 miles S of Las Cruces on I-10); Chama (just off Hwy 64/84); Gallup (I-40 exit 22); Glenrio (31 miles E of Tucumcari on I-40); La Bajada (11 miles S of Santa Fe on I-25); Lordsburg (on I-10); Raton (off I-25); Santa Fe (downtown); and Texico (7 miles E of Clovis on Hwy 70/84).

THE WILD (AND NOT SO WILD) WEST

This two- to three-day tour from Las Cruces offers a combination of scenic and technological wonders, hiking and fishing opportunities, and a glimpse into the Wild West. From Las Cruces head northeast on Hwy 70 to White Sands National Monument. This huge beach may lack an ocean, but it offers a seemingly endless expanse of sparkling white gypsum dunes. You'll drive among the dunes along a 16-mile scenic drive, which also provides access to the monument's four hiking trails. Or just take off on foot into the dunes, where kids will have endless hours of fun sliding down the mountains of sand on plastic saucers (available at the monument's gift shop). Visiting the monument is best either early or late in the day, when the dunes display mysterious and often surreal shadows.

Continue northeast on Hwy 70 to Alamogordo, a good spot to spend the night. Attractions here include the Space Center, where you can test your skills as a pilot in a Space Shuttle simulator, explore the International Space Hall of Fame, and see a show at the Tombaugh Omnimax Theater. Also in town is the Alameda Park Zoo and the Toy Train Depot, a museum containing a fascinating collection of toy trains, some dating from the 1800s. The Depot is lots of fun for kids, but its biggest fans are probably baby boomers who reminisce about their childhood trains as they examine the best and sometimes the worst electric trains of the 40s and 50s, including Lionel's tremendous marketing flop–the pink train just for girls. About 12 miles south of Alamogordo via Hwy 54 is Oliver Lee Memorial State Park, with a short, pleasant nature trail along a shaded stream, plus a rugged hiking trail that climbs up the side of a mountain and offers spectacular views. The park also includes the ruins of a pioneer cabin and a museum that tells the story of the site's often violent past.

From Alamogordo, go north on Hwy 54 to Tularosa, where you can visit Tularosa Vineyards to sample the local wine and stop at the small but interesting Tularosa Basin Historical Society Museum. Then head east on Hwy 70 up into the Sacramento Mountains to the resort community of Ruidoso, whose name (Spanish for "noisy") comes from the babbling Ruidoso Creek. Surrounded by the Lincoln National Forest, this picturesque town is a good base for hiking and fishing and is another possibility for overnight lodging. Nearby is the village of Ruidoso Downs, home of Ruidoso Downs Race Track, which offers quarter horse and thoroughbred racing, and the Hubbard Museum of the American West, with displays on horses, horse racing, and related items. Head east out of Ruidoso Downs to Hondo, then turn back to the northwest on Hwy 380, which leads to Lincoln. This genuine Wild West town, which is preserved as a state monument, was the site of a jail break by famed outlaw Billy the Kid. It's also known for the notorious Lincoln County War, in which ranchers and merchants staged a lengthy and bloody battle for beef contracts for a nearby fort.

Continue west on Hwy 380 to the town of Capitan for a visit to Smokey Bear Historical State Park, with exhibits and the grave of the orphaned bear cub who was found in a forest fire near here and became a symbol of forest fire prevention. Leaving Capitan, drive west on Hwy 380 to the town of Carrizozo and cross Hwy 54. Continue 4 miles to Valley of Fires National Recreation Site, where a short trail provides close-up views of numerous jet-black lava formations. Now return to Carrizozo and head south on Hwy 54 to the turnoff to Three Rivers Petroglyph Site, one of the best places in the Southwest to see prehistoric rock art. An easy trail meanders along a hillside where there are thousands of images, ranging from geometric patterns to handprints to a variety of animals (some pierced by arrows or spears) created by the Mogollon people at least 1,000 years ago. To return to Las Cruces, take Hwy 54 south through Tularosa and Alamogordo; turn southwest on Hwy 70. **(Approximately 349 miles)**

Acoma Pueblo (C-2)

See also Albuquerque, Grants

Population 4,000
Elevation 7,000 ft
Information Tourist Visitation Center, PO Box 309, Acoma 87034; phone 505/740-4966 or toll-free 800/747-0181
Web site www.puebloofacoma.org

On a mesa rising 367 feet from the surrounding plain is perhaps the oldest continuously inhabited town in the United States. The exact date of establishment is not known, but archaeologists have dated occupation of the "Sky City" to at least 1150. Legend says it has been inhabited since the time of Christ.

Acoma is a beautiful pueblo with the mission church San Esteban del Rey. This mission probably includes part of the original built by Fray Ramirez in 1629. Beams 40 feet long and 14 inches square were carried from the mountains 30 miles away; even the dirt for the graveyard was carried up by Native Americans. They farmed on the plain below and caught water in rock basins on top. The Acoma are skilled potters and excellent stockbreeders.

The pueblo is about 12 miles south of I-40 and is accessible from exit 102. Tours leave from the base of the pueblo at the visitor center, where a shuttle bus takes visitors to the pueblo on top of the mesa (fee). Visitors may walk down the steep, narrow "stairway" to the visitor center after the tour.

There is a museum with Native American pottery and history exhibits (circa 1400 to the present). (Daily) **FREE**

Acoma-made crafts, native foods, tours, and a cultural and historical exhibit can be seen at the visitor center below Sky City.

Once or twice a year special religious ceremonials are held at which no outsiders are permitted, but there are several festivals (see SPECIAL EVENTS) to which the public is welcome. (Daily; closed pueblo holidays, mid-July, and first or second weekend in October) Your guide will explain the rules and courtesies of taking pictures (picture-taking fee; no video or movie cameras).

Approximately 1 mile north on Hwy 23 is the Enchanted Mesa, 400 feet high. According to an Acoma legend, the tribe lived on top of this mesa until a sudden, violent storm washed out the only way up. Visitors are not permitted to climb to the mesa.

Special Events

Christmas Festivals. *San Estevan del Rey Mission, Old Acoma; I-40 W and Acoma Pueblo exit, Acoma Pueblo. Phone toll-free 800/766-4405.* Dances, luminarias. Late Dec.

Feast of St. Estevan. *Old Acoma, Acoma Pueblo.* Harvest dance. Early Sept.

Fiesta (St. Lorenzo's) Day. *Acomita, Acoma Pueblo.* Mid-Aug.

Governor's Feast. *Old Acoma, Acoma Pueblo.* Dances. Early Feb.

Santa Maria Feast. *McCarty's Village Mission, I-40 W and Acoma Pueblo exit, Acoma Pueblo. Phone toll-free 800/766-4405.* First Sun in May.

Alamogordo (D-3)

See also Cloudcroft, Mescalero, Ruidoso, White Sands National Monument

Founded 1898
Population 35,582
Elevation 4,350 ft
Area Code 505
Zip 88310
Information Chamber of Commerce, 1301 N White Sands Blvd, PO Box 518; phone 505/437-6120 or toll-free 800/826-0294
Web site www.alamogordo.com

Alamogordo is a popular tourist destination because of its proximity to Mescalero Apache Indian Reservation, Lincoln National Forest, and White Sands National Monument. A branch of New Mexico State University is located here. Surrounded by desert and mountains, Alamogordo is the home of Holloman AFB and the 49th Fighter Wing, home of the Stealth fighter. The first atomic bomb was set off nearby.

What to See and Do

Alameda Park Zoo. *11th and White Sands Blvd, Alamogordo. Phone 505/439-4290.* A 7-acre zoo with more than 300 native and exotic animals. Built in 1898, this is the oldest zoo in the Southwest. (Daily 9 am-5 pm; closed Jan 1, Dec 25) **$$**

Lincoln National Forest. *3496 Hwy 82, Alamogordo. E of town. Phone 505/434-7200. www.fs.fed.us/r3/lincoln.* This forest is known as the birthplace of Smokey Bear of "Only you can prevent forest fires"-fame. Fishing; hunting, picnicking, camping, wild cave tours, and winter sports in the Sacramento, Capitan, and Guadalupe mountains. Backpack in the White Mountain Capitan Wildernesses. Some campsites in developed areas free, some require fee.

★ **New Mexico Museum of Space History.** *Hwy 2001, Alamogordo. 2 miles E via Hwy 54, Indian Wells and Scenic Dr. Phone 505/437-2840; toll-free 877/333-6589. www.spacefame.org/museum1.html.* Museum features space-related artifacts and exhibits; self-guided tour; IMAX theater. (Daily 9 am-5 pm; closed Dec 25) **$$** Combination ticket includes Museum of Space History and

Tombaugh IMAX Theater. *New Mexico Museum of Space History, Tombaugh Planetarium, Hwy 2001, Alamogordo. Phone 505/437-2840; toll-free 877/333-6589. www.spacefame.org/plan.html.* Planetarium with Omnimax movies (daily). Features laser light shows (Fri-Sat evenings). **$$**

Oliver Lee State Park. *Hwy 54 S and Dog Canyon Rd, Alamogordo. 10 miles S via Hwy 54, E on County A16. Phone 505/437-8284.* (Dog Canyon) Mecca for mountain climbers, photographers, and history buffs. Early Apache stronghold, site of at least five major battles; box canyon protected by a 2,000-foot bluff; mossy bluffs, cottonwood trees; Frenchy's Place, a substantial rock house with miles of stone fence. Hiking, camping (hookups, dump station). Visitor center (daily), museum, tours of restored Lee Ranch House (Sat and Sun, mid-afternoon; also by appointment).

Three Rivers Petroglyph Site. *County Rd B-30, Three Rivers. 29 miles N on Hwy 54 to Three Rivers, then 5 miles E on county road. Phone 505/525-4300.* Twenty thousand rock carvings made between AD 900-1400 by the Jornada Branch of the Mogollon Indian Culture; semidesert terrain; interpretive signs; reconstructed prehistoric village; six picnic sites; tent and trailer sites (no hookups). **$**

Toy Train Depot. *1991 N White Sands Blvd, Alamogordo. N end of Alameda Park. Phone toll-free 888/207-3564. www.toytraindepot.homestead.com.* More than 1,200 feet of model railroad track and hundreds of model and toy trains are on display in this five-room, 100-year-old train depot. Also a 2-mile outdoor miniature railroad track (rides). Gift and model shop. (Wed-Sun noon-5 pm) **$**

Special Events

New Mexico Museum of Space History Induction Ceremonies. *New Mexico Museum of Space History, Hwy 2001, Alamogordo. Phone 505/437-2840; toll-free 877/333-6589. www.spacefame.org.* Call for schedule.

Trinity Site Tour. *1301 N White Sands Blvd, Alamogordo. Phone 505/437-6120; toll-free 800/826-0294.* Visit the site of the first A-bomb explosion. The site is open to the public twice a year. First Sat in Apr and Oct, 9 am-2 pm.

Limited-Service Hotels

★ BEST WESTERN DESERT AIRE HOTEL. *1021 S White Sands Blvd, Alamogordo (88310). Phone 505/437-2110; fax 505/437-1898. www.bestwestern.com.* 100 rooms, 2 story. Pets accepted; fee. Complimentary continental breakfast. Check-out noon. Pool, whirlpool. **$**

★ DAYS INN. *907 S White Sands Blvd, Alamogordo (88310). Phone 505/437-5090; fax 505/434-5667. www.daysinn.com.* 120 rooms, 2 story. Complimentary continental breakfast. Check-out noon. Pool. **$**

Albuquerque (B-3)

See also Acoma Pueblo

Founded 1706
Population 448,607
Elevation 5,311 ft
Area Code 505
Information Convention & Visitors Bureau, 20 First Plaza NW, PO Box 26866, 87125; phone 505/842-9918 or toll-free 800/284-2282
Web site www.abqcvb.org

In 1706, Don Francisco Cuervo y Valdés, then governor of New Mexico, moved 30 families from Bernalillo to a spot some 15 miles south on the Rio Grande where the pasturage was better. He named this community after the Duke of Alburquerque, then Viceroy of New Spain. With a nice sense of diplomatic delicacy, the Viceroy renamed it San Felipe de Alburquerque (the first R was dropped later), in limited deference to King Philip V of Spain. He also named one of the first structures, a church (still standing), San Felipe de Nerí.

Catholic missionaries began to build churches in the area and inadvertently brought diseases that afflicted the Pueblo Indians. The settlers fought with the Native Americans for many years, but Albuquerque now celebrates the cultural heritage of groups like the Pueblo, the Anasazi, and other tribes.

The pasturage that the governor chose proved good, and by 1790, the population had grown to almost 6,000 (a very large city for New Mexico at the time). Today, Albuquerque is the largest city in New Mexico.

Albuquerque was an important US military outpost from 1846 to 1870. In 1880, when a landowner near the Old Town refused to sell, the Santa Fe Railroad chose a route 2 miles east, forming a new town called New Albuquerque. It wasn't long before the new town had enveloped what is still called "Old Town," now a popular tourist shopping area.

Surrounded by mountains, Albuquerque continues to grow. The largest industry is Sandia National Laboratories, a laboratory engaged in solar and nuclear research and the testing and development of nuclear weapons. More than 100 firms are engaged in electronics manufacturing and research and development.

Dry air and plentiful sunshine (76 percent of the time) have earned Albuquerque a reputation as a health center. Adding to that reputation is the Lovelace Medical Center (similar to the Mayo Clinic in Rochester, Minnesota), which gave the first US astronauts their qualifying examinations. The University of New Mexico is also located in Albuquerque.

Local attractions like the annual Albuquerque Balloon Fiesta and several nearby vineyards make it a place for all to visit and enjoy. To be sure, the culture is an active one, and the people of Albuquerque enjoy as many outdoor activities as they can fit into their schedules.

Public Transportation

Buses (Sun Tran of Albuquerque), phone 505/843-9200.

Airport Albuquerque International Sunport (ABQ).

Information Phone 505/244-7700

Web site www.cabq.gov.airport

Lost and Found Phone 505/244-7733

Airlines America West Airlines, American Airlines, Continental Airlines, Delta Air Lines, Frontier Airlines, Great Plains Airlines, Mesa Airlines, Northwest Airlines, Rio Grande Air, Skywest Airlines, Southwest Airlines, United Airlines

What to See and Do

Albuquerque Biological Park. *903 Tenth St SW, Albuquerque (87102). Phone 505/764-6200. www.cabq.gov/biopark.* Biological park consists of the Albuquerque Aquarium, the Rio Grande Botanic Garden, and the Rio Grande Zoo. The aquarium features a shark tank, eel tunnel, and shrimp boat. The botanic garden displays formal walled gardens and a glass conservatory. The zoo exhibits include koalas, polar bears, sea lions, and shows. (Daily 9 am-5 pm, until 6 pm in summer (June-Aug); closed Jan 1, Thanksgiving, Dec 25) **$$**

Albuquerque Little Theatre. *224 San Pasquale Ave SW, Albuquerque. Phone 505/242-4750. www.swpc.com/~alt.* Historic community theater troupe stages Broadway productions. Sept-May. **$$$$**

Albuquerque Museum. *2000 Mountain Rd NW, Albuquerque. Phone 505/243-7255. www.cabq.gov/museum.* Regional museum of art and history; traveling exhibits; solar-heated building. Across the street from the New Mexico Museum of Natural History and Science (see also). (Tues-Sun 9 am-5 pm; closed holidays) **$**

Cibola National Forest. *2113 Osuna Rd NE, Albuquerque. Phone 505/346-3900. www.fs.fed.us/r3/cibola/.* This forest has more than 1 1/2 million acres and is located throughout central New Mexico. The park includes Mount Taylor (11,301 feet), several mountain ranges, and four wilderness areas: Sandia Mountain, Manzano Mountain, Apache Kid, and Withington. Scenic drives; bighorn sheep in Sandia Mountains. Fishing; hunting, picnicking, and camping (some fees). La Cienega Nature Trail is for the disabled and visually impaired.

Coronado State Monument. *485 Kuaua Rd, Bernalillo. 15 miles N on I-25, then 1 mile W on Hwy 44. Phone 505/867-5351.* Coronado is said to have camped near this excavated pueblo in 1540 on his famous but unsuccessful quest for the seven golden cities of Cibola. Reconstructed, painted kiva; visitor center devoted to Southwestern culture and the Spanish influence on the area. Picnicking. (Wed-Mon 8:30 am-4:30 pm; closed holidays) **$**

Indian Pueblo Cultural Center. *2401 12th St NW, Albuquerque. 1 block N of I-40. Phone 505/843-7270; toll-free 800/766-4405. www.indianpueblo.org.* Owned and operated by the 19 pueblos of New Mexico. Exhibits in the museum tell the story of the Pueblo culture; Pueblo Gallery showcasing handcrafted art; Native American dance and craft demonstrations (weekends). Restaurant. (Daily; closed holidays) **$**

Isleta Pueblo. *PO Box 1270, Isleta Pueblo. Rio Grande Valley, just 13 miles S of Albuquerque and only five minutes away on I-25 to exit 215. Phone 505/869-3111.* (Population 4,000; altitude 4,885 feet) A prosperous pueblo with a church originally built by Fray Juan de Salas. The church was burned during the Pueblo Rebellion of 1680 and later rebuilt; beautiful sanctuary and altar. Recreation area 4 miles NE across the river includes stocked fishing lakes (fee); picnicking, camping (electricity, water available, two-week limit), concession. Pueblo (daily). **$$**

National Atomic Museum. *1905 Mountain Rd NW, Albuquerque. Phone 505/245-2137. www.atomicmuseum.com.* This nuclear energy science center, the nation's only such museum, features exhibits depicting the history of the atomic age, including the Manhattan Project, the Cold War, and the development of nuclear medicine. Replicas of Little Boy and Fat Man, the world's first two atomic weapons deployed in Japan in World War II, fascinate visitors, as do the museum's outdoor exhibits of rockets, missiles, and B-52 and B-29 aircraft. Guided tours and audiovisual presentations are also offered. (Daily 9 am-5 pm; closed holidays) **$**

New Mexico Museum of Natural History and Science. *1801 Mountain Rd NW, Albuquerque. Phone 505/841-2800. museums.state.nm.us/nmmnh.* Fans of dinosaurs, fossils, volcanoes, and the like will love this museum, with exhibits on botany, geology, paleontology, and zoology. The LodeStar Astronomy Center gives museum-goers a view of the heavens in its observatory. Also on site are a naturalist center, the "Extreme Screen" DynaTheater, and a café. (Daily 9 am-5 pm; closed holidays) **$**

★ **Old Town.** *Old Town and Romero rds, Albuquerque.* The original settlement is one block N of Central Ave, the city's main street, at Rio Grande Boulevard. Old Town Plaza retains a lovely Spanish flavor with many interesting shops and restaurants.

Petroglyph National Monument. *6900 Unser Blvd, Albuquerque. 3 1/2 miles N of I-40. Phone 505/899-0205. www.nps.gov/petr.* In the West Mesa area, this park contains concentrated groups of rock drawings believed to have been carved on lava formations by ancestors of the Pueblo. Three hiking trails wind along the 17-mile escarpment. (Daily 8 am-5 pm; closed Jan 1, Thanksgiving, Dec 25) **$**

Rio Grande Nature Center State Park. *2901 Candelaria Rd NW, Albuquerque. E bank of Rio Grande. Phone 505/344-7240. www.emnrd.state.nm.us/nmparks/pages/parks/rgnc/rgnc.htm.* Glass-enclosed observation room overlooking a 3-acre pond that is home to birds and other wildlife, interpretive displays on the wildlife of the bosque (cottonwood groves) along the Rio Grande, 2 miles of nature trails. Guided hikes, hands-on activities. (Daily 8 am-5 pm; closed Jan 1, Thanksgiving, Dec 25) **$**

Rio Grande Zoo. *903 Tenth St SW, Albuquerque. Phone 505/764-6200. www.cabq.gov/biopark/zoo.* More than 1,200 exotic animals in exhibits among a grove of cottonwoods. Rain forest, reptile house, Ape Country, Cat Walk, white tigers. (Daily 9 am-5 pm, until 6 pm in summer (June-Aug); closed Jan 1, Thanksgiving, Dec 25) **$$**

Sandia Peak Tramway Ski Area. *#10 Tramway Loop NE, Albuquerque. 16 miles E on I-40, then 7 miles N on Hwy 14, then 6 miles NW on Hwy 536, in Cibola National Forest, Crest Scenic Byway, Sandia Mountains. Phone 505/242-9052. www.sandiapeak.com.* Area has four double chairlifts, surface lift; patrol, school, rentals, snowmaking, café, restaurant, bar. Aerial tramway on the west side of the mountain meets lifts at the top. Longest run is over 2 1/2 miles; vertical drop 1,700 feet. (Mid-Dec-Mar, daily) Chairlift also operates July-Labor Day (Fri-Sun; fee). **$$$$**

Sandia Peak Aerial Tramway. *#10 Tramway Loop NE, Albuquerque. 5 miles NE of city limits via I-25 and Tramway Rd. Phone 505/856-7325. www.sandiapeak.com.* From the base at 6,559 feet, the tram travels almost 3 miles up the west slope of the Sandia Mountains to 10,378 feet, with amazing 11,000-square-mile views. Hiking trail, restaurant at summit, and Mexican grill at base. (Memorial Day-Labor Day: daily 9 am-9 pm, shorter hours rest of year; closed two weeks in Apr and two weeks in Oct) **$$$$**

Telephone Pioneer Museum. *110 4th St NW, Albuquerque. Phone 505/842-2937.* Displays trace the development of the telephone from 1876 to the present. More than 400 types of telephones, plus switchboards, early equipment, and old telephone directories, are available for viewing. (Mon-Fri 10 am-2 pm; weekends by appointment; closed holidays) **$**

University of New Mexico. *Central Ave and University Blvd, Albuquerque. E of I-25, Central Ave exit. The visitor center is at the corner of Las Lomas and Redondo sts. Phone 505/277-1989; toll-free 800/225-5866. www.unm.edu.* (1889) (25,000 students) This campus shows both Spanish and Pueblo architectural influences. It is one of the largest universities in the Southwest. Special outdoor sports course for the disabled, N of Johnson Gym. On campus are

Fine Arts Center. *Central Ave at Cornell, Albuquerque. Just NW of university's Stanford Dr and Central Ave main entrance. Phone 505/277-4001.* Houses the University Art Museum, which features more than 23,000 pieces in its collection (Tues-Fri 9 am-4 pm, Tues eves 5-8 pm, Sun 1-4 pm; free); the Fine Arts Library, which contains the Southwest Music Archives; the Rodey Theatre; and the 2,094-seat Popejoy Hall, home of the New Mexico Symphony Orchestra and host of the Best of Broadway International Theatre seasons of plays, dance, and music (phone 505/277-2111).

Jonson Gallery. *1909 Las Lomas NE, Albuquerque. Phone 505/277-4967. www.unm.edu/~jonsong.* This gallery, owned by the University of New Mexico and part of its art museums, houses the archives and work of modernist painter Raymond Jonson (1891-1982) and a few works by his contemporaries. Also has exhibitions on the arts in New Mexico. (Tues 9 am-8 pm, Wed-Fri 9 am-4 pm; closed holidays) **DONATION**

Maxwell Museum of Anthropology. *Anthropology Building, University Blvd and Dr. M. L. King Jr. Blvd, Albuquerque. Phone 505/277-4404. www.unm.edu/~maxwell.* Permanent and changing exhibits of early man and Native American cultures with an emphasis on the Southwest. (Tues-Fri 9 am-4 pm, Sat 10 am-4 pm; closed holidays) **FREE**

Museum of Geology and Institute of Meteoritics Meteorite Museum. *Northrop Hall, 200 Yale Blvd NE, Albuquerque. Phone 505/277-4204.* The Museum of Geology contains numerous samples of ancient plants, minerals, rocks, and animals. The Meteorite Museum has a major collection of more than 550 meteorites. Both museums are part of the University of New Mexico. (Mon-Fri 9 am-4 pm; closed holidays) **DONATION**

Special Events

Albuquerque International Balloon Fiesta. *Balloon Fiesta Park, North Albuquerque. Phone 505/821-1000; toll-free 888/422-7277. www.aibf.org.* As many as 100,000 people attend this annual event, the largest of its kind in the world, that fills Albuquerque's blue skies with rainbows of color. Attendees can catch their own balloon rides from Rainbow Ryders, Inc. (phone 505/823-1111). First Sat in Oct through the following Sun.

Founders Day. *In Old Town, Albuquerque. Phone 505/338-2399.* Celebrates the city's founding in 1706 with traditional New Mexican festivities. Late Apr.

Musical Theater Southwest. *4804 Central Ave SE, Albuquerque. Phone 505/262-9301. www.hilandtheater.com.* This troupe produces five Broadway-style musicals each season at the historic Hiland Theater in the Frank A. Peloso Performing Arts Center. **$$$$**

New Mexico Arts & Crafts Fair. *Expo New Mexico State Fairgrounds, Central and San Pedro blvds, Albuquerque. Phone 505/884-9043. www.nmartsandcraftsfair.org.* Exhibits and demonstrations by more than 200 craftsworkers representing Spanish, Native American, and other North American cultures. Artists sell their wares, which range from paintings to sculpture to jewelry. Last weekend in June. **$**

New Mexico State Fair. *Expo New Mexico State Fairgrounds, Central and San Pedro blvds, Albuquerque. Phone 505/265-1791. www.nmstatefair.com.* Horse shows and racing, rodeo, midway, flea market; entertainment. Sept.

New Mexico Symphony Orchestra. *University of New Mexico, Popejoy Hall, Albuquerque. Phone 505/881-9590 (office); toll-free 800/251-6676 (box office). www.nmso.org.* Sept-May.

Santa Ana Feast Day. *Santa Ana and Taos Pueblos, Albuquerque. www.santaana.org.* Corn dance. Late July.

St. Augustine's Feast Day. *Isleta Pueblo, Albuquerque.* Dances. Late Aug.

Limited-Service Hotels

★★ BEST WESTERN RIO GRANDE INN. *1015 Rio Grande Blvd NW, Albuquerque (87104). Phone 505/843-9500; toll-free 800/959-4726; fax 505/843-9238. www.riograndeinn.com.* 40 rooms. Check-in 3 pm, check-out noon. Restaurant, bar. **$**

★★ COURTYARD BY MARRIOTT. *1920 S Yale Blvd, Albuquerque (87106). Phone 505/843-6600; fax 505/843-8740. www.courtyard.com.* 150 rooms, 4 story. Check-out noon. Restaurant bar. Fitness room. Indoor pool, whirlpool. Airport transportation available. **$**

★★ DOUBLETREE HOTEL. *201 Marquette NW, Albuquerque (87102). Phone 505/247-3344; toll-free 888/222-4335; fax 505/247-7025. www.doubletree.com.* Connected to the Albuquerque Convention Center, this property is located in the heart of downtown. Guest rooms feature in-room coffee, dataports, work desks, and hairdryers. Many suites offer views of the Sandia Mountains. Guests will enjoy the outdoor pool and fitness center. 295 rooms, 15 story. Check-out noon. Restaurant, bar. Fitness room. Pool. **$**

★★ HILTON ALBUQUERQUE. *1901 University NE, Albuquerque (87102). Phone 505/884-2500; toll-free 800/932-3322; fax 505/880-1196. www.hilton.com.* With its arched doorways, Indian rugs, and local art, the Southwest comes alive in this conveniently-located property. Guests will enjoy the indoor and outdoor heated pools, sauna, whirlpools, and lighted tennis courts. Accommodations feature two-line phones, data ports, in-room coffee and premium cable. 264 rooms, 12 story. Check-out noon. Restaurant, bar. Fitness room. Indoor pool, whirlpool. Tennis. Business center. **$**

★★ HOLIDAY INN. *2020 Menaul NE, Albuquerque (87107). Phone 505/884-2511; fax 505/884-5720. www.holiday-inn.com.* This full-service hotel offers guests every service they may need. Parents can play virtual golf at the Sandia Springs golf course lounge, which features two full-swing golf simulators, while the kids play in the indoor pool and whirlpool. 360 rooms, 5 story. Pets accepted; fee. Check-out noon. Restaurant, bar. Fitness room. Pool, whirlpool. Airport transportation available. **$**

★ HOMEWOOD SUITES BY HILTON ALBUQUERQUE. *7101 Arvada Ave NE, Albuquerque (87110). Phone 505/881-7300; fax 505/881-0041. www.homewood-suites.com.* 151 rooms, all suites. Check-in 3 pm, check-out noon. **$**

Full-Service Hotels

★★★ HYATT REGENCY ALBUQUERQUE. *330 Tijeras NW, Albuquerque (87102). Phone 505/842-1234; fax 505/766-6710. www.hyatt.com.* Adjacent to the convention center, this 22-story tower is centrally located near Old Town and the Rio Grande Zoo and is only 5 miles from the airport. One of the city's newest high-rise hotels, the property offers a health club, sauna, and outdoor pool. Guest rooms include hairdryers, in-room coffee, and dataports. 395 rooms,

20 story. Check-out noon. Restaurant, bar. Fitness room. Pool. **$$**

★ ★ ★ SHERATON OLD TOWN HOTEL. *800 Rio Grande Blvd NW, Albuquerque (87104). Phone 505/843-6300; toll-free 800/237-2133; fax 505/842-8426. www.sheraton.com.* With its large, open lobby and tiled floors, this property offers a casual yet elegant environment. Located in historic Old Town across from the New Mexico Museum of Natural History, it is close to more than 200 specialty stores. All guest rooms feature furniture hand-made by local artists. 188 rooms, 11 story. Check-out noon. Restaurant, bar. Fitness room. Pool, whirlpool. Business center. **$**

Specialty Lodgings

The following lodging establishments are approved by Mobil Travel Guide, but due to their unique and individualized nature have not been given a traditional Mobil Star rating. Included in this listing you may find bed-and-breakfasts, limited-service inns, guest ranches, and other unique hotel properties.

APACHE CANYON RANCH. *4 Canyon Dr, Laguna (87026). Phone 505/836-7220; toll-free 800/808-8310; fax 505/836-2922. www.apachecanyon.com.* Surrounded by nature's beauty, guests can enjoy watching the antelope, cattle and coyotes roam freely. For more hands-on adventures, guests can explore the land by hiking on the nature trails or by horseback. 5 rooms. Complimentary full breakfast. Check-in 3 pm, check-out 11 am. Fitness room. **$**

BRITTANIA W.E. MAUGER ESTATE B&B. *701 Roma Ave NW, Albuquerque (87102). Phone 505/242-8755; toll-free 800/719-9189; fax 505/842-8835. www.maugerbb.com.* "Mi Casa es Su Casa!" is the mantra of this warm bed-and-breakfast. The eight suites in this restored Queen Anne house (1987) offer fresh flowers, antique furniture, private baths, data ports with ISDN Internet connections, and air conditioning. Centrally located near the business district and Old Town. 10 rooms, 3 story. Pets accepted, some restrictions; fee. Complimentary full breakfast. Check-in 4-6 pm, check-out 11 am. **$**

CASA DEL GRANJERO. *414C De Baca Ln NW, Albuquerque (87114). Phone 505/897-4144; toll-free 800/701-4144; fax 505/897-9788. www.innewmexico.com.* This 1880 bed-and-breakfast fits its Spanish name which translates as "farmer's house." Guests will enjoy the Old West décor, huge sculpted adobe fireplace, and Indian artifacts. Suites feature hand-painted murals, kiva fireplaces, and two-headed showers. 7 rooms. Pets accepted, some restrictions; fee. Complimentary full breakfast. Check-in 11 am-2 pm, check-out 11 am. Whirlpool. Business center. **$**

CASAS DE SUENOS OLD TOWN BED AND BREAKFAST INN. *310 Rio Grande Blvd SW, Albuquerque (87102). Phone 505/247-4560; toll-free 800/242-8987; fax 505/842-8493. www.casasdesuenos.com.* Situated in the valley of the Sandia Mountains just three blocks from the Historic Old Town Area, this inn features the art of local talents. Beautiful guest rooms offer private baths, private entrances, televisions and VCRs. Enjoy a full breakfast in the sunny garden room featuring such dishes as Southwestern frittatas. 17 rooms. Children over 12 years only. Complimentary full breakfast. Check-in 3 pm, check-out 11 am. **$**

CHOCOLATE TURTLE BED AND BREAKFAST. *1098 W Meadowlark, Corrales (87048). Phone 505/898-1800; toll-free 800/898-1842; fax 505/899-8734. www.collectorsguide.com/chocturtle.* Situated on 1 1/2 acres in Corrales, guests can relish the beautiful view of the mountains. Enjoy the homemade chocolates and gourmet breakfasts. 4 rooms. Children over 6 years only. Complimentary full breakfast. Check-in 4-6 pm, check-out 11 am. Whirlpool. **$**

ELAINE'S, A BED & BREAKFAST. *72 Showline Rd, Cedar Crest (87008). 19 miles E. Phone 505/281-2467; toll-free 800/821-3092. www.elainesbnb.com.* Set in a beautiful log cabin within easy distance of golfing, hiking, skiing, bird watching and more. 5 rooms, 3 story. **$**

HACIENDA ANTIGUA B&B. *6708 Tierra Dr NW, Albuquerque (87107). Phone 505/345-5399; toll-free 800/201-2986; fax 505/345-3855. www.haciendaantigua.com.* Built on the famous El Camino Real, this 200-year-old adobe is conveniently located in the North Valley area. The warm property features traditional kiva fireplaces and antique furnishings in the guest rooms. 8 rooms. Complimentary full breakfast. Check-in 4-6 pm, check-out 11 am. Pool, whirlpool. **$$**

RIVER DANCER BED AND BREAKFAST. *16445 Hwy 4, Jemez Springs (87025). Phone 505/829-3262; toll-free 800/809-3262. www.riverdancer.com.* Located near the village of Jemez Springs, the beauty of this 5-acre property is the natural landscaping. Guests will be treated to a relaxing and refreshing getaway. Enjoy Jemez Falls, natural hot springs and hot air ballooning. 6 rooms. Complimentary full breakfast. Check-in 3-7 pm, check-out 11 am. On river. **$**

Restaurants

★ 66 DINER. *1405 Central Ave NE, Albuquerque (87106). Phone 505/247-1421; fax 505/247-0882. www.66diner.com.* American menu. Breakfast, lunch, dinner. Closed holidays. Children's menu. Outdoor seating. **$**

★ ★ ANTIQUITY. *112 Romero St NW, Albuquerque (87104). Phone 505/247-3545.* American, seafood, steak menu. Dinner. Closed holidays. **$$**

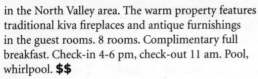

★ ★ ★ THE ARTICHOKE CAFE. *424 Central St, Albuquerque (87102). Phone 505/243-0200; fax 505/243-3365. www.artichokecafe.com.* A perennial favorite among the area's white-tablecloth restaurants, this pleasant eatery has beautiful fresh flowers and a menu that leans toward Italy. Lunch, dinner. Closed Sun; Jan 1, Thanksgiving, Dec 25. Children's menu. Outdoor seating. **$$**

★ ★ BARRY'S OASIS. *445 Osuna, Albuquerque (87109). Phone 505/884-2324.* Greek, Mediterranean menu. Lunch, dinner. Closed Thanksgiving, Dec 25. Bar. Children's menu. Outdoor seating. **$$**

★ ★ CHEF DU JOUR. *119 San Pasquale SW, Albuquerque (87104). Phone 505/247-8998; fax 505/247-8998.* International menu. Lunch, dinner. Closed Sun; holidays. Outdoor seating. **$**

★ CHRISTY MAE'S. *1400 San Pedro NE, Albuquerque (87110). Phone 505/255-4740; fax 505/265-3511. www.christymaes.com.* American menu. Lunch, dinner. Closed Sun; holidays. Children's menu. **$**

★ ★ CONRAD'S DOWNTOWN. *125 2nd St NW, Albuquerque (87102). Phone 505/242-9090; fax 505/242-8664.* Southwestern menu. Breakfast, lunch, dinner. Bar. Valet parking. **$$**

★ COOPERAGE. *7220 Lomas Blvd NE, Albuquerque (87110). Phone 505/255-1657; fax 505/266-0408.* Built like an enormous barrel; circular rooms with many intimate corners, booths; atrium dining room. American menu. Lunch, dinner. Closed Dec 25. Bar. Children's menu. **$$**

★ ★ EL PINTO. *10500 4th St NW, Albuquerque (87114). Phone 505/898-1771; fax 505/897-8147. www.elpinto.com.* Mexican menu. Lunch, dinner. Closed Thanksgiving, Dec 25. Bar. Children's menu. Outdoor seating. **$$**

★ GARDUÑO'S OF MEXICO. *10551 Montgomery NE, Albuquerque (87111). Phone 505/298-5000; fax 505/271-6628.* Contemporary Mexican menu. Lunch, dinner, Sun brunch. Closed Thanksgiving, Dec 25. Bar. Children's menu. Outdoor seating. **$**

★ ★ HIGH NOON. *425 San Felipe St NW, Albuquerque (87104). Phone 505/765-1455; fax 505/255-4505.* Original two rooms built in 1785. Southwestern menu. Lunch, dinner. Closed Jan 1, Dec 25. Bar. **$$**

★ LA HACIENDA DINING ROOM. *302 San Felipe NW, Albuquerque (87104). Phone 505/243-3131.* Mexican décor in old hacienda; antiques, Native American art. American, Mexican menu. Lunch, dinner. Closed Thanksgiving, Dec 25. Bar. Children's menu. Outdoor seating. **$$**

★ ★ ★ LE CAFE MICHE. *1431 Wyoming Blvd NE, Albuquerque (87112). Phone 505/299-6088; fax 505/332-8911. www.lecafemiche.com.* Although the French country cuisine served here is a bit old-fashioned—think veal Orloff and chicken cordon bleu—this romantic, candlelit restaurant remains a favorite because of the attentive service and welcoming ambience. Lunch (Mon-Fri), dinner (Tues-Sun). Closed holidays. Bar. Reservations recommended. **$$$**

★ M AND J. *403 2nd St SW, Albuquerque (87102). Phone 505/242-4890.* Mexican menu. Lunch, dinner. Closed Sun; holidays. Children's menu. **$**

★ ★ NEW CHINATOWN. *5001 Central Ave NE, Albuquerque (87108). Phone 505/265-8859; fax 505/266-3324. www.newchinatown.org.* Chinese menu. Lunch, dinner. Closed Thanksgiving, Dec 25. Bar. **$**

★ RAGIN' SHRIMP. *3619 Copper NE, Albuquerque (87108). Phone 505/254-1544.* Cajun menu. Lunch, dinner. Closed holidays. Children's menu. Outdoor seating. **$$**

★ ★ ★ SCALO. *3500 Central Ave SE, Albuquerque (87106). Phone 505/255-8782.* Chef Enrique Guerrero has just taken over the kitchen of this northern Italian grill, and he's already brought back favorites such as chicken cooked under a brick. Dining areas on several levels. Italian menu. Lunch, dinner. Closed holidays. Bar. Outdoor seating. **$$**

★ ★ TRATTORIA TROMBINO. *5415 Academy Blvd NE, Albuquerque (87109). Phone 505/821-5974.* Italian menu. Lunch, dinner. Closed Thanksgiving, Dec 25; Super Bowl Sun. Bar. Children's menu. **$$**

Angel Fire (A-4)

See also Cimarron, Red River, Taos

Population 1,048
Elevation 8,500 ft
Area Code 505
Zip 87710
Information Chamber of Commerce, PO Box 547; phone 505/377-6661 or toll-free 800/446-8117
Web site www.angelfirechamber.org

This is a family resort area high in the Sangre de Cristo Mountains of northern New Mexico.

What to See and Do

Angel Fire Ski Resort. *10 Miller Ln, Angel Fire. 3 1/2 miles off Hwy 64, Hwy 434. Phone 505/377-6401; toll-free 800/633-7463. www.angelfireresort.com.* Resort has two high-speed quad, three double chairlifts; patrol, school, rentals; cafeteria, restaurants, bars. 67 runs, longest run more than 3 miles; vertical drop 2,077 feet. (Thanksgiving-Mar, daily) Nordic center, snowmobiling. Summer resort includes fishing, boating, lake; 18-hole golf, tennis, mountain biking, riding stables. Conference center (all year). **$$$$**

Carson National Forest. *15160 State Rd 75, Angel Fire. 3 miles W. Phone 505/587-2255.* (see TAOS)

Cimarron Canyon State Park. *29519 Hwy 64, Eagle Nest. 15 miles NE on Hwy 64. Phone 505/377-6271.* Region of high mountains and deep canyons has scenic 200-foot palisades; winding mountain stream has excellent trout fishing; state wildlife area. Hiking, rock climbing, wildlife viewing, winter sports, camping. (Daily) **FREE**

Eagle Nest Lake. *Angel Fire. 12 miles N on Hwy 64.* This 2,200-acre lake offers year-round fishing for rainbow trout and Kokonee salmon (fishing license required). **FREE**

Vietnam Veterans National Memorial. *Angel Fire. 3 miles N on Hwy 64. Phone 505/377-6900.* This beautiful, gracefully designed building stands on a hillside overlooking Moreno Valley and the Sangre de Cristo Mountains. It is dedicated to all who fought in Vietnam. Chapel (daily). Visitor center (daily). **FREE**

Artesia (D-4)

See also Carlsbad, Roswell

Founded 1903
Population 10,692
Elevation 3,380 ft
Area Code 505
Zip 88210
Information Chamber of Commerce, 107 N First St, 88210; phone 505/746-2744 or toll-free 800/658-6251
Web site www.artesiachamber.com

Artesia was named for the vast underground water supplies that once rushed up through drilled wells and are now used to irrigate the area's farmland. The first underground school in the United States, Abo Elementary School at 18th Street and Centre Avenue, was built here for safety from the radiation effects of fallout. Potash, natural gas, oil, and petroleum products are processed near here. Artesia is the home of the Federal Law Enforcement Training Center. The area offers wild turkey, deer, bear, and upland game for hunting enthusiasts.

What to See and Do

Historical Museum and Art Center. *503 and 505 W Richardson Ave, Artesia. Phone 505/748-2390.* Pioneer and Native American artifacts; changing art exhibits. (Tues-Sat; closed holidays) **FREE**

Special Events

Bulldog Balloon Rally. *408 W Texas Ave, Artesia.* Second weekend in Nov.

Eddy County Fair. *2707 S 1st St, Artesia.* First week in Aug.

Limited-Service Hotel

★★ BEST WESTERN PECOS INN MOTEL. *2209 W Main St, Artesia (88210). Phone 505/748-3324; fax 505/748-2868. www.bestwestern.com.* 81 rooms, 2 story. Check-out 11 am. Restaurant, bar. Indoor pool, whirlpool. **$**

Specialty Lodging

The following lodging establishment is approved by Mobil Travel Guide, but due to its unique and individualized nature has not been given a traditional Mobil Star rating. Included in this listing you may find bed-and-breakfasts, limited-service inns, guest ranches, and other unique hotel properties.

HERITAGE INN. *209 W Main St, Artesia (88210). Phone 505/748-2552; toll-free 866/207-0222; fax 505/746-4981. www.artesiaheritageinn.com.* 11 rooms. Children over 15 years only. Complimentary continental breakfast. Check-in 3 pm, check-out 11 am. **$**

Restaurant

★★ LA FONDA. *206 W Main, Artesia (88210). Phone 505/746-9377.* American, Mexican menu. Dinner. Closed Jan 1, Thanksgiving, Dec 25. Children's menu. **$**

Aztec (A-2)

See also Farmington

Founded 1890
Population 6,378
Elevation 5,686 ft
Area Code 505
Zip 87410
Information Chamber of Commerce, 110 N Ash; phone 505/334-9551
Web site www.aztecnm.com

Aztec is the seat of San Juan County, a fruit-growing and cattle-grazing area. This town is filled with history; architectural and historic commentary for walking tours may be obtained at the Aztec Museum.

What to See and Do

Aztec Museum and Pioneer Village. *125 N Main, Aztec. Phone 505/334-9829.* Main museum houses authentic pioneer artifacts, including mineral and fossil display, household items, farm and ranch tools, and Native American artifacts. Atwood Annex has authentically furnished pioneer rooms, farm equipment, sleighs, buggies, and wagons. Oil Field Museum has 1920s cable tool oil rig, oil well pumping unit, "doghouse," and tools. Pioneer Village has 12 reconstructed buildings, including doctor's and sheriff's offices, blacksmith shop and foundry, pioneer cabin (1880), general store and post office, original Aztec jail, and church. (Mon-Sat) **$$**

Aztec Ruins National Monument. *Aztec Ruins Rd, Aztec. 1/2 mile N of Hwy 550. Phone 505/334-6174 (voice or TDD). www.nps.gov/azru.* One of the largest prehistoric Native American towns, it was occupied between A.D. 1100-1300. These are ancient Pueblo ruins, misnamed Aztec by early settlers in the 1800s. The partially excavated pueblo contains nearly 450 rooms, with its plaza dominated by the Great Kiva (48 feet in diameter). Instructive museum, interpretive programs in summer. Self-guided tours, trail guide available at visitor center for the 1/4-mile trail. Some portions accessible by wheelchair. Contact Superintendent, 84 County Rd 290, Aztec 87410. (Daily; closed Jan 1, Dec 25) **$$**

Navajo Lake State Park. *Aztec. 18 miles E via Hwy 173, 511. Phone 505/632-2278.* Surrounded by sandstone mesas and stands of piñon and juniper. Part of Colorado River Storage Project; reservoir extends 35 miles upstream into Colorado, totaling 15,000 surface acres of water. (Daily) **$$** Also in the area are

Pine River Site. *West side, Aztec.* Swimming, waterskiing, fishing (panfish, catfish, bass, salmon, and trout), boating (ramps, rentals, marina); picnicking (fireplaces), concession, camping (hookups). Visitor center with interpretive displays.

San Juan River Recreation Area. *Below the dam, Aztec.* Fishing (trout); camping.

Sims Mesa Site. *East side, Aztec.* Boat ramp; camping (dump station).

Limited-Service Hotel

★ STEP BACK INN. *103 W Aztec Blvd, Aztec (87410). Phone 505/334-1200; toll-free 800/334-1255; fax 505/334-9858.* Turn-of-the-century décor. 39 rooms, 2 story. Check-out 11 am. **$**

Bandelier National Monument (B-3)

See also Los Alamos, Santa Fe

From Los Alamos, 6 miles SW on Hwy 502, then 6 miles SE on Hwy 4 to turnoff sign.

A major portion of this 32,000-acre area is designated wilderness. The most accessible part is in Frijoles Canyon, which features cave dwellings carved out of the soft volcanic turf and houses built out from the cliffs. There is also a great circular pueblo ruin (Tyuonyi) on the floor of the canyon. These houses and caves were occupied from about AD 1150-1550. The depletion of resources forced the residents to abandon the area. Some of the modern pueblos along the Rio Grande are related to the prehistoric Anasazi people of the canyon and the surrounding mesa country. There is a paved 1-mile self-guided trail to walk and view these sites. The monument is named after Adolph Bandelier, ethnologist and author of the novel, *The Delight Makers,* which used Frijoles Canyon as its locale. There are 70 miles of trails (free permits required for overnight trips; no pets allowed on the trails). Visitor center with exhibits depicting the culture of the pueblo region (Daily; closed January 1, December 25), ranger-guided tours (summer), campfire programs (Memorial Day-Labor Day). Campground (March-November, daily) with tent and trailer sites (fee; no showers, hookups, or reservations); grills, tables, and water. Golden Access, Golden Age, Golden Eagle Passport (see MAKING THE MOST OF YOUR TRIP). Contact the Visitor Center, HCR 1, Box 1, Suite 15, Los Alamos 87544; 505/672-3861, ext 517 or 505/672-0343 (recording). Per vehicle $5-$10.

Bernalillo (B-3)

Special Event

Buffalo and Comanche dances. *San Ildefonso Pueblo, 2 Dove Rd, Bernalillo. Phone 505/867-3301.* Fiesta at San Ildefonso Pueblo. Late Jan.

Specialty Lodging

The following lodging establishment is approved by Mobil Travel Guide, but due to its unique and individualized nature has not been given a traditional Mobil Star rating. Included in this listing you may find bed-and-breakfasts, limited-service inns, guest ranches, and other unique hotel properties.

LA HACIENDA GRANDE. *21 Baros Ln, Bernalillo (87004). Phone 505/867-1887; toll-free 800/353-1887; fax 505/771-1436. www.lahaciendagrande.com.* Cathedral ceilings, beautiful views and an open-air center courtyard grace this bed-and-breakfast; a Spanish hacienda built in the 1750s. 6 rooms. Pets accepted. Complimentary full breakfast. Check-in 4-6 pm, check-out 11 am. **$**

Restaurants

★ ★ ★ PRAIRIE STAR. *288 Prairie Star Rd, Bernalillo (87004). Phone 505/867-3327; fax 505/867-2108. www.santaanagolf.com.* This casual fine-dining restaurant in the Santa Ana Golf Club has stunning views of the Sandias. Among the kitchen's specialties is game. American menu. Dinner. Closed Mon; Dec 25-Jan 1. Bar. **$$**

★ **RANGE CAFE AND BAKERY.** *925 Camino del Pueblo, Bernalillo (87004). Phone 505/867-1700; fax 505/867-7256. www.rangecafe.com.* Southwestern Breakfast, lunch, dinner. Closed Thanksgiving, Dec 25. Bar. Children's menu. **$**

Capitan (D-3)

Limited-Service Hotel

★ **SMOKEY BEAR MOTEL.** *316 Smokey Bear Blvd, Capitan (88316). Phone 505/354-2253; toll-free 800/766-5392. www.smokeybearmotel.com.* This roadside motel is located in the birthplace of the original Smokey Bear. 9 rooms, 1 story. Check-in 4 pm, check-out noon. **$**

Restaurant

★ **SMOKEY BEAR RESTAURANT.** *316 Smokey Bear Blvd, Capitan (88316). Phone 505/354-2253. www.smokeybearmotel.com.* Interesting Western food with a strong local following in a unique setting. American menu. Breakfast, lunch, dinner. **$**

Capulin Volcano National Monument (A-5)

See also Raton

Web site www.nps.gov/cavo

29 miles E on Hwy 64/87 to Capulin, then 3 1/2 miles N.

Dormant volcano that last erupted approximately 10,000 years ago. The strikingly symmetrical cinder cone rises more than 1,500 feet from plains, with a crater 1 mile in circumferenc e and 415 feet deep. Visitors can spiral completely around the mountain on paved road to rim (daily); five states can be seen on clear days. Picnic area. Visitor center with exhibits of geology, flora, and fauna of the area (daily; closed January 1, December 25). Uniformed personnel on duty at the crater rim (summer only). Contact the Superintendent, Box 40, Capulin 88414.

Carlsbad (E-4)

See also Artesia, Carlsbad Caverns National Park

Founded 1893
Population 25,625
Information Convention & Visitors Bureau, 302 S Canal, PO Box 910; phone 505/887-6516 or toll-free 800/221-1224 outside NM
Web site www.carlsbadchamber.com

Explorers such as Antonio de Espejo and Alvar Nuñez Cabeza de Vaca probably traveled through this area as they made their way down the Pecos River during the 1500s. Carlsbad is also on the famous Goodnight-Loving cattle drive trail.

Irrigation of the rich alluvial bottomland began with the earliest Spanish settlements in the early 1600s. In 1911, the US Bureau of Reclamation began its Carlsbad Project, building three dams and an intricate network of canals that now irrigate more than 25,000 acres. Cotton, alfalfa, and vegetables are the principal crops.

In 1925, potash was discovered by a company drilling for oil; six years later active mining began.

A Ranger District office of the Lincoln National Forest (see ALAMOGORDO) is located here.

What to See and Do

Brantley Lake State Park. *Lakewood. 12 miles N on Hwy 285, then 5 miles NE on County Rd 30. Phone 505/457-2384.* This 3,000-acre park is adjacent to Brantley Lake on the Pecos River. Fishing, boating (ramps); picnicking (shelters), camping (hookups, dump station, showers). Visitor center. (Daily) **$$**

Carlsbad Museum & Art Center. *Halagueno Park, 418 W Fox St, Carlsbad. One block W of Canal St. Phone 505/887-0276. www.nmculture.org/cgi-bin/instview.* Pueblo pottery, art, meteorite remains. Potash and mineral exhibits. Pioneer and Apache relics. McAdoo collection of paintings, bird carvings by Jack Drake, changing temporary exhibits. (Summer: Mon-Sat 10 am-6 pm; winter: Mon-Sat 10 am-5 pm; closed holidays) **FREE**

Lake Carlsbad Water Recreation Area. *Off Green St, on the Pecos River, Carlsbad. Phone 505/887-2702.* Swimming, water sports, fishing, boating; tennis, golf (fee), picnic area.

Living Desert Zoo and Gardens State Park. *1504 Miehls Dr, Carlsbad. 1 1/2 miles NW, off Hwy 285. Phone 505/887-5516.* This 1,100-acre park is an indoor/outdoor living museum of the Chihuahuan Desert's plants and animals. The Desert Arboretum has an extensive cactus collection. Living Desert Zoo has over 60 animal species native to the region including mountain lions, bear, wolf, elk, bison, and an extensive aviary. (Summer: daily 8 am-8 pm; winter: daily 9 am-5 pm; closed Dec 25) **$$**

Million Dollar Museum. *Hwy 62/108 and 7, Whites City. 20 miles SW on Hwy 62/180 to White's City, then W on Hwy 7. Phone 505/885-6776.* Early Americana collection; 31 antique European doll houses, $25,000 doll collection, first car west of the Pecos, Whittlin' Cowboys Ranch. (Daily; closed Dec 25) **$$**

Sitting Bull Falls. *114 S Halegueno, Guadalupe Ranger District, Carlsbad. 11 miles NW on Hwy 285 to Hwy 137, then 30 miles SW, in Lincoln National Forest. Phone 505/885-4181; toll-free 800/221-1224.* Day-use area near a spectacular 130-foot desert waterfall. Hiking trail to piñon and juniper forest, diverse vegetation along the trail with scenic overlooks of the canyons and plains. Picnicking. (Daily) **FREE**

Limited-Service Hotels

★ ★ BEST WESTERN STEVENS INN. *PO Box 580, Carlsbad (88220). Phone 505/887-2851; toll-free 800/730-2851; fax 505/887-6338. www.bestwestern.com.* 202 rooms, 2 story. Pets accepted, some restrictions; fee. Complimentary full breakfast. Check-out noon. Restaurant, bar. Pool. **$**

★ ★ HOLIDAY INN. *601 S Canal St, Carlsbad (88220). Phone 505/885-8500; fax 505/887-5999. www.holiday-inn.com.* Living Desert Zoo State Park and Brantley Lake State Park are just a few short minutes away. 100 rooms, 2 story. Pets accepted; fee. Check-out 11 am. Restaurant. Fitness room. Pool, whirlpool. **$**

Carlsbad Caverns National Park (E-4)

See also Carlsbad

Web site www.nps.gov/cave

27 miles SW of Carlsbad on Hwy 62/180.

One of the largest and most remarkable in the world, this cavern extends approximately 30 miles and is as deep as 1,037 feet below the surface. It was once known as Bat Cave because of the spectacular bat flights, still a daily occurrence at sunset during the warmer months. Cowboy and guano miner Jim White first explored and guided people through the caverns in the early 1900s, later working for the National Park Service as the Chief Park Ranger. Carlsbad Cave National Monument was established in 1923, and in 1930 the area was enlarged and designated a national park. The park contains 46,755 acres and more than 80 caves. Carlsbad Cavern was formed by the dissolving action of acidic water in the Tansill and Capitan limestones of the Permian age. When an uplift drained the cavern, mineral-laden water dripping from the ceiling formed the stalactites and stalagmites.

The main cavern has two self-guided routes, a Ranger-guided Kings Palace tour, and several "off-trail" trips. The "Cavern Guide," an audio tour rented at the visitor center, enhances self-guided tours with interpretations of the caverns, interviews, and historic re-creations. Also available are tours in two back-country caves: Slaughter Canyon Cave and Spider Cave. All guided tours require reservations.

Since the temperature in the cavern is always 56 ° F, be sure to carry a sweater even if it is hot outside; comfortable rubber-soled shoes are also recommended for safety. No pets; kennel available. Photography, including flash and time exposures, is permitted on self-guided trips and some guided tours. Wheelchairs can be accommodated in the elevator for a partial tour. Rangers patrol the cave. Holders of Golden Access and Golden Age passports (see MAKING THE MOST OF YOUR TRIP) receive a 50 percent discount. Picnic area at Rattlesnake Springs. Scenic 9-1/2-mile loop drive, hiking trails, observation tower, exhibits on surface, restaurant. No camping in park, but available nearby. Bat flight programs are held each evening during the summer at the cavern entrance amphitheater.

Visitor center and museum with educational exhibits and displays. For tour reservations and fees, contact the Superintendent, 3225 National Parks Hwy, Carlsbad 88220. Phone 505/785-2232 (ext 429 for reservations).

Cerrillos

See also Santa Fe

What to See and Do

Broken Saddle Riding Company. *56 Vicksville Rd, Cerrillos. From Santa Fe, take exit 278A (Hwy 14) from I-25 S. Conitinue on Hwy 14 S for 16 miles until you reach the Cerrillos business district. Turn right at the first intersection, cross the railroad tracks, and continue for about 1/4 mile. Phone 505/424-7774. www.brokensaddle.com.* Explore the high desert backcountry surrounding the historic mining town of Cerrillos on smooth riding Missouri Foxtroters and Tennessee Walkers. Broken Saddle Riding Company offers morning, afternoon, and sunset rides catering to all riding levels and private rides by appointment. Excursions can include any number of scenic and historic areas surrounding the town of Cerrillos, including old mining areas, ghost towns, and beautifully scenic desert terrain. Monthly full-moon rides are also offered. (By appointment) **$$$$**

Specialty Lodging

The following lodging establishment is approved by Mobil Travel Guide, but due to its unique and individualized nature has not been given a traditional Mobil Star rating. Included in this listing you may find bed-and-breakfasts, limited-service inns, guest ranches, and other unique hotel properties.

HIGH FEATHER RANCH BED & BREAKFAST. *29 High Feather Ranch, Cerrillos (87010). Phone 505/424-1333; toll-free 800/757-4410. www.highfeatherranch-bnb.com.* This architecturally stunning ranch on 65 private acres, features luxurious accommodations and a full gourmet breakfast. 3 rooms, 1 story. **$$**

Chaco Culture National Historical Park (B-2)

See also Farmington, Gallup

Nageezi. From Hwy 44, 25 miles S on country road 7900; 3 miles S of Nageezi Trading Post; from I-40, 60 miles N of Thoreau on Hwy 57. Check road conditions locally; may be extremely difficult when wet. www.nps.gov/chcu.

From AD 900 to 1150, Chaco Canyon was a major center of Anasazi culture. A prehistoric roadway system, which included stairways carved into sandstone cliffs, extends for hundreds of miles in all directions. Ancient roads up to 30 feet wide represent the most developed and extensive road network of this period north of Central America. Researchers speculate that Chaco Canyon was the center of a vast, complex, and interdependent civilization in the American Southwest.

There are five self-guided trails with tours conducted (Memorial Day-Labor Day, times vary), as well as evening campfire programs in summer. Visitor center has museum (daily; closed Jan 1, Dec 25). Camping (fee). Contact the Superintendent, PO Box 220, Nageezi, 87037-0220; phone 505/786-7014. Per vehicle **$$$**

Chama (A-3)

See also Dulce

Population 1,199
Elevation 7,800 ft
Area Code 505
Zip 87520
Web site www.chamanewmexico.com

What to See and Do

Cumbres & Toltec Scenic Railroad, New Mexico Express. *500 S Terrace Ave, Chama. Phone toll-free 888/286-2737.* Round-trip excursion to Osier, CO on 1880s narrow-gauge steam railroad. Route passes through backwoods country and spectacular mountain scenery; including the 4-percent-grade climb to Cumbres Pass. Warm clothing advised due to sudden weather changes. (Memorial Day-mid-Oct, daily)

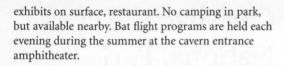

Also through trips to Antonito, CO with van return. Reservations advised; contact PO Box 789. **$$$$**

El Vado Lake State Park. *Chama. 15 miles S on Hwy 84 to Tierra Amarilla, then 13 miles SW on Hwy 112. Phone 505/588-7247.* This park features an irrigation lake with fishing, ice fishing, boating (dock, ramps); hiking trail connects to Heron Lake, picnicking, playground, camping (hookups, dump station). (Daily)

Heron Lake State Park. *640 Hwy 95, Chama. 10 miles S on Hwy 84, then 6 miles SW on Hwy 95. Phone 505/588-7470.* Region of tall ponderosa pines. Swimming, fishing (trout, salmon), ice fishing, boating (ramp, dock); hiking, winter sports, picnicking, camping (hookups; fee). Visitor center. (Daily) **$$**

Cimarron (A-4)

See also Angel Fire, Raton, Red River

Population 917
Elevation 6,427 ft
Area Code 505
Zip 87714
Information Chamber of Commerce, PO Box 604; phone 505/376-2417 or toll-free 800/700-4298
Web site www.cimarronnm.com

This historic Southwestern town was part of Lucien B. Maxwell's land holdings on the Santa Fe Trail. The St. James Hotel (1872), where Buffalo Bill Cody held his Wild West Shows, the gristmill, the old jail (1872), and several other historic buildings still stand.

What to See and Do

Cimarron Canyon State Park. *US Hwy 64, Eagle Nest. 10 miles W on Hwy 64. Phone 505/377-6271.* (see ANGEL FIRE)

Old Aztec Mill Museum. *Hwy 21, Old Town. S of Hwy 64. Phone 505/376-2913.* (1864) Built as gristmill. Chuckwagon, mill wheels, and local historical items. (Memorial Day-Labor Day, Fri-Wed; early May and late Sept, weekends) **$**

Philmont Scout Ranch. *Rte 1 and Hwy 21, Cimarron Town (87714). Headquarters is 4 miles S on Hwy 21. Phone 505/376-2281.* A 138,000-acre camp for some 20,000 Boy Scouts. Villa Philmonte, former summer home of ranch's benefactor, offers tours (mid-June-mid-Aug, daily; rest of year, call for schedule; fee). Ernest Thompson Seton Memorial Library and Philmont Museum includes several thousand drawings, paintings, and Native American artifacts (Mon-Fri; closed holidays). Kit Carson Museum (7 miles S of headquarters; mid-June-Aug, daily; fee). Camp also has buffalo, deer, elk, bear, and antelope. **FREE**

Special Events

Cimarron Days. *Village Park Hwy 64, Cimarron. Phone 505/376-2417.* Crafts, entertainment. Labor Day weekend.

Maverick Club Rodeo. *Maverick Club Arena, Cimarron. Phone 505/376-2417.* Rodeo for working cowboys. Parade, dance. Phone 505/376-2417. July 4.

Specialty Lodging

The following lodging establishment is approved by Mobil Travel Guide, but due to its unique and individualized nature has not been given a traditional Mobil Star rating. Included in this listing you may find bed-and-breakfasts, limited-service inns, guest ranches, and other unique hotel properties.

CASA DEL GAVILAN. *Hwy 21 S, Cimarron (87714). Phone 505/376-2246; fax 505/376-2247. www.casadelgavilan.com.* Peace and tranquility are the most appreciated features of this inn. Guests can relax in the library or on the porch while sipping tea or wine. The more adventurous guests can go hiking in the trails behind the inn. Southwestern adobe built in 1912. 5 rooms. Complimentary full breakfast. Check-in 3 pm, check-out 11 am. **$**

Cloudcroft (D-3)

See also Alamogordo, Mescalero, Ruidoso

Population 749
Elevation 8,700 ft
Area Code 505
Zip 88317
Information Chamber of Commerce, PO Box 1290; phone 505/682-2733
Web site www.cloudcroft.net

One of the highest golf courses in North America is Cloudcroft's most publicized claim to distinction, but this is also a recreation area for non-golfers. It is at the crest of the Sacramento Mountains in the Lincoln

National Forest (see ALAMOGORDO), among fir, spruce, pine, and aspen. A Ranger District office of the forest is located here. The area is popular with writers, photographers, and artists. Several art schools conduct summer workshops here. There are many miles of horseback trails through the mountains, and skiing, snowmobiling, and skating in winter. Deer, elk, turkey, and bear hunting is good in season. Several campgrounds are located in the surrounding forest. During the day temperatures seldom reach 80° F; nights are always crisp and cool.

What to See and Do

Sacramento Mountains Historical Museum. *1000 Hwy 82, Cloudcroft. Phone 505/682-2333.* Exhibits depict 1880-1910 life in the Sacramento Mountains area. (Mon, Tues, Fri-Sun) **$**

Ski Cloudcroft. *1 Corona Pl, Cloudcroft. 2 1/2 miles E on Hwy 82. Phone 505/682-2333. www.ski-cloudcroft.com.* Double chairlift, beginner tows; patrol, school, rentals, snowmaking, lodge, snack bar, cafeteria, restaurant. Vertical drop 700 feet. (Mid-Dec-mid-Mar, daily) Snowboarding. Elevations of 8,350-9,050 feet. **$$$$**

Special Events

Western Roundup. *1001 James Canyon Hwy, Cloudcroft. Phone 505/682-2733.* Contests, parade, street dance. Phone 505/682-2733. Mid-June.

Full-Service Resort

★★★ THE LODGE AT CLOUDCROFT. *1 Corona Pl, Cloudcroft (88317). Phone 505/682-2566; toll-free 800/395-6343; fax 505/682-2715.* Historic building (1899). 60 rooms, 3 story. Pets accepted, some restrictions; fee. Check-in 4 pm, check-out noon. Restaurant, bar. Pool, whirlpool. Golf, 9 holes. **$**

Restaurant

★★★ REBECCA'S. *1 Corona Pl, Cloudcroft (88317). Phone 505/682-2566; fax 505/682-2715. www.thelodge-nm.com.* This casual, fine-dining restaurant in The Lodge serves an American menu that includes beef, poultry and seafood. Breakfast, lunch, dinner, Sun brunch. Bar. Children's menu. **$$$**

Clovis (C-5)

See also Portales

Founded 1907
Population 30,954
Elevation 4,280 ft
Area Code 505
Zip 88101
Information Chamber of Commerce, 215 N Main; phone 505/763-3435
Web site www.clovis.org

Established as a town for Santa Fe railroad stops, Clovis is named for the first Christian king of France, who ruled from A.D. 481-511. It is surrounded by cattle ranches and dairies, alfalfa, wheat, milo, and corn farms. Cannon Air Force Base is located 8 miles west on Hwy 60. Clovis is also home of the Norman Petty Recording Studio, where Buddy Holly, Roy Orbison, and others recorded some of their first hits.

What to See and Do

Clovis Depot Model Train Museum. *221 W First St, Clovis. Phone 505/762-0066.* Built in 1907 by the Atchison, Topeka, and Santa Fe Railway, the Depot has been restored to its condition in the 1950s era. Features working model train layouts, railroad memorabilia, historical displays, and an operating telegraph station. Real train operations along one of the busiest rail lines in the US can be viewed from platform. Gift shop. (Wed-Sun afternoons; closed holidays) **$$**

Hillcrest Park and Zoo. *Sycamore and 10th, Clovis (88101). Phone 505/769-7870.* Second-largest zoo in New Mexico; more than 500 animals, most of which are exhibited in natural environments. Informational programs. Park has kiddieland with amusement rides, outdoor and indoor swimming pool, golf course, picnic areas, sunken garden. **$$**

Special Events

Curry County Fair. *600 S Norris St, Clovis. Phone 505/763-3435.* Mid-Aug.

Pioneer Days & PRCA Rodeo. *1002 W McDonald, Clovis. Phone 505/763-3435.* Parade, Little Buckaroo Rodeo. First week in June.

Limited-Service Hotels

★ BEST WESTERN LA VISTA INN. *1516 Mabry Dr, Clovis (88101). Phone 505/762-3808; fax 505/762-1422. www.bestwestern.com.* 47 rooms. Check-out 11 am. Pool. **$**

★ ★ HOLIDAY INN. *2700 E Mabry Dr, Clovis (88101). Phone 505/762-4491; fax 505/769-0564. www.holiday-inn.com.* 120 rooms, 2 story. Check-out noon. Restaurant, bar. Indoor pool, outdoor pool, whirlpool. **$**

Restaurants

★ GUADLAJARA CAFE. *916 L Casillas St, Clovis (88101). Phone 505/769-9965.* Mexican menu. Lunch, dinner. Closed Sun. **$**

★ LEAL'S MEXICAN FOOD. *3100 E Mabry Dr, Clovis (88101). Phone 505/763-4075; fax 505/763-0791.* Mexican, American menu. Lunch, dinner. Closed Thanksgiving, Dec 25. Children's menu. **$**

★ ★ POOR BOY'S STEAKHOUSE. *2115 N Prince, Clovis (88101). Phone 505/763-5222; fax 505/769-1207.* Seafood, steak menu. Lunch, dinner. Closed Thanksgiving, Dec 25. Children's menu. **$$**

Deming (E-2)

See also Las Cruces, Silver City

Founded 1881
Population 14,116
Elevation 4,335 ft
Area Code 505
Zip 88031
Information Chamber of Commerce, 800 E Pine St, PO Box 8; phone 505/546-2674 or toll-free 800/848-4955
Web site www.cityofdeming.org

This is a livestock, cotton, chiles, onions, and feed grain town in the Mimbres Valley. The old Butterfield Trail, route of an early stagecoach line to California, passed about 12 miles north of here; there is a marker on Hwy 180. Hunting enthusiasts will find deer, antelope, ibex, bear, and blue quail plentiful in the surrounding mountains.

What to See and Do

City of Rocks State Park. *327 Hwy 61, Faywood. 28 miles NW on Hwy 180, then E on Hwy 61. Phone 505/536-2800.* This 680-acre park features fantastic rock formations formed by a thick blanket of volcanic ash that hardened into tuff, and subsequently was sculpted by wind and water; extensive cactus garden. Hiking, picnicking, camping. (Daily) **$$**

Columbus Historical Museum. *Hwys 9 and 11, Columbus. 32 miles S. Phone 505/531-2620.* Housed in restored Southern Pacific Depot (1902). Memorabilia of 1916 Pancho Villa raid and Camp Furlong (Pershing expedition into Mexico); headquarters of Columbus Historical Society. (Daily; closed holidays) **FREE**

Deming-Luna Mimbres Museum. *301 S Silver St, Deming. Phone 505/546-2382.* Mining, military, ranching, railroad, Native American, and Hispanic artifacts of the Southwest. Mimbres pottery; Indian baskets; chuckwagon with equipment; photographic display; antique china, crystal; quilt room; antique dolls; bell and bottle collections; gems and minerals. Musical center; art gallery. (Daily; closed holidays) **FREE**

Pancho Villa State Park. *Hwys 9 and 11, Columbus. 32 miles S. Phone 505/531-2711.* Commemorates Pancho Villa's famous raid (Mar 9, 1916) into US territory. On site of Camp Furlong, from which Brigadier General John "Black Jack" Pershing pursued Villa into Mexico; the first US military action to employ motorized vehicles and airplanes. Some original buildings still stand. Garden of desert vegetation, hundreds of different cacti. Picnicking, playground, camping (hookups, dump station). Three miles south is Las Palomas, Mexico. (Daily) (For Border Crossing Regulations, see MAKING THE MOST OF YOUR TRIP.) **$$**

Rockhound State Park. *Hwy 143, Deming. 5 miles S on Hwy 11, then 9 miles E on Access Rd 549. Phone 505/546-6182.* This 1,000-acre park is on the rugged western slope of the Little Florida Mountains. An abundance of agate, geodes, and other semiprecious stones for collectors (free; limit 15 lbs). Display of polished stones. Hiking, picnicking, playground, camping (hookups). (Daily) **$$**

Rock hunting. *Deming Gem and Mineral Society, Raymond Reed Blvd Southwestern NM Fair Grounds, Deming. Phone 505/546-0348.* "Deming Agate," jasper, onyx, nodules, and many other types of semiprecious stones abound in area. Local gem and mineral society sponsors field trips (see SPECIAL EVENTS).

Special Events

Great American Duck Race. *Courthouse Park, 101 N Copper, Deming.* Live duck racing; duck queen, darling duckling, best-dressed duck contests; hot-air balloon race; tortilla toss; parade. Fourth weekend in Aug.

Old West Gun Show. *Fairgrounds, 800 E Pine, Deming. Phone toll-free 800/848-4955.* Western artifacts, jewelry; military equipment, guns, ammunition. Phone 800/848-4955. Third weekends in Feb and Aug.

Rockhound Roundup. *Fairgrounds, 3115 S Belen, Deming.* More than 6,000 participants. Guided field trips for agate, geodes, candy rock, marble, honey onyx. Auctions; exhibitions; demonstrations. Contact Deming Gem & Mineral Society, PO Box 1459. Phone 505/544-4158. Mid-Mar.

Southwestern New Mexico State Fair. *Fairgrounds, Deming. Phone 505/546-8694.* Livestock shows, midway, parade. Phone 505/546-8694. Early-mid-Oct.

Limited-Service Hotels

★ DAYS INN. *1601 E Pine St, Deming (88030). Phone 505/546-8813; fax 505/546-7095. www.daysinn.com.* 57 rooms, 2 story. Pets accepted, some restrictions; fee. Complimentary continental breakfast. Check-out 11 am. Pool. **$**

★ ★ HOLIDAY INN. *I-10 E exit 85, Deming (88031). Phone 505/546-2661; toll-free 888/546-2661; fax 505/546-6308. www.holiday-inn.com.* 120 rooms, 2 story. Pets accepted. Check-out 11 am. Restaurant. Pool. Airport transportation available. **$**

Dulce (A-2)

See also Chama

Population 2,623
Elevation 6,769 ft
Area Code 505
Zip 87528

A section of Carson National Forest (see TAOS) is located southwest on Hwy 64.

What to See and Do

Jicarilla Apache Indian Reservation. *Seneca Dr, Dulce. On Hwy 64. Phone 505/759-3242.* The Jicarilla Apaches came from a group that migrated from southwestern Canada several centuries ago. The reservation is at an elevation of 6,500-8,500 feet and has excellent fishing and boating; hunting (guides available; tribal permit required; phone 505/759-3255 for information). **$$**

Special Events

Go-Jii-Ya. *Stone Lake, Dulce. Phone 505/759-3242.* Rodeo, Pow Wow, foot races. Mid-Sept.

Little Beaver Roundup. *Jicarilla Apache Indian Reservation, Dulce.* Parade, rodeo, dances, arts and crafts, carnival, 62-mile pony express race; baseball tournament; archery. Phone 505/759-3242. Mid-July.

Limited-Service Hotel

★ ★ BEST WESTERN JICARILLA INN AND CASINO. *PO Box 233, Dulce (87528). Phone 505/759-3663; fax 505/759-3170. www.bestwestern.com.* 42 rooms, 2 story. Complimentary continental breakfast. Check-out 11 am. Restaurant, bar. **$**

El Morro National Monument (Inscription Rock) (C-1)

See also Los Alamos, Santa Fe

From I-40, 43 miles SW of Grants off Hwy 53. Phone 505/783-4226. www.nps.gov/elmo.

Here, on the ancient trail taken by the Conquistadores from Santa Fe to Zuni, is the towering cliff that served as the guest book of New Mexico. Don Juan de Oñate carved his name here in 1605; others followed him in 1629 and 1632. Don Diego de Vargas, reconqueror of New Mexico after the Pueblo Rebellion of 1680, registered his passing in 1692, and scores of other Spaniards and Americans added their names to the cliff at later dates.

The rock is pale buff Zuni sandstone. The cliff, 200 feet high, has pueblo ruins on its top; pre-Columbian petroglyphs. Visitor center and museum (daily; closed January 1, December 25; free).

Trail (fee), picnic facilities. Ranger on duty. Golden Eagle and Golden Age passports (see MAKING THE MOST OF YOUR TRIP). Primitive camping (fee). Contact the Superintendent, El Morro National Monument, Rte 2, Box 43, Ramah 87321; phone 505/783-4226.

Española (B-3)

See also Los Alamos, Santa Fe

Population 9,688
Elevation 5,585 ft
Area Code 505
Zip 87532
Information Española Valley Chamber of Commerce, 417 Big Rock Center; phone 505/753-2831
Web site www.espanolanmchamber.com

First settled 700 years ago by the Pueblo, then by Don Juan de Oñate in 1598, Española was claimed by the United States in 1846. Prosperity came with the railroad in the 1870s. A Ranger District office of the Santa Fe National Forest (see SANTA FE) is located here.

What to See and Do

Florence Hawley Ellis Museum of Anthropology. *Mile Post 224 Hwy 84, Española. Phone 505/685-4333.* Exhibits of Native American/Spanish history. (Memorial Day-Labor Day, Tues-Sun; closed Dec; rest of year, Tues-Sat) **$$**

Ortega's Weaving Shop. *Hwy 76 and Hwy 520, Chimayo. 10 miles NE. Phone 505/351-4215.* Near the Plaza del Cerro (plaza of the hill), an example of an old-style protected Spanish Colonial village. Generations of noted weavers make blankets, coats, vests, purses, rugs. (Mon-Sat) **FREE** Directly north of the shop is

Galeria Ortega. *55 Plaza Del Cerro, Chimayo. Phone toll-free 800/743-5921.* Contains works by artists of northern New Mexico depicting the region's unique tri-cultural heritage. (May-Oct, daily; rest of year, Mon-Sat) **FREE**

Ruth Hall Museum of Paleontology. *Mile Post 224 Hwy 84, Española. Phone 505/685-4333.* Exhibits on Triassic animals, Coelophysis, New Mexico state fossil. (Memorial Day-Labor Day, Tues-Sun; rest of year, Tues-Sat) **$**

Special Events

Fiesta del Valle de Española. Celebrates establishment of New Mexico's first Spanish settlement in 1598. Torch relay, vespers, candlelight procession, street dancing, arts and crafts, food, entertainment, parade (Sun). Phone Chamber of Commerce. Second week in July.

Sainte Claire Feast Day. *Santa Clara Pueblo, south of Española, north of Santa Fe. 2 miles S via Hwy 30. Phone 505/753-7326.* Dancing, food, market. Mid-Aug.

San Juan Feast Day. *San Juan Pueblo, Española. 5 miles N via Hwy 84, Hwy 68. Phone 505/852-4400; toll-free 800/793-4955.* Dancing, food, carnival. Late June.

Tri-cultural Arts Festival. *Northern New Mexico Community College, 921 Paseo de Onte Rd, Española.* Features local artisans and their works; including potters, weavers, woodworkers, photographers, painters, singers, and dancers. Phone Chamber of Commerce. Usually first weekend in Oct.

White Water Race. *Phone toll-free 800/222-7238.* Canoe, kayak, raft experts challenge 14 miles of white water below Pilar. Mother's Day.

Full-Service Inn

★★★ RANCHO DE SAN JUAN COUNTRY INN. *Hwy 285, Mile Marker 340, Española (87533). Phone 505/753-6818; toll-free 800/726-7121; fax 505/753-6818. www.ranchodesanjuan.com.* Situated between Taos and Santa Fe, this inn offers many tranquil spots over its 225 scenic acres. Designed in the Spanish tradition, the décor is both rustic and refined with wildflower-filled courtyards, exposed beams, tile floors, and Southwestern art and antiques. The colorful mountain and river-valley views can be enjoyed from the rooms or the award-winning restaurant (see RANCHO DE SAN JUAN). 17 rooms. Children over 12 years only. Complimentary full breakfast. Check-in 2 pm, check-out 11 am. Restaurant. **$$**

Specialty Lodging

The following lodging establishment is approved by Mobil Travel Guide, but due to its unique and individualized nature has not been given a traditional Mobil Star rating. Included in this listing you may find bed-and-breakfasts, limited-service inns, guest ranches, and other unique hotel properties.

INN AT DELTA. *243 Paseo De Onate, Española (87532). Phone 505/753-9466; toll-free 800/995-8599; fax 505/753-9446. www.innatthedelta.com.* This bed-and-breakfast is located between Sante Fe and Taos and is close to art studios, museums and local craft persons. The inn is also close to famous pueblos of New Mexico. Adobe structure with Southwestern-style furnishings, hand-carved by local craftsmen. 10 rooms, 2 story. Complimentary full breakfast. Check-in 3 pm, check-out noon. **$**

Restaurants

★ ★ ANTHONY'S AT THE DELTA. *233 Paseo de Onate, Española (87532). Phone 505/753-4511.* Many plants; courtyard with rose bushes. Dinner. Closed Jan 1, Thanksgiving, Dec 25. Bar. **$$$**

★ ★ EL PARAGUA. *603 Santa Cruz Rd, Española (87532). Phone 505/753-3211; fax 505/753-6749. www.elparagua.com.* Mexican menu. Lunch, dinner. Closed holidays. Bar. Children's menu. **$$**

★ ★ RANCHO DE CHIMAYO. *County Rd 98, #300, Chimayo (87522). 9 miles E. Phone 505/351-4444; fax 505/351-4038. www.ranchodechimayo.com.* In an old hacienda (1885); antiques, fireplace, original artwork. Mexican, American menu. Lunch, dinner. Closed Dec 25; Mon Nov-May; also the first full week in Jan. Bar. Children's menu. Outdoor seating. **$$**

★ ★ ★ RANCHO DE SAN JUAN. *Hwy 285, Española (87533). Phone 505/753-6818; toll-free 800/726-7121. www.ranchodesanjuan.com.* The elegant, cheerful dining room of this inn, situated between Taos and Santa Fe, overlooks the Ojo Caliente River valley and the Jemez Mountains. The tranquil setting is the perfect backdrop for chef/owner John H. Johnson III's Southwest-inspired, international cuisine. Each dish on the daily-changing prix fixe menu is artistically prepared and as beautiful as the patio sunsets. Southwestern menu. Dinner. Closed Sun-Mon; Dec 25. Bar. Reservations recommended. Outdoor seating. **$$$$**

Farmington (A-1)

See also Aztec, Chaco Culture National Historical Park, Shiprock

Founded 1876
Population 37,844
Elevation 5,395 ft
Area Code 505
Information Chamber of Commerce, 203 W Main St, 87401; phone 505/326-7602 or toll-free 800/448-1240
Web site www.farmingtonnm.org

The Navajos call it Totah, the meeting place at the convergence of three rivers in the colorful land of the Navajo, Ute, Apache, and Pueblo. Once the home of the ancient Anasazi, Farmington is now the largest city in the Four Corners area and supplies much of the energy to the Southwest. From Farmington, visitors may explore Mesa Verde, Chaco Canyon, and the Salmon and Aztec ruins.

Visitors to the area can also enjoy some of the best year-round fishing in the state at Navajo Lake State Park (see AZTEC) and in the San Juan River. Farmington is also the home of the Navajo Indian Irrigation Project, which encompasses more than 100,000 acres.

There are many shops offering traditional Native American crafts in the immediate area—baskets, jewelry, pottery, rugs, and sand paintings. Obtain a list of local art galleries and trading posts at the Convention and Visitors Bureau.

What to See and Do

Bisti Badlands. *Hwy 371, Farmington. 37 miles S via Hwy 371. Phone 505/599-8900.* A federally protected wilderness area of strange geologic formations; large petrified logs and other fossils are scattered among numerous scenic landforms. No vehicles permitted beyond boundary. **FREE**

★ Four Corners Monument. *Navajo Reservation, Farmington. 64 miles NW via Hwy 64, Hwy 504, Hwy 160. Phone 928/871-6647.* Only point in the country common to four states: Arizona, Colorado, New Mexico, and Utah.

San Juan County Archaeological Research Center & Library at Salmon Ruin. *6131 Hwy 64, Bloomfield. 12 miles E on Hwy 64 near Bloomfield. Phone 505/632-2013.* Archaeological remains of a 250-room structure built by the Pueblo (circa AD 1100). Museum and research center exhibit artifacts from excavation; historic structures; picnicking. (Daily; closed holidays) **$$**

Special Events

Black River Traders. *Lions Wilderness Park Amphitheater. Piñon Hills and College, Farmington. Phone 505/325-0279.* Historical drama about the Southwest's multicultural heritage, presented in an outdoor amphitheater. Contact Convention and Visitors Bureau for schedule. Phone 505/325-0279. Mid-June-mid-Aug.

Connie Mack World Series Baseball Tournament. *Ricketts Park, 1101 Fairgrounds Rd, Farmington.* Seventeen-game series hosting teams from all over the US and Puerto Rico. Aug.

Farmington Invitational Balloon Rally. *3041 East Main, Farmington. Phone toll-free 800/448-1240.* Hare and hound races; competitions. Memorial Day weekend.

San Juan County Fair. *41 Road 5568, Farmington.* Parade; rodeo; fiddlers' contest; chili cook-off; exhibits. Mid-late Aug.

Totah Festival. *200 W Arrington, Farmington.* Fine arts juried show. Rug auction; powwow. Labor Day weekend.

Limited-Service Hotels

★★ BEST WESTERN INN & SUITES. *700 Scott Ave, Farmington (87401). Phone 505/327-5221; fax 505/327-1565. www.bestwestern.com.* 194 rooms, 3 story. Pets accepted, some restrictions; fee. Check-out noon. Restaurant, bar. Fitness room. Indoor pool, whirlpool. Airport transportation available. **$**

★ COMFORT INN. *555 Scott Ave, Farmington (87401). Phone 505/325-2626; fax 505/325-7675. www.comfortinn.com.* 60 rooms, 2 story. Pets accepted; fee. Complimentary continental breakfast. Check-out 11 am. Pool. **$**

Specialty Lodging

The following lodging establishment is approved by Mobil Travel Guide, but due to its unique and individualized nature has not been given a traditional Mobil Star rating. Included in this listing you may find bed-and-breakfasts, limited-service inns, guest ranches, and other unique hotel properties.

CASA BLANCA. *505 E La Plata St, Farmington (87401). Phone 505/327-6503; toll-free 800/550-6503; fax 505/326-5680. www.4cornersbandb.com.* This Mission-style house, built in the '50s, features manicured lawns and gardens on a bluff overlooking Farmington and the San Juan River. Guests can enjoy such activities as visiting the Anasazi sites, train rides, golf, and fly fishing. 4 rooms. Complimentary full breakfast. Check-in 4-7 pm, check-out 11 am. Airport transportation available. **$**

Restaurant

★★ CLANCY'S PUB. *2703 E 20th St, Farmington (87402). Phone 505/325-8176; fax 505/325-9295. www.clancys.net.* Mexican, American menu. Lunch, dinner. Closed Easter, Thanksgiving, Dec 25. Bar. Children's menu. Casual attire. Outdoor seating. **$**

Gallup (B-1)

See also Chaco Culture National Historical Park, El Morro National Monument (Inscription Rock), Zuni Pueblo

Founded 1881
Population 20,209
Elevation 6,600 ft
Area Code 505
Zip 87301
Information Gallup-McKinley County Chamber of Commerce, 103 W Hwy 66, 87301; phone 505/722-2228
Web site www.gallupnm.org

Gallup, originally a railroad town, was established to take advantage of the coal reserves nearby and has grown into a retail center serving a large area. The Navajo reservation is north and west of town. The Navajo, Zuni, Hopi, and Acoma trade here.

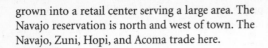

What to See and Do

Cultural Center. *201 Hwy 66 E, Gallup. Phone 505/863-4131.* Located in a restored historic railroad station; ceremonial gallery, storyteller museum, Indian dances (Memorial Day-Labor Day, evenings), kiva cinema, visitor center, gift shop, café. (Summer, Mon-Sat; winter, Mon-Fri) **FREE**

McGaffey Recreation Area. *12 miles E on I-40, then 10 miles S on Hwy 400 in Cibola National Forest. Phone 505/287-8833.* Half mile to lake. Fishing, picnicking (fireplaces, tables), tent and trailer sites. Ranger District headquarters at Grants. Fees for some activities. (May-Sept, daily) **$**

Red Rock State Park. *5 miles E via I-40 and Hwy 566. Phone 505/722-3839.* Desert setting with massive red sandstone buttes. Nature trail, boarding stable. Picnicking, concession, camping (hookups; fee). Interpretive displays, auditorium/convention center, 7,000-seat arena; site of Inter-Tribal Indian Ceremonial (see SPECIAL EVENTS) and rodeos. **FREE** In the park is

> **Red Rock Museum.** *Phone 505/863-1337.* Hopi, Navajo, and Zuni artifacts; gift shop. (Summer: daily 8 am-8 pm; winter: Mon-Sat 8 am-4:30 pm; closed holidays) **DONATION**

Zuni Pueblo. *1222 Hwy 53, Zuni. 31 miles S on Hwy 602, then 8 miles W on Hwy 53.* (see)

Special Events

Inter-Tribal Indian Ceremonial. *Red Rock State Park, Convention Center, and Aitson Amphitheater, Gallup. Phone 505/722-3839; toll-free 888/685-2564. www.gallupnm.org/ceremonial.* A major Native American festival; more than 50 tribes from the US, Canada, and Mexico participate in parades, rodeos, games, contests, dances, arts and crafts sales. Second week in Aug. **$**

Navajo Nation Fair. *Fairgrounds in Window Rock, AZ. Phone 505/871-6478.* Dances, ceremonials, rodeo, arts and crafts, educational and commercial exhibits, food, traditional events. Contact PO Box 2370, Window Rock, AZ 86515. Five days beginning the Wed after Labor Day.

Red Rock Balloon Rally. *Red Rock State Park, Gallup. Phone 505/722-6274. www.redrockballoonrally.com.* Contact the Convention and Visitors Bureau for more information. First weekend in Dec.

Limited-Service Hotels

★★ **EL RANCHO.** *1000 E Hwy 66, Gallup (87301). Phone 505/863-9311; toll-free 800/543-6351; fax 505/722-5917.* Step back in time at the El Rancho. Billing itself as the "Home of the Movie Stars," this historic hotel has welcomed visitors, including those from Hollywood, since 1937. Actors like Ronald Reagan and Allan Ladd often stayed here while filming westerns nearby. In addition to autographed photos from the hotel's past, you'll find rustic Old West décor in the form of beamed ceilings and Navajo rugs. Guest rooms are individually decorated in Southwestern style. 75 rooms. Pets accepted. Check-out noon. Restaurant, bar. **$**

★★ **HOLIDAY INN.** *2915 W Hwy 66, Gallup (87301). Phone 505/722-2201; toll-free 800/432-2211; fax 505/722-9616. www.holiday-inn.com.* 212 rooms, 2 story. Complimentary full breakfast. Check-out noon. Restaurant, bar. Fitness room. Indoor pool, whirlpool. Airport transportation available. **$**

Restaurant

★ **RANCH KITCHEN.** *3001 W Hwy 66, Gallup (87301). Phone 505/722-2537; toll-free 800/717-8818; fax 505/722-2338. www.ranchkitchen.com.* Mexican, American menu. Breakfast, lunch, dinner. Closed Dec 24-25, Easter, children's menu. **$$**

Grants (B-2)

See also Acoma Pueblo, El Morro National Monument (Inscription Rock)

Founded 1882
Population 8,806
Elevation 6,460 ft
Area Code 505
Zip 87020
Information Chamber of Commerce, 100 N Iron St, PO Box 297; phone 505/287-4802
Web site www.grants.org

A Navajo named Paddy Martinez revolutionized the life of this town in 1950 when he discovered uranium ore. More than half the known domestic reserves of uranium ore are in this area.

About 4 miles east, I-40 (Hwy 66) crosses one of the most recent lava flows in the continental United States. Indian pottery has been found under the lava, which first flowed about 4 million years ago from Mount Taylor, to the north. Lava also flowed less than 1,100 years ago from fissures that, today, are near the highway. The lava is sharp and hard; heavy shoes are advisable for walking on it. A Ranger District office of the Cibola National Forest (see ALBUQUERQUE) is located here.

What to See and Do

Acoma Pueblo. *Acoma Pueblo. 32 miles SE via I-40, Hwy 23. Phone toll-free 800/747-0181.* Oldest continuously inhabited pueblo in North America. Provides a glimpse into well-preserved Native American culture.

Bluewater Lake State Park. *Bluewater. 19 miles W on I-40, then 7 miles S on Hwy 412. Phone 505/876-2391.* Rolling hills studded with piñon and juniper trees encircle the Bluewater Reservoir. Swimming, water-skiing, fishing (trout, catfish), boating (ramps); ice fishing, picnicking, camping (electrical hookups, dump station). (Daily) **$$**

El Malpais National Monument and National Conservation Area. *11000 Ice Cave Rd, Grants. S on Hwy 53; or 6 miles SE on I-40, then S on Hwy 117. Phone 505/783-4774. www.nps.gov/elma.* These two areas total 376,000 acres of volcanic formations and sandstone canyons. Monument features splatter cones and a 17-mile-long system of lava tubes. Conservation area, which surrounds the monument, includes La Ventana Natural Arch, one of the state's largest freestanding natural arches; Cebolla and West Malpais wildernesses; and numerous Anasazi ruins. The Sandstone Bluffs Overlook, off Hwy 117, offers an excellent view of lava-filled valley and surrounding area. Facilities include hiking, bicycling, scenic drives, primitive camping (acquire Backcountry Permit at information center or ranger station). Lava is rough; caution is advised. Most lava tubes accessible only by hiking trails; check with information center in Grants before attempting any hikes. Monument, conservation area (daily). Information center and visitor facility on Hwy 117 (daily; closed Jan 1, Thanksgiving, Dec 25). **FREE**

Laguna Pueblo. *33 miles E off I-40. Phone 505/552-6654.* (Population approximately 7,000) This is one of the 19 pueblos located in the state of New Mexico. The people here speak the Keresan language. The pueblo consists of six villages: Encinal, Laguna, Mesita, Paguate, Paraje, and Seama. These villages are located along the western boundary of the pueblo. The Pueblo people sell their arts and crafts on the reservation; items such as Indian belts, pottery, jewelry, baskets, paintings, Indian kilts, and moccasins can be purchased. Visitors are welcomed to the pueblo throughout the year and may encounter various religious observances, some of which are open to the public. However, questions concerning social and religious ceremonies should be directed to the Governor of the Pueblo. As a general rule, photographs, sketches, and tape recordings of Pueblo ceremonials are strictly forbidden. Therefore, it is most important that visitors observe these restrictions and first obtain permission from the Governor of the Pueblo before engaging in such activities. Fiestas and dances are held throughout the year.

New Mexico Mining Museum. *100 N Iron St, Grants. Phone 505/287-4802; toll-free 800/748-2142.* Only underground uranium mining museum in the world. Indian artifacts and relics; native mineral display. (Mon-Sat) **$$**

Limited-Service Hotel

★ ★ BEST WESTERN INN & SUITES. *1501 E Santa Fe Ave, Grants (87020). Phone 505/287-7901; fax 505/285-5751. www.bestwestern.com.* 126 rooms, 2 story. Pets accepted, some restrictions; fee. Check-out noon. Restaurant, bar. Indoor pool, whirlpool. **$**

Hobbs (E-5)

Founded 1927
Population 28,657
Elevation 3,650 ft
Area Code 505
Zip 88240
Information Chamber of Commerce, 400 N Marland; phone 505/397-3202
Web site www.hobbschamber.org

A chance meeting between two covered wagons on a trail across the Llano Estacado (Staked Plain) led to the founding of Hobbs. James Hobbs and his family were headed for Alpine, Texas when they met an eastbound wagon of pioneers returning from Alpine because they couldn't make a living there. Hearing this, James turned his wagon north and eventually settled in what is now Hobbs. This was primarily an agrarian community until the discovery of "black gold" turned it into a booming oil town.

Oil, natural gas, and potash are the big products here; however, Lea County has long been (and still is) an important cattle ranch and dairy territory. Because there is a plentiful supply of shallow water in the ground, cotton, alfalfa, grain, and vegetables have been grown successfully.

What to See and Do

Lea County Cowboy Hall of Fame & Western Heritage Center. *New Mexico Junior College, 5317 N Lovington Hwy, Hobbs. Phone 505/392-1275.* Local memorabilia and artifacts with emphasis on the cowboy, Native American, and oil eras. Permanent displays of Lea County history. (Mon-Sat; closed holidays) **FREE**

Special Events

Lea County Fair. *101 S Commercial Ave, Hobbs. In Lovington, 20 miles NW on Hwy 18. Phone 505/396-5344.* Aug.

Noche de Espana Music Festival. *Main and Becker sts, Hobbs. Phone 505/864-2830.* Includes Mexican food booths, arts and crafts booths. May.

Limited-Service Hotel

★ ★ HOWARD JOHNSON. *501 N Marland Blvd, Hobbs (88240). Phone 505/397-3251; fax 505/393-3065. www.hojo.com.* 75 rooms, 2 story. Pets accepted; fee. Check-out 11 am. Restaurant, bar. Pool. **$**

Restaurant

★ ★ CATTLE BARON STEAK AND SEAFOOD. *1930 N Grimes, Hobbs (88240). Phone 505/393-2800.* Seafood, steak menu. Lunch, dinner. Closed Thanksgiving, Dec 25. Bar. Children's menu. **$$**

Jemez Springs (B-2)

Specialty Lodgings

The following lodging establishments are approved by Mobil Travel Guide, but due to their unique and individualized nature have not been given a traditional Mobil Star rating. Included in this listing you may find bed-and-breakfasts, limited-service inns, guest ranches, and other unique hotel properties.

DANCING BEAR BED & BREAKFAST. *314 San Diego Dr, Jemez Springs (87025). Phone toll-free 800/422-3271. www.dancingbearbandb.com.* Beautifully situated along the Jemez River. Know for gourmet breakfasts. 4 rooms, 2 story. **$**

JEMEZ MOUNTAIN INN. *Hwy 4, Jemez Springs (87025). Phone toll-free 888/819-1075. www.jemezmtninn.com.* Located within walking distance of local restaurants, sights, and attractions. 6 rooms, 2 story. **$**

Restaurants

★ ★ CONSETTA'S. *16351 Hwy 4, Jemez Springs (87025). Phone 505/829-4455.* A local favorite for freshly prepared Italian cuisine. Lunch, dinner. Closed Mon-Tues. **$**

★ ★ THE LAUGHING LIZARD INN & CAFE. *PO Box 263, Jemez Springs (87025). Phone 505/829-3108. www.thelaughinglizard.com.* Featuring distinctive regional cuisine in a country setting. Southwestern menu. Breakfast, lunch, dinner. **$**

★ LOS OJOS RESTAURANT & SALOON. *17596 Hwy 4, Jemez Springs (87025). Phone 505/829-3547.* Known for its excellent Mexican food and the only full-service bar in Jemez Springs. Lunch, dinner. Bar. **$**

Las Cruces (E-2)

See also Deming

Founded 1849
Population 74,627
Elevation 3,896 ft
Area Code 505
Information Convention & Visitors Bureau, 211 N Water St, 88001; phone 505/541-2444 or toll-free 800/FIESTAS
Web site www.lascrucescvb.org

In 1830 a group of people from Taos were traveling on the Spanish highway El Camino Real; they camped here and were massacred by the Apache. They were buried under a field of crosses; hence the name Las Cruces ("the crosses"). Situated in the vast farming area of the fertile lower Rio Grande Valley, this region is especially noted for its homegrown green chile as well as pecans, cotton, lettuce, and corn.

What to See and Do

Aguirre Spring Recreation Site. *Organ. 17 miles E via Hwy 70, 5 miles S on unnumbered road. Phone 505/525-4300.* Organ Mountain area formed by monzonite intrusions—molten rock beneath the surface. Wearing away of the crust left organ pipe rock spires. Baylor Pass and Pine Tree hiking trails. Picnicking, camping (centrally located rest rooms; no drinking water). Managed by the Department of the Interior, Bureau of Land Management, Las Cruces Field Office. (Daily) **$$**

Cultural Complex. *500 N Water St, Las Cruces. Phone 505/541-2155. www.lascruces-culture.or.* Found at the north end of Downtown Mall, includes the Las Cruces Museum of Fine Art & Culture, and the Braningan Cultural Center, which oversees the Bicentennial Log Cabin Museum. Developing is a Volunteers Memorial Sculpture Garden, five blocks west of the complex at the Historical Sante Fe Depot in the New Mexico Railroad and Transportation Museum. (Call for schedule)

Exploring by car. *Las Cruces.* There are ghost mining towns, extinct volcanoes, frontier forts, mountains, and pecan orchards in the area.

Fort Selden State Monument. *1280 Fort Seldon Rd, Radium Springs. 12 miles N on I-25. Phone 505/526-8911.* Frontier fort established in 1865. General Douglas MacArthur lived here as a boy (1884-1886) when his father was post commander. Famed Buffalo Soldiers were stationed here. Self-guided, bilingual trail. Visitor center has history exhibits. Picnicking. (Daily 8:30 am-5 pm; closed winter holidays) **$**

Gadsden Museum. *W Barker Rd and Hwy 28, Mesilla. 2 miles SW. Phone 505/526-6293.* Native American and Civil War artifacts; paintings; hand-painted china; Santo collection; history of the Gadsden Purchase. (Mon-Sat 9-11 am, 1-5 pm, Sun 1-5 pm; closed holidays) **$**

Mesilla. *Mesilla. 1 mile SW. Phone 505/647-9698. www.oldmesilla.org.* Historic village that briefly served as the Confederate capital of the Territory of Arizona. Billy the Kid stood trial for murder here and escaped. La Mesilla consists of the original plaza and surrounding adobe buildings. There are numerous specialty shops, restaurants, art galleries, and museums.

New Mexico Farm and Ranch Heritage Museum. *4100 Dripping Springs Rd, Las Cruces. 1 mile off I-25. Phone 505/522-4100. www.frhm.org.* Interactive 47-acre museum that brings to life Mexico's 3,000-year history, and farming and ranching life. Hands-on exhibits including plowing, blacksmithing, and cow-milking. Outdoor animal and plant life. (Mon-Sat 9 am-5 pm, Sun noon-5 pm; closed holidays) **$**

New Mexico State University. *PO Box 30001, Las Cruces. University Ave. Phone 505/646-0111. www.nmsu.edu.* (1888) (15,500 students) On the 950-acre campus are a history museum (Tues-Sun; free), an art gallery, and an 18-hole public golf course.

White Sands Missile Range. *25 miles E on Hwy 70. Phone 505/678-1134.* Missiles and related equipment tested here. Actual range closed to the public; visitors welcome at the outdoor missile park and museum. Missile Park (daily 8 am-4 pm; closed holidays). Museum (Mon-Fri 8 am-4:30 pm). **FREE**

Special Events

Our Lady of Guadalupe Fiesta. *Tortugas Village, adjacent to town. 3600 Parroquia St, Mesilla Park. Phone 505/526-8171.* Evening Indian dances, vespers; daytime ascent of Mount Tortugas; Mass, bonfire, and torchlight descent; fiesta. Mid-Dec.

Renaissance Craftfaire. *Young Park, 224 N Campo St, Las Cruces. Phone 505/524-6403.* Juried fair with participants in Renaissance costume. Food, entertainment. Early Nov.

Southern New Mexico State Fair & Rodeo. *Dona Ana County Fairgrounds, 12125 Robert Larson Blvd, Las Cruces. Phone 505/524-8602. www.snmstatefair.com.* Carnival midway, rodeo, concerts, food, and contests. First weekend in Oct.

Whole Enchilada Fiesta. *Downtown Mall, Main and Las Cruces sts, Las Cruces. Phone 505/524-6832. www.twefie.com.* Street dancing, entertainment, parade, crafts, food including world's largest enchilada. Last weekend in Sept.

Limited-Service Hotels

★ ★ BEST WESTERN MESILLA VALLEY INN. *901 Avenida De Mesilla, Las Cruces (88005). Phone 505/524-8603; toll-free 800/327-3314; fax 505/526-8437. www.bestwestern.com.* 167 rooms, 2 story. Pets accepted, some restrictions; fee. Check-out 11 am. Restaurant, bar. Pool, whirlpool. **$**

★ FAIRFIELD INN. *2101 Summit Ct, Las Cruces (88011). Phone 505/522-6840; toll-free 800/228-2800; fax 505/522-9784. www.fairfieldinn.com.* 78 rooms, 3 story. Complimentary continental breakfast. Check-out noon. Fitness room. Pool. **$**

★ ★ HOLIDAY INN. *201 E University Ave, Las Cruces (88005). Phone 505/526-4411; fax 505/524-0530. www.holiday-inn.com.* Enclosed courtyard re-creates Mexican plaza. 114 rooms, 2 story. Pets accepted; fee. Check-out noon. Restaurant, bar. Fitness room. Indoor pool, children's pool. Airport transportation available. **$**

★ ★ MESON DE MESILLA RESORT HOTEL. *1803 Avenida Demesilla, Mesilla (88046). Phone 505/525-9212; toll-free 800/732-6025; fax 505/527-4196. www.mesondemesilla.com.* Scenic views. 15 rooms, 2 story. Pets accepted; fee. Complimentary full breakfast. Check-in 1 pm, check-out 11 am. Restaurant, bar. Pool. **$**

Full-Service Hotel

★ ★ ★ HILTON LAS CRUCES. *705 S Telshor Blvd, Las Cruces (88011). Phone 505/522-4300; fax 505/521-4707. www.hilton.com.* This hotel is just minutes from New Mexico State University, Las Cruces International Airport, NASA, White Sands Missile Range and Historic Old Mesilla. Activities such as golfing, bowling, horse-back riding and fishing just minutes away. 203 rooms, 7 story. Pets accepted; fee. Check-out 1 pm. Restaurant, bar. Fitness room. Pool, whirlpool. Airport transportation available. **$$**

Specialty Lodging

The following lodging establishment is approved by Mobil Travel Guide, but due to its unique and individualized nature has not been given a traditional Mobil Star rating. Included in this listing you may find bed-and-breakfasts, limited-service inns, guest ranches, and other unique hotel properties.

LUNDEEN INN OF THE ARTS. *618 S Alameda Blvd, Las Cruces (88005). Phone 505/526-3326; toll-free 888/526-3326; fax 505/647-1334. www.innofthearts.com.* Built in 1890; antique furnishings. Art gallery; each room named for an artist. 21 rooms, 2 story. Pets accepted, some restrictions; fee. Complimentary full breakfast. Check-in 4 pm, check-out 11 am. **$**

Restaurants

★ CATTLE BARON. *790 S Telshor, Las Cruces (88011). Phone 505/522-7533; fax 505/521-3300. www.cattlebaron.com.* Lunch, dinner. Closed Thanksgiving, Dec 25. Bar. Children's menu. **$$**

★ ★ ★ MESON DE MESILLA. *1803 Avenida de Mesilla, Las Cruces (88005). Phone 505/525-9212; fax 505/527-4196. www.mesondemesilla.com.* This romantic restaurant in an adobe-style bed-and-breakfast is a haven of sophisticated dining. Swiss-trained chef Matthew Barton Mattox combines continental cuisine with Italian and Southwestern accents for an unusual and delicious menu. American menu. Dinner, Sun brunch. Closed Mon; Jan 1, Dec 25. Bar. **$$$**

Las Vegas (B-4)

Founded 1835
Population 14,565
Elevation 6,470 ft
Area Code 505
Zip 87701
Information Las Vegas-San Miguel Chamber of Commerce, 727 Grand Ave, PO Box 128; phone 505/425-8631 or toll-free 800/832-5947
Web site www.lasvegasnewmexico.com

Las Vegas once was a stopover on the old Santa Fe Trail. The town prospered as a shipping point, and after the arrival of the railroad in 1879 it began an active period of building and rebuilding. Consequently there are 918 historic buildings (1846-1938). A Ranger District office of the Santa Fe National Forest (see SANTA FE) is located here, as are New Mexico Highlands University and Armand Hammer United World College of the American West.

What to See and Do

City of Las Vegas Museum and Rough Riders' Memorial Collection. *Municipal Building, 727 Grand Ave, Las Vegas. Phone 505/425-8726.* Artifacts and memorabilia from Spanish-American War and turn-of-the-century northern New Mexico life. (May-Oct, daily; Nov-Apr, Mon-Fri). **DONATION**

Fort Union National Monument. *Watrous. 20 miles NE on I-25 to Watrous/Fort Union exit 366, then 8 miles NW on Hwy 161. Contact Superintendent, PO Box 127, Watrous 87753. Phone 505/425-8025. www.nps.gov/foun.* Established at this key defensive point on the Santa Fe Trail in 1851, the third and last fort built here was the largest post in the Southwest and the supply center for nearly 50 other forts in the area. It was abandoned by the military in 1891; 100 acres of adobe ruins remain. Self-guided trail with audio stations, living history programs featuring costumed demonstrations (summer). Visitor center depicts the fort's history, artifacts. (Daily; closed Jan 1, Thanksgiving, Dec 25) **$$**

Las Vegas National Wildlife Refuge. *Storrie Project, Las Vegas. 2 miles E via Hwy 104, then 4 miles S via Hwy 281. Phone 505/425-3581.* Nature trail, observation of wildlife, including migratory water fowl. Hunting for dove (permit required), Canada goose (permit required, limited drawing); user's fee for hunts. (Daily; some areas Mon-Fri) **FREE**

Morphy Lake State Park. *Mora. 11 miles N on Hwy 518 to Sapello, then 16 miles NW off Hwy 94. Phone 505/387-2328.* Towering ponderosa pines surround 15-acre mountain lake in Carson National Forest. Primitive use area. Fishing (trout), restricted boating (oars or electric motors only; ramp); winter sports, primitive camping. Accessible to backpackers; four-wheel-drive vehicle advisable. No drinking water available. (Daily) **$$**

Storrie Lake State Park. *Las Vegas. 4 miles N on Hwy 518. Phone 505/425-7278.* Swimming, water-skiing, fishing, boating (ramp), windsurfing, picnicking, playground, camping (hookups). (Daily) **$$**

Limited-Service Hotels

★ COMFORT INN. *2500 N Grand Ave, Las Vegas (87701). Phone 505/425-1100; toll-free 800/716-1103; fax 505/454-8404. www.comfortinn.com.* 101 rooms, 2 story. Complimentary continental breakfast. Check-out 11 am. Indoor pool, whirlpool. **$**

★ ★ PLAZA HOTEL. *230 Plaza, Las Vegas (87701). Phone 505/425-3591; toll-free 800/328-1882; fax 505/425-9659. www.plazahotel-nm.com.* Historic hotel built in 1882 in the Victorian Italianate-bracketed style; period furnishings, antiques. 37 rooms, 3 story. Pets accepted; fee. Check-out 11 am. Restaurant, bar. **$**

Restaurants

★ EL RIALTO. *141 Bridge St, Las Vegas (87701). Phone 505/454-0037.* Historic building (1890s); antiques. American, Mexican menu. Lunch, dinner. Closed Sun; holidays. Bar. Children's menu. **$$**

★ PINOS TRUCK STOP. *1901 N Grand Ave, Las Vegas (87701). Phone 505/454-1944.* American, Mexican menu. Breakfast, lunch, dinner. Closed Thanksgiving, Dec 25. Children's menu. **$$**

Los Alamos (B-3)

See also Bandelier National Monument, Española, Santa Fe

Population 11,909
Elevation 7,410 ft
Area Code 505
Zip 87544
Information Los Alamos County Chamber of Commerce, 109 Central Park Sq, PO Box 460; phone 505/662-8105 or toll-free 800/444-0707
Web site www.vla.com

On high mesas between the Rio Grande Valley floor and the Jemez Mountain peaks, Los Alamos offers spectacular views and outdoor activities. The city was originally the site of a boys' school; it was acquired by the government in 1942 to develop the first atomic bomb. In 1967, the city property was turned over to Los Alamos County. The scientific laboratory, where research continues, remains a classified installation.

What to See and Do

Bradbury Science Museum. *15th St and Central Ave, Los Alamos. Phone 505/667-4444.* Displays artifacts relating to the history of the laboratory and the atomic bomb. Exhibits on modern nuclear weapons; life sciences; materials sciences; computers; particle accelerators; geothermal, fusion, and fission energy sources. (Daily; closed holidays) **FREE**

Jemez State Monument. *18160 State Rd 4, Jemez Springs. 18 miles N on Hwy 4, then 9 miles S. Phone 505/829-3530.* Stabilized Spanish mission (1621) built by Franciscan missionaries next to a prehistoric pueblo. Self-guided bilingual trail. Visitor center has anthropology and archaeology exhibits. Picnicking. (Daily; closed holidays) **$$**

Los Alamos Historical Museum. *Fuller Lodge Cultural Center, 1921 Juniper, Los Alamos. Phone 505/662-4493.* Artifacts, photos, other material tracing local history from prehistoric to present times; exhibit on the Manhattan Project. (Daily; closed holidays) **FREE**
Also here is

Fuller Lodge Art Center and Gallery. *2132 Central Ave, Los Alamos. Phone 505/662-9331.* Ground floor of Fuller Lodge's west wing. Historic log building provides setting for changing exhibits. Features arts and crafts of northern New Mexico. (Mon-Sat; closed holidays) **FREE**

Pajarito Mountain Ski Area. *Camp May Rd, Los Alamos. From Santa Fe, take St. Francis Dr N, which turns into Hwy 285 N, and continue until you reach the Pojoaque turn-off for Los Alamos (Hwy 502). Continue on Hwy 502 and stay in the right lane, taking the Truck Route (Hwy 501) to Los Alamos. Continue until you reach the well-marked turn-off to the ski hill. Phone 505/662-5725. www.skipajarito.com.* Pajarito Mountain is run by the Los Alamos Ski club and situated near the town of Los Alamos and the ancient volcanic caldera at Valle Grande. Despite being a small resort (280 acres), it offers some excellent and challenging terrain, making it a well-kept secret for local ski buffs despite operating only on Friday, Saturday, and Sunday. The nearby National Labs attract a diverse group of PhDs and scientists, ensuring interesting conversations on the lifts. (Fri-Sun, 9 am-4 pm; closed Mon-Thurs) **$$$$**

Limited-Service Hotels

★★ BEST WESTERN HILLTOP HOUSE HOTEL. *400 Trinity Dr at Central, Los Alamos (87544). Phone 505/662-2441; toll-free 800/462-0936; fax 505/662-5913. www.bestwestern.com.* 98 rooms, 3 story. Pets accepted, some restrictions. Complimentary continental breakfast. Check-out 11 am. Restaurant. Fitness room. Indoor pool, whirlpool. Airport transportation available. **$**

★★ LOS ALAMOS INN. *2201 Trinity Dr, Los Alamos (87544). Phone 505/662-7211; toll-free 800/279-9279; fax 505/661-7714. www.losalamosinn.com.* 116 rooms, 3 story. Complimentary full breakfast. Check-out 12:30 pm. Restaurant, bar. Pool, whirlpool. **$**

Restaurants

★★ BLUE WINDOW BISTRO. *813 Central Ave, Los Alamos (87544). Phone 505/662-6305.* Continental menu. Lunch, dinner. Closed Sun; Jan 1, Thanksgiving, Dec 25. Children's menu. **$$**

★★ KATHERINE'S FINE DINING. *121 Longview, White Rock (87545). 9 miles SE. Phone 505/672-9661.* An upscale restaurant featuring progressive American cuisine. American menu. Lunch, dinner. Closed Sun-Mon. **$$$**

Madrid (B-3)

Restaurant

★ **THE MINE SHAFT TAVERN.** *2846 Hwy 14, Madrid (87010). Phone 505/473-0743. www.mineshafttavern.com.* Located in the small town of Madrid, population 400, the tavern was built in the 1940s at the old coal mine and has been a local favorite ever since. American menu. Lunch, dinner. **$**

Mescalero (D-3)

See also Alamogordo, Cloudcroft, Ruidoso

Population 1,233
Elevation 6,605 ft
Area Code 505
Zip 88340

What to See and Do

Mescalero Apache Reservation. *101 Central Mescalero Ave, Mescalero. Phone 505/671-4494.* Approximately 4,000 Native Americans live on this reservation. Timber, cattle, and recreation are sources of income. There is also a store, museum, and casino. Ceremonials may sometimes be observed (fee); inquire at the community center or at the Mescalero store. Most famous dances are on or around July 4 (see SPECIAL EVENT). Contact Main Tribal Office. Also on the reservation are

Silver Lake, Mescalero Lake, and Ruidoso recreation areas. *101 Central Mescalero Ave, Mescalero. Phone 505/671-4494.* Fishing; hunting for elk, deer, antelope, and bear (fall), picnicking, camping (except at Mescalero Lake; hookups at Silver and Eagle lakes only). Some fees. **$$$**

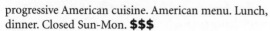

Special Event

Mescalero Apache Maidens' Ceremonial. *Mescalero. Phone 505/671-4494.* Colorful and interesting series of dances, Mountain Spirits dance at dusk, rodeo, parade. Four days including predawn ceremony July 4.

Mesilla (E-2)

Restaurants

★ ★ ★ **DOUBLE EAGLE.** *308 Calle Guadalupe, Mesilla (88004). Phone 505/523-6700; fax 505/523-0051. www.doubleeagledining.com.* Owned by C.W. "Buddy" Ritter, this historic restaurant in a 150-year-old house is filled with antiques. The menu features beef, seafood, poultry, and game. Among the specialties are locally raised ostrich and chateaubriand. Seafood, steak menu. Lunch, dinner, Sun brunch. Bar. Outdoor seating. **$$**

★ **EL COMEDOR.** *2190 Avenida de Mesilla, Mesilla (88005). Phone 505/524-7002. www.vianet.com/elcomedor.* Southwestern menu. Breakfast, lunch, dinner. Closed Jan 1, Thanksgiving, Dec 25. **$**

Portales (C-5)

See also Clovis

Founded 1890
Population 11,131
Elevation 4,000 ft
Area Code 505
Zip 88130
Information Roosevelt County Chamber of Commerce, 200 E 7th; phone 505/356-8541 or toll-free 800/635-8036
Web site www.portales.com

Irrigated with water from several hundred wells, land near Portales produces a wide variety of crops. The county is the Valencia peanut capital of the United States.

What to See and Do

Blackwater Draw Museum. *Hwy 70, Portales. 7 miles N on Hwy 70. Phone 505/562-2202.* Operated by Eastern New Mexico University. Includes 12,000-year-old artifacts and fossils from nearby archaeological site (Mar-Oct); displays, murals tell story of early inhabitants. Films, tours (by appointment). Museum (Memorial Day-Labor Day, Mon-Sat, also Sun afternoons; rest of year, Tues-Sat, also Sun afternoons). **$$**

Eastern New Mexico University. *1200 W University Ave, Portales. SW corner of town. Phone 505/562-2178.* (1934) (4,000 students) On campus is the Roosevelt County Museum; exhibits depict daily lives of early Western pioneers (daily; closed holidays; museum phone 505/562-2592).

Oasis State Park. *1891 Oasis Rd, Portales. 6 miles N, off Hwy 467. Phone 505/356-5331.* Shifting sand dunes and towering cottonwood trees, planted in 1902 by a homesteader, form an oasis. Fishing lake; picnicking, camping (hookups, dump station). (Daily) **$$**

Special Events

Peanut Valley Festival. *Portales. Phone 505/562-2242.* Late Oct.

Roosevelt County Fair. *705 E Lime St, Portales. Phone 505/356-4417.* Mid-Aug.

Roosevelt County Heritage Days. *200 E 7th, Portales. Phone 505/356-8541.* Rodeo, dance, barbecue, parade, contests, entertainment. June.

Raton (A-4)

See also Cimarron, Capulin Volcano National Monument

Founded 1880
Population 7,282
Elevation 6,666 ft
Area Code 505
Zip 87740
Information Chamber & Economic Development Council, 100 Clayton Rd, PO Box 1211; phone 505/445-3689 or toll-free 800/638-6161
Web site www.raton.info

Raton is at the southern foot of famous Raton Pass, on the original Santa Fe Trail (the main road to Denver, now I-25). The road over the pass is a masterpiece of engineering; the view from several points is magnificent.

What to See and Do

Folsom Museum. *Main Street, Folsom. 29 miles E on Hwy 64/87, then 10 miles N on Hwy 325. Phone 505/278-2122.* Artifacts and fossils of Folsom Man (circa 12,000 B.C.). (Memorial Day-Labor Day, daily; May and Sept, weekends; winter, by appointment) **$**

Raton Museum. *218 S 1st St, Raton. Phone 505/445-8979.* Collections relating to the Native American, Hispanic, ranch, railroad, and mining cultures in New Mexico. (Memorial Day-Labor Day, Tues-Sat; rest of year, Wed-Sat or by appointment; closed holidays) **FREE**

Sugarite Canyon State Park. *Sugarite Canyon, Raton. 10 miles NE on Hwy 72 and Hwy 526. Phone 505/445-5607.* This park contains 3,500 acres on the New Mexico side and offers fishing, ice fishing, boating (oars or electric motors only), tubing; seasonal bow hunting for deer and turkey, cross-country skiing, ice skating, riding trails (no rentals), picnicking, camping (fee). Visitor center. (May-Sept, daily; rest of year by appointment) **$$**

Limited-Service Hotel

★★ BEST WESTERN SANDS. *300 Clayton Rd, Raton (87740). Phone 505/445-2737; toll-free 800/518-2581; fax 505/445-4053. www.bestwestern.com.* 50 rooms. Check-out 11 am. Restaurant. Pool, whirlpool. **$**

Restaurant

★★ PAPPAS' SWEET SHOP. *1201 S 2nd St, Raton (87740). Phone 505/445-9811; fax 505/445-3080.* Lunch, dinner. Closed Sun; holidays. Bar. Children's menu. **$$**

Red River (A-3)

See also Angel Fire, Cimarron, Taos

Population 484
Elevation 8,676 ft
Area Code 505
Zip 87558
Information Chamber of Commerce, Main St, PO Box 870; phone 505/754-2366 or toll-free 800/348-6444
Web site www.redrivernewmex.com

This was a gold mining boom town with a population of 3,000 in the early days of the twentieth century. Today it is a summer vacation and winter ski center. Trout fishing, hunting (deer, elk, and small game), snowmobiling, horseback riding, and backpacking are popular sports here.

What to See and Do

Red River Ski Area. *400 Pioneer Rd, Red River. Phone 505/754-2223.* Two triple, three double chairlifts, surface tow; patrol, school, rentals; snowmaking; snack bar, cafeteria. Fifty-seven runs, longest run more than 2 1/2 miles; vertical drop 1,600 feet. (Thanksgiving-late Mar, daily) Chairlift also operates Memorial Day-Labor Day (daily; fee). **$$$$**

Special Events

Enchanted Circle Century Bike Tour. *100 E Main, Red River.* Nearly 1,000 cyclists participate in a 100-mile tour around the Enchanted Circle (Red River, Angel Fire, Taos, Questa). Sept.

Mardi Gras in the Mountains. *Red River.* Ski slope parades, Cajun food. Feb.

Limited-Service Hotels

★★ ALPINE LODGE. *417 W Main, Red River (87558). Phone 505/754-2952; toll-free 800/252-2333; fax 505/754-6421. www.thealpinelodge.com.* 45 rooms, 3 story. Check-out 10 am. Restaurant, bar. **$**

★ BEST WESTERN RIVER'S EDGE. *301 W River St, Red River (87558). Phone 505/754-1766; toll-free 877/600-9990; fax 505/754-2408. www.bestwestern.com.* 30 rooms. Check-in 3 pm, check-out 10 am. **$**

Restaurants

★★ BRETT'S HOMESTEAD STEAKHOUSE. *102 High Cost Trail, Red River (87558). Phone 505/754-6136; fax 505/754-3319.* Prime aged beef with all the fixings is the draw at this casual steakhouse. In a Victorian house with a duck pond. Dinner. Closed Easter-mid-May, Nov. Children's menu. **$$**

★★ SUNDANCE. *102 E High St, Red River (87558). Phone 505/754-2971. www.redrivernm.com/sundance.* Mexican menu. Dinner. Closed Apr-mid-May. Children's menu. **$**

★★ TEXAS RED'S STEAK HOUSE. *111 E Main St, Red River (87558). Phone 505/754-2964. texasreds.com.* Steak menu. Dinner. Children's menu. **$$$**

Roswell (D-4)

See also Artesia

Founded 1871
Population 45,293
Elevation 3,981 ft
Area Code 505
Zip 88201
Information Chamber of Commerce, PO Box 70, 88202; phone 505/623-5695
Web site www.roswellnm.org

Roswell was a cattle town in its early days, with the Goodnight-Loving cattle trail passing through and the Chisholm Trail starting here.

Farming, ranching, livestock feeding, oil and gas exploration and development as well as other industrial areas surround the town. The Roswell campus of Eastern New Mexico University is located here.

What to See and Do

Bitter Lake National Wildlife Refuge. *4065 Bitter Lakes Rd, Roswell. 13 miles NE, via Hwy 70, 285, and Hwy 380 exits. Phone 505/622-6755.* Wildlife observation, auto tour. Hunting in season with state license. (Daily) **FREE**

Bottomless Lakes State Park. *E of Roswell. 10 miles E on Hwy 380, then 6 miles S on Hwy 409. Phone 505/624-6058.* Bordered by high red bluffs, seven small lakes were formed when circulating underground water formed caverns that collapsed into sinkholes. Headquarters at Cottonwood Lake has displays and a network of trails. Beach and swimming at Lea Lake only, bathhouse, skin diving, some lakes have fishing (trout), paddleboat rentals; picnicking, camping. (Daily) **$$**

Dexter National Fish Hatchery and Technology Center. *7116 Hatchery Rd, Roswell. 20 miles SE via Hwy 285 or Hwy 2. Phone 505/734-5910.* This facility is the US Fish and Wildlife Service's primary center for the study and culture of endangered fish species of the American Southwest. (Daily) Also visitor center (Apr-Oct, daily). **FREE**

Historical Center for Southeast New Mexico. *200 N Lea, Roswell. Phone 505/622-8333.* Antiques, period rooms (early 1900s); turn-of-the-century furnishings, clothes; communications exhibits; research library, and archives. (Daily, afternoons; Fri, by appointment) Tours by appointment. **FREE**

★ **International UFO Museum & Research Center.** *114 N Main St, Roswell. Phone 505/625-9495. www.iufomrc.org.* Museum includes exhibits on various aspects of UFO phenomena and a video viewing room. Various video tapes can be viewed upon request. (Daily 9 am-5 pm) **FREE**

New Mexico Military Institute. *101 W College Blvd, Roswell. N Main St and College Blvd. Phone 505/624-8011; toll-free 800/421-5376.* (1891) (1,000 cadets.) State-supported high school and junior college. Alumni Memorial Chapel, near the entrance, has beautiful windows. Also here is the General Douglas L. McBride Military Museum with an interpretation of 20th-century American military history (Tues-Fri; free). Occasional marching formations and parades. Tours.

Roswell Museum and Art Center. *100 W 11th St, Roswell. Phone 505/624-6744.* Southwest arts collection including Georgia O'Keeffe, Peter Hurd, Henriette Wyeth; Native American, Mexican American, and western arts; Dr. Robert H. Goddard's early liquid-fueled rocketry experiments. (Mon-Sat, also Sun and holiday afternoons; closed Jan 1, Thanksgiving, Dec 25) **FREE**

Spring River Park & Zoo. *1306 E College Blvd, Roswell. Phone 505/624-6760.* Zoo and children's zoo area; small lake with fishing for children 11 and under only; miniature train; antique wooden-horse carousel. Picnicking, playground. (Daily; closed Dec 25) **FREE**

Special Events

Eastern New Mexico State Fair and Rodeo. *2500 N Main St, Roswell. 2 miles S on Hwy 285, at Fair Park. Phone 505/623-9411.* Sept-Oct.

UFO Encounters Festival. *International UFO Museum & Research Center, 114 Main St, Roswell. Phone 505/625-9495. www.iufomrc.org.* UFO Expo trade show, alien chase, alien parade, costume contest, guest speeches. July 4 weekend.

Limited-Service Hotels

★★ BEST WESTERN SALLY PORT INN & SUITES. *2000 N Main St, Roswell (88201). Phone 505/622-6430; fax 505/623-7631. www.bestwestern.com.* 124 rooms, 2 story. Pets accepted, some restrictions; fee. Complimentary full breakfast. Check-out noon. Restaurant, bar. Fitness room. Indoor pool, whirlpool. Tennis. Airport transportation available. **$**

★ RAMADA LIMITED. *2803 W 2nd St, Roswell (88201). Phone 505/623-9440; fax 505/622-9708. www.ramada.com.* 61 rooms, 2 story. Pets accepted, some restrictions. Check-out noon. Pool. **$**

Restaurant

★ EL TORO BRAVO. *102 S Main St, Roswell (88201). Phone 505/622-9280.* Mexican menu. Lunch, dinner. Closed holidays. Children's menu. **$**

Ruidoso (D-3)

See also Alamogordo, Cloudcroft, Mescalero

Population 7,698
Elevation 6,911 ft
Area Code 505
Zip 88345
Information Ruidoso Valley Chamber of Commerce, 720 Sudderth Dr, PO Box 698; phone 505/257-7395 or toll-free 800/253-2255
Web site www.ruidoso.net

This resort town in the Sierra Blanca Mountains, surrounded by the trees of the Lincoln National Forests, has enjoyed spectacular growth. It is a thriving town and an all-year resort with skiing in winter and fishing and horseback riding in summer. If planning to visit during June, July, or August, secure confirmed reservations before leaving home. Few mountain resorts have such a variety of attractions. The forested mountain slopes and streams are idyllic, the air is clear and cool, especially at night, and there are many interesting ways to spend time. A Ranger District Office of the Lincoln National Forest (see ALAMOGORDO) is located here.

What to See and Do

Hubbard Museum of the American West. *841 Hwy 70 W, Ruidoso Downs. Phone 505/378-4142.* Western-themed exhibits relating to horses and pioneer life. (Daily; closed Thanksgiving, Dec 25) **$$$**

Lincoln State Monument. *Ruidoso. 30 miles E on Hwy 70, then 10 miles NW on Hwy 380.* Lincoln was the site of the infamous Lincoln County War and a hangout of Billy the Kid. Several properties have been restored, including the Old Lincoln County Courthouse and the mercantile store of John Tunstall. Guided tours (summer, reservations required). (Daily; closed holidays) **$$**

Old Dowlin Mill. *Sudderth and Paradise Canyon Rd, Ruidoso. In town. Phone toll-free 800/253-2255.* A 20-foot waterwheel still drives a mill more than 100 years old.

Ski Apache Resort. *Hwy 532, Ruidoso. 16 miles NW on Hwys 48, 532 in Lincoln National Forests. Phone 505/336-4356.* Resort has four-passenger gondola; quad, five triple, two double chairlifts; surface lift; patrol, school, rentals; snack bars, cafeteria, bar. Fifty-two runs, longest run more than 2 miles; vertical drop 1,900 feet. (Thanksgiving-Easter, daily) **$$$$**

Smokey Bear Historical State Park. *118 Smokey Bear Blvd, Capitan. 22 miles N via Hwys 37/48 on Hwy 380. Phone 505/354-2748.* Commemorates the history and development of the national symbol of forest fire prevention. The original Smokey, who was orphaned by a fire raging in the Lincoln National Forests, is buried here within sight of the mountain where he was found. Fire prevention exhibit, film. (Daily; closed Jan 1, Thanksgiving, Dec 25) **$** Nearby is

> **Smokey Bear Museum.** *102 Smokey Bear Blvd, Capitan. Phone 505/354-2298.* Features 1950s memorabilia of famed fire-fighting bear, whose real-life counterpart was found in the nearby Capitan Mountains. (Daily; closed holidays) **FREE**

The Spencer Theater for the Performing Arts. *Ruidoso. N of Ruidoso at Alto via Hwy 48. Phone toll-free 888/818-7872.* Stunning $22 million structure offers 514 seats for professional touring musical and theater productions. Created from 450 tons of Spanish limestone, the building's design calls forth images of pyramids, mountain peaks, and sci-fi star cruisers. Inside are multiple blown glass installations by Seattle artist Dale Chihuly. (Call for schedule) Tours (Tues, Thurs).

Special Events

Arts Festival. *Paradise Canyon Rd and Sudderth, Ruidoso. Phone 505/854-2261.* Last full weekend in July.

Aspenfest. *Ruidoso. Phone 505/253-2255; toll-free 800/253-2255.* Includes motorcycle convention, official state chili cook-off, arts and crafts. Early Oct.

Horse racing. *Ruidoso Downs, 1461 Hwy 70 W, Ruidoso. Phone 505/378-4431.* Thoroughbred and quarter horse racing, pari-mutuel betting. Home of All-American Futurity, world's richest quarter horse race (Labor Day); All-American Derby and All-American Gold Cup. Thurs-Sun and holidays. Early May-Labor Day.

Smokey Bear Stampede. *8 5th St, Ruidoso. Phone 505/354-2273.* Fireworks, music festival, parade, dances, barbecue. Phone 505/354-2273. Early July.

Limited-Service Hotels

★★ BEST WESTERN SWISS CHALET. *1451 Mechem Dr, Ruidoso (88355). Phone 505/258-3333; toll-free 800/477-9477; fax 505/258-5325. www.bestwestern.com.* 81 rooms, 2 story. Pets accepted, some restrictions; fee. Check-out noon. Restaurant, bar. Indoor pool, whirlpool. **$**

★ VILLAGE LODGE. *1000 Mechem Dr, Ruidoso (88345). Phone 50/525-8544; toll-free 800/722-8779; fax 505/258-3127. www.villagelodge.com.* 28 rooms, 2 story. Check-out 11 am. **$**

Specialty Lodging

The following lodging establishment is approved by Mobil Travel Guide, but due to its unique and individualized nature has not been given a traditional Mobil Star rating. Included in this listing you may find bed-and-breakfasts, limited-service inns, guest ranches, and other unique hotel properties.

CASA DE PATRON BED AND BREAKFAST INN. *Hwy 380 E, Lincoln (88338). Phone 505/653-4676; toll-free 800/524-5202; fax 505/653-4671. www.casapatron.com.* Built in 1860; antiques. This inn was the home of Juan Patron, the youngest Speaker of the House in the Territorial Legislature. Legendary figures such as Billy the Kid and Pat Garrett are said to have spent the night here. 5 rooms. Complimentary full breakfast. Check-in 3-8 pm, check-out noon.**$**

Salinas Pueblo Missions National Monument (C-3)

See also Socorro

Web site www.nps.gov/sapu.

Approximately 75 miles SE of Albuquerque via I-40, Hwy 337, 55.

This monument was established to explore European-Native American contact and the resultant cultural changes. The stabilized ruins of the massive 17th-century missions are basically unaltered, preserving the original design and construction. All three units are open and feature wayside exhibits, trails, and picnic areas (daily; closed January 1, December 25). Monument Headquarters, one block west of Hwy 55 on Hwy 60 in Mountainair, has an audiovisual presentation and an exhibit depicting the Salinas story. (Daily; closed January 1, December 25) Contact the Superintendent, PO Box 517, Mountainair 87036; phone 505/847-2585. The three units of this monument are

Gran Quivira. Here are the massive walls of the 17th-century San Buenaventura Mission (begun in 1659 but never completed), "San Isidro" Church (circa 1639), and 21 pueblo mounds, two of which have been excavated. A self-guided trail and museum/visitor center (exhibits, seven-minute video, 40-minute video) combine to vividly portray Native American life and the cultural change that has occurred over the past 1,000 years. Various factors led to the desertion of the pueblo and the mission around 1671. Tompiro Indians occupied this and the Abó site. Picnicking. 25 miles SE of Mountainair on Hwy 55. Phone 505/847-2770.

Abó. Ruins of the mission church of San Gregorio de Abó (circa 1622), built by Native Americans under the direction of Franciscan priests. This is the only early church in New Mexico with 40-foot buttressed curtain walls—a style typical of medieval European architecture. The pueblo adjacent to the church was abandoned around 1673 because of drought, disease, and Apache uprisings. The Abó and others from the Salinas jurisdiction eventually moved south with the Spanish to El Paso del Norte, where they established the pueblo of Ysleta del Sur and other towns still in existence today. There are self-guided trails throughout the mission compound and pueblo mounds. Picnicking (no water). 9 miles W of Mountainair on Hwy 60, then 3/4 mile N on Hwy 513. Phone 505/847-2400.

Quarai. Ruins of the Mission de la Purísima Concepción de Cuarac, other Spanish structures, and unexcavated Native American mounds, all built of red sandstone. Built about 1630, it was abandoned along with the pueblo about 1677, most likely for the same reasons. Unlike the other two, this site was occupied by Tiwa-speaking people. Much of the history is related to the Spanish-Indian cultural conflict. The church ruins have been excavated, and it is the most complete church in the monument. The visitor center has a museum and interpretive displays. Wayside exhibits, trail guides. Picnicking. 8 miles N of Mountainair on Hwy 55, then 1 mile W on a county road from Punta.

Sandia Park

Restaurant

★ KOKOPELLI'S RESTAURANT AND KANTINA. *12540 N Hwy 14, Sandia Park (81082). Phone 505/286-2691.* Featuring regional American and Southwest cuisines in a family-oriented setting. American menu. Breakfast, lunch, dinner. **$**

Santa Fe (B-3)

See also Bandelier National Monument, Cerrillos, Española, Las Vegas, Los Alamos

Founded 1607
Population 62,203
Elevation 7,000 ft
Area Code 505
Information Convention & Visitors Bureau, PO Box 909, 87504; phone 505/984-6760 or toll-free 800/777-2489
Web site www.santafe.org

This picturesque city, the oldest capital in the United States, is set at the base of the Sangre de Cristo (Blood of Christ) Mountains. A few miles south these mountains taper down from a height of 13,000 feet to a rolling plain, marking the end of the North American Rocky Mountains. Because of the altitude, the climate is cool and bracing. Tourists and vacationers will find much to do and see here all year.

Santa Fe was founded by Don Pedro de Peralta, who laid out the plaza and built the Palace of the Governors in 1610. In 1680, the Pueblo revolted and drove the Spanish out. In 1692, led by General Don Diego de Vargas, the Spanish made a peaceful re-entry. Mexico gained its independence from Spain in 1821. This was followed by the opening of the Santa Fe Trail. In 1846, General Stephen Watts Kearny led US troops into the town without resistance and hoisted the American flag. During the Civil War, Confederate forces occupied the town for two weeks before they were driven out.

In addition to its own attractions, Santa Fe is also the center of a colorful area, which can be reached by car. It is in the midst of the Pueblo country. The Pueblo, farmers for centuries, are also extremely gifted craftsworkers and painters. Their pottery, basketry, and jewelry are especially beautiful. At various times during the year, especially on the saint's day of their particular pueblo, they present dramatic ceremonial dances. Visitors are usually welcome. Since these are sacred rites, however, visitors should be respectful. As a rule, photographs are forbidden. A list of many of these ceremonies is given under SPECIAL EVENTS.

The high altitude may cause visitors accustomed to lower altitudes to have a little shortness of breath for a day or two. A short walking tour taken slowly will be helpful; the tour covers many centrally located sights.

Santa Fe Fun Fact

- At 7,000 feet above sea level, Santa Fe is the highest capital city in the United States.

What to See and Do

Atalaya Mountain Hiking Trail. *Santa Fe. From downtown Santa Fe take Alameda Ave eastbound. Turn right onto Camino Cabra and continue to the intersection with Camino Cruz Blanca where you will turn left. Look for the signs for St. John's College and the parking area for Atalaya Mountain Trailhead. For the shorter trail, keep driving 8 miles past the college on Camino Cruz Blanca to the small parking lot on the left side of the road.* The Atalaya Mountain Trail, accessible from the parking lot at St. John's College, is one of the most popular and easily accessible hiking trails in Santa Fe. Hikers have the option of taking the longer route (Trail 174), which is approximately 7 miles roundtrip, or parking further up near the Ponderosa Ridge development and doing a 4.6-mile loop (Trail 170) instead. Both trials eventually join and take you towards the top of Atalaya mountain, a 9,121-foot peak. The first few miles of the trail are relatively easy but become increasingly steep and strenuous as you near the summit of Atalaya Mountain. Hikers who make it to the top will be afforded great views of the Rio Grande valley and city below.

★ **Canyon Road Tour.** *Santa Fe. Go east on San Francisco St to the cathedral and bear right to the end of Cathedral Pl. Turn left on Alameda.* Many artists live on this thoroughfare. This tour totals about 2 or 3 miles, and there is no better way to savor the unique character of Santa Fe than to travel along its narrow, picturesque old streets. On the left is

Camino del Monte Sol. *Santa Fe.* Famous street on which many artists live and work. Turn left up the hill. Off this road are a number of interesting streets worth exploring. If traveling by car, continue down the hill on Camino del Monte Sol about 1 mile to

Cristo Rey Church. *Santa Fe.* This is the largest adobe structure in the US. It contains beautiful ancient stone reredos (altar screens). (Mon-Fri; closed holidays) Return on Canyon Road to

Museum of Indian Arts and Culture. *710-708 Camino Lejo, Santa Fe. Phone 505/476-1250.*

www.miaclab.org. When the Spanish arrived in the Southwest in the 16th century they found many sprawling towns and villages which they referred to as Pueblos, a name that is still used to identify Indian communities in New Mexico to this day. The Museum of Indian Arts and Culture houses an extensive collection of historic and contemporary Pueblo art from throughout the Southwest. One of the highlights of the museum is an excellent interpretive section where you can encounter Pueblo cultures from the viewpoint and narrative of modern-day Pueblo natives and exhibit designers. The museum itself is housed in a large, adobe-style building that blends architecturally into the surroundings, and also houses many outstanding examples of Pueblo textiles, pottery, jewelry, contemporary paintings, and other rotating exhibits. An adjacent building houses the Laboratory of Anthropology, which contains an extensive library and supports continuing research into Southwestern archeology and cultural studies. (Tues-Sun 10 am-5 pm; closed holidays) **$$** Across the yard is the

Museum of International Folk Art. *706 Camino Lejo, Santa Fe. Phone 505/476-1200. www.moifa.org.* The Museum of International Folk Art, first opened in 1953, contains more than 120,000 objects, billing itself as the world's largest folk museum dedicated to the study of traditional cultural art. Much of the massive collection was acquired when the late Italian immigrant, architect/designer Alexander Girard donated his 106,000-object collection of toys, figurines, figurative ceramics, miniatures, and religious/ceremonial art that he had collected from more than 100 countries around the world. In addition to the collection in the Girard wing, you'll also find a large collection of Hispanic art in the Hispanic Heritage Wing, as well as costumes and folk art from many cultures in the Neutrogena Collection. Several smaller collections and major temporary exhibits add to a rich museum experience that can easily take several hours to explore. Two museum shops offer a wide variety of folk-oriented books, clothing, and jewelry to choose from. (Tues-Sun 10 am-5 pm; closed holidays) **$$** On the same road, less than one long block beyond the museum, is the

National Park Service, Southwest Regional Office. *1100 Old Santa Fe Trail. Phone 505/988-6011.* (1939) Adobe building with central patio. (Mon-Fri; closed holidays) **FREE** From here, go west a short distance on Old Santa Fe Trail, then south on Camino Lejo to the

St. Francis School. *Santa Fe.* Turn right across the first bridge and immediately bear left onto

St. John's College in Santa Fe. *1160 Camino Cruz Blanca, Santa Fe. Just W of Camino del Monte Sol. Phone 505/984-6000. www.sjcsf.edu.* (1964) (400 students) The first campus of St. John's College is in Annapolis, Maryland (1696). Liberal arts. Turn right across the first bridge and immediately bear left onto

Wheelwright Museum. *704 Camino Lejo, Santa Fe. Phone 505/982-4636; toll-free 800/607-4636. www.wheelwright.org.* Founded in 1937 by Mary Cabot Wheelwright and Navajo singer/medicine man Hastiin Klah to help preserve Navajo art and traditions, the Wheelwright now devotes itself to hosting major exhibits of Native American artists from tribes throughout North America. The Case Trading Post in the basement sells pottery, jewelry, textiles, books, prints, and other gift items. (Mon-Sat 10 am-5 pm, Sun 1-5 pm; closed Jan 1, Thanksgiving, Dec 25) **DONATION**

Cathedral of St. Francis. *Santa Fe Plaza, 231 Cathedral Pl, Santa Fe. Phone 505/982-5619.* (1869) French Romanesque cathedral built under the direction of Archbishop Lamy (prototype for Bishop Latour in Willa Cather's *Death Comes for the Archbishop*). La Conquistadora Chapel, said to be the country's oldest Marian shrine, is here. (Daily 8 am-5:45 pm, except during mass) Tours (summer).

College of Santa Fe. *1600 St. Michael's Dr, Santa Fe. 3 miles SW at Cerrillos Rd and St. Michael's Dr. Phone 505/473-6011; toll-free 800/456-2673. www.csf.edu.* (1947) (1,400 students) On campus are the Greer Garson Theatre Center, Garson Communications Center, and Fogelson Library.

Cross of the Martyrs. *Paseo de la Loma, Santa Fe. Access from the stairs on Paseo de la Loma. Phone 505/983-2567.* An ideal destination for history fans and anyone looking for a sensational city view, this large, hilltop cross weighing 76 tons and standing 25 feet tall honors the memory of more than 20 Franciscan priests and numerous Spanish colonists who were killed during the 1680 Pueblo Revolt against Spanish dominion. Dedicated in 1920, this cross

Santa Fe's Art and Architecture

Every tourist's Santa Fe exploration begins at the Plaza, plotted when the town was built in 1610. A square block planted with trees and grass, it's a place to sit on park benches to study a map or just watch the parade of visitors go by. Lining the Plaza on the east, south, and west are art galleries, Native American jewelry shops, boutiques, a vintage hotel, and restaurants. Facing the Plaza on the north is the Palace of the Governors, the first stop on your walking tour. Sheltered along the portal (porch) that spans the front of the block-long, pueblo-style building—which also dates from 1610—are dozens of craft and art vendors from the region's nearby pueblos. Only pueblo Indians can sell their jewelry, blankets, beadwork, pottery, and other goods here. Inside the palace, a museum exhibits nearly 20,000 historic objects, including pottery, books, documents, and artifacts.

One block west along Palace Avenue, the Museum of Fine Arts was built in 1917 and represents the Pueblo Revival style of architecture, also called Santa Fe style. Site of chamber music concerts, the museum exhibits work by local artists and by noted painters of the Santa Fe and Taos art colonies. Continue west on Palace another block, turning north on Grant Avenue one block, then west on Johnson Street one block. Stop inside the relatively new Georgia O'Keeffe Museum to see the world's largest collection of the artist's work.

Backtrack to the Plaza, heading to the Catron Building, which forms the east "wall" of the Plaza. Inside the 1891 office building are several art galleries and stores. At the building's southern end, anchoring the southeast corner of the Plaza, is La Fonda, the oldest hotel in Santa Fe. The lobby's art and décor are worth a look, and the rooftop bar is a favorite gathering place. From the plaza, walk south two blocks on Old Santa Fe Trail to Loretto Chapel. The beautiful chapel has an irresistible story in its Miraculous Staircase. Now walk east on Water Street one block to Cathedral Place, turning left (north) on Cathedral one block to the magnificent St. Francis Cathedral, built over several years in the latter 1800s.

Directly across the street, see the Institute of American Indian Arts Museum, housing thousands of pieces of sculpture, basketry, paintings, and pottery. Cathedral ends here at Palace Avenue, which you'll follow east one long block to explore two excellent bookstores, Nicholas Potter Bookseller and Palace Avenue Books. Backtracking on Palace again to the west, Sena Plaza is on your right (on the north side of the street). Inside the lovely, flower-filled courtyard, you'll find a 19th-century hacienda that once belonged to the Sena family and is now filled with art galleries, shops and a restaurant. Wind up back at the Plaza by following Palace another long block to the west; head to the Ore House on the Plaza's west side to review the day over refreshments.

shouldn't be confused with the newer one at nearby Fort Marcy Park. Vistas from the old cross include those of the Sangre de Cristos mountain range immediately northeast, the Jemez about 40 miles west, and the Sandias, 50 miles south near Albuquerque.

Dragon Room. *406 Old Santa Fe Trail, Santa Fe. Phone 505/983-7712.* The rustic Dragon Room in the Pink Adobe Restaurant is one of the best places to mingle with locals, spot celebrities, and enjoy the Santa Fe ambience while sipping on house specialty drinks like the "Rosalita" or "Silver Coin Margarita." The Santa Fe Reporter voted this the top bar in Santa Fe, and it's always a hot social spot on Friday and Saturday nights.

El Farol. *808 Canyon Rd, Santa Fe (87501). Phone 505/983-9912.* El Farol ("The Lantern" in Spanish) is the oldest restaurant and cantina in Santa Fe, dating back to 1835. Located near the top of Canyon Road, it serves up award-winning Mediterranean food and continues to be one of the most popular late night watering holes, offering patrons live music and a usually packed dance floor Wednesday through Saturday nights. The music tends towards Famenco, Latin, Jazz, Soul and Blues and usually gets hopping after 10 pm.

El Rancho de las Golondrinas. *334 Los Pinos Rd, Santa Fe. 13 miles S, off I-25. Phone 505/471-2261. www.golondrinas.org.* This living history museum is set in a 200-acre rural valley, and depicts Spanish Colonial life in New Mexico from 1700-1900. It was once a stop on the Camino Real, and is one of the most historic ranches in the Southwest. Original colonial buildings date from the 18th century, and special festivals and theme weekends offer visitors a glimpse of the music, dance, clothing, crafts, and celebrations of Spanish Colonial New Mexico. Self-guided tours. (June-Sept: Wed-Sun 10 am-4 pm) **$**

Federal Court House. *Federal Pl and Paseo De Peralta, Santa Fe.* There is a monument to Kit Carson in front.

Genoveva Chavez Recreation Center. *3221 Rodeo Rd, Santa Fe. Phone 505/955-4001.* The Chavez Recreation Center is housed in a massive, architecturally imposing solar complex covering several city blocks. Inside, for a small daily fee, visitors can get access to a 50-meter lap pool, leisure pool, spa, sauna, and therapy pool, competition-sized ice skating rink, basketball and racquetball courts, numerous fitness classes (extra charge), and a full line of state-of-the-art exercise equipment. **$$**

Georgia O'Keeffe Museum. *217 Johnson St, Santa Fe. Phone 505/946-1000. www.okeeffemuseum.org.* One of the most important American artists of the 20th century, Georgia O'Keeffe lived and worked at Ghost Ranch near Abiqui for much of her career, drawing inspiration from the colors and forms of the surrounding desert environment. This museum houses the world's largest permanent collection of her artwork and is also dedicated to the study of American Modernism (1890-present), displaying special exhibits of many of her contemporaries. (Nov-June: Mon-Tues, Thurs, Sat-Sun 10 am-5 pm, Fri 10 am-8 pm; closed holidays; daily rest of year) **$$**

Hyde Memorial State Park. *740 Hyde Park Rd, Santa Fe. 8 miles NE via Hwy 475. Phone 505/983-7175.* Perched 8,500 feet up in the Sangre de Cristo Mountains near the Santa Fe Ski Basin; used as base camp for backpackers and skiers in the Santa Fe National Forests. Cross-country skiing, rentals, picnicking (shelters), playground, concession, camping (electric hookups, dump station). (Daily)

Hyde Park hiking/biking trails. *Santa Fe. From the Santa Fe Plaza go north on Washington Ave, and continue several blocks to the light at Artist's Road and turn right. Continue on Artist's Rd for about 8.6 miles to a parking lot on the left side of the road just before you reach the Hyde Park RV campground.* One of the closest hiking opportunities to Santa Fe is available in the Hyde Park area on the road to the ski basin. From the Hyde Park parking lot, you can access a loop covering three different trails offering easy hiking that's popular with runners, hikers, dog walkers, and weekenders looking for a quick getaway. The loop consists of switchbacks, moderate grades, creek crossings, and fine views of the mixed conifer forest. If you come during the fall you can view the spectacularly colorful changing of the Aspen leaves. Start with the common trailhead at the far side of the parking lot. Look for the Borrego Trail (150), Bear Wallow Trail (182), and Winsor Trail (254) markings. A loop covering all three is about 4 miles long.

Institute of American Indian Arts Museum. *108 Cathedral Pl, Santa Fe. Phone 505/983-1777. www.iaiancad.org.* The Institute of American Indian Arts, established in 1962, runs a college in south Santa Fe in addition to a museum just off the Plaza. The museum is the only one in the country dedicated solely to collecting and exhibiting contemporary Native American art, much of it produced by the staff and faculty of the college. Inside you can view educational films, exhibits of contemporary artists, and outdoor sculptures in an enclosed courtyard. (June-Sept: daily 9 am-5 pm; Oct-May: daily 10 am-5 pm; closed holidays) **$$**

Kokopelli Rafting Adventures. *541 W Cordova Rd, Santa Fe. Phone toll-free 800/879-9035. www.kokopelliraft.com.* Kokopelli Rafting offers a full range of whitewater rafting trips to the Rio Grande and Rio Chama rivers as well as sea kayaking trips to Cochiti lake, Abiqui lake, and Big Bend National Park in Texas. Rafting trips cover Class II through IV rapids. Excursions include half-day, full-day, overnight and 2 to 8 day wilderness expeditions. Transportation from Santa Fe included. (Apr-Sept) **$$$$**

La Fonda Hotel. *100 E San Francisco St, Santa Fe. Phone 505/982-5511; toll-free 800/523-5002. www.lafondasantafe.com.* A longtime center of Santa Fe social life. Former meeting place of trappers, pioneers, merchants, soldiers, and politicians; known as the "Inn at the End of the Trail."

Las Cosas School of Cooking. *DeVargas Center, 181 Paseo de Peralta, Santa Fe. Phone 505/988-3394. www.lascosascooking.com.* Found within a beautiful store stocked with gourmet kitchen tools and elegant tableware, this cooking center offers hands-on culinary education experiences that fill a morning or evening. Taught by school director John Vollertsen and by chefs from New Mexico's leading restaurants, the classes cover a wide range of topics, such as artful risotto, Atkins diet dishes, soups and stocks, Oaxacan moles, the best in fish preparations, grilling, one-dish wonders, and fresh herb recipes. All kitchen supplies are provided, as are alcoholic beverages, and private classes can be arranged, too. (Classes usually at 10 am and 6 pm; closed Thanksgiving, Dec 25, Jan 1) **$$$$**

Lensic Performing Arts Center. *211 W San Francisco St, Santa Fe. Phone 505/988-7050. www.lensic.com.* The Lensic Theater is one of Santa Fe's historical and architectural gems, reopened after a full restoration completed in 2001. The structure was first built in 1931 in a Moorish/Spanish Renaissance style and has always been Santa Fe's premiere theater space, having played host to celebrities such as Roy Rogers and Judy Garland over the years. Since reopening, it has provided a constantly changing schedule of quality theater, symphony, and performing arts events.

Loretto Chapel. *207 Old Santa Fe Trail, Santa Fe. Phone 505/982-0092. www.lorettochapel.com.* The Loretto Chapel was built in 1873 and is one of the few non adobe-style buildings in downtown Santa Fe. Modeled after St. Chapelle cathedral in Paris, it was the first Gothic building built west of the Missisippi. The chapel itself is not particularly impressive, but what draws countless tourists is the "miraculous stairway", a two-story spiral wooden staircase built without any nails or central supports that seems to defy engineering logic. (Summer: Mon-Sat 9 am-6 pm, Sun 10:30 am-5 pm; winter: Mon-Sat 9 am-5 pm, Sun 10:30 am-5 pm)

Museum of Fine Arts. *107 W Palace Ave, Santa Fe. Phone 505/476-5072. www.museumofnewmexico.org.* Designed by Isaac Hamilton Rapp in 1917, the museum is one of Santa Fe's earliest Pueblo revival structures and its oldest art museum. It contains more than 20,000 holdings, with an emphasis on Southwest regional art and the artists of Santa Fe and Taos from the early 20th century. The St. Francis Auditorium inside the museum also presents lectures, musical events, plays, and various other performances. Free admission on Friday evenings. (Tues-Sun 10 am-5 pm, Fri 5-8 pm) **$$$**

Museum of Spanish Colonial Art. *Museum Hill, 750 Camino Lejo, Santa Fe. Phone 505/982-2226. www.spanishcolonial.org.* This small museum holds some 3,000 objects showcasing traditional Hispanic art in New Mexico dating from conquest to present day. The galleries are housed in a building designed in 1930 by famous local architect John Gaw Meem, gracefully restored with historically accurate appointments. The collection includes many early works in wood, tin, and other local materials as well as numerous works by contemporary New Mexican artists who continue the rich Hispanic artistic traditions to this day. (Tues-Sun 10 am-5 pm; closed Thanksgiving, Dec 25) **$$$**

Oldest House. *De Vargas St and Old Santa Fe Trail, Santa Fe.* Believed to be pre-Spanish; built by Native Americans more than 800 years ago.

Palace of the Governors. *105 Palace Ave, Santa Fe. Phone 505/476-5100. www.palaceofthegovernors.org.* Built in 1610, this is the oldest public building in continuous use in the US. It was the seat of government in New Mexico for more than 300 years. Lew Wallace, governor of the territory (1878-1881), wrote part of *Ben Hur* here in 1880. It is now a major museum of Southwestern history. The Palace, Museum of Fine Arts, Museum of Indian Arts and Culture, Museum of International Folk Art, and state monuments all make up the Museum of New Mexico. Free admission Friday evenings. Tours (Mon-Sat 10:15 am-noon). (Tues-Sun 10 am-5 pm, Fri 5-8 pm; closed holidays) **$$**

Pecos National Historical Park. *25 miles SE via Hwy 25, in Pecos. Phone 505/757-6414. www.nps.gov/peco.* The ruins of Pecos Pueblo lie on a mesa along the Santa Fe Trail that served as a strategic trade route and crossroads between Pueblo and Plains Indian cultures. At its peak, the Pueblo housed a community of as many as 2,000 people, and was occupied for nearly 500 years. When the Spanish arrived, it became an important missionary outpost that continued to be occupied until the 1800s when its last inhabitants relocated to Jemez Pueblo. Ruins of the original multi-story structures survive in the form of large stone walls and several ceremonial kivas that have been restored. The largest ruins are of two Spanish missionary churches that were destroyed in the Pueblo revolt of 1680. An easy 1.25-mile hike and self-guided tour allows visitors to explore the ruins at their own pace. The visitor center includes historical exhibits and shows an introductory film covering the area's history. (Daily 8 am-5 pm; closed Dec 25) **$$**

The Plaza. *100 Old Santa Fe Trail, Santa Fe.* The Santa Fe Plaza, steeped in a rich history, has been a focal point for commerce and social activities in Santa Fe since the early 17th century. The area is marked by a central tree-lined park surrounded by some of Santa Fe's most important historical landmarks, many of which survive from Spanish colonial times. The most important landmark is the Palace of the Governors, which was the original seat of local government and is the oldest public building in the US still in use. Native American artists from nearby Pueblos sell handmade artwork in front of the Palace, and various museums, shops, and dining establishments surround the Plaza, making it the top tourist destination in Santa Fe. Numerous festivals and activities are held in the Plaza throughout the year, including the Spanish Market and the Indian Market.

San Felipe's Casino Hollywood and Hollywood Hills Speedway. *25 Hagan Rd, San Felipe. 30 miles S of Santa Fe via I-25. Phone 505/867-6700; toll-free 877/529-2946. www.sanfelipecasino.com.* This multiuse complex situated midway between Santa Fe and Albuquerque on the San Felipe Pueblo brings something akin to Las Vegas-style entertainment to New Mexico. Within the casino, guests find abundant gaming opportunities, as well as showroom entertainment. (Mon-Thurs 8 am-4 pm, Fri-Sat 24 hours) Also on site is the Hollywood Hills Speedway, opened in 2002 and known as the state's premier venue of its kind. The 3/8-mile clay oval speedway for auto and motorcycle racing is viewed from a grandstand seating 10,000, as well as from sky boxes. Also look for monster truck shows, extreme sports events, and outdoor concerts, with entertainers ranging from country music acts to specialty cultural performers.

San Ildefonso Pueblo. *Santa Fe. 16 miles N on Hwy 84, 285, then 6 miles W on Hwy 502. Phone 505/455-2273.* (Population: 447) This pueblo is famous for its beautiful surroundings and its black, red, and polychrome pottery, made famous by Maria Poveka Martinez. (Daily; closed winter weekends; visitors must register at the visitor center) Photography permit may be purchased at the visitor center (fee). Various festivals take place here throughout the year (see SPECIAL EVENTS). The circular structure with the staircase leading up to its rim is a kiva, or ceremonial chamber. There are two shops in the pueblo plaza, and a tribal museum adjoins the governor's office. One-half mile west is a fishing lake. **$$**

San Miguel Mission. *401 Old Santa Fe Trail, Santa Fe. Phone 505/983-3974.* Built in the early 1600s, this is the oldest church in the US still in use. Construction was overseen by Fray Alonso de Benavidez, along with a group of Tlaxcala Indians from Mexico who did most of the work. The original adobe still remains beneath the stucco walls, and the interior has been restored along with Santa Fe's oldest wooden reredos (altar screen). Church services are still held on Sundays. (Sun 1-4:30 pm; summer: Mon-Sat 9 am-4:30 pm; winter: Mon-Sat 10 am-4 pm; closed holidays) **DONATION**

Santa Fe Children's Museum. *1050 Old Pecos Trail, Santa Fe. Phone 505/989-8359. www.santafechildrensmuseum.org.* Happy activity fills a creative space that absorbs the attention of children of all ages. Hands-on exhibits invite kids to make magnetic structures, route water streams, create paintings, illustrate cartoon movies, discover plants on a greenhouse scavenger hunt, scale an 18-foot-high climbing wall, use an old-fashioned pitcher pump, and weave beads and fabric on a loom. Local artists and scientists make appearances to teach kids in playful, inventive ways. Especially interesting are regularly scheduled events like "Music Under the Big Top" and "Ice Cream Sunday." (Wed-Sat 10 am-5 pm, Sun noon-5 pm; closed holidays) **$**

Santa Fe National Forest. *1474 Rodeo Rd, Santa Fe. Phone 505/438-7840.* This forest consists of over 1 1/2 million acres. Fishing is excellent in the Pecos and Jemez rivers and tributary streams. Hiking trails are close to unusual geologic formations. Hot springs in the Jemez Mountains. Four wilderness areas within the forest total more than 300,000 acres. Campgrounds are provided by the Forest Service at more than 40 locations; for reservations call 800/280-2267. There are user fees for many areas. Forest headquarters are located here.

Santa Fe Premium Outlets. *8380 Cerrillos Rd, Santa Fe. Phone 505/474-4000. www.premiumoutlets.com.* Shop for bargain-priced designer apparel, shoes, luggage, jewelry, housewares, and other accessories at New Mexico's only outlet center. Located on the south side off Cerrillos Road, the more than 40 stores include such well-known brands as Bass, Bose, Brooks

Brothers, Dansk, Eddie Bauer, Liz Claiborne, Nautica, Samsonite, Van Hausen, and many more. (Daily)

Santa Fe Rafting Company. *1000 Cerrillos Rd, Santa Fe. Phone 505/988-4914; toll-free 800/467-7238. www.santaferafting.com.* The Rio Grande and Rio Chama rivers north of Santa Fe provide excellent opportunities for river running and white water rafting, offering Class II through Class IV rapids. Santa Fe Rafting Company offers several rafting trips including half-day, full-day and multi-day camping excursions, some of which include a boxed lunch. The biggest rapids are found on their Taos Box full-day trip, open to anyone over age 12. All trips include roundtrip transportation from Santa Fe. (Apr-Sept) **$$$$**

Santa Fe School of Cooking. *116 W San Francisco St, Santa Fe. Phone 505/983-4511. www.santafeschoolofcooking.com.* Sign up for classes offered several times weekly in traditional and contemporary Southwestern cuisine. Culinary tours involve classes with nationally renowned chefs with trips to local farms and wineries. Call for schedule.

Santa Fe Southern Railway. *410 S Guadalupe St, Santa Fe. Phone 505/989-8600; toll-free 888/989-8600. www.sfsr.com.* Made famous by the 1940's swing tune "Atchison, Topeka & Santa Fe," a small part of this historical rail line continues as the Santa Fe Southern Railway, which still carries freight and tourists between Santa Fe and nearby Lamy, an 18-mile trip. The start of the route is housed in the old Santa Fe Depot, where you can view vintage railcars and shop for gifts and memorabilia in the original mission-style train depot. Several scenic train rides in restored vintage cars are offered to the public, following the original high desert route to and from Lamy. The rides cater to tourists and range from short scenic roundtrips to longer outings that include picnics, BBQs, and various holiday-themed events, such as the Halloween Highball Train and New Year's Eve Party Train. **$$$$**

Santuario de Guadalupe. *100 Guadalupe St, Santa Fe. Phone 505/988-2027.* Built in 1781, and the oldest shrine in America dedicated to Our Lady of Guadalupe, the Santuario has been converted into an art and history museum specializing in religious art and iconography. The holdings include a large collection of Northern New Mexican santos (carved wooden saints) and paintings in the Italian Renaissance and Mexican baroque styles. A famous rendering of Our Lady of Guadalupe by renowned Mexican artist Jose de Alzibar is also on display. (Nov-Apr: Mon-Fri 9 am-4 pm; May-Oct: Mon-Sat 9 am-4 pm; closed holidays) **FREE**

Scottish Rite Temple. *463 Paseo De Peralta, Santa Fe. Phone 505/982-4414.* Modeled after part of the Alhambra. (Mon-Fri 9 am-noon, 1-4 pm)

Sena Plaza and Prince Plaza. *Washington and Palace aves, Santa Fe.* Small shops, formerly old houses, built behind portals and around central patios.

Shidoni Bronze Foundry and Gallery. *1508 Bishop's Lodge Rd, Santa Fe. Phone 505/988-8001. www.shidoni.com.* A fantastic resource for art collectors and sculptors, Shidoni consists of a bronze foundry, art gallery, and outdoor sculpture garden set in an 8-acre apple orchard 5 miles north of Santa Fe. Artists from around the country come to work at Shidoni's 14,000-square-foot foundry, open to the general public for self-guided tours. Explore the lovely sculpture garden during daylight hours or shop for works of bronze and metal in the adjacent gallery. Gallery (Mon-Sat 9 am-5 pm). Foundry (Mon-Fri noon-1 pm, Sat 9 am-5 pm).

Ski Santa Fe. *2209 Brothers Rd, Santa Fe. Take Paseo de Peralta to Bishop Lodge Rd and turn N onto Bishop Lodge Rd. Continue one block and turn right on Artist Rd (which becomes Hyde Park Rd) and follow to the top of the mountain (approximately 16 miles). Phone 505/982-4429. www.skisantafe.com.* World-class skiing and snowboarding in the majestic Sangre de Cristo mountains is only a 20-minute drive from the downtown Santa Fe Plaza. Ski Santa Fe is a family-owned resort catering to skiers and snowboarders of all levels, from beginning to expert. In addition to breathtaking views of the city below, the 12,053-foot summit offers six lifts and 44 runs (20 percent easy, 40 percent more difficult, 40 percent most difficult), with a total of 660 acres of terrain. The longest run is 3 miles, and the mountain offers a vertical drop of 1,700 feet. The average yearly snowfall is 225 inches. A PSIA-certified ski school offers group and private lessons for adults and children, and there are restaurants, rental shops, and a clothing boutique on site. The Chipmunk Corner offers activities and lessons for children ages 4-9. (Late Nov-early Apr, daily) **$$$$**

State Capitol. *Old Santa Fe Trail at Paseo de Peralta, Santa Fe. Phone 505/986-4589.* (1966) This unique building, in modified Territorial style, is round and intended to resemble a Zia sun symbol. Self-guided tours. (Mid-May-Aug: Mon-Sat 8 am-7 pm; Sept-mid-May: Mon-Fri 8 am-7 pm; closed holidays) **FREE**

Swig. *135 W Palace Ave, Level 3, Santa Fe. Phone 505/955-0400.* This is Santa Fe's swankiest bar/nightclub. Swig offers four different bar areas (mostly nonsmoking) and a very red dance floor all set in an intoxicatingly contemporary atmosphere. Sip the expensive but refreshingly creative martinis (starting at $11) or sample the excellent pan-Asian tapas. The dance floor will keep you entertained while a fresh roster of rotating DJs spin. Be sure to dress the part: Swig does enforce a dress code. (Tues-Thurs 5 pm-midnight, Fri-Sat 5 pm-1 am)

Ten Thousand Waves. *3451 Hyde Park Rd, Santa Fe. Take Paseo de Peralta to Bishop Lodge Rd and turn N onto Bishop Lodge Rd. Continue one block and turn right at Artist Rd (which becomes Hyde Park Rd) and follow to the sign on left side of winding road (approximately 4 miles). Phone 505/982-9304. www.tenthousandwaves.com.* When you feel like being pampered, this exquisite Japanese-themed spa and bathhouse is a genuine treat. Located in a unique Zenlike setting in the Sangre de Cristo Mountains, Ten Thousand Waves offers soothing hot tubs, massages, facials, and other spa treatments to make you forget your cares. The choices here are endless: hand, foot, scalp, and full-body massages, herbal wraps, rejuvenating facials, and a variety of open-air hot tubs, including coed public hot tubs (where clothing is optional before 8:15 pm), a women-only tub, secluded private tubs, and large private tubs that can accommodate up to 20. Whichever you choose, you'll find all tubs clean and inviting (and chlorine-free), and amenities such as kimonos, towels, sandals, lotion, and lockers provided for you. Be sure to call ahead for reservations, especially for massage services. (Daily) **$$$$**

★ **Turquoise Trail.** *PO Box 303, Sandia Park. Drive S from Santa Fe via I-25, exiting New Mexico Hwy 14 S toward Madrid. Phone 505/281-5233. www.turquoisetrail.org.* Undeniably the most interesting path between Albuquerque and Santa Fe, this poetically named route is the 50-mile reach of New Mexico 14 that parallels I-25 north from I-40 and a National Scenic Byway. Cutting a course along the backside of the Sandias just north of Albuquerque, the trail winds through a rolling countryside of sumptuous, cactus-littered hills populated by tiny burgs. Along the way, watch for the mountain sun to cast spectacular purples and roses on crumbling rock houses, ancient family cemeteries, and long-abandoned ranch houses and barns. Stops include the town of Golden, where the first discovery of gold west of the Mississippi was made and where a silver boom once employed more than 1,200 workers; and Madrid (pronounced MAD-rid), once rich in coal mines but today the refuge of artists whose galleries and shops have become lucrative businesses. The wonderful Mine Shaft Tavern offers burgers, buffalo steaks, and cold beer, along with live entertainment on weekends.

Special Events

AID and Comfort Gala. *Eldorado Hotel, 309 W San Francisco St, Santa Fe. Phone 505/989-3399. www.aidandcomfort.org.* Since 1989, the organization Aid and Comfort has raised money to benefit those suffering from HIV and AIDS. The annual gala kicks off the holiday season on the Saturday after Thanksgiving with a lavish bash at the Eldorado Hotel, featuring live music for dancing, a buffet, and a silent auction. Sat after Thanksgiving. **$$$$**

Christmas Eve Canyon Road Walk. *Santa Fe Plaza, Canyon Rd, Santa Fe. Starts at the foot of Canyon Road near Paseo De Peralta. Phone toll-free 800/777-2489.* Adorned with thousands of farolitos, traditional luminaries (lights made of a single small candle inside a paper bag), the streets and homes around Canyon Road play host to a unique and colorful festival each Christmas Eve. Literally thousands of pedestrians stroll up and down the streets while singing Christmas carols, lighting bonfires, and enjoying hot apple cider. A major Santa Fe tradition not to be missed. Dec 24. **FREE**

Christmas Eve Celebrations. *Santa Fe. Phone toll-free 800/777-2489.* In Santa Fe and nearby villages, with street fires and farolitos (paper bag lanterns) "to guide the Christ Child," candlelit Nacimientos (nativity scenes), and other events. Santo Domingo, Tesuque, Santa Clara, and other pueblos have Christmas dances the following three days. Late Dec.

Eight Northern Pueblos Arts & Crafts Show. *San Juan Pueblo, Santa Fe. artnewmexico.com/eightnorthern/index.shtml.* This annual festival features traditional and contemporary Native American art at more than 500 booths. Approximately 1,500 artists attend and have their work judged for prizes before being displayed for sale. Third weekend in July.

Fiesta and Green Corn Dance. *San Felipe Pueblo, Santa Fe.* Early May.

Fiesta at Santo Domingo Pueblo. *Santo Domingo Pueblo, Santa Fe. Phone 505/465-2214.* Corn dance. This fiesta is probably the largest and most famous of the Rio Grande pueblo fiestas. Early Aug.

Indian Market. *Santa Fe Plaza, Santa Fe. Phone 505/983-5220. www.swaia.org/indianmrkt.html.* Each year in late August, the Santa Fe Indian Market attracts a swarm of national and international buyers and collectors to the largest and oldest Native American arts show and market in the world. More than 1,200 artists from over 100 North American tribes participate in the show, with around 600 outdoor booths set up in the middle of the ancient Santa Fe Plaza. The market is a great opportunity to meet the artists and buy directly from them instead of going through the usual galleries and other middlemen. Quality of work is stressed, as all sale items are strictly screened for quality and authenticity. Numerous outdoor booths sell food, and the event draws an estimated 100,000 visitors to Santa Fe during the weekend, so make your lodging reservations well in advance. Late Aug.

Invitational Antique Indian Art Show. *Sweeney Center, 201 W Marcy, Santa Fe. Phone 505/984-6760.* Largest show of its kind in the country. Pre-1935 items; attracts dealers, collectors, museums. Two days in mid-Aug.

Mountain Man Rendezvous and Festival. *105 W Palace Ave, Santa Fe. Phone 505/476-5100. www.palaceofthegovernors.org.* In early August, costumed mountain men ride into town on horseback for the Museum of New Mexico's annual buffalo roast, part of a large gathering of trappers and traders from the pre-1840 wilderness. Participants sell primitive equipment, tools, and trinkets and compete in period survival skills such as knife and tomahawk throwing, muzzleloader rifle shooting, cannon firing, storytelling, and foot races. Early Aug.

Santa Fe Chamber Music Festival. *PO Box 2227, Santa Fe. St. Francis Auditorium, Museum of Fine Arts, and the Lensic Performing Arts Center. Phone 505/983-2075. www.sfcmf.org.* Since the first season of the festival in 1973, when Pablo Casals was the founding, honorary president, this artistic tradition has grown into a major event consisting of more than 80 performances, open rehearsals, concert previews, and roundtable discussions with composers and musicians during the annual summer season. The celebrated "Composer-in-Residence" Program has hosted luminaries such as Aaron Copland, Ellen Taafe Zwilich, and John Harbison, and the festival has sent ensembles on national tours since 1980. Performances are frequently heard on National Public Radio, and the festival fosters a significant outreach program to Santa Fe schools. Check for performances scheduled at St. Francis Auditorium, Museum of Fine Arts, and the Lensic Performing Arts Center. July-Aug.

Santa Fe Fiesta. *Santa Fe Plaza, Santa Fe. Phone 505/988-7575.* This ancient folk festival, dating back to 1712, features historical pageantry, religious observances, arts and crafts shows, and street dancing. It also celebrates the reconquest of Santa Fe by Don Diego de Vargas in 1692. Make reservations well in advance. First weekend in Sept.

Santa Fe Opera. *Hwys 84/285, Santa Fe. Drive N from Santa Fe about 7 miles via Hwy 84/285; the Opera is on the W side of the highway. Phone 505/986-5900; toll-free 800/280-4654. www.santafeopera.org.* Founded in 1957, this opera company presents one of the world's most famous and respected opera festivals each summer from early July through late August. Each season, the company stages five works, including two classics, a lesser-known work by a well-known composer, a Richard Strauss offering, and a world premiere or new American staging. Possibly more dramatic and appealing, even to an opera novice, is the Santa Fe Opera's home, a breathtaking hilltop amphitheater found about 7 miles north of the city. Designed by Polshek & Partners of New York, who refurbished Carnegie Hall in Manhattan, the Opera incorporates bold, swooping lines with excellent sight lines and is known for superb acoustics. Featured stars frequently include those from New York's Metropolitan Opera, among many others, and the festival is known for offering an exemplary apprentice program to young opera hopefuls. Backstage tours (early July-late Aug: Mon-Sat at 1 pm, fee)(Performances begin between 8 pm and 9 pm) **$$$$**

Santa Fe Pro Musica. *Lensic Performing Arts Center, 211 W San Francisco St, Santa Fe. Phone 505/988-4640; toll-free 800/960-6680. www.santafepromusica.com.*

Chamber orchestra and chamber ensemble perform classical and contemporary music, also performance of Messiah during Christmas season, Mozart Festival in Feb. Sept-May. **$$$$**

Santa Fe Rodeo. *Santa Fe Rodeo Grounds, 2801 W Rodeo Rd, Santa Fe. Phone 505/471-4300. www.rodeodesantafe.com.* The Santa Fe Rodeo offers the chance to see real live cowboys and bucking broncos in action at the outdoor rodeo fairgrounds. Various professional competitions and public exhibitions open to the public are put on during the brief summer season. Rodeo events generally happen during evening and weekend matinee hours. A downtown rodeo parade takes place in mid-June at the start of the season. **$$$$**

Santa Fe Stages. *Santa Fe. Performances held at the Lensic Performing Arts Center and the Armory for the Arts. Phone 505/982-6683. www.santafestages.org.* With presentations offered primarily at the wonderfully renovated, historic Lensic Performing Arts Center, Santa Fe Stages hosts a season of dance, music, and theater with national and regional appeal. The season typically begins before Memorial Day and ends in late September, and may offer Irish folk dance, classical ballet, opera, jazz, drama, comedy, or cabaret shows. Late May-late Sept.

Santa Fe Symphony and Chorus. *Lensic Performing Arts Center, 211 W San Francisco St, Santa Fe. Phone 505/983-3530. www.sf-symphony.org.* Santa Fe's orchestral company presents works in classical and jazz music, as well as specialty programs that may include the music of Spain and Mexico. Look for a blend of genres for the season-ender, which could include Copland's *Fanfare for the Modern Man*, Ellington's *The River*, and Dvorak's *Symphony No. 9 (New World)*. The season generally runs from early October through Memorial Day, with matinee and evening performances at the Lensic Performing Arts Center. Early Oct-late May. **$$$$**

Santa Fe Wine and Chile Fiesta. *Santa Fe Opera grounds, Hwys 84/285, Santa Fe. Phone 505/438-8060. www.santafewineandchile.org.* Begun in 1991, this wildly popular festival honoring the best in food and drink brings in some 2,000 appreciative fans from around the state and across the country for four days of noshing and sipping on the last weekend in September. Roughly 30 local restaurants and 90 wineries from around the globe team up with a half-dozen or so of America's top celebrity chefs and cookbook authors to present a culinary extravaganza in a variety of venues around town. Wine seminars, cooking demonstrations, special vintners' lunches and dinners, and the gastronomic circus called the Grand Tasting, staged in mammoth tents on the Santa Fe Opera grounds, fill a palate-thrilling schedule. Late Sept. **$$$$**

Shakespeare in Santa Fe. *St. John's College, 1516 Pacheco St, Santa Fe. Phone 505/982-2910. www.shakespearesantafe.org.* Established in 1987, the Santa Fe Shakespeare Company is a professional group that presents classical and contemporary theater to the community, with an emphasis in bringing works to young people. Each season, one of the works by William Shakespeare is presented in an outdoor setting, but the majority of presentations are made at St. John's College in the Meem Library Courtyard and at the Lensic Performing Arts Center, and a few are staged at venues like the Museum of Indian Arts and Culture. Classic Fairy Tales are among the presentations arranged specifically for Santa Fe families. Look for Shakespeare works to be presented in May and June. **$$$$**

Spanish Market. *Museum of Spanish Colonial Art, 750 Camino Lejo, Santa Fe. Phone 505/982-2226. www.spanishmarket.org.* The rich and colorful Hispanic art traditions of Northern New Mexico are celebrated twice a year during Spanish Market, the oldest and largest exhibition and sale of traditional Hispanic art in the US. The smaller winter market in December is held indoors in the Sweeney Convention Center (201 W Marcy St), while the larger summer market occupies the entire Santa Fe Plaza for one weekend in July. During the market as many as 300 vendors sell and display santos (carved saints), hide paintings, textiles, furniture, jewelry, tinwork, basketry, pottery, bonework, and other locally produced handicrafts reflecting the unique and deeply religious traditional art which still flourishes in this part of New Mexico. Sponsored by the Spanish Colonial Arts Society. Dec and late July.

Spring Corn Dances. *Cochiti, San Felipe, Santo Domingo, and other pueblos, Santa Fe. Phone 505/843-7270.* Races, contests. Late May-early June.

St. Anthony's Feast-Comanche Dance. *San Clara Pueblo, Santa Fe. Phone 505/843-7270.* Mid-June.

Tesuque Pueblo Flea Market. *Hwy 84/285, Santa Fe. From Santa Fe, take St. Francis Dr N, which turns into Hwy 84/285 as you leave town. Continue N for approximately 5.5 miles. The Flea Market is located on the left side of the highway next to the Santa Fe Opera. Phone 505/995-8626. www.tesuquepueblofleamarket.com.* At the Tesuque Pueblo outdoor flea market, you'll find hundreds of vendors offering antiques, gems, jewelry, pottery, rugs, and world folk art of all descriptions at very competitive prices. Plan on devoting a couple of hours to browse all the various treasures and myriad of vendor booths stretching for several acres. Even if you don't buy anything, it's a browser's paradise well worth the 15-minute drive from Santa Fe.

Zozobra Festival. *Fort Marcy Park, 490 Washington Ave, Santa Fe. Phone 505/983-7700. www.zozobra.com.* Each year on the Thursday before Labor Day, the Kiwanis Club of Santa Fe hosts the burning of Zozobra, a 50-foot effigy of "Old Man Gloom", whose passing away is designed to dispel the hardships and travails of the previous year. Zozobra started in 1924 as part of the Fiestas celebration, when a local artist conceived a ritual based on a Yaqui Indian celebration from Mexico. Over the years, Zozobra caught on and the crowd sizes have grown, making Zozobra Santa Fe's largest, most colorful and most spectacular festival. Lasting for several hours, as many as 60,000 visitors crowd into a large grassy field in Fort Marcy Park to listen to live bands, watch spectacular fireworks displays, and cheer the ritual burning. Fiestas celebrations continue during the Labor Day weekend with all day booths and activities set up in the nearby plaza. Thurs before Labor Day. **$$**

Limited-Service Hotels

★ COMFORT INN SANTA FE. *4312 Cerrillos Rd, Santa Fe (87505). Phone 505/474-7330; fax 505/474-7330. www.comfortinn.com.* 50 rooms. Check-in 3 pm, check-out noon. **$**

★★ HOTEL PLAZA REAL. *125 Washington Ave, Santa Fe (87501). Phone 505/988-4900; toll-free 877/901-7666; fax 505/983-9322. www.buynewmexico.com.* Territorial-style architecture; fireplaces, handcrafted Southwestern furniture. 56 rooms, 3 story. Pets accepted. Check-in 3 pm, check-out noon. Restaurant, bar. **$$**

★★ HOTEL SANTA FE. *1501 Paseo De Peralta, Santa Fe (87501). Phone 505/982-1200; toll-free 800/825-9876; fax 505/984-2211. www.hotelsantafe.com.* This hotel features such extras as storytelling in front of the kiva fireplace, ceremonial dances and pottery/paintings. Guests can also relax in the swimming pool, whirlpool or with a massage. 129 rooms, 3 story. Pets accepted. Check-in 2 pm, check-out noon. Restaurant, bar. Outdoor pool, whirlpool. Airport transportation available. **$$**

★★ HOTEL ST. FRANCIS. *210 Don Gaspar Ave, Santa Fe (87501). Phone 505/983-5700; toll-free 800/529-5700; fax 505/989-7690. www.hotelstfrancis.com.* As part of the Historic Inns of America, this property was originally built in 1880 and then rebuilt in 1923 after a fire in 1922. Each room has a high ceiling and original windows, some with mountain views. The inn is one block from the historic plaza and close to museums, shops and galleries. Concierge services, an all day restaurant and afternoon tea service are available. 83 rooms, 3 story. Check-in 3 pm, check-out 11 am. Restaurant, two bars. **$$**

★ LA QUINTA INN. *4298 Cerrillos Road, Santa Fe (87507). Phone 505/471-1142; fax 505/438-7219. www.laquinta.com.* 130 rooms, 3 story. Pets accepted; fee. Complimentary continental breakfast. Check-in 3 pm, check-out noon. Outdoor pool. **$**

Full-Service Hotels

★★★ ELDORADO HOTEL. *309 W San Francisco St, Santa Fe (87501). Phone 505/988-4455; toll-free 800/955-4455; fax 505/995-4555. www.eldoradohotel.com.* The Eldorado Hotel's imposing Pueblo Revival-style building is one of Santa Fe's largest and most important landmarks. Its lobby and interiors are lavishly decorated with an extensive collection of original Southwest art. The lobby lounge is a great spot for snacking, people-watching, and enjoying live entertainment. Sunday brunch is served in the cozy Eldorado Court, voted "Best Brunch" by the residents of Santa Fe. 219 rooms, 5 story. Pets accepted; fee. Check-in 4 pm, check-out 11:30 am. High-speed Internet access. Two restaurants, bar. Fitness room. Rooftop pool, whirlpool. Business center. **$$$**

★★★ **HILTON SANTA FE.** *100 Sandoval St, Santa Fe (87501). Phone 505/988-2811; toll-free 800/336-3676; fax 505/986-6435. www.hiltonofsantafe.com.* Located within walking distance of the Plaza in a 380-year-old family estate, this property embodies the history found in Santa Fe. Guest rooms feature locally handcrafted furnishings and include in-room coffee, hair dryers, and data ports. 157 rooms, 3 story. Check-in 4 pm, check-out noon. Two restaurants, bar. Fitness room. Outdoor pool, whirlpool. Airport transportation available. Business center. **$$**

★★★ **INN AND SPA AT LORETTO.** *211 Old Santa Fe Trail, Santa Fe (87501). Phone 505/988-5531; toll-free 800/727-5531; fax 505/984-7968. www.hotelloretto.com.* Adobe building built in 1975, this hotel offers guests a heated outdoor pool, 12 specialty shops, and galleries. Guests can also enjoy skiing, hiking, tennis and horseback riding. 135 rooms, 4 story. Check-in 3 pm, check-out noon. Restaurant, bar. Fitness room, spa. Outdoor pool. **$$**

★★★★ **INN OF THE ANASAZI.** *113 Washington Ave, Santa Fe (87501). Phone 505/988-3030; toll-free 800/688-8100; fax 505/988-3277. www.innoftheanasazi.com.* Native American, Hispanic, and cowboy cultures collide at the Inn of the Anasazi, where a masterful blend of New Mexican legacies results in a stunning and unusual lodging. The true spirit of Santa Fe is captured here, where enormous handcrafted doors open to a world of authentic artwork, carvings, and textiles synonymous with the Southwest. The lobby sets a sense of place for arriving guests with its rough-hewn tables, leather furnishings, unique objects, and huge cactus plants in terracotta pots. Located just off the historic Plaza, the inn was designed to resemble the traditional dwellings of the Anasazi. The region's integrity is maintained in the guest rooms, where fireplaces and four-poster beds reside under ceilings of vigas and latillas, and guests discover toiletries made locally with native cedar extract. Artfully prepared, the meals of the Anasazi's restaurant earn praise for honoring the area's culinary heritage. 59 rooms, 3 story. Pets accepted; fee. Check-in 3 pm, check-out noon. Restaurant, bar. Fitness room. **$$$**

★★★ **LA POSADA DE SANTA FE.** *330 E Palace Ave, Santa Fe (87501). Phone 505/986-0000; toll-free 800/727-5276; fax 505/982-6850. www.rockresorts.com.* Nestled on 6 lushly landscaped acres, La Posada de Santa Fe Resort & Spa effortlessly blends past and present. The original Staab House, dating to 1870, is the focal point of the resort, and the lovely rooms and suites are scattered throughout the gardens in a village setting. Adobe casitas surround the Victorian/Second Empire Staab mansion (1882); guest rooms are either Pueblo Revival or Victorian in style. Warm colors mix with Spanish colonial and old-world style, and every amenity has been added. Relaxation is the order of the day here, especially at the fantastic Avanyu Spa with its Native American-themed treatments using local ingredients. The resort's Fuego Restaurant is a standout for its innovative food with Spanish and Mexican inflections, while the historic Staab House is an inviting setting for American classics. 157 rooms, 2 story. Check-in 4 pm, check-out noon. Restaurant, bar. Fitness room, spa. Outdoor pool, whirlpool. **$$$**

Full-Service Resorts

★★★ **BISHOP'S LODGE.** *1297 Bishop's Lodge Rd, Santa Fe (87504). Phone 505/983-6377; toll-free 800/732-2240; fax 505/989-8739. www.bishopslodge.com.* The Bishop's Lodge Resort & Spa is a Santa Fe treasure. This historic resort has been welcoming guests since 1918, and its beloved chapel, listed on the National Register of Historic Places, remains a popular site for weddings. This resort is vintage chic, with rooms decorated with a 1930s Santa Fe flair. Lush colors, Navajo rugs, and kiva fireplaces reflect local pride. While modern American cuisine is the focus at the restaurant, the ShaNah spa is influenced by Native American traditions. Each treatment begins with a soothing drumming and blessing, adding to the uniqueness of this resort. Skiing in Santa Fe and nearby Taos attract winter visitors, while summer lures horseback enthusiasts. 88 rooms, 3 story. Pets accepted. Check-in 4 pm, check-out noon. Restaurant, bar. Children's activity center. Fitness room, spa. Outdoor pool, whirlpool. Tennis. **$$$**

★★★ **HYATT REGENCY TAMAYA RESORT & SPA.** *1300 Tamaya Trail, Santa Ana Peublo (87004). Phone 505/867-1234. www.hyatt.com.* Calling 500 acres of unspoiled desert beauty home, the Hyatt Regency Tamaya Resort & Spa shares the magic of New Mexico with its visitors. Pueblo-style buildings, open-air courtyards, and striking views of the Sandia Mountains and the Bosque capture the spirit of the area. Mood-elevating turquoises and bright oranges are used throughout the public and private spaces, and distinctive artwork leaves a lasting impression. Golf, tennis, and hot air ballooning are among the recreational opportunities available at this family-friendly resort, where kids can participate in special programs geared for their interests. Like the Hyatt itself, the restaurants are a showcase of Southwestern flavors, offering sophisticated takes on local favorites. 350 rooms, 4 story. Check-out noon. Restaurant. Fitness room, spa. Pool, whirlpool. Golf. Business center. **$$**

★★★ **RANCHO ENCANTADO RESORT.** *198 State Rd 592, Santa Fe (87501). Phone 505/982-3537; toll-free 800/722-9339; fax 505/983-8269. www.nmhotels.com/html/sfranchencantado.html.* If only the walls could talk at Rancho Encantado. This legendary hideaway has played host to many of the world's most influential people, including Prince Rainier, Princess Grace, and the Dalai Lama. Once visitors catch a glimpse of this ranch nestled in the foothills of the Sangre de Cristo Mountains, it is no surprise that it has beckoned so many since the 1950's. Casitas with kiva fireplaces and outdoor hot tubs are scattered throughout the 200-acre property, offering guests the highest levels of privacy. This luxurious guest ranch-style resort is renowned for its horseback riding and equestrian center, and the Acacia spa is a relaxing addition. Western cuisine is spotlighted at The Restaurant, while the Green Room serves breakfast and sushi using ingredients from its working greenhouse. 55 rooms. Check-in 3 pm, check-out 11 am. Restaurant, bar. Pool, whirlpool. Tennis. **$$**

Full-Service Inns

★★★ **GALISTEO INN.** *9 La Vega, Galisteo (87540). Phone 505/466-8200; fax 505/466-4008. www.galisteoinn.com.* Guests can tour the area on mountain bikes, horseback, or by hiking. Located just a half hour from Pecos National Monument and nearby Santa Fe, guests can enjoy a true Southwestern vacation. Hacienda on 8 acres built in the 1750s. 12 rooms. Children over 6 years only. Complimentary full breakfast. Check-in 4-6 pm, check-out 11 am. Restaurant, bar. Outdoor pool, whirlpool. **$**

★★★ **INN OF THE GOVERNORS.** *101 W Alameda, Santa Fe (87501). Phone 505/982-4333; toll-free 800/234-4534; fax 505/989-9149. www.innofthegovernors.com.* Guests will enjoy relaxing at the piano bar or around the heated outdoor pool. Guests can venture into town for shopping, hiking, fine restaurants and even take in an opera or visit the museums. 100 rooms, 3 story. Complimentary full breakfast. Check-in 4 pm, check-out noon. Restaurant, bar. Outdoor pool. **$$**

Specialty Lodging

The following lodging establishments are approved by Mobil Travel Guide, but due to their unique and individualized nature have not been given a traditional Mobil Star rating. Included in this listing you may find bed-and-breakfasts, limited-service inns, guest ranches, and other unique hotel properties.

ADOBE ABODE. *202 Chapelle St, Santa Fe (87501). Phone 505/983-3133; fax 505/424-3027. www.adobeabode.com.* Built in 1905 as officer quarters for Fort Marcy, this property offers guests a unique stay in one of the finely decorated rooms. Visitors will enjoy the complimentary sherry and Santa Fe cookies in the afternoon. 6 rooms. Complimentary full breakfast. Check-in 2 pm, check-out 11 am. **$**

CASA PUEBLO INN. *138 Park Ave, Santa Fe (87501). Phone 505/988-4455; fax 505/995-4543. www.casapueblo.com.* 32 rooms. Check-in 4 pm, check-out 11:30 am. **$$**

DANCING GROUND OF THE SUN. *711 Paseo De Peralta, Santa Fe (87501). Phone 505/986-9797; toll-free 800/745-9910; fax 505/986-8082. www.dancingground.com.* 21 rooms, 2 story. Pets accepted. Complimentary continental breakfast. Check-in 4 pm, check-out 11 am. **$$**

DOS CASAS VIEJAS. *610 Agua Fria St, Santa Fe (87501). Phone 505/983-1636; fax 505/983-1749. www.doscasasviejas.com.* Two historical buildings in a 1/2-acre walled/gated compound; renovated to restore 1860's architecture. Set in the heart of Sante Fe's Guadeloupe District, guests can enjoy all that Sante Fe has to offer. Available activities include opera, museums, art galleries, restaurants, hiking, skiing, horseback riding, shopping, and golfing. 8 rooms. Complimentary continental breakfast. Check-in 3-6 pm, check-out noon. Outdoor pool. **$$**

EL FAROLITO BED & BREAKFAST. *514 Galisteo St, Santa Fe (87501). Phone 505/988-1631; toll-free 888/634-8782; fax 505/988-4589. www.farolito.com.* 8 rooms. Check-in 3 pm, check-out 11 am. **$$**

EL REY INN. *1862 Cerrillos Rd, Santa Fe (87505). Phone 505/982-1931; toll-free 800/521-1349; fax 505/989-9249. www.elreyinnsantafe.com.* 86 rooms, 2 story. Complimentary continental breakfast. Check-in 3 pm, check-out noon. Outdoor pool, two whirlpools. **$**

GRANT CORNER INN. *122 Grant Ave, Santa Fe (87501). Phone 505/983-6678; toll-free 800/964-9003; fax 505/983-1526. www.grantcornerinn.com.* Located two blocks from Santa Fe's historic Plaza and next to the Georgia O'Keeffe Museum, this Colonial Manor house (1905) is a picture of tranquility, with many gardens and large trees. The air-conditioned guest rooms feature hand-painted armoires, antique photographs, and four-poster beds. The full breakfast offers such dishes as Swedish pancakes. 10 rooms, 3 story. Children over 8 years only. Complimentary full breakfast. Check-in 3-6 pm, check-out noon. **$$**

GUADALUPE INN. *604 Agua Fria St, Santa Fe (87501). Phone 505/989-7422; fax 505/989-7422. www.guadalupeinn.com.* A quiet inn offering rooms with unique style and décor. Local artists display their work in the rooms and many pieces are for sale. 12 rooms, 2 story. Complimentary full breakfast. Check-in 3-6 pm, check-out 11 am. **$**

INN OF THE TURQUOISE BEAR. *342 E Buena Vista, Santa Fe (87501). Phone 505/983-0798. www.turquoisebear.com.* 10 rooms. Check-in 3 pm, check-out noon. **$$**

INN ON THE ALAMEDA. *303 E Alameda, Santa Fe (87501). Phone 505/984-2121; toll-free 800/289-2122; fax 505/986-8325. www.inn-alameda.com.* Sitting unassumingly behind adobe walls near the start of Canyon Road, this inn offers all the comforts of a luxury hotel, but with the quiet elegance of a smaller bed-and-breakfast. Guest rooms feature Egyptian cotton sheets, fireplaces, robes, hairdryers, cable television, and data ports. 69 rooms, 3 story. Pets accepted, some restrictions; fee. Complimentary continental breakfast. Check-in 4 pm, check-out noon. Bar. Fitness room. Two whirlpools. **$$$**

INN ON THE PASEO. *630 Paseo De Peralta, Santa Fe (87501). Phone 505/984-8200; toll-free 800/457-9045; fax 505/989-3979. www.innonthepaseo.com.* Located on the Paseo de Peralta in the heart of downtown Santa Fe, this recently renovated inn offers a relaxing Southwest experience. Air-conditioned guest rooms feature down comforters, patchwork quilts, and private baths. The breakfast buffet is served on the sun deck and features a collection of healthy favorites like muffins, granola, and fresh fruit. 18 rooms, 3 story. Complimentary full breakfast. Check-in 3 pm, check-out 11 am. **$**

LAS PALOMAS. *460 W San Francisco St, Santa Fe (87501). Phone 505/988-4455; fax 505/995-4543.* 40 rooms. Check-in 3 pm, check-out noon. **$$**

TERRITORIAL INN. *215 Washington St, Santa Fe (87501). Phone 505/988-2800; toll-free 866/230-7737; fax 505/982-5457. www.territorialinn.com.* This charming Victorian home is located one block from the historic Santa Fe Plaza. House (circa 1895) blends New Mexico's stone and adobe architecture with pitched roof, Victorian-style interior; sitting room, antiques; garden and tree-shaded lawns more typical of buildings in the East. Rooms offer queen-size beds, alarm clocks, voice mail, cable televisions, and telephones. Relax in the rose garden or in the whirlpool. 25 rooms, 2 story. Children over 10 years only. Complimentary continental breakfast. Check-in 3 pm, check-out 11 am. **$$**

WATER STREET INN. *427 W Water St, Santa Fe (87501). Phone 505/984-1193; toll-free 800/646-6752; fax 505/984-6235. www.waterstreetinn.com.* Located just two blocks from Santa Fe's historic Plaza, this recently restored inn, with art and photography lining its walls, features Southwestern décor. Spacious brick-floored guest rooms have private baths, cable TV with VCRs, air conditioning, and decks/patios. The courtyard offers a sundeck with great views. 12 rooms. Pets accepted. Complimentary continental breakfast. Check-in 2 pm, check-out 11 am. Whirlpool. **$$**

Restaurants

★★ **AMAYA AT HOTEL SANTA FE.** *1501 Paseo de Peralta, Santa Fe (87501). Phone 505/982-1200; toll-free 800/825-9876; fax 505/984-2211. www.hotelsantafe.com.* Southwestern menu. Breakfast, lunch, dinner. Bar. Children's menu. Casual attire. Outdoor seating. **$$$**

★★★ **THE ANASAZI.** *113 Washington Ave, Santa Fe (87501). Phone 505/988-3236; toll-free 800/688-8100; fax 505/988-3277. www.innoftheanasazi.com.* The creators of memorable cuisine at this Plaza mainstay like to point out that the Navajo definition of Anasazi has come to embody an ancient wisdom that is "synonymous with the art of living harmoniously and peacefully with our environment." That philosophy is translated in the colorful Native American weavings, petroglyph-inspired art upon the walls of beautiful rock, and mesmerizing fires that crackle and warm the rooms within this dining favorite. Executive chef Tom Kerpon devotes himself to inventive uses of locally grown, organic products, from cactus and sage to chiles and corn. Plenty of satisfaction is found in his grilled basil-marinated opah with green chile risotto, buffalo osso bucco, and soup of grilled corn, tortilla, and lime. Southwestern menu. Breakfast, lunch, dinner, Sun brunch. Bar. Children's menu. Casual attire. **$$$**

★★ **ANDIAMO.** *322 Garfield, Santa Fe (87501). Phone 505/995-9595. www.andiamoonline.com.* Three dining areas. Italian menu. Dinner. Children's menu. Casual attire. Outdoor seating. **$$**

★ **BLUE CORN CAFE.** *133 Water St, Santa Fe (87501). Phone 505/984-1800.* New Mexican menu. Lunch, dinner. Closed Thanksgiving, Dec 25. Bar. Children's menu. Casual attire. **$**

★★ **CAFE PARIS.** *31 Burro Alley, Santa Fe (87501). Phone 505/986-9162; fax 505/995-0008.* Café-style dining. French menu. Lunch, dinner. Closed Mon; also Jan 1, Dec 25. Casual attire. **$$$**

★★ **CAFE PASQUAL'S.** *121 Don Gaspar, Santa Fe (87501). Phone 505/983-9340; fax 505/988-4645.* New Mexican, American menu. Breakfast, lunch, dinner, Sun brunch. Closed Thanksgiving, Dec 25. Casual attire. **$$$**

★★ **CELEBRATIONS.** *613 Canyon Rd, Santa Fe (87501). Phone 505/989-8904. www.celebrationscanyonroad.com.* American menu. Breakfast, lunch, dinner. Closed Jan 1, Thanksgiving, Dec 25. Bar. Casual attire. Outdoor seating. **$$**

★ **CHOW'S CUISINE BISTRO.** *720 St. Michaels Dr, Santa Fe (87505). Phone 505/471-7120; fax 505/471-7120. www.mychows.com.* This little restaurant tucked away in a shopping mall offers some of the best Chinese food in Santa Fe. Offering mostly Szechwan dishes in a contemporary Asian atmosphere, Chow's consistently wins the Santa Fe Reporter's "Best of Santa Fe" award. Enjoy numerous unique and tasty dishes all prepared without MSG. Chinese menu. Lunch, dinner. Closed Sun. Casual attire. **$$**

★★★ **COYOTE CAFE.** *132 W Water St, Santa Fe (87501). Phone 505/983-1615; fax 505/989-9026. www.coyote-cafe.com.* Famed cookbook author and pioneer of Southwestern cuisine Mark Miller has enjoyed nothing but success at this bastion of trendy dining found just a block off the Plaza. Although the menu changes seasonally, patrons are assured of finding a whimsical mingling of the cuisines of New Mexico, Mexico, Cuba, and Spain in all manner of meats, fish, and vegetables. Look for chile-glazed beef short ribs with corn dumplings, pecan wood-roasted quail, and halibut in a mango-habañero blend, among many inventions, and don't miss the house drink special, a margarita del Maguey. Whether seated in the main dining room (try for a window-side table overlooking the street) or on the festive rooftop Cantina, be sure to relax and soak up the setting, decorated by magnificent folk art and artistic lighting fixtures. New Mexican menu. Dinner. Bar/cantina (May-Oct). Casual attire. Outdoor seating. **$$$**

★ **EL COMEDOR.** *727 Cerrillos Rd, Santa Fe (87501). Phone 505/989-7575; fax 505/984-8879.* Southwestern menu. Breakfast, lunch, dinner. Closed Thanksgiving, Dec 25. Children's menu. Casual attire. Outdoor seating. **$**

★ **EL FAROL.** *808 Canyon Rd, Santa Fe (87501). Phone 505/983-9912. www.elfarolsf.com.* Mexican menu. Lunch, dinner. Closed holidays. Bar. Casual attire. Outdoor seating. **$**

★★ **EL MESON - LA COCINA DE ESPAÑA.** *213 Washington Ave, Santa Fe (87501). Phone 505/983-6756; fax 505/983-1262. www.elmeson-santafe.*

com. Spanish, tapas menu. Dinner. Closed Sun-Mon; also Jan 1, Thanksgiving, Dec 25. Bar. Children's menu. Casual attire. **$$**

★ ★ GABRIEL'S. *4 Banana Ln, Santa Fe (87506). Phone 505/455-7000; fax 505/455-3866.* Southwestern menu. Lunch, dinner. Closed Late Nov-late Dec. Bar. Casual attire. Reservations recommended. Outdoor seating. **$$**

★ ★ EL NIDO. *591 Bishops Lodge Rd, Tesuque (87574). 6 miles N. Phone 505/988-4340; fax 505/988-2011.* Steak, seafood menu. Dinner. Closed Mon; Jan 1, Thanksgiving, Dec 25; also Super Bowl Sun. Bar. **$$**

★ ★ ★ ★ GERONIMO. *724 Canyon Rd, Santa Fe (87501). Phone 505/982-1500; fax 505/820-2083. www.geronimorestaurant.com.* Housed in a restored 250-year-old landmark adobe, Geronimo (the name of the restaurant is an ode to the hacienda's original owner, Geronimo Lopez) offers robust southwestern-spiked "Global Fusion Fare" in a stunning and cozy space. Owners Cliff Skoglund and Chris Harvey treat each guest like family, and this is a nice family to be a part of. Geronimo is inviting and warm, with a wood-burning cove-style fireplace; eggshell walls; sheer curtains; tall, rich chocolate- and garnet-leather seating; and local Native American-style sculpture and artwork decorating the walls. It feels like a Georgia O'Keefe painting come to life. It's not just the serene and stylish space that earns Geronimo points with its regulars. The food is remarkable, fusing the distinct culinary influences of Asia, the Southwest, and the Mediterranean. Vibrant flavors, bright colors, and top-notch seasonal regional ingredients come together in perfect harmony. While Geronimo is a great place for dinner, it is also a perfect spot to take a break from gallery hopping around lunchtime. When it's warm outside, sit on the patio for prime Canyon Road people watching. *Secret Inspector's Notes: This restaurant is a delight. Make sure to arrive early enough to have a drink in the cozy bar.* Southwestern, American menu. Lunch, dinner. Bar. Casual attire. Reservations recommended. Outdoor seating. **$$$**

★ ★ IL PIATTO. *95 W Marcy St, Santa Fe (87501). Phone 505/984-1091; fax 505/983-6939.* Italian menu. Lunch, dinner. Closed Jan 1, Thanksgiving, Dec 25. Bar. Children's menu. Casual attire. Outdoor seating. **$$**

★ ★ INDIA PALACE. *227 Don Gaspar, Santa Fe (87501). Phone 505/986-5859; fax 505/986-5856. www.indiapalace.com.* The multi-award-winning India Palace, conveniently located only a block from the Santa Fe Plaza, offers some of the best authentic Indian cuisine available in New Mexico. On the menu, you'll find an excellent selection of familiar Indian dishes, including a wide variety of meat and vegetarian offerings. The real deal, though, is the popular all-you-can eat lunch buffet, available for only $8.45. East Indian menu. Lunch, dinner. Closed Super Bowl Sun. Outdoor seating. **$$**

★ ★ ★ JULIAN'S. *221 Shelby St, Santa Fe (87501). Phone 505/988-2355; fax 505/988-5071. www.juliansofsantafe.com.* Officially called Julian's Cucina d'Italia, this bistro has long been a favorite for romantic dining in a neighborhood cluster of high-end shops and galleries. Diners are warmed by two fireplaces within the old adobe walls, where owner-executive chef Wayne Gustafson treats them to authentic dinners designed with style. Typical of his winning ways are the antipasto of oysters baked with Parmesan and his alternative to traditional escargot, a dish of pasta shells stuffed with snails, prosciutto, garlic butter, and pesto. Signature entrées include his classic osso bucco Milanese with saffron risotto and shrimp sautéed with tomatoes and graced with fresh basil and marscapone. Italian menu. Dinner. Closed Thanksgiving. Bar. Casual attire. Outdoor seating. **$$$**

★ ★ ★ LAS FUENTES AT BISHOP'S LODGE. *Bishop's Lodge Rd, Santa Fe (87504). Phone 505/983-6377; toll-free 800/732-2240; fax 505/989-8739. www.bishopslodge.com.* Rich in history, architecture, and art, the Bishop's Lodge resort introduced Las Fuentes in the spring of 2002. Executive chef Alfonso Ramirez brings a new edition of Nuevo Latino cuisine in a vibrant blend of foods that includes tostones, mariquitas, fufu de platino, and ropa vieja from Cuba, chimmichurri from Argentina, pupusas from Salvador, aropas from Colombia, and much more from Puerto Rico, Mexico, and other Caribbean and Central and South American countries. Seared plantain-crusted salmon with fennel and chipotle juice and swordfish marinated with chile guajillo have quickly become favorites. Spa cuisine choices gazpacho with roasted cumin seeds and Cuban black bean soup. American, Southwestern menu. Breakfast, lunch, dinner, Sun brunch. Bar. Children's menu. Outdoor seating. **$$$**

★★ LITTLE ANITA'S. *2811 Cerrillos Rd, Santa Fe (87501). Phone 505/473-4505; fax 505/471-6441.* Mexican menu. Dinner. Closed Dec 25, children's menu. Casual attire. **$$**

★★ MARIA'S NEW MEXICAN KITCHEN. *555 W Cordova Rd, Santa Fe (87501). Phone 505/983-7929; fax 505/983-4700. www.marias-santafe.com.* If you love margaritas, this popular restaurant offers more than 100 different varieties of REAL margaritas, made with some of the best and most exotic tequilas imported from Mexico. The margarita menu is bigger than most restaurants' food menus. Maria's also offers a great selection of Mexican beers and specializes in homemade, freshly cooked New Mexican cuisine. Try the BBQ ribs or any of the fajita dishes, along with the excellent homemade salsa. New Mexican, Southwestern menu. Lunch, dinner. Closed Thanksgiving, Dec 25. Bar. Children's menu. Casual attire. Outdoor seating. **$$**

★★★ THE OLD HOUSE RESTAURANT. *309 W San Francisco St, Santa Fe (87501). Phone 505/988-4455; toll-free 800/855-4455; fax 505/995-4555. www.eldoradohotel.com.* Supping on the culinary genius of chef Martin Rios produces a sensation much like that of falling in love—sweet, seductive, and intensely pleasurable. Taking time to prepare every element in the most fastidious fashion, Rios is known for making all sauces from stock reductions and finishing with butter and cream, and for introducing unexpected flavors in otherwise everyday items. Witness his roasted pork tenderloin, accompanied by sweet potatoes pureed with oranges that he's preserved for nine days, and his duck confit and foie gras in puff pastry with pistachios and cherry-celery compote. Take just a moment from swooning over chilled sweet corn soup and lobster soup with lobster tempura and osetra caviar to enjoy the candlelit stucco room, which is adorned with Mexican folk art and bold, oversized paintings, and is part of one of the city's oldest buildings. Southwestern menu. Dinner. Closed Thanksgiving, Dec 25. Bar. Casual attire. Valet parking. **$$$**

★★ OLD MEXICO GRILL. *2434 Cerrillos Rd, Santa Fe (87501). Phone 505/473-0338; fax 505/424-0890.* Mexican menu. Lunch, dinner. Closed Labor Day, Thanksgiving, Dec 25. Bar. Casual attire. **$**

★★ ORE HOUSE ON THE PLAZA. *50 Lincoln Ave, Santa Fe (87505). Phone 505/983-8687; fax 505/920-6892. www.orehouseontheplaza.com.* A perennial favorite on every list of great taverns in the City Different, this comfortable hangout is in its third decade of pleasing visitors with a menu of more than 40 custom-made margaritas and dozens of sipping tequila choices. The balcony, with its unbeatable setting above the historic Plaza, is open year-round, thanks to special heating during cooler weather. A regular custom of frequent pilgrims is to wind up the day over a cocktail, noshing on complimentary snacks, listening to the evening's guitarist, and watching the stars light the sky. Happy hour is from 4-6 pm daily. Seafood, steak menu. Lunch, dinner. Closed Thanksgiving, Dec 25. Bar. Children's menu. Casual attire. Outdoor seating. **$$**

★★ OSTERIA D'ASSISI. *58 S Federal Pl, Santa Fe (87501). Phone 505/986-5858; fax 505/986-3938. www.osteriadassisi.com.* Italian menu. Lunch, dinner. Closed Jan 1, Thanksgiving, Dec 25. Casual attire. Outdoor seating. **$$**

★★★ PALACE RESTAURANT AND SALOON. *142 W Palace Ave, Santa Fe (87501). Phone 505/982-9891. www.palacerestaurant.com.* Recalling images of happy decadence from the Wild West, the Palace is a place where diners might expect to see a high-rolling gambler eating and drinking with the town's prettiest painted lady. Opened as a saloon by the renowned Doña Tules in 1837, the gathering spot boasts an old-fashioned red décor, with ornate lighting fixtures and portrait frames reminiscent of the period. Devotees come for the fresh fish offerings, free-range veal and poultry, Black Angus steaks, and locally raised lamb. Tableside Caesar salad preparations make meals special, as do house-made pastries from the cart rolled through after dinner. Expect live music, and in the summer, ask for a table on the shady old patio. American menu. Lunch, dinner. Closed Thanksgiving, Dec 25. Bar. Children's menu. Casual attire. Outdoor seating. **$$$**

★★ PAUL'S. *72 W Marcy St, Santa Fe (87501). Phone 505/982-8738. www.paulsofsantafe.com.* Owner/chef Paul Huntsicker, consistently a winner of the annual Taste of Santa Fe competition, woos patrons with a contemporary cuisine selection that includes fish, lamb, beef, and fowl, all given specialized treatments with an international assortment of herbs and exotic touches. Among the favorites are red chile wontons stuffed with duck and bathed in a ginger soy, saffron-scented fish stew, and blue crab cakes crowned with a tomato-orange-chipotle sauce. A twilight menu offers less expensive, fixed-price fare. Don't miss the chance to see folk art from New Mexico, Mexico, and Central and South America. American, Southwestern menu. Lunch, dinner. Closed July 4, Dec 25. Casual attire. **$$$**

★ ★ THE PINK ADOBE. *406 Old Santa Fe Trail, Santa Fe (87501). Phone 505/983-7712; fax 505/984-0691. www.thepinkadobe.com.* Historic pink adobe building circa 1700. Southwestern, continental menu. Lunch, dinner. Closed holidays. Bar. Children's menu. Casual attire. Outdoor seating. **$$**

★ PLAZA. *54 Lincoln Ave, Santa Fe (87501). Phone 505/982-1664.* Century-old building with many original fixtures; stamped-tin ceiling; photos of early Santa Fe. American menu. Breakfast, lunch, dinner. Closed Thanksgiving, Dec 25. Children's menu. Casual attire. **$$**

★ ★ PRANZO ITALIAN GRILL. *540 Montezuma, Santa Fe (87501). Phone 505/984-2645; fax 505/986-1123.* Pranzo, which translates from Italian as "main" or "favorite" meal of the day, consistently ranks as one of the best Italian restaurants in Santa Fe. Situated in the Sanbusco Center in an old 19th century lumberyard, its hardwood floors and casual ambience serve to transport diners back to Old World Italy. The experience is further enhanced by a superb menu of pastas, wood-oven pizzas, and succulent appetizers made with fresh ingredients such as goat cheese, sun-dried tomatoes, portabello mushrooms, roasted bell peppers, and plenty of garlic. You'll also find an excellent selection of wines. Late-nighters can enjoy pizza, salad, and appetizers, served in the lounge until midnight. During warm weather, patrons can dine on the rooftop patio, which offers great views of the surrounding mountains. Northern Italian menu. Lunch, dinner. Closed July 4, Thanksgiving, Dec 25. Bar. Children's menu. Casual attire. Outdoor seating. **$$**

★ ★ RISTRA. *548 Agua Fria, Santa Fe (87501). Phone 505/982-8608. www.ristrarestaurant.com.* Barely off the beaten path, in a quiet neighborhood a short drive from the Plaza, this graceful Victorian adobe home provides a departure from typical Santa Fe in both setting and cuisine (although there are Southwestern elements in both). Diners gaze out of enormous windows at stands of evergreens while tucking into appetizers such as grilled foie gras and black Mediterrranean mussels swept with mint and chipotle. Fresh, seasonal ingredients are the key to the kitchen's successes, and a wine list of 100 French and California vintages keep local and visiting diners happy. Modern American, Southwestern menu. Dinner. Casual attire. Outdoor seating. **$$$**

★ ★ ★ ROCIADA. *304 Johnson St, Santa Fe (87501). Phone 505/983-3800; fax 505/983-8306. www.rociada.net.* A New York transplant, owner/chef Eric Stapelman brings country French cuisine to the near-Plaza environs with requisite panache. The interior's clean but mellow design is burnished in the golden light of small candles, allowing diners to be carried away by the food's rapture. Typical favorites have included octopus Provencal with roasted plum tomatoes, green olives, capers, and Yukon gold potatoes and California squab with applewood-smoked bacon, potato pavé, and red wine reduction. As icing to this gastronomic cake, there's a lovely, extensive selection of dessert wines (the '96 Chapoutier banyuls rouge is a huge hit) and vintage ports. French, Mediterranean menu. Dinner. Closed Sun. Bar. Casual attire. Outdoor seating. **$$$**

★ ★ SAN MARCOS CAFE. *3877 NM 14, Santa Fe (87505). Phone 505/471-9298.* Known for it's great Southwestern breakfasts and vegetarian cuisine. Southwestern menu. Breakfast, lunch. **$**

★ ★ ★ SANTACAFE. *231 Washington Ave, Santa Fe (87501). Phone 505/984-1788; fax 505/986-0110. www.santacafe.com.* Situated a block from the Plaza in the restored Padre Gallegos House, which was built by a colorful priest and politician from 1857 to 1862, Santacafe has been lauded by the *New York Times* for memorable works in globally influenced fish and meats. Simple but exquisite dishes include a salad of blood oranges and grapefruit with fennel and celeriac remoullade, shrimp-spinach dumplings in a tahini sauce, filet mignon with persillade and green chile mashed potatoes, and roasted free-range chicken with quinoa and a cranberry-chipotle chuntey. Patio dining in warmer weather is divine. American menu. Lunch, dinner. Bar. Casual attire. Outdoor seating. **$$$**

★ SHED AND LA CHOZA. *113 1/2 E Palace Ave, Santa Fe (87501). Phone 505/982-9030; fax 505/*

982-0902. *www.sfshed.com.* New Mexican menu. Lunch, dinner. Closed Sun; holidays, children's menu. Casual attire. Outdoor seating. **$**

★ ★ SHOHKO-CAFE. *321 Johnson St, Santa Fe (87501). Phone 505/983-7288; fax 505/984-1853.* Japanese menu. Lunch, dinner. Closed holidays. Bar. Casual attire. **$$**

★ STEAKSMITH AT EL GANCHO. *104 B Old Las Vegas Hwy, Santa Fe (87505). Phone 505/988-3333; fax 505/988-3334. www.santafesteaksmith.com.* Steak menu. Dinner. Closed holidays. Bar. Children's menu. Casual attire. **$$$**

★ TECOLOTE CAFE. *1203 Cerrillos Rd, Santa Fe (87501). Phone 505/988-1362.* Southwestern, American menu. Breakfast, lunch. Closed Mon; Thanksgiving, Dec 25. Children's menu. Casual attire. **$**

★ ★ TOMASITA'S. *500 S Guadalupe, Santa Fe (87501). Phone 505/983-5721; fax 505/983-0780.* An excellent choice for northern New Mexico cuisine, Tomasita's is housed in an old brick train station built in 1904. It's a great place to sample traditional sopapillas, puffy fried bread served with butter and honey (it comes with all entrées). Be warned about the chili, though; Tomasita's makes it HOT, whether you order it red, green, or Christmas. Other specialties include quesadillas, enchiladas, burritos, and various Mexican-inspired dishes prepared with a local twist. New Mexican menu. Dinner. Closed Sun; Jan 1, Dec 25. Bar. Children's menu. Casual attire. Outdoor seating. **$**

★ ★ VANESSIE OF SANTA FE. *434 W San Francisco St, Santa Fe (87501). Phone 505/982-9966; fax 505/982-1507.* American menu. Dinner. Closed Easter, Thanksgiving, Dec 25. Bar. Children's menu. Casual attire. **$$$**

Santa Rosa (C-4)

Settled 1865
Population 2,744
Elevation 4,620 ft
Area Code 505
Zip 88435
Information Santa Rosa Chamber of Commerce, 486 Parker Ave; phone 505/472-3763 or toll-free 800/450-7084
Web site www.santarosanm.org

In grama-grass country on the Pecos River, Santa Rosa has several natural and man-made lakes.

What to See and Do

Billy the Kid Museum. *1601 E Sumner Ave, Fort Sumner. Phone 505/355-2380. www.billythekidmuseumfortsumner.com.* Contains 60,000 items, including relics of the Old West, Billy the Kid, and Old Fort Sumner. On display is rifle once owned by Billy the Kid. (Mon-Sat 8:30 am-5 pm, Sun 11 am-5 pm; closed the first two weekends in Jan, holidays) **$**

City parks. *Santa Rosa. Phone 505/472-3404.* Fishing in stocked lakes; picnicking. (Daily) **FREE**

Blue Hole. *Blue Hole Rd, Santa Rosa. 1 mile E.* Clear blue lake in rock setting fed by natural artesian spring, 81 feet deep; scuba diving (permit fee).

Janes-Wallace Memorial Park. *1 mile S on 3rd St.* Also camping, small trailers allowed.

Park Lake. *Park Lake Dr, Santa Rosa.* Also swimming, lifeguard (June-Aug), children's fishing only; paddleboats, canoe rentals; playground.

Santa Rosa Dam and Lake. *Hwy 91, Santa Rosa. 7 miles N via access road. Phone 505/472-3115.* Army Corps of Engineers project for flood control and irrigation. No permanent pool; irrigation pool is often available for recreation. Fishing, boating (ramp, launch); nature trails, also trail for the disabled; picnicking, camping (fee; electricity additional). Information center. Excellent area for photography. Contact ACE, PO Box 345. (Daily) **$$**

Tres Lagunas. *1/4 mile N of Hwy 66, E end of town.* Fishing; hiking, nine-hole golf (fee).

Fort Sumner State Monument. *RR 1, Fort Sumner. 3 miles E on Hwys 54/66, then 44 miles SE on Hwy 84, near Fort Sumner. Phone 505/355-2573.* Original site of the Bosque Redondo, where thousands of Navajo and Mescalero Apache were held captive by the US Army from 1863-1868. The military established Fort Sumner to oversee the containment. (See SPECIAL EVENTS) Visitor center has exhibits relating to the period. (Mon, Wed-Sun; closed winter holidays) **$$**

Puerta de Luna. *10 miles S on Hwy 91. Phone 505/472-3763.* Founded approximately 1862, this Spanish-American town of 250 persons holds to old customs in living and working. Also here is

Grzelachowski Territorial House. *Phone 505/472-5320.* Store and mercantile built in 1800; this house was visited frequently by Billy the Kid. Grzelachowski had a major role in the Civil War battle at Glorieta Pass. (Daily, mid-morning-early evening; closed holidays) **DONATION**

Rock Lake Rearing Station. *2 miles S off I-40. Phone 505/472-3690.* State fish hatchery, rearing rainbow trout and walleyed pike. (Daily) **FREE**

Sumner Lake State Park. *3 miles E on Hwys 54/66, then 32 miles S on Hwy 84, near Fort Sumner. Phone 505/355-2541.* A 4,500-surface-acre reservoir created by irrigation dam. Swimming, fishing (bass, crappie, channel catfish); picnicking, camping (hookups, dump station). (Daily) **$$**

Special Events

Old Fort Days. *Fort Sumner, downtown, and County Fairgrounds.* Parade, rodeo, bank robbery, barbecue, contests, exhibits. Second week in June.

Santa Rosa Day Celebration. *Santa Rosa.* Sports events, contests, exhibits. Memorial Day weekend.

Limited-Service Hotels

★ BEST WESTERN ADOBE INN. *1501 Will Rogers Dr, Santa Rosa (88435). Phone 505/472-3446; fax 505/472-5759. www.bestwestern.com.* 58 rooms, 2 story. Pets accepted, some restrictions. Complimentary continental breakfast. Check-out 11 am. Pool. Airport transportation available. **$**

★ HOLIDAY INN. *3202 Will Rogers Dr, Santa Rosa (88435). Phone 505/472-5411; fax 505/472-3537. www.holiday-inn.com.* 67 rooms, 2 story. Check-out 10 am. Pool. **$**

Shiprock (A-1)

See also Farmington

Founded 1904
Population 8,156
Elevation 4,903 ft
Area Code 505
Zip 87420

Named for a 1,865-foot butte rising out of the desert, Shiprock is on the Navajo Reservation. The tribe is the largest in the United States, numbering about 200,000. Once almost exclusively shepherds and hunters, the Navajos have acquired some wealth by discoveries of oil, coal, and uranium on their lands—oil wells are found in the Four Corners area nearby and throughout San Juan County. The Navajo people are applying this income to urgent needs in educational and economic development. The Navajo Tribal Council has its headquarters at Window Rock, Arizona. Contact Navajo Tourism Department, PO Box 663, Window Rock, AZ 86515; phone 520/871-6659; or the Branch of Natural Resources, Shiprock Agency, PO Box 966; phone 505/368-3300.

Special Event

Shiprock Navajo Fair. *Shiprock. Phone 505/598-8213.* Powwow, carnival, parade. First weekend in Oct.

Silver City (D-1)

See also Deming

Founded 1870
Population 10,545
Elevation 5,895 ft
Area Code 505
Zip 88061
Information Chamber of Commerce, 201 N Hudson; phone 505/538-3785
Web site www.silvercity.org

The rich gold and silver ores in the foothills of the Mogollon (pronounced MUG-ee-yone) Mountains are running low, but copper mining has now become important to the economy. Cattle ranching thrives on the plains. The forested mountain slopes to the north are the habitat of turkey, deer, elk, and bear, and the streams and lakes provide excellent trout fishing.

What to See and Do

Gila National Forest. *Silver City. Surrounds town on all borders except on the SE. Contact the information desk, 3005 E Camino del Bosque. Phone 505/388-8201. www.fs.fed.us/r3/gila.* Administers more than 3 million acres, including the New Mexico part of the Apache National Forest. Also includes Gila, Blue Range, and Aldo Leopold wildernesses. Hunting, backpacking, horseback riding. Lakes Quemado, Roberts, and Snow also have fishing, boating, and camping. Fees for some activities. In the forest are

Catwalk of Whitewater Canyon. *63 miles NW of Silver City via Hwy 180, then 5 miles NE on Hwy 174. Phone 505/539-2481.* National recreation trail. Steel Causeway follows the course of two former pipelines that supplied water and water power in the 1890s to the historic gold and silver mining town of Graham. Causeway clings to sides of the sheer box canyon of Whitewater Creek. Access is by foot trail from Whitewater picnic ground (no water available); access also to Gila Wilderness. (Daily) **$$**

Gila Cliff Dwellings National Monument. *44 miles N of Silver City on Hwy 15. Phone 505/536-9461. www.nps.gov/gicl.* There are 42 rooms in six caves (accessible by a 1-mile hiking trail), which were occupied by the Mogollon circa 1300. Well-preserved masonry dwellings in natural alcoves in the face of an overhanging cliff. Self-guided tour, camping. Forest naturalists conduct programs (Memorial Day-Labor Day). Ruins and visitor center (daily; closed Jan 1, Dec 25). **$$**

Mogollon Ghost Town. *Hwy 180 S, Glenwood. 75 miles NW of Silver City via Hwy 180 on Hwy 159. (Note that Hwy 159 is closed Nov-Apr past the ghost town.) Phone 505/539-2481.* (1878-1930s) Former gold-mining town. Weathered buildings, beautiful surroundings; nearby Whitewater Canyon was once the haunt of Butch Cassidy and his gang, as well as Vitorio and Geronimo. **FREE**

Phelps Dodge Copper Mine. *Silver City. 7 miles NE on Hwy 15. Phone 505/538-5331 (24 hours in advance).* Historic mining town is home to fort and other historic buildings.

Silver City Museum. *312 W Broadway, Silver City. Phone 505/538-5921.* In restored 1881 house of H. B. Ailman, owner of a rich silver mine; Victorian antiques and furnishings; Casas Grandes artifacts; memorabilia from mining town of Tyrone. (Tues-Sun; closed holidays) **FREE**

Western New Mexico University. *12th and Virginia sts, Silver City. W part of town. Phone 505/538-6011.* (1893) (3,000 students) On campus is

Western New Mexico University Museum. *In Fleming Hall, 1000 College Ave, Silver City. Phone 505/538-6386.* Depicts contribution of Native American, Hispanic, African American, and European cultures to history of region; largest display of Membres pottery in the nation; photography, archive, and mineral collections. (Daily; closed holidays) **FREE**

Special Event

Frontier Days. *Silver City.* Parade, dances, exhibits, food. Western dress desired. July 4.

Limited-Service Hotels

★ COMFORT INN. *1060 E Hwy 180, Silver City (88061). Phone 505/534-1883; fax 505/534-0778. www.comfortinn.com.* 92 rooms. Check-in 2 pm, check-out 11 am. **$**

★ ★ COPPER MANOR MOTEL. *710 Silver Heights Blvd, Silver City (88062). Phone 505/538-5392; toll-free 800/853-2916; fax 505/538-5830.* 68 rooms, 2 story. Pets accepted. Complimentary continental breakfast. Check-out 11 am. Restaurant. Indoor pool. **$**

Restaurant

★ ★ BUCKHORN SALOON. *32 Main St, Pinos Altos (88053). Phone 505/538-9911.* Four dining rooms in house designed to look like Western opera house; melodrama performed some weekends. Steak menu. Dinner. Closed Sun; Jan 1, Thanksgiving, Dec 25. Bar. **$$**

Socorro (C-2)

Population 8,877
Elevation 4,620 ft
Area Code 505
Zip 87801
Information Socorro County Chamber of Commerce, 103 Francisco de Avondo, PO Box 743; phone 505/835-0424
Web site www.socorro.com

Originally a Piro Indian town, Socorro had a Franciscan mission as early as 1598. In 1817, a Spanish land grant brought ancestors of the present families here.

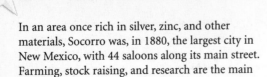

In an area once rich in silver, zinc, and other materials, Socorro was, in 1880, the largest city in New Mexico, with 44 saloons along its main street. Farming, stock raising, and research are the main income sources in this part of the Rio Grande Valley.

What to See and Do

Bosque del Apache National Wildlife Refuge. *1001 Hwy 1, San Antonio. 18 miles S via I-25 and Hwy 1. Phone 505/835-1828.* A 12-mile self-guided auto tour loop allows visitors to view a variety of wildlife. Also walking trails. Nov-mid-Feb are best viewing months (see SPECIAL EVENTS). Visitor center has brochures and exhibits (daily). Tour loop (daily; phone for hours and fee).

Mineral Museum. *801 Leroy Pl, Socorro. 1 mile W of I-25 on campus of New Mexico Institute of Mining and Technology (College Ave and Leroy) at Workman Center. Phone 505/835-5154.* More than 12,000 mineral specimens from around the world. Free rockhounding and prospecting information. (Mon-Sat) **FREE**

National Radio Astronomy Observatory. *1003 Lopez Ville Rd, Socorro. 52 miles W on Hwy 60, then S on Hwy 52. Phone 505/835-7000.* The VLA (Very Large Array) radio telescope consists of 27 separate antennas situated along three arms of railroad track. Self-guided walking tour of grounds and visitor center. (Daily) **FREE**

Old San Miguel Mission. *403 El Camino Real NW, Socorro. 2 blocks N of the plaza. Phone 505/835-1620.* (1615-26) Restored; south wall was part of the original 1598 mission. Carved ceiling beams and corbels; walls are 5 feet thick. (Daily) Artifacts on display in church office (building south of church) (Mon-Fri). **FREE**

Special Events

Conrad Hilton Open Golf Tournament. *Olive Ln and Golf Course Rd, Socorro. Phone 505/835-0424.* Early June.

Festival of the Crane. *Bosque del Apache National Wildlife Refuge, San Antonio exit and I-25, Socorro. Phone 505/835-0424.* Third weekend in Nov.

Socorro County Fair & Rodeo. *101 Plaza, Socorro. Phone 505/835-0424.* Labor Day weekend.

Limited-Service Hotels

★ ECONO LODGE SOCORRO. *713 California St NW, Socorro (87801). Phone 505/835-1500; toll-free 800/553-2666; fax 505/835-1500. www.econolodge.com.* 40 rooms. Check-in 1 pm, check-out 11 am. **$**

★ HOLIDAY INN EXPRESS SOCORRO. *1100 California NE, Socorro (87801). Phone 505/838-0556; toll-free 888/526-4567; fax 505/838-0598. www.holiday-inn.com.* 120 rooms. Check-in 3 pm, check-out noon. **$**

Taos (A-3)

See also Angel Fire, Red River

Founded 1615
Population 4,700
Elevation 6,950 ft
Area Code 505
Zip 87571
Information Taos County Chamber of Commerce, 1139 Paseo Del Pueblo Sur, PO Drawer I; phone 505/758-3873 or toll-free 800/732-8267
Web site www.taos.org

On a high plateau flanked by mountains, low, flat-roofed houses hug the ground. D. H. Lawrence said, "I think the skyline of Taos the most beautiful of all I have ever seen in my travels around the world."

Other artists and writers agree with him, for many now live and work amid this stimulating mixture of three peoples and three cultures: American Indian, Spanish-American, and Anglo-American. They like it for its clear air, magnificent surroundings, and exciting and congenial atmosphere.

Taos is actually three towns: the Spanish-American settlement into which Anglos have infiltrated, which is Taos proper; Taos Pueblo, 2 1/2 miles north; and Ranchos de Taos, 4 miles south. Each is distinct, yet all are closely allied. In the surrounding mountains are many other towns, Spanish-American farming communities, and fishing resorts. Taos Ski Valley, 19 miles northeast, is a popular ski resort.

As early as 1615, a handful of Spanish colonists settled in this area; in 1617 a church was built. After the Pueblo Rebellion of 1680 and the reconquest by

De Vargas in 1692, the town was a farming center plagued by Apache raids and disagreements with the Taos Indians and the government of Santa Fe. The first artists came in 1898; since then it has flourished as an art colony.

What to See and Do

Carson National Forest. *208 Cruz Alta Rd, Taos. Phone 505/758-6200. www.fs.fed.us/r3/carson/.* On 1 1/2 million acres. Includes Wheeler Peak, New Mexico's highest mountain at 13,161 feet, and the Valle Vidal, home to Rocky Mountain elk. Fishing (good in the 425 miles of streams and numerous small mountain lakes); hunting, hiking, winter sports, picnicking, camping (some fees). (Daily)

Ernest L. Blumenschein Home. *222 Ledoux St, Taos. Phone 505/758-0505. www.taosmuseums.org/blumenschein.php.* Restored adobe house includes furnishings and exhibits of paintings by the Blumenschein family and other early Taos artists. Cofounder of Taos Society of Artists. (May-Oct: daily 9 am-5 pm; call for winter hours) Combination tickets to seven Taos museums available. **$$**

Fort Burgwin Research Center. *6580 Hwy 518, Taos. 8 miles S on Hwy 518. Phone 505/758-8322.* Restored fort was occupied by First Dragoons of the US Calvary (1852-1860). Summer lecture series, music and theater performances. Operated by Southern Methodist University. (Schedule varies) **FREE**

Governor Bent House Museum and Gallery. *117A Bent St, Taos. 1 block N of plaza. Phone 505/758-2376.* Home of New Mexico's first American territorial governor; scene of his death in 1847. Bent family possessions, Native American artifacts, western American art. (Summer: daily 9 am-5 pm; winter: daily 10 am-4 pm; closed Jan 1, Thanksgiving, Dec 25) **$**

Hacienda Martinez. *708 Ranchitos Rd, Taos. 2 miles W of plaza on Hwy 240. Phone 505/758-1000. www.taoshistoricmuseums.com/martinez.html.* Contains early Spanish Colonial hacienda with period furnishings; 21 rooms, two large patios. Early Taos, Spanish culture exhibits. Used as a fortress during raids. Living museum demonstrations. (Summer: daily 9 am-5 pm, call for winter hours) Combination tickets to seven Taos museums available. **$**

Harwood Museum of Art. *238 Ledoux St, Taos. Phone 505/758-9826. harwoodmuseum.org.* Founded in 1923; features paintings, drawings, prints, sculptures, and photographs by artists of Taos from 1800 to the present. (Tues-Sat 10 am-5 pm, Sun noon-5 pm; closed Mon, holidays) Combination tickets to seven Taos museums available. **$$**

Kit Carson Home and Museum. *113 Kit Carson Rd, Taos. On Hwy 64, 1/2 block E of Taos Plaza. Phone 505/758-4741. taoshistoricmuseums.com/kit_carson.html.* (1825) Restored house with mementos of the famous scout, mountain man and trappers rooms, artifacts, gun exhibit. (Summer: daily 9 am-5 pm, call for winter hours) Combination tickets to seven Taos museums available. **$$** Nearby are

Kit Carson Park. *Paseo del Pueblo Norte, Taos. Phone 505/758-8234.* A 25-acre plot with bicycle/walking path. Picnic tables (grills), playground, sand volleyball pit. No camping. Graves of Kit Carson and his family. (Daily) **FREE**

Millicent Rogers Museum. *1504 Millicent Rogers Museum Rd, Taos. 4 miles N of Taos Plaza, 1/2 mile S of Hwy 64. Phone 505/758-2462. www.millicentrogers.com.* Native American and Hispanic arts and crafts. (Daily; closed holidays) **$$$**

Orilla Verde Recreation Area. *Hwy 570 and Hwy 68, Taos. 12 miles SW via Hwy 68. Phone 505/751-4899.* Offers spectacular views. Park runs along banks of the Rio Grande, offering some of the finest trout fishing in the state; whitewater rafting through deep chasm north of park. Hiking, picnicking. (Daily) **$$**

Ranchos de Taos. *60 Ranchos Plaza Rd, Taos. 4 miles S on Hwy 68. Phone 505/758-2754.* (circa 1800) This adobe-housed farming and ranching center has one of the most beautiful churches in the Southwest—the San Francisco de Asis Church. Its huge buttresses and twin bell towers only suggest the beauty of its interior. (Mon-Sat 9 am-4 pm) **$$**

Rio Grande Gorge Bridge. *Taos. 12 miles NW on Hwy 64.* Bridge is 650 feet above the Rio Grande; observation platforms, picnic, and parking areas.

Sipapu Area. *Hwy 518, Vadito. 25 miles SE on Hwy 518, 3 miles W of Tres Ritos. Phone 505/587-2240; toll-free 800/587-2240. www.sipapunm.com.* Area has two triple chairlifts, two Pomalifts; patrol, school, rentals, snowmaking; accommodations, restaurant, lounge. 31 runs, the longest more than 1 mile; vertical drop 1,055 feet. (Mid-Dec-Mar, daily) Cross-country skiing on forest roads and trails. Snowboarding. **$$$$**

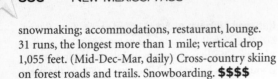

Taos Pueblo. *Taos. 2 1/2 miles N. Phone 505/758-1028. www.taospueblo.com.* With a full-time population of 150, this is one of the most famous Native American pueblos and has been continuously inhabited for more than 1,000 years. Within the pueblo, a National Historic Landmark, is a double apartment house; the north and south buildings, separated by a river, are five stories tall and form a unique communal dwelling. Small buildings and corrals are scattered around these impressive architectural masterpieces. The residents here live without modern utilities such as electricity and plumbing and get their drinking water from the river. The people are independent, conservative, and devout in their religious observances. Fees are charged for parking and photography permits. Photographs of individual Native Americans may be taken only with their consent. Do not enter any buildings that do not indicate a shop. Pueblo (daily 8 am-4 pm; closed for special occasions in spring). (See also SPECIAL EVENTS) **$$**

Taos Ski Valley. *103A Suton Pl, Taos Ski Valley. 18 miles NE via Hwy 522, 150. Phone 505/776-2233 (reservations); toll-free 800/776-1111 (reservations, except NM). www.skitaos.org.* Area has 12 chairlifts, two surface lifts; patrol, school, rentals; cafeteria, restaurants, bar; nursery, lodges. Longest run more than 4 miles; vertical drop 2,612 feet. (Nov-Apr, daily) **$$$$**

Van Vechten-Lineberry Taos Art Museum. *501 Paseo del Pueblo Norte, Taos. Phone 505/758-2690.* Houses artwork of the Taos Founders and other local artists. (Wed-Fri 10 am-5 pm, Sat 1-5 pm, Sun 1-4 pm) **$$**

Special Events

Annual Pow Wow. *Taos Pueblo, Taos. Phone 505/758-1028. www.taospueblopowwow.com.* Intertribal dancers from throughout US, Canada, and Mexico participate; competition. Second weekend in July.

Chamber Music Festival. *Taos Community Auditorium and Hotel St. Bernard in Taos Ski Valley, 145 Paseo del Pueblo, Taos. Phone 505/776-2388.* Mid-June-early Aug.

Fiestas de Santiago y Santa Ana. *Taos Plaza, Taos. Phone 505/758-2241; toll-free 800/732-8267. www.fiestasdetaos.com.* Traditional festival honoring the patron saints of Taos. Candlelight procession, parade, crafts, food, entertainment. Late July.

San Geronimo Eve Sundown Dance. *Taos Pueblo, Taos. Phone 505/758-1028505.* Traditional men's dance followed the next day by San Geronimo Feast Day, with intertribal dancing, trade fair, pole climb, footraces. Late weekend in Sept.

Spring Arts Festival. *Taos. Phone 505/758-3873; toll-free 800/732-8267. www.taoschamber.com.* Three-week festival featuring visual, performing, and literary arts. May.

Taos Arts Festival. *Taos. Phone 505/758-1028. www.taosguide.com.* Arts and crafts exhibitions, music, plays, poetry readings. Mid-Sept-early Oct.

Taos Pueblo Dances. *Taos Pueblo, Albuquerque. Phone 505/758-1028. www.taospueblo.com.* Several Native American dances are held throughout the year. For a schedule of annual dances, contact the pueblo.

Taos Pueblo Deer or Matachines Dance. *Taos Pueblo, Taos. Phone 505/758-1028.* Symbolic animal dance or ancient Montezuma dance. Dec 25.

Taos Rodeo. *County Fairgrounds, 502 Los Pandos, Taos. Phone toll-free 800/732-8267.* Late June or early July.

Yuletide in Taos. *Taos. Event held throughout city. Phone toll-free 800/732-8267.* Ski area festivities, farolito (paper bag lantern) tours, food and craft fairs, art events, dance performances. Late Nov-late Dec.

Limited-Service Hotels

★ COMFORT INN. *1500 Paseo Del Pueblo Sur, Taos (87571). Phone 505/751-1555; toll-free 888/751-1555; fax 505/751-1991. www.taoshotels.com//comfortsuites.* 60 rooms, 2 story, all suites. Complimentary continental breakfast. Check-out 11 am. Pool, whirlpool. Tennis. **$**

★ HAMPTON INN. *1515 Paseo Del Pueblo Sur, Taos (87571). Phone 505/737-5700; fax 505/737-5701. www.hamptoninn.com.* 71 rooms, 2 story. Complimentary continental breakfast. Check-out 11 am. Indoor pool, whirlpool. **$**

Full-Service Hotels

★★★ FECHIN INN. *227 Paseo del Pueblo Notre, Taos (87571). Phone 505/751-1000. www.fechin-inn.com.* Inspirational and creative, The Fechin Inn is Taos' most unique lodging. This one-time home to Russian artist Nicolai Fechin is the perfect place to enjoy the artistic spirit of Taos. Vibrant colors, woodcarvings crafted in the Fechin style by a local artisan, and prints of the artist's work that line the walls show off a funky and appealing attitude. The romance of the Southwest is celebrated in the rooms and suites, where patios, balconies, and fireplaces add comforting touches. This delightfully unique hotel is just two blocks from Taos Plaza and adjacent to Kit Carson Park, making it an exceptional place for those who want to explore the sights of this renowned city. 85 rooms, 2 story. Complimentary continental breakfast. Check-out noon. Fitness room. Whirlpool. **$$**

★★★ SAGEBRUSH INN. *1508 S Santa Fe Rd, Taos (87571). Phone toll-free 800/428-3626; fax 505/758-5077. www.sagebrushinn.com.* Built in 1929, this 100-room adobe inn houses a large collection of paintings, Indian rugs, and other regional art. The most recent addition, an 18,000-square-foot conference center, features hand-hewn vigas and fireplaces. Visitors will enjoy the outdoor pool and two whirlpools. Guest rooms feature in-room coffee, handmade furniture, and cable television. 100 rooms, 2 story. Pets accepted, some restrictions. Complimentary full breakfast. Check-out 11 am. Restaurant, bar. Pool, whirlpools. Business center. **$**

Full-Service Inn

★★★ THE HISTORIC TAOS INN. *125 Paseo Del Pueblo Norte, Taos (87571). Phone 505/758-2233; toll-free 800/826-7466; fax 505/758-5776. www.taosinn.com.* This historic inn offers a comfortable Old West experience with its blend of history and modern amenities. Guests will enjoy the outdoor heated pool and greenhouse whirlpool. The unique guest rooms feature Southwestern decor, hair dryers, and voice mail; many offer kiva fireplaces. Be sure to dine at the acclaimed Doc Martin's Restaurant. Inn consists of number of structures, some dating from 17th century. Meet-the-Artist Series in spring, fall. 36 rooms. Check-in 3 pm, check-out 11 am. Restaurant, bar. Pool, whirlpool. **$**

Specialty Lodgings

The following lodging establishments are approved by Mobil Travel Guide, but due to their unique and individualized nature have not been given a traditional Mobil Star rating. Included in this listing you may find bed-and-breakfasts, limited-service inns, guest ranches, and other unique hotel properties.

ADOBE AND STARS INN. *584 Hwy 150, Taos (87571). Phone 505/776-2776; toll-free 800/211-7076; fax 505/776-2872. www.taosadobe.com.* Located near the Historic Taos Plaza and the Taos Ski Valley, this Southwestern inn offers panoramic views of the Sangre de Christo Mountains. Guest rooms feature kiva fireplaces, private baths with terra-cotta tile, and ceiling fans. 8 rooms. Pets accepted, some restrictions; fee. Complimentary full breakfast. Check-in 4 pm, check-out 11 am. **$**

AUSTING HAUS B&B. *1282 Hwy 150, Taos Ski Valley (87525). Phone 505/776-2649; toll-free 800/748-2932; fax 505/776-8751. www.taoswebb.com/hotel/austinghaus.* Constructed of oak-pegged heavy timbers with beams exposed inside and out; built by hand entirely without nails or metal plates. 45 rooms, 2 story. Closed mid-Apr-mid-May. Pets accepted, some restrictions. Complimentary continental breakfast. Check-in 2 pm, check-out 10 am. Restaurant. Whirlpool. **$**

BROOKS STREET INN. *119 Brooks St, Taos (87571). Phone 505/758-1489; toll-free 800/758-1489; fax 505/758-7525. www.brooksstreetinn.com.* This casual inn offers a quiet environment where guests can relax while gazing at Taos Mountain. The elegant guest rooms feature fresh flowers, artwork, and handcrafted furniture, while the fireplace warms the common room. Breakfast includes an espresso bar and favorites like blue corn pancakes and pineapple salsa. 6 rooms. No children allowed. Complimentary full breakfast. Check-in 4-6 pm, check-out 11 am. **$**

CASA DE LAS CHIMENEAS. *405 Cordoba Rd, Taos (87571). Phone 505/758-4777; toll-free 877/758-4777; fax 505/758-3976. www.visit-taos.com.* True to its Spanish name (The House of Chimneys), all guest rooms in this bed-and-breakfast have kiva fireplaces as well as brass and wooden beds, private entrances and baths, down pillows, and electric blankets or down comforters. Guests looking to relax will enjoy the inn's formal gardens and courtyards, fountains, and whirlpool. 9 rooms. Complimentary full breakfast. Check-in 3-6 pm, check-out 11 am. Fitness room. **$$**

CASA EUROPA INN. *840 Upper Ranchitos, Taos (87571). Phone 505/758-9798; toll-free 888/758-9798; fax 505/758-9798. www.casaeuropanm.com.* Set on 6 acres of land, this 17th-century Pueblo-style inn offers a soothing experience with its beautiful views and walls adorned with local art. The flowered courtyards feature a fountain as well as a sauna and whirlpool. The spacious guest rooms offer private bathrooms, desks, and fans. 7 rooms, 2 story. Complimentary full breakfast. Check-in 3 pm, check-out 11 am. **$**

HACIENDA DEL SOL. *109 Mabel Dodge Ln, Taos (87571). Phone 505/718-0287; toll-free 866/333-4459; fax 505/758-5895. www.taoshaciendadelsol.com.* This inn consists of three adobe buildings set on 1.2 acres overlooking the Taos Mountains. The romantic guest rooms feature thick adobe walls, original artwork, and corner fireplaces. 11 rooms. Complimentary full breakfast. Check-in 3-6 pm, check-out 11 am. **$$**

INN ON LA LOMA PLAZA. *315 Ranchitos Rd, Taos (87571). Phone 505/758-1717; toll-free 800/530-3040; fax 505/751-0155. www.vacationtaos.com.* Formerly known as the Taos Hacienda Inn, this restored historic inn offers mountain views and spacious gardens. Visitors looking to relax can enjoy the whirlpool or take advantage of the complimentary spa, tennis, and health club privileges. Guest rooms feature private baths, fireplaces, phones, televisions, robes and slippers. 7 rooms, 2 story. Complimentary full breakfast. Check-in 4-9 pm, check-out 11 am. Pool, whirlpool. **$**

LA POSADA DE TAOS. *309 Juanita Ln, Taos (87571). Phone 505/758-8164; toll-free 800/645-4803; fax 505/751-4696. www.laposadadetaos.com.* Old adobe structure with courtyard. 6 rooms. Complimentary full breakfast. Check-in 4-6 pm, check-out 11 am. **$**

SALSA DEL SALTO BED & BREAKFAST INN. *543 Hwy 150, Taos (87529). Phone 505/776-2422; toll-free 800/530-3097; fax 505/776-5734. www.bandbtaos.com.* With the inn conveniently located close to Taos Ski Valley and Taos, guests will have the option of skiing or shopping. After a game of tennis, guests can enjoy the mountain and sunset view from the whirlpool. 10 rooms, 2 story. Children over 6 years only. Complimentary full breakfast. Check-in 3-7 pm, check-out 11 am. Pool. **$**

SAN GERONIMO LODGE. *1101 Witt Rd, Taos (87571). Phone 505/751-3776; toll-free 800/894-4119; fax 505/751-1493. www.sangeronimolodge.com.* Old adobe lodge with handcrafted furniture. 18 rooms, 2 story. Complimentary full breakfast. Check-in 3-7 pm, check-out 11 am. Pool, whirlpool. **$**

TOUCHSTONE LUXURY BED AND BREAKFAST. *110 Mabel Dodge Ln, Taos (87571). Phone 505/758-0192; toll-free 800/758-0192; fax 505/758-3498. www.touchstone.com.* This quiet, historic bed-and-breakfast is nestled among the trees on the edge of Taos Pueblo Lands. 7 rooms, 2 story. Complimentary full breakfast. Check-in 4 pm, check-out 11 am. **$**

Restaurants

★ ★ APPLE TREE. *123 Bent St, Taos (87571). Phone 505/758-1900. www.appletreerestaurant.com.* Mexican menu. Lunch, dinner, Sun brunch. Outdoor seating. **$$**

★ ★ ★ DOC MARTIN'S. *125 Paseo Del Pueblo, Taos (87571). Phone 505/758-1977; fax 505/758-5776. www.taoswebb.com/nmusa/hotel/taos.inn.* Chef Patrick Lambert serves nouvelle Southwestern in an adobe setting. Specialties include chipotle shrimp on corn cake and southwestern lacquered duck. The wine list is one of the best in the area. American, Southwestern menu. Breakfast, lunch, dinner. **$$**

★ ★ ★ LAMBERT'S. *309 Paseo Del Pueblo Sur, Taos (87571). Phone 505/758-1009.* Service is enthusiastic and friendly at this family-owned restaurant. Dinner. Children's menu. Outdoor seating. **$$**

★ MICHAEL'S KITCHEN AND BAKERY. *304 Paseo Del Pueblo N, Taos (87571). Phone 505/758-4178; fax 505/758-4088. www.michaelskitchen.com.* Mexican, American menu. Breakfast, lunch, dinner. Closed holidays; also Nov. Children's menu. **$**

★ ★ OGELVIE'S BAR AND GRILLE. *103 E Plaza, Taos (87571). Phone 505/758-8866; fax 505/758-0728.* Lunch, dinner. Bar. Children's menu. Outdoor seating. **$$**

★ ★ STAKEOUT GRILL AND BAR. *101 Stakeout Dr, Taos (87557). Phone 505/758-2042; fax 505/751-3815. www.stakeoutrestaurant.com.* Historically located adobe pueblo-style building. Steak menu. Dinner. Bar. Children's menu. Outdoor seating May-Oct. **$$**

★ ★ ★ VILLA FONTANA. *NM 522, Taos (87571). Phone 505/758-5800; fax 505/758-8301. www.villafontanahouse.com.* Italian-born chef and artist Carlo Gislimberti serves an authentic Italian menu, which includes fresh mozzarella, Parma ham, osso buco, and other favorites, in a comfortable setting. Dinner. Closed Sun; also Sun-Wed mid-Apr-mid-May, mid-Nov-mid-Dec. Bar. Outdoor seating. **$$**

Truth or Consequences (D-2)

Population 7,289
Elevation 4,240 ft
Area Code 505
Zip 87901
Information Truth or Consequences/Sierra County Chamber of Commerce, 201 S Foch St, PO Drawer 31; phone 505/894-3536
Web site www.truthorconsequencesnm.net

Formerly called Hot Springs, for the warm mineral springs, the town changed its name in 1950 to celebrate the tenth anniversary of Ralph Edwards' radio program, "Truth or Consequences."

In the early 1500s, the Spanish Conquistadores came through this area, and legends of lost Spanish gold mines and treasures in the Caballo Mountains persist today. There are numerous ghost towns and old mining camps in the area. A Ranger District office of the Gila National Forest (see SILVER CITY) is located here.

What to See and Do

Caballo Lake State Park. *18 miles S on I-25. Phone 505/743-3942.* Caballo Mountains form a backdrop for this lake. Swimming, windsurfing, water-skiing, fishing (bass, crappie, pike, trout, catfish), boating (ramp); hiking, picnicking, playground, camping (hookups). (Daily) **$$**

Canoeing, boating, and tubing. *Truth or Consequences.* On the Rio Grande, which flows through the city.

Elephant Butte Lake State Park. *Hwy 195, Elephant Butte. 5 miles N via I-25. Phone 505/744-5421.* This 40-mile-long lake was created in 1916 for irrigation; later adapted to hydroelectric power. Swimming, windsurfing, water-skiing, fishing (bass, crappie, pike, catfish), boating (ramp, rentals, slips, mooring, three marinas); hiking, picnicking, playground, concession, restaurant, lodge, camping (hookups), cabins. (Daily) **$$**

Geronimo Springs Museum. *211 Main St, Truth or Consequences. Phone 505/894-6600.* Exhibits of Mimbres pottery, fossils, and photographs, and articles on local history. Ralph Edwards Room, Apache Room, Hispanic Room, and log cabin. Gift shop. (Mon-Sat; closed Jan 1, Thanksgiving, Dec 25) **$**

Limited-Service Hotels

★ BEST WESTERN HOT SPRINGS MOTOR INN. *2270 N Date St, Truth or Consequences (87901). Phone 505/894-6665; fax 505/894-6665. www.bestwestern.com.* 40 rooms. Check-out noon. Pool. **$**

★ ★ QUALITY INN. *401 Hwy 195, Elephant Butte (87935). Phone 505/744-5431; fax 505/744-5044. www.*

qualityinn.com. 48 rooms, 2 story. Pets accepted; fee. Check-out 11 am. Restaurant, bar. Pool. Tennis. **$**

Restaurant

★ ★ LOS ARCOS STEAK HOUSE. *1400 N Date St, Truth or Consequences (87901). Phone 505/894-6200; fax 505/894-9797.* Steak menu. Dinner. Closed Thanksgiving, Dec 25. Bar. **$$**

Tucumcari (B-5)

Settled 1901
Population 5,989
Elevation 4,096 ft
Area Code 505
Zip 88401
Information Tucumcari/Quay County Chamber of Commerce, 404 W Rt 66, PO Drawer E; phone 505/461-1694
Web site www.tucumcarinm.com

A convenient stopping point between Amarillo, Texas, and Albuquerque, this is a trading center for a 45,000-acre irrigated and industrial water area. New energy is focused on carbon dioxide, petroleum, and natural gas. There is also a thriving cattle business. Tucumcari has become a transportation center with many trucking companies and much railroad traffic. Tucumcari Mountain (4,957 feet) is to the south.

Born when the railroad reached its site, Tucumcari was once known as "six-shooter siding."

What to See and Do

Conchas Lake State Park. *Conchas Dam. 33 miles NW of Tucumcari via Hwy 104, 433. Phone 505/868-2270.* Lake is 25 miles long. Swimming, water-skiing, fishing, boating; picnicking, camping (hookups, dump station). (Daily) **$$**

Tucumcari Historical Museum. *416 S Adams St, Tucumcari. Phone 505/461-4201.* Western Americana; Native American artifacts; gems, minerals, rocks, fossils; restored fire truck and caboose. (Tues-Sat) **$**

Ute Lake State Park. *1800 540 Loop, Logan. 22 miles NE on Hwy 54, Hwy 540. Phone 505/487-2284.* Created by a dam on the Canadian River. Swimming, water-skiing, fishing (bass, crappie, channel catfish), boating (marina, ramp, slips, mooring); hiking trails, picnicking, camping (hookups, dump station). (Daily) **$$**

Special Event

Route 66 Festival. *404 W Tumcari Blvd, Tucumcari.* Rodeo, car show, parade, arts and crafts, entertainment. July.

Limited-Service Hotels

★ COMFORT INN. *2800 E Tucumcari Blvd, Tucumcari (88401). Phone 505/461-4094; fax 505/461-4099. www.comfortinn.com.* 59 rooms, 2 story. Pets accepted; fee. Complimentary continental breakfast. Check-out noon. Pool. **$**

★ ★ HOLIDAY INN. *3716 E Tucumcari Blvd, Tucumcari (88401). Phone 505/461-3780; toll-free 800/335-3780; fax 505/461-3931. www.holiday-inn.com.* 100 rooms, 2 story. Pets accepted, some restrictions; fee. Check-out noon. Restaurant, bar. Fitness room. Pool, whirlpool. **$**

White Sands National Monument (D-3)

See also Alamogordo

Web site www.nps.gov/whsa/
15 miles SW of Alamogordo on Hwy 70/82.

These shifting, dazzling white dunes are a challenge to plants and animals. Here, lizards and mice are white like the sand, helping them blend in with the background. (Similarly, mice are black in the black lava area only a few miles north.)

Plants elongate their stems up to 30 feet so that they can keep their leaves and flowers above the sand. When the sands recede, the plants are sometimes left on elevated pillars of hardened gypsum bound together by their roots. Even an ancient two-wheeled Spanish cart was laid bare when the sands shifted.

Beach sand is usually silica, but White Sands National Monument sand is gypsum, from which plaster of paris is made. Dunes often rise to 60 feet; White Sands is the largest gypsum dune field in the world.

White Sands National Monument encloses 143,732 acres of this remarkable area. The visitor center has an orientation video, exhibits concerning the dunes and how they were formed, and other related material (daily except Dec 25). Evening programs and guided nature walks in the dunes area are conducted (Memorial Day-mid-Aug). There is a 16-mile round-trip drive from the center; free printed guide leaflet. Picnic area with shaded tables and grills (no water); primitive backpackers' campsite (by permit only). Dunes Drive (daily except Dec 25).

For further information, contact the Superintendent, PO Box 1086, Holloman AFB, NM 88330-1086; phone 505/672-2599.

Zuni Pueblo (B-1)

See also Gallup

Population 6,367
Elevation 6,283 ft
Area Code 505
Zip 87327

Thirty-nine miles south of Gallup, via Hwy 602 and west on Hwy 53, is one of Coronado's "Seven Cities of Cibola." Fray Marcos de Niza reported that these cities were built of gold. When looking down on the Zuni pueblo from a distant hilltop at sunset, it does seem to have a golden glow. Marcos' story was partly responsible for Coronado's expedition of the area in 1540, which found no riches for Spain.

Zuni is linguistically unique and distinct from other Rio Grande pueblos. The people here make beautiful jewelry, beadwork, and pottery. They also have a furniture and woodworking center with colorful and uniquely painted and carved items. Zuni works are available at Pueblo of Zuni Arts and Crafts. Phone 505/782-5531. Ashiwi Awan Museum and Heritage Center displays historical photos and exhibits. (Daily) Phone 505/782-4403. The pueblo, built mainly of stone, is one story high for the most part. The old Zuni mission church has been restored and its interior painted with murals of Zuni traditional figures. A tribal permit is required for photography; certain rules must be observed.

Picnicking and camping at Eustace, Ojo Caliente, Pescado, Nutria #2, and Nutria #4 lakes. Lakes stocked by Tribal Fish & Wildlife Service; a tribal permit as well as a state fishing license is required. For further information contact the Pueblo of Zuni, PO Box 339; phone 505/782-4481.

Utah

Utah is named for the Ute people, a nomadic tribe that populated these regions before the days of westward expansion. The state presents many natural faces, with arid desert and the deep, jagged canyons of the Colorado and Green rivers dominating the west and south and high, rugged mountains in the east and north. Utah contains examples of almost all water and land forms, many unique to the state. This natural diversity, though stimulating to the artistic eye, created an environment inhospitable to early settlers. Tribes of Ute, Piute, and Shoshone were the only people living in the region when the first white men, two Franciscan priests, passed through the area in 1776 en route to California from New Mexico. In 1819, British fur trappers began voyaging into northern Utah; by 1824 mountain men—people like Canadians Étienne Provost and Peter Skene Ogden, for whom some of Utah's towns and rivers are named—were venturing into Utah's wilds. Although these men traversed and explored much of the state, it took the determination and perseverance of a band of religious fugitives, members of the Church of Jesus Christ of Latter-Day Saints, to conquer the wilderness that was Utah and permanently settle the land.

Population: 1,722,850
Area: 84,990 square miles
Elevation: 2,200-13,528 feet
Peak: Kings Peak (Duchesne County)
Entered Union: January 4, 1896 (45th state)
Capital: Salt Lake City
Motto: Industry
Nickname: Beehive State
Flower: Sego Lily
Bird: California Gull
Tree: Blue Spruce
Fair: September in Salt Lake City
Time Zone: Mountain
Web site: www.utah.com

Brigham Young, leader of the Mormon followers, once remarked, "If there is a place on this earth that nobody else wants, that's the place I am hunting for." On July 24, 1847, upon entering the forbidding land surrounding the Great Salt Lake, Young exclaimed, "This is the place!" Immediately, the determined settlers began to plow the unfriendly soil and build dams for irrigation. Hard work and tenacity were put to the test as the Mormons struggled to convert the Utah wilderness into productive land. With little to work with—what the settlers did not have, they did without—the Mormons gradually triumphed over the land, creating the safe haven they were searching for.

The Mormon church was founded by Joseph Smith on April 6, 1830, in New York state. The religion, based on writings inscribed on golden plates said to have been delivered to Smith by an angel and translated by him into The Book of Mormon, drew a large following. Moving from New York to Ohio and Missouri, and then driven from Missouri and later Illinois, the church grew despite persecution and torture. When Smith was killed in Illinois, Young took over. With a zealot's determination, he headed farther west in search of a place of refuge. He found it in the Salt Lake area of Utah. Growing outward from their original settlement, Mormon pioneers and missionaries established colonies that were to become many of Utah's modern-day cities. During 1847, as many as 1,637 Mormons came to Utah, and by the time the railroad penetrated the region, more than 6,000 had settled in the state. Before his death in 1877, 30 years after entering the Salt Lake Valley, Brigham Young had directed the founding of more than 350 communities.

While the Mormon church undoubtedly had the greatest influence on the state—developing towns in an orderly fashion with wide streets, planting straight rows of poplar trees to provide wind breaks, and introducing irrigation throughout the

Calendar Highlights

JANUARY

Sundance Film Festival *(Park City). www.sundance.org.* A week-long festival celebrating independent filmmaking. Workshops, screenings, and special events.

JUNE

Utah Arts Festival *(Salt Lake City). Downtown. Phone 801/322-2428; www.uaf.org.* More than 1,000 participants, 90 performing groups; Children's Art Yard, juried show with demonstrations. Ethnic food.

Utah Summer Games *(Cedar City). Phone 435/865-8421; www.utahsummergames.org.* Olympic-style athletic events for amateur athletes.

JULY

Festival of the American West *(Logan). Phone 435/797-1143 or toll-free 800/225-FEST. Ronald V. Jensen Living Historical Farm.* Historical pageant; pioneer and Native American crafts fair, art exhibition, antique quilt show, frontier town, medicine man show, log construction; Dutch-oven cook-off.

Renaissance Fair *(Cedar City). Main St City Park.* Renaissance-style entertainment, food, and games. Held in conjunction with the opening of the Utah Shakespearean Festival.

Ute Stampede Rodeo *(Nephi). Phone 435/623-7102.* Three-day festival featuring horse and mammoth parades, carnival, PRCA rodeo, contests, arts and crafts, concessions.

AUGUST

Bonneville National Speed Trials *(Wendover). Bonneville Speedway. Phone 805/526-1805.* Held since 1914 on the Bonneville Salt Flats, which has been used as a track for racing the world's fastest cars. Car racing in competition and against the clock.

Novell Showdown *(Park City). Contact the Park Meadows Golf Club, phone 801/531-7029.* PGA invitational golf tournament.

Railroaders Festival *(Brigham City). Contact the Golden Spike National Historic Site, phone 435/471-2209; www.nps.gov/gosp.* Relive the rush to complete the transcontinental railroad and watch professional railroaders pursue the world record in spike driving.

SEPTEMBER

Utah State Fair *(Salt Lake City). State Fair Park. Phone 801/538-FAIR.* Arts and crafts, live entertainment, horse show, and rodeo.

desert regions—the church members were not the only settlers. In the latter part of the 19th century, the West's fabled pioneer era erupted. The gold rush of 1849-1850 sent gold seekers pouring through Utah on their way to California. The arrival of the Pony Express in Salt Lake City in 1860 brought more immigrants, and when the mining boom hit the state in the 1870s and 1880s, Utah's mining towns appeared almost overnight. In 1900, there were 277,000 Utahns; now the population stands at more than 1,700,000, with more than 75 percent living within 50 miles of Salt Lake City. The Mormon Church continues to play an important role, with close to 60 percent of the state's population being members.

Utah's natural diversity has made it a state of magnificent beauty, with more than 3,000 lakes, miles of mountains, acres upon acres of forests, and large expanses of deserts. Its main heights, 13,000 feet or more, are reached by plateaus and mountains lifted during the Cascade disturbance of the Cenozoic period. In northern Utah, the grandeur of the Wasatch Range, one of the most rugged mountain ranges in the United States, cuts across the state north to south; the Uinta Range, capped by the white peaks of ancient glaciers, is the only major North American range that runs east to west. In the western third of the state lies the Great Basin, a land-locked drainage area that, at one time, was half covered by a large, ancient sea. At its peak, Lake Bonneville was 1,050 feet deep, 145 miles wide, and 346 miles long. The Great Salt Lake and Sevier Lake are saltwater remnants of Bonneville, and Utah Lake is a freshwater remnant. To the east, the Bonneville Salt Flats lie where the ancient lake had retreated. To the east and west extends the Colorado River Plateau, or Red Plateau. This red rock country, renowned for its brilliant coloring and fantastic rock formations, is also home to one of the largest concentrations of national parks and monuments. With its many aspects, Utah is a land designed for the traveler who loves the Western outdoors and can appreciate the awesome accomplishments of the pioneers who developed it.

When to Go/Climate

Temperatures vary across the state, but in general, summer days are hot and summer nights are cool. Winters are cold and snowy except in the southwestern part of the state. The best time to visit Utah is in the spring or fall, when the temperatures are milder and the tourist crowds have thinned out.

AVERAGE HIGH/LOW TEMPERATURES (° F)

Salt Lake City

Jan 37/19	**May** 72/46	**Sept** 79/51
Feb 44/25	**June** 83/55	**Oct** 66/40
Mar 52/31	**July** 92/64	**Nov** 51/31
Apr 61/38	**Aug** 89/62	**Dec** 38/22

Parks and Recreation

Water-related activities, hiking, riding, various other sports, picnicking and visitor centers, as well as camping, are available in many of Utah's state parks. Day-use fee, including picnicking, boat launching, and museums: $5-$20 per vehicle. Camping (mid-Apr-Oct; some sites available rest of year), $7-$16 per site per night; most sites have a 14-day maximum. Advance reservations can be obtained at most developed state parks; phone 801/322-3770 (Salt Lake City) or toll-free 800/322-3770. Pets allowed on leash only. Senior citizen and disabled permit (free; UT residents only). For information on park facilities and permits, contact Utah State Parks & Recreation, 1594 W North Temple, Salt Lake City 84114; phone 801/538-7220.

FISHING AND HUNTING

Wildlife habitat authorization $6; nonresident deer permit $198; permit for bull elk $300; once-in-a-lifetime permit for moose, bison, desert bighorn sheep, Rocky Mountain goat $1,003. For special permits, write for information and apply from early to late January (bucks, bulls, and once-in-a-lifetime draw) and early June (antlerless draw). Small game licenses $40. Deer, elk, ducks, geese, pheasants, mourning doves, and grouse are favorite quarry.

Further information can be obtained from the Division of Wildlife Resources, 1594 W North Temple, Box 146301, Salt Lake City 84114-6301; phone 801/538-4700.

More than 3,000 lakes and hundreds of miles of mountain streams are filled with rainbow, German brown, cutthroat, Mackinaw, and brook trout; there are also catfish, walleyed pike, bass, crappie, and bluegill. Nonresident season fishing license (14 years and over) $45; seven-day fishing license $27; one-day fishing license $8.

Driving Information

Safety belts are mandatory for all persons in the front seat of a vehicle. Children under age 8 must be in approved passenger restraints anywhere in a vehicle; children ages 2-7 may use regulation safety belts; and children under age 2 must use approved safety seats.

INTERSTATE HIGHWAY SYSTEM

Use the following list as a guide to access interstate highways in Utah. Always consult a map to confirm driving routes.

Highway Number	Cities/Towns within 10 Miles
Interstate 15	Beaver, Brigham City, Cedar City, Fillmore, Nephi, Ogden, Payson, Provo, Salt Lake City, St. George.
Interstate 70	Green River, Salina.
Interstate 80	Salt Lake City, Wendover.

WALLS OF STONE

This three- to four-day tour out of Moab includes magnificent vistas, whimsical rock formations, an early "newspaper," and the upper reaches of Lake Powell. From Moab, head south on Hwy 191 to Hwy 211; follow 211 west to Newspaper Rock, a huge sandstone panel with petroglyphs that are up to 1,500 years old. Images etched into this wall of stone were left by prehistoric peoples such as the Fremonts and Ancestral Puebloans, as well as the Utes, Navajo, and European-American settlers from the 19th and early 20th centuries. From Newspaper Rock, it is an easy drive west on Hwy 211 to the Needles District of Canyonlands National Park. You probably visited the Island in the Sky District of Canyonlands during your stay in Moab, but this section of the park offers a different perspective. Although best explored by mountain bike or in a high-clearance four-wheel-drive vehicle, there are several roadside viewpoints from which you can see the district's namesake red-and-white-striped rock pinnacles and other formations. Several easy hikes offer additional views.

Retrace your route back to Hwy 191, and continue south to Hwy 95, where you will head west to Natural Bridges National Monument. This easy-to-explore monument has a scenic drive with overlooks that offer views of three awe-inspiring natural stone bridges and some 700-year-old Ancestral Puebloan cliff dwellings. There is also prehistoric rock art and a demonstration of how solar energy is used to produce the monument's electricity. The viewpoints are short walks from parking areas, and the more ambitious can also hike to all three of the natural bridges, which were created over millions of years as water cut through solid rock.

Returning to Hwy 95, head northwest to the Hite Crossing section of Glen Canyon National Recreation Area. Encompassing the northern end of Lake Powell, this is one of the least developed and also least crowded sections of the recreation area. Hite has scenic views, boat rentals, and plenty of available lodging (including houseboats). This is a good opportunity for kids who have spent too much time in the car to stretch their legs and play in the water.

From Hite, continue northwest on Hwy 95 across rock-studded terrain to Hanksville; head north on Hwy 24 to the turnoff to Goblin Valley State Park. This delightful little park–sure to be a favorite of anyone with a vivid imagination–is a fantasyland where whimsical stone goblins seem to be frozen in mid-dance. From Goblin Valley, return to Hwy 24 and continue north to I-70. Head east to the community of Green River, which offers an ample supply of motels. Here you'll discover Green River State Park, a good spot for a picnic under the Russian olive and cottonwood trees along the river or perhaps a round of golf at the park's nine-hole championship course. Nearby, the John Wesley Powell River History Museum tells the incredible story of explorer Powell, a one-armed Civil War veteran who did what was considered impossible when he charted the Green and Colorado rivers in the late 1800s. From Green River continue east on I-70 to Hwy 191, which leads south back to Moab. **(Approximately 448 miles)**

Additional Visitor Information

Utah Travel Council, Council Hall, Capitol Hill, 300 N State St, Salt Lake City 84114, will furnish excellent, extensive information about every section of the state and about special and annual events (phone 801/538-1030 or toll-free 800/200-1160).

There are several visitor centers in Utah, with information and brochures about points of interest. Major centers can be found at the following locations: Utah Field House of Natural History, 235 E Main St, Vernal; St George Information Center, Dixie Center; Echo Information Center, 2 miles east of junction I-80 E, I-80 N; Thompson Information Center, on I-70, 45 miles west of Utah-Colorado border; and Brigham City Information Center, I-15, 5 miles north.

The Utah Fine Arts Council (617 E South Temple, Salt Lake City 84102, phone 801/236-7555) provides information about local and statewide artists, museums, galleries, and exhibits.

Alta

See also Heber City, Park City, Salt Lake City, Snowbird

Population 370
Elevation 8,600 ft
Area Code 435
Zip 84092

Founded around silver mines in the 1870s, Alta was notorious for constant shoot-outs in its 26 saloons. The town became the center of a noted ski area in 1937, with the opening of Utah's first ski resort. Historic markers identify the original townsite. Unusual wildflowers are found in Albion Basin.

What to See and Do

Alta Ski Area. *On Hwy 210 in Little Cottonwood Canyon, Alta. Phone 801/359-1078. www.altaskiarea.com.* Three triple, five double chairlifts; four rope tows; patrol, school, rentals, snowmaking; lodges, restaurant, cafeteria. Longest run 3.5 miles, vertical drop 2,020 feet. Half-day rates. No snowboarding. (Mid-Nov-Apr, daily) **$$$$**

Limited-Service Hotels

★ ALTA LODGE. *State Rd 210, Alta (84092). Phone 435/742-3500; toll-free 800/707-2582; fax 435/742-3504. www.altalodge.com.* The original guest rooms of this small hotel were built in 1939, shortly after Alta's first ski resort opened. Today, the lodge is a mix of room styles, with dormlike rooms as well as newer and more luxurious rooms with mountain views, fireplaces, and balconies. Rates include full breakfast and dinner. Two saunas and whirlpools with a 30-foot wall of glass facing the slopes help guests thaw out after a day in the snow, and the private sundeck has a wonderful view of the mountain. In this city of natural beauty, there are no TVs in the guest rooms, although there's a big-screen TV in the lobby area if you must indulge. 57 rooms, 3 story. Closed mid-late Oct, May. Check-out 11 am. Wireless Internet access. Restaurant, bar. Children's activity center. Whirlpool. Tennis. Ski in/ski out. **$**

★★ ALTA'S RUSTLER LODGE. *Little Cottonwood Canyon, Alta (84092). Phone 435/742-2200; toll-free 888/532-2582; fax 435/742-3832. www.rustlerlodge.com.* With its ski in/ski out access to all of Alta's lift base facilities and a full-service ski shop on site, the Rustler Lodge is all about skiing; those with a passion for powder need look no further. A complimentary shuttle takes guests wherever they want to go in Alta and Snowbird, and the new business center offers high-speed and wireless Internet access for those who need to stay in and get some work done between runs. For extra pampering, the lodge also has steam room and offers manicures, pedicures, and other spa treatments. Organized children's programs and events keep young ones occupied while Mom and Dad hit the slopes. 85 rooms, 5 story. Closed May-Oct. Check-out 1 pm. Restaurant, bar. Fitness room, fitness classes available. Outdoor pool, whirlpool. Ski in/ski out. Business center. **$$$**

Arches National Park (D-5)

See also Moab

Web site www.nps.gov/arch.

5 miles NW of Moab on Hwy 191 to paved entrance road.

This timeless, natural landscape of giant stone arches, pinnacles, spires, fins, and windows was once the bed of an ancient sea. Over time, erosion laid bare the skeletal structure of the earth, making this 114-square-mile area a spectacular outdoor museum. This wilderness, which contains the greatest density of natural arches in the world, was named a national monument in 1929 and a national park in 1971. More than 2,000 arches have been cataloged, ranging in size from 3 feet wide to the 105-foot-high, 306-foot-wide Landscape Arch.

The arches, other rock formations, and views of the Colorado River canyon, with the peaks of the LaSal Mountains in the distance, can be reached by car, but hiking is the best way to explore. Petroglyphs from the primitive peoples who roamed this section of Utah from A.D. 700-1200 can be seen at the Delicate Arch trailhead. This is a wildlife sanctuary; no hunting is permitted. Hiking, rock climbing, or camping in isolated sections should not be undertaken unless first reported to a park ranger at the visitor center (check locally for hours). Twenty-four miles of paved roads are open year-round. Graded and dirt roads should not be attempted in wet weather. Devils Garden Campground, 18 miles north of the visitor center off Hwy 191, provides 52 individual and 2 group camp sites (year-round; fee; water available only March-mid-October). There is an entrance fee of $10 for a seven-day permit; Golden Eagle, Golden Age, and Golden Access passports are accepted (see MAKING THE MOST OF YOUR TRIP). Contact the Superintendent, PO Box 907, Moab 84532; phone 435/259-8161 or 435/259-5279 (TTY).

Beaver (D-2)

See also Cedar City, Richfield

Settled 1856
Population 2,454
Elevation 5,898 ft
Area Code 435
Zip 84713
Information Chamber of Commerce, 1603 S Campground Rd, PO Box 760; phone 435/438-5081
Web site www.beaverutah.net

The seat of Beaver County, this town is a national historic district with more than 200 houses of varied architectural styles and periods. It is also the birthplace of Butch Cassidy (1866).

Problems arose in Beaver's early days when tough gentile prospectors (in Utah, anyone not a Mormon was called a "gentile"), who came with a mining boom, derided the Mormons, who owned woolen mills. There was little harmony until the boom was over, but millions in gold, silver, lead, copper, tungsten, zinc, bismuth, and sulphur had been mined by then. Now, irrigation has brought farming to Beaver. Dairying and stock-raising, as well as recreation, hunting, and fishing, are important to the economy.

What to See and Do

Elk Meadows Ski and Summer Resort. *Hwy 153, Beaver. 18 miles E on I-15. Phone 435/438-5433; toll-free 888/881-7669. www.elkmeadows.com.* Quad, triple, three double chairlifts; one surface lift; school, rentals. Snowboarding. Shops, café, lodging. Longest run 2 1/2 miles; vertical drop 1,400 feet. Over 400 inches of snowfall annually. (Mid-Dec-Apr, daily)

Fishlake National Forest. *115 E 900 N, Richfield. E on Hwy 153. Phone 435/896-9233. www.fs.fed.us/r4/fishlake.* (See RICHFIELD) A Ranger District office of the forest is located in Beaver.

Special Event

Pioneer Day Celebration and Parade. *Beaver. Phone 435/438-5081.* Features a parade, entertainment, and horse racing, along with other events. Late July.

Limited-Service Hotels

★ BEST WESTERN BUTCH CASSIDY INN. *161 S Main St, Beaver (84713). Phone 435/438-2438; toll-free 800/780-7234; fax 435/438-1053. www.bestwestern.com.* 35 rooms, 2 story. Pets accepted; fee. Complimentary continental breakfast. Check-in 3 pm, check-out 11 am. High-speed Internet access. Fitness room. Heated outdoor pool, whirlpool. **$**

★ QUALITY INN. *781 W 1800 S, Beaver (84713). Phone 435/438-5426; fax 435/438-2493. www.qualityinn.com.* 52 rooms, 2 story. Pets accepted, some restrictions. Check-in 3 pm, check-out 11 am. Indoor pool, whirlpool. **$**

Blanding (E-5)

See also Bluff, Monticello, Natural Bridges National Monument

Settled 1905
Population 3,162
Elevation 6,105 ft
Area Code 435
Zip 84511
Information San Juan County Visitor Center, 117 S Main St, Box 490, Monticello 84535; phone 435/587-3235 or toll-free 800/574-4386
Web site www.blandingutah.org

In 1940, with a population of 600, Blanding was the largest town in a county the size of Connecticut, Rhode Island, and Delaware combined. Although it's surrounded by ranches and grazing areas, the city is a gateway to hunting and fishing grounds and national monuments. The sites can be explored by jeep or horseback along the many trails, or by boat through the waters of Glen Canyon National Recreation Area.

A Pueblo ruin, inhabited between AD 800 and AD 1200, is now a state park within the city limits.

What to See and Do

Edge of the Cedars State Park. *1 mile NW off Hwy 191. Phone 435/678-2238. www.utah.com/stateparks/edge_of_cedars.htm.* This park sits on the site of a pre-Columbian Pueblo Indian ruin. You'll find excavated remnants of ancient dwellings and ceremonial chambers fashioned by the ancient Pueblo people, as well as artifacts and pictographs and a museum of Native American history and culture. Visitor center. (Daily; hours vary by season) **$**

Glen Canyon National Recreation Area/Lake Powell. *4 miles S on Hwy 191, then 85 miles W on Hwy 95 and Hwy 276. Phone 928/608-6200. www.nps.gov/glca.* (See LAKE POWELL.) **$$**

★ **Hovenweep National Monument.** *Blanding. Approximately 13 miles S on Hwy 191, then 9 miles E on Hwy 262 and 6 miles E on county roads to Hatch Trading Post; follow signs 16 miles to Hovenweep. Phone 970/562-4282. www.nps.gov/hove.* The monument consists of six units of prehistoric ruins; the best preserved are the remains of pueblos (small cliff dwellings) and towers at Square Tower. Self-guided trail; park ranger on duty; visitor center (daily 8 am-5 pm; closed Jan 1, Thanksgiving, Dec 25). **$$**

Bluff (E-5)

See also Blanding

Founded 1880
Population 320
Elevation 4,320 ft
Area Code 435
Zip 84512
Information San Juan County Visitor Center, 117 S Main St, Box 490, Monticello 84535; phone 435/587-3235 or toll-free 800/574-4386
Web site www.bluffutah.org

Bluff's dramatic location between the sandstone cliffs along the San Juan River, its Anasazi ruins among the canyon walls, and its Mormon pioneer past all combine to make it an interesting stop along scenic Hwy 163 between the Grand Canyon and Mesa Verde national parks.

What to See and Do

★ **Tours of the Big Country.** *Hwy 191, Bluff. Phone 435/672-2281.* Trips to Monument Valley, the Navajo Reservation, and into the canyons of southeastern Utah explore desert plant and the wildlife, history, geology, and Anasazi archaeology of this area. Naturalist-guided walking and four-wheel-drive tours. Llama rentals. Half-day, full-day, and overnight trips. (Year-round) **$$$$**

Wild Rivers Expeditions. *101 Main St, Bluff. Phone 435/672-2244; toll-free 800/422-7654. www.riversandruins.com.* This tour company, in business since 1957, arranges fun and educational single-day and multi-day trips on the archaeologically rich San Juan River, framed by dramatic red rock formations and fossil beds. Licensed guides, many of whom are archaeologists, geologists, or of Navajo descent, conduct the tours, interpreting the native ruins and rock art found along the journey. Reserve well in advance. (Mar-mid-Nov) **$$$$**

Special Event

Utah Navajo Fair. *Bluff. Phone toll-free 800/574-4386.* Traditional song and dance, food, crafts, and a rodeo. Mid-Sept.

Brigham City (A-3)

See also Logan, Ogden

Settled 1851
Population 17,411
Elevation 4,439 ft
Area Code 435
Zip 84302
Information Chamber of Commerce, 6 N Main St, PO Box 458; phone 435/723-3931
Web site www.brigham-city.org

Renamed for Brigham Young in 1877, when he made his last public address here, this community was first known as Box Elder because of the many trees of that type that grew in the area. Main Street, which runs through the center of this city situated at the base of the towering Wasatch Mountains, is still lined with these leafy trees.

What to See and Do

Brigham City Museum-Gallery. *24 N 300 W, Brigham City. Phone 435/723-6769.* Permanent history exhibits, rotating art exhibits; displays include furniture, clothing, books, photographs, and documents reflecting the history of the Brigham City area since 1851. (Tues-Fri 11 am-6 pm, Sat 1-5 pm) **FREE**

Golden Spike National Historic Site. *Brigham City. 32 miles W via Hwys 13 and 83. Phone 435/471-2209. www.nps.gov/gosp.* This is the site where America's first transcontinental railroad was completed when the Central Pacific and Union Pacific lines met on May 10, 1869. At the visitor center, you'll find movies and exhibits (daily 9 am-5:30 pm; closed Jan 1, Thanksgiving, Dec 25; also Mon-Tues mid-Oct-Apr). There's also a self-guided auto tour along the old railroad bed. The summer interpretive program includes presentations and operating replicas of the steam locomotives *Jupiter* and *119* (May-early Oct, daily). (See SPECIAL EVENTS) Golden Eagle, Golden Age, Golden Access passports are accepted (see MAKING THE MOST OF YOUR TRIP). For more information, contact the Chief Ranger, PO Box 897. **$$**

Tabernacle. *251 S Main St, Brigham City. Phone 435/723-5376.* (1881) The Box Elder tabernacle, one of the most architecturally interesting buildings in Utah, has been in continuous use since 1881, gutted by fire and rebuilt in the late 1890s and restored in the late 1980s. Guided tours are given in the summer months. **FREE**

Special Events

Box Elder County Fair. *Brigham City.* Late Aug.

Driving of the Golden Spike. *Brigham City. Phone 435/471-2209.* The reenactment of the driving of the golden spike takes place at the Promontory, the site where the Central Pacific and Union Pacific railroads met in 1869. Locomotive replicas are used. Mid-May.

Peach Days Celebration. *Brigham City.* Parade, arts and crafts, carnival; car show, entertainment. First weekend after Labor Day.

Railroaders Festival. *6450 N 22000 W, Howell.* Golden Spike National Historic Site. Relive the rush to complete transcontinental railroad. Professional railroaders pursue world record in spike driving. Second Sat in Aug.

Limited-Service Hotel

★ **CRYSTAL INN.** *480 Westland Dr, Brigham City (84302). Phone 435/723-0440; toll-free 800/408-0440; fax 435/723-0446. www.crystalinns.com.* 30 rooms. Check-in 3 pm, check-out 11 am. **$**

Bryce Canyon National Park (E-2)

Web site www.nps.gov/brca

7 miles S of Panguitch on Hwy 89, then 17 miles SE on Hwy 12 to Hwy 63, 3 miles to entrance.

Bryce Canyon is a 56-square-mile area of colorful, fantastic cliffs created by millions of years of erosion. Towering rocks worn to odd, sculptured shapes stand grouped in striking sequences. The Paiute, who once lived nearby, called this "the place where red rocks stand like men in a bowl-shaped canyon." Although termed a canyon, Bryce is actually a series of "breaks" in 12 large amphitheaters—some plunging as deep as 1,000 feet into the multicolored limestone. The formations appear to change color as the sunlight strikes from different angles and seem incandescent in the late afternoon. The famous Pink Cliffs were carved from the Claron Formation; shades of red, orange, white, gray, purple, brown, and soft yellow appear in the strata. The park road follows 17 miles along the eastern edge of the Paunsaugunt Plateau, where the natural amphitheaters are spread out below; plateaus covered with evergreens and valleys filled with sagebrush stretch away into the distance.

The visitor center at the entrance station has information about the park, including orientation shows, geologic displays, and detailed maps (daily; closed Jan 1, Thanksgiving, Dec 25). The park is open 24 hours a day year-round; in winter, the park road is open to most viewpoints. Lodging is also available from April to October. There is an entrance fee of $20 per vehicle; motorcycles, bicyclists, and pedestrians pay $10. Golden Eagle, Golden Age, and Golden Access passports are accepted (see MAKING THE MOST OF YOUR TRIP). To ease traffic around the park, a shuttle system operates from the intersection of Hwys 12 and 63 and from Ruby's Inn, on Hwy 63 just north of the park. For more information, contact the Superintendent, PO Box 170001, Bryce Canyon 84717; phone 435/834-5322.

What to See and Do

Camping. *Bryce Canyon.* North Campground (year-round), east of park headquarters; Sunset Campground, 2 miles S of park headquarters. Fourteen-day limit at both sites; fireplaces, picnic tables, rest rooms, water available. (Apr-Oct) **$$$**

Hikes. *Bryce Canyon.* With ranger naturalists into canyon. (June-Aug)

Riding. *Bryce Canyon.* Horses and mules available, guided trips early morning, afternoon (spring, summer, fall). Fee.

Talks. *Bryce Canyon.* Given by rangers about history, geology, fauna, flora at campgrounds or lodge auditorium in the evening. (June-Aug)

Limited-Service Hotels

★ ★ BEST WESTERN RUBY'S INN. *Hwy 63, Bryce Canyon (84764). Phone 435/834-5341; fax 435/834-5265. www.rubysinn.com.* Rodeo in summer; general store. Lake on property. 368 rooms, 3 story. Pets accepted, some restrictions. Check-in 4 pm, check-out 11 am. Restaurant. Indoor pool, outdoor pool, whirlpool. **$**

★ ★ BRYCE CANYON LODGE. *1 Bryce Canyon Lodge, Bryce Canyon (84717). Phone 435/834-5361; fax 435/834-5330. www.brycecanyonlodge.com.* Original 1925 building. 114 rooms. Closed Dec-Mar. Check-in 4 pm, check-out 11 am. Restaurant.**$**

Restaurant

★ FOSTER'S STEAK HOUSE. *Hwy 12, Bryce Canyon National Park (84764). Phone 435/834-5227; fax 435/834-5304.* Steak menu. Breakfast, lunch, dinner. Children's menu. **$$**

Canyonlands National Park (D-4)

See also Moab, Monticello

N district: 12 miles N of Moab on Hwy 191, then 21 miles SW on Hwy 313; S district: 12 miles N of Monticello on Hwy 191, then 38 miles W on Hwy 211.

Spectacular rock formations, canyons, arches, spires, pictograph panels, ancestral Puebloan ruins, and desert flora are the main features of this 337,570-acre area. Set aside by Congress in 1964 as a national park, the area is largely undeveloped. Road conditions vary; primary access roads are paved and maintained, while others are safe only for high-clearance four-wheel-drive vehicles. For backcountry road conditions and information, phone 801/259-7164.

Island in the Sky, North District, south and west of Dead Horse Point State Park (see MOAB), has Grand View Point, Upheaval Dome, and Green River Overlook. This section is accessible by passenger car via Hwy 313 and by four-wheel-drive vehicles and mountain bikes on dirt roads.

Needles, South District, has hiking trails and four-wheel-drive roads to Angel Arch, Chesler Park, and the confluence of the Green and Colorado rivers. Also here are prehistoric ruins and rock art. This section is accessible by passenger car via Hwy 211, by four-wheel-drive vehicle on dirt roads, and by mountain bike.

Maze, West District, is accessible by hiking or by four-wheel-drive vehicles using unimproved roads. The most remote and least-visited section of the park, this area received its name from the many mazelike canyons. Horseshoe Canyon, a separate unit of the park nearby, is accessible via Hwy 24 and 30 miles of two-wheel-drive dirt road. Roads are usually passable only in mid-March through mid-November.

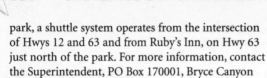

Canyonlands is excellent for calm-water and whitewater trips down the Green and Colorado rivers. Permits are required for private trips (fee; contact Reservation Office, 435/259-4351) and commercial trips (see MOAB). Campgrounds, with tent sites, are located at

Island in the Sky (fee) and at Needles (fee); water is available only at Needles. Visitor centers are in each district and are open daily. There is an entrance fee of $10 per vehicle. Golden Eagle, Golden Age, Golden Access passports are accepted (see MAKING THE MOST OF YOUR TRIP). Contact Canyonlands *NP, 2282 S West Resource Blvd, Moab 84532; phone 435/259-7164.*

Capitol Reef National Park (E-3)

Web site www.nps.gov/care

10 miles E of Richfield on Hwy 119, then 65 miles SE on Hwy 24.

Capitol Reef, at an elevation ranging from 3,900-8,800 feet, is composed of red sandstone cliffs capped with domes of white sandstone. Located in the heart of Utah's slickrock country, the park is actually a 100-mile section of the Waterpocket Fold, an upthrust of sedimentary rock created during the formation of the Rocky Mountains. Pockets in the rocks collect thousands of gallons of water each time it rains. Capitol Reef was so named because the rocks formed a natural barrier to pioneer travel and the white sandstone domes resemble the dome of the US Capitol.

From A.D. 700-1350, this 378-square-mile area was the home of an ancient people who grew corn along the Fremont River. Petroglyphs can be seen on some of the sandstone walls. A schoolhouse, farmhouse, and orchards, established by early Mormon settlers, are open to the public in season.

The park can be approached from either the east or the west via Hwy 24, a paved road. There is a visitor center on this road about 7 miles from the west boundary and 8 miles from the east (daily; closed Dec 25). A 25-mile round-trip scenic drive, some parts unpaved, starts from this point. There are evening programs and guided walks (Memorial Day-Labor Day; free). Three campgrounds are available: Fruita, approximately 1 mile south off Hwy 24, provides 70 tent and trailer sites year-round (fee); Cedar Mesa, 23 miles south off Hwy 24, and Cathedral, 28 miles north off Hwy 24, offer five primitive sites with access depending on the weather (free; no facilities). There is an entrance fee of $4 per vehicle. Golden Eagle, Golden Age, Golden Access passports are accepted (see MAKING THE MOST OF YOUR TRIP). Contact the Superintendent, HC 70, Box 15, Torrey 84775; phone 435/425-3791.

Cedar Breaks National Monument (E-2)

See also Cedar City

Web site www.nps.gov/cebr.

23 miles E of Cedar City via Hwy 14.

Cedar Breaks National Monument's major formation is a spectacular, multicolored, natural amphitheater created by the same forces that sculpted Utah's other rock formations. The amphitheater, shaped like an enormous coliseum, is 2,000 feet deep and more than 3 miles in diameter. It is carved out of the Markagunt Plateau and is surrounded by Dixie National Forest (see CEDAR CITY). Cedar Breaks, at an elevation of more than 10,000 feet, was established as a national monument in 1933. It derives its name from the surrounding cedar trees and the word "breaks," which means "badlands." Although similar to Bryce Canyon National Park, Cedar Breaks's formations are fewer but more vivid and varied in color. Young lava beds, resulting from small volcanic eruptions and cracks in the earth's surface, surround the Breaks area; the heavy forests include bristlecone pines, one of the oldest trees on the earth. Here, as soon as the snow melts, wildflowers bloom profusely and continue to bloom throughout the summer.

Rim Drive, a 5-mile scenic road through the Cedar Breaks High Country, provides views of the monument's formations from four different overlooks. The area is open late May to mid-October, weather permitting. Point Supreme Campground, 2 miles north of south entrance, provides 30 tent and trailer sites (mid-June-mid-September, fee; water, rest rooms). The visitor center offers geological exhibits (June-mid-October, daily); interpretive activities (mid-June-Labor Day). There is an entrance fee of $4 per vehicle. Golden Eagle, Golden Age, Golden Access passports accepted (see MAKING THE MOST OF YOUR TRIP). Contact the Superintendent, 2390 W Hwy 56, Suite 11, Cedar City 84720; phone 435/586-9451.

Cedar City (E-2)

See also Beaver, Cedar Breaks National Monument, Panguitch

Settled 1851
Population 20,527
Elevation 5,834 ft
Area Code 435
Zip 84720
Information Chamber of Commerce, 581 N Main St; phone 435/586-4484
Web site www.cedarcity.org

In 1852, Cedar City produced the first iron made west of the Mississippi. The blast furnace operation was not successful, however, and stock-raising soon overshadowed it, though iron is still mined west of the city on a limited basis. A branch line of the Union Pacific entered the region in 1923 and helped develop the area. Now a tourist center because of its proximity to Bryce Canyon and Zion national parks (see both), Cedar City takes pride in its abundant natural wonders; streams and lakes have rainbow trout, and the Markagunt Plateau provides deer and mountain lion hunting. Headquarters and a Ranger District office of the Dixie National Forest are located here.

What to See and Do

Brian Head Ski Resort. *329 S Hwy 143, Brian Head. 19 miles NE on I-15 to Parowan, then 11 miles SE on Hwy 143, in Dixie National Forest. Phone 435/677-2035. www.brianhead.com.* Five triple, double chairlift; patrol, school, rentals; restaurants, cafeterias, bars, nursery, ski shops, grocery, gift shops, lodging. Longest run 1/2 mile, vertical drop 1,700 feet. (Mid-Nov-early Apr, daily) Cross-country trails, rentals; snowmobiling, night skiing. Mountain biking (summer). **$$$$**

Dixie National Forest. *82 N and 100 E, Cedar City. 12 miles E on Hwy 14 to forest boundary or 17 miles SW on I-15, then W. Phone 435/865-3200. www.fs.fed.us/dxnf.* This 2-million-acre forest provides opportunities for camping, fishing, hiking, mountain biking, and winter sports. For more information, contact the Supervisor, PO Box 580, 84721. (Daily) **FREE**

Iron Mission State Park. *635 N Main, Cedar City. Phone 435/586-9290. www.stateparks.utah.gov/park_pages/iron.htm.* The museum at the park is dedicated to the first pioneer iron foundry west of the Rockies and features an extensive collection of horse-drawn vehicles and wagons from Utah pioneer days. (Daily; closed Jan 1, Thanksgiving, Dec 25) **$**

Kolob Canyons Visitor Center. *3752 E Kolob Canyon Rd, New Harmony. 17 miles S on I-15. Phone 435/586-9548.* This section of Zion National Park (see) provides a 14-mile round-trip hike to the Kolob Arch, world's second largest, with a span of 310 feet. A 5-mile scenic drive offers spectacular views of rugged peaks and sheer canyon walls 1,500 feet high. (Daily; closed Jan 1, Thanksgiving, Dec 25) **FREE**

Sightseeing trips. *Cedar City Air Service. 2281 W Kitty Hawk Dr, Cedar City. Phone 435/586-3881.* Trips include Cedar Breaks National Monument and Grand Canyon, Zion, and Bryce Canyon national parks (see all); other trips available. (Daily) **$$$$**

Southern Utah University. *351 W Center, Cedar City. Phone 435/586-7700.* (1897) (7,000 students) Braithwaite Fine Arts Gallery (Mon-Sat; free). (See SPECIAL EVENTS)

Special Events

Renaissance Fair. *City Park, Cedar City.* Entertainment, food, and games, all in the style of the Renaissance. Held in conjunction with opening of Utah Shakespearean Festival. Early July.

Utah Shakespearean Festival. *Southern Utah University campus, 351 W Center St, Cedar City. Phone 435/586-7878.* Shakespeare presented on outdoor stage (a replica of 16th-century Tiring House) and 750-seat indoor facility. Mon-Sat evenings; preplay activities. Children over 5 years only; babysitting at festival grounds. Phone 435/586-7878 (box office). Late June-early Oct.

Utah Summer Games. *351 W Center St, Cedar City. Phone 435/586-8421.* Olympic-style athletic events for amateur athletes. June.

Limited-Service Hotels

★ **ABBEY INN.** *940 W 200 N, Cedar City (01453). Phone 435/586-9966; toll-free 800/325-5411; fax 435/586-6522. www.abbeyinncedar.com.* 81 rooms, 2 story. Complimentary full breakfast. Check-in 2 pm, check-out 11 am. Indoor pool, whirlpool. Airport transportation available. **$**

★ **BEST WESTERN TOWN AND COUNTRY INN.** *189 N Main, Cedar City (84720). Phone 435/586-9900; toll-free 800/528-1234; fax 435/586-1664. www.bwtowncountry.com.* 157 rooms, 2 story. Check-in 3 pm, check-out 11 am. Indoor pool, outdoor pool, whirlpool. **$**

Dinosaur National Monument (B-5)

Web site www.nps.gov/dino

7 miles N of Jensen on Hwy 149.

On August 17, 1909, paleontologist Earl Douglass discovered dinosaur bones in this area, including several nearly complete skeletons. Since then, this location has provided more skeletons, skulls, and bones of Jurassic-period dinosaurs than any other dig in the world. The dinosaur site comprises only 80 acres of this 325-square-mile park, which lies at the border of Utah and Colorado. The back country section, most of which is in Colorado, is a land of fantastic and deeply eroded canyons of the Green and Yampa rivers. Access to this backcountry section is via the Harpers Corner Road, starting at monument headquarters on Hwy 40, 2 miles east of Dinosaur, Colorado. At Harpers Corner, the end of this 32-mile surfaced road, a 1-mile foot trail leads to a promontory overlooking the Green and Yampa rivers, more than 2,500 feet below. The entire area was named a national monument in 1915. Utah's Dinosaur Quarry section can be entered from the junction of Hwy 40 and Hwy 149, north of Jensen, 13 miles east of Vernal; approximately 7 miles north on Hwy 149 is the fossil exhibit. Another 5 miles north is Green River Campground, with 90 tent and trailer sites available mid-May to mid-September. A smaller campground, Rainbow Park, provides a small number of tent sites from May to November. Lodore, Deerlodge, and Echo Park campgrounds are available in Colorado. A fee is charged at Green River, Echo Park, and Lodore (water and rest rooms available).

Because of snow, some areas of the monument are closed from approximately mid-November to mid-April. Golden Eagle, Golden Age, Golden Access passports are accepted. Contact the Superintendent, 4545 E Hwy 40, Dinosaur, CO 81610. (Closed holidays)

What to See and Do

Backpacking. *Dinosaur National Monument.* By permit obtainable at visitor centers; few marked trails.

Dinosaur Quarry. *11625 E 1500 S, Jensen. 7 miles N of Jensen, UT, on Hwy 149. Phone 970/374-3000. www.nps.gov/dino.* Remarkable fossil deposit; exhibit of 150-million-year-old dinosaur remains; preparation laboratory on display. (Early June-early Sept: daily 8 am-7 pm; rest of the year: daily 8 am-4:30 pm; closed Jan 1, Thanksgiving, Dec 25) **$$$**

Picnicking, hiking, fishing. *Dinosaur National Monument. Phone 970/374-2468.* Harpers Corner area has picnic facilities, also picnicking at campgrounds. Self-guided nature trails (all-year), guided nature walks. State fishing license required; boating permit required (obtainable by advance lottery at the Headquarters River Office).

River rafting. *Dinosaur National Monument. Phone 970/374-2468.* On Green and Yampa rivers, by advance permit from National Park Service or with concession-operated guided float trips. Information at River Office.

Fairview (C-3)

Restaurants

★ **BIRCH CREEK INN.** *22130 N 11750 E, Fairview (84629). Phone 435/427-9578.* A local favorite with large portions and an inviting atmosphere. American menu. Lunch, dinner. Closed Sun. **$$**

★ HOME PLATE CAFE. *215 N State St, Fairview (84629). Phone 435/427-9300.* This restaurant features a baseball-inspired menu of outdoor favorites. American menu. Lunch, dinner. Closed Sun. **$**

Fillmore (D-2)

See also Nephi, Richfield

Settled 1856
Population 2,253
Elevation 5,135 ft
Area Code 435
Zip 84631
Information Chamber of Commerce, City of Fillmore, 96 S Main St, PO Box 687; phone 435/743-6121
Web site www.millardcounty.com

Fillmore, the seat of Millard County and Utah's territorial capital until 1856, is today a trading center for the surrounding farm and livestock region. It is a popular hunting and fishing area. A Ranger District office of the Fishlake National Forest is located here.

What to See and Do

Fishlake National Forest. *115 E 900 N, Fillmore. E on improved gravel road. Phone 435/896-9233.* (see RICHFIELD)

Territorial Statehouse State Park. *50 W Capitol Ave, Fillmore. Phone 435/743-5316.* Utah's first territorial capitol, built in the 1850s of red sandstone, is now a museum with an extensive collection of pioneer furnishings, pictures, Native American artifacts, and early documents; also rose garden. (Mon-Sat; closed Jan 1, Thanksgiving, Dec 25) **$**

Resort

★ ★ BEST WESTERN PARADISE INN AND RESORT. *905 N Main, Fillmore (84631). Phone 435/743-6895; fax 435/743-6892. www.bestwestern.com.* 80 rooms, 2 story. Pets accepted, some restrictions. Check-out 11 am. Restaurant. Pool, whirlpool. **$**

Garden City (A-3)

See also Logan

Settled 1875
Population 357
Elevation 5,960 ft
Area Code 435
Zip 84028
Information Bear Lake Convention & Visitors Bureau, PO Box 26, Fish Haven, ID 83287; phone 208/945-2333 or toll-free 800/448-2327
Web site www.bearlake.org

As was the case with many of Utah's towns, Garden City was settled by Mormon pioneers sent here from Salt Lake City. Today, it is a small resort town on the western shore of Bear Lake.

What to See and Do

Bear Lake. *Garden City.* Covering 71,000 acres on the border of Utah and Idaho, this body of water is the state's second-largest freshwater lake. Approximately 20 miles long and 200 feet deep, it offers good fishing for mackinaw, rainbow trout, and the rare Bonneville Cisco. Boat rentals at several resorts. On the western shore is

> **Bear Lake State Park.** *147 W Logan Rd, Garden City. 2 miles N on Hwy 89. Phone toll-free 800/322-3770.* Three park areas include State Marina on west shore of lake, Rendezvous Beach on south shore, and Eastside area on east shore. Swimming, beach, waterskiing, fishing, ice fishing, boating (ramp, dock), sailing; hiking, mountain biking, cross-country skiing, snowmobiling, picnicking, tent and trailer sites (rest rooms, showers, hook-ups, dump station; fee). Visitor center. (Daily) **$$**

Beaver Mountain Ski Area. *Garden City. 14 miles W via Hwy 89. Phone 435/753-0921. www.skithebeav.com.* Three double chairlifts, two surface lifts; patrol, school, rentals; day lodge, cafeteria. Twenty-two runs; vertical drop 1,600 feet. Half-day rates. (Dec-early Apr, daily) **$$$$**

Green River (D-4)

Settled 1878
Population 973
Elevation 4,079 ft
Area Code 435
Zip 84525
Information Green River Travel Council, 885 E Main St; phone 435/564-3526

Originally a mail relay station between Ouray, Colorado, and Salina, Utah, Green River now produces premium watermelons and cantaloupes on land irrigated by the Green River, one of Utah's largest rivers.

What to See and Do

Goblin Valley State Park. *450 S Green River Blvd, Green River. 50 miles W on I-70 (Hwy 50), then 30 miles S on Hwy 24. Phone 435/564-3633.* Mile-wide basin filled with intricately eroded sandstone formations. Hiking, camping (rest rooms, showers, dump station). (Daily) **$$**

John Wesley Powell River History Museum. *885 E Main St, Green River. Phone 435/564-3427.* This 20,000-square-foot museum sits on the banks of the Green River. Contains exhibits exploring geology and geography of area; auditorium with 20-minute multimedia presentation; river runner Hall of Fame. Green River Visitor Center (daily). Gift shop. Picnic area. (Daily; closed Jan 1, Thanksgiving, Dec 25) **$**

River trips. *Green River.* On the Colorado, Green, San Juan, and Dolores rivers.

Colorado River & Trail Expeditions, Inc. *125 E and 1000 N sts, Green River. Phone 801/261-1789; toll-free 800/253-7328.* PO Box 57575, Salt Lake City 84157-0575. **$$$$**

Holiday River and Bike Expeditions. *544 E 3900 S, Green River. Phone 801/266-2087; toll-free 800/624-6323 (except UT).* **$$$$**

Moki Mac River Expeditions. *6006 S 1300 E, Salt Lake City. Phone 801/268-6667; toll-free 800/284-7280.* **$$$$**

Special Event

Melon Days. *Green River.* Third weekend in Sept.

Limited-Service Hotels

★ BEST WESTERN RIVER TERRACE MOTEL. *880 E Main St, Green River (84525). Phone 435/564-3401; fax 435/564-3403. www.bestwestern.com.* 51 rooms, 3 story. Check-out 11 am. Pool, whirlpool. **$**

★ HOLIDAY INN EXPRESS. *965 E Main St, Green River (84525). Phone 435/564-4439; fax 435/564-3333. www.hiexpress.com.* 60 rooms. Check-in 3 pm, check-out noon. **$**

Restaurant

★ TAMARISK. *870 E Main St, Green River (84525). Phone 435/564-8109; fax 435/564-8590.* American menu. Breakfast, lunch, dinner. Closed Thanksgiving, Dec 25. Children's menu. **$$**

Heber City (B-3)

See also Alta, Park City, Salt Lake City, Timpanogos Cave National Monument

Settled 1859
Population 7,291
Elevation 5,595 ft
Area Code 435
Zip 84032
Information Heber Valley Chamber of Commerce, 475 N Main St, PO Box 427; phone 435/654-3666
Web site www.hebervalleycc.org

Located in a fertile, mountain-ringed valley, Heber City was once a commercial and livestock shipping center. Unusual crater mineral springs, called hot pots, are located 4 miles west near Midway. Mount Timpanogos, one of the most impressive mountains in the state, is to the southwest in the Wasatch Range. Good picnicking, fishing, and hunting areas abound. A Ranger District office of the Uinta National Forest (see PROVO) is located here.

What to See and Do

Deer Creek State Park. *Hwy 189, Midway. 8 miles SW on Hwy 189. Phone 435/654-0171.* Swimming, fishing, boating (ramp); camping (fee; rest rooms, showers; dump and fish cleaning stations). (Daily) **$$$**

Heber Valley Railroad. *450 S 600 W, Heber City. Phone 435/654-5601.* A 90-year-old steam-powered excursion train takes passengers through the farmlands of Heber Valley, along the shore of Deer Creek Lake and into Provo Canyon on various one-hour to four-hour trips. Restored coaches and open-air cars. Special trips some Fri, Sat evenings. Reservations required. (May-mid-Oct, Tues-Sun; mid-Oct-Nov, schedule varies; Dec-Apr, Mon-Sat) **$$$$**

Wasatch Mountain State Park. *2 miles NW off Hwy 224. Phone 435/654-1791.* Approximately 25,000 acres in Heber Valley. Fishing; hiking, 36-hole golf, snowmobiling, cross-country skiing, picnicking, restaurant, camping (fee; hookups, dump station). Visitor center. (Daily)

Special Events

Swiss Days. *55 S Center St, Heber City. 4 miles W in Midway.* "Old country" games, activities, costumes. Fri and Sat before Labor Day.

Wasatch County Fair. *2843 S Daniels Rd, Heber City.* Parades, exhibits, country market, livestock shows, rodeos, dancing. First weekend in Aug.

Limited-Service Hotel

★ HOLIDAY INN EXPRESS. *1268 S Main St, Heber City (84302). Phone 435/654-9990; fax 435/654-9991. www.hiexpress.com.* 75 rooms. Check-in 3 pm, check-out noon. Pool, whirlpool. **$**

Full-Service Resort

★★★ HOMESTEAD RESORT. *700 N Homestead Dr, Midway (84049). Phone 435/654-1102; toll-free 888/327-7220; fax 435/654-5087. www.homesteadresort.com.* Surrounded by lush gardens and the Wasatch Mountains, this historic country resort (1886) welcomes guests with Western hospitality. Quaint cottages make up the majority of the guest accommodations, which range from traditional and historic rooms to executive suites and condos that accommodate large groups. Activities are plentiful on 200 acres, with cowboy poetry readings, yard games, and a video arcade complemented by more adventurous pursuits like snowmobiling and downhill skiing. The resort rents cross-country skis, snowshoes, and bicycles to guests and offers guided horseback rides as well as buggy, wagon, and sleigh rides. It even has its own crater, in which guests can float in the crystal-clear, 90-plus-degree mineral waters. 142 rooms, 2 story. Check-in 4 pm, check-out noon. Restaurant, bar. Children's activity center. Fitness room, spa. Indoor pool, outdoor pool, whirlpool. Golf, 18 holes. Tennis. Business center. **$$**

Specialty Lodging

The following lodging establishment is approved by Mobil Travel Guide, but due to its unique and individualized nature has not been given a traditional Mobil Star rating. Included in this listing you may find bed-and-breakfasts, limited-service inns, guest ranches, and other unique hotel properties.

THE SUNDOWNER INN BED & BREAKFAST. *425 Moulton Lane, Heber City (84032). Phone 435/654-4200. www.thesundownerinn.com.* 9 rooms. Check-in 4 pm, check-out 11 am. Complimentary full-breakfast. **$$**

Huntington (C-4)

Restaurant

★ CANYON RIM CAFE. *505 N Main St, Huntington (84528). Phone 435/687-9040.* Regional cuisine in an attractive family-style setting. American menu. Lunch, dinner. Closed Sun. **$**

Kanab (F-2)

See also Pipe Spring National Monument

Founded 1870
Population 3,564
Elevation 4,909 ft
Area Code 435
Zip 84741
Information Kane County Office of Tourism, 78 E 100 S; phone 435/644-5033 or toll-free 800/733-5263
Web site www.kaneutah.com

Located at the base of the Vermilion Cliffs, this city began around Fort Kanab, built in 1864. Native Americans, however, forced the abandonment of the fort. Later, Mormon missionaries made Kanab a permanent settlement. The city's regular economy revolves around tourism. Since 1922, more than 200 Hollywood productions have used the sand dunes, canyons, and lakes surrounding Kanab as their settings. Some movie-set towns can still be seen. Kanab is within a 1 1/2-hour drive from the north rim of the Grand Canyon, Zion, and Bryce Canyon national parks, Cedar Breaks and Pipe Spring national monuments, and Glen Canyon National Recreation Area.

Kanab Fun Fact

- Kanab is known as Utah's Little Hollywood because of the large number of motion pictures that are filmed in the area.

What to See and Do

Coral Pink Sand Dunes State Park. *Yellowjacket and Hancock rds, Kanab. 8 miles NW on Hwy 89, then 12 miles SW on county road. Phone 435/648-2800.* Six square miles of very colorful, windswept sandhills. Hiking, picnicking, tent and trailer sites (fee; showers, dump station). Off-highway vehicles allowed; exploring, photography. (Daily) **$$**

Glen Canyon National Recreation Area/Lake Powell. *Page. Phone 928/608-6404.* 68 miles E via Hwy 89, at Wahweap Lodge and Marina (see PAGE, AZ); access in Utah at Bullfrog Marina (see LAKE POWELL).

Grand Canyon Scenic Flights. *Kanab. 2 1/2 miles S on Hwy 89 A. Phone 435/644-2299.* Flights to Grand Canyon during daylight hours; flight covering Bryce Canyon and Zion national parks, Lake Powell, and Coral Pink Sand Dunes. (All year) **$$$$**

Limited-Service Hotels

★ BEST WESTERN RED HILLS. *125 W Center St, Kanab (84741). Phone 435/644-2675; toll-free 800/830-2675; fax 435/644-5919. www.kanabbestwestern.com.* 75 rooms, 2 story. Check-in 3 pm, check-out 11 am. Pool, whirlpool. **$**

★ ★ PARRY LODGE. *89 E Center St, Kanab (84741). Phone 435/644-2601; toll-free 800/748-4104; fax 435/644-2605. www.infowest.com/parry.* Autographed pictures of movie stars displayed in lobby. 89 rooms, 2 story. Closed Dec-mid-March. Pets accepted; fee. Check-out 11 am. Restaurant. **$**

Restaurant

★ HOUSTON'S TRAIL'S END. *32 E Center St, Kanab (84741). Phone 435/644-2488; fax 435/644-8148. www.houstons.com.* American menu. Breakfast, lunch, dinner. Closed mid-Dec-mid-Mar. Children's menu. Casual attire. **$**

Lake Powell

See also Page

Web site www.lakepowell.com

Lake Powell, formed by the Glen Canyon Dam on the Colorado River, is located in Glen Canyon National Recreation Area. It stretches 186 miles, has more than 1,900 miles of shoreline, is the second largest man-made lake in the United States, and is located in the second largest canyon in the US. The lake is named for John Wesley Powell, the one-armed explorer who, in 1869, successfully navigated the Colorado River through Glen Canyon and the Grand Canyon and later became director of the US Geological Survey.

What to See and Do

Boat trips on Lake Powell. *Bullfrog Marina, Hwy 276, Lake Powell. From Bullfrog or Halls Crossing marinas, both on Hwy 276. Phone toll-free 800/528-6154.* Trips include Canyon Explorer tour (2 1/2 hours) and all-day Rainbow Bridge National Monument tour; also houseboat and powerboat rentals. Reservations advised. (Daily)

Glen Canyon National Recreation Area (Bullfrog Marina). *On Hwy 276, Lake Powell. Phone 435/684-2243.* Additional access and recreational activities avail at Hite Marina, north end of lake. This boasts more than 1 million acres with year-round recreation area, swimming, fishing, boating, boat tours and trips, boat rentals and repairs; picnicking, camping, tent and trailer sites (full hookups; fee), lodgings. A ranger station and visitor center are located in Bullfrog on Hwy 276 (Apr-Oct, daily).

Lake Powell Ferry. *Bullfrog Marina on Hwy 276, Lake Powell. Phone 435/538-1030.* Approximately 3-mile trip between Bullfrog and Hall's Crossing saves 130 miles driving around lake. (Daily; reduced hours in winter) Contact Bullfrog Marina. **$$$$**

Limited-Service Hotel

★★ DEFIANCE HOUSE LODGE. *Hwy 276, Bullfrog (84533). Phone 435/684-3032; toll-free 800/528-6154; fax 435/684-3114.* Anasazi motif; décor, artifacts. 48 rooms, 2 story. Pets accepted. Check-in 3 pm, check-out 11 am. Restaurant, bar. Airport transportation available. **$**

Logan (A-3)

See also Brigham City, Garden City

Founded 1856
Population 42,670
Elevation 4,535 ft
Area Code 435
Zip 84321
Information Logan Convention & Visitors Bureau/Bridgerland Travel Region, 160 N Main; phone 435/752-2161 or toll-free 800/882-4433
Web site www.ci.logan.ut.us

Logan, situated in the center of beautiful Cache Valley, is surrounded by snowcapped mountains. The city received its name from an early trapper, Ephraim Logan. Begun by Mormons who were dedicated to living from fruits of the soil, little was sold in Logan's early days except timber and farm produce. The change to a more industrialized economic base came about slowly. Now the city of Logan is the location of Utah State University, five electronics plants, space technology, book printing, plastics, baking, and meat-packing plants, as well as specialized woodworking and locally made craft and collectible shops.

What to See and Do

Daughters of the Utah Pioneers Museum. *158 S 500 W St, Logan. Phone 435/752-5139.* Exhibits depict Utah's past. 160 N Main, in Chamber of Commerce Building. (Mon-Fri) **FREE**

Hyrum State Park. *405 W 300 S, Logan. 12 miles S, off Hwy 89/90. Phone 435/245-6866.* A 450-acre reservoir with beach swimming, waterskiing, fishing, ice fishing, boating (ramp, dock), sailing; picnicking, camping (trailer parking). (Year-round) **$$**

Mormon Tabernacle. *50 N Main St, Logan. Phone 435/755-5598.* (1891) A gray limestone example of an early Mormon building; seats 1,800. Genealogy library. (Mon-Fri)

Mormon Temple. *175 N 300 E, Logan. Phone 435/752-3611.* (1884) The site for this massive, castellated limestone structure was chosen by Brigham Young, who also broke ground for it in 1877. Grounds are open all year, but the temple is closed to the general public.

Utah State University. *7th N and 7th E sts, Logan. Phone 435/797-1129.* (1888) (20,100 students) On campus is the Nora Eccles Harrison Museum of Art (Mon-Fri; closed holidays, also Thanksgiving weekend, Dec 22-Jan 2; free).

Wasatch-Cache National Forest, Logan Canyon. *1500 E Hwy 89, Logan. Phone 435/755-3620. www.fs.fed.us/r4/wcnf.* Fishing, backcountry trails, hunting, winter sports, picnicking, camping. Fees are charged at most recreation sites. (Daily) E on Hwy 89 National Forest (scenic byway). A Ranger District office is located in Logan at 1500 E Hwy 89.

Willow Park Zoo. *419 W 700 S, Logan. Phone 435/750-9893.* This small but attractive zoo has shady grounds and especially good bird-watching of migratory species, with more than 100 captive species and 80 species of wild birds visiting and nesting at the zoo. (Daily 9 am-dusk; closed Jan 1, Thanksgiving, Dec 25) **$**

Special Events

American West Heritage Center. *7700 Old Main Hill, Hwy 8991 in Wellsville. Phone 435/245-6050.* Pioneer and Native American crafts fair, art exhibition, antique quilt show; frontier town; medicine man show; log construction; Dutch-oven cooking demonstration. Late July-early Aug.

Cache County Fair. *400 S 500 W. Logan.* Rodeo, horse races, exhibits. Early Aug.

Utah Festival Opera Company. *59 S 100 W, Logan.* July-Aug.

Limited-Service Hotels

★ ★ BEST WESTERN BAUGH MOTEL. *153 S Main St, Logan (84321). Phone 435/752-5220; fax 435/752-3251. www.bestwestern.com.* 77 rooms, 2 story. Pets accepted. Complimentary continental breakfast. Check-in 2 pm, check-out 11 am. Restaurant. Outdoor pool, whirlpool. **$**

★ COMFORT INN. *447 N Main St, Logan (84321). Phone 435/752-9141; fax 435/752-9723. www.comfortinn.com.* 83 rooms, 2 story. Complimentary continental breakfast. Check-in 2 pm, check-out noon. Fitness room. Indoor pool, whirlpool. **$**

Specialty Lodging

The following lodging establishment is approved by Mobil Travel Guide, but due to its unique and individualized nature has not been given a traditional Mobil Star rating. Included in this listing you may find bed-and-breakfasts, limited-service inns, guest ranches, and other unique hotel properties.

THE ANNIVERSARY INN. *169 E Center St, Logan (84321). Phone 435/752-3443; toll-free 800/574-7605; fax 435/752-8550. www.anniversaryinn.com.* Not your typical frilly B&B, this inn's guest rooms and suites are all charmingly unique, each appointed with its own theme. From the Pyramids of Egypt to Aphrodite's Court to Lost in Space, each room is guaranteed to tickle your fancy. Most have jetted tubs, and some have fireplaces and big-screen TVs. Lobby in historic mansion (1879); Oriental rugs, period furniture. 20 rooms. No children allowed. Check-in 5 pm, check-out noon. Whirlpool. **$$**

PROVIDENCE INN. *10 S Main, Providence (84332). Phone 435/752-3432; toll-free 800/480-4943; fax 435/752-3482. www.providenceinn.com.* As part of "The Old Rock Church" building, this historic bed-and-breakfast has rooms decorated in various periods: Early American, Victorian, and Georgian. A hearty breakfast is provided and guests may sit in the parlor and enjoy the fireplace and selection of reading material or wander through the landscaped grounds. Built in 1869; accurately restored.17 rooms, 3 story. Check-in 4 pm, check-out 11 am. **$$**

Restaurants

★ BLUEBIRD. *19 N Main St, Logan (84321). Phone 435/752-3155; toll-free 800/772-3155.* American menu. Lunch, dinner. Closed Sun; Thanksgivng, Dec 25, children's menu. Casual attire. **$**

★ CABIN FEVER CAFE. *180 W 1200 S, Logan (84321). Phone 435/563-4700.* This is a favorite of Logan residents providing good food in a comfortable family setting. American menu. Breakfast, lunch, dinner. **$**

★ ★ CAFE SABOR. *600 W Center St, Logan (84321). Phone 435/752-2700.* This regional Mexican eatery is located in the historic Center Street Depot. Mexican menu. Lunch, dinner. **$**

★ THE COPPER MILL. *55 N Main St, Logan (84321). Phone 435/752-0647.* A local favorite serving family-style food in a comfortable settings. American menu. Lunch, dinner. **$**

★ ★ GIA'S RESTAURANT AND DELI. *119 S Main St, Logan (84321). Phone 435/752-8384; fax 435/750-6595.* Italian menu. Lunch, dinner. Closed Dec 25. Casual attire. **$**

★ ★ LE NONNE. *132 N Main St, Logan (84321). Phone 435/752-9577.* Located in downtown Logan, this establishment specializes in traditional Italian specialties. Italian menu. Lunch, dinner. Closed Mon. **$$**

Midway

Full-Service Inns

★ ★ ★ THE BLUE BOAR INN. *1235 Warm Springs Rd, Midway (84049). Phone 435/654-1400; toll-free 888/650-1400; fax 435/654-6459. www.theblueboarinn.com.* Utah's secluded and picturesque Heber Valley is home to the heartwarming Blue Boar Inn. The blissful quietude of this remote location is perfect for visitors wanting to unwind, yet be in relatively close proximity to the slopes and nightlife of the ski resorts of Deer Valley, The Canyons, and Sundance. During the summer months, nearby fly fishing and 54 holes of golf entertain guests. While the chandeliers are crafted of antlers and the furnishings are indicative of the region, the restaurant is a showpiece of fresh American cuisine. Decorated in a unique Austrian-influenced style, the guest rooms are enlivened with an amusing theme inspired by famous authors and poets. From the handmade willow bed of the Robert Frost and the whimsical design of the Lewis Carroll to the English cottage style of the William Butler Yeats and the exotic flavor of the Rudyard Kipling, each room attempts to capture its namesake's distinctive personality. *Secret Inspector's Notes: The Blue Boar Inn is perfect for travelers seeking a bed-and-breakfast-like experience, with a pleasant staff and quiet rooms. The location is a little odd, in the center of what appears to be a housing development and removed from other popular destinations. For those wishing to hike or fish in the Heber Valley, this may be appropriate. Amenities at this inn are limited, but the breakfasts are absolutely delicious as long as you have the patience to wait for their arrival.* 14 rooms, 2 story. Complimentary full breakfast. Check-in 3 pm, check-out noon. Restaurant, bar. Business center. **$$**

★★★ INN ON THE CREEK. *375 Rainbow Ln, Midway (84049). Phone toll-free 800/654-0892. www.innoncreek.com.* 40 rooms. Check-in 3 pm, check-out noon. Restaurant, bar. **$$**

Restaurants

★★★ THE BLUE BOAR INN RESTAURANT. *1235 Warm Springs Rd, Midway (84049). Phone 435/654-1400; toll-free 888/650-1400; fax 435/654-6459. www.theblueboarinn.com.* Well worth the 20-minute drive from Park City, this charming Tyrolean chalet offers some of the best New American cuisine in Utah. Flavors are clean and fresh as Chef Jesse Layman endeavors to accentuate the natural quality of each item. The menu changes periodically to capture the best produce and fresh seafood available. American menu. Lunch, dinner, Sun brunch. Bar. Casual attire. Outdoor seating. **$$$**

★★★ SIMON'S FINE DINING. *700 N Homestead Dr, Midway (84032). Phone 435/654-1102; toll-free 800/327-7220; fax 435/654-5087. www.homesteadresort.com.* Dine in an elegant country setting either inside the dining room by the fireplace or outside on the deck, with beautiful views of the valley. American menu. Dinner, Sun brunch. Closed Mon-Tues. Bar. Children's menu. Casual attire. Outdoor seating. **$$**

Millville

Limited-Service Hotel

★ BEAVER CREEK LODGE. *Hwy 89, Millville (84326). Phone 435/946-3400; toll-free 800/946-4485. www.beavercreeklodge.com.* Offering many outdoors amenities from skiing and hiking to snowmobiles. 11 rooms, 3 story. **$$**

Moab (D-5)

See also Arches National Park, Canyonlands National Park

Founded 1879
Population 4,779
Elevation 4,025 ft
Area Code 435
Zip 84532
Information Moab Area Travel Council, PO Box 550; phone 435/259-8825, 435/259-1370, or toll-free 800/635-6622
Web site www.discovermoab.com

The first attempt to settle this valley was made in 1855, but Moab, named after an isolated area in the Bible, was not permanently settled until 1880. Situated on the Colorado River at the foot of the LaSal Mountains, Moab was a sleepy agricultural town until after World War II, when uranium exploration and production, and oil and potash development made it boom. Today, tourism and moviemaking help make it a thriving community. A Ranger District office of the Manti-LaSal National Forest is located here, as are headquarters for Canyonlands and Arches national parks.

What to See and Do

Canyonlands By Night. *1861 S Hwy 191, Moab. Leaves dock at bridge, 2 miles N on Hwy 191. Phone 435/259-2628; toll-free 800/394-9978. www.canyonlandsbynight.com.* Two-hour boat trip with sound-and-light presentation highlights history of area. (Apr-mid-Oct, daily, leaves at sundown, weather permitting) Reservations required; tickets must be purchased at office. **$$$$**

Dan O'Laurie Canyon Country Museum. *118 E Center St, Moab. Phone 435/259-7985.* Exhibits on local history, archaeology, geology, uranium, minerals of the area. Walking tour information. (Summer: Mon-Sat 1-8 pm; winter: Mon-Thurs 3-7 pm, Fri-Sat 1-7 pm; closed holidays) **$**

Dead Horse Point State Park. *313 State Rd, Moab. 9 miles NW on Hwy 191, then 22 miles SW on Hwy 313. Phone 435/259-2614; toll-free 800/322-3770 (camping).* Promontory rising 2,000 feet above the Colorado River, this island mesa offers views of the LaSal Mountains, Canyonlands National Park, and the Colorado River. Approximately 5,200 acres in region of gorges, cliffs, buttes, and mesas. Visitor center, museum. Picnicking, limited drinking water, camping (fee; electricity, dump station). Trailer parking. (Daily) **$**

Hole 'n the Rock. *11037 S Hwy 191, Moab. 12 miles S via Hwy 191. Phone 435/686-2250. www.moab-utah.com/holeintheroc.* A 5,000-square-foot home carved into huge sandstone rock. Picnic area with stone tables and benches. Tours. (Daily 8 am-dusk; closed Thanksgiving, Dec 25) **$$**

Manti-LaSal National Forest, LaSal Division. *2290 Resource Blvd, Moab. 8 miles S on Hwy 191, then 5 miles E. Phone 435/259-7155. www.fs.fed.us/r4/mantilasal.* The land of the forest's LaSal Division is similar in color and beauty to some parts of the Grand Canyon, but also includes high mountains nearing 13,000 feet and pine and spruce forests. Swimming, fishing; hiking, hunting. Contact the Ranger District office, 125 W 200 S. (See MONTICELLO, PRICE) **FREE**

Pack Creek Ranch trail rides. *Pack Creek Ranch Rd, Moab. Just off LaSal Mountain Loop Rd. Phone 435/259-5505. www.packcreekranch.com.* Horseback rides, ranging from 1 to 1 1/2 hours, in foothills of LaSal Mountain. Guided tours for small groups; reservations required. (Mar-Oct; upon availability) **$$$$**

Redtail Aviation Scenic Air Tours. *N Hwy 191, Moab. 18 miles N on Hwy 191, at Canyonlands Field. Phone 435/259-7421; toll-free 800/842-9251.* Flights over Canyonlands National Park and various other tours. (All-year; closed Jan 1, Thanksgiving, Dec 25) **$$$$**

Rim tours. *1233 S Hwy 191, Moab. Phone 435/259-5223; toll-free 800/626-7335. www.rimtours.com.* Guided mountain bike tours in canyon country and the Colorado Rockies. Vehicle support for camping tours. Daily and overnight trips; combination bicycle/river trips available. **$$$$**

River trips. *Moab. Phone 435/259-8825.* On the Green and Colorado rivers, includes Canyonlands National Park, Lake Powell (see both), and Cataract Canyon.

Adrift Adventures. *378 N Main St, Moab. Phone 435/259-8594; toll-free 800/874-4483. www.adrift.net.* Oar, paddle, and motorized trips available; one to seven days. Jeep tours and horseback rides are also available. (Early Apr-late Oct) **$$$$**

Canyon Voyages. *211 N Main St, Moab. Phone 435/259-6007; toll-free 800/733-6007. www.canyonvoyages.com.* Kayaking, whitewater rafting, canoeing, biking, or four-wheel drive tours. (Early Apr-Oct) **$$$$**

Colorado River & Trail Expeditions, Inc. *PO Box 57575, Moab. Colorado and Green rivers. Phone 801/261-1789; toll-free 800/253-7328. www.crateinc.com.* Motor- and oar-powered raft trips down the Colorado and Green rivers. **$$$$**

Sheri Griffith River Expeditions. *2231 S Hwy 191, Moab. Phone 435/259-8229; toll-free 800/332-2439. www.griffithexp.com.* Choice of rafts: oarboats, motorized rafts, paddleboats, or inflatable kayaks; one-to-five day trips; instruction available. (May-Oct) **$$$$**

Tex's Riverways. *691 N 500 W, Moab. Phone 435/259-5101. www.texsriverways.com.* Flatwater canoe trips, four to ten days. Confluence pick-ups available, jet boat cruises. (Mar-Oct) **$$$$**

Tag-A-Long Expeditions. *452 N Main St, Moab. Phone 435/259-8946; toll-free 800/453-3292. www.tagalong.com.* One- to seven-day whitewater rafting trips on the Green and Colorado rivers; jetboat trips on the Colorado River; jetboat trips and four-wheel-drive tours into Canyonlands National Park; winter four-wheel-drive tours (Nov-Feb). Also Canyon Classics, one-day jetboat trips with cultural performing arts programs. (Apr-mid-Oct) **$$$$**

Special Events

Butch Cassidy Days PRCA Rodeo. *Moab. Phone toll-free 800/635-6622.* Second weekend in June.

Jeep Safari. *PO Box 1471, Moab. Phone 435/259-7625.* This event, sponsored by Red Rock Four Wheelers, offers 30 different trails. Easter week and weekend.

Moab Music Festival. *Suite 3, 59 S Main St, Moab. Held at various venues. Phone 435/259-7003. www.moabmusicfest.org.* This festival features classical music performed in natural settings throughout southeastern Utah. First two weeks in Sept.

Limited-Service Hotels

★★ BEST WESTERN CANYONLANDS INN. *16 S Main St, Moab (84532). Phone 435/259-5167; toll-free 800/780-7234; fax 435/259-2301. www.bestwestern.com.* 77 rooms, 2 story. Complimentary continental breakfast. Check-in 4 pm, check-out 11 am. Restaurant. Fitness room. Outdoor pool, whirlpool. **$**

★★ BEST WESTERN GREENWELL INN. *105 S Main St, Moab (84532). Phone 435/259-6151; fax 435/259-4397. www.bestwestern.com.* 72 rooms, 2 story. Check-in 3 pm, check-out 11 am. Restaurant. Fitness room. Outdoor pool, whirlpool. **$**

★ BOWEN MOTEL. *169 N Main St, Moab (84532). Phone 435/259-7132; toll-free 800/874-5439; fax 435/259-6641. www.bowenmotel.com.* 40 rooms, 2 story. Pets accepted, some restrictions; fee. Complimentary continental breakfast. Check-in 2 pm, check-out 11 am. Outdoor pool. **$**

Full-Service Resort

★★★ SORREL RIVER RANCH RESORT. *Hwy 128, Moab (84532). Phone 435/259-4642; toll-free 877/359-2715. www.sorrelriver.com.* Set amid a dramatic landscape of red rock formations, this full-service resort is just 30 minutes from Arches National Park. Many of the Western-themed guest rooms, all of which have kitchenettes, overlook the Colorado River; family loft suites are also available. Fireplaces and jetted hydrotherapy tubs are found in the deluxe suites. But outdoor recreation is really the focus in this mountain-biking mecca: from horseback riding to kayaking and whitewater rafting to basketball and volleyball, you'll find no shortage of ways to burn calories here. After an activity-filled day, while away the evening admiring the views from one of the porch swings or enjoy an upscale meal at the River Grill. 59 rooms. Check-in 4 pm, check-out 11 am. High-speed Internet access. Restaurant. Children's activity center. Fitness room, spa. Outdoor pool, children's pool, whirlpool. Tennis. **$$**

Specialty Lodgings

The following lodging establishments are approved by Mobil Travel Guide, but due to their unique and individualized nature have not been given a traditional Mobil Star rating. Included in this listing you may find bed-and-breakfasts, limited-service inns, guest ranches, and other unique hotel properties.

PACK CREEK RANCH. *Pack Creek Ranch Rd, Moab (84532). Phone 435/259-5505. www.packcreekranch.com.* 11 rooms. Pets accepted, some restrictions; fee. Check-in 3 pm, check-out 11 am. Outdoor pool, whirlpool. **$$**

SUNFLOWER HILL BED AND BREAKFAST. *185 N 300 E, Moab (84532). Phone 435/259-2974; fax 435/259-3065. www.sunflowerhill.com.* Turn-of-the-century adobe farmhouse, cottage amid gardens. 12 rooms, 2 story. Children over 10 years only. Check-in 3-6 pm, check-out 11 am. Whirlpool. **$**

Restaurants

★★ CENTER CAFE. *60 N 100 W, Moab (84532). Phone 435/259-4295; fax 435/259-0158.* International menu. Dinner. Closed Thanksgiving; Dec-Jan. Jacket required. Outdoor seating. **$$**

★ MOAB BREWERY. *686 S Main St, Moab (84532). Phone 435/259-6333. www.themoabbrewery.com.* Moab's only on-site microbrewery and restaurant with a full selection of regional specialties. American menu. Lunch, dinner. **$$**

★★ SLICKROCK CAFE. *5 N Main St, Moab (84532). Phone 435/259-8003. www.slickrockcafe.com.* A favorite local spot with adventurous Southwestern-inspired cuisine. American menu. Breakfast, lunch, dinner. **$**

Monticello (E-5)

See also Blanding, Canyonlands National Park

Founded 1887
Population 1,806
Elevation 7,066 ft
Area Code 435
Zip 84535
Information San Juan County Visitor Center, 117 S Main St, PO Box 490; phone 435/587-3235 or toll-free 800/574-4386
Web site www.monticelloutah.org

The highest county seat in Utah (San Juan County), Monticello was named for Thomas Jefferson's Virginia home. On the east slope of the Abajo Mountains, the elevation makes the weather delightful but the growing season short. Livestock raising, dry farming, and tourism are the chief industries.

What to See and Do

Canyon Rims Recreation Area. *82 E Dogwood St, Monticello. 20 miles N on Hwy 191.* Anticline and Needles overlooks into Canyonlands National Park are located here, as are Wind Whistle and Hatch campgrounds.

Manti-LaSal National Forest, LaSal Division. *62 E 100 N, Monticello. 2 1/2 miles W. Phone 435/587-2041.* (See MOAB, PRICE) The forest land of this division ranges from red rock canyons to high alpine terrain. Ancient ruins and rock art contrast with pine and spruce forests and aspen-dotted meadows. Fishing; hiking, snowmobiling, cross-country skiing, hunting, camping (fee). **FREE**

Special Events

Monticello Pioneer Days. *Monticello.* Parade, booths, food, games, sports. Weekend nearest July 24.

San Juan County Fair & Rodeo. *Monticello.* Second weekend in Aug.

Limited-Service Hotel

★ BEST WESTERN WAYSIDE MOTOR INN. *197 E Central Ave, Monticello (84535). Phone 435/587-2261; toll-free 800/633-9700; fax 435/587-2920. www.bestwestern.com.* 37 rooms. Pets accepted; fee. Complimentary continental breakfast. Check-in 2 pm, check-out 11 am. Outdoor pool, whirlpool. **$**

Natural Bridges National Monument (E-4)

See also Blanding

Web site www.nps.gov/nabr

4 miles S of Blanding on Hwy 191, then 36 miles W on Hwy 95, then 4 miles N on Hwy 275.

This 7,439-acre area of fantastically eroded and colorful terrain, made a national monument in 1908, features three natural bridges, all with Hopi names. Sipapu, a 268-foot span, and Kachina, a 204-foot span, are in White Canyon, a major tributary gorge of the Colorado River; Owachomo, a 180-foot span, is near Armstrong Canyon, which joins White Canyon. Sipapu is the second-largest natural bridge in the world. From 650 to 2,000 years ago, the ancestral Puebloan people lived in this area, leaving behind cliff dwelling ruins and pictographs that visitors can view today. Bridge View Drive, a 9-mile-loop road open daily from early morning to 30 minutes past sunset, provides views of the three bridges from rim overlooks. There are hiking trails to each bridge within the canyon.

In the park is a visitor center (daily 8 am-5 pm; closed holidays in winter) and a primitive campground with 13 tent and trailer sites (all year, fee; 26-foot combined-length limit). Car and passenger ferry service across Lake Powell is available (see LAKE POWELL). There is a $6 per vehicle entrance fee; Golden Eagle, Golden Age, Golden Access Passports are accepted (see MAKING THE MOST OF YOUR TRIP). For more information, contact the Superintendent, Box 1, Lake Powell 84533; phone 435/692-1234.

Nephi (C-3)

See also Fillmore, Payson

Settled 1851
Population 4,733
Elevation 5,133 ft
Area Code 435
Information Juab Travel Council, 4 S Main, PO Box 71, 84648; phone 435/623-5203 or 435/623-2411

What to See and Do

Yuba State Park. *30 miles S via I-15, near Scipio. Phone 435/758-2611.* Waterskiing and walleyed pike fishing are the big attractions of this lake, as well as sandy beaches. Swimming, waterskiing, fishing, boating (ramps); picnicking, camping (fee; rest rooms, showers, dump station). (Daily) **$$$**

Special Event

Ute Stampede Rodeo. *795 S Main St, Nephi. Phone 435/623-5608.* Three-day festival featuring Western and Mammoth parades, carnival, PRCA rodeo, contests, arts and crafts, concessions. Second weekend in July.

Limited-Service Hotel

★ BEST WESTERN PARADISE INN OF NEPHI. *1025 S Main, Nephi (84648). Phone 435/623-0624; fax 435/623-0755. www.bestwestern.com.* 40 rooms, 2 story. Pets accepted; fee. Complimentary continental breakfast. Check-in 2 pm, check-out noon. Indoor pool, whirlpool. **$**

Ogden (A-3)

See also Brigham City, Salt Lake City

Settled 1844
Population 77,226
Elevation 4,300 ft
Area Code 801
Information Convention & Visitors Bureau, 2501 Wall Ave, 84401; phone 801/627-8288 or toll-free 800/255-8824
Web site www.ogdencvb.org

The streets of Ogden, fourth-largest city in Utah, were laid out by Brigham Young in traditional Mormon geometrical style: broad, straight, and bordered by poplar, box elder, elm, and cottonwood trees. In the 1820s and 1830s, Ogden was a rendezvous and wintering place for trappers, who wandered as far afield as California and Oregon. In 1846, Miles Goodyear, the first white settler, built a cabin and trading post, Fort Buenaventura, here. The next year he sold out to the Mormons. During the last 30 years of the 19th century, Ogden was an outfitting center for trappers and hunters heading north. Its saloons and gambling halls were typical of a frontier town, and there was considerable friction between the Mormons and the "gentiles." With the coming of the railroad, however, Ogden became one of the few cities in Utah whose inhabitants were not primarily Mormons.

Today, Ogden is a commercial and industrial center. Hill Air Force Base is nearby. Bernard DeVoto—American novelist, journalist, historian, and critic, best known for his history of the western frontier—was born in Ogden, as was John M. Browning, inventor of the automatic rifle. Mount Ben Lomond, north of the city in the Wasatch Range, was the inspiration for the logo of Paramount Pictures. A Ranger District office of the Wasatch-Cache National Forest (see SALT LAKE CITY) is located in Ogden.

What to See and Do

Daughters of Utah Pioneers Museum & Relic Hall. *In Tabernacle Square, 2148 Grant Ave, Ogden. Phone 801/393-4460.* Old handicrafts, household items, pioneer clothing, furniture, and portraits of those who came to Utah prior to the railroad of 1869. Also Miles Goodyear's cabin, the first permanent house built in Utah. (Mid-May-mid-Sept, Mon-Sat) **FREE**

Eccles Community Art Center. *2580 Jefferson Ave, Ogden. Phone 801/392-6935.* A 19th-century castlelike mansion that hosts changing art exhibits, plus has a dance studio and an outdoor sculpture and floral garden. (Mon-Sat; closed holidays) **FREE**

Fort Buenaventura State Park. *2450 A Ave, Ogden. Phone 801/621-4808.* The exciting era of mountain men is brought to life on this 32-acre site, where the actual fort, Ogden's first settlement, was built in 1846 by Miles Goodyear. The fort has been reconstructed according to archaeological and historical research: no nails have been used in building the stockade, and wooden pegs and mortise and tenon joints hold the structure together. (Apr-Nov) **$$**

George S. Eccles Dinosaur Park. *1544 E Park Blvd, Ogden. Phone 801/393-3466.* Outdoor display containing more than 100 life-size reproductions of dinosaurs and other prehistoric creatures, plus an educational building with a working paleontological lab and fossil and reptile displays. (Daily; closed Nov-Mar) **$$**

Hill Aerospace Museum. *7961 Wardleigh Rd, Roy. 4 miles S on I-15, exit 341. Phone 801/777-6868.* More than 55 aircraft on display, some indoors and suspended from ceiling. Planes include B-29 Superfortress, SR-71 "Blackbird" reconnaissance plane, B-52 bomber, PT-71 Stearman; helicopters, jet engines, missiles; uniforms and other memorabilia. (Daily; closed Jan 1, Thanksgiving, Dec 25) **FREE**

Lagoon and Pioneer Village. *375 N Lagoon Dr, Farmington. Approximately 20 miles S on I-15. Phone 801/451-8000; toll-free 800/748-5246.* Amusement park. Thrill rides, musical entertainment, water park, food, campground. (June-Aug, daily; late Apr-Memorial Day and Labor Day-Oct, weekends) **$$$$**

Nordic Valley. *Ogden. 7 miles E on Hwy 39, then N on Hwy 162. Phone 801/745-3511.* Two chairlifts; patrol, school, rentals; snack bar, lounge. Longest run 1 1/2 miles, vertical drop 1,000 feet. (Dec-Apr, daily) **$$$$**

Pine View Reservoir. *Ogden. 9 miles E on Hwy 39 in Ogden Canyon in Wasatch-Cache National Forest.* Boating, fishing, waterskiing; camping, picnicking. Fees for activities.

Powder Mountain. *State Rd 158, Eden. 8 miles E on Hwy 39, then 11 miles N on Hwy 158. Phone 801/745-3772. www.powdermountain.net.* Quad, triple, two double chairlifts, three surface tows; patrol, school, rentals; food service, lodging. (Mid-Nov-Apr, daily) Night skiing. **$$$$**

Snowbasin. *Rte 26 and Ogden, Huntsville. 10 miles E on Hwy 39, then S on Hwy 226 in Wasatch-Cache National Forest. Phone 801/399-1135. www.snowbasin.com.* Two gondolas; quad, four triple, double chairlifts; patrol, school, rentals; food service, lodges. Longest run 3 miles, vertical drop 2,940 feet. (Late Nov-mid-Apr, daily) **$$$$**

Union Station–the Utah State Railroad Museum. *Center of Ogden, 2501 Wall Ave, Ogden. Phone 801/629-8444.* Spencer S. Eccles Railroad Center features some of the world's largest locomotives, model railroads, films, gem and mineral displays, guided tours by "conductors." Browning-Kimball Car Museum has classic American cars. Browning Firearms Museum contains the reconstructed original Browning gun shop and inventor's models. Also here is 500-seat theater for musical and dramatic productions and an art gallery; restaurant. Visitors Bureau for northern Utah located here. (June-Sept, daily; rest of the year, Mon-Sat; closed Jan 1, Thanksgiving, Dec 25) **$**

Weber State University. *3750 Harrison Blvd, Ogden. Off Hwy 89. Phone 801/626-6000.* (1889) (17,000 students) On campus are Layton P. Ott Planetarium, with natural science museum and Foucault pendulum, shows (Wed; no shows summer; fee); and Stewart Bell Tower, with 183-bell electronic carillon, performances (daily; free). Campus tours.

Willard Bay State Park. *Ogden. 15 miles N via I-15, exit 360, near Willard. Phone 435/734-9494.* This park features a 9,900-acre lake. Swimming, fishing, boating (ramps), sailing; picnicking, tent and trailer sites (fee; showers, dump station). (Daily) **$$**

Special Events

Pioneer Days. *Ogden Pioneer Stadium, 1875 Monroe Blvd, Ogden.* Rodeo, concerts, vintage car shows, fireworks, chili cookoff. Mon-Sat evenings. Mid-late July.

Utah Symphony Pops Concert. *Lindquist Fountain/Plaza, 1875 Monroe Blvd, Ogden.* Music enhanced by fireworks display. Late July.

Limited-Service Hotels

★ BEST WESTERN HIGH COUNTRY INN. *1335 W 12th St, Ogden (84404). Phone 801/394-9474; fax 801/392-6589.* 111 rooms. Check-in 1 pm, check-out 11 am. **$**

★ COMFORT INN AND SUITES. *2250 S 1200 W Ogden, Ogden (84401). Phone 801/621-2545; toll-free 800/517-4000; fax 801/627-4782. www.ogdencomfortsuites.com.* 40 rooms, all suites. Check-in 3 pm, check-out noon. **$**

★ HAMPTON INN & SUITES. *2401 Washington Blvd, Ogden (84405). Phone 801/394-9400; fax 801/394-9500. www.hamptoninn.com.* 135 rooms. Check-in 3 pm, check-out noon. **$**

Full-Service Hotel

★★ **MARRIOTT.** *247 24th St, Ogden (84401). Phone 801/627-1190; toll-free 888/825-3163; fax 801/394-6312. www.marriott.com.* This hotel is located in downtown Ogden, one block from the Eccles Convention Center and the Ogden Raptors baseball stadium and within walking distance of the Ogden City Mall. 292 rooms, 8 story. Check-in 3 pm, check-out noon. High-speed Internet access. Restaurant, bar. Fitness room. Indoor pool, whirlpool. Business center. **$**

Specialty Lodging

The following lodging establishment is approved by Mobil Travel Guide, but due to its unique and individualized nature has not been given a traditional Mobil Star rating. Included in this listing you may find bed-and-breakfasts, limited-service inns, guest ranches, and other unique hotel properties.

ALASKAN INN. *435 Ogden Canyon Rd, Ogden (84401). Phone 801/621-8600. www.alaskaninn.com.* 12 rooms. Check-in 3 pm, check-out 11 am. **$$**

Orem (B-3)

Restaurant

★★★ **CHEF'S TABLE.** *2005 S State St, Orem (84097). Phone 801/235-9111; fax 801/235-9333. www.chefstable.net.* American menu. Lunch, dinner. Closed Sun. Bar. Casual attire. Outdoor seating. **$$**

Panguitch (E-2)

See also Cedar City

Settled 1864
Population 1,623
Elevation 6,624 ft
Area Code 435
Zip 84759
Information Panguitch Chamber of Commerce, PO Box 400, 84759; phone 435/676-8585
Web site www.panguitch.org

A livestock, lumbering, and farm town, Panguitch is also a center for summer tourists who come to see nearby Bryce Canyon National Park and Cedar Breaks National Monument. The Paiutes named the city, which means "big fish," because of the large fish they caught in nearby Panguitch Lake. A Ranger District office of the Dixie National Forest (see CEDAR CITY) is located here.

What to See and Do

Anasazi Indian Village State Park. *460 N Hwy 12, Boulder. 75 miles E of Bryce Canyon National Park. Phone 435/335-7308.* Partially excavated village, believed to have been occupied from AD 1050-1200, is one of the largest ancient communities west of the Colorado River. Picnicking. Museum (daily; closed Jan 1, Thanksgiving, Dec 25). **$**

Panguitch Lake. *Panguitch. 17 miles SW on paved road in Dixie National Forest. Phone 435/676-2649.* This 8,000-foot-high lake, which fills a large volcanic basin, has fishing; resorts, public campgrounds (developed sites, fee), ice fishing, snowmobiling, cross-country skiing.

Paunsagaunt Wildlife Museum. *250 E Center St, Panguitch. Phone 435/676-2500.* More than 400 animals from North America in their natural habitat can be viewed here. Also exotic game animals from Africa, India, and Europe. (May-Oct, daily) **$$**

Limited-Service Hotel

★ **BEST WESTERN NEW WESTERN MOTEL.** *180 E Center St, Panguitch (84759). Phone 435/676-8876; fax 435/676-8876. www.bestwestern.com.* 55 rooms. Complimentary continental breakfast. Check-in noon, check-out 11 am. Outdoor pool, whirlpool. **$**

Restaurant

★ **FOY'S COUNTRY CORNER.** *80 N Main, Panguitch (84759). Phone 435/676-8851.* American menu. Breakfast, lunch, dinner. Closed Sun; Thanksgiving, Dec 25. Casual attire. **$**

Park City (B-3)

See also Alta, Heber City, Salt Lake City, Snowbird, Timpanogos Cave National Monument

Founded 1868
Population 7,371
Elevation 7,080 ft
Area Code 435
Zip 84060
Information Park City Chamber/Visitors Bureau, 1910 Prospector Ave, PO Box 1630; or the Visitor Information Center, 750 Kearns Ave; phone 435/649-6100, 435/649-6104, or toll-free 800/453-1360
Web site www.parkcityinfo.com

Soldiers struck silver here in 1868, starting one of the nation's largest silver mining camps, which reached a population of 10,000 before declining to a near ghost town when the silver market collapsed. Since then, however, Park City has been revived as a four-season resort area with skiing, snowboarding, golf, tennis, water sports, and mountain biking.

What to See and Do

Brighton Resort. *Park City. Approximately 10 miles SW via Hwy 190 in Big Cottonwood Canyon.* (see SALT LAKE CITY)

The Canyons. *4000 The Canyons Resort Dr, Park City. Phone 435/649-5400; toll-free 866/604-4171 (lodging and reservations). www.thecanyons.com.* Sixteen high-speed quad, triple, double chairlifts; gondola; patrol, school, rentals; restaurant, cafeteria, bar, lodge. One hundred-forty trails. Winter lift (daily 9 am-4 pm). (Thanksgiving-Apr, daily) **$$$$**

Deer Valley Resort. *2250 Deer Valley Dr S, Park City. 1 mile SE on Deer Valley Dr. Phone 435/649-1000; toll-free 800/424-3337. www.deervalley.com.* Eight high-speed quad, eight triple, two double chairlifts; rental, patrol, school, snowmaking; restaurants, lounge, lodge, nursery. Approximately 1,750 skiable acres. Vertical drop 3,000 feet. (Dec-mid-Apr, daily) Summer activities include mountain biking, hiking, horseback riding, and scenic chairlift rides (fee). **$$$$**

Egyptian Theatre. *328 Main St, Park City. Phone 435/649-9371. www.egyptiantheatrecompany.org.* (1926) Originally built as a silent movie and vaudeville house, now a year-round performing arts center with a full semiprofessional theater season. (Thurs-Sat; some performances other days)

Factory Stores at Park City. *6699 N Landmark Dr, Park City. I-80 and Hwy 224. Phone 435/645-7078. www.shopparkcity.com.* More than 45 outlet stores. (Daily)

Kimball Art Center. *638 Park Ave, Park City. Phone 435/649-8882. www.kimball-art.org.* Exhibits in various media by local and regional artists. Gallery (Mon, Wed-Fri 10 am-5 pm, Sat-Sun noon-5 pm) **FREE**

Park City Mountain Resort. *1310 Lowell Ave, Park City. Phone 435/649-8111toll-free 800/222-7275. www.pcski.com.* Gondola; quad, four double, five triple, three 6-passenger chairlifts; patrol, school, rentals, snowmaking; restaurants, cafeteria, bar. Approximately 2,200 acres; 100 novice, intermediate, expert slopes and trails; 750 acres of open-bowl skiing. Lighted snowboarding. (Mid-Nov-mid-Apr, daily) Alpine slide, children's park, miniature golf in summer (fees). **$$$$**

Rockport State Park. *9040 N Hwy 302, Park City. N on Hwy 248 and Hwy 40, then 8 miles NE on I-80, Wanship exit. Phone 435/336-2241.* Approximately 1,000-acre park along east side of Rockport Lake. Opportunity for viewing wildlife, including bald eagles (winter) and golden eagles. Swimming, water-skiing, sailboarding, fishing, boating (rentals, launch); picnicking, restaurant, concession, cross-country ski trail (6 miles), camping, tent and trailer sites. (Daily)

Solitude Resort. *Park City. W via I-80 to I-215 S, exit 6 in Big Cottonwood Canyon.* (See SALT LAKE CITY)

Utah Winter Sports Park. *3000 Bear Hollow Dr, Park City. 4 miles N on Bear Hollow Dr. Phone 435/658-4200.* Recreational ski jumping in $25-million park built for 2002 Olympic Winter Games. Nordic, competition, freestyle, and training jumps. Lessons followed by two-hour jumping session. Also Olympic bobsled and luge track (high-speed rides available). Day lodge, snack bar, gift shop. (Wed-Sun) **$$$$**

White Pine Touring Center. *Park City Golf Course, 201 Heber Ave, Park City. Approximately 1 mile N via Hwy 224. Phone 435/649-8710.* Groomed cross-country trails (12 miles), school, rentals; guided tours. (Nov-Apr, daily) Summer mountain biking; rentals. **$$$$**

Special Events

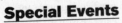

Art Festival. *Main St, Park City.* Open-air market featuring work of more than 200 visual artists. Also street entertainment. First weekend in Aug. **FREE**

Sundance Film Festival. *Park City. Events held throughout city. festival.sundance.org.* Ten-day festival for independent filmmakers. Workshops, screenings, and special events. Mid-Jan.

Uniting Fore Care Classic presented by Novell PGA Tournament. *Park Meadows Country Club, Park City. 8 miles N on Hwy 224.* PGA Invitational Golf tournament. Aug.

Limited-Service Hotels

★ HOLIDAY INN EXPRESS. *1501 West Ute Blvd, Park City (84098). Phone 435/658-1600; fax 435/658-1600. www.holiday-inn.com.* Conveniently located just off I-80 at the entrance to Park City, this hotel is well maintained and has a variety of accommodations. 76 rooms, 3 story. Pets accepted; fee. Complimentary continental breakfast. Check-in 3 pm, check-out noon. Fitness room. Indoor pool, whirlpool. **$**

★★ RADISSON INN. *2121 Park Ave, Park City (84060). Phone 435/649-5000; toll-free 800/649-5012; fax 435/649-2122. www.radisson.com.* 131 rooms. Pets accepted; fee. Complimentary full breakfast. Check-in 3 pm, check-out noon. Restaurant, bar. Indoor pool, outdoor pool, two whirlpools. Golf. Tennis. **$**

Full-Service Hotels

★★★ CHATEAUX AT SILVER LAKE. *7815 E Royal St, Park City (84060). Phone 435/658-9500; toll-free 800/453-3833; fax 435/658-9513. www.chateaux-deervalley.com.* 148 rooms. Check-in 4 pm, check-out 10 am. Restaurant, bar. Fitness room. Outdoor pool, whirlpool. **$$**

★★★ MARRIOTT. *1895 Sidewinder Dr, Park City (84060). Phone 435/649-2900; toll-free 800/234-9003; fax 435/754-3279. www.marriott.com.* This hotel is located a mile from downtown Park City and the historic Main Street. Ski packages are available if you'd like to enjoy the nearby slopes during your stay. Starbucks lovers will find a coffee kiosk in the lobby, and the hotel also rents ski equipment in winter and bicycles in summer. 199 rooms, 4 story. Pets accepted. Check-in 3 pm, check-out noon. High-speed Internet access. Two restaurants, bar. Fitness room. Indoor pool, whirlpool. Business center. **$**

Full-Service Resorts

★★★ THE CANYONS GRAND SUMMIT RESORT HOTEL. *4000 The Canyons Resort Dr, Park City (84098). Phone 435/649-5400; toll-free 888/591-5138; fax 435/615-8041. www.thecanyons.com.* This lovely mountain lodge, one of three at The Canyons Resort, has a spectacular location at the foot of Park City's ski slopes. Guest rooms, most of which have balconies and fireplaces, have excellent views of the mountains and the valley below. Down comforters help take the chill off after a day in the snow. If you need a break from skiing, check out the resort's Village Shops, where regularly scheduled concerts and other events are held. Summer brings warm-weather activities like horseback riding, hiking, and fly fishing, and the gondola remains open for scenic rides. 421 rooms, 8 story. Check-in 5 pm, check-out 11 am. Two restaurants, bar. Children's activity center. Fitness room, spa. Outdoor pool, whirlpool. Ski in/ski out. **$$**

★★★ HOTEL PARK CITY. *2001 Park Ave, Park City (84068). Phone 435/940-5000; fax 435/940-5001. www.hotelparkcity.com.* 54 rooms, all suites. Check-in 3 pm, check-out noon. Restaurant, bar. **$$$$**

★★★ SILVER KING HOTEL. *1485 Empire Ave, Park City (84060). Phone 435/649-5500; toll-free 800/331-8652; fax 435/649-6647. www.silverkinghotel.com.* This condominium hotel is close to the base of Park City Mountain Resort, which features more than 2,000 acres of ski area. It's also less than a mile from Park City's historic Main Street. Great for families, the modern guest rooms have washers and dryers and fully equipped kitchens, as well as fireplaces. Note the minimum stays apply during peak travel periods. 64 rooms, 5 story. Check-out 11 am. Heated indoor/outdoor pool, whirlpool. **$$**

★★★★ STEIN ERIKSEN LODGE. *7700 Stein Way, Park City (84060). Phone 435/649-3700; toll-free 800/453-1302; fax 435/649-5825. www.steinlodge.com.* Stein Eriksen may be a skier's Valhalla, but this superb resort delights visitors year-round. Nestled mid-mountain at Utah's Deer Valley ski resort, this Scandinavian masterpiece enjoys a magnificent alpine setting. The resort offers visitors unparalleled levels of service. Heated sidewalks and walkways keep guests toasty, while the ski valet service is heaven-sent for skiers at the end of an adventurous day. The dining is equally outstanding, and the Sunday Jazz Brunch and Skiers Lunch Buffet are local sensations. The roaring fireplace and inviting ambience of the Troll Hallen Lounge make it a cozy place for après-ski or light fare. Guests rest weary muscles at the spa, work out at the well-equipped fitness center, or unwind in the year-round outdoor heated pool at this comprehensive, full-service resort. Rustically elegant, the Lodge proudly shows off its Norwegian heritage while incorporating design elements synonymous with the American West. *Secret Inspector's Notes: You might expect a larger room or a better view of the incredible landscape at these lofty rates, but be warned that you will not receive either. The rooms are comfortable and Western-feeling, with luxurious bathrooms, but they are extremely cramped for travelers with large amounts of ski gear, and the tiny closets won't help with your frustration.* 175 rooms, 2 story. Check-in 4 pm, check-out 11 am. Two restaurants, bar. Children's activity center. Fitness room, spa. Outdoor pool, whirlpool. Business center. **$$**

Full-Service Inn

★★★ GOLDENER HIRSCH INN. *7570 Royal St E, Park City (84060). Phone 435/649-7770; fax 435/649-7901. www.goldenerhirschinn.com.* The Goldener Hirsch Inn is an Austrian wonderland in the heart of Deer Valley. Warm and inviting, this exceptional ski resort blends the services of a large resort with the charm of a small bed-and-breakfast. The guest rooms and suites are the ultimate in romance, with hand-painted furniture and whimsical touches. Ski-in/ski-out access to Utah's famous Deer Valley ski resort makes this a top destination for skiers, while a host of outdoor activities and cultural attractions lure visitors in every season. All-day dining and après-ski service are available at the hotel's Austrian-themed restaurant, where fine French food pleases palates. 20 rooms, 4 story. Complimentary continental breakfast. Check-in 4 pm, check-out 11 am. Restaurant. Whirlpool. Ski in/ski out. Business center. **$$**

Specialty Lodgings

The following lodging establishments are approved by Mobil Travel Guide, but due to their unique and individualized nature have not been given a traditional Mobil Star rating. Included in this listing you may find bed-and-breakfasts, limited-service inns, guest ranches, and other unique hotel properties.

CLUB LESPRI BOUTIQUE INN & SPA. *1765 Sidewinder Dr, Park City (84060). Phone 435/645-9696; toll-free 866/838-3533.* 10 rooms. Check-in 4 pm, check-out 10 am. Complimentary full-breakfast. **$$$**

OLD MINERS' LODGE. *615 Woodside Ave, Park City (84060). Phone 435/645-8068; toll-free 800/648-8068; fax 435/645-7420. www.oldminerslodge.com.* Established in 1889, this charming inn is located within the National Historic District of Park City. Guest rooms are graciously appointed with antique furnishings and country charm and are named after historic society members of Park City. Guests will find service informative, friendly, and attentive. Located just blocks from the Town Lift and the historic Main Street, this hotel offers something for everyone. Renovated lodging house used by miners; early Western décor, fireplace, antiques. 12 rooms, 2 story. Complimentary full breakfast. Check-in 2 pm, check-out noon. Whirlpool. **$**

WASHINGTON SCHOOL INN. *543 Park Ave, Park City (84060). Phone 435/649-3800; toll-free 800/824-1672; fax 435/649-3802. www.washingtonschoolinn.com.* Built in 1889, this historic stone schoolhouse is charming and well appointed with turn-of-the- century country décor and replete with modern amenities. 15 rooms, 3 story. Complimentary continental breakfast. Check-in 3 pm, check-out 11 am. Whirlpool. **$**

WOODSIDE INN B & B. *1469 Woodside Ave, Park City (84068). Phone 435/649-3494; toll-free 888/241-5890; fax 435/649-2392. www.woodsideinn.com.* 6 rooms. Check-in 3 pm, check-out 11 am. Complimentary full-breakfast. **$**

Spa

★★★ THE SPA AT STEIN ERIKSEN LODGE. *7700 Stein Way, Park City (84060). Phone 435/649-6475; toll-free 800/453-1302. www.steinlodge.com.* The Spa at Stein Eriksen Lodge was designed to appeal to active-minded guests needing remedies for sore and tired muscles and guests affected by the resort's high altitude. All spa services grant complimentary use of the fitness center, steam room, sauna, whirlpool, and relaxation room. Aromatic and exhilarating treatments refresh and renew at this European-style spa, where Vichy showers and kurs are de rigueur. The extensive massage menu includes Swedish, deep tissue, aromatic, stone, reflexology, and a special massage for mothers-to-be. In-room massages are available for additional privacy. Dehydrated skin is pampered with a soothing vitality treatment, where an almond-based scrub exfoliates prior to the application of a soothing aloe and azulene gel mask, while the honey body polish cleanses and nourishes skin with pure honey, almonds, and fresh buttermilk. Weary muscles are attended to with a vapor wrap, where eucalyptus oil takes the edge off soreness, and a peppermint sea twist reawakens skin by improving circulation. Melissa, wildflower, and eucalyptus herbal and thermal baths, inspired by old German remedies, help ease stress and stiff muscles, while chamomile and thalasso baths are hailed for their moisturizing, detoxifying, and nourishing benefits. Facials pay special attention to skin damaged by the sun and the drying effects of the high-altitude setting. From gentle papaya enzymes and seaweed serums to milk and honey masks, nature's best ingredients combine to revitalize skin.

Restaurants

★★★ THE CABIN. *4000 The Canyons Resort Dr, Park City (84098). Phone 435/615-8060; toll-free 888/591-5138; fax 435/615-8041. www.thecanyons.com.* Upscale rustic decor and a friendly staff bring warmth to The Canyons Grand Summit Hotel dining room. The menu is frequently changing. International menu. Breakfast, lunch, dinner. Bar. Children's menu. Casual attire. **$$$**

★★ CHEZ BETTY. *1637 Short Line Rd, Park City (84060). Phone 435/649-8181; fax 435/649-0880. www.chezbetty.com.* The warm and understated elegance of this cozy dining room creates the setting for the chef's wonderfully imaginative cuisine. The featured menu items are enhanced by daily specials that capture the freshest ingredients the market has to offer that day. The combinations of flavors and textures, as well as the visually stunning presentations, keep patrons returning again and again. American menu. Dinner. Closed Tues-Wed. Casual attire. Outdoor seating. **$$$**

★★★ CHIMAYO. *368 Main St, Park City (84060). Phone 435/649-6222; fax 435/647-0672. www.chimayoresturant.com.* Park City's best venture into Southwestern cuisine. The warm colorful atmosphere is enhanced by a fireplace at one end of the dining room. Southwestern menu. Dinner. Bar. **$$**

★★★ THE GLITRETIND. *7700 Stein Way, Park City (84060). Phone 435/649-3700; fax 435/649-5825. www.steinlodge.com.* This rich, European dining room is housed at the Stein Eriksen Lodge perched in the Wasatch Mountains at Deer Valley Resort. The excellent wine list is nationally recognized and the American continental menu features first-rate preparations including mustard-crusted rack of lamb with lentil and arugula strudel. The upbeat Sunday jazz brunch draws a crowd for a good reason. American menu. Breakfast, lunch, dinner, Sun brunch. Bar. Children's menu. Outdoor seating. **$$$**

★★★ GRAPPA. *151 Main St, Park City (84060). Phone 435/645-0636. grapparestaurant.com.* Located in a former boarding house on Park City's historic Main Street, this upscale restaurant offers dining on three levels. Many of the dishes feature just-picked herbs and flowers from the adjacent gardens. Italian menu. Dinner. Closed Dec 24. Bar. **$$$**

★★ KAMPAI. *586 Main St, Park City (84060). Phone 435/649-0655; fax 435/277-2867.* Japanese menu. Lunch, dinner. Closed Thanksgiving, Dec 25. **$$**

★★★★ RIVERHORSE ON MAIN. *540 Main St, Park City (84060). Phone 435/649-3536; fax 435/649-2409. www.riverhorsegroup.com.* For many people visiting Park City, the prospect of leaving the slopes, even for sustenance commonly known as dinner, is unappealing. But alas, even ski bunnies (and bums) must eat, and when they do, they flock to the Riverhorse on Main, a bustling, happening scene. Serving delicious contemporary fare in a swanky setting, the restaurant, set in a renovated historic Masonic Hall on Park City's Main Street, is sort of urban-modern, warmed by dark woods, soft candlelight, and fresh flowers. The Asian-influenced menu is filled with fun, easy eats like chicken satay, shrimp potstickers, crispy duck salad, macadamia-crusted halibut, grilled lobster tail, and charred rack of lamb. Note that this place is very popular, and while the dress code is informal, reservations are a must. American menu. Dinner. Closed Thanksgiving. Bar. Outdoor seating. **$$$**

Payson (C-3)

See also Nephi, Provo

Settled 1850
Population 12,716
Elevation 4,648 ft
Area Code 801
Zip 84651
Information Chamber of Commerce, 439 W Utah Ave; phone 801/465-5200 or 801/465-2634
Web site www.payson.org

Payson sits at the foot of the Wasatch Mountains, near Utah Lake. Mormons first settled the area after spending a night on the banks of Peteneet Creek. The surrounding farmlands produce fruit, milk, grain, and row crops; livestock is raised. Limestone and dolomite are dug in the vicinity for use in smelting iron.

What to See and Do

Mount Nebo Scenic Loop Drive. This 45-mile drive around the eastern shoulder of towering Mount Nebo (elevation 11,877 feet) is one of the most thrilling in Utah; Mount Nebo's three peaks are the highest in the Wasatch range. The road travels south through Payson and Santaquin canyons and then climbs 9,000 feet up Mount Nebo, offering a view of Devil's Kitchen, a brilliantly colored canyon. (This section of the drive not recommended for those who dislike heights.) The forest road continues S to Hwy 132; take Hwy 132 E to Nephi, and then drive N on I-15 back to Payson.

Payson Lake Recreation Area. *Payson. 12 miles SE on unnumbered road in Uinta National Forest. Phone 801/798-3571.* Hiking.

Special Event

Golden Onion Days. *Payson.* Includes community theater presentations, 5K and 10K runs, horse races, demolition derby, parade, fireworks, and picnic. Labor Day weekend.

Limited-Service Hotels

★ CHERRY LANE MOTEL. *240 E 100 N, Payson (84651). Phone 801/465-2582.* This is a cozy and efficient roadside motel in classic 1950s décor. 10 rooms, 1 story. **$**

★ COMFORT INN. *830 N Main St, Payson (84651). Phone 801/465-4861; fax 801/465-7686. www.comfortinn.com.* 62 rooms, 2 story. Pets accepted; fee. Complimentary continental breakfast. Check-in 2 pm, check-out 11 am. Fitness room. Indoor pool, whirlpool. **$**

Restaurant

★ DALTON'S FINE DINING. *20 S 100 W, Payson (84651). Phone 801/465-9182.* Featuring upscale regional American cuisine in a refined atmosphere. American menu. Lunch, dinner. Closed Sun. **$**

Perry

Restaurant

★ MADDOX RANCH HOUSE. *1900 S Hwy 89, Perry (84302). Phone 435/723-8545; fax 435/723-8547. www.maddoxranchhouse.com.* American menu. Lunch, dinner. Closed Sun-Mon; Thanksgiving, Dec 25. Casual attire. **$$**

Price (C-4)

Settled 1879
Population 8,402
Elevation 5,567 ft
Area Code 435
Zip 84501
Information Carbon County Chamber of Commerce, 90 N 100 E, #3; phone 435/637-2788 or 435/637-8182
Web site www.pricecityutah.com

Price, the seat of Carbon County, bases its prosperity on coal; more than 30 mine properties, as well as oil and natural gas fields, are within 30 miles. Farming and livestock are also important. Price was one of the stopping places for the Robbers Roost gang in the 1930s. Headquarters and a Ranger District office of the Manti-LaSal National Forest are located here.

What to See and Do

Cleveland-Lloyd Dinosaur Quarry. *155 E Main St, Price. 22 miles S on Hwy 10, then approximately 15 miles E on unnumbered road. Phone 435/637-5060.* Since 1928, more than 12,000 dinosaur bones, representing at least 70 different animals, have been excavated on this site. Visitor center, nature trail, picnic area. (Memorial Day-Labor Day, daily; Easter-Memorial Day, weekends only) **DONATION**

College of Eastern Utah Prehistoric Museum. *155 E Main St, Price. Phone 435/637-5060.* Dinosaur displays, archaeology exhibits; geological specimens. (Memorial Day-Labor Day, daily; rest of year, Mon-Sat) **DONATION**

Geology tours. *90 N 100 E, Price. Phone 435/637-3009.* Self-guided tours of Nine Mile Canyon, Native American dwellings, paintings, San Rafael Desert, Cleveland-Lloyd Dinosaur Quarry, Little Grand Canyon. Maps available at Castle Country Travel Region or Castle Country Regional Information Center, 155 E Main. Phone 800/842-0784. **FREE**

Manti-LaSal National Forest, Manti Division. *599 W Price River Dr, Price. 21 miles SW on Hwy 10, then NW on Hwy 31. Phone 435/637-2817.* (See MOAB, MONTICELLO) Originally two forests—the Manti in central Utah and the LaSal section in southeastern Utah—now under single supervision. A 1,327,631-acre area partially in Colorado, this forest has among its attractions high mountain scenic drives, deep canyons, riding trails, campsites, winter sports, fishing, and deer and elk hunting. Joe's Valley Reservoir on Hwy 29 and Electric Lake on Hwy 31 have fishing and boating. Areas of geologic interest, developed as a result of massive landslides, are near Ephraim. Some fees in developed areas. **FREE**

Price Canyon Recreation Area. *Price. 15 miles N on Hwy 6, then 3 miles W on unnumbered road.* Scenic overlooks; hiking, picnicking, camping (fee). Roads have steep grades. (May-mid-Oct, daily) **FREE**

Scofield State Park. *Hwy 6 and Hwy 96, Price. 24 miles N on Hwy 6, then 10 miles W and S on Hwy 96. Phone 435/448-9449.* Utah's highest state park has a 2,800-acre lake that lies at an altitude of 7,616 feet. Fishing, boating (docks, ramps); camping (rest rooms, showers), snowmobiling, ice fishing, cross-country skiing in winter. (May-Oct) **$$$**

Limited-Service Hotels

★ BEST WESTERN CARRIAGE HOUSE INN. *590 E Main St, Price (84501). Phone 435/637-5660; fax 435/637-5157. www.bestwestern.com.* 41 rooms, 2 story. Complimentary continental breakfast. Check-out noon. Indoor pool, whirlpool. Airport transportation available. **$**

★ ★ HOLIDAY INN. *838 Westwood Blvd, Price (84501). Phone 435/637-8880; fax 435/637-7707. www.holiday-inn.com.* 151 rooms, 2 story. Check-out noon. Restaurant, bar. Fitness room. Indoor pool. **$**

Restaurant

★ CHINA CITY CAFE. *350 E Main St, Price (84501). Phone 435/637-8211.* Chinese, American menu. Lunch, dinner. Closed Thanksgiving, Dec 25; July. **$$**

Provo (B-3)

See also Heber City, Payson, Salt Lake City, Timpanogos Cave National Monument

Settled 1849
Population 105,166
Elevation 4,549 ft
Area Code 801
Information Utah County Visitors Center, 51 S University Ave, 84601; phone 801/370-8394 or toll-free 800/222-8824
Web site www.utahvalley.org/cvb

Provo received its name from French-Canadian trapper Etienne Provost, who arrived in the area in 1825. Provost and his party of mountain men set up camp near the mouth of the Provo River, but skirmishes with Native Americans forced them to escape to the mountains. It wasn't until 1849 that the first permnent settlement, begun by a party of Mormons, was established. The Mormon settlers erected Fort Utah as their first building, and despite famine, drought, hard winters, and the constant danger of attack, they persisted and the settlement grew. Today, Provo is the seat of Utah County and the state's third-largest city.

An important educational and commercial center, Provo's largest employer is Brigham Young University. Beyond that, the city boasts major steel and electronic component manufacturers, health care and municipal employers, and other educational facilities. Provo lies in the middle of a lush, green valley: to the north stands 12,008-foot Mount Timpanogos; to the south is the perpendicular face of the Wasatch Range; to the east Provo Peak rises 11,054 feet; and to the west lies Utah Lake, backed by more mountains. Provo is the headquarters of the Uinta National Forest, and many good fishing, boating, camping, and hiking spots are nearby.

What to See and Do

Brigham Young University. *Provo. Phone 801/378-4678.* (1875) (27,000 students) Founded by Brigham Young and operated by the Church of Jesus Christ of Latter-day Saints. This is one of the world's largest church-related institutions of higher learning, with students from every state and more than 90 foreign countries. One-hour, free guided tours arranged at Hosting Center (Mon-Fri; also by appointment) Includes

Earth Science Museum. *1683 North Canyon Rd, Provo. Phone 801/378-4678.* Geological collection, extensive series of minerals and fossils. **FREE**

Harris Fine Arts Center. *HFAC Campus Dr, Provo. Phone 801/378-4322.* Houses B. F. Larsen Gallery and Gallery 303; periodic displays of rare instruments and music collection. Concert, theater performances. **FREE**

Monte L. Bean Life Science Museum. *1430 N, Provo. Phone 801/378-5051.* Exhibits and collections of insects, fish, amphibians, reptiles, birds, animals, and plants. **FREE**

Museum of Art. *Provo. Phone 801/378-2787.* Exhibits from the BYU Permanent Collection; traveling exhibits (some fees). **$$$**

Museum of Peoples and Cultures. *Allen Hall, 710 N 100 E, Provo. Phone 801/378-6112.* Material from South America, the Near East, and the southwestern United States. **FREE**

Camp Floyd and Stagecoach Inn State Parks. *1800 W and 1540 N, Cedar Valley. 13 miles N on I-15 to Lehi, then 20 miles W on Hwy 73. Phone 801/768-8932.* Only the cemetery and one commissary building remain as evidence of the pre-Civil War post that quartered the largest troop concentration in the US here between 1858-1861. Approximately 400 buildings were constructed for troops deployed to the west in expectation of a Mormon rebellion. The nearby Stagecoach Inn has been restored with original period furnishings. Visitor center. Museum. (Apr-Sept daily, mid-Oct-Mar, Mon-Sat) **$**

John Hutchings Museum. *55 N Center St, Lehi. 17 miles NW via I-15 or Hwy 89/91. Phone 801/768-7180.* Six main collections include archaeology, ornithology and zoology, paleontology, mineralogy, and pioneer artifacts. Most of the items are from the Great Basin area. Rare sea shells, fossils, Native American artifacts. (Tues-Sat; closed holidays) **$$**

Pioneer Museum. *500 W 500 N, Provo. On Hwy 89. Phone 801/377-0995.* Outstanding collection of Utah pioneer relics and Western art. Pioneer Village. (June-early Sept, Wed, Fri, Sat afternoons; rest of year, by appointment) **FREE**

Springville Museum of Art. *126 E 400 S, Springville. 7 miles SE via I-15 exit 263. Phone 801/489-2727.* Contemporary artists. Changing exhibits. Competition in Apr, quilt show in July-Sept. Guided tours. (Hours vary with exhibit; closed Jan 1, Easter, Dec 25) **FREE**

Sundance Ski Area. *North Fork Provo Canyon, Sundance. 15 miles NE on Hwy 189, North Fork Provo Canyon. Phone 801/225-4107; toll-free 800/892-1600. www.sundanceresort.com.* Three chairlifts, rope tow; patrol, school, rentals; warming hut, restaurants. Longest run 2 miles, vertical drop 2,150 feet. Cross-country trails. (Late Nov-Apr, daily) **$$$$**

Uinta National Forest. *88 W and 100 N, Provo. S and E of town. Phone 801/377-5780. www.fs.fed.us/r4/uinta.* Scenic drives through the 950,000-acre forest; areas include Provo Canyon, Bridal Veil Falls, Deer Creek Dam and Reservoir, Diamond Fork Canyon, Hobble Creek Canyon, Strawberry Reservoir, and the Alpine and Mount Nebo Scenic Loop (see PAYSON); roads give an unsurpassed view of colorful landscapes, canyons, and waterfalls. Stream and lake fishing; hunting for deer and elk, camping (fee), picnicking. Reservations accepted.

Utah Lake State Park. *4400 W Center St, Provo. 2 miles W on Center St, off I-15. Phone 801/375-0733.* Park situated on the eastern shore of Utah Lake, a 150-square-mile, freshwater remnant of ancient Lake Bonneville, which created the Great Salt Lake. Fishing (cleaning station), boating (ramp, dock); ice skating (winter), roller skating (summer), picnicking, play area, camping (dump station). Visitor center. (Daily)

Special Event

Freedom Festival. Bazaar, carnival, parades. Early July.

Limited-Service Hotels

★ BEST WESTERN COTTONTREE INN. *2230 N University Pkwy, Provo (84604). Phone 801/373-7044; toll-free 800/662-6886; fax 801/375-5240. www.bestwestern.com.* 80 rooms, 2 story. Complimentary continental breakfast. Check-in 2 pm, check-out noon. Indoor pool, outdoor pool, whirlpool. **$**

★ ★ COURTYARD BY MARRIOTT. *1600 N Freedom Blvd, Provo (84604). Phone 801/373-2222; fax 801/374-2207. www.courtyard.com.* 100 rooms. Check-in 3 pm, check-out 1 pm. Restaurant, bar. Fitness room. High speed Internet access. Indoor pool, whirlpool. **$**

★ FAIRFIELD INN. *1515 S University Ave, Provo (84601). Phone 801/377-9500; fax 801/377-9591. www.marriott.com.* 72 rooms. Complimentary continental breakfast. Check-in 3 pm, check-out noon. Indoor pool, whirlpool. **$**

★ ★ HOLIDAY INN. *1460 S University Ave, Provo (84601). Phone 801/374-9750; fax 801/377-1615. www.holiday-inn.com.* 79 rooms, 2 story. Complimentary full breakfast. Check-in 3 pm, check-out noon. Restaurant, bar. Fitness room. Outdoor pool. Business center. **$**

Full-Service Hotel

★ ★ ★ MARRIOTT PROVO HOTEL AND CONFERENCE CENTER. *101 W 100 N, Provo (84601). Phone 801/377-4700; toll-free 800/777-7144; fax 801/377-4708. www.marriott.com.* Nearby attractions include two shopping malls, as well as the Seven Peaks Water Park and Ice Rink, where the ice hockey competition and practices for the 2002 Winter Olympics were held. 330 rooms, 9 story. Check-in 3 pm, check-out noon. Restaurant, bar. Fitness room. Indoor pool, outdoor pool, whirlpool. Airport transportation available. Business center. **$$**

Full-Service Resort

★ ★ ★ SUNDANCE. *N Fork Provo Canyon, Sundance (84604). Phone 801/225-4107; toll-free 800/892-1600; fax 801/226-1937. www.sundanceresort.com.* Sundance is more than just a vacation destination; it is a community and a way of life. Founded by Robert Redford in the 1960s and famous for its annual winter film festival, this community of cottages and lodges is the antidote to the mega-resort. Sundance lives in harmony with its natural surroundings, and everything from the interior design to the cuisine reflects this connection to its environment. A little bit country, a little bit luxury, it appeals to families and couples who visit for its creative spirit, stunning scenery, fine dining, and endless recreation. The general store's eclectic finds are so popular that a mail-order catalog has been designed to meet demand. A fabulous spa completes the well-rounded experience available at this unique resort. 110 rooms. Check-in 3 pm, check-out 11 am. Two restaurants, bar. Children's activity center. Fitness room. **$$$**

Restaurants

★ ★ BOMBAY HOUSE. *463 N University Ave, Provo (84601). Phone 801/373-6677; fax 801/373-9377. www.bombayhouse.com.* Indian menu. Dinner. Closed Sun; Dec 25. Casual attire. **$**

★ ★ FOUNDRY GRILL. *N Fork Provo Canyon, Sundance (84604). Phone 801/223-4220; toll-free 800/892-1600; fax 801/226-1937. www.sundanceresort.com.* American menu. Breakfast, lunch, dinner, Sun brunch. Bar. Outdoor seating. **$$**

★ JOE VERA'S MEXICAN RESTAURANT. *250 W Center St, Provo (84601). Phone 801/375-6714.* Mexian menu. Lunch, dinner. Closed Sun. Children's menu. Casual attire. **$$**

★ **MAGLEBY'S.** *1675 N 200 W, Provo (84604). Phone 801/374-6249; fax 801/374-0449.* American menu. Lunch, dinner. Closed Sun; Thanksgiving, Dec 24-25. Casual attire. **$$**

★★★ **THE TREE ROOM.** *RR 3, Box A-1, Sundance (84604). Phone 801/223-4200; toll-free 800/892-1600; fax 801/226-1937. www.sundanceresort.com.* Located at the base of the Sundance ski lift, this restaurant's two-story windows offer stunning views of the rugged mountains and surrounding wilderness. The upscale, yet casual, room is filled with beautiful displays of American Indian dolls and pottery. The sophisticated new American cuisine includes wild game, steaks, seafood, and herbs and vegetables from the resort's own organic gardens. American menu. Dinner. Bar. Reservations recommended. **$$$**

Rainbow Bridge National Monument (F-3)

Web site www.nps.gov/rabr

Rainbow Bridge, which rises from the eastern shore of Lake Powell, is the largest natural rock bridge in the world. It was named a national monument in 1910, one year after its sighting was documented. Carved by a meander of Bridge Creek, this natural bridge stands 290 feet tall, spans 275 feet, and stretches 33 feet at the top. One of the seven natural wonders of the world, Rainbow Bridge is higher than the nation's capitol dome and nearly as long as a football field. The monument is predominantly salmon pink in color, modified by streaks of iron oxide and manganese. In the light of the late afternoon sun, the bridge is a brilliant sight. Native Americans consider the area a sacred place; legend holds that the bridge is a rainbow turned to stone.

The easiest way to reach Rainbow Bridge is a half-day round-trip boat ride across Lake Powell from Page, Arizona (see) or a full-day round-trip boat ride from Bullfrog and Halls Crossing marinas (see LAKE POWELL). The bridge also can be reached on foot or horseback via the Rainbow Trail through the Navajo Indian Reservation (see ARIZONA; permit required). Fuel and camp supplies are available at Dangling Rope Marina, accessible by boat only, 10 miles downlake (south). For more information, contact the Superintendent, Glen Canyon National Recreation Area, PO Box 1507, Page, AZ 86040; phone 520/608-6404.

Rainbow Bridge Fun Fact

- Rainbow Bridge, nature's abstract sculpture carved of solid sandstone, is the world's largest natural-rock span. It stands 275 feet wide and 209 feet high.

Richfield (D-3)

See also Beaver, Fillmore, Salina

Settled 1863
Population 5,593
Elevation 5,330 ft
Area Code 435
Zip 84701
Information Chamber of Commerce, PO Box 327; phone 435/896-4241
Web site www.richfieldcity.com

Brigham Young sent members of his church here to settle the area, but problems with Native Americans forced abandonment of the fledgling town for almost a year before the pioneers were able to regain their settlement. Located in the center of Sevier Valley, Richfield has become the commercial hub of the region. Today, some of the world's best beef is raised in and shipped from this area. Headquarters and a Ranger District Office of the Fishlake National Forest are located here.

What to See and Do

Big Rock Candy Mountain. *Richfield. 25 miles S on Hwy 89, in Marysvale Canyon. Phone 435/896-4241.* Multicolored mountain that Burl Ives popularized in song.

Fishlake National Forest. *115 E and 900 N, Richfield. Phone 435/896-9233.* This 1,424,000-acre forest offers fishing; hunting, hiking, picnicking, camping (fee). Fish Lake, 33 miles SE via Hwy 119 and Hwy 24, then 7 miles NE on Hwy 25, offers high-altitude angling on a 6-mile-long lake covering 2,600 acres. Campgrounds (mid-May-late Oct). Contact the Supervisor's Office.

Fremont Indian State Park. *11550 W Clear Creek Canyon Rd, Sevier. 20 miles SW via I-70. Phone 435/527-4631.* Museum and trails feature the Fremont people, who lived in the area from A.D. 300-1300 and then vanished. There is no explanation, only speculation, for their disappearance. Interpretive center highlights evolution of their culture; artifacts from nearby Five Fingers Ridge; nature trails lead to panels of rock art and a reconstructed pit house dwelling and granary. Fishing; camping (fee), picnicking. (Daily; closed Jan 1, Thanksgiving, Dec 25)

Limited-Service Hotels

★ **DAYS INN.** *333 N Main, Richfield (84701). Phone 435/896-6476; toll-free 888/275-8513; fax 435/896-6476. www.daysinn.com.* 51 rooms, 3 story. Pets accepted; fee. Check-in 1 pm, check-out 11 am. Restaurant. Fitness room. Outdoor pool, whirlpool. **$**

★ **QUALITY INN.** *540 S Main St, Richfield (84701). Phone 435/896-5465; fax 435/896-9005. www.qualityinn.com.* 79 rooms, 2 story. Check-in 2 pm, check-out 11 am. Fitness room. Outdoor pool, whirlpool. **$**

Roosevelt (B-4)

See also Vernal

Settled 1905
Population 3,915
Elevation 5,182 ft
Area Code 435
Zip 84066
Information Chamber of Commerce, 50 E 200 S 35-11, PO Box 1417; phone 435/722-4598

Roosevelt, in the geographical center of Utah's "dinosaur land," was settled when the opening of reservation lands prompted a flood of homesteaders to stake claims in the area. The town was named after Theodore Roosevelt, who had once camped on the banks of a nearby river. Nine Mile Canyon, with its Native American petroglyphs, can be reached from here. A Ranger District office of the Ashley National Forest (see VERNAL) is located in the town.

Limited-Service Hotel

★ **BEST WESTERN INN.** *E Hwy 40, Roosevelt (84066). Phone 435/722-4644; fax 435/722-0179. www.bestwestern.com.* 40 rooms, 2 story. Check-out 11 am. Fitness room. Pool, whirlpool. **$**

Salina (D-3)

See also Richfield

Settled 1863
Population 2,393
Elevation 5,150 ft
Area Code 435
Zip 84654

What to See and Do

Palisade State Park. *2200 Palisade Rd, Sterling. 20 miles N via Hwy 89, then 2 miles E, near Sterling. Phone 435/835-7275; toll-free 800/322-3770 (camping reservations).* Approximately 200 acres. Swimming beaches, showers, fishing, nonmotorized boating, canoe rentals, nature trail, hiking, 18-hole golf, picnicking, camping (fee; dump station). Six Mile Canyon adjacent. **$$**

Special Event

Mormon Miracle Pageant. *4 N 100 E, Salina. Phone 435/835-3000.* 30 miles N via Hwy 89 in Manti, on Temple grounds. Portrays historical events of the Americas; cast of 600. Early-mid-June. **FREE**

Limited-Service Hotel

★ **BEST WESTERN SHAHEEN MOTEL.** *1225 S State St, Salina (84654). Phone 435/529-7455; fax 435/529-7257. www.bestwestern.com.* 40 rooms, 2 story. Complimentary continental breakfast. Check-in 1 pm, check-out 11 am. Outdoor pool. **$**

Salt Lake City (B-3)

See also Alta, Heber City, Ogden, Park City, Provo, Snowbird

Founded 1847
Population 181,743
Elevation 4,330 ft
Area Code 801
Information Convention & Visitors Bureau, 90 S West Temple, 84101-1406; phone 801/521-2822 or 801/534-4927
Web site www.saltlake.org

On a hill at the north end of State Street stands Utah's classic capitol building. Three blocks south is Temple Square, with the famed Mormon Temple and Tabernacle. The adjacent block houses the headquarters of the Church of Jesus Christ of Latter-day Saints, whose members are often called Mormons. Salt Lake City, with its 10-acre blocks, 132-foot-wide, tree-lined streets, and mountains rising to the east and west, is one of the most beautifully planned cities in the country.

Once a desert wilderness, Salt Lake City was built by Mormon settlers who sought refuge from religious persecution. Neither the barrenness of the land, drought, nor a plague of crickets swayed these people from their purpose. Followers of Brigham Young arrived and named their new territory "Deseret." In these early days, the Mormons began a variety of experiments in farming, industry, and society, many of which were highly successful. Today, Salt Lake City is an industrious, businesslike city, a center for electronics, steel, missiles, and a hundred other enterprises.

West of the city is the enormous Great Salt Lake, stretching 48 miles one way and 90 miles the other. It is less than 35 feet deep and between 15 and 20 percent salt—almost five times as salty as the ocean. Humans bob like corks and cannot sink in the water. The lake is what remains of ancient Lake Bonneville, once 145 miles wide, 350 miles long, and 1,000 feet deep. As Lake Bonneville water evaporated over thousands of years, a large expanse of perfectly flat, solid salt was left. Today, the Bonneville Salt Flats stretch west almost to Nevada.

Headquarters and a Ranger District office of the Wasatch-Cache National Forest are located in Salt Lake City.

Salt Lake City was laid out in grid fashion, with Temple Square at the center. Most street names are coordinates on this grid: 4th South Street is four blocks south of Temple Square, 7th East is seven blocks east. These are written as 400 South and 700 East.

Additional Visitor Information

For additional information contact the Salt Lake Convention & Visitors Bureau, 90 S West Temple, 84101-1406; phone 801/521-2822; or the Utah Travel Council and Visitor Information Center, Council Hall, 300 N State St, 84114; phone 801/538-1030.

Public Transportation

Buses (Utah Transit Authority), phone 801/287-4636

Airport Salt Lake City International Airport (SLC)

Information Phone 801/575-2460

Web site. www.slcairport.com

Lost and Found Phone 801/575-2427

Airlines AeroMexico, America West Airlines, America West Express, American Airlines, Atlantic Southeast, Comair, Continental Airlines, Delta Air Lines, Frontier Airlines, jetBlue Airways, Northwest Airlines, SkyWest Airlines, Southwest Airlines, United Airlines, United Express

What to See and Do

Alta. *26 miles SE on Hwy 210 in Little Cottonwood Canyon in Alta (see). Phone 801/742-3333.*

Arrow Press Square. *165 S West Temple St, Salt Lake City. Phone 801/531-9700.* Once the city's printing district, now buildings such as Arrow Press Building (1890), Upland Hotel (1910), and Midwest Office Building Supply (1910) have been reconstructed into a retail/restaurant complex.

Brigham Young Monument. *Salt Lake City. At N side of intersection of Main and South Temple sts. Phone 801/531-9700.* (1897) This statue, first seen at the Chicago World's Fair in 1893, honors the church leader.

Brighton Resort. *12601 E Big Cottonwood, Big Cottonwood Canyon. 25 miles SE via I-215, exit 6 in*

Big Cottonwood Canyon. Phone 801/532-4731. www.skibrighton.com. Three high-speed quad, one triple, three double chairlifts; patrol, school, rentals; lodge, restaurant, cafeteria. Sixty-four runs; longest run 3 miles, vertical drop 1,745 feet. (Mid-Nov-late-Apr, daily) Night skiing (Mon-Sat). Half-day rates. **$$$$**

The Canyons. *4000 The Canyons Resort Dr, Park City. 28 miles E and S via I-80, Hwy 224 in Park City (see). Phone 435/649-5400. www.thecanyons.com.*

Clark Planetarium. *110 S 400 W, Salt Lake City. Phone 801/538-2104. www.hansenplanetarium.net.* Space science museum and library. Seasonal star shows, stage plays (fee; schedule varies). (Daily at 11 am; closed Thanksgiving, Dec 25) **$$**

Council Hall. *300 N State St, Salt Lake City. S of Capitol Hill. Phone 801/538-1900.* (1864-1866) Council Hall was once the meeting place of territorial legislature and city hall for 30 years. It was dismantled and then reconstructed in 1963 at its present location; Federal/Greek Revival-style architecture. Visitor information center and office; memorabilia. (Daily; closed Jan 1, Thanksgiving, Dec 25) **FREE**

Deer Valley Resort. *2250 Deer Valley Dr S, Park City. 34 miles E and S via I-80, Hwy 224. Phone 435/649-1000; toll-free 800/424-3337. www.deervalley.com.*

Fort Douglas Military Museum. *32 Potter St, Salt Lake City. 3 miles NE, Building 32. Phone 801/581-1251. www.fortdouglas.org.* Army museum features history of military in Utah from arrival of Johnston's Army during the 1857 "Utah War" through Vietnam. Also tours of the fort (self-guided or guided, by appointment). (Tues-Sat noon-4 pm; closed Jan, holidays) **FREE**

Governor's Mansion. *603 E S Temple St, Salt Lake City. Phone 801/538-1005.* (1902) Restored mansion of Thomas Kearns, a wealthy Utah senator in the early 1900s; decorated with Italian marble. Tours. (Apr-mid-Dec, Tues and Thurs 2-4 pm; closed holidays) **FREE**

Hogle Zoological Garden. *2600 E Sunnyside Ave, Salt Lake City. Phone 801/582-1631.* Wildlife exhibits; Discovery Land; bird show; miniature train (summer). Picnicking, concession. (Daily; closed Jan 1, Dec 25) **$$$**

InnsBrook Tours. *Suite 804, 3359 S Main St, Salt Lake City. Phone 801/534-1001; toll-free 877/210-5637. www.saltlakecitytours.org.* This is the best way to see all the famous sites in Salt Lake City. Pick-up begins at 9:15 am, and then you're off to see landmarks like the Mormon Tabernacle, the Salt Lake Temple, and the Olympic Stadium and Village. (Daily) **$$$$**

Kennecott Bingham Canyon Mine. *Hwy 48 (7200 S), Magna. 25 miles SW of Salt Lake City. Phone 801/569-6248.* Open-pit copper mine 2 1/2 miles wide and 1/2 mile deep. Visitor center, observation deck, and audio presentation explain mining operations, which date from 1906. Gift shop.(Apr-mid-Oct, daily) **$**

Lagoon Amusement Park. *Pioneer Village and Water Park. 17 miles N on I-15, exit 325, then N to Lagoon Dr. Phone toll-free 800/748-5246. www.lagoonpark.com.* Rides, water slides; re-creation of 19th-century Utah town; stagecoach and steam-engine train rides. Camping, picnicking. (Memorial Day-Aug, daily; mid-Apr-late May and Sept, Sat-Sun only) **$$$$**

Liberty Park. *1300 South St, Salt Lake City. Between 500 and 700 E and 900 and 1300 S. Phone 801/972-7800 (park).* In a 100-acre park are Chase Mill (1852), Tracy Aviary, children's garden playground (Apr-Sept), amusement park. Swimming; lighted tennis, horseshoe courts, picnicking. Park (daily 6 am-11 pm). Aviary (daily 9 am-6 pm; Nov-Mar: daily 9 am-4:30 pm). **FREE**

Lion House. *67 E South Temple, Salt Lake City. South Temple and State St. Phone 801/363-5466 (Lion House) or 801/240-2671 (Beehive House).* Lion House (1856) and Beehive House (1854), family residences, offices, and social centers for Brigham Young and his wives and children. Guided tours of Beehive House. (Mon-Sat 9 am-6 pm; closed Jan 1, Thanksgiving, Dec 25) **FREE**

Maurice Abravanel Concert Hall. *123 W South Temple, Salt Lake City. Phone 801/533-6683.* The home of the Utah Symphony, this building is adorned with more than 12,000 square feet of 24-karat gold leaf and a mile of brass railing. It has been rated one of the best halls in the US, acoustically. Free tours (by appointment). The symphony has performances most weekends.

Salt Lake City's Mormon Heritage

The centerpiece of downtown Salt Lake City is Temple Square, the city block bordered by three streets named Temple—West, North, and South—and Main Street on the east side. Utah's top tourist attraction, Temple Square, is the hub for the Church of Jesus Christ of the Latter-Day Saints, where guests are invited to join a free guided tour that offers a glimpse of several architectural and cultural landmarks, including the Mormon Tabernacle, the Museum of Church History and Art, and the Joseph Smith Memorial Building. (Tours start at the flagpole every few minutes.) If your timing is right, you can also take in a film, choir rehearsal, or organ recital here. From Temple Square, head east on South Temple to a pair of historic homes, the Lion House (63 East South Temple) and the Beehive House (67 East South Temple). No tours are available of the Lion House, which served as Brigham Young's abode during the mid-19th century, but there is a restaurant on the lower level that is a good spot for a lunch break. Next door, the Beehive House, another former Young residence and a National Historic Landmark, offers free tours every day. Just east of these houses on South Temple is Eagle Gate (at the intersection of State Street), an impressive arch capped by a two-ton sculpture of an eagle with a 20-foot wingspan. Just south of Eagle Gate on the east side of State Street are two of Salt Lake City's standout cultural facilities, the Hansen Planetarium (15 South State Street) and the Social Hall Heritage Museum (39 South State Street). The former features daily star shows and a free space museum with hands-on exhibits; the latter includes remnants of Utah's first public building and the West's first theater. From the museum, it's best to reverse course and walk north on State Street, passing under Eagle Gate. Just beyond North Temple, hop on the paths that run through the lush City Creek Park for a break from the urban bustle and head north to the adjoining Memory Grove Park. From here, it's only a two-block walk west to the Utah State Capitol (just north of the intersection of State Street and 300 North Street), an exemplary Renaissance Revival-style structure built from Utah granite in 1915. The building is open to the public daily and guided tours are offered on weekdays. Two blocks west of the State Capitol is the Pioneer Memorial Museum (300 North Main Street), a majestic replica of the original Salt Lake Theater (demolished in 1928) with 38 rooms of relics from the area's past, including photographs, vehicles, dolls, and weapons. The museum is on the eastern edge of one of the city's oldest neighborhoods, the tree-lined Marmalade District (between 300 and 500 North streets to the north and south and Center and Quince streets to the east and west), a good place to meander and gaze at historic homes.

Park City Mountain Resort. *1310 Lowell Ave, Park City. 32 miles E and S via I-80, Hwy 224. See (PARK CITY). Phone 435/649-8111; toll-free 800/222-7275. www.pcski.com.*

Pioneer Memorial Museum. *300 N Main St, Salt Lake City. W side of capitol grounds. Phone 801/538-1050.* Manuscripts, pioneer relics. Also here is Carriage House, with exhibits relating to transportation, including Brigham Young's wagon, mule-drawn vehicles, Pony Express items. One-hour guided tours (by appointment). (Mon-Sat 9 am-5 pm; June-Aug: Mon-Sat 9 am-5 pm, Sun 1-5 pm; closed holidays) **FREE**

River trips. *Moki Mac River Expeditions. 6006 S 1300 E, Salt Lake City. Phone 801/268-6667; toll-free 800/284-7280. www.mokimac.com.* Offers 1-14-day whitewater and canoeing trips on the Green and Colorado rivers. **$$$$**

Salt Lake Art Center. *20 S West Temple, Salt Lake City. In the Salt Palace complex. Phone 801/328-4201.* Changing exhibits featuring photographs, paintings, ceramics, and sculptures; school; lectures, seminars, films. (Tues-Thurs, Sat 10 am-5 pm, Fri 10 am-9 pm; closed holidays) **FREE**

Sightseeing USA. *553 W and 100 S sts, Salt Lake City. Phone 801/521-7060.*

Snowbird. *25 miles E and S via I-215, Hwy 210 in Little Cottonwood Canyon (see SNOWBIRD). Phone 801/742-2222 (resort information). www.snowbird.com.*

Solitude Resort. *12000 Big Cottonwood Canyon, Salt Lake City. SE via I-215. Phone 801/534-1400. www.skisolitude.com.* Detachable quad, two triple, four double chairlifts; race course, patrol, school, rentals; day lodge, cafeteria, restaurants, bar. Longest run 3 1/2 miles, vertical drop 2,047 feet. (Nov-Apr, daily) Cross-country center. **$$$$**

State Capitol. *350 N Main St, Salt Lake City. Phone 801/538-1563; toll-free 800/200-1160. www.utah.com/culture/capitol.htm.* (1914) Constructed of Utah granite and Georgia marble, with a modern annex, the capitol has a commanding view of the valley and Wasatch Mountains. The Gold Room is decorated with bird's-eye marble and gold from Utah mines. The ground floor has exhibits. Guided tours every 30 minutes (Mon-Fri 9 am-4 pm). Building (Sept-May: daily 6 am-6 pm; June-Aug: daily 6 am-8 pm). **FREE**

★ **Temple Square.** *Main and N,S, and W Temple sts, Salt Lake City. Phone 801/240-1245; toll-free 800/537-9703.* Visitor centers provide information, exhibits and guided tours (1/2- to 1-hour; daily, every 10 minutes). (Daily 9 am-9 pm) **FREE** The tour includes

Assembly Hall. *Salt Lake City. SW corner of Temple Square. Phone 801/521-2822.* (1880) Tours (daily), concerts (Fri, Sat evenings).

Family History Library. *35 N W Temple, Salt Lake City. Phone 801/240-2331.* Largest genealogy library in the world aids in compilation of family histories. (Mon 7:30 am-5 pm, Tues-Sat 7:30 am-10 pm) **FREE**

Museum of Church History and Art. *45 N West Temple St, Salt Lake City. Phone 801/240-3310.* Exhibits of Latter-Day Saints church history from 1820 to present. (Mon-Fri 9 am-9 pm, Sat-Sun 10 am-7 pm; closed holidays) **FREE**

Seagull Monument. *Temple Square, Salt Lake City. Phone 801/521-2822.* (1913) The monument commemorates the seagulls that saved the crops from crickets in 1848.

Tabernacle. *Temple Square, Salt Lake City. Phone 801/240-2534.* (1867) The self-supporting roof, an elongated dome, is 250 feet long and 150 feet wide. The tabernacle organ has 11,623 pipes, ranging from 5/8 inch to 32 feet in length. The world-famous Tabernacle Choir may be heard at rehearsal (Thurs 8 pm) or at broadcast time (Sun 9:30 am, be seated by 9:15 am). Organ recitals (Mon-Sat noon, Sun afternoon). **FREE**

Temple. *N, S, and W Temple and Main sts, Salt Lake City. Phone 801/240-2534.* (1893) Used for sacred ordinances, such as baptisms and marriages. Closed to non-Mormons.

This Is the Place Heritage Park. *2601 Sunnyside Ave (800 S), Salt Lake City. Phone 801/584-8392. www.thisistheplace.org.* Day-use museum park at mouth of Emigration Canyon, where Mormon pioneers first entered the valley. In the park are This Is the Place Monument (1947), commemorating Brigham Young's words upon first seeing the Salt Lake City site; a visitor center with an audio presentation and murals of the Mormon migration; and the Old Deseret Pioneer Village, a living museum that depicts the 1847-1869 era and pioneer life. Admission to the monument and visitor's center is free. (Monument and grounds (daily, dawn-dusk). Visitor center (Mon-Sat 9 am-6 pm). Village (late May-early Sept: Mon-Sat 10 am-6 pm)) **$$**

Trolley Square. *600 S 700 East St, Salt Lake City. Bounded by 500 and 600 S sts and 600 and 700 E sts. Phone 801/521-9877.* This 10-acre complex of trolley barns has been converted into an entertainment/shopping/dining center. (Daily)

University of Utah. *200 South St, Salt Lake City. 2 1/2 miles E, at head of 200 S St. Phone 801/581-6515. www.utah.edu.* (1850) (25,900 students) On campus are

J. Willard Marriott Library. *295 S 1500 E, Salt Lake City. Phone 801/581-8558. www.lib.utah.edu.* Western Americana collection, rare books, manuscripts. (Mon-Thurs 7 am-midnight, Fri 7 am-8 pm, Sat 9 am-8 pm, Sun 11 am-midnight; closed holidays, also July 24) **FREE**

Pioneer Theatre Company. *300 S and 1400 E sts, Salt Lake City. Phone 801/581-6270. www.pioneertheatre.org.* Two auditoriums; dramas, musicals, comedies. (Sept-May; closed holidays) **$$$$**

Red Butte Garden and Arboretum. *300 Wakara Way, Salt Lake City. Phone 801/581-4747. www.redbuttegarden.org.* More than 9,000 trees on 150 acres, representing 350 species; conservatory.

Self-guided tours. Special events in summer. (Apr: daily 9 am-5 pm; May-Sept: Mon-Sat 9 am-8 pm, Sun 9 am-5 pm; Oct: daily 9 am-5 pm; Nov-Mar: Tues-Sun 10 am-5 pm; closed Dec 25) **$**

Utah Museum of Fine Arts. *410 Campus Center Dr, Salt Lake City. Art & Architecture Center, S of library. Phone 801/581-7332. www.umfa.utah.edu.* Representations of artistic styles from Egyptian antiquities to contemporary American paintings; 19th-century French and American paintings, furniture. (Mon-Fri 10 am-5 pm, Sat-Sun noon-5 pm; closed holidays) **FREE**

Utah Museum of Natural History. *1390 E Presidents Cir, Salt Lake City. Phone 801/581-6927. www.umnh.utah.edu.* Halls of anthropology, biology, mineralology, paleontology, geology; traveling exhibits. (Mon-Sat 9:30 am-5;30 pm, Sun noon-5 pm; closed holidays, also July 24) **$$**

Utah Fun Dome. *4998 S 360 W, Murray. Located 20 minutes S of Salt Lake City. Go S on I-15, 53rd St S exit, W to 700 West, then N. Phone 801/265-3866. www.fundome.com.* Enclosed mall with entertainment, rides, bowling, roller skating, baseball, arcades, miniature golf; cafes. Fee for activities. (Mon-Sat) **$**

Utah Jazz (NBA). *Delta Center, 301 W South Temple, Salt Lake City. Phone 801/355-3865. www.nba.com/jazz.* Professional basketball team.

Utah Opera Company. *Capitol Theatre, 50 W 200 South St, Salt Lake City. Phone 801/533-5626. www.utahopera.org.* Grand opera. (Oct-May)

Utah Starzz (WNBA). *Delta Center, 301 W South Temple, Salt Lake City. Phone 801/355-3865. www.utah.com/sports/starzz.htm.* Women's professional basketball team.

Wasatch-Cache National Forest. *82306 Federal Building, 125 S State St, Salt Lake City. E via I-80; or N via Hwy 89; Lone Peak Wilderness Area, 20 miles SE. Phone 801/524-3900. www.fs.fed.us/r4/wcnf.* High Uintas Wilderness Area has alpine lakes and rugged peaks; Big Cottonwood, Little Cottonwood, and Logan canyons. Forest (1 million acres) has fishing, boating, deer and elk hunting, winter sports, and camping (fees). **FREE**

Wheeler Historic Farm. *6351 S 900 E St, Salt Lake City (84121). 15 miles SE on I-15, exit I-215. Phone 801/264-2241. www.wheelerfarm.com.* Living history farm (75 acres) depicts rural life from 1890 to 1918. Farmhouse, farm buildings; animals, crops; hay rides (fee). Tour (fee). Visitors can feed the animals, gather eggs, and milk cows. There is a small fee for various activities and events. (Daily dawn to dusk; no rides Sun) **FREE**

ZCMI (Zion's Co-operative Mercantile Institution) Center. *Main and South Temple, Salt Lake City. Phone 801/321-8745.* A department store established in 1868 by Brigham Young anchors this 85-store, enclosed, downtown shopping mall. (Mon-Sat) **FREE**

Special Events

Days of '47 Celebration. *300 N Main St, Salt Lake City.* Mid-July.

Utah Arts Festival. *Library Square, 400 S 200 E, Salt Lake City. Phone 801/322-2428. www.uaf.org.* More than 1,000 participants, 90 performing groups; Children's Art Yard, juried show with demonstrations. Ethnic food. Last week in June.

Utah State Fair. *Utah State Fairpark, 155 N 1000 W, Salt Lake City. Phone 801/538-8400. www.utah-state-fair.com.* Mid-Sept.

Limited-Service Hotels

★★ COMFORT INN. *200 N Admiral Byrd Rd, Salt Lake City (84116). Phone 801/746-5200; toll-free 800/535-8742; fax 801/532-4721. www.slccomfortinn.com.* 155 rooms, 4 story. Pets accepted; fee. Complimentary continental breakfast. Check-in 3 pm, check-out 11 am. Restaurant, bar. Fitness room. Outdoor pool, whirlpool. Airport transportation available. **$**

★ DAYS INN. *1900 W North Temple, Salt Lake City (84116). Phone 801/539-8538; fax 801/595-1041. www.daysinn.com.* 110 rooms, 2 story. Pets accepted, some restrictions. Complimentary continental breakfast. Check-out 11 am. Fitness room. Indoor pool. Airport transportation available. **$**

★★ EMBASSY SUITES. *110 W 600 S, Salt Lake City (84101). Phone 801/359-7800; toll-free 800/325-7643; fax 801/359-3753. www.embassysuites*

.com. Located in the heart of Salt Lake City, this downtown hotel offers guests spacious rooms, a relaxing atmosphere, and friendly service. Nearby attractions include the LDS Mormon Temple, Salt Lake City Convention Center, and guests are just 1/2 mile to the historic Trolley Square Plaza. 241 rooms, 9 story, all suites. Complimentary full breakfast. Check-in 3 pm, check-out noon. Restaurant, bar. Fitness room. Indoor pool, whirlpool. Airport transportation available. **$**

★★ HILTON SALT LAKE CITY AIRPORT. *5151 Wiley Post Way, Salt Lake City (84116). Phone 801/539-1515; toll-free 800/999-3736; fax 801/539-1113. www.hilton.com.* With views of the Wasatch and Oquirrh Mountains, this hotel is minutes from the airport. Amenities include an outdoor swimming pool and whirlpool. Other activities are paddle boats, a putting green, jogging path, fitness center and indoor pool. Grill 114 is a full-service restaurant with seating outside and great panoramas. 188 rooms, 5 story. Pets accepted; fee. Check-in 3 pm, check-out noon. Restaurant, bar. Fitness room. Indoor pool, outdoor pool, whirlpool. Airport transportation available. Business center. **$**

★★ HOLIDAY INN. *999 S Main St, Salt Lake City (84111). Phone 801/359-8600; toll-free 800/933-9678; fax 801/359-7186. saltlakeholidayinn.com.* 292 rooms, 3 story. Pets accepted. Check-in 3 pm, check-out noon. Restaurant, bar. Fitness room. Indoor pool, whirlpool. Tennis. Airport transportation available. Business center. **$**

★★ INN AT TEMPLE SQUARE. *71 W S Temple, Salt Lake City (84101). Phone 801/531-1000; toll-free 800/843-4668; fax 801/536-7272. www.theinn.com.* Nestled in the heart of downtown Salt Lake City and just blocks from the Symphony Hall and Temple Square, this Edwardian landmark offers guests a truly unique stay. From the warm and personal service to the elegant guest rooms, this hotel offers style and personal service that immediately welcomes guests. 90 rooms, 7 story. Complimentary full breakfast. Check-in 3 pm, check-out noon. Restaurant. Airport transportation available. **$**

★★ PEERY HOTEL. *110 W 300 S, Salt Lake City (84101). Phone 801/521-4300; toll-free 800/331-0073; fax 801/364-3295. www.peeryhotel.com.* Historic building (1910). 73 rooms, 3 story. Check-in 3 pm, check-out noon. Restaurant, bar. Fitness room. Airport transportation available. **$**

★★ WYNDHAM SALT LAKE CITY HOTEL. *215 W S Temple, Salt Lake City (84101). Phone 801/531-7500; toll-free 800/553-0075; fax 801/328-1289. www.wyndham.com.* Adjacent to Delta Center. 381 rooms, 15 story. Check-out noon. Restaurant, bar. Fitness room. Indoor pool, whirlpool. Airport transportation available. Business center. **$**

Full-Service Hotels

★★★★ THE GRAND AMERICA HOTEL. *555 S Main St, Salt Lake City (84111). Phone 801/258-6000; toll-free 800/453-9450; fax 801/258-6911. www.grandamerica.com.* Set against the beautiful backdrop of the Wasatch Mountains, The Grand America is a tribute to the glory of old-world Europe. This esteemed hotel is the pinnacle of refinement. The details make the difference here, from intuitive service to extraordinary amenities. The guest rooms are classically French, with plush carpets, resplendent fabrics, fine art, and Richelieu furniture. Private balconies draw guests' attention to the splendid mountain views. Several dining establishments tantalize tastebuds in a variety of atmospheric settings. Afternoon tea, with its delicate sandwiches and flaky pastries, is particularly notable here, and the seasonally inspired cuisine of the Garden Café is matched by its lovely outdoor venue. The hotel's convenient location is perfect for exploring Utah's famous great outdoors, yet the two pools, spa, salon, and fine shopping persuade many to remain within this temple of luxury. 775 rooms, 24 story. Check-in 3 pm, check-out noon. Restaurant, bar. Fitness room, spa. Indoor pool, outdoor pool, whirlpool. Business center. **$$$**

★★★ HILTON SALT LAKE CITY CENTER. *255 S W Temple, Salt Lake City (84101). Phone 801/328-2000; fax 801/532-1953. www.hilton.com.* Located in the heart of downtown, guests can enjoy all the comforts of home with spacious rooms and friendly service. 499 rooms, 18 story. Pets accepted, some restrictions; fee. Check-in 3 pm, check-out noon. Restaurant, bar. Fitness room, spa. Indoor pool, whirlpool. Airport transportation available. Business center. **$$**

★ ★ ★ HOTEL MONACO SALT LAKE CITY. *15 W 200 S, Salt Lake City (84101). Phone 801/595-0000; toll-free 877/294-9710; fax 801/990-9754. www.monaco-saltlakecity.com.* The Hotel Monaco stands out for its haute décor and personalized services. Located in the heart of downtown Salt Lake City, this boutique hotel makes a smashing first impression upon visitors with its dazzling décor. At once classic and irreverent, the rooms and suites blend a panoply of colors and designs. Creature comforts abound, from beds piled high with luxurious sheets to high-speed technology for business travelers. Pets are more than welcome to share in the high style at this hotel, and those guests who left their furry friends behind may request a goldfish to join them in their rooms. Bambara's design and menu reflect the contemporary panache of the hotel, delighting diners with flavorful and creative concoctions. 225 rooms, 15 story. Pets accepted, some restrictions. Check-in 3 pm, check-out noon. Restaurant, bar. Fitness room. Golf. Tennis. **$$**

★ ★ ★ LITTLE AMERICA HOTEL. *500 S Main St, Salt Lake City (84101). Phone 801/363-6781; toll-free 800/453-9450; fax 801/596-5911. www.littleamerica.com.* This hotel provides every possible amenity, along with elegant and spacious rooms. 850 rooms, 17 story. Check-in 3 pm, check-out noon. Restaurant, bar. Fitness room. Indoor pool, outdoor pool, children's pool, whirlpool. Airport transportation available. **$$**

★ ★ ★ MARRIOTT SALT LAKE CITY DOWNTOWN. *75 S West Temple, Salt Lake City (84101). Phone 801/531-0800; fax 801/532-4127. www.marriott.com.* Located across from the Salt Palace Convention Center, this hotel caters to the business traveler and is close to the airport and major ski resorts. 515 rooms, 15 story. Check-in 3 pm, check-out noon. Restaurant, bar. Fitness room. Indoor pool, whirlpool. Airport transportation available. Business center. **$$**

★ ★ ★ MARRIOTT SALT LAKE CITY-CITY CENTER. *220 S State St, Salt Lake City (84111). Phone 801/961-8700; toll-free 866/961-8700; fax 801/961-8704. www.marriott.com.* 359 rooms, 12 story. Check-in 3 pm, check-out noon. Restaurant, bar. Fitness room. Indoor pool, whirlpool. Business center. **$$**

Full-Service Inn

★ ★ ★ LA EUROPA ROYALE. *1135 Vine, Salt Lake City (84121). Phone 801/263-7999; toll-free 800/523-8767; fax 801/263-8090. www.laeuropa.com.* Tucked away in a residential area, the large floor-to-ceiling windows in the public areas overlook the lovely landscaped grounds punctuated with fountains and small ponds. 9 rooms, 2 story. Complimentary full breakfast. Check-in 2 pm, check-out 11:30 am. Restaurant, bar. Fitness room. Airport transportation available. Business center. **$$**

Specialty Lodgings

The following lodging establishments are approved by Mobil Travel Guide, but due to their unique and individualized nature have not been given a traditional Mobil Star rating. Included in this listing you may find bed-and-breakfasts, limited-service inns, guest ranches, and other unique hotel properties.

ARMSTRONG MANSION. *667 E 100 S, Salt Lake City (84102). Phone 801/531-1333; toll-free 800/708-1333; fax 801/531-0282. www.armstrongmansion.com.* This bed-and-breakfast is tastefully decorated with antiques and carved wood, creating a relaxing setting for guests. Built in 1893; antiques. 13 rooms, 3 story. Complimentary full breakfast. Check-in 3 pm, check-out 11 am. **$$**

BRIGHAM STREET INN. *1135 E S Temple St, Salt Lake City (84102). Phone 801/364-4461; fax 801/521-3201. www.brightonstreetinn.citysearch.com.* This appealing bed-and-breakfast is located just blocks from the scenic area of downtown Salt Lake City. This remarkable inn offers guests a relaxing stay amidst elegant surroundings. 9 rooms, 3 story. Complimentary continental breakfast. Check-in 3 pm, check-out 11 am. **$**

Restaurants

★★ ABSOLUTE. *52 W 200 S, Salt Lake City (84101). Phone 801/359-0899; fax 801/359-0559. www.citysearch.com/slc/absolute.* American menu. Lunch, dinner. Closed Sun. Bar. Children's menu. Casual attire. Outdoor seating. **$$$**

★ ARGENTINE GRILL. *6055 S 900 E, Salt Lake City (84121). Phone 801/265-0205; fax 801/265-0760. www.argentinegrill.citysearch.com.* Latin American menu. Lunch, dinner. Outdoor seating. **$$**

★★ BABA AFGHAN. *55 E 400 S, Salt Lake City (84111). Phone 801/596-0786.* Middle Eastern menu. Lunch, dinner. Closed Sun; holidays. Casual attire. **$**

★★ BACI TRATTORIA. *134 W Pierpont Ave, Salt Lake City (84101). Phone 801/328-1500; fax 801/539-8783. www.gastronomyinc.com.* Large stained-glass partitions. Italian menu. Lunch, dinner. Closed Sun; major holidays. Bar. Children's menu. Casual attire. Outdoor seating. **$$**

★★ BAMBARA. *202 S Main St, Salt Lake City (84101). Phone 801/363-5454; fax 801/363-5888. www.kimptongroup.com.* American menu. Breakfast, lunch, dinner. Bar. Children's menu. Casual attire. **$$$**

★★ CREEKSIDE AT SOLITUDE. *12000 Big Cottonwood Canyon, Solitude (84121). Phone 435/649-8400; fax 435/649-5276. www.skisolitude.com.* Overlooks a pond and the ski slopes. American menu. Dinner, Sat-Sun brunch. Closed May, late Sept-mid-Nov. Bar. Casual attire. Outdoor seating. **$$**

★★★ FRESCO ITALIAN CAFÉ. *1513 S 1500 E, Salt Lake City (84105). Phone 801/486-1300.* A winding brick walkway lined with flowers leads the way to this charming neighborhood bistro, which offers a roaring fireplace indoors and al fresco dining during the summer. Guests will enjoy the fresh and authentic flavors of Italy. Italian menu. Dinner. **$$$**

★ LITZA'S FOR PIZZA. *716 E 400 S St, Salt Lake City (84102). Phone 801/359-5352; fax 801/359-5352.* Italian menu. Lunch, dinner. Closed Sun; Thanksgiving, Dec 25. **$$**

★★★ LOG HAVEN. *6451 E 3800 S, Salt Lake City (84109). Phone 801/272-8255; fax 801/272-6173. www.log-haven.com.* Chef David Jones revived this rustic log mansion into Utah's most innovative and elegant restaurant. His sophisticated and excellent fresh specialties change daily. Check out the wine and dine program. American menu. Dinner. Closed Jan 1, July 4, Dec 25. Casual attire. Valet parking. Outdoor seating. **$$$**

★★ MARKET STREET BROILER. *260 S 1300 E, Salt Lake City (84102). Phone 801/583-8808; fax 801/582-8107. www.gastronomyinc.com.* Modern décor in historic former fire station. American menu. Lunch, dinner. Bar. Casual attire. Outdoor seating. **$$**

★★ MARKET STREET GRILL. *48 Market St, Salt Lake City (84101). Phone 801/322-4668; fax 801/531-0730. www.gastronomyinc.com.* In renovated 1906 hotel. Seafood menu. Breakfast, lunch, dinner, Sun brunch. Closed Labor Day, Thanksgiving, Dec 25. Bar. Children's menu. Casual attire. **$$**

★★ MELTING POT. *340 S Main St, Salt Lake City (84101). Phone 801/521-6358; fax 801/521-7001. www.meltingpot.com.* Fondue menu. Dinner. Bar. Casual attire. **$$**

★★★ METROPOLITAN. *173 W Broadway, Salt Lake City (84110). Phone 801/364-3472; fax 801/364-8671. www.themetropolitan.citysearch.com.* American menu. Dinner. Closed Sun; Jan 1, Thanksgiving, Dec 25. Bar. Casual attire. **$$$**

★★ MIKADO AT COTTONWOOD. *6572 S Big Cottonwood Canyon Rd, Salt Lake City (84121). Phone 801/947-9800.* Zashiki rooms. Japanese menu. Lunch, dinner. Closed major holidays. Casual attire. Outdoor seating. **$$$**

★★★ **NEW YORKER CLUB.** *60 W Market St, Salt Lake City (84101). Phone 801/363-0166; fax 801/363-0588. www.gastronomyinc.com.* Appetizers (including fruit, cheese, and seafood) are offered as guests arrive. American menu. Lunch, dinner. Closed Sun; major holidays. Bar. Casual attire. Valet parking. **$$$**

★★ **PIERPONT CANTINA.** *122 W Pierpont Ave, Salt Lake City (84101). Phone 801/364-1222; fax 801/539-8783. www.gastronomyinc.com.* Mexican menu. Lunch, dinner. Closed Jan 1, Thanksgiving, Dec 25. Bar. Children's menu. Outdoor seating. **$$**

★★ **RINO'S.** *2302 Parleys Way, Salt Lake City (84109). Phone 801/484-0901.* Bistro-style café. Italian menu. Dinner. Closed major holidays. Casual attire. Outdoor seating. **$$$**

★ **RIO GRANDE CAFE.** *270 S Rio Grande St, Salt Lake City (84101). Phone 801/364-3302; fax 801/364-1857. www.riograndecafe.citysearch.com.* In historic Rio Grande Depot also housing train museum and displays. Mexican menu. Lunch, dinner. Closed major holidays. Bar. Children's menu. Casual attire. Outdoor seating. **$$**

★★ **SAMBA GRILL.** *162 South 400 West, Salt Lake City (84101). Phone 801/456-2200. www.sambagrill.net.* Brazilian menu. Lunch, dinner. Casual attire. **$$**

★ **SQUATTERS PUB BREWERY.** *147 W Broadway, Salt Lake City (84101). Phone 801/363-2739; fax 801/359-5426. www.squatters.com.* American menu. Lunch, dinner, late-night. Closed Thanksgiving, Dec 25. Bar. Casual attire. Outdoor seating. **$**

★★ **TUCCI'S CUCINA ITALIA.** *515 S 700 E, Salt Lake City (84102). Phone 801/533-9111; fax 801/531-9633. www.tuccisitalian.com.* Italian menu-Lunch, dinner. Closed Thanksgiving, Dec 25. Bar. Children's menu. Casual attire. Outdoor seating. **$$**

★★★ **TUSCANY.** *2832 E 6200 S, Salt Lake City (84121). Phone 801/277-9919; fax 801/277-0980. www.tuscanyslc.com.* This tremendously popular place maintains a high quality of service. Italian menu. Lunch, dinner. Bar. Children's menu. Casual attire. Outdoor seating. **$$$**

★★ **XIAO LI.** *307 W 200 S #1000, Salt Lake City (84101). Phone 801/328-8688; fax 801/328-9488.* Chinese menu. Lunch, dinner. Closed July 4, Dec 25. Casual attire. **$**

Sandy (B-3)

Restaurant

★★★ **LA CAILLE.** *9565 S Wasatch Blvd, Little Cottonwood Canyon (84092). Phone 801/942-1751; fax 801/944-8990. www.lacaille.com.* An impressive country French chateau surrounded by beautiful gardens populated by peacocks, llamas, ducks, and a host of other exotic creatures are just a prelude to the authentic French menu served by a friendly staff dressed in 18th-century costumes. French menu. Dinner, Sun brunch. Bar. Casual attire. Outdoor seating. **$$$**

Snowbird

See also Alta, Park City, Salt Lake City

Population 150
Area Code 435
Zip 84092
Web site www.snowbird.com

In 1971, a Texas oil man recognized the potential of Little Cottonwood Canyon in the Wasatch National Forest and developed the area as a ski resort. Once home to thriving mining communities, the resort village of Snowbird, 29 miles east of Salt Lake City, now offers year-round recreational activities. Skiing, of course, remains the biggest draw here; with an average of 500 inches of snowfall annually, Snowbird claims to have the world's best powder.

What to See and Do

Snowbird Ski and Summer Resort. *Hwy 210, Snowbird. Phone 801/742-2222; toll-free 800/232-9542 (reservations). www.snowbird.com.* 85 runs on 2,500 acres; 27 percent beginner, 38 percent intermediate, 35 percent advanced/expert. Elevations of 7,800 to 11,000 feet. Seven double chairlifts, three high-speed quads, 125-passenger aerial tram. Patrol, school, rentals. Restaurants, cafeteria, bar. Children's activity center. Four lodges. Night skiing Wed, Fri. Heli-skiing, halfpipe. Snowboarding, snowshoeing, ice skating. (Mid-Nov-early May, daily) Summer activities (June-Oct, daily) include rock climbing, hiking, mountain biking (rentals), tennis, tram rides, and concerts (see SPECIAL EVENTS). **$$$$**

Special Event

Utah Symphony. *7350 S Wasatch Blvd, Snowbird. Phone 801/533-5626; toll-free 888/355-2787. www.utahsymphony.org.* Snowbird Ski and Summer Resort (see) is the summer home of the orchestra. Several Sun afternoon concerts. July-Aug.

Full Service Resorts

★★ CLIFF LODGE & SPA. *Little Cotton Canyon, Snowbird (84092). Phone 801/742-2222; toll-free 800/232-9542; fax 801/947-8227. www.snowbird.com.* 511 rooms. Check-in 4 pm, check-out 11 am. Twelve restaurants, bar. Ski in/ski out. **$$$**

★★★ LODGE AT SNOWBIRD. *Snowbird Ski and Summer Resort, Snowbird (84092). Phone 801/933-2229; toll-free 800/453-3000; fax 801/933-2248. www.snowbird.com.* Lodging at this condominium building in the Snowbird resort, within walking distance of the lifts, ranges from single rooms to one-bedroom studios with lofts. The mountain views are spectacular, and every room here has an exterior balcony so that guests can enjoy the vistas. Fireplaces and kitchens are available in some rooms. Note that tire chains are required from Nov-Apr, and you must have tire chains in your car. 123 rooms, 7 story. Check-in 4 pm, check-out 11 am. Restaurant, bar. Children's activity center. Fitness room. Heated outdoor pool, whirlpool. Tennis. **$$**

Restaurant

★★ STEAK PIT. *Snowbird Ctr, Snowbird (84092). Phone 801/933-2260; fax 801/933-2264. www.snowbird.com.* Snowbird's oldest restaurant, this classic steakhouse serves aged Angus beef and fresh seafood along with all-you-can-eat salad, enormous baked potatoes, and homemade nine-grain bread. The rustic interiors are exactly what you'd expect at a mountain resort, with lovely views to match. Reservations are not accepted. Seafood, steak menu. Dinner. Children's menu. **$$**

St. George (F-1)

Founded 1861
Population 49,663
Elevation 2,761 ft
Area Code 435
Zip 84770
Information Washington County Travel & Convention Bureau, 425 S 700 E, Dixie Center, 84770; phone 435/634-5747 or toll-free 800/869-6635
Web site www.stgeorgechamber.com

Extending themselves to this hot, arid corner of southwest Utah, members of the Mormon Church built their first temple here and struggled to survive by growing cotton—hence the nickname "Dixie." With determination and persistence, members of the Church struggled against odds to construct the temple. The site, chosen by Brigham Young, turned out to be a bog, but another site was not selected. Instead, hundreds of tons of rocks were pounded into the mud until a stable foundation could be laid. Mormons from the north worked 40-day missions, and southern church members gave one day's labor out of every ten until the temple was complete. The workers quarried 17,000 tons of rock by hand. A team of oxen hauled the stones to the construction site, and for seven straight days, timber was hauled more than 80 miles from Mount Trumbull to build the structure. Made of red sandstone plastered to a gleaming white, the Mormon temple is not only the town's landmark, but also a beacon for passing aircraft.

In St. George, warm summers are balanced by mild winters and a long growing season. Tourists and sportspeople bring in important business. The seat of

Washington County, St. George is the closest town of its size to Zion National Park (see). A Ranger District office of the Dixie National Forest (see CEDAR CITY) is located here.

What to See and Do

Brigham Young Winter Home. *100 West St, Saint George. 200 N and 100 W sts. Phone 435/673-2517.* (1873) Two-story adobe house where the Mormon leader spent the last four winters of his life; period furnishings, garden. (Daily) **FREE**

Daughters of Utah Pioneers Collection. *Memorial Building, 143 N 100 E, Saint George. Phone 435/628-7274.* Regional memorabilia. (Mon-Sat; closed holidays) **DONATION**

Gunlock State Park. *Hwy 8, Ivins. 16 miles NW on Old Hwy 91. Phone 435/628-2255.* Approximately 450 undeveloped acres in scenic red rock country. A dam across the Santa Clara River has created a 240-acre lake, which offers swimming, water-skiing, fishing, and boating (ramp). The park also has facilities for picnicking and primitive camping, but no drinking water is available. (Daily) **FREE**

Jacob Hamblin Home. *490 S and 300 E, Santa Clara. 5 miles W off I-15. Phone 435/673-2161.* (1863) Native sandstone house of Hamblin, Mormon missionary to Native Americans for 32 years; pioneer furnishings. (Daily) **FREE**

Pine Valley Chapel. *St. George. 30 miles N via Hwy 18, Central exit, in Dixie National Forest. Phone 435/634-5747.* White frame meeting house built in 1868 as an upside-down ship by Ebenezer Bryce, a shipbuilder by trade. The walls were completed on the ground, then raised and joined with wooden pegs and rawhide. Still in use, the chapel served as both church and schoolhouse until 1919. (Memorial Day-Labor Day, daily) **FREE**

Snow Canyon State Park. *Hwy 8, Ivins. 10 miles N on Hwy 18. Phone 435/628-2255; toll-free 800/322-3770 (reservations). www.utah.com/stateparks/snow_canyon.htm.* A flat-bottomed gorge cut into multicolored Navajo sandstone; massive erosional forms, sand dunes, and Native American petroglyphs. Hiking, biking, picnicking, improved camping areas (some hookups, dump station), trailer parking. (Daily)

St. George Temple. *490 S 300 E, Saint George. Main and Tabernacle sts. Phone 435/628-4072.* Red sandstone structure built 1863-1876 with local materials; resembles colonial New England church. (Daily; closed Dec 25) **FREE**

Temple Visitor Center. *490 S 300 E, Saint George. Phone 435/673-5181.* On grounds of temple; guided tour of center explains local history and beliefs of the Latter-day Saints; audiovisual program. (Daily; closed Dec 25) **FREE**

Zion National Park. *(see) 42 miles NE on Hwy 9. Phone 435/634-5747. www.nps.gov/zion.*

Limited-Service Hotels

★ BEST WESTERN CORAL HILLS. *125 E St. George Blvd, Saint George (84770). Phone 435/673-4844; toll-free 800/542-7733; fax 435/673-5352. www.coralhills.com.* 98 rooms, 2 story. Complimentary continental breakfast. Check-out 11 am. Fitness room. Indoor pool, outdoor pool, children's pool, whirlpool. **$**

★ COMFORT INN. *1239 S Main St, Saint George (84770). Phone 435/673-7000; toll-free 800/517-4000; fax 435/628-4340. www.comfortsuites.net.* 122 rooms, 2 story. Complimentary continental breakfast. Check-out 11 am. Pool, whirlpool. Airport transportation available. **$**

★ ★ HOLIDAY INN. *850 S Bluff St, Saint George (84770). Phone 435/628-4235; toll-free 800/457-9800; fax 435/628-8157. holidayinnstgeorge.com.* 164 rooms, 2 story. Check-out 11 am. Restaurant. Indoor pool, outdoor pool, whirlpool. Tennis. Airport transportation available. **$**

Full-Service Inn

★ ★ ★ GREEN GATE VILLAGE. *76 W Tabernacle St, Saint George (84770). Phone 435/628-6999; toll-free 800/350-6999; fax 435/628-6989. www.greenegatevillage.com.* Situated in the historic district of St. George, this quaint village offers a delightful visit for guests who wish to enjoy modern elegance and nostalgic charm. Consists of eight

Victorian and pioneer houses from late 1800s; library, sitting room, antiques, tole-painted furnishings. Guests will find a delight waiting for them in one of the elegantly restored pioneer homes. 14 rooms, 2 story. Complimentary full breakfast. Check-in 3 pm, check-out 11 am. Restaurant. Pool, whirlpool. Airport transportation available. **$**

Timpanogos Cave National Monument (B-3)

See also Heber City, Park City, Provo

Web site www.nps.gov/tica.

26 miles S of Salt Lake City on I-15, then 10 miles E on Hwy 92.

Timpanogos (tim-pa-NOH-gos) Cave National Monument consists of three small, beautifully decorated underground chambers within limestone beds. The cave entrance is on the northern slope of Mount Timpanogos, monarch of the Wasatch Range. Much of the cave's interior is covered by a filigree of colorful crystal formations where stalactites and stalagmites are common. However, what makes Timpanogos unique is its large number of helictites—formations that appear to defy gravity as they grow outward from the walls of the cave. Temperature in Timpanogos Cave is a constant 45° F, and the interior is electrically lighted.The cave's headquarters are located on Hwy 92, 8 miles east of American Fork. There is picnicking at Swinging Bridge Picnic Area, 1/4 mile from the headquarters. The cave entrance is 1 1/2 miles from headquarters via a paved trail with a vertical rise of 1,065 feet. Allow three to five hours for guided tour. No pets, no strollers, walking shoes advised, jackets and sweaters needed. Tours limited to 20 people (late May-early September, daily). Purchase tickets in advance by calling 801/756-5238 or 801/756-1679, or at the visitor center. Golden Age and Golden Access passports accepted (see MAKING THE MOST OF YOUR TRIP). Contact the Superintendent, Rural Route 3, Box 200, American Fork 84003; 435/756-5238. Cave tours **$$**

Vernal (B-5)

See also Roosevelt

Population 7,714
Elevation 5,336 ft
Area Code 435
Zip 84078
Information Dinosaurland Travel Board, 55 E Main St; phone 435/789-6932 or toll-free 800/477-5558
Web site www.dinoland.com

This is the county seat of Uintah County in northeastern Utah, which boasts oil, natural gas, and many mineral deposits. A trading center for sheep and cattle, Vernal is in an area of ancient geologic interest. Nearby are beautiful canyons, striking rock formations, and majestic peaks. Headquarters and a Ranger District office of the Ashley National Forest are located here.

What to See and Do

Ashley National Forest. *Vernal. 15 miles N on Hwy 191. Phone 435/789-1181.* The High Uinta Mountains—the only major east-west range in the US—runs through the heart of this nearly 1 1/2 million-acre forest. The 1,500-foot-deep Red Canyon, the 13,528-foot Kings Peak, and Sheep Creek Geological Area are also here. Swimming, fishing, boating (ramps, marinas), whitewater rafting, canoeing; hiking and nature trails, cross-country skiing, snowmobiling, improved or backcountry campgrounds (fee). Visitor centers. Contact the Supervisor, 355 N Vernal Ave. **FREE**

Daughters of Utah Pioneers Museum. *500 W 200 S, Vernal. Phone 435/789-3890.* Relics and artifacts dating from before 1847, when pioneers first settled in Utah; period furniture, quilts, clothing, dolls; early doctor's, dentist's, and undertaker's instruments; restored Little Rock tithing office (1887). (June-weekend before Labor Day, Mon-Sat) **DONATION**

Flaming Gorge Dam and National Recreation Area. *Vernal. 42 miles N on Hwy 191, in Ashley National Forest. Contact the Ranger District office, PO Box 279, Manila 84046. Phone 435/784-3445. www.utah.com/nationalsites/flaming_gorge.htm.* Area surrounds 91-mile-long Flaming Gorge Reservoir and 502-foot-high Flaming Gorge Dam. Fishing on reservoir and river (all year), marinas, boat ramps, water-skiing; lodges, campgrounds (fee). River rafting below dam. Visitor centers at dam and Red Canyon (on secondary paved road 3 miles off Hwy 44).

Ouray National Wildlife Refuge. *Vernal. 30 miles SW on Hwy 88. Phone 435/789-0351.* Waterfowl nesting marshes; desert scenery; self-guided auto tour (limited route during hunting season). (Daily) **FREE**

Red Fleet State Park. *4335 N Hwy 191, Vernal. Phone 435/789-4432.* A scenic lake highlighted by red rock formations. Boating, swimming, fishing; camping. Several hundred well-preserved dinosaur tracks. (Daily) **$$**

River trips. *Vernal.* Guided whitewater trips on the Green and Yampa rivers.

Hatch River Expeditions. *55 E Main St, Vernal. Phone 435/789-4316; toll-free 800/342-8243.* **$$$$**

Steinaker State Park. *Vernal. 7 miles N off Hwy 191. Phone 435/789-4432.* Approximately 2,200 acres on west shore of Steinaker Reservoir. Swimming, water-skiing, fishing, boating (ramp, dock); picnicking, tent and trailer sites (fee). (Apr-Nov; fishing all year) **$$**

Utah Field House of Natural History and Dinosaur Gardens. *235 Main St, Vernal. Phone 435/789-3799.* Guarded outside by three life-size cement dinosaurs, this museum has exhibits of fossils, archaeology, life zones, geology, and fluorescent minerals of the region. Adjacent Dinosaur Gardens contain 18 life-size model dinosaurs in natural surroundings. (Daily; closed Jan 1, Thanksgiving, Dec 25) **$**

Western Heritage Museum. *300 E 200 S, Vernal. Phone 435/789-7399.* Houses memorabilia from Uintah County's "outlaw" past as well as other artifacts dealing with a western theme. Includes the Thorne Collection, photographs, and artifacts of the ancient people of Utah. (Mon-Sat; closed holidays) **FREE**

Special Events

Dinosaur Roundup Rodeo. *134 W Main St, Vernal. Phone toll-free 800/421-9635.* Mid-July.

Outlaw Trail Festival. *Vernal.* Festivals, sporting events, entertainment, theatrical events. Late June-mid-Aug.

Uintah County Fair. *Vernal. Phone 435/781-0770.* Aug.

Limited-Service Hotels

★★ BEST WESTERN DINOSAUR INN. *251 E Main St, Vernal (84078). Phone 435/789-2660; fax 435/789-2467. www.bestwestern.com.* 60 rooms. Check-in 2 pm, check-out noon. Restaurant, bar. **$**

★ THE SAGE MOTEL. *54 W Main St, Vernal (84078). Phone toll-free 800/760-1442. www.vernalmotels.com.* Classic 1950s roadside motel owned and operated by the same family. 26 rooms, 2 story. **$**

Specialty Lodgings

The following lodging establishments are approved by Mobil Travel Guide, but due to their unique and individualized nature have not been given a traditional Mobil Star rating. Included in this listing you may find bed-and-breakfasts, limited-service inns, guest ranches, and other unique hotel properties.

HILLS HOUSE. *675 W 3300 N, Vernal (84078). Phone 435/789-0700.* Featuring a full breakfast and in-room whirlpools. 4 rooms, 2 story. **$**

LANDMARK INN BED & BREAKFAST. *288 E 100 S, Vernal (84078). Phone 435/781-1800; toll-free 888/738-1800. www.landmark-inn.com.* This small inn is located in a renovated former Baptist church. 10 rooms, 2 story. Check-in 3 pm, check-out noon. **$**

Restaurants

★ 7-11 RANCH. *77 E Main St, Vernal (84078). Phone 435/789-1170; fax 435/781-1130.* Known for its friendly, family-oriented atmosphere and large portions. American menu. Breakfast, lunch, dinner. Closed Sun; Jan 1, Thanksgiving, Dec 25. **$$**

★★ CURRY MANOR. *189 S Vernal Ave, Vernal (84078). Phone 435/789-7268.* A local favorite for authentic Indian cuisine. Lunch, dinner. **$**

Wendover (B-1)

Founded 1907
Population 1,537
Elevation 4,232 ft
Area Code 435
Zip 84083

Half in Utah, half in Nevada, Wendover lies on the western edge of the Great Salt Lake Desert. The town was settled to serve the Western Pacific Railroad, which cut a historic route through here across the Bonneville Salt Flats. Accommodations can be found on both sides of the state line, but gambling is allowed only in Nevada. Blue Lake, 30 miles south, provides water at a constant temperature of 75° F for scuba diving and is open to the public (no facilities).

What to See and Do

Bonneville Salt Flats. *Wendover. E of town.* This approximately 100-square-mile area of perfectly flat salt, packed as solid as cement, is what remained after ancient Lake Bonneville, which once covered the entire area, retreated to the present-day Great Salt Lake. The area is part of the Great Salt Lake Desert.

Special Event

Bonneville National Speed Trials. *Wendover. Bonneville Speedway, approximately 15 miles E, then N. Phone 805/526-1805.* Held since 1914 on the Bonneville Salt Flats (see), which has been used as a track for racing the world's fastest cars. Car racing in competition and against the clock. Aug or Sept.

Zion National Park (E-2)

Web site www.nps.gov/zion

42 miles NE of St. George on Hwy 9.

The spectacular canyons and enormous rock formations in this 147,551-acre national park are the result of powerful upheavals of the earth and erosion by flowing water and frost. Considered the grandfather of Utah's national parks, Zion is one of the nation's oldest national parks and one of the state's wildest, with large sections virtually inaccessible. The Virgin River runs through the interior of the park, and Zion Canyon, with its deep, narrow chasm and multicolored vertical walls, cuts through the middle, with smaller canyons branching from it like fingers. A paved roadway following the bottom of Zion Canyon is surrounded by massive rock formations in awe-inspiring colors that change with the light. The formations, described as temples, cathedrals, and thrones, rise to great heights, the loftiest reaching 8,726 feet.

The canyon road runs 7 miles to the Temple of Sinawava, a natural amphitheater surrounded by cliffs. Another route, an extension of Hwy 9, cuts through the park in an east-west direction, taking visitors through the mile-long Zion-Mount Carmel Tunnel, and then descends through a series of switchbacks with viewpoints above Pine Creek Canyon. Note: Large vehicles must pay an escort fee to pass through the tunnel.

Zion's main visitor center, open daily, is near the south entrance. Check here for maps, information about the park, and schedules of naturalist activities and evening programs. Each evening in spring through fall, park naturalists give illustrated talks on the natural and human history of the area. Pets must be kept on leash and are not permitted on trails. Vehicle lights should be checked; they must be in proper condition for driving through the highway tunnel. The park is open year-round. There is an admission fee of $20 per seven-day stay per vehicle; pedestrians and cyclists pay $10. Golden Eagle Passports are accepted (see MAKING THE MOST OF YOUR TRIP). For more information, contact the Superintendent, SR 9, Springdale 84767-1099; phone 435/772-3256.

What to See and Do

Bicycling. Permitted on roads in park, except through Zion-Mt Carmel Tunnel. Roads are narrow and no designated bicycle routes exist.

Camping. At south entrance to park: South Campground provides 140 tent or trailer sites (mid-Apr-mid-Sept); Watchman Campground provides 229 tent sites and 185 trailer sites (all year). Lava Point Campground, 26 miles N of Virgin off Hwy 9, provides a minimal number of tent sites (free; no facilities). South and Watchman campgrounds **$$$**

Escorted horseback trips. *Phone 435/772-3967.* Special guide service may be obtained for other trips not regularly scheduled. Contact Bryce/Zion Trail Rides at Zion Lodge. (Mar-Oct, daily)

Grand Circle: A National Park Odyssey. *Springdale. O. C. Tanner Amphitheatre in Springdale. Phone 435/673-4811.* Multimedia presentation encompassing four states, 14 national parks and monuments, and numerous state parks and historic sites, plus Glen Canyon National Recreation Area (see PAGE, AZ, and LAKE POWELL, UT) and Monument Valley Navajo Tribal Park (see KAYENTA, AZ). One-hour show (Memorial Day-Labor Day). **$$**

Guided trips, hiking tours. *Zion. Phone 435/772-3256.* Conducted by ranger naturalists, who explain geology, plant life, and history.

Kolob Canyons Visitor Center. *Cedar City. Phone 435/772-3256.* (See CEDAR CITY)

Mountain climbing. *Zion. Phone 435/772-3256.* Should be undertaken with great care due to unstable sandstone. Climbers should consult with a ranger at the park visitor center.

Park trails. *Zion. Phone 435/772-3256.* Trails lead to otherwise inaccessible areas: the Narrows (walls of this canyon are 2,000 feet high and as little as 50 feet apart at the stream), the Hanging Gardens of Zion, Weeping Rock, the Emerald Pools. Trails range from 1/2-mile trips to day-long treks, some requiring tested stamina. Trails in less-traveled areas should not be undertaken without first obtaining information from a park ranger. Backcountry permits required for travel through the Virgin River Narrows and other canyons, and on all overnight trips (fee/person/night).

Zion Nature Center. *Adjacent to South Campground. Phone 435/772-2356.* Junior Ranger program for children ages 6-12. (Memorial Day-Labor Day, Mon-Fri) **$**

Limited-Service Hotel

★★ FLANIGAN'S INN. *428 Zion Park Blvd, Springdale (84767). Phone 435/772-3244; toll-free 800/765-7787; fax 435/772-3396. www.flanigans.com.* 34 rooms, 2 story. Check-in 3 pm, check-out 11 am. Restaurant. Pool, whirlpool. Small local artists' gallery. **$**

Full-Service Resort

★★ CLIFFROSE LODGE AND GARDENS. *281 Zion Park Blvd, Springdale (84767). Phone 435/772-3234; toll-free 800/243-8824; fax 435/772-3900. www.cliffroselodge.com.* 40 rooms, 2 story. Check-in 2 pm, check-out 11 am. Pool, whirlpool. **$**

Specialty Lodging

The following lodging establishment is approved by Mobil Travel Guide, but due to its unique and individualized nature has not been given a traditional Mobil Star rating. Included in this listing you may find bed-and-breakfasts, limited-service inns, guest ranches, and other unique hotel properties.

NOVEL HOUSE INN. *73 Paradise Rd, Springdale (84767). Phone 435/772-3650; toll-free 800/711-8400; fax 435/772-3651. www.novelhouse.com.* This literary-themed bed-and-breakfast, which promotes itself as a romatic getaway for adults, takes full advantage of its setting, with the towering sandstone cliffs of Zion National Park on three sides. It is secluded but within walking distance of shops and restaurants. Complimentary breakfast and afternoon tea are served in the dining room with a view of West Temple Mountain, and guest rooms are named after writers like Jane Austen and C. S. Lewis. 10 rooms, 2 story. Closed mid-Dec-late Jan. Children over 12 years only. Complimentary continental breakfast. Check-in 4-7 pm, check-out 11 am. **$**

Index

B

D

M

N

X

Y

Z

Notes

Notes

Notes

Notes

Notes

Notes